TEMPESTUOUS JOURNEY

TEMPESTUOUS
JOURNEY

LLOYD GEORGE HIS LIFE AND TIMES

FRANK OWEN

WITH 41 PHOTOGRAPHS

HUTCHINSON
STRATFORD PLACE
LONDON

Hutchinson & Co. (Publishers) Ltd
London   Melbourne   Sydney   Auckland
Bombay   Cape Town   New York   Toronto

First Published 1954

Set in eleven point Monotype Fournier one point leaded
Made and Printed in Great Britain by
GREYCAINES
(Taylor Garnett Evans & Co. Ltd.)
Watford, Herts.

ACKNOWLEDGMENTS

I HAVE to acknowledge the gracious permission of Her Majesty the Queen to make use of material from the Royal Archives, Windsor Castle.

I wish, also, to acknowledge the permission which Sir Winston Churchill has kindly granted me to reproduce so many of his letters to Lloyd George. They have enabled me, I trust, to bring forth clearly his own great part in the conduct of that First World War in which Lloyd George bore the main responsibility of leadership of this country after December 1916.

For three years I have quarried in the vast papers of the Lloyd George Archives, which now belong to Lord Beaverbrook. There are 1,025 boxes of them, a treasury for a score of books upon our Welfare State, the First World War, the Allied Intervention in Russia, the Irish Republic, the National Home of the Jews, the developing constitution of the British Empire, the part of the Monarchy in the first fifty years of this tumultuous century of Britain's history. These papers were place at my disposal, and I have to thank Lord Beaverbrook for it. In the sorting and reading of these documents Mrs. Elton, the custodian of the Lloyd George Archives, gave me incalculable help.

I acknowledge, too, the access which Lord Beaverbrook allowed me to his own papers.

More than two hundred books, many of them written by Lloyd George's own contemporaries, his colleagues, friends and enemies, and others by historians and critics, have also been studied, and the newspaper files of the period consulted.

There are, too, a host of those who knew Lloyd George personally who have searched their memories of him, and given me the result. I thank them.

I also wish to acknowledge with thanks the permission of the following individuals and publishers to quote from the books listed:

Robert Laird Borden, His Memoirs; edited by Henry Borden: the author and MacMillan & Co. Ltd.

Economic Consequences of the Peace by J. M. Keynes: MacMillan & Co. Ltd.

Stanley Baldwin by G. M. Young: the author and Rupert Hart-Davis Ltd.

Contemporary Personalities by the Earl of Birkenhead: Cassell & Co. Ltd.

Down the Years by Sir Austen Chamberlain: Cassell & Co. Ltd.

Ireland For Ever by Brig.-Gen. Frank Crozier: Jonathan Cape Ltd.

Prelude to Victory by Brig.-Gen. E. L. Spears: the author and Jonathan Cape Ltd.

Twenty-Five Years by Sir Edward Grey (Viscount Grey of Fallodon): Sir Cecil Graves, K.C.M.G., M.C., (executor) and Hodder & Stoughton Ltd.

The Intimate Papers of Colonel House: Ernest Benn Ltd.

Lloyd George by Tom Jones: the author

Politicians and the Press by Lord Beaverbrook: the author

C. F. G. Masterman—A Biography by Mrs. Lucy Masterman: the author

King George V by Harold Nicolson: the author

Curzon—The Last Phase by Harold Nicolson: the author

Ordeal by Battle by F. S. Oliver: MacMillan & Co. Ltd.

The Real Lloyd George by A. J. Sylvester: the author

On Passing the New Menin Gate; Poem by Siegfried Sassoon: the author

Let Candles Be Brought In by Geoffrey Shakespeare: the author

Memories and Reflections by Lord Oxford and Asquith: Cassell & Co. Ltd.

The Big Fellow, A Life of Michael Collins by Frank O'Connor: the author

Beatrice Webb's Diaries, 1912–19 edited by Margaret Cole: the author and
     Longmans Green and Co.

Field-Marshal Sir Henry Wilson, His Life and Diaries by Maj.-Gen. Sir C. E.
     Callwell: the executors and Cassell & Co. Ltd.

Tim Harington Looks Back by General Sir Charles Harington: John Murray
     (Publishers) Ltd.

Official History of the First World War: Her Majesty's Stationery Office

Lord Riddell's War Diary: Ivor Nicholson & Watson Ltd.

Lord Riddell's Intimate Diary of the Peace Conference and After: Executor and
     Victor Gollanz Ltd.

The Private Papers of Douglas Haig (1914–19) edited by Robert Blake: the
     author and the present Lord Haig

Despatches of Douglas Haig, December 1915–*April* 1919 edited by J. H.
     Boraston: the author and the present Lord Haig

The World Crisis by Winston S. Churchill: the author

Thoughts and Adventures by Winston S. Churchill: the author

Autobiography by Margot Asquith: Eyre & Spotiswoode (Publishers) Ltd.

Peace by Ordeal by Frank Pakenham: the author

Robert Donald by H. A. Taylor: the author

                                                        FRANK OWEN

CONTENTS

ERRATA

Page 109 line 35. For "Field Marshal" *read* "General".

Page 359 line 30. For "Breshaven" *read* "Berehaven".

Page 469 line 24. Delete, "the Secretary of State for War".

Page 488 Note 1. For "1950" *read* "1930".

Page 718 line 24. For "Two only" *read* "Three only".

Page 718 line 26. For "Philip Snowden and J. H. Thomas" *read* Philip Snowden, J. H. Thomas and Lord Sankey.

Page 721 line 32. For "India" *read* "Foreign Affairs".

Chapter

LIST OF ILLUSTRATIONS

A*   9

CHAPTER I

CRAGS OF THE EAGLE

It was midnight on a wooded hillside in Wales. The moon was veiled as yet behind the clouds that tipped the ghostly peak of Snowdon. The candles had long since gone out in the cottages of Llanfrothen village, which kneels between the mountains and the sea. Now was the hour when the small, wild creatures of the earth creep out, and own it for a while.

Suddenly, S-ssst! S-ssst! Men!

Scurry. The rabbits and the moles and the frogs were gone.

A lantern gleamed between the trees. Quiet footfalls sounded. A knot of shadowy figures mounted the steep pathway to the old stone church on the shoulder of the knoll . . . six, seven, eight men . . . they went to the graveyard gate, and fumbled with the lock. It was fast secured. Over the wall, then!

"S-ssh! S-ssh! Here, man, take the spades! Evan and I will keep watch!"

Now, a couple of them were digging. They were digging a grave. Or, rather, they were shovelling away the loose soil of a lately-filled grave. In a short time, their spades struck something hard. It was a coffin. The coffin of a girl, daughter of an old quarryman.

What now? Wait! Make all tidy, and all ready! They piled the soil neatly beside the open grave, and reverently. The coffin they left where it lay. The dark visitors had not come to take away the body that was there, but to make room beside it for another one, that of a father whose last wish had been that he might be buried in the same place as his daughter.

The diggers finished. A low whistle, to tell the men beyond the churchyard wall that the job was done. Now, they would sit together upon the ground, talk in low tones, and watch until the morning broke on the mountain tops. With it, trouble might come to all of them, but they were ready to bear that. For these men preparing for another burial were also doing sentry for a living cause, and faithfully they would hold their vigil here for three more days and nights.

By then, the whole countryside would be aroused, and the police would be keeping their own anxious eye upon the Rectory. The mourners would meet in force at the home of the dead quarryman, and the funeral procession would start their three-mile trudge along the winding country lanes to Llanfrothen Church, ever-growing in numbers as they went. Another great concourse would be gathered at the churchyard to receive them. The gate would be broken open, and Robert Roberts would be laid to rest by the side of his child.

Now, what was this strange story?

Its origins went back to the bitter religious feuds which reft Wales in the childhood days of men who are still living. Then, although by a recent Act of Parliament[1] it was permitted dissenters from the Established Church of England to bury their dead in the Parish churchyard with the rites of their own denomination, this did not always accord with the Christianity of some of the incumbents, and among these was the Rector of Llanfrothen. Twenty years earlier, a local lady had offered a plot of neighbouring land to the church-yard of this parish, the gift being recorded in the Vestry Book and a wall built around it at the cost of the parishioners. Here, the daughter of the quarryman, a Calvinistic Methodist, had been buried some time ago. But in the meantime, since this new ground had never yet been formally conveyed to the Parish, the Rector persuaded the donor to transfer it to him personally on trust, with the proviso that no one else should be buried there except with the rites of the Established Church.

So, when the dying request of Robert Roberts was brought to the Rector, and he was served with a formal notice that the Methodist pastor would conduct the last service, the Rector resolved to put the issue to the test. He ordered the sexton to fill in the half-opened grave. In tears, old Roberts' son appealed to his Nonconformist pastor. The good man borrowed a horse, and rode hoppity-cloppity down the valley track to Portmadoc, where in the main street of that little fishing port he met a young solicitor whom he knew. He reined in his mount, jumped off, and besought him desperately to help.

"Carry the burial right through at once," said the solicitor, "and I will defend you."

The name of this young man was David Lloyd George.

There and then, he took note from that Nonconformist pastor of all that happened, including the evidence of the Rector locking the graveyard gate and refusing the key to the family. That night he studied the case of the original unconditional gift of the land, and of its subsequent so-called "conveyance", and next day he advised the family to break open that barred gate, and bury their dead where they willed in God's Acre.

So it was done, and in the faith by which the old quarryman had lived.

The Rector went at once to court. He sued the quarryman's son and seven others for damages for

"wrongfully entering the plaintiff's land, digging a grave therein, burying a corpse, and conducting a burial service."

[1] The Osborne Morgan Burial Act of 1880.

Mr. D. Lloyd George appeared for the defence. He immediately applied for a trial by jury.

He handled his case in masterly style, confining his legal argument to the single issue: did the ground belong to the parish as the result of the original gift, or did it belong to the Rector as trustee under the terms of the donor's later deed of conveyance? But he also made a passionate protest against the conduct of this Christian clergyman who had told the old quarryman's family that he might be buried

"not in the last resting ground he had asked, beside his daughter, but in a post, bleak and sinister, in which were buried the bodies of the unknown drowned that were washed up from the sea in this region of shipwrecks, or of suicides, or of the few Jews that died in the district."

The jury found for the defendants. Fortunately, the foreman made a note on a slip of paper of their precise finding.

Fortunately, because the Case of the Quarryman of Llanfrothen was by no means over. The County Court Judge reserved judgment. "There were," he said, "questions of law still to be decided."

Two months later he gave his decision. He paid tribute to the "ingenuity" of Mr. Lloyd George, and entered a verdict for the plaintiff for five guineas and costs.

At once Lloyd George sought leave to appeal, which was granted. He also asked the Judge to amend his note of the findings of the jury, which was refused. When Lloyd George urged that the shorthand of the court reporter would show that His Honour's note was in error, the Judge retorted that he did not care if there were fifty shorthand records. It was then that the audacious young attorney reminded him that the jury, at any rate, had taken the unusual precaution of putting their own verdict in writing, "and the sequel shows that they were right in doing so."

So to the High Court of Justice went the case of the Quarryman of Llanfrothen. When it was heard the Lord Chief Justice Coleridge gave judgment for the defendants. He also gave severe admonition to the County Court Judge for his refusal to amend his notes, despite all the evidence to the contrary. After a few pertinent observations on the legal habits of County Court Judges in general, His Lordship added,

"As for this paper and these shorthand notes, I shall simply send them to the Lord Chancellor without comment, and if he does not take some steps I shall be surprised."

When Lloyd George met that anguished pastor on horseback in the main street of Portmadoc his own name was beginning to be known in the towns and villages beneath Snowdon, where he had been brought up in a cobbler's cottage. When the case of the Quarryman of Llanfrothen had been settled, all

Wales was talking of David Lloyd George, and he had set forth on his path
to Downing Street.

.   .   .   .   .   .

David Lloyd George, the Welshman, was born in Manchester. His birthplace was No. 5 New York Place, a two-storeyed brick house in an alley off
a dull back street. The smoke of the city mingled with the first draught of
air that the boy David breathed.

The smoke entered also into the lungs of his father, William George, the
schoolmaster, who was acting headmaster of a large National School in the
suburbs, and set him off coughing. Soon, in the spring, it would finally decide
him to quit that grey wilderness of stone and return to the green land of his
fathers. This day, 17 January, 1863, was the birthday of his first son.

"A sturdy, healthy, little fellow, with fine curly hair," wrote William
the same evening.

That was more than ninety years ago, and now David Lloyd George is
part of history. Not a stone, not a sign is there yet to mark the place where
he was born. Hardly one of the neighbours even knows it. But his monument
is all around us. The shape of the society in which we dwell was largely hewn
by this man's hands. Like it or not, Lloyd George laid the base of Britain's
Welfare State.

He was the son and grandson and great-grandson of a yeoman farmer.
Great-grandfather farmed the rolling fields behind the lighthouse on Strumble
Head, near Fishguard in Pembrokeshire, when Pitt the Younger was Prime
Minister of England. Barely a mile beyond Tresinen Farmhouse, the invading
soldiers of the French Revolution landed in 1797. It was the last time that a
foreign enemy ever set foot in this island, and it ended in farce. The Welsh
women put on their tall, black, conical witch hats with their red cloaks, and
paraded round the hills above the shore. The Frenchmen thought they were
surrounded by an overwhelming force of British Redcoats, and they surrendered without striking a blow.

The next of the Georges, Lloyd George's grandfather, settled with his
wife in a nearby farm at Trecoed. Both were devout Baptists, and the wandering
preacher was ever sure of a welcome at their hearth. In their family life, the
Georges united two of the ruling passions of the Welsh people of those days—
a thirst for theology and a love of learning.

Their eldest son, William, drank deep at this well, and the more he grew
the less he liked the idea that he should spend his manhood on a farm and
"live with his nose dug into the soil".

William was clever and studious, and to be a scholar was his dream. After
some debate, his mother had him "apprenticed" (as it was then called) to a
doctor in Fishguard. But since William's days of labour were prolonged

far beyond evening in making prescriptions and rolling pills, and his nights of study were cut short by his master begrudging him a candle, he decided to quit Medicine. He took himself off to London to become a pupil teacher in a Private School. Here he remained for six beggarly years.

In 1844, when the violent anti-Corn Law agitation was shaking Hungry England, William went first to Liverpool as a schoolmaster, and most of the next twenty years he spent in Lancashire, with two interludes as Headmaster at Haverfordwest and Pwllheli. It was at Pwllheli that he met the girl he meant to marry. She was to be the mother of David Lloyd George. Her name was Elizabeth Lloyd, and she was the daughter of David Lloyd of Llanystumdwy, near Criccieth, and of Rebecca, his wife. Lloyd, dead himself long before this, had been the village shoemaker of Llanystumdwy. In Wales, this may mean something different from what it is likely to mean in other parts of the kingdom. The Lloyds of Lleyn peninsula, the shoulder that North Wales thrusts into the Irish Sea, traced their ancestors back into the morning shadows of Celtic history.

William George was at this time approaching forty years of age, a man of middle height and spare frame. His face was pale and thin, his forehead high and broad, his eye commanding. His movements were lithe and his conversation shrewd; in argument it was said he was "invincible".

Elizabeth, his wife, was eight years younger. She had a fair complexion, which appeared the fairer because of her crown of dark hair. Her eyes were a deep brown, and her expression was one of charm and thoughtfulness. It reflected a serenity and a steadfastness of character which perhaps her husband needed most as complement to his own restless moods which turned him aside from the road of practical success. That their partnership was full and happy, many who knew them in different places have testified.

Another place name was now due to appear in the log book of William's wanderings. He required a better paid post to provide for his new responsibilities, and he believed that he had found it a second time in Lancashire. So, in 1859, the young couple moved to Newchurch, where William took up his labours at the local school. Before long their first child was born, a girl whom they named Mary Ellen.

But troubles, too, began to beset the family. William's health was giving way in the moist Lancashire air, and his spirit was depressed by the lack of sympathy between him and those with whom he worked. Indeed, the social climate seemed to him to be less kindly than the weather. He made up his mind to move once more.

A good friend was the means of his release from these toils. This was John Daniel Morell, a well-known educationalist who had given up a Congregational pulpit to become an Inspector of Schools. Morell was a philosopher, who had studied under Fichte at Bonn University. He, too, had found delight in William's company, and was happy to help him now with the offer of a temporary post for three months as headmaster of a large school in Manchester. It was William George's final term in the service of Education.

It lasted long enough to give his son, David, a native citizenship of Manchester. Before the year was out, William had gone back home to Wales, to settle there as a tenant of a small farm at Bwlford, near Haverfordwest. Home-coming it was, in the last, true sense. He caught a chill while gardening one damp summer evening and died of pneumonia within the week, on 7 June, 1864. He left his widow little money, two tiny children, and another, unborn, baby under her heart. Young David had nearly been lost that previous winter with an attack of croup. One stormy night, a neighbour hurriedly saddled his horse and set off through the blinding snow to the nearest doctor, who by lucky chance had just returned from the local hospital. They rode back together in time to save the little fellow's life.

It was good that Elizabeth had a brother in that hard year, and that he was so good a brother. He was Richard Lloyd, who had followed their father as the Shoemaker of Llanystumdwy. In her lonely trouble Elizabeth sent him a telegram, "Come, Richard."

He went at once. Never before in his life had Richard slept a night away from his native village under Snowdon. He walked twenty miles through the mountain pass from Criccieth to Caernarvon. It took him another day and night to reach Bwlford in South Wales by rail, and to bring comfort to his sister. They both realized that she could not possibly remain there alone on the farm with her orphan children. It seemed right to Richard that they should all come home with him to Llanystumdwy. Together, they sought the aid of a Liverpool solicitor, Thomas Goffey, who had been a friend of William's in his schoolmastering days in that city, and asked him to arrange the disposal of the farm lease. Their clothes and personal possessions were packed and all else sold up.

So they came to Llanystumdwy, Richard, with Elizabeth his sister, and her two children, to live together in his five-roomed cottage with his mother, Rebecca. They were joined within a few months by another baby, William George's second son, posthumously born.

Llanystumdwy lies a mile or so beyond Criccieth, on the road between the mountains and the sea that skirts the north shore of Cardigan Bay. Southward, across the waters of this bay you can see the grey pile of Harlech Castle and beyond, the Merioneth hills and the far coast of Cardiganshire. Northward, behind Llanystumdwy, rises that mighty range

> "Where Snowdon night by night
> Receives the confidence of lonely stars"

which the Welsh call *Creigiau Eryri*. "Crags of the Eagle," black in storm, green when the sun shines, a magical purple when it sets beyond the Irish Sea.

Right through the middle of Llanystumdwy village there tumbles under an ancient stone bridge the sparkling trout stream called the Dwyfor. It leaps down the rocks through a deep gully to this place, and so goes cantering onward to the sea a mile away. Many a fine fish did Lloyd George take out of it as a boy, some as a man; in the evening of his stormy life it was his favourite walk beside its banks; and he is buried beneath the trees there, as he ever said he would be.

As you approach the old bridge, coming from Criccieth, there is a two-storeyed cottage on the right-hand side of the road. It is built of grey stone, and covered with rose-creeper. This was the home of Richard Lloyd, the Shoemaker, which became the home of Lloyd George, the future Prime Minister of Britain. There is no plaque or notice here, either, to mark the place today. But in those times over the door hung the sign painting of a boot and a top-boot, with the words:

RICHARD LLOYD

GWNEUTHWYR

When travellers, unlearned in the Welsh language, asked Richard what this formidable designation meant in simple English, the shoemaker translated it, with appropriate rolling sound, "MAN-U-FACT-URE-ER," which was exactly what this man was in the days when the boots and shoes of the people in the countryside were made by hand by the village craftsman.

The house consisted of a small kitchen, a smaller parlour and a scullery on the ground floor, with two bedrooms upstairs. The kitchen had a floor of slate slabs, a ceiling of wooden beams and a fine cooking range and hearth, the makings of an inviting living-room. The parlour was furnished with a formal sofa, a round table and stiff antique armchairs, and in the corner stood a glass-fronted cupboard with the Sunday-best tea service. The ordinary life of the family was lived in the kitchen, until as the boys David and William grew up they gradually civilized (or humanized) the parlour by turning it into a study for their homework.

Uncle Lloyd (as the children called him) carried on his own shoemaking business in a single-storeyed, stone-built workshop next door. Here, on three benches, sat the Master Shoemaker with his men. At his elbow, in the thick outer wall of the workshop, there was a convenient cavity. This was the place where the shoemaker kept both the book he happened to be currently reading (for the moment that his work was done his study was resumed) and also a note-book and pencil. Should he come across a striking phrase or novel idea, either in the page or in the casual conversation of a customer, he promptly wrote it down. It might come in handy for next Sunday's sermon.

For Uncle Lloyd belonged to the straitest Baptist sect of the Campbellites, who preached and practised the literal interpretation of the Scriptures as the sole creed of the Christian Church. "The Disciples of Christ" they called themselves, and like the first followers by the Sea of Galilee, they were unpaid.

The Lloyds were the only Baptists in Llanystumdwy, and to worship in their own way they had to walk that long mile to the chapel on the hill behind Criccieth. It was in the brook that runs beside it that, at the age of twelve, Lloyd George was baptized.

So six days a week the shoemaker worked at his last and on the seventh he laboured for the Lord. Twice he preached, in the morning and in the evening, and he spoke to the children at Sunday School in the afternoon. His sermons were eloquent, and though they were seasoned with doctrine to suit a congregation of sermon-tasters, they were designed to grip the heart as much as convince the head. Old Mrs. Jones (she is well beyond eighty), who lives today in Uncle Lloyd's cottage, remembers how the shoemaker preached.

"Very, very clever and convincing he was. He always made you believe whatever he said."

Mrs. Jones was herself baptized by him, though in the sea, not in the brook. Any water will do for baptism.

"He made you believe." And not only believe, but perform! Lloyd George himself never forgot what oratory is really for—not to please men or lull them, but to move them—and if they accept the message, to make them go out and straightaway do something worthwhile about it. He had learned that as a boy, sitting beneath the pulpit of the Shoemaker of Llanystumdwy.

Lloyd George ever had a purpose in his mind. It was Power—to perform. Always, the man wanted to *DO* something. If you had also to *BE* somebody in order to bring this about, well, be that, too. But the *doing*, not the *being* was the vital part, the real, true "object of the exercise", as soldiers say. Herein, Lloyd George differed from many figures who have filled the stage of politics.

Uncle Lloyd was fine-looking, as his pictures show, bearded but with a clean-shaven mouth and dark eyebrows, and bearing himself with a dignity in which strength and tenderness were compounded. One who knew him said of him that the only time he raised his voice in his house was when he cried out in prayer. He was, in fact, a noble man, a selfless character of whom every neighbour spoke well.

"Nothing must be done except what is right," Richard wrote in his diary.

He never married. Lloyd George kept a boyhood memory of a good-looking girl, obviously fond of his uncle, who would come and lean on the window-sill of the little shop and discuss the merits of the latest sermons with him. But with the responsibilities he had taken on, marriage was not possible. Resolutely he put the thought from him, and it can be truly said that from the moment when Richard Lloyd first heard of their distress, he devoted his life to the well-being of the children he had harboured.

Such a man would never be without his own good library, and to this had been added the only worthwhile possessions that his adopted orphans had brought with them—the books of their late father. Lloyd George grew up not only on the Bible but on Bunyan, on Shakespeare, Macaulay's and Carlyle's Essays, on Scott and Dickens and Defoe. In those days, he read rapidly but not carelessly, because his uncle had impressed on him that if a book was worth beginning it was worth finishing. There was even a time in his childhood when he seemed to some of his schoolfellows to be becoming "a bit of a book-worm".

To be sure, the boy stored his memory. Fifty years later, Lloyd George would analyse with knowledge the swaying fortunes of the Greek wars against the Persian Kings, or the tactics of Stonewall Jackson in the American Civil War. One of the most powerful weapons in Lloyd George's armoury was his memory.

Apart from these vigorous impulses of home education and religious instruction which he imbibed from the Baptist services, Sunday School, and from the Calvinistic Methodist Band of Hope meetings which he also attended every Wednesday evening (teaching of abstinence and singing practice), two other factors now began to shape the mind and character of the boy.

The first of these was the village school, which he first entered at the age of three-and-a-half years. Village children went to school early then, largely to have them out of the way of their hard-worked mothers. The school at Llanystumdwy stood a few yards beyond the Anglican Church, was the property of that Church and, indeed, was an annexe of it. The teachers were approved Churchmen and the teaching was the teaching of the Established Church of England, including the Catechism, though nearly all the pupils were Nonconformists. The secular education was elementary; reading, writing and arithmetic, with some history and geography. In the higher standard, which Lloyd George reached some time before he left, Euclid and Algebra were also taught. He turned out to be especially apt at arithmetic, though in later life few people would ever believe it of this most famous Chancellor of the Exchequer. His personal writing was almost from the start, sprawling, and was known as "crowsfeet".

Lloyd George was lucky in his headmaster. Mr. David Evans was an exceptional teacher, with a passion for his task and genius in discharging it. History, as David Evans taught it, became thrilling, personal adventure.

And the Bible stories! Lloyd George would recall in his mellow age how Evans described the sacrifice of Isaac by Abraham. In his outstretched hand the headmaster held a ruler, the symbol of the sacrificial knife. He raised it to strike, and then—the Lord hurled it from him to the ground! Down crashed the ruler on the floor of the schoolroom! The class sat breathless, petrified and entranced. Thus Lloyd George went early in life to the theatre.

Both his uncle and his headmaster were pleased with David Lloyd George's progress, and when Richard Lloyd decided to keep the boy on at school for a year or two beyond the customary leaving age of twelve, the wise teacher Evans placed him with two other pupils of promise in a special class. These senior boys sat at a table immediately below the headmaster's desk in the big schoolroom and learned from him the elements both of higher mathematics and Latin. They repaid, in part, his special attentions by helping to teach some of the younger boys. Lloyd George did well enough at this to make both the headmaster and the Rector of the Church try to persuade him to take up teaching as a profession and perhaps even, in due course, take Orders. Years later, Lloyd George would joke: "With care, I might have been a curate, perhaps a canon—please don't think I'm bragging."

His studies gave the authorities more satisfaction than some of his other activities. Though the school owned by the Church of England was conducted without undue attempt to proselytize its Nonconformist pupils, that Church itself was sincerely regarded by many of the children's parents as something foreign not only to the people of Wales, but even to the teaching of Christ Himself. To a man such as Uncle Lloyd it seemed an abomination (because it was a lie) that Baptist children should be made to declare in catechism that their names had been given them by their godfathers and godmothers, for they positively had neither godfather nor godmother. Moreover, the Catechism required them to affirm that their names had been given them at baptism.

"But these children," said Uncle Lloyd, pointing to his own little nephews, "have never yet been baptized"

(for the Baptists did not believe in the baptism of infants: they held that only for the adolescent could this service have a true significance). The alternative to the Church of England School was not to send the children to school at all, for there was no other place of education then in the villages of Wales. It hurt the soul of Richard Lloyd that he should make the compromise, but how could he deny these children the very tools of civilized life?

The question caused less anxiety to Master David Lloyd George at that age, but the prospect of rebellion had its own attractions. The opportunity arose on Ash Wednesday. On this day the Rector, the Diocesan Inspector and the Squire paid a visit to the school to hear the pupils recite the Apostles Creed and answer the questions of the Catechism. The rebel framed his plan, and enlisted his confederates. It was one of the few times in his life that Lloyd George organized a conspiracy of silence.

The company assembled in the Big Schoolroom. The Squire smiled benignly, the Headmaster bowed respectfully, and children shuffled and whispered fearfully, the Rector rose and asked the first question of the Catechism.

No response.

The Rector repeated the question.

"What is thy duty towards thy neighbour?"

The children trembled, stared ahead, and answered not a word.

The Rector looked startled. The Diocesan Inspector glanced at the Headmaster. Pale and bewildered, Mr. Evans stepped forward and asked the school to follow him in reciting the Creed.

"I believe," he began in a shaking voice.

Dead silence.

He stopped. He was ashen. The Squire and the Inspector stared. Then suddenly, as a distant and long delayed echo, a boy's treble pipe broke through:

"I believe. . . ."

It belonged to William George, Lloyd George's younger brother. Others began to join in. The Squire and the Rector bowed and smiled, and everyone breathed easily again. The rebellion was over.

Later, that afternoon, Lloyd George thrashed William with his fists.

There was another anvil on which the pattern of young David Lloyd George's life was welded. It was, aptly, in the village smithy. Aptly also, the smithy stood in the same lane, opposite the Church gate by the bridge. The glow of the forge on the winter nights beckoned to the boys as they trudged homeward from school. There was fire and spark of another kind there, too. The smithy was the Village Parliament.

Hugh Jones was the blacksmith, with bushy side-whiskers and a mane of white hair falling from his massive head, which he cocked on one side when he was arguing points of theology with his cronies, a thing he habitually did. Hugh Jones was a strong Congregationalist and a deacon of that sect, and though compared with the Methodists they were in a minority in the village (or perhaps because of it), he was ready at the drop of his hammer to prove that neither they nor the Baptists had the flimsiest warranty in Scripture for their tenets. As for the Church of England, that was for those who had given up religion. . . .

The time came when Lloyd George himself felt versed enough to take part in this debate, and he and the blacksmith argued the question of adult as against infant baptism. Hugh Jones began by letting the boy off lightly, but before long he found that it was taking an unnecessary risk.

"If I had not been well grounded in my matter the other evening," he confided to Uncle Lloyd, "your boy would have tripped me up."

But though the blacksmith preferred himself to stick to his favourite matter of theology he did not rule politics out of order.

When Lloyd George had become Chancellor of the Exchequer and the most formidable politician in Britain, he returned to Llanystumdwy to make a speech at a gathering of his old schoolfellows.

"Yonder smithy," he cried, pointing to the old ivy-covered building, "was my first parliament, where night after night we discussed and decided all the abstruse questions relating to this world and the next, in politics, in theology, in philosophy and science. There was nothing too wide and comprehensive for us to discuss, and we settled all the problems among ourselves without the slightest misgiving."

Politics, indeed, were coming to the people. Mr. Gladstone's Reform Act of 1867 had enfranchised the agricultural workers, and in Wales and Scotland, at any rate, the vast new vote was not moving in the main towards the party of the Tory Landlords. Thus, from roughly dividing the Welsh seats between them, after 1868 the Liberals came to outnumber the Tories by nearly two to one. The General Election of that year had been an especially bitter one in Caernarvonshire, and worse than the wounds inflicted during the struggle was the festering of them that followed it.

The Tory candidate, Mr. Douglas Pennant, had been returned to Parliament on seven previous occasions with hardly a ripple of opposition. But now the Liberal tide was rising in Wales. Three fierce currents swelled and swirled within it—social, racial and religious; it was anti-landlord, anti-English and anti-Established Church. In Caernarvonshire, the tenant farmers went in droves to the polling booths and voted defiantly Liberal for Jones Parry, "The People's Candidate". Defiantly, because voting was still open in those days, and would remain so until 1872.

There was a dramatic turnover. Jones Parry was elected by a majority of forty-eight votes. Uncle Lloyd was one of the few who did not have to fear who knew which way he had voted. His livelihood depended only on his own skill as a shoemaker and the goodwill of any customer who came. It was otherwise for the tenant farmers who had broken ranks in the phalanx of feudalism in the Welsh countryside.

In a famous speech at Queen's Hall during another fierce General Election in 1910, Lloyd George recalled:

"I was a boy at school then, and I was in the blackest Tory parish in the land. I believe that my old uncle was the only Liberal in the village, though not the only Liberal in the parish. There were three or four in the parish besides him. One or two of them refused to vote for the Tory candidate, and two or three actually went further and dared to record their votes for the Liberal. All of them received notice to quit. I remember that some lads who were at school with me in the same class in a year or two had to leave the neighbourhood. I was very young, but lads do not forget things of that sort. I knew the reason why they left—because the great Squire of the Parish had turned their fathers out of their homes purely because they dared to vote for the Liberal candidate. The next quarter day after the Election, notices were showered upon the tenants. They were turned out by the score on to the roadside because they had dared to vote according to their consciences. But they woke the spirit of the mountains, the genius of freedom that fought the might of the Normans for two centuries. There was such a feeling aroused among the people that, ere it was done, the political power of landlordism in Wales was shattered as effectively as the power of the Druids. It is my first memory of politics."

To a poor Welsh village boy what an ogre seemed this Foreign, Church of England, Tory Landlord! Anybody who does not understand this will not understand Lloyd George—and all that he would come to represent. To the end of his days, Lloyd George could never quite bring himself to banish his dislike and distrust of landlords, even when he had become one himself in two countries, England and Wales.

He passed fairly early through his Welsh Nationalist phase (it was almost Welsh tribalist in its inception; certainly it was fiercely anti-English):

"I shall not sleep in my grave until someone knocks and tells me '*Mae hi wedi mynd*'." (She has gone.)

"She" was the hated Saxon Power that young Lloyd George was in this case bitterly denouncing to his boyhood friend, Mr. D. R. Daniel. In the early days of "Chamberlain's Boer War" it certainly caused Lloyd George no private grief to hear of Boer successes; those who pretend otherwise make humbug of this man's generation and his own youth. Later, he sincerely sought to reconcile the beaten Boer enemy within the bounds of a greater British Empire. He let the years bury the old religious feud, too, over the disestablishment in Wales of the Church of England (which, in any case, was settled half way through his political career). He formed a subsequent warm personal friendship with an Anglican Bishop who had become Archbishop of Wales. He did the same with certain Tory politicians. Indeed, in the time of a far greater war, he made a Coalition Government with their Party. But landlords ever stuck in Lloyd George's throat.

The land around his village was strictly preserved. "Beyond every wood and stream there stood the silhouette of a gamekeeper," and that was a challenge to the village lads. Not only the orchards but the woods and rivers were fair field for their invasions, "marauding expeditions in quest of Nature's bounties," as Lloyd George explained in his diary.

In some ways, or rather, at some time, he seems to have been a lonely child, though this was of his own choosing, for he was also the spoilt child of the family. When, after an injury, his mother made him give up playing "bandy" (a local and rather more violent form of hockey), he used to take his exercise in long tramps and climbs alone. Not that Lloyd George cut himself off from the rest of the village boys for more than a few days. Then, after his solitary excursions (perhaps he had merely been reconnoitring) he would rejoin the gang in their forays and their fights. Another, and this a lifelong element, of Lloyd George's character, was his love of storm and the destructive force of Nature. Lloyd George was really happy, as few men are, in thunder and lightning and great winds.

Rabbiting was perhaps the fun he best enjoyed, for then he could take his dog and Lloyd George loved a dog. His favourite at this time was a nondescript black hound called "Bismarck"; he had been snatched from the quays of Hamburg and brought home by a local sailor, who was also one of the best poachers in the district.

Lloyd George himself had no need to poach, except for sport. His home was comfortable, and by comparison with their neighbours the family were well-off; for if there was a gulf between the gentry and the handicraftsman there was also a margin between the handicraftsman and the farm labourer. It was still a strain on the resources of his uncle to keep things going as well as he would have wished. Richard was never good at collecting his own accounts, and when a building society in Liverpool in which Lloyd George's mother had invested almost all her savings failed, there was a time of anxiety. Lloyd George remembered how his mother, who had been in the habit of buying a bag of meal every week from a travelling salesman, would then open her purse, look at it, and shake her head. The sight of her face in these moments haunted the boy.

But, in general, they lived fairly enough. The cheapest kinds of meat, such as sheep's head and other offals, could be bought for a few pence. Lloyd George used to point out later in life that these offals, despised by many in his youth, had now been proved by scientists to be richest in vitamins.

"Look at the lion" (he would say) "he always makes his first meal of the heart and the liver of the antelope he has killed—and leaves the joints till later. Instinct tells him which is the best part!"

For the rest, the family largely grew up on potatoes, home-made bread, an occasional egg, and buttermilk. They had bread-and-jam, or bread-and-butter, but never bread-and-butter-and-jam. It was drilled into the children that waste of every kind was sinful.

"I know what a 'squeeze' is," Lloyd George would say long afterwards, "and I resolved to do my best to lighten the load for other people."

The George brothers were rather better dressed than most of their schoolfellows. They were the only boys in the village to wear knickerbockers; they also wore red stockings, and Lloyd George sported a Glengarry cap, which perhaps enabled him to be picked out more readily by property owners who wanted to blame someone for a broken fence. The care for a distinctive appearance (was it vanity—or a calculated sense of advertisement?) developed very early in Lloyd George and never left him.

"Davy Lloyd" he was known as in those days, and that he then accepted it is shown by a carving he made when he was eight on the parapet of the old stone bridge over the Dwyfor, which read for many a year:

"D.L."

A later hand of some admirer has added the missing "G" and also the unnecessary letters, "M.P." You can see it there yet.

Lloyd George was already practising, not only how to discuss and debate, but also how to orate. At the Band of Hope on Wednesday evenings, he learned both tonic *sol-fa* singing and the art of speaking. Brother William and sister Mary Ellen could remember long before this how, at the age of four or five, he gave them a preaching one day at home, using the cottage stairs as a pulpit, and bringing home his points by banging the stair with a stick. Old school-fellows have recorded that the boy was lusty in singing, while in speaking his opinions were "but narrowly orthodox".

He was chosen to deliver the prize recitation at the *Cyfarfod Cystadleuol*, one of the annual events of the village, and he scored a triumph which delighted his family and all the neighbours. It was the first platform appearance of David Lloyd George.

He had now come to his fourteenth year. It was time to decide what he should be in life. Often, and earnestly, Uncle Lloyd pondered the problem, and there is a story of how one day Lloyd George coming home from school, ran into the shoemaker's shop and was greeted by him as he talked with a customer. Putting his hand round the curly head and looking down into the eager, upturned face of the boy, the kindly old cobbler murmured, as to himself, the scriptural phrase

"Beth fydd y bachgen hwn?" ("What shall this child be?")

What was, in fact, to happen? Many a night his uncle and his mother talked by the fireside that winter, long after the boys had gone to bed.

The choice before them was hard. The offer by the Headmaster and the Rector of a pupil-teachership carried with it the implicit proviso of regular attendance at the Parish Church. This was impossible for the boy who had been baptized only a year or so previously, on confession of faith, by his uncle in the brook that runs beside the Baptist Chapel above Criccieth. On the other hand, the Church to which they themselves belonged could offer nothing, for as we have seen it had an unpaid Ministry.

Uncle Lloyd would have liked the lad to take up medicine, but this would have meant a course of study both long and costly. Moreover, the boy himself seemed to shrink—as he was to do throughout his life—from even the presence of sickness and suffering. Lloyd George had no call for healing.

Of course, he could follow the shoemaker's own trade. He had run many an errand, delivered many a pair of shoes or boots, tramped the countryside, or driven round it by donkey-and-cart many a mile collecting overdue accounts, made himself useful in little ways in the shop. But he had no manual skill whatever. His fingers were oddly clumsy to the end of his days, and he could hardly turn a door-handle the right way or tie his own bootlaces. Lloyd George's fortunes lay in his head and in his heart, never in his hand, and this was plain both to his uncle and his mother.

The same objection held good against putting the boy on a farm, although Lloyd George himself has assured us that

"when I was from five to ten years old, it was I that wheeled the barrow, did the manuring, planted the garden and pruned the fruit trees; and I continued to do so until we left Llanystumdwy."

He may have done it, but we doubt if he enjoyed it as much as he used to claim. For it is already obvious that Lloyd George, like his father before him, did not wish to live with his nose dug into the soil.

There was one task, however, which pleased the village boy well enough, for it had in it an element of quest and adventure. Forty years on from now, at the height of the fierce storm of the people's Budget, Lloyd George would tell an excited audience at Caernarvon in those softened, almost tremulous tones of his most moving perorations:

"Yesterday, I visited the old village where I was brought up. I wandered through the woods familiar to my boyhood. There I saw a child gathering sticks for firewood, and I thought of the hours which I spent in the same pleasant and profitable occupation, for I also have been something of a backwoods man; and here is one experience taught me then which is of use to me today. I learned as a child it was little use going into the woods after a period of calm and fine weather, for I generally returned empty-handed. But after a great storm, I always came back with an armful. We are in for rough weather now; we may even be in for a winter of storms which will rock the forest, break many a withered branch, and leave many a rotten tree torn up by the roots. But when the weather clears, you may depend upon it there will be something brought within the reach of the people that will give warmth and glow to their grey lives, something that will help to dispel the hunger, the despair, the oppression and the wrong which now chill so many of their hearths."

It still seemed possible, that if things were most firmly resolved, most carefully planned and most faithfully carried out he might hope to escape from the drudgery, either of the bench or of the fields.

Richard Lloyd, and Elizabeth George, his sister, made up their minds.

They resolved to make David Lloyd George a lawyer. It was a mighty decision for them, and him, for his country and for the world.

That night the future Prime Minister of Britain, and one of its greatest, unknown to himself, began his march to power.

CHAPTER II

WHICH WAY THERE?

WHAT did Lloyd George himself want to do?

Clearly, the pulpit made its powerful appeal. Not only the matter but the manner of the preacher's business attracted the boy. After attending the three services which were held at the Criccieth Chapel every Sunday, he would walk home with his uncle at evening's close through the woods and fields to Llanystumdwy, discussing the whole way "the points" of the day's discourses. These would be again analysed at the informal meeting of deacons and elders of neighbouring churches which took place every Monday evening at the shoemaker's shop. Then, all other local sermons would be considered and judged, both by theological and artistic standards.

For in Wales, throughout the last century, the chapel filled the life of the people in culture as in faith. This was the result of an earlier and astonishing renaissance, long overdue. Whatever the Great Reformation of 1536 had done to revivify religion in England and Scotland, its principal effect in Wales had been to drug and deaden it. In the hands of the Tudor monarchs—themselves Welsh—the Church of England was used as a weapon of State to enforce uniformity, lay and clerical, in the cause of their own New Despotism. Its wielders in Wales were either Englishmen by birth, or Welsh nobles who were willing to be anglicized; and since the Welsh language was the greatest barrier to uniformity, it must needs be broken down. The new church services in Wales were ordered to be held in English.

Now the Welsh peasantry may or may not have understood much of the sense of the Latin language in which the ancient liturgy was conducted, but, at least, they were familiar with its sounds. The words of the modern one bore no more meaning for them than the incantations of a Zulu witch-doctor in a kraal. The priests and monks of the Old Order, at any rate in their daily mingling with the people, had spoken the same native Welsh tongue. The clerks of the New Order specifically did not. A Church-and-State safety curtain descended, cutting off the rural folk of Wales both from spiritual refreshment and from their only source of knowledge in those days. A winter of superstition and brutishness gripped all the land of Wales. Two hundred years after the Reformation John Wesley would write:

"The Welsh people are as little versed in the principles of Christianity as a Cherokee Indian."

But it was a winter of sleep, not of death.

It was Wesley's own mighty Methodist crusade which roused the nation from its torpor.[1] And as the Welsh people stood erect again to take up:

"a religion free enough to be strong, and strong enough to be free"

there grew up with them a vast thirst and yearning for learning. The chapel was also college, club, forum and theatre of this awakening land. So, while every other art yet languished—poetry, painting, sculpture, drama, even music —the pulpit flourished at its noonday. Indeed, it embraced so many of the rest of the arts. The sermons which found fame in nineteenth-century Wales were one-man plays, of vivid and vital words, performed with every perfected device of voice and gesture. The preachers, with the teachers, were the players of this New Wales.

Not only their names, Owen Thomas, John Elias, John Jones, Herbert Evans, rang as a trumpet's call through the land, but also the titles of their great works: The Sermon of the Day of Judgment; The Sermon of Jacob's Ladder; The Sermon of Balaam's Ass. Men told by the fireside, and by the roadside, too, how the vast voice of Owen Thomas, preaching at Bangor, could be heard in Anglesey Island beyond the Menai Straits, where the last of the Druids had died defying Caesar. How, when John Elias described the Almighty letting the arrow fly from his bow, the whole immense congregation parted in two, as by instinct, to allow passage for the shaft. How hundreds fainted from terror as John Jones warned of The Day of Judgment, or leapt in ecstasy as he proclaimed the mercy of God in Christ the Saviour.

Lloyd George himself ever remembered the electrifying effect which the Reverend Herbert Evans produced upon him as he delivered his famous sermon on Livingstone, then one of the most exciting characters in the world. The strong, deep-chested preacher kneeled to act the missionary facing a lion in wildest Africa; a prayer was on his lips; then he rose to his feet, filled with the strength of Angels.

"Never in my life have I heard anything more eloquent than this. He has a marvellous power of pathos. I was quite overwhelmed."

wrote Lloyd George in his diary that night.

These lessons in the arts of enchantment were not lost on him. Part of his hold over his schoolfellows was his power of telling stories about his own and their heroes. Chief of these was Owen Glendower, the last Welsh Prince of Wales, with whom legend has never done among the Welsh folk.

Then there was a brief Napoleonic phase (indeed, there were two!). But another and far greater hero to him, whom Lloyd George shared with his uncle, was Abraham Lincoln. The drama of Lincoln's climb from the poverty

[1] It was John Wesley who wrote to Francis Asbury, a fellow evangelist: "Men may call me a knave, or a fool, a rascal, a scoundrel and I am content. But they shall never by my consent call me a bishop!"

of a frontier shack to the Presidency of the greatest republic on earth, could not fail to stir the sons of another nation whose own history is so much the Song of its Frontier.

And then there was the tremendous issue of Liberty! All Wales had sided with the Northern States in the American Civil War, which to the outside world appeared solely as a crusade to set free the slaves. Time and again, talk in the Llanystumdwy smithy or the shoemaker's shop would turn to Lincoln the Giant, and the mighty blows that he had struck for human rights. Lincoln's assassination in the hour of his triumph had fallen upon the village argument with the force of a thunderclap from the mountains, compelling instant and awed silence.

The lad, David, read and revelled in the popular biographies that poured out about "Honest Abe". Certainly, no other figure in history so permanently impressed Lloyd George as Lincoln did. A few years after the great President's death, when Lloyd George had qualified as a solicitor and set up in practice, he came across the following precept of Lincoln, who had been himself a struggling lawyer before he had become a successful statesman:

"There's a vague popular belief that lawyers are necessarily dishonest. Let no man, choosing the Law for a calling, for a moment yield to that popular belief. Never stir up litigation. As a peacemaker the Lawyer has a supreme opportunity of being a good man."

Young David Lloyd George copied out those words, framed them and kept them on his desk to remind him; several instances are on record that he did, indeed, permit himself to be reminded during the next few hard years of litigation. He did not forget them, either, when as a politician he came to be appointed President of the Board of Trade, or Minister of Munitions, and had to mediate between the conflicting industrial claims of employers and their labour.

Last of all, in the manpower crisis of the First World War, when the only way to keep up the flow of troops to the Front was by the drastic expedient of compulsory military service, Lloyd George was inspired and fortified by the example of Abraham Lincoln in America's great hour of ordeal. To Lincoln, then, as to Lloyd George later, there came counsels to hold back from the decision; it would be politically inexpedient, even perilous; it might utterly ruin his prospects at the next election.

Lincoln had replied:

"It is not a personal question at all. It matters not what becomes of me. We must have the men. And if I go down, I intend to go like the *Cumberland*,[1] with my colours flying."

[1] An American ship belonging to the Union, sunk by the Confederate ship, *Merrimac*, during the Civil War.

Whatever the petty men of politics may say, there was this, too, in Lloyd George's heart in the most terrible hour of his own country.

There were other parallels between the lives of Lincoln and Lloyd George, besides the obvious one of the journey from Log Cabin to White House. Each had the same peculiar power of attracting and subjecting others while remaining himself untouched, not superficially but nevertheless essentially aloof. Men—and women—who had known either Lincoln or Lloyd George for years and, as they imagined, intimately, and thought that they knew his heart, were astonished and annoyed to find that they had hardly got under his skin. There was a reticence, a remoteness, even secretiveness about both of them.

There was also a curious vein of indecision, which was uncovered in the history of both men at various times. To the world they have appeared, or have been presented, as "human dynamos". Read this by John Hay, one of his private secretaries, of Lincoln at the height of the Civil War:

> "The Tycoon" (he writes) "is in fine whack. He is managing this war, the draft, foreign relations and playing a reconstruction of the Union, all at once. I never knew with what a tyrannous authority he rules the Cabinet until now. The most important things he decides, and there is no cavil . . ."

It reads like a page from the history of the Supreme War Cabinet, 1917.

But dynamos idle, too. Lincoln foozled and fumbled, even after the Confederate rebels fired upon the Union Flag at Fort Sumter and Civil War had begun. Lloyd George could not make up his mind about the First World War until after the Prussians had marched into Belgium. The energy, moral and physical, of both Lincoln and Lloyd George came not as a steady current, but in terrific tides.

There was the death of a parent during the early years of both men; Lincoln lost his mother, Lloyd George his father. Both had to mourn a beloved child; Lincoln his son Edward, Lloyd George his daughter Mair. Then, too, in youth both men experienced sudden, shattering doubt of God's existence. Lincoln's biographer has told us of his ribaldries, blasphemies. As for Lloyd George, many years later he put his feelings this way:

> "You prayed . . . but there was a sudden terrible fear that there was no one at the other end of the telephone."

He was walking home from chapel with his uncle along the coast road through the woods the very evening that he had been baptized, when suddenly the whole fabric of his religious beliefs fell away from him, as a man might shed a cloak. He passed nights of terror and years of agnosticism, appalled by the thought that the universe should be under no direction, no control and with no purpose. At last, he resolved to confide in Uncle Lloyd. To his astonishment and relief, Richard was not in the least shocked, but seemed to understand the mental and moral strife which raged in the boy's heart.

Indeed, this vacuum where faith had been was the real cause of his loneliness. It was Carlyle's *Sartor Resartus* which began to lead him back by a broad track from Doubting Castle to his own rather highly personal view of the Delectable Mountains (for it describes a man who made a similar journey). Soon after reading this book, Lloyd George spent a night in a Merioneth village with an old Methodist minister, who gave him Renan's *Life of Jesus*. He devoured it, and it brought him peace of mind. A strange thing, said Lloyd George years later, that this book by an atheist should have been put into his hands by a parson in that out-of-the-way place! Its irresistible appeal to the man who had lost faith in God was its noble portrait of Christ as a living being, a human hero, a perfect Man. So the wayfarer returned to the hearth.

But the doubts did not altogether disappear. He was driven to confess his secret to at least two other friends, D. R. Daniel and Herbert Morgan. It is a mystery of Lloyd George's almost violent grip upon the loyalty of men who afterwards parted company with him that they still kept guarded from the wider public a matter of such interest (there were others), which he had never made the slightest effort to disguise from them. So, for the next quarter of a century, Lloyd George would figure as one of the foremost fighting leaders of a fanatical Welsh Nonconformity—while at the same time he doubted its most basic spiritual tenets. This was the orator, who in the days of the People's Budget battle went down to Treorchy to deliver an address from the Chair of the Baptist Union, enshrining its message in the words:

"No hope for Democracy except in Jesus of Nazareth."

Was it hypocrisy, then, for Lloyd George to praise Jesus of Nazareth? Or could he have been saluting Christ the Man?

The truth appears to be, that whatever his religious doubts during this period, Lloyd George believed in Christian Nonconformity as a social power for good. He held that it had given a steadfast character to the nation, taught its people to think and to discipline themselves. In the darkest days of the First World War, he would discover virtue in the practice of the Roman Catholic Lent.

Indeed, Lloyd George's objection to both the Roman Catholic Church and the Established Church of England (like his acceptance of the Protestant Nonconformist Churches), was really political. For him, the Roman Catholics and the Established Churchmen had made a pact in history with "foreign" or "reactionary" forces with which Lloyd George was in conflict.

It must be added, that at all times Lloyd George went willingly to a Church Service, especially if he expected to appreciate the singing. He would travel many a mile to hear a good sermon.

Besides the Pulpit, the Press! No politician who really meant business could afford to neglect either "such an engine as possessed the power of making people think".

Many an evening Lloyd George and his younger brother, William, walked to Criccieth to fetch the day's issue of the *Liverpool Mercury*. Indeed, Lloyd George recalled tramping the fourteen miles to Portmadoc and back to get a London newspaper with a full report of one of Mr. Gladstone's speeches during the Midlothian Campaign. The fashion then required, and the cheap and abundant newsprint ensured, the publication verbatim of all the leading politicians' speeches; these, together with the newspaper's own pretty ponderous editorial comment, would be read aloud by Uncle Lloyd in sonorous tones to a little throng of listeners in the shoemaker's shop.

To be admitted to the hierarchy of famous politicians, to become such a popular god, able to hand down thunder to the whole people, why, it seemed to the boy to be the proper object of a life's labour! Thus, as a modern knight-errant of Cambria, in line with those of fabulous King Arthur's Court, a young man might still do battle with the oppressors of the land!

The influence of Lloyd George's mother clinched his uncle's opinion that the Law was the way. Elizabeth had never forgotten the Liverpool solicitor, Mr. Thomas Goffey, who had befriended her and her children in the time of their trouble. For many a year, Mr. Goffey had been the symbol to this family of a great name adorning a great profession. To follow in his steps seemed a splendid thing.

The problem was the money. It was already costing more to keep the growing children, and with the death of their grandmother the household had lost the only member with a head for figures. The shoemaker and his sister, the boy's mother, made the final anxious budget of their resources. After all, there need be no further school or college for the future lawyer: the period of preparation for the first examination could be taken at home, and then he could be articled to a local solicitor. The Bar, of course, would have suited him better, with his darting mind, his eloquence, good humour, his channelled passion and shrewd common sense. But the cost of the first inevitable lean years at the Bar would be prohibitive. So it would have to be the Desk instead of the Bar. But it would still be the Law.

Lloyd George was told that he must now prepare to learn Law. His heart leapt.

Promptly, another problem loomed. The Preliminary Law Examination required a knowledge of both Latin and French and in neither had the boy received any instruction whatever. As to the Latin, his old headmaster, David Evans, had indeed some knowledge, but neither he nor any other man or woman in Llanystumdwy had ever heard or said or read a single word in "the French".

Easily done. Or rather, hardly and bravely done. The shoemaker set himself to learn French, so that he could teach the boy.

It happened that *Cassell's Popular Educator* was then being published in serial form, and some copies were brought into the shop. They contained articles setting forth in clear and simple style a course of instruction in the

At seventeen

French language. Uncle Lloyd studied it, bought a dictionary and a French Grammar, and at close upon fifty years of age sat down every evening with Lloyd George to this new and arduous homework. Together, the boy and his uncle plodded through syntax and idiom, spelling out the words—the pronunciation must have left much to be desired.

The task did not end with the French, for the standard of Latin set up by the examiners was beyond the learning in that language even of schoolmaster Evans. So, to Aesop's *Fables*, in French was added Sallust's *Catiline* in Latin. Long after the village had gone to sleep, the lamp burned in the kitchen of the shoemaker's house as the resolute adventurers picked their way through the forest of a foreign tongue. History will find something sublime in this fireside picture of a man's love for another's child.

It was a family secret. Not even the schoolmaster knew the real purpose of the Latin lessons; Uncle Lloyd would not risk the pitying sympathy of neighbours for his nephew if the great enterprise should fail. The village folk had to contain their curiosity when, in November, 1877, uncle and nephew went off together on a long railway journey.

Their destination was Liverpool, where Lloyd George was to sit for his Preliminary Law Examination. It lasted a week, and every morning Uncle Lloyd took the candidate to St. George's Hall and every evening met him on the steps and fetched him home.

They returned to Llanystumdwy, and early in December came good news that ran like fire about the village. Uncle Lloyd's boy "had passed to become an attorney".

It was a famous day in the shoemaker's home, and proudly Mr. David Evans recorded the event by special entry in the school log-book:

"1877. 8 December.
    D. Ll George, 1st cl. pupil, successful in passing the preliminary examina- Age not tion of the Incorporated Law Society at Liverpool, and received the quite 15 certificate."

The first bastion had fallen.

. . . . . .

Lloyd George was not yet fifteen. His uncle thought it best that he should spend a few months as a junior clerk in a solicitor's office before taking up his articles. Thus, he would learn at first hand the groundwork of his profession. It was summer before this could be arranged; in July, 1878, Lloyd George took his seat on a high stool in the office of Messrs. Breese, Jones and Casson, Solicitors of Portmadoc.

Portmadoc is a small country town which is also a seaport. It lies about seven miles east of Llanystumdwy, at the mouth of the Glaslyn River that flows down from Snowdon.

B

The offices there of Messrs. Breese, Jones and Casson were, in many ways, a hub of local business. Besides having a large private practice, the solicitors were Clerks to two Petty Sessional Divisions, while Mr. Breese himself was Clerk of the Peace and also Clerk to the Lieutenant of the neighbouring county of Merioneth. Furthermore, though a Churchman he was a staunch Liberal, and held the post of Liberal Agent both for Merioneth and South Caernarvonshire. So Lloyd George entered at once, and both by a legal and a political approach, into direct and intimate touch with questions which formed the texture of the daily lives of the people; for all items of county administration fell within the jurisdiction of Quarter Sessions—rating, licensing, assessments, distraints, criminal law. A young lawyer who meant to be a People's Champion could not have studied his profession in a more useful university.

Lloyd George took to it, thirstily. He began to digest Law books from the moment he entered the office, and he carried on his labours late at night, not only in the Law but in Constitutional History, biographies and current political controversies. His fellow clerk at Portmadoc recalls that on his desk was Hallam's *Constitutional History* and that while he ate a "scrappy bread-and-cheese lunch he dipped all the time into Hallam".

It was not possible for him to go on living at home in Llanystumdwy, making a double journey of seven miles a day. So Lloyd George took lodgings with an old couple whose own children had gone out into the world; he returned to Llanystumdwy only for the week-end. Again the midnight candle burned, while the neighbouring streets lay in darkness and silence.

Practice, he considered, was still better than precept, even from the best of masters. Mr. Jones Morris, a solicitor at Portmadoc who served in those days with Lloyd George as an articled clerk, tells how after only a few weeks in the office Lloyd George made out a summons. Jones Morris warned him to be very careful in its preparation, and to see that on no account did it leave the office without being approved by one of the partners of the firm. In this particular document there turned out to be, in fact, a slight informality. When Jones Morris drew Lloyd George's attention to it and suggested that he would save himself trouble if he consulted Mr. Casson even before preparing a summons, Lloyd George replied curtly in Welsh:

"*Mae arnaf eisiau dysgu.*" (I want to learn.)

He carried that method into his political adventures.

On 28 January, 1879, eleven days after his sixteenth birthday, he was articled to Mr. Casson, the junior partner of the firm. A clerk rode over to Llanystumdwy to attest the signatures of himself, his mother and his uncle.

The senior partner, Mr. Breese, was well pleased with his showing. He saw to it that the young man was kept busy serving papers, watching cases in court, registering voters and canvassing for the Liberal cause.

The thunder of Gladstonian–Disraelian politics was shaking the earth of Britain again. In Midlothian, in December, the Grand Old Man was addressing audiences of six thousand people, while sixty thousand more clamoured to hear him. The Scottish hills were frozen, but fire roared through the glens. The woes of Ireland, of Transvaal, Zululand, even Afghanistan first transfixed, then galvanized the conscience of Liberal Britain.

"Remember the rights of the savage, as we call him!" cried Gladstone. "Remember that the sanctity of life in the hill villages of the Afghans, among the winter snows, is as inviolable in the eye of Almighty God as can be your own!"

To the Afghan village and its sorrows Lloyd George himself would shortly return, and also to the Zulus and the Boers. Meantime, the Midlothian campaign had brought on, in March, 1880, another General Election.

In Wales, the Liberal strength was still mounting and they sensed it at Portmadoc, which was one of the northern Liberal citadels. In the candle-maker's workshop behind the main street, where they moulded candles for the slate quarries of Blaenau Festiniog, Lloyd George discovered a depth and power of political feeling that matched anything he had known in the smithy at Llanystumdwy. This force was effectively deployed in Caernarvonshire in the 1880 General Election. It surprised no intelligent observer of the local contest that in the political upheaval which resulted in the dismissal of Disraeli from the Premiership and the accession of Gladstone again, the Liberal candidate for Caernarvon Boroughs, Mr. Watkin Williams, the lawyer, was returned by a record majority over the Tory, Mr. Douglas Pennant. Lloyd George himself played a junior, but an energetic part in this.

Now he added a sharp, new weapon to his armoury. This was journalism, and as often before with such political journalism, it began by being voluntary and unpaid. The writer felt that he simply had to project somewhere or other what he felt within him, or else himself explode. He looked around for the appropriate artillery, and field of fire.

There was only one cause on the march in Wales then: it was the Liberal, Nonconformist cause, to which was being added that vehement, almost violent element of Nationalism, as the revolt against what was called the Two Hundred Years of Sloth took fire and spread. The other, Tory, Church of England, cause was dug-in on the defensive, though some young and resolute spirits, headed by the Bishop of St. Asaph, were preparing a bold counter-offensive campaign.

Almost without exception, the Welsh journals of the time were radical and nationalist in sympathy. Today, it seems incredible that the ruling alliance of Church and Land should have made no serious effort to combat with the same weapons a power so hostile to their own ascendancy. Perhaps most of their leaders never realized it, which may explain why within a few more years this ascendancy had been broken.

The greatest of these "engines of propaganda", for that is frankly what they were, was undoubtedly the "*Baner ac Amserau Cymru*" (the Banner and Times of Wales—it might almost have been called the Banner and Bible of Wales), and the most vigorous of the propagandists was its proprietor, Thomas Gee, the son of an Englishman who had married a Welshwoman. Mr. Gee, senior, had come to Denbigh to manage a printing press which had been set up there to publish Welsh religious tracts in the language of the country. He learned the Welsh language himself, settled there and founded a prosperous family publishing firm of his own.

On this battlefield, Lloyd George himself was shortly due to appear and reinforce the doughty veteran, who had been born in the year of Waterloo. But for the moment, the young man called Lloyd George was unknown and alone. He wrote his first article, and sent it off to the Editor of the *North Wales Express*. He signed it "Brutus".

What the author himself thought of its chances of appearing in print is shown by this entry in his diary.

"November 1, 1880–. . . . Do not relish the idea of that refusal which Editor, overwhelmed with a redundance of such trash, will have to accord to some of them."

There followed four days of alternating hopes and fears, and then the diary tells us:

"November 5, 1880. When I eagerly opened the *North Wales Express* this morning I found my own contribution on the same page as leading article. I had first of all looked up 'Notices to Correspondents', expecting to find a refusal of my letter, but disappointed on the right side."

The article, which ran to about six hundred words, dealt with an after-dinner speech delivered by the Marquis of Salisbury at Taunton. Amongst other items, the Tory ex-Foreign Secretary (and future Tory Prime Minister) had charged Mr. Gladstone's Liberal Government with concealing or withholding information, and with proposing foolishly to prosecute certain of the Irish Nationalist leaders.

The article was entitled "POLITICAL SHREDS", and the author began it in lively personal style with an attack on the after-dinner orator.

"He is a relic of what he has been; the ruins of a character, which, if not noble, at least seemed stable. Office proved to be too much for him. It has shattered his reputation. The prejudice and rancour of his unalloyed Toryism he still retains, but the consistency and integrity of character which whilom graced these propensities have departed. . . ."

On the day that Lloyd George posted his first article to the Editor of the *North Wales Express*, there came news to Portmadoc that Mr. Watkin

Williams, Liberal M.P. for Caernarvon Boroughs, had been appointed a Judge of the High Court, which involved an immediate by-election. The rival candidates were hastily chosen, Mr. Rathbone for the Liberals and Mr. Ellis Nanney, the Squire of Llanystumdwy, for the Tories. "Brutus" sharpened his blade.

On 13 November, 1880, he noted in his diary that the Election Addresses of both candidates were that day published. The Liberal's was very long, and the Tory's very short. "Brutus" did not propose to permit his old school patron to hide his light under any bushel, however modestly or discreetly it glimmered. He sat down, and in an article twice as long and doubly as vitriolic as the one he had devoted to Lord Salisbury, he analysed the politics of Squire Nanney's Party, with appropriate reference to the contemporary Afghan and Zulu wars, which, wrote "Brutus":

"made Afghan mothers husbandless, their children fatherless and both homeless—saturated the Afghan snows with the blood of patriots, and drove hatred of our very name and presence into the heart of the Afghan nation. Whose policy made Zululand mourn the loss of its brave sons, devastated its fertile plains, turned its happy kraals into sombre mortuaries, and sacrificed its nationality upon a pyre erected with the carcases of its defenders."

He then offered a few observations on the personality of the Tory candidate himself, concluding:

"If my information be correct, you are just the man whom the electors of Caernarvonshire would delight to reject with contumely."

He had doubts about the fate of this editorial offering also:

"Am afraid its length, and I suggest its virulence will tend to its exclusion. However, it does not matter much. Pseudonyms do not blush. . . ."

The Editor did not blush to publish. He boldly displayed the article in his newspaper; and advertised it on his bill-posters throughout the constituency. "Brutus" had only one small complaint which he kept to his diary and himself: "A truculent passage has been partially left out."

Though he was so scathing about the Squire, the truth is that Mr. Nanney was personally popular in many quarters, and deservedly so, for he was a kindly and generous man. His handicap in this election was his politics.

There were bumper meetings, cheering crowds, torchlight processions. Lloyd George canvassed enthusiastically during the election, and on polling day acted as Liberal Committee man for Dolbenmaen district. Late that night, he left for Caernarvon as one of the Liberal custodians of the local ballot box. Next morning, 1 December, 1880, the result of the poll was declared. Mr. Rathbone had beaten Squire Nanney by a handsome majority. Later, the same day, Lloyd George called at the newspaper office of the *North Wales Express* and met the Editor in person for the first time. The Editor assured "Brutus" that his contributions were most acceptable. No question of payment arose.

By this time, Lloyd George was already back in his own home, though it was no longer at Llanystumdwy. His uncle's interest in his customers as a shoemaker was now quite o'ertopped by his interest in his flock as their unpaid pastor. Most of these were centred around Criccieth, and when a local iron-monger who was an Elder of the Baptist Church offered him a dwelling there at a nominal rent, Richard Lloyd and his sister resolved to move.

Their new home stood in Tanygrisiau Terrace, near the foot of the rocky hillock on the seashore which is crowned by the ruins of Criccieth Castle. It was called Morvin House, but despite its more dignified name, it was, in fact, not much more commodious than the cottage at Llanystumdwy. There was enough extra room, however, to enable them to take in holiday visitors, one of whom was the novelist, Rider Haggard. Another advantage was that though Morvin House was still several miles away from Lloyd George's office at Portmadoc it was near enough for him to come and live there. The housework was done by his mother and sister, and Uncle Lloyd still repaired the family's shoes.

Thus Lloyd George returned to the strongest influence he had known in his youth, and at a critical period of restlessness, doubt and often deep unhappiness. Now, under the eye of his uncle, he took active part in the work of the Baptist Chapel, its Sunday School and Bible Class, and also of the Temperance Society.

The last of these avenues of service seemed to offer then in Britain the most direct approach to the gravest social problem of the time, the poverty of the masses herded into the great cities and seaports, and the lure of drink to forget it for a while. Few drunkards, indeed, have had better excuse for their offence. Then, a bottle of cheap spirits was in literal truth "the quickest way out of Manchester", or out of the slum alleyways of any other great British city.

The nation has found out since, and Lloyd George himself was one of the earliest of the real social reformers to grasp it, that temperance will come soonest when the vile conditions which make temptation for excess have been removed. Many of them have now gone, largely due to the reforming zeal of Lloyd George and those whom he organized and mobilized, and today Britain is a pretty sober land. But in 1880 it was easy for the reformer to see the Demon Rum alone at the bottom of every cup of misery that mankind had to drain.

Uncle Lloyd's own household was strictly teetotal, and Lloyd George grew up in these principles. His first public addresses outside the Chapel on the Sunday School were delivered from the Temperance platform, and they lacked nothing in fervour.

Lloyd George had learned well, in both Chapel and Sunday School, to judge by the observations of his progress which his uncle made in the notebooks which he kept carefully up-to-date.

"*Wednesday night.* David read well. He has attained naturalness of voice, and expression better than ever. The singing also led by him correct and lively."

"*Today David George's* 18*th birthday.* Feel that if he makes as good progress in the next eighteen he will, by God's grace, be successful, useful and happy."

"*Wednesday night.* Excellent meeting. D. Ll. G. speaking for the first time—O, my dear boy, he did speak well!"

"*Chapel.* Good meeting—D. Ll. G. spoke excellently—a little practice, and a little more spirited delivery, and he will make a fine speaker—pluck and perseverance, that's all!"

Towards the end of this year Lloyd George paid his first visit to London, to stay there for a few days with another uncle. He quickly made his way to the House of Commons, although it was a Saturday and Parliament was not in session. He recorded his impression of the place.

"*November* 12. Went to the Houses of Parliament. Very much disappointed with them. Grand buildings outside, but inside they are crabbed, small and suffocating, especially the House of Commons. I will not say but that I eyed the Assembly in a spirit to that in which William the Conqueror eyed England on his visit to Edward the Confessor, as the region of his future domain. Oh, vanity!

At Westminster Abbey contemplated the monuments of departed genius. In the evening went with Uncle to Madame Tussaud's."

He determined to enlarge his range of operations.

On his return home, Lloyd George joined the Portmadoc Debating Society, which met every month in a room above a shop in the High Street. He meant to get more practice in speaking English. His first speech was made there early in the New Year, his most notable one the following autumn.

Lloyd George was then opposing the motion that the recent war in Egypt was justifiable. In the insurgent leader, Arabi Pasha, he discerned virtues which that bold adventurer would hardly have discovered in himself.

"The foreign control of the country was a great injustice to the Egyptians," declaimed Lloyd George. "The peasants were being driven to the greatest poverty by the shameful taxation imposed by the rotten government of the country upon them. They were glad to get any man to come and deliver them from their pitiful state."[1]

[1] There is a note-book of Lloyd George's belonging to this period, filled with notes on Egypt. They are salted with violent observations on the English, too.

The Society voted by a large majority in favour of the war, two members remaining neutral. The *Caernarvon Herald*, however, noted of Lloyd George's speech, that:

"It would probably have gained praise had it been delivered in the House of Commons. The matter, the words, and the style, together with the freedom with which it was delivered took everybody by surprise, and made a deep impression."

He drove home the impact with regular blows. Ireland, Tithes, Landlords, Peers, the Church of England were his themes. Ireland was suffering from the "sores inflicted by Satanic landlordism"; it was the duty of statesmen to "alleviate the misery of the poor before pandering to the vanity of the rich"; the House of Lords was "the lumber-room of musty prejudice and an asylum of hereditary delusions".

It read lively enough in those days. Did it sound as well? Yes, because it had been most carefully cultivated. Somebody once wrote of the "untaught eloquence" of Lloyd George. Nonsense. True, the man was born with the gift of seeing things, and of seeing through and beyond them. It was Winston Churchill who said of him: "He was always looking in the next field". True, too, he had imagination. But he had still to learn how to paint the picture, how to tell the story, how to sing the song, like the bards.

Methodically, assiduously, painfully, he did it. Mr. Beriah Evans, a contemporary Welsh journalist and close friend of Lloyd George for many a year, has told of catching up with him as he went striding along the hilly coast road at night on his homeward stretch, declaiming to himself his next speech. Alderman William George, his brother, recalls how he saw the early Lloyd George addressing his mirror. In later years Lloyd George would fasten on a member of his family, or a friend, to whom he would recite the most powerful passages. He invited criticism, and respected it. Very often, he accepted it. For the greater part of his life Lloyd George was a severe self-critic of Lloyd George speeches.

He kept his hand in at journalism. In 1882, he and his young brother William jointly won first prize at Criccieth Eisteddfod with an essay on the "Cash and Credit System". With a perfervid preference rare in young, poor men, they scorned credit and praised cash. The same summer, Lloyd George joined the local volunteers as a "Saturday afternoon soldier", attending weekly drills at the annual camp at Morfa Conway, North Wales. It appears that Volunteer Lloyd George, the future great War Prime Minister of Britain, had no more distinguished personal military record than Militiaman Abraham Lincoln, the great Civil War President of the United States, who also shouldered a Saturday musket in his lumberman youth. Both emerged without scars.

A brief, unhappy and unique experience Lloyd George did, however, undergo in his Volunteer days. One night in camp, he was induced to drink alcohol. He had never tasted it before, and with the rest of the squad, he drank too much. It made him violently ill, and confirmed him for many a year longer in his temperance habits. Undoubtedly the Devil brewed this stuff!

His civilian career was going well enough. An entry in his diary of 2 June, 1883, reads:

"Titbit in *Caernarvon Herald* refers to my 'thirst for renown', etc. Perhaps it will be gratified. I believe it depends entirely on what forces of pluck and industry I can muster."

Another year of improving labour and of increasing stature, and then, in April, 1884, the young lawyer was off to London once more, to sit for his final Law Examinations. One evening, he visited the House of Commons again, and this time heard a debate there. He was fortunate, for Gladstone spoke and then, when all seemed to be over, Lord Randolph Churchill rose and bearded the giant himself.

Age 21

"Gladstone," said Lloyd George, "simply swept the Front Opposition Bench out of existence—he cowed them into silence; no one had a syllable to say in defence of the amendment, and the Speaker was just about to put the question when a slight, stooping young man with a heavy moustache rose just below the gangway. It was Lord Randolph Churchill. He stepped out almost into the middle of the floor. He pointed scornfully at the great man, he snapped finger and thumb at him. I thought Churchill an impudent puppy, as every Liberal was bound to do. I hated him for assailing the Old Man. I hated him, but I thoroughly enjoyed his speech; *it was splendid.*"

But this enchanted evening was almost his only relaxation from a final burst of "swotting". Early and long and late, Lloyd George went at it, for this was the highest and the hardest test so far. From Uncle Lloyd came daily encouragement by post, and best of all, on Examination Day itself:

"Would it be better for us to whistle 'For we are jolly good fellows' together first, I wonder? Well, if there isn't time the spirit is in me, I know. Go to it, like a lion my boy! 'Cool as a cucumber though not so green' is the motto of a student on Exam Day. Can you legally adopt it, Dai?"

Soon, there came news to Criccieth of Lloyd George's new triumph. He had passed with honours, and was now a fully-qualified solicitor; his firm suggested that he should take charge of a new branch which they proposed to open in his town. It did not justify the expense, and within a few weeks they had decided to close it down. Instead, they offered Lloyd George a

B*

managing clerkship in their old-established and prospering branch at Dolgelly. It was an attractive prospect for a man who wished to live a safe, sure life. The name of such a man was not Lloyd George. He resolved to carve his own fortune.

The tiny back-parlour of the house beneath the walls of Criccieth Castle was rigged out as an office. He had no capital, and as yet no clients. He did not have three guineas to spare to buy the robe and neckband he needed to appear in court. But firmly and proudly, he nailed upon the front door a brass plate bearing the inscription:

D. Lloyd George, Solicitor

Now, the second bastion had fallen.

CHAPTER III

INDUSTRIOUS APPRENTICE

HE rose at six in the morning, and worked until midnight or beyond. Sunday brought no rest, for then he either preached in chapel or else listened to another's sermon.

While he listened, Lloyd George observed the art of the preacher, his gestures, postures, glances, language, intonations, pauses. The theme concerned him less. When he preached himself he practised what he had learned, and studied his congregation. Lloyd George never ceased to watch the man, or men, he talked to. "*Mae arnaf esiau dysgu.*"

He pleaded in the police courts at Criccieth, Portmadoc and Blaenau Festiniog, in the county court at Pwllheli. Soon, he found it necessary to open a "branch office" (it was a single small room in all these places). At Criccieth, it faced the Brynhir Arms in the High Street. After a time, the landlord of this snug little inn called to see Uncle Lloyd, who was in charge, and appealed to him to move elsewhere, "for the sake of my customers".

"Why? Am I a bad influence on your customers?" asked Uncle Lloyd, half-playfully.

"No, indeed," said the landlord very seriously. "You are such a good influence that I am going to lose about half of them, who are afraid you'll see them coming in or out of my pub."

Lloyd George kept up his reading, both in law and history. He kept up his newspaper writing, too; Lloyd George the journalist, still had his eye upon the Marquis of Salisbury. He also kept within his rifle sights the Tory guerilla, Lord Randolph Churchill, who he noted had that week in Parliament:

"succeeded in drawing the badger" (it was Mr. Joseph Chamberlain) "and has good reason to regret his temerity, for the brute has severely bitten him."

Joe Chamberlain was more than ever Lloyd George's hero.

"He is unquestionably the future leader of the people," he wrote. "He is a Radical, and doesn't care who knows it as long as the people do. He is convinced that the aristocracy stands in the way of development of the Rights of Man, and he says so unflinchingly, though he be howled at as an ill-mannered demagogue by the whole kennelry of gorged Aristocracy, and of their fawning minions."

What was Lloyd George like at this time? According to a photograph taken on the day of his wedding, his hair had not yet begun to flow into the famous mane that the cartoonists captured. His eyes had a questing look, his mouth was resolute and rather cruel. His face in 1888, indeed reflects the ambitious man's restless spirit, and also his resentment of the superior social set-up which then surrounded (and excluded) him. Sir David Brynmor-Jones, a well-known County Court Judge of the Mid-Wales Circuit in those days, remembered:

> "a particularly boyish-looking advocate, thin and rather pale. I was attracted by his youthful appearance and his taking voice," added this friendly Judge, "as well as by a certain earnest, eager, but yet restrained manner. I asked the Deputy-Registrar the name of the young fellow and he replied 'David Lloyd George'."

Burning the midnight oil may have induced Lloyd George's youthful pallor, and his still modest earnings preserved his youthful figure, for several days a week he walked the five miles from Criccieth to Portmadoc and then home again to save expense. It was also most useful to see people and—even more—to be seen by them! After that one "night out" in camp, Lloyd George was a more-than-ever convinced teetotaller; he still had the Temperance Question at heart, and gave much of his spare time to speaking on it.

He was by no means temperate in his opinions, most of which seemed somehow to lead back, *via* politics, to the subject of his especial abhorrences, the Squirearchy and "that old stranger, the English Church".

He was himself naturally and thoroughly detested by the leading members of both.

> "The bantam is the noisiest inmate of the farmyard," remarked one of the local gentry at a public meeting. "He is also the smallest. Mr. Lloyd George is the bantam of the political arena."

But the bantam continued both to demand and to attract more and more attention.

Age 22   Politics needed more fire, anyway, thought Lloyd George. Another General Election was approaching, and "Humdrum Liberalism won't win elections" wrote Master Firebrand in his diary.

The General Election turned out to be brisk enough despite his fears, and though the Tories claimed an early lead in the towns, when the country vote came in victory perched once more upon the Liberal banners.

> "I am convinced," wrote Lloyd George, "that this victory is all due to Chamberlain's speeches. Gladstone had no programme that would draw at all."

He made many speeches himself, and (he notes), "at Portmadoc, in a Vote of Thanks, was singled out as a future M.P."

His Tory opponents singled him out, too, as a particular target of abuse.

He attended one of these complimentary occasions, boldly stood up at questions and in no time had turned the place into a bull-ring.

Lloyd George was sharp enough with questions himself. At one meeting, a heckler kept calling out: "Where's the donkey and cart?"

He was referring to the time when as a boy Lloyd George had driven round the countryside with his mother, delivering boots to his uncle's customers.

"As to the cart I have no present information," retorted Lloyd George. "As to the donkey . . ." a pause, and a Lloyd George gesture of explanation.

Things went beyond hard words. Lloyd George's Diary notes:

"*November* 26. Ll—— warned me that they had heard from the other side that they intended stoning me on Saturday night."

"*November* 28. Took M.O.[1] and her cousin home. Was warned that the rioters threatened to kill me."

"*November* 30. Some of our weak-kneed Liberals decided not to hold meeting this evening. I was awfully annoyed at this. There were about sixty coming over from Portmadoc to assist in maintaining order."

Something like a Land War already raged in the neighbouring counties of Flintshire and Merionethshire, where the Anti-Tithe League, organized by Thomas Gee, editor and publisher of the *Baner ac Amserau Cymru*, and the Rev. John Parry, dominated the Welsh countryside.

At this time the tithe had still to be paid, not by the owner but by the occupier of the land. Since, in Wales, the tenant farmer was almost always a Nonconformist, subscribing to his own chapel, this charge for the upkeep of a church he disliked and never attended pressed hard upon him. Thomas Gee himself had chosen to have distraint levied upon his goods rather than to pay church rates. He had already launched his vigorous campaign for fair rents, security of tenure and compensation for tenants' improvements. Now he was out to nationalize the tithe, because he opposed not its collection but its appropriation for purely sectarian ends.

So great was the stir in Wales over Tithe during the 'eighties that frequently the military were called out, and more than once, in places such as Blaenau Festiniog, where a considerable number of free-spirited quarrymen were massed, there was real trouble.

Blaenau Festiniog is a town beneath Snowdon, whose mountain mists wash the great slate wall surrounding the place, and make it glitter like silver. Indeed, it is less a matter of the town being sited in the midst of the mountain than of the mountain invading the town. The rock rises out of the streets, and the sheep graze a few feet above the chimneys; a place once seen not soon forgotten.

It was at Blaenau Festiniog, in the course of this Land War that Lloyd

[1] Miss Margaret Owen, later Mrs. Lloyd George.

George began to make his mark upon National as well as upon merely local politics. These were days—two years before the Llanfrothen case—when his own reputation reached hardly beyond his own part of Caernarvon. He was **Age 23** in lively company that February night in the grey little town among the quarries. Indeed the other names upon the bill were the attraction, for his own intervention was quite unheralded. These characters were Michael Jones of Bala, and Michael Davitt of Ireland.

The first Michael, who took the chair, had gone from being pastor of an Independent church in Carmarthenshire to become Principal of the Congregational College at Bala. But neither the instruction of his flock nor the preparation of other instructors was the purpose that lay nearest to the heart of the Rev. Michael Jones. He wanted to nationalize the land.

Michael Jones had not arrived at this point via the dusty corridors of Karl Marx. He was a Radical, not a Socialist. Like Thomas Gee, he had been driven to the conclusion that the only practical way to cut through the tangle of tithe, feudal tenure, and traditional rights of game and fishing was to vest the ownership of the soil in the community under the Crown. He was an honest, fearless and self-sacrificing man, and when he realized that his life-long crusade for land reform was not going to succeed in this country, he devoted his entire savings to founding a Welsh colony in Patagonia, where it flourishes yet in a proud, irregular kind of independence. Michael Jones was not popular with the Welsh Liberal leaders of 1886.

The second Michael was a kindred spirit from Ireland, and in so far that he too, was fighting a Land War against an alien landlordism he had a kindred policy. He was himself the son of an evicted Irish peasant, and had been sentenced to an English jail for several years for his Fenian faith and works. Indeed it was while he was in jail, in 1882, that Michael Davitt had been elected Nationalist M.P. for West Heath. He was released on ticket-of-leave but not yet allowed, as an ex-convict, to sit in the House of Commons. Michael Davitt was not *persona grata*, either, with the Elders of Welsh Liberalism and Nonconformity.

When, therefore, the Rev. Michael Jones invited this turbulent and exciting rebel to address a public meeting at Festiniog on 12 February, 1886, on the subject of a Land League for Wales, the Local Whig Worthies one and all discovered that they had pressing engagements elsewhere.

Not so Lloyd George. He did, however, consult a friend, for his own family had their doubts. This friend was the daughter of a well-to-do yeoman farmer near Criccieth. Lloyd George begins to mention her in his diary about this time, and more and more so. The reader has seen her initials once, "M.O." and will remember that her name was Margaret Owen. One day soon, David Lloyd George would marry her.

Now, when he asked Margaret if he should go to the Davitt meeting, the young woman, who already held decided views, replied:

"Why not? Of course, go!"

So, though he was kept late in court that day, Lloyd George went. With Michael Davitt and Michael Jones he, too, believed that the land laws lay at the root of the social problem. Furthermore, though the official Liberal leadership was not finally committed to Home Rule for Ireland, Lloyd George was heart and soul in favour of it—and Home Rule for Wales, too!

Michael Davitt did not disappoint his audience. The quarrymen of Festiniog had not asked, unlike the town's élite, by what right this black-bearded, one-armed, passionate peasant came over the Irish Sea to speak to a Welsh gathering. They packed the Hall, and crowded far beyond its doors into the dark street under the rock. They heard a deeply-moving speech.

When Davitt had done, the chairman looked around for someone to propose a vote of thanks. His eye fell on the young solicitor from Criccieth, and he called upon him.

Lloyd George had not been notified beforehand, but he had prepared beforehand, and had waited for this chance. He spoke for five minutes, and when he sat down the audience rose and roared their applause for half as long again. The speech is early Lloyd George vintage, mingling wit, mockery, praise, abuse, and passion. The *Cambrian News* thus reported it:

"Mr. D. Lloyd George, solicitor, said that when he saw the two Michaels on the platform it reminded him of the fight that the Archangel Michael had with Satan. (Laughter.) Though that Michael, being single-handed, was unable to dispose of Old Nick, he trusted that the two Michaels would be able to bring the cause of the farmers and the working men to a successful issue. (Cheers.) Mr. Michael Davitt was a man who had not only done much for humanity, but had also suffered much for humanity, and therefore they all honoured him. (Applause.) To oppose a man because he did not belong to their nation was most narrow minded and contrary to the principles of their religion. They remembered the parable of the man who fell among thieves. His neighbour was not the man who belonged to his own nation, but a stranger from Samaria—an Irishman—who had come there to bind up their wounds. (Cheers.) Let them respect him on that account. (Applause.) The people who spoke against bringing Mr. Michael Davitt into Wales were those who on bended knees begged princes who were no better than German half-breeds to come into Wales to preside over Eisteddfodau. (Laughter and cheers.)

Not only the *Cambrian News* but other newspapers, English as well as Welsh, spread far afield the fame of the young orator. More immediate was the effect upon him of the advice which Michael Davitt offered as they sat at supper in the house of a friend that night. The Irish leader urged Lloyd George to go in wholeheartedly for politics.

"There is a future for you there, my boy," he said earnestly as he put his hand on Lloyd George's shoulder.

He was, indeed, already getting deeply into politics, led there by these very issues of local controversy and conflict. But first, there was something else in his heart.

Lloyd George was in love. Margaret Owen was the woman of his heart. She was the daughter of Richard Owen of Mynydd Ednyfed, Criccieth, who claimed descent from Owen Gwynedd, one of the greatest of the old Welsh Princes. Mr. Owen farmed about a hundred acres, and was highly regarded in the community. "Sure-footed" his neighbours said of him, and certainly "sure-headed" was a quality which he transmitted to his daughter. As long as Lloyd George listened to her advice, he made no mistakes.

Margaret met David as they walked home from chapel—but not the same one, for she belonged to the Methodists. He was welcome at Mynydd Ednyfed Farm as a Liberal and a Free Churchman, though a Baptist.

Cordiality cooled when the head of the family found that it was not *his* opinion which was really being sought about matters. Mr. Owen did not view with favour the idea of his daughter's marriage with a struggling young solicitor who was still living under his uncle's roof, and, as it appeared, was endowed with little more than a ready tongue and unbounded self-confidence. Margaret's mother was persuaded to share her husband's doubts, and there were sad nights at Mynydd Edynfed.

However, "Maggie" (as she appears from 1885 onward in Lloyd George's diary), had a mind of her own. She made it up to marry David Lloyd George, and she was fortified in her resolution by the advice of her aunt, who told her: "Don't give him up! That young man has a great prospect ahead of him!"

The reader will not be surprised to learn that for many months before David formally proposed to his Maggie, he had carefully cultivated the confidence of Maggie's aunt, and had won her over to his side. At this period, the sweethearts still exchanged their love letters (literally, a "hole-in-the-wall" correspondence) *via* a secret cranny in a stone fence around one of Farmer Owen's pastures. To complete our story of Young Love Conquering All, Uncle Lloyd also looked coldly on his nephew's suit, and according to Lloyd George's eldest son, Richard, he even sought out all the attractive Baptist young ladies he could find to tempt David away from Maggie. All in vain.

On 24 January, 1888, D. R. Daniel received a letter, dated that same day from Lloyd George. Amongst other things it said:

Age 25   ". . . I am starting for a distant land—and a better one, I trust. I am to be spliced this morning at Pencaenewydd."

It was one week after his twenty-fifth birthday. The wedding took place at the Methodist chapel in Pencaenewydd, near Chwilog. The Rev. John Owen, Methodist minister of Criccieth, and Richard Lloyd jointly performed the service in the presence of a handful of friends and relatives. The villagers along the road back to Criccieth hung out flags, and the town fêted the event. The bridal pair left by the noon train for London on their honeymoon, and that night Criccieth, defying a steady drizzle, was lit up with a bonfire and fire-works were let off.

The question of a parliamentary career was not one of those which the young pair discussed on their honeymoon. Indeed, though Lloyd George had resolved upon it, the prospect of achieving it must still have seemed far off, for in those days Members of Parliament were not paid any salary, and Lloyd George had still to build up a paying legal practice. On their return, he and Margaret were very glad to live for a time at Mynydd Ednyfed.

These were the days of the Case of the Quarryman of Llanfrothen, and the young lawyer with a newly-married wife was risking much. In this case, Lloyd George showed at the outset of his career the essential qualities of his character throughout his tempestuous days. The decision and the audacity of the challenge attracted the public attention and applause. But behind it there also lay the requisite legal knowledge and the skill in preparing and contesting the case. It has often been said of Lloyd George that he was ready: "to fight at the drop of a hat."

To be sure, he liked fighting, but he preferred to drop the hat himself, if possible, having examined its contents. The Llanfrothen case certainly did nothing to endear the cocksure attorney to the County Court. Nor did his frequent tussles with the Police Court Bench make him any more popular there. He was in no way discouraged; he reckoned that the ill-will of the Bench, especially in cases which involved the Game Laws, was well offset by the confidence of his clients that in him they had an advocate who would really fight Authority. Bearding the Justices was a bold line for a young solicitor to take in the late 'eighties, for they represented a formidable social as well as a legal power in the land. It will not now be denied that these magistrates in Wales at that time paid considerable deference to their own interests.

Nor was this bias by any means confined to the English squires who accepted the Commission of the Peace; Lloyd George himself recalled a native born Caernarvonshire J.P. who would always decide for a Welshman against an Englishman, and for a Caernarvonshire man against a stranger from Merioneth.

There were times when humour eased the tension in court. So it was in the case which Lloyd George fought before the Merioneth County Bench, presided over by Mr. Samuel Pope, Q.C., one of the leading members of the Parliamentary Bar. The young solicitor had been submitting certain legal propositions with complete assurance, when the chairman broke in:

"No, no! This won't do! Mr. Lloyd George is laying down the law as though he were a Judge in the Court of appeal. It is necessary for me to point out that we here do not believe in the infallibility of Mr. Lloyd George."

"Neither do we in these parts believe in the infallibility of the Pope," retorted Lloyd George.

Other encounters ended more sharply. The year after the Quarryman of Llanfrothen was buried, four quarrymen of Talysarn were charged with unlawfully fishing with a net in Nantlle Lake, which is the source of Llyfnwy river. There was no doubt that they had fished, or that the river was legally preserved by the district conservators; the question was whether the lake came within the definition of the word "river". For the quarrymen, Lloyd George contended that it did not, and the case had to be adjourned to get a certificate from the Secretary of State for Home Affairs, defining the Fishery District. When it arrived, it named the river but not the lake, and pending a decision in the Court of Queen's Bench Lloyd George denied the jurisdiction of the Caernarvonshire County Bench. The chairman said brusquely that it would have to be proved a higher court.

Age 26

Mr. George: Yes, sir, and in a perfectly just and unbiased Court, too.

The Chairman: If that remark of Mr. George's is meant as a reflection upon any magistrate sitting on this Bench, I hope that he will name him. A more insulting and ungentlemanly remark to the Bench I never heard during the course of my experience as a magistrate.

Mr. George: But a more true remark was never made in a Court of Justice.

The Chairman: Tell me to whom you are referring? I must insist upon you referring to any magistrate or magistrates sitting in this Court.

Mr. George: I refer to you in particular, sir.

The Chairman (rising): Then I retire from the Chair. Good-bye gentlemen. This is the first time I have ever been insulted in a Court of Justice. (*He then left the Court.*)

Another Magistrate: In fairness to the Chairman and other magistrates, I must say that Mr. George was not justified in making such remarks.

A third Magistrate: I decline to proceed with this case until Mr. George apologizes.

Mr. George: I am glad to hear it.

It was too much for their Worships. Even the rearguard now withdrew. The sporting quarrymen were wondering if the case against them would now lapse for lack of Justices to try it, when four of the magistrates marched back into court to announce the unanimous opinion of the Bench that Mr. Lloyd George's remarks were entirely unjustified and should have been withdrawn. Also, that under all the circumstances, it was better that the case should proceed.

Two of the quarrymen were acquitted, and the other two fined a shilling apiece.

.   .   .   .

Politics were calling him again.

The same month that he married Margaret Owen, Lloyd George had also entered on the troubled seas of newspaper ownership. With his ardent Welsh Nationalist friend, D. R. Daniel, he had launched at Pwllheli the periodical *Udgorn Rhyddid* (Trumpet of Freedom). Lloyd George had suggested the title himself, and also the general style of the editorial contents: "We want something stirring, never mind the bombast if the stuff is good."

"We propose raising a capital of, say £100," he explained in a letter, "and limiting our liability to that sum, so as to escape the ruinous consequences of probable libel suits. It is to be a thorough Nationalist and Socialist paper—a 'Regenerator' in every respect . . . it will work untold good."

By now, the early summer of 1888, Lloyd George's name was being canvassed as the Gladstonian Candidate for Caernarvon Boroughs.

It was not the first time that he had been mentioned as a possible Parliamentary challenger. At the General Election two years before, when Mr. Gladstone's first Home Rule Bill had brought about the secession of the Liberal Member for Merioneth, Lloyd George's name had been submitted to the local Liberal selection committee by a Harlech doctor.

Busily trumpeting the name then had been D. R. Daniel, not yet only in his capacity as editor of *Udgorn Rhyddid*, but as Secretary of the Quarrymen's Union. Urged by Lloyd George, he had inscribed a fiery anonymous appeal to the Caernarvonshire Press, setting forth the claims of his friend to be the Liberal and Welsh Nationalist candidate. Lloyd George had written him, D. R. Daniel, privately:

"You know that I am a Welsh Nationalist and have more or less studied the Church, Land and Temperance questions. Perhaps, if you would do me the kindness of placing my elocutionary powers under the microscope of your powerful imagination you might give a tolerably favourable account of my gifts of speech!"

For the moment, however, another figure had loomed larger on the Welsh scene. He was Mr. Tom Ellis, son of a Merionethshire tenant farmer, who had been one of the victims of a bigoted landlordism. Tom Ellis himself was a gifted man with already a meteoric record of scholarship through Bala Theological College, Aberystwyth University College and New College, Oxford. Now, at twenty-seven years of age, he was the undisputed leader of the resurgent Welsh Nationalist movement known as Cymru Fydd (Young Wales), which sought to unite the entire Principality by means of a Welsh National League. Tom Ellis and Lloyd George had met at Blaenau Festiniog during a temperance conference there, and struck up a firm friendship.

"Do you not think," wrote Lloyd George inviting him a few weeks later to come and speak at an anti-Tithe meeting at Pwllheli, "that this Tithe is an excellent lever whereby to raise the spirit of the people?"

This friendship, and the fact that Ellis was Merioneth-born had led Lloyd George to withdraw his own name as parliamentary candidate for the Merioneth seat, and to offer his support. Ellis had been triumphantly elected, and had started on his brilliant career at Westminster by claiming that Home Rule must come nearer home than Ireland—it must come to Wales!

Now by June, 1888, the Llanfrothen Burial Case had gained Lloyd George himself a nation-wide reputation in Wales, and the Liberal Association in three of the six Caernarvon Boroughs were pressing for him as their candidate; by August, following a vigorous speech by him there, Bangor had followed suit. That month he wrote:

"Despite all the machinations of my enemies, I will succeed. I am now sailing before the wind, and they against it."

A critical question for Lloyd George at this time was one of money. He had none of his own to finance his candidature, nor could he count even upon the expectation of success in an election to repay a loan, for members of Parliament did not yet receive any salary. So a small committee was formed of his Liberal Party supporters to raise funds. One of its members took the candidate along to see a wealthy local Methodist, and make appeal to his generosity. At first the interview did not seem to be going too well, for the prospective patron made some rather disparaging remarks about the candidate's "excessively youthful appearance".

Later, the already powerful Lloyd George personal charm must have come into play, for when they departed, the candidate and his committee man carried away with them a promise to pay the whole of the estimated £200 for the expenses of the next election.

Soon, Lloyd George had discovered a new weapon, or rather, an entire arsenal of weapons, to use in his crusade of Welsh Nationalism. For in the autumn, Lord Salisbury's Tory Administration passed the Local Government Act, setting up County Councils to administer the countryside, as City and Borough Councils already administered the towns.

Promptly, Lloyd George insisted that here was a great political chance for Liberalism—at any rate, for Radical Welsh Nationalist Liberalism! The forthcoming County Council elections must be fought on party lines, and the Tory grip upon the countryside challenged the very first time the people had been allowed to vote upon administration of their local affairs.

Lloyd George himself was offered four different Council candidatures, but turned down all of them, preferring to fight a general battle by giving his services to other candidates. He spoke up and down the country, far beyond the confines of Caernarvonshire. When the results of the elections were declared and it was found that in Wales the Liberal Councillors outnumbered the Tories by two to one, Lloyd George felt justified in accepting nomination himself as an Alderman. He was twenty-six years of age at the time. His enemies dubbed him "The Boy Alderman". It delighted him.

Soon, Lloyd George was fighting another battle, this time within the Party camp itself. The issue was Unity—and also More Energy in attacking the Enemy! For in Wales, at this time, there were two Liberal Federations, one in the North and the other in the South. Neither was representative of much more than a fraction of the real Welsh democratic opinion. Hovering vaguely above them both, was a still more insubstantial body known as the Welsh National Council, and the united results of the efforts of the three so-called "progressive" bodies in the field of social and political advance amounted to practically nil.

So when Lloyd George learned that the North Wales Liberal Federation and the Welsh National Council were due to meet together at Caernarvon in October, 1889, he and his friends prepared for action. They gave the Council immediate notice of a motion calling for its merging, with both Welsh Liberal Federations, into a single Welsh National League. The motion was powerfully supported on the day by the prospective Liberal candidate for Caernarvon Boroughs in person.

He made a passionate plea for the "Union of all Wales—in one Wales!"

One of the great historic blunders of their forefathers, he reminded his hearers, had been the division of Wales into the two provinces of North and South. They were now perpetuating this fearful folly, and with what result? The South Wales Federation met one day and passed sweeping resolutions imbued with Nationalist sentiment. Next day, the North Wales Federation met "at Chester, or some other English town", and passed resolutions of an entirely antagonistic character. In place of unity and co-operation, they had bickering and dissension. A kind of Punch-and-Judy exhibition was being made of Welsh Liberalism, which became the butt of the foe's ridicule, instead of the object of his terror. He urged the advantage of fusing the two organizations

> "if only to impregnate the timid, genteel Liberalism of the Northern Committee with the plucky and robust Liberalism of the South!"

Thus Lloyd George returned to his first theme of Unity is Strength. His motion was decisively lost.

By February, 1890, he had changed his tactics, and had shifted his operation from the obdurate Northern sector to the more promising Southern sector of the front. Now he was at Cardiff, urging the South Wales Liberal Federation to determine Home Rule for Wales—and to drag that North Wales Federation along in their wake. He argued that every plea that could be made in support of Home Rule for Ireland applied equally to Wales. Still more, every stock objection raised against granting autonomy to Ireland did *NOT* apply to Wales! He listed, and tested, both sets of arguments in what was probably the most closely and powerfully-reasoned of all his early speeches.

Perhaps it was also the most eloquent and prophetic in its wider appeal. For Lloyd George warned the Conference that while they had pledged themselves to a truly Radical programme—Disestablishment, Land Reforms, Local Option for Drink—however drastic and broad these policies might appear they merely "touched the fringes of that vast social question which must be dealt with in the near future.

> "There is a momentous time coming," cried Lloyd George, "the Dark Continent of Wrong is being explored, and there is a missionary spirit abroad for its reclamation to the Realm of Right. A Holy War has been proclaimed against Man's inhumanity to Man, and the people of Europe are thronging to the crusade."

He made a deep impact, both upon the Conference and upon the individual newspapermen who reported it. Only the Liberal Federations remained cold. Their low temperature would continue to be maintained by frigid doctrines throughout the next few years, until Nationalism had been frozen out of Welsh Liberalism. Never, in all his life, did Lloyd George get on well with Party caucuses. It may explain some of his cynicism about them and their doings in later years.

But, now—crisis!

In March 1890, the Tory member for Caernarvon Boroughs, Mr. Edmund Swetenham, Q.C., died suddenly. The news reached Lloyd George by telegram one morning, just as he and Margaret were setting off for a holiday by the sea. It meant, of course, an immediate by-election. When Lloyd George read it, Margaret said:

> "the smile vanished from his face. The thought of that election was like a nightmare about us."

They spent a worried, hurried week-end.

Hastily, too, the Tories selected their new champion. He turned out to be Lloyd George's old school patron and public enemy, Squire Nanney. The Tories made a far greater mistake when they attacked Lloyd George for lacking the Squire's own qualifications.

These qualifications were faithfully dealt with by the Liberal candidate.

> "I have read the report of last night's Conservative Meeting," he observed at one of his own gatherings, "and I see that one qualification Mr. Nanney possesses in order to become the Tory Party's candidate is that he is a man of wealth, and that the great disqualification in my case is that I am possessed of none. ('Oh' and Laughter.) The Tories forget that they are not now living in the seventeenth century. I once heard a man wildly

declaiming against Mr. Tom Ellis as a parliamentary representative; but according to that man Mr. Ellis' disqualification consisted mainly in the fact that he had been brought up in a cottage! (Laughter and loud applause.) The Tories have not yet realized that the day of the cottage-bred man has at last dawned!" (Prolonged applause.)

The heat increased as polling day approached. Tory M.P. Sir John Puleston came from Devonport to take one side, and Liberal M.P. Arthur Acland from Yorkshire to support the other. Also Ulstermen and Irish Nationalists arrived to argue their respective views of Ireland's woes. In his Election Address, Lloyd George himself laid down an opening barrage against "Balfour's baton-and-bayonet rule in Ireland," and compared it with "Mr. Gladstone's noble alternative of Justice for Ireland".

And, of course, for Wales as well! For Justice was needed here, too! They could do with Disestablishment and Disendowment in Wales for a start; also Taxation of Ground Rents, Enfranchisement of Leaseholders, the Direct Veto, One Man Vote, and, naturally, a Free Breakfast Table!

Both sides mobilized every elector that they could reach. There were no motor-cars yet, but carriages were sent as far away as Wolverhampton to collect absent voters. Everyone realized that the final result was going to be a terribly close one. Even so, there was one shrewd observer who had already made up his mind. This was the chief Tory agent for Wales, who had begun the campaign with confident hope. As it drew towards its closing phase, he reported to his Party Headquarters of the young Liberal challenger:

"A man who can make so thrilling and overpowering appeal to the emotions is absolutely invincible in Wales, and for that reason I feel compelled to warn you that in my opinion the seat is lost to our Party."

On 11 April, the votes were counted in Caernarvon Town Hall. The battle continued up to the bell in the last round. Right at the end, it appeared that Squire Nanney's pile slightly topped that of Lloyd George, and early reports of Tory victory ran around the town. Lloyd George advanced towards his old opponent to congratulate him, when Mr. J. T. Roberts, his Election Agent, spotted some Liberal votes in a bundle on the Tory pile.

"Demand a recount!" he urged.

The votes were transferred and recounted. They gave Lloyd George a majority of twenty. This time, the Tories called for a recount and one paper was returned to their pile. Then the final tale was told:

David Lloyd George 1,963
Ellis Nanney 1,945

Age 27

LIBERAL Majority . . . 18

"Three cheers for the Boy M.P.!" roared the crowd.

Dazed and excited, and deeply moved, he came forward, to speak in Welsh.

"Dear Fellow Countrymen," he said, "The County of Caernarvon today is free! (Loud cheers.) The Banner of Wales is borne aloft, and the Boroughs have wiped away the stain!" (Prolonged cheers.)

The clamouring crowd dragged his open carriage to the Liberal Club for further speeches, songs and demonstrations.

He would have dearly liked to go home then to Criccieth, where Margaret waited, with her firstborn son, Richard, and Uncle Lloyd. But only Squire Nanney caught the train that afternoon to Criccieth. The victor had to visit Bangor, and there go through the same performance. It was evening before he reached his own town, to find almost the entire population massed outside the railway station to welcome him. Another set of speeches was followed by another procession of excited supporters to his home.

Mynydd Ednyfed Farm stands more than a mile beyond the town, and upon a steep little hill. The sound of the celebrating host, and the sight of its swaying torches warned Margaret of their approach. It was now late, and she sent off Sally, the nurse, to meet them. Down the dark lane ran Sally to the closed gate, and there she waited, arms akimbo. The procession arrived, singing, shouting and laughing—and saw Sally. They stopped in their tracks, and in the middle of a bar of the Victory Song.

"What's all this going on?" said Sally. "Do you want to wake the baby?"

The Banner-Bearer of Wales Arisen stepped out of the carriage, considerably crestfallen, and discreetly made his way up the lane to bed.

CHAPTER IV

NEW BOY

WHEN he entered the House of Commons, Lloyd George came as a stranger.

Beyond the borders of Wales only a handful of people knew him yet—including the Tory M.P. for Devonport, Sir John Puleston, who had campaigned against him and who now with traditional House of Commons courtesy that afternoon sent a note along the Liberal benches, "Congratulations! Will you dine with me tonight?"

It was Budget Day, and Chancellor of the Exchequer, Mr. George Goschen, the Liberal Unionist whom Lord Randolph Churchill, in making his own dramatic resignation of that same high office, confessed he had "forgotten", was already on his way to the crowded and excited House. A policeman on duty there that afternoon has remembered how the young new Welsh Member, waiting in the Outer Lobby for Question-time to end, remarked to him: "I wonder how a Chancellor of the Exchequer feels on this day. Pretty nervous, I expect?"

He was introduced by Mr. Stuart Rendel[1] and Mr. Arthur Acland, and took the oath and his seat "amidst an enthusiastic reception by the Liberal Members of the House". For he had just captured a Tory seat in his by-election. There may have mingled with it a measure of relief on the Liberal Front Bench when the victor of Caernarvon appeared in person, though there was certainly some regret in the Press Gallery.

Wrote the famous Parliamentary journalist, Harold Spender:

"We had heard of him vaguely as a spellbinder unequalled in the power of rousing Welsh crowds in the Welsh tongue. We had been told he had the gift of the '*hwyl*' and not knowing quite what this meant we expected to see something resembling a Druid appear on the floor of the House of Commons. Imagine our surprise when we saw instead, a slim, well-groomed young lawyer in a frock-coat and with side-whiskers."

Far and away the most fascinating figure for the newcomer in this House was neither Goschen nor Lord Randolph, not even the greater giants, Joseph Chamberlain and Mr. Gladstone himself. It was Charles Stuart Parnell, "The uncrowned King of Ireland".

At this moment Parnell stood at the summit of his dramatic career. He had won his libel action against *The Times* over the Piggott forged letters and had obtained £5,000 damages, silencing both the enemies of Ireland and

[1] Afterwards Lord Rendel.

his own bitter foes *in* Ireland. In ten years' unrelenting battle in the House of Commons, playing the Liberals against the Tories and *vice versa*, and caring for nothing in British politics except the cause of Home Rule for Ireland, Parnell had forced both British parties into a situation wherein they hovered between a fearful acquiescence in some enforced action and a fear of any action at all. Those were the days—and "Irish nights"—of Tim Healy and Tom Sexton. Captain O'Shea had already filed, the previous December, his action for divorce from his wife, Catherine, naming Parnell as co-respondent. But few people outside the House of Commons knew of it, and fewer still regarded it as foreboding tragedy. Though Parnell's own appearance in the House became even more rare he was still a mighty figure in the spring of 1890, and Lloyd George regarded him with unstinted admiration.

He did not himself rush at once into the battle of words with a speech, though a week after his introduction he put his first question to a Minister, Mr. W. H. Smith, the Leader of the House. A Gallery writer noted that he had a soft, rather sweet voice and was more inclined to speak in a whisper than to shout.

Already, by post, he had advised Uncle Lloyd in Criccieth of his early voting activities: "My first division last night. I voted against Bi-metallism; but I couldn't tell you why." A month later, in his nightly report to that same ever-watchful guardian, he confided:

> "I shan't speak in the House this side of Whitsuntide holidays. Better not appear too eager. Get a good opportunity and make the best of it— that's the point."

Instead, he gave his time to study, especially of the rules of procedure in the House. He meant to master the rules he proposed to break, or else evade. When he became "Father of the House", forty years later, he would tell young Members, with a twinkling eye, "It is your absolute duty to *know* the rules."

But if Lloyd George curbed his speech in Parliament he let himself go outside it. "Coming straight from the hills," as he put it, the fiery young Welshman was about to make his first speech in England. He had accepted an invitation of the Liberation Society to speak at the Metropolitan Tabernacle in London on Disestablishment, with his future leader, Mr. Henry Campbell-Bannerman[1], in the chair. Thoroughly Lloyd George prepared his address, sending his notes for it off to Criccieth for brother William's opinion, with a request to show it also to the *esgob* (bishop), i.e. Uncle Lloyd. He added: "If you or he have any good story or joke in support, send it on."

He also went for a long walk with his wife Margaret, recited it to her and listened to her shrewd comments. It was a great Home Guard that rallied round

---

[1] Later, Sir Henry Campbell-Bannerman.

Lloyd George in those early anxious days. He was hurt and angry to find on the night of the Tabernacle meeting that his name was the last on the list of speakers.

"Stuck at the very end of the programme," he wrote home that evening, "after three or four weary and dreary speakers—and a collection—had depleted the building of a considerable part of its audience, and all but one or two of the reporters. But not a man moved whilst I spoke. . . ."

His speech was a plea for Nonconformity (especially Welsh!) couched in the form of a vehement attack on the Church of England, with scorn for such apologists of the Church as the Bishop of St. Asaph, who was claiming an Anglican revival. Any gains that could be noted in that quarter were contemptuously dismissed by Lloyd George as the result of corruption or coercion.

"The spiritual wants of the Welsh people," he flamed, "are attended to by Nonconformity. The Nonconformist chapels are crowded, but the churches of the Establishment are forsaken in every rural district in Wales. It is the same old story—it is not the people who do the work who receive the pay. In fact, it is a *very* old story! If you recollect, it was Elisha who cleansed Naaman's leprosy but it was Gehazi who secured the emoluments. It is Nonconformity that cleansed the moral leprosy which had afflicted Wales under the quack doctoring of the Established Church, but it is the Gehazi of the Establishment that is enjoying the emoluments!"

It was an effective enough entrance, but broader in its appeal was his next speech, in the following month at Manchester, when he spoke at the Free Trade Hall on the compensation clauses of the Local Taxation Bill. Lloyd George was by no means even yet at the top of the programme as speaker of the evening, but he was about to make another, and immense, upward leap. He began by reminding his hearers that he came before them as a native son of their famous city. His words held in their places some hundreds of people, who were about to leave and, as usual, only paused to see what kind of stuff the next speaker was made of. They soon found out.

"Mr. George had not been on his feet for five minutes before he fairly brought down the house," ran the newspaper report next day. "Apologizing for keeping the audience so long, he was overwhelmed with cries of 'Go on!' and a voice from the gallery saying 'We will stop with thee all night, me boy!' "

They stopped long, that night. For the words flowed "like lava from a fire burning within".

The orator climbed to his peroration. The publican had claimed equity?

"Very well," cried Lloyd George, "by the rule of equity let his case be judged! There is a grand old maxim in Equity that I wish to see applied

to that claim: 'He who comes to Equity must come with clean hands.' Let
the liquor traffic display the hand with which it means to grab compensation.
It reeks with human misery, vice and squalor, destitution, crime and death.
By that foul hand, and with Equity, let the claim be judged!"

The report ends:

"When Mr. George sat down the people became almost unmanageable;
the audience sprang to their feet, cheering, waving hats and handkerchiefs
in a paroxysm of something very much akin to madness. The Chairman
had to sit down, being unable to bring the people to order and terminate
the meeting."

His fellow-speaker on that memorable Manchester evening, Mr. W. S.
Caine, M.P., told him: "You have made your reputation in England by that
speech."

Lloyd George knew that it was true. Within a day or two Birmingham
and Liverpool were clamouring to hear him. He was especially glad to go to
Birmingham, he wrote to his uncle, "because of the representation of that
town".

Uncle Lloyd understood what he meant: Lloyd George was already in
hot and harassing pursuit of his old hero and lost leader, Joseph Chamberlain.
For "Joe", who had been Lloyd George's hero, had left the National Liberal
Party of Mr. Gladstone, quarrelling with the Grand Old Man over Home Rule
for Ireland, and had taken his own "Liberal Unionists" off to join up with
the Tories.

But Lloyd George also stuck closely to the House of Commons, making
a point of being always in his place to follow the debate from the start—and
to study the debaters and the way they shaped until the end. On 13 June, 1890,
after eight weeks' experience of Parliament he saw his chance on an issue
which he had already well explored, the compensation clauses of that Local
Taxation Bill again. He seized upon it to make his maiden speech.

The Bill provided a fund to compensate publicans whose licenses were
withdrawn as redundant. The Welsh Members proposed that in Wales, at
any rate, the moneys should be directed to Welsh educational ends. Lloyd
George rose to support this amendment. After the bishops, as we have seen,
the brewers were at this time his favourite meat.

But he made a good-humoured speech, adroitly linking the Bill under
discussion with the Coercion Act, which "Bloody Balfour", as Secretary of
State, was then sternly enforcing in Ireland. He suggested a Coercion Act for
publicans: "armed with all the modern appliances, such as Star Chamber
inquiries, 'shadows', and removable magistrates. In my belief," added Lloyd
George, "very few would survive such an inquisition."

He received the congratulations customary on a maiden speech, and, indeed, it was fair enough, though speaking of the ordeal long afterwards Lloyd George recalled: "The sense of nervousness was horrible; my mouth felt as if it were full of coal dust."

Gladstone was present to hear his terrible young man (he had had a brief brush with him already over Welsh Disestablishment at a Hawarden gathering up in Wales a fortnight before), and an Opposition Front-Bench Member who sat near him told Lloyd George later, "The Old Man was exceedingly delighted". Others who heard it were A. J. Balfour and Joseph Chamberlain, and Sir William Harcourt warmly praised it in conversation; John Morley invited the younger speaker to dinner.

The Press gave him good notice, too. *The Times* mentioned the speech in its leading article. The *Daily Graphic* rated it "rather clever". The *Pall Mall Gazette* acclaimed it "a capital maiden speech, full of promise for his future career". It was noted that he spoke fluently rather than familiarly; English was still a foreign tongue.

The next time Lloyd George addressed the House (the second time, as every M.P. knows, is a considerably more critical occasion), he earned no medals for his speech from any parliamentary quarter except, possibly, the Irish. He was well aware of the probable effect of it before he made it, for he had written home the previous evening:

"I cannot gain much in this House by my speech. On the contrary, I may lose much influence—these M.P.'s are so frightfully decorous and respectable. My audience is the country."

True, and it would remain so throughout the great, long day of his power. Lloyd George became a master of parliamentary debate, and he made one of his gravest errors when, later in life, he ceased to woo and win that ever-jealous House of Commons; but it was as a platform orator that he used to the full measure his superb gift of moving men by words to do great deeds.

This evening, the House was debating a supplementary estimate to cover certain royal pageantry. One of the items was for a fee of £439 3s. 4d. paid on the installation of H.R.H. Prince Henry of Prussia as a Knight of the Garter, a dignity, commented Lloyd George, which as a general rule was granted for some signal service rendered to the country. Now what service had Prince Henry of Prussia ever rendered to this country? ("Oh!" "Oh!"). He had not yet rendered any service to his own country ("I say!" "I say!").

Lloyd George had not quite done with the accounts. There was also a sum of £180 in respect of the funeral of the Duchess of Cambridge, but the family of the Duke of Cambridge had from the first to last received something like £3,000,000 out of the Exchequer. It was monstrous that they should be paying these sums for what was absolutely worthless to the country. Members had just read the report of the Enquiry into Sweated Labour, which showed that thousands of hardworking, thrifty men were leading a life of hopeless, ceaseless toil and yet the House was being asked to spend hundreds of pounds in adorning a mere supernumerary! Such gorgeousness, such ostentation of wealth was not necessary to maintain the Constitution. On the contrary, it did far more to repress than to promote sentiments of loyalty. ("Shame!")

The speech was considered by many Members to have been extremely bad form, though the quarrymen of Blaenau Festiniog and the coalminers of Tonypandy (whom he was really addressing) may have reckoned otherwise.

For in the closing years of the last century there was a wave of republicanism sweeping across Victorian Britain, less powerful in fact than it appeared, but strong enough to include the support of public figures as famous as Joseph Chamberlain and Sir Charles Dilke, not to say those clamant voices now rising from the dark industrial underworld and soon to be represented in Parliament itself (after the very next General Election) by that first fiery apostle of Socialism, Keir Hardie. Outside Parliament, the working masses had not forgotten either the great dock strikes of the late 'eighties or the riots in Trafalgar Square, and the use of armed police and troops. For Lloyd George, at this period, the Monarchy went into the same category as the Established Church—it was foreign to Wales. In days to come, his behaviour towards it would be governed entirely objectively and frankly, by his relations with the wearer of the crown. He bridled his tongue in public, but to the end of his life Lloyd George did not change his private view—that monarchy had merely outlived, though not outdated, feudalism.

The speech was not lost upon Queen Victoria, who later was to write to her Private Secretary that her Prime Minister:

"forgets the danger of increasing the power of the House of Commons and having no force to resist the subversive measures of the so-called Liberals, but better called 'destructors'."

A day or two later Parliament rose. The new Member for Caernarvon Boroughs had done pretty well in four months. He had learned what to do and also, if possible, what not to do. One thing to avoid was getting on to a Parliamentary Committee. He had found himself that sultry June sitting on one:

"judging some confounded Scotch Water Bill. Good practice and experience to acquire . . . but it takes up all my time, and, I fear, health now. Ten hours in an office would be preferable to the five I spend in a crowded room over this dry Scotch Bill. No more committees for me!"

As nearly as he could, Lloyd George stuck to that resolution for the rest of his life. No more committees for him!

What were his other interests, if any? According to his letters home to Criccieth, they were almost none. Occasionally, when he could afford both the time and the money he indulged his taste for the theatre—a Beerbohm Tree first night was always a favourite. On Sundays he went in the morning to the Metropolitan Tabernacle (the mighty Spurgeon reigned there—a finer actor, far, than Beerbohm Tree); or to the City Temple, to hear the great Joseph Parker; in the afternoon to Westminster Central Hall, or to St. Paul's to hear Canon Liddon. *Mae arnaf eisiau dysgu.*

For, to the young Welsh Member in those days, politics had three faces. They were (i) Social; (ii) National; (iii) Religious.

The condition of the people in his own land could not be separated from the fact that an alien aristocracy and an alien Church sat in the seats of authority there. For the next few years Lloyd George would be fighting chiefly to establish Welsh Home Rule, and to disestablish the English Church in Wales.

For the country as a whole, there remained other, wider issues to be decided and Lloyd George himself would come in good time to understand that the power of the United Kingdom to lead the world for the next fearful half-century depended primarily upon its ability to organize itself. A great empire could not develop its potential strength while its own heart was weakened by a disease. This disease was the poverty to which the crude existing social system condemned so many of the people in the homeland.

Lloyd George had caught a vivid glimpse of this in the East End of London one Saturday night when, with a fellow-Welshman, the late Sir Alfred Davies, and a Caernarvon-born Superintendent of the Metropolitan Police, he made an expedition to the scenes of Jack the Ripper's recent operations. At this time, these ghastly crimes of murder and mutilation had set people talking all over the world. They had been committed, without exception, against women of the East-End streets, pretty certainly with revenge as their motive.

Naturally, the newspapers made much of the story, which obligingly continued with regular instalments over a period of more than three months. *The Times* devoted editorials to it, as well as columns of highly intimate descriptive; the Radical Press attacked the incompetent Tory Home Secretary; there were questions in the House of Commons, and a popular panic forced a pack of bloodhounds on the Metropolitan Commissioner of Police (much good they would have been trying to pick up a scent in those stinking alleys), before it forced his own resignation for his failure to catch the criminal.

So it was with a sense of excitement that Lloyd George met his friends that evening at nine o'clock at Aldgate Underground Station, which was within a couple of hundreds of yards of Jack the Ripper's first murder. They dived at once deeply into Darkest London—for in those days the town was still hardly lighted at all beyond the main streets of the West End and the more respectable boroughs.

In the dim-lit sawdust bars they saw dockers in rags drinking with their drabs the cheapest liquor which their wretched wages could just afford, while their wives hung around outside the doors, abusing them, calling them home, and being clouted and kicked in return. They heard hungry children whimpering. They then turned into the squalid alleys and backyards of the fourpenny doss-houses, climbed the rickety stairs and pushed their way into the crowded dens where tramps and thieves lay in dozens on the floor, being introduced as "Tecs from the Yard", and invariably greeted with a friendly question, "Come for me, guv'nor?" To which the superintendent would reply genially, "Not this time, Bill." Lloyd George was fascinated by this Hogarthian picture of the nasty 'nineties, and appalled by its degradation.

Life was by no means easy for him. To his eldest son, Richard, born in February, 1889, had been added in August, 1890, his first daughter, Mair Eiluned. On coming to London, Lloyd George had rented rooms first at Essex Court, in the Temple, and later at Verulam Buildings in Gray's Inn. In those days M.P.s received no salary for their services and no free railway vouchers to and from their constituencies. It is true that the local Liberal Association insisted on paying its Member's election expenses, and when he visited other constituencies to speak there his fares were defrayed and he was entertained by friends. But while Parliament was in session, the solicitor was cut off from his practice in Wales. He would have been in serious straits if it had not been for his young brother William, who kept things going for him up there. In this, once more, came help from faithful Uncle Lloyd, who, though he had no legal training, performed as clerk a score of necessary tasks inside the office.

Lloyd George was a poor man, but he was a proud one. He earned his occasional hard coin as a writer in the political newspapers; he scorned the easy fees he could have had as a director of companies. He was offered a seat on the Board of a famous Oxford Street Welsh drapery firm with a director's three hundred guineas. Contemptuously, he rejected it.

"A guinea pig? No, it has not come to that yet."

Often Margaret sighed for home in Wales, and sometimes prayed that things would so fall out that she and her husband and her babies (another daughter, Olwen Elizabeth, was born in April, 1892) could return and settle down there. As things went, it was not easy to have children living in the Inns of Court, and for her to take them off to Criccieth meant separation from her husband. Even when they were able to afford, first a flat in Kensington, and, later a small house on Wandsworth Common, Margaret never liked London.

The children, of course, enjoyed it, and especially when Father could go with them to the Park to feed the ducks on his way to the House of Commons.

As Parliament reassembled that autumn, the drama of Parnell mounted swiftly to its climax. Roman Catholic Ireland and Nonconformity in Britain were especially shocked. A powerful movement developed to force Parnell's retirement from the leadership of the Irish Party. But Parnell refused to quit, and at this stage Tim Healy stood by him, saying:

"We'll teach these damned Nonconformists to mind their own business."

Parliamentary Candidate, 1890

Then, ten days after Captain O'Shea had been granted his decree *nisi*, Gladstone wrote his famous letter to John Morley, declaring that for the co-respondent to continue as the Leader of the Irish Party in the House of Commons would be "disastrous in the highest degree to the cause of Ireland."

It was an ultimatum to the Irish to say that unless Parnell went, the Liberal Party would no longer associate itself with them in the crusade for Home Rule. Still Parnell held on, in the face of growing revolt, which even Tim Healy now regretfully joined. With grudging half-admiration, an Irish enemy described him as: "Lucifer, the proud fellow."

Certainly, Parnell bore himself with proper arrogance. In the bitter family squabble which the Irish fought among themselves in Committee Room 15 he dared to insist that he sat in the Chair while his own case was being discussed and

"he looked so calmly," an Irish Member told Lloyd George, "that if a stranger had come in, he would certainly have thought that all the rest of us had committed adultery with Parnell's wife!"

And how he fought! How they all fought! When Healy urged that he should go before the Irish cause forfeited the goodwill of Gladstone, Parnell contemptuously dismissed the value of that "unrivalled sophist", which stung Healy to inquire if the Liberal-Irish alliance was "to perish in the stench of the Divorce Court?"

Then, during a further furious debate, John Redmond demanded to know if Gladstone was to be "the Master of the Party?" To which, Healy interrupted: "Who is to be the Mistress of the Party?"

The din from Committee Room 15 drifted downstairs to the Lobbies and the Chamber. Lloyd George himself, to judge by his letters home, began by sharing the "anger and despondency" which reigned on the Liberal benches. (He describes how the Tories, on the other hand, could hardly contain their joy. Confound it!)

Lloyd George's colleagues remained estranged from Parnell, but Lloyd George himself soon began to discover a sympathy with him (he was seldom able to withhold it for long from any lone rebel). One evening in the House, he asked Parnell if he could introduce him to a Welsh friend who was sitting in the Gallery.

"Ah," said Parnell, a smile breaking on his face for the first time for many a day, "I did not know I had a friend left in Wales."

He had two that night.

A week later Lucifer was still defying the world in Committee Room 15. By now Lloyd George was writing: "His fight is simply sublime. It shows what a leader he is, and the stuff he is made of."

But it broke the Irish Party in two, and broke Parnell himself, who within

c

a year was dead. Recalling these things long afterwards, Lloyd George used to maintain that Parnell made his fatal mistake in not resigning the leadership of the Irish Party before the divorce. He insisted that it was Morley, not Gladstone, who decided (and persuaded his colleagues) that the Liberal Party would not be able to carry the British Nonconformist vote if Parnell remained the leader of the Irish Party—Morley, who Lloyd George said was himself at this time living with a woman to whom he was not married.

It became Lloyd George's plan now to fill with a Welsh Nationalist Party the vacuum in British politics thus created by the temporary eclipse of Ireland. He had already made his stand upon three main issues. (1) Land Reform, to free the yeoman and the quarryman from the grip of landlordism; (2) Disestablishment of the Church of England in Wales, to divert its endowments to Welsh education; (3) Local Option, to reduce Welsh intemperance.

But always, Lloyd George returned to that original premise—all these objectives could be best achieved if Wales first secured her own Home Rule. It was Lloyd George's belief that this could be done if the Welsh Liberal organizations were welded into a single fighting force, and then led to battle with the consummate skill and single-minded thoroughness that the lost Irish leader had so long displayed. How sadly Wales needed it! How confidently he believed that this ambitious young Lloyd George himself could do it! How despairingly he wrote to a friend that winter:

"The Welsh Party (!) met on Tuesday to discuss Disestablishment, *and elaborately resolved to do nothing.*"

There were a handful of young Welsh Liberal Members who thought along the same lines as Lloyd George did—Tom Ellis (the future Liberal Whip), Sam Evans (the future President of the Divorce Court), and D. A. Thomas (the future Lord Rhondda). They opened their War of Welsh Independence in the House of Commons on the Tithe Recovery Bill. So envenomed had the land struggle now become in Wales over distraints, forced auctions and evictions that Lord Salisbury's Tory Government proposed to transfer the responsibility for paying the tithe from the tenant to the landlord.

Tithe was a subject which Lloyd George thoroughly knew. He and Sam Evans fought the Bill clause by clause right through the autumn of 1890, and into the following spring, staying in their places in the House day after day until long past midnight, and sometimes speaking seven or eight times.

The guerilla pair had to operate adroitly, for they did not wish to wreck the Bill. They sought rather to gain as much relief as possible for the farmers; at the same time, since they also aimed at Disestablishment and the diversion of the tithe to Welsh education, they had no desire to diminish its value. So skilfully did they manœuvre, that Lloyd George was able to report to his Bangor constituents in March that about a third of their amendments had been incorporated in the Bill.

His next big brush with Authority brought down upon his head the wrath of his own leader. The measure before the House was the Clergy Discipline (Immorality) Bill, and its purpose was to give more power to the bishops to punish offending priests. It also aimed to relieve them of the heavy costs they might incur in the process. Gladstone, a strong Churchman, entirely approved. Lloyd George, with his three Welsh Nonconformist Allies, Ellis, Evans and Thomas, as vehemently disapproved.

Indeed, as the only Opposition to the Bill, they had to make up with their forcefulness in debate for their fewness in the lobby. Lloyd George opened with an amendment affirming that it was no part of the functions of the State to attend to matters of spiritual discipline. As he sat down Gladstone rose, and faithfully he dealt with his mutinous lieutenant's arguments, one by one. He pulverized them, and him. The victim leaned forward in his seat to catch every word, entranced with the annihilating performance. He and his colleagues then transferred their operations to the Committee upstairs. They fought every line of the Bill, and the first three sessions of the Committee stage ended without even the opening clause being passed.

The Government were justifiably angry at this sabotaging by Irregulars of what they had expected to be an agreed measure (they had probably received an official promise that it would be). Far angrier was Gladstone. The Grand Old Man got himself put on the Committee, expressly for the purpose of disciplining his young rebels. It only made matters worse, for the harder he fought them the longer the obstruction lasted. In the end, he realized that he was simply playing their game.

A critic in the *Liverpool Echo* paid compliment to the Welsh Resistance, commenting that the

"misplaced ability of these Welsh doctrinaires of licensed abuse of debate ... the celerity with which they argue questions, is quite admirable as an example of casuistry. New amendments rise out of old and rejected ones with a freedom that Mr. Healy, with all his familiarity with the malignant art, cannot hope to improve or exceed."

Journalists who knew the later Lloyd George will find a familiar ring in the account which the *Morning Leader* wrote in the early 'nineties:

"To the pressmen who haunt the Lobby he is extremely genial; and there is an engaging candour about his conversation which deceives the most experienced, for when afterwards you recall what has been said you almost invariably discover it is the interviewer who had been interviewed."

From his "Brutus" days onward, via *Udgorn Rhyddid*, Lloyd George never underrated the power of the Press, or the good friendship (or odd touchiness) of pressmen.

He still earned a useful free-lance guinea himself from the *Manchester*

Guardian when opportunity served, and in the New Year of 1892 he took a leading part in setting up in Caernarvon the Welsh National Press Co., Ltd., which acquired a number of Welsh and English newspapers. These included *Y Genedl Cymreig* (The Welsh Nation), which had the largest circulation in the Welsh language, *Y Werin* (The Democracy), a Labour paper, and the *North Wales Observer and Express*. The articles of association were signed by himself and half a dozen of his Welsh Liberal colleagues, all of whom were specifically banned from sitting on the Board, so that:

> "the liberty of these papers, as representative organs of Welsh public opinion, to criticize the action of the country's representatives in Parliament should be absolutely unfettered."

It may be taken, however, that the Welsh National Press Co. Ltd. gave steady support to Mr. Lloyd George, M.P., and his associates. Also Lloyd George now himself enjoyed the privilege, which few newspaper owners have abstained from exercising, of writing in his own pages. Chiefly, he described in *Y Genedl Cymreig* the debates in the House, and lively enough stuff it was.

With sound journalistic sense he realized that the most interesting thing about debates, as of battles, is the men who make them. So Lloyd George set out to give his readers pictures of his performers. He thus describes Mr. Asquith, his future fellow minister, Prime Minister, and ultimate enemy:

> "A short, thick-set man, rather round-shouldered, with a face as clean-shaven as that of the most advanced curate, keen eyes and a broad intellectual forehead. He is only a few years over forty, and the hope of the rising generation of Radicals. There is only one man in the House who is more effective as a Parliamentary debater."

This was not Mr. A. J. Balfour, the Tory Leader in the Commons. It was Mr. Joseph Chamberlain, the Liberal Unionist and ex-Radical, who was now Balfour's rather uncomfortable First Mate. Lloyd George compared them.

> "Mr. Chamberlain is by nature much more aggressive and stubborn than Mr. Balfour. The Tory leader lacks energy and application. Those who know him best think him rather indolent. When he was Irish Secretary he worked harder than he has ever done before or since, but even then he accepted without hesitation any explanation which was offered him by the Irish Constabulary in reply to complaints of injustice. It was less trouble than to make a personal investigation. That is not Mr. Chamberlain's way. He is mercurial, always on the move, and full of life and vigour."

Not only his own newspapers could fairly ascribe to him a victory for his constituents over a Board of Trade Bill which proposed to regulate railway rates in such a way as would have penalized the Nantlle Vale quarries in his constituency. After "many pages of amendments" Lloyd George secured for Welsh slate rail transportation equal treatment with their English competitors.

"You have got to fight for what you want," their parliamentary champion told his countrymen. "The English are a strong race; they possess the qualities as well as the defects of strong people. They have a very healthy contempt for the cringing. The man who crawls and creeps about their feet and licks the dust, they spurn and kick—and from the bottom of my heart I admire them for it!"

He held up the example of the success which the Irish had achieved by their fighting parliamentary tactics, and pointed the plain moral:

"This is the policy for us! I do not believe that in the long run it pays to send our representatives crawling up the backstairs of the Government offices in Westminster to fall on their knees before every scribbler there who draws his pay from the public purse, in order to beseech as alms the concessions which we ought to demand as our right."

He did not neglect to remind them that another part of the trouble lay at their own doors—and also the remedy in their own hands.

"The most startling fact about our country is this—that you have men who have accumulated untold wealth living in gorgeous splendour in one street, and a horde of miserable, poverty-stricken human beings huddled together in the most abject penury and squalor in the adjoining courts."

He had to lay it on pretty thick, for now a General Election was approaching (July, 1892) and his new Tory opponent was his friendly critic, Sir John Puleston, who was giving up his own safe seat in Devonport to try and turn him out of Caernarvon Boroughs.

Sir John was wealthy, intelligent, and likeable, "Pleasant Puleston", they called him. As a Welshman himself he professed, and genuinely felt, sympathy with many Welsh national aspirations. For the past two years, he had been Constable of Caernarvon Castle, an appointment which Lloyd George himself would one day hold.

Sir John was certainly a serious Tory challenger in a seat which Lloyd George himself had only snatched for the Liberals at the last election by the narrow margin of eighteen votes.

It says something for his boldness and energy that Lloyd George continued to give so much time to speaking outside his own threatened base. He calculated that in fighting a general battle in populous centres such as Manchester, Liverpool, Newcastle-upon-Tyne and Cardiff, he was best defending the sector of the Liberal line which lay around Caernarvon. Certainly, it did his fame no harm to share the platform with John Morley in the great Home-Rule-for-Ireland Rally at St. Helen's, though these journeys laid heavy penalties upon his time.

Some of these charges fell upon his already considerable correspondence. From early in life, Lloyd George wholeheartedly disliked answering letters or even reading them, just as later on he would never study an official paper if he could get the author to explain it to him in conversation. Sir Alfred Davies used to recall how he returned with him to his flat in Kensington Palace Mansions one evening after a tour of speech-making, to find that they could hardly push open the door so heavy was the pile of letters which had accumulated behind it. Gathering them up, Lloyd George flung them on the table, begged Davies to read the lot for him, as he would be so busy himself on other matters—and to tell him only about those he absolutely MUST see.

Sir Herbert Lewis, a parliamentary colleague, has also told how Lloyd George once asked him to go to his locker in the House and fetch him some document he needed. When Lewis opened the locker hundreds of letters addressed to Lloyd George—very few of which had even been opened—fell on to the floor.

"Most of them will have answered themselves, anyway, by now," said Lloyd George indifferently, and possibly correctly.

If there was one thing he disliked more than reading letters, it was writing them. He confessed that he would rather submit to a dozen interviews than write one letter.

"Letters are the very devil," he said to George Riddell[1]. "They should be abolished altogether."

There was one exception—and it was not made even in favour of his wife, Margaret. It was that nightly letter to Uncle Lloyd.

In a stormy hour in the First World War, Lloyd George would tell a Trade Union Congress at Bristol:

"The first and greatest nobleman I ever met was an old British working man. He writes to me every day—at eighty-two years of age. I get his letter every morning, telling me how to put the world right. And if you will allow me to say so, however busy I am—and I am not a good letter writer— there is one letter that I do not miss; it is the one to the old British working man."

For the rest, a joke about Lloyd George's methods of handling his mail at this time said that the only way to get an answer from him was to enclose in your letter two stamped and addressed envelopes, one bearing the word "Yes" and the other "No". There were jokers, too, who swore that they had received both.

This carelessness with correspondents (or was it contempt of them?)

[1] Later, Lord Riddell, owner of the *News of the World*.

made him enemies in his own camp. The local Tory opposition was naturally
diligent to create as many more as possible. Sir John Puleston himself tried
it when he declared that Gladstone had condemned Lloyd George's attacks on
the Clergy Discipline Bill as being insincere. Promptly, and flatly, the Liberal
Leader himself denied it, adding for good measure:

"If I were an elector for the Caernarvon Boroughs I should vote against
Sir John Puleston, and in favour of Mr. Lloyd George."

The ladies of the Primrose League aimed better. They put around the
story that Lloyd George had refused to stand up at a Mansion House banquet
to the toast of "The Queen". It was untrue, but you could easily believe it
if you wanted to do so; it did not appear incompatible with the views of the
Liberal Member for Caernarvon Boroughs on the subject of Prince Henry of
Prussia's Garter.

Lloyd George stirred up violent enemies by his own pretty violent speeches.
One rowdy election night in Bangor, a gang of men flung a blazing fireball of
tarred tow, dipped in paraffin, into the carriage in which he and his wife were
driving home from a meeting. It struck him on the head, knocked off his hat
and fell into Margaret's lap. He was able to throw it out of the window, and
to beat out the flames in her dress before she was burned. Another night, when
he spoke at the Penrhyn Hall, in the same town, the windows were smashed
with stones by a threatening demonstration outside.

The uproar continued up to polling day, and beyond. The result was
declared in Caernarvon on 10 July, 1892.

Age 29

Lloyd George	.	.	.	.	.	2,154
Sir John Puleston	.	.	.	.	.	1,958
Liberal Majority	.	.	.	.	.	196

The total Liberal vote in the constituency had increased by one-tenth, and
Lloyd George's majority more than tenfold. The local Liberals were wildly
excited, and the Tories correspondingly incensed. The victor went off on a brief,
triumphal tour through the Boroughs and was finally drawn in his carriage by
cheering admirers to his new home in Criccieth. Lustily they bellowed (to
the tune of "Marching Through Georgia") the Lloyd George Battle Song:

"*Hurrah! Hurrah! We're ready for the fray!*
Hurrah! Hurrah! We'll drive Sir John away!
The 'Grand Young Man' will triumph,
Lloyd George will win the day
FIGHT FOR THE FREEDOM OF CAMBRIA!"

At Bangor, about midnight, a Tory mob broke up a Liberal torchlight
procession, whereupon the Liberal mob smashed the windows of the Conservative Club, and "tumult continued until late into the night".

All over the country, the General Election had given the Liberals and Irish Nationalists a majority of forty over the Tories and Liberal Unionists. It meant the fall of Lord Salisbury's Government.

For Lloyd George it meant that the position he had stormed two years ago had been held, and fortified. He began to plan new operations.

.   .   .   .   .

He was twenty-nine years old. He had a growing family. His political activities had advertised his name in his profession, but they had also distracted his attention from it. Lloyd George had to look both sides of a sixpence in those days. He would have found it hard to refuse a minor office if he had been offered one in the new Liberal Government.

He was not offered anything. For although he had demonstrated a very definite destructive capacity in assailing the Tory Tithe and Clergy Discipline Bills, Lloyd George had not yet established a mastery over that most difficult of all audiences, the House of Commons. He confessed to a friend long afterwards that "for the first five years of my life in Parliament I never felt happy about a speech I made there".

For the time being, the Welsh rover remained in the hills of the back benches.

CHAPTER V

WELSH COMMANDO

WHEN a guerilla soldier or a privateer sailor gets caught up in the operations of a Regular Army or Navy he feels rather like a patient in the grip of a male nurse. He finds himself being endlessly organized and disciplined to do what he does not want, and instructed that it is both necessary and good. And all the time he remains convinced that it is neither.

Lloyd George began to experience this as soon as he found himself on the Government Benches of the House of Commons. Though he had been dutiful, and even devoted, in his parliamentary attendance during the previous session, when in Opposition, it had been by his own choice. No "snap" division could possibly have overthrown Lord Salisbury's Tory majority in that House of Commons; Lloyd George had been on duty to learn his own business, and to wage his own wars. Now, he was just one serving soldier in the victorious Army of Liberalism, led by the Grand Old Man in person, and drilled by the sergeant-majors known as the Government Whips.

Gladstone himself was well aware of the restive spirit of some of his younger troops, especially the contingent from Wales. He was not permitted to overlook their parliamentary importance, either. Thirty-one of the thirty-four Welsh constituencies had fallen to the Liberal assault in the General Election, a figure which accounted for three-quarters of his total majority. Lloyd George drew due attention to it in a speech at Conway soon after his re-election, and also asked the relevant questions:

"Why is Wales so overwhelmingly Liberal at the present moment? It is not to install one statesman in office. It is not to deprive one party of power in order to put another in power. It has been done because Wales, by an overwhelming majority, has demonstrated its determination to secure its own progress. Wales has returned the men most in sympathy with its need—to fight for its rights!"

These "rights" included (i) a Suspensory Bill, to prevent the creation of any further dignities of the English Church in Wales, pending a final Dis-establishment Bill, (ii) a Welsh Land Commission, and (iii) a Royal Charter setting up a University of Wales. The Prime Minister deemed it prudent to recognize the power of his followers from the Principality (and seek to curb it) by offering Tom Ellis, the accepted Parliamentary leader of Welsh Nationalism, a post in his Administration as a Junior Whip.

This move had been foreseen by Tom Ellis, Lloyd George and the group who had worked with them in the previous Parliament, and they had agreed

c*   73

that none of them should accept office without the consent of his colleagues. They debated it now, and most of them advised Ellis to decline. They did not insist, and he entered the Liberal Government, to become Chief Whip a year a two later when Lord Rosebery took over the Premiership from Gladstone. It marked the end of Tom Ellis as First Crusader for Wales, and the emergence of Lloyd George.

Before the new Parliament had run many months, his colleagues in the House were commenting on the rare appearance in debate of the Member for Caernarvon Boroughs; the Government Whips had noted with more anxiety his abstention from the Lobby. The reason was that Lloyd George was not even in London. He was addressing large and clamorous public meetings, especially in Wales, on issues which so far had their place in the House of Commons only upon the Order Paper. The House of Commons was not yet his theatre. In the country was still Lloyd George's audience, and in the country called Wales his principal theme at this time, Disestablishment, took on a political even more than a religious cloak.

For the Welsh regarded Disestablishment almost as the Irish regarded Home Rule—as a challenge to their nationality. Were the Welsh a People? Or merely the inhabitants of a geographical sub-division of England? Angrily, Lloyd George asked it.

The way in which the new leader of Cymru Fydd ("Liberalism in Welsh costume", Lloyd George christened it) mixed his appeal to the Welsh Tribes with his agitation against the English Church is illustrated by a speech he made to his compatriots in Birkenhead. The meeting began in an atmosphere appropriately charged by the musical rendering of "Land of My Fathers", "Shy Robin", and "Men of Harlech", after which Lloyd George rose amid applause to deliver a few observations on the behaviour of Lord Salisbury's late Administration, both towards Mashonaland and Wales.

"Some English statesmen," he observed, "know less about Wales than about Mashonaland. Now, if only one could be found with daring enough to undertake a journey of exploration, he might find out facts about the customs of the natives which would be a source of wonderment to his countrymen!

He would discover how backward and primitive are the Welsh. Why, would it be believed that we have actually no race-course in the whole country, nor even a Stock Exchange? Who would credit the tale that an old festival, called the *Eisteddfod*, a relic of the Middle Ages, where such barbaric pastimes as music, poetry and literature are cherished, is still preferred to horse-racing? Nay, that in some parts the people are so steeped in savagery as to attend preaching meetings on holidays, to the utter neglect of prize-fights?"

Surely, Lloyd George urged, once the British public were awakened to a full realization of these appalling facts they could readily be convinced of the necessity of separate legislation for such a race?

He then laid about the Church of England in Wales as being equally alien in character and fraudulent in origin. For centuries, even before the Great Reformation, this Church had been a hostile garrison in Wales, bound to the wearers of the crown of England by ties of gratitude for past favours and a common hatred towards the native folk. Only the monks, by their charity, and the friars by preaching the Gospel as the religion of the poor and the downtrodden, had kept the salt from utterly losing its savour. They had been the real keepers of the ancient British Church of St. David, which, being expelled from the great Cathedrals and Bishop's Palaces, had found a home in the Monasteries. When these in turn were suppressed and plundered by the rapacity of the founders of the present Anglican Establishment this old, true Church had fled to the hills to find its last sanctuary in the conventicles of Puritanism.

He did not have it all his own way. Dr. Edwards, Bishop of St. Asaph, whom Lloyd George himself would years afterwards salute as "the doughtiest champion that the Church in Wales possesses", did not still his tongue either. He characterized the Welsh Nonconformist critics of the Establishment as: "ignorant", "unprincipled", "shrivelled, meagre, lewd and troublesome insects," who were "animated solely by sectarian spite and greed." Mr. Lloyd George, he considered, "operated on a variable plane, betwixt the noisy and the noisome."

Mr. Lloyd George, in turn, undertook before a Baptist Conference at Shrewsbury to deal deliberately but faithfully with the Bishop, "this Yahoo of political controversy". He noted that some members of the Right Reverend Gentleman's own flock had expressed surprise and disgust at one who had so far degraded his office to trail his robes in the gutter. He himself would have to be careful in approaching such an atmosphere of squalid slang lest he became infected with the contagion. He would seek, however, even with much soiling of hands and sickening of spirit to separate any grain of argument from the gross invective.

The Bishop had conducted his case, said the speaker:

"by simply latinizing the tirades of an enraged washerwoman, and then rushing out of his Palace like a common scold, brush in hand, to daub his neighbours."

As for his claim that the Church of England in Wales was a truly national institution, that rested entirely upon the argument that the Welsh people were not a nation and, therefore, not entitled to be treated as a separate entity. It was pretty bold for the Bishop to advance such a plea, since it was chiefly because he was himself a Welshman that he had obtained a Welsh bishopric, for neither his scholarship, theology nor preaching merited preferment.

The Church was not entirely without reply. It was at this time, too, that the story began to go round of the Nonconformist Deacon, introducing Lloyd George from the Chair at a meeting in Flintshire in favour of the Disestablishment Bill.

"And now," said the Chairman, "I haff to present to you the Member for Caernarvon Boroughs. He hass come here to reply to what the Bishop of St. Asaph said the other night about Welsh Disestablishment. In my opinion, ladies and gentlemen, the Bishop of St. Asaph iss one of the biggest liars in Creeashon! But, thank God, yess, we haff in Mr. Lloyd George a match for him tonight!"

The Member for Caernarvon Boroughs was already engaged in another struggle and of a more intimate, deadly nature. This was the grave and growing discontent within the ranks of his own Parliamentary Party. The demand of the Welsh M.P.s for Disestablishment—Not Tomorrow, but Today!—was threatening to end in another Liberal split, and it was Lloyd George and his friends who were the threateners.

They were in no way placated when in February, 1893, Mr. Asquith, the new Liberal Home Secretary, moved the First Reading of the Suspensory Bill. Though they had clamoured for it a year ago, the more ardent Welsh Nationalists already regarded it as now too late. Lloyd George himself did not fail to stress that it was one thing (and for a busy, harassed Government a very convenient thing) to introduce any number of desirable Bills, but it was quite another thing to find the Parliamentary time to pass them into law. The Liberal majority in the House of Commons had voted Gladstone's Home Rule for Ireland after sustained obstruction there by Joseph Chamberlain, overcome by drastic application of the closure, only to have it thrown out by the House of Lords. This Suspensory Bill, urged the leader of the Welsh rebels, would turn out to be just one more Bill to kill time.

(In the event, even the Suspensory Bill was talked out, during the last debate in which Lord Randolph Churchill graced the House of Commons.)

None of these happenings really disturbed Lloyd George half as much as he pretended. In fact, all suited him admirably—the veto of the Lords, the obstruction of the Tory Opposition in the Commons and the general Welsh frustration with the Parliament at Westminster.

Naturally, the House of Lords had done their worst! Well, let them do their worst once more! Perhaps it would also be their last! If the House of Lords threw out or mutilated the Disestablishment Bill when it came up, then the People would know what to do with them—they would very soon mutilate the House of Lords. Yes, they would *annihilate* them!

The Tory Opposition in the House of Commons came in for a different treatment from Lloyd George, who after all had made some parliamentary reputation himself as an Opposition obstructionist. But now, really! If only these Tories had discussed the Home Rule Bill with the intention of making it a piece of workable legislation he (Lloyd George) would have felt compelled to vote consistently against any motion to curtail debate. But, no, they were simply discussing the Irish measure with an ulterior motive. Their purpose, of course, was to stop Mr. Gladstone legislating upon English—and Welsh —affairs!

This brought Lloyd George to his third point—and the very bedrock of his current political thesis—Home Rule for Wales. They would never get Welsh problems settled in an Imperial Parliament, he urged. It was time, in the interests of Wales, to initiate a new policy. That policy must be—a Welsh Parliament for Wales!

There was only one barrier in the way. Some of the Welsh themselves.

To begin with, the Nonconformist churches and the powerful political and social forces which they deployed, were bent first upon Disestablishment (it was the very reason that they had entered politics), and now it seemed to them that they were actually within sight of the Promised Land. To halt, or turn aside for any cause whatever would surely be to betray the great crusade of the Army of the Covenant.

Next, there were a number of leading Liberals in Wales who, while they were Nonconformist in religious faith and Radical in social opinion, were internationalist rather than nationalist in their outlook upon world affairs. Such were Mr. D. A. Thomas and Mr. C. J. Cory, the rising young coal kings of South Wales, whose market was, indeed, the world. They wanted to be freed of trammels upon trade, whether imposed by English or Welsh authority.

David Alfred Thomas was one of seventeen children of a hard-working, hard-fisted grocer of yeoman stock in Glamorgan, who for many years had struggled just clear of bankruptcy. When "D.A." was born his father greeted the news with the comment: "Well, I see nothing for him but the workhouse."

However, by a scholarship, D.A. arrived at Caius College, Cambridge, where he boxed so well that he won the Varsity light-heavy championship, and neglected his studies so badly that he lost his scholarship. Back in South Wales, his shrewd grasp of finance and his outstanding organizing ability soon led him on the road to fortune in the Rhondda Valley mines. Here, indeed, was a man who taught himself really to "know coal". He was seven years older than Lloyd George, and had entered Parliament in the General Election before him as Liberal Member for Merthyr Tydfil. But though D.A.'s brain could master a case clearly, his tongue could not cogently expound it—in public. Persuasive in a Board room, he was incoherent in the House of Commons. Four Liberal Prime Ministers in turn ignored D.A., and after twenty disappointing years in Parliament this talented man retired from public life until his old friend, Lloyd George, called him back in 1917, as Lord Rhondda, to become the most successful Food Minister of the First World War.

Old friend, and old enemy, too. For if they began in politics as David and Jonathan, they ended up almost as David and Saul. In Gladstone's last Parliament, Lloyd George and D.A. found themselves still together, trying somehow to squeeze their favourite Disestablishment Bill into the bulging programme of the current session, and never succeeding, at any rate in the Grand Old Man's day. Now that great day was coming to an end. Sixty years without a break in service, Gladstone had sat in the House of Commons, and this last long duel with the Lords had borne heavily upon his failing strength. Suddenly, early in March, 1894, the veteran Liberal Prime Minister resigned his seals of office. The Queen let him go without regret, and without consulting him as to his successor passed over Sir William Harcourt, the Chancellor of the Exchequer, and sent for Lord Rosebery to fill his place.

The malcontents were not disposed to wait upon the new régime establishing itself before discussing grievances. When the next session opened ten days later, the *Manchester Guardian* reported that a talk in the Lobby with Lloyd George suggested that Welsh support would hinge upon whether or not the Government guaranteed an autumn session to bring in a Disestablishment Bill. They did not receive any such assurance, and when they pressed Sir William Harcourt, now Leader of the House, to promise them that Disestablishment should at any rate take precedence over the other proposed measures, he told them bluntly that he wished them and their bill in hell.

Next month, on 26 April, 1894, the Liberal Government did bring in a Welsh Disestablishment Bill, which was introduced by Mr. Asquith. The rebels had already broken away and hoisted their own flag. Two days earlier, Age 31   Lloyd George and three Welsh colleagues, D. A. Thomas, Herbert Lewis and Frank Edwards had refused the Government Whip. The large majority of the Welsh Members remained loyal to Lord Rosebery, and the new Party of Four came in for some bitter criticism, both at Westminster and in Wales. They defended themselves with equal firmness and fierceness.

Lloyd George himself attacked the Disestablishment Bill in the House of Commons. He found it far too lenient. The proposal to leave the Clergy in enjoyment of their benefices for life, he warned, would be a direct incitement to disturbance in order to get rid of them. For the longer they lived, if young, the more the local animosity against the pensioner would grow. But bad as the Bill was, still worse was the reason for bringing it in. It was simply to offer a sop to Welsh Nonconformist sentiment, for unless the Government's Parliamentary programme were drastically pruned or better still, scrapped, there was no hope of carrying it. Lloyd George concluded with a vitriolic onslaught on the Church, familiar to his audiences in Wales, but shocking to the House of Commons.

"Mr. Lloyd George's speech," wrote the *Manchester Guardian* next day, "will be a revelation to most Englishmen of the unsuspected depths of passionate animosity entertained by the Welsh masses for the English Church in Wales."

His action, nevertheless, aroused anger and resentment, even among his own local and faithful Liberals and Nonconformists, who considered that this was not the time to break the ranks. To which, Lloyd George answered contemptuously that "the 'convenient hour' never comes for doing a disagreeable job. There are always lions in the path of lazy men".

Once, Disestablishment had been second on the Government list. Now, it ranked only tenth. It was time for a show-down. Lloyd George proposed an Independent Welsh Party.

Promptly, the Rebel Four took themselves off to Wales, "over the dark, misty hills" where, at Rhyl, they persuaded a meeting of the North-Wales Liberal Federation to pass a resolution calling on the other, laggard, twenty-seven Welsh Liberal Members to join in the Great Uprising.

The new Liberal Leader, Lord Rosebery, decided to announce that when next the Liberal Government appealed to the country, they would go with Welsh Disestablishment passed through all its stages in the House of Commons.

This was more than enough to woo back the Loyal Twenty-seven, most of whom had, anyway, already clashed at some time or other with the lively personalities of Lloyd George or D.A.; so they resolved to give the Rosebery Administration "honourable and consistent support".

Lloyd George turned at once to the country. If he could not organize the Lobbies, well, he would try to mobilize the constituencies. He dealt a parting blow at his Parliamentary Leader.

Lord Rosebery had dropped his guard when he referred to the Welsh as "Natives of the Principality". Lloyd George, at Cross Keys, pounced upon the phrase.

"*Natives* of the Principality?" he queried. "Are the Welsh, then, to be considered as a tribe of Wahabees in Central Africa? The explorer Stanley and his followers, as I have been reading, used to cheat the natives by giving them empty jampots in exchange for food supplies. The same policy of empty jampots is being pursued towards the Natives of the Principality. Others have the jam; we get the pots."

He had to fight his own private Civil War. When he voted against the Liberal Party on a Tithe measure, which he regarded as inadequate, the local Liberal Press warned him: "An error not lightly to be passed over, and certainly not to be repeated."

Then there were those ancient personal enemies who, with a Welshman's memory for feud, Lloyd George vividly recalled (they had not forgotten him, either!) had sought to balk his nomination as a young candidate for Parliament six years earlier. Now, they were in the field again.

" 'You see, you see! We told you so! We *knew* he would let the Party down!' 'Too ambitious, eh?' 'Yes, and most headstrong also!' 'Thinks he knows better than Lord Rosebery, I suppose.' 'Well, didn't he think he knew better than Mr. Gladstone?'"

Lloyd George stood up to the local blast of battle, appeared in person before his Constituency Party meeting—and carried the day with a resolution expressing their wholehearted approval of their Member's conduct, and pledging support for any future action that he might take in furtherance of his policy. Lloyd George was sailing before the wind again.

When the squall had first struck his barque, and any rumour was liable to be borne like a leaf through the rushing air, he had allowed, if not encouraged, the idea to circulate that he was ready if need be to apply for the Chiltern Hundreds and then fight a by-election, either in Caernarvon Boroughs or elsewhere. It had rallied his supporters, for it indicated that he was in earnest, even if mistaken, in his fight for Disestablishment; and it had offered no ammunition to his opponents which they did not already possess.

He now seized the favouring breeze to moot officially to his constituents the question of his retiring at the next General Election. The reason put forward was not the personal expense of Parliamentary Elections, for we have seen that most of this was defrayed by local subscriptions, but that Membership of the House of Commons left him no time to *earn* more money. Lloyd George's family was still growing—on 4 December, 1894, his fourth child, Gwilym, would arrive—but his means remained as modest as before. He had entered his name for the Bar, following in the steps of his Welsh Party colleague, Sam Evans, but he went no farther with this project. Lloyd George was not the man to spend a day in the courts and then go, as a second chore, to the House of Commons. As a solicitor, he had not yet been able to establish his own office in London or to form a partnership there, and little legal work came his way.

He began by being as careless of finance as he was of correspondence. When he was a young lawyer-candidate in Caernarvon Boroughs, he declared: "I never sent in any bill of costs."

Bad business, though perhaps good politics. It was only when brother William joined the local Criccieth firm that things improved. Meantime, Lloyd George had so carried the day in his local skirmishes that the Council of Caernarvon Boroughs Liberal Association had decided to place an Election Fund upon a new, firm, popular basis.

All was now forgiven, if not forgotten. The whirlwind series of "Justification" meetings staged by the Rebel Four up and down the country had likewise succeeded, and the campaign for the Independent Welsh National Party was going great guns.

Lloyd George himself was in full blast, charging the Tory Opposition with the corruption of the electors by bribery and being aided, of course, by the Bishops! He discovered a natural affinity between Ale and Anglicanism;

both required Tied Houses. Nationalism was the violent motive power which in these days Lloyd George sought to harness. It long remained in his heart, and the student of the Versailles Peace may find a key to some of the mysteries perpetrated in the name of "Self-determination of Peoples" in 1919 if he will recall the echoes of a passionate, ringing voice one night in a crowded meeting in Chapel Street, Cardiff, 1894.

"The spirit of patriotism has been like the genii of the Arabian fable. It has burst asunder the prison doors, and given freedom to them that were oppressed. It has transformed the wilderness into a garden, and the hovel into a home. It has helped to drive away poverty and squalor, and brought riches and happiness in its train. It has raised the destitute into potentates, and bent monarchs to its will. Now this is the mighty spirit which has wandered homeless and aimlessly amongst our hills. Let us requisition the powerful aid of a force which has done so much for our fellow men in other countries!"

The force was there. It all depended how it was going to be used—and what for. There were different views in Wales. Almost everyone agreed upon the aim of Church Disestablishment, and very many favoured Temperance Reform, at any rate, as far as Local Option. Industrial South Wales was, of course, less interested than pastoral North Wales in Land Reform, but if Lloyd George wanted to scalp the gamekeepers as well as the priests and the publicans, well, D. A. Thomas and his coal trade friends were willing. There could even be Equal Political Rights for Women.

It was when it came to the question of Home Rule for Wales that Lloyd George and D.A. parted sympathies—and right now, under the dynamic drive of Lloyd George, it seemed to D. A. Thomas that the Welsh Revolt was getting uncomfortably close to it. At this moment, therefore, there arose what Lloyd George afterwards described as "that cross wind from the South."

For D. A. Thomas had reasons for not wanting Home Rule for Wales. He did not consider it necessary to set up another Administration in Britain in order to carry through the reforms which he himself genuinely believed in. Then there was the age-old antagonism between North and South Wales, further sharpened by the recent influx of Irish workers and English traders and business men into the developing coalfield of the Monmouthshire and Glamorgan valleys. A strong reaction developed among commercial circles, otherwise Liberal and Free Trader, against "Welsh domination", meaning Welsh Nationalism. Finally, if Home Rule came for Wales, what would happen to the very considerable political power which Mr. D. A. Thomas, M.P., now wielded as President of the South Wales Liberal Federation? In short, D.A. had already come to the breaking point with "that young Northman, Lloyd George."

At Cardiff, early in the New Year of 1895, he made it plain that, as far as

South Wales Liberals were concerned, the proposed merger with the North Wales Liberals and *Cymru Fydd* in an All-Welsh Union was "off". It was the beginning of an undeclared but unceasing war which raged between the Northman and the Southman for many a year. It was also the end of Home Rule for Wales.

Neither of the rivals realized it at the time, nor did Lord Rosebery, who made a declaration in line with Lloyd George's policy of Home Rule All Round. The Prime Minister considered that every one of the four countries of the United Kingdom should have local autonomy, subject only to the overriding authority of the Imperial Parliament. Lloyd George's "Federal Solution" (which had been Joseph Chamberlain's own original thought) was the subject of some celebrated backchat at one of his Welsh Nationalist meetings that Spring.

"Home Rule for Ireland! Home Rule for Wales! Home Rule for Scotland! Yes, and Home Rule for England, too!" declaimed the orator.

"Home Rule for Hell!" interrupted "the voice".

"Quite right," said Lloyd George, "let every man speak up for his own country."

Already, Lloyd George had seized upon the Liberal Government's new Parish Council's Bill (as once he had seized upon the Tory Government's County Councils' Bill) to press forward its exploitation as a political weapon. Everywhere, he urged, the men of Cymru Fydd should act as local Vigilance Committees to watch and guide the conduct of the members of these Councils —to encourage those who did well, to spur on those who flagged, and to punish those who failed. They might, indeed, also apply the same pressure to their Parliamentary representatives!

For M.P.s, insisted young Lloyd George, M.P., were just as good, or bad, as their constituents made them. They were supposed, indeed, to be leaders in the fight; but what was the fact? Some of these honourable gentlemen reminded him rather of honourable Chinese generals, lounging in sedan-chairs in the rear of the battlefield. They got the cushions and the kudos, the ease and the glory; the men up front got the bullets, the swordcuts, the hunger and the hardship.

Lloyd George was already aware of a new threat developing on his left flank. Comrade Keir Hardie, in his cloth cap, had arrived in the House of Commons almost at the same time as himself, and William Abraham, M.P. ("Mabon"), the old Liberal-Labour ("Lib-Lab") Miners' leader from South Wales, was warning him that in the Rhondda Valley and the coal ports, a body known as the Independent Labour Party was preaching the strange, new and exciting doctrine of Socialism. Yes, Humdrum Liberalism would have to get a move on!

In April, 1895, on All Fools' Day, the Welsh Disestablishment Bill passed its Second Reading and Joseph Chamberlain, the Unitarian turned Tory, voted for it. But in June the Liberal Government fell, and the Bill died with it.

They were defeated by seven votes, on a snap division over the supplies of cordite for the Army. Absent from the division, and unpaired (not for the first, or last, time), was the Liberal Member for Caernarvon Boroughs. But, though he was subsequently bitterly blamed for the Government's defeat, Lloyd George was not responsible for the Prime Minister's decision to resign on the Cordite Vote.

The truth was that Lord Rosebery was tired and bored, and he was glad of the excuse to be quit of the Liberal family feuds. At the General Election in July, 1895, the Party paid forfeit at the polls for these sad divisions, when the Tories swept forward in nation-wide triumph. With their Liberal Unionist allies, they secured more than twice as many Members as the Liberals, giving them a majority of 152 over the combined Liberal and Irish vote. In Wales, where they also improved their local position, Church of England champions claimed that their general victory was the result of Divine intervention (though Lloyd George offered the opinion that it was perhaps due less to grace than to grog).

Lloyd George's own contest was no easy ride. The Tories once again put up popular Squire Nanney, and they had much improved their local organization in the meantime. Still more were they helped by Liberal criticisms of Lloyd George. These were directed, first, to his absence on the night of the Cordite Vote, and they were not entirely answered by Lloyd George's retort that seven Ministers were themselves missing on the same occasion, for this was difficult to check. Next, he was accused of so embarrassing the Liberal Government on the Disestablishment Bill that they preferred to quit. His colleague, Mr. Bryn Roberts, M.P. for South Caernarvonshire, publicly denounced him for allying himself (with D. A. Thomas!), "in sinister coalition with the Tories and the Parnellites", to overthrow the Liberal Administration. The Ministers, declared Bryn Roberts, would surely not have resigned on a matter so trivial as the question of cartridges if they had not been previously so disheartened by seeing that they had lost control over their own followers.

There was an instant Lloyd George reaction. He at once rebutted the charge of treachery by extracting from his old friend, Tom Ellis, the Liberal Chief Whip, a statement that Mr. Asquith, the Home Secretary, had accepted Lloyd George's Disestablishment amendment in substance, and had actually so informed a meeting of Welsh Members at the House of Commons. So there was no question of causing the Government's resignation. Thus cleared, Lloyd George turned and dealt with his accuser, who happened to be unopposed at this election.

"If it is true that I am a wrecker of Liberalism," said Lloyd George, "it is very remarkable that I have had to encounter the most bitter, even savage opposition of the Tories, while Mr. Bryn Roberts has had a walk-over. Maybe, the best reply to his attacks upon his fellow Liberal is what a leading Tory in Caernarvonshire said about him. Asked 'Why don't you people oppose the return of B.R.?' he replied, 'Why should we? He is doing our work.'"

Lloyd George came to his traditional enemies. He would tell the electors what had really happened on that night of the Cordite Vote. A Tory M.P. complained that there were not enough cartridges per soldier. Mr. Campbell-Bannermann, the Liberal War Secretary, denied it. Mr. Joseph Chamberlain said that there should be 400 rounds per man. He complained that there was not enough powder and bullets to kill people, said Lloyd George, and he was anxious to know if enough orders had been given to a firm called Kynoch & Co., of Birmingham. The Chairman of that firm was Joe Chamberlain's brother. There were four Chamberlains who had large holdings in the firm, and two of Joe Chamberlain's partners in the screw trade were also shareholders in that concern. So much for Imperial Patriotism, Brummagem type! It was the first time that this charge had been levied against Joe Chamberlain.

As for Mr. A. J. Balfour, well, Lloyd George promised them to be a thorn in *his* side. He would bring Wales continually to that gentleman's notice, until he would be compelled to give them something, if only for the sake of peace—something in order not to have to pay the doctor's bill.

And their own lost Disestablishment Bill? "Buried, but buried in the sure and certain hope of a glorious resurrection."

Age 32   Polling Day, 22 July, 1895, broke in a terrific thunderstorm over Caernarvon Boroughs, which lasted until nightfall. When the result was announced, it was seen that Lloyd George's majority had been reduced by only two votes:

Lloyd George	.	.	.	.	.	2,265
Ellis Nanney	.	.	.	.	.	2,071
Liberal Majority	.	.	.	.	.	194

"The wave of Toryism which has swept over England has dashed itself in vain against the rocks of Eryri," he told the exulting Liberal crowd.

He was pretty exuberant himself. He was free! The soldier had escaped his sergeant-major!

There were one or two troubles, it was true, to clear up with Welsh Nonconformists, who feared that a further excursion into Home Rule for Wales might delay the unsealing of the Tomb of Disestablishment. There was the series of anonymous articles in the denominational journal *Goleuad* ("Light"), which were also so venomous that it seemed only a colleague could have done this thing, likening Lloyd George to Cleon, the shoemaker-demagogue of Athens, whose single talent was his brawling tongue. There was still the old family problem of "the needful". This was only partly solved when, a year or two later, he entered into a law partnership in London with Mr. Arthur

Rhys Roberts, a Welsh solicitor, and opened an office in the City at 13 Walbrook Street, E.C.1.

This late-summer of 1895, Lloyd George and his Welsh friend, Alfred Davies, with their wives, went off by steamer from Liverpool to Oban for a holiday. It was nearly the end of the Lloyd George story. For while they were there, they went for a sail one sunny day in Oban Bay. A sudden squall blew up. It struck their boat, heeled it half-over, and seemed certain to capsize it. For several fearful minutes the gunwale poised within a fraction of an inch above the water, until the skill of their boatmen righted the little craft. Not one of those aboard could swim, and no other vessel was in sight. Lloyd George never again in his life went out in a small boat.

A few days later, at Ferres, he was initiated into the mysteries of a strange game. It was golf. No spare set of men's golf clubs was available, so the novice was equipped with those of a lady, and thus learned the game which later played a notable part in his life.

When Lloyd George returned to the House that autumn it was no longer in the role of a rebel. Opposition gave him his chance again to fall into line with his leaders. Indeed, for a time, almost to lead them.

Attack! Attack! And if attacked yourself—counter-attack!

He charged the new Tory Government with squandering the £5,000,000 budget surplus left by the late Liberal Chancellor of the Exchequer. Now they were going to make the Navy, which was already twice the size of any other maritime Power, larger than ever! Of course (Lloyd George conceded), it would have the incidental advantage of providing additional berths for the impecunious sons of the aristocracy; some of them might become admirals before they had properly learned to be before the mast.

Early next year, he was able to make more direct allegations. The Government had brought in an Agricultural Land Rating Bill in relief of the farmers. At least, that was what they claimed it was! According to Lloyd George, the benefit would ultimately accrue instead to the landlords, who on account of the lower rates would be able to extort higher rents. He calculated that certain members of the Government would themselves share in the proceeds to the extent of £60,000. He listed some of them personally (Lloyd George was nothing if not personal in his politics). Mr. Henry Chaplin, who introduced the Bill, would get £700; Mr. Balfour, £1,450; Lord Salisbury, £2,000; The Duke of Devonshire (he was an ex-Liberal), £10,000. There was uproar in the House.

He kept up the fight in Committee. Rating was a subject which Lloyd George understood as thoroughly as Tithe. In his skilful framing of amendments, he outstripped the famous lawyers on the Opposition Front Bench, and he was tireless.

"Has Lloyd George been speaking all morning?" "Lloyd George *still* speaking?" "Hasn't anyone else but Lloyd George spoken?"

Such were the questions, wrote a *Western Mail* (and hostile) Press Gallery reporter, that he heard different M.P.s ask as they came in one after another, only to find the Member for Caernarvon Boroughs where they had left him when they went out, namely, on his feet and speaking.

As far as Lloyd George was concerned, the referee stopped the fight when, on Clause Four at 3.30 a.m. one May morning, Balfour moved the closure. Lloyd George, Herbert Lewis, and three Irish Members refused to obey the Speaker and leave the Chamber. They were suspended for a week, and Lloyd George got a rest at last.

He had made a remarkable impression upon the House, and through the newspapers, upon the country, and Sir William Harcourt, who had not so long ago cordially invited him "to go to hell", told some of his Scots colleagues:

"All you Scots Members together are not worth Lloyd George's little finger."

It was indeed a Soldiers' Battle as far as the Liberal Party was concerned. Lord Rosebery finally gave up the official leadership in 1896, after Gladstone had made a one-day comeback in public life to denounce the Turks for a fresh Armenian massacre and to recommend the recall of the British Ambassador from the Porte. Indeed, Rosebery genuinely feared that the G.O.M.'s condemnation would rush the country into war, "the last straw". He made his farewell the next day in a stately speech at the Empire Theatre, Edinburgh. The entry in his diary that night was characteristic: "Home for supper. What a relief!"

Sir William Harcourt, as leader of the Liberal Members in the House of Commons, thereupon became the acting head of the Party, though many still looked to Rosebery, who had a further role to play. Soon, the Grand Old Man himself would finally quit the earthly scene,

"the greatest leader of men since the days of Napoleon," said Lloyd George. "No other man has excited the same personal loyalty and enthusiasm among his followers. His death leaves a gap like that made by the fall of the greatest of the oaks of the forest."

Age 33   This summer of 1896, Lloyd George voyaged with Herbert Lewis, his fellow fighter in the Rating Bill, to the River Plate and the rich new lands of Uruguay and Argentina. In Montevideo, they ran into a fellow Welshman, Jones, who was head of the Uruguayan Telegraph System, and within a few hours they were the feted guests of the Government and all the leading clubs. Then, Lloyd George and his friend went up to the hills of Cordova, half-way to the towering Andes, and there spent a week in the land of palm groves and vineyards, where, as he wrote home, "every cottage has its fig tree, on which the fruit is ripening in the summer sun".

Lloyd George was enchanted by the scenery, the scents, the flowers, the birds, and the people. But what pleased him best of all was their visit to a camp in the hills, and their exciting ride home through the night of a great storm. Midnight in the mountains in a storm! Lloyd George's ideal of happiness! He tells the story:

"As we entered the encampment, we heard a kid, or '*gavarita*', bleat; half an hour later it was cooked ready for our eating. After mealtime, our guide or peon sang us a Spanish song to the accompaniment of a guitar which he himself played. A native minstrel (Indian?) was stirred to emulation, and responded in fine style. Here we remained until nightfall, expecting to return when the moon had risen. But instead of a moon, we had a thunderstorm. We hastily mounted our horses, and rode after our guide and the Indian through lonely glens and over narrow passes, flanked by a precipitous chasm on one side and steep rocks on the other. Sometimes, we could not see a foot in front of us; then the whole wild scene would be suddenly lit up by a vivid flash of lightning. Our two guides rode steadily ahead, nothing heeding, twanging their guitars and singing love songs. It was an experience I would not have missed for anything in the world."

Lloyd George returned from the land of the pampas, charged with fresh energy to fall upon the British Tory Government. It was as well for the Liberal Opposition that some volunteer on the Back Benches was ready to fight the enemy, for Sir William Harcourt's colleagues on the Front Bench that autumn and the following spring seemed concerned rather with fighting one another for the succession of the Party leadership.

Lloyd George did not miss the chance thus afforded by these sulks and squabbles among his own High Command. From his Back Bench, he made all the running once again in the debates on the Voluntary Schools Bill, a measure which involved a grant of money to the Denominational Schools of the Church of England. This was another subject which the Member for Caernarvon Boroughs well understood.

Soon, he showed his skill in framing an "Instruction" on the Bill, the only one accepted by the Speaker. (This is a Parliamentary device which opens up the possibilities of delay and subsequent manoeuvre on a far wider ground than a mere amendment.) It earned the tribute of the shrewdest of Parliamentary observers, Mr. Punch's "Toby M.P." He commented:

"another step in a successful Parliamentary career, achieved by sheer ability, lived up to with unvaried modesty. To frame Instruction on going into Committee has always been, for technical reasons, work of great difficulty. Tonight six Parliamentary hands essayed it. The youngest alone accomplished it."

Lloyd George followed up his successful Instruction, as he had intended, with a series of amendments,

"Bobbing up and down, down and up, like a monkey on a stick," remarked the Bishop of St. Asaph.

To which Lloyd George retorted by challenging the claim of any Welsh Bishop to set himself up as an authority on teaching (Dr. Edwards himself had taken only third-class honours in his degree at Oxford).

"No doubt they pass their examinations. But you cannot even make a first-rate bishop out of a third-rate scholar, a fifth-rate preacher, a no-rate theologian and an irate priest."

And Lloyd George himself? To a public becoming increasingly interested in politics, he was already a recognizable figure; to his fellow politicians a formidable one; to a wide circle of friends an irresistible one, with his gaiety, vitality and curious prescience. He took considerable care with his appearance in these days, always dressing neatly, almost fastidiously—one newspaper described him as: "looking a bit like a shopwalker."

He still worked very hard, for to be sure, he still had to live fairly hard. But however busy he was he rarely forgot that letter home, "the daily boon", to Uncle Lloyd.

Suddenly, thunder. In July, 1897, there appeared in the Divorce List the case of Edwards *v.* Edwards and Wilson, with an application for leave to proceed without making any co-respondent other than Wilson. But the respondent, Mrs. Edwards, the wife of a well-known Montgomeryshire doctor, alleged that a person referred to as "A.B." was the father of her child. "A.B." was David (Lloyd) George. Mrs. Catherine Edwards was herself a distant relative of Mrs. David Lloyd George.

Here was crisis, of a deep, personal and perhaps decisive nature. For in those days—and for another thirty years in British public life—to be cited in divorce proceedings was practically to close a political career, as Dilke and Parnell had proved. Lloyd George did not appear in the court in person, but a large public followed the Press reports, with varied feelings.

The story was that one night in the previous February, Dr. Edwards had invited Lloyd George to stay at his home, in Cemmaes, Montgomeryshire, and that during the night, while he was called away on a professional visit, his guest had committed adultery with his wife. In August, she signed the following confession:

"I, Catherine Edwards, do solemnly confess that I have, on the 4th February, 1896, committed adultery with Lloyd George, M.P., and that the said Lloyd George is the father of the child, and that I have on previous occasions committed adultery with the above Lloyd George."

In November, when the case came up for hearing, Lloyd George produced to Counsel the record of the Parliamentary division lists to show that on 4 February he had been until early morning voting in the House of Commons.

In August, Mrs. Edwards was in childbirth. Counsel on both sides were satisfied that the "confession" was designed to protect another man, and that there was no evidence against Lloyd George. He was therefore cleared of the charge. It was for a number of persons a most disappointing outcome of an apparently promising "scandal". In the following month, the local Executive Councils of the Caernarvon Boroughs Liberal Association passed unanimous resolutions of sympathy with Mr. Lloyd George in his "cruel position", congratulated him upon the complete vindication of his character and assured him of their unswerving loyalty.

So passed the second sudden storm of Lloyd George's life of tempest.[1] The third storm was as yet no larger than a man's hand, far off on the horizon of that illimitable *veldt* in South Africa.

That autumn, Sir William Harcourt threw in his hand and Campbell-Bannerman, an earlier and rather bolder Clement Attlee, stepped up to the Liberal leadership. Lloyd George regarded his new captain without enthusiasm, though with respect. He had outdistanced Rosebery, Harcourt, Morley and Asquith, all of them men of greater intellectual calibre than himself and with a gift of speech which he did not possess, and he had done it by sheer staying power. Now, the great figures of the Victorian Age were making their exit from the stage, with the Age itself. New men were entering, with the new century. It was going to be so much more progressive in so many things, especially wars. It was going to be so different, so dramatic, and so dangerous for everyone, in future. The map of the world was going to be redrawn, drastically, within the lifetime of this new generation. Some rough-handed draughtsmen were already at work in South Africa in the New Year of 1899.

But for a change of plans, Lloyd George himself would have been there that autumn when the first violent strokes were made, for such had been his original intention only a few weeks before. As it was, Lloyd George was in Canada, at the invitation of the High Commissioner, Lord Strathcona, studying the conditions of settlement in the Dominion for Welsh emigrants, and immensely impressed by the vast potentialities of that still almost unknown land.

"Everything that tends to make a country great is here," he told the *Toronto Globe* in an interview. "Wheat, cattle, gold, silver, iron, copper, fish, magnificent streams and untapped water-power are in abundance. The Canadians have not shouted loud enough for themselves; consequently, their voice has been drowned by the shouting of the Americans, who have attracted the trade."

As he spoke, the rattle of rifle fire from the *veldt* rose above the chorus of both.

[1] Throughout his career he was the victim of charges of this nature. In Wales the gossip related to London. And in London the rumours referred to Wales.

CHAPTER VI

"THE UNNECESSARY WAR"

THE Boer War had been coming for more than sixty years. For the greater part of this time it cannot be charged that the Boers sought it. On the whole, history offers few examples of a people so resolutely trying to march away from the fate which eventually overtook them.

They had come, first, to South Africa during Elizabethan days as a handful of settlers in Table Bay, to make a half-way station for the Dutch merchantmen sailing to the Far East. It was not until more than two centuries later that the English arrived in force at the Cape of Good Hope, during the Napoleonic Wars, to keep out the French. Afterwards, they bought the place by the Convention of London in August, 1814.

So far, colonization of the Cape had been confined to the coastal fringe. Now, driven by their dislike of British rule (especially in its Native Policy), the Boer farmers began to edge away towards the frontier lands. They were harried by the ferocious Bantu tribesmen, whom they preferred, as enemies, to the British tax-gatherer. In the late 1830's, the more adventurous of the Boer people loaded their goods and families into the great, lumbering ox-wagons and, driving their herds of sheep and cattle along with them, made the Great Trek across the Vaal River and over the Drakensberg mountains. A boy of ten years old who rode along with his parents was named Paul Kruger.

They wanted to get away and "govern themselves without interference", which was exactly what they were not going to be allowed to do.

The British at the Cape might well have been ready to wave their departing Dutch "Good-bye, and Good Luck!" But just at this hour in history when the Boers, advance guard of the White invasion from Europe, were pressing north-wards, the Bantus, last wave of the Black tide from Africa's mysterious land of the lakes, were surging south. It was a time of raid, reprisal, murder and massacre. Against their own will, and simply for the sake of the general peace in South Africa, successive Imperial Governments at Westminster found themselves extending the boundaries of their responsibility. Hard on the heels of the ever-eagerly escaping Boers trudged the ever-unwilling pursuing British.

In the 1850's both the Orange Free State and the Transvaal Republic had been granted "freedom to manage their own affairs". By the 1860's the discovery of diamonds near Kimberley, eighty miles north of the Orange River, brought the British Government there on the grounds that only the Crown was powerful enough to control the unruly diggers. In the 1870's the cost of incessant Native wars threatened to bankrupt the Transvaal, and the British Government felt obliged to take over that country, too. The burghers rose in revolt, and at Majuba Hill wiped out an Imperial force. Gladstone's Government hastily restored the independence of the Transvaal.

The Boer release from the British embrace was brief. In the 1880's gold was discovered in fabulous quantity on the Rand in the Transvaal. At once there poured in a flood of the hated adventuring Englishmen, Frenchmen, Germans, Jews, and Greeks, all eager to explore and exploit the newest Eldorado.

Along with these fortune hunters, some of them the scum of the earth, came outstanding characters like Cecil Rhodes, egotist and idealist. He was already a millionaire from his shrewd Kimberley diamond dealing, and determined now to realize his early dream of the "All-Red Road to the North".

Cecil Rhodes was reaching out his arm to other British adventurers in Uganda, East Africa and even Egypt, who were also scheming to build the All-Red Route from the other end of the Continent. The Partition of Africa was at hand, with Germany, France, Belgium, Italy and Portugal all in the game, or else about to enter it. Blocking the path of Britain to a new empire of dazzling wealth and power, there stood only a poor, primitive, bigoted community of Boer farmers, organized under a corrupt, petty oligarchy.

At least, so it seemed to Cecil Rhodes, by now Prime Minister of Cape Colony. He resolved to smash the obstruction.

There was plenty of political, as well as chemical dynamite lying around on the Rand. If President "Oom Paul" Kruger and his Kirk-going burghers could reasonably complain of the rowdy, bawdy behaviour of the cosmopolitan gang of gold miners, gamblers and dealers who had turned the Rand into an inferno by day and night, these Uitlanders, as they were known, also had real grievances.

Their 80,000 strength outnumbered the local Boer population by four to one, and though they contributed in taxes nineteen-twentieths of the total Transvaal revenue they had no voice whatever in the government of the country, nor even of Johannesburg municipality. Their industry, which had brought such unheard-of wealth to the country, was further systematically fleeced by the President's personal and political friends. Kruger had granted these favoured folk monopolies in explosives, in the transportation of coal necessary to work the mining machinery, and in liquor (with which they debauched the Native workers as thoroughly as they cheated the Europeans).

On 29 December, Dr. Jameson, administrator of the neighbouring territory already known as "Rhodesia", and the personal friend of Cecil Rhodes himself, crossed the Transvaal frontier at the head of a force of volunteers. They rode hard across the *veldt* for Johannesburg, where a body of Uitlanders waited to rise and seize the key-points of the town. But the plotters fumbled; the

Johannesburg Fifth Column stayed indoors, and four days later "Doctor Jim" surrendered to the Boer commandos who had closed in upon him. The Raid was over.

Its impact stayed many a day. Jameson was jailed. Rhodes resigned. It seems doubtful if he knew in advance of the Raid, but he was certainly privy to the plot of the Rising. He was censured both at the Cape and at Westminster, where an unsuccessful effort was made to implicate Joseph Chamberlain himself. In Pretoria, President "Oom Paul" Kruger continued in his autocratic ways as before, refusing any redress of the Uitlanders's grievances. Passions rose on either side, and South Africa raced towards war.

The ostensible point at issue was whether or not the Uitlanders were to be granted an electoral franchise.[1] Kruger made several promises, but he was determined that these foreigners should never have the power to "swamp" the votes of his own burghers. Argument about the terms of the franchise brought up the question of Britain's rather shadowy "suzerainty" over South Africa, and served only to confirm the old man's suspicions. "You mean to take my country!" he cried to Sir Alfred Milner,[2] the High Commissioner of Cape Colony.

Meantime, Joseph Chamberlain, the Colonial Secretary, and the real master of the Government, though a Liberal Unionist, thought it as well to warn the nation of the coming storm. On 26 June, 1899, he went down to his citadel at Birmingham, and there in the Town Hall declared that:

> "The British Government have put their hands to the plough . . . and having undertaken this business we will see it through. . . . We have tried waiting, patience and trusting to promises which were never kept. We can wait no more."

Queen Victoria had her Private Secretary read every word of the newspaper report carefully to her, and then sent the orator a note:

> "The Queen greatly admires Mr. Chamberlain's speech."

As summer died, the clamour for war grew even more fiercely among the Boers themselves. At this mad moment, indeed, they were the noisiest jingoes. Rifles and ammunition were freely distributed throughout the two Republics, artillery was brigaded at Pretoria, and the Burghers made ready to saddle-up and ride within the hour. Their commandants realized surely enough that all the advantages of an early start to the campaign lay with them.

On 2 October, 1899, the *Volksraad* approved war. President Kruger asked the members to read Psalm 108, verse 7, which, he declared, had come to him as a Message while he struggled in prayer. It says:

[1] While the Uitlanders demanded the rights of citizenship of Transvaal they refused to renounce their own nationality.
[2] Later Lord Milner.

"God hath spoken in His Holiness; I will rejoice. I will divide Shechem, and mete out the valley of Succoth."

It accorded with their mood. The Boers meant to carve up the lands of the enemy. Francis Reitz, State Secretary of the Transvaal, foretold that the Afrikaaner flag would fly from the Zambesi to the Cape, and that the grand-daughter of George III would have to reconcile herself to another War of Independence and the rise of the United States of South Africa. Many of the *Volksraad* members were already in the field with their commandos.

In Britain, the newspapers were hustling their war correspondents off by the earliest ship to South Africa, and on 5 October, Joseph Chamberlain wrote from the Colonial Office a letter to the High Commissioner, Sir Alfred Milner:

> "I am sending a line to anticipate a probable visit from Winston Churchill, the son of Lord Randolph Churchill, who is going out as a correspondent for the *Morning Post.* . . . He is a very clever young fellow with many of his father's qualifications. He has the reputation of being bumptious, but I have not myself found him so, and time will no doubt get rid of the defect if he has it. . . . He is a good writer and full of energy. He hopes to be in Parliament, but want of means stands in the way. . . ."

A few days earlier, Chamberlain had drafted an ultimatum to Pretoria which the Cabinet had approved. At 6.15 a.m. on 10 October he was awakened to read another ultimatum. Kruger had saved him the trouble of posting his own. The President imperatively demanded (1) that all British troops be withdrawn from the frontiers of the Transvaal, (2) that all reinforcements which had arrived in South Africa since 1 June be repatriated, (3) that no troops currently on the high seas be landed at any port in South Africa. "They have done it!" cried Chamberlain exultingly.

Even better. They had done it a little too late. An Indian Army contingent had been disembarked at Durban forty-eight hours before.

Time, however, was still on the side of the enemy. Next morning, the Orange Free State ranged herself alongside her sister Republic. The Boer commandos were already riding into the British Colonies. In Bechuanaland, south of Mafeking, they captured an armoured train and advanced upon the town. Within a few days Kimberley and Ladysmith were also invested. This put a full stop to the usual "All Over by Christmas" optimism, at any rate, on the British side. The Boers had better cause to cheer. November saw the British General French narrowly escaping capture by Commandant De Wet in Natal, and the commandos freely raiding into Cape Colony. December brought Black Week (11–16 December), with three separate, stinging Imperial defeats. The British public were stunned, and then furious.

For once, the wrath fell where it properly belonged. The blundering War

Office was on all sides condemned, and an excellent soldier, Field-Marshal Lord Roberts, was at once despatched to South Africa as Commander-In-Chief, with Lord Kitchener as his Chief of Staff. The people of Britain set their teeth, and from all over the Empire poured in spontaneous offers of help in men and money. "Imperial Joe" could hardly have dared to hope for better fortune than those first disasters of Black Week. He knew now, as he wrote to Milner, that the nation as well as the Government meant to "see the matter through, at whatever cost".

In Parliament, early in the New Year, 1900, Chamberlain would affirm that:

"the Colonies, repelled in the past by indifference and apathy . . . for the first time are now claiming their share in the duties and responsibilities as well as the privileges of Empire. . . . We are slowly but steadily advancing to the realization of that great federation of our race which will inevitably make for peace and liberty and justice."

Meantime, from every township in Canada, Australia and New Zealand thirty thousand volunteers were advancing to join the colours. It was in this political climate that Lloyd George, abandoning his Canadian tour, returned home. He did not feel at all the same way about the war.

He had already sent a warning message to his constituents from British Columbia, 18 September, 1899.

"The news from the Transvaal threatens to alter my arrangements. War means the summoning of Parliament; the former now seems inevitable. The prospect oppresses me with a deep sense of horror. If I have the courage, I shall protest with all the vehemence at my command against this outrage which is perpetrated in the name of human freedom."

The Liberal Party, its ranks still divided in several degrees over Home Rule, and its leadership distracted by the personal rivalries of Campbell-Bannerman, Rosebery, Morley and Asquith, was now faced with a fresh "split". On one side were the "Liberal Imperialists", who upheld the Government's policy while occasionally criticizing its conduct. On the other side were the Radicals, "Little Englanders", and "Pro-Boers" who condemned the whole business. There were, of course, a variable number of others who hovered above or between the battle.

The fighting in South Africa had already begun when Lloyd George landed on 16 October. He wrote a hurried note that night to his brother William.

"Not seen anyone yet as to the Transvaal. A letter awaiting me from the editor of *The Speaker*. He has been staying with Morley at Hawarden, and at his request wrote me for my opinion what should be done on opening of Parliament. Shall not reply until I have time to reflect deeply over new situation created by Boer advance. . . . The Boers have invaded our territories, and until they are driven back, Government entitled to money to equip forces to defend our possessions. In my opinion the way these poor hunted burghers have been driven in self-defence to forestall us aggravates our crime—there is something diabolical in its malignity."

The House of Commons was prorogued after ten days, Lloyd George winding-up with the last speech of the Session. It was short, but enough to disclose in which Liberal camp he was in future to be found. He had finished his reflection, and made up his mind. He was in fact to prove the principal opponent of the Government in this war.

His words were biting. This was a war to enforce a pure and honest administration in the Transvaal? What! By a Government which, under the pretence of relieving agricultural distress, had just divided £3,000,000 of public money amongst its supporters through a measure carried by a Chamber composed of Landlords (The House of Lords)—a Chamber for which no native-born British subject had the right to vote! The speech did not go down very well in the prevailing mood of patriotic rally-round.

His next one, at Carmarthen in the following month, went down hardly better. The speaker found it necessary to declare that he would be recreant before God and man if he did not make protest against what he thought an infamy. "And here I do it tonight," he cried, "even if I have to leave Carmarthen tomorrow without a friend."

At Flint, on New Year's Eve, in a burst of xenophobia, Lloyd George competed for a moment with his most rabid opponents. Had Flint no grievances, say, against the alien institutions which misgoverned her? Was Flint free? Talk about Johannesburg! Why, if there had been a colony of German Jews in Flint—and in one or two other places in Wales suffering such injustices—there would have been an Army Corps despatched to stop the business! As it was, all our righteousness, all our sense of justice, all our hatred of wrong was reserved for a community of Jews 6,000 miles distant in Johannesburg, who ran away when the fight came for their own cause. Let them seal the testament of their freedom with their own blood!

Early in the New Year, 27 January, 1900, Lloyd George was invited to Oxford to address the Palmerston Club, one of the glowing hearths of Liberalism in that University. He seized the occasion to deal with the Liberal Unionist, Joseph Chamberlain, and the Liberal Imperialist, Lord Rosebery, each of whom had conveniently provided him with a text. Age 37

Chamberlain had recently referred to "the Transvaal, the country we created". Why, this was the Birmingham version of the Scriptures, mocked Lloyd George.

"In the Beginning, Joseph Chamberlain created Heaven and Earth——including the Transvaal."

At any rate, it could be said of the Boer farmer who lined the trenches that the hand that grasped the Mauser was never soiled with a bribe. He fought for the freedom and independence of his native land, and there was no more sacred cause for which a man could die. Thank God, there was one little community where the millionaire was not omnipotent! As for Lord Rosebery:

"Lord Rosebery would sharpen England's sword, to make it more deadly? Let him rather purge the Empire's conscience to make its statesmanship more upright!"

Next month, 6 February, on a fine evening, the House of Commons was debating the Queen's Speech. About six o'clock, Lloyd George rose from his bench below the gangway. He possessed a reputation as a formidable Welsh clan fighter; when he sat down, he had made his name as a British national figure, established beyond challenge. A great company witnessed it. Asquith opened the Debate, and Balfour closed it. Chamberlain was present, but he did not speak.

Lloyd George began by reminding the House that the former Commander-in-Chief at the Cape, General Sir William Butler, had warned the Government early in the previous year that the posting of more British troops to the Transvaal Border would be regarded by the Boers as deliberate provocation; that actual war would involve reinforcement from Britain of the local garrison by at least 50,000 men; and that if the Orange Free State took sides with the Transvaal, as must be expected, then still more soldiers would be required.

The Colonial Secretary, said Lloyd George, had generously conceded the mistakes of the Government, those of the War Office, of the Generals—of everyone except himself and the Colonial Office. In truth, gibed Lloyd George, the greatest of all the mistakes had been the "New Diplomacy" of the Colonial Secretary. It was no good "deprecating" debate in Parliament as to the merits or otherwise of this war; discussion would go on in the factories, on the farms, in the homes. The whole country was stirred up about it, and rightly so. They had been told of the "intolerable" situation in the Transvaal. Well, the wages of miners over there were four times higher than miners earned here. They had an officially recognized Eight Hours Day there, but we had not yet got that here. There, the State charged the exploiting mine capitalists a royalty of 50 per cent; here, it was half of one per cent.

The chief thing that these Uitlander gentlemen wanted to exploit was labour. There was a Mr. Rudd, went on Lloyd George, who had declared at a meeting of Consolidated Goldfields that:

"if under the cry of Civilization we, in Egypt, lately mowed down 10,000 or 20,000 Dervishes with Maxim guns, it can surely be considered no hardship to compel the Natives in South Africa to give three months in the year doing a little honest work."

At the Board of Trade, 1907

"So," asked Lloyd George, "at the price of the lives of brave British soldiers we are going to renew slavery on the Rand?"

He then produced an inimitable character (Lloyd George invariably did; he had such luck in his opponents that people suspected he had invented them). This was an American businessman named Mr. Hays Hammond. He had been indiscreet enough to explain that:

"with good Government there should be an abundance of labour, and with abundant labour there should be no difficulty in cutting down wages. In any case, it is preposterous to pay the present rate of wages to Kaffirs."

"It is £3 per month," commented Lloyd George, and was himself corrected. "No! it is £2 5s."

Mr. Hays Hammond himself considered that these Kaffirs would be quite as well satisfied—in fact, they would work longer—if you paid them half as much. It would also considerably reduce the cost of White Labour.

The opinions of Mr. Hays Hammond were to Lloyd George the gift of a political goldmine. Henceforth, in Georgian banter, the hapless Hammond became (because he happened to be a citizen of the United States) "The George Washington of South Africa". If ever there was a natural word-cartoonist in the art of politics it was Lloyd George—and persons like Mr. Hays Hammond were his natural raw material.

Possibly because he could not tell a lie, South Africa's George Washington had admitted that Consolidated Gold would gain £2,199,433 as an immediate result of the war, and he reckoned that the firm would be able to increase their annual dividend by 45 per cent.

"Look!" cried the cartoonist from Caernarvon. "Here is the key to the whole picture! It is simply—L.S.D.!"

He made a good party gibe on the Uitlander Petition to the British Government to request revision of the Boer Liquor Laws.

"Well! A Government that was floated into power on Beer, going to enforce Prohibition on the Rand!"

And a better one still on the Uitlanders' plea that the Transvaal railways should be taken away from their present private owners and run by the Republic.

"What! Run by a corrupt and inefficient Government, which can't even manage its own affairs!"

The most effective part of Lloyd George's speech, in a House of Commons predominantly bent on war, was when he claimed that the Boer Liberals in the Transvaal had almost won their own fight against that "obstinate old

D

Tory, Kruger", on the question of the Uitlander franchise when war had been forced upon their country. He named the leaders of these Liberals, Joubert, Burgher, Meyer. He asked, dramatically: "Where are they now?" And answered, dramatically, "In the field. They are Boer generals now!"

And the Uitlanders? Surely, their greatest pride had been to take part in the armed conflict, and to fight for their supposed rights? No! They preferred to lounge around the hotels of Capetown while English homes were made to mourn. There was barely a battalion of them fighting for us. Such men and such grievances were not worth a drop of British blood.

It was the best fighting speech Lloyd George had ever made—against fighting—and in a hostile House. His case against what he had called in a letter to D. R. Daniel "an unnecessary, a damnable, even worse perhaps, a senseless war" was almost complete. In thirty months more of crusading for peace Lloyd George would find little to add to his original indictment, except infinite variations of expression.

"You have made a speech which Grattan himself might have envied"

wrote Harcourt, on a slip that was passed to him along the benches. Balfour told a friend that it was the best speech he had ever heard in the House of Commons, though, of course, he disagreed with every word of it. What brought from Lloyd George a typical expression of pleasure was the compliment of Campbell-Bannermann, who said that a famous London actress had been present in the gallery, and had "begged her escort to bring her again whenever the Member for Caernarvon was likely to speak".

Soon, the war was going better. While up to the end of the Old Year almost nothing had gone right for us, after the New Year almost nothing went wrong. Though the call for seven divisions had drained the United Kingdom of its trained men, the rally of the Imperial Yeomanry and the volunteers made the flow of soldiers faster than that of their equipment. And, as so often, lacking it the men on the spot "made-do", and made better.

Three days after the great debate in the House of Commons (9 February) the Imperial general advance began. Roughly, it provided (in return order to Black Week) a Red Letter Month. Kimberley was relieved; Ladysmith was relieved; General Cronje surrendered at Paardeberg; Bloemfontein fell, and the Transvaal *Volksraad* deputies fled overseas. It really began to look as if it would be All Over by Easter, anyway. The impatient British public had to hang on until 17 May, anniversary of the memorable defeat at Majuba in the First Boer War, before they could celebrate the Relief of Mafeking. Then the town went mad, and a new word was coined.

Did Lloyd George enter into this mood of exultation? Some writers have claimed that he shared in the popular pride in the success of our armies in South Africa, but they have offered no evidence of it. On the other hand, there is plenty to show that, while he was not unduly downcast over the disasters of Black Week, he was meticulous not to attack the conduct of either commanders or men in the field. Vehemently, he rebutted the charge of blackening the name of the British soldier, and turned upon those who dared to make it.

"We, whom you call pro-Boers, here have nothing to do with the blackguardly liars who have spread false reports on the continent about our British troops. I challenge all the world to find in any of my speeches a single word accusing our soldiers of brutality."

Lloyd George insisted that he was concerned only to ensure that criticism of the war should be centred upon the question of whether or not it could be justified as an act of policy. When George Wyndham, a rising young Tory Minister, made a lively speech on the conduct of the operations, Lloyd George wrote, in one of his nightly letters home:

"Wyndham made a very fine defence of the Government from a military point of view. Very glad of it, as I don't want the argument against the Government to be a military one."

Now there opened the famous series of Boer War "Lloyd George Nights". The first of these took place at Glasgow in March, 1900, when an anti-war meeting at the City Hall had provided the battlefield for rival mobs of Tory students and Socialist dockers, these last being led by the warlike pacifist, Keir Hardie. Fighting broke out long before the meeting started. The auditorium and the staircases were cleared at length of the main enemy forces, and Lloyd George and the other speakers were eventually allowed a rowdy enough hearing. Though the windows of his cab were broken as he left, Lloyd George himself escaped injury. Keir Hardie and three of his womenfolk were set upon by hooligans, and knocked about until rescued by the police.

So Lloyd George was well aware of what awaited him when he resolved to speak at Bangor, always the most hostile borough of his own constituency. The leading local Liberals did their best to dissuade him. He refused to be put off, and a letter of 22 March, 1900, to his brother William explains why:

"*I am going to Bangor*. I mean to insist upon it. I hear the bulk of the leading Liberals are strongly opposed to meeting at this juncture, and they entreat me not to go. I will not listen to them. Here are my reasons:

(*a*) There may be a general election soon.

(*b*) You may rely upon Chamberlain forcing dissolution in the height of the war fever.

(*c*) If the policy of abstaining from meeting to instruct the people is adhered to, judgment will go by default against us and we will be hopelessly beaten—and we deserve to be.

(*d*) If the Association still deprecate meetings I resign my candidature, as I cannot hope to succeed if I am shut up."

So the preparations went ahead. But the trustees of the hall insisted on being secured against damage. Lloyd George noted in his diary:

"*March* 30, 1900. Just had a wire from Bangor, that the trustees of Penrhyn Hall won't let it without substantial guarantee against damages. . . . And we are fighting for free speech and equal rights in the Transvaal! First-rate object lesson! I mean to get there."

It was a fine night in Bangor. The meeting turned out to be a near-riot. Lloyd George had been warned what to expect, and though he had duly arrived on time, looking a little pale, he showed no sign of fear on the platform.

He went out of his way to pay tribute to the Colonies. When he could make himself heard, he praised the young Empire nations, both for their splendid help to the Old Country in its time of trouble and for the reserve with which Canada, especially, had refused to be "rushed" by the Colonial Secretary into the events which led up to the war.

"They have proved their loyalty—and their independence!" cried Lloyd George.

Then he saluted the Queen, who had worn the Shamrock on St. Patrick's Day. By her gracious act of simple recognition of Irish nationality, Her Majesty had done more in a day for the real Empire of hearts than all her present Ministers had done in a lifetime.

"Mr. Chamberlain," he went on, warming to his favourite subject, "cannot understand Irish nationality, or indeed any other man's nationality than his own. He prefers the patriotism which gives a position of £5,000 a year—and ensures a dividend from the Small Arms Factory in which his relatives are interested."

It was the first time during the war that this charge had been made. Lloyd George would repeat it again, until in the end Joseph Chamberlain, almost broken by it, would rise in the most tense debate of his whole political career of unceasing strife, and deny it—but not quite.

Meanwhile, tonight the Bangor meeting was warming up.

Outside the Hall, a large mob alternately howled "Pro-Boer!" and rendered (with cornet accompaniment) " Soldiers of the Queen", and steadily flung stones through the windows. ("Another Imperial argument," commented Lloyd George as each shower landed.) A strong body of police had been brought into the town to guard against the doors being rushed and they were thoroughly needed. Inside the Hall, strong-arm squads of stewards eventually ensured some kind of order, though Lloyd George had to fight against continual interruption for more than an hour. He kept his head, and a resolution condemning the war was carried by a large majority.

After the meeting was over, he was lucky to keep his life. On arrival, someone had thrown a clod of earth at him as he drove up to the front entrance. As he left, he became separated from his party (which included Mrs. Lloyd George) and, on entering the High Street, a zealous patriot struck him a violent blow on the head with a bludgeon. Lloyd George's hat was smashed in, and he was half-stunned. He managed to make his way into a nearby café, where the proprietor slammed the door behind him in the nick of time. Police hurried there, and held off the mob until midnight. While his constituents hooted him, sang loyal songs and hymns and surged and barged against the constabulary, their M.P. made his way out by a back door.

His constituents were more civil at Caernarvon, though some of his oldest supporters there warned him frankly that they were not going to vote for him at the next General Election. To which he replied, with equal frankness, that if the local Liberal delegates wished him to stand aside then he would do so; let them make their own choice. He had made his, and he was prepared to pay for it and not only in politics. Both in his London office and at Criccieth the order of the day was often "No Business".

At a Liskeard "Peace Meeting" in July there was a repeat riot. Arthur Quiller-Couch ("Q") took the chair. The arrival of the platform party was the signal for uproar—whistling, stamping, shouting, cheers for "Tommy Atkins" and boos for "Kroojer". Then came "God Save the Queen", "Rule Britannia!" the Doxology—and "Shall Trelawney Die?" On Lloyd George rising, the crowd rose, too, and surged forward. The ladies fled. Chairs were smashed and flung at the platform, several attempts were made to storm it, and khaki-clad soldiers were chaired round the hall. After an hour or more of pandemonium, the police cleared the building.

The trouble on this occasion was incited and inflamed by the report of some supposed slighting reference by Lloyd George to the British Tommy in the House of Commons a few days previously. He had not made any such remark. What he had done was to oppose the system whereby the Colonial Volunteer received 5s. a day while Mr. Atkins was handed 1s. 3d. It was true that he had voted "No" in a War Supply Vote. But this is the traditional Parliamentary method of protest against a war which a Member deems to be wrong. Mr. Chamberlain had so voted at the time of the Zulu War which included the heroic stand at Rorke's Drift. But that did not make him a Nigger, said Lloyd George.

There was, in fact, remarkably little Pacifism in Lloyd George's opposition to the war, once he had got going. He was against it because it was "Chamberlain's War" and it was "damnable" because it was "unnecessary". Brave men's lives were being "senselessly, needlessly, callously sacrificed on the altar of one man's selfish ambition".

And, no call to drag in derogatory references to the native country of the critic of this "Brummagem-made Imperialism". If ever Britain were to be invaded, the hills of Wales would stand out for Independence long after the keys of Birmingham had been surrendered.

He then repeated, specified and amplified, his personal charge against Chamberlain. The War Office, asserted Lloyd George, had invited tenders for cordite ammunition. They had received seven tenders, the difference between them ranging from 1s. 10d. in the pound to 2s. 6d. in the pound. That of the Birmingham firm of Kynoch's was the highest—and it was accepted! The War Office privately asked Kynoch's to reduce it to 2s. 3d. and then closed the deal. What had this to do with Mr. Joseph Chamberlain? Lloyd George then reiterated the family connections of Chamberlain with Kynoch's. This was the man who had the audacity to go to war with the Transvaal because he said Kruger had enriched himself by a dynamite monopoly!

Chamberlain, in a letter, declared that it was "without a shadow of foundation".

He had sold out of Kynoch's on entering public life.

Lloyd George returned to the attack. What about Haskins & Son? This was a firm of contractors to the Admiralty. The first name on the list of share-holders was that of Mary Endicott Chamberlain, of Highbury, Birmingham (wife of Joseph Chamberlain). The second was Arthur Neville Chamberlain, same address. Then came the name of Joseph Austen Chamberlain, same address. He was described as a Member of Parliament, and held 600 Ordinary shares; he was an official at the Admiralty. (Austen Chamberlain was the Civil Lord.) There were other Chamberlains interested in the Company. In fact, the whole of the Chamberlain family owned the concern with the exception of a few shares. Yet Joseph Chamberlain had said that he had no interest, direct or indirect, in any firm dealing with the Government!

By August, it really seemed that the end of the Boer War was in sight. Cape Colony had been cleared of all its Boer invaders, and in the Transvaal the two last big towns of Johannesburg and Pretoria had fallen. "Oom Paul" himself had fled, and was soon to board a Dutch man-of-war and sail for Europe. Field-Marshal Roberts cabled home that he wished to do the same. Chamberlain considered that it was time to end the present Parliament, too.

He was determined to go to the country while the going remained good, and in the event, he was profoundly wise. A new Parliament was needed to deal with the winding-up of war and the unfolding of the mighty tasks of peace, reconciliation and reconstruction in Greater Africa. The Prime Minister, Lord Salisbury, hesitated. But the Colonial Secretary had his way.

On 17 September, 1900, the Queen signed the Proclamation dissolving Parliament. The first Khaki Election was on.

CHAPTER VII

"GO FOR JOE!"

"Go for Joe!" said Labby.

"Labby" was Henry Labouchere, the piratical Radical M.P. Editor of *Truth*, who had once shared Lloyd George's own admiration for Joseph Chamberlain and had also long since come cordially to loathe him. To the official Liberal leadership, still half-in and half-out of the war, Labby's advice was unacceptable; they knew what Joe would always do to half-and-halfers who got in *his* way. To Lloyd George, in root-and-branch opposition to the war, it was unnecessary; *he* would always go for the main target.

The Khaki Election was, in fact, a One-Man Show, and that man was not the Prime Minister, or even the leader of the Party. The event was dominated by Joseph Chamberlain, the Colonial Secretary. He, almost alone of the Ministers, was popularly held not to blame for the early military defeats and the muddle over medical supplies. Every Tory and Liberal Unionist candidate besought him to address his local electors, or at least, send him a commending letter. Totally, Joe made twelve public appearances in the General Election of 1900, all of them terrific. One of these occasions was at Oldham, in support of the young Tory candidate, Winston Churchill:

> ". . . who I think has inherited some of his father's great qualities, his originality and his courage."

The candidate got in by 222 votes.

It was everywhere a hard struggle. There was a war on, and many of those citizens who felt that they should vote for the Government were doing so, as Chamberlain privately warned his colleagues, "this time, but never again".

Enough, at any rate, were of this opinion to give the Government a majority of 134, a gain of three seats. Joseph Chamberlain had not scrupled himself to brand all opponents, whether Liberal Imperialists or Radical Little Englanders, as "Pro-Boers". He exploited to the full the alleged statement (it had been distorted in telegraphic transmission) of the Mayor of Mafeking that: *"Every seat lost to the Government is a seat sold to the Boers."*

There is no point now in inquiring who started the mud-slinging (nor any, either, in accepting Chamberlain's plea after it was all over, that the Election "had been fought with the greatest malignity by the baser sort on the other side").

The materials for a rough-house were abundant in October, 1900, and it is enough to say that the first Khaki Election set the tone for the next two.

Lloyd George was fighting his own bitter battle, on his own doorstep. The Bangor "Anti-Boer Commandos" had not forgotten how nearly they had silenced him forever only the previous spring. A local squire offered the Member for Caernarvon Boroughs an ancestral suit of armour for the next occasion on which he should visit that particular borough. All through the summer, Lloyd George's meetings in his constituency had either been howled down or, what was worse, held in a half-silence. His practice in London had almost closed for lack of clients (his City partner, Rhys Roberts, loyally stood by him and suffered considerable financial loss with him). Lloyd George himself continued to risk—some said he invited—injury of a more personal kind. He was probably lucky, as *London Opinion* subsequently noted, in that he neglected to publish in *Who's Who* the address of the solid grey-brick house, with the bay windows, which he had now rented at 179 Trinity Road, near Wandsworth Common. His eldest son, Richard, was so mercilessly baited at school as a "Pro-Boer" by his fellows, natural baiters, that Lloyd George had to bring the boy home and put him to school at Portmadoc.

In Wales, also, Lloyd George's joint legal business with his brother William suffered severely in the prevailing temperature. He himself was burned in effigy in his own constituency at Nevin, Pwllheli and Criccieth. His enemies even stuck upon their bonfire a likeness of his uncle, Richard Lloyd. But in this they succeeded only in bringing odium on themselves, for this man's character was beyond assault.

Lloyd George stood up to the blast. "These are the times that try men's souls," he would have agreed with old Tom Paine. As the General Election approached, the story was put about—it was printed in the local Press—that he was in constant touch with the Boers, through Kruger's exiled Transvaal Government in Holland. He denied it utterly, then wasted no more time in shielding himself against the renewed salvoes of the same stuff.

"Don't dig-in in defence! Counter-attack! Go for Joe!"

Joe Chamberlain had chosen to make this a One-Man-Election? All right, Mr. Lloyd George would help him to do better still. He would prove to the nation that it was also a One-Man-War. From every platform on which he spoke Lloyd George proclaimed that Chamberlain and Milner ("Joe's Man Friday") had first planned it, then provoked it, and now were pursuing it, long after the original purpose which they pretended had required it had been achieved. The Boer invasion of the two British colonies in South Africa had by this time been repelled, the two Boer Republics themselves overrun, and their Governments put to flight and exile.

At Nevin, the district in his constituency most hostile to his present cause, Lloyd George spoke before an audience which, at first, received him sullenly and stonily. He melted their resistance with a brilliant attack on the legislative record of the Government in social reform, a matter which lay nearest to their own hearts. Then, when he had warmed his hearers to him, Lloyd George made his passionate plea for peace on the *veldt*:

"All wars are so horrible in their incidence, and so uncertain in their event, that sensible statesmen recognize that as soon as you can secure the main object of a war and bring it to an end the better it is, even for the victor. . . .

In May, this year, the Boer Army was so discomfited and disheartened by Field-Marshal Lord Roberts's daring strategy that their generals utterly failed to induce them to make a stand anywhere. They were nothing but a demoralized rabble of peasants. They had been swept out of Natal. There was not a Boer in uniform left in Cape Colony, nor a single Boer Commando to be found anywhere south or east of the Orange Free State. De Wet was the only Boer leader who could persuade his followers to make even a show of fighting.

That was the time to make peace! General Sir Redvers Buller, with his downright British common sense, was of that opinion and he advised in May that terms be offered. What did Headquarters reply? 'Nothing but Unconditional Surrender!' And what was the outcome of the foolish decision? It drove the Boers to despair! They listened again to the fighting men in their own ranks, and they plucked up new courage. They went on fighting, and the war is not over yet. I say that it is time to stay the slaughter in the African sand of brave soldiers on either side."

Lloyd George paused. Then he added quietly, in Welsh:

"Five years ago, the electors of the Caernarvon Boroughs gave to me my strip of blue paper, the certificate of my election, to hand to the Speaker of Parliament as your accredited representative. If I never again represent the Caernarvon Boroughs in the House of Commons, I shall at least have the satisfaction of handing back to you that blue paper with no stain of human blood upon it."

A moment of tense silence, and then the packed audience were leaping to their feet in a gale of acclamation. They recognized courage of another kind.

It was the swing of the tide. When he went to Bangor a few days later, Lloyd George was welcomed by applauding crowds in the place where six months earlier he had come near to being lynched. So soon had sped the illusion of "glory" from the patriotic mob in the street; the truth of it lingered with the already half-forgotten dead in the field, and survived only in the fine traditions of the regiments which had served there.

Polling Day was Saturday, 6 October, 1900. In the early evening the "mafficking" was for Colonel Platt, the Tory opponent. But as night drew on in Caernarvon, where the ballot-boxes of the other boroughs had been

D*

brought to be counted, the strains of "Rule Britannia" began to be drowned in the gathering thunder of the Welsh anthem "Land of Our Fathers". Lamps shone late in every window in the town as the excited crowds surged up and down the narrow streets. Drawn and nervous now that the battle was over, Lloyd George waited in the Town Hall, his wife Margaret, calm, by his side. This was the make-or-break of a career. It was gone midnight when at last the Mayor stepped out on to the balcony.

"Lloyd George . . ." he said,

but not another word could be heard. A mighty shout that stretched up to Snowdon rose from the crowded square, echoing and re-echoing.

"When the victor appeared," wrote the staid *Manchester Guardian*, "then came delirium . . . it reached fever-pitch again when finding no carriage could come through the crowd, Mr. Lloyd George essayed to reach the Liberal Club under the escort of six constables. He might as well have relied on a set of corks to face the rapids of Niagara. . . . The love of those people was almost terrible; it was certainly dangerous. . . ."

The carriages were now assembled, and the torchlight procession round the town set forth, Lloyd George standing up, hatless, to acknowledge the uproar in his honour.

Now it was early Sunday morning, though yet dark, and it remained to get the tramping, still tempestuous, legions home. They had arrived under the walls of grey old Caernarvon Castle.

"Then," said the *Manchester Guardian*, "Mr. George called for silence and asked them to sing once more 'Land of Our Fathers'. In a moment there was utter stillness, and then they sang that great and solemn anthem. The darkness above us lent the scene a ghostly majesty; the earnest melancholy harmonies breathed an undying hope; the sea of invisible faces gave a sense of vast, indefinable strength. The great Hymn ended, and then in perfect quiet the multitude dispersed."

It would be Lloyd George's greatest hour, until that November afternoon eighteen years hence when, as Prime Minister of Britain in the most terrible of all her wars, he would walk at the head of the Members of the House of Commons across Parliament Square to Westminster Abbey, to give thanks to God for the deliverance.

On the Monday following the declaration of the poll the Liberal Press hailed the victory of "Cambria's Coeur de Lion". The figures were:

Lloyd George	.	.	.	.	.	2,412
Colonel Platt	.	.	.	.	.	2,116
Liberal Majority	.	.	.	.	.	296

The same afternoon, Coeur de Lion, with rather unknightly grace, explained to a reporter that he did not regard Mr. Joseph Chamberlain as "a cat", but rather as "a powder-monkey". The General Election might be over, but the Member for Caernarvon Boroughs was not going to Let Go of Joe.

. . . .

The war was very far from being over. Indeed, it was about to enter its most prolonged and difficult phase.

This was the far-flung campaign (it might well have been termed "Operation Net-work") to enmesh and destroy the almost independent roving commandos into which the main Boer forces had divided themselves in face of the superior manpower and warpower of the British. It was, of course, the only way in which they could continue their resistance, and since it was the natural way of fighting for men who lived in the saddle, it was far more effective than trying to take on the British in trench battles or artillery duels. Superbly, the Boers seized their last chance. For the next eighteen months, about twelve thousand hard-riding, sharp-shooting Boer "rebels" (both the Republics had been declared annexed in the summer of 1900) gave the Armed Forces of the Crown such an exercise on the *veldt* in guerilla warfare as they would hardly receive again until six thousand Malayan "bandits" repeated it in the jungle half a century later.

The Boers were exceptionally fortunate in their leaders, Botha, Smuts, De Wet, and De La Rey, and others, all daring, skilful and resourceful commanders. They enjoyed the advantages of guerilla troops fighting in their own country. While the British lines of communication stretched across vast areas, long, lonely and exposed to sudden raid, the roving Boers knew the country as they knew their own hand, and they could live on it more easily because the great majority of the *veldt* population were on their side. In fact, the scattered farms of the *veldt* provided the commandos with natural bases for food, fodder, shelter and information.

To repel this kind of warfare, General Kitchener, who had succeeded Roberts, devised the "Blockhouse System" which meant setting up a chain of fortified posts, linked by barbed wire, to contain the Boers and gradually close in upon them. If the plan had also been to use these posts as pivots of manœuvre for our own mobile forces, it would have had real and early worth. But mobile forces were exactly what we lacked; six months after the war had begun, the War Office was still replying to the offer of troopers from the eager Dominions, "Unmounted Men Preferred."

The Boer Commandos rode in and out between the blockhouses, cutting the barbed wire and the telegraph lines, and raiding where they listed.

In February, 1901, De Wet invaded Cape Colony at the head of several columns, and raised rebellion among the Dutch there. Was it going to turn into a "People's War"?

An ugly development of the "Blockhouse System" now took shape. The proper name for this should have been "Operation Waste", for it involved burning down the Boer farm-houses as a reprisal, destroying the farm crops, driving off their herds, and turning their inhabitants loose upon the *veldt*. Thus, the proclamation of Major-General Bruce Hamilton, dated 1 November, 1900:

> "The town of Ventersburg has been cleared of supplies and partly burnt, and the farms in the vicinity destroyed on account of the frequent attacks on the railway line in the neighbourhood. The Boer women and children who are left behind should apply to the Boer commandants for food, who will supply them, unless they wish to see them starve. . . . No supplies will be sent from the railway to the town."

    .   .   .   .   .   .

Meanwhile, it was the "Warmonger" Joe Chamberlain himself, and not his works, that Lloyd George had immediately in mind.

When the new House of Commons met in December, 1900, he moved the following Amendment to the Address:

> "That Ministers of the Crown and Members of either House of Parliament holding subordinate office in any public department ought to have no interest, direct or indirect, in any firm or company competing for contracts with the Crown unless the nature and extent of such interest being first declared, Your Majesty shall have sanctioned the continuance thereof, and when necessary have directed such precautions to be taken as may effectually prevent any suspicion of influence or favouritism in the allocation of such contracts."

Lloyd George then recited to the House of Commons, though in more restrained form, the case he had made on the platform against the Colonial Secretary and his financial interest in munitions. Chamberlain replied, also in subdued tone, though he was bitterly hurt. During the recent General Election, indeed, he had several times considered taking legal action against his detractors, but Counsel had advised restraint.

Now, Joe Chamberlain explained to the House of Commons, not his family's commercial dealings, but his own.

> "When I went into public life," he said, "I gave up business altogether. I withdrew my capital such as it was. I had to invest it somehow, but I have endeavoured in the whole course of my public life to be in the position in which Caesar's wife should have been—to give no cause, even of suspicion, to the most malicious of my opponents. . . . I will take one case. I was a considerable shareholder in the Small Arms Company and in another

company, Kynoch's. Now, what did I do? I sold out of both companies, and I sold out of them at a loss . . ."

He ended in his old proud, challenging style:

"It is true that nobody has made an accusation. It has been a conspiracy of insinuation—which is infinitely worse. I have never complained of any attack made upon me in a fair field and in regard to my public action; but this is not a fair fight, and I think it hard that after twenty-five years of Parliamentary service in the full light of day I should have to stand up here and explain to my colleagues on both sides of the House that I am not a thief and a scoundrel."

Lloyd George was in no way put out by Chamberlain's vindication of himself—or put off Chamberlain. He made it plain at his own public meetings that the man who was being hounded in the Press and mobbed in the country as a pro-Boer by Chamberlain's friends was less concerned with the personal integrity of the Colonial secretary than with his political character and his influence upon events. Lloyd George cared no more about the rebuke of his own colleague, Asquith, when that leading Liberal Imperialist took him to task in a debate early in the New Year, 1901, for his attitude towards the war.

In this debate Lloyd George cut short his own address to give more time to the new Tory Member for Oldham, who was waiting to make his maiden speech. There was already more political affinity between this Radical and this young Tory than there was between him and the Liberal Imperialists on his own Front Bench. It was the beginning of a friendship between David Lloyd George and Winston Churchill which would endure for the next forty years.

The political war over the military war raged in the country more violently than ever. Just at this moment the *Daily News*, the most widely read Liberal newspaper in the country, ran short of money. Lloyd George persuaded Mr. George Cadbury, partner with his brother in the prosperous Cadbury chocolate business at Bourneville, and some others to put up enough capital to buy the newspaper. Lloyd George himself became a Director, and under the new dispensation, the *Daily News* gave steadfast support to the crusade to Stop the War.

This idea, indeed, was now in the minds of the militarists, as well as the pacifists. In February, 1901, the same month as that in which Asquith chided Lloyd George for not sustaining the soldiers in South Africa, Field-Marshal Lord Kitchener, the Commander-in-Chief there, was sitting down with General Botha at Middlesburg in Cape Colony and seeking a way of peace with the Boers.

It is true that Lord Kitchener was not prepared to discuss the question of Independence, which he said had now been settled by the sword. It would have to be "Crown Colony" rule from now on. "Crown Colony" rule, however, meaning an Executive nominated by the Crown but advised by an elected Assembly, was a possibility which could lead towards eventual self-government. The Boers demanded an amnesty for all the burghers still bearing arms, and financial grants to restore their devastated farms on the *veldt*. The soldier, Kitchener, was himself strongly disposed to agree to these "reasonable" terms (the soldiers so frequently, mercifully are). The statesman, Chamberlain, absolutely refused to include the Cape rebels in the amnesty, or to do more than lend the money needed to salvage the *veldt* farms. He was determined to show who was master in South Africa; it seems probable that the Boers were not yet prepared to recognize Joe Chamberlain as boss[1]. Furthermore, there was still in the Boer hearts a faint hope of foreign intervention. The Middlesburg Truce Talks broke down.

Snapped Chamberlain, angrily: "The Boer proposals were preposterous!"

Cried Lloyd George, in another kind of passion: "There was a soldier, who knew what war meant; he strove to make peace. There was another man, who strolled among his orchids, 6,000 miles away from the deadly bark of the Mauser rifle. He stopped Kitchener's Peace!"

Lloyd George recalled then how General Sir Redvers Buller's earlier proposed armistice had been destroyed by the demand for "Unconditional Surrender".

This made at least two occasions, said Lloyd George, on which The Man Who Began the War had insisted on keeping it going. But, in fact, there had been a *third* occasion, claimed Lloyd George. This had occurred immediately after the Fall of Pretoria, when the Governments of both the Boer Republics had resigned, and the regular war had ended—and the irregular one had not yet started! Sir Alfred Milner, who had just returned to England from South Africa at this moment, gave unexpected confirmation to this story. He admitted frankly that during the uncertain period which Lloyd George spoke of, it would have taken very little to persuade the Boers to accept the Empire. The hostile element had made their appeal to arms in vain, and would have been glad to settle down again. The commandos had been thinned by disease and desertion. The inhabitants as a whole were utterly sick of war. Why had not the propitious hour been seized?

"Because," answered Lloyd George, "we had an Electioneer, and not a Statesman at the head of affairs; a man who had his eye not on the destiny of Africa, but on the polling booths of Britain!"

As the year 1901 advanced Lloyd George found at hand a new and deadlier hose to play upon "Chamberlain's War". This was fed by the stream of pity aroused in the generous British Public's heart as the story of the Concentration Camps came out. It was appalling.

The Boer Concentration Camp Policy itself was then probably as much a military necessity in 1901 as that of the Chinese Squatter Settlements in

---

[1] The word is Dutch, "baas".

Malaya in our own day. To pacify the country, it was imperative to deny supplies and information to the enemy. Having burned the Boer farms the British Army could not, in the face of world opinion (at that time extremely critical in America as in Europe), leave the farmers and their families to starve. Also, it was reckoned, wrongly, that by interning their women and children the burghers in the field would be persuaded to surrender. For, instead, by relieving them of their closest domestic anxieties, it kept them with their commandos. What they endured, as the Blockhouse campaign developed, has been vividly told by Deneys Reitz, who rode with Jan Smuts on that record raid to the Atlantic coast of Cape Colony[1].

The scandal of the Concentration Camps lay in their gross maladministration. Many of them had been sited without any regard to health, or even to water supply. Nor did it appear that any serious thought had ever been given to an adequate food supply; half-rations were the order of the (best) day. Add to this, that most of the camps were hopelessly overcrowded. The habits of the people who filled the camps had been fairly primitive to begin with, and the conditions of their confinement made them beastly. Disease leapt like wildfire among them.

In the Orange River camps (the population was averagely 90,000), the general death-rate rose from 192 per 1,000 per annum in June, 1901, to 422 in September. In the Transvaal 585 per 1,000 per annum. This was Imperial Whitehall at its block-headed worst.

"At this rate," declared Lloyd George, "within a few years there will not be a child alive on the *veldt*. And when the Boer prisoners of war return from St. Helena and Ceylon and Bermuda to see a dark patch on the bare *veldt* where once stood their homestead, to look on the black embers of the house that has been burned to the ground, to hear from the lips of their wives how their children died in the disease-stricken camps—what then? A barrier of dead children's bodies will rise up between the British and the Boer races in South Africa!

"Herod of old tried such a thing as this," he warned. "He sought to crush a little race by killing its young sons and daughters. He was not a success; and I would commend the story to Herod's modern imitator."

In Parliament, Joseph Chamberlain replied tersely: "Such pro-Boer speeches must encourage the Boers."

The British military killed in the Boer War were nearly 6,000; and 16,000 more died of wounds or disease; the Boers lost 4,000 killed. The total number of their women and children who died in concentration camps by disease was more than twice as many.

When the House of Commons rose for the Summer Recess of 1901 Lloyd George could count his gains. In the face of a fierce flood of public opinion

[1] *Commando*, by Deneys Reitz.

he had set his course, and held on it. Now the tide was turning; the war was still on, but the feeling of many people in the country about it was different, and one good reason was that a year ago they had been assured that it was already over. Even the Liberal Imperialists and the Radical Little Englanders, who had been denouncing each other at a series of banquets at the Reform Club and the Holborn Restaurant ("war to the knife-and-fork" the journalist, W. T. Stead, called it), began to discover those respectful reasons for differing which are the politician's advance notice of agreement.

The acrimonious Lloyd George–Chamberlain exchanges on the floor of the House of Commons had drawn from the pen of a *Daily Mail* Parliamentary Sketch-Writer this parallel between the Lloyd George of that day and the "Radical Joe" of twenty years before:

> "The man of now, like the man of then, has an indomitable, unquestioning, self-confidence, an irresistible pushfulness. Sprung from no exalted parentage, he has forced his way forward by the same dogged tenacity. . . . Look to him in debate, leaning forward, eager, keen, alert, hand-to-ear, ready to spring on his prey and rend him to pieces—the very reflection of what his great adversary once was.
>
> The moment he opens his mouth to speak, the same similarity is so striking as to make the listener start involuntarily. Listen! The same clear, low-pitched, cruel voice; the same keen, incisive phrases; the same mordant bitterness; the same caustic sneer; the same sardonic humour; the same personal enmity. It is the very reincarnation of the present Colonial Secretary in his younger days—a spectre of his dead self arisen to haunt him."

The writer ended on a question mark:

> "Will Time, that has had so mellowing an influence on that great Imperialist, work a similar change in the virulent Little Englander? Will he a score of years hence be the tower of strength of the Imperialist or the Parochial Party?"

He stormed up and down the land. From the Queen's Hall, London, to Liverpool, Edinburgh, Derby, North Wales, South Wales, to the dockside and the pithead and the chapel and the Cambridge Union. And always in pursuit of Chamberlain. Go for Joe!

At Llanelly, on 7 October, 1901, he accused him of plain political swindling. Hadn't the great Imperialist Colonial Secretary solicited their votes at the last General Election on a purely fraudulent prospectus? They might care to recollect the boastful beginnings of Joe Chamberlain's War:

> "*Fifty thousand Horse and Foot, going to Table Bay . . .*"

and all that. They were going to be enough to "see the job through". Then their number had been doubled, then trebled, and now quadrupled. As for the expense! . . . Then the public had been relieved to hear that the War was over—how handily, just in time for the General Election in October! Then—Hallo! What's this? Still on in November—and another little bill for a few more million pounds! That was *last* November, Lloyd George reminded them. Now, after twelve months more fighting, how did we stand? We had a Government which would not make Peace, and even yet did not know how to make War! We had been campaigning for two years with the wrong kind of troops, and the wrong kind of guns—with not enough medical supplies for the first, nor enough ammunition for the second.

Because he exposed these scandals he (Lloyd George) had been charged with "encouraging the Boers". Well, now, what about that brilliant young Tory M.P., Mr. Winston Churchill? Had he not declared, publicly, that the situation was "disquieting, and the position as momentous as it was two years ago, before the first shot was fired"?

Now, if what Mr. *Chamberlain* said was true, that every speech about Africa delivered in this country was carefully read by the Boers (it was not very creditable to our generals, who were supposed to be hustling them about!) then the Boers would say:

"Why, look what Mr. *Churchill* says! Now, we know him! This is that young fellow we caught on the armoured train, a bright, intelligent young lad he is! And he is going around Britain declaring that for the British the situation is becoming very disquieting. Well, this is *most* encouraging!"

Then there was the Unionist journal called the *Spectator*, a pretentious sixpenny humbug. It said in its usual superior, cultured fashion that our generals had not got enough brains to beat the Boers, and suggested that we should recall Lord Kitchener. If the Boers read that, they would go straight to the next field-cornet and say:

"Have you seen last Saturday's *Spectator*? They are beginning to say that the British generals have no brains; we came to that conclusion long ago."

There was another print, a raucous, jingo journal, the *Daily Express*. It had been reviling in the most malignant way the men whom it called "pro-Boers". Then it had published a cartoon representing the British Ship of State being smashed by huge waves, marked "South African War", with poor old John Bull standing on the bow and calling out for rescue in a most distracted fashion. Pro-Boer papers were not allowed in South Africa, but this paper could go anywhere and everywhere as a most patriotic, imperialist journal. In the next train that they captured, the Boers would open the *Daily Express* and say:

"Look at that! In just over two years' time, according to this jingo paper, we have wrecked their Empire for them!"

Lloyd George wound up with two barbed personal attacks. The first was upon a Cabinet Minister, who had boasted that they would finish this war triumphantly, "in spite of anything that is on earth below, or in the Heaven above". (Shame! Shame!)

The second onslaught was against the Archbishop of York, who had piously proposed a "Day of Humiliation" for the Empire,

"because we are not making sufficient progress with the subjugation of the Boers?" inquired Lloyd George. (Uproar.) "Ah! They are beginning to discover that they cannot force God to Unconditional Surrender. So we are to have that Day of National Humiliation. We are to try the other tack—Humiliation on Terms.

We are to approach the Throne and say 'We, the greatest Empire in Thy World upon which Thy sun can never set, we humble ourselves for a whole day before Thee, but on the distinct expectancy that Thou on Thy part shalt help us to finish that troublesome creature Naboth so that we may enjoy his vineyard in his place.

Gentlemen," he ended, "it needed a Bishop, an Archbishop, to dare to suggest such blasphemy to the nation. I am not going to tell you that we have no need of a Day of Humiliation. What empire is there or nation, or individual that stands in no need of it? But I tell you this: it will avail us nothing until as a people we are prepared to say 'Thy will be done in Africa, as everywhere else on this Earth'."

Age 38

It was in the political weather conditioned by such speeches—and the equally violent replies and counter-attacks from the other side—that Lloyd George set off to keep his engagement to speak in the Town Hall, Birmingham, on 18 December, 1901.

At no time during the extraordinary forty-year ascendancy of the Chamberlain caucus in Birmingham—a political machine without parallel in England, or anywhere else in the English-speaking world outside of Tammany Hall—was it ever an agreeable task to speak there against "Joe". Lord Randolph Churchill himself had painfully found this out in 1884, when he had appeared at Aston as a Tory Democrat to challenge the All-Powerful One, who at that time was still a Radical.

The Birmingham mob did not change with the years. They were not so much pro-Jingo or anti-Jingo (they had been both) as pro-Joe, whatever Joe happened to be.

Now, as the time drew near for the new David to challenge the old Goliath, protests poured in to the Birmingham Liberal Association, who had made the invitation. They also flooded across the correspondence columns of the local Liberal-Unionist newspapers, many of them amounting to open threats of violence. In the editorial columns, Lloyd George was denounced as a "virulent anti-Briton", and readers were assured that a hundred years ago he would have stood an excellent chance of losing his head; at the present time, in any Continental country, he would certainly have been arraigned for treason, and condemned to a long term of imprisonment. Mr. Lloyd George's visit was, in fact, an open insult to the city, and to every loyal citizen of Birmingham. So the patriots said; what had undoubtedly infuriated a number of them a great deal more was Lloyd George's personal, continual and vitriolic attack upon their especial and genuinely beloved hero, Joe Chamberlain.

The local Liberal Association commanded the allegiance of at least one-third of the voters of Birmingham, but their leaders began to quail before this menacing barrage. They suggested to Lloyd George that perhaps, after all, it would be wise to postpone his visit "until tempers had died down".

Mr. Rafter, the Chief Constable of Birmingham, also wrote to him courteously in this sense.

Lloyd George consulted Margaret. She hated the trouble he was getting into. She wanted her husband at home. In her beloved Wales, if possible. But she said, "You must go."

Lloyd George replied to his correspondents that he intended to keep his appointment with the public. He would be there on the night.

By the morning of the meeting, 18 December, 1901, every building in the main streets of Birmingham adjoining Victoria Square, where the Town Hall stands as an island, was heavily boarded up. Barricades had been erected, several hundred police named for duty and reinforcements drafted in from the neighbouring Midland towns. It was rumoured that a squadron of cavalry had also been ordered to stand-by in the barracks. Admission to the Town Hall was by ticket only, but by noon it became known that thousands of forged tickets were already in circulation. A mood of grim expectancy, and apprehension, settled over the great city. In a final warning the *Birmingham Mail* had written:

"There is every reason to believe that Birmingham is menaced by the prospect of serious rioting."

The newspaper published the photograph of the chief speaker. The skies all day were grey with snow-laden clouds.

A vivid scene of the prologue to the drama which was timed for 7.30 p.m. is given by Miss M. E. Wright, the Private Secretary of Mr. William Evans, a Birmingham merchant who was Lloyd George's host that night. She arrived at the Town Hall about mid-afternoon to find it was already surrounded. As her carriage drew up at a private entrance in Victoria Square, scores of angry people rushed towards it, shouting excitedly. They were looking for Lloyd George. An hour later the Square was a seething, surging mass.

Lloyd George himself walked in quietly at 6.15 p.m. He had arrived in the city by an earlier train than expected, anticipating the patriotic "reception committee" which awaited him a little later. He was met by Mrs. Evans and her four-year-old niece, and drove off with them, unrecognized, to the Evans's home in Hagley Road, the little girl on his knee. After tea, instead of coming to the meeting by road as the much larger "reception mob" expected, he had taken a local train to the centre of the city. From there, he drove through the crowded streets in a closed carriage with Mr. and Mrs. Evans. He was wearing a peaked cap and a rough overcoat, which was to be only his first disguise that day. It was successful. Some distance from the Town Hall he alighted, and made his way, still unrecognized, through the crowds.

It quickly became known, however, that he had arrived, and at once pandemonium broke out all around. Brass bands were playing patriotic airs at the four outside corners of the Hall, and men were doing a roaring trade selling half-bricks from a piece of waste-land in Edmund Street, a few yards away: "three a penny, to chuck at Lloyd George."

Inside the hall he was rapturously welcomed by his supporters. Miss Wright describes how he looked, "perfectly cool and unperturbed. I recollect it," she adds, "because it was the first time in my life that an exhibition of unconcernedness impressed itself upon me."

The forged tickets had been easily detected and their holders turned away by the police constables on duty. About seven o'clock, however, there was a terrific crash. The mob had torn down the big notice-boards outside the Victoria Square entrance, and, using them as battering rams, drove them through the police-guard and broke in the doors.

Within a few minutes about 7,000 people were jammed inside the hall. Every other one seemed to have brought a Union Jack to wave, and those who had not provided themselves with a whistle or a horn to blow were howling in chorus for Lloyd George.

He was in a Committee Room just off the platform, which fortunately stood high above the body of the hall. Miss Wright tells how he behaved within a few yards of this riot which threatened his life:

"pacing backwards and forwards without the least trace of excitement in his manner, and apparently without paying the slightest attention to his enemies, Mr. Lloyd George dictated, in the third person and ready for the Press, the speech which he saw he would be prevented from delivering."

These copies were distributed at once, and people all over the United Kingdom next morning read the speech which no single other person heard that night in Birmingham.

The time came to appear on the platform, and with his Chairman and supporting friends, Lloyd George walked quietly forward. A roar of "Pro-Boer! Traitor! Kill him!" with boos and catcalls and "Three cheers for the Boys at the Front", rose from the hall, mingled with the tuneless bellowing of the song:

"We'll throw Lloyd George in the Fountain
And he won't come to Brum any more."

Not a word of the Chairman's speech or of his own could be distinguished. Lloyd George rested his arm on the desk, and leaning forward to the reporters' bench, which was mid-way between the platform and the floor, called down to one of them: "Rather lively for a peace meeting!"

A noise like the fall of hailstones sounded from above; it was the bricks showering through the windows, and some of them were barbed. A heavy piece of stone coping fell from the roof, and smashed in a policeman's helmet. Then a solid wedge of the mob rushed forward, and bursting through the police cordon which stood below the platform, they clambered up the tall pillars which supported it to the Press bench. The reporters scattered, and as the boarding-party piled *en masse* on to the bench, it broke beneath their weight and many fell back to the floor. Others climbed on upwards and were with difficulty pushed off, to fall in turn upon the heaving, struggling mêlée below. Police whistles were shrilling, women were screaming and a furious free-fight was going on all over the hall, throughout the corridors and up and down the stairs.

By now, almost every window in the Town Hall had been broken (the Liberal Association subsequently paid for 1,198 to be replaced). With the platform-party of about thirty persons, and guarded by a police squad of almost equal numbers, Lloyd George permitted himself to be barricaded in one of the Committee Rooms. There they sat in darkness for nearly two hours by the order of the Chief Constable. Gradually, the police overcame the mob inside the hall, but by this time the mob outside had been reinforced and a fresh attempt was made to get at Lloyd George. The Chief Constable now returned from the battle-front, and insisted that at all costs Lloyd George must be got away within a few minutes, for he could no longer guarantee his life or the lives of the party. It was the suggestion of Mr. Evans, Lloyd George's host, that he should put on a policeman's uniform, with cape and helmet, and pass out of the building with a police squad.

He demurred: "It would be rather ridiculous."

But when the Chief Constable himself made the request, "For the sake of my professional reputation," Lloyd George finally agreed.

The policemen went out in a long file, marching down Paradise Street and Easy Row for two miles to Ladywood Police Station, where at last Lloyd George was in safety. It is said that one man in the square recognized him, but his shouts were unheard in the general din.

It remained to bring the rest of the party away in safety. It was done by the ruse of a carriage-and-pair, with mounted police escort, driving up to the private entrance in Victoria Square, as though to prepare for an official departure. While the mob assaulted them, the platform-party escaped across the road with another police guard into the Midland Institute Offices opposite.

Gathering final force, the rioters rushed the Town Hall and broke into every room. Too late! In frustrated fury, they smashed everything that they could lay their hands on.

Now snow began to fall. The Riot Act was read, the police drew their truncheons, and charged.

In the tumult which followed, one man was killed and many badly injured, nearly forty being detained in hospital that night. A number of the police were also seriously hurt, and one of them died later from his wounds.

So ended the great Birmingham Riot. When Mr. W. S. Caine, M.P., met Joe Chamberlain in the Lobby of the House of Commons a day or two later, he asked him in his genial, cynical way:

> "What's the matter with Birmingham? Everyone expected you would kill Lloyd George. Why did you let him escape?"

Joe stared at him, coldly, through his eye-glass. He said:

> "What is everybody's business is nobody's business."

CHAPTER VIII

AFTER THE WAR

NEITHER the war in South Africa nor the riots in Great Britain were quite over.

The *veldt* was being methodically made "horse-proof" to the roving Boers, but several thousand of them remained at large beyond the advancing line of the Blockhouses. Lord Kitchener was bitterly complaining that although the War Office had now got round to Preferring Mounted Men for service overseas, still many of those whom it sent out to him could neither ride nor shoot. Young Mr. Winston Churchill was still more sharply criticizing his own Government in the country, and writing letters to Mr. Joseph Chamberlain telling him (*a*) how to run the war intelligently, or (*b*) to make peace.

Lloyd George offered no alternatives. The Endless War Must End, and Joe Must Go. Early in the New Year, January, 1902, he went to Bristol to address a "Peace Meeting", which had been called by a number of local bodies to demand that the fighting should cease forthwith. After Birmingham, the Committee of the Vestry Hall of St. Phillips's were naturally concerned about their property, and hastened to cancel the arrangement. They relented under protest, but let the Hall only on the understanding that the promoters of the meeting should be held liable for all damage done to the building. Lloyd George was again begged by his friends to avoid trouble, and not appear. He again replied that he intended to keep his appointment.

Age 39

All day long, hand-bills were distributed in the streets of Bristol, calling on the citizens to roll up in their thousands and protest "in an orderly manner" against this pro-Boer meeting in the heart of their city.

The police guard numbered 250 constables, with mounted men in reserve. Every window of the Vestry Hall was barricaded, and barriers were thrown across the streets leading to it and strongly manned. On the steps of the Hall, the Fire Brigade assembled powerful hoses and a score of St. John's Ambulance Brigade stood by to deal with casualties.

Lloyd George, who had arrived in Bristol unnoticed earlier in the day, was escorted to the meeting by a stalwart bodyguard, largely composed of Irish Nationalists. A telegram awaited him there from frustrated members of his last public audience. It read:

"That Bristol will go one better than we did and crack your skull is the sincere wish of all Birmingham."

Admission tickets had again been forged, for two hours before the meeting a huge crowd crammed the streets around the Hall and, after a time, succeeded in breaking through the barriers. A police charge forced them back, and though another organized rush was made for the entrance it was also repelled. Inside the Hall, Lloyd George was considerably heckled but the powerful force of stewards ensured no serious disorder, and he was able to deliver his speech to an audience of about 2,000 people. He compared Joe Chamberlain with Judas, to the disadvantage of Joe. "Judas only finished himself—this man finished thousands!"

The mob remained baying outside, though without the peculiar "Brummagem" violence, and Lloyd George was able to reach his hotel with his "Shillelagh Guard" without further incident.

It was not the final chapter in the Lloyd George Boer War saga. He was, indeed, denied free public speech altogether in a number of places simply because the local authorities feared another riot if he spoke. The war itself came to an end in May, 1902, but nearly two years later there was still a hangover of hatred against the "pro-Boer". At a by-election in St. Albans in February, 1904, Lloyd George's meeting at the Drill Hall was invaded by a mob armed, according to the local newspaper report, with "eggs, onions, potatoes, stones and bottles containing prepared chemicals".

He was again assaulted in the street.

There were scenes in the House of Commons, too. They were not confined to the Party front. The rift remained between the Asquith-Grey Imperialists and the Lloyd George anti-war Radicals. An attempt in the new Session of 1902 by a well-meaning Liberal backbencher, Mr. Cawley, to bridge it by a Get-together Amendment to the Address merely served to point out to all the width of this chasm. Lloyd George did not propose to rally to what he described as "this colourless flag". According to him, one set of gentlemen were being asked to support what they regarded as a criminal enterprise as an inducement for another set of gentlemen to vote for a proposition which they did not believe to be true. He preferred an amendment to the Amendment (moved by John Dillon, the Irish Nationalist leader), which flatly condemned the conduct of the war as "contrary to the recognized usages of civilized warfare" and "barbarous". With eight other Liberal Members Lloyd George voted for the Irish amendment. It was overwhelmingly lost.

This was a bad breach of discipline, but what was considered a much worse error of taste was his personal attack on Campbell-Bannerman, the harassed and still hesitant Leader of the Liberal Party:

"He has been captured by the Imperialists, and I am afraid that his captors have treated him as the Boers treat their prisoners: they have stripped him of his principles and left him on the *veldt* to find his way back as best he can. I hope this will be a lesson to him."

It offered A. J. Balfour the chance to condole from the Government Front Bench with the leader of the Opposition on the violence with which he had been assailed by his runagate follower, and to assure him that no amount of premeditation would have enabled him (Balfour) to accumulate so much bitterness. It confirmed the Liberal-Imperialist gentlemen in their suspicion that the Welsh attorney was not quite the right kind of colleague. Campbell-Bannerman himself took it in good temper, though he observed in his reply to the debate

"I will only say that the Honourable Member for Caernarvon Boroughs might have expressed his differences with his friends quite as effectively with more respect to them."

When the main division on the Address was called, Lloyd George abstained from voting. He was joined by several other Radicals, including Labouchere and John Burns, as well as by the Irish Nationalists. At the other extreme, Asquith and Sir Edward Grey walked out of the House with a number of other Liberal Imperialists, amid an excited scene. The Cawley Amendment was also overwhelmingly defeated. The odd sequel to these events was to bring Campbell-Bannerman steadily nearer towards Lloyd George on the question of the war.

There was a far angrier night in Parliament before peace at last shone upon the *veldt*. It arose when Campbell-Bannerman accused Chamberlain of treating him with "malignant slander, as a pro-Boer", and the Colonial Secretary retorted by charging Campbell-Bannerman with "malicious calumny of his own countrymen".

Chamberlain claimed that only the obstinacy of the Boers, encouraged by the treachery of the pro-Boers, was still prolonging a hopeless struggle. He spoke of between 3,000 and 4,000 burghers, who had formerly borne arms against us, and now were fighting for us in the Corps of "National Scouts" in the hope of averting the complete ruin of their country. He mentioned the name of their commander, General Vilonel.

"Vilonel is a traitor!" snapped Dillon, from the Irish benches.

"The Honourable Member," retorted Chamberlain, icily, "is a good judge of traitors."

Instant uproar. The Irish Members were yelling and waving their fists, the Tories were cheering and jeering, and a score of Members on either side of the House were on their feet trying to make Points of Order above the din. At length, Mr. Speaker was permitted to be heard, replying to Dillon's demand for a withdrawal of Chamberlain's offending words. He ruled that the Colonial Secretary was under no necessity to make it.

"Then I desire to say, Mr. Speaker," said Dillon, very deliberately, "that the Right Honourable Gentleman is a damned liar!"

At once, his suspension from the service of the House was moved, and carried by a large majority. Six Radicals voted with the Irish, including Lloyd

George. It set the mood for the rest of the debate, and when later Lloyd George taunted the Government with its foolish talk of

"avenging Majuba—since this present war broke out British arms have suffered eighteen defeats of far greater magnitude than Majuba——"

there was a shout from the Tory benches "And the pro-Boers rejoice at it!"

For a time, it seemed certain that there would be a score more suspensions, for the Irish returned to the fray and extended the area of tumult. But Lloyd George was allowed to finish his speech, and he made it an eloquent appeal for peace with the enemy on honourable terms to both,

"for otherwise the moment we are embarrassed with any foreign nation and there is a serious war these men in South Africa will seize their opportunity. Can we then send out 250,000 troops to reconquer the country? Make peace now! . . . Once, the Orange Free State was as independent as Britain is at the present moment. The only difference is, that we are a Great Power and they are a small one. Does that make any difference at all in the inherent justice of the war? Have you a right to be unjust to a man because he is poor and weak? Every honest man would say that you should treat him with more generosity."

There was sense as well as passion in this plea. Seldom has Britain been more isolated than she was in 1902. The Dominions, indeed, stood by her side, but the Empire was still far from the Power which it might yet become. The war in South Africa had brought Britain no goodwill from the United States. In Europe, the Triple Alliance had been created of Germany, Austria-Hungary and Italy, while our older enemies France and Russia had entered into a counter-alliance. Both of the latter had several causes of serious quarrel with us, the French in Egypt, Siam and on the Newfoundland fishing coasts; the Russians in Persia, Afghanistan and Tibet. Two factors only restrained any or all of these loving neighbours from falling upon Britain in her hour of trouble, and despoiling her in Africa and Asia. The first was their own fierce rivalries; the second was the commanding strength of the Royal Navy. The moral was not lost upon the Kaiser, who thenceforth did his utmost in his own energetic, erratic way to foster European ill-will against Britain, while systematically building up Germany's sea power.

Two days after Lloyd George's speech, the Transvaal envoys rode through the British lines under safe-conduct to urge their Orange Free State allies to join with them in discussing peace terms. Some of the leaders, notably De Wet and De La Rey, were for fighting on "to the bitter end", but after two months obstinate argument they were overborne by those who looked to Louis Botha. Sadly, thus, at last, even the lion-hearted De La Rey: "Has this bitter, *bitter* end not come?"

In the event, the Boers were generously treated and near midnight on

31 May, 1902, the Treaty of Vereeniging was signed in Kitchener's house. The Endless War was over.

The transformation of the immediate scene was drastic. The week after the stormy debate in the House of Commons which had rallied the Government ranks behind the Colonial Secretary, A. J. Balfour, as Leader of the House, introduced a measure which divided Tories and Liberal Unionists on a deeper and more intimate issue than an overseas war, fought 8,000 miles away. At the same time, it reunited the various clans of the Liberal opposition who had been bitterly quarrelling among themselves ever since the departure of Gladstone. This measure was the Education Act of 1902.

The objects of the Education Bill of 1902 were simple, and necessary. It was a genuine, and overdue, attempt to bring under one hat two separate and frequently conflicting educational systems, and to the benefit of both.

The origins of this situation went back into the previous century, when both the Established Church and the Nonconformist Churches had built their own schools. In the latter, at any rate, no denominational dogma had ever been taught and when, in 1870, the Compulsory Education Act provided a school place for every child in the land, the same rule obtained in all their schools, including those which voluntarily transferred to the State. Most of the Nonconformist Schools did so, but not those of the Church of England. Nonconformist critics sometimes objected that since 1870, various State grants had been made to these Church schools to bring their standards up to the required level. But since these grants were buried in general taxation, very few citizens were aware of them. On the whole, the public seemed content with an untidy compromise, and only the fanatics on either side wanted strife.

Their opportunity was now presented.

Briefly, the Education Bill of 1902 proposed that the County Councils should take over all Primary Schools recognized by the Board of Education, and levy a local rate to run them. This set up the requisite single control. The stern Liberal *Manchester Guardian* applauded the reform, and the National Union of Teachers unanimously endorsed it.

The politicians, in general, made a more cautious approach march—with two decisive exceptions, one in either camp, the Tory A. J. Balfour, and the Liberal R. B. Haldane. Trouble occurred when Balfour agreed to let the Church of England retain the ownership of its National Schools as long as it kept them in structural repair. The Church was also to hold the right of appointing the majority of the School managers. This, of course, safeguarded their claim to appoint the teachers. The schools were still to be subsidized out of the rates.

Such a surrender at once destroyed all hope of getting the Nonconformists to agree. For Free Churchmen, it represented the ultimate of Anglican arrogance. It meant that in many parts of the Kingdom they would have to pay for their children to be taught a creed in which they did not believe.

Of course, A. J. Balfour must have realized that this would stick in the throat of the Unitarian Joe Chamberlain, leader of his Liberal Unionist allies. But despite his personally charming manner towards Chamberlain, Balfour was not at all sorry to slight him politically, and neither was that far more ardent orthodox Church champion, Lord Hugh Cecil. To the aristocratic House of Cecil this "Empire Joe" (ex-"Radical Joe") still represented a rather vulgar Brummagem materialism. Only the old Marquis of Salisbury himself, who liked him no better, had his doubts. As an Anglican Churchman, Salisbury did not want to see voluntary contributions cease (which they certainly would do once the Church Schools were put on the rates). And as a politician, he foresaw that this would alienate many Nonconformists (who formed the bulk of the Liberal Unionists), and perhaps even drive them back to their former official Liberal Party allegiance. In this, the veteran Tory Prime Minister showed more political prescience than his nephew, soon to be his successor. Balfour could understand any individual man well enough; men in the mass he understood not at all.

For the Liberals, Haldane pressed forward to praise the Bill. He was one who watched with anxiety the rising commercial challenge of Germany in the markets of the world, and was already mesmerized by the legend of her "thoroughness". Haldane believed that it was based upon a superior popular education, and this opinion was shared by men of progressive mind in all parties, including Sidney Webb and his fellow Fabians, George Bernard Shaw and H. G. Wells. This Bill, they hoped, would help to put that right. As for the Irish Party, they followed the lead indicated by the Roman Catholic Church, and upheld the Bill. So the memorable measure was launched with hardly a ripple. Before long, it was reeling in a gale.

Lloyd George entered upon the scene warily. He told a reporter at the outset,

> "I am not favourably impressed with the Bill. . . . There may be points in it which I cannot agree with, and until I have seen it in print I must reserve further opinion."

As soon as the Bill appeared, there was explosion. The militant Nonconformist forces of England, led by the redoubtable Dr. Clifford, prepared a plan of "Passive Resistance". Its tactics were to be those of the old Tithe War: refuse to pay the abhorrent education rate, submit rather to the forced sale of your goods and even of your house; if need be, go to jail!

This was an echo down the English centuries of John Hampden, and the "damnable impost" of Ship Money. History had told how that small tax to finance the King's Navy helped to bring about England's own fearful Civil War. Now, hundreds of highly respected Nonconformists, great-great-great-grandsons of the troopers who rode in Cromwell's Ironside Army, again chose defiance of the Government which outraged their religious scruples.

It did not take Lloyd George long to realize that in his Education Bill the Tory leader had presented the enemy with a sword for the execution of his own Party. Eagerly Lloyd George seized it, and he used it with deadly effect when he spoke in the four-day debate on the Second Reading of the Bill, 8 May, 1902. It was the most powerfully-reasoned speech he had yet delivered in the House of Commons.

Age 39

W. H. Massingham wrote in the *Daily News*:

> "Until Mr. Lloyd George spoke tonight Nonconformity, its intellectual attitude to Education, its historical associations with the settlement of 1870, now being torn up, and its contribution to the religious problem, had gone without a recorder and a champion. Mr. Lloyd George took that vacant place tonight."

He argued that a special privilege was being granted to the Church of England schools which had been withheld from the other schools. In places where no other educational centre existed, the machinery of the Law was being used to force Nonconformist children into the Church of England establishments, which by their own rules were, in fact, "Mission rooms to proselytize them".

Yet what was the alternative? For each sect to set up its own separate, poorly equipped little school house? Lloyd George claimed to have found the answer. It was the "Colonial Compromise". In the British Dominions (Lloyd George had seen it himself in Canada), instead of having a number of little local rural schools they built a bigger and better one and brought the children there from miles around. No religious instruction was given which could offend anyone, but the pastors of the different denominations were permitted to come there after school hours and teach their own doctrine to their own flock. There was surely a great and civilized example of what to do!

Lloyd George's powerful intervention in this battle sprang from his own deep and abiding interest in the cause of Education. He was himself the son of a schoolmaster, and he knew, as he said years later, "from painful experiences of my childhood how shabbily the teaching profession was treated . . . paid a salary that today a scavenger would regard as an insult to his trade".

He realized, indeed, that Education could never be put on a firm foundation until the teachers were given a decent security and the children proper schools; that only a national and not a sectarian system could guarantee both; and that unless Britain put this first line of her future commercial, industrial and scientific development in order, then she would fall from her proud place in the march of history.

This Education Bill turned out to be the cause of a fateful personal quarrel between Lloyd George and the Irish Nationalist Party. Fiercely, he turned upon them, and gave them a taste of someone else's nationalist passion.

Who were the men who rejoiced at the introduction of this Bill? Why, the bitterest enemies of Ireland! Who were the men who would be saddened most because they had done it? The best friends of Ireland! The people who would benefit would be those people who had coerced Ireland, and supported every measure for throwing the leaders of the Irish people into prison, for keeping Ireland down with soldiers and police. The people who would be hit would be the people of Wales, whom Joe Chamberlain had offered Disestablishment long ago if they would only give up Home Rule for Ireland. The Welsh had refused, and now they would be sold up for refusing to pay rates under this Bill, probably imprisoned. They would long remember, in Wales, that their chains were forged by the help of the Irish!

It was the twilight of the Celtic love-story, begun nearly twenty years ago in the misty mountains of Blaenau Festiniog when a young Welsh Nationalist named David Lloyd George had bowed in homage before an old Irish Nationalist, named Michael Davitt, who had spent years of his life in prison for the cause of his country. Lloyd George would continue in political alliance with the Irish Party for many a year to come, would go on advocating Home Rule for Ireland, in the end would be the Prime Minister of Britain who granted it. But he would do it with his head, as a hard bargain after a bitter struggle; his heart, for Ireland, was dead.

To the long-divided Liberal Party the Education Bill brought unity, and revival. June, 1902, saw a packed Queen's Hall meeting, presided over by Lord Rosebery, addressed by Asquith and Lloyd George, and graced by a special message from Sir Henry Campbell-Bannerman. Both the chief speakers received a tremendous ovation, Lloyd George's the more significant since only yesterday he had been the erring son, an outcast in a detested minority. He spoke briefly, but he won a rollicking cheer when he asked how we should get on if we tried to run the Royal Navy on the lines it was proposed to run National Education?

"Under good old sectarian control we should have a Roman Catholic battleship, a Congregationalist cruiser, a Methodist torpedo-boat, an Anglican destroyer, and, of course, a Baptist *submarine*!"

In a single savage sentence he dealt with Unitarian Joseph Chamberlain, who in his Radical days had been the foremost political champion of Nonconformity:

"His advocacy of this Bill is the last act of treachery in the career of one who has sold many of his convictions."

(In fact, this charge was quite untrue. Chamberlain had steadfastly opposed the Education Bill inside the Tory Cabinet. His allies were the Diehard Marquis of Salisbury and the Cobdenite Free Trade Chancellor of the Exchequer, Sir Michael Hicks-Beach.)

In the House of Commons, Lloyd George fought the Committee stage of the Bill line by line, again astonishing those who knew him best by his diligence in attendance even more than by his extraordinary detailed knowledge of his subject. Press Gallery reporters wrote that on this issue Lloyd George was leading the Opposition. He led the battle against the Bill so well that he could claim at Bangor, on 17 September,

> "after three months of struggling in the House of Commons, the Government have succeeded in placing two-and-a-half pages out of twenty-two of their Bill on the Statute Book".

Now he was seeking the powerful aid of the Press again, writing to Dr. Robertson Nicoll,[1] famous Editor of the leading Nonconformist journal, *The British Weekly*, appealing for "a more complete understanding between those who conduct the campaign in the country and the Members who fight the Bill in the Commons. . . ."

Throughout that summer and autumn of 1902, the tide was rising against the Government. In July, a Baptist Liberal candidate had won a decisive victory in the North Leeds by-election, capturing a seat which had returned a Tory for the previous five elections; in August a Tory local Gibraltar stronghold had been narrowly held at Sevenoaks; in September, the rising Trades Union Congress condemned the Education Bill by a huge majority; in October only Joe Chamberlain himself was able to quell an open mutiny of the Birmingham Liberal Unionist Association. He wrote to the Duke of Devonshire:

> "The worst of the business is that after the Bill has passed, the agitation will continue in its most serious form. What are you going to do with Town Councils that refuse to act, and ratepayers who refuse to pay? *Some will!* Damn the Bill!"

Joe was right again.

It was exactly what happened. In England, Dr. Clifford's Resistance Movement raised the ancient war-cry of "No Taxation Without Representation", and hundreds of ratepayers were sent to jail for refusing to pay for the Church of England schools. In Wales, a more elaborate and more effective campaign of Civil Disobedience was being planned.

But first, there was one more plea to be made in the House of Commons for a truly National, non-Sectarian Educational Code. It was movingly done by Lloyd George, December 1902.

> "Give the children the Bible, if you want to teach them the Christian Faith. Let it be expounded to them by its Founder. Stop this brawling of priests in and around the schools, so that the children can hear Him speak to them in His own words. I appeal to the House of Commons now, at the eleventh hour, to use its great influence and lift its commanding voice and say: 'Pray silence for the Master.' "

[1] He became Sir William Robertson Nicoll in 1909.

He had won a further real acclaim in that Parliament. Balfour, who had never lost his temper with Lloyd George (or at any rate, never showed it), paid him tribute in his winding-up speech on the Bill:

> "His part in these debates has been most distinguished and though I could wish unsaid some of his observations, by the omission of which, in my opinion, he would greatly gain in and out of the House, we must all admit on both sides of the House and in the country that he has made himself a position as an eminent Parliamentarian."

Lloyd George now showed himself to be an expert political general, too. He had already carefully chosen his battlefield—in Wales!

FIRST, he urged his countrymen, they must open action in the forth-coming Municipal and County Council Elections. The rebels must seize control of those public bodies which were due to administer the new Education Act. They could easily do this, for while in England the Nonconformists were in a minority, in Wales they outnumbered the Anglicans by three to one. By mobilizing their full strength, they could dominate all Local Government. Their purpose should not be to refuse to operate the Act, for if the Councils did so (Lloyd George warned), then the Board of Education would set up some other crude machinery in their place, and a whole generation of children would suffer. Lloyd George proposed, not to *break* the Law, but to *bend* it:

> "Let us capture the enemy's artillery, and turn his guns against him."

In an *Address to the People of Wales*, Lloyd George set forth the rest of his plan of campaign.

SECOND phase was for the Local Councils to operate the powers con-ferred upon them, to conspire together and exclude from the sixteen new Welsh County Education Committees all bodies which did not represent the ratepayers (thus pushing out an "official" Church of England element).

THIRD, they should have all the schools in their area strictly surveyed as to accommodation, ventilation, sanitation, lighting, etc., and should refuse to take them over until they had been "properly cleansed and clothed".

LASTLY, they should levy no rates to support any school, unless they had secured (*a*) complete control over the spending of the money thus raised, and (*b*) abolition of all religious and political tests for the teachers. Otherwise, don't touch these schools! NO Control, NO Cash!

Such was the programme of what was called "The Welsh Revolt". Lloyd George claimed that it was cast-iron. He had studied "every letter and comma of the abominable Act", and he was satisfied that what he recommended was "within the letter of the Law". For, Liberals in Wales should not entertain for one moment the idea of resisting the Law—only Tories in Ulster did that! Rather, they should operate the Act in the good old spirit of the British Consti-tution, which was never in a hurry to do anything! By an overwhelming vote,

At an air display at Hendon with Lord Northcliffe and Lord Reading in 1911

a tumultuous National Conference at Cardiff of political, religious and educational leaders in the Principality adopted the Lloyd George Plan.

Candidates pledged to it swept the Municipal polls and, the following year, the County Council Elections endorsed this verdict, returning Nonconformist majorities throughout the land. In every County Council in Wales, except three, the Tories were unable to form a quorum of one-third, without which no public business of any kind could be transacted. Out of thirty County and Borough Educational Authorities, twenty-eight bound themselves to resign if the Government should attempt to coerce them to levy a rate.

In alarm, the Bishop of St. Davids wrote to Balfour pointing out the dilemma in which he was placed. A resolution had been passed, he said, by the Carmarthenshire County Council, refusing to contribute anything whatever out of the rates to the maintenance of National Schools . . . there would soon be no money to meet current commitments, and he would have to face the alternative of closing down the schools or of providing a loan.

The mechanism of the Whitehall power-grid would, indeed, have been paralysed if the Welsh County Councils had stuck strictly, as Lloyd George so firmly counselled, to "the letter of the Law that killeth". But a couple of them rashly refused to administer the Education Act at all. This gave Balfour his opportunity to bring in a Local Authorities Default Bill, which enabled the Board of Education to spend the necessary money for the Church of England schools over the heads of the local Councils and then to send them the bill from the Exchequer.

Promptly it was named the "Welsh Coercion Bill". It afforded Lloyd George, in turn, the chance to brand the Tory Government (then framing a new Liquor Law to make the publican's licence a freehold, instead of a permit from the magistrates) as "the joint prisoner of the Bishops and the Brewers".

Cried the organizer of the "Welsh Revolt", about the Tory Government's own troublesome Household Troops (it was on the occasion of the Second Reading of the Welsh Bill):

"The Government found their empire tottering; and like the Roman Empire of old, they had to buy off the Goths. One day, the Goths came from Burton-on-Trent (Breweries); the next from Lambeth (Bishop's Palace). They threatened to sack the City. For a year or two, the Education Act satisfied them, but the Brewers' Endowment Act brought the hordes back! 'Our consciences will not stand this,' they said. 'I'll square that for you,' said the Prime Minister, and he put matters right with the Bill for the Coercion of Wales. It is like compounding a spree on a Saturday night by putting a threepenny bit in the plate on Sunday."

The "Coercion Bill" aroused all Wales, uniting the entire country as it had hardly been since the days of Llewellyn the Great. Whitehall was now going to try and tell the Welsh people how to run even their own village life,

E

eh? Well, Whitehall would find out! The national mood happened to be further heightened at this very moment by one of those extraordinary religious revivals which from time to time sweep across the Land of the Druids with the suddenness and violence of a typhoon. At a second, excited conference in Cardiff, Lloyd George urged that if the Board of Education should seek to exercise in any Welsh area the powers granted by the Coercion Act the Local Authority should instantly take legal steps to renounce every whit of responsibility for its schools, denominational or otherwise. It meant that Whitehall itself would have to run the whole of Welsh Education from London. This resolution was carried amid tremendous acclamation, and without a single dissentient.

The Times considered it necessary to admonish Lloyd George.

"Five or six years ago, in his callow youth, these schemes might have been regarded as promising methods of self-advertisement adopted by a young politician who must at any cost attract attention. But that time is long gone by. Mr. Lloyd George should no longer use tactics worthy of his own distant past, and of Mr. Winston Churchill's present. He has become a serious politician, and a serious claimant for high office."

He had certainly shown some marks of statesmanship besides those of an adroit political campaigner. He could understand what a fight was about, and calculate the gain to be got out of it, as well as how to conduct it. Lloyd George was also coming to realize that, if you can win it, a fair peace is often a less expensive proposition than a final victory. Earlier in the year, he had made a sincere attempt to settle the Sectarian Civil War in Wales by a direct approach between the contestants. Lloyd George himself led one delegation, and found that at the head of the other was his ancient enemy, whom he had never yet met in person, Dr. Edwards, the doughty Bishop of St. Asaph's. They played golf together, and got on famously.

But the *concordat* which they agreed, based on that old Colonial Compromise, broke down; some other Christian crusaders were not ready yet to lay aside their broadswords. Negotiations dragged on for many months, like a Korean truce talk; the quarrel also continued in desultory fashion.

The Welsh Revolt never flared. The pyre was all set. But the fire had gone out—of the Government. The "Coercion Act" was never enforced. The Ministers were too busy bitterly fighting among themselves about something even more controversial.

This was the great Protection *v.* Free Trade issue, which rent the nation and the Tory Party for the next quarter of a century. Ever since the Repeal of the Corn Laws in the Hungry " 'Forties", Protection, as Disraeli had warned the Tories of his time, had been "dead and damned". All attempts to resurrect it under the *alias* of "Fair Trade" had been easily frustrated, on the last occasion in the early " 'eighties" by a rising young Radical from Birmingham in Gladstone's Cabinet, named Chamberlain, then an uncompromising Cobdenite Free Trader. In the days when England was still outstripping every competitor in the race for industrial and commercial supremacy, it seemed economically unprofitable to prop up the Feudal landed system of British agriculture by taxing imported foodstuffs. It would certainly have been inviting electoral disaster for any political Party to advocate it. The Workshop of the World had also to be its market-place, for its cheap manufactures were based on cheap raw materials both for its machines and its men.

There were indeed already those politicians—and they were not all Tory backwoodsmen from the shires—who wondered whether or not the decay of the countryside and the draining away of the farm population to the factories and the jail-like tenements of the industrial towns, was finally worth it. It was not, however, from the old Aristocracy of the Land that the latest fiscal revolutionaries arose, but from the new Plutocracy of Trade. Nor was their programme the mere insular Protection of the industry and commerce of the United Kingdom, but a system of Preferential Tariffs, and, eventually, of free trade within a far vaster area of the world, namely, the bounds of the British Empire. They were proposing to build a tariff wall round the Mother Country in order to make loopholes in it through which the goods of the children could pass. Such was the later idea of Joe Chamberlain, by this time the outstanding Imperial Tariff Reformer.

He had arrived at this point after a curious journey. Before the South African War, as Colonial Secretary, Chamberlain had sought to convert the Dominion Prime Ministers to the policy of an All-Empire Defence. They remained unwilling to commit their citizens to wars in Europe. They feared that Imperial Defence would be run by the British Admiralty and the War Office, and these vigorous young countries were already nations in their own right. Nor were they anxious to enter on the path of a closer political federation, for this also suggested a centralizing of power in London. In matters of trade, however, there was business to be done and Canada, in particular, gave proof of her desire for it by her 25 per cent tariff preference for British goods (in 1900, it was raised to $33\frac{1}{3}$ per cent). The teething troubles of the freshly-formed Commonwealth of Australia and the war in South Africa delayed a like response from Britain. But to strengthen the trade links between the Mother Country and the Dominions at the earliest possible moment seemed to Joe Chamberlain to be the obvious and, indeed, the only available way to fortify the fabric of the British Empire.

"If England wants our help, she should call us to her Councils," Sir Wilfrid Laurier, Prime Minister of Canada, had said.

But Chamberlain, speaking at the Canadian banquet in London in 1901, had replied that nothing would be more fatal than to be premature. The movement for closer inter-Empire trade must start from the Colonies themselves.

Yet when it came, what could Britain offer in fiscal exchange for further concession of Colonial preferences? The answer was—under her existing Free Trade System—absolutely nothing. Then, suddenly, a gleam. . . . This was the Corn Registration Duty of Sir Michael Hicks-Beach's 1902 Budget.

It was not much of a tax, only 3*d*. per cwt on imported corn. It was not imposed in order to protect British agriculture, but to raise revenue; the Chancellor of the Exchequer was no Tariff Reformer; but he faced a deficit of £10,000,000. He put a penny on Income Tax, bringing it up to 1*s*. 3*d*. in the £, and reckoned that after this imposition on the well-to-do he might reasonably broaden the basis of taxation a bit. Mr. Bonar Law, a thoughtful young Glasgow M.P., calculated that it would increase the cost of a four-pound loaf by no more than half a farthing.

But Chamberlain seized upon it eagerly. Here was a small beginning which might come to a great fulfilment. When Sir Wilfred Laurier formally asked, at the Colonial Conference, for Canadian corn to be exempted from this duty, Joe Chamberlain backed him to the limit in the Cabinet. The Chancellor of the Exchequer stonily refused; he needed all the revenue that the duty would yield to help pay for that South African War.

It was the second time that the Orthodox Old Guard at the Treasury had baulked Joe Chamberlain's plans. The first had been when they denied him Old Age Pensions, and for the same half-contemptuous economy "reason". So now, he resolved to present a new political issue for the people to debate: the Greatness, Glory, Wealth and Opportunity of the British Empire. Henceforth his social and his imperial policies would run in harness together. Trade would flourish between all partners in the great free commonwealth, the foreigner would pay proper toll for entry into this fine market, and the revenue thus derived would be so rich as to finance with ease those schemes of pensions, schools and hospitals which had been the dream of young "Radical Joe" (now "Empire Joe").

It seemed to suit everyone, except a Free Trader. Those who wanted Protection for their own industry: those who wanted "Retaliation" to compel their foreign competitors to produce on equal terms with themselves: those who wanted Imperial Preferences to bind the Empire countries together in a common trade: and those who simply required revenue.

Unhappily, for Joe, not all these desires could be easily reconciled between the various kinds of Protectionists. And, still more unhappily, there remained such a large number of those obstinate Free Traders—and in all Parties!

Balfour, who had inherited the Premiership from his uncle, Lord Salisbury, in July, 1902, managed during his next three years to conceal both from his friends and his foes on which side he stood. His prime concern was to postpone any final decision on Policy, and thus avert a Party split. So, right up to the forthcoming General Election of 1906, the views (and voices) of Ministers remained at variance, and Tory disaster at the polls was thus ensured. It gave Lloyd George the opportunity to describe in his own lively fashion, the plight of the Balfour Cabinet: "like a worm, cut in half, but both ends still wriggling, blindly".

The facts of the day appeared to be against Chamberlain. No nation in the history of the world had ever yet been so rich as Britain was at the beginning of this century. Others, indeed, were rising—in Europe, Germany; in America, the United States, and Chamberlain himself warned of their coming challenge:

"Now we are face to face with great combinations, with enormous trusts, having behind them gigantic wealth. Even the industries and commerce which we thought to be peculiarly our own are in danger. These threats cannot be met by old, antiquated methods, which were good enough in their day."

This, too, was truth. But it lay upon the eyelids of tomorrow. To the nation, it was not apparent today. Trade still boomed. Employment was high. By comparison with other countries, wages in Britain were good. Joyfully, the Liberal Opposition went to work.

"Woe! Woe!" had been the jeremiad of Joe. Our financial supremacy was going! Our merchant trade was going! Our industries were going!

"In fact," jeered Lloyd George, "everything is going—except the Government, and that won't go."

With mock despair, he traced Britain's Road to Ruin.

National wealth in the country, 1885 ("the year that Mr. Chamberlain left the Liberal Party"), £10,000,000,000; 1902, £15,000,000,000. Cargoes carried in British ships, 1885, 2,700,000 tons; 1902, 8,100,000 tons. British steel production, 1885, 2,500,000 tons; 1902, 5,000,000 tons.

Wages? Lloyd George compared the weekly pay-packet of the outmoded Free Trade British workman with that of his up-to-date Protectionist German competitor. The Briton earned substantially more at engineering, coal-mining, cotton-spinning and cotton-weaving than the German, who, as Lloyd George pointed out, also worked longer hours and bought dearer food. "He lives on black bread and horsemeat sausages. They go along with Protection!"

Unemployment? In Britain, it fluctuated between 3 and 5 per cent. In Germany between 7 and 30 per cent. It gave the "pro-Boer" a certain satisfaction to reprove the "Patriotic Party" for its denigration of our national affairs.

There was another appreciation of the Lloyd George of those days. It came from a phrenologist in Ludgate Circus near Fleet Street, whom Lloyd George had called in to see one morning on his way to his solicitor's office in the City. (Lloyd George nourished all his life the idea that you could measure the capacity of a man by the size of his head—what size hat did the fellow wear? The single exception that Lloyd George would ever allow to this remarkable standard of judgment was Bonar Law.) We do not know what the Ludgate

Circus phrenologist thought of Lloyd George's own capacity, judged by the size (or perhaps, even the shape) of his head. Of his personality, he wrote:

"He lives longer in one day than most men do in a month. Yet he is perennially youthful; he will be something of a boy when many who went to school with him are grey in hair and grey in outlook . . . a Welshman's caution and secretiveness . . . craves sympathy and praise, and is not without vanity . . . tends to cultivate a brilliant but not spontaneous wittiness. . . ."

Already, as another perceptive Fleet Street critic had noted of him in the *Review of Reviews*, he had now attained the distinction of always being spoken of without the "mister".

"—a kind of knighthood which is the gift of the man-in-the-street, a knighthood more sparingly distributed than the titular 'Sir'."

It was to see more of this interesting "firebrand from Wales" that King Edward VII one evening suggested to his friend, Lord Tweedmouth, a leading Liberal Peer, that he might invite them both to dinner at Brook House, Tweedmouth's London home. (The King had dined with Lloyd George once before, in 1902, in Sir Edward Grey's company, and told Morley that he was "favourably impressed with him". Lloyd George reported that the King was "very affable".)

So duly Lloyd George went to the Park Lane palace which Lord Tweedmouth was about to sell for £60,000 to another of the King's close personal friends, the millionaire financier, Sir Ernest Cassel. What further impression the two chief guests formed of each other in these surroundings is not recorded. They had some tastes in common, but for the rest King Edward recognized in this "firebrand" one who might some day burn down the splendid mansion of that society of which he was himself so notable a pillar.

One of these common tastes was for the company, not so much of rich men but of *self-made* rich men. The King liked Sir Ernest Cassel, Sir Thomas Lipton and some of the new millionaires from the Rand; Lloyd George had rich friends in Mr. Timothy Davies, the prosperous merchant mayor of Fulham, and Mr. Charles Henry,[1] an energetic Jewish Australian who had also made a fortune in South Africa. Another was Mr. Arthur Crosfield,[2] a Warrington soap manufacturer. A fourth who shared his politics (and his golf) was Mr. Alfred Mond.[3] He was of German Jewish extraction, with a strong guttural accent, which he overrode by the vigour of his delivery. He had, indeed, an abundance of energy, plenty of business brains, a sound political understanding and no sense of political continuity. This vehement Land Reformer and Free Trader before the 1914–18 War left the Liberal Party after the war in opposition to their Land Reform policy and joined the Tory Party, to subscribe shortly

---

[1] Later Sir Charles Henry.   [2] Later Sir Arthur Crosfield.
[3] Later Sir Alfred Mond, and then Lord Melchett.

afterwards to the cause of Empire Protection. While he sat as Liberal M.P. for Swansea, and supported the struggle for the Disestablishment of the Welsh Church, Mr. Alfred Mond had to endure the taunts of Mr. F. E. Smith about this "fiery crusader" who cried out "in the wild accents of his native Wales", and when finally he deserted the Liberal Party, in 1926, he had to bear the more savage gibe of Lloyd George about this Judas, who "has gone to his own place". For some time past Lloyd George had travelled abroad in such well-breeched company to France, Italy, Austria, Switzerland, as well as making those occasional further forays to Canada and the Argentine.

He had earned his rest and change by his laborious days and nights in the House of Commons, in his office and at the innumerable public meetings which he attended up and down the land.

He made his holidays, too, profitable in experience, for Lloyd George possessed a perpetually inquiring mind, and though steady work was never congenial to him, he made it by habit a second nature in those days. Thus, he had returned from Switzerland in time for the great Education Bill debates in the House of Commons with much useful data about the model system of public education in that enlightened and business-like little republic, and from Canada with the eminently sensible and liberal example of that great Dominion in the matter of the famous "Colonial Compromise" upon the same issue.

Lloyd George had need, indeed, to apply himself to his business; for in 1902, Megan, his third daughter, had been born, bringing his young family up to five. (In deference to the respective Baptist and Methodist faiths of their father and mother they were alternately baptized or christened.)

In his own profession, Lloyd George had by this time more than recovered what he had lost during the days of his "Pro-Boer" unpopularity. His city practice of Lloyd George, Roberts and Co., flourished at Trinity Lane, and all went well now at Portmadoc.

By this time Lloyd George had leased a red-brick house, for about £65 per annum, at 3 Routh Road, a few hundred yards away from his original Wandsworth address. It was not much larger and had no pretensions to style. But it had a better garden and that meant much; the children could play there, he could keep a dog there, he could eat a meal there, and after lunch on a sunny day he could take half an hour's nap under the trees. Wandsworth Common began at his garden hedge, and he was almost half-way from London to Walton Heath, where shortly he would play golf with his political cronies, an increasingly congenial exercise.

There is a warm picture handed down to us of the Lloyd George family evenings during this period. Welsh was still the language of the home, and by the hearth sat Father, with Megan on his knee, and Richard, Mair, Olwen, and Gwilym grouped round him and their mother, Margaret. By the light of the fire, then, the spell-binder of multitudes would entrance the little company as he told them in the music of their native tongue his own, Lloyd George edition of the thrilling stories of *Ivanhoe*, of *Gulliver's Travels*, *The Tale of Two Cities* and *The Count of Monte Cristo*. Each instalment ended by Lloyd George announcing suddenly: "That's all for now. I haven't read any further." Like every good serial, this point always occurred at a particularly exciting moment.

These fireside evenings would become more rare, and almost cease, as first office, and then bereavement, altered his life. Lloyd George was able to repay to the next generation of his family only part of the rich heritage which his elders had bequeathed to a wondering village boy.

Tremendous days were near. Some more irrelevant arguments, some more sterile skirmishes, and then would come the Day of Decision, D-Day in the greatest social struggle that Britain had known since Cromwell broke the power of the Kings. The day of the cottage-bred boy would really dawn; yes, and the day of the slum-bred boy, too.

South of France. Lloyd George and Lord Devonport, with their sons

Recuperating. Beachborough, with Megan, 1911

CHAPTER IX

THE FIRST SHIFT

THE Great Conservative Administration fizzled out, in the end, as a spent squib. Rising out of the dust and din of the Khaki Election, the Salisbury–Chamberlain combination had seemed, in 1900, to offer glittering prospects. It was the time of victories in South Africa. Most precious prize of all—there was the gleam of peace on the horizon of the *veldt.*

But the war had gone wrong, and had dragged on. The glory of the fighting began to fade, and the scandals of the Whitehall military maladministration began to leak out. The public found them harder to bear than the earlier reverses in the field.

The aftermath had been worse than the war. The bill had come in, £250,000,000, or more than double the size of a Victorian Budget. There was not the money in the Treasury till to meet it. So neither the wealthy had much to look forward to in remission of taxes, nor the poor in provision of boons. The fabulous riches of the Rand lay still buried there, and meantime, its own peculiar labour troubles loomed up.

Half-way through its lifetime, the mind of the Tory Government had become as split on the Protectionist issue as ever that of the Liberal Opposition had been over the Boer War. The resignation of Tariff Reformer Chamberlain and Free Trader Ritchie from the Administration in 1903 had settled nothing, for the argument was simply transferred from the Cabinet room to the country. It brought forth the following Lloyd George gibe:

"Whenever the Government adopts any decision on policy there follow resignations of leading members: so that a Government without a policy threatens to become a policy without a Government."

In vain did Balfour exercise his own unrivalled dialectical skill to bring together, as he wrote to Chamberlain, "the reasonable free-fooders and the reasonable whole-hoggers". Not even a Tory philosopher could reasonably explain how you could be both a Free Trader and a Tariff Reformer at the same time, though, as Lloyd George did not fail to point out, Tory politicians in different places sought between them to square the circle.

"At the next election," he explained, "in the agricultural districts they will be Chamberlainites in favour of taxing corn and foreign cattle; in the industrial areas they will be Balfourites in favour of taxing the products of those areas' competitors; in the districts depending on shipping they will be Duke of Devonshire Free Traders."

At least half a dozen other troubles beset Balfour at that time, and would follow him to the grave of his party's fortunes at the next General Election. The first of these was the question of Chinese labour in the Rand mines, or "Chinese Slavery" as it soon became in the dog-fight of politics. Chinese labour certainly turned out to be a Chinese devil in the politics of South Africa.

Before the war, about a hundred thousand Kaffirs had been employed in these mines. During the war, they had gone off to the railways or the farms, or had followed in the wake of the armies as labourers, earning better money. After the war, they had returned to find that the mining companies had slashed the former wage rates in order to raise more capital for development. The capital was raised, but in the meantime labour dwindled.

Some folk (they included both Joe Chamberlain and Lloyd George) advised "Bring in White labour!" This would increase the British population in the new colony. But others (they included Sir Alfred Milner), doubted if it would solve the problem, for White labour is not, in general, suited to work in the deep, hot mines of the Rand. Still others simply wanted cheap hands, and the question was whether or not Central Africa, India or China was the best source for "indentured labour". In the end, the lot fell on China, and 50,000 coolies were duly recruited there and shipped to South Africa.

Their wages were a shilling a day. They were kept in a compound and numbered. A tiny handful of Chinese wives were allowed to accompany this vast new labour army which was encamped on the Rand. The Boers strongly objected, so did Natal and Cape Colony and, not unnaturally, the local White miners.

Cried Lloyd George:

Age 41

"They have brought back slavery to the British Empire. Of course, it is not called that. It passes under the much more attractive name of 'The Labour Question in Africa'."

And he went on to rub the Chinese labour question in to Joe Chamberlain, for had it not been *his* war, just as Tariff Reform was his own private ruse to distract public attention from its consequence? Yes, it was Joe who had "nailed the Yellow Flag to the mast of Protection".

Lloyd George admitted that there had been a certain increase in the number of Whites in the Transvaal—but the Tories did not tell them to what race these whites belonged. They were, in fact, mostly aliens, who had come in from all parts of Europe. The result was that this Colony, on which they had spent £250,000,000 to make it British was now, as far as the agricultural population was concerned, Dutch; as far as the mining population was concerned, Chinese; as far as the labourers were concerned, Kaffir; as far as the artisans and shopkeepers were concerned, Russians and Polish Jews.

It will be observed that at this period of his life, Lloyd George had little good to say for the Jewish people, the more noteworthy because in Wales anti-Semitism was, and is, almost unknown (indeed, some Welshmen claim that the *Cymru* are one of the Lost Tribes of Israel!). Certainly, Lloyd George permitted himself to speak derisively of the way in which "the British Empire is being run by Brummagem and Jerusalem!"

"Chinese Slavery" provided Lloyd George with an effective Party simile when a would-be conciliatory amendment on Tariff Reform was put down on the Parliamentary Order Paper by a Tory "near-Free Trader", approved by Balfour himself—and hurriedly withdrawn under violent pressure from the Tory "whole-hog protectionists".

"The Prime Minister tried to escape from the Birmingham Compound," mocked Lloyd George next day, "but the Overseer left in charge discovered him before he had got very far beyond the fence. He and his colleagues were brought back by their pigtails."

The debate had been marked by a less pleasant interlude than this banter. When young Mr. Winston Churchill rose to speak from the Tory benches in support of Free Trade, the Ministers on the Government Front Bench got up and walked out of the House, followed by almost the entire Party. A few days later the Member for Oldham crossed the floor and took up his place next to Lloyd George on an Opposition Bench below the gangway. That autumn, 1904, found him at Caernarvon, speaking from the same platform as Lloyd George, whom he described enthusiastically as "the best fighting general in the Liberal Army".

Lloyd George, on his part, welcomed the promising recruit. Churchill, he opined, was a good exchange for Chamberlain, who had left the Liberals to join the Tories. All the best, most vigorous, most intelligent, most useful years of that remarkable man's life he had spent abusing his present hosts. Only when he had got to the shady side of his life—in more ways than one— —had "Radical Joe" taken to defending the abuses—and the abused.

When Chamberlain professed to find something remarkable in Lloyd George of all people defending Free Trade because it had worked well for the greater part of the last century, Lloyd George took the Bible to him in his most infuriating (to the recipient) style:

"Really, is it an objection to a thing that it is old? A thing which has been tried for sixty years and has brought prosperity! Is that not all the more reason for sticking to it? Besides, there are a good many old things that we should not like to see thrown over. The Sermon on the Mount is pretty old—the first great deliverance against the policy of retaliation (cheers). Mr. Chamberlain says that we must not believe in its principles; he says that they don't work; he says that the jewellers of Birmingham cannot thrive on New Testament lines!"

The peers were not overlooked in this interchange. In rather different style, Lloyd George dealt with Chamberlain's Glasgow meeting, where he had spoken of protecting the "Little Man" smallholder.

"It was attended," said Lloyd George, "by three dukes, two marquesses, three or four earls, and as many lords as there were ministerial resignations. Mr. Chamberlain spoke of the day when every working man should have a pig. A few years ago the policy was three acres and a cow. Now it is three dukes and a pig."

At Maidenhead, in May, 1905, he developed a further opinion about peers. He said he did not care whether a man was an earl or just a man like himself, who had never been, and never would be a lord, so long as the right quality of manhood was there. He had better not have said that.

More deadly to Chamberlain's cause than the invective of his critics was the inquest on the war now so inextricably associated with his name. After the scandal of the concentration camps came the exposure of wartime profiteering by contractors and wastefulness by officials.

Lloyd George was also able to attack the War Office on their own ground, when he declared that their Military Intelligence had warned them before the war broke out the Boers had machine-guns, field-guns, plenty of rifles and millions of rounds of ammunition, as well as 50,000 of the finest mounted infantry in the world.

Debating at Cambridge Union one evening, in the autumn of 1905, he said scornfully that such was the foresight of the great Imperial Government which had sent Britain's sons to fight on the *veldt* that at one critical moment, they had got down to their last couple of boxes of rifle ammunition.

He was immediately challenged. It is typical of the rising Lloyd George of 1905 that he paused, fumbled in his pocket, and almost casually produced the Blue Book on the War. He then read out the evidence of Sir Henry Brackenbury, Director-General of Ordnance to the War Commission, that we had once actually been down to two boxes of ammunition!

The rash interrupter was floored; he should have foreseen that come-back blow. Lloyd George triumphantly concluded:

"The same with gun ammunition. The best ships in the world, and the finest sailors in the world sent out to face the navies of Europe—and suddenly, in the middle of a battle, having to retire because this precious Government had got, not insufficient cordite this time, but not a shot in its locker!"

Then, after the big mess of the war, they had made a bigger mess of the peace! There was prescience in Lloyd George's warning that if we intended to retain South Africa we must make it British, not merely in name, but in fact. If we were going to leave the country in the hands of a people whom we had exasperated and let them still predominate as a race, then sooner or later South Africa would cease to be a British Colony. As early as 1905 Lloyd George toyed with an idea of planned Empire emigration. He returned to it later, sincerely believed in it but, strangely, never pursued it.

At Finsbury by-election Lloyd George indulged in a further attack on Brummagem and Jerusalem. The Conservative Candidate, Mr. Cohen, had attacked the Liberal, Mr. Baker, as being a Canadian. Why, a few years ago, cried Lloyd George, if you had even suggested that a Colonial was not better than an ordinary Britisher, Mr. Chamberlain and his friends would have thrown a brick at you! Hadn't their Government established a Canadian at four times the worth of an Englishman—the Canadian soldier got 5s. a day in the Boer War, and Tommy Atkins 1s. 3d.?

"I do not say that a Canadian is better," said Lloyd George, thoughtfully. "But a British subject born in Ontario is no worse than a British subject who traces his ancestry from Jerusalem. As for me, in a case like that I am for Colonial Preference.

"Would you like to know how to make a fortune?" he inquired. "I will tell you. First get up a war, like Mr. Chamberlain's. Choose a country with gold in it. Get the *Daily Mail* to back you up. Take a country with very few people—a Republic, for preference; then you will have Society with you. Having got your war, go down there and start business. If you have a British name, like Jones or Smith, or Baker, change it at once. Make it Beit, Dunkelsbuhler, or, say, Cohen!

"The day of Mr. Chamberlain's ascendancy in British politics is drawing to a close," predicted Lloyd George, "and a fitting termination it is for such a career! It ends, as it began, with a split of a Party."

The thrust was cruel, but it had truth. The row between the Free Traders and the Tariff Reformers was mounting to its height, and the Free Traders were still winning because their case was still well-founded on the statistics of the day. Thus, as the General Election drew near, Lloyd George was able to show that the woe that Joe had foretold would come upon the country if it did not change its fiscal policy was still not visible. Throughout all the early years of Chamberlain's campaign, British exports went on obstinately rising, and in 1906, Britain was still selling more goods abroad than her nearest rivals, Germany and the United States, put together; and she was building more ships than the rest of the entire world. Lloyd George made great platform play with the unfulfilled story of Joe's Woes.

Nevertheless, he was not really happy on this fiscal theme. What concerned him was that the Free Traders were fighting a defensive battle. Lloyd George did not fancy himself in the role of a Conservative at any time, and he was sharply aware that the working masses were not really much interested in any economic theory. What they wanted was decent houses, better food, higher wages, shorter hours. "You cannot feed the hungry with statistics of national prosperity."

Joe Chamberlain thoroughly understood this, too. Furthermore, he fully approved of it. His old Radical faith had never wavered in this matter, and he wanted Tariff Reform at least as much for the sake of the Social Reform which he believed it could help to finance, as for the sake of Empire Unity. In these exciting years, the real prize that our David and Goliath were contending for was the heart of the British working classes. It was one reason for their rivalry —and a deeper one for the genuine appreciation which each of these men had for the other.

Lloyd George understood poverty, and he hated it with all his passion. He had not himself suffered harshly from its lash, but he had seen it at close hand. In his youth he certainly had known hard days.

The social facts of Britain, 1905, were terrible. Seven per cent of the city population of the richest nation in the world were destitute. Thirty per cent lived on or below the poverty line. The evidence given at the Old Age Pensions Committee, on which both Chamberlain and Lloyd George had sat before the Boer War, showed that if the qualifying age were to be fixed at 65 years, masses of old working people would never live to get it, so poor was the diet which they ate, so filthy were the habitations in which they lived, so decayed were their bodies with disease.

"There are conditions of poverty, destitution and squalor," said Lloyd George, "that would make the rocks weep."

Lloyd George proposed a National Inquest on this state of affairs. There were reasons for it, and he believed he had found the root of them. It lay in the Land Laws, and above all, in the Great Land Trust. He unburdened his discovery to the people of Newcastle-on-Tyne.

Other countries, he explained, also suffered from enormous trusts and combines and monopolies, which interfered with the natural growth and development of the nation's industries, even crushed them out. But such trusts as in, say the U.S.A., were ephemeral; ours were part of the social fabric. They had their beginning in the days of William the Conqueror, and the first was this Great Land Trust.

"In London alone the land is worth about £500,000,000—worth more than all the municipal debt throughout the kingdom—the money which has been sunk in great municipal enterprises, in water-works, sanitation, lighting, tramways and roads. Who created the wealth? Not the landlords! London was a swamp, and the landlords did not even create that! All the wealth of this great city has been created by the industry, the energy and the enterprise of the people who dwell in it."

Lloyd George had regarded Britain, then the greatest trading nation of all time, as the world's most powerful Missionary for Peace. He saw her, too, as the foremost pioneer of social justice; and it was increasingly in this role that he would treat her until suddenly, nearly a decade later, the thunder of artillery broke over Europe and set back all his dreams. Meantime, he cried "we mean to eliminate hunger from British civilization."

The Landlord, of course, was not the only demon in the Lloyd Georgian drama of popular politics. Indeed, he was not even the worst, for ignorance might often be pleaded in mitigation of this rich man's crimes, whereas "no poor man could afford to be ignorant". The Priest, to be sure, lurked ever in the shadows "with his black sceptre, to ensnare and enslave the souls of children". Most sinister of all, however, in the Triumvirate of Evil, was the Brewer, "the Simon Legree of the tragic slave trade of Drink".

It was not only that the nation's annual liquor bill ran up to close upon £200,000,000 or double that of the United States, and far more than our own National Budget. Lloyd George claimed that the estimate of employers of labour was that more than one-third of the permanent unemployment of the country was due to drink. It was a greater handicap to Britain's trade and industry than all the tariffs in the world put together; the 160,000 convictions for drunkenness every year went to prove that. Worst of all, though drunkenness was slightly declining among men it was increasing among women.

"A nation that is suckled on alcohol is doomed . . . as long as Drink is allowed a free hand on the hearth the result will be that although you may convert your slums into garden cities, your garden cities will in a short time be reduced to slums."

The Trade was anathema to Lloyd George for another powerful reason; it was one of the pillars of the Tory Party.

They were quite frank, and even crude about it. During the House of Commons debates on Balfour's Licensing Bill of 1904 Lloyd George quoted one of the leading Brewers as saying:

"We put them into power, and if they treat us properly we will keep them there. But if they don't we'll chuck 'em out!"

Lloyd George commented:

"The Tory Government is standing a drink to the chuckers-out . . . and begging not to be put out in such weather as this! The Licensing Bill is a Party bribe for gross political corruption—an act which Tammany Hall could not exceed "

And then he, in turn, assumed the mantle of Jeremiah, and prophesied in ringing words the coming doom of the Trade.

"The cry of the orphan has risen against it, the wild plea of the poor madman, the moaning of the myriads to whom it has brought shame and sorrow has ascended to the Throne of God against it. Now the Arm of the Most High is uplifted against it, and woe to the statesman, woe to the party, woe to the government that intervenes between the recreant and its doom!"

He was eagerly sought after to speak on every Radical platform and for Lloyd George in those days, this included the Labour. He was often to be found in company with "Mabon" Abraham, the Welsh miners' leader, with Will Crooks, and even Keir Hardie; Lloyd George was the leader of the "Keep Left" group in the Liberal Party, because he wanted to keep it abreast of the industrial movement then on the march in Edwardian England.

An interesting note came into him in the Chamber of the House of Commons one day in April, 1905, "to ask a favour". The writer said he was a young lawyer who had just been adopted as Liberal candidate at Walthamstow, and had arranged a meeting in the Baths there *before Easter*, because after it the water was let in for the summer and the space for any public gathering was thereby much diminished. So, could Lloyd George possibly come while the place still accommodated a couple of thousand people?

"I would be so very glad if you found you were able to be my sponsor at my first appearance," concluded the writer.

He signed himself John Simon, and said he would wait in the Outer Lobby for an answer. Besides being a lawyer, he shared with Lloyd George a consuming political appetite, a Welsh origin, and a Manchester birthplace.

Lloyd George still suffered at this time from serious trouble with his throat. The newspapers reported that he was "under tuition with his voice". Treatment may have been a truer word, but—it sounds almost unbelievable— nervousness played quite a part in it. The reader will recall Lloyd George's own account of the feeling of "coal dust in the mouth" which he experienced during his maiden speech in the House of Commons, not an uncommon thing during that ordeal. But Lloyd George added, that if he went for a month without speaking, he felt exactly the same sensation when he next rose to address the Chair. Indeed, to the end of his days this great orator suffered chronically, from "nerves" before he delivered any prepared speech. It may have been the compliment which every speaker owes his audience of being keyed up to make his effort for them, as the veteran fighter fusses in his corner of the ring before the bell sounds, or the sprinter quivers on his marks as he awaits the starter's pistol shot.

In the autumn of 1905, so painful did his malady of the throat become that an operation on his tonsils was necessary. But, then, as a result of it his tonsils began to bleed profusely. It was lucky for him that Mrs. Timothy Davies, his friend's wife, was at his house when this occurred. She hastily summoned a young Welsh specialist, Dr. William Lloyd. Another ten minutes, said Dr. Lloyd, and Lloyd George would have been dead.

It left him terribly weak, and in any event Lloyd George was pretty well worn out by his repeated journeys and exertions. By doctor's orders, he went on holiday to Italy to rest and regain his strength for the General Election, which could not be delayed beyond 1906. Faithful Brother William, who had borne far more than his own share of the family trials, went with him.

But hardly had they settled down at Rapallo than business called William home. There were already rumours in the air of coming political events. The brothers arranged a code, and William set off by train. Lloyd George proposing to stay another week and then return by sea. William reached London on 2 December, where he heard the certain, dramatic news. Balfour had decided to resign. At once, he cabled Lloyd George the codeword, who left that same night.

He arrived on Sunday, 3 December, 1905. Next week he was a Cabinet Minister, as President of the Board of Trade, in Campbell-Bannerman's new Liberal Government.

Fifteen years Lloyd George had been in Parliament, the "talking-shop". Now he had crossed the threshold of the powerhouse.

·   ·   ·   ·   ·   ·   ·

He was in exceptional company. There has not been throughout British history a more talented team of men in Government. The names of four of them will go down the years as famed Prime Ministers.

They represented Liberalism, under the broad cloak of Campbell-Bannerman, from the Imperialist fringe of Asquith (Chancellor of the Exchequer) and Grey (Foreign Office) to the Radicals, John Morley (India Office), Lloyd George (Board of Trade), Churchill (Under Secretary for the Colonies) and on to the "Lib-Lab" John Burns (Local Government Board). The rumbustious ex-Labour agitator of the great Dockers' Strike of the 'eighties, however, turned out in practice to be the most reactionary of all administrators, as well as the most peacock of politicians. He proceeded to snub all his old industrial associates and to surrender himself to his new officials.

It was not John Burns but Lloyd George that the audience in the great national Westminster Theatre had their eye upon, as he stepped up at the age of forty-three to his first job in Government. Friends found some relish —and critics a potential parallel—in the fact that it had also been Joe Chamberlain's first Cabinet appointment, at the age of forty-four. From a portrait on the wall in his new House of Commons room, "Radical Joe" gazed down upon his latest successor, thoughtfully, Lloyd George said. Everyone else wondered what was going to happen now.

Lloyd George began carefully. His was a highly technical task, if not the most technical in the Government certainly the most complex.

"I am an amateur," he confessed, "but so must everybody be, in some sense, in this office. For if a shipping man is chosen because it involves questions of trade and navigation, the same chap has also to deal with railways, tramways, electric lighting, industrial patents, bankruptcy and company law!"

Nothing, of course, could be settled before the General Election, for the new Liberal Government was without either a mandate or a Parliamentary majority. Balfour hoped that they would hang on long enough to embarrass themselves, and certainly he was willing to refrain from adding anything on his own account to precipitate a decision.

But by this time, Balfour held the Tory Party in very dubious discipline. It had not been possible to patch up peace within the ranks over the Tariff quarrel. Many Nonconformist Liberal Unionists had returned to their old Radical allegiance as a result of the Education Act. Many Tory working men had been alienated by the late Government's acceptance of the Taff Vale Judgment, in which the Judges had ruled that the Trade Unions could be sued for actions committed by their agents and their funds made liable for damages. Campbell-Bannerman resolved to go to the country at the earliest possible moment in the New Year.

"The best fighting general" went joyfully to war. This time he did not need to fight for his life among his own folk. His local opponent was Mr. R. A. Naylor, an amiable timber importer, who put up an unconvincing case to Caernarvon Boroughs that it would benefit them to levy a tax on all other commodities except the wood for their furniture. Lloyd George was able to roam far and wide in the country, and he did, lending reinforcement at any weak point along the Liberal front. He was able to repay at least four friends, Timothy Davies, Charles Henry, Arthur Crosfield and Alfred Mond, by speaking on their behalf. All four were duly returned to the House of Commons. He spoke, too, on "Lib-Lab" platforms.

He did not have to struggle anywhere so furiously as of old. Lloyd George said nothing memorable in the memorable 1906 General Election, though he summed up the issue in characteristic terms.

"Protectionists are fighting to increase rent-rolls; Free Traders to increase bread rolls. Free Traders are fighting for the Big Loaf; Protectionists are fighting for the Big Loafer."

Methodically, he calculated the cost of "Chamberlain's Unnecessary War" to each city that he visited. Thus, he reckoned that to Middlesborough it had added £110,000 a year as her share of the increased national expenditure. A fair summary of Lloyd George's 1906 Election Speech is: "*This* is what the Tory Government cost *you*—and it constitutes *my* case."

He added, confidently: "I believe that there is a new order coming. It is a quiet, but certain revolution, as revolutions come in a constitutional country, without doing injustice to anybody, but redressing those injustices from which the people already suffer."

At Hanley, he added at least one more to his collection of Retorts to Hecklers. He was speaking on the evils of intemperance when he was repeatedly interrupted by the catcalls of an elector, who himself afforded a first-hand example of the validity of the speaker's arguments.

"Sound like the echoes of an empty cask," suggested the Chairman. "Oh, no," said Lloyd George, "the gurgling of a very full one."

The Election was an earthquake. First warning of its nature was the overthrow of Balfour himself in East Manchester. "The dykes have been opened," exulted Lloyd George, "and reaction in all its forms will be swept away."

Certainly, organized Conservatism in the House of Commons was borne off on the flood. The Tory–Liberal Unionist Majority of 130 was replaced by a Liberal majority of 200, not including the 54 Labour Members, who invariably voted with the Liberals, and the 83 Irish Nationalist Members, who generally did so.

"Sign your X at the ballot box! Sign it deep, deep with all your hearts!"

Lloyd George had urged the electors of Caernarvon Boroughs, as he submitted himself to their judgment for the fifth time. On 25 January, 1906, they delivered the verdict:

Lloyd George	.	.	.	.	.	3,221
R. A. Naylor .	.	.	.	.	.	1,997
Liberal Majority	.	.	.	.	.	1,224

"This old nation has risen from one end to the other, and there will not be a single Conservative left this day week," said Lloyd George. "For the first time, Wales has become one in the cause of Freedom, and the nation, like the Israelites of old, has commenced its march from the land of bondage, without leaving a single tribe behind."

Every Welsh seat was either held or captured by the Liberals and their Labour Allies. The Established Church suffered almost as severe a political setback as the Tory Party. In the House of Commons as a whole, more Dissenters were returned in the 1906 General Election than at any time since the days of Cromwell.

The warrior turned to the workman's bench.

Lloyd George now gave the country a foretaste both of his energy and his capacity. Half a dozen real reforms stand witness to his work. They were framed and made Law within two years, and all these measures were carried through not by the steam-rollering of a political majority but with the cordial acceptance of both Parties in the House of Commons.

The first was the Patents Law Amendment Bill. This was designed in the main to prevent foreign patents from being registered in this country (it was done in order to secure the effective safeguard of the laws of Britain) and then being worked almost entirely abroad and even denied operation here. In 1906, more than half the patents so registered were held by foreigners and operated elsewhere. Lloyd George argued that this was an abuse of Britain's free economy.

A second, and still more considerable achievement of the new President of the Board of Trade was the Merchant Shipping Act of 1906. This was a determined and successful effort to codify the shipping legislation of the past fifty years, the revolutionary era of the shift from sail to steam. It involved a mass of technicalities, and Lloyd George made history in Whitehall by the frank way in which he summoned to his conferences the best available exponent of every powerful interest concerned. They had to hammer out between them the question of the loadline of all ships using British ports; they had to give sanction to such reforms as had already been carried out in the best of British ships as to the crews' food, fresh water, living space, medical care, remittance of wages and repatriation; they had to extend this Seamen's Charter in many ways to passengers, especially steerage. It was done to the general satisfaction.

Other measures included a new Companies Act, ensuring information to shareholders and creditors; an Employers' Liability Insurance Act to strengthen the safeguards of workmen's compensation for accidents in industry; a Census of Production Act; a drastic revision of the Consular Service overseas in the interests of British traders, and a mutual agreement with France, Belgium and Switzerland to clear trade samples through the respective Customs by a common code of marks, seals and stamps.

The British Press—in 1906 most of it was hostile to the Government, and had previously not spared criticism of Lloyd George—discovered unexpected virtue in the President of the Board of Trade.

"There has grown up a new Mr. Lloyd George," wrote *The Times*. "The keen but ever courteous Minister . . . bitterness has gone from him" (*Daily Mail*).

All pleasant enough. He told the Law Society, on their presenting him with his portrait, that when he entered the Board of Trade he was

"feeling like a mariner who has been all his life on stormy seas in a very frail craft and has suddenly been appointed to the position of Harbour Master: there is a calm about it which is most soothing."

To his friend, young Charles Masterman, he confided:

"When I came to the Board of Trade I was in a blue funk. I thought 'here am I with no business training, and I shall have to deal with all these great business men'. I found them children."

But if the sun shone on Westminster, thunder rolled in Wales. A new Welsh Revolt was in the air. And this time, it was against Lloyd George!

In April, 1906, Mr. Augustine Birrell, the new Minister of Education, had introduced a Liberal Education Bill. It was based on the Colonial Compromise, but it was still far too liberal for the House of Lords. They slashed the Bill and sent it back to the House of Commons. To the indignation of Lord Lansdowne, the Government declined to pick up the pieces. They refused to accept a single one of their Lordships' amendments. The Liberal Education Bill was buried in December.

The reaction on Lloyd George was as expected. The Lords, he said, had been up to their old trick of debasing the coinage of democracy before it was put into circulation. A bull in a china shop was much safer as beef than as bull, and a House of Lords which went mad at every show of Liberal colour would have to be dealt with "like over-angry bull". The House of Commons, whatever gibes might be cast at it, was a picked Assembly. There, the sailor who had worked before the mast, the fireman who had worked in the stoke-hold, sat side by side with the great shipowners. Workmen, professional men, men of business, combined to represent the industry of the country; the House of Lords represented the idleness of the country. They represented vested interests, privileges, monopolies.

Speaking at Oxford in December on the Rejection of the Bill by the Lords, Lloyd George concluded a lively speech with the words:

"I think that the time has come, if the House of Lords insists on main-taining a claim to reject legislation that comes from the representatives of the people, to consider another great question. If a dissolution comes sooner or later, it will be, in my judgment, a much larger measure than the Educa-tion Bill that will come up for consideration, if the House of Lords persists in its present policy. It will come on an issue of whether this country is to be governed by King and Peers or by the King and his People."

It was most strongly resented by King Edward VII. He had already, in July, had occasion to send a complaint to the Prime Minister about Lloyd George's public speeches. In October, he had again taken exception to a reference by Lloyd George to the House of Lords, and his Secretary, Lord Knollys, had written to the Prime Minister intimating the King's displeasure. Sir Henry Campbell-Bannerman undertook to convey the protest to Lloyd George, at the same time putting up a certain defence for his Minister.

". . . Lloyd George is essentially a fighting man, and he has not yet learned that once he gets inside an office his sword and spear should only be used on extreme occasions. In all business connected with his department and in the House of Commons work, he is most conciliatory, but the combative spirit seems to get the better of him when he is talking of other subjects."

Lord Knollys had replied on 18 October, agreeing that

"Your view of Mr. Lloyd George appears to me to be a fair and good one from what I have heard about him. The King will be glad to hear that you have written to him (Mr. Lloyd George) about his speech!"

After receiving the King's complaint, Lloyd George himself had written to Sir Henry Campbell-Bannerman . . .

"I am greatly obliged to you for the kind way in which you convey to me the King's rebuke.

If you wish me to make no further reference at present to the House of Lords question, of course I shall take care to avoid it."

Now, in December, the Oxford speech again aroused the Royal wrath, and again the King's Secretary wrote to the Prime Minister . . .

Sandringham,
Norfolk.
3 December, 1906.

"Dear Sir Henry,

The King desires me to point out to you that Mr. Lloyd George brought in His Majesty's name in the speech which he made against the House of Lords at Oxford on Saturday.

The King sees it is useless to attempt to prevent Mr. Lloyd George from committing breaches of good taste and propriety by abstaining from attacking, as a Cabinet Minister, that branch of the legislature, though His Majesty has more than once protested to you against them. . . .

But His Majesty feels that he has a right, and it is one on which he intends to insist, that Mr. Lloyd George shall not introduce the Sovereign's name into these violent tirades of his, and he asks you as Prime Minister to be so good as to take the necessary steps to prevent a repetition of this violation of constitutional practice, and of good taste.

The King says he has no doubt he shall be told that it was only a 'phrase', but he must really make a point of his name being omitted, even from a 'phrase' in Mr. Lloyd George's invective against the House of Lords.

Believe me, yours very truly,
Knollys."

The Prime Minister replied on 4 December:

"Dear Lord Knollys,

I deeply regret to learn that the words of one of the King's Ministers have been such as to give offence to His Majesty, and on receipt of your letter I took the earliest occasion to see Mr. Lloyd George.

As you are aware I had previously remonstrated with him as to his previous utterances in which he seemed to exceed his usual traits in condemning the actions of the House of Lords and in assailing the constitutional position of that House. . . .

Mr. Lloyd George assures me that, bearing in mind the warning and rebuke of the former occasion, he endeavoured to be moderate on Saturday and I think he did not at least greatly err. . . .

I pointed out to him that His Majesty was chiefly annoyed by his introduction of the King's name which it was of course entirely improper to bring in, as making His Majesty in some sense a participator in a political controversy.

I presume that the passage referred to was that in which he said that it was not right to be governed by 'The King and the Peers'; he would bow to 'The King and the People'. He explained to me that he would have considered it would be disrespectful to speak of 'The Peers' alone and 'The People' alone, omitting a reference to the Supreme Head of the State; and he therefore used the phrase reported out of respect without the slightest idea of employing any connivance or co-operation; and that it was so understood.

Mr. Lloyd George begged me to lay before the King the expression of his profound regret if he had inadvertently offended and I would simply express the hope that His Majesty will, in view of the great tension of opinion and following which this keen controversy has evoked, look with indulgence on any indiscretion which might have been committed. . . .

Believe me,

Yours very truly,

H. Campbell-Bannerman."

A second letter from Lord Knollys pointed out that the King realized that the Lords' action had aroused angry feelings amongst Liberal M.P.s, but his complaint about Lloyd George was that some of his speeches had been delivered before the Education Bill had even been introduced into the Upper House.

"The King says," wrote Lord Knollys, "Mr. Lloyd George appears to forget that as a Cabinet Minister he cannot, with propriety, indulge in that freedom of speech which, if he were a private Member, he would be at liberty to indulge. . . ."

When the Bill had been duly passed His Majesty did not expect Ministers to refrain from criticizing the conduct of the Lords, but he did expect them to abstain from advocating their abolition, which coming from *His Ministers* would place him in a false position, and which would be improper language for the responsible advisers of the Crown to use.

While these Palace protests were being registered, popular fury was mounting, at any rate in Wales, the area most intimately affected by the Education Quarrel. There the Nonconformists, frustrated in their quest for a "free" education, turned back to their ancient heart's desire of a "free" religion, i.e. Disestablishment of the State-endowed Church—and this time, they were determined to have their price, or be done with Liberalism! At the first meeting of the Welsh National Liberal Convention after the dissolution of January, 1906, Lloyd George, from the Chair, had pledged the Prime Minister's word that Disestablishment would be dealt with at the earliest opportunity. Nothing whatever had been done, except to set up a Royal Commission to inquire into the existing Church situation in Wales. Now, in the spring of 1907, the mutterings swelled into a menacing rumbling.

Lloyd George went up to Caernarvon to quieten it. For once, the magic failed. Sullenly, stonily, his fellow-countrymen heard him when he pleaded that the House of Lords was the real issue of the hour, that until this institution had been faithfully dealt with no worth-while Liberal legislation could be passed. Silently, the Welshmen listened when he warned them:

> "Welshmen who find the Government manœuvring its artillery into position for making an attack on the Lords, and still go on worrying the Government to attend to anything else until the citadel has been stormed ought to be put in the guard-room."

Then—crash! The rumbling broke in a black storm over the mountains. Not even Lloyd George could do this to his own people! Not even the leader of the last Welsh Revolt read *them* the King's Regulations!

Ten days later, the Congregationalist Association of North Caernarvonshire damned the recreant proposal to postpone Disestablishment. Almost every Nonconformist meeting in Wales followed suit. By the end of the month, the Liberal Association of South Caernarvonshire had unanimously rejected the suggestion of their Member. His closest colleague, Ellis Griffiths, M.P. for Anglesey, cried: "For more than a generation we have been the anvil in the politics of Britain. Now we wish to be the hammer!"

"Mabon" Abraham threatened to make the Welsh Party like the Irish Party—and Mabon was a mighty voice in Wales, especially in industrial South Wales, where already Socialist and Syndicalist agitation was outstripping the appeal of old-time Radicalism to the miners and steelworkers.

Black-bearded, broad-shouldered, deep-chested son of a miner, Mabon (the name is Bardic) had earned a boy's bread himself at the age of ten, in the pits. He had a silver tenor voice, and when he ran short of matter for a speech, which was rare, Mabon would break into song and the miners loved that best of all. He would give them the rousing tune of "Captain Morgan's March" or the mournful, majestic hymn "Aberystwyth", which sounds like the eternal beat of the sea upon the rock coast of Wales. Perhaps, he would give them both.

With Megan at Criccieth, 1913

With Colonel Seeley, Mr. Winston Churchill and Mr. Asquith, Isle of Arran, 1913

Once, in the House of Commons, during a bitter debate on Welsh Disestablishment, Mabon broke into Welsh. Some fool laughed, but Mabon went on—for half a minute. Then he stopped, and said, quietly:

"You laughed. I was saying the Lord's Prayer, in my native tongue. Can you wonder how my people feel when they hear it recited in an unknown tongue?"

Nobody laughed then.

In June, Dr. Robertson Nicoll, Editor of the *British Weekly*, wrote that a General Election would see the end of the Government. There was no need to call Nonconformists from the Liberal camp. The fire that had lit Liberalism to its triumph was dead.

In October, a great Nonconformist Convention was held at Cardiff. Strong resolutions had been set down which amounted to a vote of censure on the Government. Lloyd George was not invited. Welsh M.P.s who were Ministers had been carefully excluded. Then, two days before the Convention, it was suddenly announced that Lloyd George had obtained a nomination as a delegate and would attend! He had come to face the music, before 3,000 people.

The meeting was one of the great testing ordeals of Lloyd George's life. If he failed here, he failed everywhere, and well he realized it. He began, as he had done at Nevin in the time of his Boer War trial, gently. He spoke of the things and the people and the causes that they all knew, and loved, and which bound them together. He made them laugh at their differences, but he did not mock at old comrades now divided. He explained the difficulties of the Government, promised to seek a path through them, defended the Prime Minister.

"Let us be fair, even to our friends. Yes, be fair to us and we will be true to you."

Then suddenly, swiftly, his peroration:

"Who said I was going to sell Wales? Seven years ago there was a little country which I never saw, fighting for freedom, fighting for fair play. I had never been within a thousand miles of it, never known any of its inhabitants. I risked my seat. I risked my livelihood—it was leaving me. (You risked your life!) Yes, I risked my life. Am I going to sell the land I love?"

And in the trembling silence of 3,000 hearers: "God knows how dear to me is my Wales!"

It was the end of another Welsh Revolt.

Already a new cloud was rising out of the sea. The concentration of Capital into vast trusts, and monopolist combines, was being paralleled—after a lag in time—by the organization of Labour into closed-shop trade unions and nation-wide labour federations. And as Labour grew in strength industrially it began to think politically. Indeed, a more menacing question would soon be posed: would the new young giant exercise his power in politics constitutionally via the House of Commons, or outside it? Would the Ramsay MacDonald Socialist parliamentarians win the backing of the trade union movement, or the Tom Mann Syndicalist advocates of Direct Action?

Lloyd George was well aware of the current phases of this new Labour deployment to the Left. He understood the deep causes for it, too. He warned his Liberal colleagues:

"If at the end of an average term of office it is found that Parliament has done nothing to cope seriously with the social condition of the people, to remove the national degradation of slums and wide-spread destitution in a land glittering with wealth; if they shrink from attacking boldly the main causes of this wretchedness, notably the drink and this vicious land system; if they do not arrest the waste of our national resources in armaments; if they do not save up, so as to be able to provide honourable sustenance for deserving old age; if they tamely allow the House of Lords to extract all the virtue out of their Bills, so that when the Liberal statute book is produced it is simple a bundle of sapless legislative faggots fit only for the fire, then a real cry will arise in this land for a new Party. And many of us here in this room will join in that cry."

It was with the zest of a crusader hurrying against the hour-glass that Lloyd George flung himself into tackling, and settling, the menace of a great industrial strike as 1907 drew to a close. All the summer, trouble had been brewing between the Railwaymen and the Companies. It was admitted that the men had grievances, but the Masters refused to treat with their Trade Union because they included only a small proportion of the total staff. Things were headed for a certain clash when Lloyd George invited the Railway Directors to come and see him informally at the Board of Trade. Before meeting them, he had written to the Prime Minister to get his sanction for the general line of action which he suggested that the Government should pursue in this dispute.

Age 44

They must make up their mind, said Lloyd George, that there was going to be no strike. And they must see to it that no cause for strike was left unremedied.

"A strike at this juncture would be disastrous to our trade. It is doing well just now—extraordinarily well—but it is just on the turn here, in the

United States and in Germany, and a strike would have the effect of precipitating the slump here and postponing it in the United States and Germany.

Then there are considerations of public anxiety of the throwing out of employment in winter of hundreds of thousands of miners, iron workers, sailors, etc. We ought definitely to make up our mind that we cannot permit such a catastrophe.

It can only be obviated, if the Directors refuse conciliation—the one way. We must, when Parliament meets, at once introduce a measure making Arbitration in railway disputes compulsory in all cases where the Board of Trade consider the nature and magnitude of the dispute warrants such a course being adopted."

Lloyd George admitted that Trade Unionists were divided in their views about compulsory arbitration in general labour disputes, but generally they agreed that with the railways the case was different, for here the other industries of the country would at once be involved.

"The Conciliation Act itself is a poor thing," ended Lloyd George. "It is only the knowledge that there is something behind it that will induce the Directors to pay any attention to it."

Next week, Lloyd George saw both Directors and Trade Unionists in turn, then called them to meet together with him at the Board of Trade. He reported the same night to the Prime Minister.

> Board of Trade,
> Whitehall Gardens.
> 25 October, 1907.

"My dear Sir Henry,

I had a most satisfactory conference with the Railway Directors and Managers today. At first a little hostile—towards the end they became quite friendly.

I submitted to them a carefully thought out plan for settling disputes with their men—based on schemes actually in operation in the iron, steel and coal trades. I asked them to consider them and if they thought they constituted even a basis for negotiation we could later on discuss details. I also invited them to select six of their number to carry on further negotiations with me. This they promised to do next week and send me the names.

They parted in the most friendly spirit, thanking me with warmth for the tone of my speech to them.

They left in a conciliatory frame of mind. What they will do when they meet next week in secret conclave I cannot tell. But I am very hopeful of a settlement after today's meeting.

> Yours sincerely,
> D. Lloyd George."

There followed nearly a fortnight of hard, continuous bargaining, and then the Prime Minister was able to send this letter to the King:

10 Downing Street.
6 November, 1907.

"I have the honour, with my humble duty, to enclose for your Majesty's information memorandum just received from Mr. Lloyd George intimating the happy result of the negotiations he has been conducting between the Railway Directors and the railwaymen. He describes in a summary way the nature of these arrangements, embodied in a document signed by both parties. . . .

I would further venture to say that the country is largely indebted for so blessed a conclusion of a time of great anxiety and danger to the knowledge, skill, astuteness and tact of the President of the Board of Trade and those around him in his Department.

Henry Campbell-Bannerman."

At the Lord Mayor's Banquet, three days later, all joined in the Prime Minister's tribute

"to my friend and colleague . . . for his great gifts of unconquerable hopefulness, of unfailing courage, and of alert diplomacy".

A few days later the personal blow fell. This was the death of Mair Eilund, Lloyd George's eldest and best-beloved daughter. It was the most enduring sorrow he ever suffered. Mair was seventeen, a beautiful, gifted and sweet-natured child. He adored her, and when she died of appendicitis on 30 November, 1907, his grief almost destroyed him. He could not bear to go home, where they had been so happy together, but slept in his office. His official secretary, Willie Clark,[1] lay there beside him, for he feared for his master's reason or that he might take his own life. Lloyd George's old doubts about the existence of a God returned, and sunk in despair and misery, he would cry out wildly, denying God, condemning God, cursing God, and the wicked ways of a Providence which could take all the joy out of a man's life. Long afterwards, calling at the house of a friend, he was shown into a drawing-room to wait. When his friend came in he found Lloyd George lying on the sofa, shaking with sobs. There was a portrait of Mair on the mantelpiece.

As soon as he could he went away, taking with him to the South of France his two young sons, Richard and Gwilym. (The very day of Mair's funeral he had been summoned to settle a cotton strike.) Never afterwards did he live at 3 Routh Road, Wandsworth. Margaret made a new home for him in 5 Cheyne Place, Chelsea. Mair was buried at Criccieth, a stone's throw from her mother's old home.

Many letters came to him from friends and foes. None he valued more

[1] Later Sir William Clark, G.C.M.G., K.C.S.I., High Commissioner in Canada 1928 to 1934; in South Africa 1934 to 1939.

than the one which was written by a man who had been both his sturdy foe and his stout-hearted friend, the Bishop of St. Asaph. He had lately suffered a deep personal loss himself.

"My dear George,
"I shall not soon forget her face," he wrote of Mair. "Death cannot rob us of the memory & the spirit of such a presence. But after all the iron fact remains. When the blow first falls the hot tears that flow bring some relief, but these pass and the dull heavy weight is there, and there always. . . . I thought it brave and wise of you to plunge at once into work—work which happily gave peace to others. . . . Two thoughts have come often to me. I have dear friends who have lost their only child, and yet they go on as bravely doing their duty. Then there is a thought which it would be unreal to pass over. The 'sure and certain hope', has buoyed me up. . . .
Yours in sorrow as in joy,
A. G. Asaph."

New labours and new responsibilities awaited Lloyd George. Every morning, he strode down the Embankment two miles from Cheyne Place, Chelsea, to Whitehall. The spring evenings were already dark when he returned. That New Year he had framed his Port of London Bill, setting up a Public Authority which would become a model for future legislation. New honours came, too. He was made, in turn, a Freeman of Pwllheli, Cardiff and Caernarvon.

Sir Henry Campbell-Bannerman had long been ailing. In April, 1908, his health finally broke down. He resigned and Asquith stepped from being Chancellor of the Exchequer to become Prime Minister. To his old office, he appointed Lloyd George, whose first financial transaction was to buy Asquith's robes of office. He was forty-five years of age.   Age 45

What a wonderful, sudden exaltation for a man still young in politics, hardly yet entering upon the noonday of his career! For the Chancellorship of the Exchequer carried with its own great office the next claim to the Premiership itself. Not twenty years yet had Lloyd George been on his adventurous, tempestuous journey from the cobbler's cottage in Criccieth to the Prime Minister's home at No. 10 Downing Street.

Indeed, he was now already next door to the Prime Minister's house at No. 11 Downing Street. The Lloyd George family moved there from their own brief new home in Cheyne Place, Chelsea. A strange experience, and especially for Sarah Jones, who was Lloyd George's faithful Welsh cook and housekeeper. Taken to No. 11, on a preliminary visit to the kitchen, which was hung around in the traditional manner with myriads of copper utensils, Sarah threw up her hands in horror. "*Duw anwyl!*" she cried, "what am I to do with all these pots and pans now?"

It was on Sunday, 12 April, 1908, that Lloyd George was appointed

Chancellor of the Exchequer. Next morning, he put in his first appearance at the Treasury. On Tuesday, 14 April, the House of Commons welcomed the new Chancellor with a friendly cheer as he made his way along the Front Bench to his place next to the Prime Minister.

A parliamentary reporter records that he looked "extremely pale and worn".

Long and hard indeed Lloyd George had been labouring in these latter months. In the press of his work, he had found solace, or at least for a time, forgetfulness. He seemed to become again the same kind of man that he had been, though larger. A great tomorrow was promised to Lloyd George.

But the sorrow abided within. The evening of the day in April that he went to Buckingham Palace to see the King, on becoming Chancellor of the Exchequer, he wrote to his brother, William, describing the kindly welcome he had received.

"But I walked home through the rain crying, because I knew my little Mair would not be there to receive me."

CHAPTER X

THE PEOPLE'S BUDGET

"*Set Fair to Dull*", read the barometer at Westminster. Trade had fallen off in the New Year, although Lloyd George claimed that it was no more than a shallow and temporary depression. He proved right; as 1908 advanced, the nation's business began to pick up. Prices and wages rose, too, although it was ominous that wages rose less. The purchasing power of the £ was entering on its slow decline. Mysterious rumbling sounds began to drift up from the cellars of society.

The Irish were fairly controllable. They were still hopeful of their Liberal allies' long-standing pledge to deliver them Home Rule. The Welsh were momentarily stilled. The Tory Opposition had hardly yet recovered from the knock-out blow of 1906. But eldritch voices were rising from another quarter, and even more clamorously. The Women were demanding the Vote.

There were two elements in this movement for the enfranchisement of women. First, there was the N.U.W.S. (National Union of Women's Suffrage) Societies, organized by Mrs. Fawcett, widow of the blind Postmaster-General of a Gladstonian Government. Now sixty years of age, Millicent Fawcett had been fighting this battle for the greater part of her lifetime. These were the Suffragists. They were democratic in constitution, law-abiding in operation, and not "anti-man" in mood, for they hoped to win by reason the backing of the men for women's claims. Public meeting and petition were weapons of the Suffragists.

Secondly, came the W.S.P.U. (Women's Social and Political Union), led by Mrs. Emmeline Pankhurst, widow of a Socialist barrister, and her daughters, Christabel and Sylvia. These were the Suffragettes. Frail little Mrs. Pankhurst led an army of Amazons, autocratically organized, disciplined and commanded, trained in the tactics of direct action to exact their "rights", and in some cases so far feminist in attitude as to invite the suspicion of abnormality.

Formed at Mrs. Pankhurst's house in 1903, the W.S.P.U. had succeeded in getting a Private Members' Bill for women's suffrage as far as a First Reading in the previous House of Commons. It had then been laughed off the floor. In the present House, Emmeline's daughters had barely restrained her from creating a scene in the Ladies' Gallery.

"You have baulked me, both of you," she wept. "I thought there would have been one little niche in the Temple of Fame for me!"

There would still be time.

There would be straggling processions in the streets of women with long

Edwardian skirts, tight corsets and wide, plumed Edwardian hats and parasols, carrying the purple, green and white bannerettes of the W.S.P.U.

They would hide under the platform at Liberal Ministers' public meetings, or climb up into the rafters and heckle, or cackle, there until they had to be ejected, sometimes with the loss of half their clothes. They would assault Mr. Asquith on the golf-course, wreck Winston Churchill's most carefully prepared perorations, blow up Lloyd George's new house at Walton Heath. They would stuff paraffin-soaked rags in the pillar-boxes and set them alight, padlock themselves to the rails of the public galleries in the House of Commons, slash the paintings in the Art Galleries, smash with flints or hammers the windows of politicians' homes, West End Clubs and West End stores. They would endure forceful mob-handling by police, whom they had provoked to fury by their own insults and assaults. Some would learn the wonderful newly-popularized Japanese ju-jutsu, and throw strong men on their backs. They would be sent to prison, go on hunger-strike there, suffer forcible feeding, torture themselves to the point of death—or release, and being released, would promptly break the peace again.

The most determined martyr of them all, Miss Emily Davidson, red-haired, green-eyed, half-demented girl, denied the sacrifice of her life when she leapt from an upper floor in Holloway Prison after a hunger-strike, was killed in the end on Derby Day, 1913, when she flung herself under the flying hooves of the King's horse as it led the field, thundering round Tattenham Corner.

The day before, Emily had gone to lay a wreath at the foot of Joan of Arc's statue. Six thousand women trudged in her funeral procession to St. George's, Bloomsbury. The granddaughters of the Victorian Age surely paid their gate-money to get out of the seraglio.

The only other storm for the moment (spring, 1908) was the one brewed by the Beer Trade, who were organizing their private Public House protest against the new Liberal Licensing Bill. This Bill did not propose to revert to the conditions which had obtained before Balfour's own contentious measure. Instead, it offered the publicans a term of fourteen years' security, or else due compensation. After that their licences could be withdrawn if the local magistrates so ruled. It was reckoned that the total number of licences would be reduced by about one-third. The Trade appealed to their customers to fight the Bill as an un-British attack on Liberty and an un-Christian attack on property. "THOU SHALT NOT STEAL!" ran the placards on the brewers' drays.

For the first time, the forces of the Trade and the Episcopacy (as represented by the Archbishop of Canterbury and the Church of England Temperance Society, who supported the Licensing Bill) met in head-on and violent collision. This break in what he had once described as "the offensive and defensive alliance of rum and ritualism" impelled Lloyd George to make a fresh effort to bring about a compromise on the Education question.

Golfing with Mr. Asquith, Holyhead, June, 1914

It failed once more, but the experience persuaded him that in certain things he had better friends on the other side of the front than on his own.

There was Mr. Reginald McKenna, who became First Lord of the Admiralty as a result of the Cabinet reshuffle which had brought Lloyd George to the Exchequer. Discussing at dinner with Balfour the possibility of this event a few months before "Reggie" McKenna had confided:

> "If George ever should become Chancellor he would be a very unsound one. Of course, *you* disagree with us, but you *can* understand our principles. Lloyd George doesn't understand them and we can't make him!"

Another Cabinet colleague with whom Lloyd George exchanged cold eyes was Haldane, Secretary of State for War.[1]

It did not make for a Happy Family in the Liberal Cabinet that when Lloyd George went to the Exchequer, the two new Service Ministers (the Navy and the Army were the only really big spending Departments in those days) happened to be McKenna and Haldane.

The first clash in Asquith's Cabinet came that summer over the Army Estimates.[2] It was not Lloyd George, however, who challenged them, but the young man who had succeeded him as President of the Board of Trade, Winston Churchill. It was obvious that they had been exchanging notes.

Promotion to Cabinet rank in those days involved resubmitting yourself to the electors at a by-election, and this Churchill had done at North-West Manchester. Despite the eloquent reinforcement of Lloyd George at the Gaiety Theatre, "making in my native city of Manchester my first speech as Chancellor of the Exchequer", the Lancashire electors rejected Winston Churchill, who promptly retired northward upon Dundee, where the sitting Liberal Member had been prevailed on to accept a peerage. Next month, he got in. Flushed with triumph at his electoral vindication, the energetic young President of the Board of Trade arrived back in the Cabinet to take a deep interest in the War Office. He produced a detailed memorandum arguing that the British Army was too large and too expensive. He called for a reduction of staffs, and of the medical, transport, ordnance and engineer services. The date was 18 June, 1908, the anniversary of the Battle of Waterloo.

Haldane read it with baleful content. He had the answers.

A week later he replied in detail. Some of the "problems" which Churchill had attacked simply did not exist; the British Army staffs were proportionately lower than those of seven other leading Powers, and the total strength of our Army, compared with the armies of the Continent of Europe, was smaller than in Wellington's time (or even Marlborough's!) He pointed out that Germany possessed expeditionary forces of far greater strength than

---

[1] Later, Viscount Haldane.
[2] Before the Budget is framed in the spring, the Service Estimates are, of course, naturally discussed for many months, beginning in the previous year.

the infant one with which we were alleged to be "menacing" our neighbours. After all, we had "certain Treaty obligations which might compel us to intervene on the Continent".

Nobody appears to have noted this significant phrase. Haldane's defence of his army was complete. Churchill withdrew. When he and the Chancellor of the Exchequer challenged the next Service Estimate (for McKenna's Navy) they took care to prepare a better case.

A Tory newspaper labelled them Cleon and Alcibiades. We have seen Lloyd George already ten years earlier cast (by a Welsh Nonconformist scribe), in the role of the shoemaker demagogue of Athens; it was Churchill's *début* in print as the renegade aristocrat who joined the rabble. He much enjoyed the classical insult. He was not particularly happy at the Board of Trade, though pleased enough to be promoted. "I've got this pie too late," he complained. "Lloyd George has pulled out all the plums."

The Old Age Pensions Bill was going uneventfully through the House of Commons piloted by Lloyd George, and openly opposed only by a handful of Diehard individualists led by the Liberal Diehard, Mr. Harold Cox. The pensions proposed ranged from 5s. a week for old folk aged seventy (if their income did not exceed 8s. a week), down to 1s. a week (if their income was 11s.). Paupers and convicted persons were excluded. Lord Rosebery, who had turned aside from horse-racing to counsel Nonconformists on Law-breaking over Education, delivered himself of the economic opinion that "a scheme so prodigal of expenditure might be dealing a blow at the Empire which could be almost mortal".

The Tory leaders abstained from voting against the Bill, though Bonar Law alone had the sincerity to record his vote for it. In the end, the Bill was sent up to the Lords almost unaltered, where, in turn, with a sorrowing shake of the head at the ruin it was about to bring upon the country, Lord Lansdowne let it pass.

Lloyd George made a rare slip of the tongue as the Bill left the Committee stage of the House of Commons. Admitting that revenue was hard to come by, he said: "I have no nest-eggs. I am looking for someone's hen-roost to rob next year."

The phrase trailed him for many a year, and cartoonists blessed its author.

They were not the only careless words that bore trouble on that summer's air. In the *Bystander* of 29 July, 1908, in a column entitled "The World's Pageant", this paragraph appeared:

"Mr. Chancellor's Troubles."

"All is not going well with Mr. Lloyd George in his new and exalted sphere. Not only is he having a most uncomfortable time of it politically, as a result of certain queer intrigues conducted by him and a certain colleague in connection with a proposed reduction of Army and Navy expenditure, but rumour is now busy as to the existence of embarrassment of another kind, which is even less likely to prove of assistance to his career. Mr. George, has, of course, been overloaded with flattery of late, especially from the fair sex, which is always difficult for a man of 'Temperament' to resist. The matter may, of course, be kept quiet. Also, it may not. *Nous verrons.*"

It did not help the Editor in the action which Lloyd George promptly brought for libel that the page-heading under which the offending column as well as others appeared, read:

INDISCRETIONS—IRISH AND OTHERWISE

On 16 September, 1908, *The Bystander* printed the following:

"Mr. Lloyd George: An Apology

"In a recent issue, we inadvertently published a paragraph reflecting upon Mr. Lloyd George. The statements were made entirely without foundation and we most sincerely regret having made them. To mark our sense of the pain and annoyance which we have caused, we have made a donation of £315 (three hundred guineas) to the Caernarvon Cottage Hospital at Mr. Lloyd George's request and in his name."

The gossip went on in the London clubs and drawing-rooms. In the New Year, *The People* newspaper published several articles on the subject. The writer did not mention Lloyd George, but he left no doubt in the mind of the reader as to whom he was referring. He indicated that Lloyd George was about to be named as a co-respondent, that there was no question of his guilt and that his ruin would follow. Another article declared that Lloyd George's friends were trying desperately to stop the case, but that the injured husband was determined to go on with it. The third instalment, however (it was entitled "The Price of Peace"), said that the Chancellor's friends had finally succeeded in their efforts, and that the case would now be withdrawn; it had cost him £20,000.

Lloyd George acted at once. He briefed Mr. Rufus Isaacs, K.C., M.P.,[1] Mr. F. E. Smith, K.C., M.P.,[2] and Mr. Raymond Asquith.[3] For *The People* there appeared Sir Edward Carson, K.C., M.P., and Mr. Edward Duke, K.C. By special arrangement, the case was brought forward for hearing almost at once.

On 12 March, 1909, the court-room at the Law Courts was crowded to the gangways with Society, Politics and the Press. Lloyd George entered in frock-coat, and a hum of excitement rose as it was seen that he was

Age 46

[1] Later Sir Rufus Isaacs, and finally the Marquess of Reading.
[2] Later Sir Frederick Smith, and finally the Earl of Birkenhead.
[3] Eldest son of Mr. Asquith, killed in action in 1916.

accompanied by his wife. They took their seats in front of the Bench, and people stood up and craned to see them. This was a new climacteric in the career of the most talked-of man in Britain.

He went into the box.

"His face was very pale and grave," wrote the *Daily Express* reporter, "and his hands gripped the ledge of the witness box as he answered the questions of his leading counsel."

He had read the allegations in *The People*?

"Yes."

Were they true in substance, or in fact?

"The paragraphs are an absolute invention," said Lloyd George in a loud, firm voice. "Every line of them."

He returned to his wife's side.

Carson rose. He offered no defence whatever. The proprietors of the newspaper admitted the libel, desired to put on record their profound and unqualified regret for having published it, to offer Mr. Lloyd George:

"most sincere and frank apology, without reserve of any kind and to say that the statements were unfounded and absolutely without justification."

They also paid £1,000 damages, which Mr. Lloyd George undertook to devote to charity. This time it was Llanystumdwy Village Hall which benefited, "Not due to the greatness of my own benevolence," observed Lloyd George, "but the hatred of my enemies."

The Judge added that he considered Mr. Lloyd George had behaved with "extreme moderation". He explained that he himself had taken the unusual course of allowing the case to be heard at once, though the pleadings had only been completed the day before. The Chancellor of the Exchequer was actually framing his Budget, and he could not do his duty to his Office or his country with such a charge hanging over his head.

The Budget was, indeed, at hand, and it was to be the most controversial Budget ever introduced in the history of England. Apart from a short visit to Germany the previous August to study the model German system of social insurance, Lloyd George had been working on his Budget ever since the passage of the Old Age Pensions Bill at midsummer. He had now to find the money for these pensions, £6,000,000 in the next financial year.

There was also an extra million needed for the Navy, for the revolutionary "Dreadnought" had now arrived on the scene. The Liberal Government proposed to build four of these giant ironclads in 1909, and to make provision for four more to be laid down in the following spring if the developing international arms race could not be halted. The Admiralty Board, basing their demands on technical advice, called for six. The Tories (briefed personally by Admiral "Jackie" Fisher, himself the First Sea Lord) were clamouring for eight at once. Their slogan:

> *"We Want Eight*
> *And We Won't Wait."*

It was very effective in stirring up the people, and also by this time Jackie Fisher was about to net Reggie McKenna himself, the First Lord of the Admiralty.

There was no love lost between the Chancellor of the Exchequer and the First Lord of the Admiralty. To his friend, Charles Masterman, Lloyd George about this time described his Cabinet colleague as "a good clerk—or perhaps an accountant".

In some ways, a contradictory character was Reggie McKenna. He possessed some oratorical ability on the platform, depending partly on his cocksure attitude. He was competent in debate, if rather disposed to adopt an attitude of I-told-you-so. As a young M.P., he had attached himself to Sir Charles Dilke, and from that once great House of Commons figure he had derived the benefit of his wide knowledge of Parliamentary procedure. Yet whatever Ministerial post he held, McKenna was often selected for attack by the Opposition as being the weak link of the Government Front.

He came of a family of lawyers, and was well off, living in London latterly, in a house built by Lutyens in fashionable Smith Square, Westminster, where he basked in the warm admiration and flattery of an attractive, charming and much younger wife. Flattery was also a well-practised art of Reggie McKenna himself, and if he set his mind to win over anybody he unloaded praise, with subtlety, upon them in full measure. For persistence was also one of his characteristics, and to ram home his point of view he would address himself to the object of his attentions directly, indirectly, by intonation of voice, by look, by gesture, or by significant silence.

McKenna succeeded in building himself up a great reputation both for financial acumen and for political probity. Asquith, in forming his War Coalition Government in 1915, was happy to appoint him Chancellor of the Exchequer, and Stanley Baldwin, in forming his first Tory Government in 1923, was equally anxious to induce Reggie McKenna to accept that office again. Yet while he seemed so shrewd in money matters, McKenna got himself subsequently mixed up in what can only be described as a flight of folly. This was what became known as the "Pepper Scandal" in 1935 when, being at the time chairman of the Midland Bank, he took up several thousand shares in a company based on a prospectus which subsequently landed three of its promoters in the dock at the Old Bailey. He had done no wrong, but he had behaved without due discretion and, indeed, with folly.

Just before he joined Lloyd George in his Coalition Government of 1916, Bonar Law said of Lloyd George and of Reggie McKenna that, when he had first worked with them both as colleagues under Mr. Asquith, he liked Lloyd George most and McKenna least; and when that association ended in eighteen months' time, he liked Lloyd George least and McKenna most. But certainly neither Lloyd George nor McKenna ever liked one another.

In 1908, the Chancellor of the Exchequer was not unnaturally in favour of budgeting for only four dreadnoughts now, and four more (if really necessary), later on. In this second effort during that financial year to restrain Services expenditure, Lloyd George was again reinforced by the President of the Board of Trade, Churchill.

The First Lord and his Admirals argued for More Than Four. They urged that the Germans were already "anticipating" their own Imperial Navy building programme. Lloyd George retorted that the German Government were simply seeking to relieve current unemployment in their shipyards. What *we* really needed was a far-sighted, long-term naval building plan which would always keep us ahead of them, and not subject us to following their year-to-year fluctuations. The present "hand-to-mouth" policy was "a poor compromise between two scares—the fear of the German Navy abroad and the fear of the Radical Majority at home".

But Lloyd George and Winston Churchill were out-manœuvred in this battle, too. McKenna, like Haldane before him, carried the day in the Cabinet discussions. As Churchill has good-humouredly recalled: "a curious and characteristic solution was reached. The Admiralty had demanded 6 ships; the economists offered 4; and we finally compromised on 8."

Morley's characteristic rejoinder had been: "If *he* (Churchill) ever goes to the Admiralty it will be *sixteen* we'll need, not eight!"

Later that year, in September, a still stranger quarrel broke out, when Lloyd George asked the First Lord of the Admiralty if he could possibly speed up the construction of the agreed ships? This was, of course, the other part of Lloyd George's own suggested "Long-Term Plan", by which our own shipyard unemployment problems might be met. McKenna replied, rather pompously, that he could not increase his programme before March "without consulting the Prime Minister" and gave several reasons.

From Lloyd George he got a prompt rejoinder:

"You surely could not have imagined that Churchill and I could have proposed that you should immediately proceed to lay down two or three first class battleships without even mentioning the matter to the Prime Minister. And yet your letter clearly implies that. Even if we were capable of such disloyalty to our chief—and you must allow me to say that you have no right to suggest the possibility of such treachery—we should have been exceptionally stupid to have thought it possible that such a change in naval construction could have been undertaken without the consent, not merely of the Prime Minister but of the Cabinet also.

Churchill, being profoundly impressed by the reports about unemployment coming into the Board of Trade, suggested to me that the shipbuilding vote of next year might be anticipated as to the immediate expenditure of part of it on second and third class vessels. Before communicating this idea to the Prime Minister we both felt that we ought to ascertain your views on the subject first. What would you have said if we had written to the Prime Minister without consulting you?

I am sorry to have to write a colleague—for the first time—in such a strain. But I rather resent being lectured on my elementary duty to my chief. I have never forgotten it, and I am not likely to."

Lloyd George was a very combative man. To Charles Masterman, he confided one night during the long Budget struggle: "I would dearly like a rest, but I would rather have a fight."

Yet the statesman who became one of the greatest of all Britain's War Ministers realized the fearful hazard of war, and if he ever deemed conciliation was possible he always sought it.

At this time, he was strongly hopeful that both in Britain and Germany the parties of peace would win the day. There had been a moment of tension in October, 1908, when following the palace revolution in Constantinople and the overthrow of the Sultan Abdul Hamid ("Abdul the Damned"), Austria had seized the opportunity to annex the outlying northern Balkan provinces of the Turk Empire, Bosnia and Herzgovina. Russia had growled, and threatened. So had Germany, and Russia had climbed down. She would not forget her humiliation on this occasion.

Nor had Lloyd George forgotten either his lunch in London earlier that summer with the German Ambassador, Count Metternich, or his dinner in Berlin the month after with the German Chancellor, Dr. Von Bethmann-Hollweg. He retained a lively recollection of the deep suspicion of the German ruling caste that England's oft-expressed anxieties about the possible "challenge" of the new German Navy concealed her own sinister design, with France and Russia, of encircling Germany in an "iron ring". Lloyd George also recalled a significant scene he had witnessed at Stuttgart in 1908, where an early Zeppelin had crashed on an exhibition flight. There had been no loss of life, but the vast crowd was almost prostrate with grief and frustrated pride. Then, with their defiant chanting of "Deutschland uber Alles" over the wreckage of their great airship, he got a glimpse of the fanatic fervour of German patriotism.

With these reservations, Lloyd George was still not in favour of the Big Navy (or at any rate, the Big Battleship) School. He considered that we should concentrate less on the Dreadnought and more on smaller craft such

as cruisers and destroyers for the protection of our trade routes. In this, the
First World War proved the Chancellor's judgment sounder than that of the
Sea Lords.

As a Radical Chancellor of the Exchequer, Lloyd George was in any event
anxious to save as much money as he could from armaments to spend on
social reform. Though the political pundits of the National Liberal Club were
much concerned with Education, Temperance and Disestablishment, Lloyd
George was well aware that the masses were taking ever less interest in such
abstractions. They were looking for the prospect of material and immediate
improvement. He proposed to offer it to them in his forthcoming Budget.

It would shake the politicians out of their current complacency, too. Yes,
Lloyd George would stir the People themselves. His Budget would be something more than a mere balance-sheet. It would be more than a financial bill
of accounts. It would be a National Bill of Rights. It would be a *People's
Budget*!

> "When you find the House of Commons is lifeless and apathetic you
> must stir public opinion by violent means, so that the public will react upon
> the legislation."

The first thing was to find the new hen roosts.

He could put up Income Tax—which he did, from 1s. to 1s. 2d. Death
duties could be increased—which they were, by one-third on estates of more
than £5,000. At the same time, new concessions and a new imposition made
their appearance. Earned incomes were charged at a lower rate than unearned,
and family allowances were introduced; against this there was a Super Tax
of 6d. in the £ on incomes above £5,000. Spirits and tobacco, faithful old
shaft-horses of the revenue, were also called on to carry an extra load. Whisky
went up from 3s. 6d. to 4s. per bottle. The motor-car had now arrived, and
there were small taxes on both vehicles and petrol.

None of these items, when unfolded in the Budget of 1909, greatly upset
the country, or even the Tory Opposition. The uproar arose over Lloyd
George's new Land Taxes.

There were four of them. There was a Development tax of ½d. in the £ on
the added value realized by the sale of land where this new value was solely
due to the effort and expenditure of the community, a 20 per cent tax on
Increment value and a Reversion duty of 2s. in the £ on the enhanced value
of property when it reverted at the end of a lease. There was also a Mineral
Rights Duty of 1s. in the £.

The Tory Opposition professed to regard these Land Taxes as a revolutionary assault upon property. They certainly did not turn out to be so, for
after the war the Chancellor of the Exchequer in Lloyd George's own Coalition
Government (it was Mr. Austen Chamberlain) repealed them because they
brought in so little revenue that they were not worth levying. In introducing

them, Lloyd George had two prior purposes. He wanted to provide a financial spur to the development of land and minerals, and, even more pressing, he wanted to provide a battlefield to take on the landlords, especially the landed lords.

Lloyd George had been squaring up to the Peers even before the end of that brief honeymoon with the Opposition while he was at the Board of Trade. He thought then that it was already time to tackle their lordships when they threw out the Liberal Education Bill. For this had proved how true was Balfour, when on the morrow of the great Liberal Election victory of 1906, he had boasted:

"Whether in power, or whether in opposition, the Tory Party will control the destinies of the country."

He meant, of course, via the House of Lords. And now Lord Lansdowne underlined it when, the day before the Second Reading of the Licensing Bill, he summoned the Tory five-sixths of his fellow Peers to Lansdowne House, where they decided to throw this Bill into the Parliamentary waste-paper basket after the other one.

"In two hours," cried Lloyd George, "this nobleman arrogated to himself a position no King in England has claimed since the ominous days of Charles the First!"

To the lofty claim of Mr. Henry Chaplin, M.P., that the House of Lords was the "watchdog of the Constitution", he retorted contemptuously:

"You mean it is Mr. Balfour's poodle! It fetches and carries for him. It barks for him. It bites anybody that he sets it on to!"

It was then that Lloyd George had proposed in Cabinet to deal with this hostile majority in the House of Lords, by the simple process of creating sufficient friendly new peers. Surprisingly, it was the veteran Radical, Lord Morley, who most vehemently rejected it.

At Govan, just before sitting down to prepare his Budget, Lloyd George had told a Scottish audience:

"We have heard a great deal about self-government for Ireland. We want self-government for England—and Scotland too! We are not allowed to govern ourselves. There are five or six hundred gentlemen—I beg your pardon, NOBLEmen—in another House who have got there owing to fortuitous circumstances. From the North, from the South, from the East and the West, without anyone in particular summoning them they arrive there and begin to decree what legislation the nation shall be allowed to enact for itself. What do they represent? They do not represent Wealth as a whole, not Capital, not one-tenth of it. They represent the Landowners . . ."

He offered his public some examples of what landownership meant in a great English city, Liverpool. There, Lord Sefton received £16,000 per annum, and a premium of £70,000 for letting land which would be worth £700 but for the great industrial hive which had grown up around it. The three noble lords, Sefton, Salisbury and Derby, between them drew £345,000 per annum from ground rents in that city, while contributing absolutely *nil* to the public expenditure on the place. It must be very hard work receiving and spending £345,000 a year, even if you didn't earn it.

"The first thing to do in lifting up the people is to provide decent habitations. Before you can do that you must grapple with the land question in the towns."

Yes, and in the countryside, too! This was even more the concern of the cottage-bred boy. Everyone knew how the Landlords had acquired those commons where once the people had grazed their flocks. The Landlords considered that it would be better to put that common, waste land under the plough. So, in Parliament, which had then been largely composed of lords of the manor, they passed an Enclosure Act—naturally, purely in the public interest! They put the land under the plough—and the tenants had been under the harrow ever since.

In this mixed spirit of sincere social crusading and deliberate political provocation, Lloyd George had framed the People's Budget.

It was, indeed, a truly tremendous job, and it bore those signs of haste which were the most serious (and alas! familiar) defects of much of Lloyd George's otherwise solid achievement. Both "Willie" Clark and John Bradbury, his Treasury aides, found it necessary to hurry down to Brighton over the week-end before the Budget and stay in the busy Metropole Hotel in order to be near Lloyd George, who was then living in a house in Chichester Terrace lent by his Liberal friend, Lord Rendel.

They got to bed at 6 a.m. on Monday morning, rushed back to London by the early train with the many corrections, as well as several new ideas. Two confidential typists, a man and a woman, then went into action on the revised Budget Speech. At 2 a.m. on Tuesday, Budget morning, the woman broke down, and was sent home by taxi. The job was completed by dawn, and then faithful Willie Clark went off to bath, breakfast, and be back in the office by nine o'clock.

That afternoon, 29 April, 1909, the Chancellor of the Exchequer introduced his historic Budget in a four-hour speech, which almost everyone who heard it agrees was an incredible Parliamentary failure. For a start, he read it—and extremely badly—from an apparently interminable manuscript, stumbling over the sentences and rushing past the full stops. He appeared dead beat, and half-way through Balfour proposed an adjournment to enable him to recover. The sole enlivening incident of the entire performance was when a Tory millionaire M.P. arose as the Chancellor was reading out the graduated scale of the new taxation, and walked out of the Chamber in deep thought. "He went away exceedingly sorrowful, for he had great possessions."

In his peroration Lloyd George claimed:

"This is a War Budget. It is for raising money to wage implacable warfare against poverty and squalidness. I cannot help believing that before this generation has passed away, we shall have advanced a great step towards that good time when poverty, and the wretchedness and human degradation which always followed in its camp, will be as remote to the people of this country as the wolves which once infested its forests."

It was prophetic: this was, indeed, the true beginning of the Welfare State. But it was the Land Taxes that raised, from the Radical rank-and-file, the only real cheers on the Government benches for the Budget that afternoon, for the Labour Party disliked the extra tax on tobacco and the Irish objected to any increases on whisky.

In his lengthy and involved statement, the Chancellor of the Exchequer derived no reinforcement from any spontaneous rally to his side by his own colleagues on the Front Bench. He had had to fight his Budget through the Cabinet before he could fight it through the House of Commons, and long afterwards, he maintained that the first was the hardest battle; Asquith alone had given him steady support there. The Prime Minister did this in his own ingenious fashion, not by backing him up in argument, but summing up at the close of an almost unanimously critical discussion:

"Well, I think there is substantial agreement on this proposal. We will let it stand!"

As at that period no Minutes of Cabinet meetings were ever taken, and no votes recorded, it was left to the Prime Minister to report to the King what had happened.

As for Winston Churchill, his own Radical rash had for the moment abated, though it would come out strong again later on. A number of the Chancellor's other colleagues were not at all displeased with the Budget Speech's mixed reception. In the smoke-room that evening, Leverton Harris, a Tory M.P., suggested to Haldane that Lloyd George had read his piece like a man who didn't understand what he was reading.

"Of course he doesn't," beamed Haldane. "Why, for weeks we've been trying to make him understand clause X, and he can't!"

"A pitiful exhibition!" snorted John Burns, who suspected Lloyd George had lately been colloguing with the Fabian, Sidney Webb, whom Burns detested almost as cordially as he envied his old I.L.P. comrade, Keir Hardie.

Another colleague, "Lulu" Harcourt, son of that Sir William who had invented Death duties, said of Lloyd George at this time, "he uses figures as if they were adjectives". Professing the sternest Radicalism himself, Lulu was perhaps Lloyd George's most inveterate opponent in those Cabinet Budget Battles. His personal feelings were cordially reciprocated.

The Times found the Budget speech:

> "a chaotic welter of half-ascertained facts, half-thought out arguments and half-sincere sentimentalism."

Lloyd George himself thought that it had been a thorough "flop". He said so to Edwin Montagu, when they dined together that evening. Well, there was always tomorrow—and there would be plenty of tomorrows with this Budget! By next morning, the Chancellor had completely recovered from his ordeal, and was playing golf at Walton Heath. According to his partner, George Riddell, he did the first hole in bogey.

Lloyd George had started something, in spite of his critics and his colleagues. The "People's Budget" was not a financial measure. It was an Election Manifesto. Indeed, some of the shrewdest and hardest-hitting of his Tory opponents insisted that it was far more. Instead of presenting a book-keeping account dealing with a deficit caused by Old Age Pensions and an increased Naval Estimate, they charged that Lloyd George was proposing a "social revolution".

They did their utmost to make it seem so, from the storm that they whipped up around the Land Taxes. It was with relief and joy that Lloyd George saw the enemy was making his attack on the Landlords the main political issue; it was exactly what he himself wanted to do. Now, if only the House of Lords could be induced to interfere the Radicals would really have a battle-cry—and one which was a long, safe way away from Free Trade *v.* Tariff Reform!

The enemy again obliged.

Most of the Budget provisions passed the Committee stages rapidly enough, but the Land Taxes were fought line by line, night by night. Altogether, the House of Commons debated the Budget for 72 days and nights (and several all-nights). Members marched through the lobbies for 550 divisions.

Lloyd George stuck it out, sparing neither himself nor his lieutenants. Do the business! To Willie Clark, he remarked years afterwards: "You know, Clark, I often wondered if I could be half as tired as you looked!" To his wife, Margaret, anxiously watching their own mounting Family Budget, Lloyd George would sometimes offer solace. "Well, we'll be out next Election, I expect!"

One evening, indeed, worn out himself, he said to Clark: "I must get to bed for an hour or two. You go over to the House, and listen. If things go wrong, come and wake me."

Haldane was, rather unwillingly, holding the fort that night, on estate duties, and he was being roughly handled. After midnight, Clark went across Whitehall to Lloyd George's bedroom at 11 Downing Street. The Chancellor of the Exchequer was fast asleep, but being roused, he jumped out of bed, shaved, and hurried to the House. He was welcomed with a sympathetic cheer. "He was in splendid fighting trim," says Willie Clark, "at 7 a.m., the House was adjourned in uproar."

The debate continued still in the Cabinet. As the winds rose, there were timid counsellors who considered that it might be as well to throw overboard "this frail freight". On the other hand, Winston Churchill with characteristic enthusiasm—much to the disgust of his cousin the Duke of Marlborough—became President of the "Budget League", which had been formed to carry on propaganda in the country.

Churchill himself addressed great meetings up and down Britain, and led the singing of the rousing "Land Song", set to the tune of "Marching Through Georgia":

> *"The Land! the Land! 'Twas God that made the Land:*
> *The Land! the Land! The ground on which we stand.*
> *Why should we be beggars with the ballot in our hand?*
> *God gave the Land for the People!"*

What kind of land *was* this—the England, Scotland, Ireland, Wales of 1909? How did the people fare, and behave? Who was Who? What sort of Parliament had Lloyd George to meet, and fight?

One thing was as sure as that the Edwardians had succeeded the Victorians, The Absolutely Indestructible British Empire still blazed with sunlit glory. But it was high noon, no longer early morning. Britannia ruled the waves. The City of London ran the banks. Socially, as well as financially, the capital of England was the centre of the world. Kipling still sang. But in Africa, last of the Imperial conquests, Rhodes, best and boldest of the New Imperialists, was dead. Canada, Australia and New Zealand were all busily minding their own business, and (when they bothered to think about it) resenting the idea that Westminster or Whitehall could manage it for them. In India, British policy still tended to deal with the Princes and the proud fighting races of the mountains and the jungle, and to ignore the rising mercantile classes of the ports and cities and overlook the social problem of the labouring and factory masses herded there.

Some other, older Empires, were breaking up, China, Turkey and Morocco. Nobody in the West discerned a deeper truth, except perhaps a certain Russian exile in Geneva named Vladimir Ilyitch Ulianov, whom history will remember as Lenin. In fact, the mould of the world was dissolving.

The process could not fail to affect the country which was the heart of it. A social tide as mighty as that which marked the end of the Feudal System, four centuries before, was beginning to sweep over Britain. The first waves were there for any contemporary observer of the scene to note. So, James Ramsay MacDonald, who saw things more clearly in those days than ever he did later, wrote:

"The Age of the Financier had come. . . . The rich . . . gathered from all quarters of the earth, from American millionaires seeking vainglories which a Republic could not offer, to the scum of the earth which possessed itself of gold in the gutters of the Johannesburg market-place . . . received the homage of every dignitary in society. To the drawing-rooms and into the families of the ancient aristocracy, as to the Parliament of the people, they bought their way."

Such people, MacDonald continued, "did not command the moral respect which tones down class hatreds, nor the intellectual respect which preserves a sense of equality under a régime of considerable social differences, nor even the commercial respect which recognizes obligation to great wealth fairly earned".

The Social Revolution in which we dwell today began, in fact, not by the challenging new classes seeking to overthrow the old ruling class and their way of life, but by energetically climbing up alongside them and aping their manners, dress, language and interests. To get to Ascot, Cowes, to Court, to Parliament in the "right" company was the proper ambition of every bold young adventurer of the Edwardian Age.

You may see it all yet in the faded files of the popular newspapers, in the now-dulled, once glossy society, tittle-tattle journals, in cynical, good-tempered old *Punch*, in the tattered little booklets on "How to Behave" at luncheon, dinner, after the theatre, before marriage, in a hansom cab, at a christening or a funeral. You may read how the Young Edwardian gentleman learned to hold an umbrella correctly, or a lady in the waltz, *scottische* or quadrille; how to absorb asparagus, or brandy; how to entertain his betters, equals or inferiors; how to appear before Royalty, or his Maker.

You may also read how Edwardian Young Ladies were taught to regard marriage. . . . Thus:

"The action for breach of promise of marriage . . . is socially a dead letter for all but the ladies of the dramatic profession and the lower classes."

The manners, like the modes of the Edwardians, if not their morals, were still Victorian.

Parliament was a reflex of these various values. The House of Lords, solid, stolid and Tory, was almost a mausoleum, except that it still retained the vital power to mutilate or reject Radical legislation; a fatal power too, which it had been far wiser from its own point of view to refrain from exercising in the next few months. The House of Commons was otherwise; it was changing with the times, and taking on their mood. If it was no longer the Best Club in Europe, it was still decidedly the most interesting. Lloyd George, in his Boer War days, had thus described both Houses of Parliament:

"It is easier for a rich man to enter the House of Commons than the Kingdom of Heaven. It's still easier to enter the House of Lords! You only have to be born once—and to do nothing else in the rest of your life—to enter there."

In the Ministry itself the movement of change was more gradual. On the morrow of the great popular flood of the Liberal Revival, 1906, Sir Henry Campbell-Bannerman's team—apart from the Radical Welsh lawyer Lloyd George and the ex-Labour agitator, John Burns—had not been so very different in composition from Gladstone's last Cabinet but one. The "Grand Old Man" of Liberalism had firmly believed in a democratic franchise, an aristocratic House of Commons and an autocratic Cabinet. Only with the utmost reluctance had he relaxed his rule of having nobody except gentry for his colleagues, in favour of Joseph Chamberlain, the Radical businessman from Birmingham—and the result had not encouraged Gladstone to pursue the experiment. Twenty years later, in the Cabinet of Campbell-Bannerman there had been posts for three Earls, one Marquess, and two other Peers.

The House of Commons itself was more representative of the shift in the social climate than the House of Lords. Of course, the Old Guard of the Landed Interest were still on sentry duty there. The Tory troop included a couple of dozen elder and younger sons of the peerage. The Bar was also there in force, with Sir Edward Carson and Messrs. F. E. Smith, George Cave and Marshall Hall. The "Beerage" were represented by Messrs. Guinness, Gretton, Younger, and Big Business by the Chamberlains, Robert Houston, Frederick Banbury and the silent, still unobtrusive figure of the new Member for Bewdley, Stanley Baldwin.

With less of Squire strength, but still more of Bar and Business, were marshalled the Liberal Forces. Asquith, Isaacs, Evans, Haldane, Simon were names to conjure with in the Law Courts before ever they commanded hearing in the High Court of Parliament. And Brunner, Mond, McKenna, Markham, Lever, Guest, D. A. Thomas and Runciman rivalled in the world of politics, and for the most part out-stripped in wealth the Tory captains of industry.

There were two other Parties in the 1909 Parliament. The Irish Nationalists, numbering eighty-three, were still split within themselves after the Parnell–Kitty O'Shea scandal, but united for the purpose of harrying the English. Stolid and sonorous John Redmond, reciting his melodious monody of Ireland's woes, led the pro-Parnell Party, always a long way behind his "followers", and irrepressible "Tim" Healy was the real head of the anti-Kitty O'Shea section (Irish memories are long). Soon, indeed, the story of the Irish Party in the British Parliament would be ended, and the House of Commons is always impatient of Members who really represent nothing except themselves.

But Tim Healy continued to interest and influence the House as long as he remained there. He did it usually with wit, but also at times with passion, for Healy was a deeply religious as well as a patriotic man.

A typical "Tim piece" was when, one evening, when the House was in committee, he concluded a series of orations totalling several hours on a Parliamentary measure to deal with water and butter in Ireland, by observing: "Well, Mr. Speaker, it's now ten of the clock, and as the Irish Mail leaves at ten-thirty, I'll bid ye Good Night."

Three other stars twinkled over the stormy Irish Sea in these days—the lanky, saturnine John Dillon ("John Redmond's mother-in-law!") the benign "Tay Pay" O'Connor, and the perky, pint-pot "Duodecimo Demosthenes" Joe Devlin.

The Irish were the Party with a past. The one with a future was the Labour Party. They numbered rather fewer, fifty-three, and were not homogeneous either. A baker's dozen of them were working miners or seamen, such as Mabon or Havelock Wilson, elected on the Liberal ticket and labelled in the jargon of the day as "Lib-Labs". The rest had been selected by the Labour Representation Committee, and this requires a brief explanation.

The Labour Party, at the beginning of this century, was based upon four pillars. *First*, was the Trades Union Congress, in those days very much the preserve of the Craft Unions, bent as much on guarding the "Mysteries" of their trade against the competition of the still unorganized general worker as on protecting their wage rates against the exploitation of the boss. *Second*, was the Social Democratic Federation, which was a Marxist propagandist body founded and led by Karl Marx's own old personal friend and enemy, the top-hatted, frock-coated Old Etonian, H. M. Hyndman. *Third*, was the Independent Labour Party, created by Keir Hardie, a character from the Scottish Lowlands with the appearance and the soul of an artist. Keir Hardie had gone down the pit at the age of eight, and legend said that he had taught himself shorthand scrawling with a piece of chalk on the dim-lit blackboard of the coal-face. Certainly, he emerged from that murky university as fine a propagandist as any in his age, save perhaps one—his future journalistic colleague, ex-soldier, Bob Blatchford, Editor of the *Clarion* and author of *Merrie England*. The *Fourth* corner of the Labour camp was upheld by the Middle Class intelligentsia of the Fabian Society, which moved around Sidney and Beatrice Webb, George Bernard Shaw and H. G. Wells.

In February, 1900, these several bodies had met at the Memorial Hall, Faringdon Street, where twenty-six years later the General Strike was born, and formed the Labour Representation Committee. Its purpose: to raise funds, conduct propaganda and choose candidates to "secure a greater number of working men as Members of the House of Commons".

Thus, the most powerful Labour Party in the world first saw the light of day. Its representatives in this Parliament of 1906–10, besides Keir Hardie,

"Mabon", Will Crooks and company, included Arthur Henderson, Philip Snowden and Ramsay MacDonald. They chose MacDonald, originally as their Secretary and then as their Chairman, thus offering that astute and ambitious political actor his opening engagements on his way to stardom as the first Socialist Prime Minister of Britain.

Such were the members of that memorable assembly who lived in the fake-Gothic labyrinth of lobbies, libraries, committee-rooms, corridors and dining-rooms which is the hearth and citadel of the liberties of England. During the next few months, after the introduction of the People's Budget, the inmates ate, drank and dozed there a great deal more than they did in their own homes. It was the fiercest and the longest Parliamentary struggle since the Great Reform Bill of 1832.

On the floor of the House of Commons, Lloyd George was driven to make substantial concessions in his massive masterpiece. The original 74 clauses of the Finance Bill were expanded to 96, and their strength was much diluted. Outside the walls of Parliament the battle went better.

At Limehouse, for example.

Limehouse belongs now to the coinage of politics. It means demagogy. It conjures up a picture of rabble-rousing, of inflaming class-passions, of holding out wild hopes to the poor and, more especially, of blasting and blackening the rich. "Slimehouse" the Tories (and Whigs) of 1909 called it.

No doubt, Lloyd George's speech in the great hall of "The Edinburgh Castle" on 30 July, 1909, read that way at that time. Still less doubt that it sounded so in that sweltering hall (it was the hottest summer of the century) to that densely-packed, rowdy Cockney audience of 4,000 people, who interrupted almost every sentence with their cheers and laughter, encouraging and provoking the man as he spoke. For Lloyd George possessed the secret of the true orator, who exacts from his audience almost as much as he gives to them.

Age 46

But it does not read that way now. The atmosphere of the excited summer night has gone. (Even "Limehouse" began with a Suffragette uproar.) And the theme has been used so often since, and so much less effectively. When Lloyd George, from Limehouse, addressed the Aristocracy, it was the first time that they had been spoken to like that in Europe since Marat apostrophized *his* "betters" from his bath. Also, this was not a mob orator on Tower Hill, inciting a dock strike. Lloyd George was Britain's Chancellor of the Exchequer. The speech rang round the world.

Yet all he did was to give some examples—they were certainly very vivid, and nobody in the subsequent uproar ever controverted them—of the way in which the marsh between the River Lea and the River Thames had become valuable building sites because of the growth of the vast Port of London. Land which used to be rented at £2 or £3 per acre, had been selling lately at £2,000 an acre, £3,000 an acre, £6,000 an acre, £8,000 an acre!

"Who created that increment?" demanded Lloyd George. "Who made that golden swamp? Was it the *Landlord*? Was it *his* energy? Was it *his* brains, his forethought? It was not! It was the combined efforts of all the people engaged in the trade and commerce of that part of London—the trader, the merchant, the shipowner, the dock labourer, the workmen—of everybody *except* the Landlord!"

He came to the dukes. Ah! The Dukes! They all knew the Dukes, especially in the East End! Now there was the well-known case of the Duke of Northumberland. A County Council wanted to buy a small plot of land as a site for the school to train the children who in due course would become the men labouring on that Duke's property. The rent was insignificant; his contribution to the rates on the basis of, say, 30s. an acre. What did the Duke demand for it for a school? £900 an acre! Well, if it was worth £900, let His Grace pay taxes on £900!

There was the case of the Duke of Westminster ("Oh! these dukes! how they harass us!"). This Duke was in the West End. Mr. Gorringe obtained a lease of certain premises from His Grace for a few hundred pounds a year ground rent. He built up a great business there. When the lease ran out, he went to the Duke and asked to renew it. Oh yes, said the Duke, charging him, instead of a few hundreds a year, £4,000 a year. He also had to pay a *fine* of £50,000. "A case like that is not business," thundered Lloyd George. "It is blackmail!"

The Liberal Government proposed to tax such landlords, because the value of their property was going up by reasons of the growth of population with the increased prosperity of the community. The Landlord objected. He said:

"Doesn't the value of a doctor's business go up in the same way?"
"What! Fancy comparing themselves for one moment! Who is the Landlord? The Landlord is a gentleman—I have not a word to say about him in his personal capacity—who does not earn his wealth. He has a host of agents and clerks that receive for him. He does not even take the trouble to *spend* his wealth. He has a host of people around him to do the actual spending. He never sees it until he comes to enjoy it. His sole function, his chief pride is the stately consumption of wealth produced by others. How does the doctor earn his income? The doctor is a man who visits our homes when they are darkened by the shadow of death: who, by his skill, his trained courage, his genius, wrings hope out of the grip of despair, wins life out of the fangs of the Great Destroyer. All blessings upon him and his divine art of healing that mends bruised bodies and anxious hearts. To compare the reward which he gets for that labour with the wealth which pours into the pockets of the landlord purely owing to the possession of his monopoly, is a piece of insolence which no intelligent man would tolerate."

And then this swift glimpse of the lot of the miner in the dark, mysterious underground, then one of the poorest paid workers in the land:

"I went down a coal-mine the other day. We sank into a pit, half a mile deep. We then walked underneath the mountain, and we did about three-quarters of a mile with rock and shale above us. The earth seemed to be straining—around us and above us—to crush us in. You could see the pit props bent, and twisted, and sundered, until you saw their fibres split in resisting the pressure. Sometimes they give way, and then there is mutilation and death. Often a spark ignites, the whole pit is deluged in fire, and the breath of life is scorched out of hundreds of breasts by the consuming flame."

Meantime, that evening, as the platform party drove home westward, Lloyd George suddenly said, "I'm hungry!" They were crossing Trafalgar Square, so he decided that the restaurant of the Carlton Hotel would be a suitable place for supper. Also a suitable place to challenge the Idle Aristocracy. Willie Clark, who accompanied his master, had to explain to the Manager that these sudden guests, none of them in evening-dress, were the Chancellor of the Exchequer's special party. They were politely, if reluctantly, accommodated, and sat down at a table in the dining-room, amid much nudging and whispering from the rest of that plush company. Luckily, these ladies and gentlemen had no idea of what had just been said at Limehouse.

Next day, the Opposition Press fell upon him with a delighted fury (but Northcliffe came to see him in the morning to ask why he hadn't warned him of what he was going to say?). The Tory leader-writers were driven to the dictionary to find the right expletives for the Chancellor of the Exchequer, and the cartoonists to the wardrobes to find the right fancy-dress. In their pages, Lloyd George appeared in turn as highwayman, hen-roost robber, poacher, pirate, pantaloon, agitator, and anarchist complete with bomb. After two days' deliberation, *The Times* declared editorially that Lloyd George (and Winston Churchill!) were preparing for leadership of a new Party in which:

"those who have anything to lose, no matter what their traditional politics may be, will find no place."

Unionists, said *The Times*, must resist with all their power the thinly disguised Socialism which would shortly uncloak itself and stand forth as the enemies of Liberals and Unionists alike. In the House of Commons, Sir Edward Carson, who was to spend the next three or four years of his own life threatening civil war in Ireland, rose to inquire if such language were permissible in Ministers of the Crown? The Duke of Beaufort announced that he would "like to see Winston Churchill and Lloyd George in the middle of twenty couples of dog hounds".

King Edward VII complained to the Prime Minister. He had objected to Lloyd George's appointment as Chancellor of the Exchequer the previous year, and now it appeared that his fears were only too well-founded. It was the fourth time of his complaining.

After those earlier offences, and explanations, His Majesty had understood that Mr. Lloyd George would, in future, restrain his expressions. Now, here he was again, asking rhetorical questions which dragged the King's name into his political controversies, such as:

"Who is going to rule the Country? The King and the Peers? Or, the King and the People?"

His Majesty was thoroughly annoyed. Angrily, he inquired of his Prime Minister, Mr. Asquith, was there no way to curb the Chancellor of the Exchequer? Mr. Asquith discreetly suggested that maybe the King himself would care to talk to the offender?

A week after Limehouse, Lloyd George wrote to King Edward a letter which some may consider to be surprisingly humble and apologetic, even almost servile; others may suspect that it is subtly insolent.

"Treasury Chambers,
Whitehall, S.W.　5.8.09.

The Chancellor of the Exchequer, with his humble duty to Your Majesty, has the honour to say that he understands from the Prime Minister with great regret that Your Majesty looks with disapproval on the speech which he delivered on Friday last at Limehouse. The Chancellor of the Exchequer would be grateful if he might be permitted to lay some considerations on the subject before Your Majesty.

It is no doubt within Your Majesty's recollection that when the Chancellor of the Exchequer laid his financial proposals before Your Majesty, prior to the introduction of the Budget, Your Majesty was good enough to listen with consideration, and even on some points with sympathy, to his statement. Since then the country has had full time to consider its proposals, and according to the testimony of *The Times* and other Opposition papers this week, the tide is running in their favour.

The Chancellor of the Exchequer, however, has found himself subjected in connection with these same proposals to a storm of hostile criticism, the virulence of which, he ventures to think is without parallel in the history of financial legislation in this country. Many and substantial concessions have been granted in order to remove such inequalities and hardships as have been shown to be likely to arise, and the Chancellor thinks he may fairly say that throughout the protracted discussions in the House of Commons he is admitted to have shown a constant moderation and willingness to meet his opponents. But in spite of this attitude on his part, the violence of the attacks to which he has been and is being exposed has been in no way mitigated, and he ventures to submit to Your Majesty that in his recent speech, the first public speech which he has made since the introduction of the Budget, he was justified in retorting upon his opponents in language which fell short of much that has been said and repeated on the other side.

The Chancellor trusts that Your Majesty will excuse the length of this communication. If he might at any future date be honoured with another audience with Your Majesty, he would greatly value the opportunity for a fuller statement of his position, and for learning direct from Your Majesty what are Your Majesty's views.

D. Lloyd George."

King Edward, who was at Cowes, wrote the following answer:

"H.M. Yacht *Victoria & Albert*.

The King thanks the Chancellor of the Exchequer for his letter of the 5th instant, and for the explanation which he has given him respecting his recent speech on the Budget at Limehouse.

As regards the Budget itself, the King expresses no opinion, but he was very glad to see the Chancellor of the Exchequer on two occasions concerning it and to have had some interesting conversations with him on various details connected with the Bill.

The points on which he spoke to the Prime Minister on Monday last, were those concerning the language used by the Chancellor of the Exchequer, which the King thinks was calculated to set class against class and to inflame the passions of the working and lower orders against people who happen to be owners of property.

The King readily admits that the Chancellor of the Exchequer has been attacked by some Members of the Opposition with much violence, and he regrets it, but he must remind him that though those gentlemen may have passed the fair limits of attack, they are private members and do not hold a high office in the Government as is the case with Mr. Lloyd George.

If therefore the Chancellor of the Exchequer had been a private member, it certainly would not have been within the King's province to offer any official criticism on his speech; but it is owing to the fact that he holds one of the most important offices under the Crown and is an influential member of the Cabinet, which made him feel it his duty, with much regret, to remonstrate with the Prime Minister against the tone of the Chancellor of the Exchequer's speech, and to express to him his fear that Mr. Lloyd George was departing from the best traditions of his high office, traditions that had always been invariably observed by his distinguished predecessors.

The King, in conclusion, must give the Chancellor of the Exchequer every credit for the patience and perfect temper which he has shown, under considerable provocation, during the debates on the Budget.

Edward R. & I.

Cowes, 7 August, 1909."

Later, King Edward VII had another talk with Lloyd George. They again discussed the Budget (such talks were quite unprecedented, and have probably never been repeated). It was worth while, for the King made friends at last with Lloyd George. He said, "I am an old man, and I am giving you advice." He suggested that instead of the Land taxes the Chancellor might collect the same amount of revenue from sugar or tea. But Lloyd George explained that the Liberal Government was pledged against a sugar tax, and that the old folk depended on tea for one of their comforts.

"All right," said the King. "We won't tax their tea."

It was the last time that they met.

On 25 November, 1909, the Finance Bill passed its Third Reading in the House of Commons. Would the Lords throw it out, as Lloyd George so devoutly hoped? It would be highly unconstitutional for the Upper House to meddle with a Money Bill, as *The Times* duly warned them. There had been a great Civil War in England to settle the question of who should control the public purse. But there were dialecticians who argued that this Budget was no mere Money Bill, but a blue-print for Socialism.

Then, in case their Lordships should lag at the last moment, Lloyd George had gone up to Newcastle-on-Tyne on 9 October, 1909, and there given them Limehouse, Second Edition. It was a considerably hotter number. The King had failed to make an enduring impression on his Chancellor of the Exchequer.

The country, the Chancellor of the Exchequer reported to his audience, was doing well. It had begun to recover from the trade depression, which had first come from the United States, the land of high tariffs. Only one stock had gone down badly—there had been a serious slump in Dukes. They used to stand high in the market, especially the Tory market, but now the Tory Press had discovered that they were of no value. Recently, one specially expensive duke had made a speech and the Tory Press said, "Well, now, really, is that the sort of thing we are spending £250,000 per annum on?"— because a fully-equipped duke cost as much to keep up as two dreadnoughts: they were just as great a terror, and they lasted longer.

Then Lloyd George dealt with the Constitutional issue, and the dangerous part which the Tory Opposition was playing.

"The great Constitutional Party! If there is one thing more than another established about the British Constitution it is that the Commons— and the Commons alone—have the complete control of Supply and Ways and Means. And what our fathers established through centuries of struggle and of strife, even of bloodshed, we are not going to be traitors to!"

As long as the Constitution gave rank and possession and power, said Lloyd George, the great Constitutional Party said it was not to be interfered with. As long as it secured even their sports from intrusion and made interference with them a crime, as long as it enforced royalties, and ground rents, and fees, and premiums, and fines, "all the black retinue of exaction", the Constitution was inviolate. It was sacred. But the moment that the Constitution looked round, the moment it began to discover that there were millions outside the park gates who needed attention, then the Constitution was to be torn to pieces!

Lloyd George warned the Lords, and his words echoed ominously through the land:

"Let them realize what they are doing. They are forcing a Revolution. The Peers may decree a Revolution, but the People will direct it. If they begin, issues will be raised that they little dream of. Questions will be asked which are now whispered in humble voice, and answers will be demanded with authority. It will be asked why 500 ordinary men, chosen accidentally from among the unemployed, should override the judgment— the deliberate judgment—of millions of people who are engaged in the industry which makes the wealth of the country. It will be asked who ordained a few should have the land of Britain as a perquisite? Who made ten thousand people owners of the soil, and the rest of us trespassers in the land of our birth? Where did that Table of the law come from? Whose finger inscribed it?

These are questions that will be asked. The answers are charged with peril for the order of things that the Peers represent. But they are fraught with rare and refreshing fruit for the parched lips of the multitude, who have been treading along the dusty road which the People have marked through the Dark Ages, that are now emerging into the light."

Lloyd George went to Edinburgh to make one final gibe.

"In England every Peer is a Peer of Parliament. In Scotland he is not. I don't know why a Scottish Peer is supposed to be inferior to an English Peer. I should not have thought that it was possible."

It was more than enough for the Lords. At Glasgow, Lord Milner advised them: "Throw out the Bad Budget, and damn the consequences!"

On 30 November, 1909, after six days of angry debate, they threw it out. Asquith at once took up the challenge. He advised the King to grant a dissolution, and a General Election was decreed for the New Year. Lloyd George was radiant. "Their greed has overborne their craft," he told the National Liberal Club, "and we have got them!"

He had just time, before Christmas, to deal with the City, and in particular its spokesman, Lord Rothschild, who had addressed a meeting of a thousand merchants in that Sacred Square Mile in protest against the "Robber Budget". For this purpose, Lloyd George returned to the East End, at Walworth on 17 December, 1909. He did not spare the feelings of his Jewish friends.

He could remember a great meeting in the City in June, presided over by Lord Rothschild, who demanded that eight Dreadnoughts should be instantly laid down. The Government ordered four—and Lord Rothschild wouldn't pay. There was a very cruel king in the past who ordered Lord Rothschild's ancestors to make bricks without straw. That was a much easier job than making Dreadnoughts without money. . . .

"Now we are not to have Temperance Reform in this country. Why? Because Lord Rothschild has sent a circular to the Peers to say so. We must not have Estate Duties, and a Super Tax. Why? Because Lord Rothschild signed a protest on behalf of the bankers to say that he would not stand it. We must not have Tax on Reversions. Why? Because Lord Rothschild, as chairman of an insurance company, said it would not do. We must not put a Tax on Undeveloped Land. Why? Because Lord Rothschild is chairman of an industrial dwellings company. We ought not to have Old Age Pensions. Why? Because Lord Rothschild is chairman of a committee which says it can't be done. Is Lord Rothschild the Dictator of this country? Are we to have all the ways of reform, financial and social, blocked simply by a notice board:

NO THOROUGHFARE!

By order of Nathaniel Rothschild."

Lloyd George went off to Wales to whet his sword. On Christmas Night, he attended the Annual Eisteddfod at Llanystumdwy Village Hall. Gaily, he recalled that it was here he had made his first public appearance on a platform, in a new suit of clothes, and had given a recitation for which he had been awarded a prize: "Remember, child, to speak the truth."

"I have really endeavoured to do that all along," said Lloyd George, "in spite of the fact that I was brought up as a lawyer."

CHAPTER XI

"THE YEAR OF THE COMET"

THE year 1910 was the Year of the Comet. It was known as Halley's Comet, from the astronomer who identified it in the troubled autumn of King Charles II's reign. Long before, in 1066, it had been seen on the eve of the Battle of Hastings, again when Owen Glendower set the Welsh Marches afire from the Dee to the Wye. The Comet was believed to foretell the death of kings, or worse. It was seen again in the spring of 1910.

There were two General Elections in 1910, one in January and the other in December. They produced only a couple of stalemates as between the two great Parties. For the Liberals lost their mighty 1906 majority, while the Tories failed to gain one; the Government continued in office after both Elections by the favour of their Irish and Labour allies. There was a tragic   Age 47 moment at the first meeting of the new Parliament, when the stricken old Radical Imperialist, Joe Chamberlain, was led in by his son Austen, and was too weak to sign the roll-call on the table of the House. Twenty years of public life Lloyd George had fought him. But he admired him, and privately he praised Joe Chamberlain's "strong and forcible, but rather savage personality".

The January, 1910, General Election results were:

Liberals	275
Tories	273
Irish Nationalists	82
Labour	40

Perhaps the most significant of these figures was that which recorded the Labour strength. It showed a fall of nearly 25 per cent. The Tribunes of the People may have stirred up their masses to shout, but plainly they had not yet mobilized them to vote.

For the Trade Unionists, the Taff Vale Judgment of the House of Lords had now been reversed by a Private Members' Bill. No longer could a trade union be sued for the wrongful act of any servant. But, just before the 1910 January Election, the Osborne Judgment, by the same House of Lords Court, had ruled that trade union funds could not be used to finance any political Party. This naturally upset the politicos in the Trade Union Movement, who had just acquired Parliamentary dignity as the first product of the machine set up by the Labour Representation Committee. The worker at the lathe or the loom cared a good deal less. A fair social deal was what he wanted.

To reawaken this gentleman's interest in politics had been Lloyd George's primary preoccupation as he sat down to frame his General Election appeal.

He returned to his pre-Budget thought—that the old Liberal "moral" issues of Temperance, Education and Disestablishment had lost their once potent spell. As for Free Trade, as unemployment slowly seeped into the great basic industries and prices crept above wages, it began to appear less as a way of life than as a debatable economic method of existence. The Chancellor of the Exchequer hastened back to the question which he had posed nine months before: The Condition of the People.

On New Year's Day, 1910, he had opened his campaign at Reading, speaking in support of Sir Rufus Isaacs, the Solicitor General.

Lloyd George held up, for his audience to see, the thick tome of Mr. Seebohm Rowntree's study of *Poverty*. That painstaking social detective had discovered that 80 per cent of the children of the slum-dwellers of London and York were "below an average standard" of health. He had found old women of seventy earning 7s. per week at sweated labour, making mats and toothbrushes in their own wretched "homes", for which they paid half of this pittance in rent. He showed that hardworking men were spending on food for themselves and their families a weekly sum smaller than workhouse fare would cost. He revealed that every other would-be volunteer for the Army or the Navy was being rejected as physically unfit for service.

"Four spectres haunt the Poor," cried Lloyd George, "Old Age, Accident, Sickness and Unemployment. We are going to exorcise them. We are going to drive hunger from the hearth. We mean to banish the workhouse from the horizon of every workman in the land."

Next week, at Peckham, Lloyd George had taken Balfour to task for a speech in which the Tory leader had rather loosely spoken about "inevitable" war with Germany. Now, where before had the British public heard of "inevitable war" (for, of course, the people who believed in this monstrous concept were those who made wars)? Ah, yes! We had sent such a man[1] to South Africa who believed in this inevitability and, sure enough, within a few months it had happened.

Mr. Balfour had gone on to report that important Germans had declared that they would never allow England to adopt a Protectionist system (which made the Balfour blood boil!); furthermore, there was a belief widespread in Europe (from which he, Mr. Balfour, disassociated himself) that because of our blindness to our responsibilities, we were designed to succumb in such a contest.

Blindness? Lloyd George undertook to deal with that first! Had Mr. Balfour seen the recent figures of Britain's naval strength? Lloyd George had taken the trouble to look them up just before coming out. In battleships,

[1] Sir Alfred Milner, High Commissioner at the Cape. 1897–1901.

smaller ships, smaller craft, and submarines we were overwhelming. Ah! But the Germans were building? Yes, and so were we building, and we would build faster than they built! We would not only build Dreadnought for Dreadnought, but we would build more. We had the money. Yes, and above all, we had the men!

"After all, it is not so much the gun, as the man behind the gun. We have more than two to every one that they have. If we had only one to every two, I would be willing to fight them, for ours are the best and most tried sailors in the world! No, do not be afraid of seeing the German Army on Peckham Rye!"

The Man Behind the Gun! Is this a pacifist speaking? No, this is he who within a few years would be the greatest of all organizers in massing six million of his countrymen behind the guns, and then, with a dramatic call to back them up with enough munitions, would mobilize millions more of Britain's men and women, too, to "Stand behind the Man behind the Gun".

Then, having treated Peckham to his own particular brand of patriotic pride, the Chancellor of the Exchequer had resumed his more habitual role of peace-loving Citizen of the World, and solemnly reproved the Tory leader for

"plucking the feathers of the German eagle's tail with his war alarms—a trick played in America by the lowest type of politician, the last resort of a desperate man who sees that his game is lost."

Lloyd George had then advanced upon the Midlands. The General Election was now warming up, and he had something to contribute to the process. A New Year spurt in trade put spring into his heart, and what was in Lloyd George's heart generally came out ere long on his tongue. At Wellington, Shropshire, he developed the theme of unemployment insurance.

You could no more account for the fluctation in trade than you could account for the weather. There were seasons of trade, as there were of time. They were having a springtime in trade right now. Looking at the Board of Trade returns, he could hear the birds singing! There had been winter—now the winter of trade was past. It would come again. The true business of statesmen was to fill the granaries, so that there would be grain for the people in the dark, drear days.

Later, the same evening, at Wolverhampton, he was less lyrical. He was discussing the Peers:

"They have no qualifications—at least, they *need* not have any. No testimonials are required. There are no credentials. They do not even need a medical certificate. They need not be sound either in body, or in mind. They only require a certificate of birth—just to prove that they are the first of the litter. You would not choose a spaniel on these principles . . .

It was the most offensive onslaught yet; there was some disorder at Wolverhampton, and considerably more at Stafford the next day. At Louth, Lloyd George was the target for a shower of stones from a "turbulent crowd". At Grimsby, an even more lively mob awaited him at the Skating Rink, whence he had come to deal with the popular "German invasion" threat started by Balfour, and dished up again on this occasion by the sitting Tory Tariff Reform champion, Sir George Doughty.

Once more, the police took an anxious view, and after the speech the Chancellor of the Exchequer was persuaded to make another strategic retreat under escort. A cordon was drawn round the building and, surrounded by a police guard, Lloyd George set off from a side-door. They walked about a quarter of a mile along a deep drain cutting and, after climbing a wall and crossing the railway, entered the Fire Brigade Station, while the mob still threatened to burn down the Skating Rink. It brought him memories of Birmingham.

These Election experiences had encouraged Lloyd George to provoke his enemies further. Besides, he would much rather discuss House of Lords Reform than Tariff Reform. At York, on 14 January, 1910, he referred to these Lords who had stolen the Common Lands from the people, and had been sitting in judgment on thieves ever since in the magistrates' courts.

For his own Election contest at Caernarvon Boroughs, the Tories had produced a candidate who was a Welshman, a lawyer, and the locally popular Mayor of Bangor, Mr. H. C. Vincent. The result was as before:

Lloyd George (Liberal)	.	.	.	.	3,183
H. C. Vincent (Tory)	.	.	.	.	2,105
Liberal Majority	.	.	.	.	1,078

The morning after the General Election, the Great British Public awoke to ask themselves what it had all been about. It was not easy to say.

The Tories had increased their strength, though not enough to turn the Liberals out, and they certainly had not scored much success with their latest Tariff Reform campaign. The Free Trade party still held most of the industrial seats, and they had actually gained some in the great ports of riverside London, in Glasgow, Newcastle, Hull, Grimsby and Cardiff. Most of the country-side had gone to the Tories, a fact which was not lost on Lloyd George in considering future Radical policy. The "Irish Question", in the form of Home Rule, had also been raised, but (it must be admitted) chiefly in the areas, like Liverpool, where the Irish vote had to be considered.

Nor was the Lords v. Commons controversy much clearer in the new 1910 Parliament than it had been in the old 1909 one. In opening the Liberal Election campaign at a great Albert Hall rally Asquith had promised his cheering regiments:

"Neither I nor any other Liberal Minister supported by a majority of the House of Commons is going to submit again to the rebuffs and humiliations of the last four years. We shall not assume office, and we shall not hold office, unless we can secure the safeguards which experience shows us to be necessary for the legislative utility and honour of the Party of Progress."

Most people took it to mean that the Liberal Prime Minister, if he were returned to power, would ask the King for a guarantee that he would support him in curbing the House of Lords. The Irish Party had certainly believed this, and they now demanded that the Peers be dealt with before the Budget. The Irish were determined to hold the Liberal Party to its pledge of Home Rule, and they understood very well that the Peers were now the last barrier in the way; furthermore, there was that unfortunate whisky tax. The Irish Party itself, by the way, was as usual riven with feud, this time William O'Brien and Tim Healy against Redmond, and this made their support of the Liberal Government even more dubious at the very moment when it had become even more necessary. The Tory Opposition missed no opportunity of pointing out that the Government's "composite majority" could only be maintained by a series of "under-the-counter deals" to settle its IOUs with both its Irish and its Labour associates.

This prospect had not been lost sight of by the Liberal leaders themselves. As a matter of fact, both Asquith and Lord Crewe, surveying the political battlefield after their latest so-called victory, had come to the conclusion that the retirement of their own Government was inevitable. It was Lloyd George who vigorously argued against any such defeatist idea. These formidable allies of the Government were, after all, he urged, only pressing for policies which the Liberal Party itself had endorsed again and again—Home Rule for Ireland and Social Reform for the United Kingdom. Besides, the enemy was desperately worried himself over his own troubles.

It was true. Two General Elections, in turn, in 1906 and 1910, had the Tories fought and lost, and there were many in their ranks who blamed these setbacks upon Tariff Reform. The Tariff Reformers retorted that their policy had failed to convince the electors only because it had obviously not yet convinced their own leaders. The inquest continued. Balfour, the Tory leader, went on half-heartedly trying to damp down the Protectionist issue in the Party camp, while their latest Liberal ally and encumbrance, Lord Rosebery, set out whole-heartedly to try to revivify the House of Lords.

In February, 1910, the Government introduced into the Commons three Resolutions to deal with the Peers: (1) Excluding the House of Lords from interfering with any Money Bill whatsoever, (2) Declaring that the House of Commons should have power to pass into law, in three successive sessions during the lifetime of a single Parliament any other Bill, whatever the verdict of the Lords, and (3) reducing the Parliamentary lifetime from seven to five years.

These Resolutions were passed by the House of Commons on 14 April. The same night, the Prime Minister laid on the table of the House a Parliament Bill to give them legislative effect, with a preamble proposing to substitute for the House of Lords:

"A Second Chamber constituted on a popular instead of a hereditary basis."

The Prime Minister warned that if the Peers rejected this Bill, then he would tender advice to the Crown as to how to pass it into law. If this was not done, then either the Government would resign or recommend a dissolution of Parliament.

The House of Commons then took up the rejected People's Budget, and with a majority of the Irish Members, passed it and returned it to the House of Lords. Sullenly, their Lordships this time accepted it. On 28 April, the Budget passed through all its stages within a few hours. Next day it received the Royal Assent, exactly one year from the day it had been introduced.

On 6 May, 1910, King Edward VII died.

The Prime Minister, returning with the First Lord of the Admiralty, McKenna, from an Admiralty yacht cruise to Gibraltar, learned the news one night at sea. He has vividly described going up on deck, and there the first sight that met his eyes was Halley's Comet blazing in the sky. Asquith "felt bewildered and, indeed, stunned".

At once, the face of British politics was changed. Both the Liberal Government and the Tory Opposition leaders were anxious to spare the new King a political crisis at the outset of his reign. For now Parliament was almost evenly divided between the two great Parties. Certainly they had their political differences, but was there no common ground on which they could meet and frame an Agreed Programme for a few months? The idea of a Party truce quickly became very popular.

It does not much matter now who first thought of it, though at the time Lloyd George was widely credited with it; in certain quarters it was also suspected that he, at any rate, hoped that in the outcome it would result in overthrowing his own leader, Asquith. The truth is that Lloyd George did indeed prepare a memorandum, both proposing a truce and setting forth a basis for it. He sent it to Asquith, who consulted his closest colleagues: Lord Crewe, Sir Edward Grey and Haldane. They approved the idea, and only then was Balfour approached.

Lloyd George was at this time much under the spell of Balfour's attractive personality.

"I could work with Balfour myself," he confided to his golfing companion, Sir George Riddell, "he is kind and courteous, but his underlying sense of class superiority is the trouble with him. It makes him unpopular with his own people like Bonar Law and Carson."

Lloyd George was respectful, but not yet cordial towards Bonar Law and Carson. Much closer to him (through their mutual friendship with Winston Churchill) was that Tory buccaneering barrister from Birkenhead, the debonair, devil-may-care, F. E. Smith, who was generally in favour of any interesting coalition, being also quite genuinely in favour of obtaining office in it. To him Tim Healy once complained of Asquith, who had kissed hands with King Edward while in Biarritz on his appointment as Prime Minister.

"Would you kiss hands on foreign soil, F.E.?" demanded Healy.

"I would kiss hands in hell, Tim," answered F.E. honestly, as ever.

He possessed a lively and dangerous wit, which he did not confine to his table talk, but allowed to spill into and to spice his political, and even his legal opinions. Bonar Law used to say of F.E., quoting the Arab proverb: "Easier to keep a live coal in the mouth than a witty saying."

Thus, F.E. once had reason to believe that Sir Robert Houston, a wealthy Lancashire shipowner M.P., intended to make him one of his heirs. Sir Robert belonged to the Right Wing "Diehard" element of the Tory Party, although he was far from being one of its leading figures. He was rather vain of his appearance and especially of his fine red beard, and as the years advanced he went to some trouble to preserve its fiery colour.

"Well, of course, he's the original Dye-Hard!" explained F.E. one evening at a dinner-table. He got a great laugh, and lost a large inheritance.

Brilliant, eloquent, insolent F.E. often delivered his daring speeches without any previous preparation. Pomposity was what he adored to deflate, although, like other human beings, he had his lapses. While he was Lord Chancellor, the present Lord Beaverbrook gave a dinner-party at the Hyde Park Hotel, to which F.E., who had been to some official reception, turned up late wearing medals and the magnificent sash of some Order. Proposing the health of his host, F.E. made him the butt of his ridicule, so that everyone roared with laughter. But the Lord Chancellor did not join in the joke when Beaverbrook, in replying, assured the company that this distinguished guest had been paid a large fee to appear, provided he did so in fancy dress.

F.E. had a high, bold spirit, but his temper was uncertain and his ability outstripped his conduct. He loved Cakes and Ale, but he also loved real comradeship, and whatever changes politics might bring, F.E. stayed loyal to his friends. If he gave you his hand, he gave you his heart. Needless to say, he had an ample ration of enemies.

Already, in 1910, F.E. had that profound regard for Lloyd George's qualities which later led him to write:

"I do not believe there has ever been a man who discerned more swiftly and certainly the moods of an assembly—Cabinet, Parliament, or political meeting—with whose mental or emotional processes he was concerned."

As for Lloyd George himself, he very early on developed a personal liking for F.E. His relationship with several of his own Liberal colleagues was getting decidedly cool.

Already, in March, 1910, he had discussed with his well-liked lieutenant, Charles Masterman, the possibility of resigning one of these days, breaking-up the existing administration and forming "A Government of Business Men" under his own leadership.

For the moment, the prospect of getting something solid done over Housing, Health and Unemployment Reform, Insurance, Pensions for Widows, Home Rule (perhaps for Wales and Scotland, as well as Ireland), National Development (of the land, railways, roads, canals and electricity) and even National Military Service, strongly stirred Lloyd George's imagination. With reasonable luck, the country might also say good-bye to those hoary old hobgoblins, Education, Drink and Disestablishment. As for Free Trade or Tariffs, let there be an impartial inquiry into the working of both systems. To Masterman Lloyd George said: "I think Free Trade is defensible. But I don't regard it as sacred. Some of you chaps have got Free Trade consciences. Now, I have not!"

He never had. Years later, he asked a Liberal candidate who insisted on putting Free Trade in the forefront of his election address; "Do you want to get to Heaven, or to Westminster?"

The surprising new item in this Lloyd George 1910 agenda was National Service or Conscription, then being passionately advocated up and down the land almost alone by old Field-Marshal Lord Roberts, V.C. ("Bobs"). Surprising, that is, to most people. Lloyd George, the man the public mistook for a pacifist, was in favour of National Service, the servicemen to be selected by ballot. He had been impressed by what he saw of the Swiss Militia System during one of his journeys on the Continent. Thus, another of the great acts of the dark Year of Decision, 1916, thrust its shadow forward into the sunlit midsummer of 1910.

On 17 June, 1910, the Prime Minister summoned a Conference to his room at the House of Commons. It is typical of the unimportance which the Edwardian world attached to anyone outside the "great historic parties" that no invitation was issued to either the Irish Party or to Labour.

For the Government, the delegates were Asquith himself, Lord Crewe, Augustine Birrell and Lloyd George. The Tory team were Balfour, Lord Landsdowne, Austen Chamberlain and Lord Cawdor.

Altogether, the Conference met twenty-two times. No minutes were taken and no official report was ever issued, though some of its members have left fragmentary memoirs. Discussion ranged beyond the items already listed, to cover the idea of a Referendum to the People on selected subjects and a Joint Session of both Houses of Parliament. Asquith tells us that among the witnesses they examined on the possibility of a Joint Session were Dr. Nicholas

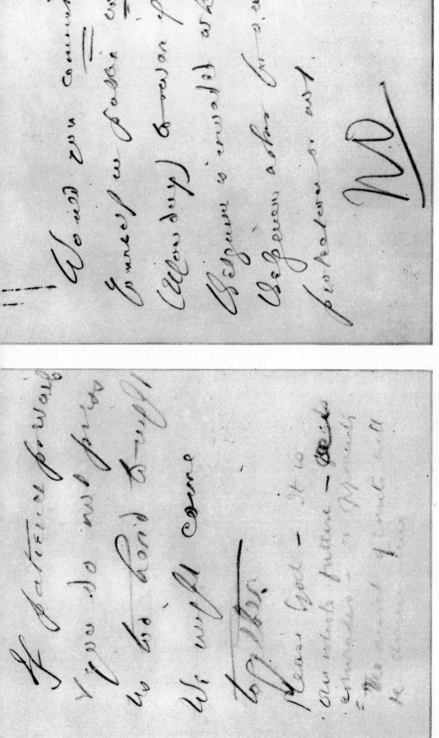

Notes exchanged between Lloyd George and Winston Churchill during Cabinet Meeting of August 1st, 1914

Murray Butler, President of Columbia University, New York, and Mr. Fielding, of Canada, the greatest living authority on the working of that Dominion's constitution. The Prime Minister later claimed that he told a friend at the time that he never expected anything to come of this Two-Party Conference, and declared that though the experiment was worth trying,

> "the conditions were never propitious. Party feeling was running very high, and the ardent spirits on both sides viewed with a certain amount of rest-lessness, if not of suspicion, what they feared . . . might be going on behind the closed doors of a *camarilla*."

Such sceptics were not entirely unjustified. For Austen Chamberlain has written that Lloyd George was so keen on a deal that he proposed a Coalition to carry it out, if necessary. He had become suddenly impressed with the growing menace of German rivalry in commerce and naval power.

Lloyd George's idea of a suitable Cabinet, at this time, is said to have included Asquith as Prime Minister, Balfour as President of a National Defence Committee, Lord Lansdowne as Foreign Secretary and Austen Chamberlain as First Lord of the Admiralty. Had he abandoned that idea of a "Business Government"—or was this first Coalition Cabinet intended to precede a second one? Churchill, though not a member of the Conference, was apparently (along with Bonar Law and F. E. Smith) taken into close confidence. He was another who strongly favoured a modern Ministry of All the Talents—though not when he was asked his view upon the feasibility of it from the standpoint of one who would be left out![1]

Later, being placated (by being associated as prospective War Secretary), Churchill became an enthusiastic salesman for the Coalition scheme, and urgently pressed it upon all customers. During this period, Churchill regarded, and reluctantly acknowledged Lloyd George as the supreme political artist of the age. The friendship of the "Heavenly Twins", as they were dubbed, con-tinued close, if intermittent, for there remained more than a suspicion of mutual jealousy between them. Mrs. Lucy Masterman recalls in her book a sharp passage-at-arms between them earlier in the year at No. 11 Downing Street. According to her story[2]:

> "Winston was here last night," said Lloyd George, "and he got up just as he did that time in the Spring. You remember, Masterman, he began to fume and kick up the hearth-rug, and became very offensive, saying: 'You can go to Hell in your own way, I won't interfere. I'll have nothing to do with your damned policy,' and was almost threatening, until at last I had to deal very faithfully with him, and remind him that no man can rat twice."

[1] *C. F. G. Masterman*, by Lucy Masterman (Nicholson & Watson).
[2] *Ibid.*

G

In this, too, as Churchill has himself observed, Lloyd George under-estimated his friend's resource.

Up to within ten days of the final breakdown of the Two-Party Conference Lloyd George still believed that a Bargain was possible. He ardently hoped so. He said:

"In some ways the Conference is more Liberal than the Cabinet. I should have much less trouble in getting the section about National Defence through the Conference than through the Cabinet. Reginald (McKenna) would not like it at all."

It was not to be. One evening, a worried-looking Balfour called to see Lloyd George at No. 11 Downing Street. Diffidently, he explained that any prospect of forming a National Coalition Government was vitiated by the objections of some of his colleagues to serving with Lloyd George. Whereupon, Lloyd George offered to stand out. It seems to have made the resistant Tories more suspicious than ever.

So that the early Coalition dream died, and with it the Ballot Conscription Plan, which might have given us a million trained men by the outbreak of war. When that war came, Lloyd George one day showed his draft scheme to Edwin Montagu. "Well, now!" exclaimed Montagu, "I always thought you weren't really a Liberal!"

When the House rose in July, 1910, for the long summer adjournment, Lloyd George went off with the Mastermans on a motor tour, via Bavaria, to Italy.

"He was an extraordinarily attractive and, at times, extraordinarily provoking travelling companion," wrote Lucy Masterman in her diary, herself an interesting and provoking woman.

Her husband, the son of an evangelical farmer, was then one of the most brilliant young men in Britain. Scholar, lecturer, author, journalist, Charles Masterman was a real Radical. He had worked as a social student in the slums of Lambeth, and Masterman not only studied the "submerged tenth"; he cared in a deeply personal way about their plight, and he fought for them. He brooded, too, for he had a strain of deep melancholy, which he hid, beneath a mask of cynical wit. While his work was precise, his personal appearance was always untidy ("dirty", complained Margot Asquith, the Prime Minister's sharp-brained, sharp-tongued wife), and his style of living was chaotic. Though a sparkling speaker, Masterman somehow never struck the public imagination. He had a host of personal friends, and ever welcome to any group in club or lobby was his gangling frame and long nose and loose lock of hair falling across his brow.

This interesting and highly unorganized trio passed on their journey south through Oberammergau, where they saw the famous Passion Play. It seized the imagination of Masterman, but Lloyd George remained obstinately determined not to be impressed. "This is not *my* Christ," he kept saying. "This is the Christ of the Theologians!" On the other hand, he considered the Oberammergau Judas very decently done!

When he came home in September, Lloyd George paid a duty visit to Balmoral to stay with the new King and his family.

It turned out to be another holiday, for life there was simple and on a fine day they all went out with the children, picnicked in Queen Victoria's hut on the river bank and afterwards played hide-and-seek in the woods, the King and Queen included. Lloyd George charmed everyone, and the King presented him with one of his father's walking-sticks while the Queen gave him some presents for Megan. He wrote to his wife, Margaret:

"I liked it much more than I ever dreamt I should, entirely owing to the unaffected and simple kindness of the two principal persons here."

Later, at Buckingham Palace, King George asked him: "When are you coming to teach that boy of mine some Welsh?"

When Lloyd George replied that he had not been invited, but would come whenever His Majesty thought proper, the King said: "You don't need an invitation. Come whenever you like."

So Lloyd George went, and taught the Prince of Wales. He developed a very fair accent.

On being told of Lloyd George's success with the Royal Family, John Burns snorted: "Yes, and he's had housemaid's knee ever since."

It had been a wonderful summer. Indeed, the Year of the Comet was rather a wonderful year to be alive in. The aeroplane had arrived from across the Channel, piloted by M. Bleriot in 1909, and now M. Paulham had flown from London to Manchester: distance 188 miles, time 4 hours 20 minutes. A telephone service connected Paris with Glasgow. More remarkable, that wife-murderer, Crippen, and Ethel Le Neve (disguised as a sailor-boy), were located in mid-Atlantic by the mysterious agency of a Marconi wireless message and arrested on their arrival in Canada. There was a terrific City boom, both in oil and rubber shares, and young Empire adventurers were prospecting for oil in Newfoundland, Australia, Africa and Burma, while others were clearing jungles to plant rubber trees in Malaya. For 18,000 motor cars were now spluttering along the roads of Britain, average price £200 at the Olympia Motor Show, where there was also on view, for £170, a "pretty 8-h.p. touring car, able to travel at as much as 30 m.p.h., given favourable circumstances".

At His Majesty's Theatre the newly-created stage knight, Sir Herbert Beerbohm Tree, was terrifying ten-year-old girls like Megan Lloyd George, who was taken by her father to see him as Fagin in "*Oliver Twist* . . . diabolical, saturnine and leery". The actor came to their box during the interval, and Megan liked him even less. There were as yet no public cinematograph theatres, but the bioscope was a popular attraction. In the great world of adventure, England's Captain Scott was setting forth on his last, heroic voyage to plant the Union Jack on the South Pole.

Lloyd George's own affairs prospered in a modest way. He had built himself, for £2,000, an attractive new house, Brynawelon, with a view on the hill above Criccieth, for which he had not yet fully paid. (Indeed, he told George Riddell that this sum represented his whole estate.) In London, he lived in No. 11 Downing Street all the week, and retired at the week-end to his Brighton rented house. Brighton was a great draw to Lloyd George in these days; he was fascinated by the rich and rather mixed company which flocked into the great hotels there on summer evenings. "I do not know where they come from," he used to say, "but I know where they are going to."

Close friends of Lloyd George's were wealthy Charles Henry, Liberal M.P. for the Wrekin division of Shropshire, and his attractive wife, Julia, who was the sister-in-law of Edna May, the original Belle of New York. Henry, who was Jewish, and had come to this country from Australia via South Africa and the United States, left more than a quarter of a million pounds in his will to found scholarships at Oxford and Cambridge, Harvard and Yale to foster friendship between Britain and America. He was interested in journalism as well as politics, became one of the proprietors of the *Westminster Gazette*, and later founded the *Jewish Guardian* as an anti-Zionist organ.

Lady Henry made herself one of the great Liberal Party hostesses at their spacious house in Carlton Gardens. Balfour and Ramsay MacDonald were also often to be found there. Summer week-ends at the Henry's country house near Henley-on-Thames brought these notable figures and many visiting American friends down from London, and every year the Parliamentary Cricket Match was played there.

Another hostess whose company Lloyd George enjoyed was Domini, Lady Crosfield, the charming Greek wife of Sir Arthur Crosfield, Liberal M.P. for Warrington. She was rich in her own right, being the daughter of a Greek merchant. She was a dear personal friend of Madame Veniselos, wife of a rising Cretan leader. An international tennis champion herself, her thirty-bedroomed "country house" (Witanhurst), built in a fifteen-acre park-land estate in Parliament Fields, Highgate, was the scene of many a tournament graced by Balfour ("he always asked for and invariably obtained a new set of tennis balls because he claimed that it helped his eyesight") and F. E. Smith ("he drank a bottle of fizz before the game because it helped his vision"). Lloyd George took no part in the tennis, but both he and his family loved to roam the garden. In particular, Lloyd George himself enjoyed the musical evenings for which Witanhurst was equally famed. There was usually a string quartet, and much fine music. But the fun began when Sir Arthur Crosfield sat down at the piano and accompanied the Chancellor of the Exchequer in Welsh songs and hymns. Lady Crosfield recalls of her guest:

"He had an intense, almost feminine fascination, great personal charm, and talked with sometimes startling insight. He acted quite a bit, and he had small feet of which he was vain."

The Great Summer passed. With it, died the last hopes of an accommodation at the Two-Party Conference. It finally broke down on 10 November, under pressure from the extremists in either Party camp. One who strove hard, from the outside, to bring about "a real and honest truce" was F. E. Smith. Bonar Law was also said to be in favour of this, though "less vehemently so". For Bonar Law had by no means given up believing that the Tory Party would win office by its own strength. Perhaps he was right, if the generalship had been better.

Rising on the other flank of the Liberal Government was that other challenge. Lloyd George put his finger on the truth in sure fashion when he spoke one Sunday in October, 1910, at the City Temple. This famous home of Preachers was then presided over by the Reverend R. J. Campbell, who was exciting and infuriating London society with his New Theology, the doctrine of the God with us.

"Jesus was Divine! So am I! So are you!" thundered this Prophet with the compelling eyes and white, waving locks (his enemies often omitted to quote that last sentence when attacking him; not that Campbell cared). To his crowded congregation, Lloyd George now delivered a speech which created as much stir as any of Campbell's own sermons.

The Problem of Destitution was his theme, and the discourse of it was the more remarkable because it was very nearly devoid of any striking illustration or analogy. With one of these rare exceptions Lloyd George opened his case:

"Humanity is like the sea—it is never quite free from movement; but there are times of comparative calm, and times of turbulence and violent commotion. Everything today points to the fact that the storm cone has been hoisted, and that we are in for a period of tempests."

What was the cause? Idle to seek it in any condition of things peculiar to one country, for trouble racked every land, from East to West. They had it in Portugal, in Germany, France, Austria, Russia, Italy and America, which were all highly-protected countries. We had it in the North of England, in South Wales and in Scotland, which were under the banner of Free Trade. What, then, was the root of the unrest which made the worker everywhere reflect upon the contrast between his own hard, grey life, and that of more favoured, though not more meritorious members of society?

Lloyd George answered that it was because men of all Parties now not only recognized the ugly fact of Poverty—much more vital, *they believed it to be remediable*! It was not hopelessness which stirred the discontent of the masses, but Hope! And if the great historic Parties were going to do nothing about it, then new and dynamic forces would be called into action to serve the time and generation.

He, the speaker, was no Tariff Reformer, but he recognized that Joseph Chamberlain's historic agitation had rendered one outstanding service to the cause of humanity. It had helped to call attention to a number of crying evils festering among us, whose existence the Governing Classes were either ignorant of, or had overlooked. What had been Chamberlain's six great propositions?

One: That ours was the most powerful Empire under the sun. *Two:* Great Britain was the heart of this Empire, strong, rich enough to send even more of its blood to the remotest member of this huge body. *Three:* In the affluent centre of this potent Empire there was a multitude of industrious men, women and children whose living, almost bare subsistence, was hard and poor and precarious. *Four:* To alter all this would need drastic and far-reaching changes (and Chamberlain had, at any rate, proposed his own drastic policy of fiscal revolution). *Five:* The fact that changes would mean losses to the fortunes of individuals, or harm to the interests of certain trades, should be no barrier to action, since the well-being of the whole community would thereby be ensured. *Six:* The time had come to seek a remedy, not in voluntary effort, but in bold and comprehensive measures by the State. With this general analysis of our desperate condition, and its promise of concerted social action as its remedy, Lloyd George agreed.

What of the still undeveloped resources of our own soil? How many million acres were sacrificed to sport that could instead be drained, or afforested? And, then, side by side with this criminal prodigality of space in the countryside, what a still more evil parsimony in the towns! Once, in the olden days of rough tracks and primitive transport, it had perhaps been necessary to crowd people together within the narrow compass of the city wall. Now, with trams and trains there was no need for it. Let the people spread out again into God's green fields!

He cited the problem of the Sudan, as a parable. There was a broad, rich river upon which both the Sudan and Egypt depended for their fertility. There was enough water to irrigate both lands, and every part of both. But, in the Upper Sudan there was a vast tract where the water had drained itself into a morass, breeding nothing but pestilence. Far down the valley, the river shrank to a stream and the land was barren because of its thirst. Properly channelled, prudently husbanded and distributed, that water would make the desert blossom like the rose.

Even then there would be some men who would do better than others— the land which had fallen to their lot may have had more bounteous qualities, or its cultivators may be better fitted to make more effective use of what they had got. Some inequalities would remain, and rightly so. But while some would have a surplus, all would be blessed with an abundance.

In its pattern and prophetic content this Temple speech of Lloyd George's (it runs to about 6,000 words) must rank among one of the most eloquent he ever delivered. It found an unusual acceptance amongst the clergy of all Churches, and though Lord Rosebery shuddered at its "*Socialism*", *The Times* boldly commended its sincerity, and the adept handling of its philosophic theme.

But by now the break-up of the Two-Party Conference had opened the sluice gates of Party passion. Furious and foaming came the dirty flood. Whether or not it is true, as Austen Chamberlain claims, that the Truce was finally destroyed by the Irish Unionist section of the Tory Party (to the distress of certain English Tariff Reformers), at any rate, all sections now united on the subject of Ireland—to blast the Irish Nationalists.

John Redmond, the Irish Leader, had just returned from a tour of propaganda in Canada and the United States, where he had succeeded in raising a substantial fund to fight his battle for Home Rule. Some of it had been subscribed by Sir Wilfrid Laurier, the Liberal Prime Minister of Canada.

Monstrous! Thundered excitable J. L. Garvin, editor of the *Sunday Observer*:

> "Last night Mr. Redmond landed at Queenstown with 200,000 dollars in his pocket—for the purpose of tearing down the British Constitution with American money!"

The cry was taken up throughout the country by the Tory Press and platform, and since it touched that strange, anti-American chord which has remained a part of the English (though perhaps not the Scots, Welsh or Irish) make-up since 1776, it aroused the utmost anger. Lord Rosebery, in a "Non-party" speech at Manchester, did not fail to grace this resentment with his approval.

Lloyd George replied to the ridiculous charge with ridicule. To deliver his speech, he returned once again to an appreciative Cockney audience at Mile End.

The Tory Party, explained Lloyd George, must always have a bogy. Like certain savage tribes, they were addicted to devil worship. At the last Election, the Germans had been the bogies. In 1900, it was the "Dutchmen"; in 1895, it was Irishmen; in 1885, "Radical Joe" Chamberlain. Now, having exhausted the list, they were going round to the Irishmen again. But this new one was a different kind of Irishman from the Irishman of '95. That Irishman was a midnight assassin—ragged, tattered, fierce. The Irishman of the day was a "gilt-edged bogy, framed in American dollars".

> "Since when," inquired Lloyd George, "has the British aristocracy started despising American dollars? Many a noble house, tottering to its fall, has had its foundations underpinned, its walls buttressed, by a pile of American dollars."

In making this last reference, the Chancellor of the Exchequer was well aware that it would cause no especial pleasure to his colleague, the President of the Board of Trade. Winston Churchill was, of course, himself a son of the House of Marlborough which had lately been so buttressed, and not for the first time.

"However, in this case," concluded Lloyd George, "a large proportion of the 'American dollars' have come from Canada. Since when has Canada been a foreign country? When Canada and Canadian statesmen are to be used as an excuse for taxing the bread of the people, then Canadians are 'our kith and kin beyond the seas', and 'our dearest relations'. But when Canadians subscribe money for the purpose of enabling Ireland to win the same measure of self-government, then Canadians are 'aliens tearing down the Constitution'."

The blow went home the harder because the British newspapers were currently reporting that these same Canadians had decided to launch and pay for their own Dreadnought to supplement the strength of the Royal Navy.

This noisy good-bye to the Truce brought back, as Asquith said, "a state of War" and, furthermore, one of immediately impending battle. It was impossible for the Liberal Cabinet to carry on the King's Government while their every legislative measure remained exposed to the veto of the hostile House of Lords. They were back to the position of April, when Asquith had warned that if the Peers did not accept the Bill restricting their powers then the Government would either resign, or dissolve.

On 15 November, 1910, the Cabinet met and drafted a memorandum, which Lord Crewe subsequently conveyed to King George.

It set forth that His Majesty's Ministers could take the responsibility of advising a Dissolution only if they understood that in the event of their policy being approved by a substantial majority of the electors, His Majesty would be ready to exercise his prerogative of creating sufficient Peers to give effect to that decision. Since the Ministers were aware of the importance of keeping the King's name out of Party strife, he would probably agree not to make this intention known to the public until the occasion for operating it actually arose.

When the King accepted this, Asquith went to the country.

The General Election of December, 1910 (it turned out to be the last one before the First World War), was fought with the utmost ill will on both sides. The Tory leaders, who were still divided about the merits of Tariff Reform v. Free Trade, did their best to keep discussion away from the subject. They were not allowed to do so, either by the Liberal Free Traders or by their own determined Tariff Reformers. The flashing sword and challenging voice of the first Imperial Crusader, Joe Chamberlain, were silent and stilled at last. But Bonar Law, giving up his safe Dulwich seat, went down to Man-

Notes exchanged across the Cabinet table between Lloyd George and Winston Churchill

August 3rd, 1914

chester to fight Free Trade in the very citadel of Cobden.[1] His desperate challenge brought to his side two new violent young warriors from the Outer Empire. There now appeared upon the warpath in Lancashire and East London, Messrs. Max Aitken from Canada and Leopold Amery from South Africa. After a tornado campaign in Ashton-under-Lyne, the future Lord Beaverbrook defeated the popular local Liberal, A. H. Scott, who had modestly described himself as the future Prime Minister. At Bow-and-Bromley, Leopold Amery failed narrowly to unseat the notorious Mayor of Poplar (and perhaps the best-loved Socialist in British politics), George Lansbury. At Manchester, Bonar Law went down bravely, firing every gun, an example everywhere to politicians who aspire to leadership of how to live dangerously.

With equal fire and fervour, Lloyd George plunged into his seventh Election. He steered off the Irish Question as far as possible, though at Bangor he repeated the Prime Minister's pledge that there would be no shirking of Home Rule in the new Parliament. He dealt with Tariffs only in so far as he sought to prove that they were a Tory trick to keep the public's eyes from the real issue of the General Election, which was: Should the Peers, or the People Rule? He was fortunate, once more, in his enemies, who obligingly supplied him with his best ammunition. Earl Curzon, for example, had just pronounced that the best work in this world had always been done by the aristocracy.

"He evidently doesn't think much of the Christian religion," mocked Lloyd George. "No doubt he would have rated it higher had it been propagated not by twelve Gallilean fishermen but by a dozen dukes.

In an aside at Mile End, which matched in the language of Billingsgate the language then being currently employed on Merseyside by the Tory candidate for Birkenhead, F. E. Smith, he declared that the British aristocracy, of which Lord Curzon was so proud, was like cheese: "the older they are, the higher".

The result of the second (December) General Election of 1910 was, if possible, even less satisfactory to all Parties than the first (January) one:

Liberals .	272
Tories .	272
Irish Nationalists	84
Labour .	42

During the Election, Lloyd George had once again spoken up and down the country; at Edinburgh, Wrexham, Cardiff, Llandrindod and Pwllheli. Before the end, his voice failed and his health broke down; his own election at Caernarvon Boroughs was never in doubt, and in the event the figures were:

D. Lloyd George (Liberal) .	3,122
A. L. Jones (Tory) .	1,904
Liberal Majority .	1,208

[1] He invited Churchill to give up his Dundee candidature and fight him at Manchester. Offer declined. But Churchill would have won!

He went off with the Mastermans again for Christmas in the sunshine on the Riviera. They left behind them a land in which political frustration was mingled with growing social turbulence. For several weeks past, South Wales had been in the grip of a violent mining dispute, which had started at D. A. Thomas's collieries of the Cambrian Coal Trust in the Rhondda Valley. The Eight Hours Act had set up peculiar problems in the Welsh coalfield, tending to diminish both output and earnings. The Liberal Government, in vain, tried to mediate. The wayward Radical, D. A. Thomas, was determined to fight it out with his old constituents.

At 4 a.m. one November morning, the strikers formed a cordon round the Valley pitheads and prevented the enginemen from going to their work. They also stopped the ventilating machinery, thus imperilling the lives of some hundreds of pit ponies in their underground stalls. The Chief Constable of Glamorganshire appealed for troops, and two squadrons of Hussars and two companies of infantry were dispatched from Salisbury Plain. At the last moment, they were halted in Swindon by the order of Winston Churchill, who had been promoted to the Home Office when the Government was re-formed after the General Election. Instead, two hundred Metropolitan Policemen on foot were sent into the Rhondda Valley.

That night, rioting broke out. The police were stoned, and shops were looted. The soldiers had to be sent for, after all.

The struggle in the coalfield was true drama, prologue of fire and thunder to the mighty play of industrial strife about to be presented in Britain, 1911–14. In the East End of London, there was melodrama. Villain: Peter the Painter. Hero: Winston Churchill.

It began one December night when police interrupted a burglary in Hounds-ditch. The robbers opened fire, and six policemen were shot dead. The murder gang vanished. The story made an immense sensation, and the victims were accorded a public funeral and their coffins, draped in Union Jacks, lay in St. Paul's Cathedral for a solemn memorial service.

A few days later, Scotland Yard picked up the trail of the assassins. They belonged to a small, alien colony in the East End, originating from Baltic Russia, and were anarchists, led by a man known in the Police records as "Peter the Painter". They were located early one morning at No. 100 Sidney Street, from which they fired on anyone who approached. The Home Office was telephoned for authority to call on the troops at the Tower of London. Winston Churchill at once agreed, and hurried himself to the scene, where he took charge of operations, ordering up Royal Engineers and Royal Artillery to sap and bombard the gunmen's nest before the infantry advanced upon it. At this point, the house caught fire and burned itself out. Two charred corpses were found in the ruins, but of Peter the Painter nobody ever heard again.

The year of the Comet went out with a bang.

CHAPTER XII

SHADOWS OVER THE LAND

THERE now unfolds one of the most exciting periods in Britain's tempestuous twentieth century. Three thunderclouds gathered over the land. They threatened trouble in three separate forms—Civil War between the Irish factions, Social War between the English classes and International War between the Great Powers of Europe.

Lloyd George was going to be in the very centre of all this turmoil. He was going to climb almost to the summit of power, and come near to being cast down utterly into the abyss. He was going to be saved in the end only by the greatest storm of all. But for the First World War, Lloyd George's star might have set in 1914.

When 1911 opened, he was still convalescing on the French Riviera, **Age 48** where he had greatly enjoyed reading in the newspapers the saga of Sidney Street. He came back in January, only to collapse once more and have to go away again. The rumours spread. "Lloyd George has cancer of the throat." "Lloyd George is going to resign." "Lloyd George is dying." When he returned the second time, for at least three months he was not fit for the rough-and tumble of those pre-war House of Commons nights. He stayed down in Kent at the country house which Sir Arthur Markham, a Liberal M.P., had lent him in Beachborough, near Folkestone, and from there he gradually resumed his work at the Treasury.

Lloyd George returned in May, 1911, to a curiously illusive political scene. He had been working off-and-on for many months on his monumental National Insurance Bill, which covered both Health and Unemployment, and was intended in due course to include provision for Widows' and Orphans' Pensions, too. Since much of this was common ground (at any rate, between the Radical wing of the Liberal Party and the more progressive Tories who followed the tradition of Disraeli, Lord Randolph Churchill and Joe Chamberlain), Lloyd George expected an easy passage for his Bill. Indeed, it started off that way, welcomed with almost rapturous praise by the Opposition Press, and registering both its First and Second Readings in the House of Commons without a division. George Riddell noted in his diary:

"Tories almost as enthusiastic as the Radicals . . . treating Lloyd George as if he was a saviour of society. . . . Balfour all smiles and cordiality."

But the Bill rapidly gathered critics, and eventually developed into a political dog-fight which lasted well into the following year.

The Parliament Bill, on the other hand, which finally clipped the wings of the House of Lords, was introduced and carried forward amid unparalleled disorder. But it was on the Statute Book before mid-August.

Trouble grew as the idea sank into Tory heads that the Liberal Prime Minister had really meant what he said about the House of Lords, and that if the Opposition majority there proposed to throw out the Parliament Bill, then enough new Peers would be created to ensure a Government majority. It was reckoned that as many as four or five hundred might be necessary, and the Liberal Whips began laboriously to compile lists of more or less willing volunteers. Lord Curzon made a further contribution to the dictionary of political phrase and fable when he defied this threat, and adapting King William III's famous *mot*, declared: "We will die in the last ditch before we surrender."

Thereupon, the Tory Party split in two. One half was the Ditchers, who professed to believe that Asquith was bluffing and would never dare to advise the King to make a mass-manufacture of Peers. The other half was the Hedgers, who suspected that it might be true, after all, and counselled strategic retreat.

The approach of the Coronation, in June, 1911, enforced a second brief armistice between the Parties. Those diverse but loyal members of the Prime Minister's own Top-level Trade Union, Asquith and Balfour, could once more be seen together, exchanging epigrams at the same Mayfair ball. As for Winston Churchill and F. E. Smith, they were divided in politics but united socially at any rate.

The House of Lords returned refreshed from the Coronation festivities to maul and mangle the Parliament Bill, so that it soon became unrecognizable. Promptly, the Prime Minister went off to see the King. Next morning, Lloyd George called on Balfour. He bore a letter from Asquith which politely made it clear that the Government meant to have their Bill and the whole of that Bill, and that if the House of Lords rejected it then His Majesty in accordance with the verbal promise he had given the Prime Minister before the General Election, would now create the necessary number of new Peers.

"Dear Mr. Balfour,

I think it is courteous and right, before any public decisions are announced, to let you know how we regard the political situation.

When the Parliament Bill in the form which it has now assumed returns to the House of Commons we shall be compelled to ask that House to disagree with the Lords' amendments.

In the circumstances, should the necessity arise, the Government will advise the King to exercise his prerogative[1] to secure the passing into law of the Bill in substantially the same form in which it left the House of Commons, and His Majesty has been pleased to signify that he will consider it his duty to accept and act on that advice.

Yours sincerely,

H. H. Asquith."

[1] That is, the Royal prerogative to create Peers. In this instance, of course, enough Liberal Peers to ensure the passage of the Parliament Bill through the House of Lords.

Not so Earl Halsbury, an aged Law Lord of angry views. (He was eighty-eight, and had been Lord Chancellor for the last ten years of the Tory régime.) He declared that if this damnable Parliament Bill became Law he would feel himself unable to take office in any future Administration. With the aid of a young sporting Peer, Lord Willoughby de Broke, the vehement veteran now set out to mobilize resistance. The main hope of this lay in the noblemen whom Lloyd George, unkindly though not untruthfully, described as the "backwoodsmen", i.e., Peers from the shires who had rarely if ever before attended their Lordships' debates.

The rebellion spread to the House of Commons. A day or two after Lloyd George had delivered by hand the Liberal bombshell, the Prime Minister rose from the Front Bench amid Government cheers to deal with the Lords' amendments. He had got no more than half-way through his opening sentence when he was interrupted by shouts from the Opposition Back Benches of "vide! vide!". The whole range of Tory seats behind Balfour (though not the exquisite-mannered Opposition Leader himself) then took up the chant. The volume of the din grew higher, and its content lower.

"Traitor! Traitor!" screamed Lord Hugh Cecil. "Disgrace to your office!"

"Treason! Treason!" "Consult your Irish bosses!" "Who killed the King?" howled those around him.

F. E. Smith exuberantly led this supporting chorus. The Liberals bawled back, the Irish and the Labour Party joined in with zest. There was social uproar in the Ladies' Gallery, where Mrs. Asquith reigned at one end and Lady Londonderry at the other. Margot hastily scribbled one of her peremptory dispatches and sent it down to Sir Edward Grey, who sat next to her husband. "For God's sake," she wrote, "defend him from the cats and the cads!"

Had it been addressed to Lloyd George, she might have had better luck. The Foreign Secretary, like the Prime Minister himself, gazed on the beargarden with composure and contempt. He had no wish to join in the bear-play. After nearly an hour of it, Mr. Speaker adjourned the House without question being put, "a state of grave disorder having arisen".

The Lords were still more steamed-up, especially the "Ditchers". They genuinely hated and despised the "Hedgers", even more than they did the Radicals. (Lord Curzon, who by this time had changed his opinion about dying in a ditch and now preferred to survive in a hedge, came in for especial reviling.)

The final, furious debate in the Upper House began one sultry August afternoon, when the temperature stood at 97 degrees in the shade, and perhaps for the last time in English history every public box and gallery and square foot of standing space in the Lords was packed. The speeches rasped on, the shadows grew, and "candles were brought in".

The House divided, and the watchers in the Galleries, tensely craning, saw the two lines of voters emerging from the Lobbies to the right and left of the Throne. Which would hold out the longest? Then at last, the Verdict.

Contents, 131; Not-Contents, 114.

So the Hedgers won. The two Archbishops, and most of the Bishops had voted for the Bill; several more Ditchers had funked it at the last moment, and abstained. "We have been beaten by the Gaiters and the Rats," said George Wyndham. Society was split, and at the Carlton Club members checked up Hansard before they spoke to one another.

Lloyd George was happy. He was back at work. Already, in April, the *Daily News* had reported:

"The Chancellor is now practically restored to health, and is able to smoke again."

Early in May, he had signalized his return to the House of Commons by introducing his National Insurance Bill. In the end, it had become a good deal of a rush job and, like the People's Budget, it bore the marks. There was need to hurry forward this next operation of the People's Battle.

The new Insurance Bill would begin the advance, claimed Lloyd George. He calculated that at least one-third of the pauperism in Britain was due to sickness, a lot more to unemployment and there was "a vast mass of unacknowledged destitution". He proposed to raise £27,000,000 funds in a full year, partly by State grant, partly by employers' and employees' contributions. Everyone earning less than £3 a week would be covered by this insurance, which was to be based on a compulsory weekly levy. (There were special provisions for soldiers, sailors, Crown servants, teachers and certain classes of casual labour.)

If Lloyd George's reputation as a social builder "with a trowel in one hand, and a sword in the other", had to rest upon the National Insurance Act of 1911 alone, it would still be secure. For this Act set the mould, and it built the base, for all the other Acts of social reform which have led our people forward since then towards the concept of the Welfare State.

The pioneer plan was not evolved overnight, as some critics have pretended, although two General Elections within twelve months and his own indisposition had delayed settling both the scale and much of the mechanism of the Bill. Lloyd George had, in fact, been working on it since his visit to Germany, in 1908, when in the towns and villages of that country he had studied what was then a model for the world. He had found the workers there, on the whole, well-enough content with the contributory basis. They turned out to be a good deal less satisfied with it over here, and though Lloyd George did his best to sell the idea under the slogan "Ninepence for Fourpence" (the State contributed 2d., the employer 3d., and the worker 4d.) there were many British workers who considered that a far better idea would have been a non-contributory scheme and a slogan of "Ninepence for Nothing".

There were critics, indeed, in all camps. Treasury officials estimated that by operating via the Post Office, Lloyd George would have been able to include Life Insurance in his scheme, yielding double the current benefits (because more than half of the private companies' takings were spent in expenses). But this, of course, would have thrown about 80,000 private-enterprise clerks and agents out of work—and many of them were Liberals.

Then there were the Socialist intellectuals of the Fabian Society, such as Sidney and Beatrice Webb, who feared that the Trade Unions might now be turned into Insurance Societies, and that their leaders would be further distracted from their industrial work, an opinion not shared by the Unions themselves. Indeed, hundreds of small trade unions now gained recruits, who preferred to register for benefit through them rather than at the Post Office. As for the Friendly Societies, who also stood to increase their membership, for several months past they had been consulted, and they were now duly invited to become "approved" agents in the new State scheme. The Chancellor of the Exchequer displayed in these negotiations the same conciliatory arts which had marked his tenure of the Board of Trade. The largest of the Friendly Societies by 10 to 1 passed a resolution to work the Insurance Act.

Now by this time the Government had come to a firm understanding with its Allies the Irish Party and the Parliamentary Labour Party, thus solidifying their majority.

They agreed to run in triple harness the three young colts—House of Lords Reform, Home Rule for Ireland, the Repeal of the Osborne Judgment. Thus the Allies were bound to the Government and to each other providing always that the Bills moved simultaneously in all stages.

Lloyd George was the intermediary with both of the Allies, and he did not neglect his friends the Labour Members. The Osborne Judgment had dealt them a hard blow—no more subsidizing by Trade Unions of Labour Party Candidates. But now, the Liberal Government, pending their dealing by law with the Osborne issue, were proposing to pay M.P.s £400 per annum. In return for this—to the Labour Party immensely valuable—offer, their Chairman, Ramsay MacDonald, was prepared to do business over the Insurance Bill. The following letters passed between him and Alexander ("Alick") Murray, the Liberal Chief Whip:

The Hillocks,
Lossiemouth.
4 October, 1911.

"Dear Elibank,

. . . I need not reassure you that the statement I made to you about the attitude of the [Labour] Party on the Insurance Bill before we separated in the summer holds good.

The Party came to its decision, and its decision will be carried out by the officers loyally and faithfully in spite of what two, or at the outside three, Members may do to the contrary.

Yours very sincerely,
J. Ramsay Macdonald."

The welcome news of this frank political deal was transmitted to Lloyd George in a letter next morning.

Juniper Bank,
Walkerburn,
N.B.
5/10/11

"My dear Chancellor,
I have received the following letter from Ramsay MacDonald.
The understanding—after the passage of Payment to Members—was that he and his friends should give general support to the Insurance Bill. . . .

Yours ever,
Alick Murray."

The Doctors were a lot less amenable than the Trade Unions or the Labour Party.

It had not been possible to consult them beforehand as a body, and many were implacably opposed to extending the contract medical system, or "Panel". They protested that it would ruin their private practices, that the patient would have to put up with a nominated "State" doctor instead of one of his own choice, that malingering would be encouraged, and that professional standards would be degraded. Lloyd George had a far livelier and longer struggle with the Doctors before the First World War than ever Aneurin Bevan did after the Second one.

The housewives who kept servants were more hostile still. Their tempers were inflamed afresh each morning by Northcliffe's *Daily Mail*, which alleged that inspectors would invade their drawing-rooms to check if servants' cards were stamped, while it warned the servants that their mistresses would sack them the moment they became liable for sickness benefit. (A Radical cartoon depicted a duchess furiously exclaiming, "What! Me Lick stamps?")

The Servants Tax Registers Defence League was organized, and took the Albert Hall for a protest demonstration. The Dowager Lady Desart graced the Chair, and ten thousand women in the Hall (and as many more outside) alternately shrilled "We Won't Pay!" and chanted:

*"Taffy was a Welshman
Taffy was a thief."*

There were cheers for "Rule Britannia" and hisses for "Men of Harlech", and Lloyd George was denounced as a "benevolent busybody", "mischief-maker-in-chief", "mongrel", "gagger", "guillotiner" and "tyrant". The orator of the evening declared that the Chancellor of the Exchequer was seeking to do what the worst kings in English history had failed to accomplish, and which their own forefathers would have died to prevent.

Lloyd George dealt lightly with this meeting "when the domestic servants drove up in their limousines to the Albert Hall to protest against their mistresses paying 3d. a week."

Later, when Northcliffe pursued his campaign in his latest acquisition, *The Times*, and advised his new public not to observe the Act, Lloyd George took on a different tone. Were there now to be *two* classes of citizens in the land—*one* class which could obey the laws if they liked; the *other*, which must obey whether they liked it or not? Some people seemed to think that the Law was an institution devised for the protection of their property, their lives, their privileges and their sport—it was purely a weapon to keep the working classes in order. This Law was to be enforced. But a Law to ensure people against poverty and misery and the breaking-up of home through sickness or unemployment was to be optional. Was the Law for the preservation of game to be optional? Was the payment of rent to be optional?

The Times persevered with its incitement, assuring its readers the penalty for breaking *this* law would be very small, only a shilling fine. With relish Lloyd George returned to his meat. There was a foot-and-mouth plague rampant in the countryside at the time, and he drew on it for a contemporary simile:

> "Defiance of the law is like the cattle plague. It is very difficult to isolate it and confine it to the farm where it has broken out. Although this has developed first of all among the Harmsworth herd, it has travelled to the office of *The Times*. Why? Because they belong to the same cattle farm. *The Times* is just a tuppeny ha'penny edition of the *Daily Mail*."

In the event, the workers accepted National Insurance without enthusiasm. They would have much preferred higher wages, and they were already setting on foot a massive agitation to get them. As the year 1911 advanced, a series of strikes threatened to halt the entire trade of the country; there were nearly nine hundred strikes or lock-outs that summer.

The Tory Opposition would naturally have liked to exploit the Insurance Bill's unpopularity, but not even the Tory Peers were prepared to attack its principle. It was much amended during the Committee stages in Parliament, and much improved as a result. At the end, during the Third Reading, Lloyd George publicly thanked those sincerely socially-minded Tory M.P.s who had helped to make the Bill what it became.

It had been a strenuous summer, as well as one of the hottest of all time. The Coronation Service, Royal Processions, State Balls, Garden Parties, Command Performances, Army and Navy Reviews filled the social programme of Britain's public men, and of the foreign potentates who had thronged here. What impressed the Kaiser more than any other event that he attended was the Naval Review at Spithead, for 165 warships were on view, including eight dreadnoughts and 24 battleships, the most formidable fleet ever yet mustered anywhere in the history of the world. All over the land there were festivals and junketings and at night thousands of bonfires blazed on the British hills.

Lloyd George was called on to play a personal part in one of the last and most picturesque of the Coronation ceremonies. This was the July investiture at Caernarvon Castle of the King's eldest son, Edward, as Prince of Wales. The Royal Family had arrived the night before at Holyhead aboard the yacht *Victoria and Albert*. As Constable of the Castle, and accompanied by the Lord Lieutenant, the High Sheriff, the Archdruid and the Mayor, with heralds and officers of the Welsh regiments, Lloyd George received the Royal Party at the Water Gate of King Edward I's great stronghold. Then he stood by the side of the three thrones, while Churchill, as Home Secretary, proclaimed the Young Edward's style and titles as Prince of Wales,

"amid the sunlit battlements of Caernarvon Castle"

(as he would himself recall on that winter afternoon of King Edward VIII's abdication of a quarter of a century later).

They sang "God Save the King" and "The Land of my Fathers", the Red Dragon flag flew from the Eagle Tower, and the Prince of Wales made a little speech in the Welsh tongue, which Lloyd George had taught him. The Welsh people took him to their heart that day, and they kept him there.

Re-enter that interesting pre-war character, the Kaiser. His Imperial Majesty had been intently watching the rather hesitant French advance into Morocco and had come to the conclusion that Imperial Germany, by being a bit bolder, could snatch something a lot larger for herself in North or Central Africa. He was encouraged in his hopes by the fact that the Prime Minister of France at this time was Joseph Pierre Caillaux, an earlier Pierre Laval. Late in June, under the pretext of protecting German merchants in Agadir, the German gunboat *Panther* anchored off that port.

Britain, as well as the real France, was roused. We had signed the Anglo-French Algeciras Convention of 1906, which had acknowledged France's paramountcy in Morocco, and had snubbed Germany. We were now ourselves concerned to see that this persistently-challenging rival did not set up a naval base on the African Atlantic coast, which could threaten our sea routes to the Cape of Good Hope and South America.

To the inquiries of the British Foreign Secretary, Sir Edward Grey, the German Chancellor returned no reply for seventeen days. Now, the week after the Caernarvon Investiture, Lloyd George was due to speak in the City of London at the Bankers' Dinner. He arrived twenty minutes late, which gave ill-disposed critics a chance to comment that the author of the People's Budget could hardly be expected to behave with any better manners to the City. The real reason was serious; the Chancellor of the Exchequer had been showing the Prime Minister and the Foreign Secretary a certain passage in the speech he proposed to make, and getting their approval of it.

When he rose, after making appropriate reference to the healthy state of the nation's finances and the improvement in its trade, Lloyd George went on to stress the paramount importance to Britain of world peace, and the need of settling the disputes otherwise than by the sword. Then followed the significant words:

"But if a situation were to be forced upon us in which peace could only be preserved by the surrender of the great and beneficent position Britain has won by centuries of heroism and achievement, by allowing Britain to be treated, where her interests were vitally affected, as if she were of no account in the Cabinet of Nations, then I say emphatically that peace at that price would be a humiliation intolerable for a great country like ours to endure. . . ."

The meaning of this passage appears to have been entirely lost upon that convivial gathering, but the British Press next morning underlined well enough what had been said and the German Ambassador understood well enough. So did the Kaiser when he got his report. He flew into a rage, dictated a vehement protest to Sir Edward Grey, complaining of Lloyd George's language. He was a good deal more put out to learn that the Chancellor's warning represented the considered policy of the British Government.

Considered, that is, by the inner circle of the British Cabinet. For, as we now know, only the Ministers who attended the newly-formed Committee of Imperial Defence (the Premier, Foreign Secretary, First Lord of the Admiralty, Secretary of State for War) really knew—or cared to know—what was going on in the International field. The Cabinet, as a whole, remained in ignorance of the country's commitments abroad, and if these were suspected and challenged, they were brazenly denied.

It was Lord Rosebery—what an awkward Liberal he was!—who warned, at Edinburgh in 1911, that Britain had entered into obligations, "which might lead to an Armageddon such as was not dreamed of by Napoleon".

Tackled in the House of Commons in March, 1911, by Socialist Fred Jowett, Sir Edward Grey had denied that we had made any undertaking beyond the terms of the Anglo-French Convention. After Agadir, certain commitments were admitted—but no precise Naval or Military arrangements. Almost up to August, the Liberal Government continued in this deceit, or rather half-deceit. For the so-called "understanding" was so vague and wide that either side understood of it just what they desired.

At this time, Autumn, 1911, Lloyd George himself was really aroused about Germany's intentions. (In his *Memoirs* he claims that one reason which drove him to urge by every means the development of British soil resources was the fear of war-time starvation; if so, it was an economic policy to which he steadfastly adhered for the next thirty years.) It was by his own initiative that he made his Agadir speech. Now a month later, he wrote to Churchill the following remarkable letter:

27 August, 1911.

"My dear Winston,

I have been reading the Foreign Office papers. They are full of menace. The thunderclouds are gathering. I am not at all satisfied that we are prepared, or that we are preparing. When the terrible character of the issue is considered, we seem to me to take it all much too carelessly. Weeks ago, when I thought War a possibility, I urged upon Grey the importance of Russia as a factor. I wanted him then to ascertain definitely what Russia would do, and could do, in the event of war. It is true that Isvolsky[1] dropped a casual observation in the course of a conversation on some other topic that Russia would give material support to France if war were declared. We ought to have a much more formal or definite assurance than that. Isvolsky is not to be trusted. . . . What about Russia's resources? Have we any precise information? . . . We ought to know what R. is capable of before we trust the fortunes of Europe to the hazard. We are even now almost at the point whence we cannot recede."

Then follows another prescient point:

"Here is another position we ought to reconnoitre. What about Belgium? 150,000 British troops supporting the Belgian army on the German flank would be a much more formidable proposition than the same number of troops extending the French line. It would force the Germans to detach at least 500,000 men to protect their lines of communications. The Anglo-Belgian army numbering 400,000 men would pivot on the great fort at Antwerp. The command of the sea would make that position impregnable. Is there no way open to us to sound Belgium? She does not want Germany as a neighbour on the Congo as well as temporary tenant of Liège and possible occupant of Antwerp. Send this along to Grey with your views. But let me hear from you also. I am inclined to think the chances of war are multiplying. . . . *'Be ye therefore ready.'*"

Churchill needed no further spur. Promptly, he sent a letter to Sir Edward Grey, urging a Triple Alliance of Britain, France and Russia "to safeguard the independence of Belgium, Holland and Denmark". These latter countries must, however, also make the utmost exertions to defend themselves. The Foreign Secretary briefly replied that the Russian assurance to France

[1] Andrew Isvolsky (1865–1919) Tsarist Minister of Foreign Affairs, 1906–1910; Ambassador to Paris, 1910–1917.

was "categorical". What he himself would like to know was what the Russians *could do*!

So Churchill pursued his inquiries at the War Office, where from Field-Marshal Lord Kitchener, he got a fairly encouraging opinion about the military quality of the French,[1] and from General Sir William Nicholson, a disparaging one about the Belgians. The soldiers appeared to agree on the strategic advantages to be derived from a British Expeditionary Force operating in Belgium on the German flank, and Churchill thereupon began to elaborate plans for defending Antwerp and blockading the Rhine. The Home Secretary had also been in touch with the Admiralty, and had found that:

"practically everybody of importance and authority is away on his holidays. . . . I cannot help feeling uncomfortable about the Admiralty. They are so cocksure, *insouciant* and apathetic, so far as one can judge from all that one sees and hears."

To be sure, there was thunder in the air. On 9 September, 1911, the Berlin Bourse went into a war panic, and the wildest rumours raced across Europe. Three days later, all leave was cancelled in the British Army and the Navy, and emergency coal stores were dispatched from South Wales to Cromarty Firth for the Fleet.

There was already enough trouble brewing within the country itself. The rise in the cost of living had brought to explosion point the labour troubles which had been rumbling all the year. In South Wales, indeed, D. A. Thomas had now whipped the Miners' Federation into advising the strikers at his own Cambrian Colliery to surrender and withdrawing their strike allowances, thus forcing that obdurate Rhondda rearguard back to their pits by the economic sanction of starvation. But as the fires of industrial revolt died in the Welsh coalfield, they flared in the English ports. Two days before the Coronation, the seamen at Southampton struck. They were quickly followed by their comrades elsewhere in Liverpool and Cardiff, and at Hull the dock labourers joined in. Soon, warehouses were going up in flames, and there was looting and rioting. Next week, the carters came out. On 8 August, the London dockers "downed bales". This set off the powder-keg in the seething, sweltering East End. Lorrymen, labourers, lightermen, bunkermen, bargemen, tugboatmen, enginemen, all came out on strike. The West End had had its fling; now the East End would take its fancy.

On Tower Hill, huge mobs of strikers massed to Ben Tillett, one of the heroes of the famous dock strike of 1889, which had won the "Dockers' Tanner". Though they still got that princely sixpence per hour's labour, the dockers had no guarantee of getting any work at all. Every morning, around dawn they trudged to the waterside, and there waited like cattle in the market

---

[1] Kitchener must have been in two minds about the French. To Lloyd George he said, "The Germans will walk through them like a covey of partridges."

for the ganger to look them over and pick those he wanted. Ben Tillett, a wisp of a man who had not yet lost the passion of his youth, pit boy at eight years of age, ship's boy, brick-kiln boy, circus-boy, and agitator with a voice that could sing like a stream or roar like a cataract, now set up on Tower Hill a tumultuous rebel Assembly, if not yet a rebel Soviet. In processions of 100,000 strong the strikers then marched in a more sinister silence through the City of London.

The women took a hand. As the strike on the Thames riverside rose to its climax, the women workers in the Bermondsey factories suddenly marched out, singing and shouting. They felt the hot breath of Liberty, too, and soon thousands more of their sisters poured into the streets. They had even better reason for revolt than their brothers.

Ben Tillett took time off from preaching revolution and the class-war to the dockers to apostrophize 10,000 of these ladies in Southwark Park. The employers both of the Port of London and of the Bermondsey factory girls deemed it best to settle.

They also settled with the dockers in Liverpool, who were under the leadership of another trouble seeker and troublemaker of genius. This was the redoubtable Tom Mann. Self-taught, self-disciplined, trained in industrial upheaval from the British coalfield to the Australian waterfront and back again, Tom Mann had deeply studied the writings of George Sorel, especially the masterpiece, *Reflections on Violence*, and was a thorough Syndicalist before he became a pioneer Communist. Tom Mann was not in favour of one strike, but of as many as could be got going in succession, or better still, at the same time. The culmination was to be a General Strike, paralysing the entire country, and leaving the Government helpless with a machine whose wheels had simply stopped going round. Then, the workers of each industry would take it over without further opposition.

Tom Mann was downcast by the employers' concession, but only for a moment. He was rescued from his depression by their folly in locking-out the men engaged on cargo work. At once all Liverpool's transport workers struck, including the railwaymen, and riots broke out on the Merseyside. The Lord Mayor appealed for military help. On Sunday, 13 August, a mob outside St. George's Hall, after hearing Tom Mann, set about the police. Two hundred people were injured. Next day, the Scots Greys and Warwickshire Regiment marched in and special police were enrolled. They did not deter Tom Mann and his men. When the soldiers appeared under arms on the street they were stoned, and when the ringleaders were arrested and sentenced the mobs attacked the prison vans and sought to free them. The troops opened fire, killing two people and wounding others. Trouble at the power station then put out the city lamps, and gangs ranged the darkened streets and looted. The cruiser *Antrim* sailed up the Mersey, and landed bluejackets to guard the docks.

The wave of unrest surged over the land.

Meantime, at the Board of Trade the new President, Mr. Sidney Buxton, wrestled each morning with some fresh industrial squabble. In Lancashire, eighteen different disputes were raging at once. In Glasgow, the tramwaymen "downed trams". In Llanelly, when a guarded train was pelted with stones, the escort replied with a rifle volley, which killed two rioters and so maddened the rest of the mob that farther along the line trucks were smashed and set on fire. Whereupon a van loaded with detonators blew up and killed five more.

The hold-up of the nation's traffic was now almost complete. The Prime Minister offered a Royal Commission to examine all grievances. But Royal Commissions take time, and the whole industrial tumult had largely arisen because, in the age of steam and petrol, the arbitration mechanism creaked along at the pace of a bullock wagon. The Railway Union leaders roughly rejected the offer. The patient but not placid Asquith lost his temper.

"Then your blood be on your head," he snapped.

From the Home Office came Churchill's telegraphic order:

"General Officers Commanding the various military areas are instructed to use their own discretion as to whether troops are, or are not, to be sent to any particular point. The Army Regulation which requires a requisition for troops from a Civil Authority is suspended."

Soon London was an armed camp, and troops had appeared elsewhere at thirty different places in the country.

"*Murder! Massacre!*" roared Tom Mann.

Lloyd George was called into the Board of Trade. The German scare was still going strong, and the entire German High Seas Fleet was due to concentrate at Kiel early in September. That same day Lloyd George tackled the Railway Companies, who had hitherto point-blank refused to recognize the Railway Unions. There was one thing alone which might move them—Lloyd George appealed to their patriotism. The railway quarrel was paralysing the power of Britain to act if need be in this international crisis, and well the Germans knew it. The Unions, he understood, were anxious to come to terms. Why not try?

The two sides sat down to talk it over. Next day, the railways were working. The Red Tide ebbed.

From King George, came a telegram to the Chancellor of the Exchequer.

"Heartily congratulate you . . . for averting a most disastrous calamity."

From the Prime Minister, came a letter acknowledging on behalf of all his colleagues, "the indomitable purpose, the untiring energy and the matchless skill", which he declared Lloyd George had brought to the settling of the trouble.

Wrote Asquith:

"It is the latest, but by no means the least, of the loyal and invaluable services which you have rendered since I came to the head of the Government three-and-a-half years ago."

There were many people in Britain in 1911 who were grateful to Lloyd George for settling the railway strike that holiday month. But many more held him responsible for the entire unrest. Hadn't he "stirred up the working classes at Limehouse"? So the Tories steadfastly maintained.

Lloyd George himself would have answered: "Yes, and it was right to do so."

One day, after a long Cabinet discussion on the Dock Strike he said to Masterman:

"I don't know exactly what I am, but I'm sure I'm not a Liberal. They have no sympathy with the people. . . . All down History, nine-tenths of mankind have been grinding the corn for the remaining one-tenth, been paid with the husks—and bidden to thank God they had the husks. . . . As long as I was settling disputes with their workmen, which they had not got enough sense to settle themselves, these great Business Men said I was the greatest Board of Trade President of modern times. When I tried to do something for the social welfare of their workmen, they denounced me as a Welsh thief."

Laying the foundation stone of a new Baptist Chapel at Seven Sisters, Neath, a few days after the Railway Strike, he returned to this theme, declaring that besides its spiritual functions the Christian Church had a duty towards the material welfare of its members. As long as there were these great contrasts between idle rich and struggling poor, there would be these outbursts. Let them cease their reviling, and consider the conditions under which the people lived. Let them realize their own responsibility.

Lloyd George still placed a deep reliance upon organized religion (or, at least, upon the cohorts of the Nonconformist Churches) to provide a dynamic impulse for the physical social betterment of the masses. Had he yet recovered any part of his lost spiritual belief? His confidences at this period do not disclose it, nor does his conduct. He was certainly less assiduous in his chapel going, though as ever he still revelled in a good sermon. Rumour said that the Devil, Golf, was edging his way in!

He was not yet invading Lloyd George's Sabbath, at any rate on public golf-courses in Britain. As late as the summer of 1913, Lloyd George was lamenting to Riddell at Walton Heath that he could not himself play golf on Sunday, "*but I should like to look at other people playing!*" When he was abroad, it seems that Lloyd George not only played golf himself on the Seventh Day, but was inclined to let his young sons do so. It is known that Margaret objected

Western Front. Watching a bombardment, 1916

Fishing with Megan in the Dwyfor. Llanystumdwy, 1916

to Sunday golf or indeed to any other Sunday games, and felt that their young sister Megan would also disapprove.

Megan (born in 1902) extended her dominion over her father, as well as over her brothers. The Chancellor relished the company of his determined and lively little daughter and, in spite of her mother's protests, often kept her up with him long after she should have been in bed. But if Megan received much attention in some ways from the interesting company who visited the Lloyd George home, in other ways her education was being neglected. Father decided to send her to a boarding-school in London; to prepare her for this he looked about for somebody to coach her in the summer holidays, now approaching.

He sought advice of his daughter Mair's former headmistress, and through her he eventually secured the services of Miss Frances Stevenson, a young teacher at a Wimbledon Girls' Boarding-School. When she went to No. 11 Downing Street to be interviewed for the post, it was not the first time that Miss Stevenson had set eyes on the famous Chancellor of the Exchequer. Several weeks earlier, on the last Sunday in June, 1911, a friend had taken her to the Welsh (Baptist) Chapel in Castle Street, near Oxford Circus. It was Lloyd George's annual custom to attend and address the congregation on this day, Flower Sunday, and Miss Stevenson had been entranced both by the mesmeric power and the personality of the speaker.

Rather nervous and pale, she now presented herself at No. 11 Downing Street, and she has penned another picture of Lloyd George as he then appeared to a young woman of twenty-three. His friendliness and charm melted her shyness in a few moments:

"I recall . . . the sensitive face, with deep furrows between the eyes: the eyes themselves, in which was all knowledge of human nature, grave and gay almost simultaneously; eyes which, when they scrutinized yours, convinced you that they understood all the workings of your heart and mind, sympathized with all your difficulties, set you in a place apart. The broad brow; the beautiful profile—straight nose, neat insolent chin. And a complexion as young and fresh as a child's. But there was something more even than this which distinguished him from all other men I had ever met—from all men whom I ever did meet thereafter—a magnetism which made my heart leap and swept aside my judgment."

It was arranged that she should go down to Criccieth as soon as possible, and spend the rest of the summer there teaching Megan.

It was late August before Lloyd George himself could get away from London, and join his family and friends in North Wales. There followed characteristically energetic Lloyd George afternoon picnics by the river (with the Chancellor of the Exchequer shinning up trees on the bank with astonishing facility), a midnight tramp up Snowdon to see the sunrise, an all-day tour in

Lloyd George's newly-acquired Napier motor-car to follow the sheep-dog trials—and, of course, golf (though not on Sunday!).

The Lloyd George household—or households—took some running. At this time he had three: the official one at Downing Street, the new home he had built himself above Criccieth and a small country house built for him (and later given to him) by his friend, George Riddell, at Walton Heath. A popular illusion survives in Wales that practical Margaret delighted in coping with all the problems of this movable Lloyd George H.Q., including sewing for the family and cooking at all hours. Practical Margaret, in fact, would not sew, loathed cooking, and though she loved a garden it was not peas or beans that she wanted in it, but rose trees and hyacinths.

What Margaret did—and with unfailing patience and resource—was to preside over the household wherever it was. The operative hand was that of Sarah Jones, who joined the family in 1900. Sarah is now over eighty, and she is still in charge of Megan's household at Criccieth. Sarah really did like cooking and housework, as well as minding the children. Furthermore, she thoroughly understood Lloyd George and all his moods, and Sarah was one of the very few people in his lifetime whom he could never either take in or upset, however much he flared and flamed in his tantrums.

On the day that Gwilym was going to be married, Sarah went early to Lloyd George's bedroom (he was then Prime Minister). She was happy, for she was very fond of the upstanding young fellow she had helped to bring up.

"Ah! He was always a good boy to me," she told Lloyd George, "and never a cross or an unkind word did he ever say to me."

"Well," commented the Master from behind the bedclothes, "have I?"

Sarah gave him one look. "God Almighty!" she said, and walked out of the room.

First of all, there were those famous breakfasts. It was Lloyd George's lifelong habit to go to bed early at night, around nine o'clock. He read himself to sleep soon, nearly always with a "Wild-West" thriller—and left the light burning by his bedside all night! But early, too, he awoke, sat up in bed, drank tea and worked for a couple of hours. About eight o'clock, he read the daily newspapers pretty thoroughly. Then he got up, dressed, and came down for breakfast at nine-fifteen.

Since he was, by now, quite a part of the way through his morning, Lloyd George did not feel as taciturn as some people do at this meal, so he invited company. Needless to say, it was useful and not merely social conversation which he sought. Talk, with Lloyd George, always had purpose. Usually there were a couple of guests, and his Engagement Book for one week at this time tells us who some of them were. (That Engagement Book, by the way, is a battlefield of scraps and scrawls. Also, it was even at the time only a remote guide to actual company; it could at any moment be added to. Sarah had to be ready for that.)

9.15	Gardiner and C. P. Scott	(Two famous Liberal journalists)
9.15	Massingham, Donald	(Two more)
9.15	Mond, Simon, Rowntree	(Mr. Seebohm Rowntree)
9.15	Ramsay MacDonald	(Mr. MacDonald would not talk freely in front of a third person)
9.15	Churchill and Addison	
9.15	Keir Hardie, Ben Tillett	(Labour morning)
9.15	Israel Zangwill	(The novelist)
9.15	Sydney Brooks	(Another, Tory journalist)
9.15	Isaacs, Riddell, Dillon, T. P. O'Connor, Devlin	(Irish morning)

When Budget business was the Order of the Day the guests would be drawn from the Civil Service, Sir Robert Chalmers, Chairman of the Board of Inland Revenue, John Bradbury, Willie Clark, Warren Fisher of the Treasury. Chalmers coined an epigram about his host, who was disrespectfully known in the Treasury as the "Mountain Goat—he leaps from boulder to boulder". Said Chalmers of Lloyd George: "At breakfast, he leaps from rasher to rasher."

Some of these breakfast parties took place in Downing Street, others at Walton Heath. The house on the heath was convenient for private conference. It stands in a leafy lane beyond the village, and within a hundred yards of the Golf Club. There is about an acre of garden there, well screened by high, thick hedges from peering passers-by. The two-storeyed house itself appears much larger than it really is, but it is a pleasant house with a little sun terrace, where some history has been made—and some narrowly averted. For in February, 1912, the Suffragettes planted a 7-lb. bomb in the linen cupboard, which exploded and wrecked four of the bedrooms. Fortunately for him, Lloyd George was in the South of France at the time and nobody else was in the house. Mrs. Pankhurst, who promptly and quite properly assumed full responsibility for the deed, was sentenced at the Old Bailey to three years penal servitude, and at once went on hunger-strike.

The other favourite place for those intimate private confidences on which public men subsist was the golf course, and in providing Lloyd George with a house nearby Walton Heath, journalist George Riddell was making an excellent investment of £2,000, which was the cost of it. A bigger Riddell investment, of course, was Walton Heath Golf Club itself. For, having got permission to lay out a links on the common, and acquired an estate on the edge of it for a song, Riddell built there some more attractive houses, and leased or let them to other prominent politicians such as Simon and Masterman, and Robert Donald, the Editor of the *Daily Chronicle*. Thus, he created an interesting colony, enhancing the value of his land-holding.

A high-developed sense of property—and especially, real estate—ever distinguished George Allardyce Riddell, the orphan boy from the Scots Border. As a young solicitor, it built him up a fortune within a few short years. He shifted his interest to newspapers, acquiring one-third of the shares in the then almost derelict *News of the World*, which he made into an immensely prosperous concern. His insatiable personal inquisitiveness about people assured his success as a journalist. "Women, Cash and Crime will always command public interest," said Riddell.

The sales of his newspaper support his theory. It was because he had got it firmly in his head that People Are News that Riddell cultivated Lloyd George, not only presenting him with the Walton Heath house but (when, later, Lloyd George became Prime Minister) leasing or lending him larger country houses for holiday periods at Great Walstead, Danny Park and Gairloch, and staffing them for him to entertain his distinguished guests in. Of course, Riddell was there himself a great deal, and not only for his good business reasons.

He had one weakness—he sighed for social recognition (he cared little for comfort, much less indulgence, ate and drank abstemiously, wore shabby old clothes and lived most of the time in the Dormy House of Walton Heath Golf Club, although possessing a beautiful London house in Queen Anne's Gate). So, while he cheerfully claimed that the *News of the World* was a highly moral organ, "it records wickedness—and its due punishment", he was delighted to get control of *Country Life*. Now, with the Walton Heath community as well, George Allardyce Riddell began to blossom forth, if not as a country squire at any rate, as an urban district squire.

He gave the Chancellor excellent newspaper advice, persuading him to reserve his most important speeches outside the House of Commons for week-ends and make them on Saturday. Thus, he would be reported in the Saturday evening Press, the Sunday Press and the Monday morning Press. When the reporters pointed out to him that if the speeches were made in the afternoon they would clash with football news, Lloyd George asked, "When would you like them—11 o'clock in the morning?" On their saying "yes" he did his best to arrange that, when speaking in some conference or at the laying of some memorial stone or in some great factory, it should be at that hour on Saturday. Furthermore, he undertook to provide them with a draft of his speech the previous day, subject only to the variation which new events or new inspiration might bring forth.

Lloyd George was making full use of the game of golf at this period, not only for exercise, but for the purposes of developing political friendships, mellowing opposition, and generally extending personal activities. He was no more than a fair player, but he was an enchanting partner, and many a politician spent a diverting and dangerous hour or two at golf with Lloyd George before Briand spent a famous fatal one at Cannes in 1922.

Lloyd George was luckier than Asquith in his golfing encounters with the Suffragettes. While they harried the Prime Minister over the links (more than once they actually assaulted him), the worst that happened to Lloyd George was to be interrupted by two women disguised in masculine garb, while he was playing golf with Alfred Mond and Arthur Crosfield (it was on a Sunday, but this was Mond's own private golf course).

"Give the women the Vote, you wicked man!" shrieked the Amazons, rushing towards him.

"Go away! We are trying to play golf!" roared Lloyd George, but taking up a defensive stance. He was much relieved when they turned out to be the wives of his companions, playing a joke on him.

Margaret also much preferred Walton Heath to Downing Street. It was in the country, and also she had a better idea of whom her lunch- or dinner- or even breakfast-table was likely to consist, for Lloyd George was liable to invite home for a meal anybody with whom he was doing business. Meals, with him, were an extension of working hours, not merely an agreeable interlude between them. It was no slip of the tongue (though it raised a good laugh) when, in giving evidence before the Marconi Inquiry Committee, he said of his close association with the Master of Elibank: "We were associated together at golf, or meals or other transactions of that kind."

Two significant new political appointments had marked the autumn of 1911. The first was that of Winston Churchill to the Admiralty in October, exchanging posts with Reginald McKenna; the second that of Bonar Law to the Leadership of the Tory Party, replacing Balfour. The one showed that the Liberal Government was at last aroused to the possibility of a European war; the other that the Tory Party were resolved to wage a more effective political war of their own.

The "cocksure, insouciant" attitude of the Admiralty, which had so stung Churchill at the time of the Agadir affair, had in retrospect alarmed the Cabinet, especially when it was found that the Navy had made no provision whatever for the shipment of the Army overseas to France if Germany attacked. The Prime Minister contemplated sending Haldane from the War Office (where he had completed his plans for creating the Territorial Army and organizing an Expeditionary Force) to take over the Navy. It was Lloyd George who induced him to give the post to Churchill, who, thereafter, to the saving benefit of his country, devotedly laboured at his task and strenuously battled all comers, including all colleagues, to have Britain's ships and sailors ready for the oncoming storm.

The supplanting of Balfour was equally inevitable, and from the point of view of the Tory Party, equally valuable. An extraordinary creature, Arthur Balfour. He was attractive, erudite and exquisite, so that in his youth he had been known as "pretty Fanny". Beneath it all lay an unpassionate personal courage, mingled with an impersonal indifference towards his fellow men or the fate of his closest colleagues. "He believed in nothing, not even the stars," said one who knew him well. Mrs. Sidney Webb, who herself had a nice sense both of character and how to draw one (in her own camp she had hit off Ramsay MacDonald as "the Parnell of the Labour Party—but a Parnell who does not believe in his Party", and George Lansbury as a "bewildered saint, alternately preaching universal goodwill and universal revolt"), has offered us in her Diary[1] this portrait of Balfour as Prime Minister in 1905:

> "A man of extraordinary grace of mind and body, delighting in all that is beautiful and distinguished, music, literature, philosophy, religious feeling and moral disinterestedness, aloof from all the greed and grime of common human nature. But a strange paradox as a Prime Minister!"

By 1911, Balfour had led the Tory Party three times to electoral defeat. Now he was leading them nowhere. A "B.M.G." (Balfour Must Go) whisper started round the clubs and week-end house parties. It soon became a chant, and appeared in print and ended in a shout. Balfour himself was not at all ready to go, and in this he was favoured by circumstances. For the awkward question remained: *Who would come?*

The Tory Party was divided in opinion again, and again almost equally. The Squires wanted Walter Long, and the business men were for Austen Chamberlain. Max Aitken[2], the young Canadian Member for Ashton-under-Lyne, plugged for Bonar Law, his fellow countryman, who had now returned to Parliament by winning a by-election at Bootle, Lancashire. When, in November, Balfour suddenly resigned (he announced, characteristically, that he "was tired"), it seemed that the Party must face a split—or else rally round Bonar Law, which was certainly the alternative which Aitken had not failed to press in every useful quarter.

This Tory trio must be introduced. Walter Long, himself a Squire, and looking like one. A cheerful man with a hot temper and a red, bald head. He made bad speeches, but with a lot of healthy noise, which sometimes carried them off successfully. He expressed the spirit of the Tory Party rather than its mind. Squire Long was not so strong as some of his friends could have wished in support of Tariff Reform, except those tariffs which applied to British agriculture. He was delighted by, and often recited to his friends a compliment from Disraeli's pages about a forbear of his, referring to: "the pleasing presence of Walter Long in the Lobby."

Austen Chamberlain, the elder son of Joe, resembled his famous sire in appearance, in his rather frigid formal manner, in his warm personal feelings, and in his devotion to what he held to be his duty. He had none of Joe's flair or fire in political battle. Tariff Reform, he truthfully said, was the mill-stone around his neck, although it was the lifebuoy of some other Tory leaders and undoubtedly helped Bonar Law to the Premiership. Austen Chamberlain

[1] Beatrice Webb's Diaries; Edited by Margaret Cole.
[2] Later Lord Beaverbrook.

SHADOWS OVER THE LAND

might still have succeeded him in 1923, but for the close personal loyalty which he had shown to Lloyd George at the time of the break-up of the Coalition Government in 1922. It was Winston Churchill who said so truthfully of Austen Chamberlain, "He always played the game, and never won it."

Bonar Law was accurately described by Max Aitken, the man who knew him best, as the "sombre raven among the glittering birds of Paradise" who then bedecked the political scene of Britain. The son of a Canadian Scots Presbyterian Minister, Bonar Law had made a successful business career in Glasgow before entering politics. He had a cool, logical brain, a clear, retentive memory, and a simple, direct style of speech. When he had thought out a problem Bonar Law would dictate his speech to his secretary, read it over once for accuracy, and never again look at it before delivering it. He had no need even to refer to a note, but he practised an effective oratorical trick in debate or during an address of taking a little notebook from his upper waist-coat pocket and apparently consulting it before announcing a set of figures. There was no entry at all in the book. His language dealt in commonplaces, not to say clichés, but Bonar Law spoke with such an earnest simplicity that the words seemed exactly fitting to the occasion, and men walked away from his meetings, murmuring: "That's exactly what I would have said."

Asquith called Bonar Law "the gilded tradesman" and said that he was "meekly ambitious", neither remark being unfair. But Bonar Law had a tart tongue, too, as when he said of the Liberal Government at the time of the Welsh Disestablishment Bill:

> "They have no more right to take away the property of the Church than I have to take away the coat of Mr. Winston Churchill" (loud cheers and laughter)—"even if he *has* turned it!" (Louder cheers and louder laughter.)

After some sharp inter-family exchanges, the Tory Party duly assembled in conference in London, where Walter Long proposed and Austen Chamberlain seconded the election of Bonar Law as the Party leader. Carried unanimously. But not without some heart-burning and indeed a measure of bitterness.

So another future Prime Minister had set off on his way.

When Lloyd George heard of it he said: "The Tories have stumbled on their very best man—the only man. He is a very clever fellow. I like him!"

Bonar Law said of Lloyd George about the same time, with equal sincerity: "I like Lloyd George. He is a very nice man. But he is the most dangerous little man that ever lived."

Lloyd George was about to become again also one of the most hated and reviled—and this time not on account of anything he had done or would do to the medical practitioners, peers, publicans or priests, but what he would do to himself.

For the moment, he was once more in full cry after both the Church and the Land, for the Welsh Disestablishment Bill was before the House of Commons, and both the Bishops and the Landlords were opposing it. Lloyd George reminded the Archbishop of Canterbury, who had lately visited Bangor to receive an Address, that the last time one of his predecessors had been there (A.D. 1289), was when Archbishop Peckham "came to excommunicate Llewellyn, the last Welsh Prince of Wales. He pursued him to the tomb, refusing him a Christian burial."

As for the Aristocracy, the family fortunes of their great houses— Cavendishes, Cecils, Seymours and the rest—had been laid in the reign of Henry VIII by the looting of the monasteries and the Roman Catholic churches. Now, when he urged that the ancient heritage of tithe should be again directed to the poor to whom it had been dedicated, they came "with their own hands dripping from the fat of sacrilege" to condemn him. In Rome, it is said that the Pope warmly appreciated the historic justice of this remark.

The Dangerous One was now preparing for the campaign of Land Reform, which he had long had in mind, and which, from his earliest years, he had held to be at the root of our economic troubles. A Land Enquiry Committee was set on foot, and the mass of statistics began to pour in. They made a powerful case against the way in which the land and agricultural population of pre-war Britain were being misused.

All the other political pots were on the boil—the Suffragettes, Labour Troubles, Ireland, Balkan Wars. Though Lloyd George belonged to that section of the Cabinet who favoured Votes for Women, he did not escape the attentions of their more fanatical supporters. The attempt to blow him up in his house at Walton Heath might fail, but a male Suffragist scored a bull's eye when he flung a steel-tipped case through the windows of Lloyd George's car as he left a meeting, striking him full in the face.

The New Year, 1912, roared in to the clangour of industrial strife. *The Times*, in an ominous editorial warned, 6 January, that

"the public must be prepared for a conflict between Labour and Capital, or between employers and employed, on a scale such as has never occurred before".

In February, the nation's coalfields were paralysed by a strike for a miners' minimum wage. In South Wales, the struggle was especially bitter. It produced yet another inflammatory, forceful Labour agitator in the ex-Baptist preacher, A. J. Cook, co-author with Tom Mann of the revolutionary Syndicalist pamphlet, *The Miners' Next Step*. Indeed, within the Labour Party at this moment there raged one of its periodic internal wars. Then, the movement was divided between the intellectual Fabian, Marxists and the industrial Trade Union, Syndicalists. The Marxists proposed to expropriate the private employers of industry and have the State take over. The Syndicalists felt the

Minister of Munitions: with M. Albert Thomas and Mr Edwin Montague, 1916

same about the private employers, but they wanted the workers in each industry to "run it themselves",

"... for what actually happens when industries and services are nationalized and run by officials having the same assumptions as the ordinary capitalist in respect of the remuneration and status of the wage earner?"

More than forty years have gone by, and now the coal mines, docks, railways and electricity undertakings of Britain have been nationalized. The Syndicalist question of 1912 is still being posed.

Meantime, the triumph of the coal kings over the miners in South Wales encouraged the Chairman of the Port of London Authority, Lord Devonport, to try conclusions again with the dockers. This was easily done, by challenging every point of the riverside union's interpretation of the previous year's settlement. Once more, strike and lock-out closed the greatest port in the world.

Or, almost closed it. For Lord Devonport did not hesitate to import other labour to break the strife. On Tower Hill now the "Soviet" reassembled, where nightly Ben Tillett summoned the men to stand fast and close the ranks, intoning in his vibrant voice, by way of Litany,

"Oh, God! Strike Lord Devonport dead!"

His lordship survived, and implacably bore upon the strike, which collapsed in August, 1912. It was followed by ruthless victimization. Sullenly and vengefully the workers' leaders retired, to plan for a General Strike in two years' time.

Fire was near to Ireland, too, as the summer of 1912 began to die. Before autumn was gone, the whole of the Balkans would be already aflame. Britain herself was still at peace, enjoying a trade boom, in spite of all, as Lloyd George claimed at the Bankers' Dinner in July. Shrewdly, he began to pose the question to his closest colleagues: What about an early General Election in the New Year? Better have it, he suggested to Asquith,

"before the trade boom cracks up, and the working classes drop into unemployment or low wages. Prosperity is fatal to the chances of Tariff Reform. On the other hand, one bad winter would revive its prospects and once more render it formidable."

Suddenly, Marconi. The Italian name began to be whispered, then mentioned with a wink, a nudge, then shouted, then printed. Finally, questions in the House, a Debate, a Select Inquiry, two Libel actions, a second and far more tense two-day Debate in Parliament, a series of political sensations exploding one after another like a chain of atomic detonations.

H

CHAPTER XIII

MARCONI

THE "Marconi Scandal" lasted more than a year, from April, 1912, until
June, 1913. It filled many thousands of newspaper columns, providing the
public with periodic (and genuine) "revelations". It supplied Opposition
orators with material for accusations and insinuations for the full period, and
far beyond it. It threatened to hound at least three leading members of the
Liberal Government out of public life, and to encompass the downfall of the
Government itself. In the end, as Lloyd George claimed, all the charges
were exploded. But as he also truthfully added, "the deadly after-damp
remained".

What was it all about? These facts emerge from the vast lumber heap of
rumour and innuendo:

The Committee of Imperial Defence had been urging the Government to
set up an Empire chain of wireless telegraphy, and on 7 March, 1912, the
Postmaster-General, Mr. Herbert Samuel, accepted the tender of the English
Marconi Company to do the job. At that time, it was almost certainly the
only company which could manage it, though there were other wireless-
telegraphy systems in existence besides that of Marconi. The Managing Director
of the English Marconi Company was Mr. Godfrey Isaacs, brother of Sir
Rufus Isaacs, the Attorney-General. The name was noted when the first
news broke.

There was another Marconi company, the Marconi Wireless Telegraph
Company of America (indeed, there were several others, in Canada, Spain,
France and elsewhere). The English company held more than half the shares
in this American subsidiary and, of course, both were operating the same
Marconi patents. Three directors of the English company, including Godfrey
Isaacs, sat on the board of the Marconi Wireless Telegraph Company of
America.

Towards the end of March, 1912, this American company was recon-
structed, and a large issue of new shares was proposed. Managing Director
Godfrey Isaacs personally undertook to market 50,000 of these shares in
England, while the English company guaranteed nearly twice as many more.
His other brother, Mr. Harry Isaacs, a fruitbroker, took up 56,000 of them.
On 17 April, the eve of the American flotation, Harry Isaacs offered some to
Sir Rufus, who being assured that the American firm had no interest in the
English one, bought 10,000 from him. The issue of this stock was, of course,
not yet public even in the United States; but news of its forthcoming flotation

over here had travelled and bidding for shares had already risen from £1 1s. 3d. to £2 apiece, the price at which Sir Rufus bought them.

He shared this knowledge with his close personal friends, Lloyd George and Alexander ("Alick") Murray, the Master of Elibank, the brilliant Government Chief Whip, offering them each a thousand of his shares on the same terms as he had acquired them. They accepted.

Within a day or two, American Marconi's had leapt to nearly £4 apiece. At this point, Sir Rufus disposed of the remainder of his shares, while his two friends each sold half of theirs. Later they all bought further shares, Lloyd George's own purchase being 1,500. It was an incredibly imprudent thing for Ministers of the Crown to have done; what is still more astonishing is that none of them seem to have considered the remote possibility of any future trouble arising out of it.

Their transactions, which were made quite openly, were not publicized for some time. Everybody seemed to be buying Marconis just then, for the drama of the loss of the *Titanic*, with the drowning of 1,500 of her two thousand passengers and crew, gave a grimly urgent advertisement to the need of harnessing wireless to the service of ocean navigation. But soon, to the knowing looks which had greeted the news of the English Marconi Company Chairman's name, there succeeded suggestions and, before long, open and published charges of corruption.

In the *Eye Witness*, a weekly journal of devoted anti-Semitic scurrility, the Editor, Mr. Cecil Chesterton, charged that Postmaster-General Samuel was about to hand over large sums of public money to the English Marconi Company for the private benefit of the Attorney-General Isaacs, the Isaacs brothers, and himself. Lloyd George did not at first figure in this libellous indictment of "the Three Jews", though in the City slander was busy with his name. In none of this was the American Marconi Company ever mentioned.

In July, 1912, the contract between the British Government and the English Marconi Company was signed. Parliament had yet to ratify it, and already there was serious criticism of its terms, besides the reckless diatribes of the *Eye Witness* and its rivals in sensation. In August, Cecil Chesterton coined the phrase "The Marconi Scandal" in denouncing "this abominable business of Samuel, the Isaacs and the Marconi Company".

Mr. Herbert Samuel, his attention first arrested by a screaming poster on a London railway station as he was about to board a train, considered taking action for libel. He allowed himself to be dissuaded from it by Sir Rufus Isaacs. At the same time, Messrs. Isaacs, Murray and Lloyd George, all personally confided in the Prime Minister that they had been dealing in American Marconi shares.

Asquith received this news calmly and indifferently. He saw no harm in it, and sensed no danger. He accepted the view that the American company had no pecuniary interest in the English company and, as he later declared, simply let the thing pass out of his mind.

But mud-slinging did not pass out of fashion. In October, the House of Commons debated the Marconi contract, on a motion by the Postmaster-General himself to appoint a Select Committee to inquire into the whole matter, and report. There was strong Tory pressure for a Judicial Committee, which would have excluded the possibility of what, in fact, happened. This was that the Select Committee was bound to be chosen on, roughly, the Parliamentary representation in the House of Commons, thus ensuring a Government (and Party) verdict. It was perhaps a real misfortune for those concerned that it was not left to a Judicial Committee. For the Opposition took the view that the Select Committee would be "packed", and did not fail to say so.

The opening speeches of the first Marconi Debate were reasonable enough. They discussed the merits or otherwise of the Marconi-Government bargain, the amount of royalty dues proposed, and certain technical questions. An ugly moment came when George Lansbury, from the Labour benches, referred to "the scandalous gambling in Marconi shares". He declared there had been grave rumours all over the City that certain people had made money out of this business who ought not to have made money out of it.

Lloyd George rose from the Government Front Bench. He was pale but composed, and he spoke with a cold, deliberate fury. He said:

"The Hon. Member said something about the Government, and he has talked about 'rumours'. I want to know what these rumours are. If the Hon. Gentleman has any charge to make against the Government as a whole, or against individual Members of it, I think it ought to be stated openly. The reason why the Government wanted a frank discussion before going to Committee was because we wanted to bring here these rumours, these sinister rumours, that have been passed from one foul lip to another behind the backs of the House."

Lansbury, having blundered into the centre of a cyclone, went on stumbling around in it, blaming the previous Tory speakers for first saying what, in fact, they had been most careful not to say.

At this point, Sir Rufus Isaacs, the Attorney-General, stood up to deal, not with any "charge", but with the "insinuations". He declared categorically that never from beginning to end, in any shape or form, either by deed, act, or word had he taken part in the negotiation of the Marconi contract. He had never discussed it with the Postmaster-General, had never been consulted, knew nothing of the tender until a few days before it had been accepted. Nor had he ever, from start to finish, had one single transaction in the shares of the company concerned, and that went equally for the Postmaster-General and the Chancellor of the Exchequer. In his turn, Herbert Samuel made personal disavowal. The Debate reverted to the lawyers and the engineers. Again, no reference had been made to the Marconi Wireless Telegraph Company of America.

The "Marconi Scandal" seemed to be yesterday's news.

In truth, it had hardly begun. This was only Act I. The Select Committee opened its Inquiry. Since this Committee had been chosen, as anticipated, roughly on the basis of Party strength in the House of Commons (i.e. 6 Tories, 5 Liberals, 2 Irish Nationalists and 1 Labour), and, currently, Party feeling had seldom run so high and fiercely, the "jury" could hardly be expected to set about their task otherwise than on good old partisan lines.

In the Press, Cecil Chesterton went forward with renewed zest. The *Eye Witness* had just died; but his *New Witness*, which had succeeded it, possibly improved on its parent in virulence. The *Spectator*, the *National Review* and the *Outlook* also rarely failed their readers weekly, nor daily did the *Standard, Pall Mall Gazette, Morning Post* and *Daily Express*.

But it was the French newspaper *Le Matin* which in February, 1913, really rang up the curtain on sensational Act II, of what was now becoming the Continuing Marconi Story. On 14 February, *Le Matin* ran a story to say that the Postmaster-General had rushed through the Marconi contract without submitting it to Parliament, and had then entered into a deal with the Attorney-General and his brother, Godfrey Isaacs, whereby they bought shares in the company concerned for £2 apiece and sold them for as much as £8. Next day, the newspaper corrected its story and apologized. But Herbert Samuel this time issued a writ for libel; he knew that he was innocent. His example exacted emulation; Sir Rufus Isaacs instantly followed with another writ.

The case was set down for hearing before Mr. Justice Darling on 19 March.

Then the first real sensation broke. As the prelude to Act II, it was announced that for *Le Matin* there would appear Mr. James H. Campbell, K.C.,[1] a former Tory Attorney-General for Ireland, and the colleague of Sir Edward Carson in the Parliamentary representation of Dublin University. Counsel for the plaintiffs would be Sir Edward Carson himself and Mr. F. E. Smith, the two foremost Tory leaders of the Ulster Resistance to Home Rule! At this point, it seemed that the bottom had finally fallen out of the year-old Marconi-Campaign.

The very opposite. For the first time, a serious foundation for it was about to be provided. For while F. E. Smith elicited from his client, Herbert Samuel, the Postmaster-General, that he had "never bought, sold, or had an interest of any kind whatsoever in any Marconi company", Sir Edward Carson stated (for the first time) that Sir Rufus Isaacs, the Attorney-General, had bought those 10,000 shares in the American company, 2,000 of

[1] Afterwards Lord Glenavy, Chairman of the Irish Free State Senate.

which he passed on to his friends, Lloyd George and Alexander Murray. Examined by his counsel, Sir Rufus said that having sold 3,750 of his shares at some profit he still held 6,430. If he sold these at the current price, he estimated he would lose on the whole transaction about £1,200. As for Lloyd George and Murray, they would each lose several hundreds. For the *Matin*, no defence was offered, and within an hour or so of the opening of the case, judgment with costs had been entered for the plaintiffs.

Next morning, the Tory Opposition Press artillery opened up almost all along the line. *Now* what about it! So there *was* something in it after all! So these immaculate Liberal Ministers *had* been investing, speculating, gambling —call it what you liked—on the Stock Exchange, and in Marconi shares at that! Did anybody any longer believe that there was no connection between English Marconi's and American? For if there was none then why had the Ministers withheld this information of their dealings from the House of Commons at the time of the Marconi Debate? How much more was there to come out?

The Labour Press joined in the onslaught on their nominal allies, the Liberals. The unflagging "witness", Cecil Chesterton himself, claimed to be a Socialist. As for the *Daily Herald*, "Labour's Own" (Editor, George Lansbury), it opined that the *Matin* trial was simply "a put-up job".

But there was one journalist, who stood then at the very top of his trade, who strangely enough sought to make no special "copy" out of this red-hot story. His name was Alfred Harmsworth, Lord Northcliffe, creator of the *Daily Mail*. Yet Northcliffe had got the inside news before any of his competitors.

Max Aitken, who was later to thrust the *Daily Express* to the forefront of the Popular Press of Britain, had an interesting experience in journalism at this time. When Mr. J. H. Campbell, K.C., was invited to appear for *Le Matin*, he had gone to see his own Party Leader, Bonar Law, to ask his advice about accepting the brief. "Take it," said Bonar Law. Mr. Campbell learned from his opposite Prosecuting number, Sir Edward Carson (who had himself refrained from seeking any Party guidance in this highly political issue), that disclosure of the American Marconi transactions would be made in court, and he was authorized to confide this news to Bonar Law. Now here was dynamite, and Aitken, who was in Bonar Law's close confidence, hurried off to ask (*a*) if Northcliffe knew about it and, if so, (*b*) what he was going to do about it.

He found that Northcliffe knew all about the scandal. He had been fully informed by Winston Churchill, who had telephoned him early that morning to ask if he could see him. A few minutes later, Churchill had arrived in Northcliffe's bedroom, and there unburdened to the newspaper proprietor what seemed to be the whole story. Furthermore, Northcliffe had pledged himself to handle it in a friendly way. He did not divulge to Aitken his source of information at the time. Afterwards, when he had real reason to feel aggrieved, Northcliffe told Riddell:

"Winston was very much agitated when he came to see me. I did not know until then how much he was attached to Lloyd George."

Indeed, Winston Churchill had done a lot for his friend, Lloyd George, for he had not only (i) muzzled Northcliffe; he had (ii) captured for his side the silver voices of F. E. Smith and Carson. Thus, he had (iii) further deprived the Tory Party of the Parliamentary and political services of two of their most formidable fighters, tying them, as it were to the tail of the (Lloyd George) devil himself. Churchill would do Lloyd George a further service later, with their own leader, Asquith. To Northcliffe now, Lloyd George wrote:

11, Downing Street,
Whitehall,
S.W.3.
21 March, 1913.

"Dear Lord Northcliffe,

I feel I must write to thank you for the chivalrous manner in which you have treated the Attorney-General and myself over the Marconi case. Had we done anything of which men of honour ought to feel ashamed we could not have approached you on this subject. But although the transaction was in itself a straight-forward one, we were only too conscious that it was capable of exciting unpleasant comment. The atmosphere is now a morbid one owing to the controversy that gathers round Marconi enterprises. I therefore appreciate deeply the generosity and largeness of view which have distinguished your treatment of the matter. I firmly believe that time, and a short time, will justify your foresight. None the less do I feel grateful for a great kindness done to me, for I know the power you wield.

Ever sincerely,
D. Lloyd George."

To which Northcliffe replied that he had acted as he had because five minutes explanation had shown him that this was the fairest way. He added that he was neither a rabid party man nor an anti-Semite.

Thus Northcliffe showed his own prescience, and patriotism.

The drama shifted next to Committee Room 12, at the House of Commons, where the Marconi Inquiry was now plodding forward into its fifth month. Until yesterday, this Inquiry had been steadily degenerating into the most boring performance in town. Now, the Marconi Ministers themselves were going to appear. There were queues outside Committee Room 12 for Act III, and when Sir Rufus Isaacs took his seat within the horseshoe table of the Court, the public were already standing six deep around the room.

Then, throughout two days there went on the close personal cross-examination of the keenest cross-examiner at the English Bar. After the evidence of the *Matin* trial had been rehashed, Sir Rufus defended with passion his non-disclosure to the House of Commons of his American Marconi dealings, saying that he was not answering that charge at that time; he had certainly intended to tell the Select Committee when he appeared before them. He had, in fact, informed two leading Liberal members of the Committee. (This disclosure was twisted by some enemies to say that he had tried to "get at" the jury.) As early as the previous August, said Sir Rufus, he had written to the Prime Minister about taking action for libel, and he produced Asquith's letter replying that to notice the "scurrilous rubbish" would only help to give it notoriety. The letter ended,

> "very little going on here, and but for Winston there would be nothing in the papers". (Loud laughter.)

The only other laugh came when the Attorney-General confessed he had also once invested £150 in a Welsh gold mine. He had not sold any shares to Mr. Lloyd George.

On 28 March, Lloyd George himself took his place before the Committee for his two-day ordeal. Like Sir Rufus Isaacs, he realized that he was now fighting for his political life, in the fiercest battle he had ever yet faced. The Chancellor of the Exchequer entered carrying a large dispatch-case full of documents.

Now, the public learned for the first time of the later Marconi transactions of the Ministers. But Lloyd George defined two rules of Ministerial conduct which he resolutely insisted he had kept (i) that he had made no private use of information which had come to him in the course of his public duty, and (ii) that he made no investment in any company which had a contract with the Government. He ridiculed the reports that he made £60,000, that he owned "mansions in Surrey and Wales, and villas in the South of France". He had one small house in Wales, built four years earlier at the cost of less than £2,000, "this is my great palace!" The one blown up at Walton Heath had been "someone else's property, before I even had the lease of it". He stoutly maintained that his two dealings on the Stock Exchange had been an investment, not a speculation, and that the total income he derived from all his investments was £400 per annum. "That is my great fortune," concluded Lloyd George. He opened his dispatch-case, and offered in evidence his own and his wife's bank pass-books; if need be, his own brother's.

It had not all been in apologetic vein. Lloyd George was a proud man, and he had been deeply wounded by the rumours and the smears. If any Member had believed them, he cried angrily, it was that man's duty to state them openly. It was dishonouring to Parliament itself to circulate such slander, dastardly to skulk behind other persons. Churchill, who sat near to the Chancellor, leaned across and patted him warmly on the back.

Fred Jowett, Labour M.P. for Bradford, drew this vivid picture at the time in the *Bradford Pioneer* of the two accused men in their dark hour ("Alick" Murray the Government Chief Whip, had resigned his post before the end of 1912, and had gone off on a business quest in Columbia, South America, for Lord Cowdray, the oil magnate).

"Sir Rufus Isaacs distinctly and obviously distressed, the most successful advocate in all England pleading in his own defence and it hurt him. His pale face was drawn and care-worn. No person who was not blind with Party prejudice or personal malice could look on this man this day without feeling deep sympathy for him. . . .

There was, on the part of the attacking Party, a wolfish eagerness to destroy the two Ministers. There were interruptions which seemed like nothing so much as the deep bay of eager wolves in a hungry pack.

Lloyd George appeared, and proceeded on quite other lines, than Sir Rufus Isaacs. He stood in the white sheet of Repentance—but he took care to clank the sword of Retaliation which he wore beneath."

April brought other, painful scenes. Mr. Harold Smith, Tory M.P. for Warrington (he was F.E.'s brother) resigned his membership of the Marconi Committee in protest against the use of what he called "the gag", which he claimed had "rendered the proceedings a public scandal". In the House of Commons, Mr. Kebty-Fletcher lowered proceedings to the level of a brawl in the following questions:

"To ask Mr. Chancellor of the Exchequer if there are any emolument or allowances attached to his Office other than his salary?"

"The answer is in the negative," snapped Lloyd George.

Then the insulting supplementary.

"Is not the Right Honourable Gentleman's salary sufficient to prevent him from wrongfully and improperly gambling . . ."

A storm of yells from either side of the House drowned the rest of it. Lloyd George rose to his feet. His face was ashen, but his eyes blazed. He gripped the table, and as a famous Press Gallery reporter wrote, "one thought him about to leap over it, in his passionate anger, and make a smashing fight of it in the middle of the Unionist ranks".

He spat the words:

"If he has anything of that kind to say about me he had better say it in a place where he will be subjected to cross-examination!"

A fresh turmoil broke out. The roar of cheers from the Government benches mingled with the Opposition howls of "Marconi Swindle!" "Gag!" "Packed Jury!"

H*

Mr. Kebty-Fletcher stood up. "Mock heroics!" he bawled.

"Cad!" "Snob!" screamed the Liberals, and from the Irish benches came the stentorian bellow, "Sit down, ye slanderin' divil!"

As for Lloyd George, he repeated now with composed passion, "Say it openly, if you dare!"

To be just, both Kebty-Fletcher and other Tory backbenchers did repeat it, outside and openly, awaiting libel proceedings. Wisely, these were not taken. The "public trial" of the "Marconi Ministers" continued in the street, in the trains, in the clubs and in the pubs.

On 28 April, 1913, Winston Churchill found himself before the Committee. He had been summoned there, within a couple of hours' notice, following the reluctant mention of his name by a witness earlier in the day, as being involved in the Marconi case. Churchill was beside himself, "quivering with anger", red with excitement, and furious with the Committee. Wrote Pengelly, the star reporter of the *Star* evening newspaper:

> "The Cyclone arrived, and like the population of an American town in the 'hurricane belt', the members of the Committee speedily took to the cyclone cellars."

Raising his voice and thumping the table, Churchill denounced the "most insulting charge" on which he had been summoned:

> "The charge that, having had dealings in Marconi shares, I sat silent while my friends came forward and voluntarily disclosed their exact positions; that I sat silent while they were subjected to gross ill-usage and covered with every kind of calumny and insult; that I skulked in the background, keeping my guilty knowledge to myself and desiring to conceal it from your Committee!"

The Chairman sought to placate him. It was simply out of justice to himself that the Committee had invited him to be heard. Churchill was in no way mollified, brushed him aside, then gave the most emphatic, exact and all-embracing disavowal of all Marconi disavowals, adding:

> "And if at any time anyone has said so, then he is a liar and a slanderer! And if anyone has repeated it, and has no evidence, the only difference between that person and the liar and slanderer, is that he is a coward as well!" He then snapped, "May I now assume my examination is finished?"

And getting no further response from the cyclone-cellar dwellers, stormed out of Act III.

It had been a most effective counter-attack, creating a complete diversion by turning attention away from the "Men in the Dock" to the "Men on the Bench". His object was further aided by events of May–June, when Cecil Chesterton was brought up at the Old Bailey on six charges of libel against

Godfrey Isaacs, whom he had variously described as a "vile conspirator", "corrupt", "a thief and knave attempting to obtain public plunder". Once more, Sir Edward Carson and F. E. Smith appeared for the prosecution. The trial lasted ten days, but produced little that was new. In the end, Chesterton failed to prove any of his charges. He was convicted and fined £100 and ordered to pay all the costs of the prosecution.

Next to be arraigned (these offenders before their own political colleagues), stood Carson and Smith. "Carrying chivalry too far", "unfortunate", were the least of the charges against them. "Selling themselves for a lawyer's guinea" was the more usual; to which F.E. replied with a long, lofty letter to *The Times* expounding the Traditions of the Bar. He quoted the Tory Erskine's classic argument for defending the rebel Tom Paine:

> "From the moment that any advocate can be permitted to say that he will or will not stand between the Crown and the subject arraigned in the court where he daily sits to practice, from that moment the liberties of England are at an end."

It is still being quoted in current politics of England, and it is still true, civilized doctrine. But *The Times* (which had itself congratulated them on the outcome of the *Matin* case) now portentously rebuked Carson and Smith for perplexing the average man, who it considered would find it rather hard to appreciate how two leading Tory Parliamentarians had been able to deprive their Party of their services in debate and in the lobbies at this critical moment.

What was really offending Northcliffe, the owner of *The Times*, was the latest Marconi "revelation", which had first appeared in another newspaper. This was the news that "Alick" Murray, the Master of Elibank, besides investing his own money in American Marconis, had invested £9,000 of the Liberal Party funds, and had failed to make an admission of it. The startling news, indeed, had been unknown to Churchill himself when he had gone to see Northcliffe. Now, to the bewildered British public, the whole Liberal Government seemed to be involved. Angrily, Northcliffe complained to Churchill.

After all, said Northcliffe, Churchill had come to see him and ask him to treat the Marconi affair on non-Party lines. Churchill had offered him an explanation, which he had accepted. But it had now turned out that there was a lot more to it. Northcliffe did not intend to restrain his newspapers from following up the story.

Indeed, Act IV was now in full and forceful unfolding, especially when every Opposition demand for the presence of "Alick" Murray before the Marconi Committee was met by the sincerely regretful Liberal reply:

"The Master of Elibank is detained on business in Bogota."

Bogota—or BOG-OH-TA-AAH! was by now on every lip, foul or otherwise. It was a terrific talking point, and from a thousand Tory platforms the name of that far-off jungle mountain city in Columbia, with its final condemnatory A-aah! rolled forth, bringing Homeric bouts of cheers and laughter. Interrupters in the House of Commons and hecklers in the country now no longer bawled "Marconi"! The word was *"BOG-OH-TA-AAH!"*

Lloyd George had always been the least implicated of the three Ministers involved in the purchase of the shares, but he was the best known and the most widely loved, or loathed. The venom of the enemy concentrated upon him. He had begun by treating it lightly, but as the months passed he took alarm. He fretted, talked of little else, would suddenly break off conversation on other matters and walk away, or stand in moody silence, brooding on the shadow that had fallen across his life. He had good friends besides his own family, especially Timothy Davies, Charles Henry, Arthur Crosfield, Charles Masterman and the wives of these men, and, of course, Churchill, most loyal in the darkest day. He had his own, highly personal secretaries, all understanding human beings. He needed every one of them. He lost weight, lost vitality, fell ill again, and his black hair grew grey, the lines began to mark his face, and for the first time in public he was seen to use spectacles. A great life poised on the edge.

At last, on 13 June, 1913, the Select Committee reported. Or rather, they presented three drafts of a Report, one being by the majority, another by the minority, and a third by the Liberal Chairman. One thing they all agreed on: that no Minister had been influenced in the discharge of his public duties by any interest he might have had in any of the Marconi or other undertakings, or had utilized information coming to him from official sources for private investment or speculation.

The Majority (Government Party) draft declared that not only were the newspaper charges made against Sir Rufus Isaacs, Lloyd George, and Mr. Herbert Samuel absolutely untrue, but that the persons who made them had no reason to believe them to be true. It was a total vindication; it was also noted to be a 100 per cent Party verdict.

In the Chairman's draft, this verdict was qualified by the opinion that it was perhaps a pity Sir Rufus Isaacs had ever bought the shares in the first place, and secondly, it would have averted much misunderstanding if the Ministers concerned had told the House of Commons in October what had come out in the *Matin* trial in March.

The Minority (Opposition Party) draft criticized the whole handling of the share issue and found "grave impropriety" in the conduct of Sir Rufus Isaacs, Lloyd George and Lord Murray, both in acquiring the shares at an advantageous price and in subsequent dealings in them. It censored them for their lack of candour, especially Murray (who had never yet disclosed anything). Their own reticence had been largely to blame for the reckless rumours of which they complained.

The same morning as the Marconi Report was published Lloyd George received this letter from next door. It came from Mrs. Asquith, the Prime Minister's wife, written in her own inimitable style:

10 Downing Street,
Whitehall, S.W.
13 June, 1913.

"Dear Mr. L. George,

I dined alone with my husband last night—he was in Derby form—he said he wanted to see you and Rufus to have a careful talk over the speeches 'If Lloyd George and Rufus play their cards *well*, show the proper spirit, *I* will let the opposition *have it* ! ! They shall sweat under what I've got to say!' I told him you said you wd. give them Hell he didn't mind except he said you must choose a good moment (*quite* between ourselves you might ask him when you are *absolutely* alone so that no one will ever know what sort of day etc., he advises). To my mind they seriously overrate what will happen—*We* shall score & why? because of the low vile charges they made without a shadow of evidence & after all is said and done the committee have proved nothing but great indiscretion. The points are these. This debate must show that nothing of the kind can *ever* happen again and that when you realized the folly you apologized (that part of yr. speech sd. be broad and simple in *no* way rhetorical it will have much more effect) and did yr best.

Yours ever
Margot Asquith."

The Report was received in the same spirit as it had been conceived. The Tory protests of "Gag!" which had accompanied the Inquiry now gave way to charges against the Report of "Whitewash!" The Liberals congratulated (or consoled) themselves that nothing worse than indiscretion had been proved.

A Paris newspaper described the Marconi drama so far as "an orgy of snobbery, jobbery and robbery, flagrant, palpable and odious".

In this atmsphere MARCONI, Act V, unfolded.

This was the two-day debate on 18 June, another Waterloo date, in the House of Commons, on a Tory motion regretting the transactions of certain of His Majesty's Ministers and their want of frankness towards the House. The moderation of the speeches from both sides could not bridge the gap between the Opposition and the Government, who were determined to go no further than accept the Minister's own regrets that the purchases were made and that they had not been mentioned in the October Debate. Not even the ingenuity of Balfour, who proposed that a formula should be found embodying both, was able to get over this divergence.

Decidedly, Lloyd George himself was not prepared to yield another inch. He had already offered the Prime Minister his resignation, but Asquith had stood by him loyally. There had been some talk that the word "indiscretion" in the Liberal amendment might be allowed, but that word, too, Lloyd George resolutely refused to accept. He told Churchill, who thereupon went to Asquith and told him that Lloyd George's mind on this matter was utterly made up and that if he did not have his way he meant to go; this would bring down the Government. Thus Churchill rendered a fifth service to his friend in this troubled year.

The Prime Minister generously conceded, and Lloyd George went back to battle. He made an admirable speech, "frank and manly", said Asquith, with truth. Lloyd George admitted that it would have been better if all the facts had been placed before the House long ago, but he pleaded that he had waited to be called before the Committee. He had sought to be called in the *Matin* trial, too. He had made all his transactions in good faith, openly and in his own name. In his speech he conceded the word "indiscreet" which he had refused in the formal amendment. He ended:

"If you will, I acted thoughtlessly, I acted carelessly, I acted mistakenly, but I acted innocently, I acted openly and I acted honestly."

And Lloyd George marched, erect and defiant, from the Chamber. The House divided:

> For the Government   .   346
> Against the Government .   268

An amendment, acquitting the Ministers of acting otherwise than in good faith, and reprobating the charges of corruption brought against Ministers which had been proved to be wholly false, was agreed without a division.

Was it the end of the muddy Marconi Story? Not quite. *The Spectator* did not miss the chance to suggest that the idea of delicacy and discretion cannot have been new to the Chancellor of the Exchequer; it recalled Joe Chamberlain and the Kynoch debate and the motion of censure which Lloyd George had moved when he had invoked the "rule of Caesar's wife":

"Members of either House of Parliament holding subordinate office in any public department ought to have no interest, direct or indirect, in any firm or company competing for contracts with the Crown, unless the nature and extent of such interest being first declared, Your Majesty shall have sanctioned the countenance thereof and, when necessary, shall have directed such precautions to be taken as may effectually prevent any suspicion of influence or favouritism in the allocation of such contracts."

Tory speakers in the country did not fail to carry forward the analogy either. They asked: Suppose Joe's own brother had launched an American Kynoch's firm, invested £10,000 in it and introduced into it Hicks-Beach and the Tory Chief Whip?

Perhaps the most apposite comment on the whole affair—and especially on the still-absent Master of Elibank's handling of the Liberal Party Fund came from the Liberal weekly, *Nation*:

"We imagine that Lord Murray's[1] investment of Liberal Funds in American Marconis will be promptly repudiated, and the transaction rigorously cut for the little that it is worth.

For the Liberal Party in Parliament, we can only express two hopes for the future. The first is that the watchword will be 'everything into the light', instead of 'as much in the dark as can be trusted not to come out' ... our second hope is that as this matter has now touched the Achilles' heel of Liberalism which is the secret Party Fund, the Party will proceed resolutely to a reform of the system. In so far as it accrues from the sale of honours a taint flows from it, and saturates the entire Party system of Britain. The purse so constituted and a distribution of titles as lavish and undiscriminating as that which Lord Murray initiated, there lie sources of evil far beyond this incidental disclosure of recklessness."

Thus, the Liberal journal cast its shrewd judgment far into future days, when Liberal Party internal funds would unfold another chapter in an unhappy story.

In October, 1913, Sir Rufus Isaacs, the Attorney-General, was appointed Lord Chief Justice of England. The promotion was sharply attacked by the *Daily Express* and the *Morning Post*. It moved Rudyard Kipling to pen the cruellest political diatribe since the "Letters of Junius", comparing Judge Rufus ("take oath to judge the land") with Gehazi, the servant of the Prophet Elisha, who ran after Naaman and by false pretences "extracted somewhat of him", for which the Prophet struck him with leprosy. (It was not printed then, but the words ran from mouth to mouth and did their deadly worst.)

Postscript to the Marconi Story is the following brief note from Sir Rufus Isaacs to Lloyd George, 27 December, 1913:

"My dear L. G.,

You have asked me so often to let you know the amount you owe me and I have so often said I would look it up that I have at last taken advantage of the leisure I am now enjoying to work it out:

I paid .	.	.	£8,129	15	0
I received	.	.	5,997	11	6
			£2,132	3	6

Of which you and Alick each owe 1/10th, namely £213 4 0. The account is simple enough, and the balance represents the amount I lost on

[1] He had been created Baron Murray in 1912.

the whole transaction. Don't bother about the amount. I would not have told it to you—but you seemed annoyed I hadn't yet ascertained it when last you mentioned it."

Needless to say, a cheque was sent immediately for the amount indicated. And Lloyd George? John Redmond said of him at that time:

"After 1,000 pages of Marconi Inquiry, after 19,000 questions and the evidence of thirty witnesses, after seventy days searching inquiry, every man in the House of Commons was obliged to admit that no single thing has been proved against the honour and good name of Mr. Lloyd George."

But in the alleyways of politics they fastened even on Redmond's friendly phrase, and for many a day repeated, "Not Proven".

Lloyd George's old sense of man's injustice to man, which he had originally felt on other men's account—and sought to redress for their sake—thus returned to him in bitter personal experience.

In the late summer of 1913 Lloyd George was in a dangerous mood, looking for trouble.

CHAPTER XIV

THAT OTHER ISLAND

THERE were those, beyond Lloyd George's own Party, who were still anxious to work with him. One of them, the Tory politician-lawyer, F. E. Smith, was perhaps the most persistent. With that other born coalitionist, Winston Churchill, F.E. had never ceased to hanker after an "agreed programme" between the parties, leading inevitably to some kind of "National" Government. So the talk across the lines continued. Within three months of the final unsatisfactory Marconi debate, he was writing to Lloyd George to propose a new Conference to deal with Ireland, House of Lords Reform and the Land.

Thus, on 26 September, 1913, after reporting that he has had "long and interesting talks with the King and with Winston", F.E. suggests that the King himself should summon the Conference, because then "the extremists on either side would not be able to reject the idea". He urges Lloyd George to make his forthcoming speech at Bedford, where the Chancellor was due to open the new Liberal Land Campaign "in a restrained way, and without unfriendliness to Landlords as a class. If things fail, you can return at any time to a War basis", and he adds, characteristically, "Do not attach too much importance to our speeches at the moment".

To which Lloyd George replied saying that he had been willing for years to work with F.E. and some others on his side. But if the Tories were now ready to talk business, why were they sponsoring a new campaign (over Marconi) "of pure scurrility"?

Nothing was done, then. The Land Campaign was duly launched with its programme of minimum wage for farm labourers, security of tenure for farmers, provision of small holdings, and—a lot less usefully—officials to "promote good farming". It got off to a bad start in the Bedford speech when Lloyd George, denouncing the tyranny of Game (and his own more especial villain, the Gamekeeper), described how a field of mangold-wurzels had been eaten by pheasants—a thing utterly unfamiliar to any farmer or ornithologist. Strube, the famous *Daily Express* cartoonist, picked up the pheasant and his mangold-wurzel and made them a national joke. For the next thirty years, Strube never drew Lloyd George without them.

In fact, despite the rousing refrain of the Land Song, and the never unpopular attack upon Landlords, the Liberal Land Campaign of pre-war 1913–14 had no happier fate than the post-war one of 1925–27. The officers of the Land Enquiry Organization were hampered by the dissensions of their leading Committee men and Chairman, funds were not forthcoming from the rich supporters of the Liberal Party ("Radical Plutocracy" the Tories called them), and for one reason and another, the Liberal Land Campaign hung fire. The Land League never commanded the ecstatic enthusiasm of the Budget League three years before.

The Tory Party, too, and in particular, the latest Tory leader, Bonar Law, had their troubles. Tariff Reform was the ghost that haunted the Tories, as Home Rule was the spectre that ever rose up to torment the Liberals. There were many in the Tory ranks (certainly there were a majority among the leadership) who had dared to hope that Balfour's last service at their head had also been his greatest, in that he had finally laid that ghost—by shoving the responsibility for introducing any Protectionist policy on to the electors themselves. He had certainly tried to do this when, in the December General Election of 1910, he declared that if the Tory Party were returned to power they would submit the question of Free Trade or Tariff Reform to a Referendum of the People.

In no way whatever did this satisfy those ardent spirits who really believed that Protection with Imperial Preference or even Imperial Free Trade, was the only way to bind the Empire economically together. One of these Tory Empire agitators was Bonar Law's friend, Max Aitken. As 1912 drew to its close, he persuaded the Tory Leader to come to his constituency at Ashton-under-Lyne, and there make a bold new declaration of faith. Lord Lansdowne, indeed, had already just told a London audience that the Referendum idea was dead. At Ashton-under Lyne, on 16 December, Bonar Law buried it.

He raised, instead, a daring, defiant flag of "Empire Free Trade". He declared that Imperial Preference and Food Taxes were inseparable, and that the day after the Tory Party took office, they would invite the Dominion Governments to an Empire Conference to discuss and settle both questions.

Aitken was delighted, and so was the crowded Aston-under-Lyne Tory meeting that evening. Bonar Law was escorted to the railway station by a cheering company and 100 torch-bearers in flaming procession.

Next morning, it was seen to be the Tory Party which had been set on fire. Manchester Conservative Club was in especial turmoil: did anybody *in his senses* suppose that Free Trade Lancashire would ever vote for FOOD TAXES? On the other hand, Protectionist Birmingham suspected that instead of placing the Tariff issue squarely before the British electorate, a new dodge had been invented by the politicians to shift the responsibility on to the Dominions.

As these fresh dissensions broke out in the Tory Party, Northcliffe took the field in his *Times* and *Daily Mail* denouncing this "fatal stomach-tax". The wind from Fleet Street fanned the flames of Tory revolt into a blaze. It was reckoned that at least 70 per cent of the Tory M.P.s were utterly opposed to the Bonar Law policy. There was a real possibility that he would be forced out of the leadership of the Party.

But, though the policy was unpopular, the man himself was genuinely liked, and trusted. A Memorandum signed by 229 Tory Back Benchers attested their loyalty both to Bonar Law and Lord Lansdowne, but besought them to leave the Food Tax Question to some future General Election—which, of course, meant putting it on the shelf. Reluctantly, Bonar Law agreed to "this bitter sacrifice". Max Aitken did not. With three other Tory M.P.s he proclaimed his utter impenitence. He had personally raised the Food Tax Flag—"Skull and Crossbones" Lloyd George called it—and now he nailed it to the masthead of his own ship for life.

A new storm was blowing, from across the Irish Sea. John Bull's Other Island was by now generating more electric commotion than anything experienced in this one for two centuries. It was getting ready to exact its own terrible tribute from its conqueror for all these years of its subjection. The eighty Irish Nationalist M.P.s in the House of Commons had already demanded, and obtained, a first payment from the Liberal Government; a Home Rule Bill (introduced in April, 1912), was now lumbering towards the Statute Book along the winding road of the Parliament Act, with its three successive sanctions of the House of Commons. It was not a very revolutionary Bill, for all Imperial matters, including the making of Peace or War, foreign relations, defence, taxation, customs duties, coinage and even Police remained under the authority of the Parliament at Westminster. On these scores, the Home Rule Bill had already been contemptuously rejected in advance by the extreme Irish Nationalist and Republican movements.

It was still too much for Ulster. The Scots Presbyterians there were not so devoted to England that they could not break away from the Westminster Parliament—indeed, they had objected ever to going there at the time of the Act of Union in 1800. What the Orangemen were bent on, was maintaining their own ascendancy in the Protestant North (naturally, they called it "freedom"). They were determined not to risk putting themselves under the Roman Catholic South, which would swamp them with numbers. Who can blame them? They were a sturdy, hard-working, independent people. Their social rule was certainly not as crude as their rhyme:

> "The crown of the causeway
> On road or street,
> And the Papishes under my feet!"

Nor is it to be forgotten that from Ulster had come some of the greatest of Irish patriots. Perhaps only the Irish themselves could explain this—as also that the new leader of intransigent Ulster, Sir Edward Carson, was a Southern Irishman.

It is true that Carson sat in Parliament for Dublin University, which (next to Dublin Castle) might be regarded as an English stronghold, or at any rate, a Protestant one. On the other hand, Carson had joined the National Liberal

Club in London after Gladstone had planted the Home Rule flag on the Liberal Party ramparts. That he was a very great advocate nobody could ever deny (least of all his old college contemporary and subsequent legal quarry, Oscar Wilde), although he possessed no capacity for polished speech and sometimes failed to finish a sentence. Yet he certainly was effective. What perhaps has not yet been appreciated is that Carson was also a consummate actor. So great, indeed, that Carson seems to have persuaded Ulster, Southern Ireland, England and even Carson himself, that rather than submit to Home Rule in Ireland, he was prepared to plunge both of John Bull's Islands into civil war.

Already (on 23 September, 1911), at a gathering of 100,000 members of the Orange Lodges assembled in Craigavon, near Belfast, Carson had proclaimed, "We will yet defeat the most nefarious conspiracy that has ever been hatched against a free people," and two days later, the Ulster Unionist Council began to prepare the setting up of an Ulster Provisional Government to take over the Province the instant that the Home Rule Act came into force.

Was the Tory Party really in favour of this? Was Bonar Law? He came of Ulster Scots stock himself, and as a Tory he could hardly be expected to hail Home Rule for Ireland. But Bonar Law was also a Canadian, an intense believer in the Greater British Empire—and had Home Rule for Canada made her less loyal in her faith or Imperial in her outlook? The South African War had answered that already, and soon a vaster conflict would re-echo it with a deeper note, and bloodier testament. Perhaps Mr. Bonar Law, who made the most vehement speeches about Ulster, was only returning Tory fire upon the Liberal camp with a Party violence made popular—shall we say it?—by Mr. David Lloyd George.

Early in 1912, Bonar Law had gone over to Belfast to pledge the Orangemen:

> "On behalf of the Unionist Party, I give you this message: that though the brunt of the battle will be yours, there will not be wanting help from 'across the Channel'."

Then there had been that immense summer fête at Blenheim Palace on 27 July of that same year, when Sir Edward Carson was presented with a golden sword by the Duke of Norfolk, and Bonar Law told ten thousand excited people that he could imagine no lengths of resistance to which Ulster might go which he would not be ready to support—and in which they would not be supported by an overwhelming majority of the British people. Whereupon, virile F. E. Smith had leapt up to cry: "If need be, appeal to the young men of England!"

These, however, were still only words being played with, menacing as they might be. (Asquith branded the Blenheim oration of Bonar Law as "a complete grammar of anarchy".) But Sir Edward Carson was already playing with arms. True, there was plenty of "theatre" here, too. One hundred thousand "Ulster Volunteers" had been raised, and some had certainly been drilled. Some had even been given guns, though certainly not enough to prevent a regiment of Regulars from massacring them if ever they met in battle. Then, on 28 September, 1912, there had been that dramatic signing of the Solemn League and Covenant at the City Hall, Belfast, on a table draped with the Union Jack, 48 feet by 25 feet wide, and beneath the very banner borne before William of Orange at the Battle of the Boyne, 1690. Sir Edward Carson (assisted by F.E.) then harangued the Orange bands as they moved through the Hall all that September day, signing the "loyal" rebel declaration to:

"Defeat the present conspiracy to set up Home Rule in Ireland. In sure confidence that God will defend the Right, we hereto sign our names.

God Save the King!"

Outside, the other King, "King Carson" as his enemies called him, was received with something like military honours. The Orange guard presented arms with dummy rifles and two pieces of artillery, made of wood and painted a steel grey, were hauled past. At this picture, English newspaper readers next morning found it difficult to repress a smile.

There were no smiles in Southern Ireland. Dublin's answer to Belfast "Ulster Volunteers" was to raise her own army of Nationalist "Irish Volunteers". The rival forces may both have provided no serious military opposition to professional troops, but perhaps they were good enough to fight each other to some grim decision? By 1914, there were probably 100,000 enrolled on each side. Twenty years later, the young volunteers of two factions of a valiant race in Spain, which is Europe's Other Ireland, were no better trained or equipped when they set out to slaughter half a million of one another.

Already, by the autumn of 1912, the temperature was rising in Parliament, too. The Government had been beaten in a snap division on the Financial Resolution for the Home Rule Bill. Two days later (13 November) the Prime Minister moved the annulment of the successful Opposition amendment. A series of violent scenes ensued. "Lulu" Harcourt, speaking from the Government Front Bench, was howled down. So great became the ensuing din that the Speaker then adjourned the House for an hour in the hope that tempers might cool. In vain. On resuming, the Opposition would not even listen to their own spokesman, but kept up a constant chant of "Adjourn! Adjourn!" The Speaker eventually conceded.

As he left the Chair, Ronald McNeil, M.P.,[1] who was standing nearby, seized a bound copy of Standing Orders and hurled it across the table at Winston Churchill, cutting open his forehead. Since the House stood technically adjourned, the Speaker could take no action. Next day, the culprit

[1] Later Lord Cushendun.

made a handsome apology to his victim, who accepted it with grace and good temper.

New Year brought no break in the lowering clouds. On 1 January, 1913, Carson moved an amendment to the Home Rule Act to exclude Ulster. It was rejected.

By September, 1913, gun-running into Ulster was going on openly and the Volunteers were drilling in the parks. The same month, the Ulster Unionist Council resolved itself into the Central Authority of the Provisional Government of Ulster (Chairman, Sir Edward Carson); a Military Council was set up; and an Indemnity Fund of £1,000,000 was opened for the relief of the wounded and disabled, and the widows and orphans who would suffer in the forthcoming struggle.

Lloyd George took little public part in this Irish storm of 1912-14. He had his hands full with his own Land Campaign, both in the country and in the House of Commons. On 10 March, 1914, in a full-dress debate, he was the target of a Tory motion condemning him for his "repeated inaccuracies" and "gross and unfounded personal attacks" (upon the Dukes). He evaded their fire, turned the assault on to them, provoking a considerable disturbance in the Ladies' Gallery, where Lady Londonderry, the great Tory hostess, again held court at one end of the front row while Miss Violet Asquith occupied the seat of honour at the other end. But Lloyd George, at the Prime Minister's request, had approached John Dillon unofficially, seeking an all-round agreement on Ulster and the rest of Ireland.

By March, 1914, the Home Rule Bill, having been twice passed by the Commons and twice rejected by the Lords, was due to receive its Second Reading for the third time, and become Law. Lloyd George himself felt a genuine sympathy for the Protestant Orange minority in Ireland—for that, of course, is what they were about to become. He strongly favoured the idea of so amending the Home Rule Bill as to exclude Ulster, if only for a period of years.

The Leader of the Irish Nationalist Party, John Redmond, was naturally reluctant to concede any such "partition". All Ireland, he insisted, must come in at once—and Irish Nationalist votes were vital to the Liberal Government in these days. For the Orangemen, Carson returned an equally emphatic No! Ulster, cried Carson, must not be condemned to death, with sentence merely suspended for six years—and by this time, Carson was being led by his own followers. It looked as though nothing could now hold up the rush over Niagara Falls.

It was not, indeed, that the nation had reached this dread point without warning. The Ulster Resistance might have started off as a "Carson bluff", as Liberals affected to believe. Perhaps, indeed, serious Tory statesmen like Bonar Law and Lansdowne intended no more than to use it so, hoping to scare the Liberal Government into a General Election which, by 1914, the

Tory Opposition could hardly have failed to win. It would have been the most bitter General Election in British history, if nothing more dangerous than mud-slinging (or even stone-slinging) had developed. Party leaders and newspaper editorials were all talking the language of armed strife—the Tories preferred to recall the Great Revolution of 1688, the Liberals found a more comforting parallel in the Great Civil War of 1642–48.

Most recent prize example had been that speech at Bradford on 14 March, 1914, when Churchill castigated Bonar Law as "a public danger . . . seeking to terrorize the Government to wreck the Home Rule Bill, and to force his way into the councils of his Sovereign." Well, Civil government and Parliament in Britain were not going to yield to the menace of armed violence; Marston Moor had settled all that! And if all the loose, wanton and reckless chatter of the last few months were now in the end to disclose some sinister and revolutionary purpose, then Churchill could only say to his hearers: "Let us go forward together and put these grave matters to the proof!"

Lloyd George was, by comparison, placatory the following Saturday at Huddersfield, though he, too, began by warning his audience that there had now arisen the greatest question in England since the days of the Stuarts and Cromwell. Then, it had been the Divine Right of Kings. Now it was the Divine Right of Aristocrats. The latest theory was that "Laws don't apply to Lords". If a Lord didn't like a Law, well, he needn't obey it. This was the new, fashionable doctrine of "Optional Obedience". Now, said Lloyd George, though he personally knew little about the thing called Fashion, he had observed that it was a habit percolating from the top, via various strata, to the bottom. What a Duke did today, a Poacher might do tomorrow. What had been the fashion for a Baron this morning might become the fashion for a Burglar tonight. The Irish peasantry had groaned for centuries under an alien tyranny enforced by Law, with all the weapons of the tyrants' armoury—gibbet, crowbar, fire, sword, eviction and starvation. Now, when by Law a free people sought to make some restitution to the oppressed, the Law was being defied. Well, if Liberalism now flinched from this challenge, concluded Lloyd George, then it would be "time for a new, sterner and more mettled body of British Progressives".

This conclusion marched with his own bitter mood at this moment. The memories of Marconi abided, the Land Campaign was faltering, and the Chancellor of the Exchequer was quarrelling both professionally and personally with his friend, the First Lord of the Admiralty, over his new Naval Estimates. In the spring of 1914, Lloyd George was about to "break loose", and to the Left. A multitude of followers awaited him.

Suddenly, on the Right, words gave way to deeds. These deeds were as ill thought-out, and foolhardy, and dangerous as ever the words had been, and their consequences came near to being far more fatal.

On 18 March, 1914, General Sir Arthur Paget, General Officer Commanding in Ireland, arrived at the War Office, being summoned to report there on an urgent matter. He received orders to move troops from the Curragh Camp, near Dublin, northward to certain points in Ulster, because, as the Government later stated, it was feared that "evil-disposed persons" might raid the Army depots there for arms.

General Paget returned to Ireland, and there, on 20 March, he made a statement to his officers which produced an instantaneous effect. According to an eye-witness account, which Bonar Law later read out in the House of Commons, the G.O.C. told them that "active operations were about to begin against Ulster, and that he expected the country to be in a blaze by Saturday". He had instructions from the War Office to say that officers domiciled in Ulster would be

> "allowed to disappear and would be reinstated in their position, but they must give their word of honour that they would not fight for Ulster. Officers who were not prepared to undertake active operations against Ulster for conscientious or other scruples were to send in their resignations, and would be dismissed from the Army."

The same evening telegrams came to the War Office from General Paget, to say that nearly sixty officers of the 3rd Cavalry Brigade, including their Commander, Brigadier-General Gough, wished to resign their commissions rather than move north on Ulster.

From the War Office, stirred to rare alarm, Colonel J. E. B. Seely,[1] the Secretary of State for War, telegraphed that the officers who had tendered their resignations were forthwith suspended from duty, relieved of their commands, and their resignations refused. Brigadier-General Gough was ordered to proceed at once to London with his offending colonels.

At 9.30 a.m. next morning, Saturday, 21 March, after this bombshell had exploded in the War Office, General Sir Henry Wilson,[2] Director of Military Operations, was round at Bonar Law's house in Kensington with the information. "Ugly" Wilson, he was nicknamed, for he had a lank, ungainly figure and not a good-looking feature in his face. He was a brilliant Staff Officer, an ardent Ulsterman, and a devoted intriguer, with a *flair* for mockery and the finally, fatally dangerous gift of a devastating tongue.

By Monday, 23 March, "Ugly" Wilson had some further information to furnish to the Leader of the Opposition. Earlier that morning, Brigadier-General Gough, who had in turn arrived in London, had been given a written reassurance from the now-excited Secretary of State for War, Colonel Seely, to placate his restive officers by saying that the trouble at the Curragh Camp

---

[1] Later Lord Mottistone, C.B., C.M.G., D.S.O. He had succeeded Haldane at the War Office in 1912, when Haldane became Lord Chancellor.

[2] Later Field-Marshal Sir Henry Wilson, G.C.B., D.S.O.

had been due to a misunderstanding, and that it was the "duty of soldiers to obey lawful commands in support of the Civil Power".

This had not quite satisfied the Brigadier-General (for, obviously when the Home Rule became Law it would be the duty of the Civil Power to operate it). In the end, for it was now near lunch-time, a further paragraph or two was added to say that the Liberal Government had no intention of using their authority over the Army "to crush political opposition" to the Bill. With this assurance in his pocket, Brigadier-General Gough went off happily back to Ireland to do his soldierly duty. And with the knowledge of it in his head, Bonar Law went off equally happily down to the House of Commons to do his Party duty. For those postscripted paragraphs were to prove political dynamite.

That afternoon, the War Secretary, having stated that the movement of troops to Ireland was confined to the "protective" operations in Ulster and that only three infantry battalions were involved, Bonar Law rose to ask the Prime Minister whether or not Brigadier-General Gough had been reinstated, and if so, on what terms? Asquith replied that Gough and his fellow officers, being satisfied that a genuine misunderstanding had occurred, had loyally accepted the Army Council ruling on their duty to support the Civil Power, and had returned to their units.

Nobody on the Tory Benches believed a word of it. But joy, not anger, was their emotion. They did not consider that the Prime Minister was telling a lie; they were simply quite certain that he had been misled—and by his own colleagues.

Perhaps, there was something else, even more sinister! Were there other, adventurist, forces at work within the Government itself? Was not this movement of troops in Ireland part of a carefully-engineered conspiracy to overawe opposition to Home Rule in Ulster by the threat of Armed Occupation, if not actual Coercion?

For, the Tories argued, if it had been merely a matter of guarding some military stores, it surely could not have been necessary to employ the Cavalry Brigade. And why had troops elsewhere been ordered to "stand by"? Why had officers who were domiciled in Ulster been originally offered the option of not serving if only a "police" operation was in prospect? Above all, what had the Navy been brought into the business for? At this point, re-enter Winston Churchill into the arena!

What had the First Lord of the Admiralty done to stir up Tory rage again? He had signalled the Third Battle Squadron, with two attendant destroyer flotillas, to sail from their station in Spanish waters to Lamlash off the west coast of Scotland. The signal had been made to the Fleet on Thursday, 19 March, the same day that the troops at the Curragh received their marching orders. Was there not in all this some design to "put these grave matters to the proof"?

No, there was not! protested Churchill indignantly. The Government had simply taken proper precautions against all possible risks. A query as to whether or not all this military and naval activity might be expected (or hoped) to lead to fighting he passionately repudiated, as a "hellish insinuation". He turned upon F. E. Smith, who had suggested that a serious invasion of Ulster was contemplated (though jeering that "the scheme was Napoleonic, but there was no Napoleon"), and had asked if perhaps the real object of it all was not to provide the First Lord of the Admiralty with a new political battlecry of: "The Army versus the People?" To which, Churchill angrily retorted that it was the Tory *Morning Post* which was boasting that it was the Army which had killed Home Rule.

Sensation Week was going well. On Wednesday, 25 March, War Secretary Seely made his contribution. He confessed that on the previous Monday, after telling the Cabinet the details of the Curragh crisis, he had gone off to Buckingham Palace to report to the King. On his return, he had found the Cabinet adjourned for lunch and, after studying the Cabinet draft statement to the Army officers concerned, he had himself added the paragraphs which gave them the assurances they sought. Brigadier-General Gough had then asked the Chief of the Imperial General Staff, Field-Marshal Sir John French,[1] if this meant that he and his Cavalry Brigade would not be called on to take any part in coercing Ulster. The Field-Marshal had replied that he would read it so himself. Then, with the initials of the Secretary of State for War, the C.I.G.S., and the Adjutant-General, Sir John Ewart, on their "Charter", Gough had returned to the Curragh. Colonel Seely now accepted full blame for this fatal postscript, and placed his resignation in the hands of the Prime Minister. When Asquith declined it, Austen Chamberlain characterized the whole event as "a hollow comedy".

Two more dramatic turns followed. The first was the revelation that the Lord President of the Council, Lord Morley, had remained behind in the Cabinet Room with the War Secretary, and had actually helped to frame the offending paragraphs. The question now was: did the Cabinet stand by the pledge which they contained, or not? The second sensation was when both the C.I.G.S. and the Adjutant-General also asked leave to send in their papers of resignation.

Now the air was rent on the other flank of the Liberal Government by the Labour Party, clamouring to know why soldiers could be ordered to shoot down strikers in riotous assembly, but not ordered to carry out the Laws of Parliament against the wish of the Tory Party and the Orange Covenanters? Tom Mann had been sent to jail for his syndicalist pamphlet *DON'T SHOOT!* distributed to soldiers during the Liverpool strike.

Exactly a week after the first storm had broken, there was another electric

[1] Later Commander-in-Chief, British Expeditionary Force, 1914–15, Earl of Ypres, O.M., K.P., K.C.M.G., G.C.B., G.C.V.O.

day in Parliament. This was on Monday, 30 March. When the House had assembled, Colonel Seely entered from behind the Speaker's Chair, walked past the Front Bench and turned up the gangway. At once, it was realized that this time he had resigned and really meant it. Asquith rose, and briefly announced the departure from the Government of his colleague, as well as the retirement of the distinguished Army leaders. He also said that for the present he proposed to take over the Secretaryship of State for War himself.

The Government's Liberal supporters, who had been utterly downcast and divided a moment before, leapt up as one man and cheered, and cheered again, frantically waving hats, handkerchiefs and Order Papers. From the Opposition Benches came the half-mocking, half-angry shout of, "Cromwell!" The most intense excitement pervaded the whole Palace of Westminster, and the waves of it spread out far over the land. In general, it was the Tories who were exultant: "We've got 'em at last!"

And, indeed, the Liberal Government were in a desperate way. They had been badly mauled over the Marconi scandal, their "finest fighting general", Lloyd George, smeared in the public mind. Nor did the enemy fail to hark back to it now. The War Secretary had got into trouble but, after all, he had resigned! That was the right thing to do. It was more than the Chancellor of the Exchequer had done! This line of censure obtained the more acceptance because it was widely put about (the *Daily Mail* published it) that Lloyd George had insisted that Seely must go—or else he himself would do so. The Government, in fact, were reeling, clawing on the ropes and about to crash. The Tories made ready for the inevitable General Election.

In Ireland the devil's cauldron bubbled. In April, at Larne, the Ulster Volunteers landed a cargo of 35,000 rifles and two million rounds of ammunition, thoughtfully provided by the Germans. The gun-runners' password was "Gough". It was shortly followed by the Irish Volunteers' counter-gun-running operation at Howth. This latter consignment, however, was not one-twentieth the size of the Ulster load, though it also came from Germany. The Southern Irish smugglers had not got the resources of a great English political Party behind them. Also, they were less lucky, for they clashed with the British Army, the Regulars opened fire in the streets of Dublin, and there was bloodshed.

If anything were needed to make the thing boil over this was it. Dublin had not yet recovered from the violent Transport Strike of the previous year, incited and inflamed by the third of the greatest storm-sowers of the pre-whirlwind age. This was Jim Larkin, the massive Liverpool Irishman, who combined in a kind of giant, Celtic dynamo the passionate oratorical power of Ben Tillett with the devoted organizational energy of Tom Mann. "My divine mission," bellowed Larkin, "is to stir up discontent."

He did his damnedest. To Hell with Home Rule or any other kind of rule—except the rule of utter destruction of present-day society! To the Devil with the Ulster Volunteers, and the Irish Nationalist Volunteers, too! The only kind of army Jim Larkin wanted to set marching was the Citizen Army of Workers. He had just come out of prison for his incitements to terror in the Dublin tram strikes of 1913, which had culminated in bloody street-battles between police and strikers. Then he had "gone over the Channel" to England, where he had communicated his passions to a strangely receptive working class. By 1914, the Triple Alliance of Railwaymen, Miners and Transport Workers had already been formed in Britain. Also, there had been formulated the Syndicalist Plan of Campaign—the General Strike.

To be sure, at last, grave matters were about to be put to the proof. But which matters—and to what proof?

In May, the Prime Minister announced that the Home Rule Bill would be passed as it stood, but promised an Amending Bill permitting any Ulster County to vote itself out for six years—a concession which would almost certainly have split the Irish Nationalist Party. The House of Lords came to their rescue by so amending the Amending Bill that it became utterly unacceptable to any Irish Nationalist who wanted to retain his seat.

Civil War loomed.

Long, men had talked about it. Was it all—words? Surely it is idle for us to say now that it was just "bluff", for if the bluff of either side had been called, remember, by this time both sides had weapons in their hands. A great civilized country could never have dissolved in war against itself? Why, a world was about to do it!

As a last desperate throw to hold off the guns, King George V himself appealed to the Party leaders to meet in conference at Buckingham Palace. Absolutely for the last time (as it seemed), Liberals, Tories, Irish Nationalists and Ulstermen met round a table, the Speaker of the House of Commons presiding at the King's suggestion, and Asquith and Lloyd George being the Government representatives. It was the 21 July, 1914.

The King himself appeared. He delivered his own moving message:

"For months we have watched with deep misgivings the course of events in Ireland. The trend has been surely and steadily towards an appeal to force, and today the cry of Civil War is on the lips of the most responsible and sober-minded of my people.

We have in the past endeavoured to act as a civilizing example to the world, and to me it is unthinkable, as it must be to you, that we should be brought to the brink of fratricidal strife upon issues apparently so capable of adjustment as those you are now asked to consider, if handled in a spirit of generous compromise.

My apprehension in contemplating such a dire calamity is intensified by my feelings of attachment to Ireland and of sympathy with her people who have always welcomed me with warmhearted affection.

Gentlemen, you represent in one form or another the vast majority of my subjects at home. You also have a deep interest in my Dominions overseas, who are scarcely less concerned in a prompt and friendly settlement of this question. I regard you all in this matter as trustees for the honour and peace of all."

Four earnest days they debated, but as Asquith sadly wrote, "Nothing could have been more amicable in tone, or more desperately fruitless in result." The delegates shook hands grimly and rather fearfully, and parted. They heard the roar of the rapids. . . .

Then, a couple of revolver shots in a far-off Balkan town. The crack of the Sarajevo bullets was the overture for the orchestra of forty thousand cannon.

CHAPTER XV

"THE CRITICAL YEAR"

ON New Year's Day, 1914, a remarkably reassuring opinion of affairs had been published in the *Daily Chronicle*. It conveyed the idea that there was hardly a cloud in the international sky. The name of the world weather-expert was David Lloyd George.

The Chancellor of the Exchequer was giving an interview on what he termed the "overwhelming extravagance of our expenditure on armaments". It was true, indeed, that the Continental Powers were also wasting their money on this "organized insanity", but please observe, said Lloyd George, that they were directing their energies more and more towards strengthening their *land* forces.

> "Even if Germany ever had any idea of challenging our supremacy at sea, the exigencies of the military situation must necessarily put it completely out of her head.
>
> Under these circumstances it seems to me that we can afford just quietly to maintain the superiority we possess at present, without making feverish efforts to increase it any further. The Navy is now, according to all impartial testimony, at the height of its efficiency. If we maintain that standard no one can complain, but if we went on spending and swelling its strength, we should wantonly provoke other nations."

Lloyd George did not apprehend any friction with France. He thought, indeed, that a new temper was rising throughout Western Europe, and that the common sense of the people was against the idea of war. It was a propitious moment for reconsidering the whole question of armaments. Liberals should seize it.

The Chancellor took occasion to mention, in the course of his observations, that a distinguished predecessor in his office, Lord Randolph Churchill, had resigned in 1887 rather than assent to the proposed Estimates for the Army and Navy. This reference did not pass unnoticed. Lloyd George, after giving his interview, went off to Algeria on holiday. But when he arrived there, telegrams were awaiting to recall him to London. Winston Churchill, the First Lord of the Admiralty, at the same time hurried home from his stay in France. There was a Cabinet crisis on—and Lloyd George was concerned in the brewing of it.

Mr. Charles Hobhouse, M.P., Chancellor of the Duchy of Lancaster, had just condemned the First Lord for his new, inflated Navy Estimates in a speech at Bristol. Said the *Daily Express*:

"These statements have created for Mr. Churchill a situation of extra-ordinary complexity. He has not only now to resist Little Navyite attacks from the back benches of his own party; but he has to resist concerted opposition from his colleagues in the Government. . . ."

F. E. Smith defended Churchill in a speech in his constituency. He was surprised that the "Chancellor of the Exchequer should have given an interview in which he expressed the view that the psychological moment had come for us to reduce our naval armaments". He referred to Lloyd George's "clumsy and maladroit statement" as being the work of a "bungling amateur whose hands are already too full, and who has never lost an opportunity in compromising and injuring this country in attempts to advertise himself".

This political quarrel between Lloyd George and Churchill (they both insisted there was absolutely nothing personal in it) had been coming for some time. Churchill had revelled in every hour of his labours since that autumn evening three years before when, as he tramped home from the golf links with the Prime Minister by the Firth of Forth, past the silhouetted battleships that lay there on the dark waters, Asquith had offered him the Admiralty. It was Lloyd George who had prompted that.

But since Churchill had entered the portals of Admiralty House there had been more than one occasion on which the two men had sharply differed. There was, for example, Churchill's appointment in 1912 of Admiral Prince Henry of Battenberg to be First Sea Lord. Prince Henry was an admirable naval officer but he had been born a German (he had taken up British nationality in 1868); Lloyd George said there would be a public outcry about that appointment one day. In October, 1914, there was, and Churchill had to part company with his chief Naval executive in painful circumstances.

Then, of course, long gone was the co-operation of those old days of 1908, when Lloyd George, the Chancellor of the Exchequer, could count on Churchill, the President of the Board of Trade, to combine with him to trim the Estimates of McKenna, then First Lord of the Admiralty.

From the moment that he climbed aboard the King's ships, the Blue Water school had no more ardent champion than Churchill. More warships, bigger warships, faster, farther-ranging, oil-fuelled and ever-more heavily armed warships—this was the Churchill programme now!

It is true that more than once Churchill proposed to the competing Germans that both countries should take a "Naval Holiday"—though only on the basis of Britain retaining her superior ratio. It is true, too, that at the time of the Agadir incident, Lloyd George was as closely concerned and convinced as Churchill about the reality of the German sea challenge.

But by the autumn of 1913, two years later, Lloyd George had moved a long way from his Agadir position. He no longer believe in the War Menace, but was again a Man of Peace, and indeed, a foremost leader of the Peace

Movement in Britain, a powerful crusade which commanded immense support. Now, besides the demands of the Royal Navy, and more urgently, the appetites of social reform in Pensions, Health Insurance and Education competed for the Chancellor's attention and his bounty. Already, at a dinner in No. 11 Downing Street on 12 November, 1913, when Lloyd George's guests were the Prime Minister, Sir Edward Grey, Lord Crewe and Lord Haldane, the Chancellor of the Exchequer had explained (according to a note he wrote that night) that on next year's Budget, with existing commitments, he would face a £10,000,000 deficit. Unless taxation was to be increased—and that was not recommended, in view of a possible General Election in 1914—then Churchill's naval construction programme would have to be cut. The Ministers present unanimously agreed that he should be pressed to save "at least one and a half millions". The Chancellor undertook to essay this task.

Lloyd George sought to do a deal with Churchill by postponing some of his shipbuilding programme until a later date. What Churchill thought about the way this arrangement looked like working out is shown by this exchange of notes, thrown across the Cabinet table a day or two later, 16 December, 1913, a curious habit which has come down the years.

Churchill: "I consider that you are going back on your word; trying to drive me out after we have settled, and you promised to support the estimates."

Lloyd George: "I agreed to the figure for this year and I have stood by it and *carried it*, much to the disappointment of my economical friends. But I told you distinctly I would press for a reduction of new programme with a view to 1915 and I think quite respectfully you are unnecessarily stubborn. It is only a question of six months postponement of laying down. That cannot endanger our safety."

Churchill: "No. You said you would *support the* Estimates. The estimates included the new programme."

When the New Year, 1914, dawned, the First Lord's Estimates stood at the then all-time record of £54,000,000, which was about £20,000,000 more than the last Tory Naval Budget of 1905–06. Lloyd George attacked and Churchill defended these figures with equal political vigour, which, as the following letters show, did not lack personal "edge".

The First Lord now resolutely rejected all compromise over his 1914 programme, and refused to give any promise over his 1915 programme either; he threatened to resign, and thus precipitate the long-discussed General Election. The equally determined Chancellor of the Exchequer then set out to mobilize the Radical section in the Cabinet and the Radical Press in the country.

But the pressure of Radical press and Pacifist public opinion failed to

Western Front. With Indian soldiers, 1916

Interlude at golf with Lord Riddell at Walton Heath

break the deadlock. Lloyd George then invited Churchill to go right ahead. It was a challenge. Haldane, now Lord Chancellor, told Lord Esher, the King's confidant, that nobody could be quite sure of Lloyd George's objectives in this family quarrel, but it might well be that he was preparing to break up the Government himself and take the leadership of a Radical and Labour Party.

The private pen war continued to rage.

> Admiralty House,
> 26/1/14.

"My dear David,

In Cabinet today it will be my duty to state that while I will do my best to work to the figures mentioned in my letter I cannot be bound by them in any extraordinary or improper sense. While I am responsible what is necessary will have to be provided. The Estimates of 14/15 have been prepared with the strictest economy; for all expenditure incurred or proposed there is full warrant and good reason. There is no act of Admiralty administration for which I am responsible which cannot be vindicated to the House of Commons. I cannot buy a year of office by a bargain under duress about the Estimates for 15/16.

. . . I recognize your friendship but I ask no favours and I shall enter into no irregular obligation.

I am now approaching the end of my resources, and I can only await the decision of my colleagues and the Prime Minister.

> Yours, etc.,
> Winston Churchill."

> Treasury Chambers.
> 27th Jan., 1914.

"My dear Winston,

I have striven hard for a friendly and honourable settlement without the slightest regard for the effect on my personal position, but your letter has driven me to despair, and I must now decline further negotiations, leaving the issue to be decided by the Prime Minister and the Cabinet.

Your letter warns me—in time—that you can no more be held bound by your latest figures than you were by your original figure of £49,966,000. This intimation completely alters the situation. I now thoroughly appreciate your idea of a bargain: it is an arrangement which binds the Treasury not even to attempt any further economies in the interest of the taxpayer, whilst it does not in the least impose any obligation on the Admiralty not to incur fresh liabilities. Such understandings are surely not worth all the time and anxiety you and I have devoted to arriving at them.

In one vital respect the task of the Cabinet is simplified by your letter, for it demonstrates that you and your critics are in complete agreement as

I

to the real value of your last proposals. The only certainty about them is that the Exchequer would this year have to find 56 millions—supplementaries included—for the Navy, whilst the reductions promised for 15/16 do not bind either the Board of Admiralty or the First Lord. Therein you and your critics agree. I have been repeatedly told that I was being made a fool of; I declined to believe it. Your candour forces me to acknowledge the justice of the taunt. You proposed before Christmas to take 50 millions. As a compromise on that you proposed Friday last to take 4 millions more this year on condition of coming down $1\frac{1}{2}$ millions next year. Not a sumptuous offer at best. Now you qualify that!

I have laboured these last few days—not to favour you or to save myself—but to rescue Liberalism from the greatest tragedy which has yet befallen it. I have a deep and abiding attachment for Liberal causes, and for the old Party, and the prospect of wrecking them afflicts me with deep distress. That is why I have been prepared to risk the confidence of my friends and to face the gibes and sneers from friend and foe alike with which I foresaw the publication of the figures would be greeted. I know too well that every paper would gloat over my humiliation. That I did not mind if the ship and its precious cargo could be saved. You decreed otherwise, and the responsibility is yours and yours alone.

Ever sincerely,

D. L. George."

The argument did not end until March, and after a score more Cabinet meetings had been held upon it. As Churchill has said, his resignation lay on the Cabinet table for many weeks. In the event, Lloyd George failed to dislodge the First Lord from his dug-in position and a "paper" agreement was patched up, largely by the mediation of Asquith. But though beaten in the Cabinet on this arms issue, Lloyd George's stock soared (for the selfsame reason) in the ranks of the pacifist Liberal Party and in the columns of the Radical Press. Winston Churchill's correspondingly sank, and he has admitted that "in order to strengthen myself with my party, I mingled actively in the Irish controversy."[1]

Lloyd George's case, indeed, appeared to be as powerful as it was popular. The Germans were then behaving more civilly, not to say considerately, than for many a day past. They had played a helpful part in the London Conference of Ambassadors to localize the recent Balkan wars, first of the Greek-Serb-Bulgar Alliance against Turkey, and then of these Allies amongst themselves. The Germans had also seemed reasonable enough over their proposed Berlin-Baghdad Railway, so that Britain had agreed to its extension as far as Basra, provided that our own rights in the Persian Gulf were guaranteed. This Convention was signed on 15 June, 1914. Finally, there

---

[1] *The World Crisis*, Vol. 1 (by Winston S. Churchill).

had been something more than mere diplomatic table-talk between the two countries in helping the Germans to secure a share in the reversion of the Portuguese colonies.

Whether or not all this would have satisfied the Kaiser's Germany one may doubt now. She wanted "a place in the sun", but not by courtesy of Great Britain or anybody else. She already possessed the best army in the world, and would hardly have been content with the second-best navy.

There were, of course, those in high places in 1914 who did not *want* to believe that Britain and Germany would ever go to war with each other. Not all of these persons were pacifists, and one of them was the All-Highest, the Kaiser himself. Though he continually fretted against what he regarded as "English insolence" in international affairs and boasted of what he would do to curb it, Emperor Wilhelm II probably never sat down and seriously worked out the equation of Germany and her Allies *v.* Britain and the Rest. It is certain that neither he nor his Imperial Chancellor, von Bethmann-Hollweg ever actually planned the war—as it is on indisputable record that the German General Staff did. From their point of view, watching ever against a French-organized war of *revanche* for 1870, those German soldiers cannot be blamed. The greatest flaw in the Kaiser's character was his anxiety to hear good news. Nobody who occupied so exalted an Imperial estate was likely to be short of agents equally anxious to supply it.

Prince Henry of Prussia was the Kaiser's brother. Twice, he led Wilhelm to believe that he had been given assurances by their cousin, King George V, that if Germany and Austria-Hungary became involved in war with France and Russia then Britain would remain neutral.

On the first occasion, Prince Henry posed this precise question to King George while staying with him at Sandringham in December, 1912: "Would Britain come to the assistance of France and Russia?" The King replied: "Undoubtedly yes—under certain circumstances." What Prince Henry reported to the Kaiser was that Britain was peace-loving; that she *might* remain neutral; but that also she *might*, under certain circumstances, side with Germany's foes. On this, the Kaiser, being thoroughly satisfied with what he wanted to hear, scrawled on Prince Henry's letter: "That settles it, we can now go ahead with France." (He meant the bullying of France, who dreaded war despite her Russian Alliance.)

The second occasion had more serious, final consequences. Early on the morning of 26 July, 1914, Prince Henry hurried into Buckingham Palace on his way home from Cowes, to say good-bye to King George. He saw a worried monarch who told him that the news looked bad, that Britain had no quarrel with anybody, and that he sincerely hoped we should be able to stay out of trouble. Certainly, he and his Government would do all they could to prevent a European War. The eager royal reporter rushed away to catch his train. Two days later, he wrote to the Kaiser from Kiel, quoting King George as

saying: "We shall try all we can to keep out of this, and shall remain neutral."
When Admiral von Tirpitz doubted the value of such an alleged remark,
the Kaiser stared arrogantly at him and said: "I have the word of a King,
and that is enough for me." [1]

The report that King George had given it reached both Captain Erich von
Muller, the German Naval Attaché in London (who promptly cabled it to the
German Admiralty), and also certain British inner political circles here, too,
where it created a lively sensation during the coming exciting days.

Britain had no quarrel with anybody, and only wanted to keep out of
war! How utterly true! And how utterly hopeless! For, in 1914, somebody
certainly had a deep if still undivulged quarrel with us. And even if we had
had no Enemies—well, we had Allies! They drew us into war just as surely.

What consternation there had been in the Liberal Cabinet that far-off day
in 1912, when most of the members learned for the first time of our joint staff
military arrangements with the French! They were hardly reassured by the
insistence of Sir Edward Grey that these "tentative proposals" left us quite
free, in the event of war, to decide whether or not we should join in it. When
War Office talks were succeeded by Admiralty talks, and the British Fleet
was concentrated in the North Sea, leaving the Mediterranean to the French
Fleet, it seemed that these arrangements in fact amounted to commitments,
and certainly they were so regarded both by the French and their Allies, the
Russians. We had, indeed, as Churchill afterwards expressed it, the obligations without the advantages of an Alliance. Though Lloyd George still resisted
it, from time to time the thought was remorselessly borne in upon him of
Lord Rosebery's warning ten years earlier, when in the first happy flush of
the successful *Entente Cordiale* negotiations of 1904, he had remarked to
him: "It will mean war with Germany in the end!"

Now it was here. Austria was threatening Serbia, because it was a Serb
bullet which had killed the Austrian Archduke at Sarajevo, and Austria had
long waited for the excuse to burn out that Slav "Wasps' Nest". Germany
wanted to see her Ally stage an easy prestige war in the Balkans; a Victory
Parade through Belgrade, even without any fighting would do, so the Kaiser
reckoned. Russia was still smarting under the humiliation she had sustained
at the time of Austria's annexation of Bosnia–Herzogovina in 1908. Now,
another little Slav folk were being bullied. Could the big Slav Brother stand
idly by once more, and watch it without protest? But if Russia marched against
Austria, then Germany was bound by treaty to come to the aid of her Ally.
And if Russia fought Germany, then France must fight her, too. After that
—could Britain permit Germany to send her Fleet through the Straits of Dover,
and attack the Channel ports, which the French had by implication left us to
guard when they concentrated their own Fleet in the Mediterranean?

The blood-and-iron logic of all this seems plain enough now. But in June,

[1] See Harold Nicolson: *King George V.*, pages 206 and 245.

1914, there was hardly a responsible statesman in Europe who was willing to face it.

Indeed, how many were there who even realized it?

On Sunday, 28 June, 1914, Miss Frances Stevenson, Lloyd George's confidential secretary, had been working in No. 11 Downing Street on a speech which the Chancellor of the Exchequer was due to make at the Mansion House in about ten days' time. The red dispatch-box came in from the Foreign Office, and at tea-time she took it to him. Lloyd George unlocked it, and drew forth the telegram announcing the assassination of the Austrian Archduke and his wife at Sarajevo, in far-off Serbia. "This means war," he said.

He meant another Balkan war. Neither he nor anyone else dreamed that day in June, that it meant World War.

The British Government were engrossed in other affairs. Lloyd George tells in his *War Memoirs* that the Cabinet never even discussed the gathering trouble in Europe until the week before the war broke out. They were sitting, indeed, twice a day, although what had stimulated this activity was not the Austrian ultimatum to Serbia, but the Irish gun-running at Howth. We had our own Balkan squabble to settle; Belfast, not Belgrade, was our storm-centre. Could we yet stave off that threatened Civil War? Churchill has dramatically filled in the picture.[1] The last bid for peace in Ireland (by excluding the Ulster counties from the operation of the Home Rule Act) might yet prevail if the contestants could agree on the boundaries of two of them, Fermanagh and Tyrone. So, that fateful Friday afternoon of 24 July:

"The Cabinet toiled around the muddy byways of Fermanagh and Tyrone. . . . The discussion had reached its inconclusive end, and the Cabinet was able to separate, when the quiet, grave tones of Sir Edward Grey's voice were heard reading a document which had just been brought to him from the Foreign Office. It was the Austrian Note to Serbia."

Even then, European War seemed impossible. Sir Edward Grey himself, the Foreign Secretary, did not believe it. A man devoted to his duty, Grey departed for a fishing holiday in Hampshire, and most of his colleagues likewise left town. The First Lord of the Admiralty, Churchill, alone seems to have scented battle. He had been scenting battle (or revolution) for several years past, and now by good fortune, well-earned by his energetic and imaginative administration of the Admiralty, Churchill's Department was the only one in the country which was prepared for war. Indeed, this very week-end he had concluded a test mobilization of the Third (Reserve) Fleet, and the First and Second Fleets—which had also taken part in the final Grand Review at Spithead—were still concentrated. Together, they made up immeasurably the most powerful naval force ever yet seen upon the seas of this world. Churchill kept them mobilized for the next few days.

[1] In *The World Crisis*.

His instinct turned out to be right. All over Europe, the Fleets and Armies rumbled into gear, and the Governments stumbled towards war.

On Tuesday, 28 July, 1914, Austria declared war on Serbia. On Wednesday the Kaiser promised to Britain that he would not annex any French Territory (in Europe) provided that we remained neutral. On Thursday, this "infamous offer" was repudiated by Sir Edward Grey in the House of Commons. On Friday, Germany demanded from France as a pledge of *her* neutrality the keys of her frontier fortresses of Verdun and Toule; the French Prime Minister, M. Viviani, replied that France would take care of her own business. On Saturday, Germany declared war on Russia.

In England, all this week there was gathering excitement. The Bill suspending the operation of the Home Rule Act as far as Ulster was concerned was due to be debated on Friday, 31 July, but the Prime Minister wisely moved its adjournment. A few days before, Home Rule had held the stage as the king piece of the British Parliamentary drama. Now, suddenly, it had become a mere sketch of parish politics. The wraiths of the ancient Irish feud faded into the Celtic mist, and there loomed instead the giant shapes of a modern World War.

Then it was that certain Cabinet Ministers, searching their memories, recalled a remarkable lecture delivered to them at the Committee of Imperial Defence four years ago by the Director of Military Operations, Lieut.-General Sir Henry Wilson. The talented Staff officer, with large map and pointer, had traced the course of the projected Schlieffen Movement (where did he get hold of it?); of a German wheel across Northern France, hinging on Luxembourg, and sweeping through Southern Belgium. Now, Military Information, sparse and tentative at first, but growing in substance and conviction, reported that the German armies were massing behind the frontier opposite these very areas. During this time, doomed Belgium not only made no appeal for protection, but insisted that she wanted to be left alone.

It was necessary to look to our own defences. As the Imperial German Army moved into position, The First Lord of the Admiralty ordered the Royal Navy to its battle stations. On the night of 29–30 July the Grand Fleet passed with darkened ship through the Straits of Dover and next day was on duty for its faithful watch of four and a quarter years.

But Churchill, as ever, did not rest content with doing his own job. His brain was busy with other vast projects, political and military. To begin with, a national emergency of such magnitude surely called for a National Government? Now, at their morning meeting on Friday, 31 July, more than half the Cabinet, and including the formidable Lloyd George, were bitterly opposed to Britain entering the war. Only two Ministers—Grey and Churchill —favoured it; Asquith appeared to support them. Perhaps, indeed, the Liberal Government would break up. Well, then, said Churchill, it might be necessary to bring the Tory Opposition into Coalition—or at any rate, those patriotic and intelligent Tories who shared his Imperial beliefs. With undisclosed but undoubted encouragement from the Prime Minister himself, the bridge builder set forth to lay hold of his old friend and partner in previous efforts of this kind, F. E. Smith.

The offer (or inquiry) of Coalition was taken by F.E. on Friday evening to the country house of Mr. Edward Goulding, M.P.,[1] at Wargrave, where Bonar Law, Carson and other Tory leaders were in private conference. Max Aitken, who was present, has recorded the chilly reception which F. E. received from Bonar Law. It was not that the Tory Leader was opposed either to the war or to the idea of wartime Coalition, though he did not consider that the uses of Party Government were yet exhausted. But he was decidedly opposed to Churchill being the medium of any getting-together. So Bonar Law declined an invitation to dine on Saturday night with Churchill, even though Grey and Asquith would also attend.

The forces against the War were also mobilizing, and for Peace. Lloyd George, their leader, received unexpected support from his own bailiwick, where he ruled over the Money Barons as Chancellor of the Exchequer.

On Saturday, 1 August, 1914, the burly, rather surly Governor of the Bank of England, Sir Walter Cunliffe,[2] called on the Chancellor of the Exchequer to inform him that the City was totally against Britain intervening in the war. Ever after this, Lloyd George denied that it was the capitalists who wanted war in 1914.

> "Money was a frightened and trembling thing. Money shivered at the prospect. Big Business everywhere wanted to keep out."

Big Business, in fact, fluctuated only between panic and paralysis. Everyone was trying to sell, everywhere prices slumped, and the London Stock Exchange had been closed the previous day. Also everyone wanted money, and the same day the Bank Rate had been raised to 8 per cent. The Governor now sought permission to exceed the fiduciary issue of notes laid down by the Bank Charter. It was granted, and the Bank Rate was pushed up to 10 per cent. There was a heavy public demand for gold, and the Chancellor of the Exchequer thanked his stars that Monday would be the August Bank Holiday. That left nearly forty-eight hours of breathing space. Hardly an hour of it would be spent in resting.

Strenuously the Radical Press supported the standpoint of the City. There was the *Westminster Gazette* in the early days of August, deprecating "the attempt to kindle a War fever".

Then there was the *Daily News*, demanding that the Government should "announce here and now its rigorous neutrality". On 4 August, the last day of peace and the night of war, that newspaper urged that "if we remained

[1] Later Lord Wargrave. [2] Later Lord Cunliffe.

neutral we should be . . . able to trade with all the belligerents. . . . We should be able to capture the bulk of their trade in neutral markets".

Most resolutely anti-war of all was the *Manchester Guardian*, the newspaper on which Lloyd George relied more than any other for unfailing support, and whose Editor, Mr. C. P. Scott, was almost the Keeper of his Liberal Conscience. For a week before Britain went to war the *Manchester Guardian* pleaded for Neutrality. "Not only are we neutral now, but we could, and ought to remain neutral throughout the whole course of the war. . . . We wish Servia no ill; we are anxious for the peace of Europe. But Englishmen are not the guardians of Servian well being, or even of the peace of Europe. Their first duty is to England and to the peace of England. . . . We care as little for Belgrade as Belgrade does for Manchester."

On 4 August, the *Manchester Guardian* would even take the Foreign Secretary to task for his speech in the House of Commons the previous day, as being "for all its appearance of candour, not fair either to the House of Commons or to the country". It must be added that next day, when Britain had declared war, though it still warned that one day we should all live to regret this step, the great Liberal newspaper wrote:

> "Now there is nothing for Englishmen to do but to stand together and help by every means in their power to the attainment of our common object —an early and decisive victory over Germany."

The Cabinet sat in almost continuous session throughout these days and nights. They were also in a state of considerable flux. No real record exists of their historic meetings, for at that time no minutes were taken. The Prime Minister used to write a letter to the King every evening, making it as interesting as possible and omitting nothing vital, but his version was necessarily short and personal. All that otherwise remains in writing is a few of those revealing pencilled notes scribbled by Ministers to one another, and flicked across the table. They reflect the conflict in the inner councils of the nation on the eve of war.

Wednesday, 29 July. Winston Churchill to Lloyd George: "Keep Friday night clear, F.E. is inquiring." (Obviously refers to F.E.'s mission to Bonar Law and other Tory leaders on a possibility of war-time coalition, and shows that Lloyd George was party to it.)

Undated. Lewis ("Lulu") Harcourt, Colonial Secretary to Lloyd George: "You must now speak for us. Grey wishes to go to war without any violation of Belgium." (The Pacifist opposition in the Cabinet.)

Saturday, 1 August. Churchill to Lloyd George: "I am most profoundly anxious that our long co-operation may not be severed. Remember your part at Agadir. I implore you to come and bring your mighty aid to the

discharge of our duty. Afterwards, by participating, we can regulate the
settlement and prevent a renewal of 1870 conditions." (i.e. intervening in
the war.)

Churchill to Lloyd George: "All the rest of our lives we shall be opposed.
I am deeply attached to you and have followed your instructions and
guidance for nearly 10 years."

Lloyd George to Churchill: "If patience prevails and you do not press
us too hard tonight, we might come together."

Churchill to Lloyd George: "Please God—it is our whole future—as
comrades or opponents. The march of events will be dominating."

Churchill to Lloyd George: "Together we can carry a wide social
policy, all *on the conference basis*. Naval War will be cheap, not more than
25 millions a year. You alone can take the measures which will ensure food
being kept abundant and cheap to the people."

Lloyd George to Charles Masterman: "What is your general view of
what we ought to do?"

Masterman to Lloyd George: "If I *had* to decide now I would guarantee
Belgium and the Fleet policy. If Germany accepts that, no war. But I am
with McKenna and Runciman in fighting for *time*, sooner than break up
the Cabinet. Twelve hours might find us united. Our collapse would be
unthinkable—what is to happen to the Empire if we break to pieces! Do
fight for unity."

Lloyd George was wrestling day and night to settle the financial crisis
which the War Storm had produced, conferring with Treasury officials,
bankers, brokers, businessmen and those politico-economists which financial
crisis ever brings forth to contradict their yesterday's nostrum. (Mr. J. M.
Keynes at this time firmly predicted national ruin if specie payment was
suspended.)

The Prime Minister summed up the whole position. He wrote in his *Diary*
on 1 August:

"Lloyd George, all for peace, is more sensible and statesmanlike for
keeping the position still open. Grey declares that if an out-and-out and
uncompromising policy of Non-intervention at all costs is adopted he will
go. Winston very bellicose and demanding immediate mobilization. . . . Of
course, if Grey went, I should go, and the whole thing would break up."[1]

How right Asquith was in that last opinion! And, if on the other hand,
Sir Edward Grey had insisted on issuing that ultimatum to the Germans

[1] *Memories and Reflections*, by the Earl of Oxford and Asquith.

I*

which he desired, warning them to keep out of Belgium, the Liberal Cabinet would certainly have split.

As it was, on the Saturday night of 1 August, when they instructed Grey to tell the French Ambassador in London that we would not stand by and see the German Fleet attack the French Channel ports, John Burns, who was one of the most vehement of the powerful pacifist group in the Government at once resigned. When the Cabinet met on Sunday morning, they faced two more letters of resignation, from Lord Morley and Sir John Simon. At least another half-dozen waited upon the effective hour.

Was Lloyd George among them? He has told us in his *War Memoirs*, written long after the event:

"I never doubted that if the Germans interfered with the integrity and independence of Belgium, we were in honour bound to discharge our Treaty obligations afterwards."

We still know that in these late July and early August days Lloyd George hesitated to involve Britain in war over Belgium. There is nothing wrong in that. Belgium herself hesitated to invoke aid, or even the firm promise of aid, until it was too late. Belgium herself hoped—and who shall blame her?—to escape the terror and the horror of war, as in the event her neighbour, Holland, successfully did. What Lloyd George argued in Cabinet (he demonstrated on the map which lay on the Cabinet table), was that if the Germans merely trespassed on a small part of Belgian soil in order to march into France (he laid his hand over that corner), and thereafter evacuated it and paid compensation, then the case for defending the neutrality of Belgium would be altered.

In truth, of course, the case would not have been altered at all. For the purpose that Britain, France and Germany had in guaranteeing the neutrality of the country was not a moral, but a military one; it was not for the sake of the Belgians, but to prevent Belgium from being used as a corridor or a cockpit of war, or as a base for it.

The argument would be settled by guns, as it was always going to be. While the Liberal Cabinet debated in London, the Germans delivered their demand in Brussels. Right of Way for the German Army—and Reply Please within twelve hours! The pacifist opposition within the Cabinet, which had included, besides Lloyd George and John Burns, Lord Morley and Lord Beauchamp, "Lulu" Harcourt and Charles Hobhouse, thereupon subsided from an organized movement into a number of individual reservations. Only John Burns and Lord Morley refused to withdraw their resignations, and passed stubbornly and honourably out of public life.

Were Lloyd George's own doubts resolved? This is what Walter Runciman,[1] then President of the Board of Agriculture, told Gideon Murray, brother of the Master of Elibank:

[1] Later Viscount Runciman.

"Right up to tea-time on Sunday, 2 August, Lloyd George told us that he was doubtful of the action he would take. In conversation with about one-half of our Ministerial colleagues on the afternoon of that day, he said he would not oppose the war but that he would take no part in it, and would retire for the time being to Criccieth. He would not repeat his experience of 1899–1902 . . . he had had enough of standing out against a war-inflamed populace."

To others, Lloyd George said that he would consult his uncle at Criccieth. He seemed relieved to be able to plunge back into dealing with the financial crisis. It was easier to settle than his own. For the moment, the ranks of the Government closed up. Asquith felt further fortified that Sunday by the letter which he received about noon from Bonar Law:

2 August, 1914.

"Dear Mr. Asquith,

Lord Lansdowne and I feel it our duty to inform you that in our opinion as well as in that of all the colleagues whom we have been able to consult, it would be fatal to the honour and security of the United Kingdom to hesitate in supporting France and Russia at the present juncture; and we offer our unhesitating support to the Government in any measures they may consider necessary for that object.

Yours very truly,
A. Bonar Law."

If Sunday had been the Day of Unrest, Monday was the Day of Decision.

That morning, Belgium rejected the German ultimatum and Albert, King of the Belgians, appealed to King George V. Germany declared war on France, and the German advance guard began marching into Luxembourg to execute the first movement of the Schlieffen Plan. All further diplomatic effort to hold up the war was now in vain, although it continued up to the last hour.

"The nations," wrote Lloyd George, "backed their machines over the precipice."

The Cabinet deliberations were resumed, and the Cabinet communications.

Monday, 3 August. Lloyd George to Churchill: "What is your policy?"

Churchill to Lloyd George: "At the present moment I would act in such a way as to impress Germany with our intention to preserve the neutrality of Belgium. So much is still unknown as to the definite purpose of Germany that I would not go beyond this. Moreover, public opinion might veer round at any moment if Belgium is invaded, and we must be ready to meet this opinion."

Lloyd George to Churchill: "Would you *commit* yourself in public *now* (Monday) to war if Belgium is invaded whether Belgium asks for our protection or not?"

Churchill to Lloyd George: "No."

Asquith has testified[1] how at this same Cabinet meeting Lloyd George made "a strong appeal" to the Ministers who spoke of retiring from the Government not to go, or at least to delay their departure. They agreed to sit in their usual places in the House of Commons that afternoon. Vitally important in the story of Britain that they did.

While the drama unfolded hour by hour in the Cabinet room, what was going on in the street? It was August Bank Holiday week-end, and probably not one in a thousand of those who strolled or played in the sun had an inkling of the vast calamity that was about to engulf them. There were meetings, indeed, in Trafalgar Square then as now, where trained speakers addressed "protest" meetings of more or less trained hearers. They denounced the idea of war. The citizens of London in general paid no more general attention to them than to the swarming pigeons.

Already, by Sunday, the crowds had begun to grow, with the rumours, as more and more folk came out to see what it was all about—and stayed out. "We could hear the hum of this surging mass from the Cabinet chamber," Lloyd George recalled.

By Monday, the multitude had grown so dense that no motor-car or even bus could force a passage through it, and the Ministers seeking to cross from Downing Street to the House of Commons could only reach it behind a spearhead of heaving, shoving policemen. By this time, too, there was a very different popular mood. There were cheers for the Ministers they recognized, patriotic songs, *God Save The King* and the *Marsellaise*. Also, it was "Poor Little Belgium", soon to be "Gallant Little Belgium". By what "bush telegraph" did those Bank Holiday crowds know about Belgium?

For when the Foreign Secretary began his speech that afternoon to the packed House of Commons, he was himself unaware either of the brutal German ultimatum ("Necessity knows no law, we must hack our way through," the Imperial Chancellor told the Reichstag the next day, announcing the invasion of Belgium), or of the sturdy Belgian defiance. It was only after Sir Edward Grey had sat down that the telegram containing this sensational news was passed along the Front Bench and he read it out to a tense House.

Sir Edward Grey's speech was the first official statement on the crisis which the House of Commons and the country had heard. His case was threefold.

In the first place, the Northern French coast was unguarded, and we could not let it be attacked. For if the French Fleet had to be recalled from the

[1] *Memories and Reflections*, by the Earl of Oxford and Asquith.

Mediterranean, from which we had ourselves withdrawn, then our own sea-lines would be exposed. Secondly, we had an historic and vital interest in the independence of the Low Countries. What would be *our* fate if they should fall, and France be beaten to her knees? Finally, was it conceivable that we could stand aside, husband our strength, and then intervene decisively at the end? For by then our trade with Europe would have dried up, and by denying our obligations we should have forfeited every friend.

Two items of high emotion spiced the Foreign Secretary's speech. The first was the telegram of the King of the Belgians to King George, which Sir Edward Grey read out:

"I make a supreme appeal to the diplomatic intervention of Your Majesty's Government to safeguard the integrity of Belgium."

The second electric moment came when the Foreign Secretary declared that the one bright spot in the whole of this terrible situation was—*and let this be marked abroad!*—that there was now no "Irish Question". The statement brought forth later a moving promise from John Redmond, the Irish Nationalist leader, that the South would join with the North to guard together their Green Island.

This famous speech of Sir Edward Grey lasted more than an hour. If you read it today, you may find it repetitive, even rambling. It has no symmetry, no imagery, not even the stark eloquence of facts (the Foreign Secretary apologized because he had so few). It bore the more deeply moving mark of a noble man's sincerity.

... Now, it was morning, Tuesday, 4 August. The Germans were marching into Belgium, and the Liège forts were already under fire of the howitzers. The British ultimatum had gone off, due to expire at midnight. It was a steaming, sultry day.

In the Treasury, Lloyd George was furiously fighting his own private   Age 51
battle with the intractable monster called Money. Sitting late with his team of advisers and officials until 2 a.m. that morning, the Chancellor had hit upon a plan for gaining financial time—put it in cold storage by declaring another Bank Holiday that Tuesday. Then, he was going to have a third Bank Holiday tomorrow, Wednesday, and for good measure one on Thursday, too!

... It was afternoon. A telegram had come to the German Ambassador in London from Von Jagow, the German Foreign Secretary. It insisted that Germany had no intention whatever of annexing Belgian territory ("sincerity of this declaration is borne out by the fact we solemnly pledged our word to Holland strictly to respect her neutrality!"). The Germans had "absolutely unimpeachable information" that the French had intended to attack the German Army across Belgium.

It did not, of course, answer the British ultimatum to Germany, which never was answered.

. . . It was evening. By now, the crowds about Westminster were immense, and ever-growing. The people were not going home this evening. They were coming out. They were not protesting for Peace. They were clamouring for War. A feverish breath swept the land like a blast from the furnace.

. . . It was night. Soon after nine o'clock Lloyd George was summoned from his financial councils to the Cabinet room. He found the Prime Minister and the Foreign Secretary there with two or three other Ministers in grave consultation. A message from Berlin to the German Embassy had been intercepted, saying that the "English Ambassador has just demanded his passport . . . declaring war". Could it be a ruse to anticipate the hour of our Ultimatum's expiry, and make some felon stroke against the British Fleet or shore? The Ministers sat round the green table, on which it now seemed that such awful hazards had been suddenly staked. They talked in subdued voices, beneath the light of the shaded lamps. Should the British Government declare war now —or wait till eleven o'clock (the ultimatum was due to end at midnight Central European Time, eleven o'clock Greenwich time)? They decided to wait.

. . . It was the hour. As it drew near, the voices of the Ministers around the table were hushed. They hardly looked at one another, but stole glances at the clock. Then Big Ben:

Boom! Boom! Boom!

A vast, excited concourse had gathered in the Mall surrounding Buckingham Palace, and spreading far across the Green Park. Their cheering swelled into a Niagaran roar as the King and Queen, with the Prince of Wales, appeared on the balcony. Then someone struck up "God Save the King" and 30,000 people sang. Farther up the Mall, by the Duke of York's Steps, another patriotic section were smashing the windows of the Germany Embassy, and the mounted police had to be fetched from Cannon Row.

Next morning, the public mood had rather changed. The Banks were still closed and many people were getting a little short of cash after this exciting week-end. Were the Banks going to stay shut, and for how long? What about credits? There was growing speculation as to a possible panic.

The Chancellor of the Exchequer was wasting no time. Already on the previous Monday, he had rushed through Parliament a Postponement of Payments Act empowering the Government to declare a general moratorium. It was followed by a Royal Proclamation deferring for a month the maturity of bills of exchange. Now, on Wednesday, 5 August, the first day of the war, Lloyd George was able to report to the House of Commons that it had been decided not to suspend the payment of specie, a bold and unique act which greatly helped to steady the nerves of the financial world. He appealed to the public not to hoard gold, and at the same time announced the forthcoming issue of Treasury notes to the value of £1 and 10s. As a measure of Britain's credit, the Chancellor reported that the emergency Bank

Rate had been reduced from 10 per cent to 6 per cent. Next day, the Currency and Bank Notes Bill passed through all its stages in both Houses of Parliament. When the Banks opened their doors again on Friday, 7 August, it was seen that business was normal, and cash was being freely paid in.

The trouble was not yet over, though now all prospect of panic was. It remained to lift the load of liability off the City, and to get the wheels of trade turning again there. The following week, the Bank of England agreed to discount pre-moratorium bills, at a cost of £100,000,000. Next, the Bank advanced funds to the great accepting houses to pay off their bills at maturity. In these matters, of course, the Bank was acting as the agent of the Government. In all, the Government (i.e. the Chancellor of the Exchequer initially, for there was little time for Cabinet consultation) guaranteed £500,000,000 in respect of overseas debts. Finally, the Courts (Emergency Powers) Acts of 31 August relieved debtors who could not pay owing to war conditions. Lloyd George was, no doubt, also relieved when the War Obligations Act was passed the following November. It was an Act of Indemnity for Ministers' doings during the previous three months.

In handling this unexampled financial crisis, Lloyd George had displayed skill, energy, courage and judgment. It may be urged as to this last matter, that he had enjoyed the advantage of excellent advice; if so, it simply serves to re-emphasize his judgment in selecting it—and his objectivity, too. The Chancellor of the Exchequer called to his councils, not only the capable Treasury officials or advisers such as Sir John Bradbury and Sir George Paish, but Bankers such as Lord Cunliffe, Sir Edward Holden and Lord Rothschild, and two Tory ex-Chancellors, Lord St. Aldwin[1] and Austen Chamberlain.

There were some other emergency measures that ran parallel with these City operations. On 8 August, Lloyd George asked the House of Commons for a credit vote of £100,000,000 for immediate purposes, and on 26 August, he brought forward a War Loan Bill, empowering the Government to raise by loan for the conduct of the war "any money required". By the end of August, 1914, Lloyd George had tamed, even trained his Monster. No panic ever arose again during the First World War over money.

His own credit bounded up. Lloyd George had started this year, 1914, in downcast, almost desperate mood. Politically and personally, his fortunes had gone astray. Sometimes, he thought he had set his back to the sun, and in that troubled week before the war Lloyd George perhaps knew his darkest hours. Now, suddenly, crisis had called forth the man's most splendid powers. Lloyd George rose with the storm. Ever Lloyd George loved storm, and he was right. He was a great captain in a rough sea. It was his element.

What wonderful, exciting days of August, 1914! War! Financial Fear! Invasion scares! Secret landings! Spies!

Rumour, suspicion and scandal ran wildfire. At the Home Office,

[1] Formerly Sir Michael Hicks-Beach.

McKenna was much denounced for not locking up many more people with foreign-sounding names or foreign-looking appearance whom patriotic neighbours had hastened to denounce. Moreover, he had just naturalized Baron Schroeder, a well-known German head of a British Banking House.

Then there were those Zeppelins! It did not need editorial aids to draw attention to this menace. Aircraft were still rare in 1914, and when to their novelty had been added the mystery of those pre-war stories of strange lights reported in the night sky, why then, public interest was already assured. Now that war had come, the people saw searchlights, as well as guns, mounted on the Admiralty Arch, on the gates of Hyde Park, on Barnes Common and Blackheath. These forerunners of radar and rockets seemed much more a part of the everynight life of the civilian; for one thing, they pierced like a glittering spear the shroud of these early black-outs. No "Zepps" actually appeared over England until well into the New Year, but our own naval airships paid several visits to test the alertness of the night-watch—and set off rumours next morning.

Finally, the U-boats! This was the most real scare of all. It was not (yet) that they would sink our merchantmen and so starve us, which three years later they nearly did. The fear was that they would sneak past the lights, under the nets, and through the sea-mines which guarded the great anchorages of the Grand Fleet, and there sink our mighty battleships while they lay at their moorings. Then, indeed, we might have lost the war, not as Churchill wrote of that day of muddle and glory at Jutland, "in an afternoon", but stealthily, in a night.

What had happened to the war in Europe? In the West, the German Army had stamped through Belgium, exactly as von Schlieffen had planned. The arrival of the British Expeditionary Force had been quite unable to halt them (though the "Contemptible Little Army" gave the Germans a lesson in aimed rifle-fire that they never forgot—they thought we had a machine-gun corps—and enriched the annals of war with an immortal name), and our retreat from Mons to the Marne had followed. There, at last, the German invasion of France had been held, and repelled. The enemy, in turn, then withdrew some distance, dug himself in, and from now onward with only one or two exceptions, the war in the West degenerated into the siege and counter-siege of two huge mud walls that reached from the North Sea to the Alps. In the East, it was the Russians who began by invading Germany. When they, too, were checked at the great battle of Tannenburg in September, the Eastern Front developed into a similar, although vaster, vaguer struggle along a shifting line that stretched from the Polish march to the Carpathians.

Two fateful things had happened in the politics of Britain.

First, on the morrow of his pledge of loyalty, John Redmond, the Irish leader, had met Sir Edward Carson, Ulster's chief, in the Speaker's Library at the House of Commons, and sought to come to terms. He found him "in an absolutely irreconcilable mood about everything", threatening obstruction all round in Parliament if the Home Rule Bill was placed on the Statute Book. Redmond wrote to Asquith, begging him not to bow before this bullying, and thus lose "the greatest opportunity that has ever occurred in the history of Ireland to win the Irish people to loyalty to the Empire". The Bill was placed upon the Statute Book, but its operation was suspended. Blood and tears would blot it.

The second deed of destiny was Asquith's invitation to Field-Marshal Lord Kitchener, on 5 August, 1914, to take over from himself the post of Secretary of State for War. There would be penalties to pay for this, too, but for Britain, infinitely worth while.

At the outbreak of hostilities Kitchener entered on his political career as Secretary of State for War with a soldierly contempt for politicians. Indeed, Kitchener regarded his post at the War Office as being military rather than political. He shrouded his operations in secrecy less because he distrusted his new colleagues (though he did, and more than once said so), than because he simply did not see what war had to do with civilians. So considerable, indeed, was the military ignorance of most Ministers that it was difficult for them even to suspect what was being withheld from them behind the Kitchener Security Screen. His great reputation with the public and his own forbidding mien did not encourage questions.

However, it was the Chancellor of the Exchequer's job to ask some, for he had to provide the money, both for the pay and expenses of the armies in the field and now being raised at home and also for the supply of their most outstanding needs, which were weapons and munitions. It was at this point that Lloyd George first ran up against the military mind—or rather the Quartermaster mind. By comparison, he reckoned the old Squirearchy resilient.

The War Office had always, up till then, handled its own supply business, from arsenals to tailoring contracts. If certain work had to be placed outside Service circles, then it was confined strictly to "approved" firms. When, in September, 1914, the Chancellor set aside £20,000,000 to finance the development of armament factories, the Master General of Ordnance, General Von Donop, considered that it was "inadvisable at this stage to inform the trade that grants of money will be made".

The General feared a rush of applicants for war contracts, which was exactly what was needed.

For as the Armies settled down in the West and dug themselves into their earthen fortresses, it became apparent that to break the opposing front required a hitherto undreamed-of weight of shells, and, especially, of high-explosive, instead of the shrapnel which had served well enough to destroy Boer commandos on the bare *veldt*. On the other hand, to repel the enemy infantry assault the requirement was machine-guns. The British Expeditionary Force had not enough of either. The Germans had ample of both. They had nearly

400 6-inch howitzers on the Western Front. By the New Year, we had accumulated 24. The German infantry battalions had 16 machine-guns apiece. Our battalions had 2. The Germans had trench-mortars which threw a 250-lb. bomb. We replied with (not many) hand-grenades, most of them made out of bully-beef tins and catapulted.

Lloyd George's own position was a curious one at this point. We have marked his hesitation at the time of the German threat to Belgium, even up to the hour that they were marching in. Then, for the next week, he was steadying the ship of Britain's credit in a great gale, and earning the astonished admiration of the City and of the business world beyond. But a month after the war had begun, at a great patriotic rally at Guildhall, the principal speakers were the Prime Minister and Bonar Law, with Balfour and Churchill also present on the platform. Lloyd George was not there.

This was the notable occasion of Asquith's famous speech, "We shall not sheathe the sword . . ." (until Belgium's wrongs were righted), an oration, as *The Times* justly wrote next morning, "of the noblest order, solemn and impressive. . . ." Bonar Law followed, briefly, but "with remarkable force and fervour". The audience next set up a clamour for both Balfour and Churchill to address them. Balfour obliged with a few eloquent words, and then (said the *Daily Express*) came a cry that could not be denied— "Churchill!" "Churchill!" So the First Lord of the Admiralty told the cheering assembly first, that they could ever trust the Navy, and then

"sure I am of this, that you have only to endure to conquer. You have only to persevere to save yourselves, and to save all those who rely upon you. You have only to go right on, and at the end of the road, be it short or long, victory and honour will be found!"

The name of the First Lord, at any rate in the popular esteem, stood much higher at this moment than that of the Chancellor of the Exchequer. It would be, indeed, for a moment only. For Lloyd George was about to make a sensational ascent to popularity and power—and Churchill to start as sudden, and as swift a descent. War multiplies everything, but above all the speed of events.

By now, in his own heart—and that was the vital place—Lloyd George was committed utterly to fight this war through to the end. This was a different kind of war from all the others, fought (on our side anyway) for entirely different purposes, as he thought. This had now become for Lloyd George a crusade. He believed in it, in the deepest recesses of his being. Lloyd George was back to his Boer War character, when his own self was merged in a great cause, although this was another cause and this time he was not against war but passionately for it. Lloyd George felt that way. He had to speak that way. He went to the Queen's Hall in London on the night of 19 September, a fortnight after the great Guildhall meeting, and there he made the most decisive utterance of his own life. It was one of the most splendid.

He had a huge mixed audience. It included many smart well-to-do London people, who had come to see and hear the "pro-Boer", and "Limehouse" orator turned patriot, "stodgy, fashionable folk who would chill enthusiasm in my own or anybody's breast", as Lloyd George afterwards described them. But he also had a considerable contingent of London Welsh there, who stirred up the meeting for him before he started by singing their Welsh hymns, or "battle-songs". Lord Plymouth, whose son had just been killed in France, presided, and on the platform sat Dr. Clifford, Dr. Jowett, Sir William Robertson Nicoll, Lord Reading, Sir John Simon, Sir Alfred Mond, Charles Masterman, Hamar Greenwood, and other M.P.s. Many women, some of them nurses, and soldiers in uniform were present, too.

For a moment, or two, before he spoke, Lloyd George paled and his eyes fell. Then, he raised them to his audience and, very quietly, he began.

Soon he held them in a spell. Tense, straining forward, silent, hardly breathing—then suddenly, clapping, cheering, laughing almost hysterically, or near to tears again. As Lloyd George spoke, he waved his hand gently from side to side. The silver magic of his voice, and the throbbing current of his passion, gradually possessed the entire audience and they swayed as one man in rhythm with the compelling hand. That night, Lloyd George spoke as one filled with the voices of millions from the dark, vast caverns of this nation's history.

He spoke of the civilized modern purpose of Britain, and how she had striven to keep the Peace of Europe in those sunlit summer days, just gone by. He told how the shadow of war had suddenly fallen across the land, and he named the cause of it.

Germany! the Law breaker! The Road Hog of Europe! She had ridden right across Belgium. She had tried to ride across France. She had been halted there! Then came Russia's turn. Russia had a special regard for Serbia, a special interest, for Serbia was a member of Russia's family, and she could not see Serbia maltreated. Austria knew that, Germany knew it, and she turned round to Russia and said, "I insist that you shall stand by with your arms folded while Austria is strangling your little brother to death!"

"What answer did the Russian Slav give?" cried Lloyd George. "He gave the only answer that becomes a man! He turned to Austria and said, 'You lay your hand on that little fellow, and I will tear your ramshackle Empire limb from limb!' And he is doing it!"

Storm swept the hall. The roar of it rolled far beyond, and people stopped in the streets far outside. Now, orator and audience were one. The word was his, and the thought belonged to every man and woman there. Then, quietly as he had begun, Lloyd George, the tempest-maker, ended.

"I know a valley in North Wales, between the mountains and the sea. It is a beautiful valley, snug, comfortable, sheltered by the mountains from all the bitter blasts. But it is very enervating, and I remember how the boys were in the habit of climbing the hill above the village to have a glimpse of the great mountains in the distance, and to be stimulated and freshened by the breezes which came from the hill-tops, and by the great spectacle of their grandeur.

We have been living in a sheltered valley for generations. We have been too comfortable and too indulgent—many, perhaps, too selfish—and the stern hand of Fate has scourged us to an elevation where we can see the everlasting things that matter for a nation—the high peaks we had forgotten, of Honour, Duty, Patriotism, and, clad in glittering white, the great pinnacle of Sacrifice, pointing like a rugged finger to Heaven.

We shall descend into the valleys again; but as long as the men and women of this generation last, they will carry in their hearts the image of those great mountain peaks whose foundations are not shaken, though Europe rock and sway in the convulsions of a great war."

Lloyd George returned to his office at the Treasury. There was a War Budget to be framed that autumn, for the £100,000,000 credit voted on 8 August had already been exhausted. Lloyd George asked the House of Commons for a second credit—of £225,000,000. But he was determined to raise a substantial part of this by extra taxation, for he feared that the inevitable big spending by the Government in war-time would bring about inflation, and that wage troubles would follow in its train.

It was a budget in the spirit of his Queen's Hall speech. Income-tax was doubled, going up to 2s. 8d. in the £1, super-tax was doubled, tea-duty was nearly doubled, beer-duty more than trebled. Lloyd George reckoned that these taxes would yield the Treasury an additional £60,000,000. He foresaw that after the war, following a seller's market in certain goods, there would be a slump, for the purchasing power of money of our former customers would be crippled. He meant to make the country pay its way as far as possible now.

A third measure was to float the War Loan, and Lloyd George fixed the value of this at £350,000,000. It was a 3½ per cent security, and was almost immediately over-subscribed.

For the rest, the Chancellor was busy arranging what would rapidly grow to be the truly enormous purchase of weapons, munitions, equipment, raw materials and food in the United States, not only for Britain but for her Allies. Out of this vast, but absolutely vital Lloyd Georgian transaction, would arise one of the prickly problems of post-war politics, the American War Debt.

Trouble was coming. On land, the war in the West had bogged-down in trenches after the Battle of the Marne and "the race to the sea". No other distinctive operation had followed, apart from the ill-fated expedition of the Naval Division to Antwerp in October. (Churchill offered to take command himself, and if he had, he might well have been trapped there, along with the three battalions who were forced to take refuge across the frontier of Holland, in which case we should quite certainly have had another Churchill "escape-from-the-Dutch" story.) In the east, the Russians had been driven back all along their front, to a depth of sometimes three hundred miles. Their armies were pitiably short of weapons, munitions, equipment, even clothing, never of courage.

At this point Churchill conceived an idea, or rather he resurrected it from the files of the Admiralty, where it had been buried after rejection in the previous century. This was to force the Straits of the Dardanelles, and seize Constantinople. Thus, we could open the seaway across the Black Sea to our hard-pressed Russian ally, and also probably persuade the Balkan races to make a real Third Front against the Austro-Germans. The project had always been turned down in the past because of the great risks of sending a fleet through narrow waters, dominated by steep shores, into so small an enclosure as the Sea of Marmora. Of course, if the shores could be secured by landing troops there, then the operation would be considerably more attractive.

According to Lloyd George, Churchill was willing to start off, at any rate, with a naval attack.

"Troops would be called for only after the Narrows had been forced and, therefore, after all the forts had been demolished."

Kitchener, Lloyd George observed, knew that this would take some time, and meanwhile there would be no demand for soldiers or ammunition. So Kitchener preferred the Dardanelles project to another one which was up for Cabinet examination, the unopposed landing at Salonika which the Greeks had offered, and which Lloyd George himself favoured as opening up communications with Serbia. Also Lloyd George and the Salonika section urged, this might be decisive in bringing in the Rumanians and, at the worst, neutralizing the Bulgarians. Thus, a landward contact would be established with the Russians. Kitchener was against Salonika, because this operation *would* require the immediate dispatch of a certain number of troops.

The Dardanelles Party won the day. They had been powerfully reinforced by the new First Sea Lord, Admiral "Jackie" Fisher, whom Churchill had recalled from retirement when popular clamour compelled him to part company with Admiral Prince Louis of Battenberg. Admiral Fisher, however, retained a proper inter-services suspicion of Field-Marshal Kitchener's motives, just as he was jealous of his ministerial rank. Fisher's enthusiasms were always sizzling, but often they were short. For a time, indeed, he nursed an alternative to the Dardanelles Plan, in his "Baltic Plan". This was to sail through the Skagerrak and land an invading force on the Baltic coast of Germany, within 100 miles of Berlin. It had this advantage over the Dardanelles operation—it had been done once, successfully, by the Russians in the Seven Years War.

At this period Fisher was still firm friends with Churchill. His letters were still inscribed "Yours till hell freezes", or "Yours to a cinder". Churchill had needed reinforcement, for although under him the Royal Navy had done wonderful things, they had been silent wonders. Thus, the Navy had brought safely home to Britain those far-off garrison troops from all over the world, as well as the Canadian and the British-Indian divisions, brought the Australian and New Zealand Army Corps to Egypt, taken troops to West Africa and East Africa, delivered the British Expeditionary Force to France, and swept the oceans of the world clear of all enemy surface-raiding craft.

On the other hand, there had been some mishaps, besides Antwerp, and these had been only too well-advertised. When, soon after the outset of war, the German Fleet had retired behind its mine-fields to the security of the German harbours, the First Lord of the Admiralty had made an unlucky speech, at Liverpool on 21 September about: "digging the rats out of their holes."

Next day, the British cruisers *Aboukir*, *Cressy* and *Hogue*, returning from close patrol off the Dogger Bank, had been torpedoed by a German U-boat, with the loss of 1,400 lives. The British public accounted this to be expensive rat-catching. Then, there had been the disastrous action on 3 November, off Coronel, Chile, "in thick and wicked weather, with rain squalls, a strong wind and heavy seas", when five German cruisers of Admiral Von Spee's Pacific Squadron sank the British cruisers *Monmouth* and *Good Hope*, with all hands. They had been avenged a month later, at the Battle of the Falkland Isles, when Admiral Sturdee's Fleet took toll of four of the enemy warships. Finally, on 16 December, there had been the bombardment by German warships of the open towns of Hartlepool, Scarborough and Whitby. Civilian casualties had been 500, and the raiders got away unscathed. In the autumn of 1914, the fortunes of the First Lord of the Admiralty, which had soared so high early in the first days of September, were steadily sinking. They were finally submerged off the Dardanelles.

Meantime, Lloyd George's reputation as steadily rose, both within the Cabinet, and beyond in the broader field of politics. He was getting on much better with many of his old colleagues, largely because he was by this time getting on so badly with his newest one, Lord Kitchener. Long before the end of 1914, Lloyd George and Kitchener were at daggers drawn, and the Chancellor of the Exchequer was the most consistent critic of the Secretary of State for War. In this, he rallied support even from such personally antipathetic quarters as McKenna, who liked still less the "military secrecy" with which the Field-Marshall shrouded his operations from his fellow-Ministers, whom he referred to as "the twenty-three gentlemen in the Cabinet with whom I am barely acquainted".

Looming even larger now, as the siege was developed, was the question of munitions. It was already something beyond the capacity of a Supply Section of the War Office to handle. The Western Front alone was in desperate straits (the Eastern Front, although this was even more successfully concealed from the Cabinet, was still worse off).

For weeks past, a trickle, a stream, and then a cascade of despairing telegrams and letters from Field-Marshal Sir John French, had descended on General von Donop's table at the War Office, asking, arguing, pleading for food to feed his hungry cannon. None of these documents, either the letters and telegrams from the Front or the replies to them, were ever shown to the Cabinet.

But rumours flitted over the Narrow Seas. Soldiers from the Front were coming home on leave; there were a number of "Hostilities Only" officers serving on G.H.Q. Staff in France who were Members of Parliament, or else their close friends; there were V.I.P. visitors; there were War Correspondents, and so on.

Early in September, Lloyd George urged that a special committee of the Cabinet should be set up to look into the whole question of guns, shells and rifles. Kitchener so violently resisted, and he still so dominated the Cabinet, that Lloyd George's proposal was turned down. But he persisted and, early in October, he so far won his point that a Committee of Seven were named to consider methods of speeding-up the manufacture and delivery of munitions. They were Lord Kitchener, Lord Haldane, Lord Lucas, Lloyd George, Churchill, McKenna and Runciman. The War in Whitehall was about to begin.

Soon, of course, it had spread into a wider circle. For a Committee of Seven, especially if they were in possession of even some of the main, appalling facts, would certainly discuss them with other interested people, Ministers, Service Chiefs, industrialists concerned with Supply. The story of War Office muddle began to get out—and also the information that Lloyd George was the man who was trying to clear it up. Important people began to repeat his own vehement arguments.

The facts were plain enough, urged Lloyd George. The enemy at the moment had more equipment than we possessed, and he had more factories. But we had more men, materials and liberty of movement about the seas of the world than the enemy, so that we could count on the factories of America and Japan. Our extra men could only be effectively deployed if our extra materials were effectively employed. If this were done, we should immensely exceed the enemy's equipment. What was holding us up? demanded Lloyd George. Only an antiquated method! Only an obsolete, inefficient information service, which resulted in this incredible wastage of the Allies' vast potential preponderance of resources, declared Lloyd George.

"What we stint in material, we squander in life!" he warned.

On 1 January, 1914, Lloyd George had signalled to the nation his Happy New Year greetings with a personal forecast of sunny skies. On the last evening of what had been the most fateful year in British history for a century he was writing a letter to the Prime Minister to warn him of the black hurricane that lowered immediately ahead.

31 December, 1914.

"My dear Prime Minister,

I am uneasy about the prospects of the war unless the Government take some decisive measures to grip the situation. I can see no signs anywhere that our military leaders and guides are considering any plans for extricating us from our present unsatisfactory position. Had I not been a witness of their deplorable lack of provision I should not have thought it possible that men so responsibly placed could have displayed so little forethought. You remember the guns and ammunition incident. When I raised the question in the Cabinet the War Office had only ordered 600 guns in all. Those were to be delivered before next September. The immense manufacturing resources of the country had not been organized for cannon, rifles, or ammunition, and America was not even explored. As a result of the activities and suggestions of the Cabinet Committee, 4,000 guns are now promised before that date. Ammunition has also been provided for these guns. . . .

Sincerely yours,
D. Lloyd George."

It had the note of an ultimatum. So far had Lloyd George's fortune advanced in this one critical year.

The next year began as a Grey New Year.

By 1 January, 1915, already gone were all the high enthusiasms of 4 August, 1914. The boys had marched away, through the cheering streets, to the jaunty strains of "Tipperary". Of course, they were going to be home by Christmas! They always are.

But, then, there had come the Retreat from Mons, and the Battle of the Marne, and the affair at Antwerp, and somehow the war in the West had got bogged down in the mud, Somewhere in France. In the East, the Russian Steam Roller had come to a standstill, too. Perhaps it wasn't going to be so easy after all to trim the Kaiser's fierce moustaches, and set "Little Willie" goose-stepping back to Berlin.

The early months of the New Year offered no encouragement. Two big stories were on the way—and both of them bad. The first was the Dardanelles disaster, the second the great Shell scandal.

The Dardanelles was Operation Disaster, because it was Doubt and Delay from the word Go. To force the Dardanelles was a daring idea, and it may well have been a feasible one, in that it all but came off. But it had been compromised even before the start, by the apparently aimless British bombardment of the Turkish forts at the entrance of the Straits in November, 1914. After having thus advertised to the enemy our interest in this area, the British Fleet withdrew for three months, while the Turks repaired the damage and increased the depth of their defences.

The Dardanelles Campaign proper opened on 19 February, 1915, with a renewed full-scale naval attack on the forts at the mouth of the Dardanelles. By the beginning of March, the outer ring had been reduced, and the British warships were able to sail six miles up the Straits. The Sultan made ready to evacuate his court to the highlands of Anatolia, and certain interesting new political developments promised in England. Since the Fall of Constantinople might be expected to bring about a decisive change in the whole course of the war (and, indeed, *after* it: Russia was to be installed there), Churchill strongly pressed the Prime Minister to invite the Tory leaders Bonar Law and Lord Lansdowne to the newly constituted "War Council" of the Cabinet for a discussion. Balfour, as a member of the Committee of Imperial Defence, had already been attending it since 4 August, a curious anomaly. Churchill hoped, and expected, that out of this closer association of the leaders of the two main political Parties in Britain a more complete and permanent partnership would develop. The two new guests at the "War Council", however, were not at all impressed or encouraged by what they saw.

They found that while the Cabinet had a mind on this, as on other matters, it was a split one. Not only were they divided in their view of general policy, but even upon individual military operations. And the Dardanelles especially, was the evidence.

If troops as well as ships had been employed throughout, it now seems possible that the British Forces would have been in Constantinople within a fortnight. But not until 25 April, or ten weeks after the Navy's opening bombardment, was the Army landed. Even then, the soldiers were not put ashore on the neck of Gallipoli Peninsula, a flat open plain, but on the beaches at the extreme tip, under the frowning cliffs. They never got beyond them. Indeed, their fate was sealed the day the great battleships of the Fleet were withdrawn because First Sea Lord "Jackie" Fisher had finally decided that they must not be wasted on such "subsidiary operations". He professed to fear that the German Navy was about to come out and fight in the North Sea. What is sure is that by this time he was utterly at odds with the First Lord of the Admiralty, Churchill.

But meantime, the second angry story was gathering. The Shell Scandal. Even older than the Churchill-Fisher feud was that Lloyd George-Kitchener quarrel. It probably actually traced back to that day early in the war when Lloyd George went down to Woolwich Arsenal and found them filling shells by hand with buckets of boiling liquid. The Ordnance Department were busy fighting the Last-War-But-One again. They resisted with all the dogged tenacity of a "clique within a clique" (as Wellington had once branded the War Office) any and every effort to modernize, speed up and expand their production. To all Lloyd George's urging to mobilize the great engineering firms who were normally outside the armament industry, the Master-General of Ordnance replied that unless they possessed that special know-how "which only years of practice could produce", they would only make faulty weapons and munitions. Hence Lloyd George appealed to his Prime Minister:

Treasury Chambers,
Whitehall, S.E.
18 February, 1915.

"My dear Prime Minister,
... After seven months' war we do not even now know approximately the position of the Russians. Sir John French told me that he had been assured by the Russian officers who visited him that Russia would have 3,000,000 men fully equipped in the field next month, and that they could then sweep back the German and Austrian armies opposed to them. The War Office compute the Russian forces now at 1,200,000. If Sir John French's information be correct the Russian reinforcements available in March would come to 1,800,000. Now we learn that the Russians have no rifles to equip their new men with, and that they can only turn out rifles at the rate of 40,000 per month. At that rate they can only bring 500,000 more men into the field by this time next year. The Germans are capturing more than 40,000 Russians with their rifles each month. What is the truth about their equipment? We surely ought to know. Our fate depends on it. ...

We ought to have a searching and candid survey of the whole military situation, with a view to devising the best means for meeting it—otherwise we shall drift into irretrievable disaster.

There has been a deplorable lack of co-ordination between East and West, and as long as it lasts the Germans will continue winning. Mere optimistic bluff is not going to float us through this hurricane.

Ever sincerely,
D. Lloyd George."

So keenly did Lloyd George feel about the need for closer inter-Allied co-operation that at this time, as Asquith recorded in his diary, he was pressing the Prime Minister to send him as Ambassador Extraordinary to Russia and the Balkan States in order to achieve that purpose.

On 6 March, 1915, Lloyd George told his friends that unless a Shell Committee which really did its job was set up forthwith, he was determined to resign, in order to compel action. The British Front, let alone those of our Allies, was being starved of vital supplies.

On 10 March, his fears were proven.

At Neuve Chapelle, on that day, Field-Marshal Sir John French went into the attack. Three days later, he wired Kitchener that his advance was held up "above all, by want of ammunition". Three days more, and he reported that he had been

"compelled to abandon further offensive operations until sufficient reserves are accumulated. I desire to say with all the weight of my authority that the object of H.M. Government cannot be attained unless the supply of artillery ammunition can be increased."

To which the War Office replied by complaining that the artillery had used up that month 200–220 rounds per gun, or 13 per day! They begged that less be used. To gain one square mile at Neuve Chapelle cost the British Army 12,892 dead. "What we stint in material, we squander in life."

Yet, on 20 April, Mr. Asquith could go to Newcastle-on-Tyne, and there, before a great industrial audience, deny all charges that the Allied Armies were being hampered by munition shortages. The truth was, of course, the Prime Minister and the Cabinet simply did not know, because Kitchener did not tell them.

"Some Ministers," said Lloyd George, "knew a bit more than others— none knew much. We had to forage for information. Sometimes we scrounged an important fact; more often, we picked a snub."

There are a score of letters, telegrams, notes, memos at this time from Lloyd George to his leader Asquith and to his colleagues, pressing for a change with all the energy and eloquence at his command.

"The Government must take some decisive measures at once to grip this situation." "I urge immediate action." "We must do the thing, *and do it now*!" "It is eight months since I ventured to draw attention of the Cabinet to the importance of mobilizing all our engineering resources for the production of munitions and the equipment of war." "All the engineering works in the country ought to be turned on to the production of war material. The population ought to be prepared to suffer all sorts of deprivations and even hardships whilst this process was going on."

The original Cabinet Committee which had been charged with the duty of looking after munitions had died an unmourned death in January, 1915, the only victory which the War Office could claim yet. But now, in March, Lloyd George, as a direct result of his own ultimatum to the Prime Minister was able to lay before the House of Commons a new and drastic edition (No. 3) of the Defence of the Realm Act.

This measure of "real war" gave the Government powers to take over and operate any factory or workshop it wanted, to shift its plan, break any contract whatever which stood in the way of the machines being used for the purpose the Government prescribed. The patriotic Tory Opposition made no demur. But Bonar Law noted, aptly:

"If this Bill is necessary today, I cannot understand why the necessity of it could not have been foreseen in August, and why it should not have been introduced then."

The Prime Minister considered appointing Lloyd George himself as Director of War Contracts, and relieving him of his duties at the Exchequer.

But once again—drift. Kitchener resisted every attempt to interfere in any way with the regular armament firms, or even to make use of labour from firms which, in future, might be registered at the War Office as a source of supply. In fact, Kitchener was against any real change in the existing set-up of the armament industry.

Deadlock.

Asquith took further counsel with Lloyd George, Balfour, Churchill and Montagu. Kitchener was not invited to this conference and when he heard of it, he threatened to resign. When the Committee was set up, however, Lloyd George in turn threatened to resign! In the end, on the powerful plea of Balfour, the new Shell Committee was duly appointed (8 April, 1915). It included Lloyd George (chairman) and Balfour (to keep Lloyd George under control), Edwin Montagu (Lloyd George's friend) and General von Donop (Kitchener's man). It is to be noted that neither Kitchener himself nor Churchill (whose political stock was continuing to decline) were named as members of this committee. Three weeks had elapsed since the War Council had resolved that its appointment was of the utmost urgency.

At this moment, the Tory Press opened up fire on the Prime Minister himself in what seemed to some of his circle to look suspiciously like a well-concerted attack. It was even suggested that the Chancellor of the Exchequer knew all about it. With tears in his eyes, so Asquith said, "Lloyd George assured me that sooner than take part in such disloyalty to his leader he would prefer (i) to break stones, (ii) dig potatoes, (iii) be hung and quartered. And I am sure that he was quite sincere."[1]

A curious political adventure of Lloyd George's at this period was an early attempted experiment in Nationalization (it never got beyond the drawing-board stage). What Lloyd George, the Blue Riband Temperance advocate of former days, was now proposing to make a State concern was—Drink! In a widely-publicized speech at Bangor on 28 February, 1915, the Chancellor of the Exchequer had declared that "Drink is doing more damage in this war than all the German submarines put together".

Reports of what was represented as being almost a tidal wave of drunkenness had been pouring in for months past from all over the country. Amongst shipyard workers, now getting really good wages for the first time, it appeared

[1] *Memories and Reflections*, by the Earl of Oxford and Asquith. Vol. II.

especially serious. Vital repairs to warships were delayed for days, sometimes weeks. From the great munition-making areas, where an army of women workers were now mobilized—and earning more money than they had ever earned before—there also came grave complaints of insobriety. In those days, public-houses opened at 6 a.m., and closed at midnight. It left a lot of time for drinking.

Lloyd George had been duly impressed by the fact that the French, in like circumstances, had prohibited the sale of absinthe and the Russians had banned vodka. He had mentioned this one day to King George V, who liked his glass of whisky as well as any of his subjects. The King considered that example would be a better way to temperance than injunction. He volunteered to give up whisky in his own home for the duration of the war. "The King's Pledge" caught the country's attention, but did not command its emulation.

So Lloyd George pondered on controlling the drinking habits of the people by controlling their liquor. Why not nationalize The Trade? He engaged Sir William Plender, head of the famous firm of accountants, to examine the finances of the whole brewery business with a view to purchase. Plender estimated that the breweries, tied houses and freeholds could be taken over for £250,000,000. A Government issue of 4 per cent stock at par would provide the capital—and show the Government an eventual profit.

Lloyd George sought Tory approval and advice for his project. He applied, with shrewd instinct, to Bonar Law, who was himself a teetotaller; also to F.E., who was not. Both, however, were willing to support the State ownership of the Drink Trade, if the Government declared that it was necessary for the better conduct of the war.

The Chancellor threw into his latest venture all the torrential energy and enthusiasm of his Budget League and Land League campaigns. To Miss Stevenson, recuperating at Brighton after a severe chill, J. T. Davies wrote early in April, reporting that Lloyd George was working himself and driving his staff night and day, and that his morning postbag now ran into four figures. One of Lloyd George's own letters to her tells:

"... Overwhelmed with work.... Tory leaders have decided to support my scheme. Am winning support on both sides, but it will be a tough job. . . .

I envy you that stormy sea. Nothing fills me with such a sense of wild exhilaration as a raging, boiling sea. . . ."

Lloyd George had no difficulty in mobilizing on his side for this new Temperance Crusade all the employers who were thoroughly disgusted with drunken workmen.

The Chancellor also sought to enlist the propaganda power of the Press. To Northcliffe he wrote:

11 Downing Street,
15 April, 1915.

"We have overwhelming evidence as to the grave mischief in the Munitions and transport areas caused by excessive drinking and we must take strong action otherwise the war will go on forever.

We cannot act unless we have practically the unanimous support of the leaders of the nation.

Your influence is essential.

Will you let your private secretary fix up a time with mine?

Yours sincerely,

D. Lloyd George."

Another "influence" was at work. Max Aitken, on the other side of Fleet Street, looked on beer as an "essential" to the working man. Under the headlines

BEER! BEER!
GLORIOUS
GOVERNMENT
BEER!

the *Daily Express* blew the froth off the beer story with a revelation of the proposed scheme, posing the question: "Is England to be drowned in beer or methylated spirits?"[1] This killed the Nationalization of Drink. For the Beer Barons, Brewers, Distillers and Publicans, the Irish Party—and naturally, the Sinners, that is, the Drinkers, joined at once in unacknowledged coalition with some of the Saints, that is, the Teetotallers. The most intemperate section of the Temperance Movement would not countenance the idea that the State should sully its soul by dealing in the evil trade of making and purveying alcoholic poison.

On 9 May, 1915, began the Battle of Festubert. Field-Marshal Sir John French has told what happened:

"After all our demands, less than 8 per cent of our shells were high explosives, and we only had sufficient supply for forty minutes of artillery preparation for this attack."

Once more, after three days—frustration, failure, and fearful losses in the Line. On 12 May, Lloyd George received a visit from the Commander-in-Chief's secretary, Brinsley Fitzgerald, and another A.D.C., Captain F. E. Guest. They brought a terrible tale, and an incriminating file. It was the first time Lloyd George had heard from the British Commander-in-Chief himself on the subject of the Shell Question. Up to this date, all vital telegrams from the Front about it had been withheld from the Chairman of the Shell Committee. Bitterly now, Lloyd George wrote to the Prime Minister. The

[1] In the wartime shortage of whisky, gin and rum a number of determined drinkers had taken to concoctions of methylated spirits.

Committee, he said, had become a farce and he would not go on presiding over it.

Not only to the most formidable Minister in the Government had the soldiers appealed. On 14 May, 1915 Northcliffe's *Times* came out with the headlines.

NEED FOR SHELLS
BRITISH ATTACKS CHECKED
LIMITED SUPPLY THE CAUSE
A LESSON FROM
FRANCE

Beneath, the Military Correspondent, Colonel Repington, wrote in his dispatch:

"The attacks were well planned and valiantly conducted. The infantry did splendidly, but the conditions were too hard. The want of an unlimited supply of high explosive was a fatal bar to our success."

That morning, the War Council met, as Lloyd George said, "for the first time after a long period of coma". Its last meeting had been seven weeks earlier. Crisis loured over Whitehall.

But it was not the one which had been creeping across the sky from the far horizon of the very first day of the war.

It was not a question of shells. It was one of ships.

It was not a Kitchener Crisis. It was a Fisher Crisis. The First Sea Lord had resolved finally to break with the First Lord of the Admiralty over the Dardanelles.

A day or two earlier, the British battleship *Goliath* had been torpedoed by a Turkish destroyer in the Aegean Sea, with the loss of more than 500 lives, another sacrifice to those "subsidiary operations", as Fisher was now sarcastically describing them. A week before that the great liner *Lusitania* had been torpedoed by a German U-boat off the coast of Ireland with the loss of more than 1,000 lives. The Sea War had become the Real War—and it was being lost!

"Jackie" Fisher had had enough. He pulled down the blinds in his office at the Admiralty, and walked across to the Treasury. In the entrance hall of Number 10 Downing Street he ran into Lloyd George. He thrust out his lower lip and set his face in a sinister frown.

"I've resigned," he said. "I can stick it no more."

Lloyd George was thunderstruck. He could not believe his own ears. "Well, I'm off to Scotland tonight, anyway!" said Fisher.

Quickly Lloyd George drew Fisher into his own room next door and sent a message to Asquith. When he arrived, the Prime Minister failed to shake the adamant old Admiral. Nor could the Home Secretary, McKenna, who had been Fisher's sincere friend in his own old days at the Admiralty and was

now also the sincere enemy of his supplanter there, Winston Churchill. By
this time, Fisher had retired to his room at the Admiralty again and had locked
the door. But McKenna observed him peeping from behind the curtain,
and he knocked patiently and steadily until the Admiral let him in. But that
evening "Jackie" Fisher let it be known that he had taken the Edinburgh
Express.

He disappeared from a London seething with rumour. He had certainly
done what he could to create it. To Bonar Law, he posted an anonymous letter
(but there was no mistaking the scrawl in which it was addressed) enclosing a
marked cutting from the *Pall Mall Gazette*, stating that "Lord Fisher was
received in audience of the King and remained there about half an hour".
Promptly Bonar Law went round to see Lord Lansdowne. After the conference
with his colleague, Bonar Law called on Lloyd George at the Treasury. He
asked if Fisher had resigned. And when this news was confirmed, Bonar Law
declared he would have to raise the issue in Parliament. Then, said Lloyd
George, that means coalition. Together the two statesmen called on Asquith.
There and then Coalition was determined. Bonar Law left Downing Street
to consult with his Shadow Cabinet.

As agreed with Asquith, a letter was sent from Bonar Law to the Prime
Minister that day.

It said that Lord Lansdowne and the writer had "learnt with dismay" that
Lord Fisher had resigned, and that they could not allow the House of Commons
to adjourn until this fact had been made known and discussed. Bonar Law
continued:

> "We think that the time has come when we ought to have a clear state-
> ment from you as to the policy which the Government intend to pursue.
> In our opinion things cannot go on as they are, some change in the
> constitution of the Government seems to us inevitable if it is to retain a
> sufficient measure of public confidence to conduct the War to a successful
> conclusion."

The situation in Italy (the Italians were about to throw in their lot with
the Allies) made it undesirable to have a controversy in Parliament, wrote
Bonar Law. The Opposition were prepared to keep silence if the Prime Minister
would take the necessary steps which had been indicated.

The Tory Opposition, however, was utterly determined not to let
Churchill remain at the Admiralty. To the Tories at this time, Churchill was
anathema.

The First Lord, meanwhile, had spent his morning composing a new
Board of Admiralty, and putting the finishing touches to his speech in the
House of Commons debate which would follow the announcement of it.
On his way round to see the Prime Minister, he looked into the Chancellor
of the Exchequer's room, and there, for the first time, he learned from Lloyd

Minister for War; with General Joffre and General Roques. Paris, 1916

George something of what was really going on. With a fresh interest in life, the First Lord hurried to see Asquith who received him cordially and confirmed that there was to be a new Government. He asked kindly, "What are we to do for you?"

It was Churchill's first knowledge that there was to be a new First Lord of the Admiralty. Incidentally, it was the third attempt to bring about a War Coalition—the other two had been made by Churchill himself. Twice he had failed. Now for the first time he would oppose a Coalition. This time it would succeed, in face of his opposition.

As the two men discussed what new post Churchill should be offered, or whether he would not prefer to take an Army command in France, Lloyd George entered and said: "Why don't you send him to the Colonial Office? There is a big job to be done there."

Churchill assures us in his *World Crisis* that he "did not accept this situation".

It is certain also that the Tories would not have accepted it either. They claimed half the new Cabinet posts, although Bonar Law, with characteristic self-abnegation, refrained from making the demand, which must have been instantly conceded him, of the Chancellorship of the Exchequer. Instead, it was Bonar Law who went to the Colonial Office. Churchill had to be content with the dignified sinecure of the Chancellorship of the Duchy of Lancaster. His first act in his new office extended the realm outside his regular duties —the Press. He recommended Asquith to commandeer *The Times*, turning it into an official Government organ after the style of Napoleon's *Moniteur*. The Prime Minister did not make a favourable response.

It took a full week to remodel the new Win-the-War Government in the midst of which Northcliffe in his *Times* and *Daily Mail* came out with a blast against Lord Kitchener, blaming him personally for the "Shell scandal". Both newspapers were solemnly burned the same afternoon on the Stock Exchange by the patriotic City brokers.

And Lloyd George? He went off to the brand new Ministry of Munitions, Number 6 Whitehall Gardens. The furniture consisted of two tables and a chair, and the same day a squad of workmen from the Office of Works arrived to take them away because they did not belong to the new Department. When an American visitor, Colonel House, came round to pay his respects to the new Minister, they had a friendly argument as to who should sit in the chair or on the table.

Wrote the Colonel that night to his friend, the President of the United States:

"He spoke again and again of military red-tape which he declared he would cut as speedily as possible. He was full of energy and enthusiasm, and I feel certain something will soon happen in his department. . . . He

J

has something dynamic within him which his colleagues have not and which is badly needed at this great hour."

Lloyd George had been hounded as a pro-Boer traitor by the mob in Birmingham and Bangor; hailed as a Workers' hero by the mob in Limehouse and Newcastle. He had been damned up to the day of war by the Bankers and Big Business men as the bandit of the People's Budget; almost deified the week that war broke out by the City as its saviour. For the first twenty-four years of his Parliamentary life he had been a pacifist. For the next four, he would prove himself to be the greatest War Minister of Britain since Pitt, the Earl of Chatham.

The days of his glory were about to dawn.

CHAPTER XVI

"CHURCHILL DOWN"

"THE problem of warfare," said Field-Marshal Sir Douglas Haig, "consists of three Ms: Men, Munitions and Movement." It was Lloyd George's fate to play a vital part in providing all these ingredients, though it was not his fortune to deal with them in that order, as he could have wished.

When Britain went to war, the men poured into the Recruiting Offices. For the first six months of the struggle shortage of manpower in the Services was not one of our problems. To equip this new Armed Horde was the task, and it was titanic.

On that May morning, when Lloyd George walked from No. 11 Downing Street across to the bare office in Whitehall Gardens he asked himself, "What are the true functions of the head of this new Department, on which so much now depends?" Age 52

He made up his mind that there were five.

First, you must have a firm idea of what you wanted. *Second*, a clear plan of how to get it. *Third*, you must choose the right lieutenants to run every branch of the business, and get the utmost service out of them by stimulating and supporting them. *Fourth*, you must master the principles of mass production (without becoming entangled in a jungle of details), so that you could swiftly discover where and what the cause was, if things went wrong. *Fifth*, you must take decisive action to put them right, and do it in time.

He set to work. There was much to be done, and the hour was late.

The British Armies—and the Allied Armies, too—were not only short of shells. (By New Year, 1915, the Imperial Russian arsenals had turned out four heavy guns.) We were short of guns, rifles, machine-guns, mortars, grenades, landmines, lorries, locomotives, barbed wire, trenching tools and signal flares. All these weapons, all this transport and field equipment they needed not tomorrow but, desperately, today—and as yet not even the machinery was there to make them, nor even the machine tools to make the machinery.

There had to be some extraordinary and speedy improvisation, and there was. But even while this hasty, hand-to-mouth work went forward, beneath the temporary structure Lloyd George had also to lay the massive foundations for a national production plant designed to deliver the goods for a continuing and ever-developing war, that threatened to go on for years. Like Nehemiah of old, Lloyd George had to build his walls with a trowel in one hand and a sword in the other.

There was no shortage of one supply. Critics. Lloyd George had not been in his new job a month before the rumours were running round of utter confusion and chaos at the new Ministry of Munitions. "The Clubs, the lobbies, the smoking-rooms are sizzling with tales of my incompetence," he remarked to his secretary, Miss Frances Stevenson.

It was McKenna's opinion that Lloyd George was suffering from megalomania.

"A house that is building is never like the house that is built," and even in war-time Britain Lloyd George found that there were plenty of people with time to spare for leaning over the fence and offering advice to the men on the job. The skeleton of the unfinished Super War Works reared itself up against the sky and the still-unused girders strewed the ground. Heads of departments sat in a corner of the factory while production went forward as the tiles were being laid on the roof, and the drains tunnelled beneath their feet. All *most* untidy! But what could you really expect from such frantic bustle and hustle? And Headquarters, which should have set an example, merely set the pace. It must be accounted more nearly a miracle than the fabled appearance of the Angels at Mons in 1914, that the Germans did not arrive at Versailles in 1916 to dictate a conqueror's peace in the West.

The face of war had changed, utterly. The mind of the War Office remained steadfast. Two mighty earthen ramparts fronted one another, each more massive than the Great Wall of China. They were garrisoned by millions of riflemen, reinforced by machine-gunners in concrete "pill boxes", fortified by all kinds of artillery in strongly-built gun emplacements and protected by an ample apron of barbed-wire. After a preliminary bombardment of the German positions for an hour or so, the British infantry rose out of their own trenches and, with fixed bayonet, resolutely plodded forward across the swamp between the lines to death and immortality. On the roads behind, the cavalry squadrons champed and pawed, waiting impatiently and always in vain, for the order to advance, to move through "The Gap" that was to be opened by the infantry, and to "exploit the break-through". The War Office was faithful to the ghost of the Boer War. "Mounted Men Preferred."

There were three alternative methods of seeking a decision and in due course, after fearful lessons, all were tried. One, was to smash down the enemy front by sheer weight and power of the metal flail of bombardment. Another, was to pierce the front by some new armoured weapon not yet invented which could ignore rifle fire, machine-gun fire and anything short of a direct hit by a field-gun. The third method was to turn the flanks, in the Baltic, or the Balkans, or, perhaps, the Alps?

When Lloyd George went to the Ministry of Munitions in June, 1915, only the first course lay within his power to aid. That settled at once No. 1 item of his five-fold programme—to decide what you want to do.

No. 2 was How to Get It? There was some rubbish to be cleared away for a start. The Objection (or the reservations) of the War Office had to be overcome. Incredible as it now sounds, although the British Army manpower target had by this time (June, 1915) been set at 70 divisions, no survey of its needs or even of its task had ever been attempted. Neither the number nor the calibre of the requisite guns and machine-guns had been assessed; no sum had ever been worked out of the ammunition required to feed those guns; no estimate of our own or of America's shell-making and shell-filling capacity, still less of the potential manufacture of machine-tools in either country.

Yet to do the job, you had to enlist the following trades and lay down for each a precise schedule of production, since all would in the end depend upon the contribution of each: Coal-mines, iron-ore quarries, gas-works, blast furnaces, foundries, forges, steel-works, metal-works, wire-works, rolling-mills, factories, chemical-works, dye-works, laboratories, transport and oil.

To mobilize this industrial phalanx and set it marching in the same direction was beyond the capacity of the Major-General of Ordnance. The new Ministry of Munitions was going into business on its own, and in a big way. But if it had been designed to do no more than co-ordinate the multifold activities required to produce sixty million shells, 40,000 lorries, and 20,000 guns, besides tanks, airplanes and ships, it would have been necessary. It could never have wrought the mighty achievements which it did unless the right men had been chosen for the job.

"Men ought to be marked like Army lorries with their carrying capacity 'Load not to exceed 3 tons',"

noted Lloyd George in those furious days. He was fulfilling the third requirement of his purpose (Pick Your Lieutenants With Care) when he got hold of Mr. Eric Geddes, the General Manager of the North Eastern Railway, whom he had made Director-General of Munitions and "who possessed the drive as well as the make of one of the N.E.R.'s own powerful locomotives".

When, after the war, Lloyd George came to write the story of the Ministry of Munitions he claimed with truth that from first to last it had been a business-man organization. "Its most distinctive feature was the appointment I made of successful business men to the chief executive offices."

It was equally a triumph that he succeeded in making a team out of such men, all of whom were captains in their own right. But Lloyd George was fortunate in some other fields when he signed on the Civil Servants, Sir Herbert Llewellyn Smith and William Beveridge;[1] the scientist judge, Lord Moulton; the rich social reformer, Seebohm Rowntree; the politician, Dr. Christopher Addison[2] and the economist, Walter Layton.[3] Over these distinguished men Lloyd George exercised to the highest degree his extraordinary power of persuasion. This charm, linked with his almost diabolical knowledge of men and their motives, and a patience which at any moment could turn into a

[1] Later, Lord Beveridge.   [2] Later, Viscount Addison.   [3] Later, Lord Layton.

terrifying and devastating impatience, made him matchless in handling people
and consummate in making them work to his will.

It was just as well that the members of the new Ministry of Munitions
were able to settle down together and form a comradely and united front.
For, apart from the natural suspicions and jealousies of older-established
Departments of State, there were already at work those personal dislikes and
distrust between various members of the Cabinet itself which, within a year
or so, would destroy it. Lloyd George soon found that his most formidable
and implacable opponent in council was not Kitchener, nor any of his old
Tory foes, but his Liberal colleague, the new Chancellor of the Exchequer,
McKenna. The fact that the Ministry of Munitions would quickly become the
greatest spending Department of all simply enlarged the field of operations for
the hostility of the official Keeper of the Purse.

"He knew the details of his job," conceded Lloyd George. "He was a
ready reckoner—a Master of Finance in blinkers."

It was at this time that Asquith noted in his diary, "Lloyd George and
McKenna fighting like fishwives again."

The new Ministry had been set up by Act of Parliament with wide (not
to say vague) powers, which were to be defined later by Orders in Council.
It was also just as well for the Minister that this was so. For otherwise the
broad directive, that the Ministry was to be guided by the general requirements
of the Army Council, could have been interpreted by the Generals as limiting
it to the status of a Supply Department. Indeed, they tried to do it. But the
Order in Council had laid it down that Lloyd George's task was "to ensure
such supply of munitions . . . as may be required by the Army Council or the
Admiralty, or *may otherwise be found necessary*". (Author's italics.)

It was in pursuance of this that the Ministry of Munitions now took over
the Government Ordnance Factories and the responsibility for executing the
orders which had been placed both with them and the "approved" private
firms. These orders included nearly six million shell-cases. Fewer than two
million had so far been delivered, and only a fraction of these had been filled.
In the next six months fourteen millions were delivered and filled.

How the Ministry of Munitions still had to fight the War Office to press
upon it the weapons which the Army needed is told by Eric Geddes, reporting
to his chief, Lloyd George, an interview he had secured with Kitchener on
26 July, 1915, in which he asked the Secretary of State for War, who at that
time was looked upon generally as our greatest soldier, how many rifles he
wanted in the next nine months and how many machine-guns:

"Eventually, he said that the proportion was to be two machine-guns
per battalion as a minimum, four as a maximum, and anything above four
was a luxury."

Eric Geddes sat down in the War Office, there and then, and wrote this out. He also astutely induced Kitchener to initial it. When Lloyd George saw it, he said: "Take Kitchener's maximum (four machine-guns per battalion); square it; multiply that by two; and when you are in sight of that, double it again for Good Luck."

By November, 1915, the War Office had raised their requirements to 16 machine-guns per battalion, and by the end of the war the average supply exceeded 80. We started off with 300 of these weapons and ended up with nearly a quarter of a million.

The War Office did not accept this profusion of gifts without a struggle. Tardily and reluctantly, the Machine-Gun Corps was created and trained to handle the deadly new arms. As for the Artillery, on hearing from the Commander-in-Chief, Field-Marshal Sir John French, his requirements in howitzers during the summer of 1915, Kitchener put in his demand to the Ministry of Munitions. When Lloyd George at once raised it, Kitchener intimated that the War Office had no use for the 600 extra guns proposed, and they could be transferred to Russia's account.

Lloyd George had no intention whatever of changing his guns to the Russian pattern, for this would mean delays and complications; he much preferred (and offered) to supply the Russians with both guns and ammunition. He wrote to Kitchener "an impenitent answer", suggesting that the Secretary of State for War might care to appeal to the Cabinet. For his own part,

> "the Minister of Munitions is not prepared to cancel the orders he has placed for the provision of heavy howitzers, unless the Government as a whole will take the responsibility of deciding that the proposed provision is excessive."

Kitchener did care to appeal to the Cabinet. He composed a memorandum entitled "Supply of Heavy Guns to the Army", which he circulated to his colleagues and called upon them to judge between him and Lloyd George. He protested that if the extra guns were delivered to the War Office, he would be unable to find the gunners to man the batteries. On this, the Prime Minister hastened to set up a Cabinet Committee, under the chairmanship of Lord Crewe, to settle the issue. It met once, at the Ministry of Munitions, when the Master-General of Ordnance, General von Donop, repeated the War Office case. Lloyd George made no statement in reply, which mystified those who were accustomed to see him fight for his corner.

> "I suppose, sir," said his Secretary, J. T. Davies, as they walked away from the meeting, "that this means the end of your programme."
>
> "No," said Lloyd George. "It means the end of the Committee."

In fact it never met again. Lloyd George went ahead with his 600 extra guns. All were needed, and more, before he left the Ministry of Munitions.

A remarkable man, this John Thomas Davies, and surely something near to the Perfect Secretary—at any rate, for a Lloyd George. He was a good-looking, gay-looking man, of no outstanding intellectual quality, but with a thirst for work and a genius for handling people. He possessed a high sense of humour and an engaging ribaldry of expression. He understood the arts of intrigue though he rarely employed them on his own account. Indeed, J. T. Davies is a vital part of the Lloyd George story.

When Lloyd George first became a Minister he had decided that he must have a Welsh-speaking Secretary. Friends had recommended to him a young London-Welsh schoolmaster, who was a member of their chapel, and in 1912, J. T. Davies took up his post. Lloyd George's habit of speaking to him in their own mysterious tongue in the company of other English people, who did not understand it, sometimes aroused suspicion. It did so with Kitchener one day when, in conference with him, Lloyd George turned aside to his secretary and rapidly exchanged words in Welsh. The story is told that Kitchener waited, glowering. Then Lloyd George jumped up, and beckoning Edwin Montagu, went into a corner of the room and engaged him in conversation in low tones. Kitchener exploded. "My God! He speaks Yiddish, too!" he said.

There was a final rearguard action to be fought with the War Secretary. Though the War Office had conceded its own Ordnance Factories to the upstart Ministry of Munitions, it had retained its responsibility for the research and design of all arms and ammunition. The folly—and peril—of divorcing design from production was finally borne in upon the Cabinet in November, 1915, and both duties were assigned to the Ministry of Munitions. But "the Guard dies, and does not surrender". The War Office set up its own Testing and Inspecting Department, to decide whether or not the Army should be asked to handle the suspect goods of the rival firm. It required three more months of inter-office feuding before the Cabinet War Committee said positively the last word on the subject, and ordered the generals to specify their requirements and allocate the results. Thereafter, the business both of production and distribution proceeded apace.

It was truly a gigantic business. Swiftly, the Headquarters Staff was organized into Departments—guns, explosives, shells, bombs, machine-guns, rifles, factory building, labour—and a Records Office established to make a weekly report to the Minister. Each Department had not only to render an account of its present actual output, but to put in an estimate of its future potential output. The one statement was regularly checked against the other by Walter Layton, the Director of Statistics, and every Saturday, this summary was packed into Lloyd George's bag and taken down to his house at Walton Heath. From there flew the notes to the Departmental heads of the kind that Churchill re-created in the Second World War.

When Eric Geddes received his first one from his new chief, it infuriated him. In a rage, he rushed round to see Lloyd George who happened to be out. To Miss Stevenson he spluttered:

"I can't work, and I *won't* work like this! I know what I'm doing, and I'm going to produce the goods! If Lloyd George doesn't trust me, I'll go!"

Lloyd George did trust him. He stayed, and Geddes produced the goods. These were to be obtained, at this time, primarily from private industry.

It was the purpose of Lloyd George's "Area Organization" to gear into a single National machinery all the local factory power everywhere which could be harnessed for the making of munitions. He entrusted this task to Mr. J. A. Stevenson,[1] who swiftly set up a network of about fifty local Boards of Management which distributed the orders for arms or munitions to the established engineering firms or to the new "National" factories built to meet the desperate demand from the front for high explosive. Since this explosive had to be cased in shells there was need to erect National Shell factories, too, and this was done with all speed. By Christmas, 1915, more than 50 of these factories never failed "the boys over there".

Finally, there were the National Filling factories. These did not call for highly-skilled labour, and the vast majority of the workers employed in them were women. But the job had its perils especially in its poisons—for T.N.T. is a ready producer of toxic jaundice. The girls dreaded far more than the risk of death or mutilation by explosive those of discoloration, which would blotch or stain their faces yellow and mark them forever as "canaries". There were casualty lists of both, but as in the Second World War, the women in the War factories never failed "the boys over there".

It so happened that in National Service the women of Britain found real national emancipation. On 18 July, 1915, a great women's War Pageant, numbering scores of thousands, had paraded for miles through the streets of London escorting a deputation to the Minister of Munitions. It included Mrs. Pankhurst, her daughter Christabel, Mrs. Drummond and Miss Annie Kenney. Now they had come to pledge their own help to the country in its crisis, and to express the demand of the women to take part in war work. They asked only for decent wage standards which would safeguard their labour. Lloyd George gave them the guarantee of a fair minimum weekly wage, and the same piece rates as were paid to men. These conditions were enforced through-out the war, and by example or competition they brought to an end the sordid exploitation of cheap female labour in this country.

Within twelve months of this meeting between Lloyd George and the Suffragettes who had once tried to blow him up, the number of women working directly or indirectly to Government order had been multiplied fourfold to close on 350,000.[2]

In the same twelve months of trial and triumph on the War-Production

[1] Later, Lord Stevenson.   [2] In November, 1918, it was nearly 1,600,000.

J*

Front, nearly 100 national factories had been established; the output of shells had been multiplied eightfold; the output of guns, light and heavy, had been multiplied fivefold; machine-guns more than twentyfold; grenades four hundredfold.

The Ministry could requisition any buildings, plant, property or stores. Indeed, in the end, as Lloyd George said, no one could start a new business in Britain or enlarge an old one except for war purposes. Yet he claimed it was not an "arbitrary bureaucracy". Many executive officials were themselves important leaders of trade and industry and wherever possible, the trade associations concerned were closely consulted.

Thus, Lloyd George returned to the methods and manners of objective inquiry, skilful negotiation and "the personal touch", which had earned him such success in pre-war days at the Board of Trade. It must be added that this concentration of power, however inevitable in time of crisis, was viewed with no enthusiasm either by Walter Runciman, who was the contemporary President of the Board of Trade, or by McKenna, who had succeeded Lloyd George as Chancellor of the Exchequer.

"Always running down somebody else's department in order to seize a slice of authority for himself,"

was McKenna's comment on the activities of his colleague, and "Wrecking before Capture", was his description of what he described as the Lloyd George technique. He naturally liked his predecessor no better because he had been required to give an undertaking to Lloyd George to restore the Exchequer to him when the war came to an end. Looking back in later years, Lloyd George thought that it was this option on a return to the Treasury which caused bad blood between them. "It poisoned his personal relations towards me. Ever afterwards they remained septic."

There was already another estate on which Lloyd George was trespassing, forced there no doubt just as inevitably by events. This was Labour. Every Minister of Supply or Production since Lloyd George's time has had to face the same problem, and it must have seemed to all of them that to separate the control of materials and machinery from the control of labour is as impractical as to divorce design from production.

Two or three days after he had been appointed Minister of Munitions, Lloyd George had made a rapid tour of the great engineering centres in Lancashire, the Midlands and South Wales. There, in urgent, emphatic terms, he addressed both the employers and the trade union leaders, appealing to them to close up together as one fist to smash down the common enemy. He exhorted his audience at Manchester on 2 June, 1915:

"Plant the flag on your workshops! Every lathe you have recruit it! Convert your machinery into battalions . . . and liberty will be once more enthroned in Europe!

"We are fighting against the best-organized community in the world,"
Lloyd George told them; "the best organized whether for war or peace,
and we have been employing too much haphazard, leisurely, go-as-you-
please methods, which, believe me, would not have enabled us to maintain
our place as a nation even in peace, very much longer."

Lloyd George pointed out that, under the Defence of the Realm Act
(D.O.R.A.), the Government had taken powers to control the output of the
workshops of the country, and to insist that Government work, "the work of
the country", must come before all else. This compulsion did not mean Conscription in the ordinary sense of the term, he said, but even Conscription was a
question not of principle but of necessity. It certainly was not anti-democratic.
France had saved the liberty she had won in the great Revolution from the fangs
of tyrannical military empires purely by Conscription. The United States, the
great Republic of the West, had won its independence and saved its national
existence by Conscription.

Lloyd George then appealed to the trade unionists to give up, for the
duration of the war, the unwritten code by which output was restricted. He
urged that the trade union rules which forbade the dilution of labour be
suspended, promising that piece rates should not be reduced. He concluded
by contrasting the refusal of unenlisted labour to submit to discipline with the
lot of the volunteer soldier at the front:

"The enlisted workman cannot choose his locality of action. He cannot
say, 'I am quite prepared to fight at Neuve-Chapelle, but I won't fight at
Festubert, and I am not going near the place they call "Wipers".' He cannot
say, 'I have been in the trenches eight-and-a-half hours, and my trade union
won't allow me to work more than eight hours.' "

The Lancashire men gave him a good enough reception. He was talking
their language, if not entirely their sentiments. Some, indeed, said that they
only wished that Lloyd George had made that speech eight months ago. It
is true that, in general, Labour remained hostile to compulsion, either military
or industrial. They had been annoyed at the unauthorized campaign for
Conscription by certain Tory Diehards "when we knew that all the time there
were hundreds of thousands of men who could not get equipment".

As a matter of fact, this time those Tory Diehards happened to be right.
If there had been Conscription from the start scores of thousands of skilled
workers whose loss at the forge and the lathe was then almost irreplace-
able, would have been held back at least until others had been trained to
do their job. As it was, they swelled the ranks of the first million who "fell
in" with the Reservists and the Territorials at the outbreak of war, or joined
Kitchener's Armies in the following weeks. At that time, we not only lacked
enough weapons and ammunition for this mighty reinforcement, but also

barracks, tents, uniforms, even boots. The War Office was compelled to
raise the physical standard of recruits in order to check the flow of men to the
Colours.

When Lloyd George came to "nationalize" munition-making, his view
began to veer sharply towards the Conscriptionists. It was not so much
that the War Office as yet required more soldiers—Kitchener's Armies were
only beginning to go overseas in the early summer of 1915, and the shambles
of the Somme had still to come—but that Lloyd George needed his skilled
workmen back. By August, he was openly and irrevocably for Conscription.

In his Diary Riddell noted:

14 *August,* 1915:
"Lloyd George said that if he could get 120,000 skilled workers back
from the Army he would then have all the men he wants, and that he can
only secure the return of the 120,000 by means of Conscription, which would
enable K. to get additional men to replace them."

Almost all the Liberal Ministers, and possibly most of the Tory Ministers
(though not the Tory rank-and-file) were still against it in the summer of 1915.
Naturally, there had been a Cabinet Committee to consider Conscription, too.
Lords Crewe, Curzon and Selborne, and Churchill and Austen Chamberlain
were its members; only Selborne and Churchill seem to have favoured it
from the start.

"The possibility of Compulsion is not within the landscape as we now see
it," Lord Crewe had told the House of Lords early in the New Year, 1915,
though in the same debate Lord Haldane had reminded them that the duty of
every citizen to serve the King rested not on Statute, but was inherent in the
Common Law.

It still appeared to be fairly well agreed among public men that it was
best for practical purposes to rely as long as possible on the voluntary principle,
and as far as volume alone was concerned it worked.

The first step in a more systematic approach to the problem of manpower,
however, had already been taken by the "Householders' Return". This was
organized by the Parliamentary Recruiting Committee, and consisted of a
form sent to every householder in the United Kingdom with a covering letter
signed by Asquith, Bonar Law and Arthur Henderson, leaders of the three
political parties, appealing to every eligible man to hold himself ready to
enlist in the Forces.

Soon after the Coalition Government was formed in May, 1915, this was
followed by a compulsory and far more comprehensive "National Register",
which required information about every male citizen, his age, address, occupation, etc. It was the first real record that the Government had of the nation's
resources of men for military service or war work. Even this was resisted in
Parliament by a handful of Liberals, and the pacifist I.L.P. group led by

Ramsay MacDonald and Philip Snowden, who correctly foresaw in it a preliminary to Conscription. The National Register showed that there were about five million men of military age in Britain not yet enlisted. Setting aside the physically unfit and those in "barred" occupations (i.e. reserved for munition making or vital civilian services), it appeared that the best part of two million men were available for recruitment.

By this time, Kitchener had formulated his demand for a 70-Division Army by the end of 1916. Lloyd George, examined by the Cabinet Committee on Manpower, declared that if he had his own way he would take

"the same powers exactly as were taken in France: I would make everybody between certain ages liable to serve in the Army at home or abroad. . . . You will not get through this war without some measure of Military Compulsion. The longer you delay, the nearer you will be to disaster. . . ."

When the President of the Board of Trade, Runciman, appeared before the Cabinet Manpower Committee, he calculated that if industry was to be left properly manned, the most that Kitchener could count on would be 35 divisions, and not more than half of these could be raised by voluntary recruiting. The Committee felt that if this were really so, then it would be an unanswerable argument for Conscription (to which Runciman was vehemently opposed). The Chancellor of the Exchequer, McKenna (who shared his views) simply said that the country could not afford 70 divisions as well as finance her Allies. Kitchener intimated that he would ask Parliament for Conscription before the end of the year. He let it be known that if his Cabinet colleagues were resolved to have none of Conscription, then they would have none of Kitchener, either. In the end, this became the majority view.

By the autumn of 1915, the rift in the Coalition ranks over Conscription was already widening to a gulf. Foremost against it were the Liberals, Sir Edward Grey, Sir John Simon, along with McKenna and Runciman. As resolutely for it, were Bonar Law, Lord Robert Cecil and Carson; they were backed to the hilt by Lloyd George, Churchill and Kitchener. This group grew steadily in strength. Asquith made a final effort to avoid the threatened earthquake.

This was the Derby Scheme, so-called after the Earl of Derby, who agreed to serve as its Director of Recruiting. The idea was that every man between the ages of 18 and 41 should attest, pledging himself to join up when called for. They would be divided into two classes, single and married, and each of these classes sub-divided into 23 age-groups.

But the Derby Scheme failed. Only about half of the two million single men took the trouble to attest and many who did so were either in the rejected or the protected category. The anticipated haul turned out to be no more than about 350,000 men. On 5 January, 1916, the Government had to face it. Asquith laid before Parliament the first Military Service Bill.

This measure had emerged at last as a decision of the Cabinet only after a prolonged and angry battle. The issues were real, for immediately behind compulsory Military Service (or perhaps even side by side!) there stalked the shadow of Industrial Conscription. The "pernicious pacifists", as Lord Derby angrily described MacDonald and his allies, did not fail to make great play with this in the industrial areas. The workers in the factories were going to be regimented too, eh? Labour, equally in the Parliamentary Party and in the Trade Unions, was strongly opposed to both forms of compulsion. Some early scandals of private profiteering in armaments provided the agitators with a powerful plea against conscripting men, either for battle or for war work. The cry went up: "Conscript Money First!" Wages were rising, it is true, but prices were rising faster. Rents were soaring, too. Food was getting scarcer. An ugly mood began to grow in the great ports and cities of Britain.

Lloyd George came face to face with it in Glasgow at Christmas, 1915. There, the Shop Stewards' movement, which represented local and "unofficial" grievances (as apart from the "official" Trade Unions, who dealt with national conditions) had assumed the most formidable size and shape. Indeed, in the Clyde Workers Committee, which was made up of delegate "shop stewards" from the dockyards, shipyards and engineering shops along Clydeside there was something very like an early Soviet in Britain. Prominent among its leaders were Mr. William Gallagher, the subsequent Communist M.P., and Mr. David Kirkwood, the present Lord Kirkwood.

The "Red Clyde" were determined to resist any dilution of labour or relaxation of trade union practices unless and until the State took over the private factories and ran them in partnership with the Workers' Committee. When, on Christmas Eve, Lloyd George, accompanied by Arthur Henderson, went down to Beardmore's Works at Parkside to urge the men to speed up the delivery of heavy guns, "Davie" Kirkwood put on his most ferocious scowl and stormed, "I am as much a slave of Sir William Beardmore as if I had the letter 'B' branded on my brow!" However, Lloyd George got on better there than he did on Christmas Morning at another gathering of Clydeside workers in St. Andrew's Hall.

Here, he and Henderson were greeted with the strains of "The Red Flag". When Henderson tried to address the audience he was howled down. When Lloyd George rose and, stretching out his hands in mute entreaty, won a moment's silence to appeal to them "in the name of my old friend, Keir Hardie", they sang "The Red Flag" again and gave him no more hearing. A hastily-prepared précis of his undelivered speech was handed to the reporters. The Independent Labour Party's journal *Forward* published a more interesting descriptive report of the actual proceedings, and was promptly suppressed under D.O.R.A.

It was thought a good idea (and was) to send representative workmen over to the trenches in Flanders to show them what war conditions were like for millions of their fellow-countrymen on duty there. Mr. J. H. Clynes was one who went, Ben Tillett was another. They returned with the resolve that, as Tillett wrote to Lloyd George, "no ignorant or callous creature here . . . should be allowed to skulk behind the dead bodies of the men who have given their lives for us".

The general industrial unrest, which was finally focused by the Conscription issue, naturally produced its own political repercussions. Conscription certainly suited the Tories best of the three Parties. If there had to be a General Election in wartime, at any rate, they could go to the country on a policy of Get On With the War. The Labour Party, with their 4,000,000 organized workers, steadfastly resisted Conscription and fought the Military Service Bill through all its stages in the House of Commons. Their three representatives in the Government (Arthur Henderson alone held Cabinet rank) resigned, and were only persuaded to withdraw their resignations by the Prime Minister's personal promise to modify the terms of the Bill. The Liberal Party were, perhaps, most profoundly affected of all. For they held many industrial seats in Lancashire, Yorkshire, the Midlands, South Wales and the East End of London. If the Liberals came out boldly for Conscription, they must expect to forfeit much of their working-class support to the mounting challenge of the Socialists.

Indeed, several other members of the Coalition Cabinet besides Henderson —and in absolute opposition to Kitchener and his Tory and Liberal backers on this issue—threatened to resign over Conscription if it *did* become law! In the event, only the Attorney-General, Sir John Simon, took himself off to lead not (as he had firmly expected) a powerful secession of Liberal M.P.s, but a forlorn fragment of about three dozen who voted with him against the Bill. Within the Cabinet itself the rift was far wider.

Lloyd George himself, once he had made up his mind, was adamant. In April, 1916, while the issue still hung in the balance, he told his old Editor friend, Sir William Robertson Nicoll, that he would not remain in a War Cabinet which was not making war. He said frankly that if the Cabinet did not accept the Army Council's recommendations for Conscription, "then I shall go out on Monday".

He meant it.

The following Sunday, Lord Stamfordham, the King's Secretary, called on the Minister of Munitions. He sought to dissuade him from his purpose. In the end, Lloyd George said to Stamfordham: "You know there is one decisive reason why I should not change my view."

When Stamfordham inquired what it was, he replied: "I have taken an oath which prevents me. I have sworn to serve my King faithfully."

But by now the main assault had really been carried. On 25 May, 1916, an Act to impose immediate and general compulsory Military Service received the Royal Assent.

It is necessary to add that while Britain relied solely on volunteers to defend her, 4,466,659 of her sons answered the call to duty. With her young men of the Empire, by 25 May, 1916, more than five million were serving with the British colours because they wanted to be there.

It had been the persistent, and sometimes violent, pressure of the war in the field that so reshaped the form of affairs at home. On the Western Front, despite the Allied offensive of the spring and autumn of 1915, the deadlock had held. Ten million shells and several hundred thousand casualties gained us an area about the size of Rutland, strategically useless. No doubt, it was good training—for other offensives of the same pattern.

On the Eastern Front, once the Russian offensive in the Carpathians was halted in April, the enemy had driven our Allies out of territories nearly a third the size of France. Russia's fearful losses (they exceeded a million and a half) continued until the Russian winter came to freeze the further movement of troops, and staunch the blood.

There was the Serbian Front. By New Year's Day, 1915, the Serbs had thrown the Austrians back to the frontier line of the Danube, where they rested, in no way anxious to resume their vaunted chastisement of these turbulent Slavs. There was deadlock here, too, though not from mutual strength but from weakness. As the year wore on, however, German troops and guns began to reinforce the Austrians, massing in the valleys which point south to the Danube. It was plain that big moves were afoot.

The attitude of Bulgaria should have been final warning. Once the irresolute diplomacy of the Allies had failed to induce the Serbs to concede to the Bulgars any part of the spoils which they had snatched from them at the time of their joint attack on Turkey in the First Balkan War of 1912, it was certain that the calculating Tsar ("Foxy") Ferdinand of Bulgaria would bide his time until the next crisis for Serbia, and then sell himself to the best bidder. By September, 1915, in the Balkans this was plainly the Central Powers, and not the *Entente*. Thereupon Tsar Ferdinand signed up with the Kaiser and Emperor Franz Josef. When, early in October, 1915, the Austro-German forces attacked, the Bulgars fell upon the Serbian flank. Within a month, the Serb Army had been rolled up, and a brave remnant of a rearguard was covering its main retreat across the snow-bound mountains of Albania to the Adriatic Sea.

All this time, there was a Franco-British Expedition of several divisions based at Salonika. Whether or not this skeleton force could have given effective support to the Serb Army is doubtful. But, at any rate, in the intervening months, since the idea of developing the road-and-rail route to Serbia had first been mooted by Lloyd George in Asquith's pre-Coalition War Council (January, 1915), *something* could have been done. *Nothing* was done.

Then, at last, in October, as a few Serb divisions, separated from the main retreat, sought to fight their way to the south, the Salonika garrison bestirred itself sufficiently to march northward to meet them. But now General Winter had taken command of the twisting, muddy tracks through the Balkan passes. The junction was never made, and the Serbs died in their mountains with their Allies helpless ten miles away. When this sorry story of our lethargy and—as it seemed to some—cynical desertion of a little nation—became known in London, Sir Edward Carson resigned from the British Cabinet in protest (2 November, 1915).

He was the first petrel flying before the gathering storm. For, though Carson complained initially of the betrayal of little "Sherbia" as he called her, he condemned our entire conduct of the war, the swollen Cabinet, the endless discussion, the lack of grip and decision in urgent issues.

South of Serbia, there was another front. The Dardanelles. The British, Australian, New Zealand and French troops were still where they had been landed—on the beach, under the cliffs. The British Fleet, rather weakened by the departure of the *Queen Elizabeth*, was still where it had been—off-shore. And the Turk enemy was still where *he* had been—on the top of those cliffs, now deeply dug-in, reinforced with Germany artillery, and led by a skilful and resourceful Commander, the German General Liman von Sanders.

The Man Who Won the Battle is always a good witness to put into the box. And Winston Churchill, to whom, despite all previous counter-claims and subsequent modest disclaimers, belongs the prime responsibility for initiating and persevering in the Dardanelles Campaign, has cited General Liman von Sanders. The German testifies that when the British Fleet broke off its action to force the Narrow Straits, the garrison was, in fact, down to its last few rounds. At this point, Churchill is anxious to thank the witness for giving his valuable evidence and dismiss him from the case (in his monumental book, *The World Crisis*, he does so).

In his own book, General Liman von Sanders says that if the British Fleet had forced the straits it would still have had to sail across the inland Sea of Marmora (where the General had arranged for some more shore batteries to welcome it). There was also in those waters (or perhaps beyond them in the Bosporus, in reserve) the German cruisers *Goeben* and *Breslau*, together with U-boats, which later took some toll of our warships in the open Aegean Sea. Of course, the British Fleet could have bombarded the Port at Constantinople. But, in the event, the Turkish Government had already made its dispositions to retire to the hinterland of Anatolia and rule from there, as Kemal Pasha did so successfully a few years later. What would the British Fleet have done then? Unless the Turks had surrendered within ten days, the sea-invaders, lacking an Occupation Force, would have been compelled to sail away again, back down the Narrow Straits. There would certainly have been a "God Speed" party on either cliff to see them off. So says General Liman von Sanders, the man who won the Battle of the Dardanelles.

When the project of forcing the Straits was first proposed to the Cabinet, Lloyd George, like Kitchener, had been seduced by the song that the sirens

of the Hellespont sang. What! At a single blow to cut off Turkey from the
Central Powers, seal the main gate on the Berlin-Bagdad Road to the East,
open the seaway to Russia by which her Allies could send her guns and the
stores of war—and bring away from there her priceless golden grain, bribe
thwarted Bulgaria with the compensation of the remaining Turkish territories
in Europe (and by doing so, provide security to sated Serbia, Rumania and
Greece), perhaps thus unite all the Balkan tribes—and muster 2,000,000
battle-worthy troops against the Central Powers! What a song! What a story!
Such seemed the golden prospects on the Golden Horn.

But what were the actualities?

The more Lloyd George looked at the project, the less was he enamoured of
it. Indeed, after the failure of the Fleet bombardment early in February, 1915, at
the War Council of 24 February, Lloyd George had urged

> "that the Army should not be required to pull the chestnuts out of the fire
> for the Navy. If the Navy has failed, we should try somewhere else in the
> Balkans, and not necessarily at the Dardanelles."

For the Balkan fever had seized Lloyd George early, and it recurred. When
we had failed to break down the German Wall in the West, even with the most
massive weight of shells, and before we had found in tanks a weapon which
might (as early as 1916) have pierced the enemy front, Lloyd George sought
constantly to find a way to turn the flank. In 1915 he would himself have
preferred to deliver the blow from the firm and friendly base of Salonika, in
Greece, the neighbour of Serbia, for he reckoned that thereby Turkey could
be at once cut off from any contact with the Central Powers. He continued
to nurse his dreams of an attack through Greece.

But these are might-have-beens of history. The Dardanelles Campaign,
unfortunately, actually happened, and Lloyd George with the rest of the
British Cabinet, must bear a share for its failure, if only for not firmly enough
opposing it. Beyond the original Bull-at-a-Gate (or Ship-at-a-Strait) idea, it
never appears to have been really thought-out at all. Like many another
great gamble, it was launched as a limited liability scheme. Certainly both the
soldier, Lord Kitchener, and the sailor, Lord Fisher, so regarded it (Kitchener,
because he understood that it was to be strictly a Naval affair; Fisher, because
if the stroke did not come off at once he had another one ready—his Baltic
Project—which he much preferred). No proper Joint Staff appreciation,
therefore was ever made for what dragged itself out to be a vast, though
unco-ordinated joint operation.

As for the campaign itself, to begin with, Churchill had conducted the
Sea War and Kitchener the Land War. Kitchener rarely consulted the Chief
of General Staff, and Churchill less and less consulted the First Sea Lord.
Both ministers occasionally consulted the Prime Minister. The Cabinet, and
its "War Council", were hardly ever asked—or told anything.

This was for the first three months of the Dardanelles operations. After the Ministerial crisis of May, 1915, and the formation of the first Coalition Government, had involved the departure of Churchill from the Admiralty, the conduct of affairs deteriorated. For now there was nobody in a position of power in the Cabinet who really "believed in the Dardanelles". Churchill himself had no authority in his sinecure office as Chancellor of the Duchy of Lancaster. There, he had no real Department of his own (certainly not one which had anything to do with the direction of the war), and therefore no foothold from which he could exert pressure upon any other Department. Nor did he any longer exercise an influence upon his Cabinet Colleagues. By the public he was blamed both for the brief misadventure at Antwerp, and for the continuing deadlock at the Dardanelles. Winston Churchill, in that luckless year of 1915, was the unhappiest man in England.

Lloyd George offered Churchill no encouragement. When it was proposed to make him Governor-General of East Africa, with the military command of the British and South African Forces operating there against the invaders from the neighbouring colony of German East Africa, Lloyd George's voice had been against the appointment. He feared the popular outcry which would certainly have been raised. It was then that the name of the Boer general, Smuts, had been proposed. Said Kitchener, who had fought him in the South African War: "My generals will not accept Mr. Smuts."[1]

Throughout the rest of 1915, the Government continued in a condition of developing disunity. Though, to the general public, Kitchener still appeared as the Great Soldier, the confidence of his Cabinet colleagues in his powers of War leadership steadily sank. More and more, the questions of Governmental machinery (such as the idea of a small and dynamic War Executive instead of a large and lethargic debating Council), and of national mobilization (such as Conscription), resolved themselves into aspects of one single, personal, master issue—what was to be done about that great, silent, secretive, dictator of Britain's military policy, Lord Kitchener?

Lloyd George, quite frankly, wanted him deposed. Lloyd George had been one of the foremost (others were Bonar Law and Carson) in urging upon the Prime Minister the necessity of setting up a Committee of the Cabinet, not less than three or more than five, to run the war day in and day out. Asquith had agreed. But who were to be the members of this Committee?

On 31 October, 1915, Lloyd George wrote to Asquith threatening him with the alternative: either Kitchener went or Lloyd George went.

Lloyd George then recited the tale of War Office delays in ordering artillery, ammunition and equipment. The failure to bring in Greece, Rumania and perhaps, even Bulgaria, on our side, and so cut off the Central Powers from the magnificent reservoir of fighting men in the Turkish Empire, although as early as July, 1915, Military Intelligence had warned Kitchener that the

[1] But they did.

Germans were likely to break through to Constantinople. In September, they had massed on the Danube, and in October had crossed it.

Now, the storm had broken over the entire Balkans—Serbia, Salonika, and the Dardanelles. Yet month after month, ever since December, 1914, the warning was obvious that unless the Government took a real hold of the war it must end in disaster—and such warning had repeatedly been made. Lloyd George concluded:

"I have very reluctantly come to the conclusion that I can no longer be responsible for the present war direction, and at the Cabinet tomorrow I propose, with your permission, to raise the real issue."

This was rebellion. And that it was about to be launched is shown by the note which Bonar Law sent to Lloyd George on the morning of that Cabinet meeting (1 November, 1915):

"Have you any objection to my telling the P.M. that you said to me that you were satisfied that nothing but disaster lay ahead of us as long as Lord K. was War Secretary, and that you were going to write to the P.M. that you could not continue to share the responsibility for the continuance of the present arrangement at the War Council and that I had replied that if that issue was definitely raised I must take the same course?"

And Kitchener? Asquith proposed that he should go out and inspect for himself the scene at the Dardanelles—the Balkan Front had by this time ceased to exist. Asquith was hoping that once he had got Kitchener out of the country, he would be able to keep him out of it—and out of the War Office—by appointing him Viceroy of the East and Commander-in-chief of all our forces in the Mediterranean and Asia. The *Globe* newspaper actually printed the story that there was serious disagreement between Kitchener and the Cabinet and that the Secretary of State for War had resigned. The heavy artillery of D.O.R.A. was rushed into action again, and the *Globe* was suppressed. With it went the idea that Kitchener should be exiled and that his office should be taken over, either by Lloyd George (who was nominated in some quarters), by Bonar Law, or by Asquith (who for a brief moment, nominated himself in addition to being Prime Minister). In the end, the Prime Minister contented himself with serving as Acting War Secretary until Kitchener returned from the wars. As for that small, effective War Executive Committee, once more nothing was done.

At the Dardanelles, Kitchener took one look at those beaches under the cliffs—and suggested that we might try a landing on the flat isthmus of Bulair! It remains to this day one of history's mysteries why the main assault had not been delivered there in April. Now, it was too late, for the Germans had at last established overland communications with the Turks, and our footing in any part of the Gallipoli Peninsula had become untenable.

There was still talk among some of the admirals of making one more final effort to "force the Straits".

But even an Asquithian War Committee would stand no more of this. Indeed, if anything of the kind had been pressed the Government itself would have foundered. On 7 November, Bonar Law, the Tory leader in the Coalition, insisted that the Dardanelles adventure be now wound up. If it were not, he made it plain that he meant to resign. Asquith bowed.

A week later came Kitchener's Report. He was for evacuation. One member of the Cabinet, at least, realized that this was the end—though he vehemently disapproved of the decision. Churchill had already written to the Prime Minister saying that he did not feel able in times like these to remain at the Duchy of Lancaster in well-paid inactivity. Now, on 15 November, he relinquished his Office as Chancellor of the Duchy, and sought a military command in the field. It was not until 23 November that the War Committee endorsed Kitchener's recommendations.

Even then, there was one last rearguard action to be fought by the Dardanelles Diehards. Lord Curzon arose, and painted a graphic and tragic picture of what the evacuation would be like, with the beaches a shambles and the bays a sea of blood, as the last boatloads of soldiers tried to get away under a pitiless enemy fire. There were, indeed, both military and naval experts who reckoned that the withdrawal might be as costly in casualties as the first landing had been, which had cost nearly half of the total force. The argument continued until 4 December, when Bonar Law entered a memorandum which amounted to an ultimatum.

Now, a winter blizzard began to blow along the Gallipoli coast, hundreds of our soldiers were drowned in the trenches at Suvla Bay, others were frozen to death, and 16,000, suffering from frostbite and exposure, had to be taken off at once.

To the end, the star of the common soldier's courage and of his officer's devotion shone through the night of the Dardanelles disaster and lit this sombre scene with a glory that will remain. The sailors had their hour, too. If the British battleships failed to force the Straits, our submarines found a way through. Twenty-seven times they nosed past the mine-loaded nets into the Sea of Marmora, where they sank more than 200 vessels.

Now it was the last act. On 19 December, 1915, the withdrawal from Suvla Bay and Anzac Bay took place—in a single night, and without a single casualty. The communiques reported that the night was calm and moonless, and the retiring army left nobody and not a thing worth while behind them —the miracle of Gallipoli.

Next day, a terrible storm broke.

There was still a word to be added. Or rather, a considerable number of words. Lord Curzon contributed them in Cabinet, offering elaborate argument, with full historical parallel, against evacuation. Kitchener listened in silence for some time, then broke in to say that it might shorten discussion if he reported that the last soldier had been withdrawn from Gallipoli the previous evening.

Lloyd George was speaking that very day in the House of Commons, 20 December, 1915, of an agreement with industrial labour to develop a new drive in factories and mines and shipyards. He said:

"I wonder whether it will be Too Late! Ah, fatal words of this war! Too Late in moving here! Too Late in arriving there! Too Late in coming to this decision! Too Late in starting with that enterprise! Too Late in preparing! In this war the footsteps of the Allied forces have been dogged by the mocking spectre of 'Too Late' and unless we quicken our movements, damnation will fall on the sacred cause for which so much gallant blood has flowed!"

The devil, Doubt, was beginning to walk abroad in the land. Could we hold on? Could we win? Was it all worth while?

There were few better barometers in British public life in 1915–16 than Lloyd George. Not that he allowed the popular weather to govern him: but, certainly, he registered it. In mid-July, 1915, while he was still deeply immersed in his labours to get the guns and munitions, Lloyd George had come up to the surface once or twice to take his bearings on the general scene. He told Dr. Macnamara that it was a "grey scene . . . of trouble on the face of the waters" that he beheld. The nation was not taking the war seriously enough, and the war was becoming very serious.

In August, dining with Riddell, he had said of Mr. Asquith himself:

"The P.M. is treating the war as if it were Home Rule or Welsh Disestablishment. He does not recognize that the nation is fighting for its life. When the subject is forced on his attention his judgment is admirable; but he never searches out weak places."

In September, Lord Murray of Elibank noted in a letter to his wife that:

"The P.M. and Lloyd George have lately been drifting apart. Lloyd George, who is super-sensitive, thought that Asquith didn't want to see him while Asquith thought Lloyd George was keeping away from him! Mischief-makers got to work, and the rift got wider. . . . Lloyd George was going to resign when I first saw him, on the ground that the nation was drifting to a catastrophe owing to the P.M. not 'taking charge'. He was very bitter against K. of K., whom he regards mainly as a 'great poster' and a man with essentially a 'put-off' mind. Arthur Balfour he regards as a dawdler, who will dawdle the nation into disaster as he dawdled his party out of existence. Many excellent suggestions are made in the Cabinet, but no decisions are taken."

Did any other troubles beset Britain in these baffling days? Yes. Ireland!

In Ireland, the ghosts of Drogheda and Limerick had risen up to mock the glib, new-found war-time Saxon talk about "the rights of little nations". Were only Belgium and Serbia on the map of history?

Ever since that emotional moment in the House of Commons, when John Redmond had pledged the Irish Nationalists to join the Ulster Orangemen in the United defence of Ireland during England's battle, the "Irish Question" had dropped out of the English news. It surprised—let us say, startled—nobody so much as the Irish.

John Redmond's sentiment was widespread throughout Southern Ireland in the early days of the war. It was believed that the fighting would be sharp and short, that the Irish would play their lively part in it, as ever—and as volunteers—and that a result would be that all the English Parties would be reconciled to Home Rule for Ireland.

At this time, Sinn Fein was still no more than an intellectual movement of a fraction of a rebel faction. Moreover, its philosophy was still passive resistance. Even so, by Christmas, 1914, no priest had declared for Sinn Fein. But by the spring of 1915, a different mood had begun to manifest itself. For one thing, Ireland's gesture did not seem to have been appreciated in official English quarters. The Ulster Division had marched off to battle under their silken flag with emblazoned on it the Red Hand of Ulster, sewn by the hands of the Ulster ladies. But Kitchener had not permitted the Irish Division to march off to battle under *their* silken flag emblazoned with the Green Harp of Ireland, sewn by the hands of the Irish ladies.[1] For another thing, the Irish recruiting platforms were being crowded with the wrong people. They did not require to be lectured on their duty to the British Empire by Protestant gentry, land agents and professional military orators, who warned that if their own eloquence failed to raise the necessary recruits a thing called Conscription might come along later.

Sinn Fein went to work. They had it all their own way. The young Irish Nationalists who felt otherwise were not there to combat it. They were in Flanders. Many, like John Redmond's own brother Willie, were soon to be dead upon that field. In Ireland, Sinn Fein pursued its path unchallenged. Remember that old Irish rebel injunction, "England's hour of peril will be Ireland's opportunity!"

On Easter Sunday, 1916, Dublin flared into rebellion.

The Easter Rising was a military farce—if the foolhardy effort of men prepared to pay with their lives for their folly can ever be said to be amusing. It became for Britain, a political tragedy. Only about three thousand rebels were engaged in a week's desultory rifle battle in Dublin. A hundred or two were killed. They might soon have been forgotten in a time when every day brought to some Irish cottage the cold, respectful letter, "The Secretary of

---

[1] It was only after a bitter quarrel with Lloyd George that he sanctioned the raising of a purely Welsh division.

State for War regrets to inform you . . ." But it was deemed necessary to shoot by firing-squad the leaders who has signed the Proclamation of the "Republic", along with some of the most resolute rebel commanders. Thus endowed with the essential asset of every successful Revolution—its martyrs —Sinn Fein strode forward to the deeper sorrow of the Irish Civil War, and official Britain to the squalid episode of the Black-and-Tans.

The Easter Rising, though it had been planned and was executed with the artlessness of a schoolboy strike, took the British authorities both in London and Dublin, utterly by surprise. Told by Bonar Law to telephone to "Tim" Healey, who was then in Dublin, and find out what was happening, Max Aitken eventually reached him on the official Government line.

"Is there a rebellion?" he asked.
"There is!" said Tim.
"When did it break out?"
"When Strongbow invaded Ireland!"
"When will it end?"
"When Cromwell gets out of Hell!"

It did not cast much light upon the current proceedings.

Asquith appears to have realized what was happening only when, following a violent outcry in the *Daily Express* for the heads of the Guilty (Government) Men, the three principal officers of the Crown in Ireland resigned —the Lord Lieutenant, Lord Wimborne; the Chief Secretary for Ireland, Mr. Augustine Birrell; and his under-Secretary, Sir Matthew Nathan. The Prime Minister himself hurried to Dublin. He found the smoking, smouldering city under Martial Law.

He turned to Lloyd George, whose sympathies with Ireland had never yet been challenged. He asked him to try his hand with these (other) incredible Celts. Here is the letter which might have changed the story of our times:

22 May, 1916

"My dear Lloyd George,
I hope you may see your way to take up Ireland; at any rate for a short time. It is a unique opportunity and there is no one else who could do so much to bring about a permanent solution.

Yours very sincerely,
H. H. Asquith."

Lloyd George's first Irish "Round Table" failed. Afterwards he said of five of the negotiators, Carson, James Craig, Redmond, Devlin and T. P. O'Connor that "they displayed a genuine anxiety to reach a settlement". That they did not do so, said Lloyd George, was largely due to the sixth man, John Dillon.

His own proposal had been that Home Rule should be granted to Ireland at once; that there should be an Amending Act to retain the Six Counties within the United Kingdom; that all the Irish M.P.s should continue to sit in the Imperial Parliament at Westminster; that after the war an Empire Conference should be called to decide the future relationship of all Empire Lands, including Ireland.

Both Redmond and Carson, as Leaders of Irish Nationalism and Ulster Unionism, had accepted this most sensible and statesmanlike solution.

But Lloyd George had not only overlooked John Dillon. He had overlooked the Peers, whose powers he thought he had clipped and curbed so many years ago. They were about to give Lloyd George grim evidence that their veto still held sway. It was a bad day for Lloyd George's own great record in history that they baulked him now, and no good day for Britain either, for their act ensured the bloody sequel of the post-war years.

On 23 June, 1916, Lords Halsbury, Salisbury, Cromer, Balfour of Burleigh and Middleton, denounced by manifesto what they loftily described as "this trafficking in the sacred principles of self-determination". On 25 June, Lord Selborne resigned from the Board of Agriculture in sympathy with their protest. On 27 June Lord Lansdowne also intervened to ask the Prime Minister what would happen to D.O.R.A. under Home Rule? Finally, there was the echoing incident of Lord Wimborne.

The Lord Lieutenant of Ireland now became the centre of a new Press storm which did the Government further damage and finally frustrated any hope of Irish Peace. Lord Wimborne had resigned as a result of the newspaper demand that he should go. But the Prime Minister had refused to accept his resignation. The attacks continued. Then Churchill stood forward to defend his friend, which was sufficient to concentrate all available Tory Diehard fire on Wimborne. So the Lord-Lieutenant insisted on resigning. In the next month came the report of the Royal Commission on the Easter Rising, which largely whitewashed Wimborne. So the Prime Minister reinstated him. In truth, he had been guilty, along with the rest of the Dublin Castle Government, of not understanding his job. So the Tory newspapers attacked him again, the more sharply because the Tory Ministers in the Government appeared to be condoning him by their silence.

These manœuvres enabled the extremists of the Irish Nationalist side to enlarge their claims. Two Tory leaders only still strove for settlement with the Green and Catholic South. They were Carson, the old Orangeman of the Ulster Covenant Days, and Bonar Law, the son of an Ulster Presbyterian Manse. They failed. The Irish Tragedy was not to be interfered with by anyone.

And Lloyd George? In August, 1916, he was a sick and thoroughly depressed man. He did not know that he stood almost on the threshold of the most tremendous days of his life.

CHAPTER XVII

"A MAN WHO HAS BEEN BEATEN ONCE . . ."

On 5 June, 1916, the cruiser H.M.S. *Hampshire*, carrying Lord Kitchener to the northern shore of Russia, struck a mine west of the Orkneys and sank within ten minutes in heavy seas. The boats that put off from her were wrecked and lost, and Britain's most famous soldier was drowned with the sailors who bore him on his last mission.

It is hard for anyone who did not live in the years of the First World War to realize what the death of Kitchener meant to the British public. For millions of his fellow-countrymen, in the field and in the factory alike, this stern-looking soldier was the embodiment of Britain's strength, her stolid power of endurance, her unconquerable will to victory. The best known and most effective recruiting poster of all time was surely that one of the man with the big military moustache and the arresting eyes and that pointing finger, saying:

"Your Country Needs
YOU"

Wherever you turned, or ducked, those eyes and that finger followed you. It was a brilliant trick of the artist who drew the portrait. But the latent power of its appeal resided in the character of the man he drew. It brought to the colours of Great Britain the vastest volunteer army that the world has ever seen. Kitchener, too, was deservedly a legend before he was dead.

"A great man, or a great poster?" inquired Miss Elizabeth Asquith.

"A great man, or a great disappointment?" asked Lloyd George, who fought him most fiercely of all Kitchener's opponents in life. He sincerely answered his own question.

> "Kitchener was certainly never an ordinary man. Even his failings were not ordinary. He held childish opinions in some matters, but they were not commonplace. When he did silly things—as the wisest men occasionally do—they were extraordinarily silly."

Kitchener, who knew nothing of European politics (indeed, of Europe), based his opinion of the French Army on the old Indian Army idea of French politicians. They had debased the "Froggies" with democracy

We have already seen what he thought about the British Territorials, those "Town Clerk's soldiers"—the man who in the end raised four million Town Clerk's soldiers. Yet of all the leaders in authority in England in August, 1914, Kitchener was the only one who goes on record as saying that the war

314

would last several years. In the very first days of it, when they laid on his desk at the War Office a figure of 50,000 for the volunteer force which was to grow into the New Armies, he struck it out and wrote in: 300,000. "Kitchener's Army" they became in history, and let this be his splendid monument.

The general public were still unaware that in the previous December, 1915, after coming home from the Dardanelles, Kitchener had in fact offered his resignation to the Prime Minister. One reason was that he sensed that he had lost the confidence of his colleagues in the Cabinet; another was that during his absence the Ordnance Department had finally been transferred from the War Office to the Ministry of Munitions; the third was that on his return he had been confronted with a demand that the functions of the War Office itself should be divided between the Secretary of State for War and the Chief of Imperial General Staff.

Briefly, the Secretary of State was to look after Army administration, recruiting, and equipment (though not munitions!), and the C.I.G.S. was to handle strategy. To make it plain that the latter was in no way to be considered subordinate, the C.I.G.S. was to have direct access to the Cabinet— a position never conceded to his opposite number in the Navy, the First Sea Lord, even in the hey-day of Admiral Fisher.

It was a thoroughly bad principle, this division of responsibility for a Service. By it, Kitchener's once mighty power was shorn. Probably, he would never have agreed to the new arrangement except that he got on so well with the new C.I.G.S., General Sir William Robertson, whom he trusted. One professional soldier was able to talk to another. It is a powerful trade union.

But now Kitchener was sunk beneath the wave in the grey North Sea, to the stunned horror of a nation. Indeed, men could hardly bring themselves to believe it. So, for countless numbers the Living Legend remained a living man.

But, meantime? For his third spell of such a duty, the Prime Minister himself was Acting-Secretary of State for War. Who was going to take over the permanent job?

It was a decisive question. For events had now come to a moment in the First World War, as they do in most great wars, when a military dictatorship seemed to many people the only way to get through to victory. To the politicians, the idea of the "soldier-statesman" was by now rather at a discount, but it was very far from being so with the general public (actually, the very poignancy of Kitchener's tragic death made it otherwise). Also, the most popular Press in Britain was backing the belief that the politicians were self-seeking rascals, whereas the generals and the admirals were men like gods. Northcliffe was on the war-path again.

The problem of the eagerly-awaited name of the new War Secretary posed itself thus:

Was he going to be (1) not even the equal, but the rubber-stamp of the

C.I.G.S. and the generals? Or (2), was he going to be a leading figure of the Government? Flattered by Northcliffe, the soldier-statesmen thought it was going to be the first. They did not know the resources of the politicians.

The Prime Minister himself regarded this military challenge with suspicion, the more so since he believed that it was sustained by Diehard Tory support. At the same time, he regarded with rather more suspicion the still-undisclosed operations of his political colleagues and fellow-Liberal, Lloyd George, who was being strongly lobbied in some unexpected quarters as the best of all possible Secretaries of State for War.

Asquith was well aware that at this juncture Lloyd George himself was not unwilling to retire from his Ministry of Munitions for, as he said, Lloyd George realized that there was no further credit to be gained there. He knew that Lloyd George, frankly, held that his task there had been done, the general plan of production worked out, the right men placed in the key positions, and that little attraction now remained in this place for a man such as himself. But where would his driving energies be best employed next? The Prime Minister was in process of developing fresh doubts about his too-talented lieutenant. In this exercise, he did not lack aides.

To Lord Stamfordham on 8 June, 1916, Asquith wrote from the War Office:

"All this canvassing and wire-pulling about the succession, while poor K's body is still tossing about in the North Sea, seems to me to be in the highest degree indecent.

We can carry on here very well for a few days, and I am sure it would be a great mistake to be hurried into taking a precipitate decision."

It would be idle to pretend that Lloyd George himself did not want to go to the War Office. There is, of course, a letter from him to Asquith dated as late as 17 June, 1916, in which he thanks the Prime Minister for the offer which by then had been made of the Secretaryship of State for War, but says that he has come to the conclusion "that I shall be rendering a greater service to the country in this emergency by not accepting it".

This letter bears all the marks of a "Document of Record", a favourite insurance policy of politicians in case things go wrong.

Not that Lloyd George was entirely without his own doubts about the attractions of the War Office post. He had borne no small part personally in the curbing of Kitchener's power by dividing it with the C.I.G.S., and he had also more than once declared that he would never accept the post himself with such restrictions. Indeed, only a day or two before Kitchener had set off on his last voyage, Lloyd George had remarked, with a sudden impulse of pity, upon the "humiliating conditions" in which the Field-Marshal now worked: "Many a time have I seen him wince under the indignity of his position."

If Lloyd George now went to the War Office how could he, as a civilian, hope to recapture the full authority which had been denied to a famous soldier?

He sought the counsel of his political friends, of whom Sir Edward Carson at this moment ranked among the closest. The man who was once more "agin the Government" admitted that in some ways he would be delighted if Lloyd George kept clear of the War Office and came out of the Government himself. "I would like to work with you, personally," Carson told him, "and together we might bring this Government down, and replace it by a sounder and more energetic body."

But Carson ended by advising Lloyd George to go to the War Office, though he insisted that he must stipulate for full powers.

The very thought of Lloyd George at the War Office was enough to marshall the generals for the fray. Here is Lord Stamfordham reporting to His Majesty, 15 June, 1916:

Buckingham Palace.

"Humbly submitted.

I saw Sir William Robertson this morning. . . .

He is much concerned about the question of a S. of S. The Prime Minister had a very long interview with Lloyd George on Tuesday evening but Robertson got nothing out of him when he came to the W.O. He expressed a hope that someone would soon be appointed. The P.M. only said 'it is a difficult matter to settle'.

What he fears in Lloyd George is interference in appointments in which as S. of S. he would have a *right* to interfere. It is known, for instance, that he has no opinion of Haig or Rawlinson though his judgment can only be the result of tittle tattle gossip. Still, as R. says, it would be difficult to stop him from meddling in such matters, whereas in those of higher policy, strategy and conduct of the war, R. would be justified in resisting any interference—But it would be disastrous to the Army and indeed might have fatal results on the war if a civilian War Minister were to attempt to tamper with the personel. (*sic*)

As to Bonar Law the War Office would not mind him though he is not sympathetic to the Army. R. is able to judge of these men by what he hears from them at the War Committee. . . ."

The C.I.G.S. was not alone in seeking to mobilize the Palace influence against Lloyd George's appointment to the War Office. There was his Tory Cabinet colleague, Walter Long, the President of the Local Government Board, writing two days later.

Local Government Board,
Whitehall, S.W.

My dear Stamfordham,

I am presuming upon our old friendship to write and ask you if you can't do something about the W.O.?

I have been there a great deal and know the feeling inside and out very well. The appointment suggested in the Press[1] would in my opinion be disastrous. I begged the P.M. yesterday to take the seals himself and make Derby his 2nd in Command. . . .

Yours ever,
Walter H. Long.

17.vi.16."

Another, and coded message from Lord Stamfordham to King George V:

"Decypher.   8.15 p.m.

17 June, 1916.

Have seen P.M. L.G. wants War Office but with former plenary powers restored, which is impossible as Robertson's present position would be compromised. Best solution is for P.M. to remain at War Office. Whole Army Council want this. Derby might be 2nd in Command.

L.G.'s proposals go beyond what a unanimous Cabinet would sanction. Some of them already kicking. . . .

Stamfordham."

Later that evening Lord Stamfordham found time to write a full letter, amplifying the situation. He explained that Lloyd George wanted the War Office post all right, but only on his own terms, to which Sir William Robertson so strongly objected that it was doubtful if he would stay on himself. Although Lloyd George declared that he had no wish to "interfere with the general military policy of the war", wrote Stamfordham, there could be no doubt that if he got the powers he was demanding he would very quickly assert his authority in matters which at present were entirely controlled by the C.I.G.S. He continued:

"The one argument in his favour, and it is rather a strong one, is, as the Prime Minister pointed out, that abroad Lloyd George is one of the few Englishmen regarded as a personality. He thinks it may fairly be said that Asquith, Kitchener, Lloyd George and Grey were the only members of the Government who were familiar in the minds of our Allies: now Lord K. is gone, only three remain and if Lloyd George went to the W.O. he would be to them a personal factor."

Lord Stamfordham reported that he had himself urged the Prime Minister to stay on at the War Office, where Lord Derby had agreed to help him ("and asked for no pay"). Asquith had told him that Field-Marshal French had been to see him and say that the whole Army at home and at the front wanted him as War Secretary, but that he realized he had his hands tolerably full already. He wanted the week-end to think things over "for he did not

[1] i.e. Lloyd George.

conceal from himself the fact that Lloyd George will not be pleased if his demands are refused".

The Prime Minister received from another quarter rather different advice. This came from a Liberal colleague, Edwin Montagu, then Financial Secretary to the Treasury. The letter was found by J. T. Davies, Lloyd George's Secretary, in a drawer in No. 10 Downing Street long after Asquith had gone and Lloyd George had succeeded him as Prime Minister. Some people wondered if it had been left behind deliberately.

> "Treasury Gardens,
> Whitehall, S.W.
> 20.6.1916.

Dear Prime Minister,

I happened to see L.G. at Rufus'[1] last night. He was of course very excited about Ireland and said the War Office must wait till we're over that.

But he still thinks that he had been offered the Office. He now quite clearly in my opinion, *will* take it without any change of status or constitution. He appears to be no better informed or differently informed as to K's position.

It would clearly be very disastrous to make any other arrangement while he thinks he has been offered it and is considering it. . . .

But all this must wait for the minute because of Ireland. I approve, but it would also be clearly advantageous to have L.G. at the War Office during the announcement of heavy casualties and a possibly unfruitful offensive.

> E. S. M."

A curious character, Edwin Montagu. He was the son of Lord Swaythling, the Jewish banker, and a man of brilliant political and social gifts, one of Fortune's favourites. He had entered the House of Commons on the Liberal flood-tide of 1906, and became at once the Parliamentary Private Secretary of Asquith when he was Chancellor of the Exchequer. Then he had been given, in turn, the posts of Under-Secretary for India and Financial Secretary to the Treasury. In 1915, he had married Venetia Stanley, the daughter of Lord Sheffield, a beautiful, brilliant woman with a brain equal to any man, and politically trained and equipped. He tried to get on well with everyone, Edwin Montagu, but up to 1916, certainly best with Asquith, who was Prime Minister. He had tried hard to keep out of the developing Asquith-Lloyd George feud by keeping a foot in either camp.

Meanwhile, Time was marching—but for Britain, the war was drifting. Should Lloyd George go to the War Office, or not? Should he haggle for terms first? Or take the job, and make of it a position of real power later?

The question was settled the day that Lloyd George and Bonar Law discovered that in this matter of the succession at the War Office they had a

[1] Rufus Isaacs, Lord Reading, then Lord Chief Justice.

common purpose. They already had some other things they shared, this Liberal and this Tory, besides both being the sons of poor men and dissenters, who had made their own way in life.

Bonar Law had no especial reason, indeed, to thank Lloyd George for his treatment at the time of forming the Coalition. As Leader of the Opposition Party—and one equal in Parliamentary strength to the Government Party— Bonar Law had been entitled to claim a great office of State, the Exchequer or the Foreign Office. He received neither, but went to the Colonial Office. He did not even get the Deputy-Leadership of the House of Commons. Lloyd George, so it seemed to Bonar Law, kept for himself whatever he wanted: He retained (1) the tenancy of No. 11 Downing Street, the official residence of the Chancellor of the Exchequer, (2) the reversion of the Chancellor's office; and (3) the Deputy Leadership of the House of Commons.

At this moment of history, however (June, 1916), Lloyd George and Bonar Law were thinking in harmony about more vital things—a really effective engine to provide a central drive for the entire war effort. This would never come from a divided control at the War Office, and still less would it come if the larger share of that divided power was yielded to the Generals. Both Lloyd George and Bonar Law were determined to see that Field-Marshal Lord Kitchener had not been drowned so that General Sir William Robertson should be crowned.

They met by arrangement one Sunday at Cherkley Court, the country home of Max Aitken, and there, strolling under the yew trees, it was agreed that one or the other of them must succeed to the War Office. It seems that though both were ready to be drafted for the job, only one, Lloyd George, was really anxious, and so it was decided. Next morning, Aitken drove Bonar Law over to Asquith's house at Sutton Courtney, where Bonar Law informed the Prime Minister of their talk about the War Office. At once, Asquith said: "I offer it to you!"

Bonar Law answered that if he had done so a week ago it might have been accepted but not now; he was pledged to Lloyd George. Asquith frowned, but gave way. The Prime Minister had made his first surrender; it would not be his last.

"A man who has been beaten once can be beaten twice," noted Aitken, as they drove to Dover on the way to France.

So, Asquith conceded the War Office to his most formidable rival in British politics, and on 6 July, 1916, Lloyd George became Secretary of State for War. The same day Margot Asquith noted in her diary:

"We are out, it is only a question of time when we shall have to leave Downing Street."

Lloyd George had taken a large risk in going to the War Office without securing a new charter. For the second time in the war, he accepted what

Passchendaele, 1917

At Criccieth with Philip Kerr and Lord Riddell, 1917

seemed to many to be a subordinate post. Time, and the event, would show how long it would remain so.

And here it may be as well to place on record the terms on which War Secretary Lloyd George and C.I.G.S. Robertson would work. The General had written him a memorandum setting out what he conceived should be the status of the C.I.G.S. vis-à-vis the Government. In a letter dated 26 June, 1916, and still addressed from the Ministry of Munitions, Lloyd George had replied to remind him of the position of the Secretary of State for War.

In placing the General Staff in direct relationship with the War Committee, Lloyd George pointed out, it did not separate them from the War Office in general or from the Secretary of State in particular. The holder of the seals of office retained his ultimate responsibility for the War Office, and the Prime Minister, Parliament and the country must hold him accountable. In fact, the relation of the Secretary of State towards the War Office on one hand and the Government on the other, was paralleled by that of the First Lord of the Admiralty towards the Board of Admiralty and towards the Government.

He went on to make three main points with the General:

1. In his memo, the C.I.G.S. had undertaken that the Secretary of State should receive "at all times full information of *all that he should know*"—that is, concerning operations. The Secretary of State, Lloyd George insisted, must receive information of *everything*.

2. The C.I.G.S. had claimed that all advice concerning military operations should reach the War Committee via himself. Very well, said Lloyd George, but the C.I.G.S. must first of all explain it to the Secretary of State, and also discuss with him the lines on which he is framing such advice.

3. The C.I.G.S. had claimed that all appointments of Commanders-in-Chief, Commanders of Armies, etc., should be made by the War Committee on his own recommendation to the Secretary of State. Lloyd George replied that while he would be grateful for any such recommendations, it was the Secretary of State's business to convince the War Committee and the Prime Minister of the worth of any officer and to gain their support for submitting his name to the King.

The General answered in a civil note, affirming that he was in no way seeking to lay down the duties of the Secretary of State, and promising the loyal co-operation of himself and the General Staff.

Thus it will be seen that Lloyd George entered on his period of duty at the War Office on substantially the same terms that he once imposed upon Lord Kitchener. His immediate circle were surprised. But it was evident that he was so anxious to make a change from the Ministry of Munitions that he deemed the concession as well worth while.

Nor did the new Secretary of State for War refrain very long before launching operations against the inner citadel of the War Office, and against the C.I.G.S., General Sir William Robertson, in particular. There was, indeed,

K

sound sense behind his suggestion that the British C.I.G.S. should pay a belated visit to the General Headquarters of his opposite number in the army of our great ally, Russia. There was much of vital confidence and of experience which these high officers had to exchange. But General Robertson was perhaps not unjust in suspecting that Lloyd George nursed other hopes when he urged this voyage upon him.

At any rate, he resisted, with Robertsonian tenacity.

"War Office.   27.9.16.
                                                                   6.15 p.m.

Dear Mr. Lloyd George,

The Prime Minister has just sent for me to discuss the Russian visit. I have thought it well over since you spoke to me this morning and have concluded that it is impossible for me to make the visit without losing entire control over the war, and this at an important time. I quite realize the force of what you say, but if I went I should be away for at least a month and that is much too long if I am to keep my hand on the many problems we are dealing with.

I am honestly very sorry not to be able to fall in with your proposal and, as I told the P.M., if I am asked to go—I shall go, but my opinion is that I ought *not* to go if I am of any use as C.I.G.S. . . .

                                                        Yours very truly,
                                                        W. R. Robertson."

Top of the War Office programme at this moment occupying the attention of the C.I.G.S. stood the plan for a British offensive on the Somme sector of the Western Front. Its aim: to relieve the enemy pressure against Verdun on the French sector. A secondary argument, subsequently advanced, was that it would also relieve enemy pressure on the Russian Eastern Front. Kitchener himself had begun by opposing it.

Was he wrong in urging restraint in our main theatre of battle in another great assault until we had tried out our new "secret weapon"? For by this time, that mechanical revolution in movement, shield and gun-power, the Tank, had arrived—so far, the most terrifying enemy to appear since man fought the armoured monsters of the Prehistoric Age. The first impact of the tank on the German soldiers of the Western Front was, in truth, tremendous, and might well have proved decisive, if, as Lloyd George urged (who had seen the Thing born and had nurtured it himself while at the Ministry of Munitions), the tank had been deployed in mass and not, as it was on the Somme, in penny packets.

As a matter of fact, the tanks had only been rushed into action there, very late in the battle, because the momentum of the infantry assault had already been halted against the enemy second and third line defences. This "bull-headed fight", as Lloyd George termed it, cost the British Army 400,000 casualties. Whether it eased the enemy weight against Verdun is problematical. It certainly did not save Russia. What it did to the British Army is soberly set out in the *Official History of the War*:

> "For this disastrous loss of the finest manhood of the United Kingdom and Ireland there was only a small gain of ground to show. Never again was the spirit or the quality of the officers and men so high, nor the training, leading and, above all, discipline of the new British Armies in France so good."

How slightly the holocaust on the Somme disrupted the higher strategy of the Central Powers may be gauged by the fact that when in September, 1916, Rumania decided at last to throw in her lot with the *Entente*, the Germans detached several veteran corps from the Western Front and sent them off to Austria to concentrate on the mountain frontier against this new enemy. As soon as they were ready, General von Falkenhayn's Army "fell on Rumania like an avalanche from the Carpathian heights".

At the same time, General von Mackensen advanced from Bulgaria across the plains towards Bukarest. By Christmas, it was all over in the Balkans once again. Rumania's wheat and oil passed into the hands of the enemy, and our world-wide sea blockade of Germany was thus smashed open on the Danube.

Lloyd George cannot be charged with being wise after the event. On 4 September, 1916, the day after the Bulgarians declared war on Rumania, he sent a memo to the C.I.G.S. Recalling the anxiety he had expressed two or three days earlier, Lloyd George wrote:

> "We cannot afford another Serbian tragedy. We were warned early in 1916 that the Germans meant, in confederation with the Bulgars, to wipe Serbia out. In spite of that fact, when the attack came we had not purchased a single mule to aid the Serbians through Salonika. The result was, when our troops landed there, owing to lack of equipment and appropriate transport they could not go inland and Serbia was crushed. . . . I hope we shall not allow the same catastrophe to befall Rumania through lack of timely forethought."

Lloyd George pointed out several "disquieting facts". These were Hindenburg's "well-known Eastern inclinations", and the certainty that the hardheaded Bulgarian Tsar, Ferdinand, would never have moved unless he had good guarantee. There was the slackening of the German attack on Verdun, which would release hundreds of heavy guns and hundreds of thousands of troops for use elsewhere. If Hindenburg now gave ground gradually on the Somme —and he could yield four or five times as much as we had won during the past couple of months without surrendering any vital positions, he would be able to spare several more divisions for the Eastern Front. Was it possible that the poorly-equipped Rumanian Army could stand up to this without real aid from us?

Later, when the Rumanian Campaign had developed as disastrously as his worst forebodings had suggested, Lloyd George found himself in a clash of arms with General Robertson during a session of the War Committee. After it was over, the C.I.G.S. told the War Secretary frankly that he would personally refuse to accept responsibility for any plan to reinforce the Balkan Front at the expense of the Western Front. The General extended his own "personal war" operations on this issue. He told the King, the Prime Minister and Northcliffe that if Lloyd George continued to make incursions into his own particular field then he would resign. He appears to have gone to the extent of putting this much in writing to Lloyd George himself.

The same day, Northcliffe strode into J. T. Davies's room at the War Office, looking like thunder. At once, "J.T." jumped up to show him into Lloyd George's room. But Northcliffe waved him down. He had not come to see the War Secretary, but to say something which could be transmitted to him. "You can tell him I hear he has been interfering with strategy, and that if he goes on I will break him."

Still swifter was Lloyd George's own reaction.

"11 Downing Street.

My dear Sir William,   12 October, 1916.

In the course of the two conversations I had with you at the War Office since Monday's Council you made no protest against my taking a line of my own on Rumania. Tonight's letter would therefore have caused me some surprise had not a leading newspaper proprietor given me the pith of it some eight hours before it was despatched to me. He had clearly been taken into counsel by someone in your close confidence, and by him acquainted with matters so confidential in their nature that they have not yet been imparted to the Cabinet and so dangerous in their character that their publication would materially assist the enemy. This great journalist even threatened publication unless I withdrew immediately from the position I had taken up. Had he done so my only defence would have been the public disclosure of equally secret and equally dangerous material to complete the story. Of course you could not have authorized such a breach of confidence and discipline. But unfortunately, this kind of thing is of frequent occurrence in the Service, and must be stopped in the best interests of the Army. I have during my short sojourn at the War Office frequently encountered this grave subversion of discipline in high places. I have found complaints against action taken by the Army Council and myself lodged with the Press—even before they ever reached me. These complaints must have emanated from fairly exalted quarters, for no one outside that circle had a right at that stage to know what was going on, or any interest in protesting.

I feel confident you must agree with me that this state of things is an outrage on all the best traditions of the Service, and must tend to impair discipline in all ranks of the Army, and I am certain that I shall receive your assistance and that of the Army Council in putting an end to this injurious practice. Privates have recently been court-martialled for complaining direct to their M.P.s and to the Secretary of State, and the Army Council have asked me to enforce discipline against M.P. Officers who ventilated their grievances in Parliament. How can I do so, when such an example of discipline is set by men in high places?"

The letter continues, that there are two things which must be settled immediately in the interest of the harmonious working of the War Office—so essential to the conduct of the War. One is this point of discipline. The other is the question of responsibility as between the Secretary of State and the C.I.G.S.

"There can be no doubt as to your supreme responsibility in all matters affecting strategy, and the direction of military operations—subject, of course, to the War Council. I have never questioned your authority in this respect. But there seems to be some doubt, I gather from your letter, as to my position as a Member of the War Council. It ought to be decided whether I have the same right—although I am War Secretary—to express an independent view on the War in the discussions which take place as any other member of the War Council—or whether, as long as I am War Secretary, I must choose between the position of a dummy or a pure advocate of all opinions expressed by my military advisers. . . . You must not ask me to play the part of a mere dummy. I am not in the least suited for the part.

Ever sincerely,

D. Lloyd George."

The General had not been spoken to like that since he was Private Robertson. He took it pretty well, the more so since on the big issue he may have been right. The autumn of 1916 was probably already a year too late (or perhaps another year too early) to do much about Rumania.

Now Rumania was a far-off place, of which the British public knew little. A farther-off place, of which they knew no more, was Mesopotamia. There was a war on there, too. And of all the wars ever fought by Britain this "Mespot" war was probably the worst bungled. If the facts had been given one-hundredth of the publicity which glared upon Gallipoli the Liberal Government would hardly have survived the day.

The story of "Mespot" began in September, 1914, when Turkey appeared about to enter the war, and the Government of India were sending troops up to Egypt to protect the Suez Canal. It was thought prudent, also, to land a brigade at Abadan to protect the oil tanks and the pipe lines of the Anglo-Persia Oil Company, on whom the Royal Navy then relied substantially for their supplies. This force was steadily built up, until by April, 1915, it amounted to an Army Corps and had occupied the entire coast of the Shatt-el-Arab. One oil-field after another came under its shield, until presently Bagdad began to loom on its horizon. To seize this fabulous city of the *Arabian Nights* had often been the dream of adventurous Indian Army Officers. Suddenly it seemed real. In October, 1915, General Townshend advanced on Bagdad. He was held up a few miles south of the city and withdrew, short of food, medical supplies and men, to Kut-el-Amara. Here, he was trapped by the Turks and stood siege for 147 days, until on 29 April, 1916, starvation forced him to surrender.

Already in February, the War Office had taken charge of the Mesopotamia Expedition. But since the troops were from India Command, it so happened that it was not until Lloyd George became Secretary of State for War that the full responsibility for events in Mesopotamia was transferred to the British Government.

The first steps that Lloyd George took was to set up, in August, 1916, a Royal Commission to find the facts of what had long been the talk of Service mess, canteen and club as "the Mespot Scandal". It was not until 17 May, 1917, that the Commission issued its Report. It repeated, officially, the dangerous earlier gossip of that record of stupidity and sloth. Typical of this appalling military muddle had been the handling of the wounded. Up country, there were not enough stretcher-bearers, and the wounded were often left on the field, to be stripped, mutilated and murdered by the savage Arabs. Downstream, at base, there was no ice, no fans, not enough medicine, drugs, splints, bandages or blankets. There were not enough doctors, surgeons, nurses or attendants. There was not enough food, and the water stank.

Such was "Mespot".

The credit of the Government sank. Not only those sitting in high financial and economic places, such as McKenna and Runciman, Bradbury and Keynes, began to wonder if our own seaborne supplies could keep us going longer than the enemy could outlast our blockade? If our finances would not fail though our defences held? Mr. Maynard Keynes had actually named the day of doom, 31 March, 1916 (a most convenient date for accountants, because of the end of the financial year). When spring arrived—and passed—and Britain still survived, he dubiously suspended sentence until autumn.

What cause, indeed, was there for Britain to cheer? The Russians were in retreat; the Rumanians in rout; the Turks had got us off Gallipoli at last and beaten us from Bagdad back to Basra; our long-planned offensive on the Somme had failed to break the German line (as their offensive at Verdun, indeed, had also failed to take the French citadel).

At sea, the greatest naval battle of the century had ended inconclusively off Jutland, in the sense that there was no discernible change in the existing situation, though what had been frustrated there will never be known. The British lost more ships than the Germans, and suffered more than double the casualties. But the German Fleet retired home to its harbours, and the British Fleet stayed at sea. More significant (and more menacing) in the sea war, was the sharp rise in the sinking of British merchant ships.

Indeed, by this time, quite a number of people in all the belligerent countries (besides well-meaning citizens of neutral countries) had had enough of War. They could see no end to it, except a stalemate, and they felt that it should be wound up now before everyone was ruined. Others feared defeat for their own country if the war went on. And, of course, there were also those who deliberately encouraged talk of Peace in the enemy's country, simply in order to weaken his will to resistance, and thus enhance their own prospects of victory.

Quite as certainly *not* flying any "peace-kite" was the Secretary of State for War. Lloyd George considered peace-talk in the autumn of 1916 was defeatist-talk, dangerous talk, devil-talk. He reckoned that the "Notes" which the President of the United States, Mr. Woodrow Wilson, was then addressing to the various Powers were to be numbered among the most mischievous of all peace-kites. To make this opinion plain, on 28 September, 1916, Lloyd George gave a newspaper interview to Mr. Roy Howard, President of the United Press Association of America. Headlined as the "knock-out-blow" interview, it set the world talking.

Lloyd George began by intimating that at this particular stage of the war, any outside interference would not be welcome. There had been no attempt at intervention when we were being hammered throughout the first two years, untrained and unequipped. We would tolerate no intervention now we *were* prepared, until Prussian Military despotism had been destroyed beyond repair. There was something more in this than a mere national demand for vengeance. The inhumanity and the pitilessness of the fighting was not comparable with the cruelty of stopping the war while the possibility of civilization being menaced from the same quarter remained.

How long would it go on? Said Lloyd George:

"There is neither clock nor calendar in the British Army today. Time is the least vital factor. It took England twenty years to defeat Napoleon, and the first fifteen of these years were bleak with British defeat. It will not take twenty years to win this war, but whatever time is required it will be done!"

It disrupted some intricate moves then being arranged by the Chancelleries of the Central Powers. Much more important, it abruptly ended a rather discursive mood which seemed to be settling upon the Asquithian Government, for it brought the issue of War or Peace down on the Cabinet table with a bang.

In Lloyd George's view, there were two alternative courses open—and no other. Either you were for waging War, or you were for making Peace. Merely to muddle on making some kind of war was, in fact, a method of bringing about peace, and not the best one at that.

On the other side, Lord Lansdowne penned his famous Memorandum. He asked frankly: *What are the chances that the enemy can be beaten?*

And he answered, in effect.

Here is the President of the Board of Trade, Mr. Runciman, who warns that our shipbuilding is not keeping up with the ship-sinking. He talks of "a complete break-down . . . much sooner than June, 1917". Next, the President of the Board of Agriculture, Lord Crawford, says that the price of bread will rise, the potato crop has fallen short and so has the fish haul. Cultivation of the soil is likely to decline, and livestock to die off. Then there is Mr. Balfour, the First Lord of the Admiralty, who warns us that although the size of the Fleet is too small, we are near the limit of our capacity for building capital ships. He says that we are already short of light cruisers and destroyers for anti-submarine work, and that the U-boats are growing in number and range. After him, comes the C.I.G.S. General Sir William Robertson, who tells us we are reaching the end of our tether in manpower, and we can only fill up the ranks of the Army by draining industry. We have lost more than a million men already. The truth is, observed Lansdowne, that we are steadily killing off the best of the male population of these islands. Finally, there is the question of the money. To our already "almost incalculable burden", we are adding at the rate of £5,000,000 per day. Generations will come and go before this debt in human beings and money and means of production will be paid. The responsibility of those who needlessly prolong such a war is not less than those who needlessly provoked it.

Lord Lansdowne then suggested each of the Allies should separately take stock as to their requirements, and then consider whether or not they would accept less than 20s. in the £ in consideration of cash down.

He expressed doubts about the "knock-out-blow". Did the last offensive in France suggest that we should be any more successful at a "break-through" than ever before? He had his doubts about the Italian Front, still more about Salonika. As for Russia and Rumania, we should be lucky to escape disaster there.

Finally, Lord Lansdowne deplored Mr. Lloyd George's interview as producing "an impression which it will not be easy to efface".

Nothing could have suited Lloyd George better than to have it understood that there was now a clear and ineffaceable distinction between (*a*) the Wage-War Party and (*b*) the Make-Peace Party.

He stood for the first party himself but he sincerely welcomed this calm, clear—and let us say it, courageous—statement of the case of the other party.

The defeatist movement was, in the event, effectively answered by the Minister of Blockade, Lord Robert Cecil, on 27 November, 1916. He admitted that the situation was grave and warned that unless "the utmost national effort is made, it might become fatal".

France was in grave plight. Italy's finances were tottering and Russia trembled on the verge of Revolution. But, Lord Robert Cecil argued, if Germany herself was not yet desperate, her Ally, Austria, was in really serious plight, and trouble was still growing in both. If our own Military advisers were correct, and we could, indeed, expect a great military success in 1916, then it was unlikely that the enemy could survive it. If we could hold on but another year, there was a reasonable prospect of victory.

And the alternatives? The best we could get would be *status quo*, with a big increase in German power in Eastern Europe. What is more, the Germans would realize that it was their U-boats which had forced peace on us, and in ten years time we should need to start preparing for battle all over again.

Gradually, and inevitably, everything came to centre upon the person and character of the Prime Minister himself. All who knew him, respected Asquith's intellect, his erudition, his lawyer's gift of tearing the "innards" out of a case in a fraction of time, his massive eloquence, his mastery of debate, his sense of justice. Many had reason to remember his loyalty and kindness, Lloyd George himself not the least among them. Those who knew him best, considered that Mr. Asquith would have made a superb judge. This impartial quality had served him admirably as the Prime Minister of those varied and talented teams who made up the peace-time Liberal Government. What these had most required was harmonizing, not energizing, and this Asquith, *primus inter pares*, perfectly provided. A judge is not required to enforce his own decisions.

The quality needed in a War leader more nearly approximates to that of a dynamo, and nobody ever mistook an appointment with Mr. Asquith for a visit to a power-house. The strain of war-time responsibility, the sharp and sometimes jagged edges which its fierce pressure puts upon human relationships, the single relentless, ruthless, almost sleepless pursuit of one objective only— these did not accord with the Asquithian character and personality. In battle, you do not have to be a judge. The battle itself is the judge. Henry Asquith was not born for battle.

Here is Lloyd George, complaining to Riddell during this summer of the serious state of national affairs, and the Prime Minister's neglect to recognize it. Writes Riddell in his Diary:

> "He described him as resembling a family doctor in attendance upon a patient who was seriously ill. If the patient appeared a little better, he would say, 'Well, you see, his condition is improving'. If he appeared worse, he would remark, 'Well, you must expect these variations'. While on the balance the patient was gradually approaching his end—a fact which the doctor failed to mention or appreciate."

Here is the C.I.G.S. General Robertson, walking to the War Office after lunch, with Sir Robert Donald, Editor of the *Daily Chronicle*. He tells him that, in council, Asquith behaves more like a judge than a president who is leading a war policy. Everything is decided "by majority". Says the

General, something has got to be done to get decisions out of the War Council, "which is far too big and talks too much".

The date is 24 November, 1916, which is after General Robertson and Lloyd George have had several more brushes with one another at the War Office. But the C.I.G.S. goes on:

"The only man who can decide quickly, say 'Yes! or No!' without hesitation, is Lloyd George. He might say the wrong Yes! or sometimes say the wrong No! But I prefer that to no decision at all. I am for more power for Lloyd George, not to interfere with military operations, but to direct War policy."

There was always Churchill, too. He had not been happy in his command of a battalion of the 6th Royal Scots Fusiliers, for the sector of the British Front which they held was a quiet one, and their role had largely been to bear periodical bombardment from the enemy. During the early months of 1916, Churchill had been urged by various people, as different in their politics as Sir Edward Carson and C. P. Scott, of the *Manchester Guardian*, to relinquish his commission and come home and help to form a "Patriotic Opposition". By August, 1916, he had come home.

The Prime Minister himself appeared to have no inkling of the earthquake which was opening at his feet. It is not hard to believe that, modestly as he invariably comported himself, Asquith shared the current myth of the "indispensability of Asquith". He read the newspapers which appealed to him, mingled a great deal in agreeable social company (which he loved), and as the testimony of innumerable letters, diaries and memoirs of his colleagues points, did not "face the facts"—or more accurately, if he faced them, Asquith did not "deal" with them. It never seems to have crossed his mind that consciously or subconsciously people were beginning to add up a toll of misfortunes—and also to ask: Who was the Man in Charge at the time? There had been the scandal of the Shells, the disaster of the Dardanelles and the tragedy of Serbia, the muddle of "Mespot", the indecision over Conscription, and now there loomed tomorrow's menace of the U-boats, and starvation.

Discontent was at its deepest in the rank-and-file of the Tory Party. It was from here that Lloyd George had drawn his most solid support in the Conscription issue. Now Sir Edward Carson, ever since his resignation over the Serbian debacle, had been moving into more-or-less open revolt against the Tory leadership as represented in the persons of Bonar Law and his colleagues in the Coalition Government, Chamberlain, Curzon, Cecil and Long. A rebel Tory vote of 65 in a House of Commons debate on 8 November, 1916, over the disposal of enemy property in the colony of Nigeria (they wanted to limit the auction bidders to British subjects) revealed how strongly feeling ran. It also persuaded Mr. Bonar Law that the safest place to have Sir Edward Carson was back inside the Government.

Bonar Law had his own reservations about Asquith, but he believed that no other public figure commanded such widespread national support. Bonar Law certainly did not want the Tory revolt to spread to such dimensions that the Party would demand that their leaders should resign from the Government, and so destroy it.

Sir Edward Carson, on the other hand, had no faith whatever in the War leadership of Asquith. He frankly wanted a break-up. At this time Carson was seeing a great deal of Lloyd George. Unkind critics of both at St. Stephens joked that Sir Edward Carson, the leader of the Opposition in the House of Commons, was in close co-operation with Lloyd George, the leader of the Opposition in the Government.

What Lloyd George still hankered for was that effective war engine with the central drive that Bonar Law had talked of. Lloyd George wanted a real *executive* committee of two or three. He had been hammering on this theme for months, even years. If Asquith would provide it, well and good. If he would not, then somebody else must do so.

What Lloyd George did not want was one more large debating society, "a Duma" such as the War Council, Dardanelles Committee and War Committee in turn had proved themselves to be. He felt keenly restriction of his powers as Secretary of State for War vis-à-vis the C.I.G.S., the restriction which he himself had helped to impose on Kitchener. He said to Max Aitken:

"I am the Butcher's Boy who leads in the animals to the slaughter. When I have delivered the men my task in the war is over."

Now, Max Aitken was the faithful servant of Bonar Law. Austen Chamberlain has testified to Aitken's sincere admiration for Bonar Law, and his desire to exalt him "in the eyes of history and in the hearts of his countrymen",[1] a purpose in which he has never faltered since. Highland qualities come out strong in the character of Aitken. He is, indeed, a son of Canada, as he boasts, but he is also very decidedly a grandson of Scotland. Enduring friendship and unforgiving enmity are two of his marks, and he carries a dirk in his belt. His mind is lively, and his talk is stimulating, and he is a man who knows what he wants. In politics, he was a flamboyant mixture of bright blue Imperialism abroad and near-red Radicalism at home. If his political judgment had equalled his political passion, he might have stamped himself decisively in his own vivid colours on the face of British history.

As a journalist, he was best when he was reporting, for he possessed what the newspaper world knows as the "seeing eye". His energy was ever demoniac,

[1] *Down the Years:* by Sir Austen Chamberlain (Cassell & Co., Ltd.).
"It is characteristic of Lord Beaverbrook's whole attitude to Bonar Law to represent himself merely as the clarifying medium which enabled Bonar Law to precipitate his own thoughts, and perceive them clearly. No one who ever saw them together, or even reads his book, can accept that account of their relationship."

and a vital part of the man himself. "Just be yourself, Max," a close friend
advised him when he took over the Ministry of Aircraft Production during
the Second World War, in the crisis days of May, 1940. The advice was
needless; Max Aitken grabbed materials, men and plant from the other departments; he robbed every supply depot joyously, and without regard for protests
or appeals to Cabinet Authority. He disregarded hostile judgments. At one
moment Ernest Bevin even considered recourse to the Law Courts in the
vain hope of restraining his intractable colleague. But Max Aitken, first Lord
Beaverbrook of Beaverbrook, kept the R.A.F. planes flying in the Battle
of Britain.

Now this November Aitken had been working on the plan of a second
challenge to Asquith ever since that first one had succeeded. *"A man who
has been beaten once can be beaten twice."* He thought he saw a chance here to
serve his friend, his Party and his country at one and the same time. He
determined to bring Bonar Law, Carson and Lloyd George together.

It was by no means easy. To begin with, though Bonar Law and Lloyd
George had worked closely together several times (over the forming of the
First Coalition Government in May, 1915, over the Kitchener crisis of
December, 1915, and over the War Office crisis of June, 1916) they had
drifted apart again. It is true that more than once they had discussed together
Lloyd George's idea of the small, supreme Executive, but they had not
pursued it. Nor were Bonar Law and Carson any longer moving in unison as
once they had.

Carson and Lloyd George were at one. But a week of coming and going,
talks and telephone calls, did not get Aitken far along his road—there was
much to do, and the new "Triple Alliance" had not yet even been signed. On
Saturday, 18 November, Lloyd George was not hopeful. He told Aitken that
he proposed to resign. He would have to go out of the Government, and meet
Carson in the wilderness.

But, urged Aitken, this would be a path beset with difficulties. Much better
bring Carson in! The problem was how to do that over the heads of the loyal
Tory leaders. From Lloyd George's point of view matters were not improved
by Bonar Law mentioning to Asquith the Lloyd George Executive Plan. The
Prime Minister said bluntly that it was merely a Lloyd George bid for more
personal power—and it was doubtful if he would be satisfied with his Plan
even if it were conceded him!

Certainly, it was true that Lloyd George was insisting that the Prime
Minister must not himself be a Member of this Executive. For if he was, by
reason of his official rank, he must dominate it. And Lloyd George held that
this would destroy its entire value. By this time, Lloyd George was well
aware of the deepening personal hostility of Asquith towards himself (which he
attributed chiefly to McKenna). "I would like to work with Asquith," said
Lloyd George, "but he won't work with me."

That week-end, the Triple Alliance got as far as meeting at Bonar Law's house in Kensington. They made further progress when Aitken produced a neat little memorandum, the purpose of which was to make it quite clear what was wanted. There were three points:

1. A small "Civilian General Staff" was to be set up to take the place of the former War Council.
2. It would consist of the Prime Minister and three other members, and Lloyd George would act as Chairman whenever the Prime Minister could not attend. (The names of the other two members were not given).
3. It would have executive authority, subject only to the Prime Ministers' right to refer to the Cabinet any questions which he considered should come before them.

Now here was a substantial measure of agreement. The Triple Alliance were unanimous on the first two points, and on the third there were only degrees of difference. Bonar Law still wanted Asquith to remain as Prime Minister if he would in fact yield some of his authority. Lloyd George wanted him to yield a great deal, as far as the day-to-day direction of the war was concerned. Carson wanted Asquith out.

Armed with this ultimatum—for that is what it was—Bonar Law went off to see the Prime Minister. He received a cautious welcome, though the Prime Minister did not conceal his opinion about either of his colleagues. He did not think much of Carson as an administrator, and there would be some difficulty in promoting him over the heads of other leading Tories. As for Lloyd George, the Prime Minister reiterated his opinion that this was Oliver Twist; he would come again, asking for more. Asquith promised to write Bonar Law a letter on Monday morning.

The letter repeated the same views, more precisely and more emphatically. When Bonar Law pointed out that this was pretty severe language to use about the two men concerned, and said that he would have to show it to his colleagues, Asquith rewrote the passages in which he criticized the administrative talents of Sir Edward Carson. He left unaltered what he had written about the qualities of Lloyd George.

"As to Lloyd George, you know as well as I do both his qualities and his defects. He has many qualities that would fit him for the first place, but he lacks the one thing needful—he does not inspire trust. . . . Here again, there is one construction and one only, that could be put on the new arrangement—that it has been engineered by him with the purpose, not perhaps at the moment, but as soon as a fitting pretext could be found, of his displacing me."

The Secretary of State for War called upon the Prime Minister that same morning. The meeting was not fruitful. The temperature in Downing Street between the next-door neighbours was not lowered when a few days later the *Morning Post*, the bugle of the Diehard Tories, came out with a fanfare for Lloyd George. The former "Footpad of Limehouse" appeared in Editor H. A. Gwynne's leader column on 23 November, 1916, as the "Necessary Man". The information that big Government changes were afoot had been conveyed to the *Morning Post* by Sir Edward Carson.

A week went by. The Prime Minister had not yet come to a decision. Events, as so often before in 1916, were now to compel action.

The first signs of it appeared, not in the Tory but in the Liberal Press. Thus Sir Robert Donald's editorial in the *Daily Chronicle* of 29 November:

> "Unless the Coalition Government shows more grip than it latterly has it seems to us in serious danger of coming to grief, in spite of the absence of an alternative . . . (its) arch defect is inability to make up its mind. It is not so much that it reaches wrong decisions, as that for weeks and even months it fails in crucial matter after crucial matter, to reach any decision at all."

The writer concluded by recommending that for the purpose of waging War, the Cabinet be reduced to four members, who should include the Prime Minister, Lloyd George and Bonar Law, and have the widest powers of action in conjunction with the Admiralty and the General Staff. It looked as though somebody had been talking. The *Westminster Gazette*, Editor, J. A. Spender, came out with a similar leading article the same evening.

In this atmosphere, the next day (Thursday, 30 November), the Tory Cabinet Ministers met—except Balfour, who happened to be ill in bed. To a highly critical meeting, Bonar Law explained the general situation, though he did not mention Carson's name, for Carson was being generally criticized for allowing himself to be made a tool of by Lloyd George. The suspicions of the meeting mounted as the members learned of this mysterious new proposed War Executive Committee—Chairman, Mr. Lloyd George! This was really too much for Lord Hugh Cecil, who thought that it was Bonar Law who had finally ruined the Tory Party by dragging it at the tail of the Footpad of Limehouse. Hostility to Lloyd George was also expressed by Lord Curzon and Austen Chamberlain. The next morning's post brought the Tory Leader an anxious letter from Walter Long, and an angry one from Lord Lansdowne, who wrote: "My dear Bonar, The meeting in your room yesterday left 'a nasty taste in my mouth'."

It seemed that, after all, the Prime Minister was in command of the battle. His own Liberal colleagues in the Cabinet appeared to be with him to a man. To the Liberal Party rank-and-file, Asquith was still their trusted and beloved Prime Minister and Leader. And now the Tory War Lords were marching their hosts into the same camp—with only two exceptions, Bonar Law, the Leader of the Party himself, and Carson, the Leader of the "Party within the Party".

For the conspirators, the news from the front was bad news from both sectors. All appeared darkness, disorder and defeat.

The very hour to launch the counter-attack!

Lloyd George thereupon wrote his challenge to the Prime Minister:

Memo. to Prime Minister. 1 December, 1916.

1. That the War Committee consist of three members—two of whom must be the First Lord of the Admiralty and the Secretary of State for War, who should have in their offices deputies capable of attending to and deciding all departmental business, and a third Minister without portfolio. One of the three to be Chairman.

2. That the War Committee shall have full powers, subject to the supreme control of the Prime Minister, to direct all questions connected with War.

3. The Prime Minister, in his discretion, to have the power to refer any question to the Cabinet.

4. Unless the Cabinet, on reference by the Prime Minister, reverses decision of the War Committee, that decision to be carried out by the Department concerned.

5. The War Committee to have the power to invite any Minister, and to summon the expert advisers and officers of any Department, to its meetings.

The Prime Minister replied the same day:

10 Downing Street, S.W.

1 December, 1916.

"My dear Lloyd George,

I have now had time to reflect on our conversation this morning and to study your memorandum.

Though I do not altogether share your dark estimate and forecast of the situation, actual and prospective, I am in complete agreement that we have reached a critical situation in the war, and that our own methods of procedure, with the experience which we have gained during the last few months, call for reconsideration and revision.

The two main defects of the War Committee, which has done excellent work, are (1) that its numbers are too large; (2) that there is delay, evasion, and often obstruction on the part of the Departments in giving effect to its decisions. I might with good reason add (3) that it is often kept in ignorance by the Departments of information essential and even vital, of a technical kind upon the problems that come before it, and (4) that it is overcharged with duties, many of which might well be delegated to subordinate bodies.

The result is that I am clearly of opinion that the War Committee should be reconstituted, and its relations and authority over the Departments, etc., more clearly defined and more effectively asserted.

I come now to your specific proposals. In my opinion, whatever changes are made in the composition or functions of the War Committee, the Prime Minister must be its Chairman. He cannot be relegated to the position of an arbiter in the background, or a referee to the Cabinet.

In regard to its composition, I agree that the War Committee should be accompanied by the setting up of a Committee of National Organization to deal with the purely domestic side of war problems. It should have executive powers within its own domain.

The Cabinet would in all cases have ultimate authority.

Yours very sincerely,
H. H. Asquith."

By this letter, Asquith disclosed his hand. The proposal in the last paragraph but one had originated with Lord Robert Cecil the previous week, and had been repeated by him at the stormy meeting of the Tory Cabinet Ministers only the day before. It plainly meant, that as far as the present Government were concerned, the Executive War Committee plan of the conspirators was dead. That night, Aitken was dining alone with Bonar Law, when the Tory Leader expressed the view that he must see Lloyd George at once. He had to decide whether or not to take up the challenge NOW, even at the risk of bringing down the Government, and perhaps of shattering his own Party in the process. What would happen then to the country, already in its deepest military crisis of the war? *What would happen if he held his hand?*

Get Lloyd George!

Now Aitken, as he wrote years later, "at that time had the means of finding Lloyd George at any hour of the day or night".

He found his quarry dining at the Berkeley Hotel, beckoned him away from his party, and took him off to the waiting taxi-cab in Piccadilly in which Bonar Law sat. They drove away together. Later, in Aitken's flat at the Hyde Park Hotel, Bonar Law told Lloyd George of the problem that racked his mind and soul. Lloyd George listened quietly. He had set his own course. He said: "You must do as you think best. I will not bring any pressure to bear on you."

Next morning, 2 December, on their front pages, both the *Daily Express* and the *Daily Chronicle* broke the news of the drama in Whitehall. The *Daily Express* told its readers:

"A great political crisis has arisen in the last twenty-four hours."

The big "splash" item was that a proposal for an authoritative War Council had been put forward and that the names were Lloyd George, Bonar Law, Sir Edward Carson. It was Instalment One, in the most sensational story since the death of Kitchener.

Northcliffe's *Daily Mail* missed the story. Lloyd George was avoiding

Northcliffe at this time, not because he nursed any grudge over the General Robertson incident, for Lloyd George rarely indulged in grudges against people who could be useful to him. Northcliffe he considered could not be, at this stage anyway. In fact, Lloyd George reckoned that in present circumstances Northcliffe's support would do him harm with the Liberals. When Aitken had tried recently to bring them together, Lloyd George had said: "I would as soon go for a sunny evening stroll round Walton Heath with a grasshopper, as try to work with Northcliffe."

He had, it is true, consented to see Northcliffe at the War Office on the Friday of this week, but when Northcliffe arrived he did not see Lloyd George himself, but only his secretary. However, Northcliffe rarely let personalities stand in the way of business either. Early on the Saturday morning (the day on which he had been "scooped") he was back at the War Office, where he was observed leaving Lloyd George's secretary's room by Edwin Montagu, who happened to be passing. By noon, Northcliffe's *Evening News* placards along Whitehall flared:

LLOYD GEORGE
PACKING UP

Not quite, yet! As the newspaper boys bawled their news-cries outside his window, Lloyd George was writing a letter to his colleague, Bonar Law, who was going to face and fight his Tory critics once more, tomorrow, Sunday. Lloyd George was sending him the evidence, in writing, of the Prime Minister's own challenge:

War Office,
Whitehall.
2 December, 1916.

"My dear Bonar,
    I enclose copy of the P.M.'s letter.
    The life of the country depends on resolute action by you *now*.

Yours ever,
D. Lloyd George."

On Sunday, Bonar Law summoned a meeting at his home at Pembroke Lodge, in Edwardes Square, Kensington. As the Ministers made their way to the meeting-place, their ears and eyes were assailed by fresh newspaper evidence of the villainy of the Secretary of State for War. This time it was *Reynolds Newspaper*. It announced that:

"Lloyd George will resign if he does not get his way, and will appeal to the country. He is allied with Carson; Bonar Law will probably go with him; Derby too."

Since Sir Henry Dalziel, Liberal M.P. for Kirkcaldy and the proprietor of *Reynolds*, was an old personal friend of Lloyd George, the Tory Ministers immediately assumed that the statement had been authorized by him; they also considered it to be a characteristic breach of faith by Lloyd George in "trafficking with the Press". In fact, Lloyd George had no personal part in it, though Max Aitken, who was at this moment acting as his Traffic Controller with the Press, certainly had, for he had given the news to Dalziel at the house of Neil Primrose.[1] However, this Sunday morning the appearance of the story in *Reynolds* certainly strengthened the Tory magnates in their determination to have done with Lloyd George. At the meeting in his own house that morning, Bonar Law was more alone than on the previous Thursday.

The Tory Ministers resolved that the Government could not continue as it was, and that "the publicity given to the intention of Mr. Lloyd George" made it now impossible to reconstruct it from within. They, therefore, urged the Prime Minister to tender the King the resignation of his Government. If Asquith felt unable to do this, then they then authorized Bonar Law to tender their own resignations.

Their plan and avowed intention was to force Lloyd George's resignation. But Asquith misunderstood the clumsily drafted words to mean that he himself must resign. It was Asquith's crowning error.

He had gone down to Walmer Castle for the week-end, but had been summoned back by Edwin Montagu. He returned to hear Bonar Law deliver that Sunday afternoon what he mistook to be a Tory threat against him. He was even more impressed by the thought of Bonar Law resigning, which would pull the lynch-pin out of the Coalition Government's coach. The effect was to persuade Asquith to begin building his bridges towards Lloyd George. He was delighted when he heard that Lloyd George, answering his telephone call to Walton Heath, had arrived at the War Office.

How did Lloyd George look, and behave in this hard hour? Here is the record of Aitken, present with Lloyd George in Whitehall that December afternoon.

"At last came the expected message and summons from the Prime Minister. Lloyd George took it very coolly. He lit a cigar, and considered impartially the interview which lay before him. I had never seen any man exhibit so much moral courage in the face of such great events. He considered that what he had to avoid was a settlement which was not really a decision. He would not be duped into accepting a position which gave the competent men no final and complete control of the conduct of the war. He must know how he stood in this matter once and for all before he left Downing Street. If this control was refused, events must take their course. He finished his cigar quietly, and left for Downing Street."

When Lloyd George and Asquith met later in the afternoon it was like old Budget League days. Forgotten was this morning's front-page story in

[1] Lord Rosebery's son. Killed in action, 1917

Reynolds News, or yesterday's scoop in the *Daily Express*, or even last week's "Necessary Man" editorial in the *Morning Post*. Instead, the plan of the Civilian General Staff was resurrected in all its brief glory, and its function agreed in general principle, only its personnel being left open. The Prime Minister much preferred to have Arthur Henderson there to Sir Edward Carson.

That evening, the Prime Minister dined with Edwin Montagu who believed that Lloyd George and Asquith had settled their differences. He persuaded Asquith that it would end the crisis if he made the reconciliation plain to everyone by announcing that reconstruction of the Cabinet would take place from within. That night, at 11.45 p.m., the following statement was issued from No. 10 Downing Street:

> "The Prime Minister, with a view to the most active prosecution of the war, has decided to advise His Majesty the King to consent to a reconstruction of the Government."

Its effect, next morning, was instantaneous, extraordinary—and, surely, utterly unpremeditated? For it was to infuriate both the Tories and the Liberal "Old Guard" (and largely for the same reason). The Old Guard was first on parade at No. 10 Downing Street that Monday morning, 4 December, led by McKenna. They declared that the real intention of Lloyd George was, first, to reduce the Premiership to a shadow title, and then to transfer the effective power to himself. "Wrecking before capture," repeated McKenna. Well, you could either accept the fact of that undoubted purpose now, and quit rather than linger on as the pitiable ghost of a Premier until it suited Lloyd George to finish the farce by taking the title himself. Or, you could fight the interloper now. McKenna personally preferred the second course. The Asquithian Old Guard would swear to be true to their old commander. The Prime Minister need have no fear that he could survive the departure of Lloyd George and also, if necessary, Bonar Law. Asquith was almost convinced.

The Tories appeared next. They were represented by Curzon, Cecil and Chamberlain, who explained that they also spoke for Long. They made it plain to Asquith this morning what he had not grasped when Bonar Law had presented him with the Tory resolution the previous afternoon—that their object was to help him to defeat the machinations of Machiavellian Lloyd George. They had insisted on the resignation of the Prime Minister and the entire Government, simply to afford Lloyd George (and Bonar Law, too, if he chose) the chance to form their own Government. They were absolutely certain that he could do no such thing, for Curzon assured Asquith that, apart from Bonar Law, no Tory Minister would serve under Lloyd George. Asquith accepted this assurance.

Mr. Chamberlain has denied that he attended the Monday meeting. He declares that he did not reject the possibility of serving under Lloyd George, or any other Prime Minister who could form a Government to carry on the war. But Lord Crewe's account records that Chamberlain did attend this meeting of Asquith with Tory Ministers on Monday. Crewe also discloses that Curzon made promises to Asquith.

The tonic effect of such a double reaction to his Sunday's midnight communiqué was now to prove disastrous to the Prime Minister's fortunes. Of course (he reasoned), one must have had a blind spot not to see that there was no need to come to terms with such a man as Lloyd George! The fellow had no friends anywhere, and no real appeal to the country, either! Asquith felt compelled to return to the idea, which he had temporarily permitted himself to doubt, of the indispensability of Asquith.

But the agreement with Lloyd George of yesterday afternoon?

Now, it was not possible to invoke the Press of yesterday morning to prove that there had been a breach of confidence of something which had taken place after those Sunday newspapers had been published and sold on the streets. Fortunately, however, *The Times* of today, Monday, would serve.

For it happened that there was an eminently hostile and apparently well-informed editorial there this very morning. It described accurately what was going on. It also ended on a note of sharp criticism as to Asquith's own personal qualifications "to force the pace of a War Council". Actually, this editorial had been written by the Editor, Geoffrey Dawson, after seeing Sir Edward Carson, who thus kept his own "traffic lines" open with *The Times*, as well as the *Morning Post*. Neither the author of the editorial, nor the Chief Proprietor of *The Times*, Northcliffe, had any idea of the significance which would subsequently be attached to it. Asquith chose to regard it as evidence of a personally hostile collusion between Northcliffe and Lloyd George. "Trafficking with the Press" again! Asquith was confirmed in his beliefs because Montagu had seen Northcliffe leaving Lloyd George's Secretary's room at the War Office the previous Saturday morning. So Mr. Asquith sent off the following letter to Lloyd George:

> 10 Downing Street,
> S.W.
> 4 December, 1916.

"My dear Lloyd George,

Such productions as the first leading article in today's *Times*, showing the infinite possibilities for misunderstanding and misrepresentation of such an arrangement as we considered yesterday, make me at least doubtful as to its feasibility. Unless the impression is at once corrected that I am being relegated to the position of an irresponsible spectator of the War, I cannot possibly go on.

The suggested arrangement was to the following effect: The Prime Minister to have supreme and effective control of War policy. The agenda of the War Committee will be submitted to him; its chairman will report to him daily; he can direct it to consider particular topics or proposals; and all its conclusions will be subject to his approval or veto. He can, of course, at his own discretion attend meetings of the Committee.

Yours sincerely,
H. H. Asquith."

Lloyd George replied with another letter. He would have liked to talk, but his secretaries had been trying all morning and all afternoon to reach the Prime Minister by telephone, and they had failed because the Prime Minister's staff claimed that their master was "busy".

War Office,
Whitehall, S.W.
4 December, 1916.

"My dear Prime Minister,
I have not seen *The Times* article. But I hope you will not attach undue importance to these effusions. I have had these misrepresentations to put up with for months. Northcliffe frankly wants a smash. Derby and I do not. Northcliffe would like to make this, and any other rearrangement under your Premiership impossible. Derby and I attach great important to your retaining your present position—effectively. I cannot restrain or, I fear, influence Northcliffe. I fully accept in letter and spirit your summary of the suggested arrangement—subject, of course, to personnel.

Ever sincerely,
D. Lloyd George."

The same afternoon, before Question Time, Bonar Law followed the Prime Minister into his room at the House of Commons. He asked him bluntly whether he meant to stand by his agreement of Sunday afternoon and settle the remaining outstanding question of personnel? Asquith returned evasive answers, and then, seizing the excuse of a question directed to him in the Chamber, he hurried off to the Front Bench. Subsequently, he vanished from the House and made his way to No. 10 Downing Street. Bonar Law, a pertinacious man, followed him across Whitehall, and bearding the Prime Minister in the empty Cabinet Room, repeated his question. Getting no satisfactory reply, he made it plain that if the War Council scheme were dropped again he, Bonar Law, was finished with Mr. Asquith.

That night, a meeting of Liberal Cabinet Ministers (Lloyd George was not present) pledged themselves not to serve in a Bonar Law–Lloyd George Government, if invited. Coupled with the assurances of Tory non-co-operation which he had received that morning from Lord Curzon and others, Asquith felt justified in observing that this would appear to seal the ring against the possibility of any Lloyd George Government. Arthur Henderson, the Labour Leader, who was also present, was shrewd enough to doubt those Tory protestations. He was also honest enough to say that Labour would join a

Lloyd George Government, too, since the terms offered would be such as to bring them in. Asquith still resolved to put the matter to the test.

From that moment, events began to move in an avalanche. Lloyd George, next morning, received from the Prime Minister a long, courteously written letter announcing that the King had given him authority to require the resignation of all his colleagues and form a new Government. Asquith then dealt with the proposed new Committee, and said that the Prime Minister must certainly be its Chairman. As to the personnel, he insisted that the First Lord of the Admiralty be a member and that he be Balfour. He did *not* think that Sir Edward Carson should be included. Finally, he wished it to be known that the Prime Minister alone would select the other members of the new Committee.

To which Lloyd George could only reply: "I place my office without further parley at your disposal."

He also asked for permission to publish the letters and memoranda which he had written urging Action Now, if his motives in resigning should be challenged. Because he fully realized the need for national unity, he proposed to give the Government complete support in the vigorous prosecution of the war: but Unity without Action was nothing but futile carnage, and he could not be responsible for that. "Vigour and vision are the supreme need at this hour."

A short, sharp exchange of correspondence about the propriety of publication then followed, ended by Asquith's announcement:

10 Downing Street,
S.W.
5 December, 1916.

"My dear Lloyd George,
    It may make a difference to you (in reply to your last letter) if I tell you at once that I have tendered my resignation to the King. . . .

Yours very sincerely,
H. H. Asquith."

The next item was the graceful attempted political suicide of Balfour. He had been on a sick-bed ever since the crisis developed and, as he professed, he did not read the Press (but his sixth sense was not impaired). Now, he had written to the Prime Minister to say that since there was to be a New War Council with Lloyd George as its working Chairman and he understood that Lloyd George did not favour him at the Admiralty (at this time Lloyd George certainly did not) he begged leave to retire, for the new system must be given the fairest possible trial. Asquith refused to let him go, but Balfour insisted, while reiterating his cordial good wishes for Lloyd George's success. Asquith appears not to have observed these danger signals, either.

While these literary interchanges were going on Bonar Law was dealing with an incipient officers' mutiny in the Tory ship, by C.C.C. and L.[1] These well-known quarterdeck figures had held a meeting that morning, and there decided (a) to assure once more Asquith that they were standing by him against Lloyd George and (b) to summon Bonar Law to attend what amounted to a drum-head court-martial in Chamberlain's room at the India Office for his part in recent proceedings.

First of all three delegates (C.C.C.) saw Asquith. They reviewed what was already familiar ground, while the Prime Minister refrained from telling them that he had decided to resign. Then Bonar Law interfered with the progress of their Court Martial proceedings by curtly informing the fourth delegate (L.), who came to see him, that he was not attending their meeting at the India Office at four o'clock. He was summoning them to one of his own at the Colonial Office at five o'clock. There, he made it plain that if there was any more trouble he would appeal to the rank-and-file of the Tory Party in the House of Commons, and if need be, in the country. Having thus restored discipline, Bonar Law was content to hear the Tory leaders once more resolve that the Prime Minister should resign forthwith, and that in any case, they themselves would. When Curzon took this resolution round to No. 10 Downing Street, he found that Asquith had already decided to surrender his seals of office.

That evening, 5 December, Bonar Law himself went to the Palace. He had already agreed with Lloyd George that he would put his (Lloyd George's) name forward to the King for the Premiership as the leader most likely to win the war. This was magnanimity rare in public life. It must be added—and the witness, the present Lord Beaverbrook, is with us to testify—that Lloyd George made a comparable reply. He said:

"No. I have not been fighting for the Premiership, but simply to get rid of the Asquith incubus. Give me the Chairmanship of the War Council, and I am perfectly content. I would prefer to serve under you."

It still looked as though neither would have the chance to serve under either. For Asquith was resolved to join no Ministry of Bonar Law's, or Balfour's or Lloyd George's. Nor would any other Liberal of Cabinet timber join Lloyd George—not even Montagu, who was still seeking to be the friend of two men for whom mutual friendship had ended for ever. Montagu has left his sad dilemma on record for the sympathy of all politicians of all time: "Shall I desert a sinking ship to board one that will not float?"

As for the Tories, had not Curzon assured Asquith, and Chamberlain and Cecil reassured him, that nobody of their Party except Bonar Law would ever join Lloyd George?

Straight from the King, charged with the task of forming a Government, Bonar Law drove to see Asquith to invite him to serve under him. He began

[1] Chamberlain, Curzon, Cecil and Long.

bluntly: "When a man has done another a serious injury no good can come from explanations."

To which Asquith answered, sincerely: "I have no feeling of hostility. You have treated me with complete straightforwardness all through."

But Asquith himself refused to serve.

Nor would he budge from this position when, next day, on the suggestion, both of Balfour and Arthur Henderson, an All-Party Conference was held at Buckingham Palace, attended by Asquith, Lloyd George, Bonar Law, Balfour and Henderson. The old Prime Minister said: "I have held the first place for eight years, and now I am asked to take a subordinate one."

As a matter of form, and of courtesy to the King, he agreed to consult his colleagues once again. The answer, as expected, was as before.

It was the last act in the drama which had now lasted the greater part of a month. For Bonar Law returned to Buckingham Palace, and advised the King to send for Lloyd George.

Age 53   That Wednesday night of 6 December, 1916, Lloyd George received His Majesty's Commission to form a Government. In the event, he succeeded, and beyond all men's expectations or his own wildest dreams. He made a Government that brought Britain safely through the greatest gale of her whole history.

But tonight, as he sat in the War Office, alone, by the window that looks into Whitehall, as his secretary closed the door she heard him saying very quietly, "I wonder if I can do it. I wonder if I can do it."

CHAPTER XVIII

MAKING A GOVERNMENT

THERE was enough to do.

The first thing was to put together a Government. The omens were not auspicious, nor the field of candidates for office very full. There were the Three Musketeers themselves—Lloyd George, Bonar Law and Carson. Who else? Ten of the former Liberal Ministers had announced that they would stand by Asquith. According to Curzon, none of the former Tory Ministers (except Bonar Law) would serve under his successor. The attitude of the Labour Party was still undefined and uncertain.

There arose the question of Churchill. Now here was one who was willing, yet was not called. Lord Beaverbrook (as Max Aitken became) has recorded[1] how on the Tuesday night, 5 December, 1916, that Asquith resigned, he was dining with Lloyd George at F. E. Smith's house in Belgravia. Earlier in the evening F.E. and Churchill had been together at a West End Club and when F.E. rang up Lloyd George to remind him of his engagement and mentioned the name of his companion Lloyd George at once suggested that he should be included in the party.

From this, reasonably, Churchill grew hopes that he was about to be included in the new Government. When, after dinner, Lloyd George drove off to meet Bonar Law, fresh from his return after seeing the King, and declining the Premiership in favour of Lloyd George himself, he took Aitken along with him. In the car journey, Lloyd George remarked that in certain Tory quarters the feeling against Churchill being brought back into office was so strong that he was not prepared to risk it. In these quarters, indeed, Bonar Law himself was to be found. He appreciated Churchill's outstanding qualities, but challenged to say whether he would rather have Churchill on his side or against him, Bonar Law had replied: "I would rather have him against me."

Lloyd George asked Aitken to return to the dinner-party and to warn Churchill that it would be impossible to give him any office at present. The opportunity came when Churchill suggested that Aitken himself might reasonably expect to be made Postmaster-General. To which Aitken, who thought that he had the Board of Trade offer already in his own pocket and therefore took a rather lofty line towards Churchill's allocation to him of the Post Office, replied:

[1] *Politicians and the War.* Vol. II. Lord Beaverbrook.

"The new Government will be very well disposed towards you. All your friends will be there. You will have a great field of common action with them."

Something in the speaker's tone, or the very restraint of his words, pulled up Churchill on a sudden. He rose: "Smith!" he said, addressing his host and friend, F.E.,"This man knows. I am NOT to be included in the new Government!" He stalked out of the room and into the street, refusing all entreaty to return. Churchill did not get a job in the Government then or, indeed, for another six months. Nor, as a matter of fact, did Aitken. They were both left out.

Most of the Tory leaders liked Lloyd George no better than they liked Churchill. Why *should* they have nursed any affection for either of them? A possible exception among them was Balfour, who at any rate entertained no hate for either of them. To Balfour, whom indisposition and discretion had combined to keep in bed over the crisis, Lloyd George now addressed himself. He had done his utmost only a few days ago to turn Balfour out of the Admiralty, a fact which we have seen Balfour well knew. Today, Wednesday, 6 December, he was inviting him to join his Government. Politicians understand these things, while they also do not fail to remember them. So Lloyd George sent Bonar Law as his envoy to enlist Balfour. He found the patient sitting in an arm-chair in his bedroom, clad in a dressing-gown. He offered him the post of Foreign Secretary. Balfour stood up. "You hold a pistol to my head?" he cried. "I must accept!"

He brought both immediate and continuing strength to Lloyd George's Government. No more loyal or, indeed, intimate colleague did Lloyd George have. But he did not forget that Admiralty incident, then or ever afterwards. He asked Bonar Law: "Why did Lloyd George want me out of the Admiralty?"

To which Bonar Law replied: "You had better ask Lloyd George that yourself."

Balfour did ask Lloyd George, but only many years later when he was himself lying ill and near to death in his Surrey home. The matter had rested in his heart all that time. Lloyd George could not bring himself to tell the old man that what had been desperately demanded at the Admiralty in those days was fierce energy and swift decision, not the calm, contemplative wisdom which was Balfour's. So he said: "I thought you were needed at the Foreign Office."

When Asquith learned that Balfour had agreed to join the new Government he was stunned. But Balfour had made Asquith no promises to boycott Lloyd George: Curzon had now made ready to repudiate his pledge. The solid front of Non-Co-operation with Lloyd George had been broken; it was about to be rolled up.

In this operation the Asquithian Old Guard alone stood fast, Edwin

Montagu among them possibly because he had been temporarily overtaken by events. He said himself that Lloyd George had tried to tempt him with an offer of the Admiralty, even the Chancellorship of the Exchequer. The best Liberal capture that Lloyd George could secure was of Dr. Christopher Addison, who had been his Parliamentary Secretary at the Ministry of Munitions, and now took over that office himself. Dr. Addison was a worth-while prize, for besides proving himself to be a capable Minister, both in his department and on the Front Bench, he was still a more skilful operator in the lobbies. By the end of Lloyd George's first afternoon as Prime Minister, Addison was able to report to him that 126 Liberal M.P.s, or almost half of the Parliamentary Liberal Party, had pledged their support.

The next objective was to secure the alliance of the Labour Party. So at noon on Thursday, 7 December, Lloyd George invited to the War Office a joint deputation of Labour M.P.s and the Executive of the Labour Party. There are differing accounts as to the Prime Minister's impact upon this gathering. Ramsay MacDonald, who with Philip Snowden and Sidney Webb were bitterly opposed to any kind of war coalition (and, indeed, to the war itself), asked as many awkward questions as they could compose, while Lloyd George answered them as adroitly as they had feared.

> "He was exceedingly amiable, but excessively indefinite. He was like a bit of mercury; when you thought you had caught him on one point he darted off to something else,"

complained Ramsay MacDonald. He personally rated it a poor performance, though he allowed that the majority of the Labour deputation were much impressed. Sidney Webb told his wife, Beatrice, who wrote it down in her diary that evening:

> "Lloyd George was at his worst—evasive in his statement of policy and cynical in his offer of places in the Government. The pro-war Labour Members drank in his sweet words, the pacifists maintained a stony silence ... the waverers asked questions to which Lloyd George gave non-committal answers."[1]

J. H. Thomas, already an outstanding figure in the Trade Union world and who had been against the last Asquith Coalition, considered that "Lloyd George's appeal was splendid, and all should now work for the nation"—whereupon Ramsay MacDonald inquired if he was expecting one of the Government jobs offered? Ernest Bevin, who was making an early appearance on the industrial horizon as a delegate of Ben Tillett's Dock, Wharf, Riverside and General Workers' Union, was sullenly hostile. To Ramsay MacDonald, Lloyd George remarked jokingly that he might have to lock him up, but

[1] *Beatrice Webb's Diaries*, 1912–24. Edited by Margaret Cole.

that he hoped Ramsay would have breakfast with him on the morning that he came out of jail.

What had Lloyd George said to them? He began by warning them that the war was going badly. The fall of Bukarest meant that for the time being our blockade of the enemy was broken. He hated war, abominated it. War was "organized savagery". He sometimes thought, "Am I dreaming? Is it a nightmare? It cannot be fact." But these were questions to ask before you went into a war: once you were in it you had to go grimly through it. Delay in war was as fatal as in illness. An operation which might succeed today was no good six weeks later, or even three days later. So in war. Action, which today might save the life of the country, taken a week later was no good. It was because he thought, rightly or wrongly, that there had been delay, hesitation and vacillation that he had made his proposals of a War Cabinet. He did not believe that any Prime Minister, even if he had the strength of a giant mentally and physically and morally, could possibly undertake the task of running Parliament and running the war. Whoever undertook to run the war must put his whole strength into it, and he must make other arrangements with regard to Parliament. Lloyd George then deplored the failure of the efforts to create "a truly comprehensive national Government of all Parties".

But if one set of politicians had not been able to measure up to the job in hand: "Well, we are a people of 45,000,000 and really, if we cannot produce at least two or three alternative Cabinets we must be what Carlyle once called us, 'a nation of fools'. I don't believe it, and I don't believe it is the opinion of the country."

Lloyd George then made his appeal for the co-operation of Labour. He outlined his plans for mobilizing the entire resources of the nation for battle. Three problems must be dealt with at once—Coal, Shipping, Food. The State must control the mines. As for Shipping, he strongly favoured taking the same kind of action. As for Food, we must produce far more of it at home. Every square foot of our soil must be planted. We must utilize both the giant steam ploughs and tractors and also the spade and fork of every gardener and allotment-holder. Finally, we must ration—or else the rising price of food would do it for us, and far more crudely.

He explained the new machinery of Government which he proposed to set up. There would be a War Cabinet of four Ministers, freed from departmental duties, of whom the representative of Labour, Arthur Henderson, Secretary of the Labour Party, would be one. Asked if that meant that we should have four dictators, Lloyd George retorted:

"What is a Government for except to dictate? If it does not dictate then it is not a Government, and whether it is four or twenty-three the only difference is that four would take less time than twenty-three."

Other intentions were to create a Ministry of Labour to handle the labour problems of both the Board of Trade and Ministry of Munitions; it would have a Labour man as head. There was also to be a Ministry of Pensions, with another Labour head. Lloyd George denied any present intention of introducing industrial conscription. As in the case of the Fighting Services, it would be wisest to exhaust the possibilities of voluntary enrolment first. Asked about the alleged Government fear of prosecuting big newspapers while harassing small ones, Lloyd George answered that he would treat Lord Northcliffe in exactly the same way as he would treat a labourer. Naturally, this remark soon got back to Northcliffe, as Lloyd George intended that it should. That "alliance" had not lasted long.

The Labour deputation retired. They had a much stormier session among themselves, in which Snowden and Bevin found themselves unwilling partners. In the end, by 17 votes to 14 they declared for alliance with the new Government. The same day their verdict was announced, and Arthur Henderson entered the War Cabinet.

There still remained the recalcitrant Tories. That afternoon, Lloyd George approached Walter Long. He promised to support the new Government from the back benches but he declined to accept any office, save in concert with his colleagues, the three C's, Lord Curzon, Lord Robert Cecil and Austen Chamberlain.

Lloyd George took thought, and counsel—with Bonar Law. He argued that unless these men were brought into the Government they would together be strong enough to do it "just as much damage and just as much mischief as Carson single-handed had done the Asquith Government". Bonar Law concurred. Of the Tory trio, Curzon had certainly been the most hostile, both to Lloyd George and to Bonar Law, who suspected him with good reason of seeking to wrest from him the Tory Leadership. Curzon, however, did not lack enemies in the Tory Party. So as Curzon was probably the most vulnerable of the three C's, Lloyd George decided to make him his target for the afternoon. In a secret message to Curzon, Lloyd George invited him to join the War Cabinet.

Curzon immediately accepted. The pistol presented to his head was so menacing that he had no time to consult either Asquith (whom he had convinced no ex-Tory minister would ever join the Lloyd George-Bonar Law Administration), or even his own colleagues, Cecil, Chamberlain and Long. By nightfall, the four of them were gathered in conference at the War Office. Of this meeting, Cyril Asquith[1], the biographer of his father, has observed: "By this time there were not enough pistols to go round."

To the Tory delegation Lloyd George confided the broad terms which he had offered to the Labour Party. He reported that his own Liberal Party following in the House of Commons was still growing. He declared his

[1] Later Lord Asquith of Bishopstone.

readiness if need be to appeal to the country in a General Election. The Conference then reviewed the mechanism and personnel of the War Cabinet. It was agreed that its four permanent members should be the Prime Minister and three others without portfolio, Carson, Curzon and Henderson. As Chancellor of the Exchequer and Leader of the House of Commons, Bonar Law could not attend regularly, though he would have the right to do so and also to be kept fully informed. Other Ministers would be called in as required—so would the Service Heads and any other departmental official deemed useful to consult, not necessarily with their Ministers; Lloyd George had not forgotten how at the time of the Dardanelles these experts had sat "silent and sullen at the War Committee while their chiefs advanced propositions with which they profoundly disagreed".

Three other items Lloyd George conceded as soon as they were broached. (1) No Minister was being committed to Home Rule. (2) He had no intention of removing Field-Marshal Sir Douglas Haig from the post of Commander-in-Chief in France. (3) Nor of inviting "either Mr. W. Churchill or Lord Northcliffe to join the Government".

With this charter C.C.C. and L. professed themselves well satisfied. Only one small doubt remained in Curzon's heart. He suggested to Bonar Law (who, of course, had been present at the Conference) that perhaps it had all better be put in writing, and sent by Bonar Law along to Lloyd George to sign. "Send it yourself!" snapped Bonar.

The adhesion of C.C.C. and L. to the new Coalition was a bitter blow to the Asquithians. Said a leading Liberal:

"Isn't this the last limit in political cynicism—men who have tried to ruin Lloyd George and turn him out of the Government, take office under him the moment it is shown that he has won out in the struggle? The most violent supporters of Asquith against Lloyd George now transfer their allegiance to the victor!"

So the loaves and fishes were divided. A totally unexpected late-comer to the feast was Lord Milner, of South Africa fame. He had been a political opponent of Lloyd George and of all that he stood for from the beginning of the Boer War to the beginning of the Great War. He was an old college mate of Asquith (to whom he was personally even more opposed; a contemporary has described him as "Asquith's lifelong devoted enemy"). So far, in this present struggle, Milner had busied himself without much effect in trying to stimulate more home growing of food. Now overnight[1] he emerged from the shadows to step into the War Cabinet in place of Carson, who as suddenly and inexplicably was relegated to the Admiralty.

There was one young man who might justly feel that he was being rather

[1] He received a summons to attend the first meeting of the War Cabinet an hour before he was notified that he was to be a member of it.

strictly rationed at this repast. This was Sir Max Aitken, M.P. for Ashton-under-Lyne, who had been at the very centre of the web, and by many has been credited with spinning it. He had been promised the Board of Trade. He wanted it because he believed he could bring to bear on the problem of transportation for the armies in France his own experience in the New World. He had duly informed his Tory chairman at Ashton-under-Lyne of his prospects, for at that time Private Members taking office had to re-submit themselves for election to the House of Commons.

Suddenly, on the very day that triumph crowned the banners of the whole War Cabinet campaign, Aitken felt himself the wrong side of the curtain where the drama of politics was still going on. For many days and nights his apartments at the Hyde Park Hotel had been the hub of activity and excitement. Now, a strange silence fell. All afternoon and evening he waited there in quietude and solitude:

"No more calls from politicians—no more agitated interviews. No special messengers arrived with notes. Even the telephone bell ceased to ring. . . . The dark drew down and no one came near me. There was no news of friend or foe."

At last, he jumped up and walked out into the shrouded street. His steps were drawn by an impelling instinct towards Whitehall, to the War Office where Lloyd George was, and where great decisions were still being made. He wanted to go in, but something held him back. . . . Round and round the stone pile of the War Office he tramped, until by chance he bumped into Sir Reginald Brade, the Permanent Secretary, who was making a late departure for home. Casually, Brade told him that Sir Albert Stanley[1] was to be the new President of the Board of Trade. Lady Aitken had already gone off to her husband's constituency to prepare for the by-election which would follow his ministerial appointment. He walked back to his Knightsbridge hotel, glad when he got there of the silence of his room.

It was not quite the close of the episode. A few days later Lloyd George offered him a peerage, saying that there were several Departments which so far had no representation in the House of Lords. Before Aitken had made up his mind, Lord Derby was round to see Bonar Law and protest that there were a number of other Lancashire M.P.s who considered that they had prior claim to be promoted to the Second Chamber. So Aitken sat down and wrote a letter to Lloyd George the same evening declining the recommendation for the peerage. Next morning, Bonar Law asked him to forget what had happened yesterday, and to withdraw his refusal. "I have too often stood in your way," said Bonar Law, "besides, we want your seat at Ashton-under-Lyne for Sir Albert Stanley."

So Lloyd George formed his Government, largely of Tory politicians who

[1] Later Lord Ashfield.

had been brought up to detest him, and of Labour politicians who were inclined to distrust him. Though Arthur Henderson (War Cabinet), John Hodge (Ministry of Labour), George Barnes (Ministry of Pensions) and J. H. Clynes (Parliamentary Secretary to the Ministry of Food) had voted for joining this new Coalition, they all disapproved of the way in which it had been brought about. Then there were the Business men, whom the refusal of the Asquithian Liberals to join his Government, had given Lloyd George the opportunity to enlist: Lord Devonport (his first Food Controller) with whom Lloyd George had not mixed much since he quit the House of Commons five years before; Lord Rhondda, who had an old and unresolved quarrel with him, yet was soon to follow Devonport in his Government as Food Controller at the very crisis of its existence: Lord Cowdray (Air Board) who had no special reason to like him, and soon would have less; Sir Joseph Maclay (Shipping) who had never met him before. Strange, that in the darkest hour of their country's storm these men believed that Lloyd George was the man to be trusted at the helm, and were ready to serve in any crew that he commanded.

Any crew, that is, remember, which did not include "Mr. W. Churchill or Lord Northcliffe". Lloyd George was committed against Churchill by his pledge to the Tory delegation. But meantime, Aitken was busy at work on Bonar Law, trying to persuade him to accept Churchill. To protect his flank against what he feared might endanger the whole position of his new Government, Lloyd George tossed this note to Bonar Law across the Cabinet table.

"Prime Minister.

My dear Bonar,
    I think you ought to know that Asquith told Winston that if he came in he would put him in the Admiralty.

D. L. G."

As for Northcliffe, he had not waited not to be invited to join the Government. He gave it out in good time (and not for the last time) that he did not propose to accept any office.

When Aitken, on Lloyd George's behalf, telephoned him a few days later that the Prime Minister would like to see him at 10 Downing Street Northcliffe returned the curt reply: "Lord Northcliffe sees no advantage in any interview between him and the Prime Minister at the present juncture."

Meantime, on Saturday, 9 December, Lloyd George held his first War Cabinet. He had been Prime Minister two days. Lady Carson that night noted in her *Diary* the report of her husband, who had been called in to attend it: "He says more was done in a few hours than used to be done in a year."

The following Monday the full list of the new Government was announced.

At Criccieth with Megan, 1917

There were 14 Tories, 7 Liberals, 1 Labour man and 3 Independents in the Cabinet. In Asquith's late Cabinet there had been 14 Liberals, 10 Tories and 1 Labour man, a comparison which impelled C. P. Scott, of the *Manchester Guardian*, to protest, and drew from Lloyd George the sharp retort:

"What makes you say this? Half the *acting* (i.e. War) Cabinet is Lib-Lab, the other half Unionist, the President still considering himself to be an infinitely better Liberal and Democrat than four-fifths of the men who now constitute the official Opposition."

Having thus delivered himself Lloyd George gave way to the fever which had been growing upon him throughout these tremendous days of strain, and took to his bed. His relaxation there? To have Wild West stories read to him. When his private secretary, Miss Frances Stevenson, pointed out at the end of the first page, that they might as well skip the rest, for the stories were all the same—the lone rider, the lovely girl, the crafty villain, the misunderstanding of two loving hearts, the vindication, the triumph of the hero and the happy ending——

"No, no! No! Go on!" cried Lloyd George.

Perhaps for Lloyd George, as for Robert Louis Stevenson, to travel hopefully was better than to arrive.

The Head of Britain's new Government had genuine need of a fund of optimism. Quite apart from the peculiar (and to most of the nation, still mysterious) circumstances by which they had come to power and the uncertainty of their support in Parliament and the country, there was no cause for any unbounded confidence in the general situation. On land, indeed, the war was looking dangerously like a deadlock. In the East, military defeat had lost us our early gains in Mesopotamia, almost the whole of Rumania, and thousands of square miles of Russia. In the West, military failure to pierce the enemy front on the Somme and in Artois had cost us the better part of a million casualties with no appreciable change in the shape of the front. At home, the two years' drain upon our man-power and money was beginning to be rivalled by a deadlier one—the drain upon our morale.

At this moment the prospect of Peace raised its ever-attractive, so often deceitful, head.

A year before almost nobody had wanted Peace. All belligerents then still believed that they could win. As for the neutrals, they were divided between their desire to keep their normal peace trade and the temptation to exploit an abnormal war trade. As late as October, 1916, Sir Cecil Spring-Rice, the British Ambassador at Washington, reported: "The publication of a peace rumour is at once followed by a general decline on the Stock Market."

Indeed, so far from being strictly "neutral" the United States by this time had (except for staking the lives of their manhood) as vast a vested interest in this war as any nation that was fighting it. This suited the Allies well—as

L

long as the American supplies were flowing towards them, and not towards the enemy. That they did so was due to one prime cause—the superior strength of the Royal Navy.

For the United States had started off the war with a strong tradition of neutrality in Europe's quarrels. The Monroe Doctrine was a two-edged Sword of Peace. It warned Europeans to keep out of America, and it warned Americans to keep out of Europe.

Britain had begun hostilities cagily enough by leaving cotton off our contraband list lest we should offend the United States. Copper was on the list, and a sharp cry of pain arose at once from the powerful Copper Trust of the United States. The problem was—and again the British Ambassador had aptly put it: "How to find a means of crippling Krupp without ruining the mining States here." (5 October, 1914.)

The danger to ourselves was twofold; the Americans might provide armed convoy for their ships; or worse still, they might totally embargo their supplies to us.

Should they do the first, Britain, and not Germany was likely to be chiefly concerned, since our naval interference with American trade was bound to be far greater than Germany's. As for the second, Germany had alternative sources of supply not easily available to us (she got copper from Scandinavia and when we did finally make cotton a contraband of war she promptly discovered a substitute). The loss of American supplies to us would have been disastrous.

The means of crippling Krupp were found. By March, 1915, we had collared almost the entire export of American copper. By the same means the cotton and the corn wealth of the United States was linked to Britain's cause. For this we must chiefly thank our maligned commercial ancestors; we had the money, and could pay cash.

British sea supremacy, indeed, was now beginning to distribute its vast dividend—and on the sea alone it looked as if a final decision in the war could be obtained. While our patrolling surface craft could afford to arrest and search neutral merchantmen the German submarine had to sink them by gun-fire or torpedo, for they could not take their prizes home to their harbours. Already, by February, 1915, the United States had delivered a strong Note to Germany about it. The sinking of the *Lusitania* in May of the same year brought forth another protest—though President Wilson at the same time in Philadelphia explained that America was "too proud to fight".

The President had to protest again a few months later. Not until April, 1916, when he threatened to break off diplomatic relations with them did the Germans undertake not to sink neutral merchantmen. Even so, the Imperial German Government reserved the right to resume its harsher methods if the U.S. Government should fail to induce Britain to abandon her blockade of Germany. Lloyd George himself has admitted the hard justice of this plan. "If sink-at-sight was barbarous, what was starve-at-long-range?"

Now things had come to a test. By December, 1916, all the embattled nations were strained almost to the limit. All had suffered heavily in the field, and all were feeling the pinch of war at home.

In total casualties, the Allies had certainly so far suffered most. The French Army were short of heavy artillery, the Italians were short of all artillery, and the Russians were short of everything. And on the Home Front everywhere, even in comparatively well-ordered Britain, food shortages, overcrowded housing, and ever-dearer prices set the current mood for talk of Peace.

The Germans were the first to exploit it. The since-published documents of the Imperial Government and the memoirs of Hindenburg and Ludendorff show that at this period the Junkers, who still controlled Germany (and effectively, through the High Command, the Central Powers) had not the slightest intention of making peace—unless, of course, the enemy quit—but that they had a very real intention of talking peace. They did this both to bemuse their own public into believing that it was only the insatiable and satanic enemy who stood between them and a Cease Fire, and also to sow pacifism and defeatism among the war-wearying public of the Allies.

The Great German Peace Offensive was launched early in December, 1916, with a letter from the Imperial Chancellor to the United States Chargé d'Affaires in Berlin. After denying the guilt of Germany in starting the war, it put forward evidence of her "indestructible strength", and expressed her sincere desire to make peace. It added no proposals, though it promised these in due course, and requested the United States Government to transmit its message to the Allies. To make sure that public opinion everywhere should be thoroughly aware of its "peace offer" the German Government took care to release it to the international Press almost as soon as it was made.

On 9 December, 1916, the British Secret Service picked up a message from the United States Chargé d'Affaires saying that what the President desired was some practical co-operation from the German Government in bringing about "a favourable opportunity for early and affirmative action by [the] President aiming at earliest restoration of Peace".

The reply declared that the German Government were "extremely gratified" to learn that they could count upon the President's co-operation in restoring Peace, as he could upon their own.

Both messages were forwarded to Lloyd George from the British Foreign Office on 14 December, so that, aided by the world Press and official advices from the Allied Governments, the Prime Minister had a very good idea of what the German Peace Note would contain long before it was presented. It was plainly a trap. But the War Cabinet agreed that to ignore it would simply be to play Germany's game: much better to make her expose her hand.

This view was expressed by Lloyd George in the House of Commons on 19 December, when he asked rhetorically what were the German proposals, and replied that there were none. To enter into a conference, at Germany's invitation, without any basis would be to put our heads into a noose with the rope in the hands of the enemy.

". . . The mere word that led Belgium to her destruction will not satisfy Europe any more. We all believed it. We all trusted it. It gave way at the first pressure of temptation, and Europe has been plunged into this vortex of blood. We will, therefore, wait until we hear what terms and guarantees the German Government offer other than those, better than those, surer than those, which she so lightly broke. And meanwhile, we shall put our trust in an unbroken Army rather than a broken faith."

This declaration was supported from the Front Opposition Bench by Asquith and his old Liberal Colleagues. No protest was raised from the back bench occupied by Ramsay MacDonald and Philip Snowden, with their pacifist Independent Labour Party group.

Next day, 20 December, President Wilson's own Peace Note was laid on Lloyd George's desk in Downing Street. It disclaimed any association with the letter of Bethmann-Hollweg. The President went on to urge that since all the belligerents professed the same object, i.e. securing small nations as well as themselves against future wars of aggression, let there be an exchange of views on their proposed peace terms.

The Allies replied with a Joint Note to Germany ten days later. They denounced the German peace "offer" as a war manœuvre, designed to stiffen public opinion in the Central Powers, to mislead the Neutrals, and to justify in advance the new U-boat campaign of unlimited savagery. The sham was proved by the fact that the Germans put forward nothing to discuss.

The Allied Joint Reply to the President of the United States required another ten days. It was much longer, and necessarily so, for it was in the nature of a Declaration to the American People—the first effective public statement of the Allied case made up to this date (10 January, 1917). It set forth the list of enemy crimes in Belgium, Serbia, Armenia, the Zeppelin raids and the U-boat sinkings and for good personal measure the shooting of Nurse Cavell[1] and Captain Fryatt.[2] It recited the full Allied terms, which included the restoration and compensation of Belgium, Serbia and Montenegro; the evacuation of the invaded territories of France, Russia and Rumania, also with due reparation; the restitution of Alsace-Lorraine; the liberation of Italians, Slavs, Rumanians, Czechs and Slovaks from their present alien yokes; the expulsion

---

[1] Nurse Edith Cavell, court-martialled and shot by German firing squad in Brussels, 12 October, 1915, for assisting refugees to escape.

[2] Captain Charles Fryatt, skipper of a British merchantman, court-martialled and shot by German firing squad the same evening at Bruges 27 July, 1916, as a *franc-tireur*, for ramming a U-boat. (In fact, Fryatt did not succeed in ramming her.) These two executions, and especially the stoic bearing of the condemned, did more to rouse British anger against the Germans than anything since the sinking of the *Lusitania*.

from Europe of the "murderous" Turks, and the liberation of their subject peoples also. In a covering letter, Balfour, as Foreign Secretary, pointed out that while the defeat of the Central Powers was the primary condition of establishing this kind of Just Peace it was not the only one. The enemy might *make* peace, but would he *keep* it? The fate of Belgium had shown that a scrap of paper was no guarantee. Therefore:

> "Behind International Law, and behind all the Treaty arrangements for preventing or limiting hostilities, some form of international sanction should be devised which would give pause to the hardiest aggressor."

In this last sentence, Balfour thus forecast a "League of Peace", in the only possible way in which it could have worked, with police power. The effect of these documents on American opinion during the critical weeks ahead was profoundly to our benefit.

Perhaps even more decisive was their personal impact upon the President. Up to this time, though as we have noted American "neutrality" was becoming more and more a fiction, in theory the United States Government took no sides in the conflict. Indeed, though Woodrow Wilson had only a month ago been swept back to power in the Presidential election on the slogan: *"HE KEPT YOU OUT OF WAR!"* his pride had been ruffled by the slick way in which the Germans had slipped in ahead of him with a Peace plan. He was still more put out by their delay in replying to his own Note—and correspondingly propitiated by the early reply of the Allies. The third offence of the Germans was when, on 31 January, 1917, they did at last take the trouble to acknowledge the President's communication (in a confidential Note written by Bernstorff, then Ambassador in Washington, to Colonel House, the President's close personal adviser), they put forward claims which plainly showed that their original Note had never been intended as a serious peace offer.

They now demanded that, so far from restoring Alsace-Lorraine to France, the French should yield a further province to Germany (it was rich in ore); the Russians were to concede Germany a more defensible frontier in the East; Germany was to get her colonies back, and some more; Belgium was to be restored, subject to "special guarantee for the safety of Germany", that is, suzerainty; there was also to be compensation for German business losses during the war. The Note concluded with the announcement of coming unrestricted U-boat warfare which "my Government believes . . . will terminate the war very quickly".

If these were "peace terms", then Carthage came off better in her *pourparlers* with Rome. No, the war was on—and in its most ruthless phase. The fighting tribes of Europe were about to grapple again in the bloodiest of all their encounters, and what slaughter could not achieve in the field perhaps hunger would compel in the home.

So Lloyd George had foreseen, and foretold, before ever he took the supreme power. Now he turned to the ploughshare, as well as to the sword.

.   .   .   .   .   .

Before the war, the British Empire owned rather more than half the whole shipping of the world. Even so, about one-third of our trade was borne in foreign ships. When war came, we had not only to carry our goods and food but to ship immense armies overseas, with the guns, transport, munitions, rations and all that armies need. We had not only to do these things for ourselves, but also for our Allies. France had to be allocated a million tons of our shipping for food, coal, ore and munitions, and Italy required half a million tons.

The war at sea was from the outset an odd game of imponderables. In 1914, the two mightiest armadas in the world, the British Grand Fleet and the German High Seas Fleet, had at once retired behind a mine-field into their own harbours, from which they ventured out on not more than two or three occasions throughout the entire war. Each was deterred from attacking the other in main force by the dread of losing in a single encounter that vast, mysterious threat of a "fleet in being". It must be allowed that the result of Churchill's one attempt to "dig the rats of their holes" in the Dogger Bank engagement of 1914, did not encourage a repeat-performance. Yet, at the same time, the Royal Navy did in actual fact command the seas, and within a few months of the opening of hostilities not a single enemy raider rode the waves anywhere in the world.

They got under the waves, though. And it must be accounted an extraordinary piece of luck for us that they took so long to get there in effective force. By the end of 1916 this had happened; in the last four months of that year the U-boats were sinking our merchantmen at the rate of 160,000 tons per month. Since we were only building ships at a third as fast, this was the arithmetic of ruin. From the Admiralty at the same time had come the grim memo about submarine warfare:

"No conclusive answer has as yet been found to this form of warfare; perhaps no conclusive answer ever will be found."

This, when we were losing 160,000 tons of British shipping a month. In the spring of the New Year the deadly toll of the drowned ships would be trebled. Yet at this time we had three thousand destroyers, auxiliary vessels, armed trawlers and motor-boats in home waters and in the Mediterranean chasing the German U-boats. In a twelve months' hunt they had caught seven; a few more were struck by mines or otherwise disabled.

The Germans realized at last that in the U-boat they had got hold of a master-weapon. They no longer believed that they could break through in the West. But if the war could not be won on land, then it must be won at sea. The order went forth to the German shipyards to concentrate all effort upon building U-boats and they reckoned they could average twenty per month. There were already 300 in commission, perhaps a quarter of them at sea.

On 1 February, 1917, the Imperial German Government gave notice that they had ordered their submarine fleet to sink on sight every merchant ship bound for or from Allied ports.

"We will frighten the British flag off the face of the waters and starve the British people until they, who have refused peace, will kneel and plead for it," cried the Kaiser, with better cause than usual for his bombast.

The Germans planned to sink 600,000 tons per month. They reckoned that four months of this would bring Britain to her knees. By the end of February, 1917, the U-boats had sent 310,868 tons of British shipping to the bottom. In March, they increased their score by another 40,000; in April it rose to 526,447[1] tons. If this rate had continued the enemy's calculation must have succeeded and the war would have ended by mid-summer. That it was checked, and that in the end the U-boat was beaten was due primarily to the energy and imagination of one man—Lloyd George. Was he The Man Who Won the War? The slogan of the party hacks of the 1918 Khaki Election has dust upon it now. The harshest judgment of History will not deny that he was the man who taught us how to win the U-boat War.

He won it on the sea, and on the land. Under Lloyd George's dynamic impulse the new Government drove through a six-point programme: (1) Adopting the Convoy System, (2) Arming the merchantmen, (3) Devising new U-boat "killing" methods, (4) Building new ships, (5) Saving precious cargo space, and (6) Growing more food at home. Every point had to be fought through in the teeth of the embattled opposition of ignorance and inertia.

The Admiralty had admitted that they were without an idea. No, they had one; and it was a great help to the Germans. It was that all shipping bound for Britain should approach our shores down one of our funnels pointed on Falmouth, Breshaven, Instrahull, and Kirkwall. These funnels would be patrolled by armed trawlers, destroyers and even cruisers. Woe betide the U-boat that came inside that death-trap! Yes, and woe betide the merchantmen still outside it, for there was another death-trap there! The German submarines did not have to waste time and fuel searching the seas for their prey. The British Admiralty collected it for them at the mouth of the funnel.

But suppose that the funnel stretched right across the Atlantic? That was not possible, for there were not enough warships in the world to guard it. Very well, could not the merchantmen be gathered together in a funnel on the American shore and brought across to the British shore in that travelling funnel? In other words, convoyed?

[1] The total losses of British, Allied and Neutral shipping in this month were 866,610 tons.

The Admirals were aghast. Merchantmen in convoy! Tramp steamers! Why, such fellows would not know how to keep in line! And even if by some (naval) miracle they could be taught to do so, then they would simply present the enemy with a larger target than ever! The Admirals forgot, while paying daily obeisance to the shade of Nelson, that after Nelson had sunk the French Fleet at Trafalgar, the Royal Navy spent the rest of the war against Napoleon successfully convoying British merchantmen.

Lloyd George persisted in his idea. When he pointed out that the big target argument was a very odd one to come from a service which had successfully convoyed all troopships, and which also refused to let a battleship go out of Scapa Flow without an escort of cruisers and destroyers, Admiral Jellicoe, the First Sea Lord, retired behind a sea-net of statistics. It would be utterly impossible to provide escort for the 2,500 merchantmen which weekly entered British ports. The requisite warships did not exist, and could not, by the wildest stretch of imagination be constructed.

Nor, indeed, could these 2,500 merchantmen. The fantastic figure had been reached by adding in every coastal steamer and fishing boat and ferry that tied up in a British harbour in the course of a week.

It was typical of the new methods of Government—the Lloyd George methods—how this truth was dragged forth. The Prime Minister himself one day invaded the Admiralty, and there demanded to see any officers who could produce the figures of weekly traffic in and out of British ports. At once, a real check-up was set on foot. Asquith would not have done that.

The First Sea Lord's ship counting thus proving faulty, he could only reiterate his own original argument that undisciplined merchant skippers could never be induced to keep station, anyway. But by this time Lloyd George had found the answer to this, too. They were already doing it. A naval officer named Commander Henderson was convoying coal-barges across the Channel to Brest, Cherbourg and Havre with armed trawlers. He was doing it successfully, and in fact, in the first three months of 1917, and with 30 trawlers, Henderson convoyed 4,000 ships with the loss of only 9. This evidence provoked a breach in the Admiralty front, Admiral Beatty declaring himself in favour of giving the convoy system a genuine trial in the open seas.

So it was done, and the success of the main experiment of the Gibraltar convoy compelled its general adoption in April, 1917. Between mid-summer, 1917, and the end of the war in November, 1918, more than 17,000 vessels came in convoy to the shores of Britain or left them; only 154 were sunk by all causes, or rather less than 1 per cent.

The arming of our merchantmen with 4-inch guns and the training of the gun-crews was pressed forward at the same time with a new vigour, and so was the development of other anti-U-boat weapons. Within a year of the forming of Lloyd George's Government the number of British merchant ships that were armed had been trebled. The new salvage ship, the new Q ship (it was a floating fort disguised to look like a tramp-steamer), the hydro-phone detector, the depth-charge and many more devices were mobilized against "the gangster of the ocean". The number of that enemy destroyed, too, was trebled. It became a risky thing for a U-boat to show its periscope

But all this was not enough, and for this reason. Convoy involved inevitable delays. The ships had to be assembled, and frequently ten would be ready to sail while two were still loading; they had to follow a devious route; and they had to move at the pace of the slowest member. Certainly, it was better to have the fleet come safely home slowly than to have it sunk. But the later it arrived the better it suited the enemy. The only answer was (a) to build more ships and (b) reduce the pressure on cargo space. To these tasks therefore, Lloyd George turned, even while he was fighting his Battle of the Convoys.

On the day that he became Prime Minister, Lloyd George rang up the Glasgow office of Sir Joseph Maclay, a well-known and well-esteemed Scottish shipowner. Although Lloyd George himself had never set eyes on the man, he was recommended by Bonar Law, who knew him well and held him in regard. Indeed, Bonar Law had been a shareholder in Maclay's shipping business—or rather businesses. For Maclay ran each of his ships as a separate company. He was a man of strong religious feeling, known widely with something more than mockery as "Holy Joe". What few people did know was that Maclay had set up a mission in Marrakesh, Morocco, and endowed it with a Presbyterian Minister and a medical staff entirely at his own expense.

Now, when Lloyd George telephoned him the line was so bad that neither of them could hear the other for more than a word or two, so Lloyd George invited him to come down to London and see him. He took the night express and, next morning at the War Office, met Lloyd George, who offered him the post of Shipping Controller. When the first War Cabinet met on 9 December the Prime Minister informed them that Maclay had accepted the appointment. Pending the setting up of the new Ministry of Shipping on which Lloyd George was determined, Maclay took over the Presidency of the former Shipping Control Committee which Lord Curzon had vacated.

The Ministry itself was constituted on 22 December. But Maclay did not wait for this. The same afternoon that he left Lloyd George and still wondering if he could pull off the gigantic job ahead of him ("I was one of the most miserable men in London," he confessed to Lloyd George later), Maclay called into conference at his hotel two leading shipbuilders and arranged for an immediate meeting of the Shipbuilders' Association. He had grasped at once the dire urgency of building ships faster than the enemy was sinking them.

Grasping the idea at once; that was the strength of Maclay. At a still more desperate crisis of the war, on the blackest day of the great German offensive of March, 1918, when unless we could bring across the Atlantic 120,000 American infantry reinforcements every week, the battle of the

Western Front might well be lost, Lloyd George sent for his Shipping Controller. He asked him:

"Can we do it?"

"When do you want to know, Prime Minister?"

"As soon as possible."

"Very well. I will let you know at six o'clock tonight."

At six o'clock that night Maclay came, and said he could do it. And he did.

The new Ministry of Shipping was regarded by the Admiralty much as the new Ministry of Munitions had been regarded two years before by the War Office.

They experienced the same kind of rude jolts. Within a week, the Shipping Controller had presented them with a programme to build a fleet of 8,000-ton tramp steamers. In astonishment, the Sea Lords agreed, and the matter was sent to the War Cabinet for approval, which was instantly given. A further surprise came for their Lordships when, on Admiral Jellicoe reporting that estimates for merchant shipbuilding did not exceed 408,000 tons for the first six months of 1917, the Shipping Controller reckoned that if the labour and material were available, 1,000,000 tons could be constructed. In the event, Maclay's figure was not reached, partly because when America came into the war in April, 1917, all ships being built in the American yards to Allied order were taken over by the United States Government for their own use. Nevertheless, in 1917 Britain added more than a million tons to her merchant fleet.

The "Action Stations!" signal flashed through Admiralty House when in February the Minister of Shipping, as he had become by then, demanded that the Transport Department of the Admiralty should be transferred to the new Ministry. There was a good reason for the request because, though the Director of Transports was a Naval Officer responsible solely to the Admiralty, his Department regulated the distribution of merchant-shipping, not only for the Admiralty service, but also for the War Office and other Ministries. In the event of any dispute about priorities it was obvious which one would get the verdict, and as the war grew in size such disputes became frequent. The Admirals viewed the idea of surrendering their lien on shipping with no more enthusiasm than the Generals had greeted the suggestion that a civilian Ministry of Munitions should take away the control of their arsenals.

The matter had to be settled in the War Cabinet. The Sea Lords turned up in what was meant to be intimidating force to fight it out. As though it were an infraction of Holy Writ, one of them demanded to know how it could be possible for senior officers of the Admiralty engaged on transport service to take orders from a shipowner? To their dismay, they were told that this was just the way it was going to be. They retired, baffled and angry, from this engagement with these pirate civilians.

In the turmoil of these Whitehall battles there arose another issue. Were vast, vital industries to be nationally controlled—or to be actually nationalized? The majority of the electors were not yet ready to consider the State permanently "taking over" even the coal-mines and the railways, much less shipping. But what the Man in the Street was already saying was that the war-time profits of these industries ought to be limited when fathers of families were being drafted to the trenches on the soldier's "bob a day". Were they wrong?

Sir Joseph Maclay did not think so. At the same time, he powerfully argued that you must give every man an incentive to exert himself, however trifling it be. To fix rates and figures arbitrarily was a mistake, for then there would be care neither of time nor money; far better take the average of pre-war profits over a period of peace and then allow an extra percentage to cover war-time costs, or else simply use the Treasury machinery of the Excess Profits Tax to level things out. The War Cabinet decided on the first of these two courses. It put an abrupt end to the scandal of ship profiteering, and thereby spiked the guns of certain Socialist intellectuals of those days, who were arguing that Peace at Any Price was better than War at the Profiteer's Price.

In all these matters, Lloyd George's was the sure and sensible touch. Of course, he relied upon the advice of the successful business man for whom he ever had a receptive ear. But he weighed their shrewd (and, generally sound) advice against other and more radical counsels. He sought—and often found—a working compromise to which both could subscribe. Why not? Almost everyone in Britain then wanted to win the war. Our people would quarrel among themselves only when it came to deal with the Peace.

Some further drastic action was required to speed up the turn round of ships, to pool railway transport and to deflect our import trade as far as possible towards the United States and Canada in order to save shipping time.

These considerable improvements were not effected without some casualties. Sir Edward Carson was not a success as First Lord of the Admiralty (administration was never his strong point and here he was in the hands of an obstinate staff, with outmoded ideas). Lloyd George, after about six months, transferred him to the War Cabinet, where he served faithfully, although he was bitterly hurt. His place as First Lord of the Admiralty was taken by Sir Eric Geddes.

We have last seen Sir Eric building railways in France behind the British Lines. Field-Marshal Sir Douglas Haig, who thought a lot of him, had made him a temporary Major-General, a sensible way of ensuring that his orders were carried out. When the great new shipbuilding programme of 1917 was launched and a man of decision and drive was required to see it through, Lloyd George resolved to recall Geddes from France and put him in charge of naval construction as an additional Civil Lord of the Admiralty. For this purpose "General" Geddes was granted naval temporary rank and became a Vice-Admiral, too. Finally, it was decided to give him control of mercantile shipbuilding as well, which thus passed officially under Admiralty authority, partly propitiating the Sea Lords for their earlier defeat over the Transport Department. They almost piped "Admiral" Geddes aboard.

But Lloyd George had now made up his mind to replace Admiral Jellicoe as First Sea Lord. Curiously, it was a talk with Field-Marshal Haig in the summer of this year which finally decided him. Haig was seriously alarmed at the depredations of the U-boats and feared, with good reason, "that the war might be lost at sea before he had an opportunity of winning it on land". He professed much admiration for Jellicoe's technical ability but, according to Lloyd George, considered him "much too rigid, narrow and conservative in his views". Since, according to his own *Diary*, the Field-Marshal breakfasted with Lloyd George and Geddes on 26 June, 1917, and they discussed the state of the Admiralty, it is probable that Haig characterized Jellicoe by the harsher name he uses in that *Diary*; it is "numbskull". To Lady Haig, the previous month her husband had confided: "I am afraid Jellicoe does not impress me. Indeed, he strikes me as being an old woman."

So Jellicoe went. Perhaps Lloyd George sometimes regretted afterwards that he had not also sought the Admiral's opinion of the Field-Marshal. It is an irony of History that in the First World War the Prime Minister who led Britain to final victory should have quarrelled with his First Sea Lord because he did not think he was fighting it hard enough, and with his Commander-in-Chief in France because he thought he was fighting it far too hard.

The Home Front had yet to be mobilized, and at the first Lloyd George War Cabinets the plans were laid both to slash imports and to raise home production. We had to save six million tons of cargo space, for that was the calculated total of British, Allied and Neutral shipping which would be lost that year. In the event, more than seven million tons were saved.

The largest single saving was in timber, which before the war made up about one-eighth of our total imports. Nearly twelve million tons of it had been brought into this country in 1913; in 1917 the figure was quartered while our home-felled timber of a million tons had been trebled. Much of the land was stripped of its trees—and they have not been replaced yet. Old, long-abandoned copper, iron, manganese and salt mines were reopened and disused quarries set working again. But it was in the growing of food that the greatest revolution took place. This last had long been talked about—as early as the summer of 1915 Lord Milner's Committee had recommended that Britain should go back to her old agricultural system of the " 'seventies", plough up the fields which had been laid down to grass and put a million more acres under wheat. But almost nothing had been done. Indeed, large tracts had gone out of cultivation.

Hunger drew near. That year the harvest failed in Canada, the United States and the Argentine by nearly one-third. Our own home yield was poor, and vile weather held up the winter sowing. It was time to tell the people the grim truth, and on 19 December, 1916, in the House of Commons, Lloyd George told them. We must produce or die. All must help in this crusade to save our country by making sacrifices of time (digging in your own back garden), of indulgence and of comfort:

". . . There are hundreds of thousands who have given their lives, there are millions who have given up comfortable homes and exchanged them for a daily communion with death; multitudes have given up those whom they love best. Let the nation as a whole place its comforts, its luxuries, its indulgences, its elegances on a national altar consecrated by such sacrifices as these men have made."

In his new Minister of Agriculture, Mr. R. E. Prothero,[1] Lloyd George had a colleague of capacity and character. These qualities brought forth rich results for the nation, and also produced a fine old rumpus or two for himself. Within the first few days of the New Year, 1917, Prothero had provided Lloyd George with a compendious memorandum on food and farm policy, man-power, women land workers, rent restrictions, putting down pheasants and foxes, fertilizers and the offer of Henry Ford to make tractors. Of Ford's plan to set up his own works at Cork, Prothero wrote that he believed Ford could turn out tractors at £50 apiece; ". . . it will revolutionize agriculture. It will also knock the English machine-makers out of trade". If that had to be, well, it would have to be.

A week or two later, By Order in Council, the Government took powers to seize land, stock and farm implements and compel the ploughing up of pastures where they deemed the soil was not being used to best advantage. The "bad farmers" could be dispossessed, and someone else put in charge. A four-fold Farm Policy of War was framed, and on 16 April, 1917, was embodied in the Corn Production Act. The four parts of this famous measure were:

I. Guaranteed prices for wheat, oats and potatoes.

II. A minimum farm wage of 25s. per week, with local Wages Boards to enforce it.

III. Farm Rent Restriction.

IV. Compulsory cultivation. Park lands could be ploughed up, ornamental gardens seeded with potatoes, and if pheasants interfered with any crops whatever (mangold-wurzels included) tenant farmers could shoot them.

No such upheaval had come to the countryside of Britain since the break-up of the Feudal System. While these decrees were being discussed in the War Cabinet, Balfour sat there silent, with a quizzical look on his face, watching

[1] Lord Ernle.

the clock. Presently he said: "As nearly as I can reckon, we have had one revolution every half-hour."

When the Bill was laid before the House of Commons no party declared against it. Opposition was provided by Runciman, whose Free Trade principles were outraged by the bounty on corn and potatoes, by R. D. Holt, whose *laissez faire* soul shrank from any interference with the freedom of the labour market, by Sir Frederick Banbury, who was disgusted by the attack on the divine right of landlords, and by Ramsay MacDonald, who was not in favour of pursuing the war. The Bill passed by a majority of ten to one. That winter and spring of 1917 more than a million extra acres came under the plough, and the energetic Minister of Agriculture made plans to multiply these gains four-fold.

The Food Controller, Lord Devonport, had a harder task and he made a good deal less success of it. He began by appealing to the public to ration themselves voluntarily in bread, meat, sugar and potatoes. He enforced a 30 per cent cut in the brewing of beer, to save barley. Soon, came meatless days and breadless days and in the taverns and hotels the order was "NO TREATING!" Eventually, after Devonport had gone and Lord Rhondda had taken his place, compulsory rationing was brought in.

Mr. Prothero, who wasted no love on either of the Food Controllers, penned the following ode, which he sent to Lloyd George:

> "My Tuesdays are meatless;
> My Wednesdays are wheatless;
> I'm growing more eatless each day.
> My home it is heatless;
> My bed it is sheetless——
> All are gone to the Y.M.C.A.
>
> The bar rooms are treatless;
> My coffee is sweetless;
> Each day I get poorer and wiser.
> My socks are now feetless;
> My trousers are seatless;
> My God! how I do hate the Kaiser."

Murder stalked towards Lloyd George in 1917. When the story was unfolded it seemed so wild that at first the public—like the police before them—could hardly credit it.

There was the Derbyshire school-teacher, Mrs. Wheeldon, and her daughter, Hettie, of the same profession. There, too, was her other daughter, Winnie, and her husband, a young chemist named Alfred George Mason. And they were arrested and charged with hatching a plot to kill the Prime Minister and his Labour colleague, Arthur Henderson, by firing poisoned darts at them! All were convicted, except Hettie Wheeldon, who was found not guilty. Her mother, who was described as the brain behind the murder plot, received ten years' penal servitude, Mason got seven years and his wife five years.

After sentence had been pronounced, Mrs. Pankhurst entered the witness-box. She denied a statement of Mrs. Wheeldon's that the Suffragettes had spent £300 concocting another plot to kill Lloyd George by putting a poisoned nail in the toe of his boot.

The Suffragettes, indeed, had every reason at this moment for keeping Lloyd George alive and well. For, speaking in the House of Commons on the Speaker's Conference, which had just been considering Electoral Reform, the Prime Minister declared that the war had made a tremendous effect upon public opinion about Women's Suffrage. He paid a warm tribute to the work of women in the munition factories while the Zeppelin raids were on. To deny these women a voice in determining their peace-time conditions would be an outrage. The Government proposed to leave this question to be decided by the House of Commons. Amid great cheering Lloyd George ended: "I have not the faintest doubt what the vote of the House of Commons will be."

Two other old opponents of Votes for Women, Liberal Asquith and Diehard Tory Walter Long, announced their conversion to the same cause that afternoon.

Next morning a Women's Deputation waited on Lloyd George. They included women in khaki, women police, women in bus drivers' uniform, nurses, women doctors, dentists, munition workers, oxy-acetylene welders and textile workers. They were introduced by Mrs. Fawcett, veteran leader of the constitutional Suffragists and were accompanied by Mrs. Pankhurst and Mrs. Despard, leaders of the militant Suffragettes. To them Lloyd George repeated his pledge. The long and sometimes savage struggle for women's emancipation was over at last.

In this and other aspects of Electoral Reform the House of Commons was mainly of one mind. Not so about some more recent controversial matters, the Report of the Dardanelles Commission, for instance. It contained some pungent observations on the conduct of that ill-fated campaign and especially on the quarrels of those in charge at the time of the War Office and the Admiralty and the failure of the War Council to settle them.

> "A tragic record of drift, disorganization and ultimate disaster for which the blame in chief must be placed on want of leadership in the head of the Government,"

wrote *The Times* on the morning of the Parliamentary debate.

Personal sorrow came to Lloyd George in deep measure this month, when in March Uncle Lloyd died. He had been ill for many weeks and Lloyd George's wife, Margaret, had gone down to Criccieth to nurse him, sending the busy Prime Minister a letter every day about him, as once Lloyd George had written his daily "boon" to the fine old man who had brought the fatherless child to his hearth half a century ago and been his best friend and counsellor ever since.

On 11 February Uncle Lloyd preached his last in the Chapel by the brook. They were grey days for Britain then, with Russia stumbling out of the war and America not yet entered into it. He took as his text the verse from the 23rd Psalm:

"Yea, though I walk through the valley of the shadow of death I will fear no evil, for thou art with me; thy rod and thy staff they comfort me."

After speaking movingly on the meaning of the Psalm and its message, Uncle Lloyd ended:

". . . I know that there is darkness ahead and that I shall some day lose sight of everyone. It will be necessary to walk along the Valley of the shadow of death. Yes, it is dark, Dark, DARK, too far from this world to get any of its light, and not far enough to see the light of the world to come; but let us not fear, little flock, in that thick black darkness—the Shepherd will come with us through the chasm. His rod and His staff will comfort us."

Some striking new figures appeared upon the British scene during this same month of March. These were the Prime Ministers of the British Empire Dominions. By the end of 1916, these countries together had raised a million men for service. Now, Lloyd George held it was high time that they should raise their voices in the councils of the War Cabinet. On 22 December, the invitations were sent out, asking the Prime Ministers of Australia, New Zealand, Canada, Newfoundland and South Africa, together with representatives of India, and of the Indian Princes, to come to London early in 1917 and there take part, not only in an Imperial War Cabinet but in a series of Imperial War Conferences covering a wide range of problems.

They made a remarkable gathering. The shrewd, sensible Borden, of Canada; the supple, subtle Smuts, of South Africa (Botha himself could not come at once); the bluff, burly Massey, of New Zealand; the majestic, magnificent Maharajah of Bikanir, and so on. Probably the most extraordinary of them all had not yet reached the scene when the first Imperial War Cabinet met on 20 March, 1917, for he had only just returned to Australia after an earlier visit here.

This was the astounding "Billy" Hughes. Son of a Welsh farm-labourer, he had emigrated as a boy to Australia. There he had tried his hand at an unusual variety of trades. In his time, Hughes had been sheep-drover, dock-hand, stage-hand, navvy, prospector, ship's cook, waiter and locksmith;

he had also sold fried fish. He had a tiny figure, a gnome-like face, a large and lurid vocabulary, a bellowing bark ("it'll peel the bark off a gum-tree," he claimed), a weak hearing (it was stronger than he often pretended), a hard head and the heart of a fighting bull. An enemy said of Billy Hughes that "he was too deaf to listen to reason, too loud to be ignored, and too small to hit".

A formidable fellow.

So they found out on the Sydney waterside. There his biting tongue, his demon temper and his real talent for organizing men were employed to build up in turn a wharf labour union, a transport workers' union and a seamen's union. Billy Hughes was a founder member of the Australian Labour Party, and entered the Commonwealth Parliament as one of its outstanding figures.

His patriotism was as violent as his politics. Long before 1914, Hughes was clamouring for Australia to have her own Army and Navy—to beat off any attempted Japanese invasion! During the first part of the war he made it very plain to Asquith that Australia having taken New Guinea from the Germans by force of arms, was not letting go of it after the war. Australia needed that place, too, as a buffer against Japanese invasion!

Not even "Tiger" Clemenceau could get a rise out of the "Little Digger". "I heard that you were a cannibal," he remarked, on meeting him.

"That was a long time ago," snorted Hughes.

It is a fact that Lloyd George got along splendidly with him. "Merlin, with his magic touch," said Billy Hughes of Lloyd George. They had more than one or two things in common.

Both the Imperial War Cabinet and the Imperial War Conference were a real success. More than a dozen sessions of each were held, and the questions discussed there ranged far beyond the current war. It was Massey, of New Zealand, who put forward the resolution to develop the resources of the Empire so energetically as to make its entire population independent of all other countries for its food and raw materials. He proposed an inter-Empire Customs Preference plan, and also a scheme to induce emigrants from Britain to settle in countries within the Empire. It was Borden, of Canada, who warned that a Customs Preference might be difficult. Nobody in Canada, said Borden, wanted a tariff arrangement "that might be felt to be oppressive or unjust by the population of these islands". But, Borden urged, since the British Empire could produce all the food and raw materials that it required—and distribute them effectively, too, if the cost of carrying them could be reduced—what was really needed was a mighty enterprise of cheap transportation within the Empire. "Transportation is quite as important to all the Dominions as Customs Preference," said Borden.

He found a ready listener in Lloyd George. The peril of dear food, Lloyd George reminded these Empire statesmen, had lately arisen in stark horror in Russia. There was a historic background for it in Britain, too. It had obsessed the minds of the working-classes here ever since the Corn Laws, and the memories of the present war might well revive that dread. For his own part, he concurred in Sir Robert Borden's statesmanlike view—it wouldn't do for the prosperity of Canada to be based on the want of the workmen in England.

"I want the working-classes to regard the Empire as something which means not only glory," said Lloyd George, "but solid, material advantage."

He declared that he was all for "Imperial Preference", but that he believed Borden's method of subsidized transport throughout the Empire would offer a more substantial preference than any Customs concession.

"I am all for the old Roman method of binding an Empire together by its roads—in our case by our shipping."

So useful, and hopeful, did these Imperial War Cabinet exchanges seem in 1917 that when Lloyd George proposed that they should be regularized as an annual session of an Imperial Cabinet after the war it was unanimously and enthusiastically endorsed by all the Dominions' representatives. It has yet to be established. "We are partners, not only in a Commonwealth, but in a Crusade," Lloyd George had told them. It has still to be realized. But the heartening effect of the presence in England of these leaders of the Empire countries in the early days of 1917, and of their going among the people, was notable. Reluctantly, in May, Lloyd George saw them depart. They had their own urgent tasks to do at home. General Smuts alone Lloyd George was able to detain.

So Smuts stayed in England and in the War Cabinet until the end of the war. He was kept fully employed. Lloyd George admired Smuts immensely, and his feeling was sincerely reciprocated. But while they understood one another thoroughly, each man retained reservations about the other. They had the same swift appreciation of the inner truth about a situation. Lloyd George arrived there by a sudden Celtic intuition; Smuts by some logical Teutonic alchemy. Lloyd George, we have seen, was moved, if not by rigid principles, by purposes which were rooted in idealism. Was Jan Smuts the idealistic philosopher-statesman that some have supposed? or was it that he thoroughly understood ideals—and idealists? At any rate, Smuts and Lloyd George were politically well suited to one another, and well matched.

There was another issue which was causing Lloyd George even more anxiety at this time. It was whether or not to apply Conscription to Ireland. The Army authorities, including Chief of Imperial General Staff Sir William Robertson, and Commander-in-Chief Sir Douglas Haig, were most strongly pressing for it. They were backed by many leading Tories and by the Ulster Unionist M.P.s. They were as strenuously opposed by the Irish Nationalists and most of the Liberal and Labour M.P.s. Perhaps the most sensible view was that taken by Mr. H. E. Duke, K.C., Chief Secretary for Ireland and embodied in a memorandum written by him on 27 January, 1917, at Lloyd George's request. He summed up the alternative thus:

"With a national settlement in Ireland, Conscription could be applied without grave risks; without such a settlement it could be done, but at a cost of much disturbance and some bloodshed now and intensified animosities henceforward."

In May, Lloyd George made one more effort to settle this eternal triangle problem of England, Ireland, Ulster. He proposed a Convention of all Parties to discuss and submit plans to the Cabinet for the self-government of Ireland within the Empire. There were to be 101 members, representing the Irish Nationalists, Southern Unionists, Ulster Unionists and also Sinn Fein. Four Roman Catholic bishops, the Protestant Primate and Archbishop of Dublin and the Moderator of the Irish Presbyterian Assembly were included. In order to be able to attend, the Irish prisoners of the Easter Rebellion of 1916 were unconditionally released from the jails in England where they had been held. These steps were noted with approval by King George V in his diary, though he also noted:

"I see it is to be announced in the House today, and I have never been asked for my approval. Usual way things are done in present day. I better join the King of Greece in exile."[1]

Headed by Eamonn de Valera, the Irish prisoners and deportees arrived back in Ireland on 18 June, and were given a terrific welcome at Kingstown. A procession was then formed, and set forth for Dublin, where the town went mad with joy. At Cork, the town merely went mad, and a violent riot developed. The windows of the County Jail were smashed, the Sinn Fein Drill Hall—which had been closed and locked up by the military authorities—was broken open and seized and the flag of the Irish Republic planted on the roof. A week or two later de Valera was returned as Sinn Fein M.P. at East Clare by-election, with a majority of nearly 30,000.

The fate of the Convention was that of every other body which had tried to bring peace to Erin since the storm and sack of Drogheda. Sir Horace Plunkett took the chair and Sir Francis Hopwood was appointed Secretary. For seven months they laboured in Trinity College, Dublin. Sir Horace was ever-hopeful, and almost to the very end sent to London "voluminous and optimistic reports". Sir Francis soon felt otherwise. He wrote, 27 October, 1917:

"There must be another episode of blood and tears and sorrow and shame before we can settle this difficult business."

Sadly, so it proved.

[1] See Harold Nicolson, *King George V*, page 311.

Other political problems loomed. Always, of course, there was that difficulty of the Prime Minister being opposed by at least half of his own Party, and depending for his Parliamentary majority on the Party of his traditional enemies. True, he commanded proportionately far more Liberal support in the country than in the House of Commons. But a letter, dated 1 May, 1917, from one of his close political friends, the Rev. J. H. Shakespeare, of the Baptist Union of Great Britain and Ireland, written to Dr. Addison at the Ministry of Munitions, expresses the contemporary opinion of the Free Churches. It speaks of

". . . a state of perplexity or suspicion towards him, especially in the North. It is partly due to the necessary alliance with Carson and Milner, and partly to lack of knowledge and false reports on what really happened when Asquith fell. . . . These strained relations have been getting a little worse lately."

Now came other signals from one who must be regarded at this time as a formidable Liberal privateer. These were offers of counsel or assistance, and the signaller was Winston Churchill. During this summer session he made several interventions in debate which, if not hostile to the Government, were decidedly critical. In July, the Report of the Royal Commission on the Mesopotamia Campaign was published, and Austen Chamberlain, the Secretary of State for India, resigned. He did so because the Government of India had been officially responsible for that desert-bogged adventure, though he personally bore little of the blame. Herein, Chamberlain behaved with that sense of public decorum which ever marked this man of moderate political capacity and of absolute integrity. His departure from the India Office made room for the arrival there of Edwin Montagu in the considerable reconstruction of the Government which took place during that month of July, 1917.

Age 54   Such was the Home Front during the first six months of Lloyd George's régime. Meantime, the whole face of the war had changed. Let us move over to the window of the world.

CHAPTER XIX

AMERICA, RUSSIA AND BRITAIN

It was not all dark outside, though the night had not so far looked blacker. The blackest hour had yet to come.

Two spears of light seemed to stab at the gloom of that grim New Year of 1917. The first of these was the mounting certainty that the Americans were about to join the Allies. The United States, "mighty Republic of the West", was about to come to war at last—the one remaining Great Power still outside it, and in the material potential of battle now by far the strongest. The second gleam was engendered by the sudden fire of moral hope arising out of happenings on the opposite, Eastern side of the world. Revolution—the liberal world believed, Freedom—had come to Russia.

The impact upon the war of these two tremendous events would turn out to be almost equal in power, and totally different in effect. But nobody knew that then.

How did the scene appear to the men in the watch-tower, January, 1917? This is how Lloyd George saw it.

America was marching steadfastly, inexorably towards war that almost none of her hundred million people wanted. No outstanding American statesman, except resolute old "Teddy Roosevelt", was in favour of it. Colonel House has recorded in his Diary that as late as 4 January, 1917, President Woodrow Wilson declared to him: "There will be no war. This country does not intend to become involved in this War."

Two or three weeks later (22 January), the President delivered his famous speech to Congress on the theme of "Peace Without Victory". This was just round the corner, he suggested, and though the people of the United States, as non-belligerents, could have no direct part in making it, yet the liberal ideas which they cherished—a concert of nations, all-round disarmament, democratic government, the self-determination of the peoples (they were the basis of the President's own subsequent "Fourteen Points"), would be the terms of this peace. How this was to be achieved without victory, while Germany was still in possession of her war-time conquests, and the Austro-Hungarian and Ottoman Empires were still in control of their pre-war subject races, does not seem to have struck Mr. Woodrow Wilson.

Ten days later, the "Peace-Without-Victory" plan was destroyed by enemy action. The Imperial German Government announced their "Sink at Sight" policy. This was the contemptuous German answer to President Wilson's Christmastide Peace Note. On 3 February, 1917, the President appeared before Congress, and announced that he had broken off diplomatic relations with Germany. He warned the Germans that if American ships and lives were sacrificed by the U-boats, he would come again to Congress and ask for all powers necessary "for the protection of our seamen and our people".

The same day, the Germans obliged the Allies' dearest hope by sending the American vessel, the *Housatonic*, to the bottom of the sea. For good measure, about a week later, they sank the *Lyman M. Law*. By 26 February, 1917, President Wilson was back in front of Congress, asking for its sanction to arm United States merchantmen.

The U-boats went on steadily sinking American ships. The Germans had objectively and carefully weighed the risk of provoking the last great Neutral to arms by the merciless piracy of their campaign—and had then deliberately and resolutely taken it, reckoning that they could starve Britain into surrender before America could mobilize for action. War was thus already a fact for America, whether it was Declared or Undeclared, and America was still almost totally unprepared for it. This was because, up to the very last hour, the President was unwilling for war. Forced to the decision by events, even as he prepared his fateful speech to Congress, he cried despairingly to his friend, Colonel House: "What *else* can I do? Is there anything else I *can* do?"

On 2 April, 1917, the United States declared war against Germany. "The world must be made safe for democracy," said President Wilson.

The Imperial War Cabinet discussed the mighty event next morning. Lloyd George had made ready for it. The same afternoon, the American Ambassador in London was sounded about the sending of a special British War Mission to the United States. He welcomed the idea, and two days later it was settled that Balfour, the Foreign Secretary, should lead it. His main and immediate business concerned the three priorities of shipping, military manpower and weapons.

1. *Shipping.* It was vital to harness the immense shipbuilding capacity of the United States, in order to win the U-boat war within the next few months.

2. *Military Manpower.* To send at once at least a token division of the United States Regular Army to France; to consider the early dispatch of drafts of recruits to train with British, Canadian or French units; to speed up at home the training and equipment of a really powerful composite force for overseas service in the late summer.

3. *Weapons.* To arm these troops with the same type of rifles and guns as the British Army, and thus save time and trouble in the production both of weapons and ammunition.

The Mission sailed a week later. They were almost overwhelmed by the enthusiasm of their welcome in the United States, and astonished at the ignorance which prevailed there about what was really going on in the war. The Americans could not believe that Britain had already financed her Allies with £1,000,000,000, besides spending more than four times that sum on her own account, and that the war was now costing her "fifty million dollars a day". Nor had the American public the faintest idea of the toll of the British casualties. These facts had to be rammed home, and not only to the public but to the President. He had some very intelligent and knowledgeable advisers round about him, but Woodrow Wilson was supremely capable of hearing the truth and not absorbing it if it did not suit his mood. Sincerely hating the idea of war, he had been thrust into it all unready. He fancied it no better when he was in it but, unlike Lloyd George, he never made up his mind that the best thing was to get through the fearful thing safely as soon as possible. So Woodrow Wilson went to war without a will to war.

Nevertheless, the potential of victory was there in the hands of the Allies at last. The final tug-of-war was on, and the superior strength was with us. We only had to hold fast, to win.

At this point, one of the three strongest members of the Allies' team fell down. The Russian Giant had quit. For a time, his weight would still hang upon the rope (the German divisions would have to stay for some months yet upon the Eastern Front). But his strength would never again haul upon it (those German divisions would not have to fight).

The calamity had long been coming, and—one might suppose—could long have been foreseen. It is just because such things are not foreseen, and their causes dealt with, that Revolution arrives.

Since August, 1914, the Russians had suffered more than six million casualties. The privations of their soldiers had been fearful. Half-fed, ragged, without boots, often without weapons (many a man waited for his comrade to be killed to grab his rifle), it was a miracle that they had fought for two-and-a-half years. Now they had borne enough. Yet, if the Eastern Front should fold up . . . ? Said Lloyd George, of Russia, that desperate winter: "We *must* keep her in, if no longer as a steam-roller, then at least as a stone-wall."

So Lloyd George had strongly and repeatedly urged that a first-class Mission be sent to Russia to find out the needs of our great Eastern Ally, and the means of supplying them. When, in December, 1916, he became Prime Minister of Britain, he was able to insist upon this. In the New Year, 1917, France and Italy were induced to join with Britain in dispatching a joint Allied Mission to Petrograd. The British Section was headed by Lord Milner, and included General Sir Henry Wilson and Mr. Walter Layton.

They arrived at Archangel on 29 January, 1917. They found in North Russia a state of appalling congestion at the ports, and of chaos on the railways. Hundreds of thousands of tons of war stores littered the quays, while the Front languished, and the civil population of the capital starved. Lord Milner was deeply depressed by what he saw.

But, since he spoke no Russian, and Lord Milner was not the kind of man to go into the streets or the taverns or the homes of the people, he did not hear

what the Russians were saying. He returned to England a few weeks later with
no inkling that a revolution was at hand.

On 9 March, 1917, it flamed, with a two-day bread riot in Petrograd.
Ordered on to the streets to quell it, the Imperial Guard joined the mob.
When the Cossacks stuck red favours in their caps, the drums had rolled
farewell for the Romanoff Dynasty. The Russian Democratic Republic was
proclaimed.

First thoughts among the Allies in the West were to welcome it, and
following a resolution of fraternal greetings to the *Duma* (the Russian Parliament) moved in the House of Commons by Bonar Law, the British Prime
Minister sent off a telegram to Prince Lvoff, the new Russian Prime Minister,
in which he declared that the people of Britain and the Empire believed:

". . . that the Revolution whereby the Russian People have placed their
destinies on the sure foundation of freedom is the greatest service which
they have yet made to the cause for which the Allied peoples have been
fighting since August, 1914. It reveals the fundamental truth that this war
is at bottom a struggle for Popular Government as well as for Liberty."

King George V, whose cousin Tsar Nicholas had just been thrust off his
throne, considered that this was a "little strong". Perhaps it was, though as
late as 1934, when he published his *War Memoirs*, Lloyd George affirmed
that he stood by every word of that declaration. To his Secretary, Frances
Stevenson, that grey afternoon in March, 1917, when she handed him the
telegram from the British Ambassador at Petrograd announcing the Russian
Revolution, after a couple of minutes' thoughtful silence Lloyd George said,
"They will be no more use to us in this war."

It is not easy for this generation to understand the surge of generous hope
which the March Revolution in Russia released in a world enchained in the
mud and iron of its third year of carnage. Yes, this really did appear as a light
shining through the murk and smoke of the battlefield. To hundreds of
thousands of men all over the earth it held out the same kind of dazzling
promise of freedom and fellowship as those first delirious, dreamlike days at
the dawn of the French Revolution, more than a century before. Among
Liberal-minded folk in all classes, but more instinctively and more passionately
among the industrial masses, the end of the régime of Secret Police and
Cossacks, the knout and the salt-mine, seemed to beckon humanity along the
path towards a golden future. How could we know then that the OGPU[1]
would inherit, and intensify, the horrible habits of the OCHRANA;[2]
or that the exile of a few thousand political offenders in Siberia would grow
into the monstrous prison camps where millions of men and women toiled
and died as slaves?

[1] OGPU The Soviet Secret Police.
[2] OCHRANA The Tsarist Secret Police.

Mr. H. G. Wells had quickly written to *The Times* (21 April, 1917) urging that the moment had now arrived for us in Britain to rid ourselves of "the ancient trappings of throne and sceptre", and referring to "an alien and uninspiring Court".

Reading which, King George V had snorted to a visitor at Buckingham Palace that morning: "I may be uninspiring, but I'm damned if I'm alien."[1]

In 1917, the leaders of the Labour Parties of the West were naturally anxious to visit Russia, and Lloyd George was ready enough to send there such representative Trade Union stalwarts as Arthur Henderson, Secretary of the British Labour Party (and a member of the War Cabinet), Will Thorn and James O'Grady.

He was not quite so ready, a little later, to provide a passport and passage for Ramsay MacDonald to proceed either to Petrograd to exchange comradely greetings with the "Soviet of Workmen's and Soldiers' Delegates" who were already beginning to challenge the authority of the new Russian Government which was based upon the *Duma*, or to Stockholm to address an International Congress of Socialists who were clamouring for a "People's Peace". But Lloyd George's anxieties about MacDonald were soon set at rest by the action of the Sailors' and Firemen's Union. Since MacDonald had lately associated himself with a Socialist resolution against demanding any compensation from Germany after the war for the families of British seamen drowned in the U-boat campaign, the Sailors' and Firemen's Union flatly refused to carry him to Stockholm. Despite the personal appeals of Ministers, they held firmly to their decision. Ramsay MacDonald remained on the strand.

At this point, the curious interlude occurred which landed Arthur Henderson on the mat. He had just returned from Russia, as Lloyd George said, "with more than a touch of revolutionary malaria".

It was suggested to Henderson that, as Secretary of the British Labour Party, he should accompany the Chairman, John Wardle, and the Treasurer, Ramsay MacDonald, to a meeting in Paris with French and Russian delegates to discuss further the ill-fated Stockholm Conference. Lloyd George himself happened to be in Paris at this time, and Henderson did not notify his other War Cabinet colleagues of his intention. They quickly found out, however, and expressed to the Prime Minister their strong disapproval, especially so did Bonar Law. But Henderson insisted, even to the point of offering his resignation, and went off to Paris arm-in-arm with MacDonald.

When he returned a few days later, Lloyd George tackled him. Apart from his personal regard for Henderson, the Prime Minister did not want to lose such an outstanding Labour figure from his Government, but he was determined to be master in his own house. The interview was terse, and tense. Lloyd George parted with Henderson, promising that he would talk

[1] See Harold Nicolson *King George V*, p. 308.

the matter over with his colleagues. He asked him to come round to the War Cabinet at No. 10 Downing Street that afternoon at 4.30 p.m.

Naturally, the other members of the Cabinet wanted to speak frankly, and it was decided to ask Henderson to wait a little while in Lloyd George's Secretary's room. The "little while" turned out to be the best part of an hour, and all this time Henderson remained halted at the doormat of the Cabinet room. When, at last, he was admitted he was in a really fine old temper. He no longer offered to resign; he challenged the Prime Minister to dismiss him. Lloyd George personally wanted to keep him, and that same evening, when Henderson had to face a very hostile House of Commons, he warmly defended him by justifying the anomaly of his dual position as Member of the War Cabinet and as Secretary of the Labour Party. But a week or so later, when Henderson, knowing that the War Cabinet had set its face against Stockholm and all that it stood for, went down to a Labour Party Conference and there passionately urged that British Socialists should send representatives across the North Sea to the meeting there, Lloyd George resolved to be rid of him. He prepared a letter of remonstrance which no man of spirit would accept, and ordered that for the time being Henderson should not be summoned to Cabinet meetings, nor have Cabinet documents circulated to him. The offending Henderson was to be kept waiting on the mat.

He spared Lloyd George the initiative of requesting his resignation by himself submitting it the next morning.

In this controversy there was much to be said on Henderson's side, or, at any rate, in criticism of Lloyd George's methods. By this time, he was already conscious of his power in the country, becoming difficult when opposed and even dictatorial (though not yet daring to deal with the Service Chiefs as he desired). Lloyd George was never an easy man to work with, or to live with either. As to the operational side of things, he frequently demanded something better than the best, and stormed if he did not get it. As to the social side of his life, while it could hardly be described as "luxurious", Lloyd George simply demanded the best that was going—and not too bad a best, at that.

He could be coldly indifferent to old colleagues who had worked with him loyally and well if they crossed him. Old friends, too. This man with the most compelling personal charm ("he could charm a bird off a bough," said F. E. Smith) had no genius for friendship with men. In politics, perhaps, he remained on personal, intimate terms with only a few—F. E. Smith himself, Churchill, Reading, Beaverbrook, Eric Geddes, H. A. L. Fisher, and Lord Lee. In the sunset of his great life, Lloyd George was left a lonely man. "The friendlessest man I ever knew," said an old Welsh follower of him.

He could be ruthless. His treatment of his fellow-countryman Major David Davies[1] at this time shows it. Here was a wealthy, intelligent and attractive young Welsh squire, who had become a Liberal M.P., and whom

[1] Later Lord Davies of Llandinam.

Lloyd George appointed as his Parliamentary Private Secretary. He had gone with Milner on his Mission to Russia. With another young officer, Major Arthur Lessing, who spoke fluent Russian (David Davies had only a smattering himself) he had mingled with all kinds and classes of people there during his brief visit, and he had come back with a feeling that a volcano was about to erupt. This he had communicated to Lloyd George.

David Davies had begun by amusing Lloyd George. He possessed a rich fund of stories about Wales and Welsh characters, and he could give wonderful imitations of Welsh preachers. One of these was a sermon on the parable of the Ten Virgins, delivered in the tongue of the Druids, and ending with the appeal: "Oh, my brethren! Where would you rather be—with the Five Wise Virgins in the light? Or with the Five Foolish Virgins in the dark?"

David Davies had an instinctive, almost uncanny art of nosing his way into a situation, of scratching away the covering soil, unearthing the quest, then pawing it and probing it, rather like one of his own hounds. He was not wise when he applied his pawing and probing methods to his political master. Nor when he developed the unhappy habit of repeating to Lloyd George all the disagreeable things which he heard people saying about him. He also occasionally attempted to lecture Lloyd George, a thing which only one man on earth had ever been able to do. That was Uncle Lloyd, who had now been gathered to his fathers. David Davies was a good man himself, and he wanted everyone else to be one.

There is a typical David Davies letter, written in December, 1916, the week after Lloyd George had formed his Coalition Government. "This is a lovely Sabbath morning," it begins, "and therefore ideal for heart to heart talk, such as your soul loveth." It goes on to recite that the destinies of the country, the Empire and the world are now entrusted to the recipient of this letter. And then David Davies warns Lloyd George that the war can be won by one force alone—the *moral sense of the nation*. He recalls the high and noble inspiration of August, 1914, says that the nation will judge him and his moral force now by the kind of men he appoints to be his Ministers. This was the strong lead that the country looked for and, frankly, in some instances, they'll be bitterly disappointed, says Davies.

"If there was one man who stands pre-eminently as the negation of the moral sense to which I have alluded that man is Rhondda—you know that better than I do, and the people know it. It makes me weep to think of all the mischief that this gentleman will bring in his train—to you and to your Ministry. I can imagine the jubilation of your enemies—and the disgust of your friends in S. Wales when this appointment is announced. He will sell you whenever he gets the chance—and if it suited his book he would shout for peace tomorrow. Surely it is a gratuitous piece of folly to bring this sinister influence into a ministry which is already composed of so many heterogeneous elements——"

Then David Davies goes on to indicate two or three other "cardinal blunders", such as the omission of J. H. Thomas from the War Cabinet ("Henderson is a dwarf compared to him"), the appointment of Wedgwood Benn as Chief Whip, and the retaining of F. E. Smith. ("He should have been dropped—no one in the House or the Country cares a tinker's curse what he says or does.") He ends his cheery Christmastide letter by saying that Donald MacLean[1] and his Asquithian Liberal friends expect that the new Government will last for not more than three months.

Because David Davies was such a good retriever of gossip from the lobbies and the clubs (especially the National Liberal Club and the Reform Club, where Lloyd George's Liberal enemies as well as his Liberal friends gathered), Lloyd George put up with a lot from him in those early, anxious days of his Coalition Government. And, to be fair, much of what Davies reported was more than mere gossip—and enough false gossip can make a "fact" in Westminster, as in Mayfair or any small town. It reflected much of the current political mood.

By 18 January, 1917, The Candid Friend is conducting his chief along the jungle paths of Fleet Street. He always addressed Lloyd George as "My dear Chief", and signed himself as "Daffyd bob man" ("David Everyman"). Northcliffe, he reports to be "at the moment incensed with G.H.Q. on account of their treatment of Canadian Officers . . . and in the mood to strafe the 'Brasshats' ".

Apparently His Lordship is now backing General Sir Henry Wilson to succeed General Sir William Robertson as C.I.G.S. Then Rothermere is asking what is the good of changing the Government if the Army is going to be run on the same old lines? Are we to have another Somme offensive this year, with all its woeful lack of imagination? Is the War Cabinet going to remodel our Army, and infuse it with fresh hope and vigour? Lord Rothermere trusts so, for he "says that he can work the whole Harmsworth Press for you if it is to be the 'War Cabinet' versus the 'Old Gang'. You know how much reliance to place upon this assurance".

Then David Davies informs the Prime Minister that Field-Marshal Haig: ". . . has been trying to get at the Press—through that little blighter [Philip], Sassoon. As Haig is a vain fellow, he will continue to give trouble through the Press and in other ways, until he is made to feel that he is not the boss, and so long as Robertson remains where he is I don't see how this can be done. . . ."

By June, 1917, Dafydd bob man was offering his Chief some further unsolicited advice about (a) Northcliffe, and a very important Mission that Lloyd George was then proposing to send to the United States under his direction, (b) the Asquithian Liberals, who David Davies asserted were rejoicing at Lloyd George's obvious abandonment of all principles:

[1] Sir Donald Maclean, one of the Asquithian Leaders in Opposition.

"If Northcliffe is to go to U.S.A. as head of the British Mission you will be making a damn bad appointment and you will raise a devil of a storm in the Liberal Party, which is just what you want to avoid just now. Northcliffe is one of the biggest intriguers and most unscrupulous people in this country. It is a gratuitous insult to the Americans to send him there —he will do more harm in a week than Balfour has done good in a month. He is not a business man—in the sense that you want for this job. If you are sending him there to be rid of him, you are making a huge mistake. The restless devil will be back here in less than two months, having in the meantime played hell all round and injured your reputation. Here it will be said that you are afraid of the Harmsworth Press. Rothermere at the War Office; Cecil [Harmsworth] in the Garden City; Northcliffe in New York! . . . We shall soon have a Government of the Harmsworths, through the Harmsworths, and for the Harmsworth Press!

What a joy and delight, what beaming faces there will be at Abingdon Street![1] Worth half a million to their Party funds! My dear Chief, I don't like writing like this. Honestly I only want to save you. You are going straight into the arms of the Tories and the Brasshats—when if you only knew it, you can do what you please with any of them provided you stick to the great principles which have made you what you are and will keep you where you are. If you will *only* have the courage and steadfastness to hang on to them at all cost . . .

Yours always,
Dafydd bob man."

The end of the month also brought the end of this chatty correspondence. What seems to have sent *Dafydd bob man* off on his last Lecture Tour was a War Cabinet decision to release some grain for brewing purposes, and to hold up the long-promised Salonika offensive. Lloyd George himself was certainly reluctant to let go of the barley and anxious to launch the offensive; but the restive British public were clamouring because of the watery quality of their beer ("swipes" they called it), and Haig's forthcoming offensive in Flanders prohibited any new commitment elsewhere. Passchendaele was about to cost us more than a hundred thousand dead. Troubles of all kinds gathered about the Prime Minister's head. David Davies's letters reflected them all, very truthfully, and only too insistently.

23.6.17.

"My dear Chief,
I have seen various people of all colours this week and the impression left on my mind is that the Govnt. stock, and yours in particular, is tumbling down. The Reform [Club] is seething with discontent, and even the Tories are beginning to ask questions. . . .

[1] Asquithian Liberal Headquarters.

It's no good, my dear Chief, you can't go on fooling the people indefinitely. They take you at your word—if you play them false they will send you to Coventry with Winston. They thought you *were* a man of his word, who would not tolerate delay, who would make a clean sweep of incompetents—ministers or soldiers. They thought you *were* out to win the war for the vindication of the principles we are fighting for. Making the fullest allowances for all the tremendous difficulties which have beset your path, have you employed the best means of fulfilling these expectations—have you run the straight course? Have you set your teeth and done what was obviously the right thing—regardless of other considerations? This was the one course which could bring you success and victory in the long run. The moral factor is the only one which counts in the end, and that is why so many brilliant people come to grief. . . .

You can call me anything you like my dear Chief—it's damned unpleasant—but it is the truth.

Yrs.
Dafydd bob man."

An answer came back by early post next morning.

24 June, 1917.

"My dear Davies,

I regret having to tell you that there is a concerted attack to be made upon me for what is called 'sheltering' in a soft job a young officer of military age and fitness. I am told that the attack is associated with the efforts made to reinforce the Army by re-examining medical rejects. It is urged that it is a scandal to force men of doubtful fitness into the fighting line when others whose physical efficiency is beyond question are shirking under powerful protection. I hear that Welsh parents—North and South—are highly indignant and do not scruple to suggest that your wealth is your shield. I know that you are not responsible, but they blame me, and as I know that you are anxious not to add to my difficulties in the terrible task entrusted to me, I am sure you will agree that I am taking the straight course intimating to the Committee set up to re-examine men in the public service that in my judgment you can render better service to your country as a soldier than in your present capacity.

I have put all this quite bluntly to you, as I have always found you preferred plain speaking, however disagreeable. My only apology is for having withheld from you so long rumours which were detrimental to your patriotism and courage, both of which I know to be beyond reproach.

Ever sincerely,
D. Ll. G."

It was an unwarranted reflection, for David Davies had commanded his battalion of the Royal Welsh Fusiliers in France.

The great 1917 "comb-out" for more man-fodder for the next "victorious offensive" on the Western Front was, indeed, in full sweep. And it was causing grave disruption on the Industrial Front of Britain. It was not only that the fit men who had so far avoided Military Service were hardly likely to welcome it now, but that their employers, already desperately short of skilled labour, joined with them in the conspiracy of evasion. Most dire of all, was the demand for Labour on the land. For the great food-production drive now required to save the country from starvation, the gaps in the Farm Front had to be filled up—and most effectively they were—by the new Women's Land Army. Indeed, in World War I the Land Girls were the civilian, woman's counterpart of Kitchener's Army.

In industry, trade union rules and customs were more rigid, and there was a different kind of problem. While the Land Girls had to face (at first) the gales of yokel mockery, the dilutees in the factories and the foundries met with resentment and resistance. Food shortages and food queues—up to 1917 both the Labour Party and the Trade Unions obstinately opposed the idea of compulsory rationing—fed fires of discontent which had been lit by the lurid flash of the Russian Revolution. The Communist Party did not yet exist in Britain, but the old Syndicalist school of Jim Larkin and Tom Mann still did, with their simple doctrine of anarchy: "*Force up wages! Force down hours! Insist on such improved conditions of labour that the capitalist will find it cheaper to retire.*"

Though strikes and lockouts had been prohibited by the Munitions of War Act, 1915 (which set up compulsory arbitration), in 1917, nearly seven hundred industrial disputes lost the nation nearly six million working days. Some of these strikes had to be broken by jailing the strike-leaders.

Perhaps the gravest of them all was settled in a more remarkable way. Trouble flared in the Rhondda Valley when the great comb-out of miners for the Army started. Within a few days, the entire coalfield was at a standstill. In desperation—and as it turned out, in inspiration—Lloyd George turned to General Smuts.

"Go down and talk to them," urged Lloyd George. "Your name is a legend in Wales."

"What shall I say?" asked Smuts.

"I don't know. But remember that *they* can sing!"

He went. At Cardiff they gave him a wonderful welcome, and made him a Doctor of the University. The same day he drove up the valleys. They were lined by sullen strike-mobs. But the mining folk were much interested in General Smuts from South Africa. "I really think they expected to see a black man, and they seemed very much astonished that I was not," he told Lloyd George later.

He came to Tonypandy. It was night. A vast meeting of many thousands of angry miners awaited him in that volcanic place. He said:

"Gentlemen, I come from far away. I do not belong to this country. I have come all this way to do my bit in this war, and I am going to talk to you tonight about this trouble. But I have heard that the Welsh are among the greatest singers in the world and, before I start, I want you first of all to sing to me some of the songs of your people."

Somebody struck up. It was "Land of my Fathers". The whole immense concourse rose, and there, under the stars, they sang. Smuts spoke:

"It is not necessary for me to say much. You know what is happening on the Western Front. You know that your comrades, in their tens of thousands, are risking their lives every hour. You know that the Front is not only in France; it is just as much here. The trenches are in Tonypandy, and I believe that your hearts are stirred by the same spirit as your brothers over there. I am sure that you are going to defend the Land of your Fathers."

He went on through the coalfield valleys, and said the same thing. Long after midnight, he caught the train to London to attend a War Cabinet meeting the next day. When he arrived there, they told him that all the men were back at work.

At that time, this nation had one week's reserve of coal for the Navy.

In Flanders the battle was on. The most fearful slaughter in all the wars ever fought by the British Army. It cost them 400,000 casualties, and at the end of it they had won a salient the size of London's Green Park, a narrower and more dangerous salient than even that at Ypres.

The name of this place and bloody battle of four months was Passchendaele, and to that story of sacrifice, of stoic courage, and of stubborn folly, we now turn.

En route for the Supreme War Council with Marshal Foch and General Sir
Henry Wilson, 1918

CHAPTER XX

MURDER IN THE MUD

WHAT happened on the Western Front in 1917 had been settled in the autumn of 1916, a month before Lloyd George became Prime Minister. This was done at the Conference of Allied Generals at Chantilly on 15 November. The politicians were meeting in Paris at the same time. Lloyd George, as Secretary of State for War, represented Britain.

He had strongly pressed, but in vain, that this political Conference should be held first, before the Generals could commit their countries to fresh military adventures in the West. Lloyd George wanted *all* the Allies to review the War situation together—a theme to which he constantly returned. What was the real united Allied position? And what was the true picture of each separate country, and of every battle-front?

The massive, menacing strength of the enemy lay, even more than in his Central position with its interior lines, in the fact that right from the beginning of the war a single supreme Command, that of the Germans, had directed all his efforts. On the Allied side, the only unifying factor had been the calendar; the Allies agreed, roughly, to launch their respective offensives on about the same date. By the end of 1916, as Lloyd George said, instead of the Central Powers being "encircled in a ring of fire, with Turkey cut off, now the German road to the East lies open from Belgrade to Bagdad".

Yet how vitally important were both Russia and Rumania to the Allies in this "war of attrition" which generals Haig and Robertson and Joffre were always talking about, was shown by the sum which the British Chief of Imperial General Staff worked out to prove that the policy of Continual Hammer Blows to Wear the Enemy Out was bound to win in the end. It went like this:

(1) Allied Forces (excluding Coloured troops)	13,838,000
Enemy Forces	9,120,000
(2) Allied Reserves	8,937,000
Enemy Reserves	3,212,000

On the basis of one-for-one casualties, this is the Book-keeping of Success, provided, of course, that you keep going on. What the C.I.G.S. appears to have overlooked is that of the Allied Forces, the Russians and the Rumanians provided 5,357,000, and of the Allied Reserves, 6,880,000 men. This is the Book-keeping of Disaster—if Russia and Rumania should decide to quit. Surely, argued Lloyd George, it was worthwhile for Britain, France and

Italy to make a concerted effort to provide the arms and equipment which their Eastern Allies were crying out for, even at the cost of a certain slowing-down in the equipment of their own. The date in the ledger is November, 1916. By December, the Rumanians were already beginning to reel out of the battle, and in March, 1917, came the Russian Revolution.

For this World War was one entire battle-front, urged Lloyd George, not half a dozen separate ones. Or even several separate wars, as some leaders seemed disposed to treat it. So, with the apparent deadlock of trench warfare in the West, Lloyd George turned again to the East.

What about the Balkans? There, encamped on a malarial plain beyond Salonika was an Allied Expeditionary Force of 350,000 men. Facing them was a not very well equipped or well disciplined Turkish army. The Greek King Constantine ("Tino") was hostile to the Allies and friendly to his brother-in-law, the Kaiser. But the Greek people were pro-Ally.

As for the armies of the Austro-Hungarian "ramshackle Empire", their Czech and Slovak soldiers were deserting in regiments to the Russians, their fellow-Slavs, marching into their lines, singing and cheering and with their bands playing. A threefold and fully concerted Allied drive on the Car-pathian, Balkan and Italian fronts in the spring of 1917 might drive Austria-Hungary out of the war, argued Lloyd George.

The Chantilly Conference of Generals (British, French and Italian) in November, 1916, had decided otherwise. They undertook instead, to launch joint offensives in the West in the first fortnight in February, 1917. They agreed, however, to set up a permanent organization of the representatives of all Allied Armies to study, prepare and report ideas. At Paris, during the same week, the politicians agreed to establish a Joint Standing Committee of Allied Prime Ministers. Thus far, at any rate, Lloyd George's "One War" idea had progressed by the end of 1916.

The political meeting duly took place at Rome in the first week of the New Year. By this time Lloyd George had come to power as Prime Minister of Britain and General Joffre had been relieved of his post as Commander-in-Chief of the French Army. Now, Lloyd George made one more effort to avoid another Battle of the Somme on the Western Front.

His hopes turned to the Italian Front. There, all the signs indicated that the Austrians themselves were assembling a "mass of manœuvre" for a big attack. Was it not possible to disrupt their plans by a still heavier counter-attack—or even by attacking them first? Hitherto, the Italians had been out-gunned by the enemy. Could not surprise be effected by concentrating an enormous Allied mass of manœuvre? So Lloyd George suggested, urging that in the Julian Alps, and not on the Western Front, was the enemy weakest, and that a sudden violent blow here would at once relieve his present pressure on the Russians and what remained of the Rumanians. Lloyd George proposed to reinforce the Italians with three or four hundred heavy guns. He argued that it would not involve any serious extra drain on our shipping, for they could go by rail.

General Robertson absolutely objected. It was impossible at this stage to postpone the arranged Allied offensives on the Western Front! We could not spare several hundred guns to send to Italy; besides, they would never get there in time. Even if they did, the enemy would take advantage of his interior lines to get more of his own guns there first. For, of course, he would very soon find out about us switching ours, because his planes would spot or his spies report the movement of so many trainloads of artillery and ammunition. So General Robertson said.

(When one remembers the vast network of roads, corduroy tracks and light railways, crowded with troops, trucks and trains, the captive balloons and the patrolling aircraft in the sky behind the Western Front for weeks before the battle of the Somme, it was surely pressing it too far to condemn the transfer of a few hundred guns to Italy because this would lack the important element of surprise? As for that well-worn "interior lines" argument, it was no farther to shift guns from the River Somme to the River Izonzo via France and Italy than it would have been to shift them there from the same place via Germany and Austria.)

Strangely, Lloyd George got very little support for his project and almost no thanks at all for the offer from the Italian Commander-in-Chief, General Cadorna. No doubt, the Italian War Lord had his own plan of victory, and did not want to share the glory with any Ally.

But there was one fine, constructive plan worked out at the Rome Conference which Italy and her Allies would one day bless. By it, on the day of overwhelming disaster after the Battle of Caporetto the following autumn, scores of thousands of men and hundreds of guns were rushed from the Western Front through the Alpine passes to the crumbling Italian line just in time to hold it. This operation would make General Robertson's January time-table look rather old-fashioned.

Meantime, thwarted in his grand design for a three-front attack on Austria-Hungary, Lloyd George eagerly took up a project which appeared to offer, at any rate, the prospect of securing unity of command upon one front. This was the bold plan of General Nivelle who, after making a military reputation by his recapture of Fort Douaumont, one of the outer bastions of Verdun, had succeeded General Joffre as C.-in-C. of the French Army.

Now, Nivelle had evolved the doctrine of the "unlimited offensive". The British were to attack first in their sector of the Front, drawing off the enemy's reserves and diverting his attention, while the French assaulted with sudden and sustained violence, breaking the enemy line and pouring through the gaps with another army held in close reserve to exploit the initial victory. This was a considerable variation of the original Chantilly arrangement, which had assigned the leading role to the British. Now the French took the first

place. The new plan by no means accorded with the ideas of the British
Generals, Robertson and Haig, but it still suited them better than any "back
door offensives" of the Lloyd George "Easterner" school. Sir William and
Sir Douglas were determined to go in from the front, even if they had to
batter down the face of the building.

Lloyd George was not so entirely dissatisfied either. If there had to be
another offensive on the Western Front, he preferred that the initiative should
rest with General Nivelle, rather than with Field-Marshal Haig. He had
taken a great fancy to the dashing new French Commander-in-Chief. For
one thing, he could express himself fluently in English, which could not be said
of either Haig or Robertson. (Nivelle's mother was English.)

The British C.-in-C. would sit for the most part in silence during a conference, unless his own particular Front was being discussed. The British
C.I.G.S. was equally inarticulate, though not equally silent; a series of varied
and expressive growls indicated his current opinions. Lloyd George was also
rather impressed by the shape of General Nivelle's head. He had retained his
youthful belief in phrenology, and developed a middle-aged fancy in his
ability as a phrenologist.

On 8 January, 1917, the morning after the Rome Conference ended,
Northcliffe's *Times* came out with a leading article entitled "The Decisive
Front". It said:

> "It is in the West, where the largest part of the German forces have
> always been posted, where the Germans have accumulated the greatest
> number of guns and the biggest stores of ammunition, and where they
> have lavished in a greater degree than anywhere else all the resources of
> military science in its most modern forms that the main decision must take
> place. It is all important, therefore, that our superiority upon this front
> should steadily increase. The victory of General Nivelle[1] shows that, with
> skilled preparation and good leading, very telling blows may already be
> delivered there at a cost which is comparatively slight. . . . We must run
> no risk by dissipating our forces."

If Robertson or Haig had written this it could not have better expressed
their point of view. There is not much doubt that one or the other of them
said it, and with view to publication, too, in order to bang that Balkan back-
door fast and forever. For though both of these stern professional soldiers
had deprecated any resort to the newspapers by serving officers (such as
Field-Marshal French in 1915, for instance) the C.-in-C., at any rate, was
as careful to maintain contact with the institution of the Press, as he was to
keep up a still closer correspondence with the institution of the Monarchy.

After serving nearly six months as Secretary of State for War, Lloyd
George had already, in the previous autumn, formed his opinion about Haig,

[1] At Fort Douaumont, see above.

and expressed it. That is why, when the Tories were preparing to join his Government in December, 1916, some of them had made the proviso that he should not harbour the intention of dismissing Haig from his command.

What Haig was thinking of Lloyd George that autumn is set forth in his illuminating diary. When Lloyd George, going to visit the C.-in-C. at G.H.Q. just after Lord Northcliffe had left him, Haig wrote of the then War Secretary:

"He is now staying in Amiens, and has a party of nine or ten people with him, French as well as British! He has just been to Verdun, where I suppose the French have stuffed him full of their notions . . . I think he means well, so we must try and put up with his peculiarities.

Lord Northcliffe calls him 'a shirt-sleeved politician' and he told me that Lloyd George does whatever he (Lord N.) advises!"

Two days afterwards, in a letter to his wife, the Field-Marshal confided that he had got on very well indeed with Lloyd George . . .

"and he is anxious to help in every way he can. But he seems to be so flighty —makes plans and is always changing them and his mind. . . .

From what I have written you will gather that I have no great opinion of Lloyd George *as a man or a leader*."

It was rather different from what he wrote in a letter to Lloyd George himself on his return to London:

"The whole Army appreciates to the full the stupendous task that has been accomplished under your able guidance in providing the enormous quantities of munitions of all sorts without which our present successes would be impossible. . . ."

Field-Marshal Haig, like Field Marshal Wilson, might well have wished his reputation would be spared the publication of both of his letters and of his diaries. These frankly tell how, while serving as a Corps commander in the British Expeditionary Force of 1914 under Field-Marshal French, he had begun to criticize and condemn the C.-in-C. even before the troops embarked for France. Thus, on 11 August, 1914, when King George V inspected them at Aldershot, Haig had expressed to him grave doubts as to whether or not French's "temper was sufficiently even, or his military knowledge sufficiently thorough to enable him to discharge properly the very difficult duties which will devolve upon him. . . . The King seemed anxious. . . ."

King George encouraged Haig to write to him, and he did so. On 15 July, 1915, being in London on leave, he lunched at Buckingham Palace. He found the King very critical of French for his dealings with the Press, and especially with Northcliffe. He learned that the King had promised Kitchener that he could count upon his support in any action he proposed to take with French. Wrote Haig in his *Diary*:

". . . The King hoped that I would write to Wigram,[1] and said that no one but he and W. would ever know what I had written."

The same afternoon, Haig had called on Kitchener, then Secretary of State for War, who also invited him to write and express his views, promising likewise to treat his letters as secret. Thus Haig established a second valuable line of communication.

A third one was with General Robertson, then French's Chief of Staff. On 15 October, 1915, Haig records how he informed Robertson that neither himself nor his officers had any further confidence in French, and a week later, when the King visited France, Haig spoke of his C.-in-C's "obstinacy, conceit . . . incapacity". In December, 1915, French was succeeded in his command by Haig.

The illuminating Haig *Diary* also affords an insight into that swift inter-Staff operation whereby Robertson became C.I.G.S. and the powers of the Secretary of State for War, Kitchener, were cut down.

Finally, Haig's *Private Papers* reveal how he made full use of the Press to further his purposes when he had himself become C.-in-C. and was opposing Lloyd George's Military policy. It will be seen that while the Soldiers complained of the Politicians and their "dirty tricks" (and especially of their "trafficking with the Press!") they were no innocents themselves in the art of intrigue.

After the Rome Conference, and the obvious evidence that the High Command were not without their resources or allies in Fleet Street, there came a series of incidents which intensified the hostility already existing between the Prime Minister and the Commander-in-Chief.

Lloyd George has made the grave charge that the unity which he was so ardently seeking to bring about between the British and French military leaders—and which was absolutely imperative for the success of the forthcoming operations on the Western Front, was so violently resisted by Haig and Robertson that the delays destroyed the effectiveness of the plan. When a final inter-Allied Conference was summoned to meet at Calais on 26 February 1917, to complete the arrangements, there were only twelve days left before the date originally fixed for the attack. Meantime, in mid-February, a trench raid by the Germans in Champagne enabled them to capture a field order of the French Second Infantry Division, dated 29 January, and plainly pointing to the great forthcoming offensive on the Aisne. Up to then, the enemy had been much mystified by skilfully planted rumours of an attack elsewhere.

Next comes the interlude of which the Haig–Robertson party have so bitterly complained. At a meeting of the War Cabinet on 24 February, 1917,

[1] One of the King's Secretaries

to which neither the Secretary of State for War, Lord Derby, nor the C.I.G.S., General Robertson, were summoned (indeed, Robertson was informed that there was no particular need for him to attend) an important decision was reached about Unity of Command in the impending Western Front offensive.

Now, in Joffre's time, there had existed a method, workable enough in practice if vague in theory, whereby the French and the British Armies on the Western Front conformed to a general plan of campaign. What was now proposed, was that for the next operation Field-Marshal Haig and the British Forces should come under the direct command of General Nivelle. It was pointed out that a precedent for this had been created during the Dardanelles Campaign when the two French divisional commanders at Gallipoli had been required to obey the orders of the British General, Sir Ian Hamilton. This was true enough, but to place a great British Army of 35 divisions (by far the greatest we had ever raised) under the orders of a foreign general was something else. Remember, Nivelle was not an "Allied Supremo"—Lloyd George would disclaim that idea even a year later—who would be responsible to all the Allied Governments equally. This early Generalissimo was merely the head of a neighbouring army (and he happened to be junior in rank to the British C.-in-C.). Nevertheless, it is plain that from the start of the Nivelle project Lloyd George was proposing to use this temporary subordination of one Allied Army Commander to another to build a bridge towards a permanent Unity of Command.

Hence the importance of that War Cabinet decision of 24 February, 1917. The mystery of it consists in how it could ever have been accepted by Curzon, Milner and Carson. It is possibly explained by the fact that they had not realized what was in the Prime Minister's mind. Lloyd George, of course, was out to clip the wings of Sir Douglas Haig, because he dared not yet openly shoot him down. As to the general proposition, it seemed sensible enough to agree that some One Authority should have the last word as to whether different troops engaged in a joint operation should march together, and where.

So to Calais, with General Robertson, went Lloyd George two days later, the General still knowing nothing of the War Cabinet's decision. There, some time was taken up with an involved discussion about the railway transportation arrangements behind the British lines. Incidentally, for the forward movement and supply of half as many divisions as Nivelle's assaulting force, Haig himself demanded twice as many trains. He did not deem it necessary to inform General Nivelle or the British War Cabinet, that the masses of men and material that he was assembling were required, not for the limited role assigned to him under the Nivelle Plan, but for the far more ambitious design he had been developing for many months, and which would go down to history as Passchendaele.

Towards the end of the first afternoon session at Calais, General Nivelle having expounded his plan of operations, Lloyd George almost casually raised the question of a unified command. "The enemy," he said, "has but a single army. We should secure for ourselves the same advantage. If we do not, we cannot hope for success."

M. Briand, the French Prime Minister, rose and duly blessed this proposition. What did General Nivelle himself think?

Thus prompted, Nivelle declared that unity of command was essential, not only during the forthcoming battle itself but during the preparation for it and also its subsequent exploitation.

The British Prime Minister showed much interest in these observations, and asked the Frenchman to produce a more detailed paper on the question later that evening. The conference then adjourned, and Lloyd George went off for a long walk round Calais with Colonel Sir Maurice Hankey, the Secretary of the War Cabinet.

After dinner, the Unified Command Plan was produced. It not only placed the British Army on the Western Front under the operational command of the French General; their rations, munitions and weapons were also to be handled under his authority. About all that was reserved for the British Commander-in-Chief was the control of personnel and discipline.

The friends of Robertson and Haig have always insisted that this dynamite document had been already drafted at Nivelle's Headquarters, and conditionally agreed by Lloyd George, and though Nivelle himself has denied it the French Official History supports them. It is certain that the two Prime Ministers, Lloyd George and Briand, discussed the idea even before the London meeting of the War Cabinet; the effect of it that night after dinner in Calais was, indeed, that of a bombshell. When he recovered from the blast General Robertson very nearly blew up himself. "Get 'Aig!" he bellowed.

Together, the Soldiers went to the Prime Minister's room.

They had not come to the end of their surprises. When Robertson demanded to know if the War Cabinet had been consulted in this matter, and was informed that they had decided it on the previous Saturday (the day he had not been invited to attend) his temper rose again. Was it lawful to place British troops under command of a Foreigner, who did not hold the King's Commission? To whom would General Nivelle be responsible for the safety of the British Army? To M. Briand? And had the Dominions been taken into confidence?

By this time, Lloyd George was angry, too. He answered harshly that he was determined—and he had the support of his Cabinet colleagues in saying so—that whatever modifications might be necessary, the main fact would stand; the French Commander-in-Chief must take charge of this battle, and must have the authority to move British troops. These were the orders of the British Government. "Have a scheme worked out and be in agreement with the French by eight o'clock tomorrow morning," concluded the Prime Minister.

Then, saying he had a headache, he showed them the door.

Enter at this point the ubiquitous Hankey, Secretary of the War Cabinet.

"Of all Cabinets, of all Prime Ministers equally trusted," said a fellow staff officer,[1] "attending every meeting, where he took down everything in longhand, prepared Minutes and dealt with every conceivable matter with the industry of a Continental housemaid, he was never ruffled, never out of temper. I have often thought in the next world he will certainly be selected to help St. Peter in his arduous duties. He will put difficult questions so as to cause the minimum of embarrassment, and always he will be writing in longhand, in an enormous book."

Now Hankey realized that the French proposals went far beyond anything which the War Cabinet had in mind. His business was to find a formula which would be acceptable both to the Cabinet and to the French. Hankey found one. It was worked out in conjunction with General Sir Frederick Maurice, the Director of Military Operations, who was present. It was that while Field-Marshal Haig should conform to the orders of the French C.-in-C., he should have the right to appeal to the British Government if, in his view, those orders imperilled the safety of his troops. This proviso had been granted to General Gouraud, in charge of the French contingent at the Dardanelles under a British C.-in-C.

It appeared to offer a basis for a reasonable settlement, and for getting on with the business. The urgent need for this was made plain when, next morning, General Maurice reported that the enemy had been withdrawing on the British Front during the night, and it seemed that a general retirement to the newly constructed "Hindenburg Line" was his plan. If so, it might well upset all our own arrangements for an offensive. It was swiftly agreed that instead of Nivelle being placed in a position where he could issue orders to Haig via a British Chief of Staff at French Army G.H.Q., the British Field-Marshal should not come under his command until the battle had actually begun. Meantime, he was allowed: ". . . a free hand to choose the means and methods of utilizing the British troops in the sector of operations allotted by the French C.-in-C."

In return, Haig agreed to "conform" his plans of operation to the general strategical plan of the C.-in-C. of the French Army. It was understood, that if within 15 days the Nivelle Offensive should not succeed, then we should seek to break off battle. A further safeguard offered was that both Haig and Nivelle, each in regard to his own army, should remain judge of when operations should be considered to have terminated. After that, the

[1] Brigadier-General E. L. Spears, C.B., C.B.E., M.C., *Prelude to Victory.*

situation would return to what it had been beforehand. To which the astute Briand proposed an amendment, that "*the British War Cabinet and the French War Committee*" should remain judge of what constituted the end of operations. He shrewdly suspected that the two Governments were likely to get on better together than the two soldiers. It was carried.

This concluded the business, and everybody made haste to get away.

As soon as the Conference was over, Lord Derby registered his protest, on behalf (he wrote) of General Robertson as well as himself, at their exclusion from the War Cabinet deliberations of 24 February.

As for Haig, he wrote at once to King George V that he feared something else was *behind* all this. Frankly, the Field-Marshal feared that he was about to be fired. If so, he besought His Majesty to let him go at once, "for the sake of the Army in France, and the impending offensive".

Haig was still conducting his own protective operation "Buckingham Palace".

He found His Majesty not very satisfied, either, with the course of events. When Lord Stamfordham, on 5 March, 1917, replied to the Field-Marshal, he said that the King himself had not received a report of that War Cabinet meeting of 24 February until 28 February, on the very day that the Calais Conference reached its ultimate decisions. His Majesty was much upset, but he begged Haig not to resign. Lloyd George might go to the country, in which case he would probably come back with a thumping majority.

A week later, on 12 March, the Prime Minister wrote to the King, enclosing him a Summary of the Conclusions reached at the series of Conferences between the British and French Governments. He was careful to point out that while "Sir William Robertson fully approved of General Nivelle's plan, and he had just heard from Sir Douglas Haig that the British Commander-in-Chief in France was also in accord and was ready to do all in his power to facilitate its being carried out", the British Cabinet had refused the French request to take over part of their front without first consulting the British C-in-C.

The King replied the following day:

13 March, 1917.

"Dear Prime Minister,

The King desires me to thank you for having so promptly sent him a full report of the interviews and conversations which took place yesterday between you, Sir D. Haig, Sir W. Robertson, General Nivelle and the other French representatives.

His Majesty is much pleased with the firm frank language which you held; and he trusts that a good understanding has now been established between the two Army commanders.

Yours very truly,
Stamfordham."

In these unblessed circumstances, the great Nivelle Plan to roll up the Western Front went forward. It was as late as 9 April, 1917, when the British diversionary attack was launched against Vimy Ridge. Five days earlier, the enemy had captured a French N.C.O. carrying in his pocket the Order of Battle of all French troops north of the Aisne, and also every Corps objective. It is hard to believe, even now, when the political passions of those days have long been dead, that there was not some treachery in this matter.

The great assault upon the Chemin des Dames started off well enough. The attacking army took about sixty thousand prisoners of war, and close upon a thousand guns. But these were deceptive gains. The enemy carried out a rapid, planned withdrawal to the prepared positions of their new Hindenburg Line. Thus, they evacuated what was, in fact, a very awkward salient and economized a dozen divisions along their shortened front. Meantime, within a couple of weeks, the French casualties had mounted to 120,000.

It started a panic among the French people. Conclaves of "fact-finding" Deputies descended upon the Front, which thereupon became France's Political Lobby No. 1. The offensive petered-out in military disaster and civilian scandal. Mutiny flamed. Entire divisions refused duty, and had to be brought back to military discipline by the most drastic methods, mutineers being shot by lot.

The French Commander-in-Chief, General Nivelle, did not survive the fearful smash of all his plans and promises. M. Briand, who as Prime Minister had sponsored him, had already fallen before these could be put to the test. Now, a new Government of Caution under M. Painlevé had taken over, and were steering the battered ship of France towards a quiet harbour.

With the Nivelle Plan died any early hope of the effective co-ordination of Allied Military Operations in the West. The "bridge" that Lloyd George had hoped would lead him towards his dream of a single Supreme Command had broken beneath him, and very nearly cast him into the ditch. The Haig Plan, however, remained very much alive, and now it was about to make its brief appearance. We have seen it conceived in deception, and here is the end of its tale in tragedy. Haig was responsible for both, and whatever the moralist may say of Lloyd George's manœuvres at Calais, their outcome had nothing of the terrible consequences of Haig's own actions both before that event and afterwards.

To begin with, no mention had ever been made, at the Chantilly, Rome or the Calais Conferences, of a British main attack in Flanders. What *had been* agreed at all places, though in different form, was that the French and British should attack together farther south, in France. It is true that in a letter to Joffre of December, 1916, Robertson had referred to Ostend and Zeebrugge

"with a view to this operation being given a place in the general plan of operations for next year".

Nothing of this was ever communicated either then, or in the first six months of 1917, to the British War Cabinet.

A less suitable area for launching a great infantry attack than the site selected north-east of Ypres did not exist between the English Channel and the Alps. For here was a reclaimed swamp, with an elaborate system of drains and ditches, which was certain to be smashed up by the massive preparatory barrage of gun-fire to cut the enemy wire and shatter the pill-boxes before the assaulting troops could advance. Of course, the Planners proposed to break-through in 48 hours, long before the drains could go wrong, or the water seep up into the soil again and make it slime. It was only after they had been going for 48 days and nights, and had not reached their first objective that the operation became, in G.H.Q. jargon, one of "attrition". •

Field-Marshal Haig did not unfold his plans to the War Cabinet until June, 1917, though both he and the C.I.G.S., General Robertson, had long been labouring on it. He then laid his maps upon the table in No. 10 Downing Street, explained how the German front would be broken, and described how the massed cavalry would pour through the gaps, and ride on till they came in sight of the North Sea. Passchendaele Ridge was the first objective; Ostend the second; Bruges the third. Lloyd George himself has vividly painted the picture of the Field-Marshal, bending over his maps, and fighting his battles before he came to them: ". . . the right hand brushing along the surface irresistibly, and then came the left, his outer finger ultimately touching the German frontier with the nail across . . . Mr. Bonar Law, Milner and I remained sceptical."

Haig did not tell the War Cabinet that both the new French C.-in-C., Pétain, who had succeeded Nivelle, and his chief of Staff, Foch, were opposed to his plan. He gave the opposite impression of their views. Yet, when Haig had gone to see Pétain the previous month (11 May, 1917) and propounded his plan to him, Pétain had told him plainly that he was not only opposed to this particular plan. He was against all such widespread offensives, and favoured only attacks upon narrow fronts and with great depth. As for Foch, he called Passchendaele "a duck's march".

The French Generals, of course, were nursing their Army very gingerly after the mutinies. The British C.-in-C. concealed from the War Cabinet the gravity of this situation, too. Later apologists of Passchendaele have pretended that Haig launched his battle to take the menacing enemy pressure off the shaky French front. The French Generals never asked for anything of the kind; all they wanted was for the British to take over more of the Allied line. For the rest, their policy now was to hold fast, and hold on for the arrival of the Americans.

Ah! But could Britain hold on? The last plea for Haig is that the Admiralty had warned that we could not survive 1917, through sheer lack of shipping, unless Ostend and Zeebrugge were cleared of U-boats. In the event, the Germans were still in occupation of both ports in 1918.

Enter the G.H.Q. arithmeticians. They now mathematically proved (1) that our standing strength on the Western Front was double that of the enemy. (2) That he would be at the end of his available manpower within six months, and (3) that our reserves would five times over replace the 30,000 casualties to be expected in our drive to the North Sea. Fortified with what Lloyd George calls this "joyous arithmetic of the optimistic Charteris" (he was Haig's Chief of Intelligence), the British C.-in-C. made his final undertaking to the War Cabinet. He said he had no intention of entering upon "a tremendous offensive involving heavy losses". Doubtfully, and despondently, the Prime Minister gave him permission to proceed. It was Lloyd George's biggest blunder of the war.

As for the General Staff, better far if they had been guided by the Meteorologists. *They* knew, that for the past 80 years the Flanders weather had broken in early August, with the regularity of the Indian monsoon. Then, for the next three months, the rains pelted. But no rain could damp nor quench the fire of the Great Offensive Idea which Haig had been burning with ever since the autumn of 1916.

So, at 4.15 a.m. on the morning of 31 July, 1917 (as the C.-in-C's Diary tells us):

"The heavy firing (of the opening barrage) woke me up. The whole ground was shaking with the terrific bombardment. During the night, the Fifth Army was to discharge 80,000 gas shells!"

The last entry on that D-Day is more significant:

"Heavy rain fell this afternoon, and aeroplane observation was impossible. The going also became very bad and the ground was much cut up."

Next day was worse:

"*Wednesday*, 1 *August*. Glass fell a tenth after midnight. Heavy rain began to fall about 3 a.m., and continued all day.

(Later) "A terrible day of rain. The ground is like a bog in this lowlying country. The light railways and roads are steadily being pushed forward. Still, in view of this terrible wet, I judge that we are fortunate not to have advanced to the extreme "Red Line" (i.e. the first objective), because it would not have been possible to supply our guns with ammunition."

Surely, remarkable reflections by the C.-in-C. on the second evening of his all-out offensive advance to the shores of the North Sea. Why was there such an item in a Plan of Operations as rain?

It went on raining.

By mid-August, General Gough, commanding the Fifth Army, was advising Haig that it was almost impossible to go on. The guns were sunk in the mud up to their axles, and men up to their knees.

"Attack!" ordered Field-Marshal Haig.

And Gough once more attacked, with more heavy losses. The graveyard of Gough's maligned Fifth Army was not at Amiens in 1918; it was at Passchendaele in 1917.

So, to the yellow, slimy swamp of Passchendaele trudged a million British soldiers. The roads across it were early smashed to rubble by the bombardment (24 million shells were poured there in a month) and buried beneath the oozing tide. Burdened with 60 lb. of "fighting kit" (water-bottles, haversacks, rolled greatcoats and blankets), sodden to the skin, holding their rifles high above their heads to keep the mud clear of the magazines, stumbling in file along the slippery corduroy tracks, every one of which was ranged by the enemy's field-batteries, mortars and machine-guns, and periodically scythed by his low-flying aircraft, the fine flower of the greatest army that Britain ever raised went resolutely up to death and mutilation and suffocation in the mud.

A mile a month they advanced, knee-deep, neck-deep in it, for four months. In September, the weather got suddenly better, but by then the ground every day got steadily worse. We took few prisoners ("we are killing the enemy not capturing him", claimed the communiqués). The truth was that we were not getting at him. With the enemy casualties, the joyous arithmeticians of General Charteris's Intelligence Staff showed an imaginative generosity (for August and September, they allowed them 255,000; German Army records prove that for August, September, October, November and December they only totalled 270,000). With our own casualties, the same firm of accountants, who should have known the real figures, informed the War Cabinet that our casualties for August and September were 148,470. They were nearly double. As for the campaign in general: "All going well," said the communiqués.

The newspapers gave inadvertent aid to the deception.

(In the First World War, few ordinary War Correspondents were permitted to go within range, much less sight, of the fighting.) Thus *The Times* wrote this version in October of the battle of Passchendaele:

"The particular task which Sir Douglas Haig set his armies has been very nearly accomplished. . . . The German defence system has been broken."

In the end, they advanced rather more than one mile. It cost the British Army 400,000 losses from their fighting strength, and while it was all going on the enemy detached ten divisions from the Western Front, and switched them to the Alpine Front where, at Caporetto, the Austro-German forces very nearly drove the Italians out of the war. So much for the "break through", and so much for the policy of "attrition".

Yet all the time, Haig held a master-weapon in his hand—the equivalent on land to the U-boat at sea. This was the Tank, the cavalry arm of the Mechanized Age. At Passchendaele, fortunately, Haig had not been able to employ them, because tanks will not float. So the ardent military "revolutionists", whose imagination and energy had created the new Royal Tank Corps, were now offered the opportunity of something very much like a private field-day of their own. Joyfully, they seized it.

On 20 November, 1917, at Cambrai nearly 400 British tanks advanced against the Hindenburg Line. They smashed straight through a five-mile deep defence zone, and between dawn and dusk, captured nearly ten thousand prisoners and a hundred guns. It was the pre-birth of the *blitzkrieg*. But the very triumph of the tanks converted victory into defeat, for the infantry reserves were held too far back, and not a single platoon was available to support and exploit this real break-through. The British tanks had to wait for nearly another year for their chance to shatter the German Front.

Meantime, the German High Command did not wait a week to close their own present wound. They launched an immediate counter-attack against the confused victors of Cambrai, and within ten days the Germans had recovered, totally, as much ground as they had lost. It created a difficult situation for Haig in more ways than one. For, when the first news of Cambrai had come through to London, the church bells of the capital were set ringing. What was to be the Order of the Day now that the later news of Cambrai had come through? The Generals were silent on this occasion, as the bells.

Indeed, the Generals had suppressed the news—even to the War Cabinet —at any rate, for several days. It could not be done much longer, because when the next war maps were published in the newspapers the painful fact would be apparent that we had actually lost a certain amount of ground. When the truth began to seep out, the Prime Minister at once demanded an explanation. The best that Lord Derby, the Secretary of State for War, could supply was that: ". . . the Field-Marshal Commanding-in-Chief was probably himself ignorant of the causes of this reverse."

Why hadn't Lloyd George called a halt to the butcher battle of Passchendaele? For long, it is true, the official communiqués had been hailing a great victory (and were aided in it by those famous War Correspondents' dispatches date-lined "On the Western Front", and meaning at G.H.Q., a long way behind the Front). But a Prime Minister, and especially a Prime Minister with the energy, judgment and sixth sense of Lloyd George, must have seen through that smoke-screen at the end of a few days. The answer is that Passchendaele could not have been stopped without dismissing the C.-in-C., Field-Marshal Haig, and Lloyd George himself has frankly admitted it.

Then why didn't Lloyd George dismiss Haig? He has explained that, too. The C.I.G.S., General Robertson, would certainly have resigned as well. If both had disappeared without a public fuss, it might have been done. But, Lloyd George claims, he could never have done it without the assent of the War Cabinet. He says:

"I sounded the members of the Cabinet individually on the subject, and also spoke to some of the Dominion representatives. They—or most of them—were under the spell of the synthetic victories distilled at G.H.Q. Nowhere was there a more ecstatic belief in these imaginary victories than at the chateau and village where the Field-Marshal and his staff were quartered.

I visited General Headquarters myself some time about the end of September. I found there an atmosphere of unmistakable exaltation. It was not put on. Haig was not an actor. He was radiant. He was quiet, there was no swagger. . . ."

They believed in their own communiqués at British G.H.Q. Is it surprising that politicians who wanted to do so just as strongly, for their own reasons, should have believed in the fairy stories, too? Not only the Tories, now, in the Coalition Government, who had made it a condition of their support of Lloyd George in December, 1916, that Haig should be retained as C. in-C. But also the Liberals, now in Opposition, under Asquith, who himself had always, and only too faithfully, backed the Service Chiefs when he had been in office. What trouble these various political elements could have made for the Prime Minister of a hybrid Government!

Lloyd George poured out his troubles to Sir Robert Borden, the Canadian Prime Minister one Sunday morning in July, 1918, as they tramped together from Danny Park to the Roman Camp on the hill. For eight months past, said Lloyd George, he had been "boiling with rage" against the High Command for these "constant mistakes, their failure to fulfil expectations and the unnecessary losses which their lack of foresight had occasioned". When Borden asked him why he had not got rid of those responsible during the previous autumn, Lloyd George replied that he had tried to do so but did not succeed in carrying the Cabinet.

"The High Command had their affiliations and roots everywhere," he explained, and added that it was to strengthen his own hand in dealing with the situation that he had summoned the Dominion Ministers to the Imperial War Cabinet.[1]

The Imperial War Cabinet did bring him reinforcement, increasingly so, and it is possible that by the end of 1917 he might have reshaped the High Command and, if challenged, taken the risk of a General Election. Looking back, Lloyd George often thought of this himself.

[1] Robert Laird Borden. His *Memoirs*. 2 vols.

"It is said that I ought to have taken the risks, and stopped the carnage," he wrote. "Let me confess that there were, and still are, moments when I am of the same opinion. But let those who are inclined to condemn me and the War Cabinet for not taking the hazard, weigh carefully the conditions at the time."

The last consideration was perhaps the most powerful of all. The Press. Said Lloyd George:

"G.H.Q. could not capture Passchendaele Ridge, but it was determined to storm Fleet Street, and here strategy and tactics were superb. The Press Correspondents were completely enveloped and important publicists and newspaper proprietors in this country were overwhelmed. Lord Northcliffe had, ever since 1916, been the mere kettledrum of Sir Douglas Haig, and the mouth organ of Sir William Robertson."

When, at last, the terrible truth came out, there was one interesting by-product of this G.H.Q. conspiracy to forbid (or frame), the news. Northcliffe, who had hitherto backed the Generals in all things—at any rate against Lloyd George—was stung into sudden revolt against their military intrusion into his own particular province. Thundered *The Times*:

"We can no longer rest satisfied with the fatuous estimates, e.g. of German losses in men and morale, which have inspired too many of the published messages from France."

The newspaper demanded "prompt, searching and complete" inquiry.
In December, 1917, the Battle of Passchendaele floundered to its futile finish. Three months before, Bonar Law had written to Lloyd George (who was then in Wales):

Treasury Chambers,
Whitehall, S.W.
18 September, 1917.

"My dear Prime Minister,
  ... The only thing at all new is that, in speaking to Robertson yesterday, I said to him that I had lost absolutely all hope of anything coming of Haig's offensive and though he did not say so in so many words, I understand that he took the same view. I do not know when the next attack is supposed to take place but I believe it may happen at any time. It is evident, therefore, that the time must soon come when we will have to decide whether or not this offensive is to be allowed to go on. ...

Yours sincerely,
A. Bonar Law."

What miracle of discipline, devotion, self-sacrifice, search of honour, sense of shame at of even seeming to be afraid, drove these young men forward to their fate? After the war was over and the victory won, we raised a splendid monument to them, a gateway on their road to death. The Prince of Wales opened it. And Siegfried Sassoon wrote his savage, satiric poem "On Passing the Menin Gate".

> "Who will remember, passing through this Gate.
> The unheroic Dead who fed the guns?
> Who shall absolve the foulness of their fate
> Those doomed, conscripted, unvictorious ones?
> Crudely renewed, the Salient holds its own,
> Paid are its dim defenders by this pomp;
> Paid, with a pile of peace-complacent stone.
> The Armies who endured that sullen swamp.
>
> Here was the world's worst wound. And here with pride
> 'Their name liveth for ever', the Gateway claims.
> Was ever immolation so belied
> As these intolerably nameless names?
> Well might the Dead who struggled in the slime
> Rise and deride this sepulchre of crime."

When General Kiggell, Haig's Chief of Staff, paid his first visit to the scene of the shambles—after it was all over—he grew more and more restive and unhappy as his car approached this desolation. At last, he broke down, and wept.

"Good God," he sobbed. "Did we really send men to fight in that?"

His companion, who had fought there, answered stonily: "It's worse farther on up."

CHAPTER XXI

THE RISE OF CHURCHILL

WE are now going to pay a visit to No. 10 Downing Street, which in 1917–18 was more intimately the heart of power in Britain than it had ever been before.

For no Prime Minister until this age of mass destruction, which came in with our twentieth century, had ever at any time been in a position to command so vast a force of manpower or machine-power. Since Lloyd George, only Winston Churchill has held such authority in the land.

But the difference between their two political situations was profound. Lloyd George began his War Premiership in 1916 with a highly critical military hierarchy and a restive Parliamentary majority, most of whom belonged to another Party. Though he headed a Coalition of the three main Parties, the one he belonged to himself had been split wide open by his own action and the Asquithian section of it regarded him with bitter hatred as the betrayer of their chief.

Churchill, on the other hand, started his great term with the generals in anxious submission, and a House of Commons predominantly of his own Party. That party was united, and its leader, Neville Chamberlain, himself accepted office under him. Churchill had been called to the Premiership, not as the result of any conspiracy, but openly and by the clamour of all Parties. In Lloyd George's day, the generals—especially Haig, who carried on a continuous Buckingham Palace counter-action against him—attempted to derive support from the King, whose influence at that time was active and important. Churchill never had to combat any Court opposition; indeed, the very opposite, he held the complete confidence of the King. Then again, Lloyd George had every day to face a fearful casualty list. Churchill was spared this, though he shared the same anxieties over the toll of the ships. Finally, Churchill enjoyed the whole-hearted confidence and goodwill of the United States of America and the intimate friendship of the President. It is not always a point of domestic strength to be so closely attached to an Ally, but in 1940 it was invaluable. America was then Britain's only friend in the world. Lloyd George possessed no such asset. And so, while Churchill was never once seriously challenged in his grip upon the Government of Britain, Lloyd George had to face and fight threats to his régime throughout its existence.

Thus, to a far greater extent Lloyd George's power was personal, and to an undefined and yet decisive degree it rested upon the relationship of trust which existed between him and the other man who shared Downing Street with him. In No. 10 lived Lloyd George, the Prime Minister. In No. 11 lived

Bonar Law, the Chancellor of the Exchequer, who was also the leader of the Tory Party. Biographers of both men, as well as historians of their times, have agreed how effective a partnership in politics they made. Lloyd George himself has paid just tribute to Bonar Law's great share in it. Bonar Law held the bridle while Lloyd George mounted the horse. But he did not say to the rider every time that he set off for the race that he was sure to win.

They were complementary in mood. Bonar Law's rather sombre and pessimistic view of events served to stimulate, even while it offset, Lloyd George's own high spirits. When the Prime Minister returned from a holiday or a Conference abroad, the Chancellor of the Exchequer would welcome him with "Well, there's lots of trouble ahead!" It delighted Lloyd George. He also knew that when the trouble arrived he would be able to count on Bonar Law's loyalty in facing it, and his common sense and courage in overcoming it.

Bonar Law never made any performance or "act" about offering advice, either in Cabinet or elsewhere. He preferred not even to sit down and discuss things over a meal. When he wanted to see Lloyd George he would stroll through the corridor between No. 11 and No. 10, and put his head round the door of the Prime Minister's office to see if he were free.

The Prime Minister was much more likely to be there, at any rate, than across the street at the House of Commons. He had declared at the time of his taking over the Government in December, 1916, that: "One man cannot possibly run Parliament *and* run the war. Whoever undertakes to run the war must put his whole strength into it, and he must make other arrangements with regard to Parliament."

So, less and less often did Lloyd George put in an appearance at the House of Commons. Since the House is a jealous god, this gave his enemies a chance (which the Liberal "Wee Free" back-bench snipers, Pringle and Hogge, did not miss) of charging that the Prime Minister was treating Parliamentary institutions with indifference and contempt.

There were other, Civil Service, critics who complained that he was behaving towards the entire Governmental system without proper regard. This happened when Lloyd George began to recruit a considerable personal secretariat around himself at No. 10 Downing Street, which presently flowed over into hutments in the garden there, and became known to Whitehall as "The Garden Suburb".

Its members were persons of discernment and capacity, whose job was to keep an eye on the various Departments, old and new, maintain close contact with their Heads, and see that the Prime Minister was informed of all that was going on. A difference from Asquith, whose "Secretariat" had consisted of his talented son-in-law, "Bongie",[1] and another secretary with a single typist! But it meant that the morning after any important inter-Departmental conference, a report of the proceedings was circulated to those

[1] Sir Maurice Bonham-Carter, who married Asquith's daughter, Violet.

concerned. The King was also glad to have a typed and detailed minute of what had gone on in the Cabinet (though offset by being occasionally a little late), instead of a laboriously handwritten report by the Prime Minister, as in Mr. Asquith's and Sir Robert Walpole's day.

Naturally, the Garden Suburbanites were not popular with "official" Whitehall (or with Westminster, either), and still less when they brought messages from the P.M. than when they bore reports back to him. Lloyd George used such methods of cutting-out customary form and ceremonial simply in order to save precious time in war. The Foreign Office, in particular, did not take easily to this short-circuit via the Garden Suburb. Any dealing with Suburbanites was deemed to be "rather like trading with the enemy".

Then there was the Lord President of the Council, Lord Curzon. He was shocked—and if his own office happened to be concerned, deeply and personally affronted—by the tendency of the Head of the Government to ride roughshod over precedent and procedure. Hero of the old Oxford University jingle

"My name is George Nathaniel Curzon
I am a most Superior Person . . ."

he had entered public life endowed with more than ten average men's fund of pomposity, and as he advanced through the years he had steadily increased his initial capital, until he had been twice named Viceroy of India. Now, at the age of fifty-eight, Curzon suffered from a permanent hangover of Viceroyalty. When later in 1920, Lloyd George appointed him as Secretary of State for Foreign Affairs, on his first morning at the Foreign Office he rang the bell for an official, and pointing to the inkstand on his desk ordered: "Remove this! The Secretary of State must have crystal and silver, *not* glass and brass!"

In saying this, Curzon used the short North Country "a", as in "dash". To the end of his distinguished career, the great Proconsul's pronunciation remained a mixture of Derbyshire and Eton. Born an aristocrat, Curzon had been brought up in the genteel poverty of a vicarage, from which he had climbed by his own talent and taste for hard work. It was his lifelong and not ignoble ambition to "add honour to an ancient name", and in pursuing it Curzon could be selfish and ruthless enough. At the age of nineteen, before going up to Balliol College, Oxford, he had developed curvature of the spine and he spent the rest of his days braced in a steel girdle. It gave him a stiffness of carriage which accorded with his public characteristics, but belied his private charm. "Curzon stories" were legion, and most of them, of course, apocryphal. One was of his visit during the war to a brewery behind the British lines in Flanders, where the Tommies were bathing in the steaming vats after they had come out of the muddy trenches. Seeing scores of them happily wallowing there, Curzon remarked, "I had no conception that the lower classes had such white skins!" Though he denied it, Curzon liked this story. It *sounded* true.

What was really true was that there was quite another Curzon, who was devoted to his wife, Grace, a lovely and charming woman, herself unsuited to Curzon's pomp: a husband who would insist on interviewing a prospective lady's maid for her: who would sit up into the small hours of the morning working over the household accounts; who could, on occasion, go to infinite pains to make more humble people feel at home; whose dazzling dinner-table wit would reduce the company to helpless laughter, and Balfour to disapproving silence. This was not the Curzon whom the world knew; whose rotund expositions of the obvious during Cabinet meetings would often provoke an impatient puncturing of them there and then by the Prime Minister ("We have listened enough to these pomposities")—and perhaps afterwards, in private, a cruelly amusing imitation of him.

Lord Curzon could hardly be expected to approve of the Garden Suburb, with its lamentable lack of protocol. Indeed, he personally and cordially detested Lloyd George's own Chief Secretary, J. T. Davies, who, of course, was the administrative Head of it and who had never treated him with excessive ceremony. Later, when J.T. was rewarded with a knighthood, Curzon's indignation boiled over: "Nothing so fantastic has happened since Caligula made his horse a Proconsul!"

There was another member of the Garden Suburb Secretariat whom Curzon could not ignore, but whom when he had himself become Foreign Secretary, he would have still better reason to resent. This was Mr. Philip Kerr,[1] a distinguished journalist, who had been one of Milner's Young Men in South Africa after the Boer War and had been Editor of the *Round Table* since 1910. Never did Curzon forgive Lloyd George for having Philip Kerr as his "liaison" officer at the Foreign Office when he went there after the war. For it meant that if Curzon wanted to discuss with the Prime Minister some question of foreign policy not yet before the Cabinet, he would often have to do it through Kerr—a humiliating procedure for a Foreign Secretary with a viceregal tradition. Also, it meant that at times Kerr would present him with Lloyd George's ruling on some other point, confronting him with a *fait accompli*. Curzon had genuine grounds for complaint.

Philip Kerr himself was a man of determined and devoted character. He possessed gifts of intelligence, sincerity and charm, which were reflected in a benign and handsome face. He judged no one harshly or, at any rate, hastily, and few folk ever saw him ruffled. To Lloyd George's tantrums he responded with an amused grin, for he realized that often they were the result of some annoyance which the Master had to distribute on someone who happened to be handy—not necessarily the one who had caused it. He understood, too,

---

[1] Philip Kerr, as Marquess of Lothian became British Ambassador at Washington 1939–40, where he died.

that at other times, they might be deliberate, in order to gain or cover up some point of argument.

Philip Kerr remained in Lloyd George's ever-arduous and never dull service until both the war and the Peace Conference had passed into history. He was one of the few outstanding men in British public life who worked with Lloyd George and never quarrelled with him right up to the end.

The system of highly "personal Government" which operated via the Garden Suburb brought results, both in speeding-up what needed pace and in getting done what otherwise would never have been done at all. But this parallel-control mechanism was not without its own serious disadvantages. Nobody in these days accused the Prime Minister of being unable or unwilling to take a decision, but he *was* charged with taking decisions without getting full knowledge of the available facts and without due forethought, and also sometimes of running what appeared two different policies alongside one another. Even so Lloyd George's own position in the summer of 1917 seemed to a shrewd observer[1] to be, "very strong, perhaps stronger than ever . . . the only dramatic figure, the personification of energy and the will to Victory". It was as well for Britain that such a captain stood at the wheel of our ship in this terrible hour.

The facts were grave. And gravest of all was the state of Shipping, the most vital service of all. For on the answer to it depended whether or not Britain could import enough food and raw materials to survive the U-boat siege and stay in the war.

Three anxious letters (all written in June, 1917) from the Minister of Shipping, Maclay, to the Prime Minister, told of the mortal danger.

The first, 18 June, 1917, warned that on basis of losses "as experienced and as expected by the Admiralty", and after allowing for all new shipbuilding and ship-buying we should start off in 1918 with only about twelve million tons of shipping, instead of the sixteen million of January, 1917. The one hope of closing the gap was by a further shipbuilding drive calling for "immediate extensions of shipyards . . . and the return of a *large number of men*".

The second letter, 27 June, said that on an average we were losing twenty ocean-going ships every week and could not, on present plans, build more than six a week to replace them. We had already cut our pre-war imports by nearly half. A new, "stupendous task" awaited us.

The third letter, 28 June, was the most alarming of all:

". . . it has come to my knowledge this morning that private meetings are being held of ship-masters and others to consider the position and there is a danger that unless something is done in connection with the Admiralty we shall have those men refusing to go to sea.

[1] Mr. F. S. Oliver, author of *Alexander Hamilton, Ordeal by Battle, The Endless Adventure, The Anvil of War*.

Statistics prove that what are called the Areas of Concentration—as now managed—have become veritable traps for our Mercantile Marine and our men are realizing this.

I am led to believe that confidence in the Admiralty has pretty well gone but the coming of a few American destroyers has given them a little heart, which is a melancholy reflection on the position."

The sea was not the only element that brought trouble in 1917. The air was charged with it, too, and in more ways than one. Neither the Air Ministry nor the Royal Air Force was born without pain.

It was as late as 1912 that the Royal Flying Corps had been created, with a military and naval wing. The War Office at first regarded the airplane primarily as an aid to reconnaissance. At the Admiralty, it was recognized at once as a new and deadly weapon. By 1913, the seaplane had already been assigned a three-fold task:

1. Coastal Defence and Patrol.
2. Scouting, as eyes of the Fleet.
3. Bomber Force, operating from battleships.

So when, in August, 1914, the British Expeditionary Force went overseas and took with them all the military airplanes for reconnoitring the advance of the German Army, the seaplanes alone were left to defend Britain from the dreaded Zeppelins. On 3 September, a month after the war had broken out, at Kitchener's request Churchill took charge of our Home air defence. In no time at all, he was bombing the enemy air bases in Flanders.

When, in 1915, he left the Admiralty, the more orthodox Sea Lords reasserted their official sway over their aircraft, which as the Royal Naval Air Service now became a subordinate branch of the Admiralty. It may be added that the formal division of our air forces between Army and Navy brought no benefit to either. For there was no single and superior authority to compel a concerted aerial strategy, and our two air forces competed fiercely with one another over priority claims for machines and weapons. Meantime, on the Western Front and at sea the Germans had the better planes, and the Zeppelins freely bombed the English coast towns.

Every attempt, however, during the Asquith Government to merge or even to co-ordinate our Air efforts was resolutely resisted by the Sea Lords. They were not going to yield one jot of their responsibility for invention, experiment, design, production or finance. Balfour, as First Lord of the Admiralty, had skilfully fought their battle for them in the Cabinet, and since at this period no minutes were kept of discussions—or even of decisions—the verdict rested where he wanted it to be, that is, with those who were for No Change.

When the new Lloyd George Government came in his successor, Carson, fought hard to retain this ruling. But Lloyd George had already had enough of it. Now it was laid down that the Ministry of Munitions should take over the design and supply of aircraft for both the Army and the Navy, who were to draw up their own programmes and submit them to an Air Board. On this Air Board would be included representatives of the two Services, and also of the Ministry of Munitions. Under the War Cabinet itself, the Air Board was to have the last say in any argument. The Chairman would be Lord Cowdray.

This decision put a full-stop to the inter-Service squabble. It also put an end to the enemy's air superiority, both in numbers and performance. By midsummer, 1917, Cowdray could report to Lloyd George that British aircraft production was multiplying and re-multiplying itself.

Just as well, and perhaps only just in time. For the public in London and on the East Coast were getting dangerously alarmed and angry about the German air raids. After a daylight bombing of Woolwich and Poplar, the War Cabinet held it necessary to bring two air squadrons back from the Western Front to give the raiders a really warm welcome should they return. They remained on guard for three weeks, and apart from a single raid on Harwich no enemy plane crossed the coast, for the weather was generally vile. So on 6 July, according to arrangement, Sir Douglas Haig recalled his two squadrons. Next day dawned fine and clear, and about 10 o'clock in the morning a large fleet of German planes appeared over the City of London and the South Bank, and bombed there for an hour or more at will. Hundreds of people were killed or wounded, and for many a day at the drone of aircraft the Tubes and the Undergrounds would be packed with panic-stricken people. Every night, too, crowds gathered there in what had become public refuges, and the scenes were not pleasant.

It was deemed necessary to hold a secret session of Parliament, and there Lloyd George set forth the facts. He showed how Britain's aircraft output was now rising, so that soon we should have enough both for the Front and the Home Defence. But the Front must come first.

". . . A sufficiency of aeroplanes means everything to the Army in France. They are the eyes of that Army, which cannot advance without them. By their means, the Army discovers the enemy's trenches, guns and machine-gun emplacements. To photograph these requires air supremacy and without that supremacy it is sheer murder to allow troops to advance. . . . The first duty of this country is to protect these men. The Germans realize the importance of this question quite as much as we do.

The second means by which they are attempting to diminish our superiority is by trying to force us to withdraw our machines from France in order to protect our own towns. If the Germans know that by bombing

English towns they can force us to withdraw fighting squadrons from France, there could be nothing which would encourage them more.

. . . If the aeroplanes can be provided for the Front and for our defence against raids, that will, of course be done. If not, the Army must come first, and it is vitally important that the Germans should know it."

This statement, says Lloyd George, satisfied the House of Commons.

There was, too, some delicate and highly dangerous business of a political character to be settled. Indeed, before it *was* settled it had very nearly resulted in the smash-up of Lloyd George's Coalition Government. The nation, of course, would know all about the public outcry which attended it, but they never realized at the time the secret drama which was going on inside the War Cabinet itself. It all arose over an intensely personal subject—Churchill.

For some time past, Lloyd George had been seeking to bring Churchill back into the Ministerial ranks. For one thing, he wished to harness to his war chariot the energetic and imaginative driving-power of Churchill, his genius for daring experiment, frequently so right if occasionally so wrong. Lloyd George would also be glad to have Churchill's cheerful personal encouragement not now and then, but continually, in his own anxious labours. Few of his present colleagues could supply that. Then again, Lloyd George naturally wanted to win over to his own Government's side a determined and dangerous fighter, who knew political dynamite when he saw it—and also how to use it. Churchill had, in fact, been doing that in recent debates in the House of Commons on the conduct of the war. Finally, Lloyd George had a personal debt of gratitude to discharge towards this man for the way in which he had stood by him, fought for him, and saved him from resignation in the sombre days of the Marconi Trouble.

But the difficulty in bringing Churchill back into the Government was the extraordinarily bitter dislike and distrust which then animated so many men in the public life of Britain. What! That man back again? Another Antwerp and Dardanelles coming? The mere mention of Churchill's possible reappearance in office was enough to start the most furious argument against it. Lloyd George, therefore, had to do some skilful kite-flying (and nobody was more skilful at this art than himself) before he could make up his mind whether or not he dared re-enlist his provocative ex-colleague. But, over a period of several weeks, no fair wind could be found for any of these kites. The more knowledgeable critics of Churchill admitted his glittering gifts, his attractive personality, his force and fervour. But the powerful mechanism of his mind (so they insisted) contained some fatal flaw which prevented it from running true. To these people, Winston Churchill was not to be regarded as a help in the hour of danger, but as a further danger. Some of them, said Lloyd George, were "More excited about his appointment than about the war".

So Lloyd George had to bethink himself of some other method of making use of Churchill's talents; some way perhaps of giving him a side-entry ticket to the Government. Perhaps this pioneer of the great new Army weapon, the Tank, might care to take over the responsibility for its mass production? Not as the Head of a Department himself, but, say, as Chairman of a Board under the Ministry of Munitions, dealing both with design and output? Dr. Addison, who was then the Minister of Munitions, personally recommended this. He also very sensibly added, in view of the swelling Noe chorus: "I feel that we should get Winston in, and the more it is talked about the more opportunity there is for opposition to gather."

But Churchill, not unnaturally, held out for a full and open recognition of his worth. So the idea then developed that he should take over the Ministry of Munitions, while Addison was to organize a new Ministry of Reconstruction to draw up plans for the post-war period. Smuts pressed for Churchill's appointment to the Air Board; he wrote to the Prime Minister on 6 June, 1917:

> ". . . In spite of the strong Party opposition to his appointment I think you will do the country a real service by appointing a man of his calibre to this Department, the vital importance of which will more and more appear."

The opposition came both from Party politicians and from Service quarters. There was Admiral Sir Charles Beresford, ancient enemy of Admiral "Jackie" Fisher. Hearing a rumour in his club that Churchill was going to enter the Government, Beresford told Bonar Law, as head of the Tory Party, that he had organized a Committee of well-known and influential people to hold meetings of protest up and down the country against this appointment, that he had already interviewed the editors of certain leading newspapers, and also officers of both Services, and that he was going to raise a national storm. The Admiral duly addressed a large gathering at the Queen's Hall, where he made the public charge that Churchill had "gambled with the lives of men in the most reckless way".

He had gambled, said Beresford, and had described it as a legitimate gamble, in the Dardanelles. The ships he lost he declared had no military value. What of the finest officers and crews in the world? Were they of no value? Admiral Beresford ended by saying that all Churchill's acts were failures, brought about disaster, shocking loss of life, and his whole record was such that he should not be allowed in any capacity whatever in the public service.

The next morning, the *Sunday Times* printed the story of an intrigue "by the powerful clique which has been working persistently to get Churchill back to office", and declared that his appointment, either to the Ministry of Munitions or to the Air Board, "would constitute a grave danger to the Administration and the Empire as a whole. . . . His public record has proved beyond all argument or doubt that he does not possess those qualities of balanced judgment and shrewd far-sightedness which are essential to the sound Administration. . . . Gambles today mean not only the jeopardizing of the Empire; they mean the sacrifice of men's lives. . . .

We say with all deliberation and with the utmost emphasis that nothing would tend more effectively to damn Mr. Lloyd George's Government in the eyes of the whole country than the co-option of Mr. Churchill. . . ."

From Cowdray, Chairman of the Air Board, whose office had been so freely mentioned as being one of the available "plums", came a note to the Prime Minister setting forth an account of the now remarkable output of British aircraft production, and also a sharp warning that if Churchill were now to be named as the Minister responsible, not only for the close-bombing support of infantry assault on the Western Front but also for the long-range bombing of the German cities, then he (Churchill) would certainly claim all the credit for the effective exploitation of this terrific new weapon. And then, suggested Cowdray, would you care to have, as one of your Ministers, a dangerously ambitious man who will believe that he was the most vital factor (in the eyes of the country) in securing final victory, and therefore the proper man to make a bid for the Peace Premiership?

As for the Tory Ministers, there was the Earl of Derby, Secretary of State for War, likewise most vigorously objecting to Churchill as either a source of weakness or of interference, and there was Curzon, Lord President of the Council, writing to Bonar Law on 4 June, 1917, expressing alarm at the statements appearing in the Press that Churchill was to be offered an important Government post. Curzon reminded Lloyd George of the promise that he Lloyd George) had given some of the Tory Ministers when they agreed to join his Government, that no post would be offered to Churchill. It will be remembered that Lloyd George had undertaken that neither Churchill nor Northcliffe should be included. Now, here he was trying to net one of these dangerous big fish. (In another three months' time he would be trying to net the other one. He would catch the whale, though the barracuda would get away.)

Four days later the Lord President returned to the attack in a letter to Lloyd George insisting that the appointment of Churchill would be intensely unpopular with many of the Prime Minister's chief colleagues, and that it might even lead to the downfall of the Government. Although Churchill was a potential danger in opposition, he would be an active danger in their midst. Was the risk worth while?

Thus Curzon. Sir George Younger, the Chairman of the Conservative Party, also signalled to Lloyd George, flashing the red light on two occasions,

8th and 9th of June. The appointment of Churchill, he said, would strain to breaking point the loyalty of the Unionist Party to Lloyd George. Younger referred to Churchill's "unfortunate record", his grave responsibility for two of the greatest disasters of the war, which had produced distrust of him inside and outside the House.

Sir George declared that he had attended a meeting of the National Unionist Council where a resolution had been moved that the appointment of Churchill would be "an insult to the Navy and the Army". The motion was seconded, and carried amidst cheers.

The following day, 10 June, came Walter Long, the Colonial Secretary, repeating in writing to Lloyd George the warning he had already uttered to him personally. The inclusion of Churchill in the Government "would bring about a grave situation in our Party".

Lloyd George was genuinely astounded at what he considered was these Tories' "insensate fury" which, he wrote, "surpassed all my apprehensions, and for some days it swelled to the dimensions of a grave ministerial crisis which threatened the life of the Government".

He drew back for a moment. Through Captain "Freddie" Guest, he made a tentative proposal to Churchill. Would he agree to accept for the time being, as a compromise for a Department directly connected with the war effort, the Duchy of Lancaster with "elaborated uses and functions"?

No, Winston Churchill would not. For by this time, Churchill felt that his personal honour was engaged; so he turned down the proposition flat, though in a friendly manner. He explained to Guest that he could serve neither a national purpose nor Guests' own purpose by being included in this manner. He was prepared, Guest reported, to forgo and forget all political considerations in order to help to beat the "Hun", in either of the following capacities: (1) in assisting the Prime Minister in council in the War Cabinet, if necessary without salary, (2) in accepting the charge and responsibility for any War Department, as long as he had powers actively to assist in the defeat of the enemy.

Rumour and counter-rumour ran wild for another month. Then, one July afternoon, Lloyd George sent for Beaverbrook and inquired of him if he still thought Churchill should be taken into the Government. When Beaverbrook answered that he did, and that he would be prepared to support it, both in public and in private, Lloyd George asked him to go round and tell Bonar Law that he had just given it out to the Press that Winston Churchill had been selected as the new Minister of Munitions.

So Beaverbrook went next door to No. 11 Downing Street to see his friend Bonar Law and let him know the news. It angered Bonar Law, who resented the fact that Lloyd George had taken this decision without consulting him, and feared that his Tory colleagues and followers would revolt, perhaps even wreck the Government, so intense was the Party passion which had been aroused. Beaverbrook spent much time that day trying to placate Bonar Law, who gradually became reconciled to what could not now be undone. Lloyd George himself kept away. He had a worried evening, too.

For, as the news flashed round the House of Commons and the political clubs, a great clamour arose. Angry knots of M.P.s gathered in the lobbies and the smoking-rooms, and for one evening the war against the Kaiser was well-nigh forgotten while tongues and knives were sharpened against Lloyd George.

"Let's have him out!" "He's tricked us!" "Down with both George and Churchill!" were the cries of wrath that resounded. As darkness fell on 17 July, 1917, Lloyd George's Coalition Government was engulfed in raging seas, and the ship rolled and pitched perilously.

Next morning, the newspapers officially announced a very considerable Ministerial reshuffle: Carson to leave the Admiralty and enter the War Cabinet, while "Vice-Admiral" Geddes took his place as First Lord; Montagu to become Secretary of State for India; and Addison to become Minister of Reconstruction (without portfolio), while Churchill took his place as Minister of Munitions.

There was fresh outcry. *The Times*, indeed, was objective in its comment; some of the appointments were good, some would require time to justify, and some (such as Montagu's) were remarkably misplaced. Churchill's return to office, however, was not condemned; as long as he refrained from interfering with the professional Service chiefs by shoving forward his own ideas of "amateur strategy".

The *Daily Express* praised the Churchill appointment, but then Beaverbrook ran that newspaper; he was known to be friendly to Churchill himself, as always, and if Bonar Law agreed now to having him in the Government, well that suited the *Daily Express*.

The *Morning Post* was vitriolic. To this extreme Tory newspaper, Churchill was "Meddlesome Matty", a "floating kidney in the body politic", and it recommended that he be imprisoned in an empty sea-mine, and anchored off the German coast. Even then he would certainly break loose, blunder into something, and cause an explosion! The Liberal and the Labour Press were hardly less hostile.

As for the politicians, Walter Long renewed his protests in a letter to Lloyd George dated the same day. While he agreed that ordinarily the Prime Minister had the sole right to select his colleagues, he insisted that these times were far from ordinary. Furthermore, when the Prime Minister had been contemplating changes recently he had been kind enough to consult him, and also to promise to do so again before any appointment was made. Now it had been done without a single fresh word. Frankly, Long considered that the inclusion of Churchill would "weaken your Government and would certainly make it extremely difficult for many of my friends to continue their support".

Now this, of course, was a threat of resignation. Walter Long, together with his disturbed friends, was finally induced to accept Churchill, though he wrote to Bonar Law warning him that if the new Minister of Munitions started either interfering in any other departments, or trying to control Government policy, then there would be serious trouble. Walter Long's own resentment at what had been done is revealed in his next sentence: "The real effect has been to destroy all confidence in Lloyd George. It is widely held that for purposes of his own, quite apart from the war, he has deceived and 'jockeyed' us. . . ."

More than a hundred Tory M.P.s supported a resolution of protest against Churchill's appointment, and many were the questions set down upon the Order Paper. The Tory "War Committee", the Tory "Business Committee", and a number of the other party organizations entered their emphatic disagreement and complaint. Innumerable angry letters poured into the Tory party headquarters.

Not only were the Tories hostile. The Coalition Liberals were jealous; they looked upon the Churchill appointment as taking the children's bread. The Wee Free Liberals were furious with what they regarded as the defection both of Churchill and Montagu (who had personally pledged himself to Asquith never to join Lloyd George's Government). The Labour Party still linked Tonypandy with Churchill's name.

Never did a Minister take office amid such widespread ill-will as Winston Churchill when he became Minister of Munitions in July, 1917. Lloyd George was truly daring when he decided to bring him back to the Government Front Bench, and it is evidence of the man's masterful character that he carried it through at this critical hour. He had bided his time, weighed the risks —then made up his mind, and acted. Thus, fully and generously, did Lloyd George repay his personal debt to Churchill. He did it, indeed, at what might have been the price of his own political ruin, for in the next few days his throne rocked.

Churchill was genuinely moved. After dinner at No. 10 Downing Street, the Prime Minister led him into the little room next door to the Cabinet room. There on the wall was a framed copy of a *Daily Express* placard of the year 1913 relating to Marconi which Lloyd George had asked Beaverbrook to send him from Fleet Street that afternoon. It read:

CHURCHILL
DEFENDS
LLOYD GEORGE

The order could now be changed.

LLOYD GEORGE
DEFENDS
CHURCHILL

It was long before most of Lloyd George's principal Tory colleagues forgave him for reintroducing Churchill to a place of power. They objected almost as much to the manner in which it had been done as to the fact itself.

It must be added that when the tumult and the shouting died, Lord Derby warmly endorsed the appointment of the new Minister of Munitions, and the decisive manner in which it had been carried through. Whatever their personal likes or dislikes, he said, the Tory Party would always react the right way to courageous leadership.

The din which had attended Churchill's appointment to the Ministry of Munitions drowned any objections which might have been made to that of Edwin Montagu to the India Office. We left Montagu, who had been Asquith's Minister of Munitions after Lloyd George in June, 1916, hesitating whether or not to accept (as he said) the Chancellorship of the Exchequer. He hesitated too long, so that ten days later the offer had been reduced to returning to one of his own earlier posts as Financial Secretary to the Treasury.

Three months afterwards, he was genuinely if still rather diffidently seeking work. Here is his note to Lloyd George dated 28 March, 1917:

> "As the desert sand for rain,
> As the Londoner for sun,
> As the poor for potatoes,
> As a landlord for rent,
> As drosera rotundifolia for a fly,
> As Herbert Samuel for Palestine,
> As a woman in Waterloo Road for a soldier
> *I long for talk with you.*"

By 1 May, Montagu is only anxious to be of service—and friendship:

> "I am constantly thinking of your position and something you said to me some time ago, that you felt your own isolation, that you had no colleagues who were your friends, who thought as you thought . . . that fond as you were of Henderson, he was really more of a delegate of Labour than an independent politician, that Bonar Law thought very much in terms of the Conservative Party, and that you had not much in common with Milner and Curzon."

On 17 July Montagu was "proud to accept" the India Office, and by 7 August he was telling his new chief of the mighty destiny which awaited him as the architect of a yet undreamed-of peace and prosperity for the great land of India: "You can save India. You can set your foot, and force England to set its foot, firmly on a path of progress on democratic lines. . . ."

It was a different note from the one which he had sounded in his last letter to his former close personal friend, Asquith, in which he had spoken of

Peace Conference, 1919. Clemenceau, Lloyd George, Bonar Law
and Lord Birkenhead

" . . . the anguish which separation causes me and the terrible sense of duty which compelled me to come to the rescue of a weak Government, and the sorrow with which I have been forced to fight the temptation to talk it over with you. . . ."

To which Asquith had briefly replied: "In view of our past relations it is perhaps not unnatural that I should find it difficult to understand and still more to appreciate your reasons for the course which you tell me you propose to take. . . ."

The only other problem had been to replace Sir Edward Carson at the Admiralty, where frankly he had failed to apply to the Sea Lords the pressure which Lloyd George wanted to exert in the matter of convoys. On 6 June, 1917, the Prime Minister wrote to his First Lord and sent the letter off to him by special messenger:

"My dear Carson,
    This morning I told my colleagues the purport of my conversation with you yesterday as to the desirability of strengthening the War Cabinet with your presence. They all agreed that an additional member was needed in view of the overwhelming character of the work both in mass and in responsibility, and they were also unanimous that you would be the most helpful choice.
    You know my opinion on the subject. I wanted you in the Cabinet from the start. My plans were then thwarted for reasons you know. The time is now ripe for reverting to my original idea. I hope therefore you will join us as a full member of the War Cabinet. We need your insight, courage and judgment. We have momentous decisions to take in the course of the next few days. I should therefore like to announce the appointment at once. Bonar foreshadowed it today. . . .
                                        Ever sincerely,
                                        D. Lloyd George."

Carson had gone off to his country bungalow at Birchington for the week-end, and the messenger arrived there in the middle of the night; Carson was awakened to read what he took to be his dismissal.

                                        Birchington,
                                        Thanet.
                                        7 July, 1917.
"My dear Prime Minister,
    Have received your letter by special messenger. Of course I am ready to fall in with your views that a change should be made at the Admiralty if you consider it in the public interest. It is vital that you should have confidence in the administration of so important a department.
    As regards my entering the Cabinet I am very grateful for all you say

N

but I should prefer not to have to give an answer today—I am suffering from a bad attack of neuralgia but hope to be all right by Monday.

Yours ever sincerely,
Edward Carson."

But Lloyd George did not want to lose Carson—or drive him into opposition, where he was really formidable. So he wrote at once:

"My dear Carson,

I am afraid from your letter that you have misunderstood mine. We sincerely want you at the War Cabinet, but if you cannot see your way to join the Cabinet and prefer to remain at the Admiralty then the suggestion falls to the ground. We must have your help in this terrible war. I have all along—and so has Bonar—wanted you here. But it is for you to decide.

The changes I wanted at the Admiralty could be effected under your leadership. You know my views about that. The present Board is unsatisfactory. . . .

Ever sincerely,
D. Lloyd George."

Of course, Carson knew that the Prime Minister was wrapping-up his dismissal from the Admiralty. But, as Lloyd George himself wrote in his war memoirs, "his intense patriotic sense prevailed over any personal feeling".

Thus, there passed the first great gale of Lloyd George's War Premiership. Within a month Churchill was already at odds with one of his two other Cabinet colleagues concerned with aircraft production, the new First Lord of the Admiralty, Sir Eric Geddes.

Wrote Geddes to Lloyd George 16 August, 1917:

"My fears as regards the Minister of Munitions are somewhat fortified by what has passed in conversation with him upon several occasions and at recent meetings of the War Cabinet and Cabinet Committees. He has shown that he contemplates an extension of his functions beyond what I have ever understood them to be.

. . . I feel so strongly on this subject, and it is evident that Churchill does not take the same view of the duties of the Minister of Munitions as I do, that I feel I must ask . . . that his functions should not be exceeded."

To which Bonar Law replied 21 August, 1917:

"With reference to your conversation with me I have spoken to the P.M., who assures me that he has already told Mr. Churchill that he must avoid anything in the nature of interference with the work of the Admiralty, and that he (the P.M.) will make sure that there is no such interference."

Right at this moment, indeed, Lloyd George had got something on his hands more important to settle than the jostling for position by any of his

Ministers. This was the question of whether or not to create both a separate Air Ministry and a separate Air Service.

For this revolutionary new arm in warfare Lloyd George himself favoured an entirely independent Air Ministry controlling its own Air Service.

To inquire into it, and also into the project of a unified Air Defence system for London, Lloyd George had set up a Cabinet Committee under the untiring General Smuts. They had already reported on the second item, and effective steps had been taken to meet and beat the enemy air attack before ever it could approach London. Their recommendations on the first item were now (17 August) before the War Cabinet. They supported the plan of a separate Air Ministry and Air Service, and despite a last, dogged battle by the Admiralty, both were adopted.

While these high affairs of State were moving to a decision a personal matter of a rather squalid kind caused anger and vexation to the Prime Minister. This was a paragraph which appeared in both the *Star* and the *Westminster Gazette* on the evening of 25 September, 1917, the day after another heavy air raid on London. It read:

MR. LLOYD GEORGE'S COUNTRY RETREAT

The *Exchange Telegraph Company* says the Prime Minister spent the night at his residence at Walton Heath, Surrey, having left Downing Street about the time it became known that the raiders were approaching London.

In the first place, it was not true. Lloyd George had, indeed, left London that night—but after the raiders had come and gone. He was due to take the train to Dover, stay there overnight, and board an early-morning boat for Boulogne, where he was meeting the French Prime Minister, M. Painlevé, and General Foch. Travelling with Lloyd George, were General Robertson and Admiral Jellicoe. Just as they were about to leave Downing Street, the warning reached them that enemy aircraft were coming in. They made their way to Charing Cross Station, which they found in darkness because of the approaching raid, and got into the train. It had barely started off when the bombing began, and they halted on the railway bridge over the Thames. From there, Lloyd George, and his companions watched the shells of the anti-aircraft fire bursting overhead. Then the All Quiet, and the train rolled on through the night to Dover.

The story in the newspapers was not only false but obviously malicious. It said that Lloyd George was running away from the bombs—of which he had special early warning because he was Prime Minister. What would the public say of such an "example"?

Of course, some of them promptly said it. The munition workers in the East End were eloquent. It was imperative to take action.

Lloyd George resolved to proceed against the *Exchange Telegraph Company* and the two newspapers concerned with an action for libel. His former colleague and current critic, Sir John Simon, agreed to appear for him. At this point, a still-unsolved little mystery begins to take shape.

8 Oct., 1907[1]

4 Brick Court, Temple, E.C.4

"My dear Prime Minister,

You do not need to be told with what pride and pleasure I accept the duty of appearing for you in these libel actions. Of course, the papers concerned will climb down unconditionally. But whoever ultimately bore the costs, I would never consent to take a fee in circumstances like these and I have told Poole[2] so.

I am just going off to G.H.Q., and have a message from Haig asking me to stay a day longer than I had expected. But I shall be back in good time for your cases. Especially, if they are fixed for Tuesday.

Ever yours truly,

John Simon."

But for reasons never yet explained (he does not even refer to the case in his book of memoirs, published in 1952[3]) Sir John Simon did not discharge the duty which he had accepted. Instead, Mr. Tindal Atkinson, K.C., and Mr. Douglas Hogg, K.C., appeared for Lloyd George before Mr. Justice Lush in the King's Bench Division. A point they made was that when the attention of the *Exchange Telegraph* was drawn to the error the Company at once expressed regret that the paragraph had been issued by them. The *Star* and the *Westminster Gazette* both published a correction the following day, but neither offered any apology. After the Prime Minister had entered the witness box and given sworn evidence of his experiences on the night of the air raid, both newspapers were profuse in their apologies and regrets, withdrew the statement unreservedly and indemnified the Prime Minister, 16 October, 1917.

Sir John Simon, still visiting Sir Douglas Haig, had a few days earlier received there a commission in the Royal Flying Corps, still at that time part of the Army. He was thus unable to take up his brief in this Lloyd George libel action, though in July, 1918, he was able to obtain leave to defend his former Liberal Cabinet colleague, Sir Charles Hobhouse, in another libel action, also, of course, without fee. The only other point to be noted is that the Chairman of the Air Board at the time of this *Star* and *Westminster Gazette* libel was Lord Cowdray, who happened to own the *Westminster Gazette*.

The birth pangs of the Air Ministry continued up to the final moment.

---

[1] The date on this letter is as printed; clearly a mistake for 1917.
[2] The Solicitor.   [3] *Retrospect:* By Lord Simon.

Lloyd George now decided to part with Cowdray in order to seize an opportunity (as he thought) to muzzle Northcliffe for a time—nobody could ever hope to do that for long. The Press Lord had that very day returned to London from a highly successful War Mission in the United States, where he had put a much-needed punch into British war propaganda. "Punching", indeed, was Northcliffe's genuine pleasure in life, and if he was not punching for the British Government, then the Prime Minister realized that he would very soon be punching at it. So he decided to invite Cowdray, who had done a good job as Chairman of the old Air Board, to take charge of another Department and to offer the new Air Ministry to Northcliffe. The second of the Forbidden men of December, 1916, was thus called by Lloyd George to join his Government.

The proposition was put to Northcliffe by the Prime Minister at luncheon in Downing Street. He said that he would think it over. Lloyd George understood that he intended to accept, and persuaded Bonar Law to approve of the appointment. But that evening, while dining at his club, Beaverbrook received news from the *Daily Express* to say that the Press Association had just issued a statement that Lord Northcliffe had declined the offer of the Air Ministry. When Beaverbrook telephoned this information to Lloyd George he could not believe his own ears. Never before had a Prime Minister been treated in such insulting fashion.

But next morning, he had to believe his own eyes. For there in the newspapers was published a letter to himself from Northcliffe which he had not yet received.

15 November, 1917

"Dear Prime Minister,

I have given anxious consideration to your repeated invitation that I should take charge of the new Air Ministry. The reasons which have impelled me to decline that great honour and responsibility are in no way concerned with the office which is rightly to be set up. They are roughly as follows . . ."

Northcliffe then went on to speak of the "fervour and enthusiasm" for the war which he had found "in the virile atmosphere of the United States and Canada", comparing America's instant enforcement of Conscription with our own "wobbling for two years" (he omitted to compare the strengths in the field at any period). He praised Canada's disfranchisement of conscientious objectors and denaturalization of all enemy aliens. Then the censorship came in for a clout. Finally, said Napoleon of Northcliffe House, there were a number of unnamed people in high authority who had bungled the job, and should have been sacked. The spirit of the men and women of Britain was still as eager and splendid as ever, we had the finest army in the world, led by one of the greatest generals; but

". . . I feel that in present circumstances I can do better work if I maintain my independence and am not gagged by a loyalty that I do not feel towards the whole of your Administration. . . .

Yours sincerely,
Northcliffe."

It is difficult to discover what was his motive in this strange manœuvre; the action itself appears rather base. But Northcliffe was not a base man, though he was a vain one, and could be a brutal one. The effect of it was to humiliate Cowdray, who took proper and deep personal offence at learning for the first time, along with the readers of the national Press, that a change of ministers responsible for Air was being contemplated. He resigned at once, and to the Prime Minister's own letter to him "explaining" how things had happened he curtly replied that he would have been quite prepared

". . . to have continued at the Air Ministry until it was convenient to you to appoint the new Minister had it not been that my doing so would merely prolong the natural unrest at the Ministry until my successor is appointed, and also that it would weaken my protest.

Further, I have to admit that my many years of intimate knowledge of America and of the present position do not permit me to concur in your expressed reason for the desired change, viz.: that Lord Northcliffe's personal knowledge of the Air Service in America would have enabled him better to co-ordinate the energies of the two countries.

Yours very sincerely
Cowdray."

He never forgave Lloyd George. In the bitter feuds which rent the Liberal Party after the war Cowdray's *Westminster Gazette* was Lloyd George's implacable enemy.

It was not the end of the troubles in the Air. For Lord Rothermere, Northcliffe's brother, who soon afterwards became the first Secretary of State for Air, and carried through the fusion of the Royal Flying Corps and the Royal Naval Air Service into the Royal Air Force, would end his brief ministerial career in storm and unhappiness in April of the New Year.

CHAPTER XXII

SUPREME WAR COUNCIL

BUT all this was happening at Westminster, or in Whitehall. We must see what was going on in the greater place called Great Britain.

In the autumn of 1917, among the work-people in the factories, shipyards, mines and shops of Britain, a tide of discontent was rising.

The war was not going well on the Western Front. The communiqués still claimed victories, but the men on leave and the swelling stream of wounded told otherwise. On the Eastern Front, the war had pretty well petered out in revolution. On the Italian Front, a new military disaster loomed and soon would break. And the silent war at sea—though few folk in Britain had ever seen a U-boat, by now most families were beginning to feel their effects—that was far from being won. On the Home Front, wage and price troubles grew.

George Barnes, who had succeeded Arthur Henderson as Labour's representative in the War Cabinet, began addressing memoranda to the Prime Minister warning him that the Pacifist element was at work among the industrial masses and might seize some "great reverse or untoward circumstances here at home" to turn the inevitably growing war-weariness into open anti-war activity. The Pacifist Press was increasing its sales and extending its activities. Barnes noted, too, that the general public were beginning to comment in unfavourable terms about the lack of any military success and to "contrast the actual achievements with the prospects held out by the Generals".

Frankly, he did not feel too happy himself with Field-Marshal Haig's latest estimates when he cast his mind back "to previous statements from the same quarter".

Dr. Addison, the new Minister of Reconstruction, who had been talking over things with the Socialist intelligentsia in Bloomsbury, reported that there, as usual in Gloomsbury (and especially in wartime) "All is Gloom".

Dr. T. J. Macnamara, M.P., Financial Secretary to the Admiralty, had been talking to the men in the industrial trenches—at Liverpool, Leeds, Birmingham and Blaenavon. He found that the vast majority wanted to "see it through" for their sons' sakes. But they were sorely tried—and the Independent Labour Party were always there, explaining that it was a "Profiteers' War".

So, Dr. Macnamara, in his illuminating and intelligent *Memorandum on the Civil Population and the War* urged the Ministers to get out into the country, and convince the people that they were determined to spare them any privations which were not the direct and inevitable consequence of war; to treat everyone alike, especially in food rationing (so that the *Daily Herald* could not make any more trouble by printing the Ritz Hotel dinner menu on its front page);

to stamp on the profiteers; to punish food hoarding; above all, to proclaim the Government's war aims and Tell the People What They are Fighting For!

All of it admirable, all sensible, all needful.

But how much could one man do? To the problems of maintaining morale at home and organizing labour here effectively, were now added those of arousing enthusiasm in America, and mobilizing her immense machine-power. From the United States, came cables complaining how ill-planned was the present American war effort, and from Mr. "Tay Pay" O'Connor, M.P., other cables warning that the Irish Americans there were still strongly and actively hostile to this country. Mr. Randolph Hearst's *New York American* had praised Lloyd George, but only in order to wound Woodrow Wilson, pointing out that the British Prime Minister was looking after Britain's interests while the American President was neglecting America's. The crafty British, as usual, were working for their own hand while the simple Americans were pulling the chestnuts out of the fire for them!

There was a time, indeed, during this summer when Lloyd George seriously thought of making a voyage himself to the United States. But that would have meant postponing the settlement of any outstanding issues in Britain. When this was pointed out to him, Lloyd George reluctantly agreed.

The Prime Minister was slogging away in these days under intense pressure. Riddell had now taken a country house for him at Great Walstead, Sussex, on Lloyd George's own suggestion, so that he could work in the garden in the clear summer air—and refresh his ideas, even if wearing down the energy of his colleagues, Bonar Law, Milner, Smuts and Lord Robert Cecil, by sudden climbs up the surroundings hills. One morning, Riddell noted,[1] after Lloyd George had gone to bed the night before "very tired" from addressing a tremendous mass-meeting at the Queen's Hall on the third anniversary of the war, he rose renewed with strength.

"Lloyd George's vitality is remarkable. This morning he was quite fresh and full of fun. At midday came a telephone message that the Censor had passed the first instalment of Gerard's[2] book for publication in the *Daily Telegraph* and that it contained a statement that the King had told the Kaiser's brother at the end of July that Great Britain would remain neutral. The editor, being nervous, had brought the article to Downing Street. On the matter being brought to the King's attention, he at once empowered the *Daily Telegraph* to deny the statement, and it was arranged that the denial should be cabled to all foreign capitals. The P.M. was very pleased with the result of his afternoon's work. . . .

Finished the evening by singing hymns, Welsh and otherwise, the P.M. being in great form."

[1] Lord Riddell's War Diary.
[2] James W. Gerard, U.S. Ambassador to Germany 1913–17.

That month, Lloyd George attended the Eisteddfod, an engagement he never missed in peace or war. It was held at Birkenhead, and a dramatic gathering it turned out to be. For the winner of the Bardic Crown, with a poem written in the trenches of Flanders, had been killed on duty there, and the Bardic Chair was draped in black. Lloyd George himself was showing the strain of his own great responsibilities, but he made a speech which sped like an arrow to the hearts of his Welsh hearers. These were the grey, drenched days of Passchendaele, when vision shallowed to a few hundred yards, to be won at a price beyond peer. Lloyd George, as so often, reminded his countrymen of their own mountains:

"On a clear day, they look as though they were near. You could reach them in an easy march—you could climb the highest of them in an hour. That is wrong. You could not.

Then comes a cloudy day, and the mists fall upon them and you say, 'There are no hills. They have vanished.' Again you are wrong. The optimist is wrong: the hills are not as near as he thought. The pessimist is still more wrong, because the hills *are* there. All you have to do is to keep on.

Keep on! Falter not! We have many a dangerous marsh to cross; we will cross them all. We have steep and stormy paths to climb; we will climb them. Our footprints may be stained with blood, but we will reach the heights.

And beyond them, we shall see the green valleys and the rich plains of the new world, which we have sacrificed so much to win."

At this time, as War Prime Minister, Lloyd George found every morning that he had both heights to climb and marshes to cross. To him, there fell the double duty of setting the main, mighty course of the greatest Empire in the world at war—and of settling the day-to-day petty expedients of a patched-up, all-party Coalition, hanging together largely for fear of something worse.

So Lloyd George had to take final responsibility for initiating the vital measures against the U-boats and the German air-raiders, for tackling the problems of Russia, now so rapidly fading-out from the battle front, and of America, still too leisurely arriving at it; for continuing or finishing the Passchendaele offensive. He also had to decide whether a Coalition Liberal, a Tory, or a Labour M.P. should be given the job of Under-Secretary at the Ministry of Pensions.

In August, indeed, he had to find a new Director-General of National Service to handle the distribution of the country's manpower. Lloyd George had entrusted Mr. Neville Chamberlain with this task on the formation of his Government in the previous December, but the relations between the two men had never been happy. Now Chamberlain's Ministry was the subject of an adverse report by a Select Committee of the House of Commons. He resigned,

N*

and a feud was made which would endure for nearly a quarter of a century; the final, fatal blow was struck by Lloyd George in a bitter speech which ended Chamberlain's own Premiership in 1940.

Enough for a day? No. There was trouble in the House of Lords about Honours. And there was always Ireland. But something—or rather, somebody —else was about to cause still more division in the War Cabinet.

There was another persistent people knocking at the door—and one with a still older history of oppression and exile. The Jews.

For nearly 2,000 years, the Jews had been wanting and waiting to return to the Land of their Fathers. ("Next Year in Jerusalem" they toasted at their Passover.) But it was not until about the dawn of the present century that the powerful Zionist Movement had been born, a world-wide organization pledged to restore Palestine as the national homeland of the Jewish people. They were not likely to overlook the possibilities of action opened up by a world war, and when the contemporary tyrant occupier of their ancient country (the Turk) took the side of the Central Powers, the Zionists naturally sought succour from the Allies. One of their leading members was a Russian Jew named Dr. Weizmann.

The reader has met him already, with Lloyd George one day in 1915 at the Ministry of Munitions, when the brilliant scientist set to work to produce the then vitally-needed acetone. In declining any honour or award to himself for his services, he had told Lloyd George of the national aspirations of his own people. Dr. Weizmann already knew Balfour, and had worked under him at the Admiralty. To him, too, the ardent Zionist confided his dreams, and Balfour had been perhaps more impressed.

Asquith, who was still Prime Minister in those days, had not been so encouraging. He had his good reasons. One was that secret Sykes-Picot Pact of May, 1916, whereby the Allies had agreed to carve up the Turkish Empire in the Middle East into Russian, French and British zones; the proposed Anglo-French dividing line cut right through Palestine. By the autumn of that year, however, a still stronger reason had arisen for revising this arrangement. This was the urgent necessity of winning over the goodwill of American Jewry to the Allied cause. For the Germans had not been idle in courting Zionism, either, notably addressing themselves to the Russian Jews.

So, under a new War Cabinet which included Lloyd George, Balfour and Smuts (another strong sympathizer with the ideas of Zionism), there had gone forth secret assurances to the Zionist leaders that Britain would support their claims, if she could carry her Allies with her. One thus addressed was Justice Brandeis, an outstanding figure of the Movement in the United States, and a close personal friend of President Wilson. A Zionist delegation, which included Dr. Weizmann, Sir Herbert Samuel and Mr. James de Rothschild, M.P., had journeyed to Paris, and there secured the agreement of the French Government.

Throughout the summer of 1917, Balfour kept up his talks with the

Zionists, and on 3 September, he laid before the War Cabinet the draft of a public statement to be made by the British Government endorsing and proclaiming all that had been promised in private.

But not everybody was pro-Zionist, and perhaps the least unanimous (in fact, they were about equally divided) were the people most concerned. Within the War Cabinet itself two more meetings were required before a bridge could be built to span the differences, and in public life, outside, the rifts long remained. Fiercest opposition of all came from wealthy Jews, who feared that if a Jewish National State were established they might lose their own status as citizens of the countries where they and their forbears had long dwelt and prospered. Lloyd George's own old friend, Sir Charles Henry, M.P., was foremost among these Anti-Zionists, and he did not delay any longer to found an anti-Zionist newspaper, *The Jewish Guardian,* to express his views.

In the War Cabinet, the new Secretary of State for India, Edwin Montagu, led the Anti-Zionist party. In a stormy meeting on 4 October, 1917, Balfour warned of a new German drive to capture the Zionist forces for the enemy side, and he claimed that though some rich Jews in Britain might oppose the idea of Zionism, it was enthusiastically backed by those in America and Russia. On whose side were those influential people to be ranged? There was no inconsistency whatever in having a Jewish National Home and Jews being members of other States. The French Government were sympathetic to the idea, and so, as he personally knew, was President Wilson.

Edwin Montagu rose. He most strongly objected to a "National Home" for Jews, insisting that the Jews were really only a religious community and that he was himself a "Jewish Englishman". He turned to Lloyd George. "All my life," he said, "I have been trying to get out of the Ghetto. You want to force me back there!"

Curzon was opposed to the proposal on other grounds. Ah! well did he recollect a journey he had made through the Promised Land, many years ago now. Alas! It was a barren land, with little cultivation even on the terraced slopes, and watered by all too few streams. How could this place of stone and sand become a home for millions more Jews? Moreover, what about the Moslems already living there?

Milner interposed to declare himself in favour of the National Home for Jews—provided nothing was done to prejudice the civil and religious rights of the non-Jews in Palestine, or the political status of Jews elsewhere.

The Prime Minister ruled that the War Cabinet had heard enough for one day. There was still a war on. Resolved: to hear the further views of Zionists, Anti-Zionists, Non-Zionists, and President Wilson.

The days passed. A week. Three weeks.

The Jews (at any rate, the pro-Zionist Jews) were getting restive. In particular, Lord Rothschild, the Head of his House. He had been in correspondence with Balfour since mid-July, and was beginning to wonder if anything was going to happen in the War Cabinet or not? Because, decidedly, something was happening in Palestine.

The British Army was marching in.

After three years' hold-up, 80 per cent of it by Turkish bluff (the considerable contribution of British Army Intelligence in accepting it must not be entirely overlooked), our far more powerful forces in Egypt had begun to take the offensive against a war-weary enemy, who now counted as many deserters as troops remaining on his battle strength.

"Jerusalem by Christmas!" Lloyd George had demanded of General Allenby, in appointing him to the Egypt Command in the summer of 1917. Now Allenby had crossed the desert from Egypt, turned the weak Turkish line at Gaza by a brilliant manœuvre and was moving on the Holy City. This he would take, entering humbly on foot a fortnight before Christmas Day.

At a third War Cabinet, 31 October, 1917, Balfour once more brought up the question of the National Home. How could its establishment possibly prejudice Jews elsewhere? Surely, on the analogy of a European immigrant in the United States, it would help that they had a recognized land of origin? As for the present poverty of Palestine, the scientific development of her resources might yet make it a land flowing with milk and honey.

Curzon followed. He delivered another reminiscent address on his travels in the Middle East, which the Prime Minister this time interrupted to ask if he agreed with some expression of sympathy? Resolved:

> "His Majesty's Government view with favour the establishment in Palestine of a National Home for the Jewish People, and will use their best endeavours to facilitate the achievement of this object, it being clearly understood that nothing shall be done which may prejudice the civil and religious rights of existing non-Jewish communities in Palestine or the rights and political status enjoyed by Jews in any other country."

Next day, Lloyd George presented this draft to the leaders of British Jewry. Of eight of them, four accepted it, including the Chief Rabbi, Dr. Hertz, one was neutral and three were hostile. Thus, the famous Balfour Declaration was delivered to the world. Next year, France, Italy and the United States all declared their accord with this policy.

But what *was* the policy? Lloyd George himself, in later years, insisted that what he had meant was that Jews should be free to go to Palestine and settle there in such strength as the land could support—or be made to support. Then, in due course, they should set up their own autonomous Jewish Administration. By no means all Jews would go there, any more than all the Irish-born return to Ireland.

It did not work out that way. The Jewish Question, like the Irish Question, had been too long part of History to be dismissed from it overnight. But the troubles this generation has known were far ahead in October, 1917.

An immediate calamity demanded all attention. Late that month, the Austrian Army, powerfully reinforced by Germans from the Western Front, struck with sudden, staggering fury against the Italian forces in the Styrian Alps. The Italians reeled, and broke. In a fortnight, they had retreated 70 miles, leaving on the field more than half a million dead, wounded, prisoners and missing (an uncounted number of these last had simply flung down their arms and made for home, where their lurid tales of military disorder and defeat multiplied the growing discontent which hunger had previously planted). The Battle of Caporetto cost the Italian Army, already short of guns, nearly three thousand more. By November, 1917, Italy, like Russia, was almost out of the war.

Time for decision. Lloyd George moved at once, the same hour that the black news of Caporetto was brought to him by General Robertson. He ordered him to put into instant operation those plans for rushing reinforcements to Italy which had been worked out after the Rome Conference in the previous spring. The C.I.G.S. started to demur; for once, he was sharply told to get on with the job. Furthermore, he was to go himself with all speed to Italian G.H.Q. and find out there what else required to be done.

To the French Prime Minister, M. Painlevé, Lloyd George proposed that both of them should together pay a visit to the Italian Front and meet the Italian Prime Minister there on the spot. It was agreed, and on 2 November, 1917, accompanied by General Smuts, Lloyd George crossed the Channel. A special train awaited them, and with M. Painlevé and his garrulous confidant, M. Franklin Bouillon, the party hurried towards the Franco-Italian frontier. There, at Modane, where they stepped out to stretch their legs, a splendid sight cheered their hearts—trainload after trainload of French troops and guns rattling through the station and vanishing into the tunnels beneath the snow-clad mountains, the first of five veteran divisions from Verdun. Within a few days more, they would be joined by five British divisions, who had learned their own hard business on the Somme.

It would have been strange if the thought had not kept drumming in Lloyd George's head: Why was this journey really necessary—*now*? For throughout all that year of 1917 he had been urging, begging, coaxing his military colleagues that if France and Britain could not spare a single man from the Western Front, perhaps, at least, they could lend some guns?

The Italians had mustered, in January, 1,500,000 troops against 650,000 Austrians. At that time, suffering had not yet come to Italy in great measure. But Austria-Hungary already knew the bitter price of war. It was the drain of casualties on the Eastern Front, and real privation at home which had induced the new young Austrian Emperor Karl to make his first stumbling steps towards negotiating a separate peace in the spring of 1917. *That* was the time to confirm his fears of final disaster by delivering him another hearty blow!

So Lloyd George had argued, and there was much validity indeed, in his contention.

But the ambitions (or the fixations) of the Allied Generals on the Western Front had prevented us from delivering an effective blow against Austria on the Southern Front, and not until August, 1917, was the long-planned and long-delayed Italian offensive eventually launched. By that time, the Russian Revolution had run nearly six months, and the Eastern Front was melting away. Now, Austria could spare ample reinforcements for her Southern Front. Even so, the Italian attack went pretty well. All that it lacked in the necessary knock-out punch was enough artillery and ammunition. Three hundred guns had been the figure Lloyd George named as being needed. Now, in one week of the enemy's counter-offensive, our Italian Ally had lost three thousand guns.

Writing to Bonar Law on 27 August, 1917, from the country (he was then staying at Great Walstead, where he could hear the boom of the futile Passchendaele bombardment), Lloyd George had noted from the reports of our British Observer on the Italian Front that the current Austrian retreat might very well develop into a rout. He went on:

". . . Austria is anxious for peace. A great military defeat would supply her with the necessary excuse. [General] Cadorna says his heavy ammunition will not last much longer . . . and this corresponds with the information we had before the action. We should never be forgiven if we allowed such an opportunity to go by for lack of prompt action, and we should not deserve to be forgiven. It may be said that it is now too late to send guns and ammunition. But . . . if Cadorna is informed that they are being sent he can then afford to draw on his reserves and fire his last cartridge . . . I cannot believe that transport difficulties would stand in the way if a real effort were made. . . .

P.S. If the Allied Armies from the North Sea to the Adriatic were under one command, I have no doubt as to the course which would be pursued. Surely our strategy ought to be based on the assumption that it is all one front."

But, says Lloyd George, Bonar Law failed to make any impression on General Robertson with this argument.

That was in the days when Victory had beckoned. No action had been taken. Every logistical artifice which War Office Intelligence could devise had been invoked to prove that nothing *could* be done.

Now Disaster glowered. And within a few days, it was found possible to shift half a dozen Allied divisions from the sodden battlefields of France and Flanders to the rock-hewn front of the Italian Alps.

At Rapallo, on 4 November, the three Prime Ministers met, accompanied by their military advisers, Generals Sir William Robertson and Sir Henry Wilson for Britain, Foch for France, and Porro, who was General Cadorna's Chief of Staff, for Italy. After some plain speaking about the panic which had marked Caporetto and the lack of higher leadership displayed there, Lloyd George said frankly that the French and British Governments were not prepared to entrust their troops in Italy to the present Italian C.-in-C. General Cadorna was thereupon relieved of his post and General Diaz appointed in his place.

But this was only the beginning of the military revolution which the British Prime Minister meant to make. He had long ago abandoned any faith in his own C.-in-C., and so had his colleague, Bonar Law.

They had to let Haig's Passchendaele offensive go on because they dared not dismiss Haig. The Field-Marshal was still in close and effective contact both with King George and "King Alfred" (Northcliffe). But if Haig's powers could be curbed it would serve the purpose just as well. The way to do it was to erect some military superstructure above him, and if at the same time it covered all other local and national Commanders-in-Chief, why, so much the better! For then the Allies would secure a single direction of the war instead of a set of separate ones.

This idea had long been germinating in Lloyd George's head, and was often expressed by him, both in his conversation and his correspondence. There is the personal letter which he wrote to President Wilson on 3 September, 1917, setting forth the advantages which the chief enemy, Germany, had held throughout the war by reason of his "despotic dominion" over all his allies, their armies and their economic resources. Lloyd George urged that we must parallel this on our side by ". . . some kind of Allied Joint Council, with permanent military and probably naval and economic staffs attached to work out the plans for submission to the several Governments concerned".

The Prime Minister hopes that the United States will freely come to this council table, as of her own high purpose she has come to the battlefield.

Lloyd George had sought the opinions of four of Britain's best-known soldiers on this matter. These were Haig, Robertson, French and Wilson. As might be expected, the first two flatly turned it down and the other two hailed it, Sir Henry Wilson replying with a detailed memorandum in which he outlined the framework of an entire organization to carry out the idea. Lloyd George had also consulted both the French Premier, M. Painlevé and the French C.-in-C., General Pétain. The Lloyd George proposals set forth in a long letter to Painlevé on 30 October, 1917, envisaged "a kind of Inter-Allied General Staff". It would be advisory to the several Governments, and would include "one or two political representatives of first-rate authority from each of the Allies", with a staff of its own, such as he had suggested in his letter to President Wilson a few weeks earlier. This plan, it will be observed, contains no mention of a Generalissimo.

M. Painlevé hurried over to London to have a final word about it with Lloyd George, who then took a draft to the War Cabinet and secured their acceptance of it the very same day as he set out for Rapallo. General Wilson was appointed British Representative on the new Inter-Allied Advisory General Staff.

Thus armed, Lloyd George had no trouble in carrying the Rapallo Conference with him. After three days' discussion, the new Supreme War Council was set up. Its powers were substantially expressed on the following three clauses:

(ii) The Supreme War Council has for its mission to watch over the general conduct of the war. It prepares recommendations for the decision of the Governments, and keeps itself informed of their execution and reports thereon to the respective Governments.

(iii) The General Staffs and Military Commands of the Armies of each Power charged with the conduct of military operations remain responsible to their respective Governments.

(iv) The general war plans drawn up by the competent Military Authorities are submitted to the Supreme War Council, which under the high authority of the Governments, ensure their concordance, and submits, if need be, any necessary changes.

The Permanent Military Representatives of France, Britain and Italy were then formally named: General Foch, General Wilson and General Cadorna.

Only one other question remained. Where was the Supreme Council to be established? Paris, naturally, said the French. But Lloyd George was not having that. He insisted that it should be somewhere else, as he said, "in order that it should not only be entirely independent of the French Government, but the fact of its independence should thereby be emphasized".

In the end, after the longest argument over any single point, he settled for Versailles.

One matter Lloyd George could not settle for, at least not at any price he was prepared to pay. This was General Robertson's rooted objection to the whole affair. For the C.I.G.S., Rapallo in the autumn smelt no sweeter than Calais in the spring. The moment that the item of the Supreme War Council was reached on the Conference table, General Robertson rose from his seat at the table and stamped forward to the door like an angry bear, eyes burning, eyebrows bristling, pausing only on the way at Colonel Hankey's desk to ask if he would send for him when the next item was reached. "I wash my hands of this present business," he growled.

It was the cannon's opening roar. General Robertson would fight this battle of the Supreme War Council to the bitter end of his own fine and honourable career, with the same devotion and tenacity as he struggled for his favourite War of Attrition on the Western Front.

Now, at last, some form of Allied unity of action had been established——on paper. Lloyd George meant to make it so in fact. He would tell the British people, for a start, and get their goodwill and support. And, in order to arrest public attention to what he considered the grave errors of the past, Lloyd George would be, as he said, "deliberately disagreeable". So, at Paris, he broke his homeward journey, and addressing the company after a luncheon there attended by all the Deputies and Senators at which M. Painlevé announced the setting-up of the Supreme War Council, the Prime Minister of Britain spoke frankly.

So far in this war, he said, Allied Unity had been pure pretence. The Generals from the various countries met every year, each bringing with him his own plan for his own Front. They all sat round the same table and, metaphorically, with needle and thread sewed their plans together; then produced them at a subsequent civilian conference as a single great strategic piece. Such make-believe might live through a generation of peace; it would not survive a week of war.

"Stitching is not strategy. So it came to pass that when these plans were worked-out on the terrible realities of war, the stitches came out and disintegration was complete."

Lloyd George then summarized the successes which our enemy Germany had gained simply because, he said, we had not realized that the entire Front was one and indivisible. Serbia, Rumania, Russia and now Italy, were the milestones on the march of the enemy's triumph and of our defeat. Then, Lloyd George permitted himself some odious comparisons, which would be the cause of considerable trouble to him in the next few days. He said:

"It is no good minimizing the extent of the Caporetto disaster. If you do, then you will never take adequate steps to repair it. When we advance a kilometre into the enemy's lines, snatch a small shattered village out of his cruel grip and capture a few hundreds of his soldiers we shout with unfeigned joy. . . . But what if we had advanced 50 kilometres beyond his lines, made 200,000 of his soldiers prisoners, and taken 2,500 of his best guns, with enormous quantities of munitions and stores?"

The Austrians had done exactly this at Caporetto.

Caporetto, said Lloyd George, was only the latest of our painful experiences, but if we had learned our lesson it would be the last. Real unity, not sham unity was the only such pathway to victory. That was why they had resolved to scrap the cumbrous and clumsy machinery of Conference, to set up instead a permanent Council to survey the whole field of the world battle, and decide where and how the resources of the Allies could be most effectively employed. Lloyd George ended:

"That is the meaning of this Superior Council. If I am right in my conjecture, then this Council will be given real power, the efforts of the Allies will be co-ordinated, and Victory will await Valour."

When the Prime Minister got back to London he was already a day or two behind General Robertson. The C.I.G.S. had called upon the Secretary of State for War, Lord Derby, and enlisted him against this new attempt "to interfere with the soldiers". Whether or not he also got in touch with Asquith and the Liberal Opposition was much questioned at the time, but certainly their spokesmen were well briefed when the memorable debate on the Rapallo decisions took place in the House of Commons on 19 December, 1917. Also, somebody had been talking to the Press.

For at once a fresh clatter broke out in Fleet Street. It is true that it was a very confused one. Some of the newspapers were crying that the Prime Minister had insulted the British Army by those "contemptuous" remarks in his Paris speech about advancing a kilometre to capture a ruined village and his suggestion of unnecessary sacrifice. Others, more intelligently (or perhaps more honestly) interpreted them as a criticism of certain British Generals, and the condemnation of a campaign which was still dragging itself out in the swamps of Passchendaele. A third kind, which really knew what they were writing about, understood that the Paris performance was simply the "Press Conference" of the Rapallo Conference, and that if actions had any meaning this was a design to create an *executive* and not merely an advisory War Council. It was on this point that General Robertson and his friends concentrated their fire; for they, at any rate, thoroughly grasped that its purpose was to curb their own power.

HANDS OFF THE ARMY!

boomed the *Globe*, and the *Morning Post* joined with the *Daily News* and the weekly *Spectator* and the *Nation* to assail Lloyd George's latest villainy.

The editor of the *Spectator* (Mr. John St. Loe Strachey) felt disgusted with this "mischievous speech" by one who was "not fit to be the Prime Minister of this country". He declared that "the risks of having at the head of affairs a man capable of such levity, such irresponsibility, such recklessness, such injustice are beyond endurance".

The *Nation* (Editor: Mr. H. W. Massingham), was equally condemnatory, and more constructive. It offered an alternative Government. In view of forthcoming events, the Head of it was especially interesting; the other names may indicate something, too:

"Prime Minister, Lord Lansdowne; Foreign Secretary, Mr. Asquith; Chancellor of the Exchequer, Mr. McKenna; Lord President of the Council, Lord Rosebery; First Lord of the Admiralty, Mr. Runciman; War Minister,

General Smuts; Minister of Munitions, Lord Robert Cecil (or Mr. Winston Churchill); Colonial Secretary, Mr. A. J. Balfour; Lord Chancellor, Sir John Simon; Secretary for India, Lord Grey; Minister for Reconstruction, Mr. Sydney Webb; President of the Board of Trade, Mr. Pringle; Home Secretary, Mr. Henderson; Chancellor of the Duchy of Lancaster, Mr. John Burns."

The Prime Minister had one firm friend in the national Press, besides the Coalition Liberal *Daily Chronicle*. This was the *Daily Express*, which hailed his "Great War Speech" as being both "eloquent and amazingly candid". The newspaper thought that it was necessary to talk frankly to the British Public, and reckoned that they could take it.

When the gossip raced round that Churchill had been in Paris at the time of the Prime Minister's speech and had helped in composing it, the signals were set for storm. Lloyd George's Parliamentary scouts reported renewed rumblings against this "George-Churchill combine".

It was not the only warning laid on Lloyd George's breakfast-table that Monday morning. There was Lord Derby, begging that the Prime Minister should give assurances that the military advisers to the new Supreme War Council would be definitely subordinate to the C.I.G.S. and would not be allowed to discuss any projects without his previous agreement (this would put General Wilson in his proper place!). Then there was Lord Curzon, urging that Lloyd George should see General Robertson himself before the debate, and come to terms with him.

On the other hand, there was Lord Esher, entreating Lloyd George from Paris to stand firm and declaring that any weakening in the face of opposition either in Parliament or the Press would be fatal to his influence with the French, who were (he said) desperately close to the complete break-down of all governmental authority: "France leans upon England, and for France there is only one English statesman whose name is an honourable one."

France, indeed, was near the edge of the abyss. On the very morrow of announcing the establishment of the Supreme War Council, the French Prime Minister, Painlevé had fallen. For several days France was without a Government and then, as a panic stop-gap measure, the various warring Parliamentary factions conceded to old "Tiger" Clemenceau, who was hated by all of them and sincerely reciprocated their sentiments with contempt. In his generation, the Tiger had respected the character of only one French politician, Jaurés (he opposed his opinions), and Jaurés had been assassinated by a demented patriot in 1914. Now, Clemenceau formed a Government which nobody else in France expected to survive until Christmas. If Lloyd George himself had been beaten in the House of Commons on 19 November, 1917, the repercussions in France would have been very grave.

So, to the Great Debate went the Prime Minister that afternoon, expecting not only to have to fight for the life of his Government but perhaps for the fate of the war. He had to meet and beat, besides what threatened to be the most determined attack yet mounted by the Official Opposition, a more dangerous possible revolt by sympathizers with the "Military Party" in the Government's own ranks. He had to placate these critics, and still preserve as much of the Rapallo Plan as would satisfy the French that its essence was intact.

In this, Lloyd George succeeded perhaps better than he had dared to hope, with a Parliamentary performance which *The Times* hailed as "a great personal triumph". It was true, for though his speech was variously described by some other speakers who took part in the debate as "camouflage", "an exhibition of shadow-boxing worthy of his distinguished fellow-countryman Jimmy Wilde", and "cheap rhetoric, savouring of the Chapel rather than the Senate", Lloyd George so took the sting out of the attack that the House did not divide. It is also true that his speech bore only a slight relation to what had actually gone on at Rapallo (and still less to what he had in mind there). It bore no relation at all to what he had said at Paris, which was that if he was right in his conjecture, then this new War Council would be given "real power". In fact, Lloyd George won his battle by evacuating most of the ground he had been expected (and originally had himself intended) to occupy.

Asquith's opening onslaught turned out to be a mild affair. He accepted the Prime Minister's assurance, in answer to an earlier question before the Debate opened, that "the Council will have no Executive power". That settled the fears, expressed in some high quarters, that Unity of Control was designed to develop into Unity of Command. For the rest, Asquith was concerned to show that as much Allied co-ordination as was possible had already been achieved during his own régime.

Lloyd George seized upon that blessed word "Co-ordination" (he used it seventeen times!) to cover all the plans evolved at Rapallo. He utterly repudiated the idea of a "Generalissimo". "It would not work," he declared. "It would produce real friction, and might really produce not merely friction between the Armies, but friction between the nations and the Governments."

Likewise Lloyd George declared against a Council with executive powers, unless we were absolutely driven to it by the failure of the present experiment. It was true (he must admit) that both France and America were willing to accept such a Council now. Indeed, some distinguished persons had thought it overdue for years. The first Allied Leader to seize upon the vital need for unity of action and to propose an Allied Council of some kind (Colonel Hankey had placed this invaluable brief in the Prime Minister's hand as he actually entered the Chamber) was—Lord Kitchener.

The Prime Minister then made a further effort to expunge prejudice from the debate by denying that Winston Churchill had taken any part in composing the speech.

As for the so-called interference by the politicians with the strategy of the generals: "Really, when I see in certain quarters 'Hands off the Army', it makes me feel as if I were crossing the Channel in a torpedo-boat destroyer on a choppy sea."

The soldiers had been backed by the civilians to the limit—and he did not mean "backing" in speeches. He meant backing in guns, ammunition, transport, shipping, railways, supplies and men. Only twice during this war had he himself acted against the advice of soldiers. The first time was over the gun programme, and the second was in appointing a civilian to reorganize the railways behind the front lines. As a matter of history, he did not regret either. For today, apart from the matchless valour of our troops and the skill in their dispositions, what were the two most conspicuous features in the great Flanders attacks? The overwhelming mass of artillery and ammunition, and the whole of the supplies running right into the firing line!

The Prime Minister sat down amid a storm of cheers and the rest of the debate fell flat. The House emptied, leaving nobody to answer the valid points raised about the machinery of this new Inter-Allied Staff and how it was to work in "Co-ordination" with the existing Imperial General Staff? Only Mr. Pringle put his finger accurately on a sore spot when he declared that: ". . . If you want to supersede Sir William Robertson, you ought to do it honestly and straightforwardly, and not in this way."

Lloyd George himself reckoned that in getting his Supreme War Council (in whatever shape) safely past what might have been a hostile House of Commons, he had scored a substantial victory. General Robertson, on the other hand, realized that he had suffered a severe defeat. A potentially superior Council *had* been set up, however shadowy its present powers; a rival Staff *had* been created, though ill-defined its functions. The temper of the C.I.G.S. was not improved by the fact that Britain's Permanent Military Representative on the new Council was the well-distrusted General Wilson.

So General Robertson renewed his grievances to the Secretary of State for War, Lord Derby, who was now about to enter what Lloyd George called his "resignation-twice-a-day" period.

But the Prime Minister thought it wise still to pour oil on the troubled waters of the War Office.

"26 November, 1917.   10 Downing Street.
My dear Secretary of State,

I am very glad to have your letter, and I appreciate greatly your efforts to make the new Inter-Allied War Council a really workable scheme. . . . With the points you set out in your letter I am in substantial agreement, but so much will depend on the practical working of the new agreement that I consider it would be a mistake to lay too much emphasis on details at the beginning. It is clear that while Sir Henry Wilson acts as one of the co-advisers to the War Council the C.I.G.S. remains the official adviser of the War Cabinet and the latter will therefore continue to advise the Cabinet on all recommendations of the Council before they are finally adopted by the Cabinet. He will also accompany the Prime Minister to the meetings of the Council. Whether any particular matter is first mooted at the Council or at the War Cabinet is really an unimportant detail, so long as it is clear that the C.I.G.S. will have his say and the War Cabinet the final decision. In fact, if the C.I.G.S. accompanies the Prime Minister to the meetings of the Council, he will have his say in both places, and the question of where a matter is initiated becomes immaterial.

Yours very sincerely,
D. Lloyd George."

A bitter east wind was blowing from Russia.

In mid-October, 1917, during the last days of the doomed Kerensky Government, the Russians had sent an envoy to the West with the demand that the policy of the Allies be based "upon the principle of no annexations and no indemnities", with the right of all nations to settle their own peaceful future. The German invaders must evacuate all occupied Russian territories; Russia would grant autonomy to Poland and the Baltic Provinces; Belgium was to be restored; the fate of Alsace-Lorraine decided by a free plebiscite; the subject peoples of Austria-Hungary to have Home Rule; the German Colonies to be returned; Disarmament and a League of Nations welcomed.

Fine words. Three weeks later, Lenin and Trotsky overthrew the tottering Russian Social Democracy in the Bolshevik uprising of 7 November, 1917.

The new men both understood what they wanted, and meant to get it. On 8 November, a resolution of the Congress of the Soviets of Workmen's, Soldiers' and Peasants' Delegates called for ". . . negotiations without delay for a just and democratic peace, such as is longed for by the overwhelming majority of the working and labouring classes in all the belligerent countries, who are exhausted, wearied and distressed by the war".

On 1 December, 1917, an uneasy armistice was signed on the Eastern Front.

In this kind of war weather, the Lansdowne "Peace Letter" fell like a cold cascade upon Lloyd George and his Government in Britain.

The Marquess of Lansdowne was earnest, intelligent and deeply patriotic. He was almost universally respected. He had been Viceroy of India, Governor-General of Canada, Foreign Secretary, War Secretary and for many years the joint and senior Leader of the Tory Party. Lord Lansdowne had been responsible for the *Entente Cordiale* with France in 1903, and when Germany threatened France and Russia in 1914 and the Liberal Government of Britain had been still undecided between peace and war, he had written, with Bonar Law, the Tory Leader of the House of Commons, that joint letter insisting that: "It would be fatal to the honour and security of the United Kingdom to hesitate in supporting France and Russia at the present juncture."

As one of the leaders of a Patriotic Opposition, Lansdowne had fulfilled his part. He had joined Asquith's Coalition Governmen⁺ in 1915, and served loyally. Then, in November, 1916, he had produced and circulated to the Cabinet his famous memorandum, in which frankly and objectively he had assessed our prospects of final victory. His conclusion, that we should reject no reasonable offer of a Compromise Peace, had been shot down by the vigorous counter-arguments of the Minister of Blockade, Lord Robert Cecil. So, though Peace talk was much in the political air that autumn of 1916, the Prime Minister, Asquith, had decided to make no approaches yet to the enemy. But he had written a private note to Lansdowne a few days later, expressing his "complete concurrence" with his views. The following month, Asquith had fallen.

Now another year of war had gone by. Was Peace by Victory any nearer? Were Passchendaele, Caporetto and the Bolshevik Revolution the signs of it? Lansdowne took up his pen again.

On 16 November, 1917, he addressed a private letter to Balfour to suggest a debate on peace in the House of Lords. He wanted the Government to put forward terms which should include the following propositions:

I. No dismemberment of the Central Powers.
II. No form of government to be forced upon their people which is distasteful to them.
III. No denial of trading facilities to the Central Powers, except as a legitimate war measure.
IV. A full examination with other Powers of the problems connected with the "Freedom of the Seas".
V. An international pact to settle disputes by peaceful means.

Balfour replied, also by private note. He dealt with this programme point by point, and the plan to debate it in the House of Lords. He politely turned it down.

Once more, Lansdowne began to write. Now it was a Letter to *The Times*, 27 November, 1917. It pointed out that the enemy, though repeatedly challenged, had never yet set forth his peace terms, while the Allies had certainly made a general declaration of theirs. The restoration of Belgium would always remain in the forefront of our objectives, but the possibility of achieving some of the others had altered with the years. For example, the redrawing of the map of South-Eastern Europe. A fresh exchange of views between the Allies was necessary, and the sooner the better:

". . . If we are to have an Allied Council for the purpose of adapting our strategy in the field to the ever-shifting developments of War, it is fair to assume that in the matter of Peace terms, also, the Allies will make it their business to examine, and if necessary revise, the territorial requirements."

The letter then argued that if certain considerations (those submitted to Balfour) were promulgated by the Allies "an immense stimulus would be given to the Peace party in Germany".

The Lansdowne letter filled very nearly two newspaper columns. But that was not the reason why the editor of *The Times*, Mr. Geoffrey Dawson, was reluctant to print it. The new Supreme War Council, with the new French Prime Minister, M. Clemenceau, in the chair, were meeting within a day or two at Versailles and the publication of such a letter now would look like a weakening of the Will-to-Win-the-War spirit at its strongest point, which was in Britain. (This, of course, was exactly why Lansdowne wanted it published, and at this precise moment.) After twenty-four hours' reflection Mr. Dawson went round to Lansdowne House to explain that for the letter to appear in any newspaper now would not be in the public interest. The writer was not impressed. He took it straight round to the editor of the *Daily Telegraph*, who printed it in his Correspondence columns the next morning, 29 November, 1917. An editorial almost as lengthy commended it.

It caused an instant, and intense hubbub. The public had lately heard from several sources, insistent rumours of peace-feelers. There was always the I.L.P. propaganda at home, and now it was reinforced by the No More War Please from Soviet Russia—as well as a brand new "peace-blitz" from Germany. The "Peace Party" which the German Government was interested in, which was the one in Britain, certainly received "an immense stimulus" from the Lansdowne Letter.

Newspaper comment ranged widely. There was the angry abuse of the *Globe*, the same evening:

". . . the lamentable letter which Lord Lansdowne has thought fit to present to the *Daily Telegraph* after its patriotic rejection by the Editor of *The Times*. . . . For him and all other politicians of his unhappy type, England has no longer any use. . . ."

and the *Daily Mail* next morning:

"If Lord Lansdowne raises the white flag he is alone in his surrender."

There was the measured condemnation of the *Daily Express*:

"Lord Lansdowne's inopportune speech . . . we fear it will harden Germany's resolve to conquer, since he may seem to imply that Britain's strength of purpose is weakening . . . a war half-won, a peace by negotiation could only mean gigantic world preparation for conflict more horrible and more hideous. . . ."

and the measured reproach of *The Times*:

". . . the letter reflects no responsible phase of British opinion . . . in all the Allied countries it will be read with universal regret and reprobation."

There were the Liberal ecstasies of the *Manchester Guardian*:

". . . a striking appeal . . . a wise endeavour . . . we have suffered too long from a timid reluctance to face facts and to declare in terms that all men can understand, the things we want and do not want."

and Mr. A. G. Gardiner in the *Daily News*:

"The torch is lighted; it will not be put out."

Of course, the Parliamentary lobbies buzzed, too. It was said that Balfour had seen the Lansdowne Letter and approved it (he had only seen it and disapproved it); that Curzon had discussed it at dinner with the author himself (so he had, but after it had been published). These two tales were designed to convey that the Cabinet was split on the question. Another rumour ran that Asquith had collaborated with Lansdowne; this suggested that a new "Peace" Coalition was in the offing. Finally, it was put about that Lansdowne was simply a stalking-horse for the Government itself. A "Peace" Plan, or even a "Peace" Election was already prepared, and would be launched if the signs seemed favourable. The same evening, as the Lansdowne Letter appeared, Lord Edmund Talbot, the Government Chief Whip, found it necessary to issue a denial to the Press:

"We are informed on authority that the rumour which was current this afternoon that Lord Lansdowne's letter was written with the knowledge of the Government is entirely without foundation."

Everybody in politics was offering an opinion—or an interview. The Socialist Ramsay MacDonald "welcomed" it. Liberal Ex-Chancellor Lord Loreburn considered it "of the highest importance". Tory Lord Parmoor[1] "rejoiced". Irish Nationalist, D. Lynch saw "surrender stamped on it".

Nevertheless, it had to be so discussed if only to be effectively condemned. Asquith essayed this when, at Birmingham, a week or so later, he categorically denied "any responsibility, direct or indirect, for its terms".

Asquith confessed that he did not read into it some meanings which had been so freely attributed, and denounced; but if Lord Lansdowne had suggested that we should slacken our efforts or indicate to enemies (who had so far refused even to hint their own terms) that we were ready to sue for peace, he would utterly dissociate himself from any such proposal.

It was Bonar Law who finally put paid to any "Lansdowne Movement" in the ranks of the Government Coalition in the House of Commons. At the Kingsway Hall, on 1 December, 1917, addressing 1,500 delegates of a special

[1] Charles Alfred Cripps, 1st Baron, 1852–1941. Tory M.P. 1895–1906; joined Labour Party; Lord President of the Council, 1924, 1929–31. Father of Sir Stafford Cripps.

Conference of Tory and Liberal Unionist organizations, he described the Letter as "a national misfortune" and declared that "a peace made on this basis would be nothing less than a defeat".

Bonar Law warned the country that if the pacifist movement should be so stimulated by the Lansdowne Letter as to imperil the Government in its task in the House of Commons, then a General Election would indeed follow, and very soon, too. It was not the last time that Bonar Law would have to bring his Party to heel by such a threat.

Lloyd George returned from Versailles to find it All Quiet on the Westminster Front. They had spent a strenuous and useful session at the Supreme War Council, where they had established unity of action as well as words, at last. Wrote General Wilson in his Diary:

"The proceedings went off splendidly. Clemenceau was an admirable chairman, Lloyd George backed him well, Hankey drafted resolution after resolution, which Lloyd George read out and which Clemenceau put and which were instantly passed. A number of things were referred to the Council, viz.: Italy, Salonika, Rumania, rail transportation, Belgian army. These are quite enough to keep us busy for some time!"

But Lloyd George was not well himself; he was desperately tired and overworked. Worse, worried. When, after Christmas his old friend and recent critic, C. P. Scott, Editor of the *Manchester Guardian* called to see him about following Lansdowne, at least, to the point of restating Britain's war aims he found a man strangely and suddenly bowed. Let him tell of the Lloyd George he met, December, 1917.

"I warn you," said Lloyd George, "I am in a very pacifist temper. I listened last night at a dinner given to Philip Gibbs on his return from the Front, to the most impressive and moving description from him of what the war in the West really means, that I have heard. Even an audience of hardened politicians and journalists was strongly affected. If people really knew, the war would be stopped tomorrow, but of course they don't know —and can't know. The Correspondents don't write, and the Censorship wouldn't pass the truth. The thing is horrible, and beyond human nature to bear, and I feel I can't go any longer with the bloody business; I would rather resign."

It comes to every leader worth a word in history. The moment of utter, black, annihilating despair, not of the troops by their leader, but of the leader by himself. The abasing thought that you, that leader, are incapable, unworthy, of calling forth from other men the last great sacrificial effort which might yet transform the shape of the battle, and so save all. Everyone in the human chronicle has been a coward at some time before some thing, if never yet before any other being. They are the blessed ones (and perhaps more blessed for mankind, even than for themselves) who catch the tide of Fortune and of Fame. But the same lucky men also knew those lonely, fearful hours when they grappled to be bigger than the size they felt themselves to be.

"I feel I am a C.3 chap," said Lloyd George miserably to Beaverbrook, one desperate night in this desperate winter. C.3 was the lowest grade of the serving soldier in the 1914–18 war. History will report that Lloyd George never showed it to the world.

Now in the East, the battle was done, though a fresh and more fearful blood-letting, by the hand of brother against brother in Civil War, was about to begin. In the West, storm gathered and darkness descended as the Old Year died. It was near midnight of the war.

CHAPTER XXIII

LLOYD GEORGE THREATENS TO GO

STEADILY, the fires in the furnace burned. The war on five fronts was faithfully fuelled. Collecting the fuel, not stoking it, was the hardest problem—a problem which the generals were inclined to dismiss, but which the politicians had to handle.

If there had been no other point at issue between the Prime Minister, Lloyd George, and the Commander-in-Chief, Field-Marshal Haig, it would have been serious enough. The soldiers were making demands for men and ever more men. But against them, Lloyd George had to set the equally insistent requirements of the sailors, shipbuilders, dockers, munition-makers, miners and farmers.

But it was *not* the only point at issue. Beyond Lloyd George's first and firm duty to allocate Britain's available manpower in the most economical and effective way between the men-behind-the-gun and the men-behind-the-men-behind-the-gun there lay his ever-deepening doubt of Field-Marshal Haig's capacity to make the best use of the manpower already placed at his disposal.

On the Western Front, in the battles most costly in casualties, the Somme in 1916, and Passchendaele in 1917, the British losses had been three men for every two of the enemy. So vast was the total that the generals' estimate (it steadily rose) was that by March, 1918, the British Army would be short of a quarter of a million infantry, and double that number by the following September. A military manpower crisis was at hand.

A national labour crisis loomed, too. To sort out the conflicting claims of the Services and of Industry, Lloyd George had set up in December, 1917, a Manpower Committee of the War Cabinet. He took the Chair himself, and the other members were Curzon, Carson, Smuts and Barnes.

From the War Office, Lloyd George had demanded an immediate appreciation of the relative strengths of the opposing armies on the Western Front. The Director of Military Operations, General Sir Frederick Maurice, obliged with the Allied figures and the Director of Military Intelligence, General Sir George Macdonogh, with those of the enemy.

At this time Lloyd George had returned from Riddell's country mansion at Great Walstead to his own house at Walton Heath. This was the place which Haig thus described in his *Diary* after a visit there ". . . reminds me of summer lodgings at the seaside—a sort of maid-of-all-work opened the door to us".

This was the old Welshwoman who acted as housekeeper there. Her idea of entertaining any guests, however distinguished they might be, was cursory and crude. She reckoned that her job was to look after Lloyd

George, and that she did. The rest did not interest her, however interesting they might be to other people. Once, when Lloyd George had been taking his afternoon nap in the sitting-room, he awoke to hear her shouting down the telephone, which was in the hall: "Who wants him? Who is it? *Who?* Northcliffe? Why can't you leave the man alone?"

A curious picture of the way in which the Prime Minister lived and worked at this time is told by Col. R. Rawlinson, O.B.E., then a young subaltern invalided home from the front and working in the War Office. One dark night in December, 1917, he and a fellow officer were told to strap on their revolvers, draw a couple of dozen rounds of ammunition apiece, and take certain Very Secret papers down to Lloyd George at Walton Heath. In high excitement, they set off, driving through the stormy night with lamps shrouded against the air raiders, and imagining possible enemy agents in every shadowy figure on the roadside.

After an hour, they reached the house, and hammered on the door. A wait of several minutes, and then with unbolting and unlocking, it was opened by the housekeeper. Fortunately, at this moment Lloyd George himself came out of the sitting-room, and welcomed them in out of the downpour. When he asked if they had had any dinner, standing stiffly to attention they mumbled something about it not mattering. "Oh, I'll find you some scrag end of mutton and some rice pudding!" said Lloyd George. "I've just finished supper myself." He then produced this repast, and a bottle of wine, and left them while he went off to read the Secret papers in the next room. Later, he joined them at the table, bringing a large box of cigars of all sizes and qualities. "They are forever forcing them on me at public dinners," he laughed. "Take a good one, now!"

Then Lloyd George began to pepper the two soldiers with questions about the real conditions at the front, about rations, weapons, organization, leave, the spirit of the troops, the behaviour of the enemy. It was nearly 11 o'clock when the Prime Minister led them out to their car and bade them good night. He had learnt much, besides what was in the Secret papers. They drove back to London more excited and keyed-up than when they had come out.

It was at this time, as Haig records in his *Diary* of 8 December, 1917, that he received an angry letter from General Robertson at the War Office.

"The Cabinet are at last scared as regards manpower, and notwithstanding the numerous Memos sent in by the Army Council during the last year, some of them, like Politicians, are inclined to say they have been misled by the Soldiers who have quite recently changed their minds. I thought I had been fairly cautious in this respect—but the P.M. was good enough to tell me the other day in Cabinet that he had been through my weekly summaries and had marked a curious collection of statements showing that I had underestimated the enemy's power. Nice occupation for him and his creatures, and a proof of the impossibility of honestly working with such a man. . . ."

But this time, the Director of Military operations, General Maurice, and the Director of Military Intelligence, General Macdonogh, stuck to their figures. They presented to the Cabinet Manpower Committee (December, 1917) the following picture:

On the Western Front, Allied strength exceeded that of the enemy by 800,000 men. On the Italian Front, by 400,000 men. But since the enemy was now practically freed from his commitments on the Eastern Front, he still disposed a slight superiority in numbers, and would be able to deploy many extra divisions in the West before the Americans arrived in sufficient force to offset them.

The Manpower Committee reckoned that British industry could possibly be raided of another quarter of a million men, and that as many more were due under the 1902 age draft. Then, what about those unemployed cavalry divisions which the British C.-in-C. was forever massing behind the lines for that "break-through" which never came? Why not re-train, and then use those magnificent horsed troops in the two new arms of the Services—the Royal Tank Corps, which was the modern mechanized cavalry, and the Royal Air Force which, in Lloyd George's vivid phrase, was "the cavalry of the clouds"? The Manpower Committee also reminded the War Office that, according to their own returns for 1 January, 1918, there were located in the United Kingdom a million-and-a-half troops and most of them were available. The rest, who were recruits in training, could be called upon if the Government's pledge not to send overseas men under the age of 19 was revoked.[1]

In the end, when first a disastrous retreat, and then a victorious advance compelled a reinforcement of the British Expeditionary Force in France, nearly 600,000 more men were sent across the Channel, most of them from this vast sit-down Army in England.

Why weren't they sent before?

Was it because the Prime Minister continued to accept the estimates of the War Office and G.H.Q. alike? (For their optimism continued up until a few days before the deadly blow of the enemy fell upon our weaker forces.)

Or was it because Lloyd George himself wanted to believe that on the Western Front in the New Year of 1918 the Allies were "over-insured"?

And if so, why did he want so hard to believe it?

Because of the inherent weakness of his own political position. *He was unwilling to place at the disposal of a Commander-in-Chief whom he distrusted, but dared not displace, the last great reserve of Britain's military manpower,*

[1] This pledge was "subject to grave emergency" and in March 1918 was indeed revoked.

because he feared that Haig would launch another Passchendaele offensive with it. And, quite apart from the frightful and apparently useless slaughter, argued Lloyd George, what would be the position of Britain then?

The Prime Minister had put the case before King George V on 18 October, 1917. Briefly, thus:

I. The Russians—and perhaps the Italians—are out of the battle.
II. The French "do not intend to do much fighting".
III. We shall not get much military support from the Americans in 1918.
IV. So the brunt of the fighting on the Western Front will fall upon the British, and we shall be expected "to sacrifice the flower of our Army in a single-handed offensive".
V. We should be mad if we attempted it.

For what would be the result when at last Victory perched upon our banners, asked Lloyd George? France would have her new armies intact; Russia might even be a Military Power again; America would claim the triumph; and Britain would be too weak to count, or "to make her voice heard and her will prevail in the momentous decisions to be come to in the Council of Peace".

This shall never be, declared Lloyd George. It was his duty to ensure that whenever the climax was reached, Britain should be at the zenith of her military strength, and in a position to hold her own among the other nations of the world. From this viewpoint Lloyd George never budged. He remembered our allies as well as our enemy—and kept his head about both.

So Lloyd George proposed to get it quite firmly from our partners in the war whether or not they would be ready to resume a serious general offensive in 1918? If not, we should ourselves remain on the defensive in the West, cut our campaigns elsewhere, and get as many men as possible at work at home, especially in shipbuilding and agriculture.

To which the King had inquired, pertinently: "What will the enemy be doing?"

Lloyd George's answer, then as ever after the event, was that if our forces in France were properly disposed, they were strong enough to hold the Germans. At that time, the British Expeditionary Force in France (including the five divisions dispatched to Italy) mustered a ration strength of more than two million men.

But the matter was far more than a simple sum in figures. There were complications of an imponderable kind. Greatest of these, was the lack of confidence between the Prime Minister and the Commander-in-Chief, and the fact that though Lloyd George would dearly have liked to dismiss Haig, even if he had felt strong enough to do it he did not know whom to put in his place.

There had been a time (it was just after the Battle of Cambrai) when

Lloyd George had thought of promoting Haig out of harm's way by making him a titular "Generalissimo" of all the British Armies. It came to nothing, because the Prime Minister found it too difficult to define just what the Field-Marshal's functions and authority would be in this new post.

Sir Douglas Haig, Lloyd George rated as dull-witted. Once, in his house at Churt long after the First World War was over, the old War Prime Minister was talking to the author about Haig. He jumped up from his chair, and strode over to a full-length portrait of the Field-Marshal, which hung at the foot of the stairs. Lloyd George placed his hand across the top of Haig's gleaming cavalry boots. "He was brilliant," he said, "up to here!"

Nor had Lloyd George reason to trust any longer even to Haig's belief in future victory. Early in the New Year, he had received a remarkable letter from General Smuts, then visiting the C.-in-C. at British Headquarters in France.

G.H.Q. 21 Jan. 1918.

"My dear Prime Minister,

I arrived here this evening and besides discussing with Haig the operations for 1918 I had a very interesting conversation with him over the question of peace which I thought I should report to you. Haig said he considered that so far the British Empire had got most out of this war, certainly a good deal more than even Germany, and he doubted whether we would gain more by continuing the war for another twelve months. At the end of that period we would be much more exhausted and our industrial and financial recovery would be more difficult, and America would get a great pull over us. There were besides the dangers from the collapse of Italy or France or both. He did not think France would continue to fight for Alsace-Lorraine; Northern France he felt certain would not continue the war for that purpose. He thought our best policy was to strengthen Austria against Germany, and to turn the latter in the direction of Russia for her future. Thus she would be taken off the path of the British Empire and would in future bump up against the greatest military obstacles. We should keep the German colonies and let Germany annex Courland &c. He was strongly in favour of an early peace on those lines. He doubted whether America would be a really serious factor even in 1919 from her present rate of progress.

This is all very significant, coming as it does from our Commander-in-Chief, and a man who has rather erred on the side of optimism in the past.

Yours sincerely

J. C. Smuts."

A note signed by Colonel Hankey, who had accompanied Smuts, dated 22.1.18, came with this letter. "Prime Minister, I fully confirm."

As for Sir William Robertson, Lloyd George regarded him as deceitful.

In Switzerland, 1920

For instance, he thought (unjustly) that he had deliberately instructed General Allenby, then G.O.C. in Palestine, to exaggerate the strength of the Turk enemy opposite him, and to apply for an extravagant reinforcement of troops from Britain before continuing his advance on Aleppo, in order that the C.I.G.S. himself, in London, could rule out the project as impracticable—and thus retain these troops for the Western Front. The Prime Minister's mind was darkened by these suspicions.

If Smuts was himself impressed by these events in January, 1918, two months before the Germans opened their terrible final offensive in the West, it may help to explain his own doubts later on.

The public scene was overcast in this New Year, too, by mutual recrimination—and more bitter than ever—between the supporters of "the Soldiers" and the friends and followers of "the Statesmen".

Both factions, of course, had their "fifth columns" in Whitehall, and especially in the War Office. The Director of Military Operations, Major-General Sir Frederick Maurice, was a friend of many leading Asquithian Liberals; the Deputy-Chief of Imperial General Staff, General Sir Robert Whigham, was in close touch with the Tory Press. Accusations of "working the Press" flew back and forth between both sets of active operators, and were the staple ammunition for almost any debate in the House of Commons.

The same charges seem to have formed the explosive element of the conversational hand-grenades which were currently lobbed between Number One British Statesman and Number One British Soldier. According to Haig, Lloyd George personally complained to him one day in the Hotel Crillon, Paris, during November, 1917, about attacks then being made upon himself in the Press, which he said were "evidently inspired by the Military".

Both the Statesmen and the Soldiers, of course, were again using the powerful batteries of Fleet Street for all they were worth.

Meantime, early in the New Year, somebody in Lloyd George's Government had sensed real danger in this war within the war, and sought to bring the argument back to facts and figures which nobody could escape. This was his Minister of Munitions, Winston Churchill, now once more in Lloyd George's close personal confidence, though not yet in the War Cabinet. He had entirely sided with Lloyd George in his struggle with the generals in the previous autumn over Passchendaele, and what appeared to be their inordinate appetite for more and more men to stuff the cannon's mouth. Now, the mounting strength of the enemy on the Western Front caused Churchill to sound an alarm. So, after studying an elaborate War Office appreciation of the battle in the West, he wrote to the Prime Minister:

19.1.18.

"My dear Prime Minister,
    I do hope you are not closing your mind to these facts. The war is fought by divisions, and I think that is a true way of counting forces. Next

o

to that, 'rifles', i.e. fighting infantrymen—are the test, and with them guns, light, medium and heavy. I do not like the tendencies displayed in these paras., which show very serious accumulation of forces and still more serious possibilities in the future.

I don't think we are doing enough for our Army. . . . We are not raising its strength as we ought. We ought to fill it up at once to full strength.

It is very wrong to give men to the Navy in priority to the Army . . . the imminent danger is on the Western Front, and the crisis will come before June. A defeat here will be *fatal*.

Please don't let vexation against past military blunders (which I share with you to the full) lead you to underrate the gravity of the impending campaign, or to keep the Army short of what is needed.

You know how highly I rate the modern defensive compared with offensive. But I do *not* like the situation now developing, and I do not think all that is possible is being done to meet it. . . . Men at once—at all costs from Navy, from Munitions, from Home Army, from Civil life. Stint food and commercial imports to increase shells, aeroplanes and tanks. Wire and concrete on the largest possible scale.

A good plan for counter blows all worked out beforehand to relieve pressure at the points of attack when they manifest themselves.

If this went wrong—everything would go wrong. I do not feel sure about it. The Germans are a terrible foe, and their generals are better than ours. Ponder, and then *Act*.

Yours always, W."

The climate was not improved by a vitriolic article in the *Morning Post* of 24 January, 1918, from the pen of Colonel Repington, who had now parted company with his old newspaper, *The Times*, because he considered that Northcliffe was not now sufficiently "supporting the soldiers". So Repington had transferred his allegiance to a newspaper which was not likely to be labelled as "friendly to the Government".

This opening barrage by the new contributor stated the manpower crisis in the British Army, and charged the Government with running away from it. The article had not been submitted to the Press Bureau, a serious offence under the Defence of the Realm Regulations. There was little doubt who had provided the figures for this brief. As Lloyd George well knew, Colonel Repington was on terms of friendship with the C.I.G.S., General Robertson, and of still closer friendship with the Director of Military Operations, Major-General Maurice. The Prime Minister wrote that same morning to Lord Derby, the Secretary of State for War:

"24 January, 1918   10 Downing Street
    My dear Secretary of State,
        My attention has been drawn to an article by Colonel Repington in

today's *Morning Post*. It is quite clear that the information which he conveys in that article must have emanated from someone who has access to the highly confidential material of the General Staff, and therefore a most grave breach of discipline must have been committed. As you are aware, the General Staff have altered their figures of enemy numbers from time to time, and a most serious change in their views on this subject has been effected within the last two or three days. But clearly Colonel Repington has been supplied with the very latest General Staff intelligence as to enemy numbers, and also as to our reserves, and he published these figures without any of the qualifications contained in the Staff report. This is a gross breach of Army Regulations, and if someone in the General Staff Department continues to supply secret intelligence to the Press with whatever object I must, after submitting the facts to His Majesty, take the House of Commons into my confidence and take stern action. The publication of confidential information of this character for the benefit of the enemy is an act of treason to the State.

I earnestly trust that in your capacity of Secretary of State you will make the necessary investigations into the divulgation of secret documents with a view to enforcing discipline.

Yours sincerely,
D. Lloyd George."

When no action followed, the Prime Minister followed this up four days later with another and more peremptory letter to the War Secretary demanding to know what had happened? He urged:

"The gravity of the offence lies in the fact that information has been given to the enemy which undoubtedly encourages him . . . If an ordinary soldier had been the offender he would have been shot without any compunction."

But the Director of Public Prosecutions said his department doubted if they could single out the General Staff as the source of Colonel Repington's information. Some of his statistics were inaccurate, but were the Government going into court to prove which? The case was dropped.

There followed much discussion in the War Cabinet on the Manpower issue, including some brusque exchanges between the Prime Minister and the C.I.G.S. who failed to understand what all these civilian fellows were needed for in the factories; couldn't machines do the work? There was more debate, too, at the next Allied War Conference, where the French Chief of Staff, General Foch, could not see why so many men were needed by the Royal Navy; had the Navy done any fighting? Finally, came the rather reluctant decision of the British Government to bring in a new Military Service Bill to call up more men, though it was not intended to draft overseas men younger than 19 or older than 41, nor was the Bill to apply to Ireland.

To carry even this limited measure, Lloyd George had thought it wise to make a most careful preliminary sounding of the now threateningly restive Trades Union Movement. On 17 January, 1918, the Bill was introduced into the House of Commons, and the next day, Lloyd George, accompanied by two of his Labour colleagues in the Government, J. H. Clynes and G. H. Roberts, addressed a joint meeting of delegates from the Trades Unions and the Labour Party in the Central Hall, Westminster. He warned:

"We cannot turn Hindenburg out of Belgium with Trade Union resolutions, but we can with Trade Union guns, and Trade Unionists behind them. . . . The story of democracy is this: to be ready to die for it. We are fighting now against the privilege claimed by Military Caste. Democracy means that the people of all classes must merge their privileges and their rights in the common stock. The People must go on, or go under."

Asked what he thought about nationalizing the production of armaments, Lloyd George replied that he was himself "entirely in sympathy with that proposition". Challenged as to why the Government did not "conscript money, as well as men", he pointed out that already war taxation was heavier in Britain than in any other fighting country.

He might have added (though it would have been decidedly undiplomatic at this moment to do so) that, with the exception of the United States, wartime wages generally in Britain were higher, too. The man principally credited (or blamed) for this was no Trade Union agitator, but his Minister of Munitions, Churchill.

He had moved into the middle of the industrial picture when, in the autumn of 1917, he had announced in the House of Commons a $12\frac{1}{2}$ per cent increase in wages for skilled time-workers in the munition factories and shipyards. This was to meet the problem which had been created when the rising wage-rates offered to unskilled piece-workers had begun to attract skilled labour from their jobs. A Cabinet Labour Committee, which included, besides Churchill, Milner, and two Socialist Ministers, George Barnes and G. H. Roberts, were dealing with it when Churchill's announcement was made. When semi-skilled workers throughout the engineering trades, building, textiles and railways also demanded a $12\frac{1}{2}$ per cent increase, and were followed by a fresh claim from piece-workers for a $7\frac{1}{2}$ per cent increase, the cost of this war bonus shot up from its estimated £14,000,000 to many times that figure. George Barnes, in the House of Commons on 26 February, 1918, admitted that £40,000,000 would be much nearer. He also said that this was "only a fraction of the cost. The real cost is the loss of output that is going on throughout the country. The people are in a ferment, and instead of working, are talking of $7\frac{1}{2}$ per cent or $12\frac{1}{2}$ per cent."

Barnes, indeed, had actually, in a public speech at Glasgow, accused his Cabinet colleague, Churchill, of "butting-in" with his $12\frac{1}{2}$ per cent increase,

which he said, had naturally gone right down the scale to all time-workers, so
that during the past few weeks the Government: "had been living on the top
of a veritable volcano."

The volcano was stirred into daily eruption by questions in the House of
Commons, Letters to *The Times*, and by the editorial of the *Morning Post*,
which declared that:

> "Mr. Churchill has a genius for exploiting his opportunities. Mr.
> Churchill's idea in entering upon his office was simple; he desired to make
> himself popular with what is called Labour. He argued thus: the working
> man has a vote; he will vote for those who please him; he is pleased with
> a rise in wages; therefore let me give him $12\frac{1}{2}$ per cent. That there was any
> other side to the wages question probably did not occur to Mr. Churchill."

The gossip in the lobbies of the House of Commons and the political
clubs was (*a*) that Churchill had threatened to resign, intending to place
himself at the head of the Radicals and Socialists who favoured Peace by
Negotiation, (*b*) that his Cabinet colleagues were insisting on his resignation,
(*c*) that the Prime Minister had formally required it. Certainly, the political
and the industrial terrain was heaving, the more so when the news came out
that the January, 1918, shipbuilding output was down by more than half.
Churchill had grown once more to be a figure of fascinating force in this New
Year. Would he fall again? Would he rise, to some strange, new height?
Would he—vanish?

Lloyd George kept Churchill firmly in his Government. He stood
by him in this crisis in our war industry—and, to be frank, he needed
Churchill in that other, still-present crisis, in our military affairs. Far more
difficult, indeed, than exercising effective control over the labour power of the
nation was getting any control at all over the military policy of the generals.
We have seen that in tracing the intricate, not to say tortuous, steps whereby
Lloyd George had secured the setting-up of the Supreme War Council with
its separate staff of Technical Military Advisers at Versailles.

At least, they had been originally intended to be a separate and independent
staff; but this idea had been largely lost when the French appointed as their
Military Representative, General Weygand, who was recognized as the mouth-
piece of Foch (the French Chief of Staff); the Italians appointed General
Cadorna, who was himself the Italian Chief of Staff; and the Americans
appointed General Bliss, who was the American Chief of Staff. As for the
British, naturally our own Chief of Staff, General Robertson, although he
detested and distrusted the whole idea of the Supreme War Council, might
have borne with it if either he himself had been named as our Military Representative there or some deputy under his command. This, of course, was
precisely what Lloyd George was determined *not* to have. As far as the British
Prime Minister was concerned, one of the principal advantages of setting-up

a Supreme War Council was to provide himself with an alternative authoritative Military Adviser and (who can doubt it?), eventually, an overriding Military Executive. It had simply strengthened Robertson's suspicions when General Wilson was given the Versailles job.

Now, unity of command had been the ultimate objective of Lloyd George's original manœuvres. But before this could be achieved there must first come unity of control. How could you begin better than by controlling the reserve forces of all the Allied armies, under the title of the "General Reserve"?

The matter had not been settled when the Supreme War Council had met on 1 February, 1918. It was then posed by "Tiger" Clemenceau, who took the chair. The Tiger put four questions. Shall we constitute a General Reserve? Will it serve the entire Front, from the North Sea to the Adriatic? How will it be disposed? And who will command it?

General Foch argued that "an inter-Allied Organ of Execution" must be set up forthwith to create and make ready this General Reserve, in agreement with the various Allied commanders. The same single authority must decide on the use of this reserve, and provide the means of transporting it to the required scene of action. General Foch considered that this authority should consist of the French and British Chiefs of Staff, with representatives of the much smaller Belgian and American armies.

General Robertson agreed on the necessity of creating a General Reserve. He added that: "Whoever commands the reserve must be in a position to issue orders immediately the emergency arrives."

Nobody, he thought, could do this better than himself and Foch.

Lloyd George was furious. Why, this would give more power than ever to Robertson, whose present power he was trying to curtail! It was his own intention to place the reserve under some delegated authority at Versailles, pending the time when he could get round to handing it over, together with all the main armies, to his cherished, not merely decorative British but truly effective Inter-Allied "Generalissimo". Lloyd George now insisted, therefore, that neither London, nor Rome, nor Washington could spare their Chief of Staff to sit permanently in Versailles—as the High Command of the Reserve must do—though he conceded that for the French it "might be rather different". (Both Rome and Washington, as we have seen, had already agreed to do this very thing.)

Since nobody was yet ready to propose an Allied Generalissimo, the Council next day unanimously agreed to create an alternative authority. An "Executive Board" of the Permanent Military Representatives was then set up. It died before it ever had time to start work. The greatest crisis of the war was about to break. Its origins lay in that ever-vexed problem of manpower.

The French had long been complaining that while they held more than three hundred miles of the Western Front, their British Allies held less than one hundred. It did not mollify the French to point out that we occupied the entire front in Palestine, in Mesopotamia, and in both East and South-west Africa, besides holding the seas of the world and, in vain, did Lloyd George urge that even in the West the British Army was containing about half of the total enemy forces, although upon a narrow front. He had also pointed out that the French *Poilus* (since the 1917 mutinies) went home on leave every four months, while the British Tommies saw "Blighty" once a year. To which the Tiger snarled: "We made a national levy on our manhood from the first day of the war."

Now, at the Supreme War Council which resolved to raise a General Reserve, the British C.-in-C., Haig, agreed to take over about thirty miles of the French front. Indeed, he and the French C.-in-C., Pétain, were already discussing the details. Nobody was more surprised to learn this than Lloyd George, since the Field-Marshal was still carrying on his clamour for more men to hold his own front. This time, indeed, Haig was justified in this demand, for the December disparity between the enemy strength and his own had already disappeared and soon that enemy would command an effective superiority.

But if Field-Marshal Haig was prepared to make concessions to the French (or to the Supreme War Council) General Robertson was not. When the resolution setting up the Reserve and its Command had been passed and the Council had adjourned, for long afterwards Robertson remained behind: "sitting alone in his place, motionless, his head resting on his hand, glaring silently in front of him."[1]

He returned to London, ahead of the Prime Minister, and went to work. General Robertson had made up his mind. He was going to fight this quarrel out, or fall in the attempt. At the first War Cabinet meeting after the Versailles Conference, Lloyd George reported the measures taken there by the Supreme War Council, especially those concerning the General Reserve. The Secretary of State for War, Lord Derby, who was accompanied by the C.I.G.S., announced that he had not yet had time to study the question, and so must reserve judgment. To which the Prime Minister snapped that it had been settled by the War Cabinet at the previous meeting, and that he had gone to the Supreme War Council invested with full authority to act. He trusted that the Army Council would now carry out the decision with no more delay. Lord Derby bowed.

But Robertson was not done yet. Like Haig, he was not without friends in Fleet Street. On 8 February, 1918, the *Morning Post* returned to the attack, with a brief message from its "Military Correspondent in Paris", who was, of course, Colonel Repington:

"The decisions of the recent Inter-Allied Paris War Council regarding the control of British troops in the field are reported to be of such a strange

[1] *At the Supreme War Council,* by Peter Wright.

character that Parliament should demand the fullest details, and a Parliamentary Committee should examine them at once and take the opinions of our General Staff and of our Commanders in the field concerning the new arrangements."

The same evening, the *Globe* newspaper reprinted its contemporary's "disquieting telegram". The newspaper editorial commented that, as Mr. Asquith had been responsible in the first place for appointing Sir Douglas Haig and Sir William Robertson, it was to be hoped that he would not now stand by and allow that arrangement to be broken at the whim of any individuals, however powerful. Nor should the House of Commons allow itself to be elbowed out of its duty of finding out what was going on behind the scenes of the Higher Command. The *Globe* demanded: "*Is there, or is there not a Generalissimo?*"

Lord Milner, who had accompanied Lloyd George to the Supreme War Council meeting at Versailles, sent this letter enclosing the hostile article round by hand to him that night:

"My dear Prime Minister,   8.2.18
        You have no doubt seen the enclosed from the *Globe*, I think the sooner we make a move the better. This kind of thing cannot be allowed to go on. . . ."

Then Milner, after frankly setting forth his own view that this was Robertson at work, went on to remind Lloyd George that Haig felt the same way as Robertson. His advice, therefore, was this:

"It is no use having a great rumpus, and getting rid of Robertson, if the policy is to be sidetracked, for quite different reasons by Haig.
        But Haig will, I believe, obey orders, if he once clearly understands that your mind is made up. And if he were to stick his toes in the ground, which I do not anticipate, it would be better to lose both Haig and Robertson than to continue at the mercy of both or either of them. . . .
                                                                                Yours very sincerely,
                                                                                Milner."

The Prime Minister slept that night on this advice. Early next morning, he sent for Haig to come over from France. Lloyd George was now proposing, in absence of that long-schemed-for "Generalissimo", to put Wilson in as C.I.G.S., and to send Robertson to Versailles as Deputy C.I.G.S. in his place. To this idea, Haig personally raised no objection. That evening Lloyd George wrote to Milner:

"I have had an afternoon of it with Haig and Derby. Haig was quite reasonable. He did not like H.W. (Sir Henry Wilson) coming here, and thought the Army might be very shocked; but he said that was a matter for the Government. In fact, his attitude was perfectly correct. Derby, Haig and

Macpherson[1] thought that to make Robertson Deputy would be to humiliate him, and they thought it quite unnecessary in view of the fact that Wilson was made Chief Adviser of the Government. Subject to that, the document was signed by Derby, and he is to see the King later on about it.

'Wully' (Sir William Robertson) is to be told tomorrow by Macpherson, who is motoring over to Eastbourne to communicate the news to him. Derby is delighted with our change of plans; and as we had only the choice of three or four doubtful second bests, I am firmly convinced that this is the best of them."

But "Wully," at any rate, was still fighting, and on 11 February, Milner wrote again to the Prime Minister:

"My dear Prime Minister,

I am still rather anxious about the W.O. situation. I hope the paper you drew up and showed to me on Saturday afternoon *still holds good* except in so far as it makes the Versailles man a Deputy C.I.G.S. and member of the Army Council, which is unnecessary and had better be abandoned. But if there is any question of Robertson having something more than the Versailles job, as defined in that paper, and retaining some overriding or even concurrent authority at the War Office, then I am sure we are heading for disaster. The whole object of the change is to make the Chief Military Adviser of the Government a man with whom we can get on. Unless that is clear, and we are free from interference between him and us, all the fuss and commotion will have been worse than useless.

We are on absolutely strong ground and, if there is to be a fight, which I don't feel sure of, we can win. But let us at least make sure that at the end of the fight we are free men and not still saddled with our Old Man of the Sea! If, to smooth matters over, we leave any ambiguity in the situation, we are done.

Yours very sincerely,
Milner."

On the same day, there came another salvo from Colonel Repington in the *Morning Post*. This one revealed that a Reserve of Manœuvre was to be created, that this Reserve was to be independent of the two existing Commanders-in-Chief, and that it would be controlled by an Executive Board, presided over by General Foch. Colonel Repington then launched a bitterly personal attack on Lloyd George and his civilian Allied associates, declaring that:

". . . Prime Ministers and others have recently resolved themselves into a Council of War, have rivalled it in strategy, and have exclusively occupied themselves in teaching soldiers how and where to make war."

[1] Mr. Ian Macpherson, M.P., then Under Secretary for War, later Lord Strathcarran.

o*

Then, defying an official warning to the Press not to discuss the deliberations and decisions of the Supreme War Council, the confidant of the General Staff continued:

". . . At present it is the duty of the Chief of the General Staff to issue the orders of the War Cabinet to the Armies. But now there interposes the Versailles soldiers, under the Presidency of General Foch, and the British General of this body is not apparently under the War Office, nor was he appointed by them. He owes his elevation to Mr. Lloyd George's favour alone. . . ."

The article went on to give full information, interesting to the enemy (it quoted the text of the "Top Secret" minutes), of what had taken place.

Namely, that the Supreme War Council had resolved to stand on the defensive upon the Western Front and to resist the expected German assault with the device of its Reserve of Manœuvre, while General Allenby in Palestine would deliver a "knock-out blow to Turkey". The Repington article concluded with a rousing incitement to the Army Council to stand up to this rotten Government ("Everybody has to go over the top sooner or later in this war"), and also to Parliament itself to "do its bit".

There were not lacking volunteers in Parliament to do, at any rate, what lay within their power to harass the Prime Minister. Not only Asquith's Liberal Opposition, but a body of refractory Tory Back Benchers known as the Unionist War Committee, were hot in pursuit of anyone who "dared to attack the Soldiers". Service Ministers, such as Lord Derby, were sedulously lobbied to join in the movement, which Lloyd George said: "For several days threatened the life of the Ministry itself."

Lloyd George had, indeed, to fight. He did not mind that, but his power to enforce his purposes was limited in the spring of 1918. The Prime Minister put the point squarely to Lord Salisbury at this time, when he came to see him, bearing a wad of resolutions from the rebel Unionist War Committee, including one forbidding the Prime Minister to take Churchill into the War Cabinet. The trouble in War, said Lloyd George, was that you had to create for the people a dazzling hierarchy of Gods of War, the Generals. When you found out privately that they had feet of clay, you still had to go on with their public worship—or else the people would lose faith. So would the ordinary soldiers. The mutiny in the French Army taught us what to expect from troops who had ceased to trust their leaders.

Meantime, it remained to deal with the rebel Press. The War Cabinet considered the case of Colonel Repington the same day as his latest dispatch was published. There was no doubt of his serious, indeed, deliberate offence. This last dispatch, unlike the first one, had been duly submitted to the Press Bureau censors the previous evening, and had been ruled by them to infringe Security, for it plainly contained information of a highly secret character. In spite of this, the editor of the *Morning Post*, Mr. H. A. Gwynne, had published it. This was open challenge, it could not be ignored. The War Cabinet resolved to prosecute both Repington and Gwynne.

The trouble, again, was that if too much importance was attached to this case the enemy would realize that "Repington's revelations" were the truth. The editor, and his contributor, were therefore charged at Bow Street with a mere technical breach of the Defence of the Realm Act, and on 21 February, found guilty and fined £100 apiece, with fifty guineas costs. As it was, the case aroused enormous interest and, as Repington gloated, "no such crowd at Bow Street since Crippen!"

Where had the Colonel collected his confidential information? According to his own account, General Maurice wrote Repington a letter at this time to say that he had been ordered not to talk to him about the war, and General Robertson was credited with the remark that he and Repington "could no more afford to be seen together just now than we could afford to be seen walking down Regent Street with a whore!"

By now Parliament was furiously afire. Already, sparks had been flying in the previous month when Lloyd George had been accused, on the one hand, of not daring to dismiss generals in whom he had lost faith because he was afraid of the "Fleet Street Opposition" and, on the other hand, of "nobbling the Press" to smear our distinguished military leaders. Indeed, for the first six months of this Year of Victory, 1918, Lloyd George was battling day and night for his own political life in the House of Commons. Though nominally the entire Tory Party, most of the Labour Party, and at least half of the Liberal Party stood behind him, with the Irish in fairly friendly neutrality, yet there were deep and dangerous rifts within this majority. It was not war with the Opposition, but mutiny in the ranks of the Government that caused the Prime Minister's anxieties. The debates of those memorable days and nights are marked by a personal rather than a political intensity and hostility, for fundamentally they centred around the personality of one man, Lloyd George.

On 12 February, 1918, in a debate initiated by the Liberal Opposition to draw from the Prime Minister what executive powers, if any, had now been conferred on the Versailles Supreme War Council, Asquith had opened with a eulogy of the "two great soldiers", Sir Douglas Haig and Sir William Robertson, the implication being that their powers were being somehow diminished by the new set-up. Next, Lord Hugh Cecil had recalled certain newspaper attacks which had preceded the sacking of the First Sea Lord, Admiral Sir John Jellicoe, in the previous December. Then Chamberlain, who had been out of office since the 1917 debate on the "Mespot" scandal, voiced some Back Bench Tory anxieties, though in a more friendly way.

When Lloyd George rose to reply, he had adroitly surrounded himself with the barbed wire of security—he could not tell Asquith details of the General Reserve mechanism without also telling the enemy. He must speak with caution, because he was talking about vital military decisions made in the War Council of the Allies. How sincerely he wished there had been someone in Germany or Austria whose ears were glued to the keyhole when the War Council of Austria and Germany sat, and that he had published their decision in the newspapers!

The Prime Minister had ended with an appeal to the House of Commons, and also a challenge that, if need be, he would take the issue to the country in a General Election.

"... If the House of Commons and the country are not satisfied with the conduct of the war, and if they think there is any Government which can conduct it better, then it is their business, and in God's name, to put that other Government in! But as long as the House of Commons retains its confidence in the Government, then I say it ought to allow the Government a full and free hand in the direction of the war."

For the moment—it was only for a moment—this wound-up the trouble with the official Opposition in Parliament. There remained General Robertson, in the War Office. Would he accept Lloyd George's offer to go to Versailles as the British Military Representative there? Would he even prefer to remain in Whitehall as C.I.G.S., though with the clear understanding that this office would have no authority over the other one?

Since he was himself laid up in bed with a chill, Lloyd George sent Balfour round to see the General. He found him adamant. General Robertson objected to the entire system, and he objected to it whether he was himself to be C.I.G.S. or British Military Representative. The post of C.I.G.S., he insisted, must be the superior of the two, and that if that were settled, then he was willing to take on either. From this rock position, the honest and obstinate old soldier refused to budge.

Anxious as ever to avoid trouble, or at any rate, decisive trouble, Lord Derby, the Secretary of State for War, sought out Lord Stamfordham, the King's Secretary. Could he not persuade General Robertson to remain on as C.I.G.S. under the new dispensation?

(According to his *Diary*, on 11 February Haig had urged King George himself that day to insist on Robertson going to Versailles:

"In the first place, it was necessary for all good soldiers to work together at this time, and secondly, Robertson might save us from defeat by opposing Lloyd George's desire to send troops to the East against the Turks.")

Lord Stamfordham did his best to urge Robertson to stay on. But the General replied that "even for the King" he could not work an unworkable proposition. Lord Stamfordham made a last appeal to the Prime Minister.

His Majesty, he stated, "strongly deprecated the idea of Robertson being removed from the post of C.I.G.S."

This was too much for Lloyd George. Too long, he reckoned, had he put up with this frustrating and infuriating War Office–Palace intrigue. Field-Marshal Haig was forever at it, though he conducted it largely on a personal basis. Also, he was in the field. General Robertson was the administrative head of the War Office, in close and daily communication with the Prime Minister, to whom, Lloyd George felt, he had never shown the least loyalty. Very well, if His Majesty preferred him, he could have him! There was not room for Lloyd George and General Robertson in the same Government.

So the Prime Minister replied to Stamfordham that he did not share His Majesty's extremely favourable opinion of Sir William Robertson, and that if the King insisted on retaining his services, "the Government could not carry on and His Majesty must find other Ministers. . . . The Government must govern, and this was practically military dictation."

Thus, decisively, Lloyd George threw down on the royal table his own resignation from the Premiership. Stamfordham hastened to assure the Prime Minister that His Majesty "had no idea of making any such insistence". It was the last time that Lloyd George and King George came into clash.

Well, what was going to happen now between the Prime Minister and the Military Party? For, plainly, this was the show-down. One, or the other, was going to be master in England.

Naturally, both invoked the Law.

General Robertson claimed that under the Army Act no person who was not invested with the authority of the Army Council could issue orders to British troops, and that ruled out an independent "Executive Board" at Versailles. Lloyd George asserted that the Cabinet was the supreme political authority under the British Constitution, that it had made a decision, a debate had been held in Parliament on this very issue and the action of the Government had not been challenged in the Division Lobby.

It had embarrassed certain Ministers, however, and at least two of them threatened to resign. (Needless to say, Lord Derby was one of them; now Lord Robert Cecil was the other.) Neither of them, however, was a member of the War Cabinet, who were quite unanimous in their determination to resist what they regarded as an attempt at something like "Military Dictatorship". With the agreement of his colleagues, the Prime Minister offered Robertson's post of C.I.G.S., first to General Plumer, then commanding the British Forces on the Italian Front, and when Plumer prudently declined it, to General Wilson.

Lloyd George, who personally preferred Wilson to any other candidate, was well aware of the risks he ran in appointing him. Sir Henry's talents were manifold and manifest, though trustworthiness was not one. In a few, swift, sure strokes his sometime enemy and short-time friend, Lloyd George has drawn a portrait:

"He possessed intellectual gifts which justified admiration. But he also had attributes which explained, and, to a large extent, gave warrant for the suspicion and lack of confidence so widely felt in him. He was whimsical almost to the point of buffoonery. . . . Habitually, he jested over questions of life and death. . . . He had undoubtedly the nimblest intelligence amongst the soldiers of high degree. He had also a lucidity of mind, and therefore, of expression which was given to none of his professional rivals . . . but he had no power of decision. That is why he failed in the field. For the same reason . . . he shrank from the responsibility of the final word in counsel."

Now, at any rate, Wilson expressed his willingness to take over Robertson's job. One thing more remained to be done. Settle with Haig.

On Sunday, 17 February, 1918, the Field-Marshal and Lord Derby drove down to see Lloyd George at Walton Heath. Once more they thrashed it out, and the Prime Minister was astonished to find that the C.-in-C. put up no further fight for his old ally, the C.I.G.S., whom (as he confided in a letter to Lady Haig) he considered had not been firm enough in standing up to "his political masters", that is, Lloyd George & Co! Now that Robertson had refused to be side-tracked to Versailles, Haig had no intention of resigning himself, and when he heard that Derby talked of doing so, Lloyd George said "he sniffed it aside with an expression of contempt". Later that evening, at his own house in Kingston-on-Thames, Haig told Wilson that all these quarrels had nothing to do with him and that he was prepared to abide by the Cabinet decisions and would "play up all he could".

So ended the war inside the War Council between General Robertson and Lloyd George. The appointment of Wilson was confirmed as C.I.G.S., and Robertson read in the newspapers a day or two later that he himself had "resigned", and had been gazetted G.O.C. Eastern Command in the United Kingdom. He growled and, like a good soldier, fell into line.

Less resolute were some of his other political allies. When Haig left Walton Heath on Sunday evening, Derby remained behind to resign for the third time that week-end. This time, he insisted, it was final and irrevocable. Lloyd George sincerely hoped so. When Beaverbrook went over to see him that day at Walton Heath he found him jubilant, joking and laughing with Riddell. "But Derby must promise to stick to his decision this time!" he said to Beaverbrook. He really thought at last he had got both Haig and Derby where he wanted them! He consulted Bonar Law as to who should be the new Secretary of State for War, and between them they agreed to offer the post to Chamberlain. According to Riddell, though Lloyd George that night was still uncertain what the new "Coalition Opposition", as he called them, between the Asquithian Liberals and the Military Party might bring forth in the next few days, he was happier than he had been for many a long day. "We then sang Welsh hymns to the accompaniment of the guns in the distance repelling an air raid."

Alas! The Prime Minister's rejoicing was premature—at all events over Derby! For after he left Lloyd George, the War Secretary called in at Kingston-on-Thames to see Haig again, who advised him to hang on to his job. The Field-Marshal duly recorded: "He said he would accept my advice. If he left, Lord Northcliffe would probably succeed him. This would be fatal to the Army and the Empire."

Lloyd George was not able to get hold of Chamberlain that joyful Sunday evening because he happened to be away from London for the week-end. But next morning at Bonar Law's urgent request, Chamberlain motored to town. Before he could reach Downing Street, Macpherson, the Under-Secretary of State for War, called on Bonar Law to tell him that Derby had withdrawn his resignation. None of the other threatened Ministerial departures took place, either.

An interesting new arrival, however, shook things up sharply again in politics, just as they seemed to be settling down. This was the appointment of Beaverbrook as Minister of Information and Chancellor of the Duchy of Lancaster in February, 1918. It was a new office, although Sir Edward Carson, as a member of the War Cabinet, had previously been responsible for our War propaganda. The new appointment had been clinched on that Sunday at Walton Heath. Promptly, Beaverbrook urged that Northcliffe should be given the job of organizing our propaganda in enemy countries. The Prime Minister agreed. But Bonar Law cried out when he heard that Lloyd George was preparing to take into his Government yet another Press Lord: "One was enough! Now here are two! Well, you'll have some fun."

So it shortly proved. But highly necessary was some such flow of propaganda towards friends, if not towards enemies. Northcliffe's own urgent letters from the United States to the Prime Minister during his Mission there in the previous year had underlined this need.

It was then that Lloyd George had bethought himself of his friend, Beaverbrook, the engineer who had built those vital political bridges between Bonar Law and himself in November–December, 1917, across which he had marched to the Premiership. For, as "Eye-Witness" with the Canadian Army, in 1915, as Canadian Government Representative at the Front in 1916, and as Officer-in-Charge of Canadian War Records in 1917, Beaverbrook had put over an immense propaganda for his native land. (We have just seen that America realized that, at any rate, the Canadians were fighting!) Now Lloyd George reckoned that he would harness the power of this Canadian cataract to the greater purposes of the British Empire.

There were objections. One came from Buckingham Palace. It was the appointment of Beaverbrook to the Duchy of Lancaster, not to the Ministry of Information, that was making His Majesty a little anxious. The Chancellor of the Duchy had to deal with a certain number of ecclesiastical preferments, and Beaverbrook was a Presbyterian. (As a matter of interest, the Prime Minister had even more preferments to handle, and he was a Baptist.) Lord Stamfordham wrote to say, 8 February, 1918, that His Majesty:

". . . expressed much surprise, that considering past circumstances, he should now be asked to agree to Lord Beaverbrook's presiding over the Duchy, which, as it were, is the personal property of the Sovereign and entailing closer relations between the King and its Chancellor than with many of his Ministers.

I must again assure you that the Prime Minister in merely saying to me that he was thinking of employing Lord Beaverbrook in the Propaganda Department, never referred in any way to the Duchy of Lancaster. . . ."

To which the Prime Minister replied to Lord Stamfordham, adroitly emphasizing the value of the appointment to the Propaganda services of the Government, 9 February, 1918.

". . . I am confident that I shall receive a great accession of strength in Lord Beaverbrook's appointment. His organization of the Canadian Propaganda Department entrusted to him by Sir Robert Borden has been a conspicuous success. On the other hand our propaganda has been a conspicuous failure. I have sought in vain for months for a man to put it right. So far I have not succeeded. Propaganda at home and abroad is becoming increasingly important. I consulted members of the Propaganda Committee, and they thought Beaverbrook would be the best available man. I cannot get him without offering him Ministerial rank. He is a first-rate business man, and will administer the Duchy well. In these circumstances, I trust the King will be graciously pleased to approve the recommendation which I have thought fit to make to him. I wish you to assure His Majesty that I attach great importance to the appointment of Lord Beaverbrook to this post."

Another loud "NO!" came from the Unionist War Committee, who were ardent for Generals having power against Politicians, but reluctant to have Press Lords exercising authority, anywhere. So the Unionist War Committee now produced a ponderous resolution against all, or any, newspaper proprietors holding Government office.

To this Lord Salisbury retorted that the Government had long sought "high and low" for the right man to handle Britain's case to the world, and now at last they had found him. Derby also defended Beaverbrook by urging that he was just the man for the job; he knew the exact time and place to plant the necessary propaganda; he understood how to issue the circular to the shareholders the night before the voting. Captain Guest, Government Liberal Chief Whip, advised the Prime Minister to pay no attention whatever to the Unionist War Committee's plaint.

Some powerful pro-war propaganda—and especially pro-Ally propaganda—was in dire demand. Pacifism was enjoying a new popularity, partly because of Russia walking out of the war, partly because of a genuine war-weariness among our own people, but perhaps even more because it became known that two British Government representatives, General Smuts and Mr. Philip Kerr, had around Christmas again renewed peace-talks in neutral Switzerland with Count Mensdorff, the envoy of the Austrian Government. These talks had come to naught for two reasons, (i) because Austria was not yet convinced that her ally, Germany, was beaten in the field, (ii) because Austria herself remained contemptuous of the enemy Italians, and would concede nothing to them.

But Lloyd George felt that the mood of Britain was such that the Government should set forth our own conditions of peace, if only to demonstrate to the public that the enemy's terms were so utterly at variance with them that no reconciliation of the two was possible. He went to much trouble over drafting this "Peace" document, and secured approval for it not only from Asquith's Liberal Opposition and the Trade Unions, but also from the Dominion Governments. Its terms included the restoration of independence and payment of compensation to Belgium, Serbia and Rumania; the evacuation of all Allied territories, occupied by the enemy; the return of Alsace-Lorraine to France; the granting of self-government to the various races under Austrian and Turkish rule; reparation for war injuries and the setting up of a new International Authority to guard the peace.

The Germans obliged, via the Imperial Chancellor, Count Hertling, in the Reichstag by replying that the occupation of Belgium, Serbia, etc., was Germany's business; that she would keep Alsace-Lorraine, and that the Home Rule problems of the Austrian and Turkish Governments would be settled by them.

This put an end to any more talk of a "negotiated peace", and the new Minister of Information was able to assure his public that the only way to get peace was to win the war.

Some of the Prime Minister's House of Commons public continued to be restive about his own activities, and the relations in general of the Government with the Press. On 11 March, 1918, Austen Chamberlain brought up the question of the personal connection between certain Ministers and the newspapers closely associated with their names, and also of the recent attacks by one of those newspapers (the *Daily Mail*), on naval and military leaders (Jellicoe and Robertson). Chamberlain referred to the "insolent and offensive patronage of the Prime Minister" by Northcliffe in publishing his own letter to him declining the Air Ministry, and his "equally insolent and offensive criticism of the Rt. Hon Gentleman's colleague". Chamberlain thought it an unfortunate coincidence that people who were guilty of such practices should shortly afterwards be found indispensable to the Government in particular offices. He suggested that it would be rather invidious for a Minister, who was recognized as a great newspaper proprietor, to remain a Minister if any question should arise of the prosecution of the newspaper which he owned. It must also be invidious for a Minister of Information, while in his Ministry, to receive the most confidential information and be expected to forget all about it the moment he returned to his newspaper office.

How invidious it could be for a Minister of Information who owned a newspaper to have even his Editor publish "scoop" news without his own knowledge is shown by the interlude which occurred a few weeks later when, on 18 April, 1918, the *Daily Express* published the news that Derby had resigned his post as Secretary of State for War and become British Ambassador to Paris. His place in the War Office had been taken by Milner.

The same morning, Stamfordham rang up the Prime Minister to say that the King was very indignant that this news had been published in a newspaper before it had been officially released; that His Majesty had made the appointments, and he hoped that Mr. Lloyd George would discover how the leakage came about.

A few days later Lloyd George received a letter from Beaverbrook at the Ministry of Information. Every working journalist, at any rate, will appreciate the problems which it forcefully sets forth:

April 22, 1918.

"My dear Prime Minister,

I am writing to you on the subject of the *Daily Express* announcement of Thursday morning on the Government changes and my own position in the matter. I understand that you showed some concern over this announcement. . . .

As principal shareholder, I enquired of the Editor how he had obtained the news. He replied that he went to the War Office on Wednesday and was told of Lord Derby's resignation and Lord Milner's appointment then: further, that he took part at dinner that night in a conversation with two Members of Parliament who also were aware of the changes and discussed them freely. Neither of these facts is altogether surprising because I understand that Lord Derby said 'Good-bye' to his heads of Departments on Wednesday and told his friends the news at lunch. Mr. Evelyn Fitzgerald says that the whole War Office down to the Doorkeeper knew of the change on Wednesday and that any reputable journalist who happened to be there that day would almost certainly have been told the facts. . . .

On the Thursday morning I had to consider this question. Knowing that his principal shareholder was also a member of the Government, was the Editor right or wrong in publishing the news? The Editor had come by the news in his professional capacity and he was absolutely right in publishing, and he would be justified in doing the same thing again under similar circumstances.

The Editor points out to me that . . . if he goes on refraining from publishing advance news, professionally acquired, in deference to my position in the Government he damages the position of his paper and his own reputation together. Suppose at a time when I have ceased to be a member of the Government I turn round on him and point out to him that the position of the paper is going down, perhaps on this very account, and that I shall dispense with his services, how is he placed then in getting a new post?

I have consulted with three other journalists of eminence, and they all told me that not only was the Editor right in publishing, but that he would have been justified in resigning had any impediment to publication been placed in his way. You will see then that it is impossible for me to interfere in such a matter, particularly now that I am *ex-officio* debarred from taking part in the management of the *Daily Express*.

I come to the more delicate question of how far [these facts] affect the Government and my own status in it.

I am still strongly of the opinion that newspaper proprietors ought not to be debarred from office. In fact, this seems now to be the general view, since the agitation against it never had any real strength in the country and has completely fizzled out, while Mr. Austen Chamberlain, after making two strong speeches in the contrary sense in the House of Commons has now joined a Government which includes Lord Rothermere and myself.

At the same time, such incidents as the *Daily Express* announcements are certain to recur from time to time and I am anxious to obtain from you your opinion as to whether I am embarrassing the Government by remaining in office under the circumstances. . . .

Yours faithfully,
Beaverbrook."

Meantime, Chamberlain's reasoned objections commanded considerable support in the House of Commons. There followed a good-tempered speech by Spencer Leigh Hughes, who declared that to do the job of propaganda you needed practical and experienced newspapermen who were not likely to be hampered by what Dr. Johnson termed "needless scrupulosity"; a bad-tempered one by Mr. Pringle, who underlined his favourite reference to the Government's Kept Press by defining the newspapers of any Ministerial Press Lord as "a sort of *maison tolérée*, they are the same thing, they are inspected"; a lively defence of the new Minister of Information by the Prime Minister and the latest campaign against the Government for trafficking with Fleet Street was over. Lloyd George was able to turn back to the real job in hand and "get on with the war". Nobody knew it yet, but the long night was over. Red would be the dawn.

For, suddenly, disaster.

CHAPTER XXIV

"RED DAWN"

AT a little short of a quarter to five a.m. on the morning of 21 March, 1918, while darkness still mingled with the fog, the Germans launched their offensive of a million men against the weakened Front of the British Third and Fifth Armies, 62 divisions against 24. The defenders reeled and retreated, but they did not break. Clerks and cooks and bottle-washers stuffed the gaps in the line, and answered with their lives the problematic question which the politicians would raise at the National Inquest in the House of Commons, later on, of "What is a combatant (or non-combatant) soldier?"

Are sappers "fighting troops", the men who build (or blow) the bridges under the concentrated fire of the enemy? Are signallers, the men who lay the field-telephone lines within the sniper's gun-sight? You had better not inquire of the Royal Engineers, or the Royal Corps of Signals.

Forty miles deep the enemy drove. Far more dangerously, he threatened to divide the British and French Armies—"to roll up and smash the British and Belgians", as the German Chief of Staff, General von Ludendorff, wrote and planned—pressing the British back into their shallow rear upon the Channel ports and compelling them to do an earlier "Dunkirk", forcing the Belgians to quit or drown, then sweeping forward round the broken left flank, as old Von Schlieffen had prescribed, and enveloping Paris, after all.

Who was responsible for the greatest British defeat of the whole war?

For long, the attack had been expected, and in the very place where it was ultimately launched. Three weeks before the first wave of grey-green storm-troops flooded across No Man's Land towards the British trenches, an immense activity had been observed in those enemy lines opposite. Men and guns were being massed, ammunition dumps piled up, aerodromes laid out, roads and railways built. Field-Marshal Haig himself wrote in his dispatches:

> "As the 21st March approached it became certain that an attack on this sector (held by the Third and Fifth British Armies) was imminent, and counter preparation was carried out nightly by our artillery on the threatened front."

Only one thing worried Haig, as late as 2 March, 1918. He was afraid that the enemy would not attack, after all.

> "*Saturday, March 2nd.* . . . I presided at Conference of Army Commanders. I emphasized the necessity for being ready as soon as possible

to meet a big hostile offensive of prolonged duration. I also told Army Commanders that I was very pleased at all I had seen on the fronts of the three Armies which I had recently visited. Plans were sound and thorough, and much work had already been done. I was only afraid that the enemy would find our front so strong that he will hesitate to commit his Army to the attack in the almost certainty of losing very heavily."

The British C.-in-C.'s preparations did not include concentrating his available troops on the threatened sector; it did not include digging, wiring and siting the battle-zone immediately in the rear of the Fifth Army positions; and it did not include any contribution whatever to that Reserve of Manœuvre which should have been ready to repel and counter-attack the German onslaught wherever it fell.

In his dispatches, Haig claims that:

". . . plans were drawn up in combination with the French Military Authorities and were worked out in great detail to meet the different situations which might arise on different parts of the Allied Front. Measures were taken to ensure the smooth and rapid execution of these plans."

This statement is either inaccurate, or it constitutes one of the most remarkable military mysteries of all time why these plans were not used when the expected enemy defensive was delivered, for never were they brought into operation. Indisputable, is the fact that neither Haig nor Pétain made any effort to carry out the explicit orders they had received from the Supreme War Council to create a Reserve.

Here is an extraordinary letter written by Lord Milner, the Secretary of State for War, to Lloyd George on 14 March, 1918, one week before the great battle in the West actually opened:

"My dear Prime Minister,

I hear that Haig is quite obdurate about the Reserve. He will have none of it.

Desperately stupid and very awkward for us. The fact that *after all the fuss* there is no Reserve, when we have announced to all the world, that it was so vital and that all statesmen and generals and chiefs of staff were agreed about it, will look very bad indeed. Of course, it will be known very soon to everybody, including the Germans—and the hostile critics here will have us in this unanswerable dilemma: 'Either what you said about this great new system was all humbug invented to serve an immediate purpose of personal intrigue, or, *if you really meant it*, you are risking disaster by your incapacity to carry it out.'

My one hope is that you may yourself yet succeed in inducing Haig to agree to the principle, if we are content for the time being with a smaller reserve. That might not mean much *militarily*, though it would be of some use, but it would save our faces and preserve an important principle. A General Reserve, once established, will, I believe, grow upon everybody, as experience shows its value and its working becomes better understood. But if Haig (or Haig and Pétain?) kill it now, I doubt if it will ever revive. And we shall have once more passed under the yoke of the generals.

As I say, I think *you* may be able to make Haig see reason. I never thought that at this juncture anybody else could. If you can't, I hope the three Prime Ministers will agree among themselves how to get out of the mess and announce it to the Meeting *as their decision* right away. Of course that will only save appearances, but it will be better than having to listen to a rambling, incoherent, and totally illogical statement from Haig and then pretend to be convinced by it!!

Yours very sincerely,
Milner."

The importance of having such a mass of manœuvre at hand was exactly because, although the total Allied rifle strength of 1,500,000 on the Western Front exceeded the enemy's 1,370,000,[1] he would naturally take care to outnumber us at the point he selected for his assault. In the event, the Germans concentrated a three-to-one superiority for what Lloyd George described in those days as "the most stupendous battle ever fought on this earth".

It was the last and greatest gamble of the German High Command in the First World War, this plan to split the Allied Armies while the German Army drove through the gap and forced France out of the war before the Americans could arrive. The Crown Prince boasted that he would be in Calais a week after the attack had begun, and would dine in the Champs-Élysées in the first fortnight in April. It was touch and go that "Little Willie" did not keep either appointment.

On the second day, 22 March, the new C.I.G.S., General Wilson, reported to the War Cabinet that there was no cause for anxiety. Enemy losses were very heavy (this was true), and we had the battle well in hand (this was not true).

On the third day, Britain's "Black Saturday", the scene was one of gathering calamity. The plans which Haig and Pétain were supposed to have worked out in detail to succour one another at need, were obviously not operating at all.

Lloyd George went to the War Office early that morning and took charge himself. He summoned to his desk the Adjutant-General and the Controller of Shipping. How many troops were available in Britain, and how rapidly could they be sent to France? Within the hour, the figures were supplied. There were 170,000 men on draft, and they could be shipped overseas at a rate

[1] These figures were given to the War Cabinet by the Director of Military Operations, General Maurice on 13 March, 1918, eight days before the battle began.

rising from 8,000 to 20,000 a day. Within the month, indeed, nearly a quarter of a million reinforcements reached the battle front.

Why weren't they there when the battle began?

The Military Party at the time, and apologists for their cause ever since have laid the blame upon Lloyd George for the March Retreat. Certainly many men had been held back. But Lloyd George's case is that *according to the War Office estimate*, as late as 23 March, 1918, the Allies still had a slight superiority of 1,468,000 against 1,402,000. If Haig had been actively building up the General Reserve, as he had been ordered, he could not have been denied the troops he demanded.

Meantime, the gravest peril of all now threatened. As the German attack rolled towards Amiens, the French High Command were proposing to withdraw before it with one object alone—to cover the road to Paris, even if it meant parting company with the British on their flank. The French had not yet (24 March) informed their ally of their intention. Soon, the British would have to make their own hard decision. Should they fall back with the French (and thus uncover the Channel Ports and their own vital line of communication with Britain)? Or, should they evacuate their army now, and retire into their island until the giant from America was ready to return with them and reconquer Europe?

Lloyd George was calm and cheerful. The day after Black Saturday, he sent Milner to Paris—to find out the worst. Full of conflicting versions are the scores of memoirs written by men who took a prominent part in the First World War, but upon one point no one has yet differed—that in this crisis of his country's fate the Prime Minister's spirit soared to its supreme height. Churchill, who saw much of him during these terrible hours has given us this picture of Lloyd George as he dined with him that night:

> "I never remember in the whole course of the war a more anxious evening. One of the great qualities in Lloyd George was his power of obliterating the past and concentrating his whole being upon meeting the new situation. . . . The resolution of the Prime Minister was unshaken under his truly awful responsibilities."

General Wilson, who was also present, found the Prime Minister "buoyant". He said to him: "You will come out of this bang top or bang bottom."

That same Sunday, 24 March, 1918, about midnight, Haig met Pétain at Drury and there for the first time learned of the fateful orders which the French C.-in-C. had just received to retire towards Paris and split the Allied Front. In alarm, the British C.-in-C. telephoned at once to London.

The next day the C.I.G.S., General Wilson, followed Milner to France. He saw Haig, and according to his account, suggested that Foch should "co-ordinate" the action of both Commanders-in-Chief. Haig's friends have claimed that this was his own idea; if so, it was a complete reversal of his previous policy, and desperately late at that. Wilson did not miss the opportunity to remind Haig that it was he (Haig) who had killed the plan of the General Reserve.

The Battle of the West surged and swayed. A break at any point in the Allied Front, and all was over.

Another hurried meeting, this time at Doullens, at which Clemenceau, Poincaré, Milner, Foch, Pétain and Haig attended, and then at last it was agreed:

"General Foch is charged by the British and the French Governments to co-ordinate the action of the Allied Armies on the Western Front. He will work to this end with the Commanders-in-Chief, who are asked to furnish him with all the necessary information."

On this occasion, it was Haig who proposed that the original draft, which spoke only of co-ordinating "the operations of the Allies around Amiens", should be amended to cover "the action of the Allied Armies on the Western Front". The Field-Marshal was now fervently in favour of a step which went a long way towards setting up that "Generalissimo" which he and his former ally, General Robertson, had so long and so resolutely resisted.

They were still a long way off Unity of Command. General Bliss, the American Chief of Staff (who was not invited to Doullens), noted that Foch had not been made Allied C.-in-C. His functions were limited to the British and French Armies, and did not extend to the American, Belgian or Italian Armies. Moreover, Foch had no actual power of command: he could only consult and advise.

Lloyd George thought it wise to have on the spot a man whom he could trust. He chose Churchill, who was Minister of Munitions but still outside the magic inner circle of the War Cabinet. At this hour, the most critical of the whole war, Lloyd George placed his faith in Churchill, whose return to the forefront of British politics was thus reassured.

Thus, the week after the German blow fell, Churchill found himself at Headquarters on the Western Front, acting as the personal Deputy of the British Prime Minister. He urgently reported, 29 March, 1918:

"Every fighting division will be needed in the battle, for the German reserves are by no means exhausted . . . Loucheur[1] asserts that the Germans have a million men to replace casualties this summer, and the conclusion is inevitable unless we can draw on the manhood of America."

[1] M. Loucheur had been deputed by Clemenceau, the French Prime Minister, to act for him at French Army G.H.Q. exactly as Churchill was doing for Lloyd George at British Army G.H.Q.

Two days later, 31 March, Churchill was repeating his pressing appeal for vital reinforcements NOW.

"Our armies require strengthening by every conceivable means. I wonder if there are any spare brigades of Home Defence troops? In the M.G. (Machine-Gun) Schools there are a great many officers and men. You ought to scrub your whole Military organization and the Navy also, in order to diminish the enemy's superiority. . . . There are very large training establishments in England, the personnel of which should be scrutinized. . . . Remember, after I left, the Navy increased its complements by 25 per cent above the approved War Establishment. Their whole use of manpower is luxurious. The fighting line is the weakest part of our immense organization. . . ."

Churchill found the French Prime Minister, Clemenceau: "A tower of strength and courage . . . splendid in his buoyancy and resolution. He insisted on smelling blood and powder today, and only my prudence prevented him from doing more."

The battle for Amiens continued. The battered British Fourth Army were holding it. They made it Britain's Verdun. Anxiously, in the Cabinet Room in Downing Street, Lloyd George waited with Colonel Hankey on Good Friday morning to hear the latest reports from the Front. The tension became unbearable. So:

"We decided at last to go to St. Anne's, Soho, to hear Bach's Passion Music. As we took our seats we heard the clergyman intone that poignant supplication, 'Oh God make speed to save us'. How fervently we joined in the response, 'Oh Lord make haste to help us'. When we returned to Downing Street we heard that the Germans had been beaten off by the Third Army with heavy losses and that their advance was slowing down opposite Amiens."

But now something more was needed. Foch said it. He reminded his political masters that he was charged with the task of *co-ordinating* the action of the Allied Armies on the Western Front. But if there was no action there was nothing to co-ordinate. What he required was the power to *create* action.

Lloyd George agreed. One further meeting was summoned. This time Lloyd George himself went, and there at Beauvais on 3 April, 1918, with Clemenceau and Foch the matter was finally thrashed out. Even at this late hour the British Prime Minister could not persuade his War Cabinet to accept the solution of a "Generalissimo". Especially hostile to the proposal was General Wilson, who had taken over some of General Robertson's opinions, together with his post. Surprisingly, Haig agreed with Lloyd George, and Foch's powers were extended. His charter now ran:

"The British, French and American Governments . . . entrust to General Foch the strategic direction of military operations. The Commanders-in-Chief of the British, French and American Armies have full control of the tactical employment of their forces. Each Commander-in-Chief will have the right of appeal to his Government if in his opinion the safety of his Army is compromised by any order received from General Foch."

A few days later, 14 April, 1918, Lloyd George, at last induced the War Cabinet to make Foch General-in-Chief of the Allied Armies. By then, the Germans had launched another great offensive, but they had been forced to abandon their deadly design of driving a wedge between the French and the British Armies. Though we did not know it yet, the Battle in the West was won.

"With our backs to the wall, and believing in the justice of our cause, each one of us must fight to the end."

So Field-Marshal Haig had written in his famous Order of the Day, 12 April, 1918. His dogged troops fought on, earning again that old glory which has ever marked the British soldier in the midnight of retreat.

Lloyd George at the time was working, according to a record kept by J. T. Davies, as much as 21 hours a day. There had been further Cabinet changes, in which Milner was taking the place of Derby as War Secretary (Derby had been appointed Ambassador to France) and Austen Chamberlain had returned to the War Cabinet. Once more, in the urgency of a desperate hour the Prime Minister cut short the traditional formality of consulting the King until the announcement of the new Ministers was almost due to be made. (Even then, the news was conveyed to Buckingham Palace by telephone.) Lord Stamfordham wrote, 16 April, 1918, that it had "greatly surprised His Majesty", adding that "His Majesty is not only surprised, but hurt". Replying with due expression of regret, J. T. Davies pleaded the terrific pressure under which the Prime Minister was working, and then offered him the evidence of that "21 hours' day".

Not much encouragement did Lloyd George derive from another envoy whom he had dispatched to the Western Front. This was Smuts, who on his return to Britain went so far as to express publicly in a speech at Glasgow, in May, his doubt as to whether "an out-and-out victory is possible for any group of nations in this war, because it will mean an interminable campaign". The result might be, said Smuts, that the civilization we were out to save and to safeguard would be jeopardized itself. To this opinion he held fast, even as late as 14 August, 1918, when at a meeting of the Imperial War Cabinet he declined to accept the assumption "of the complete defeat of the enemy".

Lloyd George never accepted Smuts' despondent view. In the very middle of that "most stupendous battle" the greatest contribution to the final victory was being made. It was the pressure which Lloyd George himself applied to the war effort of our American Ally. Though the United States had been a belligerent for nearly a year, by the time that the March Offensive opened they had only about 300,000 troops in France, of which more than a third were Supply units. Only one American division was in the firing line.

Both the British and the French had long been urging the Americans not to wait until their divisions, and even army corps, were complete with headquarters staffs, artillery, sappers, signallers, and transport, but to send them over at once and brigade them for the time being with British or French units. Naturally, the American soldiers did not want to merge their national identity in any foreign army, and in this they were strongly upheld by their public men led by their President.

Woodrow Wilson, in particular, Lloyd George complains, was still "saturated with American suspicion and distrust of Europe".

But despite his pleas and plaints to the Government at Washington, General Pershing could not get his American Army in Europe organized.

Lord Reading had written to Lloyd George from Washington, 12 January, 1918:

> "The raising of new armies is a tremendous task for any country, and although one might expect that America, with her two previous experiences and her supposed great business and hustling qualities, would do better than other countries, the fact is she is doing very badly. . . . The Americans are proceeding as if they had years in which to prepare. They have laid out cantonment areas for 10 Divisions and are building the most luxurious huts to supplement billets . . . each man has a *bed* and 3 blankets. . . ."

While Lloyd George had dispatched a Mission to America to tell them over there what it was all about, Beaverbrook, as Minister of Information, now took action to bring over leading citizens from the United States—journalists, and ministers of the Gospel—to find out for themselves. Lloyd George was delighted when the President personally decided to send over a Mission to London, headed by his friend and confidant, Colonel House.

They were invited to the War Cabinet, and welcomed in the very room, as the Prime Minister told them, where 130 years before Lord North had decided and directed the policy which had driven the American Colonies into revolt. There and then, Lloyd George took these envoys of the New World into the heart of the problems which then perplexed the Allies in Europe. Manpower and shipping were the vital issues. Desperately, now, we needed at least 150,000 American infantry troops, and to bring them over the Atlantic right away Britain would be willing even to let her food supplies run down. These American troops could be trained in battalions with British divisions in France, then formed into their own divisions.

With these ideas, General Bliss, the United States Chief of Staff, had been in general accord. Not so General Pershing, their C.-in-C., who stubbornly held to the dictum that American troops could only be commanded by American officers.

The lightning storm of March, 1918, shattered these conventions. By the order of Mr. Baker, United States Secretary of War, four American divisions in France were placed at the disposal of the French C.-in-C., and shipping was mobilized to bring over the infantry of six more divisions.

Now, on 18 April, 1918, urgently Lloyd George wrote to Lord Reading:

"... It rests with America to win or lose the decisive battles of the war. But if it is to be won, America will have to move as she has never moved before, and the President must overrule at once the narrow obstinacy which would put obstacles in the way of using American infantry in the only way in which it can be used to save the situation. ..."

By cutting all other imports, 700,000 American troops were brought to Britain in May, June and July, two-thirds of them in British ships. By the end of the war, the American Army in France numbered nearly two million men. It must be added that with all her mighty manufacturing power, the United States Air Force relied for half its planes on the factories of Britain and France, and no American field artillery or tanks ever went into battle.

At this moment, General Smuts came forward with his own contribution to the problem of the American Command, written in another remarkable letter:

"My dear Prime Minister, 8th June, 1918.

The Higher Command of the American Army has given me much concern, and once before I have already spoken to you about it. I do not know how the following will strike you, but ask you to give it some thought.

It is doubtful whether the war will last till next summer, and it may be that peace overtures are made by the enemy next winter and that popular pressure for peace will be such that a general peace discussion with the enemy could not be avoided. The enemy may even, in view of his Russian victories, be inclined to conclude a reasonable peace in the West. He may begin with an offer to evacuate Belgium and Northern France, which we perhaps could not directly and openly refuse.

The result would be that we go to a peace conference under the shadow of the great military achievements of the enemy in the spring and summer of this year, and conclude a peace which, however favourable to us in other respects, leaves the German military prestige dominant for the future. That would in reality be a great disaster for us and the world. How is this to be avoided?

The American Army will in the late autumn be a first-class instrument of action, and an unexpected blow could be struck with it before the end of the year, which might regain the initiative for us and reverse the military situation completely. The effect on the enemy after their efforts this summer might be far-reaching, and they might be anxious to conclude a really good peace—good for us—before it becomes too late.

The American Army will be there, but it will be without a reliable Higher Command. Pershing is very commonplace, without real war experience, and already overwhelmed by the initial difficulties of a job too big for him. It is also doubtful whether he will loyally co-operate with the Allied Higher Commands. He could not get together a first-class Staff either. I fear very much that with the present Higher Command the American Army will not be used to the best advantage; and victory for us depends on squeezing the last ounce of proper use out of the American Army. . . .

What is to be done?

I would propose that we suggest to President Wilson a reorganization of the American Command. Their Army is becoming a business too large for one man to control if he is to direct operations in the field. Let Pershing remain in charge of all organizations in the rear (bases, supplies, training camps, transport, etc.) but let the fighting command over the American Army be entrusted to another commander.

This is a very delicate matter, as every risk of hurting American pride should be avoided. But I do not think they have the man, and we cannot afford to waste time on experiments. It is doubtful whether they will be willing to accept an English or French commander. They will urge that Foch is already in command of general Allied strategy, but that is really no answer as the American commander may not even be able to carry out Foch's general ideas or handle his army properly and efficiently.

I am naturally most reluctant to bring forward my own name, as you can well understand. But I have unusual experience and qualifications to lead a force such as the American Army will be in an offensive campaign. I think if American *amour propre* could be satisfied, I could in that capacity render very great service to our Cause.

But of that as well as of the question whether it is expedient to make any such suggestion to President Wilson you will be a better judge than I am, and I must leave the matter in your hands. Of the necessity of dealing with the American Higher Command, either on the above or some other line, we can have no doubt if we mean to win the war.

If you do not yourself look upon my suggestion favourably, I trust it will not go beyond you.

> Believe me,
> Yours very sincerely,
> J. C. Smuts."

It did not go beyond Lloyd George.

This summer of 1918 was a strenuous one for the Prime Minister. Besides the deep anxieties of the military situation which called him repeatedly to France, there blew up a storm in politics over Ireland again, and also over internal troubles both at the Air Ministry and the War Office once more.

The Irish Question was this time embrangled in that other almost insoluble Problem of Manpower.

When the great German attack began in the West, a new Military Service Bill had been rushed through Parliament, making men liable to be called up at $18\frac{1}{2}$ years and raising the Service age from 45 to 50 years. The War Cabinet had long and gravely debated whether or not they should apply this new Conscription measure to Ireland. Yes, said Lord Curzon and General Wilson. No, said Mr. H. E. Duke, the new Chief Secretary for Ireland, and Sir James Campbell, the Lord Chief Justice for Ireland. In this, to the surprise of Lloyd George and Bonar Law, they were supported by Sir Edward Carson. The Dublin Castle authorities gave it as their view that Conscription *could* be enforced in Ireland, but that at least two more brigades of British troops would be required to do it. Since there were already 60,000 in garrison there, it hardly seemed worth while to collect every Irish recruit at the cost of the services of another enlisted man. Finally, why stir up more Irish ill-will in the United States?

With considerable misgivings its sponsors introduced the Military Service Bill. Meantime, the Government proceeded with a hardly less contentious measure, a new Home Rule Bill. In the midst of the political confusion thus created, another Irish Republican plot to raise a rebellion in Ireland with German aid was unearthed, with another mysterious Irish emissary landing on the lonely West Coast from a German submarine. The Sinn Fein leaders, who had been released from prison after their 1916 Easter adventures to attend the Irish Convention but had ostentatiously boycotted it and openly continued to drill, had now to be rearrested and reinterned.

In Whitehall and Westminster another crisis broke when Lord Rothermere, the Air Minister who had succeeded Lord Cowdray in that office, fell out with General Sir Hugh Trenchard, the Chief of Air Staff. On 19 March, 1918, Trenchard resigned (or was sacked), but remained at his post until 12 April. A couple of days later, Rothermere made it known that he had gone. Much had happened in that three weeks' interval. The matter had engaged the continual attention of the War Cabinet, even during the desperate days of the March Retreat.

It was revealed that considerable unrest reigned at the Hotel Cecil, where the Air Ministry was located and a very large staff had been assembled. Lord Rothermere had tried to get the machine in working order, but, unused to Civil Service ways, had decided on some drastic changes without consulting the Heads of Departments concerned. Besides this, and the usual inter-departmental jealousies, the Army and Navy representatives in the new Royal Air Force were lustily fighting out a good rival inter-services battle for control of the entire machine. Thoroughly mixed up in this free-for-all were the respective Under-Secretaries, Major Sir John Simon, M.P., and Lieutenant Lord Hugh Cecil, M.P., who were on General Trenchard's Royal Air Force Staff, and Major Evelyn Wrench, who was on Lord Rothermere's Air Ministry Staff. A general uproar was now ensured. The Politicians had shoved overboard the Great Sailor, Jellicoe; they had stabbed the Great Soldier, Robertson; and now they had shot down the Great Airman, "the Man who made the Air Force", Trenchard!

For a fortnight, the Government resisted the clamour of its critics. Then, suddenly, on 23 April, a few days before the Air Estimates were due to be debated, Rothermere himself resigned. In his letter to the Prime Minister, he pleaded that his failing health did not permit him to give to his office the energy and vitality which it demanded (in February, he had suffered the loss of another son in battle). Rothermere said that, anyway, the immediate job he had set out to do was now accomplished; the blending of the Royal Naval Air Service and the Royal Flying Corps into the Royal Air Force had gone through on 1 April without a hitch. He added that the new young Service had lately received all the publicity required, and perhaps more. There was Major Sir John Simon "sequestered into the Hotel Cecil . . . an assistant or clerk to Major-General Sir H. Trenchard", and also Lieutenant Lord Hugh Cecil "holding a Junior staff appointment," both now demanding a Parliamentary debate on Air Ministry affairs.

Rothermere wondered: "Why, in the House of Commons, should they flout disciplinary codes where elsewhere similar conduct by any other Staff Officer would form the subject of inquiry by his superior officers?"

When the Prime Minister replied, generously praising Rothermere for his pioneer work as the "First Secretary of State for Air Force", he gave Lieutenant Lord Hugh Cecil the opportunity to observe (on the Air Force Estimates Debate, 29 April, 1918) that this letter constituted "the effort of a strong Celtic imagination. It was not a statement of fact, but an essay in hagiology, and as often in hagiology, the legendary element very strongly predominates in it."

General Trenchard's value, on the other hand, said Cecil, was that "he will not always listen to the idea of every amateur strategist in the Cabinet quite as sympathetically as that strategist might desire."

When the Prime Minister angrily interrupted to say that no amateur strategist in the Cabinet had ever suggested anything to General Trenchard and that Lord Hugh Cecil had no right to say so, Cecil snapped back: "The Right Honourable Gentleman needn't get so sensitive! He seems to care about nothing except his own retention in office—himself personally."

Which Lloyd George, amid pandemonium, characterized as "a most offensive suggestion". He went on to challenge the idea of serving officers,

who happened also to be M.P.s, making political use of information acquired
in the course of service. They should choose whether they wanted to be officers
or M.P.s. Lord Rothermere had already made way for Sir William Weir as his
successor at the Air Ministry. Rothermere himself stepped up, in due course, to
a Viscountcy for his services. Not right away, because on 25 April, the day
on which his resignation was announced, Stamfordham wrote to the Prime
Minister:

> ". . . The King hopes you will not raise the question of Lord Rother-
> mere's promotion in the Peerage. The newly constituted Air Force, of
> which he was Minister, has only been in existence twenty-four days when he
> resigns. Rightly or wrongly, his administration has been sharply criticized
> and is to be discussed in both Houses of Parliament. . . . His Majesty is
> not very favourable to making Sir W. Weir a peer."

Rothermere's Viscountcy waited until May, 1919.

So the rows over the Royal Air Force—and even over Ireland—buried
themselves. The one over the Western Front went on. After the national
near-disaster of March followed the national inquest of April–May. Lloyd
George says that this controversy, too, "could have destroyed the Government".

Leading the clamour this time came the *Westminster Gazette* (owner,
Cowdray, ex-Air Minister). The Liberal newspaper called for a full Parliamentary Inquiry, declaring that there must be a drastic change in the conduct
of affairs and that if this involved a change of Government, well, that must
come, too. *The Times* (owner, Northcliffe, present Director of Propaganda
in Enemy Countries) also hastened to join in the current commotion. Manpower, the Versailles Council and Unity of Command must also come under
review, said Northcliffe.

Trouble broke wide open on 7 May, 1918, with a letter to the Press by
General Maurice, who had just been relieved of his post at the War Office
as Director of Military Operations. He challenged statements which had
recently been made in the House of Commons, both by the Prime Minister
and by the Chancellor of the Exchequer, concerning the strength of the
British Expeditionary Force and the extension of the British Front. According
to the General, both these statements were untrue.

Lloyd George had said that, despite the heavy casualties of 1917, the
British Army in France was stronger on 1 January, 1918, than on 1 January,
1917; also that the proportion of British, as compared with Indian troops in
Palestine and Egypt, was very small; and that therefore they could not have
contributed much to the total strength on the Western Front had they been
moved there. Bonar Law had declared that the extension of the British line had
been a matter which the Allied generals had settled for themselves, not the
interfering politicians.

With Lord Derby. Downing Street, 1921

Now, from the Opposition Front Bench, Asquith rose to demand a Select Committee of the House of Commons. He disclaimed any intention of attacking the Government. To which Bonar Law countered that, in any case, the Government could not submit secret military documents to a Parliamentary body, inevitably partisan in its composition. He offered instead a tribunal of two judges. Lloyd George himself was for taking the issue straight to a Vote of Confidence in the lobbies of the House. The fall of the Government was freely canvassed.

What was the Prime Minister's case? It was General Maurice's own figures. The Director of Military Operations had attended a meeting of the War Cabinet the very day after the speech in the House of Commons which he now challenged. He had said not a word at that time, nor had he ever afterwards asked for any correction of that statement. In fact, said Lloyd George:

> "The figures that I gave were taken from the Official Records of the War Office, for which I sent before I made the statement. If they were incorrect, General Maurice was as responsible as anyone else. But they were not incorrect."

Lloyd George then argued that the total manpower on the British Front was, as he had stated, greater in January, 1918, than in January, 1917. General Maurice was now, however, making a false distinction between "combatant" and "non-combatant" strength.

> "Who are the combatants? Are these men who stopped the advance of the German Army to Amiens the other day combatants? (Hon. Members: 'Yes!') They are not—if you begin to make a distinction between combatants and non-combatants! Are the men who are under fire every day making and repairing roads and tram-roads and railways, and who suffer severe casualties, combatants or non-combatants? In most lists that have been drafted they are non-combatants.
>
> Does anyone mean to tell me that they are not part of the fighting strength of the British Army?"

Lloyd George asserted that his statements about the strength of British troops in the Middle Eastern Fronts were based upon other War Office information presented to the War Cabinet, and sent to General Maurice to be checked. The message had been telephoned back that Maurice "had no remarks".

Then the Prime Minister flatly denied that "a single yard" of the Western Front had been taken over by the British Army as a result of the Versailles Conference; the extension had been agreed between Haig and Pétain before the Supreme Council ever met; it had also been carried out; and the fact was reported by Haig to the Council. General Maurice, incidentally, had not been there himself.

P

Lastly, Lloyd George turned on the Cadbury newspapers of the Liberal Press which had been attacking him. For years, he said, he had "been drenched with cocoa slop".

Now they were egging on Asquith, prodding him to refuse a judicial, secret tribunal. Very well, the public had now been given all the facts that could possibly be disclosed. These were enough to let the public judge. Let the House of Commons that very night judge, too. This was a Vote of Censure upon the Government, and if it were carried the Government would fall, and Asquith would have the responsibility for the new one.

Nobody else rose from the Liberal Front Bench, though the irrepressible Pringle got up from the Liberal Back Benches and Lord Hugh Cecil, from the Tory Back Benches, delivered another lecture to the Prime Minister on political morality. Asquith's Motion to set up a Select Committee to inquire into the allegations of General Maurice was then put to the vote:

AYES 106
NOES 293

So ended the Maurice Debate. The General himself was placed on retired pay, and perhaps was fortunate not to face a court martial. Now, but for one brief flicker in 1922, he passes out of history.

But not the gash he made upon it. The Maurice Debate marked the final division in the First World War between Lloyd George's friends and enemies, and drove a cleavage into the ranks of the Liberal Party which to this day has never yet been bridged.

The bloody grapple on the Western Front continued. A hundred miles from the lobbies of Westminster the fate of the world was being shaped.

Not with satisfaction, but with angry impatience, Lloyd George walked from the House of Commons to Downing Street that night.

CHAPTER XXV

VICTORY

N EXT morning there were some other problems on the Prime Minister's desk.

The Soldiers, the Sailors and the Airmen were not alone. The Press Lords were there, too, and in particular Rothermere's big brother, Northcliffe.

On the day after the Air Minister resigned, Beaverbrook, the Minister of Information, forwarded to Lloyd George a letter to him from Northcliffe, the Director of Propaganda in Enemy Countries. Plainly written with the intention that the Prime Minister himself should read it, this letter announced that his lordship did not propose to remain in office a moment longer than was necessary (it is a moot point whether Lord Derby or Lord Northcliffe resigned—or declined—office most times during the First World War), because the writer wished to escape from any connection with the "alleged War Cabinet", so that he could say what he really thought about it. Would Beaverbrook, therefore, kindly let the Prime Minister know of Northcliffe's decision, because he proposed to publish it and did not want to embarrass him unnecessarily. *Age 55*

There was a plain threat here. Northcliffe was dissuaded from resigning. He did not go, in fact, until 12 November, 1918, the day after the Armistice.

A couple of months later it was Beaverbrook himself who was writing to the Prime Minister to say that he wanted to walk out. But Beaverbrook's plea was not that he wanted to leave the Government so that he could attack it, but that he wanted to leave it because under existing arrangements he could not effectively serve it.

24 June, 1918.

"My dear Prime Minister,

I am writing to you to resign my office as Minister of Information and Chancellor of the Duchy.

. . . The Ministry of Information is the Ministry of Publicity abroad. Its object is to state the British case to the world. Its business is to study popular opinion abroad and to influence it through all possible channels. But since our appeal lies not to the diplomatic representatives of Foreign countries but to the public opinion of those countries, our methods must be different from those of the Foreign Office. We have a diplomacy of our own to conduct—a popular diplomacy—and for this we must have our own special organization. Unofficial propaganda of this character has been the most potent of enemy weapons and it can only be met by similar propaganda on our part.

The Foreign Office has, however, both in principle and practice refused to recognize this duty of the new Ministry from its very inception. It says in effect that the doctrine of popular diplomacy implied the setting up of a Second Foreign Office at home with a new set of representatives abroad and a policy possibly divergent from that of the Foreign Secretary. The consequences of this clash of views between the two departments has been friction and delay and for the Ministry which I represent an intolerable clog on its operations. Of the various missions I have tried to send abroad, missions to be headed by people of the status of Ministers, all save one have been blocked. . . .

It seems to me that only two things can be done. One is to abolish the Ministry of Information as a separate Ministry and make Foreign Propaganda a section of the Foreign Office: the other is to authorize the Ministry to operate abroad on equal terms with the Foreign Office, consulting and as far as possible accepting its views but with power to take its own line of action.

Nothing less than this last course in my opinion will meet the urgent needs of the situation and since I cannot make my view prevail, I must with sincere regret place my resignation in your hands and ask you to act immediately.

Yours faithfully,
Beaverbrook."

But Beaverbrook, too, was placated. It was not until his own health broke down temporarily in November that he relinquished his office. By then, Victory was at hand.

That steaming summer of 1918 there was trouble not only in the inner circle of politics; it sizzled all around the rim. Besides rebel Ireland and revolutionary Russia to confuse the straight issue of "getting on with the war", there was rising unrest in the factories of Britain against labour conditions, prices, rations. Led by their shop stewards—and flouting their official trade unions—300,000 workers in Leeds threatened to down tools. In Birmingham, 100,000 workers did it. The Government replied by declaring that the protection which these men had hitherto enjoyed by being reserved from military service would be withdrawn and they would be called up under the Conscription Acts. The men returned to their benches.

Then the women came out, demanding equal pay for equal work. The busmen and tramwaymen came out. As soon as they could be coerced or cajoled to get back on the job, the cotton-spinners came out. In turn (there was no General Strike, but a general wave of strikes), the miners, the Clyde ship-workers, the railwaymen, and, finally, the London Metropolitan policemen came out.

This last was really grave. For if policemen were allowed to strike, so might soldiers, and sailors. The shadow of the Soviets loomed.

The "National Union of Police and Prison Officers" were demanding a new war bonus. They also wanted official recognition. When these terms were rejected, at midnight, 29 August, 1918, the London bobbies walked off the beat. Next day, headed by a piper and singing lustily, they marched in column of fours, through the City to Tower Hill. The stockbrokers and their office staffs treated them to a good-tempered cheer.

The War Office, and particularly the C.I.G.S., General Wilson, wanted to put a rough stop to this business. It was getting dangerously near to their own. Lloyd George thought it more sensible to settle matters round a table. At No. 10 Downing Street, he received the strikers' representatives, not as the Executive of the National Union of Police and Prison Officers, but as policemen with a grievance. They had a genuine one over their pay and widows' pensions, and it was met. Next day, London returned to the care of its policemen.

A far more serious element in the mood of public unrest was the sudden revival of the handling (or what the noisier newspapers called the "coddling") of enemy aliens. Many were the questions set down in the House of Commons, "exposure" articles appeared in the Press, and "Down-with-the-Hun-in-our-Midst" demonstrations were held in Hyde Park.

The Government brought forward a British Nationality and Status of Aliens Bill. It tightened up existing restrictions, and laid it down that no alien was to be employed by the Government. An Aliens Advisory Committee was set up as official watch-dog, but certain zealous Parliamentary back-benchers deemed it necessary also to inaugurate an unofficial committee of the House of Commons, calling itself the "Aliens' Watch Committee", chairman, Sir Edward Carson.

Prominent among its Members was the ever-exuberant Independent M.P. Mr. Pemberton Billing, sailor, actor, inventor, airman and crank. He had lately gained himself much further notoriety by his clamour for air reprisals against the Germans. "Bomb the Hun Homeland!" bawled Billing. He now invited equal public attention to the witch-hunt against Aliens here. And promptly, Pemberton Billing unmasked an Alien in the Cabinet itself! This was Sir Albert Stanley, President of the Board of Trade. In the House of Commons, Pemberton Billing declared that though this gentleman was described in *Dod's Parliamentary Guide* as the son of Henry Stanley, of Detroit, U.S.A., wasn't his real name Nuttmeyer?

Sensation! Alarm! Strangers within the Gates! The Hidden Hand of the Hun! The Aliens' Watch Committee set up instant and insistent watch-dog barking.

An embarrassed business man rose to explain.

His name was not Nuttmeyer, but his father's name had once been Knatriess. That was originally a Scandinavian name, but the family had settled in Derby-shire for several centuries, and the President of the Board of Trade had been himself born there. When his father emigrated to Canada, he had changed this foreign-sounding name to an English one, and what more natural for a Derby-bred boy than to choose "Stanley"? Snarling, and growling, the watch-dogs retired.

The Opposition did not let up. (The Opposition in Parliament, 1918, was not by any means only the official, Asquithian Liberal one; it was almost as often—and always far more formidably—an unofficial Tory one.) Early in August, another attack was launched against the much-bruised Ministry of Information. Mr. T. Leif Jones, a Cornish Liberal M.P. and strong teetotaller, opened fire with charges of extravagance in spending public money, from Petrograd, via Paris, to Buenos Aires, and including Dublin. There, indeed, had occurred the scandal of entertaining a dozen American visitors on a two-day party, at a cost of £31 (£5 for cigars!). Other critics attacked the Government control of radio, films, and even of a special "Troops' newspaper". For what sinister electioneering purpose had this organ been devised?

The Financial Secretary to the Treasury, Stanley Baldwin, rose to defend the Minister of Information, Beaverbrook. It was his first big Front Bench occasion as the Government spokesman. He began by defending those "dollar-a-year" business men who were said to be at the Ministry of Information in such strength.

"When you are founding a new Ministry, you are between the Devil and the Deep Sea. If you fill it with people who are Civil Servants the cry goes up that the Department is filled with bureaucrats, and if you do not do that but appoint business men then along come critics who say, 'Look at him: he is surrounding himself with blackguards.' If you have an efficient man of business he is a blackguard!"

Baldwin then spoke up for Beaverbrook. "He is a man of strong personality. Men with strong personalities have this in common—that magnetism which comes with that personality either attracts or repels."

It was the first time (and it turned out to be the last time) that Baldwin and Beaverbrook were at one politically.

Beaverbrook had taken the precaution of providing some other counsel for the defence of his Ministry. The week-end before the debate, he telephoned to Ireland to invite his friend Tim Healy to come and spend it with him at Leatherhead. He had duly arrived after Mass on the Sunday. All day long, Beaverbrook sought to place his arguments before his guest, who tried, in turn, to deflect the conversation towards any subject whatever except the forthcoming debate. He sipped his wine, and smoked his cigar, and simply refused to be seriously interested in that issue. Though Beaverbrook had arranged that Healy should be called third in the debate (after the opening statements from either side of the House of Commons), he had to abandon his efforts that Sunday to marshal his case.

Now Tim Healy rose in the Parliamentary debate. A Select Committee, he said, had recently been inquiring into the new Ministry of Information. Why hadn't it looked into its predecessor, a Department which had been "staffed and stuffed" with the friends of Sir Edward Carson? Then Healy launched a passionate denunciation of the Chief Secretary for Ireland, Mr. Edward Shortt, for his brutalities towards the Irishmen he had jailed without trial. Vainly, did Shortt intervene to defend himself against this unexpected and unprovoked attack. Joe Devlin followed, and pummelled him again. The debate, having been thus turned into an old-fashioned Irish Night, nothing further was heard of the Ministry of Information.

Lloyd George himself had borne all these summer storms with good heart, and on the whole, with good temper. (Didn't the man *enjoy* rough weather?) He had reason to be, for the moment, fairly well content. He had fought his own enemies off in the House of Commons, he had never wavered for one hour, even during the most desperate days of Ludendorff's latest and greatest offensive, in his faith that Britain would win through in the end. Scores of leading men, in all walks of life and service, who worked with Lloyd George through this crisis of history have freely testified to his unflinching resolve, and not one, whom later years may have embittered, has ever since said otherwise.

It was Bonar Law, who stood nearest to him in these days of fate, who has told us of this man in the test of his life:

"He thought of nothing, and aimed at nothing, and hoped for nothing, except the successful end of the war. That was his life, and he had no other life. In good report and evil, we saw what courage meant. It was not merely the courage of dogged determination, but was accompanied by a brilliant hopefulness which was an example and inspiration to everyone who worked with him."

Now, by midsummer, on the Western Front, the Germans had made their last furious drive on Paris. They had surged up to the Marne again, and beyond it. And there, again, they had been held. The City of Paris itself, they ranged with their long-distance howitzer gun, "Big Bertha", but this intermittent bombardment served rather to stimulate the French to counter-attack and drive them back than to make further withdrawal.

There were difficult, even dangerous, hurdles still to surmount along the road to Victory. As late as 14 July, 1918, Lloyd George is writing rather anxiously to Lord Milner about Clemenceau. He is not quite sure that "that queer-tempered old gentleman" is as satisfied as he might be with the contribution of his devoted Allies to the Battle of France, or as willing as they want him to be to fall in with their plans.

"We must take no chances," says Lloyd George. "I have, therefore, come to the conclusion that it would be as well that a deputation should go to

France. . . . Borden and Smuts are coming down this afternoon. . . . I mean to press both to go over to France immediately. I think they are more likely to prevail with Clemenceau, coming as they do from the Dominions, who have made such a fine contribution to the defence of France; and Borden more especially, I am told, will have special influence with Pershing, the Americans being rather anxious to stand well with Canada, which is becoming year by year a more formidable neighbour."

At this time, according to Borden,[1] the special committee of the Imperial War Cabinet set up to find out what further effort, where, when and how, was required to win the war, could not find the answer. From first to last in this investigation, they did not find one man, either soldier or civilian, who suggested "or even dreamed" that victory could be won that year. This, although by now the Americans were swarming across the Atlantic at the rate of a quarter of a million a month. It may be added that neither Haig nor Foch then realized the grave straits to which the failure of the enemy's three offensives had reduced the German Army. A week later, the Allies advanced in general attack and on 8 August, at Amiens, the British tanks shattered the front and the heart itself of our terrible enemy in what Ludendorff described as the "Black Day of the German Army". That night, the victorious British counted 16,000 prisoners and 200 German guns, and the Kaiser told a confidant: "We must sue for peace".

The victors (as often) were slower to realize it. The German offensive power had plainly been contained at last, but how long would it take to deliver our own decisive blow on the entrenched Western Front? Lloyd George still had his eyes ranging those Italian and Balkan Fronts, and he had been encouraged by the petering-out of the Austrian Army's summer attack to hope that a way might yet be forced into the bastion of Central Powers via that "back door". Haig's masterly advance in the West this time removed any serious temptation to try it. At last, the war could be left to the generals.

Already, indeed, by midsummer of 1918, the Prime Minister had permitted his mind to roam over the possibility of a General Election. Barely a week after the Maurice Debate a Conference of Coalition Liberal Ministers at Downing Street, which included Churchill, Montagu, Illingworth, Dr. Addison and Sir Gordon Hewart, with Captain Guest in the chair, had reported to the Prime Minister that it was now time to prepare "a Liberal Policy for presentation when advisable to the Country". To Riddell on 17 June, Lloyd George confided his idea "that before long there must be an Election. We must have a Parliament which represents the views of the people."[2]

Nor was Lloyd George saying this in any fractious spirit. The last General Election had been in 1910, and on a comparatively narrow and restricted

[1] Speech to Professional Institute of the Canadian Civil Service, 21 November, 1950.
[2] Lord Riddell's War Diary.

franchise. But early in 1918, Lloyd George's Government had brought in a Representation of the People Act, conferring manhood suffrage and votes for women at the age of thirty if they were householders or the wives of house-holders (that is, occupying land or premises worth £5 a year). Plural voting, except for business or University representation, was abolished. The Local Government franchise was made practically universal. This measure, perhaps the most revolutionary of all the great Reform Bills in the history of Britain, had been carried through both Houses of Parliament almost without opposition. So far had the first "People's War" advanced the People's power.

The Prime Minister, who had sponsored this Act, was not unaware of the weapon which it placed in his hands, at any rate, against those diehard rebel Tories, and probably against the Asquithian Opposition Liberals, too. If it came to making appeal to the broad masses, Lloyd George had no rival in either of those camps. Less now than at any time for twenty years, did he care about the cliques and cabals of Westminster, but returned to the idea of his Radical youth: "*My audience is the country.*"

On 29 July, 1918, Riddell records another conversation which took place at Danny Park, near Hassocks, Sussex, a fine Elizabethan mansion which he had taken for the summer to serve as a country retreat for the Prime Minister. What Lloyd George said on this occasion undoubtedly expressed his true mood at the time. It was not that of a man who despaired of victory in the field, but rather of one who saw it possible within a measurable time. If it could be brought about soon, then the General Election could wait upon it; if not, then it seems that Lloyd George was ready to face a war-time Election to give a new mandate to his Government.

"Lloyd George is now full of it, and palpitating with energetic enthu-siasm. His vitality is wonderful. He is like a skilful prize-fighter in the ring. He is all over the arena, defending here and attacking there."[1]

He kept to his early habits. Off to bed soon after nine o'clock where he read himself to sleep, leaving the light on all night. His reading there? Much as before. "I like a good, bloodthirsty novel, with plenty of fighting and plenty of killing. I love R. L. Stevenson and Anthony Hope . . . I don't care for serious books nowadays. I have too many official documents to read!"

Bad news never disturbed Lloyd George's sleep. He did his worrying in the daytime. About half-past six in the morning, he awoke, and started that "official" reading. The maid brought him a cup of tea. At eight o'clock, the morning newspapers arrived. Most of them he skimmed through rapidly, and threw on the floor. Certain articles by certain writers he read carefully and noted. Then he got up and dressed. If he was at Danny—which lacked only a view—and the morning was fine, he climbed to the top of a hill nearby to see the country beyond. At breakfast, the Prime Minister's public day began.

[1] Lord Riddell's War Diary.

p*

After lunch, Lloyd George always took a nap for an hour on a settee. "You must relax every muscle. You can stretch full out, or curl up like my chow! It will very nearly double your working day!"

It was a habit which Clemenceau shared, and Churchill has copied (though Churchill has carried it further; he climbs into bed for an hour or so). Lloyd George developed other restful devices during these arduous years. If he could, he always put his feet up in a motor-car, and slept on a journey, which was one reason why he never liked travelling at speed.

He fancied a cigar after his meals, and he always possessed a good selection. Sometimes, at this period of his life, he still smoked a pipe. But you have to pack your own pipe, and Lloyd George was never adept with his hands. If Sarah was around, he would be only too glad to let her lace his boots up for him. With drink, he was always abstemious; a glass or so of Irish whiskey was his day's limit.

By now, he was putting on a little weight; a man of 5 feet 7 inches, he weighed 13 stone, and he took a size 17½ collar. His hair he let lengthen with his age (he always insisted that his head had increased half an inch in circumference during the time that he was Prime Minister!). He was thoroughly aware of the importance for a public man of a distinctive dress or accoutrements (had not Joe Chamberlain sported a perennial orchid and an eyeglass, and would not Baldwin provide himself with a perpetual pipe, and Churchill a cigar?). Lloyd George had his flowing mane which showed off his fine head, and his Tyrolean cloak, and his wide, open-winged collar. He went to a Cork Street tailor for his suits, his shirts were made to measure, and so were his boots (he never wore shoes, even with evening-dress).

He needed to keep his health and strength at this hard time. Though the war was now going better—indeed, no doubt because it was going so well—the prospects of Peace threatened to divide the unity of the War Cabinet. At one of its meetings on 13 August, 1918, the Canadian Prime Minister, Borden, came out with the opinion that after the victory had been won, the British Empire should make no annexations, but should hand over our conquests in South-West and East Africa, Palestine, Mesopotamia, Persia and the Pacific Islands to the custody of the United States. This was vigorously resisted by New Zealand's William Massey, and volcanically by Australia's Billy Hughes. Spluttered Billy, and the message was meant for all comers: "If you want to shift us, come and do it!"

Naturally, there were some difficulties with our Allies, too. Though the American armies were being transported to the Western battlefields largely in British ships, at the cost of withholding food and raw materials to Britain, the French were seeking to use these reinforcements to rest their own troops (who had borne far less of the 1918 battles than ours), while refusing to relieve us of any part of the British sector of the Western Front. On the eve of the arrival in London of the two French Cabinet Ministers (Clemenceau and

Tardieu) to meet the Prime Minister's protests about this situation, Lloyd
George set forth his own strong views in a letter to Lord Reading, who had
played the leading part in arranging the transportation of the Americans.

This letter, which is dated the very day of the great British tank triumph at
Amiens, forcefully expresses the Prime Minister's determination to bring
Britain out of the war, not only victorious over the enemy, but also, at
least equal to her Allies. Moreover, Lloyd George reckoned that he had the
means.

"26 August, 1918.   Danny Park,
                                                       Hassocks.
My dear R,

. . . I am anxious to use the shipping lever for the purpose of bringing
pressure to bear on the French and the Americans to take over a part of
our line, and thus enable us to give a rest to our troops. Clemenceau and
Foch mean to compel us to keep up our numbers on the British front by
refusing to take over the line. This policy would be fatal to the British
Empire, as we have no reserve of men here which would enable us to keep
up anything approximating to the number of divisions we now maintain in
the field, and if we endeavoured to keep up that number until the summer
of next year we should be left with no army at all for the rest of the war. I
cannot conceive of a more disastrous plan from the British point of view.
I mean, therefore, to fight it with every available resource. Shipping is one
of those resources, and until the French and Americans come to terms with
us on the question of the line I do not propose to give any further assistance
in the matter of shipping.

There are, therefore, two points which I am anxious you should impress
upon Tardieu. (1) That our pledge to carry American troops does not
extend beyond December and that, as we are losing 250,000 tons of essential
cargo per month owing to the diversion of ships to the American troop
business, we cannot possibly undertake any further extension. (2) That the
Americans say that they cannot build up and maintain an army of 80 divisions
in the field next summer unless we give them something like the equivalent
of 8,000,000 tons of cargo space. This we cannot do unless France and Italy
are prepared between them to surrender the shipping we have placed at
their disposal.

If we have anything in hand, I am extremely anxious that it should not
be given at this stage. It must be used for bargaining. . . .
                                                       Ever sincerely,
                                                       D. Lloyd George."

A day or two afterwards, Lloyd George went off to Manchester to receive
the freedom of the city where he was born. He fell victim to the extraordinary
influenza wave which was then sweeping across England with a casualty rate

almost equal to that of the Western Front, and spent the next week in bed at the Mansion House of the Lord Mayor.

He returned to face a fresh quarrel which had broken out over the question of the responsibility for Government propaganda. There was also a new row raging between the Zionist and the anti-Zionist Jews. His Foreign Secretary, Balfour, was no Jew, but he was the foremost and certainly the most famous Christian Zionist.

What angered the Prime Minister a great deal more than either, however, was a leading article which appeared on 29 August in the *Daily Express*, the newspaper owned by his Minister of Information, Beaverbrook. It was headed:

SOME QUESTIONS ON A GENERAL ELECTION

It said:

"We do not want a new Khaki Election. We cannot vote in the dark. If the Prime Minister seeks re-election as head of a Coalition Government which is to endure, he must satisfy those who are to vote for him that his views and theirs are the same. . . .

What, for instance, is the Prime Minister's Programme on TARIFF REFORM and IMPERIAL PREFERENCE? . . . What would be the IRISH POLICY of the Government which hopes to be returned? . . . Is the WELSH CHURCH to be sacrificed simply because the Party of Spoilers just tottering to its fall over the Irish Crisis of 1914 was saved for a moment by the outbreak of the Great War?"

Beaverbrook was in full pursuit of his own "Holy Grail", which he calls Empire Free Trade or Empire Commercial Union, or Imperial Preference, according to the time of day. So far, there have been 16,060 days since the clamour began.

Furiously, Lloyd George wrote to Bonar Law that morning:

"Have you seen the leader in today's *Express*? That is Max. Having regard to the risks I ran for him and the way I stood up for him when he was attacked by his own Party, I regard this as a mean piece of treachery. It explains why no man in any Party trusts Max.

The reference to the Welsh Church is deliberately introduced to make it impossible for me to arrange matters with the Unionist leaders.

I am sorry, for I have sincerely tried to work with him."

Already, by mid-July, 1918, a small "General Election" sub-committee of Coalition Liberal Ministers under the chairmanship of Dr. Addison had been set up on the basis that

(i) A form of agreement with the Tory Coalitionists should be prepared forthwith;

(ii) A common programme should be drawn up and jointly signed;

(iii) A general statement of policy by the Prime Minister should be made at a favourable opportunity.

From one important quarter, however, there now developed a resistance to any war-time General Election. This came from Buckingham Palace, and opened with a letter from Lord Stamfordham to the Prime Minister saying that King George V should see a letter written the day before to him (Stamfordham) by the Bishop of Chelmsford.

In this letter, the Bishop declared that all the powerful arguments adduced in favour of a General Election paled into insignificance against the fact that it would divide the country, and he quoted as examples, the results of war-time General Elections in Canada and Australia. There might, indeed, be a similar verdict for pursuing the war but it would be purchased at the price of raising all other kinds of issues. He concluded that the Khaki Election of the Boer War offered no safe parallel. There had not been a Labour Party then!

Lloyd George replied tartly, that the Bishop's letter was "surely outside his functions?" He suggested that though the Bishop was himself a stout supporter of the war, he was very much in touch with Pacifist and semi-Pacifist elements in the country.

He concluded: "These people are naturally alarmed at the prospect of an appeal to the electorate and they are working every conceivable agency to avert what they regard as a disaster to their cause. The Bishop, I fear, is their unconscious tool—hence this unconstitutional appeal to the Sovereign over the head of his Ministers."

Certainly, there was much Election talk from now on, many comings and goings, so that even had the War gone on into the New Year, 1919, it would have been difficult to hold it back. Some of the Tory leaders may have had strong feelings about Tariff Reform, but only a brace of them were still prepared to quarrel with Lloyd George any longer about the Welsh Church.

Irresistibly now, the Allied battle was rolling forward. In the East, Damascus had fallen, and with it the last buttress of Turk military power in Palestine. Bulgaria and Austria were making ready to retreat. In the West, the Allies advanced, not in sudden rushes, but by a time-table march. Riddell tells of one of those closing September days, when the news came through to Danny Park of a great new British victory: "The P.M. full of glee. On the arrival of the message, he began to dance a hornpipe."

Less than a week later, 4 October, 1918, the German Imperial Chancellor, Prince Max of Baden, asked for an armistice on the basis of President Wilson's Fourteen Points. Austria and Turkey, the remaining two of the enemy Grand Alliance, associated themselves with this request.

It confirmed Woodrow Wilson in his opinion that he was now the arbiter of the world. Omitting to consult his Allies, the President now began to treat privately with the enemy he had only just begun to fight. In the Supreme

Council at Versailles on 6 October, Lloyd George sharply protested that all the other Allied and Associated Powers did not have to pander to the President of the United States. On 9 October, he insisted that they tell him frankly that they could not agree to Point Two (the Freedom of the Seas) being made part of the basis of any truce, and that the evacuation of all occupied territory by the enemy must take place before the Allies would even discuss it. The argument continued more acidly among the Allies than between the belligerents.

The war also continued. The Germans withdrew methodically towards the Rhine, and the Austro-Hungarians tumbled back in disorder across the Piave; at Vittorio Veneto the Italians avenged Caporetto. The Czechs rose in revolt, seized Prague and proclaimed a Republic; the Croats and Slovenes joined the Serbs, and turned upon their ancient oppressors from Vienna; the Hungarians declared their independence of Austria at Budapest. The "Ramshackle Empire" had broken up. On 29 October, 1918, the Austrians surrendered. The Turks laid down their arms the same day.

Would the Germans fight on in the West? Their armies still maintained good order, and the further they retired, of course, the shorter they made both their front and their line of communication to Fortress Germany itself. As late as 27 October, Lloyd George being asked by a friend what were the chances of peace, replied: "A slight shade of odds in favour of an armistice before Christmas!"

The Allied Supreme Command prepared for the Campaign of 1919, ordering scores of thousands of tanks and scores of thousands of airplanes. They were working out the supply problems for an army of three million men to force the passage of the Rhine when, suddenly, on 7 November, a German delegation, half-military and half-civilian, appeared under a flag of truce before the French lines. Next day, they applied for an armistice.

They waited . . . waited. . . .

They had to wait. The Allied generals were arguing.

The British wanted to make the terms as easy as they dared demand. They had at their head commanders who, twenty years before, had seen on the *veldt* what the blank demand of Unconditional Surrender could do to a race as proud in spirit and far poorer in strength than were the Germans of 1918.

The French wanted to make the terms as hard as they could get. They knew the Germans.

The Americans wanted to make the terms the hardest of all, and were prepared to go on fighting as long as need be to exact them. They had no manpower problem, either at home or in the field.

The German plenipotentiaries waited. . . .

They had to wait. The Allied politicians were arguing. There was a General Election coming. Where would everybody be—and still more important *who* would everybody be in the new Administration?

There was Churchill, Minister of Munitions, writing to Lloyd George, the Prime Minister, wanting to know the composition of the new Government which Lloyd George proposed to form before he decided on his own course. Churchill was strongly of the opinion that as soon as the war was ended, they must return to the orthodox Cabinet system in which all the principal Ministers shared in a collective responsibility. He was especially anxious that this Cabinet should not contain any unrepresentative or reactionary elements. He assured the Prime Minister of his personal goodwill.

He got a sharp answer from Lloyd George—and but for the restraining advice of Bonar Law—he would have got a sharper one. Was he dissatisfied with his own personal prospects? demanded Lloyd George. Because there appeared to be no other reason for choosing this critical moment for deserting the Prime Minister, just as he was about to enter on a great new national task. It couldn't be policy, because Lloyd George had not asked him to commit himself to anything to which Asquith had not already committed the Liberal Party, and Churchill had not objected to that, either at the time or subsequently! Did he object to any of his associates in the present Government? It was a Coalition Government, and Churchill had known that when he joined it. Now, before associating himself with the new Government, he was insisting on knowing who else was going to be in it.

"Surely," wrote Lloyd George, "that is an unprecedented demand. The choice of the Members of the Government must be left to the Prime Minister, and anyone who does not trust his leadership, has but one course, and that is to seek leaders whom he *can* trust."

If Churchill was dissatisfied with his present position, Lloyd George continued, might it be pointed out that it was better than his position had been in the Asquith Coalition Government. For Churchill knew very well that instead of appointing him to the Ministry of Munitions, Asquith had sent him to the Duchy of Lancaster: it was Lloyd George himself, "at the cost of a great deal of temporary dissatisfaction" amongst many of his supporters, who had placed him in the Ministry of Munitions. The Prime Minister also would regret severing a political and personal friendship which had extended over fourteen years, but this was no time for half-hearted support. So if Mr. Churchill was assailed by any personal doubts, well, better make up his mind now!

That same day, 8 November, 1918, the sailors of the German High Seas Fleet, on a report they were about to be ordered to put to sea in one last Prussian form of *hari-kiri*, swarmed up the ladders from the lower decks in mutiny, and murdered their officers. Next day, the Kaiser and the Crown Prince fled to Holland. And the day after that, came an urgent wire from "Tiger" Clemenceau to Lloyd George.

Better close the deal with the German Army now! The Land of the

Hohenzollerns was dissolving into anarchy and communism, as the Land of the Hapsburgs had already disintegrated into rival nationalisms. In Germany now, the Bolshevik, not the Boche, was the Enemy.

But still it was not Peace. At the Mansion House, that Saturday evening, Lloyd George had to tell the eagerly expectant company: "I have no news for you."

Sunday passed.

One more dawn, and then at 5 a.m. on Monday, 11 November, 1918, the Armistice was signed in a wayside railway-station in France, to come into effect in six hours' time. A few minutes before the Cease Fire! sounded along the blood-soaked front, the Canadians marched into Mons.

At 11 a.m. the maroons went up in London, the sirens screamed, and the guns thundered. It was all over, at last. It was a grey, drizzling day, but the people poured on to the streets, sang, danced, cheered, and went mad with joy. In the House of Commons, when Lloyd George entered, all the Members stood up. He read out the terms of the Armistice. Then, in a voice, which once or twice almost broke, he said: "This is no time for words. Our hearts are too full of gratitude, to which no tongue can give adequate expression."

In quiet dignity, and with thoughts that each man keeps to himself in such an hour, the Speaker led the House of Commons across the street from the Palace of Westminster to the Abbey. Lloyd George walked with Bonar Law, his colleague and old opponent, and with Asquith, his old leader and his present opponent.

It was the highest and the humblest moment of his life.

CHAPTER XXVI

KHAKI ELECTION

LLOYD GEORGE sat down to his Armistice dinner at No. 10 Downing Street with Churchill. The guest has not forgotten that memorable evening.

"We were alone in the large room from whose walls the portraits of Pitt and Fox, of Nelson and Wellington and—perhaps somewhat incongruously—of Washington then looked down. One of the most admirable traits of Mr. Lloyd George's character was his complete freedom at the height of his power, responsibility and good fortune from anything in the nature of pomposity or superior airs. He was always natural and simple. He was always exactly the same to those who knew him well; ready to argue any point, to listen to disagreeable facts even when controversially presented. One could say anything to him, on the terms that he could say anything back."[1]

That is a friendly, and a fair picture of Lloyd George at this time. The account which Churchill gives of their talk that night rings true, too. He recalls that at this moment of absolute victory the Prime Minister had no feeling that the job was done but, rather, that a new and perhaps still more difficult effort lay ahead. They spoke of the mighty battle which the Germans had waged for four years, in the end against the main part of the world; how you could not hope to rebuild Europe without them; how under the double hammer of defeat in the field and hunger at home they might now break up in revolution. Churchill, especially, wanted to save them from that.

Next day, 12 November, by decision of the War Cabinet, Sir Auckland Geddes, Director-General of National Service, suspended all recruiting. General Wilson, C.I.G.S., was furious and not unnaturally. Generals always want more soldiers, and this one realized that before long he was likely to be rather short of them. The clamour for demobilization had begun.

Thus, the day after the war ended there arrived the immediate and most menacing problem of Peace; how to bring the millions of men in the Forces back to civilian life. They had done four years of fighting in foreign lands, in the trenches of France and Flanders, across the deserts of Egypt, "Mespot" and Palestine, through the jungles of Africa and the swamps of Salonika, on the seas of the world and in their depths, in the skies.

[1] *The World Crisis: The Aftermath*, by Winston S. Churchill. (Author's Note: According to Lloyd George's engagements, Bonar Law and F. E. Smith were also at the dinner.)

The hearts of few of these men were any longer reconciled to wounds and death in this New Year, and despite some talk of a "few hundred thousand American troops, who were longing to play a part in events" (Churchill), and of "volunteer units from the French and British Armies", within six months the Americans had all gone home to the United States, the French Army and the French Fleet intervening in South Russia had mutinied, the ugly temper simmering in the ranks of the British Armed Forces (it had several times boiled over in the camps, and even in the streets of London) had compelled a rapid demobilization of all arms and the ending of Conscription.

"*We were the masters of the world. What went wrong?*" Thus Churchill, rhetorically.

The answer is, simply—we weren't.

A New World had been born in the torment of war. The old symbols of authority had fallen into the dust. In Britain, women had won their rights. The wage-earners were claiming an ever larger share in the profits of their trade, and a real improvement of the conditions in which they worked. Indeed, organized labour was demanding a great share, if not the actual control, of industry and transport, of Government itself. Lloyd George was not ready to deny all these demands. He was in favour of many of them. There was no man in British politics who more sincerely or more ardently desired to see higher wages established, better housing, wider education, and a fuller opportunity secured for the worker than the Prime Minister who now set before the nation this ideal: "To make Britain a fit country for heroes to live in."

Now, swiftly, and acutely, there arose that question of an early General Election. The existing Parliament was eight years old, and the electorate had meantime increased from eight to twenty millions. Seven millions of these were the newly-enfranchised women, and as the Parliamentary candidates would find out, many of them were amongst the most vocal of the voters. Millions of the fighting men had never yet cast a vote; it was impossible that the Government which was to frame the Peace should do so without a fresh mandate from the nation. The case for a General Election in 1918 was overwhelming.

In deciding to go forward to the polls, Lloyd George was well aware that the voting would largely be for or against himself personally. And if he should secure a majority, he did not overlook the fact that it would free him from the shackles which his present dependence on the Tory Party in the House of Commons imposed upon him. It was a blow to Lloyd George's hopes when the Labour Party decided to withdraw from the Coalition.

On Thursday of Armistice Week, 14 November, 1918, Bonar Law, as Leader of the House, announced that Polling Day would be in one month's time and that the votes would be counted on 28 December. That same day, the Labour Party Emergency Conference resolved to withdraw its members from the Government. In the evening amid tumultuous scenes at the Albert

Hall, Labour's Election Campaign was launched. Said J. H. Thomas, M.P., the Railwaymen's leader: "Our battle-cry, above all else, will be NO MORE WAR!"

Bob Williams, Secretary of the Transport Workers Union ("I hope to see the Red Flag flying over Buckingham Palace"), warned that if the workers' grievances were not redressed by constitutional process, then organized labour would resort to "other means". Next, "Willie" Gallacher, who proudly described himself as "a Bolshevik from Glasgow", admitted that he was out for revolution; he frankly considered that though it might come through the ballot-box, the best argument would be "a six-inch howitzer gun". J. H. Clynes (who wanted the Coalition to continue), was howled down, and George Bernard Shaw (who had lately boasted that he was paying super-tax), advised him to go back to Lloyd George and tell him from embattled Labour, "Nothing doing!"

"Mr. Lloyd George," added G.B.S., "said the other day that he was as good a Free Trader as he had ever been. We can all accept that!"

The gathering then sang "The Red Flag" and gave hearty cheers for "The Bolsheviks", "Lenin and Trotsky", and (with much laughter) "The Bloody Revolution".

On Saturday, 16 November, Lloyd George unfurled the Coalition flag at the Central Hall, Westminster. The Prime Minister was accompanied by Bonar Law, his Chancellor of the Exchequer, and George Barnes, Labour's last leading representative in the War Cabinet, who had defied his own Party's orders to quit the Government.

The tasks of reconstruction were the Prime Minister's theme: better wages for the ordinary worker, a decent deal for the ex-servicemen, housing, industry, transport—and Peace were the problems that had to be solved. The Coalition Government, which had carried the war to a close, now asked the nation to entrust them with the duty of settling the legacies which war had left behind. The meeting at the Central Hall was as enthusiastic as the one at the Albert Hall, and immeasurably more united.

Swiftly, the Coalition Government programme was shaped, and on 22 November, the joint Lloyd George–Bonar Law Election Manifesto was issued.

It set forth plans for increasing the national production; for developing scientific farming; for land reclamation and afforestation; for a new housing drive; above all, for bringing the ex-servicemen back into useful employment. There were to be no new taxes on food or on raw materials, but a preference for the Empire countries on existing import duties. Key industries were to be safeguarded against unfair competition or dumping (Bernard Shaw's gibe was not so badly aimed, after all). The House of Lords was to be reformed, India was to be set upon the path towards responsible self-government, Ireland was to have Home Rule, the Six Counties of Ulster being excluded.

The Labour Party replied with a counter-blast. It called for No Conscription, the nationalization of the land, a capital levy (not on war fortunes only), Freedom for Ireland, and a "Peace of Reconciliation".

Support came for Lloyd George from another quarter. The Women.

Or, at any rate, the Women's Social and Political Union, whose co-founder, co-organizer and editor of their journal, *Britannia*, was Miss Christabel Pankhurst. On the outbreak of war, this most militant suffragette had declared a "suffrage truce" with the Government. Throughout the war she had worked unremittingly in the national effort. Now the Women had got their votes, and Christabel Pankhurst sought to enter Parliament. She proposed to stand as an Independent, though offering general support to the Coalition Government.

The week after the Armistice, Miss Pankhurst went to see Lloyd George who had just gone off to the country to get some golf after issuing his manifesto. He wrote to his Tory partner in the Government:

"My dear Bonar,   21 November, 1918.

I shall be very much obliged if you can find time to see Miss Christabel Pankhurst. She has a proposition to put before you in reference to the Westbury Division. On the face—as given to me—it seems sound. . . .

Northcliffe is also specially keen and promises to run a special edition of the *Evening News* in that area to promote Miss Pankhurst's candidature.

I am not sure that we have any women candidates, and I think it is highly desirable that we should. The Women's Party, of which Miss Pankhurst is the Leader, has been extraordinarily useful, as you know, to the Government—especially in the industrial districts where there has been trouble during the last two very trying years. They have fought the Bolshevist and Pacifist element with great skill, tenacity and courage, and I know especially in Glasgow and South Wales their intervention produced remarkable results.

I wish you would see Miss Pankhurst.

                                                     Ever sincerely,
                                                     D. Ll. George."

To which Bonar Law replied to Miss Pankhurst that he would, personally, be glad to see her returned to the House of Commons. But meantime, Christabel had found herself a place with what appeared to be brighter prospects at Smethwick. In the General Election, she was beaten there by the Labour candidate by 775 votes.

Altogether, sixteen women went to the polls, and only one was returned to Parliament. She was the Irish-born Countess Markievicz, who won St. Patrick's division, Dublin, with a 4,000 majority. Being a Sinn Feiner, the Countess refused to take the Oath of Allegiance, and never did this glamorous woman set foot in the House of Commons.

As the General Election of 1918 warmed up, its moral tone had steadily gone down. After NO MORE WAR! the most popular slogans of the day were HANG THE KAISER! and MAKE GERMANY PAY!

All more easily said than done. Soon after the Armistice, the Attorney-General, Sir F. E. Smith, had strongly recommended to the War Cabinet that the Kaiser should be brought to trial. For unless the All Highest was arraigned, argued "F.E.", how could you possibly deal with any subordinate who was guilty of crimes against humanity? (It was at this time that the dangerously all-embracing phrase was coined.) The Attorney-General insisted that if ever a stop was to be put to "frightfulness" in war, now was the time. The highest legal authorities in the land agreed with the opinion that it was right and proper to proceed with the trial of the Kaiser.

Make Germany Pay? To a people burdened with a mountainous debt for a war which the Germans had certainly started, what an attractive idea! But *how* could Germany pay? With gold, or goods, or services? Why, all the Central Powers together had not got, and could not get, enough gold! If they paid in goods, well, they would simply put their competitors in Britain out of business, for it would amount to "dumping" on a national scale. As for services, the only one they could render—short of mobilizing mass labour brigades to clear the jungles of Africa, or to irrigate the plains of India—would be to provide free ocean transport, which would spell ruin for the British Mercantile Marine.

Such thoughts were in Lloyd George's mind when at Walton Heath that week-end of 30 November, 1918, he said to Riddell: "Of course, the Germans must pay to the uttermost farthing. But the question is how can they be made to pay beyond a certain point. It could only be done with gold or goods—and goods would prejudice our trade."

The financiers, and even the economists, had more optimistic ideas. Their figures of how much the Germans could be made to pay ranged from £2,000,000,000 to £20,000,000,000! That peace-time Business Man Sir Eric Geddes, war-time First Lord of the Admiralty, told a cheering London Election audience: "We will squeeze the German lemon until the pips squeak!"

To the War Cabinet, Lloyd George put it that we must secure from the defeated enemy the greatest possible indemnity, consistent with the well-being of the British Empire and world peace, and without having to keep an Army of Occupation in Germany to collect the money.

In his early public speeches, during the General Election campaign, the Prime Minister was careful to say that we should make Germany pay "to the limit of her capacity".

He was rash enough, however, in addressing an excited overflow meeting at Bristol a few days later, while using those words again about the payment to the uttermost farthing, to add, "and we shall search their pockets for it!"

Hang The Kaiser! Make Germany Pay! Search Their Pockets! These ghosts of the second "Khaki Election" would be around for many a regretted day. Even the staid Nonconformist, Sunday-preaching Trade Unionist, George Barnes, was ready with a rope for the Kaiser—who had not yet, by the way, been brought to trial, much less found guilty of any crime.

The Election was embittered by the feud which split the Liberal Party into Lloyd Georgian and Asquithian factions. Lloyd George himself would have been willing to invite Asquith to join both the British Peace Delegation and the Government, the latter perhaps in the role of Lord Chancellor, and some talk went forward on this line. But on one side there were old Liberal Cabinet colleagues who argued against reconciliation with the "rebel" of 1916, and there was Asquith's own understandable reluctance to associate himself with Lloyd George's Coalition Government except in the independent role of Leader of what was still the official Liberal Party. On the other side there were Tory voices roused against the inclusion of Asquith. Certainly, too, Northcliffe would have opened up a violent clamour of dissent, for apart from his political dislike of Asquith, Northcliffe was desperately ambitious to go to the forthcoming Peace Conference himself as a delegate. Lloyd George was not prepared to concede him this, any more than he was willing to inform his lordship, in advance, of the composition of his new Government, as he had demanded. But while the General Election was approaching, Lloyd George was not anxious to drive the most powerful Press Lord in Fleet Street into the arms of his enemies. The moment for making things up with Asquith passed.

So, very shortly, did the always precarious prospect of placating Northcliffe. He had already, a few weeks before, made approaches to the Prime Minister to join the War Cabinet (employing, as was his practice, two separate sources of communication, Beaverbrook and Reading). Northcliffe thought he had only to ask, and be gratified. Lloyd George had said No! Now, Northcliffe was talking about a place at the Peace Conference. Bonar Law was strongly against giving him one, and so advised the Prime Minister. But after conversation with Lloyd George, Northcliffe formed the mistaken impression that he was going to be included in the British Delegation. This happened because Lloyd George had suggested to him that he should establish himself in a house at Paris for the forthcoming Conference. So Northcliffe told his staff to make ready. When he found out that he was not to be included on the British Delegation, Northcliffe was furious, and bitterly he turned against Lloyd George. By the time the General Election of 1918 came along, Northcliffe was already working devotedly for the downfall of Lloyd George.

There were some other people who had an interest, at any rate, in doing nothing to heal the wound in the Liberal Party. These were the members of the Tory Party. For twelve years they had been in a minority in the House of Commons, though probably at any time after 1912 a General Election would have returned them to power. Now, there appeared to be a real chance of winning a majority of seats, if only they were allowed to fight. It would vanish if, because the Liberal factions had patched up a truce among themselves, the Tory candidates had to stand down in more than a hundred constituencies at present held by Asquithian Liberal M.P.s.

The Tories were assisted in their not unnatural desire to keep the Liberal family feud alive by the bitter memories of the last time it had flared up in the House of Commons—the famous Maurice Debate. The Coalition leaders now agreed that the voting on that occasion should be made the test of loyalty to the Government in the approaching Election. Anyone who had gone into the wrong lobby on that critical night would not get an official letter of recommendation to the electors signed by Lloyd George and Bonar Law, dubbed by Asquith in the language of war-time rationing as the "coupon"; on the other hand, his Coalition candidate opponent *would* get it.

More than five hundred of these Coalition candidates now advanced to the polls. They were opposed by considerably larger numbers of Labour and "Wee Free" Liberal candidates, as well as Co-operators, Independents, National Democrats, Irish Nationalists, Sinn Feiners, the Discharged and Demobilized Soldiers and Sailors Federation, and some extraordinary freaks. The Election days were enlivened by mass deputations of women munitions workers in Whitehall, 10,000 at a time, by threatened strikes on the railways and in the cotton trade, and by mounting disorder in Ireland.

Northcliffe made a last determined bid to dictate policy to the Prime Minister. To Leeds, where Lloyd George was speaking on 7 December, he sent him a telegram warning him that the public were expecting him to give a definite account of cash reparations to be got from Germany as they were dissatisfied with the phrase "limit of her capacity", which they said could mean anything or nothing. He (Northcliffe) feared serious trouble in the country on this score.

To which he received the following telegraphed reply:

> "Northcliffe *Daily Mail* London
> You are quite wrong about France stop no ally has named figure stop allies in complete agreement as to demand for indemnity stop inter allied commission will investigate on behalf of all on identical principles don't be always making mischief—Lloyd George."

Lloyd George fell foul of two of his own Ministerial colleagues during the General Election. There had been delay in completing the arrangements to register the servicemen's votes, and the Prime Minister was disposed to blame Milner, the War Secretary, that "lank, saturnine figure", dull in speech, flat in voice, halting in delivery, but gifted with a fertility of ideas and a marshalling brain that made him outstanding as a counsellor. Later, it came out that Mr. Hayes Fisher,[1] the President of the Local Government Board, was responsible. Lloyd George drafted an angry letter, demanding his resigna-

---

[1] Later, Lord Downham.

tion, but in Cabinet Bonar Law pressed him to modify its terms. Scrawled in red crayon, this note was tossed back across the table:

"The P.M. doesn't mind if he is drowned in Malmsey wine, but he must be a dead chicken by tonight."

In the event, a colourless little note was composed, and Hayes Fisher exchanged his office for the Chancellorship of the Duchy of Lancaster and a subsequent peerage.

With Milner, the disagreements continued. Lloyd George had developed a disconcerting habit of "dressing-down" Ministers in the presence of others and Milner resented it. Sharply, one day, he protested.

"My dear Prime Minister, 7.12.18
. . . My desire to withdraw from the arena has been quickened by the impatience which you have of late frequently manifested, of my conduct of affairs at the War Office. . . . The obvious remedy is to put someone else in my place, and I am most willing that that course should be adopted.

What I am not willing to accept is a position in which I am exposed to such vehement charges of dilatoriness and neglect as you made yesterday in the presence of a large number of people, many of them not Ministers, in connection with the discharge of miners from the Army.

To submit to that sort of public rebuke without a protest, or to expose myself to a chance of its repetition, is, I feel, not consistent with self-respect. . . ."

The quarrel was patched up, and Milner accepted the Colonial Office in the Government reconstruction after the General Election. But a certain sharpness remained between the two men.

When the votes were counted, three days after Christmas, it was seen that the second Khaki Election had brought an outstanding personal triumph to the leader who had been hailed in the popular Press as "The Man Who Won the War". Almost every Coalition candidate had been elected, and the new Government claimed 526 out of 707 seats.

It was double the majority which Lloyd George had expected. Very significant, however, was the total Opposition vote; it was four-fifths of that of the Government. Asquith and Arthur Henderson, the two most formidable Parliamentarians of the Liberal and Labour Oppositions, were numbered among the casualties. But far more important than any personal misfortunes in the 1918 General Election were four broad and fateful results. They were:

First, the near annihilation of the Asquithian Liberals (33 M.P.s); thus sounded the death-rattle of the Liberal Party.

Second, the rise of the Labour Party (59 M.P.s) to be the official Opposition and the alternative Government.

Third, the end of the Irish Nationalist Party (7 M.P.s).

Fourth, the sweeping victory of Sinn Fein (73 M.P.s) which now took the place in politics (though not in the House of Commons, which its members refused to attend) of the historic party of Redmond and Parnell. The Irish Republic was just around the corner.

The Russian Republic was already here. And of all the mighty things which had happened in the world since the Kaiser first launched the German Armies across the plains of Belgium, the Revolution which brought this Republic into being was by far the most tremendous. It was not like one terrific blast, wrenching human society from all its old moorings, but then leaving the survivors of the storm to clear up the debris and, in time, to build anew. This Revolution rather resembled a vast atomic explosion, fearful enough in its own effects, but in turn setting off a chain of fresh explosions, so that the face of the earth could never settle down again. The explosions are going on still.

When the old order broke down in Tsarist Russia, our great ally was holding on the Eastern Front half the entire forces of the Central Powers. Her losses had been frightful; more Russian soldiers had been slain in battle, or had died of wounds and privation, than all the dead of all the other Allied armies. Transport, supply, discipline, military organization had utterly broken down. So had civil government, and except in its most primitive forms, the economic life of the whole, vast Russian area. When the Bolshevik revolutionaries, led by Lenin and Trotsky, made an enforced peace with the Germans at Brest-Litovsk in February, 1918, the mighty empire of All the Russias was already only a memory. The Baltic States, Poland, Finland, the Ukraine and the Caucasus had hived off from Muscovy. A quarter of the entire population of pre-war Russia, more than half her mineral wealth and three-quarters of her land area were for the moment lost to Russia, and for the time being the Revolution had to accept it.

To whom did these prizes pass? To the triumphant German enemy, dictating a conqueror's peace to our defeated ex-ally? It would have been desperately serious for us, indeed, if this had happened; if the corn of the Ukraine and the oil of the Caspian had fallen into the hands of the Germans. For it would have finally broken wide Britain's blockade of the Central Powers. So, when in succession, the former Tsarist generals Kornilov, Alexeiev and Denikin, raised the standard of counter-revolution against the Bolsheviks— or what it really amounted to, of continued resistance to the Germans—the Allies had naturally supported them. We had already unloaded a million tons of coal and war stores on the quays of Murmansk and Archangel in North Russia, and built up another well-stocked base at Vladivostok on the Far Eastern shore of Siberia. Also, marching through the high Caucasus, four British brigades from the Army of Mespot had occupied the oil-ports of Batum and Baku on the Black Sea and the Caspian. It was vital to deny all this military equipment and that far vaster mineral and oil potential to the enemy.

In this, of course, the only forces which could help us were those in Russia which were in rebellion against the new Bolshevik Government at Moscow. They included the "White" Government of North Russia, several other "White" Governments scattered across Siberia, and a "White" Russian Volunteer Army operating on the Don River in South Russia.

There were also those Czech and Slovak "prisoners-of-war", some of whom had been captured by the Tsarist troops, but most of whom had deserted in masses to the Russian lines from the Imperial Austro-Hungarian Army. When the Russian Revolution broke out they had been formed into a Legion 60,000 strong, and by the Allied Powers, at any rate, had been recognized as a separate Czechoslovak Allied Army. After the Brest-Litovsk Peace had closed down the Eastern Front, they had demanded to be transported to the Western Front, there to go on fighting for the independence of their nation, which they believed the victory of the Allies would bring.

The Bolshevik Government would have been only too glad to see them go. The Germans, for obvious reasons, took a different view. Either by pressure upon the Bolsheviks, or by direct action of their own forces, they succeeded in blocking the evacuation of the Czechoslovak Legion, who by mid-summer, 1918, had entrenched themselves along the Trans-Siberian Railway, from the Ural Mountains to the Pacific Ocean.

By this time, an inter-Allied Expeditionary Force of Japanese, Americans, British, French, and Italians had landed at Vladivostok. The authority over all the various White forces in Siberia was now being gathered into the hands of the former Tsarist Admiral Kolchak. Finally, another Allied Expeditionary Force, under British command, was disembarked at Murmansk and Archangel to protect our stores there. It naturally entered into friendly relations with the local White North Russian Government.

Such was the set-up in the land of the Soviets on the morrow of peace in Europe. What were the Allies to propose now? What did Lloyd George say? We had intervened in Russia simply to harass our German enemy. Now that enemy had surrendered. Was there any reason for our remaining in Russia?

Some statesmen said, Yes!

One of the most positive was Clemenceau, Prime Minister of France. On 27 October, 1918, a week before the Central Powers' resistance on the Balkan Front collapsed, Clemenceau had sent the following orders to General Franchet d'Esperey, Allied C.-in-C. there, then preparing to advance into Rumania:

"The main line of the plan of action which should be adopted is not only to continue there the struggle against the Central Powers, but also to bring about the encirclement of Bolshevism, and to provoke its downfall."

Besides the Allied loans to Russia during the war, the pre-war Tsarist Debt to France amounted to 25,000,000,000 francs (then £1,000,000,000). Also, there were very substantial French investments in Russia's banking, railways, coal-mines, oil and heavy metals; perhaps one-third of that country's entire industrial capital came from French sources. There were many folk in France who not only wanted to make Germany pay for the war debt, but also to make Russia pay up her peace debt. Clemenceau upheld this view and he believed that it could be enforced by economic pressure, if not by direct military action. Marshal Foch favoured the latter; he talked fervently of an "Army of Liberation", composed of Americans, Poles and Russian ex-prisoners-of-war, which was to invade Red Russia from the West.

Then, on the English side of the Channel, fierce for the new crusade was Lord Curzon, who in his roaming youth had visited the lovely lands of the Caucasus—Georgia, Dagestan, Azerbaijan (how lovingly the Foreign Secretary rolled his tongue around Azerbaija-a-an, though it was Georgia, which gave birth to Stalin, that Curzon particularly wished to preserve from the ravages of Bolshevism).

And there was Churchill, who had been promoted to Secretary of State for War in the new Administration. He genuinely loathed the Communist creed, which he described with characteristic vigour and vividness as "the foul baboonery of Bolshevism", and unceasingly he denounced the cruelties which marked the Red Terror in Russia. ("His ducal blood," wrote Lloyd George, afterwards, "revolted against the wholesale elimination of Grand Dukes in Russia.") Churchill held that just a little resolute joint action by the five Allied Great Powers—or even without America, if she did not choose to come in—would suffice to settle Bolshevism. He was convinced that it did not represent more than a tiny fraction of the Russian people, and that it would be swept away at a free General Election held in that land under the Allied auspices.

Indeed, Churchill was prepared even to take a risk with Germany (he did not think it would amount to much of one) in order to deal with Red Russia. As early as 10 January, 1919, before he had been appointed to his new office, Churchill was urging the War Cabinet to consider seriously "whether we should not now decide to bolster up the Central Powers if necessary, in order to stem the tide of Bolshevism".

Lloyd George took the opposite view. He believed that though the vast majority of the Russian people were not Bolsheviks, they preferred the Reds to the Whites, for they were certainly sick of the war and they did not want the old landlords back, either. As for the propertied classes in the Allied countries, though they hated and feared Bolshevism they were not, in general, prepared to pay the cost of another war to crush it, or to invite a clash on this issue with organized labour at home. Nor, frankly, was there the man-power available for the job. To hold up demobilization now would create widespread disorder, and to draft troops from France, who had just finished fighting the four-year war on the Western Front, to Odessa and Archangel might provoke open mutiny in the British Armed Forces. So Lloyd George feared.

As things were, it came fairly close to it.

On 3 January, 1919, several thousand British troops quartered in Rest Camps at Folkestone and Dover refused to re-embark for France, and marched into the centre of these towns to demonstrate against the delay in demobilization. At Osterly Camp, Royal Army Service Corps drivers got into their lorries and drove to London, where they staged a mass protest meeting in Whitehall under the windows of the War Office. In the camps at Kempton Park and Grove Park, "Soldiers' Councils" were set up. At Luton, a military mob set fire to the Town Hall. At Calais, the leave boats returning from England were picketed and angry soldiers, broken loose from all discipline, took over the town. General Byng was ordered to move two divisions towards it. Thanks to the good temper and the good sense of the officers, who pleaded with the mutinous men not to end a fine war comradeship in a quarrel, there was no shooting. But meantime, trouble had spread to the Navy in the mine-sweeper flotilla at Rosyth; it flared into the Royal Air Force, too, on the Kent airfields.

The Prime Minister issued an appeal to the great armies and fleets which had won the war. We must stay at "strength of safety", he said, until a fair settlement had been made with the enemy. At the same time, demobilization of the men who had "done their bit" was proceeding at the rate of more than 10,000 per day, on the fair basis of Age-and-Service.

In this task, Churchill, as War Secretary, although he personally urged Lloyd George to hold the British Army strength at a million men, discharged a vital duty. The British Isles were not a placid place in the spring of 1919, with a general strike in Belfast, and a bloody riot in Glasgow, but it was not the ex-servicemen who made the trouble. The Boys came home quietly. And criminologists noted that as the soldiers and sailors and airmen re-entered civilian life, crimes of violence decreased.

Indeed, there was much to be said both for Churchill's demand for a powerful post-war British Army, and for Lloyd George's own determination to squander no part of our strength on any new adventure in Russia. Already, we were committed to the military occupation of the Rhineland, Palestine, the Turkish Straits and Mesopotamia. Now India and Egypt were in gathering ferment, and soon Ireland would be so again. We had quite enough on our hands to keep order (or to restore it) in all these places. Lloyd George had reminded the War Cabinet, at their meeting on the last day of December, 1918, that even after the Peace of Brest-Litovsk had formally ended all organized fighting on the Eastern Front, the Germans had still been unable to disentangle a million sorely-needed soldiers who were stuck in that Russian morass. It had probably cost Germany the war in the West.

As for Bolshevism itself, it was Lloyd George's view in January, 1919, that if it was left alone it would either solve the social and economic problems of Russia, or else would fail and simply disappear. Unless the proposed intervention was on a really decisive scale, the only result of it would be to identify the Bolsheviks with the defence of the country against foreign invaders—Lloyd George had not forgotten his youthful reading about the French Revolution, the Jacobins, The Committee of Public Safety, "the country in danger" and the Napoleonic Imperialism that rose out of the attempted foreign intervention in La Vendée and elsewhere.

So at the first meeting of the Peace Conference on 16 January, 1919, Age 56 Lloyd George brought up the question of Russia again. He was against both the policy of intervention and the policy of insulation, known as the *cordon sanitaire*. The Allies could not find the troops to depose the Bolsheviks, and the "White" rebels were not strong enough to do it themselves. He had just been looking at a map which showed that General Denikin, with a force of perhaps 40,000 men, occupied "what might be described as a little backyard near the Black Sea".

Thus General Denikin, in South Russia, was unable even to make contact with Admiral Kolchak, in Siberia. Even the Czechoslovaks, according to General Knox, the knowledgeable British Representative on the spot, were tainted with Bolshevism and not to be relied upon. In Lloyd George's opinion, the sensible course was to invite the various Russian Governments to come to Paris and make peace among themselves. With these thoughts, President Wilson concurred.

Not so Prime Minister Clemenceau. The "Tiger" bared his teeth. He was not having any Bolsheviks in Paris. If they were invited, he would resign. In vain, did President Wilson produce a remarkable Secret Report, which he said his agent in Stockholm had sent after a most intimate conversation with a certain M. Litvinov. This report claimed that the Soviet Government of Russia really earnestly sought peace, and were prepared to protect existing foreign enterprise in Russia, to grant new concessions, and even to discuss the Tsarist Debt. To which the Tiger snapped:

"*Who* is Litvinov?"

Who *was* Litvinov? At that time, he held no official position in the Russian Government, though he was powerful in the counsels of the inner circle of the Bolshevik Party. Almost certainly, these Soviet gentlemen were stalling for time, and counting on dividing their enemies.

The same evening, at his apartment in the Rue Nitôt, Lloyd George talked frankly with his colleagues of the British Empire Peace Delegation. At least, he urged, let all the nations of the Empire speak tomorrow with one voice. Balfour assured the family party that President Wilson would certainly send no American Army to Russia. The Prime Minister, who had spent the afternoon talking to General Franchet d'Esperey, C.-in-C. of the French forces which had by this time arrived in South Russia, said that he had been informed by him that the Red Army, having now restored its discipline, numbered nearly a million men. Britain had already more than 15,000 troops tied up in Russia, and could spare no more. Would Canada send some?

Sir Robert Borden answered, No!

Would Australia care to be there?

Billy Hughes: "No!"

That settled it. Or almost so. It was agreed that the British Empire should not go on intervening in Russia, nor subsidize other Allies in doing it. Also, that we should try and get the contending Russian parties together, if not at Paris, then at some other place, perhaps Prinkipo, in the Sea of Marmora.

At the next meeting of the Peace Conference only the Italian representative, Baron Sonnino, wanted to wage war. He was another statesman who thought that a volunteer Army could be raised for the purpose.

Asked by Lloyd George what contribution Italy would make, he replied: "None."

To clinch the matter, the British Prime Minister then engagingly put the same question to Clemenceau.

"None!" snarled the Tiger.

President Wilson proceeded to draft a proclamation inviting

"every organized group that is now exercising, or attempting to exercise, political authority or military control anywhere in Siberia, or within the boundaries of European Russia as they stood before the war just concluded (except in Finland) to send representatives . . . to the Princes Islands,[1] Sea of Marmora, where they will be met by representatives of the Associated Powers, provided, in the meantime, there is a truce of arms among the parties invited . . ."

A prompt reply was requested, and every travel facility, including transport across the Black Sea, was offered to the delegates, who were asked to arrive at the appointed place by 15 February, 1919.

This well-meant effort came to nought. The Whites would not treat with people whom they regarded as traitors, robbers and murderers. The Reds would not admit that these "reactionaries, rebels and foreign hirelings" had any status. The Russian Civil War dragged on until, at last, the Allied Intervention dragged out to its inglorious end.

For the failure of Prinkipo provided the Interventionist partisans in France and Britain with the powerful plea that, having called these anti-Bolshevik (or what they had originally been, anti-German), revolts into being to serve our own war purposes, we could not, with honour, abandon our Allies there now that we were about to dictate peace to our enemy. Thus Lloyd George on his dilemma:

[1] Also known as Prinkipo.

"There were powerful and exceedingly pertinacious influences in the Cabinet working for military intervention in Russia, and as I was not on the spot in London to exercise direct influence and control over the situation, for a while I was out-manœuvred, and Mr. Bonar Law, who presided in my absence, was overridden. Mr. Winston Churchill in particular threw the whole of his dynamic energy and genius into organizing an armed intervention against the Russian Bolshevik power."[1]

Now complications at home called both the Prime Minister and President Wilson back to their own capitals. The post-war Elections had been kinder to Lloyd George than to Woodrow Wilson, whose failure to placate Republican opposition to his policies (and perhaps even more, to his personality) had resulted in the Democrats losing control of Congress at the end of 1918. Now, early in February, 1919, the President found it imperative to make a hurried voyage to the United States to deal with the growing hostility to his Administration.

Labour troubles—and the ominous march of several hundred troops on leave to Whitehall in what was known as "The Horse Guards Revolution"— brought Lloyd George hurrying home from Paris. He left Balfour in charge of the Peace Talks there, but he afterwards charged that

"Mr. Churchill very adroitly seized the opportunity created by the absence of President Wilson and myself to go over to Paris and urge his plans with regard to Russia upon the consideration of the French, the American and the British delegations."[2]

Lloyd George suspected that his Secretary of State for War was proposing (and planning) a new one, this time against Bolshevik Russia. He told Riddell so, adding that this really *would* cause a revolution. The British people would never stand it.

The previous day, the Allied invitation to Prinkipo having just expired, Churchill had telegraphed the Prime Minister twice and proposed (i) sending to the Bolsheviks what amounted to an ultimatum, proposing a new Conference, but also (ii) the setting up of an Inter-Allied Military, Civil and Economic Commission on Russia. The Bolsheviks had only replied before, as he says, "in ambiguous terms" to the Prinkipo invitation. Churchill protested that meantime the Reds had launched vigorous attacks on all their Civil War fronts, and had lately called up fresh age-groups to the colours.

But what did he expect them to do? The ultimatum suggested in the first Churchill telegram was a 10-day one, to say that unless all these offensives were halted and the Red Army everywhere withdrawn five miles from the White positions, then the Prinkipo proposals would be deemed to have lapsed. The Inter-Allied Commission suggested in the second Churchill telegram was

[1] *The Truth about the Peace Treaties.* David Lloyd George.
[2] *Ibid.*

to include not only the Big Five Allied Powers, but also the White Russian Governments and the new Border States, and they were "to examine the possibilities of Allied Military Intervention in Russia".

Churchill has published both of his own telegrams[1] (they appear as one however); he has published the Prime Minister's reply only to the first one. The reader here is offered both Lloyd George's telegrams. They were addressed via Philip Kerr, Lloyd George's trusted Secretary at the Peace Conference. As to Number 1 Churchill message:

"Prime Minister to Mr. Philip Kerr
(London)—16 February, 1919.

See Churchill and tell him I like the telegram which it is proposed shall be sent to Bolsheviks. As to alternative programme I trust he will not commit us to any costly operation which would involve any large contribution either of men or money. The form of his telegram to me looked rather too much like that. I had understood from his conversation with me that all he had in mind was to send expert details who volunteer to go to Russia together with any equipment we can spare. I also understood that our volunteer Army had not to be drawn upon for that purpose and that effort made to secure volunteers would not be on such a scale as to arouse vehement opposition in this country. . . .

All these things ought to be made clear to all the other powers before an agreement is arrived at otherwise they might either depend too much on us or subsequently reproach us with having failed in our promises. The main idea ought to be to enable Russia to save herself if she desires to do so; and if she does not take advantage of the opportunity then it means either that she does not wish to be saved from Bolshevism or that she is beyond saving. There is only one justification for interfering in Russia—that Russia wants it. . . ."

To Number 2 Churchill message, Lloyd George replied:

"Am very alarmed at your second telegram about planning war against the Bolsheviks. The Cabinet have never authorized such a proposal. They have never contemplated anything beyond supplying Armies in anti-Bolshevik areas in Russia with necessary equipment to enable them to hold their own, and that only in the event of every effort at peaceable solution failing. A military inquiry as to the best method of giving material assistance to these Russian armies is all to the good, but do not forget that it is an essential part of the inquiry to ascertain the cost; and I also want you to bear in mind that the War Office reported to the Cabinet that according to their information Intervention was driving the anti-Bolshevik parties in Russia into the ranks of the Bolshevists."

[1] *The World Crisis: The Aftermath.* Winston S. Churchill. (Thornton Butterworth.)

Salmon fishing at Gairloch, 1921

Lloyd George begs Churchill "not to commit this country to what would be a purely mad enterprise, out of hatred of Bolshevik principles". An expensive war against Russia, he says, is the way to strengthen Bolshevism in Russia, and to create it at home. Britain cannot afford the burden, anyway, for here is Austen Chamberlain (newly-appointed Chancellor of the Exchequer) telling him that even at the present crushing rate of taxation, we can hardly make both ends meet on a peace-time basis. To start a war against a continent like Russia "is the direct road to bankruptcy and Bolshevism in these islands". If it were known, says the Prime Minister, that Churchill had "gone over to Paris to prepare a plan of war against the Bolsheviks, it would do more to incense organized Labour than anything I can think of; and what is still worse, it would throw into the arms of the extremists a very large number of thinking people who now abhor their methods".

Lloyd George warns Churchill not to be guided by the French in this matter. Their opinion is biased by the enormous number of small investors who put their money into Russian loans, and now would like to see us "pull the chestnuts out of the fire for them". The Prime Minister hopes that Churchill will stick by his first proposals ("subject to the comments I have passed upon them"). Please show these telegrams from London to the Foreign Secretary.

Churchill retorted next day with another telegram to the Prime Minister in which he reminded him that he had said himself in Cabinet that we were actually making war on the Bolsheviks at the moment. All that the War Secretary sought to do was to "assemble possible means and resources for action in a comprehensive form and to submit this report to the Supreme War Council".

In a letter to Lloyd George a few days later, Churchill made the point that his proposal was that a full military inquiry should be set on foot and a plan based upon it which the Government could either accept or reject. Up to now the Allies had not decided whether they wish "to make war upon the Bolsheviks or to make peace with them".

At no time, did Churchill conceal which his own preference would be.

The activist anti-Bolshevik forces received a sharp stimulus when an attempt was made on Clemenceau's life. The would-be assassin was a half-crazy anarchist, but everybody believed he was a Bolshevik agent. ("Where was Lloyd George?" asked mocking, indomitable Clemenceau, and jeered: "My enemies never could shoot straight!") Lloyd George, and those in the British Cabinet who thought with him—both Bonar Law and Balfour were firmly opposed to further interventionist adventures—had to fight hard to get it agreed that British Empire policy should be fourfold.

(i) No foreign troops should be sent to Russia, unless volunteers went of
    their own accord;

Q

(ii) Foreign troops already in Russia should be withdrawn as soon as possible;

(iii) Material aid should be supplied to the various White Governments to enable them to defend themselves in the areas where the people were non-Bolshevik;

(iv) The new Border States should be placed under the League of Nations, which would both protect them if invaded by Soviet Russia and restrain them from aggression on their own part.

These views Lloyd George set forth at length in a personal letter to Philip Kerr, addressed from Number 10 Downing Street, and dated 19 February, 1919. Expressing his shock at the news of the attempted assassination of Clemenceau and his delight that the Tiger had escaped ("He is a gallant old boy—one of the bravest men I have ever met"), the Prime Minister insists that Russia must save herself. If she is saved by outside intervention, then she is not really "saved" at all. "That kind of parasitic liberty is a sham, and in this case it would be a very costly one for the Powers."

Lloyd George says that he hears rumours of fantastic French schemes to raise armies of Russian prisoners-of-war in Germany supported by Czecho-slovaks "and other odds and ends", even of mobilizing German units that have been left behind in the Baltic States. He wants to know who is going to pay for these new mercenary armies. How much will France contribute? Or, perhaps, America is going to bear the expense? Lloyd George ends firmly: "Pin them down to the cost of any scheme before sanctioning it!"

It was not too soon. Already, events threatened to take charge of policy. On the day after the Armistice, 12 November, 1918, Allied warships had sailed up the Dardanelles and occupied Constantinople. They advanced into the Black Sea, and by Christmas, French troops were being disembarked at Odessa. At this time South Russia, as North, West, and East Russia, was the scene of savage Civil War—with the added complication that besides Reds fighting Whites there was a Red-and-White army of Left-wing Ukrainian Nationalists under an ex-priest and revolutionary adventurer named Petlura, which was fighting both the Russian Bolshevists and Tsarists for their own independence.

It was not very long before—exactly as Lloyd George had foreseen—the French "Army of the East" at Odessa became disaffected and the troops were fraternizing with the enemy, while the French Black Sea Fleet broke into open mutiny and all the Allied Forces in this area had to be withdrawn. When the mutineers were court-martialled, it set off a fresh wave of disorder through the great French naval ports. Many observers thought that France was going Red in 1919.

It simply added to the current political confusion of that excited summer that for the moment the White forces were everywhere in the ascendant in

Russia. From Siberia, Admiral Kolchak was daily advancing westward. Could he establish contact with General Denikin, in the South, and with the growing White armies in the North? At this point, re-enter Britain—and especially, the British Secretary of State for War, Churchill.

In announcing the policy of the British Government towards Russia when he introduced his Army Estimates (about £500,000,000) in March, Churchill had already warned that the British Expeditionary Force in North Russia could not leave "that ice-bound shore" until late summer opened the seas for their evacuation. Meantime, since they had got to stay there, they must be properly sustained. He told the House of Commons, 20 May, 1919:

> "Fighting is still going on in this region, and I speak with great reserve about the future. But this much may be said, that Admiral Kolchak's advance in the northern sector, coupled with the growth and improvement of the Russian local troops at Archangel and Murmansk, offers us the prospect of a far better solution of our own problems than we could ever see before. Whereas a few months ago our only plan was to withdraw our troops and carry with them as refugees 30,000 or 40,000 inhabitants upon whom the Bolsheviks would have wreaked vengeance—people, that is to say, who have been friendly to us and who had worked for us at the time of the German war—there is now good prospect of the whole of North Russia becoming self-supporting within a reasonable time, and of purely Russian Forces maintaining themselves against the Bolsheviks in that theatre."

The confusion of politics in May, 1919, was not confined to the ordinary Man-in-the-Street. It had invaded the Supreme War Council at Versailles, and for this Lloyd George, Prime Minister of Britain, must bear his full share of the blame.

For, three days before Churchill offered the House of Commons his optimistic picture of events on the Archangel Front, the Supreme War Council had sent their own extraordinary Note, 26 May, 1919.

It began by setting forth the "cardinal axiom of the Allies", not to interfere in the private affairs of Russia; their only reason for intervening had been to help those elements who were willing to go on fighting the Germans. Then, after the war, the Allies had tried to bring all parties together, but the Bolsheviks had refused to make a truce. Now, the Allies sought to restore peace in Russia by means of a "freely elected Constituent Assembly", based on a secret and democratic franchise. There was to be no restoration of the former privileges of any class, Poland and Finland were to be recognized as independent, and the League of Nations was to arbitrate on all frontier disputes. So far, so good. But as the experience of the last twelve months has convinced the Allies that there is no hope of dealing with the Bolsheviks, they now express themselves willing to help Admiral Kolchak and his forces "with munitions, supplies and food, to establish themselves as the Government of All Russia".

On 4 June, 1919, Admiral Kolchak accepted this offer of the Supreme War Council. Churchill was naturally delighted, for it thus appeared that British Official policy was moving into line with the course which he had consistently advocated.

Lloyd George was less happy. Weeks before, he had confided to Bonar Law at Paris that sometimes his Secretary of State for War had "Bolshevism on the brain" and now he wanted to raise a German Force to undertake operations in Russia. Lloyd George had himself to thank for the momentary encouragement that Churchill and those who thought with him now received, for if he had held with undeviating firmness to his expressed view that the Russians must settle their own post-war problems Churchill must either have conformed, or resigned.

Momentary, indeed, was the lapse, and Bonar Law gloomily agreed that Lloyd George had been right in his general appreciation of the dangers of meddling in Russia. For by July, Admiral Kolchak was in full retreat, and early in this same month White Russian troops in North Russia revolted, and murdered their officers. Mr. Churchill had to face a restive House of Commons when, on 29 July, 1919, he stood up to ask for a Supplementary Vote of £107,000,000.

There was the Parliamentary Asquithian leader, Sir Donald Maclean, inquiring how much our gifts to the anti-Bolshevik cause were costing the taxpayer? There was the Socialist Mr. J. H. Clynes, warning that the rising Labour resentment against any more war-like escapades had just resulted in the Triple Alliance (of Miners, Railwaymen and Transport Workers), "a very formidable organization", passing a resolution which called for a General Strike to bring them to an end. There was the Tory, Lord Robert Cecil, who had only just resigned from being Minister of Blockade, begging him to speak "with the utmost candour and frankness".

Churchill was conciliatory, and adroit—and he had need to be both on this occasion, for public opinion was now thoroughly aroused. He explained that about £20,000,000 of war stores had been sent to Russia, but most of it was material left over from the World War, and "unmarketable" anyway. If it had been kept, it would have had to be housed and caretakers hired to watch over it. As for Britain getting embroiled in the Russian Civil War, it was precisely because the Red Army was so busy fighting the Whites that they had found no time to fall upon these hapless Border States, which were the wards of the League of Nations, and which must have succumbed to such an attack unless sustained by Allied reinforcements! Thus, beamed Churchill, but for those White armies we might not have been able to proceed so satisfactorily with our own demobilization! He then spoke of the latest victorious offensive of General Denikin, on the Russian Southern Front. He had "taken an enormous area of country, where he has been welcomed by great masses of people".

The War Secretary's optimism was not shared by the C.I.G.S. (though his abhorrence of the Bolsheviks certainly was). As early as February of this year, 1919, General Wilson had lost faith in both Kolchak and Denikin, and he had advised the Cabinet that we should clear out of Russia everywhere, lock, stock and gun-barrel. Strange, remembering Lloyd George's own instincts, that he had not preferred this advice to what he had apparently accepted at the time of the Supreme War Council Note to Kolchak in May. Indeed, now on this very day of Churchill's Parliamentary speech (29 July, 1919), the Cabinet, while agreeing to limit further aid to Kolchak to "small missions" resolved to go on sending supplies to Denikin. The explanation of this odd, uncharacteristic, half-hearted policy must be sought in the Prime Minister's immense other absorptions at Versailles.

One project about Russia, at any rate, was firm. The British Expeditionary Force to Archangel was coming home. Most of the British public thought that it was high time, too. Dispatched to this place on the Arctic rim during the late summer of 1918, these troops had known no armistice in November. For many more months, they had borne themselves well in that desolate, icy land through the long winter of almost endless night. Now, on 10 August, 1919, General Ironside launched a sharp offensive astride the River Dwina, and drove the Red Army forces opposite him back in rout. Under cover of this well-executed diversion, the last British Expeditionary Force of World War I began to embark for home.

But it was far from "Farewell, Russia!" for Lloyd George. On the Siberian Front, Kolchak was still retreating. But on the Southern Front, Denikin was still advancing. Also, a new White Knight had appeared upon another Baltic Front. This was the ex-Tsarist General Yudenitch, leading a mixed force of White Russians and Esthonians against the city of Petrograd. Perhaps the Crusade to rescue Holy Russia was going to succeed after all?

Churchill believed so.

Not any longer did Lloyd George. From Deauville, where he had gone with Bonar Law for a brief holiday after the six-months' Peace Conference, the Prime Minister replied to his War Secretary, who had sent him an enthusiastic memorandum on General Yudenitch, asking him what he was doing to cut down the cost and numbers of the British Army.

Manior de Clairfontaine,
30 August, 1919.

"My dear Winston,

    I have dictated a Memorandum in reply to yours about Yudenitch. I will say no more about that. . . .

    I am rather anxious about the Bolshevik movement on Denikin's right. It has penetrated dangerously far and if it continues might menace his communications with the Don.

    . . . But what about other economies . . . ? I beg you to look into these matters immediately. I had hoped to have heard something from you on your return as to your reflections on our conversation, but I get nothing but Russia! You will I am sure forgive me for saying that I think Russia has cost us more than the hundred millions odd we have spent on it; for an impression is left on my mind that the best thoughts of the War Office have been given to these military ventures in Russia, and that the important administrative questions upon which so many scores if not hundreds of millions depend have not received the same intense study.

When are you coming over? I shall be here up till the 10th Sept.

> Every sincerely,
> D. Lloyd George."

With this letter, went the Prime Minister's own Memorandum (copies to Balfour and Curzon).

"Notes on Secretary of State's Memorandum on the N.W. Russian position. 24.8.19.

30 August, 1919.

I earnestly trust the Cabinet will not consent to committing British resources to any fresh military enterprises in Russia. They have decided to withdraw from Siberia, from Archangel, from the Baltic, and after furnishing General Denikin with one more packet, to let the Russians fight out their own quarrels at their own expense. I hope nothing will induce the Ministry to deviate from this decision.

As to the 'great opportunities' for capturing Petrograd which we are told were 'dangling at our finger-tips', and which we never grasped, we have heard this so often of other 'great opportunities' in Russia which have never materialized in spite of lavish expenditure on their prosecution. We have already this year spent over 100 millions in Russia. We have sent some excellent troops there. Early in the year there were 'great opportunities' of liberating Moscow, and we were assured it was within our grasp. We sent every assistance in our power to Admiral Kolchak to exploit these opportunities, not merely by helping him to equip his forces but by sanctioning a military expedition which was to penetrate far into Russia in order to join hands with him. The Liberating Army—or at least what is left of it—is now running as hard as it can back to Omsk, and is mediating a further retreat to Irkutsk. The failure was certainly not due to any default on our part. It is due to the facts which are none the less stubborn because some of our advisers have habitually refused to take cognizance of them.

General Yudenitch never had a chance of taking Petrograd. The Esthonians, so far from co-operating with him, distrusted him as much as the Bolsheviks, and the result of his operations up till now has been to drive the Esthonian Republic to make a separate treaty with the Bolsheviks. . . ."

The Memorandum went on that if the Esthonians and Latvians had really been eager to join in a War of Liberation, by now there would be an Army of hundreds of thousands sweeping over North-West Russia—not twenty or thirty thousand, as in fact there were. If Russia herself was anxious to overthrow Bolshevik rule, the help we had given her would have provided a full opportunity.

General Denikin went marching on.

By September, he had advanced more than 400 miles. Before he should arrive at Moscow and re-establish there the old Imperialist Russia, Churchill hastened to plead with the Prime Minister (20 September, 1919) that Britain should recognize at once the independence of the Baltic Border States which had broken away from Russia. For in a little while, it would be too late to secure decent terms for those small, free states which had given aid against Bolshevism. Nothing now, Churchill insisted, could preserve either the Bolshevik system, or the Bolshevik régime. He begged the Prime Minister not to brush aside the convictions of one who wished to remain his faithful lieutenant, and looked forward to a fruitful and active co-operation.

Lloyd George replied at length, and frankly.

> 10 Downing Street,
> 22nd September, 1919.

"My dear Winston,

Your letter distressed me. You know that I have been doing my best for the last few weeks to comply with the legitimate demand which comes from all classes of the country to cut down the enormous expenditure which is devouring the resources of the country at a prodigious rate. I have repeatedly begged you to apply your mind to the problem. I made this appeal to all departments, but I urged it specially upon you for three reasons: the first is that the highest expenditure is still military; the second that the largest immediate reduction which could be effected without damage to the public welfare are foreseeable in the activities controlled by your Department. The third is that I have found your mind so obsessed by Russia that I felt I had good ground for the apprehension that your great abilities, energy and courage were not devoted to the reduction of expenditure.

I regret that all my appeals have been in vain. At each interview you promised me to give your mind to this very important problem. Nevertheless the first communication I have always received from you after these interviews related to Russia. I invited you to Paris to help me to reduce our commitments in the East. You there produce a lengthy and carefully prepared memorandum on Russia. I entreated you on Friday to let Russia be for at least 48 hours and to devote your week-end to preparing for the Finance Committee this afternoon. You promised faithfully to do so. Your reply is to send me a four-page letter on Russia, and a closely-printed memorandum of several pages—all on Russia. I am frankly in despair. Yesterday and today I have gone carefully through such details as have been supplied about the military expenditure, and I am more convinced than ever that Russia has cost us not merely the sum spent directly upon that unfortunate country, but indirectly scores of millions in the failure to attend to the costly details of expenditure in other spheres.

You confidently predict in your memorandum that Denikin is on the eve of some great and striking success. I looked up some of your memoranda and your statements made earlier in the year about Kolchak and I find that you use exactly the same language in reference to Kolchak's 'successes'.

The Cabinet have given you every support in the policy which they have laid down, and which you have accepted. I am not sure that they have not once or twice strained that policy in the direction of your wishes. . . .

You proposed that the Czechoslovaks should be encouraged to break through the Bolshevik armies and proceed to Archangel. Everything was done to support your proposal. Ships were promised for Archangel if they succeeded. Denikin has been supplied with all the munitions and equipment that he needed. Still you vaguely suggest that something more could have been done and ought to have been done.

I abide by the agreed policy. We have kept faith with all these men. But not a member of the Cabinet is prepared to go further. The various Russian enterprises have cost us this year between 100 and 150 millions, when Army, Navy and Shipping are taken into account. Neither this Government nor any other Government that this country is likely to see will do more. We cannot afford it. The French have talked a good deal about Anti-Bolshevism, but they have left it to us to carry out the Allied policy. Clemenceau told me distinctly that he was not prepared to do any more. Foch is distinctly and definitely opposed to these ventures at the Allied expense. Their view is that our first duty is to clear up the German situation. I agree with them.

I wonder whether it is any use my making one last effort to induce you to throw off this obsession which, if you will forgive me for saying so, is upsetting your balance. I again ask you to let Russia be, at any rate for a few days, and to concentrate your mind on the quite unjustifiable expenditure in France, at home, and in the East, incurred by both the War Office and the Air Department. Some of the items could not possibly have been tolerated by you if you had given one-fifth of the thought to these matters which you devoted to Russia."

A word about the Baltic States, adds Lloyd George. You want us to recognize their independence in return for their attacking the Bolsheviks? They would ask us to (i) *guarantee* it, (ii) supply them with equipment and cash to fight with. And in the end, whoever won in Russia, the Government there would promptly recover the old Russian Baltic ports. Are you, Mr. Churchill, prepared to have a war with perhaps an anti-Bolshevik Government of Russia to prevent that? If not, it would be a disgraceful piece of deception on our part to give any guarantee to these new Baltic States that you are proposing to use to reconquer Russia.

Lloyd George ended that he was well aware that Churchill was willing to spend hundreds of millions of pounds on these projects

"for that is what you really desire. But as you know that you won't find another responsible person in the whole land who will take your view, why waste your energy and your usefulness on this vain fretting which completely paralyses you for other work?

I have worked with you now for longer than I have probably co-operated with any other man in public life and I think I have given you tangible proof that I wish you well. It is for that reason that I write frankly to you.

Ever sincerely,

D. Lloyd George."

The end, in Russia, was tragedy. When the rearguard of the British Expeditionary Force retired, they took with them about 7,000 refugees. The White Government resolved to fight on, hopelessly, but where was hope of any kind of mercy in surrendering? At the end of the year, the Red Army entered Archangel, and a bloodier shooting began.

General Yudenitch, and the Petrograd White Front had already disappeared. Admiral Kolchak, and the Siberian Front died this December, when a Red *coup d'état* at Irkutsk overthrew the remnants of his authority; the Admiral himself was arrested and murdered in his cell. General Denikin, and the Southern Front lived hardly longer. The White tide turned at Tsaritzyn, a fortress on the Volga, where a resolute Georgian, known to history as Stalin, commanded the Red resistance. Now Tsaritzyn itself is known to history, not unjustly as Stalingrad. On 3 January, 1920, as ice bridged the great river, his assault troops crossed and fell upon Denikin's flank, rolling up the whole White Army.

The fighting was finished on the steppe, along the Arctic rim, and in Siberia. The Russian Civil War descended into the colder horror of mass-executions.

CHAPTER XXVII

PEACE AT A PRICE

LLOYD GEORGE had not favoured Paris as the place to make peace; it was too full of memories.

Paris was the capital of a country which mourned a million-and-a-quarter dead; of all France's sons in arms under thirty years of age, only about half had come home from the battlefield. The city itself had been bombed and bombarded. Not fifty years had passed since the Prussian Guard had stamped in arrogant triumph down the Champs-Élysées after another war, and had sent Montmartre up in flames under the eyes of its Mayor. His name was Clemenceau.

There was the formidable Press to be considered, too. These journals were not likely to develop an unusual restraint in their handling of Peace Conference news, or their comment on it. So Lloyd George would have much preferred to hold council in Geneva; the City of John Calvin seemed to him to offer a more promising site for constructing the Temple of Peace than the City of Georges Clemenceau. But Lloyd George was overborne, amongst others by President Wilson, who would live to regret this.

It is easy to exaggerate the effect which the moods of Paris, 1919, exercised upon the form of the Peace Treaty. It is true that by this time almost everybody was weary of war, and genuinely wanted peace. But almost everybody wanted his own particular peace. What was the general temper of the Allied nations as the Day of Settlement drew near?

Were they drunk with victory—and vengeance? Lloyd George has reminded us that all classes within these nations had taken part in this war, unlike the struggles of the mercenary armies of other days. Every section of the people had borne its share of those long absences from home, of casualties, taxation, restriction, frustration, high prices and hard rations. Indeed, the war could not have gone on unless all ranks *had* backed it. (When they ceased to do so in Russia, it had been brought to an untidy end.) All the same, Lloyd George's own well-founded opinion was that the vast majority of all the belligerent nations would have welcomed a reasonable peace long before the war was half over.

Two factors had kept the fighting going, at any rate, on the Allied side. The first, negative one, was that not even the leaders could see how to end it (short of surrendering) until almost the moment that victory hove in sight. We have already set out what Haig wrote and Smuts said and that special committees of the Imperial War Cabinet reported on the prospects of the war in the first half of the year 1918.

The second, positive reason for going on with the war had been the fear that if the enemy was not thoroughly knocked out, then he would resume his aggression the moment he had recovered his strength. None of the Allies wanted to continue the appalling sacrifices of war merely to punish the culprit.

"We shall never sheathe the sword, which we have not lightly drawn, until Belgium recovers in full measure all and more than all that she has sacrificed," Asquith had cried in his famous Guildhall speech in 1914, adding: "until France is adequately secured against the menace of aggression, until the rights of the small nationalities of Europe are placed upon an unassailable foundation, and until the military domination of Prussia is wholly and finally destroyed."

As the war went on, it was the second part of this pledge which appealed most strongly to the real feeling in the hearts of the people, British as well as their allies. Justice, yes! Reparation for the damage he had done, of course! But, above all, Security for tomorrow! Freedom from Fear! That was it! *No More War!*

Throughout the four-years' struggle this central thought had been shaping. It underlay the entire agglomeration of ideas and demands which showered upon the still-astonished victors when, suddenly, in the autumn of 1918, Peace hammered on the door of the Supreme War Council.

These other items included the claims of nationalism (most urgently in relation to the sundered empires of Austro-Hungary, Turkey, and Russia); the needs of strategy, for defence against any resurgent ex-enemies; the requirements of economics, how to make the new States and the new settlement of Europe *viable*, as the French said; yes, and idealistically, the noble concept of a higher universal authority, a League of all Nations, a Supreme Court of the World, the Parliament of Man—all these things were mingled in that public dread of a return to the anxieties and alarms of what was called power politics, and a passionate hope that some new, and better, society might be born out of the travail of the World War.

Such were the general ideas that buzzed in the heads of the peacemakers of 1919, and collided with the particular purposes of the separate nations.

Thus, on the immediate, practical plane the French wanted two things. First, security against any more attacks by the Germans; second, reparation for the last one.

Two great wars France had fought against this terrible modern Germany. After the first one, Germany had torn from her body the provinces of Alsace and Lorraine, with their rich mineral resources, as well as exacting an indemnity. During the second war, besides the inevitable ruin of her cities, factories and farms in the combat area (a belt of about 40,000 square miles), France had been despoiled by organized loot and deliberate sabotage of industries, power-plant and mines to the extent of about one-quarter of her entire productive capacity. Besides her fearful military casualties, the civilian population of enemy-occupied France had been subjected to four years of Boche brutality, insult and extortion. There was a dagger's point in Clemenceau's retort to President Wilson's inquiry at the Peace Conference: "Pray, M. Clemenceau, have you ever been to Germany?" "No Sir! But twice in my lifetime the Germans have been to France."

It was with the purpose of preventing a third call (which duly came) that the French sought to halt the unwelcome guest somewhere short of their doorstep. They resolved to make the Rhine their rampart. This could be done, either by permanently occupying the Rhine bridgeheads, or by detaching the West Rhineland from the Reich. Powerfully, did the soldiers and statesmen of France argue that this provision alone could guarantee the safety of their country. For if the German invaders should again suddenly flood across the Lowlands and seize the Channel ports, no Allied overseas armies could be disembarked to reinforce the French in the defence of Paris. And France would surely need reinforcement in that hour; her population in 1919 numbered 40,000,000, and it was static; the population of Germany was 65,000,000, and it was growing. As Churchill noted in his brilliant *History of the First World War*, written ten years before the Second World War, "it should be sufficient to state that after 1940 Germany will have about twice as many men of military age as France."

With a detail striking in its prophetic accuracy, Marshal Foch, the victorious Allied Generalissimo warned, 31 March, 1919, what would happen if the Allies did *not* remain on the Rhine:

"... the battle which we will have to face in the plains of Belgium will be one in which we shall suffer from a considerable numerical inferiority, and where we shall have no natural obstacle to help us. Once more, Belgium and Northern France will be made a field of battle, a field of defeat; the enemy will soon be on the coast of Ostend and Calais, and once again those same countries will fall a prey to havoc and devastation. . . . There is no English and American help which can be strong enough, and which can arrive in sufficient time to prevent a disaster in the plains of the North, to preserve France from a complete defeat, or, if she wants to save her armies from this, to free her from the necessity of withdrawing them behind the Somme, or the Loire, in order to await there the help of the Allies. . . ."

It was a blue print of the Battle of France, 1940.

But in 1919, the demands of the French for the effective possession of Rhineland territory brought the Peace Conference near to deadlock.

As for the second requirement of the French, which was reparation from the Germans for the damage they had wrought, the French claimed that for a start the rich coal basin of the Saar Valley should be detached from Germany to make good the losses of the ruined mines of Northern France. Within the next four years the French insistence on their security and their reparations would bring the *Entente* itself near to break-up.

Not that the British themselves neglected to take certain precautions.

They had demanded, and obtained, the surrender of the German High Seas Fleet, together with their still more formidable U-boat force. When this captive armada, in June, 1919, scuttled themselves in Scapa Flow to salve their own pride, they also solved a British problem. *We* did not want their warships, only that *they* should not have them. Nor, indeed, did we want their captured colonies (at least, Britain and Canada did not want them, though South Africa, Australia and New Zealand meant to claim some). But it was put forward, and plausibly enough, that this was to prevent those particular ex-enemy territories from being again used as a base for attack on British Dominions. It required no vehement persuasion to induce both Lloyd George and Borden to accept this argument at the Imperial War Cabinet, and as the Peace Conference unfolded at Versailles, Britain and all the Dominions would speak upon the question with one voice.

President Wilson took a loftier view. America's spokesman asked for neither territory nor indemnity for his country's exertions in the war. All he wanted was to make it America's Peace. The President was going to confer upon the world, if not the new Tables of Stone, at any rate the original Fourteen Points. These, he had first enumerated in his Address to Congress a year before, 8 January, 1918.

They included: (1) open diplomacy; (2) freedom of the seas; (3) equality of trading; (4) reduced armaments; (5) liberal rights for colonial peoples; (6) self-determination for Russia; (7) evacuation and restoration of Belgium; (8) evacuation and restoration of France, and return of Alsace-Lorraine; (9) Italian frontier adjustment, to include *Italia irredenta*; (10) autonomy for the various peoples of the Austro-Hungarian Empire; (11) evacuation and restoration of Serbia, Rumania, and Montenegro; (12) autonomy for the various peoples of the Ottoman Empire, and freedom of the Dardanelles; (13) independence of Poland; and (14) "a general Association of Nations".

In view of some illusions which have gathered around Lloyd George's part in framing the Versailles Peace Treaty, it may be noted that more than twelve months before President Wilson produced his Fourteen Points, the three Prime Ministers of Britain, France and Italy, meeting in London on Christmas Day, 1916, had put forth their own ideas of what would constitute a just peace. They were only seven in number, but in form they covered all the specific problems set out above and included the general proviso that

"behind international law and behind all the Treaty arrangements for preventing or limiting hostilities, some form of international sanction should be devised which would give pause to the hardiest aggressor".

When, in March, 1917, Lloyd George had invited the Prime Ministers of the

British Dominions to the first Imperial War Cabinet, he found that they held substantially the same views as those of the Allied Premiers. For the time being, it is true, they had devoted no great attention to the idea of a league of nations. But already, in January, 1917, before their arrival in London, Lloyd George had set up a body of experts, supervised by Lord Robert Cecil (then Under Secretary for Foreign Affairs), and a committee presided over by Lord Phillimore, a former and an outstanding Judge of the High Court, to work out a practicable method of operating such a league to ensure world peace. Later, Lloyd George set Smuts to co-ordinate these labours, and in the course of that summer he produced quite an elaborate scheme, which amongst other things, proposed to (i) abolish conscription (except for Powers with overseas commitments!), (ii) set up a Mandatory system to administer back-ward colonial areas, (iii) nationalize all armament industries, and (iv) launch a League of Nations in permanent function. Wrote Smuts:

> "The old Europe is being liquidated, and the League of Nations must be the heir to this great estate."

Nor were the French idle in this exercise of world constitution-mongering. (A "Council of Europe" had been mooted on the Continent since the sixteenth century.) On 5 June, 1917, by overwhelming vote, the French Chamber of Deputies had adopted a resolution in favour of securing guarantees of peace and independence for all nations "by association in a League of Nations, already in preparation".

Then a French Committee, headed by an ex-Premier, M. Leon Bourgeois, also drafted a League charter, laying a code of sanctions, diplomatic, legal, economic and military against any state which should go to war without first submitting its case to arbitration. Not unjustly, was it subsequently claimed by Lloyd George that, for good or ill, the idea of the League of Nations received the backing of all the Allied Governments in Europe, and of the Governments of the British Dominions, too, before President Wilson had uttered a word in public about that League.

It is also on record that these same statesmen were the first openly to challenge the sacrosanctity of the Wilsonian Fourteen Points. (It was Clemenceau who jeered, "The good God himself could think only of Ten Commandments; Woodrow Wilson has got Fourteen!")

Even before the end of the war Lloyd George had vigorously challenged No. 2 of the Fourteen Points (freedom of the seas). Had this been in operation, he said at the Supreme War Council on 29 October, 1918, the British Navy could never have imposed its blockade on the enemy, and both food and vital military material would have poured into Germany via neutral Holland and Scandinavia. When the American representative (it was Colonel House, President Wilson's confidant) half-threatened a separate peace between America and Germany, Lloyd George had retorted that we should go on fighting

(Clemenceau: "Yes"). Britain could *never* agree to give up this power, the one power which had enabled the American troops to be brought to Europe!

At a second stormy meeting, when House insisted that the President could not recede from the "essential American terms", Points 1, 2, and 3, Lloyd George declared that if he were to accept, then it would only mean that in a week's time a new Prime Minister would be there—and he would have to say No!

On report of this, the President bowed. Point No. 2 (freedom of the seas) was not mentioned again. Colonel House also reckoned it wise to offer his own "interpretations" of his master's Points 1 and 3. Point No. 1 (open diplomacy) did not preclude confidential discussions, and Point No. 3 (equality of trading) did not prohibit protection of home industries; it meant the Open Door for raw materials.

With this much of the inter-Allied battleground cleared, the victors advanced upon Paris to prepare for the Peace. On 11 January, 1919, exactly two months after the bugles sang Cease Fire on the Western Front, Lloyd George and the British Empire Delegation, including the Prime Ministers of the five Dominions, arrived in Paris to prepare for the Peace Conference. Critics have charged that there was undue delay, both in its inception and its course, for the Treaty of Versailles, which settled the First World War, was not signed until 28 June, 1919. The Peace Conference over the Second World War, which ended on 14 August, 1945, has not met yet. (August, 1954.)

Even so, between Armistice Day and the official opening of the Peace Conference at Paris, which took place a week after the British delegation had installed themselves at the Hotel Majestic, a number of significant events had occurred.

In Britain Lloyd George had won a sensational Parliamentary General Election, and in America, Woodrow Wilson had lost a decisive Congressional Election. Since the Republican Party Opposition already commanded a majority in the Senate, the Democratic Party President was literally a politician without power. He was still determined to be the plenipotentiary of his country at the Peace Conference, and to come there at the head of a narrowly partisan delegation. Thereby, Wilson probably threw away the final adherence of the United States to the Versailles Peace Treaty.

Lloyd George, who admired, as well as suffered, him has drawn this picture of a President, who he thought stood in the towering line of Abraham Lincoln ("he was genuinely humane, but completely lacked the human touch of Lincoln"):

"All men and women have dual natures. But Wilson was the most clear-cut specimen of duality that I have ever met. The two human beings of which he was constituted never merged or mixed. They were separate and distinct contrasts, but nevertheless on quite good terms with each other. It is not that he had feet of clay. He stood quite firmly on his feet, unless he was pushed over entirely. But there were lumps of pure unmixed clay here and there amidst the gold in every part of his character. And both were genuine. . . . Spiritually, he dwelt beyond the snow line, high above his fellows, in an atmosphere pure, glistening and bracing—but cold. Suddenly, he was precipitated into the swamps of petty personal or party malignity down below . . . the most extraordinary compound I have ever encountered of the noble visionary and the implacable, unscrupulous partisan."

President Wilson had come to Europe at the end of 1918, much in the same spirit as Peter the Hermit set forth on his mission to Christendom in 1095; that is, not so much to preach a crusade as to create a Crusader army to fight it. The President was over here less to make a peace than to establish a League of Nations to preserve it. He was even prepared, as we have seen, to barter some of those sacred Fourteen Points, in practice, if he could get them written into the Peace Treaty in the form of the Covenant of the League. It will be remembered that Moses, also, had to make some concessions to the prejudices of his followers. Moses had happier fortune than Woodrow Wilson. If he did not live himself to see the Promised Land, at least he was spared the sight of his own people turning their backs on it and marching away.

The British, in 1919, were much more taken up with the idea of the League of Nations than even the Americans were. They had endured a lot more of war, and this institution seemed to promise peace. Among the British Empire Delegation to the Peace Conference, according to Lloyd George, the most fervent believers in the League included not only himself, Bonar Law, Milner, and Lord Robert Cecil, but also the Dominions' Borden, Botha, Smuts and Sir Joseph Cook. He found one or two who did not disguise their opinion that it would all come to nothing. Amongst them was Billy Hughes, whose view was, as he said, that: "The League of Nations should be the gilded ball in the dome of the cathedral, not the foundation stone."

The British Empire, in fact, had been for some time past by way of creating its own League of Nations. Remember, as far back as 1897, before the Boer War, the Canadian Prime Minister, Sir Wilfrid Laurier, had told the folk in the Old Country: "If you want our aid, call us to your councils."

No one then had called the sons of the Empire to the councils of peace. They had, however, invited themselves to the fields of war, on the *veldt* of South Africa. Then it had ended, and the boys had gone home. During the next dozen or so years, from 1902 to 1914, there had been an increasing amount of Empire talk, and very little real "Empire do".

Once more, the drums had rolled—and the most part of a million men had crossed the seas to fight under the old flag, every one a volunteer. Ypres! Anzac! Messines! Gaza! Names of battlefields that would clang down history, until History was done. When Britain had wanted aid in war, she had no need to call her sons; they came. The soldiers of the Dominions, and their statesmen, too.

Sir Robert Borden, Prime Minister of Canada, had arrived in London during the first few months of the war, and on 14 July, 1915, had attended a Cabinet Meeting at the invitation of Asquith, who spoke of his presence as creating a precedent. Sir Robert recalled that "he greatly enjoined me as to the tradition which forbids one to make any note of the Cabinet proceedings".

Billy Hughes, Prime Minister of Australia, had been the next Dominions' leader to appear. Asked by Asquith to attend an important inter-Allied Economic Conference in Paris, he had agreed—provided that he was not expected always to vote with the British delegation. "If you think I'm going to sit there like a stuffed mummy while there's a war to be won, then I'm afraid you've picked the wrong man."

At no time in his life did Billy Hughes sit through any discussion like a stuffed mummy.

Borden had a less aggressive manner than Billy Hughes, but he had an equally determined character. This quiet, purposeful man was resolved to establish a new concept of the Dominions' status in the British Empire and when, in 1917, Lloyd George summoned the first Imperial War Cabinet, he had discussed it with his fellow Prime Ministers of the Empire. Together, they had drafted a motion, which Lloyd George and his own Cabinet had at once accepted. On 16 April, 1917, the Imperial War Conference formally resolved that though the question was too important and intricate to deal with during the war a special Imperial Conference should be summoned as soon as possible afterwards to discuss and settle matters. Meanwhile, there should be placed on record "the full recognition of the Dominions as autonomous nations of an Imperial Commonwealth, and of India as an important part of the same".

The right of the Dominions and of India to an adequate voice in foreign policy was affirmed, and the purpose declared of holding continuous consultation in all questions of Imperial concern—and of continuous action, too.

It must be listed as one of the casualties of the Peace that, after the First World War, this Imperial Conference never took place. It has not yet taken place after the Second World War.

Military crisis in the spring of 1918 closed the Dominion Prime Ministers even more closely together into one fist. None of them sat like stuffed mummies. Hughes says that they drove home their criticisms of the High Command "by most striking examples of its inefficiency". Lloyd George might well have found from these Empire statesmen the reinforcement he needed in his personal conflict with the Generals if the war had not almost suddenly come to an end.

The role and status of the British Dominions at the very moment of the birth of Peace had not been overlooked. As early as 20 October, 1918, Borden had written to Lloyd George from Quebec:

"... The Press and people of this country take it for granted that Canada will be represented at the Peace Conference. I appreciate possible difficulties over the representation of the Dominions, but I hope you will keep in mind that certainly a very unfortunate impression would be created and possibly a dangerous feeling might be aroused if these difficulties are not overcome by some solution which will meet the national spirit of the Canadian people."[1]

In London, the Imperial War Cabinet discussed, and decided it. Milner was most strongly backing the Dominions' claim for equal representation, and he was happy to advance the marshalled arguments of a resolute opponent of other days, General Louis Botha, now Prime Minister of South Africa, a man who commanded attention without seeking it, whose eyes sometimes lit fire but who had never need to raise the level of his husky voice. If there had existed any doubt about this recognition of the Dominions' nationhood, Billy Hughes was quite ready to make an issue of it at the 1918 General Election. No such doubt did exist. Borden, who had arrived back in London during Armistice Week, has testified that from the British Prime Minister and his colleagues he received "full sympathy and unfailing support, from first to last". It was on Borden's suggestion that they created a "panel" for the forthcoming Peace Conference, from which, when matters affecting the British Empire arose, Dominion and Indian members were to be drawn to serve on the British Delegation of five. Otherwise, the Dominions and India were to have an equal representation of two apiece with the smaller nations.

The first item on the policy of the United British Empire was the disposal of the captured German colonies.

Lloyd George himself, as we have seen, was not anxious to add any more undeveloped territory to the British flag. But—were those lands in East and South-West Africa now to be handed back to the enemy to serve him as U-boat bases and the recruiting-ground of huge Black armies the next time he made war? Lloyd George vividly recalled those German maps of the new "Mittel-Afrika" which they planned to make, stretching across the heart of the Dark Continent, an Empire of 50,000,000 Negroes and 50,000 picked German settlers, covering an area twice the size of India. It would act as a massive road block athwart our All-Red route from the Cape to Cairo; it would plant our rivals in sea-power on both the South Atlantic and the Indian Oceans; it would make Germany overnight a mighty Mohammedan Power.

If Lloyd George had any hesitation about the future of the former German South-West Africa, at any rate, the South African delegates, Botha and Smuts, had none. This colony had been made the base of the abortive rebel Boer uprising of 1914, and these loyal ex-enemies of old days had conquered it almost entirely with South African troops. Now Smuts had invented the

[1] *Robert Laird Borden: His Memoirs.*

attractive idea of "Mandates", but both Botha and himself had a firm view as to who was going to be the mandatory Power in the former German South-West Africa. Hughes, of Australia, had also left no room for doubt about his opinions on the future of the ex-German colonies in the Pacific Islands. New Guinea was only eighty miles from Australia, and whatever else the Australian people differed about they were united on at least two things: (i) Their attitude towards Japan, and the "white Australia" policy; (ii) The retention of these ex-German Pacific Islands, which they had won in the war.

Borden, by contrast, wanted no new territories anywhere for Canada. (He was not even attracted by the suggestion which Lloyd George one day threw out, that Canada should take a guardian's interest in that other Empire estate in the New World, the West Indies.) For the Canadian Prime Minister reckoned that the very best assets which we could secure would be the goodwill and good understanding of the American people. If the British made no land-grab, took no prize-money from the great contest in which they had poured out their blood and treasure it would confound and confute those powerful and ever-hostile elements in the United States, the Irish and the German communities.

The British Empire delegates agreed to speak and act unitedly at the forthcoming Peace Conference on this question of the ex-German colonies. Meantime Lloyd George himself undertook to see President Wilson, who had just arrived in London on his way to Paris, and to tackle him upon it.

He found that Wilson's ideas were no more clear-cut on the ex-enemy colonies than on the League of Nations. He thought that the Turks should be expelled from Europe, and independent states set up of the non-Turkish peoples in Asia Minor whom they had formerly oppressed. But President Wilson was unwilling that the United States should accept a mandate for them. At the same time, he was disposed to deny Australia any control over the German islands which she had conquered south of the equator. When Lloyd George pointed out that by our war-time treaty with the Japanese, we had promised them the German islands which they had seized north of the Equator, the President had replied that he was not sure that he would recognize that treaty.

When Billy Hughes heard, he uttered a shrill scream.

Who were the United States to decide whether or not indubitable facts were or were not to be recognized? Australia had been in the war more than four years, not like the United States, less than two! And these islands below the Equator had been captured by Australians while the Americans were still out of the war! Australia, with a population about one-twentieth the size of America, had suffered casualties as great. This war had cost every man, woman and child in Australia at least £75 per head. The citizens of the United States had made no monetary sacrifice at all; they hadn't even used up the profits they had made in the first two-and-a-half-years! President Wilson had been glad to make off for the comparative calm of Paris.

There was the question of the British Empire policy on Reparations also to be settled before the British Empire Delegation followed. President Wilson had conceded that "restoration" included reparations, but what were "reparations"? The President considered that they should be limited to compensation for material war damage.

This would have meant a very substantial sum to France, whose lands had been devastated and plundered. But not a yard of Britain or the British Empire had been overrun, and the damage done to our cities and ports either by bombardment from the sea or by bombing from the sky, was not comparable. True, we had lost 8,000,000 tons of our merchant shipping. Did that come into the bill? Then, according to Lloyd George's own calculations the war had cost us £7,000,000,000, without counting £3,000,000,000 in war pensions. Were these items to be included in the bill?

It was the subtle Smuts who argued that "material war damage" must cover compensation to civilians for the losses which they had sustained, also the expenses of the citizen turned soldier, i.e. his family separation allowance or his disability pension on return to civilian life (or the pension to his widow and orphaned children if he did not return), these could legitimately be collected.

Hughes agreed with Smuts. Lloyd George was not so sure. Still less sure was he of the budgeting on which Hughes based his findings.

Lloyd George himself approached the problem of making peace between the nations much in the same way as he had sought to make it between employers and workers in his old Board of Trade days. What were the rights in the case, and how near could you get to them in framing the settlement which absolutely must be made somehow? Also, how soon, for there were other things to be done in the world? In this instance, the victorious Allied armies, which were the only final sanction that we could apply to the defeated enemy, had set up a continuous clamour to be demobilized and were already melting away. As for "Making Germany Pay", Lloyd George tackled this problem like a practical lawyer. How much could the defendant actually afford? Throughout the almost interminable argument over reparations, Lloyd George stuck to the policy he had enumerated in the discussions at the Imperial War Cabinet. Germany must pay to the limit of her capacity—but in such a way that the payment did no harm to the recipient.

The three lions of the Conference were, of course, President Wilson, Lloyd George and Clemenceau. (Orlando, the Italian Prime Minister, a distinguished and attractive person, did not possess the same political fame or power.) At first, the President was hailed with general acclaim. He was lent a splendid mansion, and everyone hastened to minister to his comfort. Alas! The honeymoon was brief. The fact that his residence was guarded by American sentries was resented by the Parisians, and very soon it also became apparent that at the Conference, so far from supporting the drastic demands of the French Delegation, Woodrow Wilson was strenuously opposing them. The lady who had lent him her house demanded it back, on the grounds that the Conference was lasting longer than had been expected. The Paris Press began to assail him with obloquy and—what pained the President much more —with ridicule. Clemenceau was diplomatic—and secured certain rewards of his diplomacy—when he induced some of the more virulent newspapers to hold their fire upon the President.

Lloyd George came in for his share, too, but it worried him a lot less for, as he said, he had been brought up on it. When Wilson consulted him, Lloyd George advised the President to refuse to move out of his residence, which was exactly what he was doing himself with his own impatient landlady, and continued to do until the end of the Conference in June, 1919. She took her revenge then, by presenting him a personal Reparations Bill for dilapidations.

As for the Press, Lloyd George had foreseen and feared what the result must be of the President's Point 1 (open diplomacy), or, as Lloyd George himself preferred to put it, "peace by public clamour".

So on the eve of the formal opening of the Peace Conference, 17 January, 1919, the Prime Minister had been responsible for the statement issued by the Council of Ten (which had by then taken the place of the Supreme Inter-Allied Conference, and included two members from each of the five great Powers: Britain, France, the United States, Italy and Japan):

> "The essence of democratic method is not that the deliberation of a Government should be conducted in public, but that its conclusions should be subject to the consideration of a popular Chamber and to free, open discussion in the Press."

Lloyd George had appointed his friend, Riddell, of the *News of the World*, to be British Press Liaison Officer at the Peace Conference, and Riddell did his best to feed the ravening wolves, both with political information and with personal gossip. It was a good best, but he still had to face a daily barrage of complaint against "official secrecy". It is true that far more of the Peace Treaty was framed in Lloyd George's flat in the Rue Nitôt than ever was decided (or even discussed) in either the plenary sessions of the Peace Conference or the comparative privacy of the Council of Ten.

For within a week of the official opening of the Conference, Saturday, 18 January, 1919, all was turmoil.

To begin with, nobody seemed quite sure as to whether the terms which the Plenipotentiaries were drawing up were to be preliminary, or final; in other words, whether the Peace Treaty was to be imposed, or negotiated. The whole thing was further complicated by that insistence of President Wilson on having the Covenant of the League of Nations established and accepted. He was quite possessed by this purpose. He was going to have a League of Nations, and he would sign no peace treaty which did not embody one in its articles. If the Covenant were written into the Treaty, all trouble might subsequently be solved, said Wilson. Great was the power and the prestige of the United States in Europe, January, 1919, and the President had to be placated. Lloyd George, on behalf of the British delegation, moved a resolution at the conference setting up the League of Nations as an essential part of the peace treaty, and creating a permanent Secretariat, and also establishing an International Labour Office. Wilson put himself forward as the chairman of the Committee appointed to deal with it.

In February, 1919, trouble which had long been brewing broke out in the United States Senate, and the President had to return to Washington to deal with it. There, he learned that on many points his proposed draft of the Covenant would have to be revised, or else the Senate would refuse to ratify it. The President had told the plenary session of the Peace Conference that not one word ("nor even a period") could be altered. The warning he now received merely confirmed the obstinate idealist in his determination to force his Covenant on the Senate, by rooting it even more rigidly in the Treaty. Though he did not realize it, the President thus ensured the rejection of the Treaty itself by the Senate. He would have done better to hearken to "Teddy" Roosevelt, who told him that the Fourteen Points rang no big bell in the United States. When President Wilson returned to the Versailles arena, the bell which he himself rang there was smaller than before, for it was plain to all that he did not possess the power which had been supposed.

Had Lloyd George, Clemenceau and Orlando postponed "coming to grips with the President until the President himself had lost his grip"? These three colleagues of Woodrow Wilson on the Council of Four (which had succeeded the Council of Ten) were subtle men, but they cannot fairly be credited with the responsibility for the delays in getting on with the peace. These were due, firstly, to Wilson's own refusal to agree to a working plan; secondly, to the pre-eminence which he accorded to the League of Nations (it was the direct cause of that absence of his for a month at Washington); thirdly, the industrial storms which blew up in Britain in February, and necessitated Lloyd George's presence there; fourthly, the attempted assassination of Clemenceau in Paris.

Business did not progress more evenly when all had returned to the Peace Conference, for by this time troubles were multiplying all round and tempers were rising. Quarrelling broke out.

Much of Lloyd George's success in politics had been due to his natural ability to talk "man-to-man", and in Paris, 1919, as he said himself, "we were all feeling our way". Great things there hinged upon the play of personalities. Thus, Clemenceau was infuriated by President Wilson's "Sunday School talk" and fought bitterly with him almost to the end. He said of him: "Mr. Wilson has lived in a world that has been fairly safe for Democracy; I have lived in a world where it was good form to shoot a democrat." Or again: "Wilson talked like Jesus Christ—and acted like Lloyd George!"

To the President himself, after a violent argument, Clemenceau said:

"Mr. Wilson, if I accepted what you propose as ample for the security of France, after the millions who have died and the millions who have suffered, I believe—and indeed, I hope—that my successor in office would take me by the nape of the neck and have me shot before the *donjon* of Vincennes!"

Hughes cordially disliked Wilson, who despised him. The President and his own Secretary of State, Robert Lansing, loathed each other. Then, Clemenceau detested and distrusted his own President, M. Raymond Poincaré ("Can't you lend me your George V for a bit?" he asked Lloyd George despairingly). Lloyd George himself thought Poincaré "A fussy little man who mistook bustle for energy".

At the Council table one day, Clemenceau observed that while Lloyd George objected to the territorial exactions in Europe proposed by France he did not himself offer to appease the Germans with any "commercial, colonial or naval bones" in the way of concessions at the expense of Britain.

To which Lloyd George retorted that he had been under the delusion that France was also interested in compensation, colonies, Syria, shipping and a British guarantee to stand by France if attacked. Sorry about this mistake. He would not repeat it!

Another time, after a stand-up row with Wilson, Clemenceau strode out of the room. Next day, the President gave orders for his official liner, the *George Washington*, to be made ready at Brest to return to America. He did not actually go. But the Italian Prime Minister, Orlando, after President Wilson had addressed the Italian people over his head on the question of annexing Fiume, packed his bags and left Paris for Rome.

Another source of continuing trouble in these early days of the Conference was the growing hunger of the defeated enemy. Under the terms of the Armistice, the blockade of Germany still continued. The grey, horrible figure of starvation began to stalk through the German streets.

It was not easy to awaken sympathy in the Allied countries for "the starving Germans". Let 'em starve! There would be fewer of 'em, then, and the fewer Jerries the better! Such was the "popular" mood, the cheap line. It was from the British Army of the Rhine that the first protest arose. The decent word came from the soldiers who had fought the Germans. They were now the Army of Occupation, but they were not fighting the German children. In the House of Commons on 3 March, 1919, Churchill, the War Secretary, told of anxious and also angry reports which had been coming in to the War Office for some time past from officers in Germany. They spoke of the privations which the people there were suffering, and warned of the danger "of a collapse of the entire structure of German social and national life under the stress of hunger and malnutrition".

It was exactly what Lloyd George had feared, that through harshness or neglect, the Allies might drive the Germans into the arms of Bolshevism. Fiercely now, in Paris, he turned on M. Klotz, the French Finance Minister, who had just completed a lengthy argument against sending any food, *or gold*, to Germany. Making deadly play of Klotz' Semitic appearance, Lloyd George portrayed him as a modern Shylock, mimicked him clutching his money bags, ridiculed him and his policy, and ended by prophesying that if ever a Bolshevik State was set up in Germany, three statues would be erected there—to Lenin, Trotsky and Klotz.

General Plumer, Commander-in-Chief of the British Army of Occupation in Germany, had already sent a telegram to the War Office, which had been forwarded to the Peace Conference, urging that food should be supplied to the hungry people in order to avert public disorder, as well as for pity's sake. He warned of the effect upon the Army itself of this sea of human misery by which they were surrounded; the British soldiers would certainly share their rations with the hungry families and, indeed, their own physical fitness was being affected. This telegram was now produced. "No one," remarked the Prime Minister, "can say that General Plumer is pro-German!"

In the middle of the discussion which followed, another telegram was handed to Lloyd George. It was a fresh appeal from Plumer to the Conference, pleading once more for food to be sent to Germany without delay. It read:

> "The mortality amongst women, children and sick is most grave, and sickness due to hunger is spreading. The attitude of the population is becoming one of despair, and the people feel that an end by bullets is preferable to death by starvation."

Actually, this telegram had arrived before the meeting but Lloyd George, with his sense of theatre, had arranged for it to be handed to him during the debate. It was "curtains" for Klotz—and food for the German children.

After this public bout, the Big Four abruptly withdrew into strictly private —or rather, secret—deliberation, often at the Rue Nitôt. Not even secretaries were admitted. The newspapermen fumed, and Riddell noted in his diary, 9 April, 1919: "No four kings or emperors could have conducted the Conference on more autocratic lines."

It gave Northcliffe his chance. He had his own sources of information, and day after day his *Times* and *Daily Mail* published an "inside story" of what was going on, and how Lloyd George was letting the side down to the Germans.

The quarrelling, certainly, was continuing *in camera*. The walls of the flat in the Rue Nitôt must almost have bulged. Everybody in turn again

threatened to go home. At this, Churchill said, Lloyd George, was "first
and by far the most artistic". He gave no special reason of disagreement for
his threatened departure. It was just that time was going on, and he had a lot
of things to do at home. If there developed any prospect of getting something
done in Paris, of course, he would try and come back. His colleagues beseeched
him, in a joint letter, to remain. Lloyd George yielded.

But one week-end, he went off to Fontainebleau Forest with General
Smuts, General Wilson, Philip Kerr and Colonel Hankey for "the hardest
48 hours' thinking I have ever done". As a result he wrote this shrewd and
far-sighted appreciation.

*"Some Considerations for the Peace Conference before they finally draft
their Terms."*

Lloyd George begins, that when nations are exhausted by war they are
tempted to patch up a peace which will last their own generation. For the
next one, things may be different. So though the peace terms may be hard,
they must be just.

Thus, the victors of today should transfer no more Germans to the rule
of other peoples than can possibly be avoided. To place more than two million
Germans (in the Polish Corridor) under the Poles will, "sooner or later, lead
to a new war in the East of Europe". No, the guiding principle, as far as
humanly possible, must be to allocate the various races to their own Mother-
lands, "even beyond the considerations of strategy, or economics, or communications, which can usually be adjusted by other means".

Next, Reparations should end with this generation, and they should be
bearable. If they are not, there is real danger that Germany will throw in her
lot with Bolshevism. Her present Government is weak and without prestige,
and the alternative to it is her own brand of Communists, called the Spartacists.
If they take over, for a couple of years there will be turmoil and trouble but
the land of Germany will remain, the people will remain, roads, railways
and the greater part of the houses and the factories will remain. Germany will
wipe the slate, and make a fresh start. By this time, under the Spartacists, she
will have joined the Bolsheviks. Then we shall see a union of 300,000,000
people and a Red Army with German generals, Reichswehr instructors and
Krupp's artillery and machine-guns! Better offer Germany some peace terms
which are preferable to Bolshevism, says Lloyd George.

He concludes, that we must hold Germany responsible for the war, and
the way in which it was waged; we must impose peace terms which can be
kept without a future *revanche*; and we must ensure our ally, France, against
any such attempt.

Clemenceau read it carefully. He observed that the Maritime nations,
"which have not known an invasion", were getting "total and definite guarantees", while the Continental nations were getting "partial and temporary

solutions". Britain was to be rewarded with the German colonies, the German fleet, a large part of the German mercantile marine and considerable exclusion of German commercial competition from the markets of the world. France was to be satisfied with reduced German frontiers, and temporary occupation of the Saar and some defensive agreements.

The row in the Rue Nitôt continued.

At this moment, internal rumblings shook a much bigger building. The House of Commons. To Lloyd George, on 8 April, there came the following telegram, signed by 370 Tory Coalition M.P.s:

"The greatest anxiety exists throughout the country at the persistent reports from Paris that the British delegates, instead of formulating the complete financial claim of the Empire, are merely considering what amount can be exacted from the enemy. This anxiety has been deepened by the statement of the Leader of the House on Wednesday last.

Our constituents have always expected—and still expect—that the first action of the peace delegates would be, as you repeatedly stated in your Election pledges, to present the bill in full, to make Germany acknowledge the debt, and then to discuss ways and means of obtaining payment.

Although we have the utmost confidence in your intention to fulfil your pledges to the country, may we, as we have to meet innumerable inquiries from our constituents, have your renewed assurance that you have in no way departed from your original intention?"

Lloyd George knew who was behind this telegram: Kennedy Jones, M.P. He also knew who was behind Kennedy Jones. It was Northcliffe, who was Kennedy Jones's old newspaper chief. For Northcliffe had added to his grievances against Lloyd George for refusing him a place (i) in the War Cabinet (ii) on the Peace Delegation, a third one for rejecting his offer to take the Hotel Majestic in Paris and there organize the whole of British official propaganda for the home and foreign Press during the Peace Conference. Northcliffe had persisted, and had gone to see the Prime Minister personally to argue the matter. Lloyd George had lost his temper, and told Northcliffe angrily to "go to Hell!" (and as Lloyd George said, Bonar Law afterwards told him "He came straight to see me at the Treasury"). So after Lloyd George's rebuff, the Chief Proprietor of *The Times* had set himself up in Paris to organize propaganda *against* the British Government, or at any rate against the head of it. Northcliffe was personally the source of a good many of the "inside stories" of the Conference which had graced the pages of *The Times* and the *Daily Mail* within the last few weeks. Lloyd George was, therefore, delighted when almost with the rebel Tory telegram itself Bonar Law arrived, to discuss with him how to deal both with this latest Tory Revolt and with Northcliffe. They quickly agreed this reply:

"My colleagues and I mean to stand faithfully by all the pledges we gave to the constituencies. We are prepared at any moment to submit to the judgment of Parliament, and if necessary of the Country, our efforts loyally to redeem our promises."

The challenge was down. If the majority of the House of Commons did not like the way Lloyd George was handling the Peace Conference, well, they could get someone else. He returned to London to face them.

On 16 April, 1919, the Prime Minister rose to address the House in the most critical debate for the Government since the famous Maurice Affair. Very quietly, he began to unfold the scene of the Peace Conference. No other gathering had ever assembled in the history of the world faced with problems of such variety, complexity, magnitude and gravity. The Congress of Vienna, said Lloyd George, had been the nearest approach to it, and that was to settle the affairs of Europe alone. But this present Conference was to settle the fate of five continents. Ten new States had been born, and the boundaries of fourteen countries recast. Territories! Armaments! Economics! Indemnities! International questions of trade, transport and labour! You were not going to solve these problems by telegram!

Had they wasted time at the Conference? It would have been necessary to take even more time if they were not setting up, in the League of Nations, "a machinery which is capable of readjusting and correcting possible mistakes".

Lloyd George then claimed that, in these labours, no body of men had ever worked harder, or in better harmony (!). He also doubted whether any body of men with a difficult task had worked under greater difficulties:

". . . stones clattering on the roof, and crashing through the windows, and sometimes wild men screaming through the keyholes.

I have come back to say a few things, and I mean to say them. (An Hon. Member: 'Save you from your friends!') I quite agree, and when enormous issues are depending upon it, you require calm deliberation. I ask for it for the rest of the journey. The journey is not at an end. It is full of perils, perils for this country, perils for all lands, perils for the peoples throughout the world. I beg, at any rate, that the men who are doing their best should be left in peace to do it, or that other men should be sent there."

They were devoting much attention to small states? Yes, it was the quarrel of small states which had made the war. But they were also dealing with great empires—and three great, ancient empires had broken up—Russia, Austria, Turkey.

Russia! What was the Government going to do about Russia? Some people said "Make Peace!" Others said "Use Force!" One of the difficulties was that, in the summer of 1919, there seemed to be no "Russia". No single authority ruled over the various divided areas, and from day to day their boundaries advanced or receded.

The Prime Minister then dealt with the question of military intervention. Did anyone propose it? (Churchill sat blushing by his side on the Front Bench.) It was a very sound principle not to interfere in the internal affairs of any country, however badly governed. The British people had thoroughly disapproved of Tsarism—its principles, corruption and oppression. They certainly disagreed with the present Bolshevik experiment, deplored its horrible consequences, starvation, bloodshed, confusion, ruin. But that didn't justify committing this country to a gigantic military enterprise there. "Russia is a country which it is very easy to invade, but very difficult to conquer . . . very easy to get into, but very hard to get out of." And Lloyd George recited the fate of the Germans, who had broken through the Russian Front, rolled up the Russian armies, captured millions of prisoners and masses of guns—and entangled themselves in a morass.

Suppose we conquered the place now with an overwhelming army. What kind of Government would you set up? What kind did the Russian people want? Was Britain going to have an Army of Occupation there, too?

"I share the horror of all the Bolshevik teachings, but I would rather leave Russia Bolshevik until she sees her way out of it than see Britain bankrupt. And that is the surest way to Bolshevism in Britain. . . . I entreat the House of Commons and the country not to contemplate the possibility of another great war. We have had quite enough bloodshed."

The Peace terms—and his own Peace pledges at the last General Election? The Prime Minister extended an open invitation to "any enterprising newspaper" to publish them in parallel columns when the Treaty was signed. Those terms, by the way, had not been framed at the last moment in response to "the great agitation and the various communications we have received", but had been put forward by the British delegation from the start. They stood by them, because they thought them just.

"We want a stern Peace, because the occasion demands it. The crime demands it. But its severity must be designed, not to gratify Vengeance, but to vindicate Justice."

He asked for the confidence of the House in order that he could go back to Paris and make such a Peace. He could not always be correcting misstatements and clearing up misconceptions. He did not object to that telegram the other day, but he did object to the information on which it had been based. He was told that the telegram was sent because of information which came from a "reliable source".

Kennedy Jones rose to say that the information was put forward in an interview in the *Westminster Gazette*.

Lloyd George knew better. He recommended Mr. Kennedy Jones to compare notes with Lieut.-Colonel Claud Lowther, M.P., who had stated that the "reliable authority" was a telegram from Paris to Kennedy Jones himself. (It came, in fact, from Northcliffe, and the Prime Minister was well aware of it, because the French *Sûreté* had shown it to him in Paris before it had been sent off.) He now promised the House that he knew this "reliable source", and would tell them something about it. He left nobody in any doubt as to whom he was referring. He said:

"There were some Peace Terms published in November as a model for us to proceed upon. [They had appeared in the *Daily Mail*.] In those Peace Terms there was not a word about indemnities, not a word about the cost of the war. Reparation—yes, in the strictest and narrowest sense of the term, but no reparation for lost lives, no reparation for damaged houses, not even at Broadstairs [Northcliffe's country house]. That was in November. We were not at that time to try anyone responsible for the war. We were to try those who had been guilty of offences against the law, but the tribunals must be German. That is the 'reliable source'! Now, we must have everything—the cost of the war, damage to all sorts of property, hanging everybody all round, especially members of the Government!" . . .

At the beginning of the Conference, said Lloyd George, there had been appeals to all to support President Wilson and his great ideals. Where did these come from? From the same "reliable source" that was now hysterically attacking all these great ideals. Then, a few weeks ago, there had been a cartoon in these newspapers representing Bolshevism as a mere bogy—and Lloyd George as a man trying to frighten the working-classes with it. Now it was no longer a bogy; it was a Monster—and Lloyd George was doing his best to dress it up as an Angel! That was the same "reliable source".

Still, he was prepared to make allowances, said Lloyd George. When a man was labouring under a keen sense of disappointment, however unjustified and however ridiculous his expectations may have been, he was always apt to think the world was badly run. When a man had deluded himself—and all the people he ever permitted to go near to him, helped him into the belief that he was the only man who could win the war—and he was waiting for the clamour of the multitude that was going to demand his presence there to direct the destinies of the world, and there was not a whisper, not a sound, it was rather disappointing; it was unnerving, upsetting!

"Then the war is won without him," gibed Lloyd George. "There *must* be something wrong! Of course, it *must* be the Government! Then, at any rate, he is the only man to make Peace. The only people who get near him tell him so, constantly tell him so. So he publishes the Peace Terms, and he waits for the 'call'. It does not come. He retreats to sunny climes, waiting, but not a sound reaches that far-distant shore to call him back to his great task of saving the world. What can you expect? He comes back, and he says, 'Well, I cannot see the disaster, but I am sure it is there. It is bound to come!' Under these conditions, I am prepared to make allowances; but let me say this, that when that kind of diseased vanity"—here, Lloyd George paused and significantly tapped his head—"is carried to the point of sowing dissension between great Allies, whose unity is essential to the peace and happiness of the world . . . then I say that not even that kind of disease is a justification for so black a crime."

The Prime Minister apologized to the House for taking up its time. He had felt bound to do it, and he would tell the House why. He had been in France for weeks. Here, nobody took any notice of this thing—everybody knew it. But that was not the case in France. There, they still believed that *The Times* was a serious organ. They did not know that it was merely the threepenny edition of the *Daily Mail.*

Lloyd George ended this vitriolic counter-attack on his great Fleet Street enemy by a lofty appeal to the supreme duty of "statesmen in every land, of the Parliaments upon whose will statesmen depend, of those who guide and direct the public opinion which is the making of all—not to soil this triumph of right by indulging in the angry passions of the moment, but to consecrate the sacrifice of millions to the permanent redemption of the human race from the scourge and agony of war".

He sat down amid thunderous applause. He had gained one of the greatest Parliamentary triumphs of his time. A few formal, and mostly congratulatory speeches from the Labour Opposition and then the debate petered out. But not before Pemberton Billing had remarked that the Prime Minister had declared war against the strongest Press combine that the world had ever known. Certainly, never in the history of that House had a Napoleon of the Press been so thoroughly trounced. Mr. Lloyd George, added Pemberton Billing, "is a greater actor than an orator, and his charm is as much in gesture as in words. . . . I am sure that if it were not for the privilege of this House an action for libel by gesture might almost lie."

The Parliamentary Correspondent of *The Times,* describing the Prime Minister's speech, wrote: "It was as though a versatile performer had abruptly stepped down from a Cathedral organ to conduct a jazz band."

In the course of his hour's speech, Lloyd George, explaining the problems of settling the New Europe, had mentioned Teschen, a great coal district of Poland then in dispute, and had confessed that he had never before heard of the place. Had any other Member of the House? *The Times* editorial scolded:

"Everybody has heard of it, who knows the later history of Maria Theresa, of Frederick II, and of Catherine II; . . . but Mr. Lloyd George

evidently judges the knowledge of Members of Parliament by the standard
of his own. . . . It is currently said by his colleagues that, while he can read
and write, he does neither."

Lloyd George, refreshed by his visit to the Home Front, returned to the
battlefield of the Peace Conference. He found four separate and full-scale
actions raging. They concerned Reparations, Annexations, Colonies and
Mandates, and the League of Nations.

Reparations. Towards the end of 1918, Lloyd George had appointed Billy
Hughes as chairman of a committee of experts under the Imperial War Cabinet
to inquire into the whole question of reparations, and Germany's capacity to
pay. Other members were Walter Long, Colonial Secretary; Sir G. E. Foster,
Canadian Finance Minister; Lord Cunliffe, Chairman of the Bank of England;
Sir Herbert Gibbs, another banker; and Mr. W. A. S. Hewins, M.P., the
economist. Lloyd George had counted on a down-to-earth report from these
hard-headed gentlemen, but he afterwards sadly confessed that he had never
seen trustfulness so completely befooled by the sequel.

They recommended putting in a bill to Germany at once for
£24,000,000,000, and they saw no reason to suppose that she could not pay
£1,200,000,000 per annum as interest on that amount when normal conditions
were restored. This indemnity was to be delivered in cash, kind, securities
and by means of a funding loan.

Lloyd George says that both Bonar Law and himself regarded the conclusions of this Report as "a wild and fantastic chimera".

"It was incredible that men of such position, experience and responsibility should have appended their names to it. What is still more remarkable
is that it represented the opinions formed and expressed by the Associated
Chambers of Commerce and the Federation of British Industries. So much
for the infallibility of business men in business matters which go beyond
their day-to-day transactions!"

The Hughes Report was not the only estimate which lay on the Prime
Minister's desk in these days before the Peace Conference had even opened.
The Board of Trade (backed by a shrewd memorandum subscribed by Professor
Ashley and Mr. J. M. Keynes) thought that if the reparation could be largely
extracted in kind, and the cash payments spread over a number of years, we
might get £2,000,000,000 worth in all. Nearly half of this could be paid by
handing over merchant shipping, river barges, railway rolling-stock, minerals,
etc., and by transferring her external interest-bearing securities. The Treasury
Report reckoned that perhaps as much as £3,000,000,000 could be collected.
The United States multiplied this by anything between two and four, bringing
it up to £12,000,000,000. The French put the figure at anything between
£13,000,000,000 and £30,000,000,000! With such variable arithmetic, the

Peacemakers, early in the New Year, 1919, had converged upon Paris for the Conference and the Treaty signing.

What did Germany really owe, and what could she actually pay? A rough division of the total sum had by now been agreed: France, 50 per cent; Britain, 30 per cent; the Rest, 20 per cent; but what had not yet been settled was the total sum itself. Lloyd George now proposed, and carried, a resolution in the Peace Conference to set up a Reparations Commission to assess this bill for damages and decide the method of paying it. He well understood that the two parties were unlikely to agree any figure at the moment. Said Lloyd George: "For the Supreme Council to fix the sum now, with so many other pressing questions to be settled, is like asking a man in the maelstrom of Niagara to fix the price of a horse."

He insisted that you could not both cripple Germany, and expect her to pay her debts. He questioned the wisdom of detaching the Saar from her, though he ultimately agreed to give France a kind of "economic mandate" there for 15 years. Germany was also required to deliver to France, in compensation for her war-time sabotage, a tonnage of coal equal to the balance between the pre-war and the post-war output of the French mines. In the event, Germany did not deliver it, whereupon in 1923 the French Army marched into the Ruhr.

But while Lloyd George retained his doubts about Germany's intention or capacity to pay her penalty in full, he was as determined as Clemenceau to place upon the record Germany's offence.

The first of these "War Guilt Clauses" of the Treaty (Articles 231 and 232) affirmed the responsibility for all the loss and damage which had been caused by this war imposed on the world by "the aggression of Germany and her Allies".

The second clause recognized that the resources of Germany were not enough to make full reparation. But the Allies required, and Germany undertook, to make compensation for all damage done to the civilian population of the Allied Powers and to their property by such aggression "by land, by sea and by air".

The Reparations Commission eventually fixed the German bill for the war at £6,600,000,000. According to their books, the Germans actually paid £1,050,000,000, in cash and in kind. They borrowed from foreign banks—and defaulted on—about £1,500,000,000 so that Northcliffe was not so far wrong, after all, when he warned every day in his *Daily Mail*:

THOSE JUNKERS WILL CHEAT YOU YET!

Fantastically wrong about the final results (the more remarkable since he had been so near the truth in estimating what the Germans could be made to pay), was the economist, J. M. Keynes. Writing his provocative and immensely popular book, *The Economic Consequences of the Peace*, Keynes

Prime Minister, 1922   *Olive Edis*

charged that it "reduced Germany to servitude . . . perpetuated her economic ruin". Nay, worse. This Carthaginian Peace would "sow the decay of the whole civilized life of Europe", which would henceforth suffer "a long, silent process of semi-starvation and gradual, steady lowering of the standards of life and comfort".

Ten years after the Treaty of Versailles the productivity of Europe was greater than before the war, and the standards of living had never been higher. As for Germany, her national income was up by 50 per cent.

Reparations? For the next thirty years, said Keynes, Germany could never pay more than £100,000,000 per annum. But between 1933 and 1939, under Hitler, Germany managed to pay every year more than seven times as much for armaments.

Equally remote from the facts was Keynes's statement that the real problems which confronted the victors at Versailles (and were ignored by them) were not political or territorial, but financial and economic: ". . . the perils of the future lay not in frontiers or sovereignties but in food, coal and transport".

Such as the sack of Smyrna? Chanak? Abyssinia? The Spanish Civil War? The Reoccupation of the Rhineland? The rape of Austria? The Munich crisis over the seizure of the Sudetenland of Czechoslovakia? Danzig, and the Polish Corridor?

If Keynes had written that the problems to which civilized men *should* apply their energies were food, fuel, and transport, how right he would have been! Unfortunately, they have not realized it yet. Meantime, the truth about the Treaty is that it was not at all "Carthaginian" in its treatment of the most barbarous tribe in Europe, and Lloyd George was largely responsible for that very fact. (History, indeed, may find him to have been at fault for it!) Lloyd George always feared the prospect of a "peace" which would leave a seeping wound in Europe, and twenty years later he still sometimes cherished hopes of Germany.

Thus, in the next issue which engaged the attentions—and the dissensions —of the Big Four at Versailles, which was No. 2, or

Annexations. Lloyd George vigorously opposed any occupation of the Rhineland, except as a short-time sanction to exact reparation payments. Nor did he accept the plea that France herself was not asking either for territory or overlordship, but only for an "independent" Confederation of the Rhine to be set up. For he knew full well that such a State must either become the satellite of France, or else collapse and be annexed by her.

Instead, Lloyd George proposed a joint military guarantee by Britain and America to France against any future aggression by Germany. President Wilson agreed, and in further discussions both statesmen accepted the demilitarization of a zone on the eastern bank of the Rhine. It still did not satisfy the French.

It was over this proposed treaty of guarantee to France that a final issue

R

was raised between Britain and the Dominions. It was set forth in a letter from Botha, dated 15 May, 1919, in which he noted that "the Dominion point of view has been fully and frankly met, and no obligation is laid on us to ask our Dominion Parliaments to ratify the proposed treaty". Then Botha pointed out that one result of this, indeed, might be that in some future Continental war, Britain might be involved, and "one or more of the Dominions may stand out and maintain their neutrality. But that result is inevitable," he added, "and flows from the status of independent nationhood of the Dominions."

It brought a startled protest from Milner, who wrote to Lloyd George on 28 May, 1919, that if these words were allowed to stand unchallenged and unqualified they would appear "to embody a view of the relations between the United Kingdom and the Dominions which is incompatible with the existence of the British Empire as a political unit".

For in constitutional theory, declared Milner, when H.M. the King was at war no Dominion of the Crown could remain neutral, except by proclaiming its independence of His Majesty. Now, it was admitted that the Dominions had obtained a status in which they were "virtually independent of the United Kingdom. But I have yet to learn that they are independent of His Majesty, or that any of them would even contemplate so grave a step as that of severing itself from the British Commonwealth of Nations by repudiating its allegiance to His Majesty, which is the bond that still holds . . . all the self-governing portions of the Empire together."

There were certain obligations, said Milner, which no Dominion could escape "so long as it remains in any sense part of the Empire, and the chief of these is that the enemies of His Majesty are, *ipso facto*, the enemies of all his subjects". Each Dominion, he conceded, could, of course, decide for itself the measure of the contribution which it chose to make towards any war.

But Lloyd George, in a letter to Botha, dated 26 June, 1919, accepted the view which the South African Prime Minister had put forward. He urged that the proposed guarantee to France would be a safeguard of peace, and he hoped that all the Dominions would adhere to it. "But the British Government recognize that each Dominion has special circumstances of its own, by which its judgment must be largely influenced. It is, therefore, the intention and desire of the British Government that each Dominion should be perfectly free to add or withhold its guarantee as it thinks right."

Another difficulty on the Annexations question arose among the Allies because, although annexation had been banned by President Wilson in his Fourteen Points, before these had been proclaimed to the world the Allies had drawn up among themselves a number of extremely private treaties. Those which concerned the Russians, such as the 1915 Constantinople Agreement, promising the Tsar Constantinople, had already been publicly denounced by the Bolsheviks. But there were at least four other secret treaties, and now they were produced.

There was first of all the undertaking entered into towards the end of 1914 by our High Commissioner in Egypt with the Sherif of Mecca, later King Hussein of the Hedjaz. He certainly believed that we were backing a united Arab Empire, with its capital at Damascus. The British had not informed their French allies of this arrangement at the time.

Nor had we informed our Arab allies of the Sykes-Picot Treaty of 16 May, 1916. This had shared out most of Asia Minor between Britain, France and Russia. We got Mesopotamia, the French got Syria and Lebanon, and the Russians got Armenia and Kurdistan. Farther south, the Arab lands were divided into British and French zones. The Italians got nothing.

But wait! By the Treaty of London, 26 April, 1915, we had promised Italy a share in the carve-up of the Ottoman Empire. Later, in the Treaty of St. Jean de Maurienne, 17 April, 1917, we allotted Italy the region of Smyrna and Adalia. Italy was also to get considerable territories from Austria, certain Adriatic ports, the Dodecanese Islands and a protectorate over Albania.

Finally, there was the British–Japanese Treaty over Shantung of 16 February, 1917 The beginning of that year had marked the full unleashing of the U-boat campaign, and Britain had been desperately in need of destroyer escorts in the Mediterranean. The obliging Japanese were ready to lend a flotilla—in return for the possession of the German colonies North of the Equator and Sovereign rights over Kiao Chau and Shantung. We had to agree. As Sir Edward Grey said: "In war you will have secret treaties, and you cannot help it. Many things generally regarded as criminal are regarded as inevitable in war."

Now, not only did some of these treaties conflict with one another, but both the scenery and the *dramatis personae* of the plot had changed. For instance, in October, 1918, the Emir Feisal had galloped into Damascus with Colonel Lawrence by his side. Lloyd George, who had not engineered the Sykes-Picot Treaty with the French, but had certainly taken an active interest in the operations of Colonel Lawrence, could not see why, when Syria had been conquered by British arms, we should withhold it from the Arabs, who had helped us, and hand it over to the French, who had not been there. The French, on the other hand, asked why they should release Britain from her 1916 Treaty obligations because of our previous 1914 obligations, of which we had never informed them?

Then there was Rumania. By our Treaty with her of 17 August, 1916, she had been promised the whole of Transylvania, and much else. Ten days later she had declared war on Germany, and before the end of the following year Rumania had quit. Had the separate peace which she signed with the enemy in May, 1918, invalidated the Treaty of August, 1916? While the statesmen argued in Paris, the Rumanian Army marched over the mountains and occupied Transylvania.

Italy was trumpeting, too. Fearing the march of Socialism at home, her

Liberal Prime Minister, Orlando, was proclaiming a feverish Imperialism abroad. He not only demanded the military line of the Brenner Pass, but the naval command of the Adriatic. He must have his Albanian protectorate, the Dodecanese islands and the Adriatic ports.

"Fiume—or Death!" roared the Roman mob, who ten years later would echo for a more rabid rabble-rouser, "Nice! Corsica! Tunis!" And the poet D'Annunzio, half-hero and half-pantaloon, stormed into Fiume with a band of Italian irregulars and seized the city.

The Czechoslovak case is an example of the difficulty of reconciling the conflicting claims of nationality and "viability" in drawing the future frontiers of the New Europe. Before the Supreme Allied Council, the Czech leader, Dr. Edouard Benes, argued for retaining the existing Bohemian-German border, although this would bring a very substantial German minority within the Czechoslovak Republic. He offered both historical and political reasons. But most powerfully of all, he argued on economic grounds. The Czech-inhabited heart of old Bohemia was the industrialized area; it could not live without the German-inhabited outer rim, which was the agricultural area. The new "Czecho-Slovakia" must include both.

The eloquent Benes carried the day.

Here, at any rate, economics prevailed over self-determination, and three million Sudeten Germans were incorporated into Czechoslovakia. They created there a festering and smouldering unrest.

The simple trouble was of course, that whereas in Western Europe, the "self-determination of peoples" practically coincided with their nationality, in Eastern Europe it did not. Thus, the Sudeten Germans who lived in old Bohemia had nothing in common, of race or language, with their neighbours and co-citizens, the Czechoslovaks. Indeed, even people of the same race and tongue do not always want to live together—and more than once President Wilson was sharply reminded that President Lincoln had waged the most bloody war in American history to compel the Confederate Southerners back into the Union.

There was Poland. Now an independent Polish State, "assured of a free and secure access to the sea", really was in the Fourteen Points. Colonel House, for the President, had frankly admitted the problem which this had brought with it.

"The chief question is whether Poland is to obtain territory west of the River Vistula which would cut off the Germans of East Prussia from the German Empire, or whether Danzig can be made a Free Port and the Vistula internationalized."

It was not, however, the only Polish Question. There was that place called Teschen, and who should have possession of Upper Silesia and its precious mineral wealth? Poland claimed it, but most of the people there were Germans.

Were they to be placed under Polish rule? Oddly enough, in this case President Wilson was rather in favour of doing so. Was it Poland's subtle and charming Prime Minister, M. Paderewski, who talked him over? It could hardly have been her strong-arm soldier, General Pilsudski, who was already defying the Supreme Allied Council over Russia. Unkind critics suggested that the substantial Polish vote in the United States had something to do with it. The sensible course was to settle the problem by plebiscite, which was what Lloyd George urged, and which was eventually done. Upper Silesia voted itself back to its German motherland. The rest of the Polish Question was less satisfactorily solved. Danzig became a Free City, and the Polish Corridor was created, an alleyway to future certain war.

Not that wars were lacking at the moment. Borden and Botha on May Day, 1919, counted up eighteen fronts, in two continents, where fighting was still going on.

"Force settles nothing!" persisted President Wilson, "even Napoleon admitted that on his death-bed."

"Left it a bit late, didn't he?" suggested Clemenceau.

Closely akin to the question of annexations was No. 3 on the list before the Council of Versailles,

Colonies and Mandates. Now, if so-called "national territories" ought not, in President Wilson's view, to be stripped away from its motherland, what about colonies? What, in fact, about New Guinea?

The ingenious General Smuts stepped forward. He had a plan for this problem, too. *In the interests of the native peoples themselves* and for future peaceful precaution, ex-enemy colonies could be placed under the mandatory authority of the League of Nations, who would select an appropriate guardian.

Lloyd George leapt at it. Australia, New Zealand and South Africa had already, in the Imperial War Cabinet, expressed their determination to keep their hands on the neighbouring territories that they had captured. As head of the British Empire Delegation, Lloyd George was most anxious to carry the President of the United States along with him. He now succeeded in convincing Woodrow Wilson that there was a difference between these ex-enemy territories which had been conquered by the Empire forces as a whole, such as German East Africa, Mesopotamia, Palestine and those which had been won by the British Dominions themselves and which lay next door to them, such as German South-West Africa and New Guinea.

With his own Empire colleagues, Lloyd George had more trouble, and a downright row with Billy Hughes, because he was pressing to the limit over the islands northward beyond New Guinea itself.

"I have been fighting Australia's battle for three whole days," he told Hughes, angrily, "and I am not quarrelling with the United States of America over the Solomon Islands!"

"The ring of these South Pacific islands encompasses Australia like a chain of fortresses," snapped Hughes, "and any Power which controls New Guinea, controls Australia!"

In no way loath, he took up the cudgels again with Wilson himself, to hammer it into the Presidential head that Australia was not letting go of those islands whatever anybody else, ally or ex-enemy, thought.

"Are we to understand, Mr. Prime Minister," inquired the President in his most schoolmasterly and reproving tones, "that in the very face of world opinion, nay in defiance of the conscience of civilization, a nation of five million people from your southern sub-continent propose to retain their hold upon these islands, which do not belong to them?"

"Dead right, Mr. President!" rasped Hughes. "You took the very words out of my mouth!"

The President expressed the lofty hope that, at any rate, religious freedom would be established, and missionaries encouraged. Hughes again assented. Why, of course! The natives had been very short of food lately, and had not had enough missionary.

After much negotiation, during which Wilson threatened to retire to the United States, Lloyd George brought about a compromise. Several different kinds of mandates were devised. The Union of South Africa got one which was tantamount to annexing the former German South-West Africa, though it left the future incorporation of the territory open for decision by plebiscite: South Africa's only obligation was to furnish the League of Nations Council at Geneva with an annual report. As for Hughes and the mandate he secured for Australia, he admitted that the difference between this and outright possession was "the difference between freehold and a 999 years' lease".

Australia meant to stay there. When, in the middle 'thirties Hitler's Germany demanded the return of her old colonies, Hughes flew to New Guinea to say: "On this rock we have got our mandate and built our church, and all Hell is not going to take it away from us!"

Another World War would justify Hughes. In 1942, instead of New Guinea becoming a Japanese base, it stood fast as an Australian barrier.

Even the genial William Massey, Prime Minister of New Zealand, had a sharp brush with Wilson over mandates. He asked the President how George Washington and Alexander Hamilton would have liked to have a Mandatory Power appointed to look after the rest of North America after the successful revolt of the Thirteen Colonies in the War of Independence—or how even the ex-colonists themselves would have fancied such a mandate?

There was still Mesopotamia, Palestine and the other Asia Minor lands of the dissolved Ottoman Empire to be allocated. Not very willingly, Lloyd

George agreed that Britain should take care of the first two. Perhaps the United States could be persuaded to accept a mandate over Armenia, or even Constantinople? The President pondered. He would have liked to say yes. He knew what Congress would say.

The Council passed to their fourth problem.

The League of Nations. Trouble had already arisen in the Committee set up to deal with the League, presided over by President Wilson. It began when Hughes, fighting as ever to Advance Australia, came into collision with the Japanese delegate, Baron Makino, who proposed a resolution be embodied in the Charter of the League of Nations:

> "The equality of nations being a basic principle of the League of Nations, the High Contracting Powers agree to accord, as soon as possible, to all alien nationals of States members of the League, equal and just treatment in every respect, making no distinction in law, or in fact on account of their race and nationality."

This, of course, would have deprived any state of the right to regulate its own immigration, and Hughes promptly pointed it out. It certainly would not square with "White Australia!" In vain, did Makino urge that the motion was purely technical, and would never be evoked. When Wilson, from the chair, appeared to side with Makino, Hughes delightedly turned his guns on him. He promised to go himself and personally raise hell in the Western States of U.S.A. on this matter in the course of the next few months. Billy Hughes was well aware that 1920 would be Presidential Election Year, and that the ratification of the Peace Treaty was likely to be the chief Election issue. He confided to a colleague that when he was fighting a fellow he believed in "hitting him where he lived".

The President put the offending resolution to the vote of the Committee. When it was carried by 11 to 5, he ruled that it had failed, because the voting was not unanimous.

A graver issue occurred over the representation of the British Dominions on the League of Nations Assembly. Under the proposed Covenant, the members not only recognized the authority of a Permanent Court of International Justice to arbitrate disputes between nations, but also ensured sanctions to implement the decisions of that Court. These sanctions were to be financial, economic and military.

There was also the International Labour Organization to be dealt with. This was, in many ways, the most sensible idea which had emerged from the war. As the entire world became industrialized, labour conditions in every country had passed through the same kind of hard, haphazard ways that had marked the making of industrial Britain as the first workshop of the world. A British Consular Report of 1924 tells how, in both British and Japanese-owned mills in Shanghai, the employees worked a 12-hour shift; in other

Chinese cities it was 16 hours; in Persia, herded into stuffy hovels and squatting on planks, children of eight years old stitched until they fell dead of weariness —or else became permanently deformed.

These damnable conditions the International Labour Office sought sincerely and—over the years—successfully, to mitigate by agreed and civilized labour codes. Not much political good ever came out of Geneva, but millions of working families the world over have lived to bless the Washington Convention on the Eight Hours' Day, the Forty-Eight Hours' Week, and the protection of women and child labour.

These things were not achieved without resolute effort. When the Labour Convention was set up to settle these things, Borden drew immediate attention to the Article (No. 4) which said that "No Member, together with its Dominions and Colonies, whether self-governing or not, shall be entitled to nominate more than one delegate."

Borden demanded the deletion of the words referring to (and effectively excluding) the Dominions. He emphasized that, even in the Empire lands, labour conditions differed from those in the United Kingdom. Was it feared, also, that Britain with her Dominions might dominate the Labour Convention while, of course, the United States would have no kind of association with, should we say, Cuba, Haiti, Nicaragua, Panama, San Salvador, Colombia or Venezuela? Said Borden, bluntly:

"It is now proposed that Canada should become a party to a treaty by which she shall undertake to engage in active operations against Germany, in case that country at any time in the future shall be guilty of aggression against France.

I am not aware that any similar undertaking is proposed for Spain, or Brazil, or Greece, or Belgium, or for any of the smaller states whose representatives are not debarred from election to the Council of the League, or to the Governing Body of the Labour Convention.

Canada is asked to make way for all these states, except when effort and sacrifice are demanded. Then, but not until then, she is accorded full—and even prior—representation. Canada is to be in the first line of the battle, but not even in the back seat of the Council!"

The Prime Minister of Canada handed this, in memorandum, to Lloyd George. The Prime Minister of Britain had no intention of having a second Declaration of Independence on his hands. At once, he summoned Wilson and Clemenceau to the Rue Nitôt, and the same day the answer was devised, and dispatched to the rebel Canadians.

"The question having been raised as to the meanings of Article IV of the League of Nations Covenant, we have been requested by Sir Robert Borden to state whether we concur in his view, that upon the true construction of the first and second paragraphs of that Article, representatives of the self-governing Dominions of the British Empire may be selected or named as Members of the Council. We have no hesitation in expressing our entire concurrence in this view. . . ."

Dated at the Quai D'Orsay
the sixth day of May, 1919.

Signed   Georges Clemenceau.
Woodrow Wilson.
D. Lloyd George.

One final fight Borden put up for the sovereign independence of the British Dominions. By the time that the Peace Treaty was actually signed, 28 June, 1919, the Canadian Parliament had been prorogued. What about Canada ratifying the Treaty? Milner expressed the view that there was no more need for the Canadian Parliament to ratify this deed than there was for the British Parliament to do so. "Oh, yes, there is," said Borden. "Any Treaty which imposes any new burden on the people of Canada requires the approval of the Parliament of Canada."

So the Declaration of (Empire) Independence was delivered after all.

There now came a desperate last-minute rush to complete the Peace Treaty. Indeed, on 7 May, 1919, when it was due to be handed to the German plenipotentiaries, who had been waiting in Paris to receive it since 30 April, rather like apprehensive animals outside the veterinary surgeon's door, it had not left the printer's hands before noon. At three o'clock that afternoon they learned their fate. The Peace Terms were handed over in the Trianon Hotel, Paris.

Sullenly, the Germans received them, their chief plenipotentiary, Count Brockdorff-Rantzan, tactlessly sitting down while he read his protesting reply. (It was argued afterwards that he was too terrified to stand up.) But the only question now was: would they sign?

For a time, it seemed that they would refuse. "Those who sign this Treaty will sign the death sentence of millions of German men, women and children," said Brockdorff-Rantzan. He was no more accurate than Keynes.

But in that summer of 1919, he no doubt believed it. Many thought that neither he nor any other accredited envoy of Germany would put his name to this Treaty. And, then? Should the Allies march across the Rhine and occupy Berlin? The French were fully prepared for it. Not so Lloyd George. He told the French Foreign Minister, Tardieu, frankly:

"What I want is Peace, and England wants it, too. . . . I am prepared for any concession which will enable us to conclude. . . . If by our demands we cause the German Government to be upset we shall have nobody before us to sign. . . . They *must* sign, and with concessions, they *will* sign."

Lloyd George himself was ready to plead for a more generous peace. Six months had passed now since the Armistice, in some ways as destructive

and disastrous as the four years of war. It was time to wind up the story.
"Bring the Boys home!" roared Northcliffe, and for once Lloyd George
thoroughly agreed. He would have been prepared to concede Germany a better
Eastern frontier, to curtail the Allied occupation of the Rhineland, and to
press for the early admission of Germany to the League of Nations. The
British Empire Delegation prepared to confront Clemenceau for one last
battle.

They were spared it, by a last enemy surrender. When the German Chancellor refused to sign, and the German High Command pressed the delegates
from South Germany to support him, they flatly refused. If the Allied armies
march, they said, it will be our land which will be the first to be invaded.

Dr. Tom Jones, who was an important member of Lloyd George's
Secretariat, has remarked that this historic six-months' gathering at Versailles
"has been called a Conference which never met, and a Treaty which was a
myth. There is some basis for both statements."[1]

There is, in fact, no basis for either. From January until the end of June,
1919, the representatives of more than thirty States attended between them
more than 2,000 meetings, private and public, subsidiary and plenary, of 60
Commissions and Committees. Holding high debate were the Supreme War
Council, the Inter-Allied Conference, the Council of Ten, then the Council of
Four, and half a dozen plenary sessions of the entire Peace Conference
Delegations. The war was formally ended, and the Peace Terms signed by
both the victors and the vanquished. Disarmament and Reparations were
imposed—it is true that the extent of both were subsequently vastly varied
—the map of Europe and the Middle East redrawn, nearly a dozen New States
set up and scores of millions of people transferred from their old allegiance
to a new one.

There were some concessions made to awkward but unavoidable facts
(even President Wilson one day cried, "to hell with logic!"), and some more
to hard political pressure. In other cases, the conflict between the claims of
race and language, the desires of the populations concerned, and the requirements of strategy, economics and national politics produced results which
were neither admirable nor, as it turned out, even workable. Even so, only
about 2 per cent of the people of Europe were placed by the Treaty of Versailles
under a sovereignty which they disliked. Few Peace Treaties in history have
approached this record, and the Congress of Vienna, 1815, which had been
the last great "Settlement of Europe", does not come within comparison.

Lloyd George himself declared that the Treaty had two sets of critics: (i)

"Those who regard it as a cauldron of hatred, revenge and rapacity . . .
who regard President Wilson as the poor dupe of a couple of expert political
gunmen, who alternately bullied and cajoled, hoodwinked and flattered him,

[1] *Lloyd George.* By Thomas Jones, C.H.

until he ultimately signed on the dotted line," and (ii) "those who consider that the Treaty was not a stern enough sentence on the culprits . . . who depict Clemenceau and myself as the converts of an American revivalist. Clemenceau was not the material out of which penitent forms are made."

On 28 June, 1919, the anniversary of Sarajevo, the Peace Treaty was signed in the Hall of Mirrors of the Palace of Versailles.

CHAPTER XXVIII

THE CURSE OF CROMWELL

ON the same day, Mr. Eamon de Valera stepped ashore at New York. Within a few hours of his arrival, he was being hailed by the American people as the "President of the Irish Republic".

While Lloyd George was signing peace in Paris, war had been declared in Dublin. The Irish Republic, shot down in the flames of the Post Office during the Easter Rising of 1916, had soared up again from the ashes and proclaimed itself defiantly at the Mansion House during the first week of the New Year, 1919.

On 7 January, twenty-six of the seventy-three Sinn Fein Members who had been returned to the Imperial Parliament at the General Election of December, 1918, gathered in the Mansion House, Dublin, and took steps to convene Dail Eireann (the "illegal" Republican assembly) as the independent Constituent Assembly of the Irish Nation. Of the rest of the Sinn Fein M.P.s, three-quarters were behind prison bars in Ireland or England.

The first Dail met on 21 January, 1919. In the absence of Mr. De Valera, President of the Sinn Fein Convention (who was in an English jail), and of Mr. Arthur Griffith, Vice-President (who was in another one), Mr. Cathal Brugha, Chief of Staff of the Irish Republican Army, took the chair. The Clerks of the Day were appointed, and the roll was called. Thirty-six times the answer was made in Irish: "*Fe ghlas ag Gallaibh*" (Imprisoned by the foreign enemy).

In Irish and English then, the Declaration of Ireland's Independence was read, all the delegates and people standing, many cheering, some weeping. Proudly and passionately the proclamation rolled. It set forth Ireland's claim to be "by right a Free People", which had "for seven hundred years protested in arms against foreign usurpation". The Provisional Constitution of Dail Eireann was approved unanimously, and also the political programme it proposed to carry out. A final gesture of independence—the appointment of three "Delegates" to the forthcoming Peace Conference at Versailles, De Valera, Arthur Griffith and Count Plunkett—and then the first public session of the Dail was over. . . .

Next day, in private session, the Dail elected De Valera as *Priomh-Aire* (First Minister), an office which corresponded to that of the President of the United States of America, its bearer being both nominal Head of the State and its Chief Executive Officer. He had the power to choose the other three members of the Cabinet.

Meantime, the President himself was planning to get out of Lincoln Jail, where he had been locked up since the previous May. This he accomplished on the night of 3 February, 1919, by means of a key which was smuggled into him by a man called Michael Collins, then Director of Intelligence of the Irish Republican Army, and its real brain. De Valera made his way to Manchester, and there for several weeks the "President of the Irish Republic" vanished into the mists of the Irish underground in England. It was early April before he slipped secretly into Dublin in time to attend a series of private sessions of the Dail. The constitution of the Republican Government was then debated, and decided.

Three tasks awaited the revolutionaries to tackle at once: (i) set up the machinery of an independent, "illegal", native government; (ii) find the fuel to drive it, that is, finance; (iii) wreck the machinery of the existing, "legal", foreign government.

Within the next few weeks, Dail Eireann, meeting in almost continuous session, had set up an entire "Shadow Administration" in Ireland, with law courts, a Consular Service, Commissions of Inquiry into the industrial and natural resources of the country, and had floated a Republican Bond Loan.

Their war-like operations began with the "outlawing" of the Royal Irish Constabulary, that famous Crown-controlled Police Force which hitherto had been almost entirely recruited from the Irish people themselves, but were now branded by Sinn Fein as "the eyes and ears of the enemy". It went on to the brigading of all Sinn Fein armed units within the Irish Republican Army, and their effective training; and, finally, the organizing of sabotage, the shooting and terrorizing of all hostile forces, and the supply by secret channels of arms, ammunition, explosives, and vital military information to the forces of the I.R.A.

Nor did Dail Eireann neglect the Peace Front. It was obvious to men who had been trained in trouble that at Versailles England would have more of it with her allies than with her ex-enemies. The Irish Republic would do the uttermost to mix matters there for her still further.

Now, two of the three Irish "Delegates to the Peace Conference" being in prison at the time, it had been deemed wise to accredit Alderman Sean O'Kelly forthwith as "Envoy of the Irish Republic" in Paris to try to secure them admission to the Conference. Though he addressed a letter to Clemenceau himself, as President of the Peace Conference (and to every other Delegate, too), asking for international recognition of the Irish Republic and a public hearing for its representatives, Mr. O' Kelly received no reply.

The Sinn Fein Propaganda Department did not lose hope, as they had not lacked enterprise. They had other Irish irons in the fire of American politics. There were still enough Irish activists operating in America to stage, in February, 1919, a monster Irish Race Convention at Philadelphia claiming to represent millions of Irish-American citizens. They called upon President

Wilson to support "Ireland's right of self-determination" at the forthcoming Peace Conference and to secure for her delegates there "the same status and recognition which have been accorded to those of other small nations".

The Irish Race Convention also appointed (just to jog Woodrow Wilson's elbow) three delegates of their own to go to Paris and get an "Irish" hearing before the Peace Conference.

On 4 March, 1919, the eve of the American President's departure for Europe, the United States House of Representatives, by 261 votes to 41, passed a resolution expressing the earnest hope that the Peace Conference would "favourably consider the claims of Ireland to Self-Determination".

On 6 June, 1919, the United States Senate swelled the chorus. It was then late in the proceedings at the Peace Conference, but still time enough for action. The resolution before the House requested the American Peace Delegation at Versailles to seek for De Valera, Arthur Griffith and Count Plunkett a hearing before the Peace Conference so that they might "present the case for Ireland". It was passed with a single dissentient.

The Irish agitation was more successful in America than in Europe, a fact which did not escape De Valera's notice. When the three Irish Race Convention delegates from the United States arrived in Paris, they requested President Wilson to obtain from the British Government safe-conducts to the Peace Conference for De Valera, Arthur Griffiths and Count Plunkett. The President was too busy to see them, but Lloyd George readily provided the Irish-American delegates with passports to visit Ireland, hoping, as Birkenhead[1] explained in the House of Lords, "to help to allay the growing prejudice against England in the United States".

In Ireland, at a special session of Dail Eireann, on 9 May, De Valera welcomed the visitors. With true De Valera tact he saluted their visit as a sign that America was going to regard the official assurances of her President not "as mere scraps of paper".

It was not until after the resolution of the United States Senate supporting the claim of the Irish to be heard at Versailles that Wilson himself consented to receive the envoys. He then informed them that the Big Four (Clemenceau, Lloyd George, Orlando and himself), at that time sitting in almost continuous session as a Committee, had agreed that no small nation should appear before them without the unanimous consent of the whole Committee. One of the envoys reminded the President of his own declaration that every nation had a right to self-determination, "Words," he said, "which voiced the aspirations of countless millions of people".

Looking extremely embarrassed, Woodrow Wilson had to explain that the speaker had "touched on the great metaphysical tragedy of today". When he had given utterance to those words about self-determination, said the Presi-

[1] Sir F. E. Smith was created Baron Birkenhead, 1919, Earl of Birkenhead, 1922.

dent, he had not known that "nationalities existed which are coming to us every day". Ireland was the outstanding case of a small nationality.

"You do not know, and cannot appreciate the anxieties I have experienced as the result of these many millions of people having their hopes raised by what I have said," confessed the crestfallen President.[1]

If Ireland was an embarrassment to Woodrow Wilson in dealing with England, Ireland was also a delicate subject for Lloyd George to handle in dealing with the United States. Even in 1919, America held the key to European credit, and the successful launching of the League of Nations depended largely on American goodwill. (When America refused to enter, the League of Nations was already doomed to impotence and ultimate death.) Throughout the next three years of Anglo-Irish troubles, the influence of America upon the event would be profound.

De Valera's instinct was right when, having failed to steal the show at Versailles, he insisted on staging a one-man act in the United States. As he had been born in New York, the son of a Spanish immigrant father and an Irish immigrant mother, a reporter asked him on arrival if he were not an American citizen? He got the prompt answer: "When I became a soldier of the Irish Republic I became a citizen of that Republic."

De Valera then went forward to terrific public receptions, such as only Americans can give. In New York, Boston, Chicago, and elsewhere the legend of Easter, 1916, ran ahead of him, "the last soldier to lay down arms in the Dublin Rising".

At State Legislatures, City Halls, baseball parks, with public processions, official banquets, civic freedoms, with meetings of Women's Conventions, Rotary Clubs, Trade Union leaders and Red Indian tribal chieftains, with salutes of twenty-one guns and escorts of airplanes, De Valera did a superb job of putting Ireland on the world map of American politics.

Now, by midsummer, 1919, war scorched the Irish earth again. But this war did not blaze; it burned like one of those sinister, almost secret fires that creep beneath the dead leaves of a forest and only spasmodically burst into flame. For this war was Civil War, most evil of all, and not even open civil war. For the most part it was not even guerilla civil war, where pitched battle takes place between rival flying columns, or between the attackers and the garrisons of military posts. The Irish Civil War was a murder duel in the dark between two Secret Services.

The Troubles, as they were known, began in January, 1919, with the ambush outside Dublin by the I.R.A. of a quarry cart containing gelignite and escorted by two policemen. They were shot dead. Soon it was shooting in the streets of Dublin, on the quays of Cork, in some lonely house amid the hills of Kerry. The crackle of the gunmen's fire ran round the Green Island,

[1] Evidence of Frank P. Walsh: Hearing on the Peace Treaty, 30 August, 1919.

and dyed it with blood. Policemen were murdered, magistrates were murdered and many were the bodies found dead with the placard pinned on them:

EXECUTED BY ORDER OF THE I.R.A.
SPIES AND INFORMERS
BEWARE!

The "execution" had probably been carried out by a special G.H.Q. unit of the Irish Republican Army, known as "The Squad". They operated on the information supplied by the secret counter-spy organization created by Michael Collins to fight the activities of those ubiquitous plain-clothes agents known as the G Division of the Dublin Metropolitan Police.

Michael Collins was Minister of Finance in President De Valera's Irish Republican Cabinet. He was also (and much more actively) Director of I.R.A. Organization and Intelligence.

A handsome, broad-shouldered, six-foot of Irish manhood, possessed of a resolute will and a darting, daring spirit, Collins was the type that every Resistance movement longs for, and is lucky when it gets one. Born in West Cork not thirty years before, he had gone to London as a lad to work as a clerk in the post office. He had graduated as far as the lower reaches of the Guaranty Trust Company when the first rumblings of the Easter Rising reached him in some Irish cellar in the East End.

Michael Collins made off for Ireland, and arrived in time to join the rebel band who seized the Post Office. At the end of that week, he had walked out grimly from the smoking ruins behind Padraic Pearse, the first President of the Irish Republic and the commander of the little garrison which had just surrendered. Padraic Pearse was on his way to the execution wall, and for all he knew so was young Collins. One who stood there in the blazing street recalls him looking back at the bullet-riddled flag-pole from which the Irish tricolour still drooped.

"The flag is still up, anyway," he said, defiantly.

He was shipped back to jail in England, and subsequently sent to Frongoch internment camp, to be released at Christmas, 1916. Three years later, the British Government were offering £10,000 for Michael Collins, alive or dead.

By then, Collins had become a myth. Scores of stories were handed round about him and his mad adventures and miraculous escapes. More than once, when the police or troops were ransacking a building for the Man Behind the Gunmen, Michael Collins got away by joining in the search himself. Yet he was a figure once seen, never forgotten, this "Big Fellow" as he was known, and loved to be known. He behaved exactly as a conspirator is traditionally supposed not to behave. He wore no disguise, went to his office openly and regularly, kept business-like files and when, after his long day's work was done (twelve to fifteen hours was his strength), he went to a tavern to relax and enjoy himself, Collins would carouse, sing, swear and wrestle on the floor with the strongest of his companions. But if his heart was fire, his brain was ice; and if he organized killing, Michael Collins did not rejoice in it.

Typical both of his capacity and his audacity was Collins's organization of the supply of tools for the killing. He did this with his "Irish Mail". This was the tunnel whereby arms and ammunition, procured in England and Germany, passed into Ireland. Sometimes, the rifles and revolvers were bought, sometimes they were raided from armouries. The gelignite was stolen from the Welsh coalfield, or the Midland engineering shops. It would arrive in Ireland in baskets marked "CHINA. FRAGILE". Then Collins would ride down to Kingstown Harbour on his bicycle and oversee the cargo unloaded and piled on to lorries, to be driven openly into Dublin. So it went on for months under the eyes of the police and military, for the Customs Service was already riddled with I.R.A. agents.

The pace quickened.

In March, 1919, more than twenty Sinn Fein prisoners escaped over the wall of Mountjoy Jail, Dublin, in broad daylight.

In August, police barracks all over Southern Ireland were attacked, and many were captured, with their coveted military stores.

In September, a party of British soldiers were ambushed in Fermoy on their way to church, and one of them was killed.

Next morning, about 200 armed soldiers stormed into the town and sacked the shops in the main street. The Military Authorities turned their heads the other way.

Two days later, the British Government, through its Executive at Dublin Castle, declared Dail Eireann a dangerous association and proscribed it. The effect of this suppression was to start a fresh wave of anti-British feeling in the United States; in Ireland, merely to drive the Republican movement still more underground, where it operated more dangerously.

By autumn, the British Army of Occupation in Ireland numbered 43,000 troops, and was costing England nearly £11,000,000 a year. The Royal Irish Constabulary strength was nearly 10,000 men. Already, on Midsummer's Day, the Irish Bishops, meeting at Maynooth, had denounced this state of affairs as "the rule of the sword, utterly unsuited to a civilized nation".

To which Lloyd George, immersed in the woes of the Peace settlement of Europe and, frankly, neither yet closely informed nor immediately interested in Irish affairs, had rather impatiently replied that he had tried to apply the principle of self-determination to Ireland, but without success.[1] He was still waiting for Irishmen to agree among themselves.

Meantime, the troops who had sacked Fermoy were posted to Cork, where, on 10 November, they looted the chief shops there. Many Irish people believed that Dublin Castle was seeking to provoke another Rising, which would provide the pretext for widespread executions.

[1] He was referring to the ill-fated Convention of 1917.

Public opinion in England was deeply stirred. Liberal Party feeling was expressed by Lloyd George's old cabinet colleague, Sir Herbert Samuel, who said at St. Albans on 8 December, that if what was now going on in Ireland had been going on in the Austrian Empire all England would be ringing with denunciation of the Tyranny of the Hapsburgs.

The Times Special Correspondent in Ireland wrote, 13 December:

> "The citadel of Sinn Fein is in the minds of the young. The prospect of dying for Ireland haunts the dreams of thousands of youths today. . . . You can neither terrify nor bribe Sinn Fein."

Michael Collins was busy planning a visit to London, to see President Wilson there in person—and (according to his biographer) perhaps kidnap him! He had also arranged to have the Viceroy of Ireland, Field-Marshal Lord French, ambushed at Ashdown by "The Squad". This was duly done on 19 December, but Lord French's escort were too strong for the would-be killers, and drove them off after a brief encounter on the roadside, shooting one of them dead.

Three days later, Lloyd George himself introduced into the House of Commons a "Bill for the Better Government of Ireland". It proposed to set up separate Parliaments for the twenty-six Southern Counties and the six North-eastern Counties, with authority to create a joint "Council of Ireland" to deal with certain subjects. Ireland was still to be represented in the Imperial Parliament, though by a reduced number of Members, and considerable powers were reserved. In British politics, this Bill recorded a remarkable compromise, accepted by Tory Unionists who had bitterly opposed Irish Home Rule before the war. But for Irish Nationalists, it simply meant a concession that had come too late. When Lloyd George, with one eye on America, warned that "any attempt at secession will be fought with the same determination, with the same resource, with the same resolve as the Northern States of America put into the fight against the Southern States", the Irish tartly retorted that Lincoln had fought to abolish slavery, not to maintain it.

In the New Year, Ireland spoke. Polling for the Municipal and Urban District Councils took place on 15 January, 1920, and everywhere the issue of "The Republic—Or Not?" was squarely put to the voters.

Out of 206 Councils elected throughout Ireland, 172 were returned with a majority of Republicans. Of the twelve cities and boroughs of Ireland, eleven declared for the Republic, the Unionists holding only Belfast. Also in Ulster, two of the six counties, Fermanagh and Tyrone, voted in a majority for Sinn Fein. In Londonderry, the "maiden city" of the Covenanters, a Catholic Nationalist became Mayor.

Raids, arrests and shootings were by now the order of the day, and they were everywhere increasing. In several Southern Counties martial law was proclaimed, and in Dublin a curfew was imposed between midnight and 5 a.m.

On the night of 19 March, following the shooting of a policeman that afternoon near Cork, intruders with blackened faces broke into the house of Thomas MacCurtain, the Lord Mayor of Cork, and shot him dead.

A coroner's jury found that he had been murdered by the Royal Irish Constabulary "officially directed by the British Government", and they returned a verdict of "Wilful murder" against the Prime Minister, Lloyd George; the Viceroy, Lord French; and the Chief Secretary for Ireland, Ian Macpherson. It is necessary to add, that besides being Lord Mayor of Cork, Thomas MacCurtain was also Commandant of the Cork Brigade of the I.R.A. His place as Lord Mayor was immediately filled by his Second-in-Command of the brigade, Terence MacSwiney.

In London, Lloyd George was pressing on with his Bill for the Better Government of Ireland. It was known in Ireland itself by a briefer title, "The Partition Bill". And, indeed, this accurately defined it, with its two separate and subordinate Parliaments and its All-Ireland Council based on the equal representation of the Six Counties and the Twenty-six. For Lloyd George had made up his mind that the solution of the Irish Question lay in dividing the country, and in keeping both parts within the British Empire as far as external matters were concerned, however much internal independence of British authority was conceded.

From this position Lloyd George never really budged, although throughout these difficult post-war years he sometimes allowed other folks to suppose he had, a trick he frequently performed. He laid it down now that the Imperial Parliament reserved its control over all things concerning the Crown, Peace and War, Foreign Relations, the Armed Forces, Customs and Excise, Trade outside Ireland, Merchant Shipping and Navigation. The Oath of Allegiance was to be that in use in the Dominion Parliaments.

If, within fourteen days of the date fixed for the opening of either Parliament, the majority of the Members elected to it had not taken the Oath, that Parliament would be dissolved and the part of Ireland it represented would be administered as a Crown Colony by the Lord Lieutenant.

The Partitition Bill continued its much-debated passage through Parliament throughout the greater part of 1920. The American Presidential Election was going on, and some critics of the British Government said that the Parliamentary proceedings were being adroitly stage-managed to create among the American electorate the impression that a mighty effort was being made to settle the ancient Anglo-Irish feud. Lloyd George certainly still needed all the co-operation he could get from the United States in dealing with our other post-war allies. Meantime, in Ireland the situation was every day deteriorating.

The Sinn Fein policy of treating the Irish policemen as national blacklegs was paying off handsomely. Already, several hundreds had resigned from the

R.I.C., by far the greatest number being among the younger men. It was found necessary to reinforce the R.I.C. with a new kind of recruit.

These were British ex-servicemen, and not of the best type. They were, indeed, required to do work to which neither the British Army nor the R.I.C. were accustomed, and they were paid ten shillings a day and "all found" to do it. When the first company of them arrived in Limerick in March, 1920, police uniforms being insufficient to equip them all, they had been fitted out with either black or khaki tunics and trousers and black caps and belts. They were promptly given the nickname of "Black-and-Tans", after a famous local pack of hounds. It was not long before they had made it one of terror.

In April, the Chief Secretary for Ireland, Ian Macpherson, resigned, and his place was filled by Sir Hamar Greenwood.[1] Macpherson's nerve had gone; he lived in continual terror of assassination (and, frankly, there was a large likelihood of it). Of very different stuff was the man who succeeded him. A Canadian who had started life as a Temperance lecturer in England, then a militiaman and a barker in a travelling show before he became a lawyer, Greenwood was a man of most determined character who did not know what nerves meant. Lloyd George believed that he was the right man for a hard job. He set to work resolutely, in his own words, to "get the murder gang (the I.R.A.) on the run".

It was a formidable task. If the Crown Forces commanded superior resources of manpower, armaments and money, the I.R.A. possessed the intimate knowledge of their own countryside and the sympathy and support of the people.

Sheltered in their cottages, or hidden in dug-outs in the hills, these guerillas operated in small, flying columns of fifteen to thirty men. They moved by unfrequented paths and under the cloak of darkness, wearing soft hats and trench-coats, suddenly appearing to attack a police barracks, or opening fire on a military convoy from an ambush. They blew up bridges, tore up railway-tracks and cut telephone lines. They burned barracks and also, in counter-reprisal for the reprisals of the troops and Black-and-Tans for their own sabotage, the country houses of Unionist supporters of the British Government. And, of course, they murdered both armed and unarmed members of the Crown Forces with merciless and mechanized regularity.

Their own lines of communication the I.R.A. maintained with the aid of the women and girls of *Cumann nam Ban* (League of Women), who travelled all over the land on secret errands and also nursed the wounded I.R.A. volunteers in makeshift hospitals in the slums of the cities and in cottages among the hills.

By midsummer, 1920, more than three hundred police-stations had been evacuated by the R.I.C., who were almost everywhere withdrawing to the towns, where they concentrated in larger barracks which they fortified with

[1] Under-Secretary for Home Affairs, 1919–20, later Viscount Greenwood.

barbed wire and sandbags and sited with machine-guns. The *Irish Times* declared on 1 May: "The King's Government has virtually ceased to exist south of the Boyne and west of the Shannon."

The Irish Resistance was being carried on, not only by the "men in the trench-coats" on the run, but by those in convict garb in the jail. They demanded prisoner-of-war treatment or release, and when they got neither sixty men locked up in Mountjoy Jail went on hunger-strike. Night and day, vast crowds gathered outside the gates reciting the Rosary and singing Fenian songs for the prisoners to hear. British troops, in full war equipment stood to arms within the walls and at strategic points surrounding them. Royal Air Force planes circled overhead.

After a week, the Irish Labour Party and Trades Union Congress called a General Strike in support of the hunger-strikers. At the end of the third day of it, the Government gave way and the prisoners were released.

The war was getting into full stride, and going well for the rebels. Lord French told the *Daily Express*: "The best brains in Ireland are behind the Sinn Fein movement. . . . They have organized an army numbering 100,000 men. They are properly organized in regiments and brigades, led by disciplined officers. . . ."

This estimate was far too high. It is probable that the I.R.A. did not number 10,000 in the spring of 1920, and they were being rapidly reduced by capture, casualties and shortage of available arms. Michael Collins afterwards set his strength at 3,000 fighting men.

They included certain citizens of debatable character, not only from the shadowland of the Irish cities but from London, Liverpool, Glasgow and perhaps, as some said, from Chicago, too. The official Sinn Fein doctrine declared that any "traitor" or "spy" was liable to execution, that is, to be shot at sight (a "traitor" was any Irishman, whether policeman or civilian, who actively assisted the Crown Forces; a "spy" was any agent, Irish or English, who gathered and passed on information likely to be of use to the Crown). While these were the rules of the game, according to the I.R.A., it was inevitable that personal, not to say criminal, interests would get mixed up in the underground struggle. But on the general level the quality of the I.R.A. killers remained remarkably high, as some of the leading British officers who fought against them have testified.

One of these was General Sir Nevil Macready, who had been appointed C.-in-C. in Ireland in March, 1920, and who loathed them as assassins of soldiers; Macready bore witness to "the strict sobriety among all men working for Sinn Fein".[1]

The same could not have been said, with truth or knowledge, about the Black-and-Tans. Still less so about the newest force arrived in Ireland to "get the murder gang on the run". These were the Auxiliaries, or Cadets, another

[1] *Annals of an Active Life.* By General Sir Nevil Macready.

supplementary body to the ever-diminishing R.I.C. The Auxiliaries were supposed to be recruited from ex-officers of the war-time armies, selected, Churchill said, "for intelligence, their characters and their records in the war".

If so, the Orderly Office was decidedly in need of a fresh staff. For the Auxiliaries, who wore dark blue uniforms and Glengarry caps, were paid double the wages of the Black-and-Tans, elected their own officers and were not amenable to trial by the civil courts, were a hard-bitten company. Nobody ever doubted their courage and, as Michael Collins's biographer has admitted:

> "In a curious way, the Irish, who like a good fighter, respected them. Time and again, the Irish Volunteers testified to their bravery, but too often the mangled corpse of a woman or an old man did as much for their savagery."[1]

Churchill defended them by saying that, in grappling with murder, they "developed within themselves very strong counter-terrorist activity". He claimed that they acted with the same freedom as the Chicago police permitted themselves in dealing with armed gangs. The only real defence for such conduct, he argued, was the kind of attack to which it was a reply.

But the most serious charge of all against the conduct of this early kind of SS. Guard (the Auxiliary Division numbered 7,000 men) was that it simply was not succeeding in its purpose.

Brigadier-General Frank Crozier, who was appointed in July, 1920, to command the Auxiliaries, has reported how he found them. According to his account, the British Army in Ireland was well behaved, but the R.I.C., which these special units were reinforcing, was demoralized. They were carrying out irregular reprisals (which they attributed to Sinn Fein). They were being employed, wrote Crozier, "to murder, rob, loot and burn up the innocent, because they could not catch the few guilty on the run".[2]

They were not the only licensed hooligans on the side of "Law and Order".

"I am sick of words without action," cried Carson, addressing a great gathering in the capital of Ulster, on Orange Day, 12 July, 1920.

A week later, armed mobs rushed upon the Roman Catholic quarter of Belfast, shooting, looting and burning. During four days and nights, fighting continued and nearly a score of people were killed. The rioting spread throughout Ulster, and before it was ended as many more people had been killed and about 200 badly mauled.

In Dublin, the Dail was in secret session (forty-six deputies only were available, almost all of them being on the run). In the absence of De Valera, still in the United States, Arthur Griffith presided. He reported that the "Shadow" Republican Government was rapidly becoming the real one.

[1] *The Big Fellow: A Life of Michael Collins.* By Frank O'Connor.
[2] *Ireland for Ever.* By Brig.-Gen. Frank Crozier.

The Crown Courts were practically deserted, and even the Unionists of Southern Ireland were accepting the judgments of the Republican Courts. The rebel Revenue, too, was soaring. Michael Collins, in his civilian capacity as Minister of Finance, proposed now to close subscriptions for the Internal Loan and to institute a regular system of income-tax. When a Revolution can collect income-tax it has come to stay.

What were the British Government doing about these things? Where was the Prime Minister, Lloyd George, and what was he up to? Immersed, still, in affairs abroad and industrial disputes at home, Lloyd George had entrusted Ireland almost entirely to his ministerial colleagues and military advisers, Ian Macpherson (Chief Secretary for Ireland until April, 1920), Hamar Greenwood (his successor in that office), Lord French (Viceroy of Ireland), Field-Marshal Wilson (Chief of Imperial General Staff) and General Macready (Commander-in-Chief in Ireland).

Field-Marshal Wilson's own policy, by the way, was strongly opposed to indiscriminate reprisals by the Crown Forces in Ireland, which he feared would break down military discipline; he preferred, "shooting by roster", that is, to compile a careful list of the principal opponents of British rule, and then execute them in turn.

As late as June, 1920, however, Lloyd George held to his belief that order could be restored in Ireland, and the "murder gang" not only got on the run but put behind prison bars by police action alone. What was the alternative, he asked, to "official" reprisal and the execution of hostages? It could only be to surrender to murder, and let Sinn Fein have its Republic.

Lloyd George would never have been allowed to do this, even if he had wished. He was himself the prisoner of at least three forces in holding on to Ireland as an integral part of the British Empire.

There was Ulster, which would not have submitted to the South—and never has done so to this day. There was the Tory Party, which made up the principal part of his Coalition Government majority. And there was the broad mass of British public opinion, which would not have moved beyond the grant of Home Rule to Ireland, with adequate safeguards that she would remain within the British Empire. This, indeed, was Lloyd George's own purpose and policy.

Consistent with this attitude was his next move. Though the Prime Minister was not prepared to proclaim the Twenty-Six Counties as a war zone and to hand over their entire administration to the British Army (his Bill for the Better Government of Ireland was even now on its way through Parliament), in August, 1920, the Royal Assent was given to another measure, the Restoration of Order in Ireland Act.

It conferred emergency powers upon the Military Command. They could arrest and imprison, without trial or even charge and for an indefinite time, anyone suspected of dealing with Sinn Fein. Prisoners could be tried by court martial; potential witnesses could be held in custody and heavily fined, or jailed for six months for failure to produce the evidence; Military Courts of Inquiry could be substituted for Coroners' Inquests.

It was under this code that, three days later, the new Lord Mayor of Cork, Terence MacSwiney, who had followed the murdered Thomas MacCurtain into that office, was arrested while presiding over an I.R.A. meeting at the City Hall. He was court martialled on a charge of being in possession of treasonable documents.

Terence MacSwiney, teacher, poet, scholar, had dedicated himself when in his inaugural speech as Lord Mayor he had declared that, on the Irish side, this was a contest not of vengeance but of endurance. It was not those who could inflict the most, but those who could bear the most who would conquer. "Those whose faith is strong will endure to the end in triumph."

Here was one who would endure to the end. He refused to plead, and in protest against the arrest of public representatives throughout the country, declared that he would refuse food while in jail. On the third day of his hunger strike the Lord Mayor of Cork was put aboard a British warship, and deported to London. He was lodged in Brixton Jail.

Now thick and fast came raid and reprisal, murder and counter-murder. The shooting of British police and army officers in Ulster at the end of August provoked another outbreak against the Roman Catholic minority there which lasted fourteen days, and accounted for the lives of three times as many men and women. In the towns and country-side of the South, unarmed policemen on their beat were sniped at and ambushed night and day, so that they took to carrying hostages with them in their lorries and drove around with rifles at the "ready". Also, by this time, the policy of "hitting back and harder" was openly, though still unofficially, the working rule.

At the little town of Balbriggan one night in September, 1920, a Black-and-Tan was shot dead and another one wounded after a brawl in an inn. Later, lorry-loads of uniformed men arrived from the nearby Training Camp. They ranged the darkened streets, firing through the windows, smashing in the doors, setting fire to the furniture of the shops and houses, dragging out and beating-up the inhabitants, some of whom they bayoneted. Many families fled to the fields, and hid in ditches.

Lloyd George himself admitted that the Crown Forces sometimes got out of hand, when he addressed his constituents at Caernarvon on 9 October, 1920. During the last year, he said, 283 policemen had been shot in Ireland, and 109 killed. Nearly a hundred soldiers had been shot. Sixty-seven courthouses had been burned down. The police had endured this violence with discipline and restraint for two or three years. There was no doubt that "at last their patience has given way, and there has been some severe hitting back".

Lloyd George claimed that there had been no protest from Sinn Fein.

They said it was a state of war, he said. That the Police were a foreign garrison, and that they were entitled to shoot them. Very well, if it was a war, it was a war on both sides! You could not have a one-sided war! But, really, it was not war, it was murder. Policemen and soldiers were being shot in the back by gunmen who wore no uniform.

"Let us be fair to these gallant men who are doing their duty in Ireland," cried Lloyd George. He said that when prisoners attempted to escape and refused to halt, then undoubtedly the police fired on them. He wanted only peace himself, and believed that the vast majority of the Irish people sought it too. But a small gang of assassins were dominating the country and making it impossible for reasonable men to come together and agree on the best way of governing their country.

Lloyd George claimed that he had been a Home Ruler all his life, but the idea of complete Home Rule for Ireland was ridiculous. If they decided to have Conscription there, why, you would have to have it here! And what about submarines? And mines? Our ports in Ireland were the sea gateway of Great Britain. Complete Home Rule? Was there ever such lunacy proposed by anybody! (Asquith had just proposed it.)

On 25 October, 1920, Terence MacSwiney died in Brixton Jail. It was the seventy-fourth day of his hunger-strike. For weeks past, the world had watched his self-imposed ordeal with compassion and respect. In silence, vast crowds lined the streets in London as his coffin passed on its way to Ireland. Bishops in their vestments and a Guard of Honour of I.R.A. volunteers in their forbidden uniform followed the bier, draped with the flag of the Republic.

The event made the most tremendous effect upon public opinion in Britain. It was as though a curtain had suddenly been drawn aside upon a scene of horror. A great wave of generous sympathy and pity swept over the English people, and the Government was much condemned.

This mood might have been very different if it had been known that Cathal Brugha, the Sinn Fein Minister of Defence, was now planning to extend terrorist counter-reprisal to England, where secret Irish branches existed in all the great seaports.

Docks, railways, bridges, power-houses, reservoirs and warehouses were listed to be blown up—and, in fact, one night in November a dozen warehouses roared up in flames in Liverpool alone. More would have been burned if the plans had not been captured in Dublin, which enabled the police to arrest over a hundred suspected persons in England. It is said that Cathal Brugha also proposed to bomb and machine-gun civilian crowds in cinemas and theatres over here, but was overruled in the Irish Cabinet.

On 9 November, 1920, at the Lord Mayor's Banquet in London, Lloyd George reiterated his charge that the cause of the Troubles in Ireland was merely a murder gang, and claimed that this gang was about to meet its doom.

"There," said Lloyd George, "we have witnessed a spectacle of organized assassination, of the most cowardly character. . . . But, at last, unless I am mistaken, by the steps we have taken we have murder by the throat."

The Prime Minister asked the British people not to credit the slanders being uttered against brave men who, at the peril of their lives, were tracking down murder in the dark. There would be no real peace in Ireland until this conspiracy was scattered.

He spoke of "men in civilian clothes, armed with murderous weapons", and described how they were being summarily dealt with. He repeated that he himself sought conciliation, and had appealed to anyone who could "speak for Ireland" to come and discuss proposals with him. There had been no response, because of intimidation.

Lloyd George ended with a fresh appeal. We were offering Ireland not subjection but equality, not servitude but partnership, "a partnership in the greatest Empire in the world, in the greatest day of its glory".

On Armistice Day, 1920, the Bill for the Better Government of Ireland passed its Third Reading in the House of Commons. No Irish vote, either from North or South, was cast for it.

Now came Bloody Sunday.

Seventeen Irishmen had been killed in October in circumstances which made Michael Collins believe that Field-Marshal Wilson's policy of "shooting by roster" had been officially adopted. He now authorized reprisal "execution" of fourteen British officers in their beds at their Dublin billets on the morning of Sunday, 21 November, 1920.

It was a horrible deed, some of the officers being shot before the eyes of their wives, even children, whose pitiable pleading was contemptuously ignored. With cold horror, the world read next morning of that mass-murder as the sun broke through the windows and the church bells rang.

Meantime, the same Sunday, a bloody reprisal was organized. At the Dublin *v.* Tipperary football match that afternoon in Croke Park, Dublin, troops drove up in lorries and surrounded the stadium, intending to search for arms. Suddenly, the Black-and-Tans arrived in force. Over the fences, they opened fire on the densely-packed crowd of spectators. They killed a dozen people, wounded five times as many more. Hundreds of others were injured in the stampede.

Next, suddenly, Cork was back in the news. On the night of 11 December, shortly after 9 p.m., Auxiliaries and Black-and-Tans appeared on the streets, and at the revolver point, drove people home before the official curfew began. There had been an ambush of British troops outside the city earlier in the day, and now the apprehensions of the citizens were thoroughly aroused. Soon, fires broke out and shop after shop burst into flames. Then, beyond the river, the City Hall itself suddenly blazed up. There could be no doubt that it was deliberate arson. Though only police and troops were allowed on the streets, the Fire Brigade were shot at and their water-hoses slashed. It was estimated by the British insurance companies (who refused to pay out for "malicious injuries") that the damage done amounted to about £3,000,000's worth. A Military Inquiry was held, from which the Press were excluded. Black-and-Tans marched through the streets of Dublin with burnt corks stuck in their caps.

Yet across the waste of desolation that lay between the rival camps signals were now passing which could mean Peace.

This had begun with a letter written to *The Times* on 6 October, 1920, by a Tory M.P., Brigadier-General Cockerill, urging a truce and a conference "unhampered by preliminary conditions" between representatives of the British Government and of Dail Eireann. Then Arthur Griffith took part in certain secret and strictly unofficial exchanges with the Foreign Office which followed, but which came to an end when he and Professor Eoin MacNeill were arrested towards the end of November.

On 10 December, 1920, Lloyd George himself tried again. Speaking in the House of Commons, he declared his confidence that the great majority of the people of Ireland were anxious for peace and for a fair settlement. He reiterated his own earnest wish to hold open every channel whereby those in Ireland who desired such a settlement with Britain could find expression. The British Government, therefore, were prepared to meet certain members of the Dail, to whom they would offer safe-conduct. At the same time, the British Government were also regretfully convinced that the Party—or the faction —which "controls the organization of murder and outrage in Ireland", was not yet ready to talk peace on the only basis which could be contemplated, a basis "consistent with the unbroken unity of the United Kingdom". They were still talking like an independent belligerent Power.

Lloyd George then firmly laid down the lines of the "dual policy" which his Government proposed to follow:

I. To seek peace unremittingly with those who genuinely desired it.
II. To intensify their campaign against that small but desperate minority whose crimes would bring peace neither to Ireland nor to Britain. The British Government would, therefore, proclaim Martial Law with its death penalties over large areas, and make the surrender of all arms by a certain date compulsory.
III. It should be clearly understood that in any negotiations as to the future government of Ireland the following points are agreed: The Six Counties must have separate treatment; neither Ireland nor any part of it may secede from the United Kingdom; naval and military safeguards for the security of Great Britain must be given.

The same day Lord French, as Viceroy, proclaimed martial law in Cork, Kerry, Tipperary and Limerick and executions under the new ordinance began. They were at once avenged by ambush and assassination of the Crown

Forces. In the first three months of 1921, casualties in Ireland were estimated thus:

> Crown Forces: killed 174, wounded 288.
> I.R.A. and civilians: killed 317, wounded 285.

Now, in Ireland, curfew stretched from dark till dawn and the only sounds at night were the rumble of military lorries, the shouted challenges, the smashing-in of doors, shots, groans. . . . The Lord Mayor of Limerick was murdered at midnight in his own house; in County Cork a night battle between several hundred men lasted for hours to the wild music of Irish pipes.

In England, locally organized branches of the I.R.A. were starting fires in the cities and a window-smashing campaign in the capital itself. Nevertheless, public opinion was steadily growing against the Government policy in Ireland, and powerful newspapers like *The Times*, as well as the Liberal *Manchester Guardian*, *Westminster Gazette* and *Daily News*, tirelessly attacked it. So did Asquith in the House of Commons. He was backed from the Labour benches and from the Tory benches by Oswald Mosley, Lord Robert Cecil and Lord Hugh Cecil. It was Lord Hugh who gibed of the alternate Ministerial denials of Government outrages and claims that order was being restored in Ireland: "There is no such thing as reprisals, but they have done a great deal of good."

In the House of Lords, the Archbishop of Canterbury rose to make an impressive protest, and both the Roman Catholic and Nonconformist Church leaders subsequently spoke out publicly of the anxiety throughout the Empire. King George V was disquieted by the contradictory reports which he received from the Viceroy, Lord French, who considered the situation "shocking and lamentable", and the Chief Secretary, Sir Hamar Greenwood, who assured him that "the Republican movement is crumbling. . . ." The King did not like the policy of reprisals, and he liked still less the character of the Special Forces who were carrying them out.

In May, 1921, Lord Stamfordham wrote to Greenwood:

> "The King does ask himself, and he asks you, if this policy of reprisals is to be continued and, if so, where will it lead Ireland and us all? It seems to His Majesty that in punishing the guilty we are inflicting punishment no less severe upon the innocent."[1]

Within the Cabinet, considerable and conflicting stresses had developed. There were those who took the view that Field-Marshal Wilson was always urging in his capacity as C.I.G.S. This was to confiscate all motor-cars, bicycles and horses, making the rebels immobile, close every post office and bank, then "sweep up".

Churchill, who, as Secretary of State for War, would be the Minister

[1] Harold Nicolson: *King George V*, p. 347.

responsible for this new "drive" policy, has told us in his book, *The Aftermath*, what this would have involved. A hundred thousand new special troops and police; thousands of armoured cars; the building of cordons of blockhouses, linked with barbed wire, throughout Southern Ireland; the "rummaging" and questioning of the entire civil population. He thought himself that it could be done, and that the existing Parliament would have been ready to uphold the Government in doing it. Churchill was opposed to any attempt at treating with rebels. They must surrender, or be destroyed.

But once Sinn Fein, which he believed to be irreconcilable, had been removed from the scene, then Churchill was in favour of offering the people of Southern Ireland the widest possible measure of self-government within the British Empire.

Thus, it was in method rather than in purpose that at this period he differed from the Prime Minister. Lloyd George's own strong combative instinct certainly inclined him, too, to fight the thing out. (His own life was, of course, at hazard every hour.) But there had now emerged within the Cabinet a party who were not prepared to carry to the limit a policy of ruthless repression in Ireland. To them—and they included some powerful Tory members—the "dual policy" proposed by Lloyd George made a strong appeal.

Their cause was now aided by an unexpected memorandum from General Macready, C.-in-C. in Ireland, to say that unless the present state of affairs in Ireland were ended by October next, then steps must be taken "to relieve practically the whole of the troops, together with the great majority of the commanders and their staff".

For some time past, curious things had been going on. There had been the very private visit of Lord Derby to Dublin towards the end of April, 1921, where in horn-rimmed spectacles and known as "Mr. Edwards" he had put up at the Shelburne Hotel. During this slightly comic-opera interlude, Derby had seen De Valera, and given him to understand that the British Government might be ready to offer something "more generous" than the status provided by the Government of Ireland Act—something in the form of say, a limited form of Dominion Home Rule. Did De Valera insist on the principle of complete independence being first conceded? De Valera, after five days' mediation, replied by putting a question to the Prime Minister:

"Will he not consent to meet me or any representative of the Government of Ireland unless the principle of complete independence be first surrendered by us?"

It was still unanswered when in May, at the request of Lloyd George, Sir James Craig, the Prime Minister of Northern Ireland, also met De Valera. He was led, under the guidance of two I.R.A. men, by devious routes, to a secret rendezvous in the hills outside Dublin, a courageous venture in keeping with the character of Craig. The meeting, however, resolved itself into a four-hour recital of Ireland's woes by De Valera before Craig broke it off (with four centuries still to go).

On 3 May, 1921, the Government of Ireland Act came into force at last, and a fortnight later the first Catholic Viceroy of Ireland, Lord Fitzalan, succeeded Lord French in that office. It had been hoped that this appointment would be accepted as a conciliatory gesture. It was not. "We would as soon have a Catholic hangman" was the comment attributed to Cardinal Logue. What was this talk of "goodwill" in Ireland? At the end of the month came the Irish General Elections, North and South.

In the North, the Unionists secured 40 seats out of the 52, the rest going to the Nationalists or Republicans. Among those elected for Ulster constituencies were the Sinn Fein leaders, De Valera, Michael Collins and Arthur Griffith. No elections were contested in the South, but Sinn Fein made full use of the machinery set up by the Act in order to elect the second Dail Eireann. Of 128 seats, 124 were filled by Republicans and the remaining four were Unionists returned by Trinity College.

The Irish General Elections were preceded in the South by an audacious I.R.A. raid on Dublin Customs House, which they seized and burned to the ground, destroying all the files of the Government taxation departments and the records of local administration. In the North, the Elections were followed by bloody riots in which a score more people were killed.

But under the waves of terror and counter-terror the secret lines were still operating.

There was Sir Alfred Cope, then Assistant Under-Secretary for Ireland, once a detective in the Customs Service and with none of his old skill or contacts forgotten now that he was an official at Dublin Castle. Whom Cope met in those summer days and nights of 1921, and by what strange paths, would make a fascinating tale. Through Cope, Lloyd George kept a secret channel of communication with certain Sinn Fein leaders until the end.

On the other side, there was Tom Casement, brother of Sir Roger, who knew General Smuts and went to London to see him as the Imperial Conference was assembling in June, 1921. Both Smuts, by now Prime Minister of South Africa, and Arthur Meighen, the new Prime Minister of Canada, who strongly (though privately) urged Lloyd George and his colleagues to make every effort for peace with Ireland, played an important part in bringing it about.

So the unofficial "buzz" went on.

But now events were to be lifted on to a loftier plane.

On 22 June, 1921, King George V was due to go to Belfast and open in person the first session of the new Ulster Parliament. While Smuts was lunching with him at Windsor Castle on 13 June, 1921, they discussed this ceremony, and Smuts suggested that the King should seize the opportunity to deliver a message of peace and goodwill to the whole of Ireland. He was invited to put his ideas in writing, which he did the same evening.

He also wrote next day to Lloyd George about the "unmeasured calamity" of the present situation in Ireland, "the negation of all principles of government which we have professed on the basis of Empire, and it must more and more tend to poison both our Empire relations and our foreign relations".

Smuts suggested that in his speech the King should foreshadow the grant of Dominion Status to Ireland, Ulster being safeguarded against coercion by the establishment of the very Parliament which he was that day inaugurating. He enclosed in his letter a suggested Declaration concerning a future agreement between the North and South, which he said would "be supported by all the Dominion Prime Ministers".

A day or two later, Lloyd George prepared a speech appropriate to this memorable occasion. He took it down himself to the King at Windsor, and submitted it to him. His Majesty was delighted.

So were a vast number of people, who heard or read his speech, which he made at the Belfast Parliament opening, after driving there with the Queen beside him in an open carriage through the city streets amid wildly cheering crowds. Himself obviously and deeply moved, King George spoke of "this great and critical occasion in the history of the Six Counties", but reminded his audience—and an infinitely wider one beyond Belfast—that it was not so for the Six Counties alone, for everything which interested them touched Ireland, "and everything which touches Ireland finds an echo in the remotest part of the Empire".

"The eyes of the whole Empire are on Ireland today," said the King, "that Empire in which so many nations and races have come together in spite of ancient feuds, and in which new nations have come to birth within the lifetime of the youngest in this Hall. I am emboldened by that thought to look beyond the sorrow and anxiety which have clouded of late my vision of Irish affairs. I speak from a full heart when I pray that my coming to Ireland today may prove to be the first step towards the end of strife amongst her people, whatever their race or creed.

In that hope I appeal to all Irishmen to pause, to stretch out the hand of forbearance and conciliation, to forgive and forget, and to join in making for the land they love a new era of peace, contentment and goodwill."

The King closed by expressing the fervent wish that in Southern Ireland, too, ere long there would take place a parallel to what was passing at that moment in the Ulster Parliament.

Next day, King George returned to London, and was welcomed at the railway-station by the Prime Minister and members of the Cabinet. From the tremendous acclamation which the citizens of London gave him as he drove to

Buckingham Palace, it was plain that peace with Ireland was the most popular policy of the day.

When, on the morrow, Stamfordham called round to see the Prime Minister on the King's behalf to press him not to "miss the psychological moment . . . a very fleeting one, especially when dealing with a quick-witted, volatile and sentimental people . . ." Lloyd George was able to assure him that a letter was already being drafted, to be signed by him personally, inviting both De Valera and Sir James Craig to come to London and meet the British Ministers in conference, and to bring with them any colleagues they chose. The British Government, said the Prime Minister's letter, were deeply anxious that so far as they could assure it, the King's appeal for reconciliation should not have been made in vain.

Several days later, De Valera replied coldly to Lloyd George's invitation. He said that he and his colleagues ("such of the principal representatives of our nation as are available") also desired to secure a lasting peace between the two countries. But not if the British Prime Minister denied "Ireland's essential unity".

Thus, in a single sentence, De Valera defined that "Rock of the Republic", independent and indivisible, from which he never budged throughout the Truce, the Treaty, the Peace, the Second World War and anything that has ever happened since.

To be fair, Lloyd George on the other side did not shift, either, from the basic tenets of his own position. These were: the utmost measure of Home Rule for Ireland consistent with the strategic security of Britain, the supremacy of the Crown in all external affairs, and the non-coercion of the Six Counties by the Twenty-six.

The last two of these reservations could by no kind of casuistry be reconciled with De Valera's demand for a sovereign Republic of Ireland. But before any advance could be made in any direction, first there must be a truce of arms. With some doubts (and not without some opposition in the Cabinet), Lloyd George conceded it.

At noon on Monday, 11 July, 1921, the tanks, armoured cars and lorries of the Crown Forces converged upon their barracks in the cities of the South. The armed troops, who for two years had garrisoned the streets, were marching off to their own quarters. People sang, danced, and went wild with joy. That night, bonfires blazed over the Twenty-six Counties.

Now it was going to be Peace, and Prosperity! That was the opinion of Smuts, whom De Valera had already invited over from England, and who had come—with the cordial approval of Lloyd George. ("Just the thing to follow up the King's speech, and the very man to do the job—no Englishman, an outsider, a Boer.")

So Smuts arrived, but also secretly, as "Mr. Smith". In Dublin he met De Valera, Arthur Griffith and Erskine Childers. He argued with them that

York Cottage,
Sandringham,
Norfolk.

Oct: 16th 1922.

My dear Prime Minister

I write to thank you for your letter which I have just received. I shall anxiously await your report of Thursday's meeting. It is my hope that the result will not cause the break up of my

Government for many reasons, especially when questions like Ireland & the Near East are still unsettled. I trust you will be able to remain my Prime Minister.

Believe me

very sincerely yours

George R.I.

Letter from King George V to Lloyd George. October 16th, 1922

it was useless to go on with the rebellion; it would get them nowhere, and in the end England was bound to crush it. Besides, it was senseless. The South African Republic itself had been almost annihilated in war with Britain, but under Dominion status it had regained its independence.

"Ireland," said Smuts, "would have more privilege, more power, more peace, more security in such a sisterhood of equal nations than in a small, nervous republic having all the time to rely on goodwill, and perhaps the aid of foreigners."

De Valera said that if the status of a Dominion was offered to him he would do his best to get the Irish people to accept it.

On the Day of the Truce, the Sinn Fein Delegation arrived in London, headed by the President De Valera himself. On the afternoon of 14 July, the President went to Downing Street and there met the Prime Minister. Lying on the table of the Cabinet room, there was the letter in which he had accepted Lloyd George's invitation, and a conversation ensued on the meaning of the words *Saorstaat Eireann* which it bore.

"Now, what does that mean exactly?" inquired Lloyd George.

"Irish Free State," he was told. Then what was the Irish word for "Republic"? They had no word for it in Welsh; were the Celts ever republicans? De Valera answered, in the same vein, that the Irish had another word, *Poblacht*, which might cover it, but the Gaelic purists preferred *Saorstaat*, "Free State". There would be no need to change the name, smiled Lloyd George.

By now, they were seated side-by-side at the Cabinet table, so that they could both see a large map of the world which hung on the opposite wall. The parts of the British Empire were vividly marked in red.

Lloyd George spoke meditatively of the contributions to it made by some of his predecessors who had sat in the Prime Minister's chair. Pitt, Palmerston Disraeli . . . and what changes in these years in the relationship of the Colonies to the Mother Country! Right now, there was an Imperial Conference in daily session in this very room. He pointed to the chairs which the various Prime Ministers occupied. There had been Smuts, there Meighen, here Hughes and so on. Twice, as he came to a particular chair, he paused, then passed on. He seemed to be inviting a question. With an expressive gesture, he turned to De Valera. . . . They then talked together for three hours.

They met again next day, and later. These sessions went off "reasonably well", Lloyd George reported to the King. "On the whole, I think De Valera saw the force of what I said, but he constantly seemed to draw back while I was speaking to him."

Or, at any rate, he never seemed to get any nearer. To other people Lloyd George complained of De Valera, and the difficulty of talking to

S

him. It was like being on a merry-go-round. Up and down you bobbed, round and round you went—but you never caught up with the horse ahead of you!

On 20 July, the Prime Minister presented him with the British proposals. They offered to Southern Ireland full Dominion status, with complete control of her own finance and taxation, law-courts and police, defence forces, trade, and all home affairs. The only conditions attached were designed either to ensure facilities for the Royal Navy and Royal Air Force, to permit British recruitment in Ireland and to limit Irish Territorial forces to "reasonable" strength, or else to forbid tariffs on British goods and to accept for Southern Ireland a share of the British National Debt. The proposed settlement also safeguarded the existing powers of the Ulster Parliament.

Next day, De Valera rejected it. He told Lloyd George that he would not recommend such terms to the Dail, nor even take them back for discussion. He did not consider that these terms amounted to Dominion status at all!

Another almost interminable argument ensued, laced with recriminations and threats, too, on either side. Eventually: "Here! Put it in writing," said Lloyd George.

On 11 August, the reply arrived. It was the opening salvo of a long and wearisome bombardment and counter-bombardment.

"Dominion status" would be an illusion for Ireland, argued De Valera. The freedom which the Dominions actually enjoyed was due, not to any legal enactments, but to their distance from Britain. The most explicit guarantees, including the Dominions' acknowledged right to secede, would be necessary to secure for Ireland an equal freedom. But there was no mention here of any such guarantees.

Indeed, it was the very opposite, insisted De Valera. It was Ireland's nearness to the United Kingdom which was made the cause of "denials and restrictions", unheard-of in the case of the Dominions, such as military safeguards and guarantees which would reduce her to "a helpless dependency". In these circumstances, De Valera suggested, the only thing to do was to agree on an "amicable but absolute separation", and let the questions of Ulster and the Irish share of the National Debt be settled, if need be, by "external arbitration".

Lloyd George at once refused both secession and arbitration. The British Government had said their last word, and it had offered Ireland such a prospect as had "never dawned in her history before".

For the moment, anyway, murder was stayed, ambush and assassination stilled. The Truce held between the two rival military commands. Only a paper war raged between the two civilian leaderships, in which ghosts of Grattan, Emmett, and Parnell jostled with Burke, Pitt, and Gladstone, and history wrestled with geography.

By 26 August, the Prime Minister was writing:

"We are reluctant to precipitate the issue, but we must point out that a prolongation of the present state of affairs is dangerous. Action is being taken in various directions which, if continued, would prejudice the truce and must ultimately lead to its termination. Whilst, therefore, prepared to make every allowance as to time which will advance the cause of peace, we cannot prolong a mere exchange of Notes."

By 30 August, the President was retorting:

"Threats of force must be set aside. . . . The respective plenipotentiaries must meet untrammelled by any conditions save the facts themselves, and must be prepared to reconcile their subsequent differences not by appeals to force, covert or open, but by reference to some guiding principle in which there is common agreement."

De Valera suggested it should be "Government by consent of the governed".

In the Summer Recess, on the orders of his doctor, Lord Dawson of Penn, who "did not like the look of him", Lloyd George had gone off for a long holiday and rest in a remote spot. This was at Gairloch, in Ross-shire, on the beautiful bay that faces the Isle of Skye. But it rained nearly every day, he caught a chill, developed an abscess in his tooth, and added to it a towering temperature. The Prime Minister did not have much time off to view the Scots scenery.

Soon he had less.

Every day came dispatch-boxes full of disquieting news from Ireland. De Valera's defiant letter induced him to summon a Cabinet meeting, which he arranged to hold at Inverness Town Hall on 7 September. Thither, in no very amicable temper after their long train journey, his available Cabinet colleagues proceeded. After a long talk—and a visit by Lloyd George himself to King George, who was staying as a guest at Moy Hall nearby—a letter which was very near to an ultimatum was composed and sent to De Valera.

This correspondence, it said, had lasted long enough. His Majesty's Government must therefore ask for a definite answer. Was Mr. De Valera ready to enter a conference

"to ascertain how the association of Ireland with the community of nations known as the British Empire can best be reconciled with Irish national aspirations?"

If the answer was Yes, as he hoped, Lloyd George suggested that they meet at Inverness on 20 September.

It was handed that afternoon to Robert Barton, the Sinn Fein envoy, who took it across the Irish Sea that night.

If this present correspondence had already "lasted long enough", now a fresh flood of it was loosed. Altogether fifteen long letters and telegrams were exchanged before the Irish plenipotentiaries and the British eventually sat down in conference. On 12 September, in accepting the Prime Minister's invitation to Inverness, De Valera did not fail to point out that Ireland had formally declared its independence, and recognized itself as a Sovereign State. It was only as its representatives that he and his colleagues had any authority to act on its behalf.

Michael Collins had feared that this last statement would put an end to all further negotiations and, surely enough, when the Sinn Fein envoys, Harry Boland and Joseph McGrath, handed the letter to the Prime Minister at Gairloch, Lloyd George said at once that as this stood it "finished everything". For to accept the letter, declared Lloyd George, would commit the British Government in advance to recognition of De Valera's claim for sovereign independence. He offered to treat it as never being delivered, and to send it back. The Irishmen explained, in some embarrassment, that the President proposed to read it to the Dail tomorrow.

With that impelling urgency which he ever commanded, Lloyd George induced them to leave for Inverness at once (it was a five-hour journey) and telephone from there across the Irish Channel to De Valera in Dublin, explaining the position and asking him to hold up any public announcement until their return. De Valera's response was to summon the Dail to meet in secret session next day, secure their unanimous approval of his letter, and publish it in the evening newspapers.

Lloyd George, now laid up in bed at Gairloch, immediately telegraphed him cancelling the Inverness Conference.

It looked like the last chapter.

After several days' silence, Lloyd George sent one more, and final, invitation to De Valera to appoint delegates to attend a conference in London on 11 October, expressly not "upon the basis of this correspondence" but, in a phrase already coined,

"as spokesmen of the people, whom you represent, with a view to ascertaining how the association of Ireland with the community of nations known as the British Empire may best be reconciled with Irish national aspirations."

On the last day of September, 1921, De Valera accepted. On 8 October, the Irish Delegation arrived in London where, at Euston Railway Station, immense crowds greeted them and cheered them all the way to their quarters in 22 Hans Place, Kensington.

The five delegates were headed by Arthur Griffith, who had been a newspaper compositor before he became editor of the propagandist *United Irishman*. He was the founder, philosopher and principal propagandist of Sinn Fein, and had worked out the policy of a Dual Monarchy for England and Ireland, based on the former Austro-Hungarian union. Arthur Griffith was dour, downright, dead honest—and as Churchill said of him—"that unusual figure, a silent Irishman".

Next came Michael Collins, "Irish through and through", wrote Lloyd George, "in every respect a contrast to his taciturn neighbour, vivacious, buoyant, highly strung, gay, impulsive, but passing readily to grimness and back again to gaiety, full of fascination and charm—but also of dangerous fire."

The other three delegates were Gavan Duffy, a distinguished lawyer; E. J. Duggan ("a sober, resolute man" Churchill called him), a solicitor by profession, who had fought alongside Collins in the Post Office in 1916; and Robert Barton, a Protestant landowner from Wicklow, an ex-officer of the Royal Dublin Fusiliers. He was a cousin of Erskine Childers, the principal secretary of the delegation, who was also its most fanatical counsellor.

Anglo-Irish, ex-Haileybury and Cambridge University, a British officer in the Boer War, then a Clerk in the House of Commons and author of that best-selling spy thriller, *The Riddle of the Sands*, Erskine Childers in his yacht had been the gun-runner of the Irish Volunteers at Larne in 1914. When war came, he had served in the R.N.V.R. as a lieutenant-commander, gaining the D.S.O. He had then been assigned to the ill-fated Irish Convention of 1917, and had embraced Sinn Fein with the ardour of a late-comer.

The British Delegation numbered seven. They were Lloyd George, Austen Chamberlain, Birkenhead, Churchill, Sir Hamar Greenwood, Sir Laming Worthington-Evans, and Sir Gordon Hewart, the Attorney-General. The two principal secretaries of the delegation were Tom Jones and Lionel Curtis. They, too, both played influential parts.

Such were the opposing teams who faced one another across the table of the Cabinet room in Number 10 Downing Street at 11 a.m. on 11 October, 1921, for the opening session of one of the most momentous meetings ever held there. Passing through the dense crowds which thronged Whitehall, the Irish delegation had been welcomed at the front door by the Prime Minister himself, and the rolling thunder of the cheers from the street had followed them in. Now the great game was to begin.

The British were determined to yield nothing on three vital points:

I. Ireland must remain within the British Empire.
II. Irish Ministers and officials must swear an Oath of Allegiance to the British Crown as the symbolic head of the British Empire.
III. Ireland must grant satisfactory safeguards to ensure the imperial communications and the strategic defences of Britain in that area.

The Irish had two objects, in return for which they were willing to concede a third point. The first was the full independence of Ireland in all internal affairs. The second was "the essential unity" of Ireland; Northern and Southern Ireland must be treated as one. If these points were conceded, they would accept "external association" with the British Commonwealth. The Irish meticulously avoided using the word "Empire", as they did "Republic".

The Conference opened amiably enough, and continued so, at one point Michael Collins picking an eighteenth-century musket from the wall and gravely asking Lloyd George what this display of force might mean? But after a fortnight of "clarifying" (that is, arguing their respective cases), no real progress had been made. For example, there was interminable argument about whether or not the two Border counties of Fermanagh and Tyrone were truly "Ulster", or otherwise.

So Lloyd George proposed that at the close of the plenary session every day, he and Austen Chamberlain, together with Arthur Griffith and Michael Collins, should meet in "sub-committee". By this, he really meant secret session, the chosen Lloyd George man-to-man method of doing business; official committees he always considered admirable places to plant (and forget) pompous people.

The negotiations had now reached a point when the Prime Minister felt that he could put to the Irish delegation a vital question. A satisfactory answer would ensure the British Navy's control of the Irish coast and of the Western approaches. The question, conveyed by letter, was: "Do you concede the foreshores and the harbours of Ireland?"

For the Irishmen, it was a Devil's two-pronged fork.

If they had said "No!" then Lloyd George would there and then have called off any further talks. But if they had said "Yes!" then they would have given away at the very outset any bargaining power which they possessed (and would have been at once disowned, and quite likely executed, by their own extremists).

They were wondering what to do when "Tim" Healy, who was in their counsels, on 22 October, 1921, paid a Saturday morning call upon Beaverbrook. Now Beaverbrook, unlike Birkenhead and Churchill, was strongly in favour of keeping the negotiations going and of reaching a settlement with Sinn Fein. Though himself a former Unionist M.P., he cared not a whit whether Fermanagh and Tyrone were included in the Southern Irish State or not, provided only that this state itself remained within the British Empire. He thought that the great ship of the British Empire "ought not to be wrecked on the rocks of Fermanagh and Tyrone!"

So now, with Healy he frankly discussed Lloyd George's barbed question to the Irish delegation. And, as the outcome of their long talk, Healy hit upon the adroit answer: "What *is* Ireland?" meaning, what counties are to be included in the area referred to as "Ireland". This would enable the Irish delegation to avoid an immediate reply to that embarrassing opening gambit about the foreshores of Ireland, by opening up that interminable dispute about the two counties. Happily, Tim Healy hurried off to his Irish friends.

Beaverbrook drove down that same afternoon to Lord Wargrave's week-end party at his country house on the banks of the Upper Thames. Gathered there were Bonar Law, Birkenhead and Churchill.

"Shall we tell him the question which the Cabinet have put to the Irish delegation?" suggested Churchill.

"Don't bother to do that," said Beaverbrook, before anyone else could reply. "I'll tell you myself not only the terms of Lloyd George's letter, but also the answer which the Irish have sent!"

On this Saturday, Beaverbrook found that both Birkenhead and Churchill were still resolutely opposed to doing any kind of deal with the Irish unless they first surrendered their position. But when Beaverbrook went round to Birkenhead's house in Belgravia on the following Thursday, and found Lloyd George in conference with both of them, it was obvious that a dramatic change had taken place. For now all were agreed to go forward with the Anglo-Irish talks. What had happened in four days?

This: Lloyd George had put it frankly to Birkenhead and Churchill that they should all agree upon this policy of still keeping the door open, which he believed would bring successfully to an end this bitter, bloody Anglo-Irish strife. Thereafter they could form together a new Triumvirate of Power within the Cabinet. Lloyd George, Birkenhead and Churchill did in fact, from this moment, steer the great ship, with Austen Chamberlain in the position of a Very Important Passenger.

Now the Prime Minister's line of approach with the Irish delegates was this: to try and win them over to accepting allegiance to the Crown, while he would try to win the Ulster leaders over to accepting an All-Irish Parliament. Both Birkenhead and Churchill went with him to the limit.

On Sunday night, 30 October, Lloyd George met Arthur Griffith privately at Churchill's house in Sussex Gardens. The Prime Minister had to face a diehard Vote of Censure moved by Colonel Gretton in the House of Commons next day. If Griffith was prepared to recommend to the Irish "recognition of the Crown . . . and free partnership with the British Commonwealth", then Lloyd George himself would seek to carry a measure making the Six Counties subordinate to an All-Ireland Parliament, and he believed that he would succeed. "He would go down to the House and smite the diehards, and would fight on the Ulster matter to secure 'essential unity'," wrote Griffith to De Valera that night, reporting their three-hours' talk.

Lloyd George himself was delighted. He told Geoffrey Shakespeare, M.P., one of his secretaries, as they drove home that night: "Arthur Griffith and I talked business upstairs, while downstairs Michael Collins related to Birkenhead his hair-breadth escapes from the police. In the end, they became real buddies. . . ."[1]

Churchill and Collins became reconciled too, when, Collins complained

[1] *Let Candles Be Brought In.* By the Rt. Hon. Sir Geoffrey Shakespeare.

that Churchill had been responsible for putting a price of £10,000 upon his head. The hero of the Boer War escape went off to another room and returned with a framed placard. It was the Boer offer of reward for his own capture. "They only thought me worth twenty-five pounds," he said sorrowfully.

Next day, in the House of Commons, the diehards were duly smitten. While Colonel Gretton denounced the Government for Surrendering to Assassins, the Prime Minister warned the House of the difficulties of dealing with guerilla war in a mountainous country "where the population is entirely in sympathy with the guerilla". He recalled "how gigantic were the forces which had to be put into South Africa" to handle a similar problem. The "murder gang" had certainly grown up. By 439 votes to 43, the House of Commons upheld Lloyd George.

Ulster was not so easy to manage, and Lloyd George was the more anxious about the situation because he believed that Bonar Law was about to return to active politics as Ulster's champion. He saw Sir James Craig twice in the next few days, and found him adamant against going in with the South. When, on 8 November, 1921, Tom Jones went round from the Prime Minister's office to see Griffith and Collins at the Grosvenor Hotel, Victoria, he assured them that if Lloyd George failed finally in this purpose at his meeting with the Ulster Government that week, he would stand up in the House of Commons, announce his resignation, and retire altogether from public life. Birkenhead and Chamberlain, so Tom Jones surmised, would also resign. There would be no Dissolution. Instead, Bonar Law would come in, and form a war Government against Ireland!

It was then that Tom Jones suggested that, to avert this calamity, suppose a Boundary Commission were set up to delimit the frontier line between North and South, in accordance with the wishes of the inhabitants? This could not fail to interest Arthur Griffith, who reckoned that it would yield the South, not only most of Tyrone and Fermanagh, but parts of three other counties as well. So Griffith undertook to do nothing to queer Lloyd George's pitch, if he should put this forward.

For Lloyd George was playing on a particularly difficult pitch at this moment. Sir James Craig had flatly refused to bring Ulster into an All-Ireland Parliament. Instead, Sir James suggested that the Six Counties should be set up on the same basis as the proposed Home Rule Dominion in the Twenty-Six Counties, even if it meant losing their representatives in the Imperial Parliament. In fact, that there should be two Dominions, though he did not use the word.

Meantime, the National Unionist Conference at Liverpool was approaching, and the undismayed diehard Colonel Gretton was going to move the main resolution condemning "the long-continued ascendency of crime and rebellion in Ireland" and censuring the British Government for negotiating with Sinn

Fein at all. "Shaking Hands with Murder" was the Diehard taunt, and passions were rising. The Tory leaders of the Coalition were far from happy about the outcome of events, and both Chamberlain and Birkenhead sought urgently but vainly to bring to London for secret council the powerful boss of the Lancashire Tory Party caucus, Sir Archibald Salvidge.

So Birkenhead, three days before the Conference, sent off the telegram:

"Whitehall—O.H.M.S. Absolute Priority. Am making special and secret journey to see you. Arriving Adelphi Hotel 9.30 tonight. Leave communication there whether you can see me tomorrow morning about 10.30. . . . B."

Next morning, the Lord Chancellor received Sir Archibald in his bedroom and "under bond of secrecy" took him swiftly through "the inside story of the Irish Conference". He spoke of the Prime Minister's strong desire to set up an All-Ireland Parliament (with adequate safeguards for Ulster) but he promised that if Ulster still declined to co-operate over Dominion Home Rule for the South she would not be coerced by Britain, nor would Britain let the South attempt coercion. He assured Sir Archibald that Ireland would be kept within the Empire, and with adequate safeguards for the defence of Britain. He demanded a clear mandate from the Party Conference for continuing the Irish negotiations.

Then, with his coat collar turned up and his hat pulled down over his eyes, the Lord Chancellor hurried out to a waiting taxi (almost the only principal active agent in the time of the Troubles who does not appear to have gone about in disguise was Michael Collins). At the Unionist Party Conference the hostile resolution was overwhelmed.

On 1 December, 1921, Lloyd George sent to Arthur Griffith what he was resolved, and Griffith understood, should be the final British word. "I enclose," he wrote, "a draft of the Treaty which we are prepared to submit for the approval of Parliament."

Next night, the Irish delegation hurried back to Dublin for a Cabinet consultation, colliding with a trawler in the dark, stormy Irish Sea. They quarrelled bitterly, and returned to London, some of them not on speaking terms with one another. Their orders, however, were clear enough: To reject the Oath of Allegiance, to insist on External Association only; to break on Ulster—and not to sign, but refer back to Dublin.

A miserable meeting took place at Downing Street that Sunday afternoon, which Michael Collins refused to attend. He was bitterly unhappy, and it is fortunate for Irish history that in these dark hours he found steadfast encouragement to go forward with his task from Lady Lavery, the lovely red-haired wife of Sir John Lavery, the Irish painter. Hazel Lavery was herself Irish-born in the West, where Collins came from. She was a friend of both Birkenhead and Churchill, and her influence on Collins was profound. The picture of the colleen on the currency notes of the new Irish Free State would be that of Hazel Lavery, and the honour was deeply earned.

In Downing Street, now, his Irish colleages and the British Cabinet were once more going over that old argument about the Oath of Allegiance. . . . Then: "Our difficulty is about coming into the Empire," blurted Gavan Duffy.

"That ends it," snapped Chamberlain, jumping to his feet.

All the other Ministers sprang up, too. It was agreed that the Irish should send a formal rejection of the British Draft Treaty, and that the British Government should notify Sir James Craig, for the Belfast Parliament was meeting on Tuesday. The curtain was about to fall.

But very early next morning, Lloyd George sent Tom Jones round to see Michael Collins, and bring him privately to Number 10 Downing Street. There, Lloyd George offered Collins reassurances about the Boundary Commission, which both believed could not fail to benefit the South. That afternoon, the final session of the two-months' Conference began. The Oath, External Association, strategic safeguards . . . yes, all over again they came.

But surprisingly, a large measure of agreement, even on the Oath, which Birkenhead and Collins, those "buddies", concocted between them. But not on Ulster.

Yes Ulster was the very point for which the Irish delegates declared they had conceded so much. To bring Ulster into an All-Ireland Parliament, to preserve that precious "Essential unity" of Ireland, they claimed that they had made immense sacrifices. At this point, Lloyd George sharply intervened. Wasn't *he* seeking by every means in his power to make Ulster come in? Hadn't *he* thought of that pressure-engine, the Boundary Commission? *And hadn't Mr. Arthur Griffith promised to do nothing to upset his plan there?*

The British Delegation withdrew for a few minutes. When they returned, the Prime Minister was not among them. The debate turned upon naval safeguards.

Suddenly, dramatically, Lloyd George reappeared. In his hand he brandished a crumpled envelope, from which a letter half stuck out.

It was a written copy of what Tom Jones had put forward to Arthur Griffith on the Prime Minister's own account that morning nearly a month ago. (Lloyd George and his secretaries had been frantically searching for it for the last ten minutes because, characteristically, he had mislaid it; it was found in the pocket of another suit which he had been wearing at the time.) Now, was Mr. Griffith going to let him down?

"I have never let a man down in my whole life, and I never will," growled Griffith.

The Prime Minister nodded. Now he spoke very quickly, and solemnly. The British Government could concede no more, and discuss no more. The

Irish must settle now—or depart. For time was racing. Lloyd George held up two letters.

"I have to communicate with Sir James Craig tonight," he said. "Here are the alternative letters which I have prepared, one enclosing Articles of Agreement reached by His Majesty's Government and yourselves, and the other saying that the Sinn Fein representatives refuse to come within the Empire. If I send this letter it is war, and war within three days. Which letter am I to send?

Whichever letter you choose, travels by special train to Holyhead, and by destroyer to Belfast. The train is waiting, with steam up, at Euston. Mr. Shakespeare, the envoy, is ready. If he is to reach Sir James Craig in time, we must know your answer by 10 p.m. tonight. You can have until then, but no longer, to decide whether you will give Peace or War to your country."

Arthur Griffith rose. He said: "I will give the answer of the Irish Delegates at nine tonight; but, Mr. Prime Minister, I personally will sign this agreement, and will recommend it to my countrymen."

He was asked by Lloyd George: "Do I understand, Mr. Griffith, that though everyone else refuses, you will nevertheless agree to sign?"

Arthur Griffith, one of History's granite characters, replied: "Yes, that is so, Mr. Prime Minister."

He walked out, followed by Michael Collins.

The hour is 7.30 p.m. The Irishmen retire to 22 Hans Place, where for many another hour there rages the most bitter of all quarrels, between comrades. Four or five times they think that they have found agreement, argue again upon the stairs, return to the smoke-laden room to thrash it out once more. . . .

In Downing Street, the British Ministers wait. They expect that Arthur Griffith alone will agree to their terms—and they, too, realize that they themselves have strained to breaking-point the loyalties of their own supporters in going thus far. The hours dawdle by, they joke and laugh to ease the tension. . . . Nine o'clock, ten, eleven, twelve. Big Ben reminds them with his boom. In Whitehall, the reporters are hanging on, and the fog is closing in. Across the dark sea, in Dublin the Black-and-Tans are on the move again in their lorries.

The door-bell rings. The Irish delegation have returned. A long, it seems an interminable, pause. Then, Arthur Griffith speaking quietly: "Mr. Prime Minister, the Delegation is willing to sign the agreements, but there are a few points of drafting which perhaps I should mention. . . ."

The British delegates rise and retire, except Birkenhead, the lawyer, who sits down again at the table with the Irishmen to settle the final form of words. Lloyd George takes Churchill with him to Miss Stevenson's office, a room shut off from the Cabinet by large folding doors.

An hour passes . . . more. . . .

The doors open, and Birkenhead comes out. "I think we are practically agreed," he says, "but there is a clause that needs re-typing."

He waits while it is being done, then re-enters the Cabinet Room. Lloyd George and Churchill continue talking quietly.

Another hour—and then Birkenhead is back again. "We are agreed," he says.

The other Ministers follow him into the Cabinet Room. It is half-past two o'clock in the December morning. All sign the Treaty. "Michael Collins," said Lloyd George, "looked for all the world as if he was signing his own death-warrant."

He was.

As the Irishmen rise to go, the British Ministers jump up and spontaneously walk round the table to shake hands for the first time. Peace has come, at last.

When it was all over, exhausted, but triumphant, Lloyd George went back into Miss Stevenson's office. To win this battle, one of the greatest in his life he had used every weapon in his armoury—charm, voice, flattery, logic, irony, solemnity, anger, yes and bullying, too. He handed her the Irish Treaty, with its historic signatures and seal.

"Lock it up carefully," he said.

She did so, in a dispatch-box. There it lay, for twenty-five years, until one day after Lloyd George had gone to the land of his fathers, she was looking through his papers and found it again.

CHAPTER XXIX

INDIAN SUMMER

THE Irish Treaty provided much of the explosive which, within a year, blew apart Lloyd George's Government. There were a number of other destructive elements already at work on the fabric, and by the end of 1921, its collapse appeared to be both inevitable and imminent.

Many observers marvelled that this Coalition had lasted so long. They wondered how even the ingenuity and resource of that master of accommodation, David Lloyd George, could go on reconciling the opposite opinions of his Liberal followers and his Tory associates on such issues as trade with Russia, Indian Reform, Egyptian Independence, reparations, economy at home, and the Safeguarding of British Industries act—to say nothing of Home Rule for Ireland?

The breaking of the Union between Britain and Ireland and the setting-up of the Irish Free State, which went far beyond the modest measures of Home Rule which Gladstone and Asquith had proposed, and which the Tory Party had strenuously resisted for nearly forty years, was bound to leave behind far deeper wounds. And here again, the injury appeared the harder to endure since it was old friends who were inflicting it. Some of the most famous leaders of the Unionist cause of 1914 had now taken an active part in what their Orange allies branded as the betrayal of Ulster, Britain's historic friend in Ireland; Ulster, the loyal garrison; Ulster, which they had boasted "will fight, and will be right!"

Yes, the fine friends of Ulster yesterday had fled from the field today. With passion and scorn, the old Orange Leader, "King Carson", rose in the House of Lords on 14 December, 1921, to denounce and damn the deserters —Balfour, Curzon, Austen Chamberlain and, above all, Birkenhead (once his own A.D.C., "Galloper Smith"). It was Carson's first utterance in this assembly, for he had just been made a Law Lord, and with gaunt face and vibrant voice he delivered such a maiden speech as the House of Lords never heard before, or since:

> "I speak for a good many. I speak—I can hardly speak—for all those who, relying on British honour and British justice, have in giving their best to the service of the State seen themselves now deserted and cast aside without one single line of recollection or recognition in the whole of what you call Peace Terms in Ireland."

To Curzon, Foreign Secretary and Leader of the House of Lords, who had pompously reminded him, as a newly appointed Judge of the supreme appeal court, to have proper care for "the equipoise of his judgment", Carson contemptuously retorted that he had received "A long lecture from the noble Marquess which, may I say, I hope in the future he will spare me, because the man—let me speak plainly—who, in my opinion at all events, has betrayed me, had no right afterwards to lecture me."

Of Chamberlain, Leader of the House of Commons, Carson cried:

"The other evening I saw with disgust that Mr. Austen Chamberlain, the son of Mr. Joseph Chamberlain, having agreed to put Ulster into these terms, then said he made an appeal to the comradeship of his old friend Sir James Craig to come in and submit to the domination of Sinn Fein. I could not help thinking that it was very like after having shot a man in the back, going over to him and patting him on the shoulder and saying: 'Old man, die as quickly as you can, and do not make any noise.' "

To Birkenhead, Lord Chancellor, who sat near on the Woolsack, Carson spoke his cruellest words, for once he had been his closest friend:

"Of all the men in my experience that I think are the most loathsome it is those who will sell their friends for the purpose of conciliating their enemies and, perhaps still worse, the men who climb up a ladder into power of which even I may have been part of a humble rung, and then, when they have got into power, kick the ladder away without any concern for the pain, or injury, or mischief, or damage that they do to those who have helped them to gain power."

The Lord Chancellor did not spare his own language when he rose to reply: "As a constructive effort of statecraft," he commented on Carson's speech, "it would have been immature upon the lips of a hysterical schoolgirl."

The debate was further enlivened when Lord Farnham, recalling that Lord Birkenhead had now signed both the Ulster Covenant and the Irish Free State Treaty, speculated as to whether or not "Galloper Smith" would end up as "canterer" to Michael Collins. These amenities were continued in the New Year, 1922, when at a Londonderry House gathering, Carson confessed his predilection for "diehards" as opposed to "livehards", a reference to Birkenhead's convivial habits which did not escape the Lord Chancellor's attention.

The Irish Treaty was approved by both Houses, 401 to 58 in the Commons, 119 to 47 in the Lords, on 16 December, 1921. It was the heaviest tax on Tory loyalty that Lloyd George had yet imposed upon his colleagues. In Dail Eireann the strain on Sinn Fein solidarity was too great to be borne; the Party of the Republic broke into two pieces. De Valera, still President of Sinn Fein, declared that the Treaty document was the most ignoble that could be signed. It would not bring the Irish peace, he prophesied, but would lead to war and bitter internal strife. In this ominous weather, the Dail adjourned.

Simultaneously with the Irish negotiations a notable conference had been going on at Washington between the four great naval Powers. Britain, France, the United States of America and Japan, with China also in attendance to discuss Far Eastern affairs. Its primary object was to secure a limitation of naval armaments, but Britain had not entered it entirely unfettered, for at the Imperial Conference the previous June the Canadian Prime Minister, Arthur Meighen, had taken a particularly strong line against the Anglo-Japanese Alliance, which, he urged, stood in the way of establishing closer relations with the United States. On the other hand, Hughes of Australia and Massey of New Zealand strongly favoured the Anglo-Japanese Alliance; emphasizing the grave situation which would have developed in the Pacific Ocean during the war if Japan had been on the enemy side. It was a result of these discussions that the idea of a Four-Power Conference had emerged and the plan began to take shape for exchanging the Anglo-Japanese Alliance for a larger arrangement. This Four-Power Pact was duly concluded at Washington in the New Year, and the other, older alliance was abrogated. Thus, the influence of a British Dominion again shaped Empire and world policy.

Lloyd George turned to consider his own personal political prospects. What kind of future, if any, had the Coalition Government?

There had been that day of inspiration in July, 1919, when Churchill had returned from a visit to Criccieth, following the signing of the Peace Treaty, to proclaim that "the democratic forces in Conservatism and the patriotic forces in Liberalism can no longer be kept apart". He had also heralded "a Central Combination, ending the old Party System and all its evils". The British public were still awaiting the arrival of this political phenomenon.

Then, in March, 1920, Lloyd George himself had convened a gathering of Coalition Liberals to discuss the formation of a "National Democratic Party", with a Liberal wing and a Unionist wing. In 1921, "Fusion" had been the chosen name, though still the birthday of the infant was delayed. After Bonar Law's retirement from the Coalition Cabinet in the same year, the new, nominal Tory Leader, Austen Chamberlain, was a loyal though rather reluctant assenter.

From the Prime Minister's own point of view there was much to recommend an early General Election. The Irish Treaty would alter the composition of the House of Commons more drastically than any Reform Bill since 1832. The Irish Members from the South had disappeared. If Ulster opted to go into the Irish Free State, it would lose its representation in the Imperial Parliament, too. There was a case for submitting such sweeping constitutional changes to the electorate. Some other pure electioneering issues were con-

sidered by Lloyd George. The repeal of the Corn Production Act, with its
bounty on wheat growing, was making the Coalition Government increasingly
unpopular with the British farmers, and the forthcoming Report of the Geddes
Committee on Economy, with its inevitable recommendations of dismissals,
was bound to antagonize all those concerned. What about forestalling it by a
nation-wide appeal for retrenchment?

On Boxing Day, 1921, Charles McCurdy, Coalition Liberal Chief Whip,
who had been reconnoitring in the North of England, reported from Harrogate
to the Prime Minister, who had just arrived in Cannes for an International
Conference on the ever-unsettled state of Europe, and more especially on the
threatened default by Germany on her January and February instalments of
reparations (amounting to nearly £40,000,000).

McCurdy most strongly recommended "an immediate Election". He
believed that the great bulk of the Tories would still follow Lloyd George,
but a dangerous "breakaway movement" was growing, and might develop
into a "stampede". Already, some of the Liberal Coalition seats were being
attacked by the Tory diehards. Go to the country now, urged McCurdy,
and thereafter begin the "resolute building-up of the Centre Party".

By this time, the British Press had also got going on the General Election
story. When, next day, the Lloyd George newspaper, the *Daily Chronicle*,
supported a rumour that it would be held in February the issue seemed to
be settled. True, the Prime Minister himself had said nothing, but the
political wags recalled the story of the bishop who was offered a much-
better-paid diocese. Would he accept? Inquirers were answered by his young
daughter: "Pa is in the study, praying for guidance, but Ma is upstairs,
packing!"

On 5 January, 1922, McCurdy wrote to the Prime Minister at Cannes,
"The newspapers are boiling over with the question of the General Election.
It is the universal topic of conversation. I am informed today that in *The
Times* office the view is that an early Election will mean a large majority for
the Prime Minister. . . ."

But McCurdy notes that the leading article of the *Daily Telegraph* is
hostile to a General Election, and he believes that this is due to a warning
from Chamberlain to the editor that if a General Election is rushed he
will retire from the Government. The Coalition Liberal Chief Whip also
discusses the interviews which the chairman of the Conservative Party
Organization, Sir George Younger, M.P., has been giving to the *Press
Association*, the *Evening Standard* and the *Evening News*. Sir George, too, is
most strongly opposed to a General Election. He told the newspapers that
the Coalition Government have not yet fulfilled the two main pledges on
which it appealed to the country in 1918. These were (1) to reform the House
of Lords, "and restore the balance of the Constitution"; (ii) to steer the
nation into calm waters after the storm of war.

The most hostile expressions employed by the Tory Chairman were, not unnaturally, reproduced in the *Evening News*, a Northcliffe newspaper:

"A General Election . . . would be a complete betrayal of the Conservatives—the most powerful wing of the Coalition.

I am certain that if a General Election is decided on a number of Conservative Members will decline to go to their constituents as Coalitionists —I shall most certainly be among them."

Austen Chamberlain, the Prime Minister's official Tory partner in the leadership of the Coalition, had posted him a letter to the same effect ("Please forgive the dogmatic way in which I write; it is an attempt at brevity"). Chamberlain had made his own "neutral inquiries" of various people. Almost everyone was strongly against a General Election.

". . . All this confirms my opinion," he wrote, "and I most earnestly press you not to pursue the idea.

First, our work is not done. It is not safe to leave the Irish question half-way through. My party would be fiercely indignant if we do not first carry reform of the House of Lords.

Second, we are very unpopular in the country districts.

Third, unemployment will play havoc with us. Many of our men would be defeated, and many others will come back monstrously pledged.

Fourth. Disturbance to Trade, high taxation and high expenditure will all tell against us with business men.

Fifth, and lastly. You will probably have many three-cornered fights and many more Unionists will break away from the Coalition."

It was obvious that there was a serious revolt. Chamberlain's own hand was forced by Sir George Younger when he took steps to make public his leader's private views, so that he could not recede from them without embarrassment, or even humiliation. The signals were set at Danger! Lloyd George hurried McCurdy round to see Chamberlain personally.

A coded cable on 10 January, 1922, from the Coalition Liberal Chief Whip to the Prime Minister at Villa Valetta, Cannes, warned him that Chamberlain was probably in complete agreement with Younger, and thought "Fusion" was impossible. Certainly he could not assent to an Election after the newspaper disclosures of his personal views. The Chief Whip considered that a split of the Tory Party was inevitable "and a revolt possible whenever Parliament ends".

Angrily, Lloyd George wrote to Chamberlain. He was furious with Sir George Younger, who was now noisily mobilizing Tory M.P.s, Chairmen and Agents against this "Liberal Coalition stunt" of a General Election. The Prime Minister said he had not made up his own mind about it yet, and that his opinion would depend both on trade and electoral prospects.

He had no doubt, however, about the moral justification of asking the King for a dissolution. Meanwhile, it would be as well if responsible Ministers would refrain from public statements:

10 January, 1922

> ". . . Younger has, in my judgment, behaved disgracefully. He was consulted confidentially on a most confidential subject. He was shown a document prepared by the Chief Coalition Whip. When you informed me that you meant to send a copy to him I certainly relied that, as a man of honour, he would not reveal it. He rushed to the Press; carried on an active campaign; disclosed the most intimate and secret information which would never have been imparted to him unless we had depended upon his being gentleman enough to keep counsel. His action has caused serious damage which it will be difficult to repair. His suggestion that the General Election is a Coalition Liberal stunt is absolutely untrue. The suggestion came, in the first instance, as you are aware, from Unionist quarters. Prominent Unionists were the first to urge it upon us . . . notably F.E. . . ."

Austen Chamberlain replied by telegram 12 January, 1922. He had his problems, too:

> "I do not think you realize immense difficulties created for us by premature revelations of nature of our private discussions. These breaches of confidence almost make me despair. . . . Dissolution talk produced great reaction in Unionist Party against Coalition and I feel my effort to secure ultimate union has received an immense setback."

He added that there had been grave danger of a large section of the Tory Party hiving-off into an Independent Group. This would certainly be the result of an Election, leaving himself leading only a minority. As it was, it was reported that a "round-robin is being signed calling for Party meeting."

Lloyd George sent swift orders to his Private Secretary, J. T. Davies, to consult those two now closest-of-all colleagues, Birkenhead and Churchill. From Birkenhead, came the opinion that if the backing of Bonar Law could be secured, the rebels could be routed. From Churchill (who did not always favour an early Election, though he was consistently in support for going ahead with the creation of that New Party), a more detailed appreciation of events set forth that the Tory Press were unanimously opposed to a General Election, that Chamberlain was inclined to blame the Prime Minister himself for the original newspaper leakage, that Lord Derby had told him that, "though in favour, he now considers he must take up against", and that undoubtedly Tory opinion had been made very hostile.

Lloyd George was much incensed against Chamberlain, whom he condemned, not for any duplicity in dealing with him, but for weakness in yielding to Younger. How the Prime Minister longed for those good old days of the Coalition when Bonar Law had been both his loyal and his resolute partner!

Now, it so happened that at this very moment, Bonar Law was staying in Cannes. Could Lloyd George recapture him, and rid himself of the incubus of Chamberlain? Their mutual friend, Beaverbrook, was at the Carlton Hotel, and there in his sitting-room they met again. Lloyd George offered Bonar Law the Foreign Secretaryship—the titular Foreign Secretary, Lord Curzon, was at the time staying at the Grand Hotel, just up the street. But Bonar Law said no. His health was not yet recovered, and he was unwilling to return to the labours of Office. So, unable to enlist Bonar Law, Lloyd George dropped the idea of a General Election. At Westminster, the political scene remained one of confusion.

At Cannes, the international scene came near to being one of chaos. Lloyd George and Briand had agreed in December to make a supreme effort in the New Year to resolve the rivalries and divisions of Europe, and to reconcile victors and vanquished in an enduring peace. It was decided that the Supreme Allied Council should confer at Cannes with three main objectives:

(i) Deal with Reparations.
(ii) Discuss a Pact of Security with France.
(iii) Draw up the agenda for a subsequent Conference of Europe to settle all outstanding political and economic problems. Both Germany and Russia were to be invited and Dr. Walther Rathenau, the German Foreign Minister,[1] was also asked to attend at Cannes for the talks on Germany's war indebtedness.

So the thirtieth of the post-war Peace Conferences was staged at Cannes. The British Delegation included, beside the Prime Minister, the Foreign Secretary (Curzon), the Chancellor of the Exchequer (Sir Robert Horne), the War Secretary (Sir Laming Worthington-Evans), the Colonial Secretary (Churchill) and Lord Riddell, whom Lloyd George was especially anxious to sound about election prospects. Indeed, there was considerable election talk at the Villa Valetta, the attractive house which Sir Albert Stern had placed at Lloyd George's disposal, during the days before the Conference opened. It was in the course of one of these discussions when Worthington-Evans paused to draw breath for a further spell of a rather lengthy argument that a voice, which sounded intensely human, bawled: "You bloody fool!"

The well-timed interruption came from Sir Albert Stern's pet parrot in an unnoticed cage in the corner.

The story raced round Cannes. A few days later, when the Conference had assembled, Dr. Rathenau was subjecting the delegates to a similarly detailed recitation of the woes of Germany. Suddenly, Lloyd George felt a

[1] Assassinated June, 1922

sharp nudge from his neighbour. It was Briand. "Can you lend me that parrot?" he asked.

The opening days of the Cannes Conference were calm and sunlit. Lloyd George laid before the assembled delegates a series of proposals designed to protect the private investor in foreign countries against Government confiscation of their property, or the repudiation of public debts. Also, the nations were to agree to cease both acts of aggression and hostile propaganda against their neighbours. If the Russian Soviet Government accepted these conditions, it was to be officially recognized.

French opinion was not unfavourably disposed to any of these terms, for the heavy French investment in pre-revolutionary Russia could only be recovered now by coming to terms with the new Bolshevik régime. All Lloyd George's resolutions were adopted. Also, French interest was genuine in the British Prime Minister's offer of a Security Pact, pledging Britain to full naval and military support of France in the event of any fresh aggression by Germany.

It was the Jonah of reparations which wrecked the Cannes Conference. The French diehards were determined to have their transfusion of blood money even if it meant that Germany perished. Indeed, so much the better, said some! That were well aware that Lloyd George favoured a more moderate course, and they suspected that he was talking Briand into it. The whispers and murmurings in Paris rose to a shrill scream. For the time being, Briand ignored it.

But at this moment, Tragedy dressed as a clown stepped in.

On Monday, 9 January, 1922, there was no session of the Conference, so Lloyd George seized the opportunity to talk things over privately with Briand. He invited him to lunch at the Cannes Golf Club. Other guests at the meal included Signor Bonomi (the Italian Prime Minister), Bonar Law, Curzon, Riddell and Sir Edward Grigg. In high spirits, enjoying the sunshine, the good company and the apparent success which had so far attended the Conference, Lloyd George evolved the prank of challenging Briand and Bonomi, neither of whom had ever touched a golf club before in their lives, to play a round with him. In the same mood, they accepted.

Out of the club-house marched the party, watched by an amused little crowd who included several Press correspondents and photographers. Briand and Bonomi drove off, strangely, well down the course. Riddell and Grigg followed, and then came Lloyd George and Bonar Law. After this good start, pantomime took over, Briand in particular, swinging and swiping, missing and missing, churning up turf and sand like the track of a small tornado. According to one who watched the performance, nothing that the late Sid Field, the comedian, ever did in "gagging" the game of golf on the music-hall stage has equalled it.

Lloyd George and Briand went off to tea together, and for hours talked out their problems in the personal way that both of them liked best. They reached complete accord. Once more in Lloyd George's life a game of golf had played a part in shaping history.

But not the part which he had supposed. Next day, the Paris newspapers reached Cannes. There were ludicrous pictures, and columns of descriptive reporting of the most barbed kind, holding the French Prime Minister up to scorn and ridicule as the butt of the British Prime Minister. Editorial articles branded this man who could so neglect his duty, as being utterly unfit to represent his country, and in the Chamber of Deputies there was storm. Next morning, 11 January, 1922, after the plenary session of the Conference in Cannes, during which the most alarming messages kept pouring in from Paris, Briand told Lloyd George that he would have to leave that night and return to the capital and face the music.

"Don't resign!" Lloyd George urged him, as he saw him off at the railway station.

"I shall be back here within thirty-six hours," Briand promised.

He never returned to Cannes. Next day, after a further and still fiercer tumult in the French Chamber and a series of intrigues in the lobbies which culminated in his betrayal to Raymond Poincaré by his own Foreign Minister, Barthou, Briand did resign. Coming out of the Council after he had handed in his papers, he turned to Barthou and inquired: "Can you tell me, M. Barthou, what is the equivalent of thirty pieces of silver at the current rate of exchange?"

Lloyd George heard the news of Briand's fall with deep dismay. He had believed that the French Prime Minister meant to fight. "Briand," he said, "is like myself. When in doubt what to do, he is depressed and miserable. But when he has made up his mind, he is full of confidence and determination. His Breton blood is up!"

And Lloyd George had believed that Briand would win, and would bring back to Cannes a victory for a more reasonable and practicable method of handling reparations. That very afternoon in Cannes at the British Prime Minister's invitation, the German Foreign Minister had addressed the Conference on this problem, explaining the difficulties in which the Germans found themselves. He was still on his feet when the sensational news from Paris began to buzz around the delegates. Lloyd George, as chairman, at once adjourned the meeting.

There was nothing more to be done in Cannes. The Prime Minister and the British Delegation left for home the same evening.

Had *anything* been done? Yes. Out of the conference wrecked by a golf ball there still remained an agreed Allied plan for a fresh effort to set Europe on its feet again. Britain and France were to rebuild their *Entente*, to form the basis of an Alliance for Peace of all nations, including Germany and Russia.

"It is essential that the division of the European Nations into two mighty camps should not be perpetuated by narrow fears on the part of the victors or secret projects of revenge on the part of the vanquished. It is essential that the rivalries generated by the liberation of nations since the war should be averted from the paths of international hatred and turned to those of co-operation and goodwill. It is essential also that the conflict between rival social and economic systems, which the Russian Revolution has so greatly intensified, should not deepen the fears of nations, and end in International War."

Then followed the warning that another struggle of this kind would smash the civilization of Europe into final ruin. So Britain besought France and Italy to join with her in cutting down national armaments and building up international accord. If the proposed Economic Conference was agreed to, it would

"create an opportunity for the great Allied Powers—France, the British Empire and Italy—to inaugurate an era of Peace in their own continent, whose war-sodden fields record a history more terrible than that of any other continent in modern times."

This was the language and thought of Lloyd George, and perhaps of Briand. But Briand was gone, and in his place there reigned a legalist bigot, Raymond Poincaré. It was not that he stood for French diehard nationalism —Clemenceau had been no fervid internationalist—but Poincaré's was a mind that haggled over every comma of a contract. The beaten enemy owed so much money: he would either pay on the nail, or else the bailiffs would move in. Poincaré had ruined Lloyd George's European reconstruction policy at Cannes, and he would complete its demolition at the forthcoming Conference of Genoa. But Lloyd George could not know this last item yet, he still had hopes, and meant to fight for them—and even plead with Poincaré.

The two men met in Paris on 14 January, 1922, when Lloyd George broke his journey home for a day or two. Their encounter took place in the British Embassy, since Poincaré had not yet formally assumed office as Prime Minister of France. It lasted an hour-and-a-half, and from the first minute the barometer was set for storm. Neither of them had any reason to regard the other with goodwill, but Lloyd George tried his utmost to conciliate Poincaré in the interests of future co-operation.

He found the French Premier adamant against any more conferences on reparations: the Commission had been set up to deal with them. When Lloyd George renewed the offer he had made to Briand of a Security Pact, guaranteeing that Britain would come to the aid of France if she were attacked, Poincaré asked for it in writing.

Also, in detail. He got down to figures. How many men would Britain actually send to fight alongside France? How many guns? How many planes? How many ships?

"Everything we have, all our force, just as we did in the late war," answered the British Prime Minister.

It did not satisfy Poincaré. He wanted a Military Convention, with precise undertakings. These, Lloyd George was frankly not prepared to deliver. He did not believe that the British people would agree to it and, according to Tom Jones, then one of his Secretaries, the British Prime Minister was already acting in advance of Cabinet approval in offering France a general guarantee.[1] For this very reason, the draft of it had to be couched in general terms.

When Poincaré insisted on detail, a painful scene ensued. A. J. Sylvester, Lloyd George's Secretary, has recorded of Poincaré's demand:

"Lloyd George regarded this as an insult, not only a personal one to him, but an insult to the whole British race. He flew into a rage. Banging his fist on the table, he exclaimed:

" 'If you cannot take the pledged word of the British people, you had better consider the Draft Treaty withdrawn. Britain's word has always been her bond. There was no military Convention in existence before the Great War. Merely our word. We kept it, as France and the world knows. There are some things which cannot be set down in black and white. Britain gives you her word. If you don't accept that, then consider the Draft Treaty at an end. Choose between the two!' "[2]

They parted. Lloyd George returned to London, rather depressed and miserable. He was in doubt what to do.

His first task on arriving home was to decide what to do first. Unemployment was rising, trade was falling, Ireland was sub-dividing and criticism of the Coalition Government was everywhere multiplying.

The fundamental reason for going to Cannes had been to try and restore the conditions in which trade between the nations could flourish. This was vital for Britain, with her huge war debt, and crushing taxation, still upon a war-time scale. As for unemployment, unless the idle two million workers could be got back on the job at the lathe or loom or forge, the only other way to use their labour was to provide vast schemes of public development, dealing with roads, reservoirs, afforestation and land settlement. However admirable and desirable these were, they cost a lot of money, and at this moment in 1922 the loudest newspaper and political clamour in Britain was to save money. The shadow of the Geddes Axe was over every Ministry.

Ireland? The prolonged and passionate debates in the Dail over the Irish Treaty had come to an end on 7 January, 1922, when it had been narrowly

[1] *Lloyd George*, by Thomas Jones, C.H., LL.D.
[2] *The Real Lloyd George.* By A. J. Sylvester.

approved by 64 votes to 57. Two days later, De Valera resigned his presidency of the Dail, and Arthur Griffith became the head of the new Executive which was to carry through the establishment of a Provisional Government. Michael Collins arrived a few days afterwards in London, where a Committee presided over by Churchill, the Colonial Secretary, was dealing with the transfer of services and the evacuation of British troops. Within a week or so, the regiments were marching out, with colours flying and bands playing, as their favourite tune, "Let Erin Remember!" Erin has not forgotten yet.

But for the moment, the guns were silent. The Prime Minister turned his attention to his own private civil war inside the Coalition. Lord Derby had by now pronounced against a General Election, and the Tory diehards had undoubtedly won the day.

Lloyd George was equal to it. *What* day? he inquired, in bewildered innocence. On 21 January, 1922, he attended a Coalition Liberal Conference at the Central Hall, Westminster. "Who started this talk about a General Election?" he demanded. "I did not! I never started the idea!"

However, he made an effective electioneering speech. The Coalition Liberals, Lloyd George assured Sir George Younger, were just as anxious to reform the House of Lords as any other Liberals. As for newspaper attacks on "the failure" of Cannes, no one conference could settle the peace of Europe, but each was "a rung in the ladder" to it.

"The Washington Conference is establishing peace in the great West, and I am looking to the Genoa Conference to establish peace in the East. They will be like two wings of the Angel of Peace hovering over the world."

He spoke of the forthcoming and long-awaited Geddes Report, and warned that "drastic and ruthless" retrenchment in the public services was required if the risk of national bankruptcy was to be avoided.

Rumour set the target at £150,000,000, and the most popular pastime of the political world was speculating on whose necks the Geddes Axe would fall.

When, on 10 February, 1922, the first two volumes of the Report were published, it was seen that only about half of this estimated figure had been reached, and that most of the cuts, £46,000,000, were in Armed Services expenditure. But Education also felt the sharp edge of the blade; the cost of teaching was to be reduced, the superannuation of teachers made contributory, and there was to be a review of the system of free and state-aided Secondary Education for those whose parents could afford to pay. Economies in the Health Service were applied to Maternity and Child Welfare. The Ministries of Transport, Mines and Petroleum and the Overseas Trade Department were to disappear into the Board of Trade.

These recommendations of the Geddes Report were quite enough to set off a first-rate political fireworks display. On one hand, they infused fresh life into the Anti-Waste campaign of the Northcliffe Press, and on the other, stirred the Labour Party to rage against this "attack on the children".

Trouble had flared again, too, on the Ulster Border, and bloody reprisals with gun and bomb followed in Belfast. In the House of Commons, Churchill was having no easy passage for the Irish Free State Treaty Bill, with which he had been entrusted as Colonial Secretary. Riot and murder ran loose in Egypt and India, and in the Near East the Greek-Turk feud swelled into ominous new shape.

At Westminster, an interchange of incivilities between the chairman of the Conservative Party Organization, Sir George Younger, and the Tory Lord Chancellor, Birkenhead, exposed again the seeping wound in the body of the Coalition.

Addressing the Women's Branch of the National Unionist Association on 22 February, 1922, Younger declared that the present political combination resembled "A matrimonial alliance that I want to get rid of. A Bill of Divorcement would be the best means of accomplishing that end. It would be a divorcement but, as our American friends say, it would leave the parties concerned friendly."

Birkenhead, addressing the Junior Carlton Club next day, retorted to Younger (who had referred to his own [Younger's] impending retirement): "When the tempest rages, and when the Captain would naturally be on the bridge, I would not give any particular encouragement to the Cabin Boy to seize the helm. And I am more than ever of that opinion when the Cabin Boy has announced that he does not intend to make another voyage."

Lloyd George himself had been wondering how much longer he could keep the ship (or the marriage) off the rocks. Should he quit now, and let the Tories try to deal with all these troubles? They had available Chamberlain, Balfour, and perhaps even Bonar Law (whose health appeared much improved). It might be a good time for Lloyd George to move out. To Riddell he confided that he was strongly tempted to resign, and that if he could get his doctor (Lord Dawson) to say he must, then he would.

> "He [Dawson] says that I need to take care of myself, but will not give me a clean bad bill of health. . . . When I returned from Cannes, I told Chamberlain that my mind was in a state of suspense. I should like to retire to write a book. I have been offered £1 a word for 80,000 words. That is a lot of money. It would make my position secure."[1]

By the end of February, Lloyd George felt still more firmly that it was time to go—or, at any rate, to threaten to go and mean it, unless his own authority was restored. The Washington Treaty had now been signed, and on 25 February Lloyd George had paid a one-day visit to Boulogne to meet Poincaré again and try to settle the programme for the approaching conference

[1] Lord Riddell's *Intimate Diary of the Peace Conference and After*.

at Genoa. There had been some further plain speaking. Lloyd George bluntly told the French Prime Minister that if France was not going to work with Britain and the other nations to rebuild the peace and trade of the world, then they would manage without her.

Lloyd George did not much enjoy the meeting. But the journey to it was after his own heart. He had disembarked at Calais, to drive to Boulogne. The French Government had provided a battered, ramshackle old car that looked as if it had been in the historic taxi-drive to the Battle of the Marne, and probably had. But it started off from the quayside in lively style, rattling and bouncing over the cobblestones so that Lloyd George and his party flew off their seats and bumped their heads against the roof. Then, suddenly, with a grinding screech, the car came to a stop. "It needs oil," said the driver, and poured a huge canful into its thirsty throat. But when he started up the engine again, though the machinery whirled round and round, the vehicle stood still. The clutch was burned out. "It needs sand," said the driver and, picking up handfuls from the side of the coast-road, he flung them into the engine. When he engaged the gears, the veteran of the Marne moved off in good order.

Returning to Sir Philip Sassoon's house at Lympne, that night, Lloyd George remained in bed next day until lunch-time, busily writing. He continued it by the fireside in the afternoon. He was still at it next morning when he drove to Downing Street. It was his letter of resignation to Austen Chamberlain.

> 10 Downing Street,
> 27 February, 1922.
>
> "My dear Chamberlain,
>   "The present political position is one which calls for immediate decision on the part of the Government, otherwise the country will be plunged into hopeless political anarchy at a moment in its fortunes which, beyond all other, demands stability and steadiness."

Lloyd George then recites that the industrial crisis of the nation is the most severe since the years after the Napoleonic Wars. Unemployment is beyond compare in recent times. Trade is bad—and there is the Irish trouble. Yet the Government are working through this maze of difficulty with unity and concentration, and our financial state is better than any country in Europe. The international atmosphere itself has improved into one of general confidence, says Lloyd George, "and confidence breeds business!"

Thus, in spite of troubles, so firm was the Government's position that when some talk arose of a General Election, the Opposition were in a state of panic. Now, there is a complete change for the worse. It is not due to the Government. It is the result of the unfortunate activities of some people who are supposed to be its supporters. The control, says Lloyd George,

> "has been ostentatiously taken out of our hands by men who have no responsibility for the effects of judgment. There is an appearance of our

having been overridden on an important question of policy by bluster or menace from outside".

To submit to such a dictatorship, he continues, would be quite inconsistent with the self-respect which the nation expects from its public men. . . . So he has been driven to the conclusion that he cannot any longer render useful service to his country by retaining office under existing conditions. He had never sought his present position, and during the crisis of the war had been willing to serve under either Bonar Law or Balfour. It had been under pressure from them that he had formed his own Government.

But Chamberlain was unwilling to make the break, and he prevailed upon Lloyd George not to do so, either. Thereby, Austen Chamberlain threw away his own finest chance to become Prime Minister of Britain.

For the moment (and for the most part), the Coalition ranks closed up, unwillingly and uneasily. Fear of Labour was probably the principal solder. Within the last few days, the Socialists had scored two notable by-election victories at Manchester and Camberwell. Questioned privately by Lloyd George himself as to what he attributed their triumph, Philip Snowden, leading light of the I.L.P., replied: "To the threat of the Geddes Axe against Education. All the schoolmasters and schoolmistresses have been working like blacks for the Labour man."

The Prime Minister took due note. It accorded with his own assessment. When Volume III of the Geddes Report was published and it was seen that altogether the axe-man proposed to chop £86,000,000 from the national expenditure, the Government prepared to settle for considerably less. In the House of Commons Debate of 1 March, 1922, the Chancellor of the Exchequer, Sir Robert Horne, announced that there would be no reduction of teachers' salaries and no exclusion from the State-aided schools of children under the age of sixteen. Instead of £18,000,000, the savings to be made from Education would amount to only about one-third of this sum.

Personal trouble was coming up for the Prime Minister on the Liberal flank of his Coalition. It arose out of that fated minefield in Asia Minor where soon he and his Government would be entrapped.

The stern terms of the Treaty of Sèvres, imposed by the Allies upon the Turks in 1920, had never been enforced and instead the French were playing a curious game with the new Turkish dictator, Mustapha Kemal. Amongst other things, they were supplying him with arms and ammunition to fight the Greeks in the highlands of Anatolia. Now, in February, 1922, as Britain was faced with fresh disorders both in Egypt and India, the Viceroy of India, Lord Reading, and his Government thought it prudent to make a conciliatory gesture towards the Moslem world by recommending a formal revision of the Treaty of Sèvres. They proposed that the Allies should evacuate Constantinople, giving back to the Sultan his former suzerainty over the Holy Places, and also restore Thrace and Smyrna to Turkey.

The telegram containing these recommendations had reached the Secretary of State for India, Edwin Montagu, early on Wednesday morning, 1 March, 1922. He did not order copies to be circulated to his Cabinet colleagues until Friday and, in fact, this service was not completed until the following afternoon. The same day, Montagu received a second telegram from the Government of India, requesting permission to publish their recommendations forthwith. Later, from the country he privately telegraphed his consent, saying that he would confirm it officially and fully on the following Monday. On that day, 6 March, the Cabinet met. The Prime Minister himself was indisposed, and Austen Chamberlain took the chair. Before business began, the Secretary of State for Foreign Affairs, Curzon, protested to Chamberlain against any publication, and at the close of the meeting he expressed the same view to Montagu.

But Montagu replied: "I have already authorized it; I authorized it on Saturday."

He gave no hint that there was still time to stop publication. Indeed, he seems not to have realized it, though in fact the India Government telegram was not published until the following Wednesday in India and the day after that in Britain. Nothing more was said in Cabinet, either that evening or at any time before the storm broke in the British Press on Thursday morning. That afternoon Chamberlain rose in the House of Commons to say:

> "His Majesty's Government are unable to reconcile the publication of the telegram of the Government of India on the sole responsibility of the Secretary of State with the collective responsibility of the Cabinet, or with the duty which all Governments of the Empire owe to each other in matters of Imperial concern. Such independent declarations destroy the unity of policy which it is vital to preserve in foreign affairs, and gravely imperil the success of the impending negotiations.
>
> "The Secretary of State has tendered his resignation to the Prime Minister, and His Majesty has been pleased to approve its acceptance."

The announcement was greeted with loud and prolonged cheers from the Tory benches. Montagu and his policy of India Reforms were exceedingly unpopular with the diehards.

But he was not going down without a fight. That week-end, Montagu betook himself to his Cambridgeshire constituency to give his electors his own version of events. Both Lloyd George and Curzon came under the lash of his tongue.

"The Head of the Government," said Montagu, "is a Prime Minister of great if eccentric genius, whose contributions to the well-being of his country and of the world would have been so well advertised as to require no stress from me. He has demanded the price, which it is within the power of every genius to demand—and that price has been the total, complete, absolute disappearance of the doctrine of Cabinet responsibility ever since he formed his Government."

The latest evidence of this, Montagu added, was the Admiralty Memorandum knocking down the Geddes Report. "Cabinet Responsibility" had become a joke. The real cause of the disturbance, of course, was the diehard dislike of himself. The Prime Minister had done for them what they could not do for themselves, and had presented them with his (Montagu's) head on a charger.

He would now tell them what had happened in the Cabinet, and especially the part played by Curzon. When Montagu had informed him that he had already given the Government of India permission to publish, the Noble Lord had kept silent, and contented himself "with writing to me one of those plaintive, hectoring, bullying, complaining letters which are so familiar to his colleagues and friends, which ended with a request—not to discuss the matter in the Cabinet, but in future not to allow the publication of such documents without consultation with him".

Curzon hit back angrily. In the House of Lords on 14 March he declared that it was intolerable that he should have to negotiate over Turkey while "a subordinate branch of the British Government, 6,000 miles away, dictated to the British Government" what lines it should pursue in Thrace.

He said that when Montagu spoke to him in Cabinet he had been so dumbfounded at his avowal that he had closed the conversation forthwith. Montagu had held out not the faintest hope on that Monday evening that there was still time to cancel or postpone publication. Now he had been down to his constituency and there had publicly referred to, and travestied, a private conversation and private letter. Curzon certainly had the best of this argument, as next morning Chamberlain wrote to Lloyd George, who was in Criccieth recuperating after something very near a breakdown in health. For Montagu's reply from the House of Commons to Curzon the same evening had been bogged down with "explanations" of what he had said Curzon had said. But if the Government escaped fairly lightly in both Houses over the Montagu affair, in the corridors and committee-rooms and clubs a bitter argument raged, and chiefly around the personality of the Prime Minister.

The Tory rebellion was going strong.

On the very day that Curzon was trouncing Montagu in the House of Lords, a meeting of pro-Coalition Tory M.P.s was held at the House of Commons to discuss and pass a resolution in support of the Government. The organizers made the mistake of inviting every Tory M.P., and more than 200 turned up. After an aggressive minority of about forty diehards had staged a pandemonium, the loyal resolution was not put to the vote, a fact of which the hostile Press made full use next morning.

On the other hand, an immediate reaction was to bring in a shoal of supporting resolutions from local Tory branches all over the country. And when, at the Constitutional Club, a proposal came before the Political Committee to have Sir George Younger address the members, Mr. Petersen, one of the most popular, arose and amid cheers launched a broadside against that mutinous Cabin Boy, accusing him of almost every crime in the calendar, including the brewing of bad beer. Sir George was not invited to address the Constitutional Club.

But, in the continued absence of the Prime Minister at Criccieth uncertainty reigned at Westminster, and some intricate personal manœuvres were going on. The friends of "Fusion" continued to press their case, particularly Churchill who, in a speech at Loughborough on 11 March, declared that the historic Parties must merge to provide an effective Government, for the Labour Party was "unfit to govern" a phrase which followed him for many a year.

Critical comment was that Churchill was getting ready to ally himself with the Tory Party, with or without Lloyd George.

From a Fleet Street friend, Lloyd George received this assessment of the situation:

March 13, 1922.

"My dear Prime Minister,

. . . My opinion has been for some time past that the continuance of the Coalition, and of your headship of it in the form of 1918, has become impossible.

You have before you two alternatives: (1) To become the absolute head of a 'Fusion Party'; leaving out the Diehards and Wee Frees on each side (2) to move definitely to the Left with your own supporters and to secure in time a Liberal reunion, of which you must ultimately possess the leadership.

Until about a fortnight ago, I think my inclination would have been to advise the movement to the Left. In many ways, it is much the best plan. It would mean the rehabilitation of the Liberal Party as a potent force in the national life and an Opposition ready to take office in rotation with the Conservatives. I am tempted towards it myself because I think I should have found myself in sympathy with the policies which a Liberal Party would undertake under your leadership. . . .

Unfortunately, it appears to me that very serious obstacles to this course have arisen recently. Winston evidently does not mean to go in such a direction if he can help it. His tendency is all to the Right and his principles becoming more Tory. I am sure he would not fancy being shut up in a coop with you even for a short time. And such feelings may be natural.

But if he remains behind, several other Liberal members of the Government would do the same.

It follows that Austen Chamberlain or whoever was your successor if you left the present Coalition, would simply be at the head of a new Coalition, differing from yours in being more Tory and less Liberal—much on the lines of the Coalition of Salisbury and Joseph Chamberlain in the '80s and '90s. Your own Liberal following would be sensibly diminished and divided and, in consequence, the prospect of re-fusion with the Wee Frees greatly postponed and perhaps actually endangered. All kinds of practical difficulties I need not elaborate would also crop up.

(2) I therefore return to the 'Fusion Party' as the best alternative today. Here time is the essence of the contract. Two years ago I believe the task would have been comparatively easy. But the whole tendency recently has been adverse. In this matter I have no definite knowledge but I believe that Bonar Law is far more likely to find himself in agreement with you than is Austen Chamberlain, who will reflect the pressure of some of his official followers. It is obvious that the whole proceeding means an intense wrench and supersession of a separate Conservative leader.

None the less, I believe it to be the best plan. But if it is to be done, it has got to be done immediately. If your mind moves in this direction, you ought to forfeit your holiday and come back almost immediately to set the negotiation on foot. . . .

> Yours ever,
> Max."

From Criccieth came the reply:

> 15 March, 1922.

"My dear Max,

Thanks for your letter. Your thoughts are very much mine, but I am trying to keep off thinking about politics, but when I do, I will write to you. You may expect a letter one day next week.

A tired judgment is no judgment; I am therefore resolved not to make up my mind until I feel fit.

I am now enjoying a sun cure, but it is very hard to do nothing. I have almost lost the habit of it. I have not had a whole day's holiday for eight years.

> Yours sincerely,
> D. Lloyd George."

He really was almost exhausted, much annoyed with advisers like Sir Edward Grigg, who kept telling him from Downing Street that people were saying that either his illness was "diplomatic", or that he must be gravely afflicted to account for his silence at such a time—and quite furious with his friend Churchill for his dogged, undeviating opposition to recognizing the Bolsheviks as the *de jure* Government of Russia. (Russia was the issue upon which Lloyd George and Churchill came nearest to a final parting than any other in their lives.)

Unemployment in Britain was another, ever-present anxiety, for it was the subject of widespread condemnation of the Government, and of much bitter reproach of himself from the Left. The man who had promised "a land fit for heroes to dwell in", eh? Bah! Lloyd George had kept unemployment ever in his mind in seeking to restore peaceful trading conditions to the world, but he seems to have doubted if, in the most favourable circumstances, unemployment could be absolutely abolished—and if it were, whether or not it might bring other problems in its train. His feelings were not smoothed by King George's recurrence to the painful subject when Lloyd George had visited him at Moy, in Scotland, at the time of the Gairloch talks. The King had said then that something must be done to alleviate unemployment during the coming winter. The Prime Minister said that he liked a certain amount of it. His Majesty replied that there was, anyhow, now a great deal too much of it, and that it might lead to serious trouble. The Prime Minister informed His Majesty that it was to be discussed at the Cabinet meeting.

Then, too, Ireland was aflame again, with outrages in Dublin, Belfast and Limerick, and the Border was being wired, sandbagged and sited for battle. It was a serious question whether or not the British Government should move back in again, and occupy a "Neutral Zone" between the Irish Free State and Ulster.

How Lloyd George himself felt is revealed by these letters from Criccieth to Frances Stevenson, who had remained on duty in Downing Street.

March, 1922
Wednesday.

". . . How slowly the first week goes! It just drags along incessantly. The weather is simply wonderful and that does in a measure compensate. . . .

As for myself, I find that I am more at rest, and took it only just in time. My head is still bad—those racking pains now and again, but my cough is much better.

I have not thought too much about the political situation. I try to keep it off by reading tales of adventure, etc. I do not get up until noon, then I spend the rest of the day in the open air. . . . Montagu is a swine and a sneak. . . ."

March, 1922
Friday.

". . . Here is a completed week of our separation, and glad I am that it is gone. I know how the first few days always drag. The weather is still a marvel. J.T. and I walked down to Llanystumdwy stream this morning. It was like a June day. . . .

"The pains in my head are gradually disappearing, and I feel the last

With Mr. Asquith at Sutton Courtenay, 1924

Speaking at King's Langley, July 1924 (seated is Mrs. Asquith)

two days for the first time definitely better. I realize how much I needed
a rest. . . . But the moment I feel fit, I shall be difficult to restrain. Everything I care for is up there. I want you, however, to persuade me not to
return next week, otherwise I shall have a superficial mend which will
soon wear out and leave me a hopeless wreck. I cannot ask for a second
holiday, and whatever decision I come to I am in for an exciting time for
the first few weeks after my return.

Next week I shall be putting my thinking-cap on in real earnest—that
is if I continue to improve as I have done the last two days.

I hope you are taking advantage of my absence:
(a) To leave the office early;
(b) To play golf on Saturday and Sunday;
(c) To go to bed early. . . ."

But the world of politics did not stand still. From Beaverbrook came two
more urgent letters on the latest moves.

"My dear Prime Minister,   15 March.

I intended to add a postscript to my letter—not altering its tenor in
any way but developing one particular line of argument—that relating to
Winston. He is counting absolutely at the present moment on the formation
of a new Coalition in which Austen Chamberlain would occupy the position
of Lord Salisbury and he would possess the relative influence of Joseph
Chamberlain on Conservative Governments. Or, to put it otherwise, he
would be to Chamberlain as Premier what Chamberlain has been to you.

The Conservative rank and file may not see this at all. The Diehards
would have to be included in the negotiations for a new Coalition Government, because they might be able to turn such a Government out on a
critical division. In addition, there would be a strong view held by older
members with claims that, in the event of a reshuffle, the offices should go
entirely to Conservatives. I would not pronounce absolutely on this point,
for Winston's recent attitude has undoubtedly conciliated some of the
Diehards, and many of the men who might not forget his change of sides
in 1903. None the less, if an agitation against the inclusion of the Liberals
began in the Tory ranks, it would spread very far.

On the other hand, there would be considerable influences brought to
bear to keep Winston in the new combination. Certain members whose
seats are shaky and depend on Coalition Liberal votes would be in favour
of it. The Lord Chancellor (Lord Birkenhead) would certainly urge the
policy of inclusion and would find a ready listener in Chamberlain.

I put the probability of Conservative opposition to Winston's retention
of office to him the other day. He was obviously immensely surprised, and
had not thought of it. However, he soon persuaded himself that the danger
was negligible. I did not agree if, as I have just said, a campaign was started

T

against him. It appears to me very doubtful whether the Tories would be ready to kill the King merely to put a lesser Prince in his place, even if under their suzerainty.

Yours ever,
Max."

19 March, 1922.

"My dear Prime Minister,

In continuation of my previous letters, I may say that I think that the time is now ripe for an immediate move on your part.

Too violent action has resulted in a reaction in your favour. In particular the hostile Press has been writing you down to such an extent that your position has been strengthened on the rebound. My advice to you is to come back at once, and to go down to the House of Commons and say that in view of all this agitation and recrimination, you intend to demand a vote of confidence in your Government. It is, however, I think, most important that if you decide on this course, there should on no account be any disclosure of your intentions, otherwise your Conservative opponents will counter you by demanding a Tory Party meeting.

Twenty-four hours' notice of the Vote of Confidence would, I suggest, be quite sufficient.

I would make one further suggestion. In the course of your speech the main object of attack should be the opposing newspapers. The Press is always unpopular with members of the Commons and you would rally a lot of sympathy. If you want some stuff on this line I will give it to you.

Yours ever,
Max."

From Austen Chamberlain, there came an appeal to Lloyd George to make a decisive declaration soon—that he meant to go on with the Coalition:

". . . I beg, therefore, as a friend speaking in your own interest, as a colleague speaking on behalf of your colleagues, and as the leader of one of the Parties whose fortunes are inseparably bound up at the present time with your decision, to take the earliest opportunity of definitely declaring your resolution to continue as Prime Minister the leadership of the Coalition. . . ."

The Genoa Conference was drawing near, and it was urgent for the Prime Minister and the Government to make up their minds about it, especially about the proposed recognition of Russia. Lloyd George had already made up his own. He had told his intentions to Sir Robert Horne, the Chancellor of the Exchequer, who had been down to visit him at Criccieth.

Letter to Frances Stevenson: ". . . I mean to fight on Genoa. The Diehards all loathe it. It is the real test of whether a Coalition is to be progressive or reactionary. If I am beaten on it, I retire on a Liberal issue which I can go on fighting. . . . If I win, the Coalition is definitely Liberal in the real, and not the Party, sense. . . . Heavy snow showers all day. I love them and I am lying outside now on the verandah with the snow whirling around. . . ."

To Beaverbrook:

23 March, 1922.

"My dear Max,

I am back on Monday but leave for the country again on Tuesday. Could I see you during that interval? I mean to go wherever the policy of European pacification leads me. There is nothing else worth fighting for at the present moment. Office is certainly not worth a struggle apart from what you can accomplish through it. It is the policy that matters and not the premiership.

Ever sincerely,
D. Lloyd George."

He made his purpose publicly known when a series of articles written from Criccieth by a Special Correspondent of the *Daily Chronicle* appeared in that newspaper on the subject of Genoa, and Russia. The Correspondent wrote (Lloyd George subsequently denied that he had actually given any interview): "Mr. Lloyd George will part from his dearest political friend rather than abandon this great fundamental issue of politics." Nobody could mistake who was meant. Everybody in politics knew where Churchill stood with regard to the recognition of the Russians.

Chamberlain hastened to write to the Prime Minister urging that before he faced the House of Commons on the question of this forthcoming Genoa Conference the whole Cabinet should thoroughly discuss it, for

"If there are any differences of opinion among our colleagues, we should be in a very weak position if we dealt with so large a question in a mere Committee of Ministers, especially at this moment when public opinion has been concentrated by the Montagu episode on Cabinet responsibility.

"As you know," continued Chamberlain, "Winston is the person who has taken the strongest line on this subject. The Lord Chancellor and I have done our best to restrain him; but he has said to both of us that he could not remain a member of the Government if *de jure* recognition were granted by this country to the Soviet Government. Putting aside any feelings of our own, you will readily perceive that our position would be impossible if Winston retired because he was more Tory than the Tory Ministers. It is, therefore, very important that you yourself should see Winston and have a quiet personal talk with him before the Cabinet meeting takes place.

"As for the recognition of Russia itself, would it be wise for Britain to grant it alone of the great democratic Western Powers. The United States Government had decided not to recognize, and had refused to attend at Genoa. Surely, we should concert our own action in this matter with France? Isolated recognition by us would in any case raise great difficulties among our followers in the House of Commons, and if it led to a breach with Churchill it would be quite fatal to us. . . ."

Lloyd George replied by return post to the Tory Leader. He noted:

". . . the alarming information that unless the British Delegation tie themselves to the chariot wheels of France and go to Genoa to do what they are told by Poincaré, there is no hope of getting the Unionist Party to agree to the Genoa programme. Of course, I could not agree to such instructions, and as far as I am concerned, there is an end of it."

He insisted that the conditions of recognizing Russia had been laid down at the time of Cannes, and "never challenged by the Cabinet". He was not suggesting that Britain should take isolated action, but that France must not be placed in the position of dictator. If the Russians wanted to return to the community of civilized nations, it would be folly not to help them, and

". . . If Winston, who is obsessed by the defeat inflicted upon his military projects by the Bolshevik Armies, is determined that he will resign rather than assent to any recognition, however complete the surrender of the Communists and whatever the rest of Europe may decide, the Cabinet must choose between Winston and me. . . ."

Lloyd George concluded his ultimatum, for such it amounted to ("it is essential that there should be no misunderstanding about this matter"), by affirming that he had never believed that the restoration of European trade and business was possible without bringing Russia into the circle.

"And if with all this great unemployment in Britain, which will last for some time in spite of all we do, there is through our own fault a failure in the project of European co-operation to restore trade, there will be such a revolt amongst the working classes that no Government could withstand it. Our great industrial leaders will sympathize with it. . . ."

Lloyd George meant to go if he did not have his way. The difference between him and some other "resigning" politicians was that when Lloyd George threatened it he was prepared to do it. Those who worked closest to him realized it.

So, next day, Austen Chamberlain was offering appeasement. He had looked up the Cabinet minute of 16 December, 1921, which dealt with the Cannes Resolutions. He admitted that they went fairly far (they had authorized the Prime Minister to discuss with Briand the forming of a syndicate of the Western Powers, and possibly the United States, for the economic reconstruction of Russia). But both Churchill and Curzon had, on that occasion, requested fuller consideration before recognizing Russia, and Chamberlain now begged the Prime Minister to "take trouble with Winston", who might be awkward and remind the Cabinet that they had agreed to reserve this question.

"He is of course, at times very much a man of one idea," wrote Austen, "and his vehemence sometimes makes him a difficult partner in Cabinet. But he is not unreasonable at bottom; he is not impervious to a personal appeal; and he is, as I have said, your follower, and therefore doubly dangerous to me and my colleagues if he parts from us on a question where he would have the sympathy of a large section of Unionist opinion."

Lloyd George made no promises. He insisted again that Europe, including Russia, must be pacified or unemployment in Britain would get worse. France did not depend on international trade, being an agricultural rather than an industrial country, but it was Britain's life-blood. We had already surrendered too much to French politics. Were we now to let the French drag us along the streets of Genoa to exhibit our vassalage to the world? Their reparations proposals were likely to produce a catastrophe, and to drive Germany, either into Bolshevism, or back to Imperialism. Well, Lloyd George was coming up to London to deal with these problems.

Now all his doubts had been resolved, and he told Miss Stevenson that he was going to get "the worry blown out of my veins. I want to be in such condition that even John Simon won't upset me!"

The Prime Minister had need to be in his best fighting fettle. In industry, 400,000 members of the engineering trade unions were entering their third week of a disastrous national lock-out. In Ireland, while De Valera denied the legal existence of either the Ulster Government or the Irish Free State Provision Government, I.R.A. troops marched through the streets of Dublin and seized the Four Courts. Now the most savage shootings in Ireland were between men who only yesterday had been comrades in action. A civil war within a civil war was about to torture the tragic face and form of Ireland. In England, Churchill made a long-awaited speech at Northampton, in which he declared that "it would be a great disaster if the Conservative Party were broken up" and urged the importance of a united stand by Tories and Liberals against the "Bolshevist and Communist menace", which hardly accorded with Lloyd George's Genoa policy.

Not without difficulty were the differences of opinion in the Cabinet reconciled, and a Motion of Confidence drafted to be submitted to the House of Commons, approving the Cannes Resolutions as a basis for Genoa.

When Lloyd George rose to speak in the Debate on 3 April, 1922, he was careful to point out that the conditions for recognizing Russia would include that the Russians should (i) recognize their own national obligations to other countries; (ii) restore the property of foreign nationals, or pay compensation for its destruction; and (iii) guarantee to launch no aggressive action against the frontiers of their neighbours. The Prime Minister took the opportunity to castigate the "grotesque conglomerate" of the Opposition Press, which had been regaling its readers during the last three weeks of his own enforced absence with tales of the "Tottering Coalition" (it was *The Times* which coined this phrase). Lloyd George could only suppose that their new Government

"would have its principles enunciated and expounded by the *Morning Post*, the *Daily Herald*, the *Westminster Gazette*, the *Daily Mail* and *Comic Cuts*.[1] (Loud laughter.) I do not mention *The Times*, because that is only a tasteless rehash of the *Daily Mail*. (Laughter.)"

He did not himself entirely escape. Bonar Law observed rather tartly that some people were inclined to "over-deify the Prime Minister as an electioneering agent". Lord Hugh Cecil, who had long ranked amongst his severest critics, was quite sure that no other Prime Minister could be so bad as the present Prime Minister, and that so long as he was Prime Minister the condition of the country would go on getting worse and worse, as it had gone on getting worse and worse ever since the Armistice. By a majority of 278 the House of Commons, without undue enthusiasm, voted that without this Government things could be considerably worse.

Chamberlain, Churchill, Curzon, Bonar Law, the Tory diehards and the City bankers were not the only folk who thought of Genoa with a question mark. King George V, too, had his doubts. Indeed, he had been nursing them for some time past. In Chamberlain's letter to Lloyd George at Criccieth he had mentioned that His Majesty was

"very anxious to see you when you come up. I have told him that you have very critical decisions to take with your colleagues, and that you will be very busy on Monday evening and Tuesday morning. He is a little disturbed that it is so long since he saw you, and rather hurt that you left Town without giving him any notice. I made such excuses as I could and in particular, heaped the blame on your secretaries. I hope there are enough of them to bear the burden!"

Nor was King George very happy about the company his Prime Minister might keep in Genoa.

"I suppose you will be meeting Lenin and Trotsky there?" he said when Lloyd George went to see him at Buckingham Palace before leaving.

"Your Majesty," was Lloyd George's reply, "I have to meet all kinds of people in Your Majesty's service. Quite recently I had to meet a man of exceedingly ill-repute, the emissary of Mustapha Kemal, himself a man of ill-repute. I had to do so in Your Majesty's service."

[1] *Comic Cuts* had been one of Northcliffe's first journalistic ventures.

Neither Lenin nor Trotsky did attend Genoa for Russia, which was represented there by Chicherin. Nor did Poincaré appear; instead, he sent Barthou, with instructions to take no decisions but to refer all matters to Paris. Thirty-four nations sent delegations, including the Germans (headed by Dr. Rathenau), but not the Americans. The British Delegation numbered ninety-two persons, a figure which aroused the derision of *The Times*.

The tasks which awaited them were huge enough—to sign a Treaty of Peace with Russia, and to make the one already signed with Germany really work. To do this, when the Conference met on 10 April, 1922, it at once set up four Sub-Commissions to deal with political, financial, commercial and transport problems. Lloyd George had arranged that much of the vital preparatory work should be already executed in London by an Inter-Allied staff of experts. One of their labours had been to make out a bill for the Russians to pay in compensation amounting to £2,000,000,000. They also devised a scheme to issue interest-bearing bonds, and begin payment in five years' time. It took the Russians three or four days to digest this, and then they produced a counter-account for damage done during Allied Intervention in Russia which added up to £5,000,000,000.

Genoa began badly, with a sharp Britain *v.* France tussle over the admission of the Germans and the Russians to the various Commissions and Committees. Lloyd George fought Barthou hard on this issue of equality. He did not want to force these two outsiders into fierce friendship, and to have a hungry Russia rebuilt by an angry Germany.

"At this Conference," he cried, "we meet as equals. There is no victor, no vanquished: we are here on equal terms to do our utmost to rehabilitate Europe. Is Germany, a nation of 63,000,000 people, and Russia, with 120,000,000 people to be left standing on the door-step until we call them in? That is not equality, and such a thing as you suggest cannot be tolerated for one moment!"

He might have spared himself some trouble. For on Easter Sunday, 16 April, 1922, Rathenau and Chicherin signed the draft terms of the dual Treaty of Rapallo, whereby Germany recognized the Bolsheviks as the *de jure* Government of Russia. All claims and counter-claims between them were wiped out, and the Most Favoured Nation principle mutually adopted. Something else: Germany's renunciation of all claims against Russia was explicitly subject to the proviso that Russia should compensate no other claimant.

This Easter Egg had an instant and profound effect, not only upon the Conference but upon the political situation in every capital of Europe. When Lloyd George learned of it in Genoa, around midnight, he simply could not believe it. He had to do so next morning.

Immediately, a fresh Press barrage broke out in Britain against the Prime Minister, Northcliffe's *Daily Mail* and *Times* providing the most powerful and persistent fire. The Blunder of Genoa was every day attacked and Genoa's author, Lloyd George, held up to public opprobrium. Our "amateur diplomatists in the playground of European conferences" had been duped and trapped, and taken for a ride. (In fact, this criticism was so much nonsense; the Russians and Germans had been negotiating together since January. That is, ever since Poincaré had sabotaged the Conference of Cannes.) The French Premier now made a devoted effort to shipwreck the Conference of Genoa. In a speech at Bar-le-Duc, he suggested that the Russo-German Treaty meant that Germany was getting ready to make trouble for Poland, France's Eastern ally. Poincaré would like to make it plain to Germany that if she defaulted on the reparations due from her under the Treaty of Versailles, it was she who would get into trouble. The air grew thick with menacing rumours, so that Lloyd George asked the journalists in Genoa to publish an appeal to the British public "not to believe any statements about the Genoa Conference that are made in *The Times* or in the *Daily Mail*".

A few days later the Prime Minister was able to deal Northcliffe a blow which left its mark on him for the brief remainder of his life. This happened when Wickham Steed, the editor of *The Times*, whom Northcliffe specially sent to Genoa to cover the Conference, reported under heavy headlines

WRECKING THE ENTENTE
PREMIER'S THREAT TO FRANCE
STORMY INTERVIEW

that Lloyd George had informed M. Barthou that if France insisted on taking up the same intransigent attitude over Russia's debts as Belgium had, then the *Entente* between Britain and France was at an end. The Prime Minister had said, wrote Steed, that

"Great Britain considered herself henceforth free to seek and cultivate other friendships. His advisers had long been urging him to make an agreement with Germany, even at the cost of abandoning British claims to reparations. France had made her choice between British friendship and Belgian friendship. She had opted for Belgium, although the help she had received from Belgium was not comparable to the help she had received from Great Britain. . . .

. . . British opinion was hostile to France, and his (Mr. Lloyd George's) advisers, especially Lord Birkenhead, the Lord Chancellor of England, had been constantly advising him to break with France. Letters from all parts of the country gave him the same advice. . . ."

Wickham Steed had been careless, or unlucky. His informants had mixed up two interviews, one between Lloyd George and Barthou and another between him and Philippe Millet, a French journalist. At once Lloyd George saw Barthou, and prevailed on him to write a letter denying that he had ever uttered the alleged words. The Frenchman agreed, though the general sense of what Lloyd George had said was perhaps not so very far different from Steed's version. But the hostile tone of his dispatches and the continuous nagging of the Prime Minister by *The Times* had aroused resentment in England, and sympathy for the victim. There were loud cheers in the House of Commons when Austen Chamberlain, in answer to a question, said:

"I have seen the report published by *The Times* this morning, a summary of which appears to have reached the Prime Minister. . . . He has asked me to say that the account in *The Times* is a deliberate and malicious invention, and to contradict it at once. The Lord Chancellor, who is also mentioned in *The Times* report, has already repudiated it."

But at Genoa the ship was slowly sinking, despite the giant efforts which the captain was still putting forth. Probably, never in his whole life, including the most desperate days of the war, did Lloyd George labour with more devotion or determination than during the six weeks of the Genoa Conference. He was fighting to bring back work and wages and hope to two-and-a-half million workless, wageless and near-hopeless unemployed men and women in Britain.

How did he face the storm-tossed seas of trouble which beat upon the Conference? These extracts from his private letters to Frances Stevenson tell the story:

Villa D'Albertis
Genoa
(19 April)

". . . The Conference is once more in serious peril. Damn German stupidity!

I am working as I never worked in my life to save it. Every art and device my simple nature is capable of. You ought to know all about it. . . ."

(23 April).

". . . Had to sacrifice my Sunday rest to smooth over another French crisis. I am so glad you are not *all* French otherwise you would be difficult to handle. As it is, I get a French crisis now and again, don't I? Even with our *entente*!

The Conference is still labouring heavily and without a boast, I am the only man who can put it through—but it is going to take such a lot of life out of my frame. If my health holds out, I shall win. So far I am holding out, but I have had a fortnight of nerve-racking work. . . ."

Wednesday (26 April).

". . . I have had a simply diabolical day, all work and worry. The Con-

T*

ference is trembling on the edge of a precipice and I am doing all I can to save it—and I am just now very tired. . . . I am still sanguine."

(30 April).

". . . The French I could overcome were I certain of the Russians. But I am far from sure of them. They are fanatical Orientals. Benes thinks they do not mean to settle and no doubt he knows them well. Never mind I will go on fighting as long as the muzzle of a gun is out of the water. Then I shall have nothing to reproach myself with. . . .

I have come to the end of my shilling shockers. The consumption is unparalleled! Can you send some Byron's poems (unexpurgated please) and such Ridgwell Cullum as I have not read—and any other tales of adventure? . . ."

(2 May).

". . . I am having the struggle of my life. Foot to foot and face to face. But I am still on the hopeful side. In a few days I can tell you whether I am off next week or whether I am booked for another three weeks. . . .

No cloud without a rift—if you wait long enough! Just had one little patch of blue this morning. Rothermere sent his confidential man to me this morning (I had already had a pleasant talk on the boat with Rothermere) to place the whole of his papers at my disposal to support and defend me! . . . He has come to the conclusion there is no one else worth backing up!
. . . The Villa Albertis is beautiful—lizards crawling on the balcony. Grigg encountered one in his bath. I like the little fellows."

Wednesday (3 May).

". . . Don't you ever apologize again for sending too long a letter. . . .
I want *all* gossip, political and otherwise. The political news is valuable to me—and the rest is most entertaining. . . .

After a desperate struggle I got the document through to the Russians. It is substantially mine. I kept out of it most of the obnoxious stuff the French and others wanted to insert in it. . . .

I see from the *Sunday Express* that the attacks made upon me by the hostile Press both in France and England are specially vicious—'and of a personal character', 'on my honour and integrity'. What are they? I have not seen them. They are out to down me if they can—they are getting desperate. . . ."

(4 May).

". . . What warm days we have had! Hot fly-infested days. Eaten with flies. I am waiting for the return of Barthou and the reply of the Russians. This morning I had a couple of hours with the German Chancellor, Von Rathenau. Germany is in a mood of despair and it is too early to predict what the Russians will do. They do not know themselves. They are very divided and distracted.

F.E. came here last night. His eyesight is still very bad. Rothermere left early this morning. He is most friendly. He told me some illuminating things about the intrigues of the past few months.

Chamberlain was undoubtedly at one time tempted to try his luck. 'There is no friendship at the top.' I am enveloped in intrigues. I hate this waiting. . . .

I am in a mood to chuck politics altogether and retire to Italy like Byron and Shelley who told the world to go to the devil. I pass Byron's house every day. . . . I am in a very bad temper with everyone round me. . . ."

Sunday morning (7 May).

". . . I am off to Kirk! No time to write!

Had two hours with the German Chancellor—after three hours with the American Ambassador and several interviews before that. . . .

The struggle is *acharné—à la mort*. I am not done yet, although beset by enemies of all kinds. Many more enemies, open and secret, than friends —at least that is the case here. . . ."

Tuesday (9 May).

". . . It is very hard to go through all the worry and perplexity without you. . . .

I have no one here who thinks it is worth their while to cheer me up when I am oppressed and almost overwhelmed with anxieties.

The Russians difficult—hesitating—with their judgment warped in doctrine. The French selfish—Germans impotent—the Italians willing but feeble—the little countries cowed. *The Times* devilish!

The Russians are replying tomorrow. I have no notion—not after several interviews with them—what they mean to say, but I am far from hopeful. The French are seeking every chance to break the Conference. There are many others who would like to join them. But they are still rather afraid of me. I have a certain hold on Liberal opinion throughout the world, and I can thus make trouble for them in their own countries.

I am fighting the most difficult battle of my life—and the most decisive, for better or for worse.

Your letters give me a strength you can hardly appreciate. . . ."

11 May, 1922.

". . . I am working so hard so as to get back as soon as possible. . . . I had a real success yesterday. Saved the Conference by a 'bantering' speech. . . ."

Saturday night (13 May).

". . . Very hard day but a very good day. Beat French hip and thigh. Looks as if we were going to get something substantial after all. It has been, and still is, a terrible fight. . . ."

(15 May).

". . . The fight is still desperate but I am hopeful of saving my last scheme. That means the Conference will go on at the Hague. The fight for peace will continue. Next week I shall have to make a speech in the House. That bothers me. . . ."

Lloyd George returned home from Genoa to a tumultuous popular welcome at Victoria Station, rivalling that of another great day, three years before, when he had brought back the Treaty of Versailles. But he owed it less to what he had been able to achieve at Genoa than (as Bonar Law frankly reminded him) the vitriolic Press attacks he had been subjected to while representing his country abroad, which had disgusted many people. "Things are really very bad," Bonar concluded, sadly.

To which Lloyd George retorted gaily: "Yes, Bonar, but they will get worse. They are always getting worse!"

But Bonar Law was right about the actual achievements of Genoa. Nothing had been done to improve the handling of the Reparations problem. For Poincaré, by long-distance from Paris had rejected Lloyd George's proposal for an early meeting of the Supreme Allied Council for this purpose; he wanted to keep his hands free to invade the Ruhr in the expected event of a German default. So, on 25 May, when Lloyd George gave the House of Commons an account of the Genoa Conference, he kept off German reparations, and concentrated on Russian debts, for these had been referred to a mixed Commission of experts who were to meet at the Hague the following month. He described the Conference scene:

"They sat around that table the representatives of thirty-four nations. Over there, sat the Russian delegation, representing more human poverty, wretchedness, desolation, hunger, pestilence, horror, and despair than all the other nations represented round the table. That was the first fact to realize. The other fact was this, that without the assistance of the other nations, it was hopeless for Russia, whatever its Government, to extricate itself from that pit of squalid misery.

. . . There—it was no use questioning it—sat the men who represent the unchallenged masters for the time being of the fate of that formidable, but very distressed people. The millions of Russia could only be dealt with through them. They could only be brought into contact with the outside world through them. They could only be rescued from hunger or death through them. The treasures of Russia could not be unlocked to the outside world except through them. Peace or war with Russia could only be made through them, and whether Russia marched forward or retreated, whether the 1,500,000 men she has under arms marched today, and whether the 4,000,000 she has in the background in reserve would march tomorrow, is a question whether they obey them or not. That was the first fact that you had to get well into your mind before you began with the business of Russia."

There were several methods of dealing with this situation, said Lloyd George. One, which had been tried, and had failed, was of using force. No one at Genoa had suggested that. Another, was to leave Russia to her fate until she had reformed herself; this involved the risk that Russia might not wait while her children perished but might embrace an even more extreme and violent form of Communism, or make a partnership of desperation with some other pariah nation, and let loose a new phase of Militarism. A third course was that which William Pitt had sought to pursue with the French Revolution, namely, of dealing with it, even though he did not like it. Surely it was better to try and bring Russia back into the comity of civilized nations?

Such was Lloyd George's case, and though Asquith found the results of the Prime Minister's labour at Genoa "depressingly, and even distressingly, meagre", and it was attacked from both the extreme Right, and the extreme Left, fewer than thirty Diehards and I.L.P.-ers together mustered in the lobby against it. Independent Tory Mr. Oswald Mosley, who did not vote at all, observed that the only result that he could recognize was that the Prime Minister appeared to have reconciled the Colonial Secretary (Churchill) with his pristine enemies, the Bolsheviks. Napoleon, his hero, had been forced by an adverse fate to retreat *from* Moscow—Mr. Churchill had been made to retreat *to* Moscow. (In actual fact, Churchill was in no way at all reconciled even to the recognition of the Russians. He was furious with Birkenhead —whom he considered had been "nobbled" by Lloyd George at Genoa—and lay fulminating in bed with a bruised rib, which he had got from falling off his horse.)

The day after the Genoa debate, twenty-five Tory Peers under the chairmanship of Lord Long, and including the Earls of Derby, Balfour and Birkenhead, attended a dinner in honour of the Prime Minister, the statesman whom the chairman said had been "pursued by calumny and abuse of an unparalleled character".

Was the crisis of the Coalition now over? No. It was about to begin a new chapter of misfortune. . . .

First, Ireland. Grave doubts had suddenly arisen over the draft Constitution of the Irish Free State which Arthur Griffith and Michael Collins proposed. The Constitution of the Dominion of Canada had been regarded as the acceptable model, but this draft would give the Irish Free State complete freedom in Foreign Affairs and independence in Imperial ones. The British Cabinet on 2 June, 1922, decided to say no, and to send some searching questions to the Sinn Fein leaders. Both they and the Ulster leaders had come to London for conference, and now this warm June evening as the anxious hours passed, the drama of that misty December night of the Treaty signing was being re-enacted. Then, at last, a conciliatory answer. It was not to be war between England and Ireland again. The Conference agreed that the Irish Free State was to be a co-equal member of the British Commonwealth of Nations. A General Election in the Irish Free State immediately afterwards confirmed this agreement between the Provisional Government and the British Government, giving the Pro-Treaty Party a substantial working majority. War between England and Ireland was over, at last.

It was not over between Irishmen.

As the Ulsterman, Field-Marshal Wilson, entered his house in Eaton Square, London, after attending a memorial service to British ex-servicemen, two Southern Irish gunmen (one was himself a wounded ex-serviceman) shot him dead. In Dublin, Southern Irishmen slaughtered each other. An I.R.A. garrison still occupied the Four Courts, an extraordinary defiance of the official Government. It drew from Bonar Law the melancholy—and for the Coalition, menacing—confession that though he had voted for the Irish Treaty, he would never have done so if he had realized what was going to happen. Now, after a sharp warning from Lloyd George that if this scandal continued, H.M. Government must regard it as a violation of that Treaty, Free State artillery opened fire on the Four Courts. The I.R.A. garrison held out for several days, and destroyed with a land mine the remaining buildings and their store of public records before surrendering. Fighting then broke out all over South-West Ireland, with the blowing-up of police barracks and burning-down of coastguard stations. Before summer ended, Michael Collins had been killed in a road ambush.

This revival of Irish violence brought down upon Lloyd George's Government the condemnation of Lords Salisbury and Carson for "handing Ireland over to anarchy". But far more damaging to the reputation of the Coalition (for the tragedy of Ireland was the heritage of every party), was the latest development in the Honours scandal. This happened when Lord Harris, on 22 June, 1922, in the House of Lords asked whether the grounds on which Sir Joseph Benjamin Robinson, of South Africa, had been recommended for a peerage were National and Imperial services in connection with the Robinson South Africa Banking Corporation?

Lord Harris recalled the House of Lords Debate of August, 1917, and the Resolution which Lord Curzon had then accepted on behalf of the Government (i) that the reasons for conferring any Honours should be made public, and (ii) that the Prime Minister must satisfy himself that there was no payment of money, or expectation of it. He then outlined the Robinson story.

In 1908, said Harris, this Robinson had been made a baronet. What services to the State had merited this honour Lord Harris did not inquire, for that was over. But what had the gentleman done since to deserve public recognition? Harris next disclosed that as the Chairman of the Randfontein Estates Co., Robinson had bought certain mining property freeholds for himself and re-sold them to his company "at an enormously higher price". This "illicit profit", which he concealed from the shareholders, was condemned in scathing terms by the High Court some years later, when it was made the subject of litigation. The Lord Chief Justice of South Africa ordered Robinson to pay £500,000 compensation, and the British Press branded him as "a fraudulent trustee". When, in November, 1921, he appealed to the Judicial Committee of the Privy Council to alter the High Court findings, they had dismissed his petition. How came his name now on the Honours List?

Lord Buxton thought that it had been "received with universal astonishment and mystification. I will not use a stronger or uglier word."

The Earl of Selborne used both. After saying that the Parliament and Press of the Dominions were talking about "a public scandal of the first magnitude", while over here both had been cynically indifferent, he added:

"It is not an exaggeration to say that immense sums of money continue to flow into the coffers of the political Party in power at the moment. The whole world knows that. It is the subject of general discussion in society, in the club, wherever you meet men. It is a matter of general notoriety. . . ."

For the Government, Lord Crawford scored no marks when he said that he had never heard of the Randfontein Estates transaction. The debate continued, with Sir William Vestey's peerage also under fire. It was alleged that, during the war, Vestey had domiciled himself in the Argentine to avoid British income tax.

This was only Round One. There were four more to come. A week later, 29 June, 1922, the Lord Chancellor, Birkenhead, admitted in the House of Lords that the Colonial Secretary, Churchill, had not been consulted about the peerage recommended for Sir Joseph Robinson, whom he described as "a pioneer of the South African gold and diamond industries, and now about eighty-two years of age". It was General Botha who had advised his baronetcy, in 1908. Birkenhead then read a letter, which he said the Prime Minister had received from Sir Joseph Robinson.

It expressed the writer's surprise at the previous debate in the House of Lords over the proposed peerage for himself, an honour which he had not personally sought. He had come to an age when honours no longer interested him, and while he appreciated the suggested one he now begged His Majesty's permission to decline.[1]

[1] This letter had been sent by Robinson to Lloyd George six days earlier, 23 June, 1922. On 29 June, a National Liberal Party official called on Robinson at the Savoy Hotel to deliver by hand the Prime Minister's reply. It said that His Majesty agreed to Robinson's request to decline the proposed honour. Robinson misunderstood this message, reached for his cheque-book, and inquired "How much more?" When he realized its meaning, Robinson complained of a breach of faith, and said he would now be covered with ridicule. It seems that he was expecting his withdrawal to be declined, and the peerage conferred on him.

Lord Lansdowne, who followed the Lord Chancellor, emphasized that it was what had happened in 1915 (the Randfontein case) that weighed with most of the objectors. Why hadn't someone in that Garden Suburb Secretarial "constellation of ability" of the Prime Minister's, with a keen sense of discrimination and perhaps a little of the flair of a private detective, been able to offer advice? Lansdowne agreed that

> "the difficulty of drawing a line between the legitimate payment of money to Party and political funds and the corrupt payment for such a purpose is great. The frontier almost as puzzling a frontier as the frontier of Ulster."

Lord Buckmaster thought that the best way to keep politics clean was to publish full details of all Party Funds. Lord Carson declared that the papers which as a lawyer he had to examine in his chambers, showed that there was "a regular brokerage . . . for carrying out and obtaining honours".

King George V himself shared in the widespread public uneasiness, both about the number of honours which were being conferred and the qualifications of some of the recipients.

The question of honours, indeed, was a continuing one between Lloyd George and the King. Press Lords, political Lords, financial Lords, and even medical Lords were involved. Thus, there was the case of the doctor, Sir Bertrand Dawson, who became Lord Dawson of Penn.

Physician Extraordinary to King Edward VII, he had been made K.C.V.O. in 1911 for services to the Royal Family, and in 1914 had been appointed Consulting Physician to the British Expeditionary Force with the rank of Major-General. When Lloyd George formed his Coalition Government in 1916, Dawson had written him a letter of warm congratulation, saying how the men in the trenches had been cheered to hear this splendid news. He had himself attended Lloyd George during one of his earlier visits to France as War Minister. Later, in August, 1918, when Lloyd George was beginning to make plans for the days of peace, he invited Dawson to visit him at Criccieth, and there with Addison and Milner, discussed with him the creation of a Ministry of Health. When the war ended, Dawson became Lloyd George s own doctor.

In 1919 the Prime Minister put his name forward for a peerage. But King George V demurred; although he held a high opinion of Dawson's professional capacity, he thought that senior doctors might feel they had been passed over and that, anyway, surgeons should have precedence. No physician had been ennobled since Lister, who had done so great a service to humanity.

Lloyd George answered diplomatically. This peerage was not for services rendered but for services to come. It was prospective, not retrospective. He wanted Dawson in the House of Lords to lend his experience and counsel there when the new Health Measures were debated. The doctor was made a peer the following year. Thus a precedent was created for the subsequent creation of Lords Horder, Moynihan, Moran and Webb-Johnson.

But now this latest case of a proposed financial Lord (Robinson) was a little too much for His Majesty. Indeed, he expressed the opinion that it came pretty near to being an insult to the Crown and to the House of Lords, and would do much harm. He took the unusual step of writing a personal letter to his Prime Minister, expressing his anxieties.

Lloyd George replied deprecating any accident or error which may have occurred in the recommendations for honours. These, of course, were prepared by the Party Whips, upon a Party basis, which was coeval with the existence of the Party System, and on the whole gave few causes for complaint. With regard to Sir J. B. Robinson, it must be borne in mind that he had rendered considerable services to his country after the South African War, and had so far won the esteem of General Botha that he had recommended him to two British Prime Ministers, Sir Henry Campbell-Bannerman and Mr. Asquith. But the present Prime Minister was most anxious to protect the Crown and the Government from any abuse of such honours, and was now engaged with his colleagues in seeking further safeguards.

On 17 July, 1922, once more in the House of Lords, the Earl of Salisbury opened Round Three. Banging the box in front of him, he demanded a Joint Committee of both Houses of Parliament to examine the present methods of submitting names for honours. There were swindlers going about, it was said, suggesting that they had the power to get honours which they did not possess. If there were a proper handling of Honours they would never be listened to. Nobody believed that you could get a job as General of a Division, or as a Bishop, in return for money. Lord Salisbury then traces the "downward steps", or "Rake's Progress" in the award of honours.

i. Public Services.
ii. Public Services plus Donations.
iii. Public Services plus Large Donations.
iv. Donations plus Public Services.
v. Donations.

Lord Salisbury said they all knew now who had *not* recommended Robinson for a peerage. It was none of those men distinguished in British and South African public life—Mr. Churchill, Lord Selborne, Lord Buxton, Lord Milner or General Smuts. Who *had* done it? The ghost of General Botha?

The Duke of Northumberland then advanced to the attack. His Grace delivered some dangerous punches. He began by a general charge that the record of the Coalition Government in the matter of honours differed from that of any previous Government on four separate counts.

i. The "immense scale on which honours have been lavished".
ii. The "utterly reckless disregard of the services and character of the recipient".
iii. The "systematic attempt made to obtain control of the Press by selling honours in return for newspaper support".
iv. One of the two Parties of the Coalition Government had profited to an extent out of all proportion to its numbers.

The Unionist Party funds were at a low ebb, said the Duke, while

"the Prime Minister's Party, insignificant in numbers and absolutely penniless four years ago, has in the course of those four years amassed an enormous Party chest, variously estimated at anything from £1,000,000 to £2,000,000. The strange thing about it is that this money has been acquired during a period when there has been a more wholesale distribution of honours than ever before, when less care has been taken with regard to the services and character of the recipients than ever before, when whole groups of newspapers have been deprived of real independence by the sale of honours and constitute a mere echo of Downing Street, from where they are controlled."

The Duke of Northumberland then demanded an inquiry into the conditions under which this great fortune had been amassed with such extraordinary rapidity, and the people who had subscribed. Were they all Liberal Coalitionists? Because there was reason to suppose that the purchase money for these honours was sometimes paid by wealthy Unionists.

"It is quite extraordinary how many gentlemen who buy newspapers and run them in favour of the Coalition Government's policy are rewarded with honours . . . forty-nine Privy Councillors, Peers, Baronets and Knights created since 1918, all of whom are either proprietors, principal shareholders, editors, managing directors or chairmen of groups of newspapers. This figure does not include a multitude of others who have been made Companions of Honour, C.M.G.s and the like, nor does it include certain other gentlemen who have been similarly honoured and who, without having this direct connection with the Press, have very obligingly provided the money to purchase a newspaper or a group of newspapers."

Could it be coincidence, asked the Duke, that three persons connected with the principal newspaper in South Wales, the *Western Mail*, Cardiff, were all honoured with titles, the proprietor, one of the largest shareholders, and the editor? He then quoted from a letter (he gave no names) which had been addressed to two separate people. The second of these, said the Duke, had been assured on another occasion by one of H.M. Ministers that the Knighthood under discussion would cost £10,000, "which need not be paid down all at once, but could be spread over a period of four years."

Another tout had written:

"I am authorized to offer you a Knighthood or a Baronetcy, not of the Order of the British Empire—no nonsense of that kind, but the real thing. A Knighthood will cost you £12,000 and a Baronetcy £35,000."

The writer had added that there had been some difficulty in the past through people paying in advance, and then failing to get the honour. This could now be overcome by arranging for a deposit in joint names. Instructions followed.

"You will be asked to meet someone in high authority, probably in Downing Street, and after the introduction but not until, say, three or four days before the List is announced you will be asked to pay £10,000 or £30,000, as the case may be . . . and I am permitted to take the balance, which represents the fees. Nothing need be paid until you are absolutely assured that the honour will be given. . . .

There are only five Knighthoods left for the June list—if you should decide on a Baronetcy you may have to wait for the Retiring List. The Retiring List refers to the honours which a retiring Prime Minister is allowed to recommend on a change of Government. This may take place at any time now. It is not likely that the next Government will give so many honours, and this is really an exceptional opportunity, but there is no time to be lost if you wish to take it. I assure you that all inquiries regarding yourself have been made and satisfactory answers received, so that you may be sure there will be no difficulty. It is unfortunate that Governments must have money, but the Party now in power will have to fight Labour and Socialism, which will be an expensive matter."

The Lord Chancellor, after pleading that the Prime Minister had been overwhelmingly busy with great affairs of State, entered a general defence of Party honours. But he offered a Royal Commission on the question.

On the same day, in the House of Commons, Ronald McNeill attacked the peerages bestowed on Lord Waring (formerly Sir Samuel Waring) and on Lord Forres (formerly Sir Archibald Williamson). He said that Waring had made a fortune out of Government contracts at the White City, while debenture holders lost their money. He accused Forres of trading with the enemy in Chile during the war, when he had sold fuel oil to German nitrate firms. As McNeill made this charge, from the Distinguished Strangers' Gallery came a stentorian shout: "That's a false statement!"

It was Lord Forres. The facts appear to have been that the Germans in Chile had managed to get an embargo laid on British oil, and we had to induce the Chilian Government to remove it. But the House of Commons was now so thoroughly stirred up by the "Honours Scandal" that Godfrey

Locker-Lampson and Sir Samuel Hoare had no difficulty in getting 300 fellow-M.P.s to sign their motion for setting up a Select Committee of both Houses to inquire into it.

The Prime Minister rose. He granted that mistakes may have been made, but he denied that the percentage of error in recent awards of honours was higher than in other days. "Political honours", in any case, formed a very small fraction of the total list, and payment to the Party funds played no part at all. He had already refused a Committee of Inquiry, for this would appear to be an admission by the Government of a serious state of affairs, but he now proposed a Royal Commission to consider future procedure. Of the alleged trade in honours by political Parties, Lloyd George said:

> "If it ever existed, it was a discreditable system. It ought never to have existed. If it does exist, it ought to be terminated, and if there is any doubt on that point every step should be taken to deal with it. . . ."

From the Liberal Opposition benches Asquith entered a plea that contribution to Party funds ought not to *disqualify* a citizen from receiving public recognition. Indeed, it was the duty of those well-endowed with the world's goods to support the political causes they believed in.

So ended the Parliamentary affray over honours. It lingered on in the Press for a little longer—and then, suddenly, a flash above the murk of parish pump politics, the fire of war again between the nations.

Four troubled years of the tumult of Peace, and now it threatened that the world was going up in flames once more. What had happened while we were quarrelling in the soot and ashes of the last inferno—and what was going to happen next?

CHAPTER XXX

CHANAK

OF all the débris of modern war the most dangerous is debt. For it is not only that this pile of rubbish holds bitter memories and breeds new hatreds; it is strewn with unexploded bombs, which can go off at any time and set the whole lot blazing. Four years after the First World War, the ex-enemies were as busy bullying (or cheating) each other as on the first day of the Armistice. The ex-allies had started squabbling almost the following day.

Lloyd George wanted to wipe the entire slate clean. At least, he wanted to do so as soon as he realized the mess that inter-allied debts and enemy reparations were creating in the post-war world. Unfortunately, Lloyd George had signed his name to the stern treaties imposed upon the enemy, and before that, he had given his word to still more unfortunate promises to "search their pockets for the uttermost farthing".

Britain's financial problem was threefold: (i) to collect the reparations due to her from Germany; (ii) to collect the war debts (and in the case of Russia, perhaps also the pre-war debt) due to her from her late allies; (iii) to pay her own war debt due to the United States.

Lloyd George took the view that these inter-allied war debts were, in fact, mere paper transactions recording the contributions in goods or money which each Allied country had made towards their joint victory; they were no more required to be paid in full than the casualties which each country had incurred in the field were to be compensated by transferring population. Britain was owed in war debts and reparations a total sum of £3,400,000,000; she owed America £850,000,000; she was ready to cancel the whole account.

As Chancellor of the Exchequer, Austen Chamberlain had already broached this proposition to the United States Government in 1921, when it had been turned down. Now, 1 August, 1922, as a new London Conference on war debts and reparations drew near, Balfour issued his famous Note on behalf of the British Government. The vital paragraph declared:

"The policy favoured by His Majesty's Government is . . . that of surrendering their share of German reparations, and writing off, through one great transaction, the whole body of inter-Allied indebtedness. But if this be found impossible of accomplishment, we wish it to be understood that we do not in any event desire to make a profit out of any less satisfactory arrangement. In no circumstances do we propose to ask more from our debtors than is necessary to pay our creditors. And while we do not ask for more, all will admit that we can hardly be content with less. For it should not be forgotten, though it sometimes is, that our liabilities were incurred for others, not for ourselves."

The Balfour Note was severely criticized by *The Times*, though it was not Northcliffe's hand that was responsible this time. That formidable figure lay stricken in his house at No. 1 Carlton Gardens, and on 14 August, 1922, he died. He had been, as Beaverbrook said: "The greatest figure who ever strode down Fleet Street."

The death of Northcliffe did not alter the antagonism of *The Times* to the Prime Minister—even when for a brief moment the word went round that Lloyd George was proposing to buy it. *The Times* remained, then and ever, hostile to Lloyd George and all his works.

Political crisis was now mounting for his Government. The London Conference, which assembled on 7 August, 1922, met with no better fate than Cannes or Genoa. Poincaré was still in pursuit of his prey—reparations from Germany. While he welcomed the Balfour Note proposals to cancel inter-allied debts (France owed them both to Britain and the United States), Poincaré would not hear of remitting enemy reparations to France. When Lloyd George proposed a moratorium until December to enable the Germans to meet their obligations, Poincaré refused to consider it without fresh German guarantees. He demanded control of Germany's finances, foreign currencies, export licences, the revenues from her mines and forests, a Customs barrier between her and the occupied zone of the Rhineland, and 60 per cent share of her factories. The argument could not be settled, and was referred to one more expert committee, which once more failed to agree. Meantime the German mark began to fall. The highways of European trade—and of Britain's own economic recovery, as the greatest trader of all—remained choked with the rubble of reparations.

Thus, though the Chancellor of the Exchequer, Chamberlain, told the House of Commons that while Germany had so far paid the Allied Powers £415,000,000 in Reparations, Britain's share of this (£56,000,000) just about squared what our Army of Occupation had cost us. As for our own débris of debt to ourselves, it now stood at £7,766,000,000, compared with the United States' National Debt of £5,147,000, 000, or £181 per head of the population compared with £47.

For the rest of the general outlook, the Russian situation appeared no brighter than before—and with members of the British Cabinet no more seeing eye-to-eye on it than before.

Churchill, in particular, was still vehemently opposing Lloyd George's own desire to recognize the Soviet Government, and he threatened to resign if such an issue ever arose again. In Churchill's stated opinion there had been no improvement of any kind in the character and behaviour of the Bolsheviks, and there never would be.

Britain's relations with Bolshevik Russia were not the only point at variance between the Prime Minister and his Colonial Secretary. There was the question of the Greeks and the Turks.

In the quarrel between these two nations, Lloyd George was unreservedly on the side of the Greeks. It is not to be explained that he was mesmerized by Veniselos, that great Greek Liberal and romantic ex-rebel leader of Crete. Nor that Lloyd George derived his anti-Turk prejudices from his own old Liberal Leader, Mr. Gladstone. It was that Lloyd George believed that the Greeks were the rising Power in the Eastern Mediterranean, an intelligent and energetic people, growing rapidly in numbers, better soldiers than our British brass-hats could possibly imagine, and such good sailors that they would soon possess all the most important islands in that sea, islands which would be the potential submarine bases of tomorrow, and which lay along the flanks of Britain's own line of communication via Suez Canal to the Far East and Australasia.

Churchill once more took the opposite view. The British Empire was the greatest Mohammedan Power in the world, he argued, and any prolonged anti-Turk policy would produce grave rifts within it. The Tory Party was pro-Turk in bias, and the British generals had learned a fresh respect for these redoubtable warriors. Besides, did you really want to drive the Turks into the arms of the Bolsheviks?

In these opinions, Churchill had formerly found strong support from his fellow Liberal, Edwin Montagu, when he was Secretary of State for India. His Conservative colleagues were naturally ranged on his side. Curzon took up a midway position; he was for making a friendly peace with the Turks, but he thought that they should be expelled from Europe and Constantinople. When, on a majority vote, the British Cabinet decided not to turn out the Turks, they accompanied this decision by no positive action to come to terms with them. By the Treaty of Sèvres, a neutral zone under an International Commission had been set up, covering both shores of the Sea of Marmora, and including Constantinople. Then King Constantine had returned to the Greek throne, the Greek advance into Asia Minor had been halted, and for months a sullen, unofficial truce reigned between the Greek and the Turk armies. Nothing much seemed to be happening. Things could wait in the Near East . . . so some people said.

The trouble is that things do not wait there, any more than they do in the Near West; only that one does not hear of them so soon. Genoa, and the Russo–German deal at Rapallo, was filling the headlines on 26 April, 1922, when Churchill wrote to Curzon, complaining that the Prime Minister's policy would end in alienating France and leaving Britain without a friend in Europe.

Throughout the summer of 1922, reports of earlier Turk atrocities against the ill-fated Armenians, and of the present slaughter of Greeks in the Black Sea ports of Turkey, began to flow into Europe. Perhaps encouraged by the wave of anti-Turk feeling which these stories created, King Constantine of Greece and his Prime Minister, Gounaris, demanded permission from the Allies to enter Constantinople. To back their demand, they recalled two Greek divisions from Anatolia, in Asia Minor, and sent them to reinforce their army in Thrace, on the European shore.

It was a fatal move. For the Allies said No, and British, French and Italian detachments on duty in Constantinople made ready to move up to the Chatalja Lines, the famous defensive outworks of the great city on the Bosphorus.

The Greeks stood back. They did not want to engage the Allies as well as the Turks. Perhaps they still hoped that Britain would do something more for them than "simply hold the balance", as Lloyd George claimed that we were doing.

"Tilting the balance" would have been nearer the truth. For though the British Government were providing the Greeks with no physical aid, the Prime Minister, at any rate, was offering them moral support. In the debate on the Adjournment, 4 August, 1922, Lloyd George said of the Greek campaign in Asia Minor:

> "I do not know of any army that would have gone as far as the Greeks have gone. It was a very daring and a very dangerous military experiment. They established a military superiority in every pitched battle."

The Greek High Command thought so much of this unsolicited tribute that they reproduced it in their Orders of the Day.

But now, whatever balance had existed between the Greeks and the Turks was suddenly upset. Mustapha Kemal decided to strike in Anatolia. On 26 August, the Turkish Army advanced. By next day, the Greek line had been broken and the whole army was in full retreat. Soon it was in rout, a demoralized mob rushing back upon Smyrna. They fled so fast that the Turks never caught up with them until they reached the crowded port. There, every Greek, man or woman, soldier or civilian, was struggling to scramble aboard any kind of craft to get away from the horror that was to come.

It came. On 9 September, despite the presence of British battleships in the bay, the Turks burned Smyrna to ashes, robbing and raping in a style that the world has not seen since their forefathers had smashed in the gates of Constantinople nearly five centuries earlier, and finally massacring every Christian they could lay hands on in the city. Then, drunk with blood and victory, the Turkish troops turned north towards the Straits and Constantinople itself. Were they going to repeat history?

An inter-Allied Occupation Force of about 12 battalions was stationed in the neutral zone, under a British C.-in-C., Lieut.-General Sir Charles ("Tim")

Harington, a resolute and sagacious soldier. The triumphant Turks mustered
100,000 troops. It would not be possible to hold Constantinople if they
advanced upon it.

It was realized that against attack from the East, the true defence of Constantinople, which stands on the European shore of the Straits, was on the
Ismid Peninsula of the Asiatic shore—just as the true defence of the Dardanelles
was at Chanak on the same shore. But the Allied garrison on the Ismid Peninsula
at this grave hour consisted of only two British battalions; at Chanak, there
was one.

This was because General Harington was not allowed by the French and
Italian Governments to employ their troops on the Asiatic mainland. Now,
as the Turkish advance guards moved up towards the neutral zone, General
Harington appealed to the French and Italian commanders to send detachments of their troops to Chanak and Ismid so that the Allies could thereby
"show three flags instead of one".

They agreed, as fellow-soldiers. So the French and Italian detachments
arrived, and amid rousing cheers from the Tommies, were played in by the
British bands. General Harington then warned the Turks, exactly as he had
warned the Greeks at Chatalja a few weeks before, that any infringement of
the neutral zone would be resisted by Allied arms. A firm, united stand now
by Allied diplomacy would have more than made up for any immediate
military inferiority.

But already, by 2 September, 1922, the Man-on-the-Spot, General Harington, had reported that the French were congratulating the Turks on the
success of their operations against the Greeks. The next day, he had wired
that the situation was very serious and called for immediate action. Anything
might happen at Smyrna, Harington had warned.

A week later, after setting forth the disposition of the three Allied units,
General Harington reported that if he could show the Three Flags then
Chanak would be safe from the Kemalist threat which was gathering on the
Bosphorus; if not, we should have to take on its defence unaided. To his
dismay, he received a telegram in reply from the War Office saying that it
was not the intention of the Government to hold Chanak, and that he could
evacuate at his discretion.

General Harington stuck to his guns (or, as he then still hoped, to his
Three Flags). He replied that both the French and Italians were sending
troops to the threatened frontiers, and that to recede from the position would
be fatal. He was now making "Allied arrangements for Allied defence in
perfect harmony".

He went on to urge that even if the Allies did not intend to hold Chanak
then, at least, let them keep a rearguard there until a withdrawal across the
Dardanelles to Gallipoli was compelled.

Next day, General Harington's news was worse, and he wired that if, as was rumoured, Mustapha Kemal had declared war on the Allies, it was more necessary than ever that they should stand firm and make Allied unity apparent. They were up against a fact which admitted of no delay.

This fact was that the Turks were already drawing a net around the British position. General Harington still believed that they would not attack if only the Allies stood firm.

But, as a good soldier, Harington had made ready to receive the Turk assault. Our little garrison had been reinforced, a strong defensive position selected which could be covered by the guns of the British warships which lay in the Sea of Marmora, and night and day the troops had toiled to dig-in and to wire their front and flanks. Outnumbering them ten times over, the Turks approached.

By now, mid-September, the political commotion inside the British Cabinet was almost as considerable as that within the area of military conflict itself. Characteristically, Churchill, who had consistently opposed Lloyd George's Greek adventure, rallied to his side when it appeared that Turk intransigence would imperil the entire rewards of the World War victory of the Allies in the Near East, to which Britain had contributed more military effort, man-power and money than any other nation. Both Churchill's pugnacity and loyalty were aroused, a formidable combination. Also loyally standing by the Prime Minister were Balfour, Birkenhead, Chamberlain, Horne and Worthington-Evans.

On Friday, 15 September, the Cabinet debated the grave situation. Before them lay the telegram of Field-Marshal Lord Plumer, who by chance had been holidaying in the Eastern Mediterranean and had called in to see his old comrade, General Harington. The Field-Marshal had inspected the Chanak defences, and found them in good order. He urged that the garrison be immediately reinforced. In his view, the Turks meant business.

On the other hand the strategic situation was favourable to us, especially if we could keep that foothold at Chanak on the Asiatic shore. British battle-ships rode the Sea of Marmora, and while they did so no hostile army could cross to the European shore and Constantinople.

The British Cabinet decided to warn Mustapha Kemal not to violate the neutral zone, and to take all necessary steps to strengthen our forces both on the coast and Sea of Marmora. The French and Italian Governments at this time, 15 September, still seemed to be in line with us. The British Cabinet resolved to try and bring the Dominion Governments into active accord, too, and Churchill was instructed by Cabinet minute to draft a telegram to them from the Prime Minister, informing them of the crisis and inviting their aid.

Miss Stevenson recalled that afternoon when the door of her office at No. 10 Downing Street suddenly opened and in walked the Prime Minister and Churchill from the Cabinet Room and began discussing the form which the telegram should take. She remembered, too, that she was horrified at what she heard, conveying as it seemed to her the prospect of another Great War. When Lloyd George and Churchill returned to the Cabinet Room for further discussion, she wondered if she should not send him in a personal note, warning him of her fears. She did not do so, but soon they were being shared by a large part of the English-speaking world.

The telegram was approved early the same evening and duly ciphered and sent off before midnight to the Prime Ministers of Canada, Newfoundland, Australia, New Zealand and South Africa.

It started by setting forth the policy of Britain.

"Secret:
Following for your Prime Minister from the Prime Minister, begins:
Decision taken by Cabinet today to resist aggression upon Europe by the Turks and to make exertions to prevent Mustapha Kemal driving the Allies out of Constantinople and in particular and above all to secure firmly the Gallipoli Peninsula in order to maintain the freedom of the Straits."

The telegram then declared that both the French and the Italians were in accord with Britain in resisting any violation of the Neutral Zone around Constantinople and the Straits. The British Government were also hoping for military aid from Greece, Rumania and Serbia "in the defence of the deep water line between Europe and Asia".

Then followed the proposal of an early Conference at Venice or Paris to make an enduring peace, but meantime the Allied position must be maintained. The telegram warned:

"Very grave consequences in India and among other Mohammedan populations for which we are responsible might result from a defeat or a humiliating exodus of the Allies from Constantinople."

Would the Dominions associate themselves with Britain in this action, and say if they desired to be represented by a contingent?

"Not only does the Freedom of the Straits for which such immense sacrifices were made in the war involve vital imperial and world-wide interests," it continued, "but we cannot forget that there are 20,000 British and Anzac graves in the Gallipoli Peninsula and that it would be an abiding source of grief to the Empire if these were to fall into the ruthless hands of the Kemalists."

The very announcement of an offer from the Dominions, urged the telegram, would probably be enough to prevent actual hostilities.

Indeed, despite the obvious risk of unloosing war, it is hard to resist this conclusion. All the more oddly ill-informed, in the light of such determined words, was the editorial comment of *The Times* next morning, 16 September. It declared that

> "the time for speeches and attempts at bargaining is already past. If we mean to defend genuinely British interests such as the freedom of the Straits, we must be prepared to take the necessary military precautions. . . . If at the twelfth hour, the British Government show wisdom, coupled with energy and firmness, they may receive a greater measure of public support than that to which the demerits of their past policy would entitle them. . . ."

The Government, in fact, were showing plenty of energy (perhaps more of it than prudence). For that Saturday morning, at the request of the rest of the Cabinet—though not of Curzon, who was down at his country seat and had not attended the critical meeting of the previous day either—Churchill's literary talents were again enlisted. This time, it was to draft a communiqué for publication.

After affirming that the advance of the Turk Nationalist Army upon Constantinople and the Dardanelles jeopardized the entire results of the Allies' victory over Turkey in the Great War, the communiqué added the further warning that if Mustapha Kemal's challenge succeeded it would set off a chain of reactions not only throughout the Moslem world, but among all the enemy states defeated in the late war. It concluded with the statement that besides the Balkan Powers concerned, the Dominions had been invited to send contingents "in defence of interests for which they have already made enormous sacrifices and of soil which is hallowed by immortal memories of the Anzacs".

One trouble about this statement was not, as *The Times* would pretend on Monday morning, that the British Government did not mean what they had said, but that the French and the Italian Governments did not. For on this very same day, 18 September, the French and Italian contingents received their orders to retire from the Asiatic shore of the Sea of Marmora. Two of the three flags were lowered. With shame and anger, and watched in silence by the British, these Allied troops marched out.

Lloyd George's indignation had hitherto been concentrated on the earlier conduct of the French and Italian Governments for providing the Turk Nationalists with arms to fight the Greeks—and also, in the case of France, of signing a secret treaty with Mustapha Kemal which had allowed him to withdraw his troops from his Syrian and Armenian frontiers and concentrate them against Greece. Now, these, our Allies of the Great War, had deserted their British comrades and left exposed a vital flank at Chanak, "a treacherous part" of a "wretched business".

But, in the meantime, a much more serious trouble had arisen. This was over the moment and method of publishing that fateful Press communiqué which Churchill had drafted. Although it was not released in Britain until so late on Saturday evening, 16 September, 1922, that most of the Sunday newspapers did not carry it, yet for overseas it had been issued in time enough to be flashed "in clear" round the world that afternoon. The Prime Minister's original official message, despatched during the previous (Friday) night, had not been decoded and delivered in the appropriate Government offices until about the same time. Both in Canada and Australia, the Prime Ministers concerned read the news in the newspapers before the official message reached them. The consequences were profound.

The Prime Minister of Canada, Mackenzie King, was exceedingly annoyed and angry. For this incident, both by its very nature and by the way in which it had happened, abruptly brought up again the awkward question of the real status of the Dominion in relation to the British Crown. We have seen how Mackenzie King's predecessor, Sir Robert Borden, had insisted at the Versailles Peace Conference that Canadian representatives be included in the British Delegation (which thus became the British Empire Delegation), and that Canada should sign that Treaty as a fully fledged member of the League of Nations. It is true that Borden also believed in a common, single Empire foreign policy, and before going to the Washington Disarmament Conference in 1921 as the delegate of Canada, he had argued that

". . . the voice of the British Commonwealth in foreign affairs must not be the voice of the United Kingdom alone but the voice of all the British self-governing nations . . . the precise method by which it shall be worked out in actual practice has not yet been fully determined and is surrounded by difficulties of undoubted gravity, but it is not incapable of solution."

Unfortunately, no practical method of furnishing the Empire with a common single foreign policy, while safeguarding the sovereign independence of each self-governing Dominion, had ever been devised. There had, indeed, been that notable occurrence at this same Washington Conference when, under Canadian pressure, the British Government had abandoned the Anglo-Japanese Alliance because the United States so disliked it.

Now, was this present move to commit Canada to war in the Near East, an attempt to return to the days of "Colonial Rule" by London? Mackenzie King had ever a suspicious mind, and so he now replied to Lloyd George that the Government of Canada could not think of sending troops to Chanak without first consulting the Dominion Parliament, and it was by no means sure that the situation even justified this.

Telegram from the Governor-General of Canada:

"17 September. Following from my Prime Minister for your Prime

Minister begins: Before communication could be sent to myself or other members of the Government of Canada of the contents of your cable sent through Governor-General, dispatches from England appeared in our Press announcing the British Government's invitation to Canada to participate in resisting Turkish Forces by dispatch of troops. This has caused a most embarrassing situation and Press representatives are enquiring of me if any, and if so, what, communication has been received from the British Government. Seeing that your message takes the form of a secret cypher telegram your sanction seems to be necessary before disclosure of its contents. I should be glad to receive immediate reply by telegraph as to your wishes in the matter stating whether I am at liberty to disclose the contents of the communication the British Government desires to have made public as coming from them to the Government of Canada. . . .

Byng."

Next day, came a second telegram from Ottawa. It reaffirmed that the public opinion of Canada would demand the authorization of their Parliament before dispatching any contingent "to participate in Near East conflict", and Parliament would have to be summoned for that purpose.

Churchill hastened to assure Mackenzie King personally that same day that there was no serious probability of war, but that it was essential to stop the Kemalists from crossing the Straits and entering Constantinople. He thought it unlikely that they would try, but Great Britain must take a firm attitude and

"anything that your Government can contribute towards the sense of Empire solidarity would be of the utmost value. At this juncture, a statement to the effect that the Dominion of Canada associates itself with the general position of the Allied Powers in insisting upon the Freedom of the Straits and would be represented by a contingent if the need arose, would be quite sufficient."

This contingent, added Churchill, could be "of very moderate size". Australia and New Zealand had already replied "in a favourable sense".

In a second, official, Prime Minister-to-Prime Minister telegram dated 19 September, Churchill urged that the British Government were not asking for any immediate decision to send troops from Canada. If the need arose, a message would be sent.

"Presumably it is not necessary for you to summon Parliament till then and we hope it may not be necessary at all. A definite statement, however, that in the event of the terms of the Armistice being broken Canada will stand by the Empire will do much to ensure that peace is maintained."

Mackenzie King maintained his unenthusiasm,[1] and it was left to his Tory rival, Mr. Arthur Meighen, then Leader of the Opposition, to demand that Canada should tell Britain: "Ready aye, ready: we stand by you." It was typical of Meighen's own courage, but quite certainly Mackenzie King's prudent attitude conformed more closely to the current mood of Canada.

Nor had Australia's reaction been quite so cordial as Churchill had suggested. Indeed, Prime Minister Billy Hughes's reply may have had as much effect in restraining rash action in London as Mackenzie King's. For while the Australian Government did not refuse (indeed they at once agreed) to contribute troops to fight again if need be on that Anzac battlefield, Hughes made it plain in his own fashion that the Commonwealth of Australia was not going to be led by the nose into any purely British adventures.

The Prime Minister of Australia also began by noting that the British Prime Minister's telegram to him had arrived after his communiqué to the Press. This, in so grave a matter, was most unfortunate, for it precluded that full and judicial consideration "which was Australia's clear right as a national Government". It was wrong, said Hughes, that a Dominion should be stampeded into action by newspaper disclosures about something which it had not been consulted on, or even informed. Foreign Office dispatches, many weeks old, he agreed, contemptuously, had been received from time to time, but nothing to suggest that the Empire was likely to be involved in war. Lloyd George's own telegram had come as "a bolt from the blue".

Now (after the Australian public had already been apprised by the Press), the Australian Government were being invited, not to decide between Peace and War, but to join Britain in a war which she had decided on. Billy Hughes thought that the Dominions should be consulted *before* such irrecoverable decisions were made; if they were only to be consulted *afterwards*, then all the talk about them having a real share in framing Foreign and Imperial Policy was just "empty air". Worse.

"I feel that I ought to speak quite frankly, and say that the unity of the Empire is gravely imperilled by such action."

Australia would take her place beside Britain in defending the neutral zone

[1] Six years later, during a bitter debate in the Canadian Parliament, Mr. Mackenzie King claimed credit for having averted a European War over Chanak. He said:

". . . the British Cabinet as a whole had never considered the Communication which was sent to the Government of Canada and which was broadcast in the Press at that time. Not only the British Cabinet as a whole had not considered that appeal, but leading members of the Government and leading public men in England took the position that it was one of the most dangerous appeals that had ever been made by any Government in any part of the world. More than that, we were told that but for the action of Canada in taking the position which she did at that time, in asking that the facts be first brought out and that the Parliament of Canada should have its say before contingents were sent abroad, a second great European conflict might have taken place."

in Turkey. But just how much farther was the policy of Britain leading? How did it bear upon events in Egypt, Arabia, India and the Empire as a whole?

"The Empire," said Hughes, "is a world in itself, composed of many countries peopled with different races holding widely different religions and other opinions. Is Britain's policy satisfactory to the Moslems in Turkey and throughout the British Empire? If not, is any modification compatible with vital Imperial interest possible and contemplated?

"We are a Peace-loving democracy," he ended. "We have been through a dreadful ordeal in which we hope that you and the world will agree we played our part worthily. In a good cause, we are prepared to venture our all; in a bad one, not a single man. In our defence and that of the Empire we are ready to fight but we must know where we are going."

Lloyd George and his friends did not have much better luck in South Africa. There, the Prime Minister, General Smuts, was away from home on a visit to Zululand, and though two telegrams had been forwarded to him, as late as 19 September, he had not replied.

The second telegram, sent by Churchill on Sunday evening, 17 September, was also in the nature of a reassurance.

Following for General Smuts, private and personal begins: With reference to my Secret telegram of 15 September we do not contemplate prolonged or serious fighting near Constantinople; it is much more probable that nothing will occur, as pending the Conference the firm attitudes of the Allies will restrain the Kemalists. The position as regards the Gallipoli Peninsula of Australia and New Zealand is a special one on account of their heavy losses there during the war. We certainly do not expect South Africa to make similar exertions, but we have made the invitation common to all the Dominions from the point of view of the importance of Imperial solidarity. Even if South African representation were almost nominal any response that you could make in this sense will be very helpful.

Churchill."

Smuts did not hurry back from Zululand.

Very different, however, was the response both of New Zealand and Newfoundland. New Zealand replied within hours, associating herself with any action taken, and promising a contingent. Three days later, the New Zealand Prime Minister telegraphed Lloyd George inquiring whether "immediate dispatch of small contingent is required for sake of moral effect, to be followed if necessary by reinforcements?"

And the day after this, New Zealand's Governor-General, Admiral Lord Jellicoe, signalled:

"20 September. Unanimous resolution was passed last night by House of Representatives endorsing action of Government communicated in my

With Lord Beaverbrook (standing behind him), Lady Beaverbrook and Canadian friends, 1926

telegram 16 September after amendment of Labour Party to the effect that Parliament and People should have been consulted was defeated by 57 to 7. Over 5,000 had registered their names up to last evening although no volunteers yet called for. Imperial spirit strikingly exhibited throughout the Dominion. Prime Minister would appreciate telegraphic review of the general situation from time to time.

Jellicoe."

To which Churchill replied, expressing the "deep emotion" with which this country, "and especially my colleagues in the Cabinet", had received this prompt and generous response.

Newfoundland was almost as prompt, and equally willing, the Acting Prime Minister replying that he and his colleagues were "in fullest sympathy" with the position taken by the British Government.

So to Newfoundland, too, went the Prime Minister's grateful acknowledgment.

But gratifying as the swift replies of the two smallest Dominions had been, they hardly justified the statement which was circulated by the Government on Tuesday, 19 September, to the effect that "The Cabinet is well satisfied with the support accorded to it, not only in this country, but in the Dominions."

Indeed, as an essay in "Imperial solidarity", to quote Churchill's words, the Call to Arms over Chanak had served rather to underline, not the existence of a common, single, Empire foreign policy, but the sovereign independence of each self-governing Dominion.

The very next day, 20 September, the Colonial Secretary thought it wise to send out another explanation of British policy, and further reassurance that it was not leading to war. It was cabled to the Governments of each of the five Dominions, and also to the High Commissioner for Iraq. The Moslem world was already on the fringe of this gathering storm.

The Prime Ministers of the greatest Dominions were not the only people who watched the unfolding drama with deep disquiet. From his Scottish home at Balmoral Castle, the titular Head of the British Empire, King George V, was anxiously following its course. Indeed, he had ordered his special train to be held ready at Ballater Station in case his presence should suddenly be required in London. On 18 September, the Prime Minister had written to the King, giving him the latest news of the developing crisis.

"September 18, 1922   10 Downing Street.
Sir,

The Cabinet held another important meeting this morning, and will meet again this afternoon at five. . . .

In the first place, the Navy are prepared to guarantee the freedom of

U

passage through the Dardanelles, even in the event of the Kemalist troops occupying the Chanak side. . . .

In the second place, it was pointed out that the only two roads by which the Kemalists could bring up guns and transport to the Chanak and Karakui positions are by roads which can be shelled from the sea, and which are also open to effective attack from the air. . . .

In the third place, we decided that it was important from the military point of view to produce an immediate impression in the Gallipoli Peninsula area by arranging for the display at the earliest possible moment of British Naval, Military and Air power. The Navy is already doing its utmost in this respect—I think with excellent effect. We also decided to put a brigade under immediate orders for the East. . . . The Air Force are under orders to send a squadron immediately from Egypt, and to have two other squadrons of fighting and bombing aeroplanes ready for immediate departure."

The Cabinet are hopeful, says Lloyd George, that these dispositions will produce the diplomatic effect which is sought, of Allied Unity. The French have discovered that all the Balkan States are unanimous about one thing— they do not want the Turk back in Europe. Lloyd George hopes that the King will agree that even if Britain stood alone in the Empire in taking this line her position would be sound and promising, but to this she could now add

"the enthusiastic support of Your Majesty's Government here which is coming from New Zealand and Australia. Nothing could be finer than the immediate response of those two Dominions, and I hear today that the recruiting offices in New Zealand are already being besieged by men anxious to fight for holding the achievements of the Anzacs if these should be threatened."

The Prime Minister suggested that the King might send a telegram of appreciation to the Governor-Generals of both Dominions.

On the whole, the attitude of the British Press was satisfactory, he noted, though many had seized the opportunity, naturally, of pointing out that the need for action was due

"to the blindness and incompetence of Your Majesty's Government, and particularly of Your Majesty's Prime Minister."

Later, Lloyd George reports that Lord Curzon (who had gone to Paris) was having a little difficulty with M. Poincaré, who was saying that French naval co-operation was impossible, and France could not consent to military co-operation if the Greeks were included. Lloyd George comments that the absence of the French Navy will make no difference, and that nobody is proposing to invite the Greek Army to take part. He praises General Harington as our "very steady and efficient Commander on the spot".

Lord Stamfordham replied two days later.

Balmoral Castle
20 September, 1922.

"My dear Prime Minister,

... His Majesty entirely agrees with the Government's decision, believing as he does that immediate naval and military action is the best means to ensure successful diplomacy: and it is everything that in General Harington we have so level-headed and efficient a military Commander-in-Chief.

Although the French Press is antagonistic to our policy, the King believes, for the excellent reasons you quote, that it is very unlikely that the French Government will refuse to co-operate with us. . . .

While congratulating you and the Government upon the prompt and complete measures that have been taken to deal with this grave emergency, the King is sure that you all are as averse as he is to a renewal of war and that everything will be done to avoid such a calamity, consistently with what we hold to be true to British justice and good faith.

The King rejoices that his Government is receiving the enthusiastic support of Australia and New Zealand. He will think over your suggestion of sending a message to their respective Governors-General: but His Majesty sees a danger that his doing so may give rise to an invidious discrimination between them and the other Dominions who, so far, have not offered their assistance.

His Majesty is delighted that the Board of Trade are moving so energetically to provide the necessary ships for the transport of the refugees from Smyrna, where the Turks seem to have maintained their traditional atrocious reputation. . . .

Yours very truly,
Stamfordham."

The scene now shifted to Paris, where the British Secretary of State for Foreign Affairs, Curzon, was at grips with Poincaré. The Prime Minister, who, as Sir James Grigg says, often treated Curzon "with something very close to open contempt", had on this occasion proposed to send Birkenhead over to Paris along with him to deal with Poincaré. But Curzon vehemently protested, and it was agreed that he should go alone.

From Poincaré, he demanded an immediate explanation of the "astonishing news that France, after suggesting the solemn warning to Kemal, upon which we at once and loyally acted, has withdrawn her troops from Chanak".

Poincaré defended the French withdrawal on the grounds that, in crossing to the Asiatic shore, the French local commanders had exceeded their orders. He said that any French Government who ordered a shot to be fired would not survive for a day. Whatever Britain did, France would refuse to involve herself south of the Straits. She wanted to come to terms with Kemal.

Curzon retired.

His next meeting with Poincaré two days later was more stormy, "of quite unprecedented description", as he telegraphed to the Cabinet that evening. He opened by explaining the British position, especially regarding Thrace, where he was anxious that Mustapha Kemal should realize that Turkey was not going to be automatically yielded her pre-war frontiers and authority. Possibly, in the disputed zone of Eastern Thrace, the League of Nations might even set up a temporary buffer State between Greece and Turkey? Perhaps . . .

Poincaré rudely interrupted Curzon's disquisition by quoting several French G.H.Q. appreciations of the situation, all of the most menacing character. The only way, said Poincaré, to avoid disastrous war was to meet Kemal at once, and concede him the former Turkish frontier in Europe, including the historic fortress-town of Adrianople. The French Prime Minister demanded that this unqualified affirmative be made the very next day. When Curzon sought to discount his military fears, and added that if General Harington were forced to evacuate Chanak the reproach would not lie upon him, but upon the Allies who had abandoned him, at this word Poincaré flared up.

First, he launched a bitter personal attack on General Harington, whom he accused of having deliberately misrepresented the attitude of the French and the Italians. When Curzon indignantly rebutted the charge, Poincaré lost all command of his temper, and for a quarter of an hour shouted at the top of his voice, refusing to allow the slightest interruption or correction, and generally behaving, as Curzon reported, "like a demented schoolmaster screaming at a guilty schoolboy. I have never seen so deplorable or undignified a scene."

After putting up with it for some time, Curzon got up and walked out of the room. Perhaps it was a pity, after all, that Birkenhead had not accompanied him to Paris.

And events in the Near East? Enter a newspaper reporter. Beaverbrook.

He had lately been staying at Deauville, where he had encountered the Aga Khan, whose special interest in the Moslem world was being sharply stirred by these events. With him, Beaverbrook had discussed what he calls "the disastrous character of the relations of the British Government with the *de facto* Turkish Government",[1] and had resolved to go himself to Angora and discover what were the real intentions and strength of Mustapha Kemal. Through the Aga Khan, he arranged a meeting with that formidable figure, but before setting out he sought to get hold of the Prime Minister and, if possible, obtain from him some authority to negotiate if the opportunity arose. He deemed it wise to associate the other two Triumvirs, Churchill and Birkenhead, in this enterprise.

"Dear P.M.

Now that you have joined the 'Men of Property' where Winston is a

---

[1] *Politicians and the Press*. By Lord Beaverbrook.

pillar of the Temple, I want very much to entertain you at Cherkley on 26 August. The only poor man that will be tolerated is F.E.—and he has a right to move in the company of the rich for reasons which I won't give.

I have been very ill for days. At one moment I thought that I might at last get ahead of Lord Northcliffe. It all came from drinking first and swimming afterwards—instead of the other way about. . . .
Yours ever,
Max."

The party met, but Lloyd George and Birkenhead, at any rate, had on their minds this week-end that question of the possible purchase of *The Times*, and perhaps for this or other reasons Beaverbrook found the Prime Minister "indefinite and evasive". However, Lloyd George encouraged him to go to Turkey, saying he would be ready to listen to what he had to say after seeing Kemal.

But when Beaverbrook arrived at Constantinople, the blow had already fallen. The Greek Army was in rout, and streaming back towards Smyrna, which was soon in flames. The reporter betook himself speedily to Athens, where he was just in time to witness, and vividly describe, the return of that armada of defeat and despair from Smyrna. That day of 16 September, 1922, he had sat

"fascinated by the panorama of incoming ships . . . crowded to the brim with infantry, old men, women, girls, so that the only method of sitting was to dangle your legs over the side.

This packed mass of humanity had stood upright all through the long journey from Smyrna . . . and this is only one ripple of the great wave of refugees and disheartened troops which is breaking on every Greek island and coast in the Aegean."

Beaverbrook had observed how the Port authorities carefully landed the troops in tugs by little companies.

"as though they were afraid of having a whole mass on shore together. The disembarkation was a painful sight. As each haggard infantryman limped on shore he was deprived of his rifle; but every second man had no rifle left. . . . The men drifted off into the town with two months' leave (in the middle of a war!) in a hopeless, disorderly stream, with nothing to distinguish them but a dirty uniform and a transportation pass to some distant home.

Here and there a little group of civilians gather round some Athenian soldier, anxiously asking for news or explanations, but they look over their shoulders the while, for Athens is stunned by the severity of the blow.

. . . One liberty of speech the Athenians still retain—the right to damn all the Allies, collectively and separately. They blame the English and they curse the French."

Beaverbrook explained how these embittered people believed that it was England which had led them into this adventure, and then let them down. As for France, the returning soldiers swore that Kemal's army, even down to companies, was commanded by veteran French officers who had learned their trade on the Western Front against the Germans.

"Will there be a revolution?" asked Beaverbrook, and answered significantly: "Bread is the crux of the political situation. There is not enough bread to go round."

Well, *were* we to blame? Certainly, the British Government—or, at any rate, the dynamic head of that Government—had backed the wrong horse originally in the Greek–Turk race for power. Lloyd George had done this in the face of the almost universal opinion of Allied professional military men —Marshal Foch, even, among them. So strong had been the hangover of Haig and Kitchener in Downing Street.

But after Veniselos had fallen, in 1920, and King Constantine and his reactionary régime had returned to Athens, hadn't the British Government rather disinterested themselves in the Greek Crusade? Hadn't the Prime Minister himself, along with his Foreign Secretary, Curzon, as early as January, 1922, advised the Greek Prime Minister, Gounaris, that the wisest thing for the Greeks to do would be to quit Smyrna? Hadn't Lloyd George himself at that time urged Gounaris to place himself in the hands of Curzon?

Yes, all these things had happened. But though the Greeks received no official encouragement from the British Foreign Office—and, indeed, had received, instead, considerable discouragement and warning from the War Office—they believed that the British Prime Minister's heart was really with them, and they thought that somehow, in his own way, he would bring them aid. It was a fatal hope.

Thus, throughout that truce of 1921–22, though Gounaris kept coming to London to beg for arms and money to get on with the war, or help to get out of it, he got neither. Instead, Churchill says, Curzon "soused him in sonorous platitudes". When, in February, 1922, Gounaris wrote to Curzon that the Greeks must either have reinforcement, re-equipment and refinancing or else evacuate Asia Minor before the Turks drove them out, Curzon replied that he trusted that the forthcoming Conference in Paris would be able to settle matters.

There would develop, later, a bitter personal issue in both the House of Lords and the House of Commons, as to whether or not these letters were ever placed before the Cabinet. At least half a dozen leading members of the Cabinet, including the Prime Minister himself, would subsequently deny in public that they had ever even set eyes on this Gounaris–Curzon correspondence.

More serious was the fact that the Prime Minister, and his Foreign

Secretary, were once more out of step with one another. A second political sensation in December, 1922, would bring to light a remarkable exchange of telegrams between Athens and London at the moment of the supreme crisis on the Asia Minor front.

It was midnight, 18 July, 1922, when at the invitation of Sir Edward Grigg, one of the Prime Minister's Political Secretaries, "a certain person of military experience connected with the Greek Legation" called at his office in No. 10 Downing Street, and was asked point-blank if the Greek Army could hold on throughout the coming winter? The Turk offensive had not yet opened, and the representative of the Greek Legation had replied Yes, if the necessary credits and war materials could be obtained from Britain. No formal undertaking had been made, but the officer certainly departed that night under the impression that business would be done, and a message in that sense had been transmitted via the Greek Legation to Athens. Neither money nor munitions had, in fact, subsequently materialized.

Then, towards the end of August, the Turk Army suddenly attacked. On 2 September, as the Greek Army was in full flight towards Smyrna, the following telegram had come from Athens for Lloyd George:

> "In view of the military situation, the Greek Government are prepared to accept a proposal for an armistice conditional on the immediate evacuation of Asia Minor. They beg the British Government to take, with all possible dispatch, such steps as they may consider expedient to that effect. And the Greek Government express the hope that this request will be acceded to."

This message, in typewritten form, was delivered at No. 10 Downing Street by the same officer as before. He took back with him a copy of the following telegram:

> "We are prepared to support the Greek Government if it thinks it absolutely necessary to apply for an armistice, but in Prime Minister's opinion, the Greek Government should be very careful to avoid the mistake made by the Germans in November, 1918, namely, concluding an armistice on abject terms in a moment of panic.
>
> The best thing they can do is to hold up the Turkish Army outside Smyrna; if they can do that they can negotiate on much better terms regarding evacuation and everything else. If they really cannot stop the Turks, which is unbelievable, we shall support an application for an armistice."

This telegram was not transmitted via the Foreign Office, and Curzon appears to have had no knowledge whatever of it. History will say that when those angry Greeks in Athens harbour blamed Britain for their plight, they had some basis for their gossip.

Now, in that despairing capital, Beaverbrook's warning to his *Sunday*

Express readers that Revolution might be at hand, became fact just ten days after he had made it. On 27 September, 1922, Greek military airplanes flew over Athens and dropped leaflets declaring that the Army and People had uprisen and overthrown the guilty Government. The same day King Constantine abdicated his throne, for the second time in five years.

Meantime, trouble was mounting at Chanak.

We left General Harington energetically directing operations to strengthen the defences of that British outpost. By 19 September, he had been deserted by his French and Italian allies, but as their combined detachments did not amount to one battalion, from a military point of view the general bore their retirement with equanimity. That same day he gave orders to Major-General Marden, Officer Commanding at Chanak:

"You should hold Chanak as long as possible with the forces I have available. I am communicating the decision to the Government. In my opinion, in view of the French withdrawing from Chanak, Kemal will challenge British policy there. In all probability he will stop to reflect, if you hold him there with naval support. Your stand there may avert further trouble."

Next day he reported both his assessment of the effect of our allies' desertion and news of a decisive Council of War of the enemy's.

"If we continued to show our determination, I am of opinion that the British will be able to carry through the task without them (i.e. the other Allies), so that I do not consider you need feel concern for their action. According to my information his (Kemal's) Ministers are being summoned to Smyrna tomorrow for a Conference. Evidently this is to decide whether he will take England on with her Dominions. My own opinion is that they will not dare to do so."

The British Cabinet, with the report before them of Curzon's own battle with the obdurate Poincaré, were inclined to be rather more cautious that day. The War Office telegram to General Harington reflects it.

It advised the C.-in-C. that a summary of the political situation was being sent to the British High Commissioner there which would show the importance of avoiding anything which might precipitate hostilities. At the same time it was of the highest importance that Chanak should be held effectively. It had now become a point of immense moral significance to the prestige of the Empire, besides its military importance. It would be invaluable to retain it.

Next day, General Harington received Hamid, the Turk Nationalist envoy, and handed him a message for Mustapha Kemal. It made it plain that while the British Government were for peace and would welcome a conference at the earliest moment, if the Turkish troops crossed the frontier into the Neutral Zone they would come up against "the full might of Britain and the Dominions."

At Criccieth with H. G. Wells

The General assured the Cabinet at home that the British garrison at Chanak would do nothing to provoke trouble, but he noted that military reports which he had received indicated that the enemy might launch an attack on about 30 September.

Actually, at dawn on 23 September, the Turkish cavalry patrols entered the neutral zone. They were immediately challenged, and warned that if they advanced any farther the defenders would open fire and war between Britain and Turkey would begin. There were some awkward few minutes, in which bridles were seized and men were hustled, but no fighting actually broke out. By nightfall, the enemy troops had massed in strength along the frontier Menderes River. The banks, however, were too steep for them to force a crossing under fire at any point, the British had blown the only bridge, and all through the bitterly cold, starry night they stood to arms, watching the fords.

But it was All Quiet along the Menderes. On the morrow, clouds of dust beyond the river showed that considerable numbers of men were on the move. They were Turkish infantry, marching up to relieve their cavalry. During the next few days, the British withdrew from the river-line to their prepared position near Chanak. The Turks followed, right up to the barbed wire, where they squatted, grinning at the garrison, and with the good-tempered sauce of soldiers, inviting Tommy Atkins to lend 'em pots and pans and firewood to cook a meal.

While these front-line amenities were going on, Curzon's labours in Paris had resulted in a joint Allied invitation to Mustapha Kemal on 23 September to a conference at Mudania, on the shores of the Sea of Marmora. It was proposed to restore to Turkey the greater part of Eastern Thrace, including Adrianople, and to withdraw Allied troops from Constantinople as soon as peace was established and Turkey safely stabled within the League of Nations. The unfortunate Greeks were largely ignored.

On the danger spot itself, Harington and Kemal were now exchanging more or less friendly messages in which the Turk, while innocently inquiring what *was* this so-called neutral zone (which the Angora National Assembly had never yet recognized), and expressing regret at the demolitions which the British had carried out "in the neighbourhood of our town of Chanak", appeared to show a genuine desire to avoid a clash of arms. Nobody was more relieved than Harington. He cabled the War Office, 28 September:

". . . I do not think Mustapha Kemal wants to attack us, and I feel myself that if we go quite straight now we may remove all danger of attack. I want to reach a Conference, with British troops standing unaided at Chanak, without losing a life and with British troops in Constantinople having kept order and calmed the Christian population. . . ."

If the Man on the Spot was keeping cool, the Government in London were
U*

getting more than a little heated. Churchill, who had been asked by the Prime Minister to preside over a Cabinet Committee for concerting our naval, military and air force movements, has noted[1] that by 28 September, when we had landed artillery from the Gallipoli shore and our air ascendancy was complete while the Turks possessed neither tanks nor poison gas, the tactical situation was strongly in our favour. He has also reproduced a military appreciation, which he composed on 30 September, in which he argued that the strategical advantages lay with us even more so. If Mustapha Kemal wanted to "finish off the Greeks" he must now cross that deep-water line to Europe and do it in Thrace. Since our fleet commanded the Straits, his only practicable route lay across the Bosphorus into Constantinople. Why should he turn aside on his march from Smyrna to Constantinople to attack our flank position at Chanak? On the other hand, if Kemal *did* commit his main forces to a campaign in Thrace, what a key position we should retain, threatening his line of communications by land and sea!

All sound enough from a military point of view, and in his appreciation of 30 September, Churchill shrewdly points out that Kemal might well resolve to adopt neither course, but negotiate instead.

However, this calm, firm assessment of events was hardly the tone of the telegraphed instructions which General Harington had received on the previous day, 29 September:

> "The Kemalists are obviously continuing to move up troops, and are making efforts to net you in. General Staff advises that the defensive position will be seriously endangered if this is allowed to continue, and that time has come to avert this disaster. It has therefore been decided by the Government that immediate notification is to be sent to the local commander of the Turkish troops around Chanak that unless his troops are withdrawn from a time fixed by you, at which time our combined forces will be in their proper positions, all the forces at our disposal, naval, military and air will open fire on the Turks. The time limit should be short. It should not be forgotten that we have been warned by Intelligence Reports of the 30th September as the date of possible attack."

These orders gave Harington a good deal more licence than he had either expected or desired. He hastened to deny the necessity for strong-arm action, and begged that the matter be left to his own judgment. General Marden had reported that his position could be held against anything except a full-scale attack. He had six fine British battalions, supported by terrific artillery, both military and naval, and by air. He deemed it unwise just when the Allied generals and Kemal were due to meet that the British C.-in-C. "should launch [an] avalanche of fire which will put a match to [the] mine here and everywhere else, and from which there will be no drawing back."

[1] *The World Crisis: The Aftermath.* By Winston S. Churchill.

For, as Harington pointed out, the repercussions of any action at Chanak upon the Christian population in Constantinople might be fearful. Meantime, the C.-in-C. was becoming increasingly confident about the situation. "It was never danger," he added, and asked the War Office for an immediate ruling on his opinion.

It must be added that Harington's own earlier telegrams hardly harmonize with the latter appreciation. They had, in fact, been the cause of the War Office telegram of 29 September. On 1 October, the reassuring message reached him that the Cabinet were much relieved to find that the Chanak position was now quite different from that which the Joint Services Staffs had gathered from his reports and on which they had advised immediate action. As the C.-in-C. considered that things were daily improving, the Cabinet agreed that he need not act on the instruction of 29 September unless and until he considered events demanded it.

By now, reinforcements of troops from Egypt, Malta and England, together with the bulk of the Mediterranean Fleet and some air squadrons were arriving at Chanak. General Harington sensibly decided to keep that ultimatum in his pocket. As he wrote in his Dispatch:

"I was convinced that I was acting in the interests of peace, and in accordance with what I felt would be the wishes of H.M. Government, in withholding the warning, as I was alone in a position to judge the situation on the spot."

So, instead of fighting the Turks, "Tim" Harington kept talking with them, and on 3 October, accompanied by the French and Italian commanders, he met General Ismet Pasha on the quay at Mudania. Greek bodies, recently pushed off the pier by the Turks, washed up against the walls of the Conference room. Also mooching around Mudania was the French politician, M. Franklin-Bouillon, who had negotiated that Franco-Turkish Pact the previous year behind the backs of his British Allies. He now came round to see Harington, and offer him his assistance. It was not accepted.

For three or four days, the Allied and Turk generals sat every afternoon and evening, seeking to come to a settlement, "days of incessant work, in a network of political intrigue", reported Harington, who could deal with his French soldier colleague but loathed "Boiling Franky", as Field-Marshal Wilson had long ago christened the politician Franklin-Bouillon. Harington was well aware that this man was responsible for what he termed "the black treachery" which was making the French General prepare to quit our side.

Harington had his orders, and he stood fast. He warned the Turk General, Ismet Pasha, that Britain had gone to the limit of concession, and that he was boarding H.M.S. *Iron Duke* for Constantinople that night. He did so, reporting to the High Commissioner that in his view the situation had become hopeless. He warned Major-General Marden, at Chanak, to stand by for the worst, and made ready himself to defend Constantinople.

Next day, 10 October, Harington returned to Mudania. He had informed the British Government in the meantime of the grave deterioration of affairs, and from them had received two telegrams giving him authority to start operations if he deemed it necessary. As he entered the Conference room, Harington was handed another telegram. It came from Major-General Marden, at Chanak, and it said that he was being enveloped. Could he be given leave to open fire? Harington named the zero-hour.

He entered the Conference. The fateful argument began. Long afterwards, Harington recalled it:

"The scene is before me now—that awful room—only an oil lamp. I can see Ismet's Chief-of-Staff—he never took his eyes off me. I paced up one side of the room, saying that I must have that area and would agree to nothing less. Ismet paced up the other side saying that he would not agree. Then, quite suddenly, he said 'J'accepte'. I was never so surprised in my life! . . . I wired to General Marden, who got my message 75 minutes before he was going to open fire. I did not think of the telegram in my pocket. I only thought that our nation did not want another war so soon."[1]

They sat for fifteen hours more and then, at 7.15 a.m. on the morrow, 11 October, 1922, the Pact of Mudania was signed. The next World War had been postponed.

The political crisis in Britain could not be averted. Already on 30 September, *The Times* had published a letter from Tory M.P.s demanding the recall of Parliament. It was reported that eighty of them were opposed to the continuation of the Coalition.

Indeed, everyone was "writing to *The Times* about it"—the Liberal Earl Grey, the Tory Marquis of Salisbury, the Socialist Ramsay MacDonald, the first two insisting that we stand and work with France, the third that we hold an immediate General Election.

Most important letter of all came from Bonar Law on 7 October, 1922. (It appeared simultaneously in *The Times* and the *Daily Express*.) Dismissing any need for criticizing, or even considering, the circumstances which had led up to the current crisis, Bonar Law inquired what was to be done now? When the Greeks had been driven into the sea at Smyrna, it had seemed to him that unless a decisive warning had at once been issued the Turks would have tried to enter Constantinople and march into Thrace. Our withdrawal in such circumstances would have been regarded throughout the Moslem world as the defeat of the British Empire. Probably, the Turk occupation of Constantinople would have re-enacted the horrors of the sack of Smyrna, and set off another

[1] *Tim Harington Looks Back*. By General Sir Charles Harington, G.C.B., G.B.E., D.S.O.

Balkan war. The British Government had been right, said Bonar Law, to seek to prevent such consequences.

But the prevention of war and massacre in these places was not only a British interest, but the interest of humanity. So was the Freedom of the Straits. All the Allied Powers were involved, including America. What ought we to do? Clearly, the British Empire, the greatest Moslem Power, should be fair to the Turks. The proposals put forward in Paris by Curzon had, in fact, been fair and beyond these terms we should not go. We could not alone "act as the policemen of the world". The financial and social condition of this country made that impossible. We should say plainly to our French Ally that the position in Turkey was much a part of the Peace settlement as anything to do with Germany, and that if they were not prepared to support us there we should have no option but to imitate the Government of the United States and look after our immediate affairs.

When the ex-Leader of the Tory Party wrote this, the crisis of Chanak was at its peak. Lloyd George and his colleagues had resolved, in view of French shuffling, that they either now ranged themselves openly with us in resisting Mustapha Kemal's threats to invade Thrace or else the British garrison would evacuate Constantinople. In a last desperate effort to line up the French along-side Britain, Curzon had gone off to Paris and was bearding Poincaré again. Bonar Law's letter was apparently intended to strengthen Curzon's hand in negotiation, by showing Poincaré that the most respected veteran statesman of the powerful Tory Party held that our French Ally (indeed, *all* our Allies) must play their part in safeguarding the hard-won fruits of Allied victory in the Great War.

We say "apparently", because Beaverbrook, who was in closest touch with Bonar Law, declared at this time that in reality this letter was

"a root and branch condemnation of the Chanak policy".[1]

Certainly, Beaverbrook himself regarded it as such, and his *Daily Express* interpreted it so. He had returned to England from his Near East journey convinced that it was possible to make an honourable deal with the Turks, if the British Government really desired it. He had done his best to persuade the Big Three of the Cabinet, Lloyd George, Birkenhead and Churchill, that this was so. It was Birkenhead who explained to him that in this matter of Chanak, the British Government were fighting the "battle of Christianity".

Beaverbrook had gone to Bonar Law, and said, "These men mean war." When Bonar Law's letter came out in the newspapers, Beaverbrook believed, as he subsequently wrote, "that a new potential Premier had taken the field, and that an alternative Administration had at last become possible".[1]

So it proved. In the event, Bonar Law's letter would not affect the crisis

[1] *Politicians and the Press*. By Lord Beaverbrook.

at Chanak. It would bring down the Coalition Government at home—over Chanak.

By this time Bonar Law was finally convinced that the continuation of the Coalition would be as fatal to the Tory Party as it had already been to the Liberal Party. Bonar Law also knew that the inner Cabinet circle of Lloyd George, Churchill, Birkenhead, Balfour and Chamberlain had been discussing over Churchill's dinner-table an early General Election, and an appeal for a new mandate for the Coalition Government.

Indeed, three days after Bonar Law's letter had appeared, Chamberlain in Cabinet proposed a dissolution, the only dissident being the President of the Board of Trade, Stanley Baldwin. A meeting of the National Union of Conservative Associations had been planned for the following month, and it was deemed wise to anticipate this. The very next evening, again at Churchill's house in Eccleston Square, the aforementioned Big Five, plus Curzon, made the decision to go at once to the country. Churchill recalls how Curzon stood up and said, "All right, I'm game." Next day, it is true, he changed his mind, without telling anyone.

On 13 October, Chamberlain took the field, on his native heath of Birmingham, where he launched a pre-election onslaught on Socialism. Everyone, at any rate, took it as the opening volley, especially when the following day Lloyd George himself moved into action in the place of his own birth, Manchester. There, at the Reform Club, "in my native city", he addressed a powerful appeal to the nation. "We have been assailed," said the Prime Minister, "with misrepresentation, with abuse, with innuendo such as no Government, in conducting international affairs, has ever been subjected to before."

Lloyd George then set forth, and vigorously defended, the policy of his Government in the Near East conflict:

"Our objects were three-fold. The *first* was to secure the Freedom of the Straits for the commerce of all nations. The *second* was to prevent war from spreading into Europe, with all the inconceivable possibilities of a conflagration. The *third* was to prevent the repetition in Constantinople and in Greece of the scenes of intolerable horror which had been enacted in Asia Minor during the last six or seven years.

Since 1914, the Turks, according to testimony—official testimony that we have received—have slaughtered in cold blood a million and a half Armenians—men, women, and children—and half a million Greeks, without any provocation at all."

Lloyd George turned upon the Independent "Wee Free" Liberals, and especially Lord Gladstone:

"I am told, I think by a Liberal newspaper, that I must not invoke the name of Gladstone. I can well understand the reluctance to call that great spirit from the vasty deep to witness the spectacle of Liberal leaders and Liberal newspapers attacking a Government because it is doing its best to prevent the Turks from crossing into Europe and committing atrocities upon the Christian population.

Lord Gladstone . . . has excommunicated us from the Liberal Party. Well, Papacy is not an hereditary office. What service has *he* rendered Liberalism that gives him that right? I know of no service, except one. He is the best living embodiment of the Liberal doctrine that quality is not hereditary. . . . There is no more ridiculous spectacle on the stage than a dwarf strutting before the footlights in garments he has inherited from a giant."

He had a word for Asquith, too:

"Mr. Asquith has asked why we did not emulate the patient, forbearing policy which Lord Grey displayed in 1914 towards the Germans, instead of indulging in the amateur tactics of Downing Street today? Well, the old patient and forbearing policy of 1914 ended in the most disastrous war which this world has ever seen. The amateur diplomacy of 1922, has at any rate, brought peace."

Lloyd George denied that he had improvised the policy of guarding the Freedom of the Straits and protecting the Christian populations against Turkish misrule. As Prime Minister, he had inherited the war-time agreement with France, Russia, Italy, and Greece partitioning Turkey. Who had made that agreement? Lord Grey and Mr. Asquith. True, he had approved it, but he had not designed it. Indeed, it had been approved by Liberal, Tory, and Labour leaders—by Balfour, Bonar Law, Lansdowne, Chamberlain, Grey, Asquith, Churchill and himself. As for the Treaty of Sèvres, that had been the work of a Committee of Foreign Ministers and Ambassadors, sitting at the Foreign Office and presided over by Curzon.

He threw down his notes. He spoke to his fellow-citizens, as man to man, appealingly, as Lloyd George ever could:

"Office is a great shackle. I have never sought my present position. Mr. Bonar Law, Lord Balfour, Lord Carson can tell you. I was willing in the war to serve in any office, however humble. I gave up one of the most powerful positions in the Government in 1915 to take up an absolutely new—and what was then, a very humble office, because I thought I could serve my country better. And in 1916, if they had said to me, 'That is your job,' inside or outside, I would have done it because there were millions who were facing death for their country, and it was not for a man to pick his job.

I never said 'Make me Prime Minister!' On the contrary, I begged Lord

Balfour, Mr. Bonar Law, or anybody to take that position. I begged Mr. Asquith to remain, so long as the conditions were assured in his Premiership that I thought were necessary to conduct the war efficiently.

Three years ago I was anxious to get out. I felt that I could render better service to my country in a more independent position, and I begged Mr. Bonar Law to take charge. He declined."

Now, the Prime Minister would welcome freedom. It would be very interesting to watch others handling difficulties which they seemed to think could be solved so easily. He would watch, for instance, to see how we were to forgive Germany reparations—and still make France love her more; how we were to pay the United States of America what we owed them—and forgive every other country everything they owed us; how we were to have a better Army, Navy and Air Force, have more houses for everybody, improve our Educational system, give more to the unemployed—and yet make the taxation of this country lighter.

There were some things that he would be proud of in his "thirty-two years of strenuous public life".

"I shall be proud of the fact that I have attempted things which even yet have not reached maturity or complete success, and if this were the last day I held this high position, I should be prouder than ever of the fact that it was given me in the last days and weeks of my Premiership to invoke the might of this great Empire to protect from indescribable horror men, women and children by the hundred thousand who were trusting to the plighted word of France, Italy and Britain as their shield and their defence and who are thanking God at this hour that Great Britain has kept faith."

The Times did not consider the Prime Minister's speech very tactful in view of the forthcoming Conference with the Turks, in its references to their barbarism. But Lloyd George was not addressing Angora; he was appealing to the British electorate.

He had warned the King on 13 October, that he might have to ask for an immediate dissolution. On 16 October, he wrote saying that the Tory Ministers proposed to call a meeting of their followers on the 19th and that "upon the decision taken at that important gathering will depend the continued existence of the Coalition".

King George V replied:

"It is my hope that the result will not cause the breakdown of my Government, for many reasons, especially when questions like Ireland and the Near East are still unsettled. I trust you will remain my Prime Minister."

The same day, Lord Salisbury declared war on the Coalition Government. He attacked what he called the system of "one-man rule", declared that the

Coalition had "lowered the whole standard of public life", denounced its attempt to create a "Bolshevik bogy", and demanded independence for the Conservative Party.

Every Party warrior was now sharpening his knife. Leopold Amery, at the Admiralty, was busy lining up all the Tory Under-Secretaries (and the Tory Party Chief Whip) to insist on Tory independence both at and after the forthcoming General Election. Utterly refusing to serve any longer under Lloyd George (though he had supported his Chanak policy) was Stanley Baldwin, that emerging figure of whom Balfour would shortly comment that he had never yet heard the sound of his voice during a Cabinet meeting. Lloyd George himself reciprocated Baldwin's dislike, but the President of the Board of Trade had a more powerful friend at the moment. His name was Bonar Law.

What was Bonar Law going to do? He was getting every day more and more hostile to Lloyd George, whom he saw as the destroyer of the Tory Party, though Churchill, Chamberlain, Birkenhead and Horne were still telling him: "You are the natural leader!"

Bonar Law was very much annoyed both with Birkenhead and Chamberlain. For Birkenhead had promised that before the Cabinet made any decision to go for a General Election, he would inform Bonar Law, through the medium of Beaverbrook. He had not done so, and being now taxed with his failure he excused himself by saying that Chamberlain had specifically pledged him not to do so!

Then there was Curzon, who had at last decided to quit, escape from his indignities and had written to the Prime Minister to say so. Lloyd George had asked him to hold up his letter for three days. Now, on 17 October, according to Curzon, at No. 10 Downing Street:

> "With moving sentences and in a voice charged with emotion, he begged me not to abandon my old comrade in arms and asked me not to forget the great scenes in which we had jointly taken part and the common comradeship of the war, and thanked me for the loyalty which I had consistently shown, both in speech and action, to him. I could not, or at least I did not, question the sincerity of these utterances, sharply as they contrasted with the treatment I had so often received at his hands. They enabled us to part in the most friendly fashion."[1]

An event in the country decided the date of the meeting. This was the by-election at Newport, Monmouthshire. Here, an Independent Tory, Mr. Reginald Clarry, was contesting a seat which had been Coalition Liberal, against a Liberal (with Coalition goodwill, though not official recognition) and a Socialist. Because Chamberlain firmly expected this Government supporter to be returned he had postponed a meeting of Tory M.P.s which

[1] *Lord Curzon: The Last Phase.* By Harold Nicolson.

had been arranged at the Carlton Club, London, until the result of the poll should be declared. That would show these rebels!

So The Day was fixed: 19 October, 1922.

The evening before, while Beaverbrook was sitting in his home at The Vineyard, his telephone-bell rang. He had deliberately kept away from Bonar Law all day. Now it was Bonar Law on the line. He asked his friend to come and see him. When Beaverbrook arrived, Bonar Law showed him two letters. One was to the Chairman of his constituency, saying that he was resigning his seat in the House of Commons. The other was to give notice that he would not be attending the Carlton Club meeting next day.

"Well, you've made up your mind," said Beaverbrook. But after a talk, Bonar Law decided to cancel both letters. Beaverbrook has always claimed he had no part or share in reaching this decision.

He then returned home. And promptly, at 9.10 p.m., Beaverbrook telephoned to the Press Association, for release to all newspapers, the official news that Bonar Law would be at the Carlton Club next morning. At 7 a.m. Bonar Law was on the line again.

"Pretty mess you've made for me!" he declared.

But he went. So did Chamberlain, Curzon, Birkenhead and Baldwin. So did a milling mass of excited Tory M.P.s, all buzzing with the sensational news of the Newport by-election.

R. Clarry (Independent Tory)	. .	13,515
T. W. Bowen (Labour)	. .	11,425
Lyndon Moore (Liberal)	. .	8,841
Independent Tory majority	. .	2,090

Chamberlain's speech evoked little enthusiasm, but his statement that there was no difference of policy between the two wings of the Coalition aroused much dissent. Bonar Law, plainly torn between loyalties, thought his way aloud to the firm conclusion that the Tory Party must now quit the Coalition. This really settled the question. But the most remarkable performance of all had been that of Baldwin, who in a short, brilliantly effective speech, warned his hearers that the Prime Minister was "a great dynamic force". That force had already broken up the Liberal Party. If they did not take care, he would break up the Tory Party, too. Thus, Stanley Baldwin dealt Lloyd George his first deadly blow of an astonishing series.

By 187 votes to 87 the meeting decided to be done with the Dynamite. That afternoon, Lloyd George resigned the Premiership of Britain. His years of power had been more memorable for Britain than any for a century.

Before he left 10 Downing Street four days later, he bade a cheerful good-bye to all his Secretaries in the Cabinet room where he had made History.

He chaffed them and said it would be the last time he would ever be there again.

"Unless I come back as the head of a deputation to see Mr. Bonar Law (and Lord Curzon), to ask for a grant for Welsh Education."

As he left, his faithful handyman, Newnham, presented him with a new golf club. He drove away with his son, Gwilym, to Churt.

"I am sorry he is going," wrote King George V, "but some day he will be Prime Minister again."

No. The book was closed.

CHAPTER XXXI

THE CHANCE HE MISSED

WHAT was Lloyd George going to do now?

Perhaps, even more urgently, what were his supplanters going to do? For long, the revolt against Goliath had been growing, and though at least two other experienced and determined men, Churchill, Birkenhead, and to a lesser degree the third man, Chamberlain, shared in the supreme direction of affairs, it had become the popular line of the critics to blame the "One-Man Government" of Lloyd George for all that went amiss. His own highly personal methods of doing business had helped to build up the story. Now he, and his Coalition Government had retired from action, *The Times* hailing it as "the most salutary event of the season".

So the coast was clear for a return to good old Party politics—and, as the Tory Party was undoubtedly the strongest of the three main parties, to a sound old Tory Government?

No. The coast was oddly be-fogged, and the course for any ship uncertain.

At five o'clock on the afternoon of the Carlton Club meeting, Lloyd George had gone to Buckingham Palace and tendered his resignation. Lord Stamfordham had been sent off at once to see Bonar Law at his Kensington house and to summon him to an audience; for unless a new Government were constituted immediately and elections held, it would be impossible to ratify the Irish Treaty by 6 December, and therefore the Treaty would lapse.

But Stamfordham found Bonar Law very reluctant to come and see the King, as he was not at the moment the official Leader of the Tory party, and until he could count upon their undivided support he would not take office. Also, Bonar Law felt that his own frail health would not permit him to remain there beyond twelve months.[1] When Stamfordham pressed him, telephoning the King for further instructions and being told that His Majesty still wanted to see the man who he thought should be his next Prime Minister, Bonar Law went. He promised the King that, whatever happened, the Irish Treaty would be ratified in due course.[2]

Even allowing for Bonar Law's own habitual pessimism these things hardly added up to a mood of victory. The Tory Party by itself, remember, had not won a General Election since the first "Khaki Election" of 1901, more than twenty years before. Moreover, this time they were divided in their leadership. Birkenhead gibed about this Government of "second-class brains",

[1] In fact, he resigned within six months.
[2] Royal Archives.

and with a dozen other Tory ex-Ministers including Chamberlain, Balfour, Horne, Worthington-Evans and Lord Lee, wrote a letter to Lloyd George publicly repudiating the Carlton Club decision.

But Polling Day, 15 November, 1922, yielded the Tory Party all they needed, and more than they expected. Bonar Law's slogan of "Tranquillity" proved to be a winner, after the alarums and excursions of Chanak. The British electorate upheld it by giving the new Tory Government a clear majority of seventy-seven over all other Parties. With rather more Peers in his new Cabinet than he could have wished (so many of the "first-class brains" of the Tory Party in Parliament were still in the wilderness), Bonar Law made do. Several of the successful "rebels" of the Carlton Club *coup d'état* got high office, the chief being the up-and-coming Member for Bewdley, Stanley Baldwin, who now advanced from the Board of Trade to the Exchequer.

The Labour Party did well to increase their Parliamentary strength to 138, thus becoming the official Opposition. Among them were those leading I.L.P. pacifists of other days, Ramsay MacDonald and Philip Snowden. There were, too, the new Red Clydesiders—"Jimmie" Maxton, "Davie" Kirkwood, "Geordie" Buchanan and John Wheatley. They took the place of the old Irish Party in staging disorder in the House for the next nine years. An unobtrusive new-comer was the Labour M.P. for Limehouse, Major Clement Attlee.

The Liberal Party were still divided into two factions—in some constituencies they had actually fought one another. They returned to the House of Commons: Liberals (Asquithians) 60, National Liberals (Lloyd Georgians) 55. In November, 1922, a Lloyd George coupon was no longer a passport to Parliament. In some places, it was a danger-signal.

Among the ex-Ministerial casualties were Churchill, Hamar Greenwood and Captain Guest. Churchill, who had just undergone an operation for appendicitis, was submerged at Dundee by a majority of more than 10,000 votes given to Edwin Scrimgeour, a Total Prohibitionist, and thus as he said: "In the twinkling of an eye I found myself without an office, without a seat, without a Party, and without an appendix."

He was not long in finding a new Party, though he had to wait some time for a seat and an office. For Churchill, like Guest, his close friend and cousin, was about to leave the Liberals and set his course for the Tory harbour. He found this the easier because at a General Election meeting, Bonar Law had given a pledge that in the new Parliament there would be "no fundamental change in fiscal policy".

As for Lloyd George himself, in this Election he played a strangely indeterminate part—for the first time in any such contest during his entire political life. He addressed huge meetings up and down the country, with immense acclamation, so that Lord Birkenhead was assuring his friends that, if only Lloyd George could be a Presidential Candidate as in the United States, the Victory was already his. In fact, that though his Party might fail, his own personal success would be stupendous.

But though the people flocked to see and hear the most famous man in Britain, he made no clear political appeal to them. Lloyd George was beginning to lose his great grip upon the nation. It is true that the position was confused, some Liberals standing with Tory support. There were a number even running in double harness with them. Churchill and others, it was said, were asking which way the "Little Man" was going—so that they could make off in the opposite direction! It is true, too, that Lloyd George himself was tired, and often during the previous months had spoken to his closest friends of "taking a holiday from public life".

It did not last. Only three days after the General Election, 18 November, Riddell noted in his *Diary*:

"The change in the atmosphere since he has been out of office is amazing. Now he is working like a little dynamo to break up the Conservative Party by bringing the more advanced section to his flag, to join up with the 'Wee Frees' and to detach the more moderate members of the Labour Party—this with the object of forming a Central Party of which he will be the leader."

Age 59   Lloyd George had arrived now at one of those cross-roads in his life, and was making up his mind which turning he should take. As usual, some of those who reckoned they knew him best believed that he would go one way, and others that he would go another way. And, as usual, Lloyd George allowed them to cherish their illusions, and even encouraged them.

The General Election of 1922 was still in full flood when the United Press Associations of America approached him with the proposition that he should write a fortnightly article for them dealing with current affairs. He was already committed to write his *Memoirs* on his retirement from office, but as nobody could yet be sure that "retirement" was going to be permanent or not, he was able to postpone writing history and go ahead with journalism. He asked his Private Secretary, Frances Stevenson, if in lieu of salary she would care to take 10 per cent of the net profits on these articles. She accepted, and was astonished and delighted to receive at the end of twelve months a cheque for £3,000. Lloyd George continued this well-rewarded labour with the United Press Associations for many years, and when his contract ended, with the Associated Press of America until after the outbreak of the Second World War.

He was further fortified against that fear of poverty which threatens politicians who, in their prime, fall from office and lose overnight the ministerial salary and amenities on which they have come to rely; Andrew Carnegie, in admiration of the splendid service which Lloyd George had rendered the free world in 1914-18, had settled on him an annuity for life of £2,000. If he had needed it, a lecture tour in the United States would have set Lloyd George up financially for the rest of his life.

This was not what worried him as the year 1922 drew towards its close. Lloyd George was fifty-nine, but that is young as the world of politics goes. He had been thrown out of office, but that, too, had already been the fate of his fellow-architects of the Victory: Clemenceau, Woodrow Wilson, Orlando. Lloyd George did not indulge in self-pity. But it would not have been him if he had not turned his misfortunes to account. Years afterwards, receiving the Freedom of a remote little township in South Wales, after thanking the burgesses for still remembering him ("some great cities have forgotten"—— How the civic breasts swelled!), he excused his failure to come and claim this honour earlier.

"I could not accept in person all those splendid honours then, for right after the war had ended, I was a very busy man. There was the Peace Treaty, Russia, Poland, Ireland, unemployment. . . . But I have the time now. Yes, now I am myself Genuinely Seeking Work. . . ."

The Unemployed ex-Premier!

He became reminiscent, taking the tightly crowded audience in that little Town Hall along the vivid lanes of his memory, in the intimate way that Lloyd George could. . . . He began to recite the great names of the Great War, solemnly:

"Asquith—dead! Kitchener—drowned! Haig—dead! Fisher—dead! Foch—dead! Bonar Law—dead! Woodrow Wilson—dead! Clemenceau —dead! . . ."

It was like the Roll of the Ships. As each name rang out, men caught their breath in their throats, in a choking stillness. And then (naming the great current film success of the Gish Sisters), Lloyd George bubbled:

"There are only two of us left—the Kaiser, and myself—the Orphans of the Storm!"

It brought down the house, in laughter, to drown tears.

But for the moment, December, 1922, Lloyd George's thought was simply to get away, not only from the recriminations which followed the break-up of the Coalition in 1922, but from those which still persisted from the break-up of the Liberal Party in 1916. Lloyd George did not know that he was going to have to live with this devil six-year-old feud for the whole of the rest of his political life.

He set off on a voyage for Algeçiras in time for Christmas. The change and the sunshine re-energized him, and Riddell, who was also at Algeçiras, tells how Lloyd George walked twelve miles one morning a few days before his sixtieth birthday. He had quarrelled with Riddell for his "Pro-Turk" attitude, and now greeted him as "Riddell Pasha, I presume?" It became a gay company when Lord and Lady Birkenhead and family joined them. To their hearts' content, Lloyd George and "F.E." then discussed the shortcomings of Bonar Law's Government.

Early in the New Year these became apparent, and none more glaring than the disastrous American Debt settlement made by the new Tory Chancellor of the Exchequer, Stanley Baldwin. The Americans, who had rejected Lloyd George's proposals to cancel War Debts all round, were pressing for an early payment of Britain's obligations to them, which amounted to £1,000,000,000 in gold. The Balfour Note of July, 1922, which had informed our European debtors (of course, it was really addressed to Washington) that as we had to pay our American creditor we were reluctantly compelled to ask them in turn to pay us, had also laid it down that we should claim no more than we had to disburse. This statement had not improved the climate of Anglo-American relations, but it happened to represent the realities of the situation. Bonar Law himself put it another way when he said in the House of Commons on 14 December, 1922: "I am convinced that to make this payment (to U.S.A.) without receiving anything from outside sources would reduce the standard of living in this country for a generation."

But Baldwin, accompanied by Montagu Norman, the Governor of the Bank of England (the British banks and the City of London backed the Chancellor's attitude), went off to Washington and hurriedly concluded an agreement to pay the United States £34,000,000 annually for ten years and £40,000,000 annually thereafter until the debt was redeemed. The bankers and the City were anxious to restore the pound to parity "to make the pound look the dollar in the face", as the expression went. Thus, they hoped to restore London as the money mart of the world, and their own power in commanding it. When Bonar Law heard the news he said in an interview with an American journalist: "If I sign the terms suggested at Washington, I shall be the most cursed man in England."

It required a formal deputation from his Cabinet colleagues next day to induce him not to resign.

In the New Year, too, occurred another incident to cheer and amuse the exile in Algeçiras. At the very end of the old year, 29 December, 1922, the Royal Commission on Honours set up by Lloyd George while he was still Prime Minister, had issued their Report. It recommended that a Committee of three Privy Councillors should assist the Prime Minister to study the claims of future aspirants, together with the names and addresses of the original proposers (and a guarantee that no money had passed).

Now, in January, 1923, came the news that Lord Farquhar, Treasurer of the Tory Party, was refusing to hand over certain funds to them on the grounds that this money had been collected for Coalition Party purposes, and since the Coalition had ceased to exist he had no authority to pay them.

In March, Farquhar was requested to resign, refused and was sacked.

Explaining the "New Deal"
to Jennifer, 1935

The Tory ex-Coalitionist Ministers, Chamberlain, Birkenhead, Balfour and Horne supported him, and all dined together at Birkenhead's house in Belgravia to discuss things. It was supposed that Farquhar might hand over some contribution to their cause. He did not.

An interesting figure, and perhaps characteristic of his epoch was his lordship. Queen Victoria had created him, first a baronet, and then a baron. Her son, the Prince of Wales, later King Edward VII, had faith in Farquhar as a banker, and used to consult him about investments for the estate of the Duchy of Cornwall. It appears that the advice was sound, for he in turn appointed Farquhar to be a Lord-in-Waiting, while King George V later hoisted him to Viscount and then Earl. Farquhar made generous gifts to many members of the Royal Family, and when he died on 30 August, 1923, it was seen that he had made fantastic bequests. Thus, £100,000 to Princess Arthur of Connaught and an equal amount to her son; £50,000 to Princess Maud; and substantial sums to the King's own Private Secretaries, Lord Stamfordham and Sir Clive Wigram. When Farquhar's will was proved, it was shown that these bequests were figures of imagination. He died in debt. The Party Fund had disappeared.

Lloyd George returned from Algeçiras full of vitality, to take part in a series of moves designed to restore unity in the Liberal ranks. In the debate on the King's Speech at the opening of the new Session in February, H. A. L. Fisher, his own ex-Minister of Education, moved an Amendment to the Address on behalf of both factions in the Party. But old wounds are some men's dearest treasures, and there were enough men in the Asquithian camp who remembered 1916, and more particularly, 1918. If the Lloyd Georgians now wished to "rejoin the Liberal Party", they must appear in a white sheet at the penitent's stool, and with their gate-money in their hands.

This did not suit Lloyd George, who did not even *feel* penitent, and preferred to keep the money. On 14 March, at a meeting of National Liberals, he claimed that he had held to his Liberal faith every whit as firmly as Asquith—not forgetting the days of the Boer War! As for the record of the Liberals who had supported the Coalition, he was proud of it and would like to compare it with that of any Liberal Government that had ever existed.

Liberal reunion might have been still more difficult but for the arrival at the Tory summit of Stanley Baldwin. This occurred in May, 1923, when Bonar Law resigned the Premiership. Already, in April, he had been ordered to take a sea voyage on account of his health. During his absence, Curzon (who, in the new Administration, had returned to the Foreign Office, and was also Leader of the House of Lords) acted as deputy Prime Minister, while Baldwin became Leader of the House of Commons. On Bonar Law's return to England, his doctors diagnosed his complaint as cancer of the throat. On 20 May, he wrote to King George V and tendered his resignation.

The question was: who would now succeed? Usually, there is no doubt who commands the allegiance of the majority of the strongest Party in the House of Commons. Balfour had almost automatically followed Lord Salisbury (the last peer Prime Minister) in 1902, as Asquith had succeeded Campbell-Bannerman in 1908.

Bonar Law's own view was that there were only two possible alternatives —Lord Curzon and Mr. Stanley Baldwin—and the case for each was "very strong". Curzon had held high office, and had long experience; Baldwin, on the other hand, had risen very rapidly, indeed, his progress had exceeded the expectations of his best friends. He was liked in the House of Commons, and enjoyed the confidence of the City.

There were two things that tipped the scales against Curzon. There was his own character, which though upright and devoted in duty, did not inspire the confidence of his colleagues in judgment or decision. He might discharge the tasks of deputy Prime Minister in the absence of the Head of the Government. But Curzon himself as leader in a time of tempest? No.

Secondly, there was his position as a peer, and as one regarded, particularly in the public eye, as the representative of Privilege. Could anyone imagine how Lord Curzon, as Prime Minister, would handle a truculent deputation from the Miners' Federation, or the Triple Alliance? No. Bonar Law did not offer his advice to the King—he had not been asked for it. But he recommended that Lord Salisbury be consulted.

Salisbury considered that Curzon's claims could not be overlooked. But it seems that His Majesty paid more heed to Balfour, who though still out of office and then lying on a sick bed with phlebitis at Sheringham, Norfolk, had been summoned to Buckingham Palace to advise. He took this view:

> "You cannot have a Prime Minister who is unable to face his Opposition. The Opposition to the Government is the Labour Party; the Prime Minister must be in the House of Commons."

King George's mind was made up after his talk with Balfour that Stanley Baldwin was the man. But realizing the distress that his decision must bring to Curzon, the King wished to warn him in advance. So Stamfordham telegraphed to him at his country house in Somerset, asking him to come to London next day, 22 May. Curzon replied: "I will be at Carlton House Terrace at 1.20."

He believed that he had been "sent for" by the King. As he travelled up to town next morning with his wife, he discussed his future plans as Prime Minister; how they would continue to live at Carlton House Terrace but would use No. 10 Downing Street for official purposes, and so on. At Waterloo Station, the Press photographers swarmed round to snap the smiling Man of Destiny. He and Lady Curzon drove away amid cheers to his house for a happy private luncheon. About 2.30 that afternoon, Stamfordham called on him. He recounted the events which had led to this point, and then to a stunned man explained that with full appreciation of his own great qualities and his splendid services to the State the King felt compelled to choose the new Prime Minister from the House of Commons. When Curzon learned that it was to be Baldwin he repeated, despairingly, again and again, "a man of the utmost insignificance".

Stamfordham returned to Buckingham Palace, and reported. He wrote in his diary that night: "His Majesty immediately afterwards saw Mr. Baldwin and offered him the post of Prime Minister."

Curzon took his shattering disillusionment sorely, weeping like a child at the time. But he rallied, and thereafter bore it like a man. At the Party meeting he made a generous speech, congratulating his successful rival and pledging him the united support of his colleagues. In personal things, Curzon could be much bigger than ever he appeared in public.

The new Prime Minister did not call upon the exiled Tory "first-class brains" to reinforce his Cabinet. Chamberlain, Birkenhead, Balfour, Horne, and the rest remained outside, though Baldwin afterwards invited the Liberal first-class brain of "Reggie" McKenna to preside over the Exchequer, a curious appointment in the light of coming events.[1]

The uneasy Tory Government continued through the summer of 1923. In the spring, on a German default over reparations the French, no longer restrained by a Lloyd George in office, had marched into the Ruhr. The Germans played passive resistance, and proved that the enemy occupation of a country, except under the most ruthless terms, can be a most expensive interlude for the occupiers. By September, the mark had fallen to 20,000,000 to the £ sterling, the "pacification and rehabilitation of Europe" was in ruins, and British unemployment figures were stuck obdurately around a million and a quarter. Something had to be done, for Tranquillity was plainly not the key to the problem.

As the Summer Recess approached, Lloyd George was immersed in preparations for a forthcoming tour of Canada and the United States. Invitations poured in from almost every city and township in both countries, for civic visits, addresses, lectures, many of them offering a huge "honorarium". The lecture agencies, in particular, besieged him not only with letters and cables but with personal representatives, who quoted terms running into thousands of pounds for a single appearance. All these monetary inducements Lloyd George turned down. He was not going "to wear himself out in a circus".

In the event, he came near to exhausting his strength in something which resembled a Royal Progress.

The voyage itself was a typical Lloyd Georgian expedition, with the ship's

[1] McKenna expected a City of London seat, but Sir Frederick Banbury, a Diehard Tory, who it was hoped would make way for him, refused to budge. After being Chancellor of the Exchequer designate for a month, McKenna retired. He was succeeded by Neville Chamberlain.

radio almost choked by messages streaming in for Lloyd George, and by queries streaming out from Lloyd George. In particular, he wanted to know whether on landing he should wear a lounge suit and a trilby hat or formal morning dress and a top hat, and for the last twenty-four hours that the *Mauretania* was at sea this question flashed through the Atlantic air with almost the urgency that had attended the S O S signals of the sinking *Titanic*. It was eventually solved in favour of the "topper".

The passage up the Hudson River was a New York version of a Roman Triumph, with an immense fleet of welcoming launches and ferry-boats escorting the great liner, and a squadron of aircraft circling above and dipping in salute. More than a hundred newspaper reporters, and as many more photographers, swarmed aboard the *Mauretania* to interview and snap the legendary Man Who Won The War. A 10,000-ton steamer, chartered by American Greeks and crowded to the riggings with them, sailed alongside. It was labelled from stem to stern: "Welcome to Lloyd George, great friend of the Greeks!"

A brass band on deck blared continuously "Yes, we have no bananas", "How dry am I" and "Rule Britannia". On the other quarter, steamed a ship packed with cheering Jews.

At 12 o'clock noon, Lloyd George stepped ashore to the most thunderous reception ever accorded a visitor to the United States. On the quayside, a choir of Welshwomen in their national costume sang the songs of the land of his fathers. The drive through the streets to the City Hall to receive the Freedom of New York was the traditional coloured snowstorm of ticker-tape. Lloyd George was entranced, and in his speech he responded with genuine emotion to this wonderful welcome. He praised the mighty country of his hosts, and made a warm and moving plea for their understanding of the problems of his own.

"Don't be hard on the Old Country," said Lloyd George, in the hush which he compelled at the close of his most moving speeches. "We each have our own problems. But we have all got one problem in common—and that is Peace, World Peace."

He won New York with that speech, and at lunch-time at the Biltmore Hotel, he went far to win the hearts of a thousand seasoned newspaper owners and editors. Wrote Arthur Brisbane, then the most famous columnist in America:

"He looks like a composite picture of Michael Angelo's Moses and a two-year-old baby. Every child is a genius—every genius a child. Lloyd George, the earth's dominating genius of statesmanship, is a child in simplicity of manner, charm and truth. He gazes at you through his big, light grey eyes set far apart. They seem to say, 'I like you; you like me; let's talk.' Your impulse is to say kindly, 'Come and sit on papa's knee.'"

Next day, Lloyd George took train for Montreal. *En route*, in a wayside station in Vermont, he met Robert Lincoln, son of Abraham Lincoln, supreme of all Lloyd George's heroes. He was as excited and as delighted as a child, and the train had to wait on the track while they talked. All along the railway line crowds gathered, and whenever the train stopped, they swarmed around it and aboard. Lloyd George delivered fifteen speeches that day from the observation car, and attended a reception in Montreal the same night.

It was in Montreal, at the great Arena Hall which was packed with 15,000 people, that he made his successful début speaking through amplifiers, the first British public man to do so. He was not persuaded to try the experiment without due difficulty, for he had long held violent objections against any kind of microphone. It was only after a rehearsal with a dozen anxious members of the Reception Committee in the vast empty hall, that Lloyd George agreed to make the attempt. He, and the packed audience whom he stirred to their core with his speech on the glory of the British Empire, had no reason to regret it.

The Canadian Government Railway System had placed a special train at his disposal for his tour of the Dominion, and the party practically lived in it. They were crowded days (on some of them Lloyd George made twenty speeches from his tribune of the observation car). He had brought his golf clubs with him, but he only managed to squeeze in one game during the whole of the tour in Canada and the United States. At Ottawa, he warmly espoused the plan put forward by the American Secretary of State, Mr. Charles Hughes, that an International Commission of economic experts (it included an American), should be set up to agree on the amount of Germany's indemnity and how she could pay it. The British Government had turned it down. "One of the greatest blunders in history," said Lloyd George. His speech made a sensation in America. He got small thanks in the British Press, and less in the French. But a few days later, 10 October, 1923, President Coolidge repeated the proposal, and this time it was accepted.

It had been a personal pleasure to Lloyd George during his few hours in Ottawa to learn that the Prince of Wales was arriving later in the same evening, and readily he delayed his own departure in order to greet him. The Prince opened the State Ball with Megan Lloyd George as his partner. After Ottawa, there followed visits to Toronto, Niagara, Winnipeg, and as the train raced across the wide rolling prairie, Lloyd George sat for hours gazing out of the windows, enthralled by the scene as it unfolded.

"It's like passing through an endless, wonderful picture gallery," he said, and then asked: "Why have we put up with all those wretched, over-crowded slums at home when there's all this wonderful, abundant space and wealth here in the Empire?"

The party crossed the border into the United States, and at Minneapolis,

Lloyd George was initiated into the famous Sioux Tribe as Chief "Wambli Nopa", or Two Eagles (Peace and War). He puffed the pipe of peace, and put the long feathered head-dress over his white flowing locks. Lloyd George made rather a good Red Indian.

Chicago lit up the town for him. The citizens were determined to outdo New York, and they had their way. More than 20,000 people jammed the stockyards when Lloyd George spoke there. At St. Louis, he broke back sharply into current politics when he answered General Georges Dumont, the French Military Attaché at Washington, who had made some bitter references about British policy towards France.

"May God protect us from our friends" the General had piously declared, and added, "tomorrow, you are going to hear from one of our friends."

The whole of America duly heard.

"On the question of friendship for France," said Lloyd George tartly, "I have the right to call myself the sincere friend of France. Nay, more, I *proved* it, not by empty phrases, but by deeds.

"For four and a half years I devoted the whole of my strength to organizing the forces of Britain to helping France in her agony."

He paused, then speaking very quietly and slowly, repeated: " 'May God protect us from our friends'?" He raised his eyebrows, and with an air of puzzled surprise, added: "I never heard that prayer between 1914 and 1918!"

At Louisville, he took the opportunity to go out to the village where Lincoln was born in a log cabin. Round and round the outside of this little shack Lloyd George tramped, entered it and examined it intently, went down to the tiny stream nearby, knelt there, cupping his hands to drink from the spring which is half hidden in the rock. "A glorious day," he kept repeating. He counted it one of the most memorable of all his life.

At Indianapolis, he made a speech which recalled the art of his finest hour. It recaptured its superb simplicity. As he came to the end of it, he said:

"The question is often asked 'Who won the war?' "

Lloyd George walked forward to the edge of the platform and, gazing into the sea of faces, said in a gentle voice:

"There are many claimants, who never saw the War! Now I will tell you who won the War. The Man who won the War was the humble man in the steel helmet. God Bless the Man in the Steel Helmet and His Children."

In Cleveland, he addressed an outdoor meeting of 400,000 people, then a world's record. He lunched with President Coolidge and his Cabinet at the White House, Washington, and visited the now partly paralysed ex-President

Woodrow Wilson; he toured the battlefields of the great American Civil War, and was thrilled to talk to a veteran who had fought in it. He was at Philadelphia when the news reached him of the death of his old opponent and loyal friend, Bonar Law, on 30 October, 1923. Lloyd George was profoundly moved. He had worked with Bonar Law better than with any other man in British public life.

The very next day, the political pundits began to predict an early General Election in Britain. The issue to be decided had been already indicated by the surprise speech of Baldwin, the Tory Prime Minister, in the annual Conference of the National Unionist Association at Plymouth on 26 October, 1923. There, after recalling Bonar Law's pledge of the previous year that there would be no fundamental change in the fiscal laws of the country during the present Parliament, Baldwin had turned to unemployment, "the most critical problem of our country," and affirmed his faith:

> "I can fight it. I am willing to fight it. I cannot fight it without weapons. . . . If we go on pottering along as we are, we shall have grave unemployment with us to the end of time. And I have come to the conclusion myself that the only way of fighting this subject is by protecting the Home market."

It may have been during his summer holidays at Aix-les-Bains when, as his biographer tells us, "in solitary walks Baldwin had meditated deeply on his own discomforts as Prime Minister and the precarious condition of his Party",[1] that he decided that tariffs were the answer to unemployment. It can hardly have been when he asked the Free Trader, McKenna, to take over the Treasury in the previous summer. Perhaps he had then been seeking to drive a new rift in the ranks of the Liberal Party? He was certainly now seeking to guard against a possible one in the ranks of his own. To Tom Jones, years later, Baldwin confessed:

> "Rightly or wrongly I was convinced you could not deal with unemployment without a tariff. After the war, opinion was more fluid and open. On political grounds, the tariff issue had been dead for years, and I felt it was the one issue which would pull the Party together, including the Lloyd George malcontents [the 'first-class brains'].
> The Goat [Lloyd George] was in America. He was on the water when I made the speech, and the Liberals did not know what to say. I had information that he was going Protectionist, and I had to get in quick. . . .
> Dished the Goat, as otherwise he would have got the Party with Austen and F.E., and there would have been an end to the Tory Party as we know it. . . . It was a long calculated, and not a sudden Dissolution. Bonar Law had no programme, and the only thing was to bring the tariff issue forward."

[1] *Stanley Baldwin*, by G. M. Young.

It will be noted of this self-revealing statement that it contradicts itself. After saying that "the Goat" was on the water (presumably returning from America) and so it was necessary to "get in quick" in order to dish him, it goes on to claim that the Dissolution on the Tariff issue which followed shortly afterwards was "long calculated and not sudden".

What *is* certain is that most of the members of Baldwin's Cabinet were as astonished as the general public by his Protectionist proclamation, and that Baldwin himself firmly believed that Lloyd George was planning to come back from his tour of Canada and the United States and launch a great Empire Crusade, as Joe Chamberlain had done on his return from South Africa twenty years before. It is not known how Baldwin "got the information", as he said, that Lloyd George "was going Protectionist", but a letter indicates what was in the air. It is from Charles McCurdy to Lloyd George while he was still in the United States, and it reached him at least a week before Baldwin made his Plymouth speech.

This letter, dated 12 October, 1923, tells how the writer lunched on successive days the previous week with Lord Long and the Agent-General for South Australia. Both had expressed the same idea—that either the bonds of Empire must be drawn closer or else they must inevitably relax. Both said that this was the psychological moment for a great statesman to give the lead to Empire Federation—and the ideal leader would be a Free Trader who was prepared to sacrifice something for a greater Imperial ideal.

"I naturally said not one word which would suggest that I knew your views," writes McCurdy, ". . . but I pointed out, in the picture which they both drew, of the possibility of Mr. Lloyd George returning from America with strong views on Imperial Federation, one factor must be taken into account."

This was the general feeling of the country as a result of the Imperial Conference, which was then sitting. Up to now it had been held behind closed doors, and such meagre news as had reached the public had fallen utterly flat. McCurdy went on to say that the advocates of Imperial Preference had made no attempt to link up their policy with any promise of effective help for unemployment.

On 3 November, 1923, Lloyd George boarded the *Mauretania* at New York, bound for Britain. From the hour that he set sail, the ship's radio was once more busy with Lloyd Georgian messages, to and from the Very Important Passenger. The General Election was already under weigh at home, and the issue was Protection *v.* Free Trade.

At least, that was what *appeared* to be the issue. In truth, the real battle was not between the Protectionist and Free Trade Parties, but was going on inside one of them. The Protectionist camp was now divided against itself.

Baldwin had already, in a declaration made at Manchester on 2 November—and no doubt, to placate the Lord Derby Free Trade following there—

Berchtesgaden. Hitler greets Lloyd George, 1936

retreated from the Empire Protectionist policy of Joe Chamberlain, with its duties on foreign imported meat and wheat and free admission of these products from the Dominions. Instead, Baldwin had limited his programme to a purely insular Protection of home industries, like iron and steel. Thereby, he promptly forfeited the support of the Imperialist school, and the powerful Press backing of Beaverbrook's *Express* newspapers.

Now, before Lloyd George had started off on his voyage to America, he had substantially agreed with Beaverbrook, in a number of confidential conversations, that some form of Empire economic union was the necessary policy of tomorrow. His experiences in Canada appeared to confirm this opinion, and certainly there were many influential people in England who reckoned that Lloyd George would return home to launch a great Imperial Plan. Among them, as we have seen, was Baldwin, and that is exactly why he had "jumped the gun" with his own Protectionist proclamation.

But the chance still remained for Lloyd George to trump this trick with a far wider concept of Empire inter-trade, as against mere local Protection. This is what Beaverbrook urged Lloyd George to do, in a series of telegrams which he fired at the *Mauretania* as she bore her homeward track to Britain. Beaverbrook himself had every reason to believe that Lloyd George would land at Southampton to make a declaration of his new faith which would change the face of British politics and the future of the British Empire. Rumour of this was reflected in the newspapers of the day. Excitement mounted, and every editor hurried his star political reporter down to Southampton.

But there were other bidders for the possession of Lloyd George, and one of the most determined of them was the Free Trader, Churchill. He wrote him a most grave and fervent appeal, begging him to stand fast for their old Free Trade cause, and sent it down by the hand of Sir Archibald Sinclair to meet the ship at Southampton. It is one of the ironies of our story that within a twelvemonth Churchill himself would be the Chancellor of the Exchequer in the next Tory Government of Baldwin.

Also hurrying to the scene of Lloyd George's landing, went an anxious Liberal deputation which included Sir Alfred Mond, Dr. Macnamara, Mr. McCurdy, Sir William Edge, Mr. Geoffrey Shakespeare and Sir Alfred Cope. They meant to get aboard the *Mauretania* before the mob of journalists who had gathered on the quayside to meet the returning pilgrim.

"Pilgrim", perhaps, is hardly the word. Lloyd George's extraordinary triumph in America had made headline news in Britain, the onset of the General Election and his dramatic return to take part in it had made him bigger news, and biggest of all was the now widespread belief that he was going to provide the liveliest political sensation of the hour. Napoleon was returning from Elba, and drama had come back to politics.

Certainly, if sudden change and surprise are the necessary elements, they were now provided. At sea, Lloyd George had flirted with Empire Protection.

V

On the quayside, he reverted to Free Trade. As the *Mauretania* docked, the journalists rushed aboard. But ahead of them in reaching Lloyd George, were Archibald Sinclair, with Churchill's letter, and the Liberal deputation headed by Alfred Mond. Our tale will also tell how within four years, Mond had also found a haven in the Tory Party, and acquired a peerage there. On this day, 9 November, before Lloyd George gave his fateful interview to the British Press at Southampton, these two men, Churchill and Mond, exercised decisive influence on his fate.

For fateful that interview turned out to be. Lloyd George told the journalists who crowded into the ship's ball-room to see him that Baldwin had committed an act of "unutterable folly". He made his criticism, not from the Empire Protectionists' view-point, but as an "unrepentant and convinced Free Trader".

In doing this, Lloyd George made his choice, not so much between Protection and Free Trade as between Toryism and Liberalism. In his heart, he now saw his own future only as a Liberal, and he believed that on this traditional fiscal issue the long divided Liberal factions could be re-united (it turned out that they would only put up with one another for the lifetime of a single Parliament).

Age 60   Thus Lloyd George slammed the door for the second time upon all prospect of a "Centre Party". Perhaps, that also might never have come off. Undoubtedly, it never could after this. Napoleon had come back from exile to what might have been another age of empire. Instead, there would be another Hundred Days. Too late, did Hamar Greenwood motor down to the country next day to see him.

"Baldwin knifed me and I am going to knife him," growled Lloyd George, throwing away, as he spoke, the weapon by which at that hour he might have done it. So came Waterloo for our great Corsican, and the effective end of a human force in the politics of Britain as galvanic as that of Napoleon Bonaparte had been in the life of France. Only once again, for a brief, dazzling flash in 1929, did Lloyd George even look like gripping power in this land, though he lived nearly another quarter of a century.

Now drama turned to farce. Down to Beaverbrook's country house at Leatherhead within three days went a curiously assorted company. It included Lloyd George himself, the reclaimed Free Trader; Churchill, his triumphant gaoler; Austen Chamberlain; and Birkenhead, the Imperial Protectionists. They were united only by their common detestation of Baldwin. And while the Free Traders were as diverse in their real feelings about the Cobdenite cause as we know Lloyd George and Churchill were, the Empire Free Traders were divided into those like Beaverbrook, who wanted a tax on foreign foodstuffs and free entry for Dominion products, and those like Austen Chamberlain who thought that a bounty for Dominion goods in the form of a ship and railway rebate would meet the case, as Borden had once urged.

The Leatherhead gathering came to nothing politically, but it certainly provided splendid copy for the Press. It had been an inquest, but Fleet Street made it appear a birthday party.

The *Morning Post* inquired if the dinner table talk had touched on the revival of the "Centre Party"? Was Lloyd George going to "scupper" Mr. Asquith while Lord Birkenhead did the same for Mr. Baldwin? Two days later, the same newspaper was again asking if Lloyd George had a plan to reconstruct that interesting Centre Party "on the views of both Liberalism and Conservatism"? The *Daily Herald* revealed a "Great Conspiracy" to thrust aside Asquith and Baldwin in favour of Lloyd George and Birkenhead, and foist a new Coalition on the country. Behind this sinister plot were the Press Lords, Beaverbrook and Rothermere, who were bent on smashing Labour.

The General Election of 1923 now rolled forward on traditional Party lines. The Tory programme contained just enough Protectionist policy to arouse all the old antagonisms, and not enough to create any new enthusiasm. One thing only Baldwin had achieved. It had been his act which had provoked Lloyd George into hoisting once more that Free Trade flag under which he was never happy for long, and thereby Baldwin had effectively separated him from any serious Tory support. It was the second time Baldwin had outpaced Lloyd George when it came to moving fast.

Hardly less embarrassed than Lloyd George to find himself again in the Cobdenite camp were those strictly orthodox, not to say strait-laced, members of the Liberal Party who had never wanted to welcome him back. But their voices were overborne by those of the vast majority of the rank-and-file, and when Parliament reassembled on 13 November, and the Prime Minister announced its Dissolution in three days' time, a notice was issued at once to the Press to say that the Liberals would fight the General Election as a united Party.

Now all was peace and Party solidarity for the moment, even in the National Liberal Club, where the portraits of Lloyd George and Churchill, long consigned to the cellar, were recovered and reinstated in the places of honour in the smoke-room. Churchill himself had hurried back to the Liberal Party fold on this fiscal issue, and was contesting West Leicester as a Liberal Free Trader. Within a day or two, the official Liberal Election Manifesto was published over the signatures of Asquith and Lloyd George. It proposed a number of sound minor reforms, and plumped for Free Trade. On this main issue, traditionally favourable to Liberalism, on Polling day, 6th December, 1923, the electorate returned its chief champions a moderate third.

Conservatives	258
Labour	191
Liberals	158
Independents	8

Was it St. Helena now for Napoleon?

CHAPTER XXXII

THE BARREN YEARS

THE inquest on the Liberal Party, on the morrow of the 1923 General Election, should have established two things. (i) That Liberalism's bid for power on traditional lines had failed finally. (ii) That the Labour Party had taken their place as the alternative Government to that of the Tory Party.

But there were many people in the Liberal and Tory Parties who did not realize it. Leading Liberals could not believe that their day was done, and leading Tories were reluctant to admit that someone else's day was coming. The thought of Labour taking office was still an abomination to Conservative minds in 1923; they could not imagine how much conservatism lingered in the minds of Labour's leaders.

So, it seemed quite natural to Lord Hunsdon, Chairman of the London Conservative and Unionist Association, to propose that the Liberals should form a Government and that the Tories should support them on an agreed programme of No Tariff Changes.

Churchill was a Liberal Free Trader who wanted to go much farther, declaring that since the fiscal issue had been settled by the General Election, no difference of opinion now divided the two older Parties and they should forthwith unite to fight Socialism. (He was describing himself at this moment to his friends as "a Tory Democrat, as I have always been"; in the event, he arrived back in the Tory Party the following year in the guise of a "Constitutionalist".) Churchill, at any rate, however much he disliked the Labour Party, had grasped the fact of its challenge, and for his part, he was off to the Right.

What about Lloyd George?

Long, he had foretold the rise of Labour, if Liberalism should fail to tackle "the social problem". He had tried to forestall that rise, with his Health and Unemployment Insurance, Education Acts, Land Reform and Housing. But that crusade, which once he led with such vehemence and imagination, had been interrupted by another, bloodier one of a World War. Then, since the armistice in Western Europe five years ago, turmoil had gone on raging in Poland, Russia, Turkey, Egypt, India. Lloyd George had not been able to take up again the struggle which he really wanted to wage—against poverty and social injustice.

Now he had burned his boats with these political forces on the Right who until yesterday had been willing to join him in a Centre Party, with Empire economic union and development as its broad policy. Though Lloyd

George had several more brief flirtations with powerful persons in the Tory Party after 1923, there was never again a hope of real alliance.

In this New Year, 1924, neither Lloyd George nor Asquith had the least doubt that, since the Tories had been rejected by the country on the fiscal issue, they must now go out of office. Lloyd George, in particular, would have been no more willing to support a Baldwin Tory Government in the lobbies than Baldwin would have been to cast a vote for a Liberal Government of which Lloyd George was a leading member. Their dislike of one another had already coloured British politics, and would continue to do so for the next dozen years. Each man failed to understand the other. But if Baldwin was wrong in always mistrusting Lloyd George, then Lloyd George made a far greater error in invariably underestimating Baldwin. For Baldwin's suspicions made him wary, while Lloyd George's contempt made him careless.

No Tory-Liberal Pact being possible, therefore, when Baldwin resigned on 21 January, 1924, Ramsay MacDonald took office as Prime Minister of the first Labour Government of Britain. Although Labour was itself a minority Party in the House of Commons, with Liberal and Independent support the new Administration commanded a Parliamentary majority of about a hundred.

The fascinating new question of British politics was this:

Was Lloyd George going to move to the Left, not merely in nominal alliance with the forces of Labour, but in increasing and effective command of them? For, as his closest friends knew, Lloyd George was painfully conscious that there had been no inspiration or dynamism in his own recent Election campaign. The people had flocked to see and hear him, as in 1922, but where was the policy to grip, and move, a nation? Lloyd George had not produced one; he had relied too much upon his own personal appeal to the electors.

But now, as there had not been in those old pre-war, People's Budget days, there were other powerful competitors for the leadership of the Left, and in the post-war years they had staked their claims. Chief among them, of course, was the new Labour Prime Minister, Ramsay MacDonald.

He was a dignified, eloquent, leonine-looking man who had fought a private battle with himself all his life because of his own obscure origin. Intelligent and gifted in many ways, Ramsay MacDonald had risen, first to the Secretaryship and then to the Leadership of the Labour Party, largely through his power to rouse working-class audiences by his fervid idealistic speeches. He had read Marxism and he sometimes spoke it, though it is doubtful if he ever believed it, or really understood it. His dignity could descend into pomposity, and his eloquence into verbiage. Lloyd George said of him, slightingly, to the author: "Ramsay uses words as though they were sounds, not weapons", and if his head was lionlike, his heart was lamblike.

But Ramsay MacDonald had earned the respect of many who disagreed with the unpopular Pacifism of his during the early days of the war. In 1924, the first Labour Prime Minister of Britain appeared an impressive figure. He regarded Lloyd George, not unjustifiably from his point of view, with proper Celtic suspicion.

His Government was not a happy one. It was something new in British politics for a minority Party to take office, without having come to any arrangement with allies, without any previous experience in charge of affairs, and also with deep differences in their own ranks. Ramsay MacDonald reinforced his team with a number of ex-Liberals, like Lord Haldane (Lord Chancellor) and Mr. Noel Buxton (Minister of Agriculture), and assumed responsibility himself for the Foreign Office, as well as the Premiership. The Tory Opposition treated the new men with tolerance and fair play. But the new Administration was only one month old when mutiny broke out in the ranks of the Labour Party over the Admiralty proposal to lay down five cruisers.

These new ships made no addition to the strength of the Fleet, being replacements (the Tory Government had planned to lay down eight), and it was urged that their construction would help to relieve unemployment in the shipbuilding trade. But it offended the pacifist principles of some of the Labour Left, as well as the economist principles of W. R. Pringle and a number of his Wee Free Liberal colleagues. On this occasion, the Tories rallied round the Government, and Stanley Baldwin marched through the lobby alongside "Geordie" Buchanan, the Clydesider.

In general, of course, it was the Liberals who helped and hauled the Labour Government through their troubled times. Troubled, indeed, they were. In January, the railwaymen came out on strike; in February, the transport workers; in March, the London busmen, and also this same month the miners clamoured for a Minimum Wage Bill. People were saying that Labour could not even control their own folk, and were justifying Churchill's gibe that Labour was "not fit to govern". Although Ramsay MacDonald had claimed at the General Election that his Party alone had the answer to Unemployment, it remained a Party secret.

In April, his Chancellor of the Exchequer, Philip Snowden (an I.L.P.-er who did understand Marxism, but practised Cobdenism), brought in a deflationary Budget and repealed the McKenna protectionist duties, which promptly increased the out-of-work queue in the motor-car trade. Challenged to bring forth the Socialist panacea, Tom Shaw, Minister of Labour, protested that he could not "produce schemes like a conjurer pulling rabbits out of a hat."

The Prime Minister's political reticence was matched by his personal pride, which was perpetually affronted by the fact that his position depended upon the support of the Liberals. Asquith had proclaimed publicly that the experiment of putting a Socialist Government in office could not be tried under safer conditions, and perhaps it was a happy thing in the history of Britain that at this stage Labour should be brought to play its proper role as one of the great constitutional Parties in the State. Asquith was subjected, all the same, to some pretty severe political pressure to prevent it, being, as he said, "cajoled, wheedled, almost caressed, taunted, threatened, browbeaten, and all but blackmailed to step in as the Saviour of Society". By which was meant, of course, making a swift deal between the Liberals and the Tories to keep the Socialists out, and thus spare the country a spate of rash experiments.

In the event, the trouble was not in bridling a headstrong team but in goading a timid one into action.

It was a thankless task for the Liberals and long before summer came, Lloyd George, at any rate, was thoroughly weary of it. He told his Caernarvonshire constituents on 22 April, 1924, of the Liberal Parliamentary Party's unfortunate experience in keeping Britain's first Labour Government in office.

How had that support been acknowledged? With unmitigated hostility in Parliament, out of Parliament, in the constituencies! If Liberals dared to criticize the Labour Government, they were visited with "peevish resentment". Liberals were expected to be "the oxen to drag Labour over the rough roads of Parliament for two or three years, and at the end of the journey, when there is no further use for them, they are to be slaughtered".

It was to break this political yoke of "the patient oxen", and to try to wrest the leadership of the Left from the Socialists, that Lloyd George now set out to frame an economic policy that would tackle the problem of Britain's shrunken trade and swollen unemployment at its very roots.

Where could you start better than with Coal, which provided the fuel and the driving power of Britain's factories and foundries? Coal, which had been the cause of so much social strife between the men who owned it and the men who mined it?

So, in March, 1924, Lloyd George had formed a committee of M.P.s, industrialists, economists and engineers to investigate and report on the British coal industry. Their findings, published in the report, *Coal and Power*, a few months later, form the basis of every development in the British coalfield from that day forward until now.

The broad facts were that, though the value of our coal exports had doubled since before the war, their volume had diminished. As for the electric power derived from coal, the United States, Canada and almost all our industrial competitors in Western Europe, including vanquished Germany, had developed their output far more than we had.

The miners of Britain were poorly paid, and they dwelt in squalor. Bitterness burned into their hearts, for they had no say whatever in the handling of the hard conditions in which they worked. Big strikes in 1920 and 1921 had brought agreement between them and the coalowners to give the miners a much larger share of the proceeds of the business. But the industrial warfare of recent years had scared off the investor, and now the coalmines were in urgent need of new capital. Still more imperatively did the whole industry require reorganization. There were 4,000 separate royalty owners, and an equivalent horde of surface landlords owning way-leaves and water rights. There were more than a thousand separate mining concerns.

Lloyd George's *Coal and Power* rejected both the current Left-Wing panaceas, Syndicalism (the Mines for the Miners) and Nationalization (the Mines for the State). The function of the modern State, said this document of the New Liberalism, was not itself to produce or to direct production, but to create the necessary conditions in which "the enterprise and energy of its citizens can most effectively operate".

So *Coal and Power* proposed that the State should buy out the royalty-owners and other landlords, and grant leases to companies or co-operatives who would work the pits more efficiently, thus providing a better deal for the miners and cheaper coal for the consumers.

So much for Coal. And Power?

It was reckoned that by building super-power plants where fuel and water supplies were near at hand, we might save ourselves 55,000,000 tons of coal a year, and vastly cheapen the cost of light and power. An Electricity Commission would set up a nation-wide system of generating stations and trunk lines, pouring cheap electric power and light into the countryside and energizing its transport, too.

Thus, rural industries would be stimulated, village life revolutionized, and the trek of the country population to the great cities halted. We had drifted, or stumbled, into the first Industrial Revolution, the Age of Steam. It left a legacy of dirty, smoky, overcrowded towns. Now, the second Industrial Revolution was here, the Age of Electricity. If only Britain would seize her opportunity, she could make the lives of her children clean and healthy and spacious beyond the dreams of any who had gone before. So Lloyd George said.

Ramsay MacDonald—and Stanley Baldwin, who was shortly to succeed him—paid no attention at all to *Coal and Power*. The Miners' Federation, to their own cost, also turned it down; they were by this time committed to one policy only for all the problems of the British coal industry—an arid State nationalization. As for the problem of British trade generally, MacDonald had his own solution for that—more business with Russia.

One of his first acts as Foreign Secretary had been to send, on 1 February, 1924, a Note to Moscow stating that Britain "recognized the Union of Socialist Republics as the *de jure* rulers of those territories of the old Russian Empire which acknowledged their authority".

It invited the Soviet Government to send plenipotentiaries to London to settle outstanding questions between the two countries at an Anglo-Russian Conference. When this opened on 14 April, 1924, Ramsay MacDonald took the occasion to deprecate certain "hostile propaganda" which had been going on, in particular, a bitter anti-British diatribe recently delivered by G. Zinoviev, head of the Third International, a Communist-controlled organization. Rakovsky, Russian *Chargé d'Affaires*, made a conciliatory reply. They had come to seek understanding, peace and trade.

The Labour Government encouraged their supporters to expect great things from these negotiations, which dragged on all summer. Lloyd George viewed them with ever-growing doubt. In June, the Prime Minister assured questioners in the House of Commons that on no account would Britain guarantee a loan to the Russian Government. In August, it was suddenly announced that such a loan would be submitted to Parliament as part of the proposed Anglo-Russian Commercial Treaty, which was signed the very next day. From the Liberal benches, Lloyd George angrily denounced it as a "fake".

When the House rose for the summer recess, he carried the war into the country. On 10 September, at Penmaenmawr, he declared that in such a time of national trade depression, Britain needed all her spare cash to finance her own business and develop her own resources (he had not forgotten MacDonald's contemptuous dismissal of *Coal and Power*). To guarantee huge sums now to be spent in another country by another Government, said Lloyd George, was "an act of criminal recklessness", and a challenge which the Liberal Party dare not shirk from taking up on the floor of the House of Commons, unless it wanted to forfeit the respect of the nation. When, a few days later, both Asquith and Grey joined in condemning the Russian Loan guarantee, it seemed that the fate of the first Labour Government was sealed.

So it was, though not by this particular piece of folly. It was a local, not foreign, Communist quagmire into which Ramsay MacDonald sank. This was the historic Campbell Case.

J. R. Campbell, disabled ex-soldier of 1914–18, was acting-editor of the *Workers' Weekly*, a newspaper which described itself as the "official organ of the Communist Party of Great Britain". In July, 1924, it published an article exhorting soldiers, sailors and airmen to refuse to fire on their fellow-workers, either in a military war or a class war, on the lines of Tom Mann's famous 1913 pamphlet *"Don't Shoot!"*

The Director of Public Prosecutions drew the attention of the Attorney-General, Sir Patrick Hastings, to this incitement and the editor was brought up at Bow Street under the Mutiny Act of 1795. This roused Labour M.P.s to protest in the House of Commons, and at its second hearing the case against Campbell was dropped. It had been represented, said the Prosecution, that the article was not an attempt to seduce men in the Fighting Forces from their allegiance, but was only comment on armed military force being used by the State to suppress industrial disputes.

The editor was not disposed to forego his martyrdom so tamely. He issued a statement to say that he himself had entered no "representation", nor any apology or plea except one of justification, but that the Labour Government themselves had called off proceedings as the result of pressure by their own Left-Wing followers. From Downing Street—silence.

v*

When Parliament reassembled at the end of September, both the Attorney-General and the Prime Minister himself came in for some rough handling. On 1 October, MacDonald angrily denied in the House of Commons that he had given orders for the charge against Campbell to be withdrawn; he had not been consulted, he said. This was not quite what he had reported to Lord Stamfordham on 22 August, on learning that the King was rather disturbed about the Bow Street prosecution and its outcome.

"Pray assure him that I am equally disturbed," wrote Labour's Prime Minister. There had been a muddle somewhere. He knew these Communists far too well to pay the least attention to what they did. "They are a miserable lot of creatures, out for notoriety and mischief, and the mere fact that we prosecuted them played into their hands."

Of course, he said, what the Communists had done was criminal, but it was a question of using common sense, not just red tape and law. He had sent for the Attorney-General and the Public Prosecutor, and given them a piece of his mind. Then he had been told that the Editor was going to write a letter of apology, and he had agreed that the charge might be dropped. But the letter had not arrived. . . .

As MacDonald said, there had been a muddle all right, and now there was to be a mess.

The Tory Opposition promptly put down a Vote of Censure on the Labour Government for having "interfered with the course of justice". The Liberals moved an amendment to set up a Select Committee to inquire into all the circumstances. When Baldwin adroitly dropped the Tory Party's own motion and marched his followers into the lobby with the Liberals the Government found themselves defeated by 364 votes to 198.

The Prime Minister insisted on treating it as a vote of No Confidence. Next morning, he tendered his resignation to the King and asked for an immediate dissolution. Neither Baldwin nor Asquith had been anxious to take office alone, or to form a coalition with each other in the present state of the Parties in Parliament. The country entered upon its third General Election within two years.

MacDonald had led the Labour Party on to an unfavourable electoral battlefield in the matter of the Russian Loan. He had placed them at a tactical disadvantage there by his bungling dispositions over the Campbell case. Now, as the fighting in the constituencies mounted to a peak, his disastrous handling of the "Zinoviev Letter" completed the rout of his Government.

On 25 October, 1924, there appeared in the newspapers a Note sent by the Foreign Office to Rakovsky, Russian *Chargé d'Affaires*, protesting against a letter alleged to have been addressed on 15 September by Zinoviev, head of the Third International, to the Central Committee of the Communist Party of Great Britain. This letter, which was also published, gave instructions how to mobilize "the Army of the Unemployed", to create Communist cells among the Services and the munition workers, to organize uprisings in Ireland and the British Colonies. Only thus, the letter concluded, would it be possible "to count upon the complete success of an armed insurrection . . . or turn an imperialist war into a class war."

Both the ideas and the language in which they were couched come straight out of the Communist handbook of revolution, though whether or not this particular letter was genuine, in the sense of being actually written or authorized by Zinoviev, remains to this day a matter of dispute.

The experts of the Foreign Office, to whom a supposed copy of it had been handed on 10 October, believed in its authenticity. Sir Eyre Crowe, Permanent Secretary to the Foreign Office, thereupon on 15 October communicated with the Prime Minister, who was electioneering somewhere between Scotland and Wales. MacDonald replied that if its authenticity were undoubted it should be published, together with a protest Note to Rakovsky against such subversive foreign interference in British affairs. While drafts of this Note were passing between the itinerant Prime Minister and Whitehall, it was learned that the same source which had supplied the Foreign Office with its copy of the "Zinoviev Letter" had also given one to the *Daily Mail*, and the newspaper was going to publish it next day. Sir Eyre Crowe decided to issue both "Letter" and Note to the Press that evening. Next morning, the sensational story streamed into headlines.

The "Red Letter", claimed the Opposition Parties, was the final proof that the Labour Government were the tools (or the dupes) of revolutionary extremists. The Russian Loan, the Campbell intervention, the Zinoviev secret instructions—all were part of the same sinister Communist conspiracy to overthrow the existing order of society.

Angrily, the Labour leaders denounced the "Red Letter" as a fake, and they were fortified in this by the prompt denial issued in the Sunday Press by Radovsky, who declared it was a "clumsy forgery", and offered to submit it to the investigation of an impartial tribunal. The Russian Government demanded the "punishment of official persons concerned in the forgery".

The Labour Party, as a whole, hailed these disavowals as proof of a "capitalist plot" against the Labour Government. As November, 1924, approached, the air was thick with new "gunpowder plots".

In this weather, the nation went to the polls. The Red Letter Election result was an electoral landside to the Right.

Conservatives	413
Labour	151
Liberals	40
Others	11

It will be seen that though the Labour Party lost forty seats, the Liberal Party lost more than a hundred. They were blamed for putting the Socialists into office, and blamed for keeping them there. They were given no credit for pushing them out. The total Liberal poll fell by more than a million votes. On the other hand, though the Socialist strength in the House of Commons had been reduced, their electoral strength in the country had increased by more than a million. It was plain that Labour would come again.

Would the Liberal Party ever form a Government again? Churchill had decided that the chances were remote. He had already rejoined the Tory Party which he had left twenty years before. In coming days, other ex-Liberal Ministers would follow—General Seely, Captain Guest, Alfred Mond, and Hamar Greenwood, while Dr. Addison would cross to the Socialist camp.

There was nothing in the Liberal Party conduct of the General Election to encourage hope. They had put no Liberal issue before the voters (which, of course, was exactly why they roughly divided themselves into the Tory and the Socialist camps). Lloyd George himself again played no outstanding part, and Asquith lost his seat at Paisley in a straight fight with Labour. This now brought up, in acute form, the question of the leadership of the Liberal Parliamentary Party.

On Armistice Day, 1924, an angry meeting of about a hundred defeated Liberal candidates assembled at the National Liberal Club; W. R. Pringle presided. Their principal grievance concerned the failure of Lloyd George to place the resources of the "Lloyd George Fund" more generously at the disposal of the Party during the recent General Election. At the previous one, in 1923, the Trustees had contributed some £100,000 for the contest. But this time, they had made no more than half that sum available to Liberal Headquarters, although negotiations had been going on between them since the beginning of 1924.

It appeared that Lloyd George, not being satisfied with the efficiency of the Party machine, had decided that until this was remedied he was not parting with the money. Mond had been deputed by him to look into the organization, and though he personally had recommended that Liberal candidates be got into the field without delay, Lloyd George still held back. He had even expressed the doubt if more than 300 candidates were necessary. At the National Liberal Club post-mortem on 11 November, a number of those Liberal candidates who had struggled through to victory expressed their own determination not to recognize Lloyd George as their leader in the new Parliament.

Age 61
On 2 December, the Liberal M.P.s met at the House of Commons to elect a sessional Chairman. The anti-Lloyd George group proposed that the Chief Whip, Sir Godfrey Collins (a devoted Asquithian) should act as Chairman at Party meetings, pending the return of Asquith himself. This was rejected by 26 votes to 9, and an amendment carried to appoint Lloyd George. Next day, ten Liberal M.P.s, with Walter Runciman as their Chairman,

formed a "Radical Group", pledged to work with the rest of the Parliamentary Party, but as Runciman pointedly gave out:

"The distinctive characteristic of the Radical Group is that they are not embarrassed by compromise in any direction either Right or Left. They do not regard politics as a game, and they do not wish to arrive at understandings with their opponents for the compromise of their principles."

The Liberal Civil War was on again.

The Tory feuds were over. Austen Chamberlain was now installed at the Foreign Office, Birkenhead at the India Office, Worthington-Evans at the War Office. In his second Government, Baldwin had found room for the former Tory dissidents. He had also been able to accommodate the latest Liberal dissident, Churchill, whom he invited to join his Administration as Chancellor.

"Chancellor of the Duchy of Lancaster?" [the lowest office] inquired Churchill politely.

"No, Chancellor of the Exchequer," [the highest office, barring Prime Minister] answered Baldwin, to his new Party Member's astonishment and delight.

In the Labour Party, too, the ranks were closed. Defeat had done that, for when, at the first meeting of the I.L.P. Members of the House of Commons after the General Election, the Clydesider, Maxton, proposed that George Lansbury be elected Parliamentary Chairman instead of MacDonald, he secured not a single vote. It was reckoned invidious to discard a leader on the morrow of a setback.

But the Liberals had suffered a far worse fate at the polls. Why was healing and recovery denied to them? The answer was not their personal rivalries and rancours. These existed, but they exist in all Parties. Immediately after the Election results were known, Lloyd George had gone to see Asquith and assured him that his temporary exclusion from the House of Commons would not impair his "unchallenged leadership"; Asquith had replied that, in his opinion, Lloyd George himself should be elected Chairman of the Parliamentary Party, and after his own return to the House, should be his deputy. But Lloyd George believed that ill-disposed persons were still bent upon making trouble between them, and the sessions in the National Liberal Club did nothing to allay his suspicions.

A few days later, in a memorandum which he dictated and sent to Mrs. Asquith in reply to a letter, Lloyd George insisted that the reason for contesting so few seats in the Election had not been shortage of funds but of "eligible candidates". The reason for not putting up a better fight was bad organization; he had guaranteed to pay half the cost of a new, good one, but nothing had been done because of "the absence of real unity". He had seen one or two rifts in the Liberal Party before, said Lloyd George.

"Mr. Asquith and I were in opposite camps in the old Campbell-Bannerman and Rosebery days. In those days, Morley did his best to promote a split. I strongly resisted it, believing that the quarrels were largely petty and personal. I am still of that opinion."

He ended (and there is no doubt that, both on personal and on political grounds, in this Lloyd George was sincere):

"If we can genuinely decide to forget past grievances—and, believe me, the grievances are not all on one side—Liberal revival is a certainty. If not, then neither of us will live to see the day when Liberalism will become again a dominant force in the national life."

Lloyd George was right about the fate of the Liberal Party. Its feuds would destroy it. But he was wrong about the cause of them. It was not "past grievances" which kept alive the Liberal vendetta, but current jealousies and greeds. The seed-bed from which these sprang was the Lloyd George Fund.

The reader will recall the charges levied by the Duke of Northumberland during the 1922 Debate on the alleged sale of honours. He had talked of the Coalition Prime Minister's own "enormous Party Chest, variously estimated at anything from £1,000,000 to £2,000,000". He had also named a notable collection of newspaper proprietors, principal shareholders, editorial and managerial executives who had been awarded honours, presumably for their services to the Government.

Actually, it would have been difficult to differentiate between these and any other "political and public services" for which honours are customarily bestowed, and harder still to discover if any money had passed.

Northcliffe, whose newspaper politics generally accorded with the Tory cause, had been first ennobled by Balfour's Tory Government in 1904, then raised in rank by Lloyd George's Coalition Government in 1917. Nobody would deny that he earned his war-time promotion.

His brother, Lord Rothermere, who professed Liberalism, owed his ascent both to Asquith's Liberal Government and to Lloyd George's Coalition Government. He had done a good turn to the Liberal cause, not in "capturing" Northcliffe at the time of the Marconi Case, for Churchill had done that, but in sustaining his sympathetic treatment of that scandal. Later, as Secretary of State for Air in 1918, Rothermere found himself the centre of another kind of ministerial storm, and the manner of his resignation might have gravely embarrassed the Government if he had chosen to make it so.

There was Beaverbrook, a peer of 1917. His part in bringing about Lloyd George's Coalition Government in December, 1916, was called by some "an act of genius" and by others "a dirty political intrigue", depending upon how you felt about things. It had certainly been effective, anyway.

Then there was Lord Dalziel, who was raised to the peerage in 1921. He had played a decisive part in clinching the deal at the end of the war whereby

Lloyd George had bought the *Daily Chronicle*, and he was now its chairman. But Henry Dalziel had also sat for many a year as a Liberal Member of the House of Commons, and long and loyal service there is recognized as entitling one to be translated to the House of Lords.

A very large shareholder in the *Daily Chronicle* at this time was the Marquis of Bute. He was also a rather critical shareholder, and on 18 October, 1922, had written a letter to Lloyd George saying that he was getting alarmed about the financial position of the Company, and urging that the chairman should retire and make way for "some capable business man" before things came to a head. For if the Company were pressed at the moment, said Lord Bute, it would be impossible to raise the required capital. Lloyd George received the letter on the morning of the Carlton Club meeting. The day he left No. 10 Downing Street, he wrote to the Marquis to say that now this political trouble was over he would be able to go into the matter with him. Meanwhile,

"I had the honour to recommend your name to His Majesty the King for the vacant Thistle,[1] and he was graciously pleased to accept my recommendation. It is a pleasure to do that as the last act of my Premiership."

What is more interesting than the honours which these prominent newspaper personalities received is the money which newspapers subsequently earned Lloyd George.

It was (as he claimed) through Lloyd George's own shrewd investment in the Press world that the Fund came at one time to surpass even the figure which the Duke of Northumberland had set upon it.

Since this Fund was going to bedevil all hopes of Liberal reunion and revival, and therefore of Lloyd George's own possible return to political power, it may be as well to dispose of its origins at once, and then to trace its path of evil fortune.

In a letter to *The Times* on 16 February, 1927, Lord Rosebery posed the awkward questions as sharply as any member of the inquiring public who sought the same information, both before and after he wrote. At this moment, one more vain effort was being made to patch up the Lloyd George–Asquith quarrel, which had broken out again over the events of the General Strike of 1926. Asked Rosebery:

"Sir,
Will you assist an embarrassed old fogey to understand the present position, for he hears in the newspapers it is reported that negotiations are going on with regard to a certain Electoral Fund in the possession of Mr. Lloyd George, which appears to be the main asset in the business.
Now the question which is never asked, but which must occur to us all, is, what is this sum, how was it obtained, and what is its source? Cer-

[1] The Order of the Thistle.

tainly, it is not from Mr. Lloyd George's private means; it comes from some other direction. What is this? It surely cannot be the sale of the Royal Honours? If that were so, there would be nothing in the worst times of Charles II or Sir Robert Walpole to equal it. But what amazes me is this: no one seems to think there would be anything unusual in such a sale. If so, all the worse, for it would be the prostitution of the Royal Prerogative, and so the ruin of the British Constitution.

On such a matter there should be no possibility of doubt. Scores, nay, hundreds of 'Honours' have been distributed. Have any been sold and helped to produce the sum in question? An authoritative statement should be furnished as to the source of this Fund."

Lloyd George's office next day returned the curt reply:

"We do not think it necessary or desirable at the moment to comment on Lord Rosebery's letter further than to say that the Fund which Mr. Lloyd George controls was raised in a way that does not differ from that followed by the Conservative Party or by the Liberal Party in the days before the Coalition, and that all along it has been devoted to legitimate Party purposes."

It remained for long the official Lloyd Georgian defence of the Fund that it was no better and no worse than any other Party Fund, in its origins, content or purpose. Thus, on 3 December, 1927, Lloyd George himself issued a statement replying to what he called "cowardly slander privately circulated as to my use of the Party Funds".

In this, he referred to his own war chest as "the National Liberal Political Fund", and he claimed that it had been collected by the Whips of that Party "in exactly the same way as every other political fund, Whig and Tory, Liberal and Conservative, for well over a century".

During the Coalition Government, said Lloyd George, the Conservatives continued to maintain their own fund, and when the Coalition ended, they kept whatever money had been subscribed. The Coalition Liberals had equally retained theirs, and had devoted it to financing elections, inquiring into coal-mining and industrial conditions generally, both here and abroad, inquiring into agriculture, and in publicizing the results. Also, in maintaining a Bureau to look into the grievances of ex-Servicemen who, he said, had written to him in "scores of thousands" since he left office. It was proposed to devote the rest of the money to similar purposes. "Not one penny of the Fund," declared Lloyd George, "has ever been handled by me."

He said that up to the General Election of 1923, it had been administered by the Parliamentary Whips of the Coalition Liberal Party, without reference to him. When the Party was dissolved (or reunited into the main Liberal Movement), the management of the Fund passed to a committee on which there were three ex-Whips, Charles McCurdy, William Edge and Gwilym Lloyd George. Most of the Fund, the amount of which had been "fantastically exaggerated", was derived from the appreciation of newspaper properties. When their sale had been completed, the proceeds were paid over to a new and enlarged committee, of which Lord St. Davids was chairman and on which the Chief Liberal Whip, Major-General Sir Robert Hutchison,[1] served.

Lloyd George repeated that he had never touched the Fund himself. Since leaving office he had worked hard as a journalist to earn his livelihood——and with some success.

But a year or two later, Lloyd George decided to change his ground. This was after another General Election (in May, 1929) had failed to settle the Liberal Party quarrel. At this time, according to a letter written on 9 July, 1929, by Lord St. Davids to Sir Herbert Samuel, the Fund stood at £765,000 (there were some expense items still outstanding from the General Election of that year). There was also, in addition to this capital, 279,000 *Daily Chronicle* Ordinary Shares, which to that date, had not paid a dividend. The income of the Fund, after tax deductions, amounted to £30,000 a year, but certain liabilities under "personal arrangements" required £6,750 of this. Now, on 14 August, 1929, in the course of a long letter to the Marquis of Reading, Lloyd George insisted that the Lloyd George Fund was not a Party Fund at all!

"The usual Party Fund represents an accumulation of gifts made through the Party Whip for Party purposes. My Fund does not represent gifts made to any Party. It started with donations made through my Whip to me when I was a non-Party Premier to be used for such political purposes as I thought desirable to spend them upon. At that time, there was a very large body of non-partisan opinion which rallied around me and was convinced that my direction of affairs was essential, not only to the winning of the war, but afterwards to the clearing up of the mess that follows war."

The Bolshevik scare was very strong in those days, said Lloyd George, and these people had trusted him to see the country through this anxious time. If he were now to hand over to *any* political Party his own control of the Fund which they had subscribed, he would be betraying a trust. This did not mean that he could not make grants from time to time for political purposes consistent with its creation.

There were other persons who took an interest in this matter. There was Captain Guest, the Coalition Liberal Chief Whip, who had been

"the chief instrument in gathering together this Fund, and he maintains that in so far as it has any purpose beyond affording me political support it was anti-Socialist in its aims, and both he and Winston claim that I have

[1] Later Lord Hutchison.

no right to part with it for any other purpose. Winston has repeatedly said so in public.[1]

I feel certain that Freddie [Guest] is watching carefully my action with regard to that Fund. As long as I keep the control of it in my own hands he cannot move, for he knows that the personal element was the dominant motive in all the donations. The moment I depart from that position and hand it over to a purely Party organization, he will strike."

When Asquith and himself had rejoined forces in 1923, said Lloyd George, there was no suggestion of the Fund being handed over. Nor ever afterwards did Asquith make such a demand, though often he was strongly pressed to do so.

There was another important factor in considering "the personal character of this Fund", Lloyd George reminded Reading.

"No one knows better than you that the existing Fund has almost entirely been created by me. The original cash has been spent long ago, and a good deal more. What is in hand now is due entirely to my handling of the *Daily Chronicle* business. When the paper was in low water I bought a number of shares. I agree it was a great risk to take, but I put the whole of my strength and my experience in the newspaper business[2] into improving the value of the investment. I took in hand the supreme direction of the business policy of the enterprise, and owing to great savings, changes and improvements which were the direct result of my intervention, the property increased enormously in value so that I was able to sell it at several times the sum I paid for it. As you know I conducted all the negotiations for the sale, but it took years of careful handling and direction to create that value. The Fund, therefore, is not merely a Lloyd George Fund in its inception, but it is specially so in its present form. It is rather a cool proposition to ask me now to hand it all over to men who have done nothing but criticize and cast mud at this Fund, when I was sweating hard to increase it."

As a fact, claimed Lloyd George, the Trustees had in the last few years "subsidized the Liberal Party munificently" and neither the National Liberal Federation nor any other representative body of the Party had ever sent a word of thanks. It had simply been "Hand me your dirty money!" The truth

[1] On 9 May, 1929, during the General Election, Churchill had asserted that the Lloyd George Fund,

"raised for the express and avowed purpose of enabling both Liberals and Conservatives to make common cause against Socialism, is now being used for the purpose of securing the return of as large a number of Socialists as possible. It is an unjustifiable action, a breach of faith, of moral faith, although it may not be amenable to legal process."

[2] His actual experience in newspaper business was modest, in fact, though Lloyd George liked to think otherwise.

was that no cleaner money existed in the political market. It had been made entirely out of perfectly honest trading, and as the result of exceedingly hard work on his own part.

This view of the Lloyd George Fund as a Trust rather than a Party Chest certainly accords with a Deed signed on 5 May, 1925, by D. Lloyd George, J. T. Davies, C. A. McCurdy, W. Edge, and H. Fildes ("hereinafter called the Trustees").

It sets forth that the money and securities invested or standing in their joint names form part of and represent moneys subscribed in 1917–22 by political friends of Mr. Lloyd George, for the furtherance by political action of certain causes: Peace, Empire unity, increased production, better transport, land settlement, forestry, housing, education, better wage standards, etc., etc. In the event of Lloyd George's death, the moneys to be administered by the Trustees for these purposes. The Chief Trustee named was J. T. Davies, and with one other he was to be responsible for all payments, allowances and transfers. Always not less than three Trustees were to be nominated by Lloyd George himself.

More changes were to come. In the summer of 1931, when the Liberals split again over joining Ramsay MacDonald's "National Government", and Lloyd George once more (and finally) parted company with the official organization, he changed the name from "National Liberal Political Fund" to "Lloyd George Political Fund". He then laid down terms that on instructions from himself, approved by the Trustees, grants should be made from it for "political purposes which would advance Liberalism in this country".

There was a curious interlude in December, 1937, when Lloyd George sought to enlarge the committee of Trustees by including Dr. Christopher Addison and Miss Megan Lloyd George. Though Addison had parted company with Lloyd George many years ago, left the Liberal Party and joined the Socialists, serving in the Labour Government of 1929–31 as Minister of Agriculture, they had mended their quarrel and were again on the friendliest terms. But J. T. Davies now wrote to Lloyd George to say that the chairman of the Trustees, Lord St. Davids, while raising no personal objection to Addison, whom he knew only by name, feared that if he should again become a Minister in a Labour Cabinet and a by-election took place at a time when Lloyd George might not approve of their policy, the committee might be asked to vote money to put up a candidate in opposition to Labour. That might be awkward. Lord St. Davids cordially approved of Megan's nomination, said J. T. Davies. In the event, it appears that neither was appointed.

The Fund was not yet in its final form. Ten years after Lloyd George had explained to Lord Reading that it was not a Party Chest but a Trust, it was being claimed as personal estate. This happened in 1939, when the contemporary Liberal Party leaders, spurred on by Mr. Harcourt Johnstone and Sir Hugh Seely, who had been subsidizing the Liberal Party themselves for a considerable time out of their own purses and were getting a little tired of it, set up a private inquiry into the Lloyd George Fund to see if any contribution could be obtained from that source.

Now the previous year, two of the remaining Trustees, Lord St. Davids and J. T. Davies, had died within three days of one another, and for a short time the money had resided in Davies's name alone. It then amounted to about £470,000.

One of Davies's executors sought to resist its transfer back to Lloyd George, but he failed. Mr. Cyril Radcliffe, K.C.,[1] said that the expression "political purposes" (to which the Fund was supposed to be directed), was too wide and uncertain a definition to constitute a Trust, and that no persons were capable of enforcing the presumed intentions of those who had originally contributed to the Fund. Sir Wilfred Greene[2] had previously given it as his opinion that the money was Lloyd George's own to do what he liked with: if he chose he could "gamble the Fund away at Monte Carlo".

How much had been spent of it by this time, 1939? The following items may be taken as fairly well agreed among the Parties:

1923	£100,000 for General Election expenses.[3]	
1924	£50,000 „ „ „ „	
1927	£300,000 „ forthcoming (1929) General Election.	
1929	£20,000 „ extra Election expenses.	
1927–30	£60,000 „ Liberal Headquarters expenses.	
	£530,000	

There were undoubtedly other considerable outgoings, and Major Gwilym Lloyd George, as a Trustee in 1939, though he refused to attend the Liberal Party's private inquiry in person, forwarded a statement setting out these additional disbursements:

£105,000 towards the official Liberal Party Million Pound Fund (receipt of this was disputed).

£240,000 (approximately) over several years for the Land and Nation League.[4]

£400,000 for the Council of Action.[5]

£100,000 for 1935 General Election expenses.

£845,000

[1] Later, Lord Radcliffe.

[2] Later, Lord Greene, Master of the Rolls.

[3] Lloyd George, in his letter of 14 August, 1929, to Lord Reading, put the figure at £160,000.

[4] Lloyd George's Inquiry into British Agriculture 1925-26 and subsequent propaganda.

[5] Lloyd George's "Non-Party" organization 193.

These figures bring the total expenditure from the Lloyd George Fund over about seventeen years to £1,375,000. To this must be added the cost of the ex-Servicemen's Inquiry Bureau, set up after the First World War, and the fairly expensive political organization which Lloyd George ran. He reckoned himself that it cost him £20,000 a year in salaries and expenses.

When Lloyd George died in 1945, the trustees of his will asked for particulars of the Fund, which now stood in the name of Gwilym Lloyd George. The Bank refused to disclose any information, saying that as far as they were concerned it was nobody else's business, apparently because the Fund was *not* part of David Lloyd George's estate. Later, the Inland Revenue asked for particulars, and appear to have been duly satisfied that the Fund was, in fact, a Trust.

So, within a quarter of a century, the thing had borne two different names, the National Liberal Political Fund and the Lloyd George Political Fund, and had been a Party Chest, a Public Trust, and a personal property.

What it did to the great life of Lloyd George and to his memory is undoubted. It did him deep, if disproportionate and undeserved harm. Lloyd George's adventurous countryman, the great buccaneer, Sir Henry Morgan, was bitterly reviled in his day, not for the sack of Panama, but because the loot was so unevenly distributed. Both the Liberal Party and the Tory Party were willing enough to get hold of the Lloyd George Fund, even as "gate-money" to admit to their councils the man they condemned for collecting it. His offence, it seems, was like Henry Morgan's, for holding on to it himself.

The origins of the Lloyd George Fund were, no doubt, as Lloyd George insisted, neither better nor worse than those of any other Party Fund.

Now what of the remarkable newspaper enterprise which played so large a part in building up the Fund?

It began with the purchase in 1918 of the *Daily Chronicle* and *Lloyd's Sunday News*, together with a controlling interest in the *Edinburgh Evening News* and the *Yorkshire Evening News*. In clinching this deal, Henry Dalziel was Lloyd George's principal agent. The owning Company was United Newspapers (1918).

Control was vested in the Ordinary Shares, the majority of which were held by Trustees of the Fund. Shareholders included Dalziel, Lord Inchcape, Lord Bute, and Andrew Weir (later Lord Inverforth). An undated memorandum in the United Newspapers Ordinary Shares file of Lloyd George (it obviously belongs to the early years) states that the Trustees held 525,251 of the 616,498 Ordinary Shares in issue, the remaining 91,247 being distributed among a number of people, including Lloyd George and Dame Margaret Lloyd George.

In July, 1924 Lloyd George received a suggestion to sell his controlling interest in United Newspapers (1918).

Soon after this a tussle arose over the *Daily Chronicle*. Lloyd George's second son, Major Gwilym Lloyd George, was then acting as Manager. As a rule, they got on splendidly, for Gwilym could calm "the Old Man" out of his most typhonic rage by a funny story, delightfully acted. But Gwilym resisted one of his father's appointments to the Board of Directors and threatened his own resignation. Lloyd George stood firm, saying that he would rather go out of public life altogether than submit to such dictation of his affairs. The crisis was resolved when Lloyd George decided to dispose of the newspaper itself. To Frances Stevenson, as her *Diary* records, he said one day: "I wish I could consult someone with some experience of these matters, and whose judgment I could trust."

"Why not ask Max (Beaverbrook)," she suggested. "I feel sure he would give you an impartial opinion."

"I believe you are right," said Lloyd George. "If I put myself in his hands and ask him to advise me as a friend, I'm sure he would give me disinterested advice."

And so, as Frances Stevenson tells, he went to Beaverbrook, and the latter did advise him, "and so well that Lloyd George never had any cause to regret the sale of the *Chronicle*."

A number of schemes were considered, but it was not until 22 November, 1926, that agreement was reached for the sale of the United Newspapers (1918) Ordinary shares to Sir David Yule and Sir Thomas Catto, representing the Calcutta Discount Company. This agreement was finalized by the formation of the *Daily Chronicle* Investment Corporation in July, 1927. The Corporation was registered with a share capital of more than £3,000,000. To this Company, Lloyd George then sold 614,003 United Newspapers (1918) Ordinary Shares, for which he received a total of £2,888,642, paid as to £1,743,307 in cash and as to £1,145,335 in £1 Ordinary Shares. He agreed to pay £100,000 towards the preliminary expenses of the Company.

A little more than a year later, September, 1928, the Inveresk Paper Company Ltd., whose chairman was Mr. William Harrison, took over the controlling interest of the *Daily Chronicle* Investment Corporation. For these shares Inveresk paid £392,500 in cash and 750,000 in 6½ per cent First Preference Shares in the Inveresk Paper Company Ltd. It is difficult to discover exactly how many *Daily Chronicle* Investment Corporation Shares Lloyd George sold under this deal, but it is generally assumed that the original interest in the United Newspapers (1918) brought Lloyd George £2,500,000, about £2,000,000 in cash, as well as a block of Inveresk shares. He also retained a block of *Daily Chronicle* Investment Corporation Ordinary Shares, after the second transaction.

While these newspaper operations were being planned Lloyd George went off on a brief holiday in the New Year, 1926, to Naples. His companions included McCurdy, Macnamara and Sir Martin Conway, art collector and explorer. They were warned that Mount Vesuvius was beginning to erupt again.

This was enough to stir up Lloyd George. The party set off for the top of the crater. By the time they reached it they were enveloped in black, sulphurous clouds, and every few minutes came a deep roar out of Vesuvius and flames followed. Most of the visitors made off hurriedly for the terminus of the funicular railway. Not so Lloyd George, who, with Martin Conway insisted on going right up to the lip of the volcano, where they stood singing with exhilaration. Why, this was more violent than any storm! Reluctantly, Lloyd George allowed himself to be recovered by his companions.

He returned home to take up a tremendous task—and challenge.

The near-annihilation of the Liberal Party at the General Election of 1924 had convinced Lloyd George, more than ever, that either Liberalism must evolve a new economic and social policy, more at grips with the urgent problems of the day, or else disappear from the political scene.

He had made a good start with his report, *Coal and Power*, on Britain's fuel resources. Now he turned to his old love again—the land—and the resources of Britain's soil. So, he set up a Lloyd George Land Inquiry.

Age 62

It delved first of all into the decay of British farming and the drift of the country population to the towns. It asked if both misfortunes could not be averted. For Lloyd George, that ever-unconvinced Free Trader, believed that Britain's early nineteenth-century lead in the industrial markets of the world had gone, and that a day was at hand when many more people must grow their own food on her soil. So the Land Inquiry sought to find what was needed to restore "the great estate of England".

For a start, more capital. But few landlords could any longer provide it. Nor were their tenants ready to risk losing any money which they might themselves have invested by having their rents raised—or even being dispossessed through a change of owners. So it was proposed to set up a system of "cultivating ownership", whereby the State should resume the possession of agricultural lands as in feudal days, paying off existing landlords and giving farmers security of tenure at fixed rents, provided that they kept their land in good heart.

These findings were set forth in a report called *The Land and the Nation* (popularly known as the "Green Book" from the colour of its cover). Alas! It fertilized nothing, except a new Liberal quarrel.

For it was at once denounced by Runciman and his "Radical Group" as smacking of land nationalization and State farming. Lord Oxford[1] did not regard it so, and with Lloyd George he worked to summon a three-day Land Convention at the Kingsway Hall, London, to try and hammer out an agreed policy. The meeting was enlivened when Sir Alfred Mond turned up to attack the Green Book. He had already resigned from the Liberal Party, and he had a thoroughly unhappy reception before finally retiring on his new base. "He has gone to his own place," said Lloyd George, bitingly.

[1] Mr. Asquith had become Earl of Oxford and Asquith in 1925.

A second incident occurred when W. R. Pringle, dedicated Wee Free Liberal enemy of Lloyd George, remarked on the platform to Major Leslie Hore-Belisha,[1] a spirited young Liberal M.P., who was also a journalist, "Thanks for the boost you gave me in the *Evening Standard*! Were you well paid?"

The newspaper had reported Pringle as being howled down the previous day. Hore-Belisha, who had nothing to do with the *Evening Standard* (he contributed to its sister morning newspaper, the *Daily Express*!) invited him to apologize, "or come outside!" When Pringle did neither, Leslie Hore-Belisha slapped his face on the platform in front of a thousand delegates.

At this time, Lloyd George lived, when in London, at No. 2. Addison Road, a pleasant house with a large garden near Holland Park, and of course he kept his home in Criccieth. But where he liked best of all to retire to from town, either for work or relaxation, was his new country house at Churt, in Surrey. He had acquired this by what he described as "a blessed accident".

For some time before he resigned his Premiership, he had been looking for a house fairly near to London and with a good view. For Lloyd George loved a view, and this he had not got at Walton Heath or at Chequers. He thought he would search out a good site, buy it and build on it. By chance, one day while Lloyd George was in Scotland at Gairloch, in 1921, Frances Stevenson heard of an estate on a Surrey hill-top, near Churt, that was about to be sold. She hastened to it, forty-five miles from London, that same September afternoon, and there in the sunshine she found herself high upon a heath, with bracken and heather and pine all around, gazing across a lovely scene; it seemed to her that this was the appointed place.

The auction was due to be held, so she wrote off to Lloyd George that evening, giving particulars of her discovery and waxing eloquent about its charms. He wired back, asking what was the aspect of the site? Frances Stevenson replied that it faced south. Whereupon, the order was given to go ahead, and the hilltop with its sixty acres of heath was bought for £3,000.

About a month later, Lloyd George arrived at Churt to inspect his new property. Alas! the day was raw and misty, and the landscape was almost veiled from sight. When Frances Stevenson pointed out to him where the view should be, Lloyd George took out his watch, which he would use as a compass, and setting it, said: "It is due North!"

She was reduced to the verge of tears, and hurriedly tried to work out whether or not she would be able to muster enough money to buy the land back from him, leaving him free to go on without loss in his quest for the ideal site. But Lloyd George burst out laughing, and promptly began to plan to build the house. "We will call it *Bron-y-de*," he said, "which means 'slope of the South'."

[1] Later Lord Hore-Belisha.

It was finished in time for him to take his first rest there when he retired from No. 10 Downing Street twelve months later.

At Bron-y-de, there dwelt Lloyd George's characteristic animal and bird pets. There was Chong the Chow, who during his Premiership had lain on duty on the doormat outside the Cabinet Room at No. 10; if it was the Prime Minister speaking inside (and only if it was he) she wagged her tail. There was also Romulus, the Alsatian. But Chong the Chow had a lifelong romance with another Alsatian belonging to Mrs. Philip Snowden, who lived nearby in Churt, the result being an admirable mongrel.

Then there was Doodie, the white pigeon presented to Lloyd George in Richmond, Virginia, during his American tour in 1923. Her cage was in the drawing-room, and every night after dinner Lloyd George would take her out of it and let her fly around the room. She would then perch on his shoulder, stick her beak into his moustache, and coo. Doodie did not like her master's steel-rimmed pince-nez, and would methodically take hold of the rim of them and flick the hated things off. Then she would caress his eyebrows. He never seemed to have the least fear that she might peck his eyes.

Then there was Bill the Airedale, so hard for anyone to handle, except Lloyd George. He once kept Lord Riddell petrified in a chair in Lloyd George's study for an hour or more, unable even to reach for the bell by the fireside while Lloyd George was strolling in the garden, unaware of his visitor's terror of moving. When Lloyd George returned and saw the petrified, exhausted prisoner, he burst into a shout of laughter. Lord Riddell never forgave him, and their long friendship, which had been threatened for some time, now came to an end.

An interesting balance sheet could be made of this twenty-years-old Lloyd George–Riddell association though, of course, no bargain was ever struck, or could have been. There were mutual advantages in working together.

Lloyd George received from Riddell an early gift of the house at Walton Heath, which he afterwards sold for £7,000, and the free tenancy of two country mansions, at Great Walstead and Danny Park, during the war-time summers of 1917 and 1918. He also enjoyed Riddell's hospitality and defraying of travelling expenses when they went abroad together. From Riddell, too, Lloyd George got shrewd newspaper support.

From Lloyd George, Riddell gained first of all a close contact with an outstanding politician who became a pre-eminent Prime Minister. Thus, the journalist had a steady source of interesting items for his personal column in the *News of the World*. He met on intimate terms the inner circle of Lloyd George's friends: Churchill, Birkenhead, Beaverbrook, Reading, Masterman, Lee, and so on. He received in reward for his public and political services a knighthood in 1908, baronetcy in 1918, and a peerage in 1920.

There was trouble with the King over this last promotion. For Riddell had never disclosed in *Who's Who* the fact that he had been divorced, but in 1915 it came out as the result of a quarrel between him and another publisher, Sir Hedley Le Bas. Both were then competing for the attentions of Lloyd George, and Riddell wrote a paragraph about Le Bas in the *News of the World* which provoked Le Bas to make the revelation. When, in 1920, Riddell's name was put forward by the Prime Minister for a peerage, King George strongly objected on the grounds of his divorce. Lloyd George was driven to collect a number of letters from the Press Lords of Fleet Street as a testimony in praise of Riddell's admirable work on behalf of the Newspaper Proprietors Association. The resistance of Buckingham Palace was overborne and the master of the *News of the World* took his place in the House of Lords, the first commoner to enter its portals after being adjudged the guilty party in the Divorce Court.

Nor was this the end of the entries of the Lloyd George ledger account in favour of Riddell. When Lloyd George was "Prime Minister of Europe" after the war, he appointed Riddell as his chief Press officer at all the Peace Conferences which he attended from 1919 to 1922, and Riddell received the French Legion of Honour (Lloyd George, indeed, afterwards charged him with being too "Pro-French") and the Grand Cordon of the Order of the Crown of Italy for his outstanding services. Throughout these years, Riddell rarely missed dining every Sunday evening with Lloyd George, whom he amused with his dry comment and his well-informed personal gossip. In fact, each found the company of the other a stimulant.

He wasted little time or attention on the House of Lords during the fourteen years that he graced the peerage. In Hansard, the chief proprietor of the *News of the World* occupied four columns and forty words in all.

The estate of sandy heath around Bron-y-de provided a ready-made challenge to Lloyd George. An earlier land crusader, William Cobbett, author of *Rural Rides*, had regarded these barren acres with contempt. Farmer Lloyd George would show him—and all the current critics, too! So he acquired in due course about ten times his original holding, and over the next few years he experimented in turn with stock-raising, arable farming, poultry and, above all, fruit farming.

He had his hard times, like every other successful man who takes up farming late in life. But he stuck at it, and years afterwards was able to compare notes, exchange sad experiences and offer good advice (shades of any Farmers' Club on Market Day!) to a new fellow-adventurer in agriculture who had only entered the business in the nineteen-thirties, Winston Churchill.

"I am going to make farming pay, whatever it costs," Churchill told Lloyd George, resolutely. He found an echoing spirit. They both became very good farmers, indeed.

Of course, Lloyd George told tall stories, as farmers sometimes do.

One day, he drove with the author over to Cherkley Court to see Beaverbrook, who had just started a large chicken farm there.

"How many chickens have you got, Max?" Lloyd George inquired.

"Oh, I suppose about twenty-five thousand," replied Beaverbrook casually. "But how about your farm? How many pigs have you got, L.G.?"

"Couldn't say exactly," shrugged his visitor. "Perhaps five hundred." The farmers exchanged sidelong glances.

On his journey home by car, Lloyd George suddenly asked his companion:

"How many pigs did I say I had?" and, being told, chuckled. "Of course, I haven't got anywhere near as many as that," he said. "But he hasn't got twenty-five thousand chickens, either!"

Bron-y-de was very much Lloyd George's workshop, as well as his farm and home and playground. Here, took place much of the top-level planning of the Reports, *Coal and Power*, *Land and the Nations*, *Towns and the Land*, then, later, *Britain's Industrial Future* (the "Yellow Book") and most arresting of all, *We Can Conquer Unemployment*. Economists like J. M. Keynes, Sir Josiah Stamp,[1] Walter Layton[2] and Hubert Henderson, and industrialists like Seebohm Rowntree crowded into Lloyd George's study; the technical experts and the secretaries overflowed into hutments in the garden—so that a new Garden Suburb was born.

Here, too, Lloyd George's own six volumes of *War Memoirs* and two volumes on the Peace-making were written, as were most of the fortnightly articles on current events which he produced for many a year to come.

Like his proprietorial experiences in the newspaper world, Lloyd George's editorial adventures were themselves a story.

A new chapter in the history of that long-ago "Brutus" had begun while he was still Prime Minister. On 12 August, 1922, the *Evening Standard* announced that a contract for £90,000 had been signed between Curtis Brown (agent for Lloyd George) and Sir William Berry[3] (acting partly for himself and partly for Messrs. Funk and Wagnall, the American publishers, who would issue the book after serializing it in the *New York Times* and the *Chicago Tribune*). Sir William Berry had the controlling interest in Cassell's Publishing Co., in the United Kingdom. The sale of Lloyd George's book was described as "the biggest deal in the history of publishing", and was made up thus:

Serial rights in the United States and Canada .	£40,000
Book rights „ „ „ „ „ „ .	£20,000
Serial rights in Britain and rest of Empire .	£15,000
Book rights „ „ „ „ „ „ .	£15,000
Total	£90,000

[1] Later, Lord Stamp.   [2] Later, Lord Layton.   [3] Later, Lord Camrose.

The *Daily Express* compared this with some recent "best-sellers"; Hindenburg (£10,000), Ludendorff (£14,000), the Kaiser (£40,000) and A. S. M. Hutchinson's *If Winter Comes* (£70,000).

The news that a Prime Minister was about to write his *Memoirs* while still in office raised an immediate uproar in the Opposition Press. The *Yorkshire Post* said that it had been "received with amazement even by persons who have only an ordinary regard for the old proprieties of public life".

The *Morning Post* commented: "What could be more fitting than that the Man who had won the War should also be one of those who have done so well out of it?"

The *Daily Mail* observed that it was easy to see why Lloyd George, expecting the early collapse of his Government as the result of his failure to get any money for Reparations from Germany, should be writing his £90,000 book of *Memoirs* for Sir William Berry. "As he has not made Germany pay he is going to make Sir William Berry pay."

As a result of this outcry, on 28 August, it was given out that

"Mr. Lloyd George has decided that the £90,000 which he will receive for his book on the war shall be devoted to charities connected with the relief of suffering caused by the war. He feels unable to take any personal advantage for himself out of the story of the struggle and suffering of the nation."

On 15 September, £5,000 was paid down to the author in advance. It was understood that he might retire from office, as he had contemplated at the time of signing the contract, but that even if he remained Prime Minister the first half of the book would be delivered by New Year's Day. As for the rest, he was allowed two years in which to finish it.

On 19 October, 1922, Lloyd George's Government fell.

Three days later, the *Sunday Express* reported from New York "an extraordinary slump in the demand by American newspapers for Mr. Lloyd George's forthcoming *Memoirs*".

Offers had that day been telephoned to editors in all parts of the country, and the replies were largely rejections.

The slump in Lloyd George was briefer than most American slumps.[1] On 23 November, it was learned that he was about to enter into a contract with the United Press Associations of America to write weekly or fortnightly articles on current events over a period that might be extended to two years. At once, the *New York Times* and the *Chicago Tribune*, who had bought an interest in the *Memoirs*, vigorously protested. Next day, however, Lloyd George signed the United Press Associations contract. On 1 December, he wrote to the *New York Times* to say that he did not consider that these articles would in any way encroach on the material of his book. He said:

[1] See also the extraordinary offers made to him to deliver lectures during his American tour the following year.

"I have my living to earn. After seventeen years in office, I have retired a poor man, and it is absolutely imperative that I should turn to writing as a means of livelihood. The proceeds of the book for which you hold the serial rights are, as you know, to be given to charity."

It was not unreasonable that Lloyd George's interest in collecting the money on his *Memoirs* should have declined when he undertook to give it all away.

On 16 December, 1922, after a High Court action had been entered by the newspapers concerned, *The Times* reported that Lloyd George had agreed to release the *New York Times* and the *Chicago Tribune* from their contract. The deal with Sir William Berry also lapsed, and in March, 1925, the advances were returned.

So, for ten years more the historian shelved his *War Memoirs*. The journalist began his articles at once. They made him one of the highest-paid newspaper contributors in the world.

Lloyd George's Press writings were frank, not to say provocative. His critics—and there were plenty in his own Party—made much of the fact that he did not spare the British Government (whether Tory or Labour or "National") in the newspapers of twenty foreign countries where they appeared. Lloyd George replied that he was exercising his knowledge and his judgment in expressing his opinions, in exactly the same way as any reputable journalist is expected to do by his public.

It was Lloyd George's journalism which set off a fresh display of fireworks in the Liberal Party leadership. This occurred during the General Strike of 1926.

The origin of the General Strike, the greatest upheaval in British industrial history, may be firmly traced to the disastrous decision of Baldwin's Tory Government to put Britain back on the Gold Standard, that is, to restore the pre-war parity of the sterling pound with the gold sovereign. Churchill, the Chancellor of the Exchequer, had announced this in his Budget Statement on 28 April, 1925, the result of continuous and heavy pressure on the Treasury by the bankers and especially by Montagu Norman, the Governor of the Bank of England.

Lloyd George, who had been away on a short health cruise to Madeira with throat trouble, had hurried home to be in his place in the House of Commons when his old friend and former colleague brought in his first Budget. He had warmly praised Churchill's plans to extend National Insurance benefits to widows and orphans, and severely condemned the decision to return to the Gold Standard. Lloyd George had repeated his denunciation of this "premature and precipitate policy" up and down the country. Thus, at Wisbech on 10 July, 1925, he declared:

"It has made sterling dearer, and thus artificially put up the price of British goods in the neutral markets where we were already competing on very narrow margins with our trade rivals. At this very hour, coalowners and miners have been driven to the brink of a yawning chasm of strife, largely through this deed of egregious recklessness by the Chancellor of the Exchequer."

In his sustained opposition to the return to the Gold Standard, Lloyd George was supported by his former critic, J. M. Keynes, who wrote later in this same month of July, 1925, a series of challenging articles in the *Evening Standard*, entitled "The Economic Consequences of Mr. Churchill". They bore nearer on the facts than his *Economic Consequences of the Peace* (or of Mr. Lloyd George!) had done half a dozen years before. The Chancellor of the Exchequer had asserted that the return to gold was no more responsible for the state of things in the British coal industry than was the Gulf Stream. "Feather-brained", commented Keynes.

"The value of sterling abroad has been raised 10 per cent," he argued, "while its purchasing power over British labour is unchanged . . . the deliberate act of the Government and the Chancellor of the Exchequer . . . and the present troubles of our export industries are the inevitable and predictable consequences of it."

The Churchill policy, wrote Keynes, amounted to reducing British wages by 2s. in the £. It also meant, in effect, "the deliberate intensification of unemployment", by restricting credit, so that employers would not hire men at existing rates. The unhappy event bore him out.

Thus ran the logic of woe: British coal at once became dearer in terms of foreign currencies. In order to hold export markets, its selling price had to be cut. The coalowners sought to cheapen the cost of production. In this sum, of course, by far the biggest item was the miners' wages. The miners refused to take any wage-cut, and when the coalowners gave notice to terminate the existing National Wage Agreement, the Trades Union Congress declared that they would back the miners. Trouble on a vaster scale than ever was threatened by the old Triple Alliance now glowered over the whole of British industry.

At first, the Prime Minister, Baldwin, would not hear of a subsidy in aid of wages, and a strike was due within two days when he suddenly gave in, promised the money and set up a Royal Commission under Sir Herbert Samuel to investigate the coalmining situation. If both owners and miners accepted its findings, Baldwin undertook to implement them.

Age 63   Lloyd George had already set forth his own radical proposals in *Coal and Power*, and he now urged that these be carried out forthwith. He also branded the Tory Government as yielding at the last moment to intimidation. On 6 August, 1925, he rose in the House of Commons to declare: "Democracy is doomed if it surrenders to the compulsion of a minority."

It was not until March, 1926, that the Royal Commission finished their job, and reported unanimously. The wages subsidy was due to end on 30 April, and had already cost the country £20,000,000. The Commission recommended a small reduction in miners' wages (though no increase in working hours) and a considerable reorganization of the coal industry, much on Lloyd George's lines. The owners wanted bigger wage-cuts (while insisting on longer working hours). The miners refused to budge an inch on either issue. Through the clamant voice of a great agitator, A. J. Cook, Secretary of the Miners' Federation of Great Britain, they demanded "Not a minute on the day, not a penny off the pay!"

Nobody was really looking for trouble. Unemployment was already rife in the coalfield; the miners did not want to add to it the ravages of a strike. The coalowners were being edged out of their markets by their foreign rivals; why exclude themselves utterly by a stoppage in their pits? The Trade Union Congress had committed themselves to call on the workers in other industries to support the miners in their quarrel; hadn't they got enough worries of their own? As for the Government, who could believe they really wanted to have the coal dispute come to an open clash between the two sides, even though they had themselves been steadily preparing a National Emergency Service to handle transport and supply in the event of it?

Yet, during the remaining few weeks of the Coal Subsidy, the Government made no effective effort to bring the opposing parties together, until almost the last day of April. When no further subvention from the Exchequer in aid of wages was forthcoming, the miners came out on strike at midnight, 30 April. Next morning, the T.U.C. informed the Government that unless settlement was reached in three days' time, they would call out the workers in other industries.

Lloyd George, who was speaking in Cambridge that day, flayed the Ministers for their dawdle in the face of the oncoming storm. "All talking and no tackling", he said, contemptuously. He dismissed as mere panic-talk, the rumours of revolutionary plans of violence. This was a well-ordered country, claimed Lloyd George, "with a deep discipline in the hearts of the people". The threatened General Strike was not a conspiracy, but a lunacy, into which an ordinary trade dispute had been allowed to drift by those in power.

"But apart from the merits of the dispute," said Lloyd George, "every citizen will feel it is his duty to support the Government of the day in the maintenance of order and in the organizing and facilitating of essential services. The country must come first, always and all the time."

Throughout the week-end, the Government and the T.U.C. continued in negotiating at Downing Street, and about midnight on Sunday, 3 May, 1926, were near agreement, with the T.U.C. willing to press the miners to accept.

Then, suddenly, the news came through to the Cabinet that the compositors in the *Daily Mail* offices in Fleet Street had refused to set up a leading article, entitled "For King and Country" and denouncing the miners' strike. The Prime Minister and his colleagues chose to regard this incident as the beginning of the General Strike, and demanded that the T.U.C. at once repudiate it. The Cabinet then broke up, and Baldwin retired to bed. When a worried T.U.C. delegation sought further information, they found the house in darkness. Twenty-four hours later, the General Strike began.

Lloyd George took a different view, and in spite of much nonsense that has been said (and written) about his conduct during the General Strike, he stuck to it throughout. It was in sharp contra-distinction to both the "do-nothing" and the "strong-arm" policies advocated by different sections of Baldwin's Cabinet (the Prime Minister practised both himself, which was the immediate cause of the outbreak of the General Strike). On the very evening of it, Monday, 4 May, 1926, Lloyd George pleaded in the House of Commons for one more effort to reach a settlement.

Now the Liberal "Shadow Cabinet" had agreed that afternoon that while the Government must be upheld in resisting a General Strike—as Lloyd George himself had urged at Cambridge the previous Friday—yet they themselves bore a large share of responsibility for its onset. Lord Oxford at first appeared as anxious as Lloyd George that the door should be kept open. But on Wednesday, 6 May, came a decisive speech by Sir John Simon in the House of Commons declaring that the General Strike was illegal, and the funds of the Trade Unions concerned liable to be confiscated. It had a profound effect—especially upon the T.U.C.

Then, on 8 May, according to messages published in the *British Gazette* (the Government newspaper, controlled by Churchill), both Lord Oxford and Lord Grey lined themselves up with the Government in insisting on the unconditional withdrawal of the hastily issued strike notices. If this decision was due to Lloyd George's special emphasis on the Government's own precipitancy in breaking off negotiations, then their choice of date was not a happy one. For on 8 May, also, the *British Gazette* announced that the Armed Forces of the Crown would receive the full support of the Government "in any action that they may find it necessary to take in an honest endeavour to aid the Civil Power".

It was a provocation which drew forth an immediate protest from King George V to the War Office. Lord Stamfordham wrote: "His Majesty cannot help thinking that this is an unfortunate announcement, and already it has received a good deal of adverse criticism."

So it should, for the General Strike had not so far required strong action by the Police, much less the Military.

Two days later, the Liberal "Shadow Cabinet" met again; but Lloyd George excused himself, writing to the Chief Whip to say that the Party had been committed to a point of view from which he dissented. He deprecated

With Dame Margaret and Megan at Addison Road, 1937

the General Strike and would support the Government's emergency measures, but he would not agree to a dictated settlement, nor would he

"abstain from condemning the Government for breaking off negotiations after the T.U.C. had accepted a formula drafted by the Government, and whilst they were actually engaged in pressing its acceptance on the miners. . . . The action of the Government was precipitate, unwarrantable and mischievous. But for that, we might now have had peace. . . . For if the miners had refused the terms pressed upon them by the T.U.C., the latter could not have called a General Strike in support of them."

Then, categorically and decisively, Lloyd George reaffirmed his attitude, and made it known that he was prepared to take the consequences:

"I, therefore, cannot see my way to join in declarations which condemn the General Strike while refraining from criticism of the Government, who are equally, if not more responsible; and I certainly think that if we support the Government in an absolute refusal to negotiate until the General Strike is called off, the struggle may be a prolonged one and the damage to the nation may well be irreparable. I prefer the Liberal policy of trusting to conciliation rather than to force."

Now the latest breach in the Liberal Front—it was almost the last before it broke forever—was made, and immediately registered for the benefit of all foes. Lloyd George's own bitter personal enemies hurried to assure Lord Oxford, still the titular Leader of the Party, that Lloyd George was playing his own hand again. He had seized upon this grave crisis of his country to ingratiate himself with the "Red" faction which he calculated was going to win.

Lord Grey, one of the most characterful of Lloyd George's Liberal critics, wrote that he and his colleagues felt that Lloyd George was expecting the General Strike to last for some time, that he reckoned it was

"going to produce a great political upheaval, throwing everything into the melting-pot, and that he wanted to have his hands completely free and thought it desirable that he should not be politically associated with us any more."

These differences might have escaped the publicity they received but for the article which Lloyd George had written for the *United Press Associations* on the General Strike. He was accused of sympathizing with it, colloguing with it, supporting it (though not even Churchill's *British Gazette* charged him with fomenting it). Defending his article, Lloyd George quoted its concluding words:

"Up to now it is in essence an industrial dispute over wages, unfortunately complicated by this 'sympathetic strike'. There is no revolutionary

W

purpose animating the Union Leaders who are now in charge. There has so far been no bloodshed. There has been no interference with property, and no personal violence. The whole influence of the strike leaders will be exerted in the interests of law and order. Let us trust that a settlement will be reached whilst calm and restraint are being maintained on both sides. There are grave risks in the whole situation. I put my faith on British coolness and in the British Parliament."

It is a fair historical record of the way Britain behaved in her one and only General Strike. It did no harm that these words went out to the world at the time, when every panic-monger, local and foreign, was babbling about the break-up of this country.

On 12 May, 1926, the General Strike ended, after an orderly and good-tempered course—and a moving speech by Baldwin. "Give us peace in our time," said the Prime Minister. The miners, rejecting all compromise that meant longer hours and lower wages, held out for six more hopeless months while the Government did nothing to bring peace.

No peace was possible among Liberals. Lord Oxford publicly reproached Lloyd George with disloyalty, both to his Party and his country. Lloyd George retorted that he had never shifted from the original policy laid down by the Liberal "Shadow Cabinet" (though *they* had!). This was (i) Back up the Government in maintaining order and essential services; (ii) Hold them primarily responsible for drifting into such a crisis; (iii) Keep the door open to make a reasonable settlement. Surely, said Lloyd George, both in the Boer War and the Great War "Unconditional Surrender" had been regarded not as a Liberal, but a Diehard policy? He offered to meet Lord Oxford and his colleagues and discuss the whole matter.

Instead, Lord Oxford wrote to the Liberal Chief Whip to say that since Lloyd George had declined to attend the "Shadow Cabinet", he had, in effect, resigned from it. Twelve other leading Liberals, including Grey, Cowdray, Simon and Runciman, wrote to *The Times*, associating themselves with Lord Oxford's opinion of Lloyd George.

"We have done our best in the interests of Liberalism to work with Mr. Lloyd George in the councils of the Party, but we cannot feel surprised at your feeling that confidential relations are impossible with one whose instability destroys confidence."

They did not like him and did not trust him, and no doubt Lloyd George had been wondering what the morrow would bring forth for himself—not for the first time or the last time in his life's tempestuous journey. But what had he *done* wrong?

He was entirely unabashed himself. Indeed, he was injured innocence. He told the Manchester Reform Club: "I was walking peaceably along my path when suddenly I was assailed by an angry Bull of Excommunication!"

He was back now in the camp at any rate. He was still Chairman of the Liberal Parliamentary Party, he retained his powerful propaganda machine, and he kept control of that Lloyd George Fund. It was Lord Oxford who went. On 14 October, 1926, he resigned the Liberal Party leadership.

Lloyd George succeeded him. There was no other giant in this camp now. Was it the end of the quarrel in the Liberal Party at last? No. While the Fund remained, the Feud remained.

This Fund was the tragedy of Liberalism in Britain.

It was the political tragedy of Lloyd George. In part, perhaps, it was a tragedy for Britain.

It is true that the money provided the sinews of finance for at least half a dozen Reports on the trade, industry, agriculture, transport and resettlement of the country, which had they been amplified and made the basis of national policy of any ruling Party might have helped them to set her on the road to recover her lost industrial leadership. Yet the possession of this personal Fund, poured out as it was for several years upon many admirable social projects, brought no real gain to its owner, Lloyd George, the human driving force almost alone of British political leaders at that time capable of the action required. Instead, it bred scandal and suspicion, and continued to divide and debilitate his own Party. You cannot build a great democratic movement upon a patron.

Better far, for Lloyd George, too, if he had made the Fund over to the publicly elected officers of Liberalism, and become again a soldier—a commander, if destiny willed, but not a paymaster. Perhaps then these years of organized research, of bold imaginative planning for a nation, would not have been barren of all fruit, as, sadly, they were.

Not that the man himself ever idled, or lost his vitality or purpose. He kept up his travels in Europe and the Mediterranean, and also voyaged again to South America, this time to Brazil. But they were working travels. Lloyd George genuinely toiled away at his newspaper articles while on such holidays, writing them out in his own hand for later typing as he sat wrapped up in a rug on the deck.

He did not spare the British Government, in spite of (was it even because of?) the complaints of Baldwin, who said that these criticisms of British policy by an ex-Prime Minister were making his own job "incomparably more difficult", or of Churchill, who said that they largely consisted of "vilifying his successors in office".

As the New Year, 1929, began to grow and it became plain that the Tory Government were planning to go to a General Election before summer, Lloyd George set out to force them to fight this time on an issue thoroughly disadvantageous to themselves. It was also one which he had been thoroughly examining for some time past, and for which Lloyd George believed he had found the key.

This was Unemployment.

The Gold Standard and the General Strike had exacted their price. For four years, a time almost as long as the Great War, more than a million workers in Britain had been in the Army of the Dole, costing the country a huge annual total sum, though the individual allowance was a pittance, and sapping the strength and fibre of those reduced to living on it.

Here was a scandal, a social shame if ever there was one. The tale of men and women, citizens of the Mother Country of the richest empire in the world, condemned to dwell in idleness and wretchedness. To rot their lives away, while all around them there waited useful, vital tasks undone.

Here was a challenge, too.

For the Man of the People's Budget! Yes, for the Man of the People still! At last, after these lost years, there was something again worth while fighting for!

Lloyd George advanced to battle.

CHAPTER XXXIII

THE LAST CHALLENGE

THE strategy of Lloyd George's electoral attack was soundly planned.

Point One. To begin with, the battle-ground chosen absolutely prohibited any joint operation of the Tories and the Labour Party to out-manœuvre the Liberals. For during the last few years, the woes of the workless men and women in the dole queues had been the chief ammunition of the Socialist opposition against this Tory Capitalist Government. They could not now unite to tackle unemployment.

Otherwise, a Tory-Socialist coalition was by no means so remote a possibility as some supposed. Lloyd George had warned the Liberal Party Conference at Yarmouth the previous October:

"Believe me, if there is a combination of Socialists and Tories in the next Parliament, it will not be the first time you have had it, either in Parliament or out of Parliament. You will not hear very much said about that, but it would be the realization of the dream of Mr. Ramsay MacDonald, who once upon a time said he had a natural affinity for the Tories. . . ."

Point Two. Was a Tory-Liberal coalition a possibility, either during or after the 1929 General Election?

No. Baldwin had settled that.

On 18 February, Lloyd George had made a reconnaissance in a long talk with Churchill. He had suggested that if, as he himself foresaw, the Tories lost the forthcoming contest, they might consider coming to terms with the Liberals, and not at once resigning. The Liberals would require that no general tariff system be imposed, that the voting system be reformed, and that unemployment be tackled as a great national crusade. If this was agreed, Lloyd George and the Liberals would give general support to the Tory Government.

Baldwin was not interested. He wanted nothing to do with Lloyd George. He was quite sure that he could win the forthcoming election on the characteristic slogan of "Safety First!" His only present worry was how to satisfy various claimants for office in his next Cabinet.

"Torpid, sleepy, barren," Lloyd George had called the Baldwin Administration. One of Baldwin's own backbenchers, the sprightly Lieut.-Colonel Moore-Brabazon,[1] Tory M.P. for Rochester, did better. "The snores of the Government," he cried, "reverberate through the land."

[1] Later, Lord Brabazon of Tara.

So there was nothing else to be done with the Tories but to fight them.

Point Three. Was it possible—or worth while—to arrange a Liberal-Labour alliance to defeat the Tory Government, and set up a Labour one, with Liberal support?

Lloyd George's view of this plan was set forth in a letter which he wrote to C. P. Scott, editor of the *Manchester Guardian*, on 30 April, 1929, as the General Election approached. Could Liberals co-operate with a Labour Government? had been the theme of one of Scott's articles.

Lloyd George replied that it all depended on the interpretation of the word "co-operation".

> "If it means that the Liberals in the House of Commons are to carry the ladder and hold it in its place for five years whilst the Socialists are up on the scaffolding doing all the building, then I am utterly against it. It would be the final blow to the Liberal Party.
>
> An agreed programme would not save the situation if the Socialists make a mess of the job, and I feel certain they would because they have no man capable of handling a big task. The consequence would be that the discredit would fall more hardly on the Liberals than on the Socialists. They would always have a solid trade union vote to fall back on. . . .
>
> On the other hand, if you can conceive the possibility of the Socialists doing the job well, the young men of our Party would leave us and join the Party which was carrying through a Liberal programme successfully.
>
> Either way the Liberal Party would be done for."

It reads like a record of what actually happened, not an appreciation of what was about to do so.

Point Four. Could the Labour Party themselves so rouse the nation that they would gain a very great number of Parliamentary seats, if not an absolute majority?

Lloyd George suspected that for all the Socialists' propaganda on this great question, they had not got a plan, or a single practical idea in their heads. He was right, but they had a well-organized emotion about it, which ensured them a mass support. This great creator of emotion himself did not yet realize that Labour had now become the inheritor of the old Radical Crusade of the "Condition of the People".

Lloyd George deployed his forces for the great offensive. At a gathering of prospective Liberal candidates in London on St. David's Day, 1929, he declared that if a Liberal Government were returned to power they would put in hand immediate schemes of work, not merely useful in themselves but essential to the well-being of the country. And this work would, he pledged,

> "reduce the terrible figures of the workless, in the course of a single year, to normal proportions, and will, when completed, enrich the nation and equip

it for competing successfully with all its rivals in the business of the world. These plans will not add one penny to national or local taxation."

It sounded a tall order. Indeed, it was. Lloyd George went on:

"It will require a great and sustained effort to redeem this pledge. But some of us sitting at this table have succeeded in putting through even greater and more difficult tasks in the interests of the nation."

A few days later, the fifth Liberal Report, *We can Conquer Unemployment*, appeared upon the bookstalls. This sixpenny booklet sold by hundreds of thousands, and made Lloyd George again for a time one of the most talked-of men in British politics.

We Can Conquer Unemployment set forth three main propositions: (i) That there was an immense amount of work which urgently needed doing if ever we were to prosper again; (ii) That the labour and materials were available; and (iii) By preparing for prosperity we should actually lead to prosperity. Thus Lloyd George:

"Innumerable things cry out to be done, and a very Niagara of fine labour-power is running to waste! Can it be beyond the wit of man to harness this power? We should—we must—seize this Great Opportunity to raise the whole level of efficiency and amenity of our national life.

The Unemployment Fund will save money when its present recipients are at work in the forge or the foundry, instead of standing idle at the street corner; the National Exchequer will gain in taxes; and trade and industry, in general, will benefit when the purchasing power of a million families is raised from the dole-level to the wage-level. There is plenty of money awaiting investment.

Put our idle money, our idle men, and idle materials to earn their keep! Cash spent on vital national development is the soundest national investment. The nation freely lent for Destruction; we mobilized for war. Let the nation lend for Prosperity; let us mobilize for peace!"

This was the mood and the language and the argument of *We Can Conquer Unemployment*. The broad plan was to put in hand at once, and with real energy, many of the recommendations of the earlier Reports. But, especially, it concentrated on the building of roads, bridges, houses, telephone systems, electrical power-plants and the draining and reclaiming of "bad", that is, waste land.

The imperative need for a modernized trunk road network was most strongly urged—and the fact drummed home that Churchill, the Tory Chancellor of the Exchequer, had in the last three years raided the Road Fund of £30,000,000 and otherwise appropriated another £10,000,000 from road users which should have gone to build better roads, and give useful employment. The ever-growing, and ever-costlier congestion of London traffic was dealt with in *We Can Conquer Unemployment*, and schemes put forward not only to develop circular roads round such great cities but to drive "spoke" roads from these rims right through into the heart of them.

It was claimed that in all, directly and indirectly, three-quarters of a million people might find useful employment, at a saving to the Unemployment Fund of £30,000,000 a year, and also to the Exchequer of £12,000,000 in taxes.

Lloyd George's pamphlet and his policy were at once assailed, with vigour and variety. Its proposals were ridiculous; they would not meet the problem. They were ruinous; they would deepen it.

Churchill considered Lloyd George was suffering from some kind of road-fever, comparable with the frenzied enthusiasm which had seized the pioneer railway promoters in the early years of the previous century: you would not solve unemployment by building race-tracks across the country along which millionaires could scorch in their Rolls-Royces. Neville Chamberlain said that, of course, Lloyd George knew very well that there was not the least chance of his ever being called on to redeem his pledge, so he could (and did) say what he liked. The general Tory view was that *We Can Conquer Unemployment* had not got a good idea in it. The Socialists claimed that all the best ones had been lifted from their own *Labour and the Nation*.

But in the wider world, Lloyd George's dramatic focusing of public attention, even of argument, upon "the social shame, and crime, of unemployment" had a different effect.

After a tremendous launching of the campaign at the Albert Hall at the end of March, Lloyd George made perhaps the greatest election effort of his life. Mass meetings all over the country, floods of propaganda from his organization, a huge poster advertising campaign, more than five hundred Liberal candidates in the field and the Fund this time pouring out the money, made Lloyd George the Man of the Election.

Lloyd George himself spoke in many places, and received a public acclamation which had hardly been exceeded in 1918. Even the Liberal Council ceased from strife, and alongside the huge poster (like a cinema bill) of Lloyd George, the White Knight, slaying the Dragon, Unemployment, there appeared another of equal size (but looking like a Happy Family album) of the United Liberals, Lloyd George, Lord Grey, Herbert Samuel, John Simon, Walter Runciman and Lord Beauchamp.

And the end of all this mighty effort? On 31 May, 1929, the results of the poll were known:

Labour	288
Conservatives	260
Liberals	59
Independents	8

The Liberal half-company was almost immediately further reduced by one,

In his orchards, 1938

With his second wife, 1943

because Mr. William Jowitt, K.C., M.P.,[1] took himself off to join the Labour Government as their Attorney-General. The vagaries of the British electoral system gave the Liberals less than one-tenth of the representation in the House of Commons although they had polled more than 5,000,000 votes.

What had gone wrong? Was it that Merlin had lost his magic touch? Or that the people had lost their faith in Merlin?

Lloyd George's own bitter disappointment was partly assuaged by two facts: (i) The return of his son Gwilym as the Member for Pembroke, and of his daughter Megan as the Member for Anglesey—it must have been one of the proudest moments of Lloyd George's life when he introduced his young daughter to take her seat in the House of Commons. Their relationship had ever been happy, and he had given her in full measure that father's love which once he had lavished upon his lost child, Mair; (ii) Even with its modest Parliamentary strength, the Liberals held the balance between the Parties. After all, this was the general situation which Lloyd George had anticipated. Much might yet be done with it.

As things turned out, he was able to do little with it. Baldwin shied away from the prospect of being kept in office on Lloyd George's terms, and four days after the General Election was over he resigned and advised the King to send for Ramsay MacDonald. When the new Parliament assembled, the Tory Amendment to the Address advocated Protection, which the Liberals could not accept, and the Labour Government thus secured a majority in their first Parliamentary test.

Promptly, the new Prime Minister began to talk of the House of Commons making itself a "Council of State" for tackling the grave problems of the day, and the Liberals could hardly oppose that reasonable attitude of a Minority Government. Thus, from that initial vote on Protection, they found themselves jockeyed into a position of giving general support to Labour, without ever having been consulted themselves on any part of this Government's policy. It was the "patient oxen" situation all over again. It was also the third time that "simple" Stanley Baldwin had outwitted "crafty" Lloyd George.

That summer of 1929, Lloyd George went off with his family on a tour of the battlefields of France and Italy, both for a needed rest and change, and, as he said, "to get first-hand knowledge for my *War Memoirs*" (for which he had now received several fresh tempting offers). Lloyd George loved a battlefield almost as much as a storm. He had often gone many a mile out of his way to revisit the scenes of Tewkesbury, Bosworth, Naseby, or Crecy, Agincourt, Waterloo, and now he revelled in Mons, Verdun, and Passchendaele. He returned to Britain to find a developing economic and financial crisis.

In October, an extraordinary and prolonged boom on Wall Street suddenly broke. It was followed by a slump which dragged the United States down into the worst trade depression of its history. Soon, it had spread far beyond

[1] Later, Lord Jowitt.

w*

the shores of America, and the whole of world trade was in its grisly grip. So it would remain for several years, changing the face of our times, as orthodox Governments toppled and revolutionary régimes rose upon their ruins.

In Britain, the effect of these events was almost as calamitous as upon the countries who were concerned. Unemployment soared to two million. The puny Public Works programme, which, despite Lloyd George's ceaseless goading, was all that J. H. Thomas, the Minister in charge, seemed capable of producing, had failed utterly to cope even with the original problem.

Now, in the voting lobbies of the House of Commons, where, after all, the Liberals really held the whip hand, Lloyd George resolved to draw a lash across the back of the Labour Government. They had brought in a Coal Mines Bill to reduce working hours in the pits, regulate the output and sale of coal by a system of production quotas, and impose a levy on home-sold British coal (thereby inevitably raising prices here) to provide a subsidy for export coal. It was a muddled measure, open to attack as conferring something like monopolistic price-fixing powers on the coalowners, and backed by the miners only because it appeared to offer some immediate increase of wages. It did not tackle the basic problems of the British coal industry. Lloyd George condemned this outrage on Free Trade (!), and on the Second Reading he led the Liberals into the lobby against the Government, who narrowly survived by eight votes.

Lloyd George that night also settled a score with his late, strayed follower, the new Attorney-General, William Jowitt. Demanding to know why the name of no single Minister not connected with the Department concerned was on the Bill, Lloyd George recited those who *were* there.

The President of the Board of Trade, yes, of course! The Minister of Mines, naturally! The Attorney-General, well, he was bound to be on! He had himself said, in substance, in the discussion on unemployment, that "those who were genuinely seeking work, cannot discriminate in the jobs which are offered them".

This Liberal "Parliamentary strike" against the Labour Government started a widespread rumour that Lloyd George had decided to destroy it. The story was strengthened by the fact that Churchill had also played a prominent part in the attack on the Coal Bill, so that when the debate continued in the New Year, Aneurin Bevan, then a young Miners' M.P., could speak of Lloyd George and Churchill as being "in a temporary re-alliance, which may be carried right through to the division lobby in their capacity as joint executioners".

There followed a scene of drama when, with passionate voice and pointing finger the young Welshman assailed the Father of the House across the floor.

"Better to have slightly dearer coal than cheaper colliers," flamed Bevan. ". . . We say that you cannot get from the already dry veins of the miners new blood to rivivify the industry. Their veins are already shrunken white, and we are asking you to be, for once, decent to the miners . . . not to use all your Parliamentary skill, all your rhetoric, in an act of pure demagogy to expose the mining community of this country to another few years of misery."

Lloyd George sat opposite, listening intently, crossing and re-crossing his legs. It was one of the very few times that veteran journalists of the Press Gallery could ever remember having seen Lloyd George obviously disconcerted. Said one of them: "He was confronted with the ghost of his own angry youth."

When he rose at once to reply, Lloyd George expressed his regret "to have fallen foul of a young countryman of mine, for whom I have a great deal of admiration". But he reaffirmed his criticism of the Coal Bill, and at the risk of a split within the Liberal Parliamentary Party, led the majority of them into the Opposition lobby once again.

Indeed, the Liberals very nearly did break up, and the Chief Whip, Major-General Sir Robert Hutchison, actually resigned. But Lloyd George's sharp, short break with the Labour Government compelled the Ministers in charge of the Coal Bill to drop the obnoxious export bounty, and it brought the Prime Minister himself apparently to heel on general policy. For MacDonald (who always held that words were as good as deeds) offered to set up a Committee of Inquiry on unemployment on the lines of the Committee of Imperial Defence, that is, representative of all Parties. It gave Churchill, now no longer in any kind of alliance with Lloyd George, the chance to warn the Prime Minister to think twice "before inviting Mr. Lloyd George to take charge of the Labour Government".

The trouble was that Lloyd George was *not* in charge. Nor was he ever able to get any Minister in the Labour Government really "in charge" of unemployment, which in the end took charge of the Labour Government.

In June, 1930, MacDonald sought to call a Three-Party Conference on the subject. But if he was anxious thereby to weaken Lloyd George's hold on him, Baldwin was determined to elude it altogether, and the Tories declined to attend.

The Liberals, therefore, arrived alone. For the next six months Lloyd George, Lord Lothian[1] and Seebohm Rowntree sat in more or less continuous session with MacDonald, Philip Snowden (the Socialist Chancellor of the Exchequer) and Vernon Hartshorn (Lord Privy Seal). They achieved nothing.

It was in February, 1931, that George Lansbury, "the most sincere Socialist in Britain", wrote to Lloyd George, begging him to join the Labour Party. Their official programme as set forth in *Labour and the Nation*, said Lansbury, was only Socialism reduced to "every day expedients", and Lloyd George was willing to help Labour to put those expedients into action. "*As one of us,*" urged Lansbury, "your help would be invaluable, for as things stand, we gibe,

[1] Formerly, Mr. Philip Kerr.

humour, abuse, coax each other, to the bewilderment of all who read or hear us. . . ."

Britain was in a great transition period, and on her handling of it would depend the future of Western Civilization. Economic changes would not wait, and either we continued down the road to decay, or else replaced the existing muddle by a national and international co-operative effort. All the Liberals in the House of Commons would not come with Lloyd George, but those who counted, the young in mind, those who had faith in our common stock would come. Lansbury ended:

"Your coming would crown a professional life with the knowledge that as the world of thought and action moved on, you never closed your mind, and when the hour came and you were needed, you flung aside all thought of self and came over to the new groupings of true liberalism."

Lloyd George replied on 16 February, welcoming Lansbury's frank and cordial letter as offering some prospect of clearing up "the atmosphere of suspicion which has hitherto confined and hindered co-operation between progressive minds in both our parties". But let them tackle now the immediate problems before them—and the Liberals had pledged themselves to back the Government in their unemployment plans as sketched in *Labour and the Nation*. "Coming over" was not the best way to help; it would antagonize millions of Liberals with traditional party loyalties who would gladly support any Government from another party who were putting through a real policy of reconditioning Britain. So let the Government go ahead on these lines. Lloyd George then reaffirmed his loyalty to this purpose:

"I can and will give effective assistance to the Government—if they mean business. At present I am genuinely perplexed and disappointed by the stickiness of some of your colleagues. They are always finding reasons for not doing things. They are too easily scared by obstacles and interests. Unless you inoculate them with some of your faith and courage, your Party and ours will be landed in an overwhelming catastrophe."

By spring, 1931, the high cost of keeping two million men and their families on the dole was beginning to land the Labour Government in difficulties. On 11 February, a Liberal amendment to a Tory Vote of Censure resulted in the setting-up of an Economy Committee under the chairmanship of Sir George May to sharpen a new Geddes Axe. The very next day, Sir Herbert Samuel moved a resolution calling on the Government to put in hand the joint Liberal-Labour plans for tackling unemployment. There was not yet deemed to be any contradiction in these two policies, and Samuel's motion was accepted by the Government and carried without a division.

In the debate, Lloyd George begged Snowden not to be scared off the necessary expenditure by the "money barons" of the City of London, whom he recalled had once received him when he was himself Chancellor of the Exchequer in the days of the People's Budget, "with the frigid silence of a row of penguins in the Antarctic".

But now, indeed, an economic blizzard was approaching. The darkening scene, and the growing uneasiness about the capacity of the crew to handle the ship in heavy weather, had already set a section of the Liberals, led by Sir John Simon, with Hore-Belisha as his first lieutenant, off in search of some alternative. They opened talks with the Tories.

At the same time, the captain of the ship himself, Ramsay MacDonald, was considering a change of company—or, at any rate, the introduction of some fresh personnel. Through his friends, Lord and Lady Londonderry, he also was in touch with the Tories.

By June, 1931, the slump was rocking Europe. The *Credit Anstaldt*, National Bank of Austria, was threatened with bankruptcy because the French had failed to furnish their share of support for Austrian finances, and but for a rush loan from the Bank of England would have had to close its doors. In July, France and America agreed to suspending for a year all reparations from Germany and all war debts to the United States. A Seven-Power Conference in London decided to convert Germany's short-term borrowings to long-term, to save her from total financial collapse.

The uneasy association of the Lloyd George Liberals with the Labour Government still held, and as late as the last days of July, 1931, Lloyd George was dictating the following memorandum to Frances Stevenson on his return from seeing the Prime Minister:

> "Generally speaking, Labour would like an alliance. They would be willing to drop certain of their present Ministers. . . .
>
> Ramsay would be Prime Minister. Lloyd George would be Leader [of the House] at the Foreign Office or the Treasury. Ramsay thinks he can adjourn early in August and resume late in the autumn, and then continue till the next Budget. No fear of immediate Election. It might be contemplated that the Army, Air and Navy join up under one Ministry. . . ."

At this critical moment, Lloyd George was suddenly taken ill and had to undergo a most serious operation for the removal of a prostate gland. During recent weeks he had paid several visits to the Hampstead studio of the painter, Philip de Laszlo, for a portrait which Lord Devonport had commissioned. Lloyd George was not a patient sitter, at any time, and though Frances Stevenson had accompanied him and kept him engaged with conversation, he had been unusually restive and would seldom stay even an hour. Lord Dawson said afterwards that this portrait shows the signs of his approaching illness.

Lloyd George's family were in Wales, and he was alone at his London house in Addison Road when the seizure occurred. It was August Bank Holiday, and only with some difficulty was Frances Stevenson able to bring his son-in-law

Age 68

doctor, Sir Thomas Carey-Evans, from the country to his bedside. Lord Dawson also hurried to town, arriving in time to superintend the operation.

The May Committee had just reported, on the previous Thursday, with the warning that there would be a deficit of £120,000,000 on the Budget. To meet it, they recommended drastic limitations of all Government spending programmes for arms, agriculture, Empire development, etc., and also a 10 per cent cut in the pay and pensions of the Armed Services, Civil Service, Police, Teachers; and in unemployment benefit and health insurance allowances. Next day, 31 July, Parliament adjourned for three months.

A dangerous flight of gold from sterling now followed. As the financial crisis deepened, the choice presented itself of mortgaging the country's overseas assets or borrowing from the American banks. When the loan was decided on, the Prime Minister told his Cabinet that it could only be negotiated if drastic economies were guaranteed. The bewildered Ministers were willing to swallow most of those proposed, but not the 10 per cent dole cut. On this, Ramsay MacDonald collected their resignations and hurried off to Buckingham Palace, 24 August, 1931. His colleagues made ready to depart together on his return.

To their astonishment, MacDonald obtained the King's authority to form a National Government to meet the crisis. It was collected the same day. It included Baldwin, Neville Chamberlain, Sir Samuel Hoare and Sir Philip Cunliffe-Lister from the Tories; Sir Herbert Samuel (acting Liberal Leader) and Lord Reading from the Liberals. Two only of his own Socialist Cabinet colleagues were included in MacDonald's new National Government, Philip Snowden and J. H. Thomas. "Tomorrow," cried the Prime Minister to Snowden, "all the duchesses in London will want to kiss me!"

To Lloyd George, who acquiesced in what he could not prevent from his sick bed, MacDonald wrote:

"26 August, 1931.   10 Downing Street.

My dear Ll. George,
    We have just been at the Palace and the new venture has been launched. Its weather will be stormy, but I should certainly not be on board did I not feel that there was nothing else to do in face of the critical position of our finance. At this moment, you are first in my thoughts. Samuel has reported his interview with you, but we all feel what a loss is your absence, and how provoking the cause of it is. I hope with all my heart that you will soon be back not only alive but kicking lustily as before you went away. We shall have to do things that neither your folks nor mine will like but we must see this thing through.

                                    Always yours,
                                    Ramsay MacDonald."

Lloyd George replied with a letter, which was perhaps about as sincere.

"30 August, 1931. Bron-y-de.

My dear Prime Minister,

For some reason or other your nice letter did not reach me until late last night. The attitude you have taken is truly a heroic one. The alternatives —or shall I say both alternatives—were disastrous; and therefore when it was intimated to me that you would probably be forced to throw your hand in I was in despair. But equally did I rejoice when I heard the following morning that you had decided to take the hazard and form an administration.

I am sorry I have not been able to give you any real help, but if the promise of the doctors is redeemed I may be of some use later on.

I sincerely hope there is nothing in this talk of an early dissolution. That would undo all the good work which I hope will be accomplished.

The strain upon you must have been at certain times almost beyond endurance, and I am glad that you have pulled through without any impairment to your health.

Ever sincerely,
D. Lloyd George."

MacDonald had publicly declared on 25 August in a broadcast pledge that the National Government had been formed to deal with the emergency only, and that when this had been done it would be dissolved. He added: "The Election which will follow will not be fought by the Government." It was acting on this assurance that Lloyd George's son, Gwilym, had joined the Government as Parliamentary Secretary to the Board of Trade.

Now the Westminster air hummed with intrigue. The "Simonite" Liberals had received no offices at all as yet and now they made open approaches to the Tories. For by this time, it was the Leader of the Tory Party who was really in control of events. On 25 September, Herbert Samuel wrote to Lloyd George that only five days earlier MacDonald had assured him that he was against an election, but "today he is on the point of surrender".

Stanley Baldwin, at any rate, was quite sure what he wanted. He was going to have a General Election, while everything so favoured the Tories. The Labour Party were discredited by their failures, and deserted by their leaders. The Liberal Party were divided again, and their own formidable chieftain laid low upon a sick-bed. Baldwin did not fail to point out to MacDonald that this was the time to settle with their mutual enemy, Lloyd George.

Lloyd George, who had by now made a considerable recovery in health, was well aware of what was going on. He realized that but for his own sudden illness he, and not Baldwin, would have been dominating the Government. (How history might have been changed!) On 4 October, he invited Herbert Samuel and Walter Layton down to Bron-y-de to discuss things. He persuaded them to stand fast against a General Election. On his way home by car that even, Samuel looked out of the window at a traffic hold-up, and saw a huge red sign, KEEP LEFT! He telephoned Lloyd George to tell him the story.

A day or two later, MacDonald went down to see Lloyd George. He was not at all pleased to meet the "invalid" walking briskly into the house from the garden in his Tyrolean cloak, with his white mane blowing in the summer breeze. ("How Ramsay's face fell when he saw me!" said Lloyd George afterwards). But the Prime Minister insisted that he was not committed to give the Tories their General Election—naturally supporting the "National" Government. When he had left, Lloyd George telephoned to Samuel to get his reassurance that he and Reading, at any rate, would continue to stand firm against any rush election. But by midnight, Samuel had GONE RIGHT.

Lloyd George was beside himself with rage. He had been betrayed! From then onwards, his resentment of Samuel was never assuaged. As for the Liberal M.P.s who had agreed with Samuel's decision and were rash enough to pay a visit to Lloyd George immediately afterwards, the gale of his denunciation nearly blew them out of the house. "You have sold every pass that we held!" he shouted at them.

Worst of all, he had been tricked again by Baldwin! It was the fourth time.

At once, Gwilym resigned from the Government. And now the Liberal Party broke into *three* parts. Those who followed Simon, those who followed Samuel, and those who followed Lloyd George. The Liberal Party has never even looked like reuniting ever since that stormy day.

Lloyd George knew it in his heart. The bell had sounded.

Bitterly, he broadcast on 15 October that this Election was "a partisan intrigue under the guise of a patriotic appeal".

On 27 October, 1931, the nation polled. The result was an overwhelming victory for the National Government. The Labour Party (52) were almost annihilated in the House of Commons, but they kept their troops in the field throughout the country. The Tories (417), fighting under the "National" colours, had a huge success. The Liberals (72; in three factions), increased their total numbers, and irreparably destroyed their remaining strength.

CHAPTER XXXIV

THE LONG EVENING

ONE day in the House of Commons, during the Government of the Snores, Baldwin had been lounging on the Front Bench, deeply immersed in a handbook and paying no attention whatever to the debate. A colleague edged up to him to see what he was reading. It was *Dod's Parliamentary Companion*, which contains a detailed record of elections. "I think," said the Prime Minister, reflectively, "if the Old Man goes, we should stand a very good chance of winning Caernarvon Boroughs."

He was right. In June, 1945, within a few months of Lloyd George's resignation of the seat, it had become Tory, and has remained so ever since. Lloyd George himself held it for fifty-five years, and he had to fight hard for it the whole of that time.

He had to fight in 1931. Or rather, Dame Margaret had to do so on his behalf, and that the seat was held for him was very largely her own personal triumph. The voting was:

D. Lloyd George (Liberal)	.	.	17,101
F. P. Gourlay (Conservative)	.	.	11,714
Liberal Majority	.	.	5,387

His majority had been more than nine thousand in 1929.

Now, Lloyd George was planning to take a health cruise to Ceylon. But before he sailed, a decision had to be made about the leadership of the Liberal Party. He was out of sympathy with almost every prominent member, and out of touch with the rank-and-file. On 3 November, 1931, he wrote to Herbert Samuel, declining to stand again for the Party leadership. The following day, the Liberal M.P.s elected Samuel to the vacant post. The "Liberal Nationals", as the Simonite group called themselves, did not attend the meeting. The Liberal Party was already and finally split, this time without the assistance of Lloyd George, although both factions were represented in the new "National" Government.

Of the Samuelites, Sir Herbert himself was Home Secretary, Sir Archibald Sinclair, Secretary of State for Scotland, and Sir Donald Maclean, Minister of Education. Of the Simonites, Sir John himself became Secretary of State for India, Walter Runciman, President of the Board of Trade, and Hore-Belisha, Parliamentary Secretary to the Board of Trade.

Lloyd George's own thoughts about these events are reflected in a letter which he wrote while still at sea to his friend, Sir Herbert Lewis, who had urged him to stay clear of all party politics on his return to England, and to devote himself to world issues. Lloyd George reminded Lewis: "As you know, I have always found it difficult to keep out of a 'scrap', more particularly so when I find causes in which I am interested being so inadequately and ineptly defended."

He then repeated that the leaders responsible for directing the battle after he had himself been placed *hors de combat* had surrendered all the passes to the enemy.

"The heights are now in command of the Protectionists: we are entirely at their mercy. The poor abject mob of Liberals are there cowering down in the swamps. They have ceased entirely to count. No one talks now of exterminating the Liberal Party: for all practical purposes it is annihilated. . . ."

He added a good report of his own health. The voyage had done wonders.

"I am now able to play about five games of deck quoits a day, and walk three or four miles up and down without tiring. . . . Meanwhile, I am at it working hard on material for my book."

Before leaving England for the East, Lloyd George had what he described as an "illuminating" talk with Gandhi, who was then lecturing at Morley College. With bare legs and sandals, but swathed in a heavy blanket like a bath-robe, for it was pelting with rain, Gandhi arrived at Bron-y-de. He had dined on the way down in the car, from a bottle of goat's milk and a handful of dates. Lloyd George welcomed him warmly, and they talked for hours.

Or rather Gandhi did, for he had much to say, and Lloyd George, as ever, was a good listener. "There was really no need for me to do any of the talking," he remarked afterwards to Frances Stevenson, who had been present throughout. "But I think L. G. underestimated his own share of the conversation," was her comment.

They ranged the vast field of Indian politics, and Gandhi, said Lloyd George,

"was very definitely against giving separate votes to the Hindu, or Moslem, or Pariah. He was also against Missionaries, whom he thought did a great deal of harm by buying their converts by giving them medicine and free treatment for their illnesses. The Indian Princes he described as being nothing more than British nominees."

They discussed village industries in India, Gandhi saying he favoured them. The concentrating of machinery in the towns was the cause of much trouble in India, certainly of ill-health (Lloyd George: "In England, too!").

They talked about "women who did not wear any clothing on their chests and the upper portion of their backs nowadays" and they agreed that this had much to do with the decrease of pneumonia among women. Clothing was not necessarily protective. Look at the Polynesians, who were the finest and the healthiest race of men in the world, until they started wearing European dress.

When they came to British-India relations, Lloyd George put the same question to Gandhi that he had asked the Irish envoys. Was he willing to remain within the British Empire and to acknowledge the King as the head of that Empire? When Gandhi answered that he did not accept the word "Empire", Lloyd George asked him if he was in favour of remaining within the British Commonwealth of Free Nations. To which Gandhi said, "Yes."

"Have you ever said so in a public speech?" demanded Lloyd George, and when Gandhi said Yes again, Lloyd George shook his head, and declared that he had never himself seen or heard of such a statement being reported. It was profoundly important that Gandhi should make it publicly and in the most definite terms. It would form the basis of a settlement between Britain and India. Gandhi undertook to do it.

"He may be a saint," said Lloyd George to Frances Stevenson, "but he's also a very shrewd politician! He wants the best of both worlds."

Lloyd George had a stormy voyage to India. It did him good. At Bombay, he had a great reception, and made his first public speech since his illness. It showed that he had not lost his touch on land. He had ten busy days in Ceylon, visited the sphinx in Egypt, and on his way home ran into another splendid storm in the mouth of the Channel.

By now, he was ready to get down to the huge task of his *War Memoirs*. But first, before the Lausanne Conference on reparations and war debts met in June, 1932, Lloyd George was anxious to get his own views upon these matters published. Begun as a well-documented pamphlet, it grew into a large book, *The Truth about Reparations and War Debts*. Lloyd George argued once more for the total cancellation all round of these hoary liabilities. He thought, however, that the United States might reasonably insist that if they wiped out the debts due to them, the relieved debtor countries should refrain from joining in a fresh armaments race.

That summer, there began a movement in the Liberal Party towards Lloyd George. The world depression still continued, and unemployment had climbed to a gaunt peak of nearly two and a half millions. After all the fuss to "save the pound", the pound slid off gold with no trouble to anyone. Financial stability was restored, not to say financial immobility. Hundreds of millions of pounds piled up on deposit in the banks, while grey processions of "hunger-marchers" tramped from the depressed areas, smugly renamed "Special Areas", to the House of Commons and Trafalgar Square in futile protest.

Age 69

Lloyd George's own ineradicable sympathy with the underdog was fiercely roused.

"Do not let this country be like that Pompeian slave just discovered in Italy who was found among the ruins clutching the leather bag of his savings," he pleaded in the House of Commons, 12 July, 1932. "Utilize them! The Empire is not a hollow drum to beat; it is a gigantic estate to be cultivated."

But it was a hostile, or worse still, an indifferent House, and though by the end of September, 1932, the Samuelite Liberals had resigned from the National Government over the Imperial Preference resolutions of the Ottawa Conference, Lloyd George felt that he was simply wasting his time there. He concentrated his energies on producing his *War Memoirs*.

An immense amount of preliminary sorting and indexing of the mass of letters, documents and State papers in his possession had already been done. Malcolm Thomson, who lived at Bron-y-de while the work was going on, and Frances Stevenson did much of the research, and helped with the *Memoirs*. When the manuscript was completed Sir Maurice Hankey read it through, and Captain Liddell Hart studied the military chapters, and offered suggestions. But the work as it appeared was Lloyd George's, and a very great deal of the original drafts and redrafts of these six volumes was written by Lloyd George's hand, in pencil, for he rarely used ink.

He would start in bed, as soon as he awoke, often as early as 6 a.m. About seven-thirty, he would have a cup of tea and some fruit, and then get up and dress. After reading the newspapers at breakfast, he would organize the day's literary work, and perhaps revise the typescript copy. Then, for an hour or so, he would march round his farm—for the *War Memoirs* were almost entirely written at Bron-y-de. After lunch, he took a nap and another walk, and then returned to work. He dined early, and was off to bed by nine-thirty.

The first two volumes were published in September and October, 1933, and the remaining four were completed by 1936. They are a lively defence of his own part in the war by the only leading British Minister who held high office throughout it. Lloyd George's *War Memoirs* are also his tale of his own personal wars with other Ministers, British and Allied, and with leading military and naval officers, Kitchener, Haig, Robertson, Pétain, Pershing and Jellicoe—and newspaper proprietors such as Northcliffe, Beaverbrook and Cowdray. He tells it in a vigorous style, though less arresting than his oratory, and the story is sometimes marred by personal vengefulness. He gives no quarter, but it must be said that he offers more substantial evidence for his main contentions than most of those with whom he quarrelled have done. Naturally, Lloyd George's *War Memoirs* stirred up violent controversy at the time.

The author came off less successfully on this occasion with the financial yield of his *War Memoirs*. The British rights brought him £50,000 (the *Daily Telegraph* paid £25,000 of this sum for serialization), and the American rights only $12,000. Two subsequent volumes, *The Truth About the Peace Treaties*, brought in another £9,000 for British rights and $2,000 for American rights. Finally, some years later, an accumulation of royalties brought in some £3,000 from Russia, making a total of about £65,000. Lloyd George was either too late, or too early, to make a really big plucking with his memoirs. However, after the withdrawal of his original contract in 1922, he was no longer bound by his undertaking to hand over all the proceeds to war charities.

His rare appearances in Parliament during these many months caused rumours to be spread that he was a sick man, and no longer to be feared. Another report ran that he was "going Protectionist" at last, and that a new Lloyd George Policy was on the way, including Food Taxes. He had himself provided some grounds for this suspicion, which excited the Liberals and alarmed some Tories. He had done this in a speech in the House of Commons on 26 July, 1933.

Lloyd George had then declared that, if under the Ottawa Agreements Free Trade was to be abandoned and taxes levied on the imported goods which the British farmer bought, then that man should have the same protection for what he sold. Sir Percy Harris, a prominent Samuelite, in a letter to the *Manchester Guardian*, called him a "chameleon". In a scathing reply, Lloyd George reminded him that Sir Herbert Samuel and Sir Percy's other Liberal leaders had helped to return this Protectionist Parliament, which had now erected a high tariff. He, Lloyd George, was simply putting in a plea

"for fair and equal treatment to the cultivators of the soil. They are having a very hard struggle. I only wish to temper the wind to the shorn lamb. Sir Percy ought to help, for after all his leaders furnished the shears".

To Edward Marjoribanks, a lively young Tory M.P., who jeered at the Liberal dissensions, "in the Liberal Party there are many mansions", Lloyd George retorted, "and in the Conservative Party there are many flats", to the delight and loud laughter of the cowboy film star, Will Rogers, who sat in the public gallery. But Lloyd George went no farther along the path of Protection.

Now the shadows of a new storm were gathering on the horizon of the world. In 1931, Japan had surged into Manchuria and seized that rich province. Next year, she grabbed Shanghai. In 1933, Adolf Hitler arrived in power in Germany. In 1934, the Disarmament Conference in Geneva broke down and the World Economic Conference in London was indefinitely adjourned; millions of words had been uttered, and no single deed accomplished. Britain drifted, while in the dictator lands of Russia, Germany and Italy, purposeful and ruthless Governments drove through their Five Year Plans, their schemes of reafforestation and *autobahn* building, their land reclamation from the Pontine marshes and Alpine hydro-power development.

Yet Democracy could do great things, too, as the United States under the imaginative leadership of President Franklin Delano Roosevelt had just proved in the successful outcome of their bold New Deal. Lloyd George believed that Britain also could shape her own future, instead of wallowing along in the trough of the world trade depression. Not unnaturally, he believed that a man called David Lloyd George could supply the energy required to do that job on this side of the Atlantic. By the autumn of 1934, he was busy with a British "New Deal".

Age 71

So Bron-y-de became once more the workshop of ideas. Many of the original plans of capital development were redrafted, and much new was added concerning the iron, coal, steel and cotton trades. The vast opportunities of developing trade within the Empire, of planned migration by whole colonies of people from those living graveyards of the "Special Areas", of a new Elizabethan kind of enterprise in trade with the awakening lands of the Far East, especially China, were set forth in vivid and energetic language. He demanded a National Development Board to survey Great Britain's own needs in agriculture, industry and shipping, and to direct the requisite labour and finance to the task of satisfying them. The Bank of England was to be brought under public control—and a small inner Cabinet created on the lines of Lloyd George's own war-time model, to press through the policy.

Ramsay MacDonald's National Government would have much preferred to continue its siesta, but unfortunately for them their peace was now disturbed by trouble on either flank of the Tory Party.

On the Right, was Churchill with his India League, objecting to "handing over India" to the Indians. He had been firmly kept out of the National Government on the insistence of Baldwin in the 1931 crisis, who reckoned that with Lloyd George laid low at the time he could afford to let Churchill go loose; the two would not be getting together. On the Left were the group of go-ahead young Tories led by Mr. Harold Macmillan, who were clamouring for a programme much akin to Lloyd George's New Deal in their own *Next Five Years*' movement.

Lloyd George's labours at Bron-y-de during this time were enlivened by the steady flow of important people in all walks of life who still paid court to a man who they believed might one day "come again". Lloyd George was a charming host, and his visitors were ever sure of a good welcome—and if they happened to be journalists, of a good story! Especially interesting to Lloyd George were travellers who had just returned from journeys in China, Japan, Russia or Germany, for there, sensed this stormy petrel, fresh storms were brewing. One who came, straight from Moscow, offering a very disparaging account of Russia's military capacity, was Charles Lindberg, hero of the first solo trans-Atlantic flight. Lloyd George closely questioned him, cross-examined him as to whom he had seen, and was not at all impressed with his evidence.

As for the politicians at his table, they ranged from Churchill to Harry Pollitt, Secretary of the British Communist Party (Lloyd George found him "a surprisingly reasonable man").

He had congenial neighbours, the Sidney Webbs at Passfield, the H. A. L. Fishers at Thursley, the Philip Snowdens at Tilford. Snowden and Lloyd George were on intimate, though not always agreeable terms. Mrs. Snowden one day snapped at dinner: "You put Philip in jail in the Great War!" "I was not responsible for locking him up for his violent Pacifism," retorted Lloyd George, "though I didn't disapprove of it!"

Afterwards, she played the piano, and Lloyd George and Philip Snowden sang "On Ilkley Moor baht 'at" and "the Red Flag".

On Sunday nights, a cinema show was held in the Library—always a film about cowboys and Indians in the Wild West—lassoos, mustangs, revolvers and tomahawks!

Politics were sharpening their blade again in Britain. Who, indeed, could expect to avoid the mood of the world in those Angry 'Thirties—the mood of Japan in Manchuria, of Hitler in Germany, of Italy in Abyssinia, of the Spaniards in their Civil War?

At this moment, General Smuts turned up on a visit to England. He tackled Baldwin on the idea of working with Lloyd George, and as Lloyd George was now in full vigour again and thoroughly capable of making serious difficulties for the Government, Baldwin professed himself willing.

Early in December, 1934, Sir Edward Grigg, who had become a "National Conservative" M.P., sought to arrange a personal interview between Lloyd George and Baldwin, and again Lloyd George, at any rate, awaited action.

But, on 4 December, at a Tory Party Conference on India at Queen's Hall, Westminster, Baldwin secured a huge majority over Churchill and his diehard policy, which put that formidable rebel out of the field for the time being. The need for placating Lloyd George had thus become less urgent.

MacDonald was equally relieved at the prospect of not having the dynamo from Wales in his Cabinet. He and his colleagues preferred to proceed at their own measured pace, and as he put it in one of his illuminating phrases, to go moving "up, up and up and on, on and on, without experiencing the disastrous effects of sudden breaks in continuity".

Lloyd George, therefore, had to move on his own. At Bangor, on 17 January, 1935, he celebrated his seventy-second birthday by a lively launching of his "British New Deal". *Age 72*

"I am going back to Wales, where I began my crusading", he said, and he was not really joking, "to start the biggest one of the lot—and Wales is the proper place for it to be born!"

Lloyd George, at this time, reverted much to his native land, its legends and its history. One dinner party at Leatherhead with Beaverbrook he held the company while he expounded on a number of famous characters whose Welsh origin was not generally known. Among them was Oliver Cromwell— who, Lloyd George claimed, was really named Williams. "Good God!" interjected H. G. Wells, "Is he going to include Williams the Conqueror, too?"

The British New Deal professed to be "Non-Party" but, as Lloyd George did not disguise from certain of his political friends of other days, its object was to secure by an organized effort "a Parliament of the Left, pledged to an advanced progressive policy of Peace, Liberty and Reconstruction". Naturally, it would appeal to Liberals, but Lloyd George's hope was that its influence would extend far beyond the confines of one Party. True to this concept, he now addressed his crowded audience at Bangor:

> "I am not here tonight to launch a Party campaign. I am neither a Party Leader, nor have I any desire to become one. I have had enough of that misery! Whatever happens, I have no intention of manœuvring, or being manœuvred into it again. . . ."

Of course, it was another bid for power. As such, as well as because of its own merits, it made headlines throughout the Press. Besides the Macmillan Group, orthodox leading Tories like Sir Arthur Steel Maitland, Lord Eustace Percy and Lord Londonderry hailed it. As for Churchill, he was still more enthusiastic.

> "Mr. Lloyd George's proposals deserve the closest attention", he cried. "They are at once virile and sober. . . . He is a little hard on Mr. Neville Chamberlain, who has done most of the collar work of this administration . . . it is the more refreshing to read such a speech in contrast with the recent utterances of the deplorable politician who now maunders at the head of the Government (MacDonald)."

Neville Chamberlain, the Chancellor of the Exchequer, was not at all excited about the New Deal. He had not forgotten its author's treatment of himself in 1917. Neither were the Simonite "Liberal Nationals" in the Cabinet, Simon and Runciman. They had not forgotten the author's treatment of themselves in 1916. Nor was he without his critics among the Samuelite Liberals, who considered that this new Lloyd George programme smacked of "economic nationalism", whereas the real need was to get world international exchange back on a Free Trade basis.

But the genuine interest of the public had been aroused in the New Deal, and so much was the pressure upon the Cabinet from outside that, in March, 1935, MacDonald wrote to Lloyd George, inviting him to submit his proposals. So Lloyd George sent him a draft scheme of one hundred pages and, in April, he attended in person a number of meetings held by a Cabinet sub-

Last resting place

committee set up for the purpose of cross-examining him. It did not take him long to come to the conclusion that, as in MacDonald's previous Labour Government, his Ministers were simply talking out time to evade action.

"Our meetings were studiously pleasant," said Lloyd George, "but they knew in their hearts that they were going to knife me. What they didn't know was that I had a dagger in my sheath for them, too!"

This dagger was the new organization which he planned to set up. The Prime Minister himself was much more interested in the forthcoming Silver Jubilee of King George V, with the State pomp and panoply which it entailed. Attendance at Court delighted MacDonald, as it never did Lloyd George, who rarely put in an appearance at Buckingham Palace. However, at the King's request, he willingly accompanied the Prince of Wales to Cardiff on 11 May, 1935, when Prince Edward addressed a huge, wildly cheering Welsh audience. The next time Edward went to Wales, it would be as King himself, and fateful would be the outcome of his words on that occasion.

The Silver Jubilee provided all the alternative interest to the New Deal that Baldwin and MacDonald could have wished for. On 7 June, the one had succeeded the other as Prime Minister, with no change in policy or pace in the conduct of public affairs. MacDonald, indeed, had long been failing in health, and his grip was becoming weaker, almost embarrassingly so, over his own utterances. The *Daily Express* one day reproduced "word for word" what he had said during a speech in the House of Commons the previous afternoon; it was unintelligible.

Lloyd George now resolved to unsheath his knife, and stab back at Baldwin. He had been much impressed by a nation-wide "Peace Ballot", organized by the League of Nations Union, in which overwhelming public support had been voted for disarmament and the League itself. Lloyd George's own belief was that another great war was far off, and the arrival of the demoniac Hitler at the helm of power in Germany had not, in 1935, persuaded him that the world was already rushing towards a terrible fate. He resolved to launch a programme of both international and domestic policy, a combined campaign for peace and prosperity.

Promptly, he set to work to mobilize his "non-Party" (it was really an all-Party) movement. He christened it "The Council of Action for Peace and Reconstruction". Lloyd George was well aware that Baldwin was now contemplating a new General Election, and he meant, as he had promised from the start, to make this movement a powerful weapon for influencing its course. A Tory friend, who still hoped that Lloyd George would join the National Government, warned him that the Prime Minister was very angry when he heard of his intention, thinking he was out to wreck. "That is precisely what I *am* out for", was his retort.

The Council of Action was inaugurated on 1 July, 1935, at the Central

Hall, Westminster. The Archbishop of Canterbury had warned off certain Anglican bishops who had proposed to attend, but the Free Churches were well represented, headed by Dr. Scott Lidgett. From the Tory and Labour Parties came Lord Robert Cecil, Harold Macmillan and George Lansbury, and of the Liberals, Lord Lothian rejoined his old chief.

But although a blaze of publicity accompanied the passing of the resolution approving the manifesto, "*A Call to Action*", by the end of the first month a string of "regrets" was coming in from prominent people who had promised support. The wedding feast had become a frost.

The National Government now issued a reply to Lloyd George entitled "*A Better Way to Better Times*" (Neville Chamberlain was credited with the authorship). It set out to show that the wisdom of the Government had already been proved by their tackling of unemployment. It was not happily timed, for almost at once out came the Report of the Commissioner for the Special Areas, Sir Malcolm Stewart, which told of the dismal ineptitude of the policy of the National Government.

The Prime Minister, however, was content. He had "dished Lloyd George" again. It was the fifth time.

By the end of August, it was clear that the Free Churches, too, were running away from the Council of Action. Dr. Scott Lidgett, Dr. Sam Hughes and other members of the Free Church Council made their doubts plain to Lloyd George personally. He turned and rent them.

"Gideon knew how to distinguish between the funks and the brave men," he flamed. "I wish someone would give me that power."

"He only had three hundred left at the finish," ventured Hughes.

"But he won!" retorted Lloyd George.

The British public had hardly finished voting enthusiastically for peace and the League of Nations, when Benito Mussolini, the dictator of Italy, resolved to defy it and annex Abyssinia. He had no trouble in picking a quarrel with her over some wells on the frontier between Abyssinia and Italian Somaliland. It seemed that he would have even less trouble with the League of Nations.

For France, having done a deal with him whereby Italy withdrew her opposition to the French retaining Tunis, was ready to let him have his own way over Abyssinia. As for Britain, she was busy looking the other way. MacDonald and Simon, his Foreign Secretary, had gone to Stresa in April, 1935, to meet Mussolini and Laval, the French Foreign Minister. Although all of them were thoroughly well aware of what was developing, no mention had ever been made of Abyssinia, which led Mussolini to believe that both Britain and France would stand aside when he invaded that country.

Now Abyssinia raised piteous appeal to the League of Nations to protect her. The League responded by doing its feeble best to conciliate Mussolini.

He replied, arrogantly: "Italy will pursue her aims—with Geneva, without Geneva, or against Geneva."

On 2 October, as the summer rains died, Italian troops advanced across the frontier while Italian aircraft showered bombs upon the open and undefended Abyssinian towns and villages. The League of Nations Assembly denounced this barbarous aggression, and Sir Samuel Hoare, who represented the British Government, warmly associated himself with the condemnation. At this point, Baldwin resolved to go to the country in a General Election.

This took place on 14 November. The Prime Minister's election manifesto declared:

"The League of Nations will remain, as heretofore, the keystone of British Foreign policy. . . . We shall continue to do all in our power to uphold the Covenant and to maintain and increase the efficiency of the League. In the present unhappy dispute between Italy and Abyssinia there will be no wavering in the policy we have hitherto pursued. . . ."

At the polls, the National Government and their satellites—they were now practically indistinguishable—secured a majority of 242. The Labour Party made a large recovery, with 153 Members. The official Liberal Party (Samuelites) fell to 16, and lost their leader himself, while the Lloyd George family group of four held their seats.

Lloyd George's personal triumph at Caernarvon was complete, his majority mounting towards ten thousand votes, or nearly double that of the 1931 General Election.

D. Lloyd George (Independent Liberal)	19,242
A. R. du Cros (Conservative)	9,633
Independent Liberal Majority	9,609

Fourteen times now had he submitted himself to the verdict of his constituents—and never once failed to gain it. Half a dozen other famous politicians who also rose to be Prime Ministers of Britain could not say as much—they had all known the bitterness of defeat—Balfour, Bonar Law, Baldwin, Asquith, MacDonald and Churchill. Soon Lloyd George would celebrate his half-century's unbroken service in the House of Commons.

But Baldwin's political position was now unassailable. Though Lloyd George kept his Council of Action in the field under its capable Organizing Secretary, Victor Finney, and effectively intervened at a number of by-elections, the National Government could afford to take its own line at home and abroad.

A week after the new House of Commons assembled, Sir Samuel Hoare, who had succeeded Simon as Foreign Secretary, signed in Paris the Hoare-Laval Pact whereby large tracts of Abyssinian territory were to be transferred to Italy, and much of the rest placed under Italian "protection" for exploitation. The Prime Minister and his Cabinet endorsed this act of opportunism.

But the country and the House of Commons rose up in righteous revolt. A real storm swept through Parliament, and might well have swept the Government out of office if Baldwin had not sacrificed his Foreign Secretary and confessed his own fault.

Lloyd George was holidaying in Morocco, and working away on his *War Memoirs*. By the time he had got back to England, the National Government had made a weak pretence of levying sanctions against Italy—but not of cutting off her oil supplies, which would have grounded the planes from which the Italians were spraying poison gas by bombs upon Abyssinia. It was this savagery—as well as the fact that the Abyssinians were a poor, primitive people fighting for their freedom against a powerful modern state— that before long brought Lloyd George fiercely out on the side of the defenders.

He heard with equal anger and indignation of Il Duce's warships sailing insolently past the British Mediterranean Fleet as it lay anchored off Port Said, jeering and spitting at the Union Jack. Lloyd George would have blown them out of the water, and there were many in Britain on the so-called "Left" of politics who would have agreed with him.

When, on 18 June, 1936, the National Government abandoned even its half-hearted commercial sanctions against Italy, Lloyd George lashed them with his tongue in a speech which Churchill afterwards described as "one of the greatest Parliamentary performances of all time". Cried Lloyd George:

> "I have been in this House very nearly half a century. . . . I have never before heard a British Minister, speaking on behalf of the Government . . . say that Britain was beaten—Britain and her Empire beaten—and that we must abandon the enterprise we had taken in hand."

He quoted the Prime Minister's message to the Peace Society, "Let your aim be resolute, and your footsteps firm and certain". And he went on:

> "Here is the resolute aim; here is the certain footstep—*running away*! . . .
> The Right Hon. Gentleman has boasted today and he boasted in the last speech of his that I heard in the House, that we led the nations. That increased our responsibility. We led in the imposition of sanctions; we led also in the denunciation of the aggressor. We led, too, in proposing, I think, oil sanctions in principle; and we also led in selling oil in practice.
> What were we doing? We were leading! We dawdled for weeks before taking any action at all, everybody knew what Mussolini was after. He never concealed it. We dawdled. Why? We were leading! We put an embargo on arms for Abyssinia when we knew she was going to be attacked, and when the Italians were massing armies and piling up arms such as have never been landed by an invader on the coasts of Africa. What were we

doing? We were leading the nations in the way of showing how an aggressor—a well-equipped aggressor—could be effectively dealt with! We tried to compound a felony. We said: 'This is a crime—the robbing of a nation of its liberty. It is a crime; we condemn it!' And then we entered into negotiations to give the burglar half the goods! What were the Government doing? They were just leading the nations, they were just leading civilization in the right way to deal with crime!"

He turned to Neville Chamberlain, the Chancellor of the Exchequer and reminded him what *he* had said at the last General Election:

"The choice before us is whether we shall make a last effort at Geneva for peace and security, or whether by a cowardly surrender we shall break all the promises we have made and hold ourselves up to the shame of our children and their children's children."

Pointing dramatically to the unhappy figure of the Prime Minister, and those who sat next to him on the Government Front Bench, Lloyd George cried in a voice of scorn: "Tonight, we have had the cowardly surrender, and *THERE* are the cowards!"

Baldwin rose shakily to reply to what he described as "the extraordinarily brilliant speech of the Rt. Hon. Gentleman, the Member for Caernarvon Boroughs, which showed me that he has not lost the least atom of vigour which I remember in this House nearly thirty years ago, and I congratulate him."

He went on to make what sounded like a rather pitiable plea for mercy, and to the consternation of his followers, offered no real defence of the policy which his Government had pursued.

But if Lloyd George came out strongly and well from the shoddy affair with Mussolini, what is to be said about the next span of his ever-exciting and varied voyage through this world?

This was the strange interlude of a great British Liberal leader—with Führer Adolf Hitler.

Since the spring of 1936—about the time that Hitler was marching his troops into the demilitarized Rhineland—his ambassador to Britain, Joachim Ribbentrop, had been making attempts to persuade Lloyd George to visit Germany. Now, in September, Lloyd George had finished the last volume of his *War Memoirs*. He made up his mind to make the journey.

"I want to see the great roads, the development around the towns which has provided work for all the unemployed; to see the reconditioning and reclamation of the land and the great agricultural enterprises," he told A. J. Sylvester, his secretary. "I am not interested in the armament work the Germans are supposed to be doing. I would like to talk to the German

workers, to visit the factories and find out how the ordinary man is represented in the new Germany; to see how their needs and grievances are met."

He also wanted to meet Hitler himself, and to have a talk with von
Ludendorff about the Great War. His chosen intermediary was Mr. T. P.
Conwell-Evans, a Welsh professor at Königsberg University who knew both
von Ribbentrop and Hitler and had been recommended to him by Philip Kerr.
It was arranged that with Gwilym, A. J. Sylvester, and Conwell-Evans,
Lloyd George should leave London for Munich on 2 September, dine with
Ribbentrop in Berchtesgaden on the 3rd, and that he should meet Hitler
alone next day. Lord Dawson and Tom Jones, now deputy-Secretary of the
Cabinet and a close confidant of Baldwin, would join the party later.

Before he went off, Lloyd George lunched with Ivan Maisky, the Russian
ambassador to Britain, with whom he was on friendly terms. Maisky heard
the news of his proposed visit to Germany with dismay. Moscow, he said, was
convinced that Nazi Germany was going to build a great Mittel-Europe State,
that she would attack Czechoslovakia, overrun the Polish Corridor, annex
the Baltic States, and then go for Russia—a shrewd appreciation of the Hitler
Plan. But neither Maisky's dissuasions nor the warnings of anyone else were
going to keep Lloyd George out of Germany that summer.

He believed that France and Germany could come to terms, and two
years later there were many leading statesmen in Europe who still believed it.
Ever remembering his own efforts to put the unemployed of Britain to useful
labour, Lloyd George was specially interested in the Nazi New Deal for
the even greater army of German unemployed which Hitler himself had been
required to handle when he came to power—indeed, which had largely brought
him there.

Lloyd George found Ribbentrop pretty tiresome at dinner on the night
of their arrival. He wanted to talk of nothing but the Red Menace, a subject
to which Hitler himself would repeatedly return during the two meetings
which Lloyd George had with him. The first of these took place next afternoon
between the two men at Hitler's fabulous mountain chalet, 4,000 feet above
sea level, with its suberb panorama view of the Bavarian Alps, seen through
a wall of plate glass at the far end of his vast study. When Lloyd George's
car drew up at the foot of the great flight of stone steps leading to this eyrie,
Hitler descended them and ran forward to greet him with a warm handshake.

Lloyd George was fascinated by the man, "his gestures, his eyes, his
voice, his talk". "Führer is the proper name for him," he said enthusiastically
of him when he got back to his hotel. "He is a great and wonderful leader.
He is a man who can not only plan, but can put his plans into execution. He
is the Saviour of Germany."

Lloyd George added that he had found Hitler "not in favour of rearmament or conscription"! Building roads and developing agriculture, the Führer

declared, interested him far more. He insisted that the future of civilization depended on the co-operation of England and Germany, and said that the recently signed Anglo-German Naval Treaty was proof of German willingness to be friends.

Lloyd George replied that both countries must do their utmost to ensure the real success of the forthcoming Locarno Conference. England, Germany, France, Italy and Belgium (which, though not a Great Power, held a key frontier position) must meet and talk there on terms of complete equality. The question of Spain (just then in the opening throes of her fearful Civil War) set the Führer off again on Bolshevism, as also did the mention of Czechoslovakia. Russian Communism he compared with the great historical migrations, or the Mohammedan invasion of Europe.

Over the tea-table, when they talked about the new German *autobahn*, Hitler told Lloyd George that Germany was short of both petrol and rubber, and he spoke of the need of Germany recovering her lost colonies and her access to vital raw materials. The official Nazi interpreter diplomatically left this out of his translation to the visitor.

Lloyd George returned to his party convinced that Hitler wanted peace, based fundamentally on a better understanding with Britain. Hitler had certainly done his best to indicate that he was much impressed with Lloyd George, too.

Next day, Lloyd George and his friends all went to take tea with the Führer at his home again. Taking his guest by the arm, Hitler showed him his paintings, tapestries and a bust of Wagner. But it was the view through that huge window which entranced Lloyd George. After tea, Hitler presented Lloyd George, "the Man Who Won The War", with a signed photograph of himself in a frame. Much moved, Lloyd George jumped up from the easy chair in which he had been sitting and grasped his hand while he thanked him for this gift from "the greatest living German".

"Would you mind," he asked, "if I placed it on my desk beside those of the great War leaders, Clemenceau, Marshal Foch, and President Wilson?"

"I should raise no objection to that," replied Hitler, "but I should object very much if you put it beside such men as Erzberger and Bauer!"[1]

This caused general laughter, but it also launched the Führer off on a vehement and obviously favourite onslaught on the politicians whom, he claimed, had let Germany down at the end of the war and in the peace which followed. He and Lloyd George then exchanged further compliments on the great parts which each had played in his own country, and the tea-party ended with Lloyd George inviting Hitler to visit England.

"Possibly," said the Führer, thoughtfully.

Next day, Lloyd George had tea with Rudolf Hess, then Deputy-Leader of the German Reich, at his house near Munich, and questioned him

[1] German Socialist leaders in 1918.

closely about the functions of the local Gauleiters and their part in helping to frame Nazi Party policy, and also about German rearmament and military service. At Munich, Lloyd George laid a wreath on the War Memorial. He inscribed it:

> "A respectful and sincere tribute to the memory of the very brave men who fell fighting for their Fatherland.
>
> D. Lloyd George."

There followed a busy tour of factories, land reclamation schemes and labour camps. Lloyd George failed to see Ludendorff, but he spent a valuable and instructive morning with General Wetzell, who had been Ludendorff's Chief of Staff. He returned to England on 16 September, 1936. The following day, a remarkable article by him appeared in the *Daily Express* about the Germany he had just seen.

Of Hitler himself, Lloyd George wrote:

> "He is a born leader of men. A magnetic, dynamic personality with a single-minded purpose. He is not merely in name, but in fact the natural leader. He has made them safe against potential enemies by whom they are surrounded. The old trust him. The young idolize him. . . .
>
> The idea of a Germany intimidating Europe with a threat that its irresistible army might march across frontiers forms no part in the new vision. The Germans will resist to the death every invader of their own country, but they have no longer the desire themselves to invade any other land. The leaders of Modern Germany know too well that Europe is too formidable a proposition to be overrun and trampled down by any single nation, however powerful may be its armaments. They have learned that lesson in the war. Hitler fought in the ranks throughout the war, and knows from personal experience what war means. . . . The establishment of a German hegemony in Europe, which was the aim and dream of the old militarism, is not even on the horizon of Nazism.
>
> It is now an avowed part of the Hitler policy to build up an army which will be strong enough to resist every invader from whatever quarter the attack may come. I believe he has already achieved that measure of immunity. No country, or combination of countries, could feel confident of overwhelming the Germany of today.
>
> But it will take Germany at least ten years to build up an army strong enough to face the armies of Russia or France on any soil except her own.
>
> Her conscript army is very young—there is a gap of years to fill up in the reserves, and particularly in officers. As an offensive army, it would take quite ten years to bring it up to the standard of the great army of 1914.
>
> Everywhere I found a fierce, uncompromising hostility to Russian Bolshevism, coupled with a genuine admiration for the British people, with

a profound desire for a better understanding with them. The Germans have definitely made up their minds never to quarrel with us again. . . ."

How wrong can a great man be!

And Lloyd George remained wrong about Hitler for another twelve or eighteen months. In December of the following year he was writing to Conwell-Evans:

"Hotel du Cap, Antibes, A.M.   27 Dec., 1937.

My dear Conwell,

. . . I shall never forget the extraordinarily interesting tour which you organized for me and my friends in Germany last year, when I had the privilege of meeting the great Leader of a great people.

I have never doubted the fundamental greatness of Herr Hitler as a man even in moments of profound disagreement with his policy. You will observe that during the last few months, when I have felt it to be my duty to criticize his activities in Spain, I have never withdrawn one particle of the admiration which I personally felt for him and expressed on my return from Germany. I only wish we had a man of his supreme quality at the head of affairs in our country today.

I told you repeatedly during that visit that I had grave misgivings as to the effect which the Spanish situation might have upon our relations with Germany. It is a great misfortune that we did not compose our differences before the Spanish crisis ever arose. It could have been done quite easily at that date. It is not Herr Hitler's fault that a friendly arrangement was not reached. He made us two or three offers, which I urged the Government to act upon promptly. The present muddle is entirely due to the hesitancy and the nervelessness of the Baldwin Administration. They never saw an opportunity until it was too late to act upon it.

Things are much more difficult now. It looks as if the Führer had committed himself to Mussolini—that adds enormously to the obstacles in the path of a friendly accommodation of the troubles of Europe. Mussolini is temperamentally an aggressor. I have never thought that Herr Hitler was, and I do not believe it now. But I wish to God he could be persuaded to leave the two Spanish factions to fight their own battles as we did in the great Civil War which practically settled our Constitution.

With best Christmas wishes,

Ever sincerely,

D. L. G."

In December, 1936, while Lloyd George was avoiding the English fog in sunlit Jamaica, a different kind of crisis suddenly developed. This was the affair of the Abdication. It very nearly brought Lloyd George hurrying home. Before he left England there had already been gossip of King Edward

x

VIII's friendship with Mrs. Wallis Simpson, but, acceding to the King's request that her divorce case at Ipswich Assizes should receive no special prominence, and believing that no subsequent marriage was intended, the British Press had made almost nothing of it. The American Press were less reticent; in fact, they were having the time of their lives with the story. It broke into the news in Britain with a statement by the Bishop of Bradford, rebuking the King for his remiss conduct in other matters. Within a matter of hours, a deadlock had arisen between King Edward VIII and his Ministers over his proposal to marry the lady.

Lloyd George learned of the Constitutional crisis only on 3 December, when he was cabled that the Cabinet had decided to resign unless the King accepted their advice, which was against the marriage. The Opposition had agreed not to form an alternative Government if the King persisted with his plan. Lloyd George's private opinion was that "the nation has a right to choose its Queen, but the King also has a right to choose his own wife. If Baldwin is against them, I am against Baldwin!"

He dictated a telegram to Gwilym and Megan saying that he trusted that they were not intending to "join the harriers in hunting the King from the throne".

Lloyd George pointed out that if the King had not decided to marry the woman of his choice, probably not a word would ever have been heard from the "Scribes and the Pharisees". He went on that had not Edward, both as Prince of Wales and King, exposed neglect by the National Government of the deep distress among the unemployed, the Government themselves would not have been in such haste to dethrone him.

This, of course, referred to the visit of King Edward to South Wales, when, inspecting a Guard of Honour of ex-servicemen, in a mining town, he had asked man after man as he passed down the ranks of the veterans he had served with himself in the 1914–18 war: "What are you doing now?" and had received the reply: "I'm out of work, Sir." The King had hardly been able to go on, and then the whole concourse in the square of the little town had broken spontaneously into the hymn, "God Bless the Prince of Wales". Near to tears, he had hurried from that "Special Area", repeating to those with him, over and over again: "Something must be done. *Something* must be done."

It was commonly believed that members of the Government had taken deep offence at this "political interference". Lloyd George, in sending his private telegram, made it plain that he had no objection to publishing every word of it.

Next day, he received further information from London regarding the suggestion of a "morganatic marriage", which had been put forward only to be at once rejected by the Cabinet. Lloyd George was furious to learn, on 6 December, 1936, that the North Wales Liberal Federation had passed a resolution strongly supporting Baldwin, in his policy (as Lloyd George said contemptuously) of "polite assassination".

He was personally truly distressed over the trouble which had gathered around King Edward, whom he had seen invested as Prince of Wales at Caernarvon Castle when a boy of seventeen years of age in the Coronation Year of 1911, and who had been his special protégé and friend for the next quarter of a century.

Lloyd George was preparing to sail for home (his passage was booked and his luggage packed) when a cable arrived for him from Gwilym, saying that the crisis was over. On 10 December, followed the news that King Edward VIII had abdicated. Lloyd George was genuinely upset, and listening in far-off Jamaica to Edward's farewell broadcast, he nearly broke down in tears. On Christmas Eve he sent the ex-King a cable:

> "Best Christmas greetings from an old Minister of the Crown who holds you in as high esteem as ever and regards you with deep and loyal affection, deplores the mean and unchivalrous attacks upon you, and regrets the loss sustained by the British Empire of a monarch who sympathized with the lowliest of his subjects."

On Christmas Day, he received this reply:

> "Very touched by your kind telegram and good wishes, which I heartily reciprocate. Edward. *Cymru Am Byth.*"[1]

In the New Year, Lloyd George took a lively interest in the Civil List, especially in regard to the financial affairs of the ex-King, who had become Duke of Windsor. He made many inquiries as to the establishment which would be required for the departed monarch. Lloyd George held that adequate maintenance was essential for the honour and dignity of the Crown, and he was pleased to learn of the £25,000, free of tax, which King George VI undertook to pay his brother. The most varied estimates of the Duke's fortune were current at the time; it was Lloyd George's opinion that it was somewhere in the region of £1,000,000.

Lloyd George came home to find Europe divided into two armed camps, with Spain as the civil war battlefield on which the Great Powers (or rather, the challenging ones), fought out their scarcely disguised international war. France and England, anxious only to keep out of the *mêlée* themselves, backed a League of Nations resolution in favour of non-intervention in Spain, which in the light of events everyone recognized as plain hypocrisy.

Whatever Lloyd George still felt about Hitler, he now felt compelled to condemn the German-Italian aggression in Spain. The Council of Action prepared a series of maps for public lectures, showing vividly how Fascist

[1] Wales For Ever.

x*

Italy was steadily closing in on the Mediterranean, Britain's own main seaway to her Empire in the East and to Australasia.

On 28 May, 1937, Baldwin resigned the Premiership and retired to the House of Lords. He was succeeded by Neville Chamberlain. There now began a "positive" foreign policy which was even more disastrous than the drifting of MacDonald and Baldwin, for it involved continous concessions to the two Fascist dictators in the hope of "appeasing" them.

By the spring of 1938, Chamberlain was prepared to go to very great lengths to placate Mussolini, in the vain hope of detaching him from Hitler's side. In the course of his concessions, Anthony Eden felt it incumbent upon himself to resign from the Foreign Secretaryship, a loss which the Prime Minister accepted with equanimity. The difference between them was not so great, and rested more on Eden's resentment of Chamberlain's personal overriding direction of foreign policy than on any irreconcilable opinions as to the policy itself.

But whether or not the resignation of Eden appeased Mussolini, it did nothing to discourage Hitler, who, on 11 March, 1938, poured his armies into Austria and annexed it. He then stirred up the Sudeten Germans in Czechoslovakia to make an outcry about their grievances, and would have marched into that country, too, if the Czechs had not ordered a lightning mobilization, which persuaded the Führer to hold his hand.

Age 75
At the beginning of this year, Lloyd George had been in the South of France with his wife and family, celebrating his Golden Wedding. He had hardly got home to England when Hitler made his Austrian *coup d'état*.

Later that month, Lloyd George paid a second visit to France.

> "We took with us to Paris," wrote Frances Stevenson in her *Diary*, "my small adopted daughter, aged 8, to whom L.G. was greatly attached. He took her to Versailles and showed her the scene of his former triumphs, and to the tomb of Napoleon in *Les Invalides*."

Lloyd George was furious when Daladier, the French Liberal leader, refused to see him. There had been a time, said Lloyd George, when French leaders were very glad, indeed, to see him.

He really had little to complain of, for the Prime Minister, Leon Blum, invited him to meet a number of leading French politicians of all shades of opinion, including Paul Boncour, his Foreign Minister; Herriot, President of the French Chamber; Reynaud, Pierre Cot, and Jouhaux. He urged them to agree to end the farce of "non-intervention" in Spain. He produced his maps, showing how many Allied ships had been torpedoed in the Mediterranean by U-boats in the 1914–18 War. What would be the toll in another one, with all the Spanish ports to serve as enemy bases, as well as the Italian?

Lloyd George continued his French journey on to Cap d'Antibes again. While he was sunning himself one day on the beach, a London telephone call was relayed from his hotel to a kiosk there. It was news of the sudden death of J. T. Davies, so long one of Lloyd George's trusted secretaries and (since Lord St. Davids had died only three days earlier) the sole Trustee of the Fund. Lloyd George was deeply grieved.

Back once more in England, in a series of speeches over the next twelve months, Lloyd George warned the Government that their policy of Appeasement was leading not towards the pacification of Europe, but straight to war.

"You have retreated so often before these Dictators that they have come to the conclusion that there is no point at which you will stand."

"They are convinced you won't fight. So am I."

"We have constantly lowered our flag, and no nation will follow us when it is permanently at half-mast."

Events upheld his gloomy diagnosis. Throughout the summer of 1938, Hitler kept up his pressure on Czechoslovakia.

In September, at the Nuremberg Congress, he suddenly increased it. His patience was exhausted. The Czechs made ready for the expected onslaught. France was pledged to come to their aid, and Russia to support France. A general war appeared inevitable, when Chamberlain suddenly decided to fly to Berchtesgaden and see Hitler himself. A second visit, to Godesberg, was required before the surrender of Munich purchased a dear peace for a year, when Hitler was ready to launch his next aggression, this time against Poland.

Lloyd George had viewed the Sudeten-German crisis at first with some indifference. He had little sympathy with the way in which the Czechs had insisted, first of all, in 1919, on incorporating into Czechoslovakia the Sudeten-Germans on the old German-Bohemian frontier, and, secondly, in subsequently denying them any real form of local autonomy. He considered the Sudeten-German crisis a ready-made one, and only wondered why it had not exploded before. Also Lloyd George intensely disliked Prime Minister Benes, whom he had once dubbed "that little French Jackal".

But when Hitler pushed his demands to the verge of unloosing a European War—and, incidentally, of humiliating Britain—Lloyd George had finally made up his mind about Hitler. The honeymoon had been brief. More and more now, Lloyd George had addressed his hopes towards Russia.

Of Munich itself, Lloyd George had bitter words when on 26 October, 1938, he addressed a luncheon meeting of Free Churchmen at the City Temple, which was broadcast to the United States.

"We have only one excuse for what we have done, and that is that years of fussy, futile and very expensive preparations for the defence of the country have ended in a muddle—what might have been, if put to the test, a ghastly muddle. We were not ready to defend ourselves, let alone others.

That is our only excuse for not standing up to the Dictators, and history will ask but one question over that episode. Is incompetence a justification for the bad faith?

. . . China, Abyssinia, Spain, Czechoslovakia! We have descended during these years a ladder of dishonour, rung by rung. Are we going, can we go, any lower?"

When the House of Commons reassembled after the recess on 1 November, 1938, Chamberlain rebuked him. Lloyd George was not present at the time.

"It is not one of the characteristics of Totalitarian States, at any rate, that they are accustomed to foul their own nests. I do strongly deprecate all the statements made by persons in responsible, or even in irresponsible positions, who take opportunities of broadcasting to the world or in other countries in particular that their own country is in a state of decadence."

It was not what any Opposition critic said, however, but what the Prime Minister actually did, that weighed with the Dictators. Lloyd George was nearer to the realities of politics when, on 3 February, 1939, he condemned the democracies of the West for their boycotting of Russia—and especially for their exclusion of her from the Munich Conference. They had alienated the greatest Military Power in the world, he said, "by persistently snubbing her".

Certainly, they had driven the country potentially the most anti-Fascist of all to consider whether or not she should make her own bargain with the Dictators.

A few days earlier, though Lloyd George did not know it, the Chamberlain policy towards the Dictators touched its zero. According to Count Ciano, the Italian Foreign Minister, the British Prime Minister had submitted through our Ambassador at Rome the draft of a speech he proposed to deliver in the House of Commons, and offered to make any alterations which the Duce deemed desirable. On 27 February, Chamberlain announced that he proposed to recognize General Franco's Government in Spain, where "non-intervention" had now ensured the triumph of the Fascist forces.

Lloyd George and Miss Stevenson were staying in the South of France at this time as the guests of Beaverbrook at Monte Carlo. There was much talk of war, and he was unusually gloomy and depressed at the prospect. Beaverbrook, on the other hand, was cheerful and full of high spirits. "There will be no war", the *Daily Express* was assuring its readers. And if only all shouted "No War!" loud and long then the prospect of war would be lessened, said Beaverbrook.

Age 76   On 14 March, 1939, Lloyd George packed up, to go and spend a few quiet days at Cap d'Antibes before returning to England—"*But Hush! Hark! A deep sound strikes like a rising knell.*" Hitler's legions were stamping into what remained of Czechoslovakia after Munich. That entire country was now annexed by the Reich and "ceased to exist". Lloyd George hurried home to what he believed must be war.

At the end of this same month, Chamberlain, who had spoken of the Czechoslovak crisis as "a quarrel in a far-away country between people of whom we know nothing", offered guarantees of British aid if attacked to Poland and Rumania, of which we knew no more and which were, if anything, still less accessible. On 8 April, Mussolini invaded Albania, and began to bully Greece. When Chamberlain extended his promises of protection to Greece, too, Lloyd George declared on 8 May:

"Without Russia, these three guarantees to Poland, to Rumania and to Greece are the most reckless commitment that any country has ever entered into. I will say more. They are demented pledges that cannot be redeemed with this enormous deficiency, this great gap between the forces arrayed on the other side and the forces which at the present moment we could put in."

When Chamberlain at length invited the Russians to share with us in underwriting the defence of Poland and Rumania, they reasonably enough sought to include the Baltic States in the pact. The Russians wanted to build up their own buffer. Hitler was now clamouring for the return of Danzig and the Polish Corridor to the Reich. It was obvious that he had much bigger eventual designs much farther east, as Maisky had long ago indicated to Lloyd George.

The Anglo–Russian negotiations dragged on all summer and then, suddenly, on 23 August, a new Russo–German Treaty was signed. Stalin, also, had decided to "buy time".

At dawn, nine days later, the *Panzer Korps* and the *Luftwaffe* roared into action across the Polish frontier, and the Second World War had begun.

On Sunday, 3 September, after two more very restive days in the House of Commons, during which Chamberlain seemed to many Members to be still seeking some way out, Britain declared war on Germany. After the Prime Minister had spoken and the die was cast, and there had followed speeches by Arthur Greenwood, Sir Archibald Sinclair and Churchill, Lloyd George rose to add his voice in support.

"The Government could do no other than what they have done," he said. "I am one out of tens of millions in this country who will back any Government that is in power in fighting this struggle through, in however humble a capacity we may be called upon to render service to our country."

Briefly, then, he recalled the ordeal and the triumph of the First World War, and added:

"The nation closed its ranks then. By that means, we went through right to the end, and after four-and-a-half years, terrible years, we won a victory for Right. We will do it again."

What service could Lloyd George do now? Chamberlain had brought back Churchill from the wilderness where he had been foraging for ten years, to take over his old post as First Lord of the Admiralty. Anthony Eden had rejoined the Government as Secretary for the Dominions. The leaders of the Labour and Liberal Parties declined to associate themselves with it, though they had pledged themselves to support as a "Patriotic Opposition". Between Lloyd George and Chamberlain there remained a gulf of distrust and personal dislike.

"This man Neville is not the man to wage war," said Lloyd George contemptuously, to his friends. "In his first speech of the War, he said that he did not know what would happen to him!"

And then, reverting to his old phrenology prejudices, Lloyd George added: "Look at his head! The worst thing Neville Chamberlain ever did was to meet Hitler and let Hitler see him."

But Lloyd George himself was full of doubts.

The worst of them were quickly confirmed. As in 1914, a small but admirable British Expeditionary Force was landed in France within a few days, and took up its pre-allotted post on the Western Front. But this time, there came no German attack. The Führer was busy elsewhere, and the Western Allies allowed him to be so.

Soon, Poland was crumpling under the savage *Blitzkrieg*, while we could get no reinforcement, even of planes, through to her. After Warsaw had been heavily bombed, and the Nazi armies had advanced half-way across Poland, the Russians marched in from the other side of the country to claim their share of the loot—and also to hold the Germans as far as possible away from their own frontier; they had no illusions about the ultimate objectives of their new Treaty associates. On 29 September, the body of Poland was carved up between the two.

In the West, the "phoney war" remained unchanged, apart from some naval actions. It was accompanied by an effort to arrange a "phoney peace". On 6 October, Hitler in the Reichstag addressed an appeal to the Western Powers to join in making a settlement in Europe and thus save the millions of lives that would be sacrificed if they persisted in a quarrel which was not theirs, and had anyway been already decided.

"I make this declaration," cried Hitler, "only because I very naturally desire to spare my people suffering. But should the views of Churchill and his following prevail, then this declaration will be my last."

On 12 October, he got his answer—from Chamberlain. The Prime Minister had come at length to the point of No More Appeasement. In the

House of Commons, he made it plain that there would be an end of trying to deal with Hitler, who would now have to fight for his life.

Strangely at odds with this attitude was the conduct of Lloyd George. Already, in debate on 3 October, before Hitler spoke, he had urged the Government not to reject out-of-hand any offers which might come from the other side. Indeed, he called for a conference of Britain, Germany, France, Italy, Russia and the United States to discuss all issues in dispute.

On the same day that Chamberlain proclaimed the resolve of the British Government to have done finally with the Führer, Lloyd George staged a special meeting of the Council of Action at Caxton Hall, Westminster, in which he proposed that we should invite Hitler to state his peace terms. If they were intolerable, we should be justified in the eyes of the world in going on with the struggle.

He repeated this plea at a great meeting in his own constituency at Caernarvon on 21 October, attended by about 8,000 of his constituents, though acting on shrewd advice from the scouts whom he had sent in advance to test public opinion there, he resolved to make it sound not so much like a plan to try and come to terms with Hitler as one to put him in a corner. In his railway compartment, before leaving Euston Station, Lloyd George had entered into a long conversation with Maisky, the Russian Ambassador, and was fully persuaded that we could still have Russia as an Ally, if we took enough trouble to make the proper advances.

Met at Caernarvon by his Association chairman, Mr. E. P. Evans, who posed the question "Wouldn't another meeting now with Hitler be another Munich?" Lloyd George replied: "No! Stalin will be there this time!"

He added this second shrewd thought. "If you simply crush Germany—what about Russia afterwards? She may become the next enemy."

An interesting example of Lloyd George's capacity "to look into the next field".

At the critical public meeting next day, Lloyd George developed the theme that if all the Great Powers could now sit down together, those who really sought peace could negotiate from strength, and not, as recently, from weakness. He scored a tremendous triumph that afternoon, at a time when many, including himself, had been prepared for a tempest.

But in the country as a whole, as well as in the House of Commons, during the following months Lloyd George remained something of a puzzle. Where was that inspiring, indomitable spirit, those burning words, the unquenchable passion for victory, of the Man of the Great War? Alas! There never was a trace of either faith or fervour from Lloyd George in this present fight. Either he said nothing, or else he talked his own version of appeasement.

The truth was that this was not Lloyd George's war, and it never became so. Until the Russians were drawn in, he frankly could not see how the Allies could possibly win. He believed that the war could have been averted, and he feared that if it now dragged on for years, at best to a stalemate, Britain would emerge bankrupt.

These thoughts coloured the weekly articles which Lloyd George was still writing. They were shrewd in estimate of events, and sharp in well-earned criticism of those in charge of British policy who were supposed to be directing those events. But there were complaining critics who spoke of "defeatist propaganda".

For the moment, Lloyd George concentrated his energies on growing food, both at Bron-y-de and on the new farm which he had acquired at Llanystumdwy, near Criccieth, called Ty Newydd. He called together a number of agricultural experts, and started to draw up a war plan for food production. Three or four times, he spoke in the House of Commons on the same subject.

Age 77 On 12 April, 1940, Lloyd George celebrated his Jubilee of fifty years' unbroken service there. He received a flood of congratulations, and a huge gathering at Caernarvon in his own ever-faithful constituency marked the historic day. His speech, which was broadcast, reviewed all the dramatic developments in British politics over this half-century of tremendous history. Of the grim testing-time which now faced the country once again, he repeated his offer.

"If there is any service, be it great or small, which I can give to help the nation out of its tribulation and to lead the world again into the paths of peace, justice and freedom, I will do so."

By now, at last the war was moving in the West. Chamberlain, early in April, had expressed the opinion that Hitler had "missed the bus". He was referring, of course, to the apparent deadlock between the armies facing one another in the Maginot and the Siegfried Lines. Deadlock is no part of the plan of an aggressor.

There were other places than France to go, however, and on 9 April, Nazi troops swarmed into Denmark and Norway. A British Expeditionary Force was rushed to reinforce the Norwegian resistance, but within a month it had been forced to withdraw.

In the House of Commons debate which followed (7–8 May, 1940), Lloyd George was in two minds as to whether or not he should take part He was reluctant to make any attack on Churchill for the Navy's share in the campaign, though privately he blamed him; he did not want to bind Churchill to Chamberlain by attacking both. As it was, the Government did not lack critics, the most dangerous being on their own back benches. There was Admiral Sir Roger Keyes, a hero of the St. George's Day, 1918, raid on Zeebrugge; more deadly in the venom of his attack on Chamberlain was Leopold Amery, who ended with Oliver Cromwell's last, scathing words to the Rump Parliament: "You have sat here too long for any good you have been doing. Depart, I say, and let us have done with you! In the name of God, go!"

When the Prime Minister rose to reply, he was rash enough to claim that he would see his friends in the division lobby. During his speech, Lloyd George had been absent from the debate in his own room behind the Speaker's Chair. When these words were reported to him by Clement Davies, M.P., he hurried to the Chamber. There, in grave voice and with warning, upraised finger, he set forth the peril of the issues raised by our defeat in the Norway campaign, which he described as "half-baked", and lacking in naval co-operation. Then, after warning Churchill not to "allow himself to be converted into an air-raid shelter to keep the splinters from hitting his colleagues", Lloyd George struck at Chamberlain, with all the fire and fury of his greatest days.

"It is not a question," cried Lloyd George, "of who are the Prime Minister's friends. It is a far bigger issue. . . . He has appealed for sacrifice. The nation is prepared for every sacrifice so long as it has leadership. . . . I say solemnly that the Prime Minister should give an example of sacrifice, because there is nothing which can contribute more to victory than that he should sacrifice the seals of office."

In a scene of mounting tension and excitement, the House divided:

For the Government . . . 281
Against 200

The Government's immense majority had sunk to eighty-one votes, and nearly forty of their own supporters had gone into the lobby against them. Chamberlain walked out of the Chamber like a man half-stunned.

For the next two days he sought desperately, but in vain, to reconstruct his Government on a broader basis. Neither the Labour Party nor the Liberal Party would serve under him. On 10 May, 1940, Chamberlain resigned the Premiership, and the same evening Churchill set about forming a new Government. He persuaded Chamberlain to join, and with Lord Halifax and two Labour leaders, Clement Attlee and Arthur Greenwood, these five formed a War Cabinet on the Lloyd George model. Other Labour and Liberal leaders accepted Departmental Ministries, and a real War Coalition was created, which endured until victory in 1945.

Left out was Lloyd George. Why? Was he not approached? Did he not want to go in? Indeed, after his dramatic part in the overthrow of Chamberlain, was it not possible that the Man of the First World War might himself return to direct the Second?

There were old admirers who believed that Lloyd George could still do mighty things. They wanted to see him in the Government, if not in charge of a Department with its day-to-day routine, then in the inner circle of the Cabinet, giving his advice, his inspiration, his stimulus.

No. If he had been ten years younger, the answer might have been different. Frances Stevenson wrote in her *Diary* that week-end:

"L. G. realizes that Churchill must be chosen, and that he himself is out of the running."

According to the *Diary* of A. J. Sylvester, when Churchill had asked Lloyd George a day or two earlier whether he would join him if he should form a Government, Lloyd George had said that he would. On 11 May, the morning after Churchill took over, Lloyd George said, referring to the new Cabinet, that it suited him *not* to be included. "It would be an impossible position to be in a Cabinet like that. They would be fighting me."
Next day, Whit-Sunday, 12 May, Lloyd George reaffirmed this.

"I do not think Winston will approach me. I think it will be the old Coalition . . . a Coalition of Parties and their nominees. In that I would not have a place. . . . I would simply be there fretting and fuming, and having no real authority, and then that would do me no good. . . . Neville would have infinitely more authority than I would have, and he would oppose everything that I proposed."

Lloyd George's suspicions of Chamberlain's feelings towards him were confirmed when, on 28 May, Churchill, in the Prime Minister's room at the House of Commons, offered him a position in the War Cabinet, subject to the approval of Chamberlain! Lloyd George was not going in on those terms.

"29 May, 1940.   Thames House,
                                                                                    London, S.W.
My dear Winston,

You were good enough yesterday to ask me if I would be prepared to enter the War Cabinet if you secured the adhesion of Mr. Chamberlain to the proposal. It is the first time you have approached me personally on the subject and I can well understand the reason for your hesitancy, for, in the course of our interview, you made it quite clear that if Chamberlain interposed his veto on the ground of personal resentment over past differences, you could not proceed with the offer. This is not a firm offer. Until it is definite, I cannot consider it.

I am sure you will be just enough to realize that the experience I have already had in this war justifies my reply to your conditional inquiry. Since the war began, I have in public thrice offered to help the Government in any capacity, however humble. No notice has been taken of my tenders. I have never been consulted. I have never been invited even to sit on a committee.

Since you became Prime Minister I offered to do my best to help in organizing the food supplies of this country. I have acquired considerable knowledge and experience both in Peace as well as in War on that line. At the request of your personal friends I put forward alternative proposals for the reorganization of this essential branch of national service, and the extensive production of food in this country, and I suggested the part I might play in directing this. Nothing came of this scheme. I have not even been informed of the reason for its rejection.

I say this in order to show that it was due to no unwillingness on my part that you found it impossible to utilize my services. I apprehend that Party and personal considerations frustrated your wishes. I cannot be put in that position again. I am no office seeker. I am genuinely anxious to help to extricate my country from the most terrible disaster into which it has ever been plunged by the ineptitude of her rulers. Several of the architects of this catastrophe are still leading members of your Government, and two of them are in the Cabinet that directs the War.

Like millions of my fellow-countrymen I say to you that, if in any way you think I can help, I am at your call. But if that call is tentative and qualified, I shall not know what answer to give.

Ever sincerely,
D. Lloyd George."

Mr. Churchill replied the same day.

"29 May, 1940.   10 Downing Street.

My dear L.G.,

I have just received your letter today. I am sorry that the same difficulties in regard to persons which you mentioned to me are also only too present elsewhere. I cannot complain in any way of what you say in your letter. The Government I have formed is founded upon the Leaders of the three Parties, and like you, I have no Party of my own. I have received a very great deal of help from Chamberlain. His kindness and courtesy to me in our new relations have touched me. I have joined hands with him, and must act with perfect loyalty.

As you say, the inquiry I made of you yesterday can only be indeterminate, and I could not ask you to go further than you have done in your letter.

With regard to the organization of food supplies of this country of which my personal friend had some talk with you, I can assure you that no personal or party difficulties have frustrated its considerations. The Ministry of Agriculture was discussed and one of my friends[1] made representations to you. It was only after you had taken the decision that you did not at that time contemplate sharing responsibilities involved in joining the Administration, that I made another selection without making any stipulation with the new Minister. The alternative suggestion of the supply of organization of food supplies can well be taken up on another occasion. I have simply been so overpressed by terrible events that I have not had life or strength to address myself to it.

[1] It was Beaverbrook.

Thank you very much for what you say in your last paragraph, and I trust that we shall keep in personal contact so that I may acquaint you with the situation as it deepens. I always have the warmest feelings and regard and respect for you.

Yours ever,
Winston."

The new Prime Minister, who was genuinely anxious to enlist Lloyd George's immense experience and enthusiasm in the desperate war effort now required, appealed to Chamberlain on patriotic grounds to agree to his inclusion in the War Cabinet. If, after trial, the association did not work out, then he could ask the Prime Minister to end it.

On 16 June, "in scepticism and dismay" Chamberlain agreed. That evening, Churchill saw Lloyd George at Number 10 Downing Street, and made him a firm offer. He retired to Bron-y-de to think it over. Beaverbrook went down to see him there, and pressed him hard to accept. Once more Lloyd George's attitude suggested that this time he really did intend to do so.

He came to London one morning shortly afterwards and spent three hours talking about it with Beaverbrook in his office at the Ministry of Aircraft Production. Then, Beaverbrook certainly believed that he meant to join the Government, and at noon triumphantly he telephoned Churchill across the street to that effect. But when the three met at lunch an hour and a half later, as Beaverbrook firmly believed as colleagues, Lloyd George once more changed his mind and withdrew.

It was not only that at seventy-seven years of age, what he described as "the infinitude of control and supervision of detail" of any departmental job were beyond his powers, as Lord Dawson warned him. For Churchill's offer had made it plain that he would not be required to attend an office regularly. Had Lloyd George chosen to give his main attention to Food ("the dangerous flank", as he always called it, remembering the near success of the U-boat siege of 1917–18), it would not have been as Minister of Agriculture; he would have been a Member of the War Cabinet, who was chairman of a Council generally responsible for a group of departments dealing with nutrition, food production, distribution, rationing, etc.

Lloyd George had other reasons besides his advanced age for declining office. He kept saying to those who worked closest to him: "I am not going in with this gang. There will be a change. The country does not realize the peril it is in."

Indeed, in October, 1940, he vigorously (though privately) condemned the holding of secret sessions of Parliament which Churchill had initiated, and which Lloyd George said were designed to suppress criticism. He declared that he would himself have nothing to do with "such a pernicious sham".

On 30 September, 1940, Chamberlain resigned from the Government on account of his failing health. Within six weeks he was dead. The personal *was* "a bonnie fechter", like Alan Breck, there was no vanity or boastfulness in saying so.)

Back in Llanystumdwy now, he showed his wife the tree in the garden of old Uncle Lloyd's cottage, in whose branches he used to sit to learn his Euclid; the orchard with the cherry trees; the island in the river, where they used to play the war game of "Napoleon"; the wood on the bank above it which was his favourite haunt in late years; and Cwm Pennant, of which the bard, Eifion Wyn, wrote: *"Why, Lord, didst thou make Cwm Pennant so beautiful, and the life of an old shepherd so short?"*

In Europe and the Far East now, alike, the Allies were rolling forward irresistibly to victory. Lloyd George's interest in the war had almost vanished. But he would still have liked to take some part in shaping the peace.

And then came the offer of the Earldom. It seemed obvious that a General Election would take place before many months were out, and it was equally clear that Lloyd George's health would not allow him to fight it. Tentative inquiries were made of the two other Parties, both at Headquarters and locally, as to whether it would be possible for him to be returned unopposed; but no guarantee of this could be obtained. Some of his oldest friends thought that it would break his heart if he were defeated after his fifty-five years of uninterrupted membership of the House of Commons.

When Churchill asked him if he would accept an Earldom, Lloyd George reckoned it would relieve him of the worry which was looming ahead of having a hard election fight. He would still be in Parliament, though in that once-hated Upper House. He could not know that he would be dead before the bugles sounded the "Cease Fire" again along the battle line, much less before the victorious nation need go to the next General Election.

So he accepted. In the New Year Honours List, 1945, Lloyd George was granted an Earldom, and took the title of Earl Lloyd-George of Dwyfor and Viscount Gwynedd. Many, who loved and honoured him, will regret that David Lloyd George did not die as he had lived, and as history will ever know this great Briton.

In the early part of 1945 he became much weaker. He had lately reread Macaulay's *History of England* from cover to cover. Then he had tackled his beloved Dickens once again, *Oliver Twist, David Copperfield, Tale of Two Cities, Pickwick Papers, The Old Curiosity Shop, Christmas Carol.* Lloyd George was reliving his exciting, ever-challenging, defiant youth. But the process of reading now became so slow that at last it had to be abandoned altogether.

His children, his grandchildren, his brother, and many friends paid him frequent visits and gathered round in the great bay window looking across the sea. He would be lively yet, though he tired soon. But always "Who is coming today?" he would ask first thing in the morning when he awoke. At other times, he would sit silent, deep in thought, and oblivious to all those around him.

that of woman. And despite the cynicism which the hard battle of public life brought him, Lloyd George remained in the depths of his heart a deeply emotional person. After the War of 1914–18, in which he played so great and fateful a part, the village folk of Beria, near Criccieth, invited him to unveil a memorial in the little chapel to its members who had fallen in the field. Some of them he had known intimately. He excused himself, almost abruptly.

"I cannot do it," he wrote, "I am sure I would break down. The strain would be too much for me".

After Margaret's death, Lloyd George returned to Bron-y-de and stayed there. Though he still interested himself in such old favourite questions as the reclamation of the marsh and the tilling of marginal land, both now made desperately needful by the stringencies of the new "siege" of Britain by enemy submarine and bomber, and spoke on them in the House of Commons with effect, his appearances there became even more rare.

In the country, for hour upon hour, he would sit by the window of his study, gazing silently across the Surrey hillside. He became more and more unhappy and critical about the war, to which he could see no end but exhaustion, and perhaps revolution. On 7 May, 1941, he expressed his real thoughts in the House of Commons, where his diatribe against the set-up of the Higher War authority in Britain drew from Churchill the sharp retort: "It was the sort of speech with which, I imagine, the illustrious and venerable Marshal Pétain might well have enlivened the closing days of M. Reynaud's Cabinet."

The words stung Lloyd George. Certainly he did not forget them. More than once, when a too-pressing friend urged him to come forward even now and lend his name and reputation to Churchill's war-time Government, Lloyd George put on his most surprised look, and inquired sharply: "What? Old Papa Pétain?"

Then, on a June dawn that same year, of 1941, Hitler suddenly flung his armies against Russia. Surely, now at last, here was hope that the deadlock of the war would be broken, and in our own favour?

But Lloyd George, who had so lamented the political errors which had lost us the early alliance of the Russians in this struggle, appeared to derive no comfort as to the final outcome even now that Hitler's mad mistake had driven Soviet Russia into the Allied Camp. Certainly, for long the news from the Eastern Front continued to be principally of Nazi victories and Russian retreats; but seldom have victories been so dearly bought. The Third Reich bled to death on the Russian steppe.

Lloyd George was weary of the war, and even when America had come into it and the tide had turned for us and the victorious end was sure, he worried about the duration of it—and the cost. Vehemently, he condemned the Roosevelt–Churchill pronouncement of Unconditional Surrender, which

Y

Battle of France was over, and the great country of Danton and Clemenceau was suing for a pitiful peace. The Battle of Britain had begun, and our own cities were under the flail and fire of German bombs, welding all classes into more of a united nation than we had ever been before.

At Criccieth or Churt, Lloyd George listened for hours to the radio, both British and German, reporting Allied disaster and defeat. He spent his mornings and his evenings with the voice of that wicked, brilliant broadcaster for the Nazis, William Joyce, "Lord Haw-Haw". He should have been in Cockney London; he would have heard through the roar of the bombs and the rattle of the ack-ack fire, the steady beat of the British heart.

On 12 December, 1940, Lord Lothian, the British Ambassador to the United States, died at Washington. He had been a close and ever-loyal friend of Lloyd George, and the news of his sudden end "numbed" the old statesman, as he said. But immediately the question arose of replacing him, and Lloyd George's name as promptly suggested itself. The Prime Minister asked him to come down to London from Criccieth and discuss it with him. Lloyd George went, calling on his doctor, Dawson, ostensibly for his advice. He got assurance there that he was perfectly fit for his age, but also advice that he should decline such an onerous job.

Lloyd George had not the slightest intention of accepting it, anyway, he told Frances Stevenson. But once again, he permitted a number of people to believe that he was seriously considering it.

Early in the New Year, news came from Criccieth that Dame Margaret Lloyd George was seriously ill. She had slipped on a polished floor while paying a visit to a friend's house, and had cracked her hip bone; then complications had set in, with heart trouble. Lloyd George made ready to set off for North Wales to be beside her.

Age 78

But in January, 1941, terrible winter weather gripped the whole land, and Dawson, who travelled by train from Euston to Bangor, at Lloyd George's urgent request, could not get through the snow-drifts in the Snowdonian mountain passes to Criccieth. Lloyd George himself, coming by road from Churt, had to be twice dug out of drifts upon the Welsh Border. Next day and all night long, forty or fifty of his fellow-countrymen, who included the local vicar and the Wesleyan minister, the schoolmaster, doctor, policeman, with quarry workers and Home Guardsmen, and using both plough and spade, toiled to clear a path for him along the mountain road so that Lloyd George might reach his dying wife in time. But the blizzard howled on, piling up in their path new blocks of frozen snow. Margaret died before her husband could come to her. He did not reach Criccieth until the following day. He was utterly broken, and so remained for many a day.

For all his character, so much composed of elemental thunder and lightning, capable of such ruthlessness, Lloyd George had a strange strain of gentleness, which especially came out in his relations with his family, a tenderness almost

One afternoon, when his wife thought he was asleep, he suddenly opened his eyes, and called out: "The Sign of the Cross! The Sign of the Cross!"

Age 82   On a spring evening of a cloudless, windless day, 26 March, 1945, he died. His wife, Frances, and his daughter, Megan, held his hands as his spirit passed.

.   .   .   .   .   .

Now a last journey, to the little wood that leads into a glade, the one Lloyd George loved best; and the rough meadow beyond, with its great stones that look as though they were hurled there by some angry river god, though it must have been long, long ago, for many are deep-buried and their crusts covered with an outcrop of fern.

There are the ancient tree stumps of what were once the giants of a forest; the dank green moss on the rocks that have somehow escaped the claw of the river; the foxgloves in the wood nearby, and the beeches which are the perches of the birds; the bustling stream itself, with the white foam it always makes a few feet before it tumbles over the rapids; and beyond, the bubbles and the strong undertow which the boy swimmers know; the roar of it, coming out of the great hills, that still bow before the majesty of Snowdon; the rustle of it (as it seems), when you lie down and the tall grass screens your ears.

The sun in the evening, smiling yet beyond the ridge of the gentle-rising green hill beyond, and striking a cloud with a last ray and lighting it up, like a red ball in the sky; the mist of the coming night rising out of the far mountains, like smoke from some mystic Druid fire.

They took him there, his body borne on a farm wagon, covered with flowers and the spring leaves, followed by thousands of his countrymen, who had come from every corner of the United Kingdom to say good-bye.

There David Lloyd George is buried. There is no inscription on his tombstone. There is no slab, standing up like a sentinel, at the head of his grave.

But they put on top of him one of those great, and, as it seems, living green stones out of the river.

"Fleet foot in the corrie
Sage council in cumber
Red hand in the foray
How sound is thy slumber"

he believed would prolong the struggle and multiply the bill. When people sometimes complained to him at Churt about war-time shortages, Lloyd George would say grimly: "You just wait till *after* the war!"

Age 80   On 23 October, 1943, he married Frances Stevenson at Guildford Registry House. She had joined his staff at the Treasury in 1913, when he was Chancellor of the Exchequer, and for many a year now had been his trusted Personal Secretary. He had truthfully said to her at Christmas, 1942, when they discussed marriage: "I have spent more time with you than with any other person in this world."

In the copy of his *War Memoirs* which he gave to her, he had written:

> "To Frances, without whose sympathetic help and understanding I could not have carried through the burden of the terrible tasks whose story is related in these volumes."

It is certain that for very long she had given him much devotion, and more than ever now he needed her.

The marriage had been kept a close secret, but when the news was released congratulations poured in from every quarter.

Their married life was destined to be sadly brief. In the spring of 1944 his health began to fail, and he was losing weight. So Frances ensured that a doctor friend should make excuse for a more careful examination of him than usual. The doctor diagnosed the existence of cancer, which Dawson himself subsequently confirmed. Though Lloyd George himself did not know, he seems to have had some understanding that the fires of his great life were dying down. He began to talk continually of returning to the village under Snowdon where he had lived his boyhood.

There was a pilgrimage to be made first.

On the morning of D-Day, while Lloyd George was shaving, his wife turned on the eight o'clock radio news. She was late, and did not grasp at first that something quite exceptional was going on. But soon, both of them were following the Allied "Liberation of Europe" Army as they waded ashore, covered by the bombarding fire of a mighty Fleet and Air Force. Lloyd George was excited, and at last he seemed genuinely happy about this war. They drove together up to London to the House of Commons, and there he spoke a few words of warm congratulation to his now oldest friend and colleague, Churchill. It was Lloyd George's last sight of Churchill, and his last visit to the scene of his own supreme triumphs.

And now the shadows began to fall. It had been a long road from the village smithy at Llanystumdwy to the Prime Minister's house at No. 10 Downing Street in London. Yes, and a grand, tempestuous journey. David Lloyd George had travelled well, and truly, and unafraid. He had borne his battles on the way with courage, with eagerness, and with joy. ("Am I no a bonnie fechter, Davy?" was one of his favourite quotations—and he always laid it down that if a man *was* "a bonnie fechter", like Alan Breck, there was no vanity or boastfulness in saying so.)

Back in Llanystumdwy now, he showed his wife the tree in the garden of old Uncle Lloyd's cottage, in whose branches he used to sit to learn his Euclid; the orchard with the cherry trees; the island in the river, where they used to play the war game of "Napoleon"; the wood on the bank above it which was his favourite haunt in late years; and Cwm Pennant, of which the bard, Eifion Wyn, wrote: *"Why, Lord, didst thou make Cwm Pennant so beautiful, and the life of an old shepherd so short?"*

In Europe and the Far East now, alike, the Allies were rolling forward irresistibly to victory. Lloyd George's interest in the war had almost vanished. But he would still have liked to take some part in shaping the peace.

And then came the offer of the Earldom. It seemed obvious that a General Election would take place before many months were out, and it was equally clear that Lloyd George's health would not allow him to fight it. Tentative inquiries were made of the two other Parties, both at Headquarters and locally, as to whether it would be possible for him to be returned unopposed; but no guarantee of this could be obtained. Some of his oldest friends thought that it would break his heart if he were defeated after his fifty-five years of uninterrupted membership of the House of Commons.

When Churchill asked him if he would accept an Earldom, Lloyd George reckoned it would relieve him of the worry which was looming ahead of having a hard election fight. He would still be in Parliament, though in that once-hated Upper House. He could not know that he would be dead before the bugles sounded the "Cease Fire" again along the battle line, much less before the victorious nation need go to the next General Election.

So he accepted. In the New Year Honours List, 1945, Lloyd George was granted an Earldom, and took the title of Earl Lloyd-George of Dwyfor and Viscount Gwynedd. Many, who loved and honoured him, will regret that David Lloyd George did not die as he had lived, and as history will ever know this great Briton.

In the early part of 1945 he became much weaker. He had lately reread Macaulay's *History of England* from cover to cover. Then he had tackled his beloved Dickens once again, *Oliver Twist, David Copperfield, Tale of Two Cities, Pickwick Papers, The Old Curiosity Shop, Christmas Carol.* Lloyd George was reliving his exciting, ever-challenging, defiant youth. But the process of reading now became so slow that at last it had to be abandoned altogether.

His children, his grandchildren, his brother, and many friends paid him frequent visits and gathered round in the great bay window looking across the sea. He would be lively yet, though he tired soon. But always "Who is coming today?" he would ask first thing in the morning when he awoke. At other times, he would sit silent, deep in thought, and oblivious to all those around him.

One afternoon, when his wife thought he was asleep, he suddenly opened his eyes, and called out: "The Sign of the Cross! The Sign of the Cross!"

Age 82   On a spring evening of a cloudless, windless day, 26 March, 1945, he died. His wife, Frances, and his daughter, Megan, held his hands as his spirit passed.

.   .   .   .   .   .

Now a last journey, to the little wood that leads into a glade, the one Lloyd George loved best; and the rough meadow beyond, with its great stones that look as though they were hurled there by some angry river god, though it must have been long, long ago, for many are deep-buried and their crusts covered with an outcrop of fern.

There are the ancient tree stumps of what were once the giants of a forest; the dank green moss on the rocks that have somehow escaped the claw of the river; the foxgloves in the wood nearby, and the beeches which are the perches of the birds; the bustling stream itself, with the white foam it always makes a few feet before it tumbles over the rapids; and beyond, the bubbles and the strong undertow which the boy swimmers know; the roar of it, coming out of the great hills, that still bow before the majesty of Snowdon; the rustle of it (as it seems), when you lie down and the tall grass screens your ears.

The sun in the evening, smiling yet beyond the ridge of the gentle-rising green hill beyond, and striking a cloud with a last ray and lighting it up, like a red ball in the sky; the mist of the coming night rising out of the far mountains, like smoke from some mystic Druid fire.

They took him there, his body borne on a farm wagon, covered with flowers and the spring leaves, followed by thousands of his countrymen, who had come from every corner of the United Kingdom to say good-bye.

There David Lloyd George is buried. There is no inscription on his tombstone. There is no slab, standing up like a sentinel, at the head of his grave.

But they put on top of him one of those great, and, as it seems, living green stones out of the river.

"Fleet foot in the corrie
Sage council in cumber
Red hand in the foray
How sound is thy slumber"

BIBLIOGRAPHY

AMERY, JULIAN: *Life of Joseph Chamberlain* (Vol. 4).

AMERY, L. S.: *My Political Life.*

ARMSTRONG, H. C.: *Grey Steel: J. C. Smuts.*

ASQUITH, EARL OF OXFORD AND: *Memories and Reflections* (2 Vols); *Fifty Years of Parliament.*

ASQUITH, MARGOT: *Autobiography.*

BACON, ADMIRAL SIR R. H.: *The Life of Lord Fisher of Kilverstone.*

BARKER, SIR ERNEST: *Reflections on Government.*

BEAVERBROOK, LORD: *Politicians and the War; Politicians and the Press.*

BEVERIDGE, LORD: *Power and Influence.*

BIRKENHEAD, EARL OF: *Contemporary Personalities.*

BIRKENHEAD, 2ND EARL OF: *Frederick Edwin, 1st Earl of Birkenhead* (2 Vols.).

BLAKE, ROBERT: *Private Papers of Douglas Haig, 1914–1919.*

BORASTON, J. H.: *Sir Douglas Haig's Command.*

BORDEN, HENRY: *Robert Laird Borden: His Memoirs* (2 Vols.).

BONSAL, STEPHEN: *Unfinished Business.*

BRETT, MAURICE V.: *Journal and Letters of Reginald Viscount Esher* (4 Vols.).

BROCKWAY, FENNER: *Socialism Over Sixty Years; Fred Jowett.*

BROWN, FRANK C.: *They Called Him Billy.*

CALLWELL, MAJOR-GENERAL SIR C. E.: *Field-Marshal Sir Henry Wilson: His Life and Diaries* (2 Vols.).

CHAMBERLAIN, SIR AUSTEN: *Politics from the Inside; Down the Years.*

CHAMBERLIN, W. H.: *Russia's Iron Age.*

CHURCHILL, WINSTON S.: *The World Crisis* (6 Vols.); *Thoughts and Adventures.*

CLARKE, TOM: *My Northcliffe Diary; Northcliffe in History; My Lloyd George Diary.*

COLE, G. D. H.: *Persons and Periods; The British Labour Movement: A History of the Labour Party from 1914.*

COLE MARGARET: *Beatrice Webb's Diaries; Makers of the Labour Movement.*

COWLES, VIRGINIA: *Winston Churchill: The Era and the Man.*

CRESWICKE, LOUIS: *Live of Joseph Chamberlain* (Vols. 3 and 4).

CROZIER, FRANK PERRY, BRIGADIER-GENERAL: *Ireland For Ever.*

CRUTTWELL, C. R. M. F.: *A History of the Great War, 1914–1918.*

D'ABERNON, LORD: *Portraits and Appreciation.*

DALTON, HUGH: *Call Back Yesterday.*

DANGERFIELD, GEORGE: *The Strange Death of Liberal England.*

DARLOW, T. H.: *William Robertson Nicoll: Life and Letters.*

DAVIDSON, MAJOR-GENERAL SIR JOHN: *Haig: Master of the Field.*

DAVIES, W. WATKIN: *Lloyd George (1863–1914).*

DEUTSCHER, E.; *Stalin.*

DILNOT, FRANK: *Lloyd George: The Man and His Story.*

DUGDALE, BLANCHE: *Arthur James Balfour.*

DU PARCQ, H.: *Life of David Lloyd George.*

EDWARDS, MOST REV. A. G. (ARCHBISHOP OF WALES): *Memories.*

EDWARDS, JOHN HUGH: *Life of D. Lloyd George* (4 Vols.).

ERVINE, ST. JOHN: *Craigavon, Ulsterman.*

EVANS, BERIAH: *Lloyd George.*

FULLER, GENERAL J. F. C.: *Last of the Gentlemen's Wars.*

GALLACHER, WILLIAM: *Revolt on the Clyde.*

GARDINER, A. G.; *Pillars of Society.*

GEORGE, DAVID LLOYD: *War Memoirs* (6 Vols.); *The Truth About The Peace Treaties* (2 Vols.); *Is It Peace?*

GEORGE, RICHARD LLOYD: *Dame Margaret.*

GOLDRING, DOUGLAS: *Marching with the Times.*

GORDON, ALBAN: *Russian Civil War.*

GREEN, JOHN: *Mr. Baldwin: A Study in Post-War Conservatism.*

GREY, SIR EDWARD: *Twenty-Five Years.*

GRIGG, SIR P. J.: *Prejudice and Judgment.*

GWYNN, DENIS: *Eamon De Valera.*

GWYNN, STEPHEN: *The Letters and Friendships of Sir Cecil Spring Rice; John Redmond's Last Years.*

HALPERIN, VLADIMIR: *Lord Milner and the Empire.*

HAMMOND, J. L.: *Life of C. P. Scott.*

HARINGTON, GENERAL SIR CHARLES: *Tim Harington Looks Back.*

HARROD, R. F.: *Life of John Maynard Keynes.*

HAYWARD, JOHN: *Silver Tongues and Famous Speeches, from Burke to Baldwin.*

HENDRICK, BURTON J.: *Life and Letters of Walter H. Page.*

HER MAJESTY'S STATIONERY OFFICE: *Official History of the First World War.*

HISTORY OF THE TIMES.

HODGES, ARTHUR: *Lord Kitchener.*

HOLLIS, CHRISTOPHER: *Two Nations; Lenin.*

HUGHES, WILLIAM M.: *Policies and Potentates; The Price of Peace; The Splendid Adventure.*

HUTCHISON, BRUCE: *The Incredible Canadian.*

HUXLEY, JULIAN: *On Living in a Revolution.*

HYDE, MONTGOMERY: *Carson.*

IRONSIDE, EDMUND: *Archangel 1918–19.*

JONES, JACK: *The Man David.*

JONES, TOM: *Lloyd George.*

JENKINS, ROY: *Mr. Balfour's Poodle.*

JERROLD, DOUGLAS: *England: Past, Present and Future.*

JOHNSON, ALAN CAMPBELL: *Viscount Halifax.*

KENWORTHY, J. M.: *Sailors, Statesmen and Others.*

KEYES, SIR ROGER: *The Fight for Gallipoli.*

KEYNES, J. M.: *Economic Consequences of the Peace.*

KIERNAN, R. H. *Lloyd George.*

LANSING, ROBERT: *My Diary; The Peace Negotiations: a Personal Narrative.*

LASKI, H. J.: *A Grammar of Politics.*

LONG, R. C.: *Mythology of Reparations.*

MACARDLE, DOROTHY: *The Irish Republic.*

MACDONALD, J. RAMSAY: *The Social Unrest.*

MACKENZIE, F. A.: *Lord Beaverbrook.*

MACKINDER, SIR HALFORD: *Democratic Ideals and Reality.*

MACREADY, GENERAL SIR NEVIL: *Annals of an Active Life.*

MALLET, SIR CHARLES: *Mr. Lloyd George (A Study), 1930.*

MANN, TOM: *Tom Mann's Memoirs.*

MANTOUX, ETIENNE: *The Carthaginian Peace, or the Economic Consequence of Mr. Keynes.*

MARJORIBANKS, EDWARD AND COLVIN IAN: *The Life of Lord Carson.*

MARTIN, HUGH: *Battle: The Life Story of Winston Churchill.*

MASTERMAN, LUCY: *C. F. G. Masterman.*

McKENNA, STEPHEN: *Reginald McKenna; While I Remember.*

MILLIN, GERTRUDE: *General Smuts.*

MORRISON, HERBERT: *The Peaceful Revolution.*

MURPHY, JOHN THOMAS: *Preparing for Power.*

MURRAY, BASIL: *L.G.*

MURRAY, LT.-COL. HON. ARTHUR C.: *Master and Brother; Lord Grey of Fallodon, K.G.; At Close Quarters.*

NICOLSON, HAROLD: *Curzon: The Last Phase; King George V: His Life and Reign; Peacemaking.*

NOWAK, KARL FRIEDRICK: *Versailles.*

O'BRIEN, W.; *Recollections.*

O'CONNOR, FRANK: *The Big Fellow: A Life of Michael Collins.*

OLIVER, F. S.: *Ordeal by Battle.*

PAKENHAM, FRANK: *Peace by Ordeal.*

PEARSON, HESKETH: *Labby.*

PEEL, MRS. C. S.: *How We Lived Then: 1914–18.*

PETRIE, SIR CHARLES: *Life and Letters of Sir Austen Chamberlain.*

POSTGATE, RAYMOND: *George Lansbury.*

RAINE, G. E.: *The Real Lloyd George.*

RAYMOND, E. T.: *Mr. Lloyd George; Uncensored Celebrities.*

READING, MARQUESS OF: *Rufus Isaacs.*

REITZ, DENEYS: *Commando.*

REPINGTON, LT.-COL. C. A.: *The First World War.*

RIDDELL, 1ST BARON: *War Diary: Intimate Diary of the Peace Conference and After*

ROBERTSON, J. M.: *Mr. Lloyd George and Liberalism.*

ROWNTREE, SEEBOHM: *How the Labourer Lives.*

SALTER, ARTHUR: *Personality in Politics; Recovery.*

SCHUMAN, PROFESSOR FREDERICK L.: *Soviet Politics at Home and Abroad.*

SEVERN, MARK: *The Gambardier.*

SEYMOUR, CHARLES: *The Intimate Papers of Colonel House* (4 Vols.) (arranged as a narrative by Charles Seymour).

SHAKESPEARE, SIR GEOFFREY: *Let Candles Be Brought In.*

SIMON, LORD: *Retrospect.*

SMILLIE, ROBERT: *My Life for Labour.*

SMUTS, J. C.: *Jan Christian Smuts.*

SOMERVELL, D. C.: *British Politics Since 1900.*

SOUTAR, ANDREW: *With Ironside in North Russia.*

SOUVARINE, BORIS: *Stalin.*

SPEARS, BRIGADIER-GENERAL E. L.: *Prelude to Victory.*

SPENDER, HAROLD: *The Prime Minister.*

SPENDER, J. A.: *50 Years of Europe.*

SPENDER, J. A. and ASQUITH, CYRIL: *Life of Herbert Henry Asquith, Lord Oxford and Asquith.*

STRACHEY, JOHN: *The Coming Struggle for Power.*

SYLVESTER, A. J.: *The Real Lloyd George.*

SYKES, SIR FREDERICK: *From Many Angles—An Autobiography.*

TAYLOR, H. A.: *Robert Donald.*

THOMSON, MALCOLM: *David Lloyd George* (Official Biography); *Life and Times of Winston Churchill.*

TILLETT, BEN: *Memories and Reflections.*

TROTSKY, LEON: *The History of the Russian Revolution.*

VANSITTART, LORD: *Lessons of My Life.*

WALTERS, E. W.: *The New Lloyd George.*

WAVELL, SIR ARCHIBALD (EARL WAVELL): *Allenby.*

WAVELL, COLONEL A. P. (EARL WAVELL): *The Palestine Campaigns.*

WEBB, SYDNEY AND BEATRICE: *History of Trade Unionism.*

WEIR, N. MACNEILL: *The Tragedy of Ramsay MacDonald.*

WERTHEIMER, EGON: *Portraits of the Labour Party.*

WILLIAMS, FRANCIS: *Ernest Bevin: Portrait of a Great Englishman; Fifty Years' March: The Rise of the Labour Party; The Labour Movement.*

WINDSOR, DUKE OF: *A King's Story.*

WINTERTON, EARL: *Orders of the Day.*

WRIGHT, PETER: *At the Supreme War Council.*

YOUNG, GEORGE MALCOLM: *Stanley Baldwin.*

YPRES, EARL OF: *1914.*

ZAC, WILLIAM: *Notes on Events in the Black Sea.*

INDEX

A

E

F

opposition to Lloyd George within the War Cabinet disappeared with him. Still the Man of the First World War held back.

Had he ever really meant to take an active part in this Second World War? This letter, written by Lloyd George in his own handwriting, dated 11 March, 1941, to Jennifer Stevenson at school, casts a light upon this mystery.

"Darling Jennifer,

... Your letter interested me very much. You put your points intelligently and clearly. You want to know why I have declined to join the War Cabinet when I was given the offer. I have asked Mummy to tell you my reasons when you meet this week-end. But I can give you just a hint—for yourself alone. You are not to repeat it to anyone else—except of course your Mummy.

1. I do not believe in the way we entered the war—nor in the methods by which it has been conducted. We have made blunder after blunder and we are still blundering. Unless there is a thorough change of policy, we shall never win.

2. I do not believe in the way or in the persons with which the War Cabinet is constituted. It is totally different to the War Cabinet set up in the last war. Mummy will explain. It is not a War Directorate in the real sense of the term. There is, therefore, no real direction.

I am convinced that unless there is a real change in these two matters, it would be useless for me to join up with the present lot. If I entered the Cabinet I should have soon to resign because of total disagreement with the plans and methods, and that would do no good.

There in brief you have my reasons.

I had experience in conducting a great war and I helped to win the victory. I am unhappy at the way things are done today, and I wish I was in a position to alter the course of events.

Love and kisses,
From,
Taid."

Did Lloyd George have another thought? Might not a day come when all the other great public figures had been discredited by personal failure, or by the general hopelessness of an apparently Endless War, and a call come for a statesman who had never wanted it, or waged it, but who was able and willing to wind it up?

Desperate things had happened since that day when Mr. Churchill took the helm. The Germans had launched their biggest onslaught yet, upon the hinge of the Maginot Line. They smashed it, and split the Allied Front wide open. Holland and Belgium had been overrun, the British Expeditionary Force driven off via the Channel ports, and the French Army rolled back in rout along a wobbling line which stretched from Paris to the Alps. Soon, the